EUROPE SINCE 191

IN ITS WORLD SETTING

By

F. Lee Benns

Indiana University

EIGHTH EDITION

New York

APPLETON-CENTURY-CROFTS, INC.

TO JESSIE

WHOSE HELP MAKES THE
TASK OF WRITING EASIER

PREFACE TO THE EIGHTH EDITION

This volume aims to provide the general reader and student of history with a brief, clearly-written, well-organized introduction to the significant events and changes which have occurred in Europe since 1914. It makes no claim to be a final and complete history of the period. The writing of such a volume must remain the task of future historians who, doubtless, will rank the period alongside that of the French Revolution and the Napoleonic Era for dramatic events and for rapid and far-reaching institutional changes. The desire of the present generation to obtain as clear an understanding as possible of the profound developments which have taken place in the political, economic, and social life of Europe in the twentieth century is the justification for this work.

In this eighth edition the chapters in Part Five have been rewritten and a new chapter, "Collective Security on Trial," has been added to provide discussion of the Korean War and the various diplomatic, economic, and military measures taken by the Free World in an effort to obtain collective security against the threat of Communism. As in earlier editions, events in Europe constitute the core of this history, but the increasing involvement of Europe and the United States in affairs throughout the world has inevitably made this volume a global history. As in earlier editions, too, I am indebted to my wife for valuable assistance in preparation of the manuscript and in checking of the proof.

F. L. B.

CONTENTS

PART TWO: THE PARIS PEACE SETTLEMENT AND ITS AFTERMATH

PART THREE: NATIONAL PROBLEMS AND EXPERIMENTS BETWEEN TWO WORLD WARS

PART FOUR: THE SECOND WORLD WAR

PART FIVE: ANOTHER POSTWAR PERIOD

MAPS AND CHARTS

ILLUSTRATIONS

Part One

THE FIRST WORLD WAR

Chapter I

THE BACKGROUND
OF THE FIRST WORLD WAR

IN the years before the outbreak of the First World War hopes and plans for international peace ran high. For more than four decades prior to 1914 Europe had largely escaped the horrors of war; in fact, during that period no armed conflict had occurred between any of the great powers of Europe. Although some of the countries had carried on wars outside Europe, those who longed for world peace hoped that, once all the unclaimed areas on other continents had been appropriated and all the "backward" regions of the world had been Europeanized, war might finally be banished from the face of the earth.

Hopes of Peace

These seekers after peace—the pacifists—pointed to many circumstances which seemed to indicate that the world might outgrow war. The nineteenth century, they argued, had witnessed the rise of businesses on such a scale that nations could no longer exist economically as isolated units but had become dependent upon one another for their economic well-being. The very magnitude of foreign investments, the rapid development of international credit and exchange, they declared, inevitably worked to promote mutual confidence among the nations. The improved means of communication and the introduction everywhere of cheap newspapers, they asserted, tended to create a world community and made possible the development of a world opinion against war. The interchange among the nations of professors and students and the spread of scientific discoveries across national borders helped to provide the peoples of the world with a common cultural background. In fact, the nineteenth and twentieth centuries, they pointed out, had gone far toward the development of a world community with increasingly uniform ideas and ideals.

They pointed out also—these advocates of peace—that the nations were becoming more and more accustomed to co-operation in spheres which were nonpolitical. In the seventies of the nineteenth century, for example, thirty states had organized the Universal Telegraph Union; twenty-three states had agreed to use the metric system of weights and measures; and sixty states had created the Universal Postal Union with its headquarters in Bern, the capital of Switzerland. Thanks to this last step, uniformity of postal laws, low rates, and speedy delivery had resulted for international mail. Soon hundreds of millions of letters and packages were being delivered throughout the world with a degree of safety that was remarkable. Other international agreements which helped to bring world solidarity were entered into by many nations. During the eighties conventions to standardize patent laws and copyright laws were ratified by a number of states.

The tendency toward world co-operation and world solidarity appeared, also, in many spheres of activity outside the control of national governments. Catholic Christians in 1881 began a series of eucharistic congresses, which were held successively in different parts of the world and were attended by clergy and laymen of many countries, and Protestant Christians likewise convened in world gatherings. In 1889 the Socialists organized the "Second International," and thereafter they held congresses of the workers of the world. In 1889, too, an international Parliamentary Union was set up to aid in spreading throughout the world the idea and practice of parliamentary government. Organizations such as the Rotary Club and the Boy Scouts extended across national lines, and they, also, held their world congresses. Especially significant were the numerous world gatherings of scholars and scientists with their resultant exchange of ideas in all realms of knowledge. By 1914 there were more than thirty international organizations that concerned themselves with "international science." It was hoped by pacifists that enlightened leaders everywhere might come to have a world outlook and that they, in turn, might exert their influence to lead mankind to think not merely in terms of one country but internationally.

To facilitate the growth of internationalism and to aid in the movement for world peace, the pacifists had begun early to organize. Prior to 1870 various peace societies had been established in Great Britain, the United States, Switzerland, and France. By 1914 the number of organizations of this type had increased until there "were 55 in Italy; 36 in France; 22 in Great Britain; 17 in the United States; 8 each in Austria and Sweden; 7 in Latin America; 4 in Australia; 3 each in Hungary, Norway, Russia, Spain, Japan, and Denmark; and 1 in Canada—a total of 160 organizations with many branches and an enormous membership." Probably one weakness in the peace movement was its failure to crystallize into one great international society with a definite and uniform program. After 1889, however, peace advocates held yearly international congresses, and in 1891 they located the permanent headquarters for their international peace movement at the capital of Switzerland.

Many were drawn into the peace movement not merely because of their hatred of the brutality and suffering which always accompany war, but also for economic reasons. In an effort to be "prepared" against an attack by another country, each of the great powers levied ever-increasing taxes. If war could be abolished, it was argued, a heavy financial burden could be lifted from the shoulders of mankind. Furthermore, it was maintained, the cost of a great war in the twentieth century would be so tremendous as to stagger the imagination. Writers of keen vision pointed out that such a conflict would be disastrous for even the victors. Ever since Bismarck had made the Franco-German War "pay" by successfully collecting an indemnity of five billion francs from defeated France, it had been thought in many quarters that, if a war was won, the cost of waging it could be placed on the shoulders of the defeated. In 1898, however, Ivan Bloch, a Polish Jew, revealed the futility of this fond hope by pointing out in his book, *The Future of War,* that war under modern conditions would inevitably bring general bankruptcy and starvation. His thesis received added support in 1910 when Norman Angell, an Englishman, asserted in his volume, *The Great Illusion,* that the economic and social conditions of the twentieth century made a military victory in war a mere illusion so far as improvement in the national well-being was concerned.[1] Other men like Alfred Nobel, a Swedish chemist and manufacturer of dynamite, Andrew Carnegie, an American steel manufacturer, Count Leo Tolstoi, a Russian novelist and social reformer, and Baron d'Estournelles de Constant, a French senator and publicist, gave abundantly of their wealth, their ability, and their time to advance the cause of peace.

Of course, it was realized that differences among nations would inevitably arise to cause ill feeling and friction. But, it was argued by peace-lovers, no differences could arise that could not be peaceably adjusted through diplomatic channels, use of arbitration, or resort to the mediation of other powers. A number of famous international controversies had been thus settled without recourse to war, perhaps the most famous being the *Alabama* case (1871–1872), the Bering Sea controversy (1892), and the Alaskan boundary dispute (1903), all between the United States and Great Britain; the colonial differences between Germany and Spain (1886); the dispute over the Samoan Islands (1899), between Great Britain, Germany, and the United States; the boundary dispute between Argentina and Chile (1902); and the differences between France and Germany over Morocco (1905–1909). By 1909 some eighty treaties making arbitration compulsory had been concluded between the various countries, and it has been estimated

---

[1] Of course certain individuals—the war profiteers—might profit.

that during the century preceding 1914 arbitration in some form had been used to settle nearly three hundred international disputes.

In 1899 what was considered to be a notable step forward in the cause of international arbitration occurred when the first Hague Peace Conference created the Permanent Court of Arbitration, popularly referred to as the Hague Court because it met at the capital of the Netherlands. This court was hardly a permanent tribunal in the full sense of the term, for it consisted merely of a list of the names of 132 distinguished jurists from which disputing states might, if they wished, select arbitrators. It had, moreover, no compulsory jurisdiction over any state and no way to enforce its decisions. The court was eventually housed in a magnificent peace palace erected at The Hague with funds provided by Andrew Carnegie. By 1914 eighteen important cases and a number of lesser ones had been settled by this tribunal.

On the other hand, even after the establishment of the Hague Court the great powers—Russia and Japan—resorted to war to settle their differences (1904-1905), Italy waged war against Turkey to gain colonial territory in northern Africa (1911-1912), and the Balkan states rose in arms against the sultan to advance their nationalist programs (1912-1913).

Causes of War

It is obvious from the foregoing statement that, at the very time when more and more attention was being given to the matter of preventing war, in the very years after machinery had been set up at The Hague for the pacific settlement of international disputes, wars were being fought in rapid succession by the nations of Europe. Why was this? In the first place, it was because the more deeply engrained spirit of competitive nationalism proved to be stronger than the more recently awakened ideal of international conciliation. In the second place, it was because various types of competition had developed among the nations, each of which was determined either to attain some objective or to prevent another power from attaining its objective, regardless of the justice of either's cause, and even at the cost of war if a reasonable chance of victory seemed present. And in the third place, it was because the nations of the world in their international relations lived in a "state of anarchy."

Although since 1914 much has been written on the subject of "international anarchy," it may be well to explain what is meant by the term and what its significance was—and is—in the history of the world. In 1914 Europe consisted of some twenty-five sovereign states, each in theory the equal of every other. They were called sovereign states because each refused to recognize any authority higher than its own will and its own interests.

Each claimed the right to make its own decisions and steadily refused to accept or adopt any procedure which seemed to encroach upon its complete independence—independence to enter into alliances, to make war, to conclude peace, to do as it pleased. None would concede the right of any higher international authority to make decisions binding it, and none would admit its obligation to appeal to any arbiter except force where matters of "national honor" or "territorial integrity" were involved. In other words, the states of Europe lived in a condition of anarchy in the sense that each recognized no authority outside itself.

In such circumstances war was very likely to occur whenever some ambitious "sovereign" power believed that the situation was favorable for it to obtain some objective for which it was competing with other powers. And in the realm of imperialism rival national plans clashed in many places.

Undoubtedly the major reason for the vigorous imperialistic impulse which existed after 1870 was the rapid rise and spread of the industrial revolution.[2] Whereas Great Britain had long been the predominant industrial and commercial power of the world, other countries after 1870 embarked upon an industrial expansion and began to enter into competition with her. With the spread of the industrial revolution and the consequent beginning of a keener economic competition among the powers, the demand for colonies again began to be heard. Colonies were now desired in order (1) that raw materials might be easily and surely obtained for manufacture into finished products in the homeland, (2) that monopolistic markets might be at hand to absorb the surplus of manufactured goods produced in the homeland, (3) that fruitful avenues might be provided for the investment of the surplus funds accumulated by the capitalists of the homeland, and (4) that added food supplies might be obtained for the sustenance of the increased millions at home who were devoting themselves no longer directly to the raising of foodstuffs but to the production of manufactured goods.

In consequence, there followed a spirited contest among the powers of the world, more especially among the great powers, for possession of the unclaimed areas of the earth's surface. By the opening of the twentieth century no habitable portion of the globe remained unclaimed by some state.

[2] Other influences of course also played a part. Patriots in landlocked countries sought expansion of their national control over territories which lay between them and the high seas so that they might not be cut off from free communication with other parts of the world in time of international crisis. They sought the comfort which came from the belief that overseas colonies provided added reservoirs of man power as well as naval bases for use in future wars in defense of the homeland. They sought, too, the satisfaction derived from their ability to point with pride, on the map of the world, to the various territories which were controlled by their country.

But, unfortunately for the peace of the world, in 1914 many imperialistic programs still remained unfulfilled to constitute a disturbing element to the course of international relations.

Austria-Hungary still sought to push her way into the Balkans in order to check the anti-Habsburg propaganda emanating from Serbia. Germany was inclined to support Austria-Hungary's Balkan program, for she herself planned to exploit the rich resources of Asia Minor and for the latter purpose needed a railway route through friendly territory in the Balkans as well as predominance in Constantinople. Obviously the German and Austrian plans for a *Drang nach Osten* conflicted with Russia's desire to accomplish her "historic mission" of acquiring Constantinople and the Straits, together with domination in the Balkans. The ambitions of the two Teutonic empires militated, also, against the realization of Italy's hopes for territorial expansion, for the latter—in addition to her ambitions in Africa and Asia Minor—desired to control the eastern coast of the Adriatic in order that she might transform that sea into an Italian lake. And Great Britain and France, despite the fact that they possessed the first and second largest overseas empires respectively—or because of that fact—were disturbed lest some power might seek to obtain a "place in the sun" at their expense. Imperialism thus produced conflicting national aspirations, bred mutual fears and suspicions, and created an atmosphere which made a great war possible.

Not unrelated to the clash of imperialistic programs had been the construction of numerous entangling alliances. By 1914 Europe had come to be divided, in a general way, into two rival groups of heavily armed, ambitious powers. On the one hand, there was a system of defensive alliances centering around Germany. As a result of the latter's annexation of Alsace-Lorraine after the Franco-German War of 1870–1871, the German chancellor, Bismarck, had feared lest French desire for revenge might lead to the creation of an alliance of states hostile to Germany and an ultimate attack upon her. To safeguard the peace of the newly established German Empire, therefore, he himself began the building of a succession of alliances which should center about Germany and leave France isolated in Europe. In consequence of Bismarck's endeavors, Germany became linked in a dual alliance with Austria-Hungary (1879) and in a triple alliance with Italy and Austria-Hungary (1882). Since these two alliances were still effective in 1914, their terms merit consideration. In the Dual Alliance it was agreed that if either Germany or Austria-Hungary were attacked by Russia or a third power backed by Russia, the other would aid; and that if either were at war with any power except Russia, the other would maintain benevolent neutrality. The Triple Alliance stipulated that (1) if Germany were attacked by France, Italy would aid Germany; (2) if Italy were attacked by France, both Austria-Hungary and Germany would aid Italy; and (3) if any member of the alliance were attacked and at war with two or more powers, the other two members would aid.

These alliances Bismarck supplemented with others. A treaty between Germany and Austria-Hungary on the one side and Rumania on the other (1883) provided that if either Austria-Hungary or Rumania were attacked by Russia, the other would aid. A few years later a reinsurance treaty with Russia (1887) provided, on the other hand, that if either were at war with a third power, the other would remain neutral, except in case Russia attacked Austria-Hungary or Germany attacked France. By these treaties Bismarck provided Germany with protection against both France and Russia, and completely isolated France.

But with Bismarck's dismissal from office (1890) and William II's subsequent policy came a change in the international situation. The new Kaiser refused to renew the Reinsurance Treaty with Russia when it expired (1890), so that Russia was cast adrift and, like France, stood isolated in Europe. The inevitable consequence was that these two states, both fearful of the increasing power of the German Empire, came together in an entente (1891), culminating two years later in a military convention which created the Franco-Russian Alliance of 1894. In this convention it was provided that if France were attacked by Germany, or by Italy supported by Germany, Russia would aid France; and that if Russia were attacked by Germany, or by Austria supported by Germany, France would aid Russia.

Meanwhile Germany's rapid strides in industry and commerce, her adoption of a policy of vigorous naval expansion, and her increasing demand for a "place in the sun," began to alarm Great Britain, especially after the latter's proffer of an alliance with Germany had been declined and Germany's apparent unfriendliness had been revealed during the Boer War. These circumstances led Great Britain to abandon her previously unfriendly attitude toward France, and resulted in the establishment of the Entente Cordiale (1904) between these two powers. Although a number of questions which had disturbed Anglo-French relations were adjusted in the treaty signed at this time, perhaps the most important agreement was that Great Britain should have a free hand in Egypt and France a free hand in Morocco. No definite alliance nor military convention was entered into, but an era of good feeling began which led Great Britain and France into closer and closer co-operation in international affairs.

France, united with Russia in the Alliance of 1894 and with Great Britain in the Entente Cordiale, naturally desired to bring about more friendly relations between these two states. The possibility of doing this, however, seemed at first to be rather remote, for Great Britain had long been the traditional enemy of Russia. The latter's southward expansion and her intrigues in the Near East, in Persia, and in Afghanistan had seemed to threaten the security of India and Great Britain's most direct route thereto, while her increasing activity in the Far East had constituted a challenge to Great Britain's commercial position in that part of the world.

Nevertheless, in her endeavors to bring about a friendly understanding between Russia and Great Britain, France was assisted by several circumstances. In the first place, Russia's disastrous defeat in the Russo-Japanese War (1904–1905) considerably lessened Great Britain's fear of the former's menace to India, while at the same time it disturbed the military balance of power in Europe to the decided advantage of the Triple Alliance. In the second place, Germany's gradual acquisition of a preponderating influence in Turkey, coupled with her project for a railway from Constantinople to Bagdad, led Great Britain to believe that a German menace to British interests in the Near and Middle East had been substituted for the previous Russian threat. These facts, especially in view of Germany's apparent determination to enter into naval competition with Great Britain, convinced the statesmen of the latter country that British interests demanded a shift in foreign policy. Such a shift was finally made when Great Britain and Russia signed a convention (1907) adjusting their differences in the Middle East and dividing Persia between them. Again, no binding alliance was consummated between the two powers, but the good feeling and close understanding which followed led to the designation of France, Russia, and Great Britain as the powers of the Triple Entente. Thus by 1907 the great powers of Europe had come to be pretty definitely divided into two groups, the Triple Alliance and the Triple Entente.

Italy's alignment with Austria-Hungary, however, was unnatural. *Italia Irredenta*—territory in Europe inhabited by Italian-speaking people but not included in the Italian Kingdom—lay chiefly within Austria-Hungary's political boundaries, and the interests of the two powers conflicted in the Balkans and in the Adriatic. In the closing years of the nineteenth century, Italy's ill will toward France subsided and she began to gravitate toward the Triple Entente. In 1900 she agreed to give France a free hand in Morocco in return for which the latter gave her a free hand in Tripoli and Cyrenaica. Two years later the two powers further agreed that should either be the object of a direct or indirect aggression on the part of one or more powers, or should either, as a result of a direct provocation, find itself compelled in defense of its honor or its security to take the initiative of a declaration of war, the other would maintain a strict neutrality. In other words, should Germany attack France or should France "in defense of her honor or her security" declare war upon Germany, Italy would remain neutral. A few years later Italy moved still nearer the position of the Triple Entente. At Racconigi (1909) she agreed with Russia to attempt to maintain the *status quo* in the Balkans to the exclusion of all foreign domination, and in return for Russia's favorable attitude toward Italian interests in Tripoli and Cyrenaica, she further agreed to consider favorably Russian interests in the question of the Straits at Constantinople. It is apparent therefore that, although on paper the Triple Alliance seemed more closely and more definitely knit together than the Triple Entente, such was not the case.

These ententes, alliances, and counteralliances, though defensive in their original character, eventually created an atmosphere favorable to war. Naturally, the number of "danger spots" which might embroil all Europe in a serious international conflict was increased as states became more and more entangled in the plans and aspirations of their allies. At the same time, believing that if attacked they would have the active assistance of their allies, states became less willing to make concessions in times of diplomatic clashes. Finally, as the international situation became more tense, members of each alliance became reluctant to concede anything to members of the other lest their action be interpreted as weakness and their group suffer a loss of prestige.

Accompanying the rise of entangling alliances, and undoubtedly accelerated by the fear engendered by these alliances, was the growth of huge national armaments. After the Austro-Prussian and Franco-German wars, the system of conscription which seemed to have enabled Prussia to gain an easy victory in each case was rapidly adopted by the other states on the Continent. One after another the national armies were reorganized on the Prussian model. Year by year the number of young men called to serve in the various national armies was increased until Europe came to be a veritable armed camp. All of this was done in the name of peace, for it was argued that the best insurance against war was national preparedness. Many taxpayers complained, however, of the ever-increasing tax burden laid upon them for armaments which some pacifists maintained would not assure peace but might rather provoke war. The latter viewpoint was well presented by H. N. Brailsford, an Englishman, who in *The War of Steel and Gold* (1914) asserted that preparedness inevitably brought war.

At the close of the nineteenth century a feeble attempt was made to limit armaments by international agreement. In 1898 Tsar Nicholas II of Russia invited the powers to assemble at The Hague to consider the possibility of some such agreement. Whether he was moved to this step by a sincere personal desire to promote the cause of peace or merely because the financial burden which armaments entailed was becoming too great for Russia to carry, is not clear. It soon became apparent, however, that some of the statesmen of the great powers were opposed to any international limitation on armaments. When the Hague Peace Conference convened in 1899 with delegates from twenty-six states present, no agreement was reached on this subject. In general, Germany stood out as the power most opposed to limitation of land armaments, and Great Britain blocked all steps which might weaken her control of the seas.

A second Hague Peace Conference, held in 1907, was attended by the representatives of forty-four states, but again the nations failed to agree upon any limitation of armaments. A number of rules were adopted to regularize and make more humane the conduct of war, but these, as the succeeding pages disclose, were largely ignored when the First World War finally came. Attempts to arrive at some agreement limiting naval armaments were also carried on by direct negotiations between Great Britain and Germany, but these, too, proved futile. And so the armaments race went madly on. By 1914 the five major continental powers had millions of men in their peace-time standing armies, to say nothing of other millions trained and organized in the reserves.

Such a situation did much to create an atmosphere favorable to war. In the first place, it engendered international fear and suspicion. Although each power professed to be preparing merely to defend itself against aggression, each in turn suspected the others of preparing *for* aggression. In the second place, the knowledge that great military establishments were back of them undoubtedly increased the reluctance of statesmen to make concessions which might appear in the nature of national diplomatic defeats and, conversely, increased their determination to press for some advantage which might appear to be a national diplomatic triumph. In the third place, in all countries to some extent, but more particularly in Germany, the growth of armaments contributed to the development of a state of mind usually summed up in the one word "militarism." [3] In the fourth place, with the growth of great military machines there developed in each country a general staff of leaders and experts, one of whose chief concerns was to prevent the army of another power from "getting the jump" on them in time of international crisis. These general staffs worked out carefully calculated "timetables" of what must be done if war should break out, and in every international crisis there was always the danger that some chief of staff, in an effort to maintain the schedule on his "timetable," might force an order for mobilization and thus precipitate a war. Finally, the existence of great military establishments produced a group of arma-

---

[3] "Militarism is an attitude of approval of war as an elevating, ennobling occupation, as the purifying salt in the otherwise nauseous human compound; ... usually, the approval rises to a desire for national glory as the product of military success, welcoming quarrel in order that war's beneficent influence may have full operation; and ... the approval and desire have, as a result, the endowment of the military profession with a rank and worthiness higher and more meritorious than attaches to avocations of civil character." J. S. Ewart, *The Roots and Causes of the Wars (1914–1918)*, Volume I, pages 479–480.

ment manufacturers in all of the important countries who were at times not averse to the spread of warlike ideas as a means of increasing their own profits.

A fourth factor which disturbed the course of European international affairs and constituted an ever-present potential cause of war was the increasing desire of certain groups of people of the same race, speaking the same language or kindred dialects, having in general the same customs and traditions, and inhabiting contiguous territories, to unite into one state independent of foreign domination. This was the goal of nationalism. The years before 1914 had witnessed a considerable advance toward this nationalist ideal in the creation of the German Empire and the Italian, Greek, Belgian, Serbian, Rumanian, and Bulgarian kingdoms. Nevertheless, in 1914 national statehood was as yet unattained or only partly attained in various parts of Europe. In general, Austria-Hungary and Russia constituted the chief obstacles to its consummation.

Although the desire for national unity was a force in Italy, which since her consolidation had cast longing eyes upon the Trieste and Trentino territories of Austria-Hungary wherein dwelt "unredeemed Italians," and in France, where the desire to regain the lost provinces of Alsace-Lorraine was still strong in the hearts of many, it constituted a more active factor in the Balkans. Here, though considerable advance toward national statehood had been made, each state was possessed of nationalist dreams as yet unfulfilled. Greece desired to obtain Thrace, some of the Aegean islands, and parts of Asia Minor in order to reconstruct the ancient Byzantine Empire. At the same time Bulgaria hoped to secure most of Macedonia and Thrace in order to round out her territory and gain an adequate outlet to the Aegean. Rumania longed to bring within her boundaries the millions of "unredeemed" Rumanians dwelling in Transylvania, Bukowina, and parts of Bessarabia. Serbia aspired to liberate her kinsmen who dwelt within the Habsburg empire and to gain a foothold on the Adriatic. Naturally, this unrest in the Balkans constituted a standing menace to the peace of Europe, the more so since states like Russia and Austria-Hungary sought to turn the Balkan aspirations to their own advantage. The possibility that some Balkan group would attempt to complete its "unification" and thus precipitate a war in which the great powers might participate was always present.

And if the statesmen of any power—great or small—led their country into war, they were almost certain to receive the enthusiastic support of the great majority of their fellow citizens. Patriotic history and literature magnified the former glory and future promise of each nation, while patriotic writers devoted themselves to extolling the superiority of their own racial group. "Patriotic state education taught unquestioning loyalty to state or dynasty as the first principle of moral conduct, carefully obscured any questionable occurrences or policies in the national past, and frowned on national criticism and proposals of radical reform." In every country some jingo or venal newspapers stood ready upon the least pretext to inflame public opinion by criticizing and misrepresenting the acts or policies of other states. In many countries international antipathies had been assiduously cultivated, with the result that national suspicions, fears, and hatreds were deep-seated. Such was the spirit of this type of nationalism that in each state the people felt that their government was always honest and upright in its dealings with others, that if war occurred it was because some other state was the aggressor.

Recurring International Crises

Many careful observers of the course of international events during the decade before 1914 were not altogether surprised by the outbreak of the First World War, for a series of international crises accompanied by an increasing tension among the great powers had revealed a noticeable drift toward war. The first of these was precipitated in 1905 when William II, the German Kaiser, landed at Tangier in Morocco and proclaimed his support of the political sovereignty and territorial integrity of Morocco.

As pointed out above, France had made agreements with Italy and Great Britain giving her a free hand in Morocco, which she aimed to transform into a French protectorate.[4] She had not, however, consulted Germany. The latter seized upon the Moroccan situation as an opportunity to reveal to France that she was dependent upon German good will and as an occasion to break up, if possible, the Entente Cordiale which had been reached by France and Great Britain in the preceding year. Since the status of Morocco had been fixed by the Madrid Conference in 1880, Germany demanded that France should permit her position in Morocco to be decided by an international conference. This France was reluctant to do, and the international atmosphere for a time became exceedingly tense.

War between France and Germany might have resulted, but it was avoided because the French government gave way and permitted the Moroccan situation to be settled at the Algeciras conference in 1906. Although the outcome of this conference was largely favorable to France, the latter deeply resented Germany's interference in French plans. At the same time Germany was disturbed by finding herself and Austria-Hungary almost isolated in the deliberations of the conference, for Italy voted in favor of France against her own ally. Apparently this fact was not lost on the Kaiser, who, at the close of the conference, sent a telegram to Francis Jo-

[4] She had made a similar agreement with Spain, also.

seph referring to Austria-Hungary as his "faithful ally," evidently implying that Italy had proved unfaithful to the Triple Alliance.

If the German government's plan in precipitating the crisis had been to destroy or weaken the recently consummated Entente Cordiale between France and Great Britain, it failed miserably. At the very outset of the crisis British public opinion supported France, and the German ambassador at London notified Berlin that British newspapers were even "more French than the French." In fact, during the crisis Sir Edward Grey, British foreign secretary, went so far as to inform the German ambassador that, if Germany actually attacked France, Great Britain could hardly keep out of the war. Furthermore, after consulting the prime minister and the minister of war, Grey permitted British army leaders to work out with French and Belgian military men provisional plans for British aid against a German attack in case Great Britain should ever decide to go to the aid of these two countries. The crisis therefore served to consolidate the Franco-British entente, while increasing the tension between France and Germany.

The next event which placed a severe strain upon the peaceful course of international relations came in 1908 when Austria-Hungary announced her annexation of Bosnia and Herzegovina. In 1878, by the treaty of Berlin, Austria-Hungary had been given the right to occupy and administer these two provinces, the sovereignty of which, however, still resided in the sultan. At that time it was believed by many that this right to occupy constituted only a thinly disguised annexation, and the Habsburgs in the succeeding years had conducted themselves as though this were true. Planning to take advantage of the weakness of Turkey just after the Young Turk Revolution of 1908, Austria-Hungary consulted Russia regarding the possibility of annexing Bosnia and Herzegovina outright. Izvolski, Russian foreign minister, agreed that Russia would assume a friendly attitude toward Austria-Hungary's annexation of the two provinces, and Aehrenthal, Austro-Hungarian foreign minister, agreed that his country would in turn adopt the same attitude toward Russia's application for a modification of the agreements regarding the Straits.

When the Habsburg government announced the annexation of Bosnia and Herzegovina, the Serbs, who had hoped themselves to secure the provinces and "liberate" their kinsmen, protested vigorously against the illegal action. Apparently Izvolski, when he had thought that by co-operating with Austria-Hungary he might gain for Russia the coveted freedom of passage through the Straits, had cared little about the national aspiration of the Serbs. When he found that Great Britain would not consent to a change in the status of the Straits at that time and after he had received specific instructions from Premier Stolypin not to abandon Serbia, he altered his position and came to the support of that country. Great Britain and Russia then demanded that Austria submit her action to an international conference just as France had been compelled to do in the preceding crisis. This Aehrenthal absolutely refused to do unless the powers promised in advance to approve his government's action. Germany, seeking to advance her international prestige, strongly supported the Habsburg position. It appeared for a time that war might result.

Russia, however, had not recovered enough from her war with Japan to be in a position to fight successfully, and France at that time appeared to be little concerned in a Balkan question in which she was not directly involved. When, therefore, Germany in a practical ultimatum demanded that Russia recognize Austria-Hungary's annexation of the provinces, the Russians were forced to yield, and the crisis passed. Serbia was forced not only to accept the annexation but to admit that it was not detrimental to her interests. In addition, she was compelled to agree not to carry on propaganda inimical to Austria-Hungary.

There is little doubt that in this crisis the Teutonic powers gained a decisive diplomatic victory. But the price they paid was high. Serbia now hated Austria-Hungary more bitterly than ever. By her promises to Austria-Hungary she had gained immunity from immediate attack; but in the following years she pushed the reorganization of her army with feverish activity, obtaining from France guns, munitions, and military advice. Although she had officially undertaken not to carry on propaganda inimical to Austria-Hungary, the promise had little likelihood of being fulfilled so far as the secret agitation of the various Serbian patriotic societies was concerned. The Yugoslav threat to the territorial integrity of the Dual Monarchy was not destroyed by the annexation of Bosnia-Herzegovina.

In the second place, Russia, after her humiliation, definitely began to make preparations for a war which she regarded as inevitable. In order to block the plans of the Teutonic powers and at the same time strengthen her own position in the Balkans, she at once turned her attention to the creation of a Balkan league. In 1909 she proposed to Bulgaria a military convention designed to protect each against the Teutonic powers and Turkey. Although the convention seems never to have been actually signed, Russia's attitude is disclosed in one article which stipulated "that the realization of the high ideals of the Slavic peoples in the Balkan peninsula ... is possible only after a favorable outcome of Russia's struggle with Germany and Austria-Hungary." In 1912 the Russo-Bulgarian understanding was expanded into something resembling a Balkan league when, under Russia's guidance, alliances were entered into between Bulgaria and Serbia and between Bulgaria and Greece. In France, at the same time, Russia began a campaign to "Balkanize" the Franco-Russian alliance, that is, to convert the French to the view that developments in the Balkans which were vital to Russia were important likewise to France.

In the third place, the annexation strained relations between Italy and Austria-Hungary and led the former to take one more step toward the Triple Entente. During the crisis, when anti-Austrian agitation in Italy was feverish, Austria-Hungary had concentrated forces in the Trentino. Apparently the Habsburg chief of staff had even contemplated an attack on Italy as well as on Serbia. Russia took advantage of the increasing anti-Habsburg feeling in Italy to come to an agreement with that power (at Racconigi, October, 1909) in which each promised to attempt to maintain the *status quo* in the Balkans. Apparently both had in mind the possibility of checking further Habsburg expansion to the southeast. Italy's double-dealing at this time becomes obvious when it is pointed out that only a few weeks later (December, 1909) she signed another Balkan agreement with Austria-Hungary in which each renewed professions of loyalty to the Triple Alliance.

Within less than three years after the settlement of the Bosnian crisis Europe was again pushed to the verge of war by developments in Morocco. Despite the events of 1905 and 1906, France had continued her efforts to secure control of that country. In 1911 she took steps which, if permitted to go unchallenged, the Germans believed, would convert Morocco into a French protectorate. Germany therefore decided to secure compensation for herself, and when France delayed in making an offer the German gunboat *Panther* was sent to Agadir, a Moroccan port on the Atlantic.

Although, apparently, Germany did not expect to obtain her compensation from France in Morocco, Great Britain jumped to the conclusion that this was the German object and at once feared for the safety of British communication with South Africa and India. In the midst of the crisis Lloyd George, a member of the British government, declared in a public address that Great Britain would not allow herself to be excluded from negotiations on subjects which touched her vital interests, that peace at such a price would be too great a humiliation. The natural effect of this speech was to convince both the French and the Germans that Great Britain would support France. But the Germans felt themselves to be in a position from which, in the face of what they considered to be a British threat, they could not retreat. Fortunately, neither France nor Germany wanted war, and eventually a settlement was reached in which, in return for the acquisition of territory in the French Congo, Germany gave up all claims in Morocco.

But so strong was the feeling caused in France by this crisis that the pacific Caillaux ministry was overturned and was succeeded by one headed by the strong nationalist, Poincaré. The latter immediately set out to strengthen the ties between France and Russia. In Germany many felt that their government had been blocked in its demands for compensation by Britain's control of the sea and consequently demanded that the German navy should be increased until it should be powerful enough to dissuade the British from interfering with German plans. An act was at once passed by the German Reichstag providing for the construction of a number of new ships. When Great Britain sought through the so-called Haldane mission to arrange a naval holiday with Germany, the latter declined except on condition that Great Britain would promise to remain neutral in case Germany were forced into war. This Great Britain refused to do, with the result that Germany and Great Britain became more suspicious of each other's intentions.

Hardly had the statesmen of Europe regained their breath after this crisis before another equally grave was precipitated when, despite the opposition of the great powers, the so-called Balkan league made a concerted attack upon Turkey in 1912. The Balkan allies were at once successful. The Bulgarians drove southeastward through Thrace toward Adrianople and Constantinople; the Greeks moved northward in Macedonia toward Saloniki; and the Serbs and Montenegrins swept the Turks before them westward and southwestward toward the Adriatic. Although Russian and British sympathy was with the Balkan states, the Teutonic powers were greatly disturbed by Serbia's advance to the Adriatic. In fact, the chief crisis had to do with Serbia's seizure of northern Albania and her determination to secure a foothold on the Adriatic. Russia, France, and Great Britain were at first ready to support Serbia's claim, but both Austria-Hungary and Italy were resolved to prevent a new rival from appearing on the Adriatic. In the face of their joint opposition, the Entente powers conceded that a railway connection through Albania without the territorial access itself must satisfy Serbia, and the latter eventually agreed to yield to the decision of a conference of ambassadors which sat in London.

The London conference was not without its critical moments. Both Austria-Hungary and Russia carried out a kind of mobilization, the former being particularly restless. Throughout the crisis, however, Germany and Great Britain worked in perfect accord in the interests of peace. The treaty of London which was signed on May 30, 1913, restricted European Turkey to Constantinople and a mere foothold in eastern Thrace. The status of Albania and the Aegean Islands was left to a later decision of the great powers. The rest of the territory previously included in European Turkey was ceded to the Balkan allies.

The victors almost immediately proceeded to quarrel over the spoils. On June 29, the Bulgarians suddenly attacked the Serbian forces in Macedonia and at the same time advanced against the Greeks in Saloniki. In order

to prevent Bulgarian hegemony in the Balkans, Rumania now joined Serbia and Greece; and Turkey seized the occasion to reoccupy Adrianople. The Second Balkan War was soon over, and a new treaty was signed at Bucharest (August 10). As a result of the wars Serbia gained central and part of southern Macedonia and half of the Sanjak of Novibazar; Montenegro got the other half of the Sanjak; Greece secured Crete and most of southern Macedonia, including Saloniki; Bulgaria obtained a strip of Macedonia and western Thrace, but was obliged to return eastern Thrace, including Adrianople, to Turkey and to cede a strip of the southern Dobrudja to Rumania. Albania was eventually organized as an independent principality with William of Wied, a German prince, as ruler.

The Balkan wars had far-reaching effects on the general European situation. They nearly doubled the area and population of Serbia, greatly increased her self-confidence, and strongly stimulated her hope of a speedy realization of that dream of a "greater Serbia" which envisaged the ultimate acquisition of Bosnia-Herzegovina, Dalmatia, Croatia-Slavonia, and the Serb-inhabited districts of southern Hungary. They greatly increased the size and importance of Greece, where enthusiasm for a further advance toward the realization of its aims led the Greek government to purchase two warships from the United States in preparation for seizing any future opportunity which might present itself for the reconstitution of the Pan-Hellenic empire. They converted Bulgaria into a defeated and humiliated power which was eager for revenge upon her erstwhile allies and was therefore prepared to join with any great power that seemed in a position to bring to her the Macedonia which she had twice lost within a single generation.

They turned over to Greece and Serbia former Turkish territory through which Austria-Hungary had planned to secure railway connection with the Aegean, at the same time placing in more powerful hands her existing railway route to Constantinople. They obviously made more difficult of realization the proposed Berlin-Bagdad railway under German influence. They revealed that Rumania was no longer a trusty satellite of the Teutonic powers, and at the same time smashed Russia's recently created Balkan league. The net result seemed unfavorable to the Teutonic powers. In fact, so alarmed was the Austrian government over developments in the Balkans at this time that in the summer of 1913 it seriously contemplated a preventive war against Serbia in order to keep that country from becoming too powerful and too attractive to the Yugoslav people within the Dual Monarchy. The latter was on the point of launching an attack against the little Slav kingdom and was deterred only by the opposition of Germany and Italy.

Increasing International Tension

During the years 1912–1914, when the governments and peoples of Europe displayed an "excessive nervosity," existing alliances and ententes were tightened up and new ones were projected. Definite steps were taken, for instance, to bring France and Great Britain into closer relations. After the failure of the Haldane mission, Great Britain transferred most of her Mediterranean fleet to the North Sea in order quickly to balance there the increase in strength which Germany was planning to gain in the ensuing years by the execution of her naval program. In view of the weakening of the Entente naval power in the Mediterranean by the withdrawal of British ships, Great Britain urged France to station most of her navy in that sea. Naturally, the latter was reluctant to leave her Atlantic coast undefended unless she received some guarantee from Britain. Eventually, with the consent of the British cabinet, personal notes were exchanged (November, 1912) between Grey and Cambon, the French ambassador at London. Grey explicitly stated, that, if either country suspected that it was about to be the victim of an unprovoked attack, "it should immediately discuss with the other whether both governments should act together to prevent aggression and preserve the peace, and, if so, what measures they would be prepared to take in common." This correspondence, obviously, went far toward transforming the Entente Cordiale into a Franco-British alliance against Germany. Apparently the French government so regarded it, for it soon transferred its Atlantic fleet to the Mediterranean. Furthermore, Marshal Joffre later stated that French military plans were developed with the assumption of active British support.

In 1912, too, steps were taken to bring France and Russia into a closer understanding regarding the Balkans. Although in August of that year Poincaré informed Sazonov, Russian foreign minister, that France would not go to war over a Balkan question, he qualified his statement by adding the clause, unless Russia is attacked by Germany. Later in the year Izvolski, now Russian ambassador at Paris, reported to St. Petersburg that Poincaré realized that an attack upon Serbia by Austria might force Russia to give up her passive attitude and take diplomatic steps followed by military measures against Austria. According to Poincaré, Izvolski reported, Russia could count on French diplomatic support and, if Germany should come to the military aid of Austria, military support as well. Whether Izvolski exaggerated or truly reported what Poincaré had said is not clear, but the effect upon the Russian government at St. Petersburg would have been the same in either case. The statement seemed to indicate that the Russian ambassador at Paris had at last succeeded in "Balkanizing" the

Franco-Russian alliance. At the same time, in order to make the French people "Balkan-conscious," the French press was extensively subsidized by Izvolski with funds secured from Russia. Meanwhile, to implement the alliance more effectively, a Franco-Russian naval convention was concluded, and the general staffs of the two countries conferred annually to perfect their plans for a joint offensive against Germany in case of war. Finally, in 1914 Russia was informed of the exchange of letters between Grey and Cambon in November, 1912, and negotiations were opened between Russia and Great Britain looking to a naval agreement.

Nor were the powers of the Triple Alliance inactive. Although that alliance was not due to expire until July, 1914, the treaty was renewed in December, 1912, and extended until July, 1920. Italy announced, however, that in case of war she would be unable to send any of her military forces north of the Alps, as she had always promised to do during the preceding quarter of a century. France's transfer of her whole navy to the Mediterranean, however, frightened her enough so that she was willing to sign a naval convention with the other partners in the Triple Alliance. In June, 1913, agreements were reached defining the action of the Mediterranean fleets of Germany, Austria, and Italy in case of war. Provision was specifically made for attacking French troop ships operating between North Africa and France. And in the spring of 1914 Italy once more promised to send troops into Germany to fight against France in case Germany should be attacked by the latter. So far as agreements on paper were concerned, therefore, the powers of both the Triple Alliance and the Triple Entente were more closely bound together in 1914 than they had ever been before.

In the Balkans, meanwhile, both Russia and Austria-Hungary were busily engaged in trying to construct or reconstruct alliances. During the wars of 1912–1913 Count Berchtold, Austro-Hungarian foreign minister, had managed to destroy Russia's Balkan league, but he was not content with this achievement. He next sought to overcome the threat of a "greater Serbia" by the creation of a Balkan alliance against Serbia, with Bulgaria as the pivot but with Greece, Turkey, and possibly Rumania also included. Negotiations carried on between the Dual Monarchy and Bulgaria had progressed far enough by July, 1914, so that Bulgaria was able to secure a loan from Berlin. On the other hand, Russia, whose diplomacy had received something of a blow by the destruction of her Balkan league, was desperately attempting to reconstruct the league by substituting Rumania for Bulgaria.

In 1913 and 1914 both sets of great powers were also attempting to improve their positions at Constantinople, where the Turkish government was trying to reorganize its military and financial departments after the Balkan wars. An Englishman was invited to reorganize the empire's finances; a Frenchman was asked to train the gendarmerie; a German general, Liman von Sanders, was invited to reorganize and train the army; and a British admiral was asked to do the same for the navy. The growing international tension in Europe is clearly revealed by the fact that, as soon as Sazonov learned of the Sanders mission, he entered a determined protest against giving a German command of an army corps in the Ottoman capital, where, he declared, the sultan would be deprived of all liberty of action. The Russian foreign minister wished to use the occasion to force Germany to draw back. But Great Britain, whose admiral's powers over the Ottoman navy were probably greater than those of Sanders over the army, declined to support Russia, and France likewise refused to exert pressure at Berlin.

In January, 1914, at a Russian council meeting Sazonov urged an immediate attack upon Germany unless the latter abandoned the Sanders mission. The council, however, decided for peace. The German government, in order to appease Russia, offered a compromise arrangement by the terms of which Sanders was not to command troops in Constantinople but was to function merely as inspector of the Turkish army. But Sazonov was still dominated by the idea that Russia must not permit Germany to secure control of Constantinople and the Straits, and during the early weeks of 1914 Russian military and naval officers worked on plans for seizing the Straits in case of necessity. In a council meeting in February of that year it was decided that Russian operations against the Straits could not be inaugurated with any assurance of success without a general European war.

Meanwhile, Russia's willingness to support Serbia in order to block Austria-Hungary's advance into the Balkans continued unchecked, as was indicated by the tsar's statement to Premier Pashich of Serbia when the latter had a conference with him in St. Petersburg in January, 1914. "For Serbia," declared Nicholas II, "we shall do everything." Russia directed her immediate efforts toward securing a union of Serbia and Montenegro and in 1914 began to bring pressure to bear on the ruler of the latter state. Such a union not only would increase the size and population of Serbia, but would at the same time provide the latter with an outlet to the Adriatic. The Austrian government, however, had come to the conclusion that, if this union were ever consummated, it would demand that the coast of Montenegro should go to Albania. Such a transfer of territory would have at least two significant results. It would again prevent Serbia from securing an outlet to the sea, and it would extend Albania's territory northward to the Austrian frontier. The latter possibility was particularly alarming to the Italians, because they believed it would increase Austria's influence over Albania, which the Italians themselves wished to dominate. Consequently, in the late spring of 1914 Italy again wavered in her loyalty to the Triple Alliance.

These brief glimpses of the diplomatic situation in Europe in 1913 and 1914 somewhat resemble the pieces of a jig-saw picture, none of which alone gives a complete or true idea of the picture as a whole. Possibly enough of the pieces have been fitted together, however, to indicate that just before the crisis of 1914 international rivalry and friction in Europe were being more and more localized and centered in the Balkans and the Near East. And as the fears and suspicions increased, so did the measures for expanding the various national armies and navies. Europe as a whole was perhaps never so well prepared to wage war as in the summer of 1914.

Gradually the international situation became more tense. In Austria-Hungary "the feeling that the nations are moving toward a conflict, urged by an irresistible force," grew from day to day. In Russia the military began to realize that "we are preparing for a war in the West. Not only troops but the whole nation must accustom itself to the idea that we arm ourselves for a war of annihilation against the Germans, and the German empires must be annihilated." In France the nationalists argued that Germany's threat to French security must be met by increased preparedness. "Russia is ready. France must be ready too," proclaimed the headlines of an article in the St. Petersburg *Bourse Gazette* in June, 1914, whereupon the Kaiser wrote: "Any German who still disbelieves that Russia and France are working full steam for an early war against us ... is fit for the madhouse." "The whole of Germany is charged with electricity," wrote Colonel House, after visiting Berlin in May, 1914. "Everybody's nerves are tense. It only needs a spark to set the whole thing off." "Peace," the German ambassador in Paris reported, "remains at the mercy of an accident."

The Austro-Serbian Crisis of 1914

Such was the atmosphere in Europe when Francis Ferdinand, nephew of the Habsburg emperor and heir to the Austrian and Hungarian thrones, set out for his visit to the capital of Bosnia. In going to Sarajevo at this time the archduke took his life in his hands, for Bosnia was honeycombed with propaganda by two Serbian societies, "National Defense" and "Union or Death," and men were not lacking to undertake his assassination in the interest of the "greater Serbia" movement.[5] Even before the announcement of the proposed visit of the archduke, the latter of these societies had marked

[5] Many Serbs feared that the archduke's scheme for transforming the Dual Monarchy into a Trial (triple) Monarchy with autonomy for the Slavs might wean their kinsmen in the empire away from the "greater Serbia" movement.

him for assassination. His presence in Sarajevo provided the sought-for occasion, and plans were laid under the direction of Colonel Dimitriyevich, a member of the society and chief of the intelligence division of the Serbian general staff. Three Bosnian young men who volunteered to carry out the plot were furnished with the necessary pistols, ammunition, and bombs in Belgrade, and smuggled back across the frontier into Bosnia. Apparently still others were in Sarajevo on that fateful day as "reserves" in case the attempts of these three should fail.

On the morning of June 28, 1914, the archduke's party arrived in Sarajevo shortly before ten o'clock. A few minutes later, when the party was on the way to the town hall to be welcomed by the mayor, a bomb was hurled by one of the trio of conspirators. It missed its mark, however, and exploded under the car behind the one in which Francis Ferdinand and his wife were riding. Later, when the archduke was returning from the town hall, a second conspirator suddenly jumped on the running-board of the car and assassinated both the archduke and his wife.

Once more events in the Balkans precipitated a European crisis. Count Berchtold determined to use this occasion for that final reckoning with Serbia which had been desired but postponed in 1913. The Austro-Hungarian government held that Serbian propaganda, seeking to unite all Yugoslavs under the Serbian flag, must encourage such crimes and endanger the Habsburg dynasty and empire if not stopped. Austria-Hungary's efforts must now "be directed to isolating Serbia and reducing her size." Austria-Hungary consulted her ally and learned that Germany would fully support her in *whatever* action she might decide to take. This promise, given shortly after the assassination (July 6), constituted what was later called Germany's "blank check" to Austria-Hungary. Germany, naturally, was anxious to have her one dependable ally maintain her strength undiminished, and concurred in her belief that this necessitated military action against Serbia. Austria-Hungary desired only a local war between herself and Serbia, and Germany in the beginning urged rapidity of action in order to forestall intervention. Both recognized, however, the possibility that Russia would intervene in Serbia's behalf.

Berchtold now proceeded to pave the way for the desired military action. On July 7 at a ministerial council [6] meeting in Vienna the foreign minister proposed a surprise attack upon Serbia. To this Count Tisza, the Hungarian premier, objected, and so the matter was postponed. One week later, however, Tisza consented to a short-term ultimatum purposely designed to be so severe that Serbia could not accept it. Said Berchtold after the ulti-

---

[6] Matters of foreign policy were usually settled by the ministerial council, which included the Austro-Hungarian joint ministers of foreign affairs, war, and finance, the prime ministers of both Austria and Hungary, and sometimes their finance ministers.

matum had been drafted, "The text of the note, to be sent to Belgrade, as it was settled today, is such that we must reckon with the probability of war."

The ultimatum asserted that Serbia had broken her promise "to live on good neighborly terms" with Austria-Hungary by encouraging propaganda aimed against the Dual Monarchy, and declared that the latter was thus compelled to abandon its attitude of benevolent and patient forbearance in order to put an end "to the intrigues which form a perpetual menace to the tranquillity of the monarchy." The ultimatum then made several peremptory demands, the most important of which were: (1) that the Serbian government officially condemn the anti-Austrian propaganda of its citizens; (2) that it suppress all publications and societies which incited hatred and contempt of the Dual Monarchy; (3) that all anti-Austrian teachers and books be eliminated from the public schools; (4) that the public officials implicated in the anti-Austrian propaganda be dismissed; (5) that two Serbian officers, named in the ultimatum, be arrested at once; (6) that Serbia accept the collaboration of Austrian officials in the suppression of the anti-Austrian propaganda within her borders; and (7) that Serbia accept the help of Austrian officials in the investigation of those implicated in the Sarajevo crime. On July 23 the ultimatum, with a demand for an answer within forty-eight hours, was presented to Serbia.

The Entente powers' request that Austria-Hungary extend the time limit beyond the stipulated forty-eight hours was bluntly refused. Serbia consequently submitted her reply within the designated period. She offered to accede to all the demands of the ultimatum except the ones referring to the participation of Austro-Hungarian officials in the suppression of anti-Austrian propaganda and in the investigation of the Sarajevo crime. These, she asserted, would be a violation of her rights as a sovereign state. Serbia offered, however, to refer the whole matter to the Hague Court or to a decision of the great powers, if Austria considered the reply unsatisfactory. The reply was conciliatory, and most of the powers considered that it laid the basis for negotiation. The Kaiser himself believed that it removed "every reason for war." Nevertheless, Austria-Hungary asserted that the reply was unsatisfactory, severed diplomatic relations with Belgrade, and ordered partial mobilization against Serbia—which had already mobilized her army. "Vienna burst into a frenzy of delight, vast crowds parading the streets and singing patriotic songs till the small hours of the morning."

The Futile Efforts to Prevent War

Serbia's attempt to prevent war by having Austria-Hungary's ultimatum referred to the Hague Court or to a conference of the great powers had failed because of the Habsburg government's unwillingness to accept that means of settlement. Perhaps the latter still remembered how Germany had fared at the Algeciras conference. The great powers now offered various plans and made various proposals for a pacific settlement. On the day after the ultimatum was delivered to Serbia, Grey, British foreign secretary, proposed that Great Britain, France, Germany, and Italy should exert a moderating influence simultaneously in Vienna and St. Petersburg. Nothing came of this plan, however, largely because of the attitude of France and Russia, which demanded pressure on Austria-Hungary.

In this crisis Russia was determined to support Serbia and asserted that she would agree to a settlement only in so far as it involved no humiliation of the latter as an independent state. Furthermore, she believed that her own position in the Balkans demanded a strong and independent Serbia to block the way of her rival, Austria-Hungary. Apparently the tsar's foreign minister, Sazonov, hoped to prevent war by bluffing Austria-Hungary into moderation by a show of force. On July 25 the Russian government issued orders for the "period preparatory to war," and on the next day notified Austria-Hungary that, if the latter's forces crossed the Serbian frontier, the Russian army would be mobilized against the Dual Monarchy. At the same time Sazonov requested Berchtold to discuss the ultimatum with him. Meanwhile, in St. Petersburg there were many who felt that war was inevitable and that now was Russia's chance for a final reckoning with Germany and the acquisition of Constantinople and the Straits. Sazonov characterized the Austrian ultimatum as highly provocative and expressed the hope that Great Britain would proclaim her solidarity with Russia and France.

As in 1913, so now, however, Grey was chiefly interested in mediation in the interests of peace. He believed that France, Germany, Italy, and Great Britain—the powers which had no direct interest in Serbia—might act jointly in Vienna and St. Petersburg. On July 26, therefore, he proposed that these governments instruct their ambassadors in London to meet in conference with him for the purpose of discovering an issue which would prevent complications. He contemplated a procedure similar to that followed during the Balkan crisis of the preceding year. France and Italy promptly accepted the proposal, but Germany declared that she could take part in mediation only at Austria-Hungary's express wish. The latter had no such wish, and so the plan was rejected.

Germany, in turn, advocated direct conversations between Russia and Austria-Hungary, and on July 26 such conversations were initiated between Sazonov and the Austro-Hungarian ambassador in St. Petersburg. Sazonov requested that the latter be authorized to discuss a redrafting of certain points in the Austro-Hungarian ultimatum in such a way as to satisfy

Austria-Hungary's chief demands and at the same be acceptable to Serbia. Berchtold, who was resolved not to enter into negotiations regarding issues between Serbia and Austria-Hungary, at first evaded Sazonov's request and later rejected it on the ground that war had already been declared against Serbia. The declaration of war had been issued on July 28 for the specific purpose of evading further proposals for mediation. Opposed to war to the very last, Emperor Francis Joseph was tricked into giving his consent by a forged telegram stating that Serbian forces had already entered Austria-Hungary. The bombardment of Belgrade, an unfortified city, began on July 29.

This action on the part of Austria-Hungary furnished further basis for Russia's belief that the former was planning "to gobble up Serbia." At the same time it gave Russian military officers an opportunity to exert pressure for war preparation. They felt that a war between Austria-Hungary and Serbia was necessarily a war between Austria-Hungary and Russia, and therefore between Germany and Russia; while Sazonov believed that Germany was supporting Austria-Hungary and would continue to do so unless Russia made it clear that she would threaten Austria-Hungary with force in order to protect Serbia. On July 29 Russia declared mobilization against the Dual Monarchy. France approved the Russian policy and, far from exerting a moderating influence, telegraphed the promise of full French aid.

On July 29, also, Russia requested Great Britain again to press for mediation with a view to the suspension of military operations. The latter then suggested to Germany as a good basis for mediation that Austria should occupy Belgrade or other towns as pledges, while mediation should seek "to procure for Austria all possible satisfaction." This same plan had already been proposed by the Kaiser, and came to be known as the "pledge plan." Information on Russia's action together with Great Britain's attitude now caused Germany at once to address sharp warnings to Austria-Hungary, pointing out that the latter's refusal "to exchange views with St. Petersburg would be a grave mistake." Berchtold thereupon permitted the renewal of conversations at St. Petersburg the next day, but limited them to an explanation of the ultimatum and to a discussion of Austro-Russian—not Austro-Serbian—relations.

On July 30 the German ambassador at Vienna presented to Berchtold Great Britain's "pledge plan," together with the urgent request of the German chancellor, Bethmann-Hollweg, that it be accepted. "If Austria refuses all intervention, we are thus faced with a conflagration in which England would go against us, and, according to all indications, Italy and Rumania not with us, and we two would have to face four great powers. . . . Austria's political prestige, the honor of her arms as well as her legitimate demands on Serbia, could be amply preserved by the occupation of Belgrade or other places.... Under these circumstances we most urgently and earnestly submit to the considerations of the Vienna cabinet that it should accept mediation under the honorable terms specified. The responsibility for the consequences which will otherwise result would be uncommonly serious for Austria and for ourselves." Later in the day the Kaiser also sent a telegram of somewhat the same tenor to Francis Joseph. The German government thus—a little late, perhaps—finally brought a moderating influence to bear upon its Habsburg ally.

The Habsburg foreign minister, however, declined to commit himself on the thirtieth, but ordered a meeting of the ministerial council for July 31. But before the council met on that day, the Austro-Hungarian government had received other messages from German officials. When on July 30 Moltke, the chief of the German general staff, learned that the tsar had declined to stop Russia's military preparations, he at once advised Austria to mobilize against Russia and promised German aid. When Berchtold saw Moltke's telegram, he exclaimed, "Who is in charge, Bethmann or Moltke?" After news of Russia's order of general mobilization reached Berlin on the morning of July 31, Moltke again urged Austria-Hungary to proceed at once with general mobilization.

When the Austro-Hungarian council met on the morning of July 31 to formulate its own plans, therefore, it had two types of messages from Germany to consider: Bethmann-Hollweg's urgent advice to accept Great Britain's pledge plan and Moltke's equally urgent advice to order immediate general mobilization. Berchtold himself believed that warlike operations against Serbia must continue, that Austria-Hungary could not negotiate concerning the British offer so long as Russian mobilization had not been stopped, and that Austria-Hungary's demands must be accepted integrally without negotiation. The council of ministers adopted Berchtold's views, and practically repudiated the mediation proposals, as Francis Joseph clearly realized when he wrote to the Kaiser: "I am aware of the implication of my decisions, and have made them with entire confidence in the justice of God and with the certainty that your armed forces will range themselves with unalterable fidelity in favor of my Empire and the Triple Alliance." On that day Austria proclaimed mobilization against Russia, some hours after the latter had herself ordered general mobilization against Austria and Germany.

As early as July 26 Russia had begun to take far-reaching measures preparatory to general mobilization. Three days later, after news of the bombardment of Belgrade, mobilization had been ordered against Austria-Hungary. Finally, in the afternoon of July 30, the consent of the tsar to general mobilization was obtained, and on the following morning public announcement of the mobilization was made. According to Russian army orders of 1912, mobilization was not the signal for beginning hostilities. Nevertheless, it was generally understood between the French and Russian experts that mobilization was equivalent to a declaration of war, and Great Britain had warned Russia as early as July 25 "that if Russia mobilized, Germany would not be content with mere mobilization or give Russia time to carry out hers, but would probably declare war at once." On July 30, France, her ally, had urged Russia to "take no immediate steps that may give Germany any pretext for the total or partial mobilization of her forces." Germany herself had warned Russia that mobilization was a highly dangerous form of diplomatic pressure since "the purely military consideration of the questions by the general staffs would find expression, and if that button were once touched in Germany, the situation would get out of control." Yet, despite all these warnings, and at a time when Germany was at length endeavoring to restrain her ally, and when the Kaiser and the tsar were in telegraphic communication, Russia proclaimed general mobilization.

Apparently Germany had at first decided to remain quiescent unless Russia actually attacked Austria-Hungary or actually commenced war preparations against herself. But Germany's chances for success in war depended upon rapidity of action, while Russia, because of her area and her deficient transportation facilities, needed time for mobilization and concentration of her troops. In the words of Jagow, German secretary for foreign affairs, Germany "had the speed and Russia had the numbers, and the safety of the German Empire forbade that Germany should allow Russia to bring up masses of troops from all parts of her wide dominions." The German military leaders naturally failed to see the wisdom of the tsar's suggestion that both Russia and Germany carry out their mobilizations without recourse to war, while the diplomats continued "to negotiate for the welfare of our two countries and the universal peace which is so dear to our hearts." Upon receiving news of Russia's general mobilization, therefore, Germany immediately proclaimed a "threatening state of war," and later the same day, upon the demand of Moltke, presented an ultimatum demanding that Russia stop every measure of war against Germany and against Austria-Hungary within twelve hours, or German mobilization would follow. No answer was forthcoming, and on August 1 Germany declared war upon Russia.

The system of entangling alliances now began to operate, for Germany well understood that France was bound to come to the aid of Russia in just such a contingency as now existed. The German general staff had years before planned that in case of a war against Russia and France, Germany's first thrust must be against France because the latter could mobilize much more rapidly than Russia. With France defeated by an overwhelming attack, German forces could then turn against more slowly moving Russia. It was the essence of the German military plan, therefore, that attack on France should not be delayed. Germany could not wait for France to decide to attack in accordance with the latter's treaty obligations. As early as July 31 she inquired from France what course the latter would pursue in the event of war between Germany and Russia. It is now known that she was prepared to demand the handing over for the duration of the war of Toul and Verdun in case France promised neutrality. Even if the French government had aimed to stay neutral, this demand for the two fortresses would have forced France into the war, for no French government would have consented to hand over to the Germans the fortresses of Toul and Verdun, even temporarily. Germany had no opportunity to make her second demand, however, for on August 1 France replied that she would consult her own interests, and began to mobilize. On August 3 Germany declared war on France.

Meanwhile, on July 31 Great Britain had asked France and Germany whether, in case of war, they would engage to respect the neutrality of Belgium, and France had given the desired assurance. Germany, however, had declined to state her attitude. Both France and Germany had signed treaties to respect the neutrality of Belgium and Luxembourg, but, as pointed out above, German military leaders years before had decided that in order to crush France quickly it would be better to violate the neutrality of Belgium than to make a frontal attack on the French fortified eastern frontier. On August 2 German troops occupied Luxembourg despite the protests of that little state. On the same day Germany presented an ultimatum to Belgium demanding within twelve hours permission to move her troops across that country into France. She promised, if permission were granted, to guarantee Belgian independence and integrity and to pay an indemnity. On the other hand, she threatened that, if any resistance were encountered, she would treat Belgium as an enemy, and the "decision of arms" would determine her subsequent fate. Belgium refused to grant Germany's request and appealed at once to Great Britain for diplomatic support in upholding her neutrality. On August 4 German troops crossed the Belgian frontier, and Bethmann-Hollweg admitted to the Reichstag that "this is a breach of international law . . . ; the wrong we thereby commit we will try to make good as soon as our military aims have been attained."

The invasion of Belgium had its immediate effect in Great Britain, where up to this time public opinion had strongly opposed entrance into the war. Although Sir Edward Grey himself believed that Great Britain's interests demanded that she should range herself beside France and Russia if war came, the British cabinet was divided on the question. For a time, therefore, Great Britain kept her hands free and refused to commit herself regarding future action. On July 29 Bethmann-Hollweg made a strong bid for Great Britain's neutrality, promising that Germany if victorious would take no territory from France in Europe, would respect the neutrality of the Netherlands, and—if Belgium did not take sides against Germany— would respect her neutrality after the war. Grey's immediate reaction was that he could not for a moment entertain the chancellor's proposals.

Germany having failed in her effort to secure a promise of British neutrality, France next sought to attach Great Britain more closely to herself. On July 30 Cambon, the French ambassador at London, reminded Grey that their two countries had agreed in 1912 that, if peace was threatened, they would immediately discuss with each other what should be done. Cambon declared that now was the time for such discussions and suggested that the British government might promise to come to the aid of France in case of aggression by Germany. On the next day Grey stated that his government could not then give any pledge, and on August 1 he informed Cambon that "France must make her decision without reckoning on an assistance that we are not now in a position to promise."

On August 2, however, in view of Germany's declaration of war on Russia and her anticipated attack on France, Great Britain assured the latter that the British fleet would undertake to protect French coasts and shipping, should the German fleet come into the Channel or through the North Sea to attack them. This she did because as a result of her request in 1912 the French fleet was in the Mediterranean, and the northern and western coasts of France were undefended. Great Britain felt in honor bound to protect the latter, though the offer brought the resignation of two members of the cabinet.

On the following day came news of the German ultimatum to Belgium. This action threatened a cardinal principle of British foreign policy, namely, that the little countries across the narrow seas should not be absorbed by any great imperial system which might be hostile to Great Britain. In part because of this determination, Great Britain had fought against Louis XIV and Napoleon I, and had insisted during the Franco-German War that both sides respect Belgian neutrality. When, therefore, on August 4 news reached London that German troops had actually crossed the frontier into Belgium, Great Britain dispatched an ultimatum to Germany demanding assurance by midnight that Germany would respect Belgian neutrality. Germany, while admitting that Belgium's protest was just and that a wrong was being committed, refused on the ground that "necessity knows no law," and accused Great Britain of making war "just for a scrap of paper." The next day Great Britain announced that a state of war existed between herself and Germany.

By August 24 Austria-Hungary had declared war on Russia and Belgium; France and Great Britain had declared war on Austria; Serbia had declared war on Germany; and Montenegro had joined Serbia against Austria and Germany in another struggle to fulfill their common political aspirations. Early in September Russia, France, and Great Britain transformed their entente into a wartime alliance by signing the pact of London, in which each agreed not to conclude peace separately nor to demand peace terms without a previous agreement with the others.

The Question of War Guilt

Much time has been spent in trying to determine which country was primarily responsible for the outbreak of the First World War. Probably no decision will ever be reached which will satisfy all. It is obvious that the crisis of 1914 was precipitated as a consequence of propaganda carried on within the Dual Monarchy by Serbs who ardently sought to attain the national unification of all Yugoslavs. It is equally clear that fear of alienating the Magyars deterred the Habsburg government from giving the Yugoslavs within Austria-Hungary a place co-ordinate in political power with Austria and Hungary and led rather to repressive measures. The latter, in turn, made the Bosnians a fertile field for pro-Serbian propaganda, and from these disaffected Bosnians came the assassins of the archduke.

There is little doubt that after the assassination Count Berchtold and Conrad von Hötzendorf, the Habsburg chief of staff, determined to end the Yugoslav menace by crushing Serbia with military force, and that Germany definitely encouraged Austria-Hungary to take military measures against the small Slav kingdom. It seems reasonable to believe that, if Austria-Hungary had not early in the crisis received this encouragement from Germany, she would never have dared to be so intransigent in the succeeding days. At the same time it is very clear that Russia, in order to thwart Austria's further advance into the Balkans, to enhance her own prestige, and to bring herself nearer the accomplishment of her "historic mission," was determined from the outset of the crisis to go to war if necessary to prevent Serbia from being weakened in her political sovereignty or territorial integrity. And early in the crisis Russia, in turn, was encouraged by the French government, which stated that it approved of Russia's stand and that it would give her loyal support.

Great Britain, while declining to commit herself to either set of powers, sincerely sought, as in 1912–1913, to find some way out of the crisis short of war, and offered a number of plans for settlement. It appears, however, that this time Germany refused to co-operate with Great Britain as closely and as wholeheartedly as she had done in the previous crisis. Nevertheless, it must be admitted that eventually—perhaps after it was too late to influence Russia effectively—Germany did apparently exert considerable pressure upon Austria-Hungary in favor of moderation and mediation. This is more than can be stated in regard to French influence upon Russia.

On the other hand, so far as mediation is concerned, both Russia and France appeared generally more willing to accept the various plans offered than did Austria-Hungary and Germany. Whether Russia's willingness to accept mediation was dictated by her belief that thus she might gain more time for her mobilization is not clear. What is clear, however, is the fact that Austria-Hungary steadily declined to accept any and all schemes for a pacific settlement of her dispute with Serbia, even when toward the end of the crisis her own ally, Germany, strongly urged her to accept, and even though she knew her attack on Serbia would probably precipitate a general war.

It is, of course, undisputed that Russia—perhaps seeing in Austria-Hungary's actions nothing but a determination to crush Serbia and in Germany's stand nothing but a decision to support her ally—was the first great power to order general mobilization with its inevitable fatal effect on the general staffs of all the other countries. On the other hand, it is perfectly evident that Germany was the first great power to declare war on another great power, thus automatically and unavoidably transforming the Austro-Serbian war into a great European conflict. There is so much evidence which may be used against at least four of the great powers that the decision as to primary responsibility seems to be largely a matter of arranging the evidence according to the already existing bias of each investigator.

Probably the truth is that each statesman and each country did about what could be expected under the circumstances, that the sole responsibility cannot be placed on any one person or state, that they were all being driven into the abyss of war by certain fundamental or underlying forces. Anyone who will carefully study the crisis cannot help seeing that those who directed the destinies of the nations were largely the victims of the forces about them. Nationalism, imperialism, militarism, and entangling alliances all played a part in the final denouement, and the development of a great war out of the crisis was made easier because the countries of Europe—and the world generally—lived in a state of international anarchy.

The Alignment of the Powers in 1914

Two of the countries which were linked with Germany and Austria-Hungary did not join the Teutonic powers in the First World War. Berchtold had not taken Italy into his confidence in respect to his plans for sending an ultimatum to Serbia, and thus antagonized Italy at the very outset. Immediately upon learning of the ultimatum, however, the latter began to demand compensation under Article 7 of the Triple Alliance [7] and intimated that the Trentino might be considered as acceptable. Although Germany urged Austria-Hungary to offer some compensation to Italy, Berchtold was reluctant to cede any Austrian territory. In view of the Habsburg foreign minister's attitude, Italy informed her allies, just before the outbreak of hostilities between Germany and Russia, that, since the impending war was aggressive on the part of the Dual Monarchy, Italy was released from her obligations to them under the terms of the Triple Alliance. Although Berchtold stated that Austria-Hungary would be willing to consider a partition of Albania if Italy would join the Teutonic powers, the Italian government on August 3, 1914, formally declared its neutrality.

The secret Franco-Italian treaty of 1902 provided that in just such a contingency as existed in August, 1914, Italy should remain neutral. Nevertheless, it was not Italy's treaty obligations that dictated her policy so much as what her prime minister, Salandra, called "sacred egoism." In this respect, of course, she differed little from the other powers. She had always feared to lay her coasts open to attack by the British navy; her own army and navy had not yet recovered from the exhausting struggle in Tripoli; and *Italia Irredenta,* which she longed to incorporate within her own frontiers, lay within the territory of Austria-Hungary. During the opening weeks of the war Italy continued to carry on negotiations with both sets of powers to determine what she could gain from each, but her neutrality during this period contributed very materially, if indirectly, to the German defeat on the Marne by releasing French troops from the southeast for use against Germany.

Even before the outbreak of the First World War the Austrians had decided that, despite the treaty of 1883, Rumania could hardly be counted a loyal ally. She was, of course, in an advantageous position to receive bids for her aid from both sets of powers during the crisis. Russia started by offering Transylvania and a guarantee of the territory in the Dobrudja which Rumania had recently taken from Bulgaria. Austria-Hungary countered by offering Bessarabia. Although King Carol apparently advocated Rumania's entrance into the war on the side of Austria in accordance with her treaty obligations, Rumanian statesmen preferred a policy of watchful waiting. On August 3 the crown council decided in favor of neutrality, but

[7] This provided that, should Austria or Italy be obliged to change the *status quo* in the Balkans "by a temporary or a permanent occupation, such occupation would take place only after previous agreement between the two Powers, which would have to be based upon the principle of a reciprocal compensation for all territorial or other advantages that either of them might acquire over and above the existing *status quo,* and would have to satisfy the interests and rightful claims of both parties."

Rumania, like Italy, continued to negotiate with both sides. Eventually, in fact, Rumania and Italy agreed (September 23, 1914) to follow the same course during the war.

Before the year was over, however, each set of belligerents was reinforced by one more power. Early in August Great Britain asked Japan for assistance under the terms of an alliance concluded in 1902 and renewed in 1905 and 1911. Germany was already busy with warlike preparations in Kiaochow, her naval base in the Shantung peninsula, and her warships in the Far East constituted a serious menace to British commerce. One of the objects of the Anglo-Japanese alliance was the defense of the special interests of the contracting parties in eastern Asia, and Japan decided to comply with the British request and, if necessary, declare war upon Germany. Doubtless in reaching this decision Japan was more especially actuated by the desire to lessen by one the number of powers competing with her in the exploitation of China. On August 15, therefore, Japan sent an ultimatum to Germany demanding that the latter should withdraw all warships from Chinese and Japanese waters and deliver up the entire leased territory of Kiaochow before September 15 "with a view to the eventual restoration of the same to China." When Germany refused to comply with the demands of the ultimatum, Japan declared war on August 23.

The last country to be drawn into the conflict in 1914 was Turkey. In the years just preceding the First World War, German influence—political, military, commercial, and financial—had steadily increased at Constantinople, so that it was almost inevitable that Turkey should enter the struggle on the side of the Teutonic powers. This was particularly likely in view of the fact that her traditional foe, Russia, was one of the Entente powers. Upon the assassination of the archduke the Ottoman government at once sought to connect itself with the Triple Alliance. The German government, at first reluctant to consider any definite commitment to Turkey, ultimately came to look with favor upon such an alliance; and a treaty, hurriedly drafted, was accordingly signed by Germany and Turkey on August 2 at the very height of the diplomatic crisis. Drawn up before the conflict had become one between the great powers, it provided that Turkey should enter the war on the side of the Teutonic powers in case Russia intervened.

While the Entente powers, unaware of this secret alliance, sought through diplomacy to secure Ottoman neutrality, the Turks utilized the weeks spent in futile negotiations to carry out extensive military preparations. Gradually Turkey's connection with the Teutonic powers became evident. Upon the outbreak of the war two German cruisers in the Mediterranean took refuge in the harbor at Constantinople. When their officers refused either to put to sea or to be interned, the Entente powers protested, but to no avail. Later in the year Turkey closed the Dardanelles to commerce, thereby cutting Russia's communication with the Mediterranean, and again protests had no effect. On October 29 one of the German cruisers, masquerading as a Turkish ship, shelled Russian towns on the Black Sea, and three Turkish torpedo boats raided the port of Odessa. In consequence Russia, on November 3, declared war on Turkey and was followed in this action two days later by both France and Great Britain. At the close of the year, therefore, the military alignment stood: Germany, Austria-Hungary, and Turkey against Russia, France, Great Britain, Japan, Belgium, Serbia, and Montenegro. The two conflicting groups soon came to be generally called the Central Powers and the "Allies."

Chapter II

THE PERIOD

OF TEUTONIC ASCENDANCY

THE First World War differed from previous conflicts not only in the gigantic size of the armies directly engaged and the appalling numbers of casualties suffered, but in the tremendous mobilization of men and resources behind the lines for war purposes. The struggle was not confined to the battlefields alone, but was waged in factories, laboratories, and banks, on farms, railroads, and merchant ships. In the First World War nations fought nations, and strained every nerve, utilized every resource for victory.

Mobilization of Men and Resources

Even before the declarations of war were issued, mobilization of the various national armies had begun. In the belligerent countries on the Continent millions of men were under arms in time of peace, but they were scattered about the countryside and at the outbreak of the war had to be rushed to protect threatened frontiers or concentrated for the purpose of opening projected offensives. Other millions in the reserve armies had to be called to the colors. From the farm, the factory, the store, from every walk of life, men were summoned for military service. The problem of transportation was tremendous; nonmilitary service on the railways was temporarily set aside as thousands of trains hurried men and supplies to the fronts.[1]

In a war where more ammunition was used in two weeks on some of the sectors than in the whole Boer War, the men at the front required scores of thousands of field guns, hundreds of thousands of machine guns, millions of rifles, billions of shells, hundreds of billions of rounds of ammunition for small arms, besides high explosives, gases, airplanes, and tanks.

---

[1] Of the principal belligerents, Great Britain alone had no system of conscription. Lord Kitchener, veteran of many wars, was appointed head of the war office, and immediately laid plans for creating an army of seventy divisions. In the First World War British divisions consisted of about 15,000 men each; French and German, of about 12,000.

Existing armament firms were not equipped for the tremendous demands made upon them. Old factories had to be extended, new ones built, and others converted into war work. In Great Britain, especially, new factories had to be erected, new machine tools made and set up, material assembled, and labor gathered and instructed.

But the mobilization of resources was not limited to munitions. The millions at the front had also to be fed and clothed. Gradually agriculture, manufacture, transportation, and commerce became submilitary activities. As the military needs became more pressing, national boards were established, section after section of industry and transportation was brought under the direction of the governments, and standardization of products was introduced. In order to supply war requirements, production was diverted into new channels, new processes were initiated, wages and prices were fixed, strikes and lockouts were forbidden, and millions of women were mobilized for war work in factories.

The financing of the war was a task in itself and required sums far greater than any ever before raised. Eighty per cent of the total war expenditures was met by borrowing, the belligerent powers repeatedly resorting to great bond issues. National bonds were offered in amounts in some cases as low as ten dollars, and millions of people in each of the principal belligerent countries participated in the loans. Single issues were brought out and successfully floated which a few years earlier would have been considered impossible by even the best-informed financiers. Single loans of different governments ranged from $3,500,000,000 to nearly $7,000,000,000. Extensive advertising campaigns and methods of "high pressure" salesmanship were used to arouse the patriotism of those in a position to subscribe. For those who were unable to buy bonds except with borrowed money, special credit facilities were established. It soon became obvious that the prewar statements of financiers that it would be impossible for any country to finance a modern war for many weeks were in error. When the Central Powers finally collapsed, it was not because of lack of money but because of the lack of essential commodities.

War Propaganda

The prospect of a war in which the casualties might mount into the millions led each belligerent government to seek to throw the responsibility for the conflict solely upon its foes. Soon after the outbreak of hostilities each government published what purported to be the diplomatic documents exchanged during the crisis. These volumes, which took their names from the distinctive colors of their covers, became known as the white book

(Germany), the blue book (Great Britain), the orange book (Russia), the red book (Austria-Hungary), and the yellow book (France), and are sometimes referred to as the "rainbow books." Of them all the British blue book was probably the most truthful and nearly complete. By each of the other great powers documents unfavorable to its own cause were frequently suppressed or altered in order to mold the minds of its own citizens as well as those of neutral countries.

Before the war was many months old, agencies were organized by most of the belligerent countries to carry on systematic campaigns of propaganda. These campaigns usually had at least three major objectives: (1) to keep up the morale of the country's own citizens so that they would willingly make the sacrifices of men and money which would be necessary in order to bring victory; (2) to gain the good will, benevolent neutrality, or active participation in the war of those neutral countries whose assistance would be valuable in winning the struggle; (3) to weaken or destroy the morale of the citizens of the enemy countries so that the latter would be seriously handicapped in their conduct of the war.

On both sides stories of atrocities were widely circulated. When actual atrocities were not available, stories were frequently fabricated to serve the same purpose. The treatment of Belgium by the Germans, their reference to treaties as "scraps of paper," and their destruction of the lives of women and children by submarine warfare were eagerly seized upon by Allied propagandists to arouse enthusiasm for the war at home and to turn sentiment against the Central Powers in neutral countries. The severe hardships which fell upon the noncombatant population in the Teutonic countries as a result of the Allied blockade, on the other hand, were not so spectacular for propaganda purposes. Nor, apparently, did the Teutonic propagandists understand the psychology of the neutral peoples so well as did those of the Allies.

As the war progressed, each government sought to explain to the world and to its own people why it was fighting. In every case the war was defensive. The Germans, for example, were told that they were fighting to keep back the Slavic hordes of "freedom-slaying tsarism," whose triumph would bring the "end of the German people," that they were struggling to break the iron ring which the Allies had forged round Germany for the purpose of crushing the fatherland. The Allied peoples, on the other hand, were informed that they were fighting to protect the world from an aggressive and brutal militarism, to defend the sanctity of treaties and the rights of small nations. Eventually the Allied governments maintained that they were engaged in a "war to end war," a struggle "to make the world safe for democracy."

Relative Advantages of the Belligerents

For waging the war each side had certain distinct advantages. To begin with, the Central Powers possessed a much closer unity of command than did the Allies. Almost from the opening gun, and certainly after 1916, Germany overshadowed her allies, whose plans she came to direct, whose armies her officers frequently came to command. Among the Allies, on the other hand, until the very closing months of the war, lack of unity existed, and diversity of plans and lack of co-ordination resulted. The Central Powers, too, possessed a distinctly strategic advantage in their geographical position. Its compactness and the splendid network of railways made possible the prompt and efficient transfer of troops from one military front to another. Without interference from the Allies, troops could readily be shifted from the German front in France to the Austrian front in Galicia or, after 1915, even to the Turkish front in Mesopotamia. The Allies, on the other hand, were widely separated geographically. From the beginning, Russia was almost completely isolated from her allies in the west. The resources of Great Britain's far-flung empire could be utilized only after they had been gathered from the seven seas and transported through the perils of the sea to the front where they were needed. Japan was thousands of miles from the main theaters of the war and confined her activities chiefly to the Far East.

Nevertheless, the Allies possessed several very important advantages, especially in the case of a long war. They greatly outnumbered the Central Powers in man power and economic resources. If the war dragged on long enough to enable the Allies to tap their unlimited human reservoirs, the Central Powers might be overwhelmed by sheer weight of numbers. Especially was this true since the wealth of the Allies greatly exceeded the total wealth of the Central Powers. Moreover, the Allies possessed a naval supremacy which enabled them not only to marshal their own resources but to trade with neutral countries overseas. Thus they were able to utilize the food-producing and munition-producing facilities existing in extensive regions outside their own frontiers. At the same time Allied naval supremacy brought with it the power to blockade the coast lines of the Central Powers and, to a large extent, force them to depend on their own resources for the sinews of war. Throughout the conflict the Allies cheered themselves with the thought that time was on their side.

The Breakdown of German Plans for 1914

But Germany did not intend that the war should be of long duration. She aimed to strike a decisive blow at France immediately, then to wheel upon the slower-moving Russians and to defeat them in more leisurely fashion. With this end in view the "Schlieffen plan" called for the delivery of the blow not on the Franco-German frontier, which was lined with impregnable fortresses and defended by the Vosges Mountains, but through the neutral buffer states of Luxembourg and Belgium. The best railways and roads from Berlin to Paris ran through Belgium, and the French fortifications on this frontier were feeble compared with those at Belfort, Toul, and Verdun. The plan, therefore, held out the promising possibility of rolling up the French left by a wide encircling movement.[2]

On August 5 German troops attacked the Belgian fortified city of Liége, and, though temporarily halted by the stubborn defense of the Belgian army, they entered the city two days later. For a week longer some of the outlying forts held out, but on August 15 the last of them was captured, and German troops poured into the country in overwhelming numbers. On August 23 the Germans won the first resounding success of the war when they captured the reputedly impregnable fortress of Namur after a three days' bombardment by heavy howitzers. The way was at length cleared for a German invasion of France, but, because of Belgian resistance, eighteen days had been required for the march to the French frontier.

Meanwhile the French and British prepared to meet the German advance. France had failed to concentrate her forces on the Belgian frontier and so was now faced with the necessity of shifting some of her armies to that front. The British Expeditionary Force crossed the Channel without mishap and on August 22 took up positions on the French left in accordance with prearranged plans. But French fighting at Charleroi and British at Mons failed to stop the German advance, and the Allied armies began a general strategic retreat. The Germans disregarded the Channel ports, which might easily have been seized at this time, and rushed on toward Paris, their goal.

Not until September 5, at the very gates of Paris, did Joffre give up his Fabian policy of retreat. On the next day came his order "to attack and repel the enemy." For seven days (September 6–12) the first battle of the Marne raged over a front extending from Paris to Belfort, engaging more than two millions of men. But now, at length, Germany's long-planned scheme broke down under the burden of overworked troops and the impossible task of co-ordination and control which was placed on general headquarters. In the end—thanks to Joffre's strategy and the heroic efforts of Gallieni, Foch, Castelnau, and others—Paris was saved, the first German plan of campaign was wrecked, and the forces which were to have crushed France in a month were hurled back.

The main German armies now retreated to a strong position on the river

2 For the French front, see the maps on pages 42, 93, and 105.

Aisne, where trenches had been prepared for the infantry and concrete foundations for the big guns. From this position the Allies were unable to dislodge them in the first battle of the Aisne. Meanwhile, the lines of both armies were extended westward and northward, the French in an

THE WESTERN FRONT IN 1914

effort to outflank the Germans, the latter in an effort to protect themselves and to seize the Channel ports. Though the Germans succeeded in occupying Ghent, Bruges, and the coast towns of Zeebrugge and Ostend, their attempt to push on to Dunkirk, Calais, and Boulogne was thwarted by the determined resistance of the Allies, especially the British in the terrible first battle of Ypres. Thereafter the conflict in the west ceased to be a war of movement and maneuver, and settled down to trench warfare over a line extending some six hundred miles from the Channel to the Alps. For nearly four years, since there were no flanks to be turned, the aim of the strategists on both sides was to force a "break-through" by frontal assaults against heavy guns and concrete "pill-boxes" bristling with machine guns.

Although the Germans had failed to carry through their plans in the west, they had made conquests which were later of tremendous assistance to them in carrying on the war. They were in complete possession of most of Belgium and of a fairly large strip of northern France. These regions of Europe were highly developed industrially and were now added to the resources of the Central Powers. Especially valuable to Germany were the coal fields of Belgium and northern France and the iron mines of French Lorraine. In proportion as the Central Powers were strengthened by these conquests, France and the Allies were weakened. In fact, had the paths of commerce not been kept open for France by the British navy, it is difficult to see how the French could long have waged an effective war.

Meanwhile, in the east the Russian armies were mobilized more rapidly than Germany had expected. Even before German troops had reached the French frontier through Belgium, Russian soldiers were pouring into East Prussia and threatening Königsberg.[3] In alarm, the German government summoned from retirement General Paul von Hindenburg, reputed to be a specialist in the strategy and geography of a war with Russia, and appointed General Ludendorff, chief quartermaster of the Second Army in the west, as chief of the general staff of the Eighth Army in the east, with Hindenburg in command. The battle of Tannenberg which followed (August 26–31) put an end to Russian plans in East Prussia even more completely than the Marne did to German plans in the west. The bulk of the Russian army in this area was captured or destroyed; less than a third escaped. Hindenburg at once became the popular idol of the Central Powers.

But one defeat, no matter how decisive, did not mean that Russia was out of the war. Her man power was so great that she had planned to press her attack on more than one front. Simultaneously with her advance into East Prussia came her drive against the Austrians in Galicia. By September 3 the Russians had captured not only the outposts at Tarnopol and Halicz but also Lemberg, the capital of Galicia. They then promptly followed up their victory by driving the Austrians back into Jaroslav and Przemysl. To the latter, a strongly fortified city, the Russians laid siege; the former they captured on September 23. By the end of the year Russia was in complete occupation of nearly all of Galicia.

Russian successes in Galicia interfered disastrously with the Habsburg

[3] For the Russian front, see the map on page 48.

plan to punish Serbia in 1914. Austria opened the war by bombarding Belgrade on July 29, and thrice attempted a conquest of the kingdom. Although in their third attempt the Austrians succeeded in capturing Belgrade (December 2), they had held it less than two weeks when a crushing defeat at the hands of the Serbs and Montenegrins drove them out of the country. The year ended with not a single Austrian soldier on Serbian soil. But, on the other hand, Serbia's attempts to "liberate" her kinsmen in Bosnia-Herzegovina from Habsburg control had likewise met disaster. For the next few months the Austro-Serbian front was comparatively inactive.

But fighting was not restricted to Europe. Great Britain was not in a position in 1914 to be of great assistance to her allies with her armies, but she played a vital role with her fleets. Almost immediately her naval superiority swept Germany's merchant marine from the seas, and thus largely prevented the latter from importing foodstuffs and munitions of war and from marketing her products. Furthermore, the British navy, by hunting down and destroying isolated German warships, by forcing others into neutral ports, where they were interned, and by blockading the German battle squadron in its own home waters, gradually cleared the seas of these threats to Allied shipping, and made possible the gathering of Allied troops and supplies from the uttermost parts of the earth. All this was not done without some losses, however. At least ten British warships were sunk in 1914 by German submarines and mines. A number of minor naval engagements also occurred. Off the coast of Chile near Coronel (November 1, 1914), a superior German fleet defeated a British squadron, sinking two ships; but a few weeks later (December 8) a more powerful British squadron sighted the same German fleet off the Falkland Islands and destroyed every ship but one.

Not only on the seas but overseas events went against Germany, owing largely to the fact that the British navy made it impossible for her to send assistance to her colonies. Immediately after her declaration of war on Germany, Japan had begun a blockade of Kiaochow; a few days later troops were landed and a siege was begun. By November 6, 1914, the forts had been silenced, and on the tenth the German base was surrendered to Japan. By this time, too, Germany's various island possessions in the Pacific had been captured by Japanese or British colonial forces. In Africa, where the chief German colonies were located, operations were begun by Allied forces, and Togoland was soon conquered by Anglo-French armies. The other colonies held out longer, but it was only a question of time until they too would be captured.[4]

[4] German Southwest Africa was conquered in 1915, Kamerun in 1916, and German East Africa finally on November 14, 1918, after the signing of the armistice.

German Successes of 1915

In 1914 it had been Germany that had taken the offensive against France; in 1915, upon Russia's suggestion, Great Britain and France decided to undertake an offensive at the Dardanelles.[5] A successful outcome here would be especially advantageous for the Allies. In the first place, it would open a much desired communication with Russia from the Mediterranean and would relieve her from Turkish pressure on the Caucasian front. It would diminish the danger of attack on the Suez Canal and Egypt. Obviously, it would isolate Turkey from her allies and at the same time cut Germany's proposed Berlin-Bagdad railway. Finally, a decisive Allied victory here might have considerable influence in converting Greece, Rumania, or Bulgaria to the Allied cause.

The first plan called for a naval attack on the Dardanelles in the hope of forcing the heavily fortified strait. For this purpose a powerful fleet of British and French battleships was gathered, and on February 19, 1915, they began a heavy bombardment of the forts at the entrance to the Dardanelles. These forts were more or less in the nature of outposts and were soon silenced. But when, on March 18, the Allied fleet attempted to force the narrows, a Turkish minefield in an unsuspected location led to the loss of three battleships and some two thousand men. Although, unknown to the Allies, the Turkish defenders of the strait were on the verge of collapse, Admiral de Robeck became alarmed at his losses and immediately ordered a general retirement.

It was next decided that the strait must be opened by troops rather than ships. Unable to persuade any of the Balkan states to espouse their cause, the Allies were forced to provide an army of their own. At length a force made up chiefly of Australian, New Zealand, Indian, and French colonial troops was gathered together for the purpose. On April 25 the Allied troops began their Gallipoli campaign, forcing a landing on the peninsula at terrible cost. But the Turks had used the interval since the naval failure at the Dardanelles to strengthen the fortifications on the hills, so that the Allied soldiers were called upon to drive from almost impregnable positions a much stronger Turkish army under the command of a skillful German general. The Allies had expected that Russia would help divide the Turkish forces by landing 100,000 men from the Black Sea and seizing the northern outlet of the Bosporus, but this she was prevented from doing by a terrific Austro-German attack near Gorlice.[6] Three costly attempts to capture the peninsula netted the Allies nothing but the loss of some 55,000 men. The strait remained closed until the end of the war.

[5] See the map on page 50.
[6] See page 48.

While the Dardanelles and Gallipoli campaigns were being waged, it had been hoped that Italy might be persuaded to join the Allies and not only relieve Russia by engaging Austrian troops in the south but also contribute some forces for use against Turkey. At the time of the outbreak of the war in 1914 Italy, as already pointed out, proclaimed her neutrality on the ground that the Central Powers were waging an offensive war and also on the ground that Austria-Hungary had not lived up to Article 7 of the Triple Alliance. Even as early as the crisis of 1914 Italy had sought to obtain part of *Italia Irredenta* by demanding compensation of Austria in accordance with this article. Austria, however, had refused to discuss the question. On February 21, 1915, Italy forbade further Austrian operations in the Balkans until an agreement had been reached, and Austria on March 9 finally announced that she was willing to discuss the cession of territory. Then followed a period of bargaining, for, late in February, the Allies also began to offer Italy inducements to join them against the Central Powers. Naturally, the advantage in the bidding lay with the Allies, for they could generously offer Italy larger slices of Austrian territory than Austria herself was disposed to concede.

On April 26, 1915, Great Britain, France, and Russia signed with Italy the secret treaty of London. In this treaty the Allies promised Italy the Trentino and southern Tirol up to the Brenner Pass, Gorizia and Gradisca, Trieste and the Istrian peninsula, North Dalmatia and the islands facing it, Valona in Albania and a military zone about it, the Dodecanese in the Aegean, rights to the province of Adalia in case Turkey should be partitioned or divided into spheres of influence, and the extension of her possessions in Eritrea, Somaliland, and Libya in case Great Britain and France should gain colonial territory in Africa at the expense of Germany. The Allies further promised Italy a loan, a share in the war indemnity, and their support in preventing the pope from taking any diplomatic steps for the conclusion of peace or the regulation of questions arising from the war.

On May 23 Italy declared war on Austria, but not until fifteen months later did she declare war on Austria's more powerful ally. On September 5, 1915, she signed the pact of London, further binding herself not to make peace except in concert with the Allies. But the military hopes of the latter, based on Italy's entrance into the war, were sadly disappointed in 1915. Italy sent no troops to aid in the Gallipoli campaign, asserting, like France, that they could not be spared from the home front. Furthermore, in spite of her field army of a million and her reserve force of two million, Italy's attacks along the Isonzo and in the Trentino made little headway because of the difficult terrain [7] and apparently contributed not at all to relieving the increasing Teutonic pressure on Russia.

[7] For the Italian front, see the map on page 74.

And Russia, by this time, was in need of all the assistance she could get. At the opening of the year her prospects had, indeed, looked bright. During the preceding months she had occupied nearly all of Galicia, and on March 22, 1915, she had finally captured the powerful Austrian fortress of Przemysl, besieged since the preceding November. In Allied countries it was believed that the year would see Russian troops pouring over the Carpathians onto the Hungarian plains. By 1915, however, Russia's supply of munitions was getting low, and the possibilities of adequate replenishment were scant. Russia was primarily a peasant country; her factories for the manufacture of munitions were few; and her means of importing and transporting war material to the front were inadequate. Corruption, too, had already begun to undermine her armies and to sap their strength.

On the other hand, the Central Powers were generously supplied with heavy guns, shells, rifles, and other war material. This year, trusting the trench system to hold with fewer men in the west, they transferred thousands of seasoned German troops to the east until, by April, 1915, they had a combined Austro-German army of two million men, with heavy batteries numbering at least 1500 guns. This force they entrusted to General Mackensen. Suddenly, on May 1, the tables were turned on the eastern front; Russia ceased to be the attacker and became the attacked. The heavy Teutonic batteries were loosed against the Russian lines near Gorlice in Galicia, and the Russian trenches were simply blown out of existence. The Russians, inadequately equipped with heavy guns, could not check the attack. With the capture of Gorlice, their defense collapsed. In less than two months nearly all of Galicia, with its oil wells, mines, and other resources, was regained by the Central Powers. With it, too, came the temporary abandonment by Rumania of her thought of joining the Allies.

But the reconquest of Galicia was only one phase of the projected Austro-German campaign to put the Russian armies out of action. Success in this phase, however, rendered the next step more easy, for the Russian armies in Poland were now open to attack from both the north and the south. Pressure from both directions was brought to bear by the Central Powers, whose consistent successes led, on August 4, to the Russian evacuation of Warsaw and Ivangorod. Not content with the capture of these strongholds, the Teutonic troops pushed on, taking Kovno, Brest-Litovsk, Grodno, Pinsk, and Vilna, finally driving the Russians behind the Pripet marshes. With winter coming on, the Central Powers had no desire to court the fate of Napoleon, so they now halted their advance. At the close of the campaign, therefore, the Central Powers had driven the Russians out of most of Galicia, all of Poland and Courland, and part of Lithuania. Thanks largely to the masterly retreat conducted by Grand Duke Nicholas, the Teutonic forces had neither captured nor destroyed the Russian armies;

but they had rolled them back a safe distance and had inflicted tremendous casualties. Moreover, the region seized constituted one of Russia's important industrial areas, and its loss greatly lessened her ability to wage a large-scale war.

THE EASTERN FRONT IN 1915

By September, 1915, the Central Powers were free to look for other fields to conquer. As a result of their campaigns against Russia they had shortened and straightened their eastern front so that they could now hold that advanced position with fewer men than the old line required. The developments on the western front during the year had proved that the German entrenched positions there could not be broken by the Allies with the men and munitions which they then had at their disposal. Italy's efforts along the Isonzo and in the Trentino were being defeated largely by the terrain. In these circumstances, the Central Powers determined to administer to Serbia her long-delayed chastisement. Before the end of August they had begun to shift troops from the Russian to the Serbian front.

Meanwhile, under pressure from Teutonic general headquarters negotiations were being pushed with Bulgaria looking toward her joining the Central Powers in the contemplated attack upon Serbia. It proved to be not particularly difficult to win this country to the cause of the Central Powers, for in 1915 the latter seemed to be the winning combination in the war, and the territory which Bulgaria desired to annex in Macedonia lay chiefly within the Serbian frontiers. At length, on September 3, a military convention was signed, according to which the Central Powers and Bulgaria were to have their troops on the Serbian frontier ready for operations early in October, and General Mackensen, who had been largely responsible for the German success at Gorlice, was to take supreme charge of all troops. Bulgaria promised to allow absolutely unrestricted transport of Teutonic troops and material to and from Turkey as soon as the way through Serbia should be open; while Germany, on the other hand, agreed to grant Bulgaria a loan and to supply her with munitions to the extent that her own needs would permit. Bulgaria was to receive Serbian Macedonia; Saloniki and Epirus, in case Greece joined the Allies; and a large portion of the Dobrudja, if Rumania attacked her. Furthermore, in order to neutralize possible offers of the Allies, the Central Powers compelled the Ottoman government to promise Bulgaria territory in eastern Thrace.

On October 7, 1915, the forces of the Central Powers crossed the Danube into Serbia. Four days later the Bulgarians crossed the eastern frontier, striking the Serbians on the flank. The latter were overwhelmingly outnumbered in men and material, and within the next two months Belgrade, Nish, Novibazar, Prisrend, and Monastir were taken by the Central Powers. The Serbian army, reduced to scattered bands of retreating refugees, fled into Montenegro and Albania. But even there they found no safety, for the Austrians pushed on into the former and completely conquered it. By the end of February, 1916, Austrian and Bulgarian forces had expelled the Serbs and Montenegrins from northern Albania, capturing Tirana, the capital, and Durazzo, one of the chief Adriatic ports. Only on the Greek island of Corfu, where they were protected by Allied naval batteries, did the Yugoslavs eventually find a safe refuge from the Central Powers.

The Allied attempt to come to the aid of Serbia had been an inglorious failure. Trusting until too late that Bulgaria would not join the Central Powers or that, if she did, Greece would carry out her part of the Greco-

THE BALKAN AREA IN THE FIRST WORLD WAR

Serbian alliance,[8] the Allies had made no preparations to aid Serbia before September, 1915. As soon as Bulgaria actually mobilized, Greece did likewise, and the Greek premier, Eleutherios Venizelos, asked the Allies to send a force of 150,000 men to co-operate with Greece in support of Serbia. But King Constantine later decided that the interests of Greece could best be served by neutrality, dismissed Venizelos, and refused to enter the war. The Allied forces which landed at Saloniki on October 5 were not only too few to render effective aid to Serbia; they were so few that their own position soon became precarious in view of the successes of the Central Powers. After repeated and loud appeals for help from General Sarrail at Saloniki, the Allies eventually permitted the forces at Gallipoli to be transferred from that disastrous venture to one which, till that moment, had been only a little less disastrous.

Not only on land but on the sea as well Germany launched an offensive in 1915. Her naval leaders, during the early part of the war, held the view that an offensive by the German battle fleet was advisable only under extraordinarily favorable circumstances because the risk of a decisive action against the infinitely superior naval forces of the Allies was too great. An offensive with a view to forcing a decision by this means was therefore not undertaken. The Allies, however, were using their naval superiority to prevent the importation of war materials by the Central Powers, whose merchant ships had been swept from the seas. Great Britain not only seized and searched neutral vessels which might be carrying contraband, but gradually extended the definition of contraband. The United States, the chief neutral country of the world, was concerned with preserving open routes to the neutral countries of Europe and an open market in Europe for noncontraband goods, and accordingly proposed that the declaration of London (1909) regarding contraband should be generally accepted. This declaration had left such articles as copper and rubber on the noncontraband list and would have permitted the importation of foodstuffs by the Central Powers. But Great Britain had never ratified this declaration and refused the American suggestion.

Early in 1915, therefore, Germany decided upon the unrestricted use of submarines against all vessels of the Allied countries. Her naval staff believed that the submarines would prevent Great Britain from bringing her military forces to play on the Continent to the same extent as hitherto, and that this would have the effect of breaking the fighting spirit of the other members of the Entente. Accordingly, on February 4, 1915, Germany

[8] In 1913 Greece and Serbia had signed a treaty and military convention in which it was provided that "in case of a sudden attack by . . . the Bulgarian army against the Hellenic or Serbian army, the two states . . . promise to each other mutual military support, Greece with all her land and sea forces, and Serbia with all her land forces." Constantine maintained that this applied only to a Balkan war, not to a general European war

designated the waters about the British Isles as a "war zone" in which
enemy merchantmen would be sunk, and in which even neutral merchantmen might accidentally suffer a like fate. This step she justified on the
ground of self-preservation and as a justifiable countermeasure against "the
war of starvation which had been initiated against the noncombatant population of Germany" by Great Britain's classifying as contraband all foodstuffs intended for consumption in that country.

In response to an American note on the subject, Germany asserted that,
if Great Britain would permit the importation of food and raw materials
in accordance with the declaration of London, Germany would abandon
her unrestricted submarine campaign. Great Britain, while willing to permit the importation of food in case Germany lifted the submarine blockade,
refused to allow the importation of raw materials, and announced on
March 1 that she intended to intercept all overseas trade with Germany,
to detain all goods, and to bring neutrals into British ports for search. The
situation for neutrals came to resemble that at the time of the British and
Napoleonic decrees in the early years of the nineteenth century. Anti-
British feeling, which was rising in the United States, subsided, however,
when a German submarine sank without warning the great British liner
Lusitania, with a loss of some twelve hundred lives, of which over one
hundred were American. The fact that the ship was carrying cases of munitions for the Allies (denied at the time) in no way lessened the horror
which the deed evoked, and a wave of anti-German sentiment swept over
the United States.

Within a week an American note demanded that Germany disavow the
sinking, make reparation, and take immediate steps to prevent the recurrence of such acts. When the German government sought to extenuate the
tragedy, a second American note convinced Bethmann-Hollweg that the
United States was determined to resist the submarine campaign as then
being waged. Allied countermeasures, moreover, and the scarcity of submarines had prevented the campaign from exerting any perceptible influence on Great Britain's warlike operations. Germany therefore decided that
the slight results did not warrant a policy which might bring the United
States into the war, and ordered her submarine commanders to cease attacking passenger vessels. No public announcement of this decision was
made at the time, however. It was only in September that Count Bernstorff,
German ambassador to the United States, promised that liners would not
be sunk without warning by German submarines, provided the liners did
not try to escape or offer resistance.[9] Although nearly a thousand Allied

[9] Early in 1916 the German government finally expressed regret for the death of Americans
caused by the sinking of the *Lusitania,* recognized Germany's liability therefor, and promised
reparation by the payment of an indemnity.

and neutral ships were put out of use by the submarine campaign during 1915, Germany's counteroffensive on the seas during this year was a failure and was so recognized by German headquarters.

Teutonic achievements in 1914 and 1915, however, had done much to realize the German dream of a *Mittel-Europa* and a *Drang nach Osten*. The industrial regions of Belgium and northern France, Poland, parts of Lithuania and the Baltic provinces, Serbia, Montenegro, and northern Albania had all been successively conquered and held. Bulgaria and Turkey had become subsidiary allies, and the latter's repulse and final capture (Kut-el-Amara, April 29, 1916) of the British force which, under General Townshend, had attempted to conquer Bagdad, augured well for the future. All that seemed to remain to be done was to defeat decisively the Allied forces in the west, and then dictate a peace commensurate with Teutonic achievements. German headquarters clearly realized that Germany could not be content to stand on the defensive, because the Allies, thanks to their superiority in men and material, were increasing their resources much more than the Central Powers. If this situation continued, the time would come when the balance of numbers itself would deprive Germany of all remaining hope. The German people, too, were growing impatient of victories which brought no decision in the war. A decisive blow must therefore be struck in 1916.

German Failure to End the War in 1916

During the winter of 1915–1916 the Teutonic powers considered which of the principal Allies should be their victim. Austria pressed for an overwhelming Austro-German attack upon Italy, but German headquarters vetoed this proposal, pointing out that victory on this front would have no effect on the attitude of France and Great Britain. Besides, it was argued, domestic conditions in Italy would soon make her further active participation in the war impossible. The same argument held good for Russia, whose rapidly multiplying domestic difficulties were expected to force her to give in within a relatively short time.

The western front was therefore chosen as the area of attack, and Verdun was selected as the objective. The French lines at this point were only about ten miles from the German railway communications. An Allied drive here might conceivably render the whole German front in France and Belgium untenable. Furthermore, the German leaders felt that France had already strained herself almost to the breaking point; the breaking point might be reached if Germany could convince the French that in a military sense they had no further ground for hope. Verdun was an objective for the retention of which the French would be compelled to throw in every man they had. If they did so, Germany argued, the forces of France would bleed to death; if they did not do so, and Germany captured the city, the effect on French morale would be disastrous.

On February 21 the German attack was opened by a bombardment even more terrific than that which had preceded the campaign against Russia in the spring of 1915. "For twelve and a half hours guns of every calibre poured 100,000 shells per hour on a front of six miles. History had never seen so furious a fire. It blotted out the French first lines, it shattered the communication trenches, it tore the woods into splinters, and altered the very shape of the hills." [10] Then, after scouts had ascertained that the bombardment had accomplished its work of destruction, after the German guns had changed their range and placed a "curtain of fire" behind the French trenches, the German infantry at a quarter to five in the evening moved forward and occupied the French first line with comparative safety. The Germans expected to be in Verdun in four days.

But the Germans had miscalculated the date of their entrance into Paris in 1914; they soon discovered that they had again erred in 1916. Pétain, who had been successful in conducting French offensives at Arras and in Champagne in 1915, was immediately put in command, and reinforcements were rushed to the scene. Responding to the battle cry, "They shall not pass," the French held on while the conflict raged back and forth about the city. With only a slight slackening of effort on either side, the struggle continued through March, April, and May. With a determination little less than that of the French, the German troops fought doggedly on toward their objective. In June, when the Germans got within four miles of the city, even Joffre doubted whether Verdun could be held. But the French, now led by Nivelle, struck back and on June 30 recovered ground and neutralized the German advantage. On the following day the British launched a drive on the Somme, and the center of activity shifted farther to the west, where the Germans, in turn, were now forced to stand on the defensive. Intermittent fighting continued in the Verdun sector during the summer and fall, but for all practical purposes the battle of Verdun was ended.

The result was a distinct victory for the French. The Germans had failed to achieve any of the results which they had expected from their attack. They had not broken the French front, nor entered the city of Verdun, nor bled France to death. They had not even lured the British into a premature offensive, as they had hoped. They had won a few square miles of territory, but the price they had paid in the irreparable loss of troops was out of all proportion to the gain which they had made.[11] Fighting against

[10] John Buchan, *A History of the Great War,* Volume II, pages 547–548.

[11] German casualties at Verdun were 427,000 killed, wounded, or missing; French casualties were 535,000.

THE GERMAN HIGH COMMAND IN THE FIRST WORLD WAR

Hindenburg, William II, Ludendorff

the French in the west, they discovered, was quite different from fighting against an ill-equipped foe in the east. Falkenhayn was dismissed, and Hindenburg was elevated to the supreme command of the German armies, with Ludendorff as his assistant.

While the struggle for Verdun was in progress, the most important naval engagement of the war was fought in the North Sea. As already pointed out, German naval policy was not to risk a decisive action until, by the process of attrition, British forces had been so weakened as to give the German fleet good prospects of victory. With a view to destroying part of the British fleet, Vice-Admiral Hipper with scouting forces was ordered to demonstrate off the southwest coast of Norway in the hope of luring a British squadron out. The German battle fleet, under Vice-Admiral Scheer, was to remain out of sight until the British squadron appeared, when it would rush in to annihilate it. Early in the morning of May 31, 1916, the German fleet sailed forth.

Unknown to the Germans, however, the British battle fleet on May 30 was ordered to concentrate in the North Sea. Early in the following afternoon the British scouting squadron under Vice-Admiral Beatty and the German squadron under Hipper made contact. The latter, hoping to draw the British on, fell back toward the German battle fleet some fifty miles distant. A running engagement occurred until Beatty discovered that he had encountered the more powerful German battle fleet, whereupon the British light squadron turned and attempted to draw the Germans toward the British high-seas fleet. Late in the afternoon the latter came in sight and succeeded in placing itself between the German fleet and its home base. The scene seemed to be set for a gigantic naval engagement, more than 250 ships being present in the two fleets.

But the German fleet maneuvered with the sole object of avoiding an engagement and returning to its base. This the British prevented so long as it was light, and planned on a decisive engagement on the following day. During the night, however, the German fleet managed to cut its way through a weaker section of the British battle line, and returned to Helgoland. The question of victory was a matter of dispute at the time, and the battle of Jutland is still being fought by experts. Nevertheless, although the British lost fourteen ships to the Germans' eleven and suffered more than twice as many casualties, they were left in control of the sea. Only once afterward did the German high-seas fleet venture forth from its base, and then, upon being warned of the approach of the British battle fleet, it at once fled.

Meanwhile, although German headquarters had vetoed the Austrian suggestion of a combined Austro-German attack upon Italy when the proposal had been made during the preceding winter, the Austrian general staff determined to carry out the plan with its own resources. It chose as its point of attack the salient of the Trentino, which ran down to the Lombard plain, threatening the Italian left flank. The Austrian objective was to be the Venetian plain, through which ran the two railway lines which were the main communications with the Isonzo front. If they could cut one, the Isonzo army would be crippled and compelled to retreat; if both, it might be pocketed and disastrously defeated. For the projected drive a force of about 400,000 men was gathered in the Trentino and placed under the command of Archduke Charles, heir apparent to the Habsburg thrones.

On May 14 the preliminary bombardment began with over two thousand guns on a thirty-mile front. The Italians fell back, suffering heavy casualties. Cadorna, commander-in-chief of the Italian armies, immediately summoned his reserves to assemble around Vicenza, a stronghold protecting the northern railway line to the east, but the transfer of a new army of nearly a half million from the reserve lines of the Isonzo required time. The Italian brigades strove heroically to hold back the Austrians in the ensuing days, in some places sacrificing more than half of their strength. Nevertheless, on June 4 the Austrian troops were only eighteen miles from Vicenza. But by this time Cadorna had received his reinforcements, and soon thereafter the Italian troops repulsed what proved to be the last of the great Austrian attacks. Within a few days Cadorna began to move forward in a counterstroke. The Austrian plan to force the retirement or capture of the Italian army on the Isonzo front had failed.

One of the chief reasons why the Austrians were forced to relax their efforts against the Italians in the Trentino was the unexpected launching of a Russian attack on the eastern front on June 4. The Austrian lines in the east had been weakened not only by the withdrawal of troops for use in the Trentino offensive but by the withdrawal of artillery as well. When, therefore, the Russians suddenly attacked along almost the entire front from the Pripet marshes southward to Rumania, they met relatively little resistance. Near Lutsk they broke through the Austrian lines and within two days opened a gap fully thirty miles wide. By June 16, in twelve days of fighting in this vicinity, they had taken Lutsk and Dubno, had advanced some fifty miles from their original lines, and had reached the Galician frontier. Thousands of men had been captured, together with numerous guns and great quantities of war material. Meanwhile, in Bukowina, Czernowitz had been taken on June 10; and a week later the Russians were in possession of most of the province.

The Russian headquarters had not anticipated such a sweeping success, however, and failed to have at hand adequate reserves to take advantage of their opportunity. Teutonic forces were rushed to the threatened area from the French, Italian, and Balkan fronts, and Austrian operations were put more completely under the control of German headquarters. Opposed by German and more trustworthy Austrian divisions, the Russian advance slackened. Some Russian gains were made during July and August, but by the middle of the latter month the drive had spent itself, and it came to an end principally for lack of war materials with which to carry it on. Nevertheless, the effect of the Russian drive had been favorably felt by Allied armies before Verdun, on the Somme, in the Trentino, and along the Isonzo.

Just before the conclusion of the Russian offensive, the Italians succeeded in pushing back the Austrians a safe distance in the Trentino, and then transferred their heavy guns to the Isonzo front, where they launched an attack on August 4. Five days later, in spite of stubborn resistance by the Austrians on the heights beyond the river, Gorizia fell and the immediate Italian objective was attained. Because of the difficult terrain in which they operated, however, they were still a long way from capturing the coveted port of Trieste.

By now the western front was once more ablaze, this time the Allies taking the offensive. The British had chosen to wait until ample reserves of troops and munitions were at hand for a prolonged effort. In the first months of the Verdun drive, therefore, no great counterblow was delivered on the western front, much to the consternation of German headquarters. But when, at length, Italy had checked the Austrians in the Trentino, the Russians had put nearly half a million Austrians out of action by their unexpected drive in the east, and the British forces were well equipped with all the materials of war and thousands of reserve troops,[12] then, finally, the Allies determined to make a supreme effort in the west, and chose as their field of operations the valley of the Somme.

The aims of the Allies were threefold: to relieve the pressure on Verdun; to prevent the transfer of large bodies of troops from the western front to meet the Russian advance in the east; to exercise a steady and continuous pressure for a long period of time on one definite section of the German lines for the purpose of depleting the Teutonic forces. The Allies had created a military machine which they believed at last to be superior to that of the enemy. During all the last week of June they subjected the German lines in the Somme valley to a terrific bombardment in an effort to wipe out the opposing trenches. In that week more munitions were used by the big guns each day than the total amount manufactured in Great Britain during the first eleven months of the war. Then, on July 1, along a twenty-five-mile front the Allied infantry leaped to the attack. From then until November 18, when the weather finally rang down the curtain on the

---

[12] Dissatisfied with the results of the system of voluntary enlistment, Great Britain in January, 1916, had adopted a system of conscription.

drama in the west, the battle raged with only one intermission in September.

To the general public the Allied drive on the Somme seemed a failure, for it wrested only about 120 square miles of territory from the enemy. Nevertheless, it did succeed in doing three things. It relieved Verdun, and transferred the offensive in the west from Germany to the Allies; it held the bulk of the German army on the western front; and it wore down the German forces tremendously, for the latter suffered some 445,322 casualties to the British 419,654. The major purpose of the campaign, the acute attrition of German forces, was attained. Still more tangible evidence of the success of the drive was to be given in the spring of 1917.

The German failure at Verdun and the Austrian failure in the Trentino, followed by the Russian advance into Galicia and Bukowina, the Allied drive on the Somme, and the Italian capture of Gorizia, all had their effect on Rumania, which, up to this time, had remained a restless and uneasy neutral. In 1914 King Carol had urged Rumania's intervention on the side of Austria in accordance with the treaty of 1883, but the Rumanian crown council had overruled him in favor of neutrality. Germany's suggestion that Francis Joseph should offer Rumania territorial compensations was vetoed by the Hungarian premier, Tisza. On the other hand, Russia's offer of Transylvania and a guarantee of the territory in the Dobrudja which Rumania had recently taken from Bulgaria likewise failed to bring about her intervention. Russia's disastrous defeat in 1915, followed by the intervention of Bulgaria and the Teutonic conquest of Serbia, soon drove from the minds of Rumanian statesmen any thought of immediate entrance into the war on the side of the Allies.

But with Russia's spectacular drive against the Austrians in June, 1916, came another change, and during the summer Allied statesmen negotiated with Rumania in the attempt to gain her support. In the end a secret treaty was signed between Great Britain, France, Russia, Italy, and Rumania, promising to the latter the Banat of Temesvar, Transylvania, and Bukowina. In addition the Allies promised the simultaneous assistance of both the Russian forces in Bukowina and the Allied forces at Saloniki. On August 27 Rumania declared war on Austria, asserting that "Rumania, governed by the necessity of safeguarding her racial interests, finds herself forced to enter into line by the side of those who are able to assure her the realization of her national unity."

On August 28 Rumanian troops, in an effort to close in on the Austrians from the north and the south, crossed the frontier into Transylvania at eighteen different points.[13] But, for several reasons, they advanced not to victory but to defeat. In the first place, they were fatally short of heavy guns,

---

[13] For the Rumanian front, see the map on page 50.

airplanes, machine guns, and even rifles, and they had no great reserve of ammunition. Russia had guaranteed an ample supply of munitions, but the promise was not fulfilled. In the second place, they failed to receive the promised co-operation of the Allied armies. Russia's progress in the Carpathians was counted upon to divert the Austrian left wing in Transylvania, and Sarrail's advance from Saloniki was expected to engage the attention of Bulgaria; but neither of these developments occurred. Exhaustion of men and munitions, after a four months' campaign against Teutonic troops, prevented the Russian armies from carrying out their part of the bargain; and Sarrail, with a large but heterogeneous and poorly equipped army at Saloniki, hesitated to strike northward in a vigorous offensive lest a hostile Greek army attack him suddenly from the rear.

During the first three weeks of her campaign Rumania conquered about a quarter of Transylvania. But Mackensen was immediately dispatched to command a Bulgar-Teutonic army on the southern frontier of Rumania, while Falkenhayn took charge of the Austro-German forces facing the Rumanians in Transylvania. Heavy guns and immense supplies of munitions were rushed to the east. A simultaneous advance on the Transylvania and Dobrudja fronts then followed, and the Rumanian armies were soon in flight for safety. By the middle of October Transylvania had been cleared of Rumanian troops, and the invasion of Rumania itself began. Constanza fell on October 22, Bucharest on December 6. By the middle of the following month, the Central Powers had occupied all the Dobrudja, all Wallachia, and a portion of southern Moldavia, and had driven the Rumanian government to Jassy.

The net result of Rumania's entry into the war thus seemed favorable to the Central Powers. The fertile grain fields and rich oil wells of that unfortunate country were added to *Mittel-Europa's* economic resources. The menace of Rumania's long-delayed intervention was removed, and the Central Powers now held their lines in the east with actually fewer men than had formerly been required. Teutonic prestige, which had been badly shaken by earlier events of the year, was once more restored. The Central Powers determined to capitalize this latest achievement and to seize the favorable position created by the fall of Bucharest to make a peace offer.

Peace Proposals of the Central Powers

For some months Germany had been hoping that the President of the United States would propose mediation. Almost from the beginning of the war President Wilson had considered mediation, and in January, 1915, he had sent Colonel E. M. House to Europe as his private and personal representative to discover, by conversations with persons of high authority in the belligerent countries, the possible attitude toward mediation. In 1915 Colonel House had found, however, that, although everybody seemed to want peace, nobody was willing to concede enough to get it; that none of the belligerents was willing to yield an iota of its aspirations; that France and Germany especially wanted annexations; and that both the Allies and the Central Powers expected to win the war and to impose their own terms. "Mothers and wives, fathers and brothers," he had discovered, desired peace, but not the governing groups.

A year later Colonel House again sounded out opinion in Berlin, Paris, and London, but in none of these capitals were the leaders disposed toward a compromise peace. In a move toward possible mediation, in February, 1916, he informed the British government in confidence that President Wilson was ready, on hearing from France and Great Britain that the moment was opportune, to propose that a conference should be summoned to put an end to the war; and that, should the Allies accept this proposal and should Germany refuse it, the United States would probably enter the war against Germany. And, since the United States was not offering assistance merely for the sake of enabling the Allies to satisfy their national aspirations and to destroy Germany politically and economically, Colonel House outlined what he considered reasonable terms of peace.[14] But the Allies were determined to fight until the utter collapse of Germany, were confident of ultimate victory, and stated that the time was premature for mediation.

Although the Allies were not interested in President Wilson's proposed mediation, the Central Powers had reached the place where they were favorably disposed toward peace proposals. When, for various reasons, President Wilson delayed making any open proposal of mediation, therefore, the Central Powers at length decided to make one themselves. They believed that, in view of their decisive defeat of Rumania, they would run little risk of damaging their prestige or showing signs of weakness, and that, if the Allies rejected their offer, the odium of continuing the war would fall upon them.

Accordingly, on December 12, 1916, less than a week after the fall of Bucharest, Germany transmitted a note to France, Great Britain, Russia, Japan, Serbia, and Rumania. Animated "by the desire to stem the flood of blood and to bring the horrors of war to an end," the Central Powers proposed peace negotiations. Although the latest events had demonstrated that the war could not break their resisting power, they professed to have no desire to crush or annihilate their adversaries. They felt sure that the

---

[14] These included: (1) complete restoration of Belgium and Serbia; (2) return of Alsace-Lorraine to France; (3) cession of Constantinople to Russia; (4) surrender of *Italia Irredenta* to Italy; (5) creation of an independent Poland; (6) compensation for Germany outside Europe; (7) abolition of competitive armaments; (8) guarantees against military aggression.

propositions which they would bring forward in the negotiations would be such as to serve as a basis for the restoration of lasting peace. But if, in spite of this offer of peace and conciliation, the struggle should continue, the four Central Powers were resolved to carry it on to the end, "while solemnly disclaiming any responsibility before mankind and history." As to the final outcome in the latter case, there could be little doubt, for Germany and her allies had already given proof of their indestructible strength in winning successes at war.

The weak feature of the German note was the absence of any definite terms of peace. In respect to this matter Germany was in an embarrassing position. If she proposed terms which would be moderate enough to invite serious discussion by the Allies, the German people would question the much-advertised success of the Central Powers, and their morale might be weakened or destroyed. On the other hand, if she formulated terms in accordance with popular expectations and the demands of her military leaders, the Allies could assert that peace with victorious Germany would mean a Germanized world, and Allied morale would be enormously strengthened.[15]

An official reply to Germany was presented on December 30 in the collective name of Russia, France, Great Britain, Japan, Italy, Serbia, Belgium, Montenegro, Portugal, and Rumania. The mere suggestion, without statement of terms, that negotiations should be opened, was not, they asserted, an offer of peace but a war maneuver, a calculated attempt to influence the future course of the war, and to end it by imposing a German peace. The object of Germany's overtures, they declared, was to create dissension in public opinion in Allied countries, and to stiffen public opinion in the

---

[15] The terms upon which the Central Powers would have been prepared to take part in peace negotiations were later transmitted in confidence to President Wilson in a telegram of January 29, 1917, and are quoted by Count Bernstorff in *My Three Years in America,* page 377. They were:

"The restitution to France of that part of Upper Alsace occupied by her. The acquisition of a strategical and economic safety-frontier-zone, separating Germany and Poland from Russia.

"Colonial restitution in the form of an understanding which would secure Germany colonial possessions compatible with the size of her population and the importance of her economic interests.

"Restoration of those parts of France occupied by Germany, on condition that certain strategic and economic modifications of the frontier be allowed, as also financial compensation.

"Restitution of Belgium under definite guarantees for the safety of Germany, which would have to be determined by means of negotiations with the Belgian Government.

"Economic and financial settlement, on the basis of exchange, of the territory invaded by both sides, and to be restituted by the conclusion of peace.

"Compensation for German undertakings and private persons who have suffered damage through the war.

"Renunciation of all economic arrangements and measures, which after the peace would constitute an obstacle in the way of normal commerce and trade, with the conclusion of corresponding commercial treaties.

"The freedom of the seas to be placed on a secure basis."

Central Powers, "already severely tried by their losses, worn out by economic pressure and crushed by the supreme effort which has been imposed upon their inhabitants." They denied that the Central Powers had won the victory; the "war map" of Europe represented nothing more than "a superficial and passing phase of the situation, and not the real strength of the belligerents." The Allied governments, therefore, fully conscious of the gravity of the moment, but equally conscious of its requirements, refused to consider a proposal which was "empty and insincere."

The rejection of the German proposal was followed by a new German note to the neutral governments, stating that the Central Powers had made an honest attempt to terminate the war and pave the way for an understanding among the belligerents; that it had depended solely on the decision of the Allies whether the road to peace should be taken or not; that the latter had refused to take this road, and on them fell the full responsibility for the continuation of bloodshed. As for the Central Powers, they would prosecute the fight with calm trust and confidence in their good cause until a peace had been gained. "In your just anger at the boundless frivolity of our foes," the Kaiser proclaimed to his troops, "in your firm will to defend our holiest possessions, your hearts will turn to steel. Our enemies have not desired the hand of understanding I have offered them. With God's help our arms will compel them to accept it."

Chapter III

AMERICA'S INTERVENTION
AND RUSSIA'S WITHDRAWAL

ALTHOUGH the Central Powers had presented a bold front in their proposals for peace negotiations in December, 1916, they realized that time was running against them. They had hoped by a tremendous blow to capture Verdun in 1916 and force the Allies to consent to a peace. But their blow had been parried, and they in turn had been forced to take the defensive on the Somme, on the Isonzo, and on the Sereth. Their attempted submarine campaign had failed and had had to be abandoned; their high-seas fleet had met the British at Jutland and been forced to flee for safety to the protective guns of Helgoland. The Allied blockade had already created such an alarming food situation within their territories that riots had begun to break out and a practical food dictatorship had been established. In the face of all these developments the Central Powers realized that their spectacular triumph over Rumania counted for little; hence their desire for immediate peace negotiations at the close of 1916.

Germany's Unrestricted Submarine Campaign

The Allied reception of their peace proposal brought little comfort to the Central Powers, and still less did the subsequent announcement of the Allied war aims. In December, 1916, shortly after the Central Powers had made their peace proposals, President Wilson invited the various belligerents to state "their respective views as to the terms upon which the war might be concluded." While the Central Powers in their reply to the President did no more than "propose an immediate meeting of the delegates of the belligerent states at some neutral place," the Allied Powers went into greater detail. Their war aims, they said, implied: (1) the restoration of Belgium, Serbia, and Montenegro, with the compensations due them; (2) the evacuation of the invaded territories in France, Russia, and Rumania, with just reparation; (3) the restitution of provinces formerly torn from the Allies by force or against the wish of their inhabitants; (4) the liberation of the Italians, the Slavs, the Rumanians, and the Czechoslovaks from foreign domination; (5) the setting free of the populations subject to the bloody tyranny of the Turk; (6) the expulsion from Europe of the Ottoman Empire as decidedly foreign to western civilization. The prospect of such terms drove the German government to a new decision.

For some time both Hindenburg and Ludendorff had been urging the resumption of unrestricted submarine warfare. They had come finally to the conclusion that only by this means could Germany force the Allies to accept peace. But Bethmann-Hollweg had wished to try first his peace proposal, and general headquarters had consented. Toward the close of December, however, Hindenburg again insisted that Germany's dangerous economic and military position made the unrestricted submarine campaign absolutely essential. The chancellor at length gave way, and on January 9 a German crown council decided that unrestricted submarine warfare should be resumed on February 1, 1917. That this move on the part of Germany would force the United States to join the Allies, they had little doubt; but they believed that the war would be ended long before the United States could raise, train, equip, and place in Europe any great number of troops. Furthermore, in an attempt to embarrass the United States in case of war, Zimmermann, secretary for foreign affairs, instructed the German minister in Mexico to propose an alliance with that country as soon as an outbreak of war appeared certain. He was to propose that Germany should give general financial support, and Mexico should "reconquer the lost territory of New Mexico, Texas, and Arizona."

On January 31, 1917, Germany announced that beginning the next day all sea traffic within certain zones adjoining Great Britain, France, and Italy and in the eastern Mediterranean would, "without further notice, be prevented by all weapons." All vessels, neutral or belligerent, were to be sunk by German submarines. Special permission was granted for one regular American passenger steamship to sail in each direction between the United States and Great Britain each week, provided a number of hard and fast rules were observed. Germany was confident that this measure would "result in a speedy termination of the war and in the restoration of peace which the Government of the United States has so much at heart."

American exasperation with the Central Powers had been increasing for some months. Both groups of belligerents had been eager to influence public opinion in the United States and had carried on an active propaganda by means of subsidized newspapers and public speakers. But the Central Powers had not been content with propaganda; their diplomatic representatives had further proceeded to organize and support a staff of conspirators. Passport frauds had been committed, strikes had been instigated in munition plants, and bombs had been manufactured for the destruction of factories and ships. Late in 1915 the United States had demanded the recall of the Austro-Hungarian ambassador and the military and naval attachés of the German embassy because of their improper activities. Now, on February 3, the German ambassador was handed his passports, and

THE ZONE OF UNRESTRICTED SUBMARINE WARFARE,
FEBRUARY, 1917

President Wilson announced to Congress the severance of diplomatic relations with Germany.

President Wilson did not believe that Germany would actually do with her submarines what she had announced, and preferred to await "overt acts" before taking further steps. Nevertheless, the immediate result of the German decree was a practical embargo on American shipping, since most shipowners refused to risk the loss of their vessels. During the first week following the break in diplomatic relations not a single American ship left New York for the war zone. On February 26 the President pointed out to Congress this practical embargo on American shipping and asked for authority to maintain armed neutrality "to protect our ships and our people in their legitimate and peaceful pursuits on the sea," but the measure was defeated in the Senate by the obstructionist tactics of a few members.

Meanwhile, the British steamship *Laconia* was sunk without warning on February 26 with the loss of eight American lives. Three days later the "Zimmermann note" to Mexico, which had been intercepted and deciphered by the British government, was published in the United States. The President was therefore accorded popular support when, on March 12, the government issued an order for arming American merchant ships by executive authority. Then followed within a week the sinking (March 16–17) of three homeward-bound American ships with the loss of American lives; and by the first of April thirty-five more Americans had been drowned. These attacks undoubtedly constituted "overt acts," and anti-German sentiment rose to a high pitch in the United States.

Entrance of the United States into the War

On April 2 President Wilson went before a joint session of the Senate and the House of Representatives and advised that "Congress declare the recent course of the Imperial German Government to be in fact nothing less than war against the government and people of the United States." During the next two days Congress adopted a declaration of war by large majorities, and on April 6, 1917, President Wilson issued a proclamation declaring that "a state of war exists between the United States and the Imperial German Government."

The United States now began the task of preparing to aid the Allies and to defeat Germany. French and British missions to America pointed out that the United States could best assist by contributing (1) money, (2) food and ships to convey food, (3) help against the submarines, (4) men. In respect to the first, Congress on April 24 passed the War Finance Act authorizing the raising of seven billion dollars and the lending to the Allies of three billion. These funds were raised by "Liberty Loans." By the end of June over one billion dollars had been advanced to the Allies—chiefly for the purpose of purchasing food, cotton, metals, and other war materials. By October the amount appropriated to cover loans to the Allies had risen to the immense sum of seven billion dollars. America's entry into the war saved the Allies serious financial difficulties during the early part of 1917.

Every effort was made to increase the quantity of foodstuffs and war materials which could be shipped to the relief of the Allies and to expedite their transportation to Europe. In July the President made Herbert Hoover "food-controller"; in August Congress passed food-control and shipping acts. To counteract the menace of the submarine, the United States imme-

AMERICA'S LEADER IN THE FIRST WORLD WAR
Woodrow Wilson

diately seized all enemy merchant ships in American waters and inaugurated, under the direction of the United States Shipping Board Emergency Fleet Corporation, a tremendous shipbuilding program which called for the rapid construction of great numbers of standardized steel ships. In addition, a considerable flotilla of American destroyers was soon dispatched to co-operate with the British fleet against the German submarines in British waters.

At the time of the declaration of war upon Germany, the United States regular army consisted of only slightly more than 165,000 men, of whom more than 25,000 were scattered in outlying possessions and overseas posts. In consequence, less than five full divisions [1] were available for dispatch to the front in Europe, where divisions were numbered by the hundreds. To remedy this situation the Selective Service Act was passed in May, authorizing the President (1) to increase the regular army by voluntary enlistment to the maximum war strength, (2) to draft into federal service the national guard, and (3) to raise by conscription a force of 500,000 men, with 500,000 more if deemed necessary. On June 5 some nine and a half million men between the ages of twenty-one and thirty years were registered, and on July 20 the drawing of 625,000 men to form the first selective army took place at Washington. During the summer the national guard was mobilized, but not until September was the mobilization of the new national army begun. Germany was correct in her calculation that it would be months after the resumption of the unrestricted submarine campaign before the military forces of the United States could play an effective role in Europe.

The Allied Offensives of 1917

Meanwhile, on the western front the year opened with the voluntary relinquishment of about one thousand square miles of French territory by the German armies. As early as November of the preceding year the retreat had been decided upon, and for various reasons. The Allied drive on the Somme had struck a deadly blow at Teutonic strength and had badly dented the German line. Further Allied gains at this point might endanger the whole Teutonic western front. Allied superiority in troops in the west had risen to thirty or forty divisions, and retirement to a shorter and more defensible line would enable the Central Powers to meet this situation more readily. Finally, a strategic retreat to a stronger line might nullify the extensive preparations which the Allies were making for a gigantic offensive in 1917. During the winter, therefore, a fresh system of trenches was constructed in front of Cambrai and St. Quentin, and the new bulwark of

[1] A division in the United States army consisted of 28,000 men.

defense was christened the "Siegfried Line." The Allies, however, persisted in calling it the "Hindenburg Line." In March the Germans began to withdraw to their new position, devastating the surrendered territory as they went.

But the Germans were not left long undisturbed in their new positions. On April 9 the British opened a drive against the north end of the new line along a forty-five-mile front in the vicinity of Arras. During the first three days of the battle they advanced rapidly, capturing one of the most cherished German observation posts, Vimy Ridge, and part of the new Hindenburg Line itself. Thereafter, however, the advance slowed down in the face of stiffened German resistance. At the end of the battle the British had gained some seventy-five square miles, had taken more than 20,000 prisoners, and had captured hundreds of heavy guns, trench mortars, and machine guns. The Hindenburg Line had proved to be no more impregnable than the old one, but the British had had to pay a terrific price to prove this—30,000 killed and 75,000 wounded.

While the battle of Arras was in progress, a new experiment was tried by the French in the second battle of the Aisne. Certain groups in France had become impatient with the slow, costly tactics used by Joffre, and clamored for a change in leadership. As a result, Joffre on December 16, 1916, had been succeeded as generalissimo by Nivelle, hero of the Verdun counteroffensive of that year. The latter believed that new methods might be discovered and that the enemy's strength might be broken by some other means than slow sapping. He envisaged "limitless objectives, the end of trench fighting, victory within two days." The capture of Laon he looked for as a result of the first day's fighting. Although his plan appeared doubtful to Painlevé, minister of war, and to Foch and Pétain, he was finally authorized to try it.

But certain circumstances rendered success almost impossible. In the first place, the terrain was difficult, and practically everywhere the Germans held the dominating positions. In the second place, the enemy through the capture of prisoners with documents was fully forewarned. In the third place, Nivelle's scheme demanded fresh, enthusiastic, loyal troops, but "the French armies were weary, dispirited, out of temper, doubtful of their leader, and in the mood to listen to treasonable tales." Finally, Nivelle's purpose was to break through a strong enemy defense, but his methods differed little from those already used for less ambitious objectives.

The first day's battle, April 16, ended in driving sleet; the second day's began in a hurricane of wind and snow. By the close of the fifth, the French had taken all the banks of the Aisne from Soissons to Berry-au-Bac and all the spurs of the Aisne heights. They had captured 21,000 prisoners and

183 guns. But the French themselves had suffered 75,000 casualties, of whom 15,000 were dead. And they were still very far from Laon. An abrupt reversion of feeling in favor of the cautious tactics of Pétain and Foch resulted. Nivelle's tactics had failed, and he fell from command as suddenly as he had risen. In May, Pétain was appointed to succeed Nivelle as commander-in-chief of the French forces, Foch becoming chief of the general staff.

The needless sacrifice of men provoked a near-crisis in the French army. No adequate preparation had been made for the care of the wounded, who were sent to various parts of France where they spread despondency by the tale of their needless sufferings. The depression which resulted found vent in mutiny, which, beginning about May 20, broke out in ten divisions. Pétain immediately set to work to remedy this menacing situation. For the remainder of the year, however, the French limited themselves on the western front chiefly to the policy of attrition, seeking by minor attacks to wear the Germans down in man power, war materials, and morale.

Throughout most of the summer and fall the British carried on operations in Flanders, and eventually they succeeded in capturing the important German observation point, Passchendaele Ridge. Late in November, with scarcely any artillery preparation but aided by a large number of huge tanks, they started a drive toward Cambrai. Several villages were captured, and German occupation of Cambrai was rendered most precarious. But before the British had consolidated their newly won position, they were compelled to meet a German counteroffensive which forced them to surrender about two thirds of the territory they had gained. The battle of Cambrai closed the campaign of 1917 on the western front. While all these offensives brought the Allies comparatively few miles of new territory, they did strengthen the Allied lines, and, more important than all, they inflicted serious losses upon the Teutonic armies, which, for almost the entire year, were compelled to stand on the defensive in France.

Allied disappointments in the West were to some extent balanced by successes in Mesopotamia and the Near East. To retrieve the British disaster at Kut-el-Amara early in 1916, the British forces at the head of the Persian Gulf were strengthened by reinforcements from India and Great Britain and put under the command of General Sir Stanley Maude. The latter part of the year was spent in preparing for an advance up the Tigris, and in December the march began. In February, 1917, Maude recaptured the city of Kut-el-Amara, where a British army had been forced to surrender to the Turks only ten months before. The British pursued the retreating Turkish army and on March 11 entered the coveted city of Bagdad. By so doing they restored British prestige in the East, deprived the Central Pow-

ers of one of the famous goals of their *Drang nach Osten,* raised the morale
and enthusiasm of the Allies, and correspondingly depressed the spirits of
the Turks.

Events elsewhere were similarly depressing for Germany's ally in the
East. In November, 1916, the Sherif of Mecca proclaimed the independence
of the Arab kingdom of Hejaz and received the prompt recognition of the
Allied powers. The moving spirit in the negotiations leading to the Arab
revolt was T. E. Lawrence, a young Oxford University graduate who had
learned colloquial Arabic while working in excavations in Syria and Mesopotamia before the war. Late in 1916 Lawrence had joined the Arabs, had
won their confidence, had helped them organize their armies, and had
persuaded them to co-operate with the British against the Turks. Beginning in 1917, the sultan's forces were compelled to fight not only against
the invading Allies but against the revolting Arabs as well.

The latter were of considerable indirect assistance to General Murray in
his efforts to protect the Suez Canal and to build a railway across the Sinai
peninsula, preparatory to an advance into Palestine. The railway was at
length completed, but attempts to capture the strongly entrenched Turkish
position at Gaza were repulsed in April and May. During the summer
Murray was succeeded by General Allenby, who renewed the offensive in
October. On November 1, Beersheba was taken by a surprise attack, and
five days later Gaza fell. The British continued to push northward, took
Jaffa, the port of Jerusalem, on November 16, and on December 11 occupied the Holy City itself. The year closed with the British holding a line
running from the Mediterranean to the Dead Sea north of Jaffa and Jerusalem, while in Mesopotamia they had advanced to within a hundred miles of
Mosul. Turkey was beginning to crumble, and, in response to the urgent
pleas of the distressed Turks, Teutonic headquarters rushed to their assistance a German "Asia corps" under the command of Falkenhayn.

For a year and a half the Allied forces at Saloniki had been practically
impotent to advance against the Central Powers largely because of their
fear of the possible action of Greece in their rear. The year 1917 saw the
Greek situation finally clarified and the Saloniki army freed from this
handicap. In the closing months of the preceding year Greece had been
subjected to various coercive acts of the Allies. Her navy had been seized,
her coasts had been blockaded, and Constantine had been compelled to
transfer most of his military forces to the Peloponnesus. Early in June, 1917,
Allied forces occupied strategic points in Thessaly to safeguard the rear of
the Saloniki forces, and French troops seized the isthmus of Corinth. On
June 11 an Allied high commissioner demanded both the abdication of
King Constantine and the renunciation of the crown prince's right of succession. Constantine bowed to the inevitable and on the following day ab-

The Ottoman Empire in the First World War

dicated the throne in favor of his second son, Alexander. Venizelos was recalled as premier, and early in July Greece joined the countries at war with
the Central Powers. In the eyes of the latter the Allied treatment of neutral Greece differed little from their own treatment of Belgium.

War-Weariness

Meanwhile, three long years of fierce and bloody fighting had called
into the trenches tens of millions of men. Over four million had already
been compelled to lay down their lives, and other millions had been
wounded or crippled for life.[2] National bankruptcy stared each country
squarely in the face.[3] And to the masses it all seemed futile and empty.
Although the Central Powers had spectacularly defeated Russia, Serbia,
and Rumania, and now held territories which produced an impressive
"war map," Allied control of the seas and of the world's chief sources of
raw materials made that war map of little real significance. And although
the Allies in 1916 had finally succeeded in gaining superiority in man
power and war materials, had been able to wrest the offensive from the
hands of the Central Powers, and were seriously damaging their military
machine, victory now seemed to be slipping from their grasp because of
the collapse of Russia. In all the belligerent countries the spring and summer of 1917 saw the masses war-weary and yearning for peace.

In the Austrian Empire this war-weariness was reflected in the report
of the foreign minister, Count Czernin, to Emperor Charles[4] (April,
1917), pointing out that "the burden laid upon the population has assumed
proportions that are unbearable," that the "dull despair of the population
increases day by day," that "our military strength is coming to an end,"
that "another winter campaign would be absolutely out of the question,"
that "in the late summer or in the autumn an end must be put to the war
at all costs," and that it "will be most important to begin peace negotiations
at a moment when the enemy has not yet grasped the fact of our waning
strength." It was seen in the downfall of the ministry, in the weakening of
the Dual Monarchy's loyalty to Germany, and finally in Emperor Charles's
secret overtures to France (March–May) looking toward a separate peace,
even at the expense of granting Serbia access to the sea.

Within the German Empire the same feeling was revealed by the increase
in the number of Socialists who opposed the war, by the Bavarian Prince
Rupprecht's desire for peace, by the conversion of the Center Party's leader,

[2] The loss of life in the first two years of the war was greater than the total death toll of all
the important wars from 1790 to 1914.

[3] The total cost of the war for the first three years was about $90,000,000,000.

[4] He had succeeded Francis Joseph in November, 1916.

Erzberger, from a peace of conquest to a peace without annexations, by un-official statements in London and Paris that the Kaiser was disposed to peace, and finally by the Reichstag's resolution (July 19) that it strove "for a peace of understanding and the permanent reconciliation of the peoples," and that with such a peace "forced acquisitions of territory and political, economic, or financial oppressions are inconsistent." But the Pan-German-ists and the general staff disagreed with the Reichstag resolution and re-fused to accept it as coming from the entire country. And since Germany, in the words of Bethmann-Hollweg, had now come to be governed by a military dictatorship, no definite steps were taken to give the resolution substance.

War-weariness in the Allied countries was manifested during 1917 in what has been called the "defeatist movement," the essence of which was that peace could not be won through victory, but must be attained through negotiations—a "peace without victory." Anti-imperialist Socialists, bank-ers and capitalists who feared the effect of endless war on the world's finan-cial structure, religious leaders, pacifists, and even some aristocrats were won over to the movement, which naturally had a tremendous appeal to the suffering, heartsick masses. In France and Italy the tendency was espe-cially strong. The mutiny in the French army in 1917 has already been men-tioned. But behind the lines newspaper proprietors, financiers, senators, and deputies became interested, and ex-Premier Joseph Caillaux was ex-tremely active in spreading the doctrines. The reaction ultimately came, however, valiantly led by the aged veteran, Georges Clemenceau, who insisted upon a "peace through victory." Two ministries fell as a result of his fierce attacks, and he himself finally became premier and minister of war on November 16, 1917. Not many weeks later Clemenceau, in order to crush defeatism in France, took the drastic step of ordering Caillaux's arrest on the charge of having endangered the security of the state.

In Italy the defeatist movement was encouraged by secret agents of the Central Powers and by representatives of the Russian Bolsheviks. Both the illiterate peasants and the radical proletarian Socialists became imbued with the doctrines. Even the army became infected. In August rioting occurred in Turin, one of the chief munition centers, and mutiny broke out among the troops sent to quell the disorder. In consequence, exemption from mili-tary service was canceled for many of the munition workers, who were or-ganized into battalions and sent to the Italian front. By chance they were placed in the very sector where the Central Powers had decided to strike in an effort to cut off the Italian Second Army, on the Isonzo north of Go-rizia, and the Third Army, which held the line from Gorizia to the Adri-atic.

On October 24, 1917, the Central Powers launched an attack in the Julian

Alps. A breach was made in the Italian lines at Caporetto, and Teutonic troops rushed through. Cadorna was forced to move his headquarters from Udine to Padua. By the twenty-eighth the Austro-German troops had reached the Friulian plain, had taken Cividale, and were menacing Udine. The Italian Second Army, weakened by the discontent and treason of its recently acquired Turin battalions and broken by the impact of new Teutonic tactics, became "a fugitive rabble." The Italian Third Army, in a desperate effort to escape capture by retreat, precipitately withdrew from Gorizia.

THE AUSTRO-ITALIAN FRONT IN THE FIRST WORLD WAR

The plight of this Third Army was most serious. The Tagliamento River was the first halting-place for Cadorna's retreat, and the Third Army was as far from that river as were the advance forces of the enemy. For a time it seemed doomed. "A million of men were retreating along the western highways, encumbered with batteries and hospitals and transport, while by every choked route peasants and townsmen fled for refuge from the Austrian cavalry." But the Third Army was not captured; with heavy losses and by the narrowest margin it escaped. On November 1 it was in position on the western bank of the Tagliamento with the river between it and the enemy. Its successful retreat made an Italian stand possible and deprived the Teutonic forces of their expected triumph. But on November 3 the enemy crossed the river and began to move west along the edge of the hills. On the seventh the Italians abandoned the Tagliamento, halted temporarily on the Livenza, and by the tenth were back on the Piave. Here the retreat ended.

French and British reinforcements were at once dispatched from the western front. Diaz supplanted Cadorna as commander-in-chief. Italian boys of seventeen and eighteen, many with little military training, were rushed to the battle line. Italian monitors off the coast contributed their constant shelling to the defense. During November and December desperate fighting continued, but the Teutonic advance was finally checked. The disaster had cost Italy some 600,000 men in addition to great quantities of war materials. Yet in the end it aroused Italy's fighting spirit, brought reforms in her commands, and forced the government to give more attention to the "civil front." The aid of the British and French troops and the work of the American Red Cross impressed the Italians with the extent and good will of the alliance of which they were a part. Finally, out of it came the movement for a unified western command. Early in November the premiers of France, Great Britain, and Italy met at Rapallo, and from their conference developed the Supreme War Council of Versailles.

Growing Unrest in Russia

Meanwhile, developments in Russia were becoming more and more discouraging to the Allies. At the outbreak of the First World War various groups were already at work in that country preparing to bring about a change in its institutions. The most moderate were the Octobrists, so called because they demanded that the tsar carry out his proclamation of October 30, 1905, in which he had promised that no law would thereafter be considered binding without the consent of the national legislature, the Duma, and that to the people would be given "the power to exercise an effective supervision over the acts of the officials." The Octobrists consisted chiefly of liberal nobles who favored a government in which the Duma, though more powerful, should play a subordinate role somewhat like the Landtag in Prussia. More definitely liberal were the Constitutional Democrats or "Cadets," who were drawn chiefly from the professional classes, university men, capitalists, and more progressive nobles. They demanded a wider franchise, increased power for the Duma, ministerial responsibility—in short, a democratic, parliamentary monarchy like the British. These two groups desired to take progressive steps toward constitutional rule, but preferred to do this peaceably by means of the existing representative system which, although imperfect, nevertheless provided a legislative body. They still believed that the "unifying influence of tsardom" was essential for the preservation of Russian national unity.

More radical in their aims for Russia were the Social Democrats and the Socialist Revolutionaries. The former consisted for the most part of urban workingmen who, deprived of any real voice in the government and oppressed by an industrial system which forbade the organization of trade unions, were a fertile field for socialist propaganda. In consequence, they came to dream of the time when political power might be theirs, when factories might be seized, the capitalists turned out, and a millennium of shorter hours, increased wages, and better conditions ushered in. They therefore sought to overthrow the empire in order to erect in its stead a socialist republic. Back in 1903 this party had split into two wings, the *Bolsheviki* or "majority" and the *Mensheviki* or "minority." Originally they had differed only in matters of party organization, but in the course of years they came to differ fundamentally on the question of party tactics as well. The Bolsheviks were the extremists, opposed to any co-operation with bourgeois parties, opposed to the policy of gradual reform, in favor of a cataclysmic upheaval which should establish the regime of the proletariat. The Mensheviks, on the other hand, were the moderates, willing, if necessary, to bring in the socialist regime gradually through the slow education of the masses, even with the co-operation of the moderately liberal groups. In other words, the Bolsheviks were more "revolutionary," the Mensheviks more "evolutionary." Because of the repressive measures of the government, however, most of the leaders of the Bolsheviks were dispersed in foreign countries before 1914.

The Socialist Revolutionaries comprised the mass of the peasants under the leadership of a few radical intellectuals. They were chiefly interested in the land problem, and sought to transform the land from private property into "the property of the whole people." The lands which the peasants had been permitted to buy at the time of their emancipation were in 1861 inadequate to support them. And though in 1914 about three fourths of the Russian land was in peasant occupancy, the steady increase in population and consequent subdivision of estates left the peasants by 1917 with only about half the land per capita which they had obtained at the time of their emancipation. Millions of land-hungry peasants gazed enviously upon the remaining estates of the crown, the church, and the aristocracy and longed for the time when they might be seized and parceled out. The Socialist Revolutionary platform, therefore, sought the destruction of the existent political and social regimes in Russia for the benefit of the peasant masses.

The outbreak of the war, however, had temporarily unified the Russian people. A wave of patriotic loyalty to the tsar swept over the empire, and in the Duma party opposition seemed to disappear. But the unanimity was not for long. When in the following year the Russian armies were driven back out of Galicia and Poland, patriots began to denounce the incompetence of the military leaders and the inefficiency and corruption of the government. And, as defeat succeeded defeat, as the number of killed and wounded mounted into the millions, as the vast crowds of homeless refugees poured eastward before the retreating armies, denunciations became louder and angrier. The vigorous prosecution of the war and the punishment of criminally inefficient commanders and officials were openly demanded. Serious riots in the cities and strikes in the munition factories occurred.

Nevertheless, the tsar in February, 1916, elevated to the premiership Boris Stürmer, an ultraconservative landed aristocrat, a man of German descent and of suspected pro-German sympathies, later accused of deliberately planning the Rumanian defeat as part of his scheme for a separate Russo-German peace. Furthermore, the imperial family fell beneath the spell of the long-haired, illiterate scoundrel, charlatan, and reputed monk, Gregory Rasputin, who was thought by many to be in close contact with a pro-German organization in Petrograd.[5] Gradually the conviction gained ground among men of widely different classes that certain "dark forces" were attempting to paralyze the country, that, if the German staff itself were in control of Russia, it could not have brought to pass conditions more to its advantage than those created by the Russian government. During 1916 both conservative and liberal groups in Russia gradually came to the conclusion that victory in the war was impossible so long as the methods of autocracy prevailed. In the fall of that year preparations for a *coup d'état* were begun in various circles which included military men of both Petrograd and Moscow, and Duma members of as high standing as Rodzianko, the president. Most of the plans envisaged the abdication of Nicholas II.

At the same time the army with its millions of peasants from every part of Russia was discouraged, discontented, and weary of the futile struggle, which seemed to be waged not only against the Central Powers at the front, but against the forces of inefficiency, corruption, and even treason in the rear. By the winter of 1916–1917 the army was already in process of dissolution. "Unwillingness to fight, decline of discipline, distrust and suspicion of officers, desertion in the rear" were present. One of the essentials for successful revolution—a discontented and disloyal army—thus existed in Russia by the spring of 1917.

Among the masses, meanwhile, discontent and unrest were greatly accentuated by the economic conditions. The relative cost of living increased

[5] In September, 1914, the name of the capital was changed from St. Petersburg to Petrograd.

during the war by leaps and bounds. During the winter of 1916–1917 a coal shortage developed which made itself felt in the progressive closing down of industries in which its use was essential. The transportation system, none too efficient at best, collapsed under the strain of the war. Passenger traffic had to be stopped for weeks at a time to enable military and supply trains to go through to the front. Finally, the shift of millions of peasants from the farms into the armies, the tremendous demand for food to feed these armies, the peasants' unwillingness to part with food for depreciating paper currency, and the collapse of the transportation system, all conspired to produce an acute food shortage in the larger towns and cities. Short rations and bread lines became more and more frequent. In a winter which was bitterly cold, many Russians were hungry. "Bread!" became the dominant cry.

The Collapse of Russian Autocracy

On March 8, 1917, spontaneous riots occurred in Petrograd when crowds of people marched through the streets, shouting "Bread!" On the same day between eighty and ninety thousand workmen went on strike and joined the demonstrating masses in the streets. The more radical elements at once sought to turn the situation to their advantage, and soon red flags and revolutionary placards began to appear. On Sunday, March 11, one of the companies of the Petrograd garrison mutinied when ordered to fire upon the people, and had to be disarmed by the Preobrashensky regiment, the flower of the household troops. During the day the military governor of Petrograd posted notices ordering the strikers to return to their work; and Premier Galitzin sent Rodzianko an order proroguing the Duma. But the strikers, instead of returning to work, established the Soviet (Council) of Workmen's and Soldiers' Deputies and began organizing the masses and converting the soldiers to their cause. Even the Preobrashensky regiment now mutinied and shot some of its officers. Other regiments followed suit until by noon 25,000 soldiers had thrown themselves on the side of the workmen. By evening of the twelfth, revolutionary workers and soldiers were in control of the capital.

Meanwhile the Duma, while not venturing to defy the tsar's order officially, had met "informally" and had authorized the appointment of a temporary committee with limited powers. The latter, headed by Rodzianko, on the thirteenth undertook to assume executive functions and began to issue orders to the Petrograd garrison. At the same time the Petrograd soviet, representing the "revolutionary democracy" of the factory workers and soldiers of the city, elected a temporary executive committee and began doing the same thing. Thus there were, almost from the beginning of the revolution, two centers of authority; the temporary committee of the Duma and the temporary executive committee of the soviet.

An attempt was made to amalgamate the two groups in a provisional government which was projected on March 14, when the temporary committee of the Duma proposed a government consisting for the most part of bourgeois ministers, but with two places reserved for representatives of the soviet. The executive committee of the soviet, however, declared that representatives of the soviet could not take office in the provisional government because the government and the whole revolution were "bourgeois." But the executive committee was overruled by the soviet delegates, and Alexander Kerensky, a Socialist Revolutionary member of the Duma, was permitted to enter the new provisional government, which was composed, however, primarily of members of the Octobrist and Constitutional Democratic parties.

On the fourteenth the tsar attempted to reach Petrograd, but his train was compelled to stop because workmen had pulled up the tracks. Meanwhile, he had dispatched an army under General Ivanov, the hero of the first Galician campaign, to take Petrograd, but most of his troops went over to the revolution. On March 15 the tsar decided to give way and grant a responsible ministry, but it was too late. The demand was now for his abdication. As to what should follow his abdication, there were differing views, but the majority of the temporary committee favored the regency of Grand Duke Michael during the minority of the tsar's son, Alexis. Confronted with the information that his troops had deserted him, advised by his generals that abdication was his only possible course, Nicholas II at length surrendered his throne, requesting only that it go directly to his brother Michael rather than to his young son, Alexis.

But by this time the Petrograd soviet was demanding a republic. A delegation of the Duma thereupon visited Grand Duke Michael and informed him that the popular demand was for his renunciation of the regency and his surrender of all powers to the provisional government until a constituent assembly could decide upon the future. The grand duke in turn bowed to the revolution and requested all Russians to obey the provisional government until the meeting of a constituent assembly.

With the appointment of the first provisional government of Russia the bourgeois stage of the revolution began. The ministry represented a coalition of the moderate parties. The new premier was Prince George Lvov, creator and president of the Union of Zemstvos. Associated with him as foreign minister was Paul N. Miliukov, eminent historian and leader of the Constitutional Democrats. The war minister was Alexander Guchkov, leader of the Octobrists and formerly chairman of the military commission of the Duma. Kerensky, a Socialist Revolutionary, became minister of justice. The ministry was chiefly representative of the landowning, capitalist, manufacturing, and professional classes—obviously a bourgeois group. And the aims of the first provisional government were distinctly bourgeois aims: the establishment of constitutional, democratic, parliamentary government, perhaps even a monarchy; the active prosecution of the war in close co-operation with the Allies; the protection of the rights of private property; the settlement of the land question by a constituent assembly, but no alienation of land without compensation; the accomplishment of all changes in Russian institutions only through a legally elected constituent assembly. To the onlooker, Russia had at length apparently become one of the liberal democratic states of the world. Formal recognition of the new regime was soon forthcoming from the United States, Great Britain, France, Italy, and Japan.

The Soviets

Meanwhile, the Russian masses had begun to organize in order to make themselves articulate. Following the example of the workmen of Petrograd, they established throughout the country extralegal soviets, chosen in the towns by the factory workers, in the rural districts by the peasant communes, in the army by military units. These soviets were controlled largely by the Socialist Revolutionaries and the Menshevik Social Democrats, groups which were practically unrepresented in the provisional government.

The aims of the groups which found representation in the soviets were radically different from those of the provisional government. Both the urban proletariat and the peasants desired a thorough-going social revolution in addition to political change. Both sought the overthrow of the bourgeoisie. Specifically, the peasants wanted the great estates seized and divided up without compensation to the owners, while the proletariat hoped for the expulsion of the capitalists and the introduction of a socialistic scheme of workers' control in the factories. All were war-weary and discouraged; while not at once demanding the immediate cessation of the war, they did desire a revision of its aims and a final peace "without annexations and indemnities." They were eager for the early convocation of a constituent assembly, which they expected to provide the panacea for all their wrongs.

The masses had an opportunity to express their views on something like a national scale for the first time when an "All-Russian Congress of Soviets," composed largely of Menshevik Social Democrats and moderate Socialist Revolutionaries met early in April, 1917. The congress demanded the abandonment of imperialism, the acceptance of the principle of self-determination, and the conclusion of peace without annexations and indemnities. It voted to continue the war and to support the provisional government only if it adopted the views of the congress.

On May 1, however, Foreign Minister Miliukov sent a note to the Allied governments stating Russia's resolve to conclude no separate peace, but to carry the war to a "decisive victory" in conformity with her past agreements with the Allies. This note immediately evoked the disapproval of the Petrograd soviet. Meetings of protest were held in the capital and in Moscow. Workmen marched in processions bearing red flags with inscriptions hostile to the government, and "Down with Miliukov!" was the cry. A number of regiments also paraded with banners demanding the resignation of Guchkov, minister of war. As a result of the crisis both Guchkov and Miliukov resigned.

Up to this time the Menshevik leaders in the Petrograd soviet had declined to assume any responsibility for policies of the provisional government, had refused to co-operate with it, and had sought merely to exercise upon it the pressure of an opposition. Now, however, the provisional government demanded that the soviet should be officially represented, and in the new government which was organized the Mensheviks and moderate Socialist Revolutionaries each had three representatives. Lvov remained as prime minister and Kerensky succeeded Guchkov as minister of war. The immediate result of the change in the government was a reversal of Miliukov's earlier announced war policy. Imperialism was definitely repudiated in a manifesto of the new provisional government.

Lenin and the Rise of the Bolsheviks

One explanation of the Petrograd soviet's decision to enter the government and to give active support to its policies was the alarm with which Menshevik and moderate Socialist Revolutionary leaders viewed the increasing activity of the Bolsheviks. Although the outbreak of the revolution had found the latter's organization practically broken up, although they had taken no serious part in the overthrow of the tsar, they had finally been galvanized into action by the arrival of Nicholas Lenin on the evening of April 16 and by his dramatic speech at the railway station demanding a second revolution.

The real name of this "plump little man, with a high bulbous forehead, a snub nose, and bald head," whose tremendous will power and boundless energy so dominated the Bolsheviks that he might well have said, *"Le parti c'est moi,"* was Vladimir Ilyich Ulianov. He was born in Simbirsk (now called Leninsk) in 1870, the son of a district inspector of schools whose family descended from a stock of impoverished nobles. His elder brother,

Alexander, was executed for his part in the attempted assassination of Alexander III in 1887, and doubtless Lenin was in sympathy with his views, for he himself was soon expelled from the University of Kazan because of revolutionary agitation. Later he passed the bar examinations in Petrograd, but soon gave up the practice of law, joined a secret organization of professional revolutionists, became a Social Democrat, and was even exiled for a time to Siberia because of revolutionary activities among the working classes of the capital. The split in the Social Democratic Party which occurred in 1903 was largely due to Lenin, who repudiated co-operation with the liberals and sought a violent outbreak of class war. To a certain extent, therefore, Lenin may be considered the father of Bolshevism. During the revolution of 1905 he was again in Petrograd, but his role was rather unimportant, his chief endeavor being to incite violence and hostility against the Duma and the Constitutional Democrats. At the conclusion of the revolution he left the country, and from 1906 to 1917 lived abroad as a professional revolutionary, giving himself exclusively to the work of revolutionary organization and secret propaganda.

The revolution of 1917 found Lenin in Zurich, Switzerland, but the general pardon of political offenders proclaimed by the provisional government opened the way for his return to Russia. Refused the right to pass through territory of the Allies, he at length secured permission to cross Germany from the Kaiser's government, which hoped to weaken Russia by sowing dissension behind the lines. Upon his return to Petrograd, Lenin immediately began his attack. The food difficulties, the protracted war, the delay in summoning a constituent assembly, all these he exploited for his own ends. Upon the provisional government he placed the blame for all that went wrong.

Gradually Lenin gathered about him a group of followers: doctrinaire fanatics, masters of intrigue and propaganda, ambitious opportunists, sentimental visionaries, crazy degenerates, sincere idealists—yet withal many extremely energetic and capable men whose names, Zinoviev, Bukharin, Chicherin, Kamenev, Rykov, Stalin, Dzerzhinsky, later became prominent in Russian affairs. While Lenin unquestionably held first place in the Bolshevik Party, second place soon went to a new recruit, Leon Trotsky, who did not finally join the Bolsheviks until after the March revolution. Trotsky, whose real name was Leon Davidovich Bronstein, was a Russian middle-class Jew who had early become imbued with revolutionary ideas. Twice he had been exiled to Siberia, and twice he had escaped. The revolution found him in New York City, where he had recently gone after having lived in exile for several years in Vienna and Paris. When he attempted to return to Russia, he was arrested in Halifax, but on the application of

THE LEADER OF THE RUSSIAN BOLSHEVIKS
Nicholas Lenin

Kerensky, upon whom the Petrograd soviet brought pressure to bear, he was released and permitted to sail for Russia.

The program which these Bolshevik leaders offered was bound to make a tremendous appeal to the masses, who, with the sole exception of the announced change in war aims, could see little difference between the policies of the old and those of the new provisional government. No order for the confiscation and subdivision of the great landed estates was forthcoming. No step toward the overthrow of the capitalistic system of industry was taken. Not even a call for the early meeting of a constituent assembly was sent out. Instead of these, what they saw were vigorous efforts to prepare for a renewed military effort at the front. On the other hand, the Bolsheviks drafted a program which called for what the mass of the people wanted: (1) immediate conclusion of a general peace; (2) immediate confiscation of landed estates without compensation and without delay for legal forms; (3) possession and operation of factories by the workmen; (4) national control of production and distribution; (5) the substitution of soviets of workmen, peasants, and soldiers for all existing agencies of government; (6) the exclusion of the propertied classes from political rights.

Meanwhile, War Minister Kerensky was bending every effort to prepare for a successful offensive against the Central Powers, believing that a Russian victory would strengthen the provisional government and raise the morale of both soldiers and civilians. An offensive was projected for July. The plan called for local attacks to hold the German troops in the north while the main blow was delivered against the weaker Austrian lines. But Russian deserters betrayed the plan to the enemy, and German reinforcements were sent to the Austrian rather than to the German front. After weeks of feverish activity on the part of Kerensky and his assistants, the Russian advance began at the very close of June. For a few days all went well. Thousands of prisoners and vast quantities of war material were captured, and an advance of some twenty miles was made. Wherever the Austrian lines were not stiffened by Germans, they gave way. But on July 19 a heavy concentration of German troops began a drive in the direction of Tarnopol. Not yet recovered from the exhaustion of their own attack, the Russians fell back under German pressure. Discipline and organization broke down; entire regiments shot their officers and refused to fight. The whole Russian line in Galicia precipitately took to flight, and the Russian gains of 1916 were completely wiped out.

And behind the lines things were going no better. On July 16 the Bolsheviks made their first serious attempt at an armed uprising in Petrograd. Part of the Petrograd garrison, honeycombed with Bolshevik propaganda, revolted. In company with armed workmen they paraded through the city with banners inscribed, "Down with the capitalist ministers," "Down with the war," "All power to the soviets." Red flags appeared among the crowds, and speeches by Trotsky and Zinoviev were greeted with thunderous applause. From the front, Kerensky telegraphed demanding that the government take active steps to suppress the Bolsheviks, and dispatched sixty thousand loyal soldiers to assist in this task. After two days of desultory fighting in the streets, both the disloyal troops and the Bolsheviks were defeated. While their support in Petrograd was strong, the Bolsheviks were still weak in the country and in the army as a whole. Lenin therefore abandoned his cry for the immediate overthrow of the provisional government, and decided that special efforts must now be made to win not only the Petrograd garrison but the whole army to the Bolshevik program.

In the midst of defeat at the front and uprising in the capital, the provisional government itself passed through a crisis, as the result of which Kerensky succeeded Lvov as prime minister. Although the former at once took steps to strengthen the government, it was soon menaced from another direction. The July rising of the Bolsheviks gave a great impetus to the activities of the extreme Right. "Pale and trembling with indignation, the respectable citizen now called for the strong man," and the forces of reaction and militant monarchism raised their heads. The Bolsheviks had sought the "dictatorship of the proletariat"; the conservatives now sought the dictatorship of the military. Early in September, under orders from General Kornilov, troops advanced from the front upon Petrograd. At the same time Kornilov dispatched an ultimatum to Kerensky demanding the proclamation of martial law in Petrograd and the resignation of the provisional government. But Kerensky refused to accept the ultimatum, was given dictatorial power by the cabinet, and in the end arrested Kornilov himself.

The Kornilov affair brought a distinct reaction toward the Bolsheviks. The mass of the people—peasants, proletariat, soldiers—were in deadly fear lest "tsarist generals" might immediately bring about the restoration of the repressive system of the old regime. It was rumored that Kerensky had been in sympathy with the plot and had turned against it only under pressure from the soviet. Whether or not this was true, the Bolsheviks seized upon the rumor and used it so effectively that within a few days the confidence of the bulk of the people in the provisional government was completely destroyed. The soviets became more revolutionary. Within a week after the crushing of the Kornilov rebellion, the Bolsheviks gained control of the executive committee of the Petrograd soviet for the first time.

The moderates were waging a losing fight. The odds against them were too great. Russia was falling into chaos. The military situation became more and more desperate. Desertions were on the increase, and the mass of soldiers threatened to leave the trenches, whole regiments at a time. The Germans continued to advance, captured Riga, and threatened Petrograd. Kerensky's government prepared to move to Moscow. In the villages a general seizure of land was going on. Food riots in the cities were frequent. Russia's finances and industries were sinking into a state of collapse. Reactionary propaganda, Bolshevik propaganda, German propaganda, separatist propaganda were everywhere present and flourished in proportion as the domestic situation became more chaotic. Meanwhile, with redoubled energy the Bolsheviks sounded their slogan: "Peace to the army, land to the peasants, control of the factories to the workmen!"

The inevitable result was that the Bolsheviks rapidly increased in numbers and strength. Throughout the country land-hungry peasants, who cared not so much for victory over Germany as for the overthrow of the landlords, began to approve the Bolshevik program. In the cities the workers, so long at the mercy of their government-protected employers, became enamored of the Bolshevik promise of complete control of industry. And the active soldiers, maltreated, betrayed, defeated in the war, compelled to endure untold hardships, and at the same time yearning for the war to end in order that they might return to claim their share of the confiscated lands, gladly enlisted under the Bolshevik banner of peace.

The November Revolution

Lenin now made up his mind that the time to strike was at hand. Late in October he held a "conspiratory meeting" of the central committee of the Bolshevik Party. By an almost unanimous vote an armed insurrection against the government was decided upon. The occasion was to be the assembling of the All-Russian Congress of Soviets, which was set for November 7. A large majority of those who had been elected to this congress were Bolsheviks, and there was thought to be little doubt that the congress would declare itself in favor of handing over power to the soviets.

With everything ready for the coup, therefore, the Bolsheviks proclaimed to the masses on the evening of November 6: "The counterrevolution has raised its criminal head. The Kornilovists are mobilizing forces in order to annihilate the All-Russian Congress of Soviets and the Constituent Assembly." During the night the public buildings of Petrograd were occupied by Bolshevik troops. Railway stations, telegraph and telephone offices, bridges, power plants, and even the Bank of Russia came into their control. On the morning of the seventh another Bolshevik proclamation announced that the provisional government had been overthrown. "Long live the revolution of the workers, soldiers, and peasants!" Late in the day the members of the provisional government, with the exception of Kerensky, who escaped, were arrested and imprisoned. That same night the All-Russian Congress of Soviets approved the *coup d'état* and passed a resolution formally taking over the government, which thereupon became the soviet government. On the next day the same congress established a new provisional government, called the "Soviet of the People's Commissars," of which Lenin was chairman and Trotsky commissar for foreign affairs.

The Treaty of Brest-Litovsk

Within two weeks after the November revolution Commissar for Foreign Affairs Trotsky sent to the foreign diplomats in Petrograd a note stating that the Soviet government intended "to propose to all peoples and their respective governments an immediate armistice on all fronts, with the purpose of immediately opening *pourparlers* for the conclusion of a democratic peace." The Allies ignored Trotsky's note and refused to have anything whatever to do with the Bolshevik peace proposal. On the other hand, the Central Powers, which were naturally eager to have Russia withdraw from the war, responded with alacrity. Negotiations for an armistice were begun at Brest-Litovsk on December 3, and twelve days later a definite truce was signed between representatives of Russia on the one hand and of Germany, Austria, Bulgaria, and Turkey on the other.

On December 22, 1917, the first peace conference of the war was formally opened at the same place. The task of the Russian delegates was not an easy one. They realized well enough that military force was on the side of the Central Powers. They doubtless clearly saw that, if they resisted a peace dictated by the Central Powers, Russia would continue to be invaded and the Bolsheviks themselves might be confronted by a rebellion at home on the part of those who had been promised an immediate peace. On the other hand, if they yielded too much or too easily, they might prevent further German invasion, to be sure, but they might also bring upon themselves the wrath of Russian patriots for having betrayed the national interests. Faced by this dilemma, they played for time. They first secured a suspension of the peace conference on the pretext of enabling the Allies to participate, and then in the meantime they attempted by propaganda to incite the German people to revolt against their "imperialistic" government. But the Allies did not participate, nor did the Germans revolt, and the Bolsheviks failed to benefit by their procrastination.

The Bolsheviks next desired to transfer the negotiations to Stockholm, where they would be less under the domination of the Central Powers, but the Germans objected, and the conference was at length resumed on January 10, 1918, at Brest-Litovsk. The chief obstacle to an agreement was the treatment of the Russian territory occupied by troops of the Central Powers.

The Bolsheviks demanded that the forces of the latter should evacuate Poland, Courland, and Lithuania and permit plebiscites to determine the fate of these regions. This the Central Powers refused to do, the Kaiser ordering the German delegates to demand without plebiscites not only Courland and Lithuania but Livonia and Estonia as well. As a result of the consequent impasse the conference broke up again four days later and adjourned *sine die,* the only positive achievement being the extension of the armistice to February 12.

But Germany was determined to have a signed peace. On February 18, therefore, German armies on the eastern front once more began to advance into Russia. The following day Lenin and Trotsky capitulated and agreed to sign. The German government now made a new offer of peace, more drastic than the first, and attached a forty-eight-hour time limit for its acceptance. Although some of the more fiery Bolsheviks counseled armed resistance, Lenin advised acceptance in order that Bolshevism might have time to organize and strengthen itself within Russia.

Peace negotiations were, accordingly, once more resumed and resulted in the treaty of Brest-Litovsk, signed on March 3, 1918. Russia agreed: (1) to give up Poland, Courland, and Lithuania, and to let Germany and Austria determine the future status of these territories in agreement with their populations; (2) to evacuate Livonia, Estonia, Finland, and the Åland Islands; [6] (3) to evacuate the Ukraine and to recognize the treaty signed between the Ukrainian People's Republic and the Central Powers; (4) to surrender to Turkey the districts of Ardahan, Kars, and Batum; (5) to discontinue all Bolshevik propaganda in the territory of the Central Powers and in the territories ceded by the treaty.

Thus the Bolsheviks gained peace for Russia, but for a Russia reduced to an area less than that which Peter the Great had inherited back in the seventeenth century. Profoundly altered both politically and territorially, Russia was finally "at peace" with the world; and the Bolsheviks were now free to try their great experiment—the "dictatorship of the proletariat." For the Central Powers, Russia's withdrawal from the conflict ended the necessity of waging a war on two fronts and opened the way for the transfer of troops to the west, where the decisive battles of the war were to be fought in 1918.

---

[6] These regions were soon brought within the orbit of the Central Powers. In April, 1918, German troops landed in Finland, and not long afterward the throne was offered to Prince Charles of Hesse, brother-in-law of the Kaiser. On April 21 the Kaiser himself "accepted" the invitation of Estonian Balts to be the ruler of that country. In March Germany recognized the independence of Lithuania, which in July received Prince William of Urach, a younger member of the ruling house of Württemberg, as king. In April German and Austrian troops, entering the Ukraine as allies, occupied the whole country and established a military dictatorship under the pro-German General Skoropadski.

Chapter IV

THE COLLAPSE

OF THE CENTRAL POWERS

EARLY in 1918 the Central Powers confidently announced that that year would see the final conclusion of the war and that the end of the conflict would be achieved by the decisive victory of Teutonic arms. Their prediction of the end of the war was truly fulfilled, but their expected victory proved to be only a mirage which faded with the passing of the months. In 1918 the overwhelming resources of the Allies were at last successfully brought to bear against the Central Powers, already weakened economically by long years of blockade and undermined politically by nationalist propaganda in Austria-Hungary and liberal and radical propaganda in Germany. The outcome of the conflict was the final and decisive defeat of the Teutonic armies and the utter collapse of the Central Powers.

Renewed Optimism of the Central Powers

The opening of the year 1918 saw in German circles a spirit of optimism which was entirely lacking in the previous year. During the summer and autumn of 1917 the Central Powers had passed through a critical period of discouragement and war-weariness. They had even talked of a peace "without annexations and indemnities." But that had been at a time when they were losing their superiority in man power and war materials on the western front, when they were being compelled to stand on the defensive on nearly all fronts, when it was beginning to be apparent that their unrestricted submarine campaign was not going to bring Great Britain to her knees in a few months, if ever.

For the submarine campaign had proved to be a bitter disappointment to the Central Powers. In the early months of 1917 Allied shipping losses were tremendous, and the Teutonic threat to the sustenance of the British people and to the munitioning of the Allied armies was extremely grave. But gradually in two ways the menacing blow was countered. In the first place, shipping losses were ultimately cut down. This was accomplished by weapons of offense against the submarine itself—the submarine chaser, the destroyer, the decoy ship, the submarine, the airplane, the bomb, and the depth charge; and by methods of defense—the camouflaged ship, the convoy system, and the barrage. In the second place, Allied shipping losses were made good by the rapid construction of new tonnage, particularly in the United States, where the construction of standardized steel ships reached such a degree of efficiency that a completed vessel could be turned out in seventy days. In the end, German submarines were being destroyed about as rapidly as they could be built, and Allied shipping was being constructed faster than submarines could sink it.

Nevertheless, the Italian disaster in the fall of 1917 and Russia's withdrawal from the war during the winter restored the German hope of ultimate victory in 1918. The disappearance of the eastern front nullified the Allied campaign of attrition, and the Central Powers could once more confront the Allies in the west with a numerical superiority. The defection of Russia, furthermore, had completely isolated Rumania, which was finally compelled to sign the unusually harsh treaty of Bucharest on May 7, 1918. This left Austria-Hungary free to concentrate practically her whole army for what should be a decisive blow against the recently defeated Italians, while German troops should finally smash the Allied line in the west and compel exhausted France to sue for peace.

The Allies, it appeared, would be unable to duplicate the sudden increase of Teutonic man power in the west. France was so nearly exhausted that she could not even keep her units at full strength. The gaps in the British armies occasioned by the late offensives of 1917 had not been adequately filled; in fact, British infantry strength in March, 1918, was 180,000 less than in the same month of the previous year. American forces, since the landing of the first contingent in France on June 25, 1917, had increased slowly; but at the rate of approximately 25,000 men a month it would be many months before they could offset the sudden increase of Teutonic effectives in the west. These facts led Hindenburg and Ludendorff to lay their plans for 1918 with every expectation of final victory for the Central Powers in that year. It was this expectation of a speedy triumph, in turn, that led the political leaders of the Central Powers to treat so cavalierly the Allied announcements of war aims.

German Repudiation of Allied War Aims

Early in 1918 the Allied war aims were further clarified and formulated as a result of two notable addresses—that of Premier Lloyd George before the British trade unions on January 5, 1918, and that of President Wilson before the United States Congress three days later. The two statesmen were in general agreement, and their aims may be discussed in the order of President Wilson's famous Fourteen Points, destined to play such an important part in the final settlement. They were:

1. "Open covenants of peace, openly arrived at."
2. "Absolute freedom of navigation upon the seas, outside territorial waters, alike in peace and in war."
3. "The removal, so far as possible, of all economic barriers and the establishment of an equality of trade conditions among all the nations."
4. Reduction of national armaments "to the lowest point consistent with domestic safety."
5. "A free, open-minded, and absolutely impartial adjustment of all colonial claims, based upon a strict observance of the principle that in determining all such questions of sovereignty the interests of the population concerned must have equal weight with the equitable claims of the government whose title is to be determined."
6. "The evacuation of all Russian territory and such a settlement of all questions affecting Russia as will secure the best and freest co-operation of the other nations of the world in obtaining for her an unhampered and unembarrassed opportunity for the independent determination of her own political development and national policy."
7. The evacuation and restoration of Belgium without any limit to her sovereignty.
8. The evacuation and restoration of French territory, and the righting of "the wrong done to France by Prussia in 1871 in the matter of Alsace-Lorraine."
9. A readjustment of Italian frontiers "along clearly recognizable lines of nationality."
10. "The freest opportunity of autonomous development" for the peoples of Austria-Hungary.
11. The evacuation and restoration of Rumania, Serbia, and Montenegro, with "free and secure access to the sea" for Serbia.
12. Secure sovereignty for the "Turkish portions" of the Ottoman Empire; security and autonomous development for "the other nationalities which are now under Turkish rule"; the permanent opening of the Dardanelles "as a free passage to the ships and commerce of all nations under international guarantees."
13. The erection of an independent Polish state including "the territories inhabited by indisputably Polish populations" with "a free and secure access to the sea," and with an international guarantee of her "political and economic independence and territorial integrity."
14. The formation of "a general association of nations ... for the purpose of affording mutual guarantees of political independence and territorial integrity to great and small states alike."

The British premier, in his address, did not include within his war aims anything covering the first three of President Wilson's points. Neither did he take a stand in behalf of Russia such as President Wilson did in his

sixth point. Here Lloyd George apparently let disappointment and vin-
dictiveness dominate his statement that "if the present rulers of Russia
take action which is independent of their Allies we have no means of intervening to arrest the catastrophe which is assuredly befalling their country."
On all the other points of President Wilson's program, however, he held
a practical identity of views, and concluded by laying down "three conditions" for a permanent peace:

First, the sanctity of treaties must be re-established. Secondly, a territorial
settlement must be secured, based on the right of self-determination or the consent of the governed. Lastly, we must seek by the creation of some international
organization to limit the burden of armaments and diminish the probability
of war.

These announcements of Allied war aims evoked no enthusiasm among
the leaders of the Central Powers, whose views were set forth on January
24 in addresses by Count Hertling, the German chancellor, and Count
Czernin, the Austrian foreign minister. On the first four points they admitted that "an understanding might be reached without difficulty." The
fourteenth point Czernin accepted much more whole-heartedly than did
Hertling, the former stating his belief that it would "nowhere meet with
opposition in the Austro-Hungarian Monarchy," the latter only grudgingly
conceding that "the Imperial German Government is gladly ready, after all
other pending questions have been settled, to approach the examination of
the basis of such an association of nations."

But not even a grudging acceptance was vouchsafed the remaining points.
The fifth would have to be discussed "at the reconstitution of the world's
colonial possessions, which we ... absolutely demand." Great Britain must
"come to terms with this proposal" of President Wilson. The question of
Russia was one which concerned the Central Powers and Russia alone,
and Germany declined all interference. She also refused to agree in advance in regard to the treatment of Belgium; this question belonged "to
the complex of questions ... which will have to be settled by the war and
peace negotiations." Under no circumstances would Germany countenance
the cession of Alsace-Lorraine, and even the evacuation of France "must
take into account Germany's vital interests." The future of Poland was a
question for the decision of Germany, Austria-Hungary, and Poland. In
regard to the remaining points Germany was prepared to "do everything
for the attainment of peace by Austria-Hungary, which takes into account
her just claims," and to give her energetic support to her "loyal, brave, and
powerful ally, Turkey." The Allied war aims, Count Hertling asserted,
reflected the Allies' belief that they were the victors and that it was the
Central Powers who were the vanquished.

The leaders of the Entente must therefore free themselves from this point of view and this self-deception. And in order to facilitate this aim I would like to recall what the position really is. They may take it from me that our military position has never been so favorable as it is at the present time. Our brilliant military leaders face the future with undiminished confidence in victory. Unbroken joy of battle inspires the entire army—officers and men. . . . God is with us, and will continue to be with us.

Germany's Final Military Effort

In February Hindenburg and Ludendorff explained their military plans for 1918 to a secret session of the Reichstag, which approved the undertaking even though it called for Germany's loss of a million and a half men. Their aim was to obtain a decision in the field in four months, before the United States could bring her tremendous resources and man power fully to bear. As the first step in their campaign, they proposed to isolate the British army by rolling it up from its right and then driving it into the sea or holding it in an entrenched camp between the Somme and the Channel. The first drive, therefore, was to be directed against that point in the line where the British and French forces met, on the supposition that the lack of unified command among the Allies would lead to confusion here at the moment of attack. German divisions were withdrawn from the Italian and Balkan fronts, half of the 1920 class of recruits was prepared for service, and some half million men were transferred from the east. By March Hindenburg was on the western front with the "whole German manhood for the first time united in a single theater of war, ready to strike with the strongest army that the world has ever known." In addition to superiority of forces, the German high command counted further upon new tactics the effectiveness of which had been proved at Riga and Caporetto in 1917. The essence of these new tactics was the absence of preliminary massing of troops near the front and of long artillery preparations, the use of highly specialized shock troops, and the assault in open order by a method called "infiltration."

After preliminary threats on the Champagne and Ypres fronts, the Germans on March 21, 1918, suddenly hurled a force of over half a million men against a fifty-mile sector between Arras and La Fère. The British, outnumbered three or four to one, gave way and on the second day lost contact with the French on their right. It appeared that the Germans would succeed in breaking through the line as they had planned. But on the twenty-sixth the gap was again bridged, and, although the British continued to retreat, their line was neither broken nor pushed back into the sea. Nevertheless, when the battle finally ended in the latter part of April, the

British had retreated some thirty-five miles and had suffered over 300,000 casualties.

One reason for the extent of the British disaster on the Somme was Pétain's reluctance to shift immediately sufficient troops from the French lines to the British sector. One result of the defeat was the realization of the absolute necessity for a unified command of all Allied forces. In the midst of the retreat British and French statesmen met and unanimously decided,

THE GERMAN OFFENSIVE OF 1918

on March 26, to entrust at once the control of all forces in the west to General Foch, by universal consent the master mind among the Allied generals. Four weeks later he was given added authority by being made "Commander-in-Chief of the Allied Armies."

At the same time strenuous efforts were made to overcome the Allied inferiority in man power. Great Britain passed a more drastic conscription act, subjecting every British man between the ages of eighteen and fifty-five to military service, and within a month sent across the Channel 355,000 British troops which had been kept in England to meet a possible invasion. By herculean efforts, during May, June, and July over 675,000 American soldiers were rushed across the Atlantic to France—more than twice the number sent in the whole preceding year. On April 28 the first American regular army division, after long training in quiet sectors, began active fighting on the Picardy front.

Meanwhile, on April 9, shortly after the first offensive died down, the Germans struck their second blow against the depleted British left wing between La Bassée and Armentières, where there seemed to be a possibility of breaking through to the Channel ports. But the British troops responded to General Haig's plea that "there must be no retirement. With our backs to the wall ... each one of us must fight on to the end." And, although in some places they retreated from fifteen to twenty miles, the British stemmed the German flood, kept their lines intact, and held the enemy far back from the coveted Channel ports.

These two tremendous drives with their spectacular results temporarily encouraged the German people to make still further sacrifices, although the German armies had already incurred something over half a million casualties. Ludendorff's attempts to rebuild his forces with men returned from hospitals and with boys of the 1920 class were suffered in silent anguish in the hope that a "German peace" would be won before autumn. By the last week of May Ludendorff had succeeded in replacing more than 70 per cent of his losses. On the twenty-seventh he struck his third terrific blow, this time against the French between Soissons and Reims. Within two days the Germans captured Soissons, and on the thirty-first they reached the Marne valley, down which they hoped to advance toward Paris. Now at length the American forces began to play a decisive role. The second division and parts of the third and twenty-eighth divisions were thrown into the line and helped to bring the German drive to an end. Not only did they halt the Germans; they recaptured from them some of the positions which they had already taken.

But again the Germans had made a tremendous advance of over thirty miles in three days. They had seized the Marne bank for ten miles and had taken between 30,000 and 40,000 prisoners. But their position was such that it offered no safe resting place. They must continue the battle or relinquish their gains. So far they had established two salients threatening Paris; they now sought to convert them into one by a fourth attack (June 9–15) on a front of twenty-two miles between Montdidier and Noyon. But this time the French army, expectant and reinforced, resisted firmly and stopped the drive after an advance of only six miles. In this they were assisted by the American first division, which had proved its mettle earlier (May 28) by capturing and holding Cantigny.

No sooner had this offensive subsided in the west than the Austrians launched what they hoped would be a decisive drive against the Italians on the Piave. But General Diaz learned of the Austrian plans, and knew even the hour set for the attack, which was to begin at three in the morning of June 15. He therefore anticipated the assault by an Italian bombardment of the Austrian troops and succeeded in seriously upsetting their assembly. Nevertheless, promptly at the designated hour the advance began, the Austrians attempting to use the tactics which had been so successfully employed by the Germans in France. They had succeeded in crossing the river with nearly 100,000 men when suddenly, on the afternoon of the seventeenth, the flooding of the Piave turned that broad, shallow stream into a raging torrent which swept away ten of the fourteen bridges upon which the Austrians depended. On the next day Diaz with reinforcements began the counterattack. Within a week the whole of the west bank of the Piave was once more in Italian hands. Austria, instead of putting Italy out of the war, had lost 20,000 prisoners and had suffered at least 150,000 casualties. It was Austria's last great effort. She was broken in spirit, and great numbers of her people were starving. Mutinies and desertions menaced her armies, and disruptive nationalist aspirations threatened the empire. Germany must now continue the struggle practically alone.

But in the west the Germans were preparing to do this. They planned a great *Friedensturm,* or "peace offensive," which was to strike the French line to the east and west of Reims, capture that city, split the French front, cut the vital railway from Paris to Nancy, and enable German troops to sweep down the Marne valley to Paris. At midnight on Sunday, July 14, the sound of great guns to the east told Paris that the final struggle for her capture had begun. Four hours later, at dawn, the Germans began an advance, the importance of which was recognized by both sides. "If my offensive at Reims succeeds, we have won the war," said Ludendorff. "If the German attack at Reims succeeds, we have lost the war," admitted Foch. The Germans succeeded in crossing the Marne between Château-Thierry and Dormans, but they got little farther. On the southeast an Italian corps blocked their way, while on the southwest they encountered American troops who stopped them and pushed them back across the Marne. East of Reims French and American troops held back the German rush and prevented the capture of the city. In the three days' battle the Germans advanced barely six miles at the farthest point. The day of their terrific sledgehammer blows was past. Paris was again saved, and thereafter the offensive rested in Allied hands.

For Foch was now in a position to undertake a general advance. Thanks to American reinforcements, the Allies once more had superiority in rifle strength, a superiority which continued to increase during the rest of the war. The decisive turning point in the conflict had come. Thereafter the collapse of the Central Powers was speedy and sure. A series of Allied offensives rolled back the German armies without cessation until their final surrender in November. Château-Thierry fell on July 21; in August, Sois-

sons, Fismes, Montdidier, Bapaume, and Noyon were recaptured, and the
Allies crossed the Somme. In six weeks they captured 130,000 German
prisoners, 2000 heavy guns, and 14,000 machine guns.

On August 8 a terrific British attack convinced Ludendorff that the war
could not be won, and at a conference at general headquarters at Spa five
days later he advised the initiation of "peace feelers." The German chancellor was given a free hand to act at his discretion. Early in September the
German army chiefs informed Chancellor Hertling that they must have
peace as soon as possible. On September 15 Austria issued an appeal "to all
belligerents to send delegates to a confidential and nonbinding discussion on
basic principles," an appeal which was declined by President Wilson on the
ground that his terms had already been stated.

The Disintegration of Austria-Hungary

By this time the Habsburgs were in dire straits, for they were waging a
struggle not only against foes without their empire but also against disintegration within. The long pent-up national aspirations of the various
subject peoples were seeking concrete expression. In January, 1918, Czech,
Polish, and Yugoslav deputies in the Reichsrat had drafted a program calling for the establishment of a sovereign constituent assembly for every local
area in which a specific language was spoken, the settlement of boundary
disputes by means of plebiscites, and the right of each nation to form whatever political ties it desired. Three months later Czechs and Yugoslavs in a
great public meeting in Prague had taken a solemn oath to "persist in the
struggle for independence in all circumstances and unto the end."

Meanwhile, abroad, energetic steps had been taken to present the claims
of the various subject nationalities. Before the war was a year old, national
leaders of the Czechoslovaks, Yugoslavs, and Poles were busily at work
seeking to gain the sympathy of the Allies and the official recognition of
the justice of their cause. Representing the Czechoslovaks abroad were
Thomas G. Masaryk, professor of philosophy in the Czech University of
Prague and long the leading exponent of the Czech nationalist movement,
Eduard Beneš, one of his young colleagues at the university, and Milan
Štefánik, a distinguished Slovak scientist. By them the Czechoslovak Na-
tional Council was organized in Paris, and "bureaus" were established in
France, England, Italy, and the United States to create a sentiment favorable
to Czechoslovak national aspirations.

Similarly, under the leadership of Ante Trumbich, a deputy in the Austrian Reichsrat, the Yugoslav Committee was organized in London. The
aim of the Yugoslav leaders was set forth later in the declaration of Corfu

(July 20, 1917), drawn up jointly by Trumbich and the Serbian premier, Pashich, and forecasting the "Kingdom of the Serbs, Croats, and Slovenes." These three peoples, according to the declaration, constituted a single nation, and it was definitely agreed that they should become united under the Karageorgevich dynasty in a constitutional, democratic, and parliamentary monarchy, the constitution for which should be drafted, after peace had been attained, by a constituent assembly elected by universal suffrage.

In the early years of the war somewhat less vigorous steps were taken abroad in behalf of the Poles under the leadership of Paderewski, world-renowned pianist, and Sienkiewicz, the famous Polish novelist. Eventually the Polish National Committee, seeking the resurrection of a free and united Poland, located its headquarters in Paris and appointed Paderewski to represent it in Washington. By the middle of 1918 the subject nationalities had succeeded in winning from the Allied governments official recognition of the justice of their cause.

But the military collapse of the Dual Monarchy was a necessary prerequisite of the final independence of the subject races, for the Habsburg government steadily refused to consider any such eventuality. To this collapse the subject nationalities contributed both directly and indirectly. On the one hand, they offered their regiments to swell the Allied forces; by 1918 Czechoslovak, Yugoslav, and Polish legions were fighting on the Allied side. On the other hand, they persistently sought to undermine and weaken the Teutonic forces from within. Munition plants were blown up, mutinies became frequent both in the army and in the navy, and desertions by the thousands continued unchecked. Leaflets bearing the Allied assent to the freedom of the subject nationalities, which were scattered by airplanes over the Austrian armies in 1918, undoubtedly contributed to the destruction of the morale of the troops.

Military developments in the Near East also contributed to the undermining of that morale. On September 15 the Allied forces on the Saloniki front finally began their oft-delayed advance. In the battle of the Vardar, Serbian, French, British, and Greek troops attacked the Bulgarians, who were routed and forced to retreat. As soon as the latter's territory was actually invaded, the Bulgarian government sued for an armistice, and on September 30 the first of the Central Powers went out of the war. Her means of transportation, now placed at the disposal of the Allies, opened the way for an attack upon Turkey from the west. But Turkey did not wait for any such eventuality. Cut off from the Central Powers, driven back three hundred miles by a rapid Allied advance which captured Damascus, Beirut, Tripoli, and Aleppo in the single month of October, fearful for the safety of Mosul in Mesopotamia and Adrianople in Thrace, the Turks likewise appealed for an armistice, and withdrew from the war on October 31.

The defection of Bulgaria threw the burden of maintaining the Balkan front on weakened Austro-German forces, which were further demoralized by events within the Dual Monarchy. Early in October the German-Austrian deputies of the Reichsrat constituted themselves a provisional national assembly and proclaimed the establishment of a new Austrian state. On October 5 representatives from all Yugoslav territories of the empire met at Zagreb and elected a Yugoslav national council to defend their interests. Two days later at Warsaw Polish representatives issued a manifesto promising a national government and a freely elected diet for a reunited Poland. On October 14 Beneš informed the Allied governments that the Czechoslovak National Council in Paris had been transformed into a provisional government with Masaryk as president, Beneš as foreign minister, and Štefánik as secretary for war; and France recognized the provisional government on the next day.

In a last desperate effort to save his realm from complete disintegration Emperor Charles issued a manifesto on October 16, 1918, announcing the policy of federalization. Austrian Poland might freely unite with an independent Polish state, but the rest of Austria was to be transformed into a federal state in which every race should "create its own constitutional status" in the territory in which it dwelt. In Hungary the issuing of the imperial manifesto was regarded as the destruction of the *Ausgleich,* and the Hungarian government at once declared that the Dual Monarchy was dissolved. This resulted, in turn, in the immediate assertion of the right of self-determination by the Rumanians and Slovaks of the Hungarian kingdom. Nor did the emperor's program win the approval of the various Slav peoples; the day when federalization would satisfy the subject nationalities had passed. Their aim was now absolute independence. During the succeeding ten days the empire went completely to pieces, and the various districts came under the political control and administration of different national councils—Ukrainian, Yugoslav, Czech, German, Magyar, and Rumanian. National popular governments supplanted the Habsburg dynasty.

On the field of battle, meanwhile, the Habsburg forces were being relentlessly driven back. On October 12 they lost Nish, and two days later Durazzo and Novibazar. By the nineteenth their line near the Rumanian frontier was back on the Danube. On the twenty-fourth the Allies launched an attack in the Trentino and on the Piave, which resulted a week later in the complete routing of the Austrian forces on these fronts. On November 1 the Serbians recaptured Belgrade; two days later the Italians made their triumphal entry into Trieste. On that same day (November 3) the

Habsburgs, beset behind and before, capitulated and signed an armistice with the Allied Powers. Eight days later Emperor Charles formally surrendered his Austrian throne. Of *Mittel-Europa,* Germany alone remained a belligerent.

Downfall of the German Empire

Meanwhile, in the west the Germans by September had been driven back to the Hindenburg Line, having suffered a million and a half casualties since they had left it less than six months earlier. But the Allies continued their attacks unceasingly. In the middle of September over half a million American soldiers wiped out the long-standing St. Mihiel salient. Farther west the Allied troops smashed through the Hindenburg Line and drove the Germans back out of Péronne, Lens, and Dixmude. By September 28 Ludendorff concluded that all was lost and so informed the Kaiser at a conference at Spa the next day. On the thirtieth Hertling resigned as chancellor, and the Kaiser announced that "the German people shall co-operate more effectively than hitherto in deciding the fate of the Fatherland." On October 1 Hindenburg insisted that a peace offer should be made at once, and two days later made his demand more peremptory.

The Kaiser now appointed Prince Max of Baden German chancellor, with a coalition ministry admitting two Socialists into the government for the first time in the history of the empire. On the following day the new government sent a note to President Wilson appealing for a cessation of hostilities, and announcing Germany's readiness to accept the President's Fourteen Points together with his later pronouncements as a basis for the discussion of peace terms.[1] But the obtaining of an early armistice was not the only nor perhaps the most important task which rested upon the shoulders of the new chancellor. He had also to attempt to preserve the Hohenzollern empire against the forces which were by now apparently determined to bring about its downfall.

For the situation within Germany in 1918 was very different from that which had existed four years earlier. Then, firm in the belief that the fatherland was being maliciously attacked by an overwhelming coalition of opponents, the German people of all parties had sprung forward as a nation to repel the foes. Even the Social Democrats, who had long denounced all war as in the interest of capitalists alone, recognized the duty of defending the homeland against tsarist Russia, whose triumph their leader, Haase, declared "would be the end of the German people."

But to the Germans the war had brought ever-increasing hardships, pr-

[1] On July 4 and September 27 President Wilson had restated the purposes of the war and in the latter address had laid down five principles for the foundation of a league of nations.

vations, and sorrow. These in turn had led to disappointment, disillusion-ment, and a loss of faith in the government. In consequence, the succeeding years had witnessed a gradual decline in enthusiasm for the war and for those who in the popular mind had come to be held responsible for its continuance. In 1916 this feeling had split the Social Democrats when Haase denounced the continuance of the war and was in consequence read out of the party. In the following year he and his followers had organized the Independent Social Democratic Party. Thereafter they had devoted their efforts to denouncing the war as a crime and had even begun to work for the overthrow of the empire.

Even more destructive in their activities than the Independents were the Spartacists, led by Karl Liebknecht and Rosa Luxemburg, both of whom spent a considerable part of the war period in prison. This group had developed on the left wing of the Independents and took its name from the so-called Spartacus letters, the first of which had appeared in 1916 on the Kaiser's fifty-seventh birthday. These letters had denounced the war as one of imperialistic aggression and had summoned Germans to employ all possible obstructive tactics against it.

For the revolutionary agitators in Germany during the closing years of the war, a fertile field for propaganda was created by the dire distress of the urban masses, caused largely by the Allied blockade. Millions lived on the verge of starvation, while the death rate steadily climbed. Bread, butter, milk, sugar, meat, eggs, and potatoes were rationed out in very limited quantities, while pork, bacon, ham, fresh fish, cheese, coffee, tea, and spices gradually disappeared altogether. For weeks during the "turnip winter" of 1916–1917 potatoes were not to be had, and coarse fodder turnips had to be substituted. The discontent with such conditions was greatly magnified by frequent breakdowns in the government's rationing system, which resulted in profiteering and in an inequitable distribution of the foodstuffs that were actually available. In consequence of this, the wealthy could usually obtain most of the necessaries and some of the luxuries of life, while the poorer people were forced to suffer privation. Cold, miserable, dispirited, many recalled the prewar Socialist doctrine that all wars are the work of the capitalist classes, that existing governments everywhere are obstacles to the coming of a true universal brotherhood of men.

After the Russian Bolshevik revolution and subsequent peace of Brest-Litovsk the "poison gas of Leninism" was wafted back upon Germany. The leaders of the Spartacists and Independent Socialists were supplied with money, arms, and literature, and from the Russian embassy a staff of men worked to overthrow the very government to which it was accredited. The Spartacists now became definitely imbued with communistic doctrine and began to advocate the immediate socialization of industry and a world revolution of the proletariat. In preparation for the latter they sought to establish revolutionary workmen's and soldiers' councils throughout Germany and even at the front.

By the beginning of 1918 the influence of these revolutionary groups had reached such proportions that a great political strike was called in Berlin and Essen. For over a week a half million men refused to work. In Berlin they presented an ultimatum to the government demanding a speedy peace without annexations or indemnities, the participation of workingmen's delegates of all countries in the peace negotiations, the release of all political prisoners, freedom of assembly and the press, democratization of state institutions, and woman suffrage.

The government's ruthless suppression of this pacific strike convinced the Independent Socialists that only an armed revolt of the proletariat could free the nation from the menace of imperialism and capitalism. They therefore made the definite decision to overthrow the government. A further disastrous result of this January strike came from the punitive measures adopted by the government. Many of the strikers were promptly drafted into the army in punishment for their activity during the strike. This practice of "using the army as a prison establishment, and the trenches as cells" proved most unwise, however, for the men thus punished became ardent propagandists of socialism and peace, and carried to the front lines not only rifles but germs of revolution as well.

In the army, too, during 1918, revolutionary propaganda found a fertile field among men who were beginning to be hungry and ill-clad, and who were dispirited by complaints from home folks of increasing privations and suffering. The doctrines of Bolshevism, which the troops transferred from the east brought with them, found ready listeners in men who were subject to the discomforts of mud, vermin, and crowded quarters of the front-line trenches. This discontent was immeasurably increased when the tremendous wastage of men during the first half of 1918 brought only military defeat. Even in the highly disciplined German army desertions by the thousands occurred in the closing three months of the war.

The German defeat in the second battle of the Marne and the fearful collapse of the entire western front during the following months had an effect not only in the army itself but behind the lines as well. Everywhere was the belief that the nation had been duped and deceived, and that there was but one road to salvation—the overthrow of the regime which had brought this immense misery upon the people. The destruction of the military dictatorship of general headquarters and the democratization and parliamentarization of the empire became the program, late in September, of the National Liberals and Centrists, who signified their desire to work toward this end in co-operation with the Majority Socialists.[2]

A menacing situation thus confronted Prince Max when he assumed the chancellorship early in October. But the government went desperately to work to avert revolution by transforming the former quasi-autocratic state into a parliamentary monarchy. The new chancellor hoped that by rapidly democratizing the constitution and the government he might save the Kaiser and the Hohenzollern dynasty. Reform was now the order of the day. Ministerial responsibility was established, the sanction of war and peace was placed in the hands of the Reichstag, the military was brought under the control of the civil authority, amnesty was granted to political prisoners, and freedom of press and assembly was established. Prince Max thus ended the personal regime of the Hohenzollerns and gave the German Empire its first parliamentary government. The Kaiser remained merely as the symbol of German unity.

But by this time William II was doomed. The Kaiser's position, already undermined by Socialist and enemy propaganda, became altogether untenable when President Wilson demanded, as the prerequisite of peace negotiations, "the destruction or reduction to virtual impotency of the arbitrary power which has hitherto controlled the German nation." When the German people learned "that the nations of the world do not and cannot trust the word of those who have hitherto been the masters of German policy," that, if the United States "must deal with the military masters and the monarchical autocrats of Germany . . . , it must demand, not peace negotiations, but surrender," a revulsion of popular feeling set in against generals, emperors, and kings. Early in October the question of the Kaiser's abdication began to be discussed among the people, and by the end of the month the demand had apparently gained the support of the bulk of the nation as the only means to assure a cessation of hostilities and bearable terms of peace. On the evening of October 29 the Kaiser, feeling insecure in Berlin, fled from the capital to general headquarters at Spa.

The final crisis was precipitated when the admiralty, realizing that the armistice terms would undoubtedly demand the surrender of the German navy, ordered the fleet to steam out to engage the British in a final decisive battle. When the men realized that, with armistice negotiations actually under way, the lives of 80,000 subordinates were to be recklessly sacrificed, their bitter opposition was aroused. "If the English attack us," they declared, "we will defend our coasts to the last, but we will not ourselves attack. Farther than Helgoland we will not go." This of course constituted only mutiny, not revolution.

[2] After the founding of the Independent Social Democratic Party, those who remained in the original Social Democratic Party became known as Majority Socialists.

But it soon became revolution. On November 4 the sailors' revolt became general. Soldiers' councils were elected, the red flag was hoisted, and the cry "Long live the Republic!" was raised. On the next day the workers of Kiel joined the revolt and formed workmen's councils. What had originally been a naval mutiny now became a great revolutionary movement, which spread rapidly through the coast towns, where the proletariat united with the sailors. Hamburg, Bremen, Lübeck, Wilhelmshaven, and Hanover soon joined the revolt, and by the close of the first week in November the revolution had triumphed along the German coasts. The success of these uprisings became known in the interior, and town after town raised the revolutionary standard. The contagion swept swiftly through the empire, claiming Munich, Frankfort, Cologne, Düsseldorf, Leipzig, Stuttgart, Magdeburg, and Brunswick by the evening of November 8.

By this time Prince Max had come to the conclusion that the only way to save the monarchy and to preserve the Hohenzollern dynasty was to have both William II and the crown prince abdicate in favor of the former's young grandson, and he so informed the Kaiser. But the latter flatly refused to consider the chancellor's proposals; announced that his intention not to give way was unshaken; that at the head of his army he would reduce his country to order.

That night the Majority Socialist leaders instructed the workers that, if the Kaiser's abdication was not announced in the early morning papers of the ninth, they were to leave their work and hold big demonstrations. The Independent Socialists, likewise, decided to begin their revolution on the same morning, announcing, "We do not demand one person's abdication, we demand the republic." By ten o'clock on the morning of the ninth, therefore, thousands of unarmed workmen were marching toward the center of the city, carrying placards inscribed, "Brothers, no shooting!" But the appeal was hardly necessary, for the troops in Berlin were already mutinying and forming soldiers' councils.

All these facts were passed on to Spa by telephone, together with the insistent demand for immediate abdication. Shortly after eleven o'clock came the message that the Kaiser had resolved on abdication in principle, that he was now simply engaged in the formulation of the statement which would be received in half an hour. The half-hour passed without the promised announcement. The Majority Socialists resigned from the government, and talk of deposition was in the air. In order to forestall the latter, the chancellor now took the decisive step of notifying the press that William II had decided to abdicate his thrones, that the crown prince had resolved to renounce his rights of succession, that a regency would be set up, that Prince Max intended to propose the appointment of Friedrich Ebert, leader of the Majority Socialists, as chancellor, and that a German constituent assembly would be convoked. When the Majority Socialists demanded that the government be entrusted to men who had the full confidence of the German people, Prince Max surrendered the chancellorship to Ebert. At two o'clock that afternoon the Majority Socialist leaders proclaimed the German Republic.

At general headquarters, on the same day, the Kaiser learned from the army heads that the troops would no longer fight either abroad or at home, that they would not defend the Kaiser's life against German republicans, and that there was little chance, therefore, of his being able to reconquer Germany with their help. Confronted with these facts, the Kaiser at length agreed to a conditional abdication. In the afternoon came the message that 'His Majesty is ready to abdicate as German Kaiser, but not as King of Prussia." That night in a special train he fled to the Dutch frontier.

The End of the War

Meanwhile, during October, the Allied troops had completed their smashing of the Hindenburg Line by an "arpeggio" of attacks, which forced the Germans almost completely out of France and compelled them to surrender the Channel ports and a considerable portion of Belgium. At the same time, farther east a disastrous blow had been struck by the American forces in their Meuse-Argonne offensive, "beyond compare the greatest ever fought by American troops." [3] For nearly seven weeks the battle raged, with 1,200,000 American soldiers advancing through tangled woods and underbrush toward the Sedan-Mézières railway. This was the principal line of supply for most of the German forces in the west, and, if it were cut, a German retirement on the whole front must result. Slowly American troops pushed back the best of the German divisions until, on November 6, they reached the outskirts of Sedan, cut the Sedan-Mézières railway, and made the German line untenable.

The day before the Americans entered Sedan, President Wilson finally informed Germany that she might apply for an armistice to Marshal Foch. On the following day a delegation headed by Matthias Erzberger was dispatched to receive the terms which on November 8 were laid down by Foch, subject to rejection or acceptance without amendment within seventy-two hours. The position of the delegates was most difficult. Mutiny had already broken out in the navy. Even while they considered the armistice terms, the government of Prince Max was forced to give way to a Socialist ministry headed by Friedrich Ebert, and the Kaiser fled precipitately from

---

[3] "The actual weight of the ammunition fired was greater than that used by the Union forces during the entire Civil War."

general headquarters to Holland. Behind them was a Germany in chaos; before them, a document most severe.

According to the thirty-five clauses of the terms, Germany was to evacuate Belgium, Luxembourg, France, and Alsace-Lorraine within two weeks, and all the territory on the left bank of the Rhine within one month. Allied troops were to take over all of this territory and were to occupy the bridge-

THE FINAL ALLIED OFFENSIVE OF 1918

heads of the Rhine at Mainz, Coblenz, and Cologne to a depth of thirty kilometers on the right bank. A neutral zone ten kilometers wide was to extend along the right bank of the Rhine from Holland to the Swiss frontier. All German troops in Russia, Rumania, and Turkey were to be withdrawn. Within two weeks 5000 locomotives, 150,000 railway cars, and 5000 motor trucks in good working order were to be delivered to the Allies. A specified number of submarines and warships were to be surrendered, and the rest, together with the naval aircraft, were to be disarmed. There was to be an immediate repatriation, without reciprocity, of all Allied prisoners. Finally, the existing blockade of Germany was to continue unchanged, though the armistice stated that the Allies "contemplate" such provisioning of Germany as should be found necessary. These terms were in no sense peace terms. They were designed merely to bring about a cessátion of fighting, and to render it utterly impossible for Germany success-fully to resume hostilities. At five o'clock on the morning of November 11 the news was flashed to an anxious and expectant world that in a little clearing in the former royal forest of Compiègne these armistice terms had been accepted and signed by the German delegates, to take effect at 11 A. M.

The Cost of the War

Undoubtedly the First World War was the bloodiest that had ever been fought. The conflict mobilized the tremendous total of 65,000,000 men.[4] Of these millions of the most able-bodied of the nations, nearly 9,000,000 lost their lives and about 22,000,000 were wounded in battle. In addition, it is estimated that the loss of civilian life due directly to war or to causes induced by war equaled or perhaps exceeded that suffered by the armies in the field. Nor does this take into account the terrible effects of war, famine, pestilence, and disease on the sufferers who did not die.

The First World War was also unquestionably the costliest that had ever been fought. The total direct war costs for the principal belligerents amounted to about $186,000,000,000,[5] and when to this are added the in-direct costs due to destruction of property, depreciation of capital, loss of production, interruption of trade, and the like, the real economic cost is raised to the stupendous sum of $270,000,000,000. If to this is further added the estimated capitalized value of the human lives lost in the war ($67,000,-000,000), the astronomical figure of some $337,000,000,000 is reached.[6] The statesmen who had been responsible for the war might well stand aghast at the cataclysm which they had brought upon Europe, and at the stupen-dous task of reconstruction and reorganization which confronted them when, at eleven o'clock on the morning of November 11, 1918, firing finally ceased on the battlefields of the First World War.

[4] See statistical tables in *Current History*, Volume XXII, pages 355–357.

[5] The direct cost of the First World War to the United States was nearly enough to pay the entire cost of running the United States Government from 1791 up to the outbreak of the First World War.—U. S. General Staff, *The War with Germany: A Statistical Summary*, page 135.

[6] As distinct from the money cost or actual expenditures of the belligerent governments for war purposes, the British economist and statistical authority Edgar Crammond estimated that the war actually decreased the national wealth of Great Britain 12.7 per cent, of France 25 per cent, of Italy 20 per cent, and of Germany 26 per cent.—*The Economic World*, July 3, 1920, page 19.

Part Two

THE PARIS PEACE SETTLEMENT AND ITS AFTERMATH

Chapter V

THE TREATIES ARISING
FROM THE FIRST WORLD WAR

THE signing of the armistice was not followed immediately by the drafting of the peace treaties. For various reasons, two full months elapsed between the cessation of fighting and the first preliminary meeting of the peace conference. In the first place, even with modern means of travel it required several weeks for the duly appointed representatives to gather from all the belligerent powers, for this had been a world war. In the second place, the heads of the delegations of two of the most important states were unable to come to the conference immediately. President Wilson decided to lead personally the peace delegation from the United States, and it was impossible for him to arrive in Europe before the middle of December. Premier Lloyd George decided that his government ought to appeal to the British people for a vote of confidence before it represented them at the conference, and so called an election for December 14. This and the subsequent reorganization of the government prevented him from attending until four weeks later.

The Paris Peace Conference

In the meantime, however, attempts were made to gather up and organize the great mass of information—historic, geographic, ethnographic, economic, and the like—which had been prepared by the various elaborate research agencies of the chief Allied states for use at the inevitable peace conference. Great numbers of experts had been working for months gathering facts which might have a bearing on the solution of the many intricate and complex problems which would have to be met. For the tasks which confronted the Allied statesmen at the close of the First World War were incomparably greater than those of any previous peace conference, and the need for an adequate knowledge of the facts in connection with the various problems was imperative.

In recognition of the heroic part played by France in the war, Paris was designated as the seat of the peace conference, and early in 1919 the national delegations began to arrive. In some cases their members numbered into the hundreds—"trained diplomats, soldiers, sailors, airmen, civil administrators, jurists, financial and economic experts, captains of industry and spokesmen of labor, members of cabinets and parliaments, journalists and publicists of all sorts and kinds"—together with their clerks and typists. Whole hotels—sometimes several—were needed to accommodate the various groups. At the head of each delegation were the plenipotentiaries, of whom there were seventy representing the thirty-two Allied and Associated Powers. Although there was a noticeable absence of crowns and gold lace, the plenipotentiaries constituted a distinguished assemblage of the responsible statesmen of the world, including besides the President of the United States at least eleven prime ministers and twelve foreign ministers. Among them were such outstanding men as Clemenceau, Pichon, Tardieu, and Cambon of France; Lansing and House of the United States; Lloyd George, Balfour, and Bonar Law of Great Britain; Orlando and Sonnino of Italy; Hymans of Belgium; Dmowski and Paderewski of Poland; Pashich and Trumbich of Yugoslavia; Bratianu of Rumania; Kramář and Beneš of Czechoslovakia; Venizelos of Greece; and Smuts and Botha of South Africa. The Soviet government of Russia, which had signed a separate peace with the Central Powers in March, 1918, and which was not in good repute with the Allies because of its repudiation of capitalism, was not represented. Nor were any delegations from the defeated powers present during the drafting of the peace terms, for theirs was a role which called merely for the signing of the completed documents. This was to be a dictated, not a negotiated, peace.

On January 12, 1919, the two ranking delegates of the United States, of Great Britain, of France, and of Italy in an informal meeting decided that those states which had declared war on, or had broken off relations with, Germany should be represented at the conference, and that the number of plenipotentiaries of each state should vary from one to five, the five great powers to have the latter number.[1] A plenary session of the conference was to consist of the plenipotentiaries of all the powers, but the main organ was to be the Council of Ten, in a sense an outgrowth of the Supreme Inter-Allied War Council which had acted on matters of military policy during the last year of the war. This council should consist of two representatives of each of the five great powers,[2] and should have the right to decide what

[1] Belgium, Brazil, and Serbia had three each; Australia, Canada, China, Czechoslovakia, Greece, Hejaz, India, New Zealand, Poland, Portugal, Rumania, Siam, and South Africa, two each; Bolivia, Cuba, Ecuador, Guatemala, Haiti, Honduras, Liberia, Nicaragua, Panama, Peru, and Uruguay, one each.

[2] At the peace conference, the United States, Great Britain, France, Italy, and Japan were designated as the "Principal Allied and Associated Powers," the rest being designated merely as the "Allied and Associated Powers." For the sake of brevity, the former will be referred to as the "principal Allies" or the "great powers," the latter as the "small powers."

THE "BIG FOUR" AT THE PARIS PEACE CONFERENCE IN 1919

Orlando, Lloyd George, Clemenceau, Wilson

questions were to be referred to the general conference, and to reserve to itself all questions which it considered needed preliminary treatment. It was further decided that the great powers should be represented on all committees or commissions, the others being represented only when questions directly affecting them were being discussed. Although in theory all decisions of the conference required the approval of a plenary session, as a matter of fact only six plenary sessions were held before the treaty with Germany was signed. For all practical purposes, therefore, the Council of Ten constituted the peace conference during the first two months. Its meetings were secret, but representatives of the other powers were given an opportunity to appear before the council in order to present their claims.

The intricate facts that underlay most of the problems which it was called upon to solve, facts which were constantly being made more difficult to ascertain because of the steady stream of propagandist pamphlets, treatises, ethnographic maps, and petitions which flooded the conference, soon convinced the Council of Ten that it must be assisted in its investigations. The result was the appointment of special commissions, varying greatly in size, to which difficult questions were referred for preliminary study and report. France, Great Britain, Italy, and the United States always had representatives on each commission, and other powers had seats on some of the larger ones. Before the treaty with Germany was completed, fifty-two of these commissions had been appointed to consider various problems. Although their reports were in no sense binding upon the council, many of the articles in the final treaties were taken bodily from the reports of commissions.

By the middle of March, two months after the opening of the conference, the only parts of the treaty with Germany which had been finally agreed upon were the military, naval, and air terms. None of the important and complex territorial questions had yet been decided, and commissions were still considering the financial and economic settlement. It must not be forgotten, of course, that the necessity for dealing with a great many of what may be called executive matters, in connection with bringing order out of chaos in central and eastern Europe, prevented the Council of Ten from devoting its whole attention to treaty-making. Nevertheless, the alarming conditions in Europe urgently demanded greater speed on the part of the conference. The resultant demand for an early peace and a definite ending of the war was most insistent.

The desire for greater speed in the drafting of the treaty together with the need for secrecy during the period of compromise between the great powers led to a change in the organization of the conference. On March 25 it was announced that informal conferences of the chief plenipotentiaries would take the place of the former meetings of the Council of Ten. The "Big Four"—Wilson, Lloyd George, Clemenceau, and Orlando—ceased to attend the sessions of the Council of Ten. Since thereafter the first ranking delegate of Japan also ceased attending the sessions of that council, the latter from March on consisted of only five men. It came to be known as the Council of Five and sank to the position of a sort of superior commission. As such it considered the reports of the commissions already appointed, and transmitted them with its findings to the "Big Four." The latter, beginning with purely personal and informal conversations, finally constituted themselves the supreme Council of Four, which made almost all the important decisions of the conference in respect to the treaty with Germany.

It was an interesting personnel which composed this council: Clemenceau, the dauntless Tiger, stolidly silent save when some remark disclosed his dry humor or stinging sarcasm, inclined to be cynical and dogmatic, inflexibly and courageously fighting for one object, the security of his beloved France; Lloyd George, the nimble-minded, responsive politician, shrewd, alert, dynamic, ingenious, more and more inclined to be lenient with the defeated powers, seeking by compromise and adjustment to bring speedily a peace which would facilitate Britain's much-needed revival of trade; Wilson, idealistic spokesman of the moral and spiritual forces of the world, clear-minded and resolute, tirelessly working to construct the League of Nations which he firmly believed would be the salvation of mankind; Orlando, learned, warm-hearted, eloquent, destined to play a relatively subordinate part in the general settlement, nevertheless struggling to satisfy the ambitions of his enthusiastic compatriots.

Almost inevitably conflict arose among these four statesmen when the time came for the various personal and national programs to be presented for fulfillment, for the abstract Fourteen Points to be transformed into definite treaty provisions. In the latter case, the very elasticity and vagueness which had made it easy for the powers to accept some of the points in principle made it likewise easy for differences in interpretation to arise when they came to be examined from the conflicting nationalistic points of view. In fact, even before the peace conference the Allies had made a number of reservations. The chief problem of the statesmen at Paris was to draft terms which would reconcile the opposing viewpoints of the Allied powers. No one man could dominate a group like the "Big Four." Agreement was possible only through compromise, though frequently affairs had to reach an actual crisis before a settlement was finally effected. On one occasion President Wilson in despair ordered his ship, the *George Washington*, to come for him; on another Orlando and his delegation went even so far as to withdraw from the conference and return to Rome. Despite the strain and stress which prevailed at such times as these, however, the peace conference managed to hold together and eventually completed its work.

The Treaty of Versailles

Although more than a dozen treaties and conventions were eventually drafted and signed in the attempt to settle the many and complex problems raised by the First World War—treaties between the Allies and the defeated powers, between the principal Allies and some of the newly created states, and even between some of the Allies themselves, undoubtedly the treaty with Germany was the greatest single achievement of the peace conference.

THE LEAGUE COVENANT

At the very outset of the conference an acute difference of opinion arose as to whether the Covenant of the proposed League of Nations should be included in the treaty with Germany or should constitute a separate document. There was little doubt, of course, that the conference was expected to create such an organization. Even before the war much thought had been given to the possible prevention of international wars, and various societies had been organized both in Europe and in America to work toward that ultimate goal. The First World War with its terrible bloodshed and suffering gave a great impetus to the movement, and during the final year of the conflict the idea of creating an international organization to prevent war made a tremendous appeal. By the time the peace conference assembled in Paris there was a general demand that this great international assembly should create some common agency for the prevention of war. The spokesman of world opinion on this subject was President Wilson, who had asserted early in 1918 that for a just and stable peace a "general association of nations must be formed under specific covenants for the purpose of affording mutual guarantees of political independence and territorial integrity to great and small nations alike."

Wilson maintained that the League Covenant should be an integral part of the treaty with Germany. Others, however, in view of the serious European situation, desired the speedy conclusion of a preliminary treaty of peace, which need not wait for the drafting of the Covenant. This treaty could settle such important questions as the boundaries and military establishment of Germany, could definitely end the war, and make possible the raising of the blockade of the Central Powers. Wilson, on the other hand, felt that the preliminary treaty would in reality be the main treaty and that to leave the Covenant out would be to weaken the League, if not to postpone its creation indefinitely. Only by making it necessary for the nations to adopt the Covenant of the League in order to gain the benefits of the peace treaty, he believed, was it possible to secure their immediate and unanimous approval of the various provisions of the Covenant.

The second plenary session of the conference, on January 25, 1919, voted that the Covenant should be an integral part of the peace treaty, and entrusted the drafting of it to a special commission of which Wilson was chairman and upon which sat ultimately the representatives of fourteen states. This commission considered a number of drafts, among which the most important were undoubtedly those of General Smuts and Lord Robert Cecil, and at another plenary session of the conference, on February 14, Wilson presented the report.

The draft Covenant of the League at once encountered considerable criticism. From the United States, especially, came an insistent demand that the Monroe Doctrine be safeguarded. In order to satisfy this demand, Wilson, after consulting various political leaders in the United States, brought forward an amendment to the Covenant, which he so worded as to avoid placing the United States in the position of asking a special favor. He proposed that:

Nothing in this Covenant shall be deemed to affect the validity of international engagements, such as treaties of arbitration or regional understandings like the Monroe Doctrine, for securing the maintenance of peace.

The French, desiring a more exact definition of the Monroe Doctrine, objected to this amendment. The British and Italians, however, gave it their support, and Wilson, after an impassioned speech, secured its adoption by the commission. The amendment became Article 21 of the Covenant of the League, and for the first time in history the European powers gave their official diplomatic recognition to the Monroe Doctrine. The Covenant in its final form was definitely approved at a plenary session of the conference on April 28, and became the first twenty-six articles in the treaty with Germany as well as in the treaties with the other defeated powers. These articles are discussed in the next chapter.

TERRITORIAL PROVISIONS

When the statesmen came to consider the territorial provisions of the treaty with Germany, it was readily agreed that, in order "to redress the wrong done by Germany in 1871 both to the rights of France and to the wishes of the population of Alsace and Lorraine," these two territories should be restored to French sovereignty. Clemenceau demanded, in addition, that in the interest of French security [3] Germany's western frontier

[3] The original French program of security as presented at the peace conference has been summarized as follows:

"(1) French military control of the Rhine: (2) a permanent alliance of the Great Powers should be fixed at the Rhine, that the ten thousand square miles of territory lying on the left bank of the Rhine between Alsace and Holland should be detached from Germany and erected into an autonomous and neutral state. A secret treaty of 1917 with Russia had, in fact, stipulated that such a state should be created and that it should be occupied by French troops until all the terms of the final treaty of peace had been fulfilled by Germany. Although it was admitted that the inhabitants of the territory were thoroughly German in speech and life, Clemenceau argued that the Rhine constituted the one advance line which could not be turned and which guaranteed France against invasion.

From the outset Lloyd George opposed the creation of such a buffer state, and repeatedly insisted that "another Alsace-Lorraine" must not be created. The French plan was also consistently opposed by President Wilson. In the end Clemenceau surrendered his demand for the creation of a separate state on the left bank of the Rhine. In return, however, he secured the occupation of this territory by an Inter-Allied force for at least fifteen years, as a guarantee of Germany's execution of the peace treaty, and the permanent demilitarization of the left bank together with a strip of territory fifty kilometers wide on the right bank. Finally, and in addition, Lloyd George and Wilson promised France a guarantee treaty of security which provided that their two countries would come to the aid of France in case of an unprovoked attack by Germany.

Clemenceau also advanced a claim to the Saar basin, a highly industrialized and densely populated area of about seven hundred square miles, most of which had been French before the second treaty of Paris had taken the whole district from France and given it to Prussia and Bavaria in 1815. The basin was of great economic value because it included one of the richest and most concentrated coal beds on the Continent. Furthermore, the Saar mines lay on the outer edge of Germany, they were within a dozen miles of the new French frontier, they were already linked with the industries of Lorraine which were to become French, and with two exceptions they were the state property of Prussia and Bavaria. Clemenceau demanded the political annexation of the territory which had been French before 1815 and the full ownership of the mines but not the political sovereignty of the rest of the basin.

In view of the deliberate destruction of French coal mines by the Germans in 1918, and in view of the fact that prewar Germany had a large

to help France hold it: (3) a group of smaller allies to menace Germany from the east: (4) territorial reduction of the German Empire: (5) crippling of the German political organization: (6) disarmament of Germany but not of the Allies: (7) a crushing indemnity: (8) deprivation of economic resources: (9) a set of commercial agreements preferential to France, prejudicial to Germany."—R. S. Baker, *Woodrow Wilson and World Settlement,* Volume II, page 20.

surplus of coal, the Allied statesmen looked with favor upon French acquisition of the Saar coal mines. The acquisition of these mines might justly
balance the destruction of the French mines, and any excess value might
be credited to Germany's reparations account. But neither Lloyd George
nor Wilson favored the political annexation of the district by France. Again

THE RHINELAND

a compromise resulted. Germany for the time was to retain the political
sovereignty of the region, but was to hand over the government of the district to a commission under the League of Nations for fifteen years. The
coal mines were to be ceded to France, and the district was to be within
the French customs boundary. After fifteen years the people of the basin
should vote as to their future political status—reunion with Germany,
union with France, or continuance under the League of Nations; but only

those should vote who were resident in the territory at the time of the signing of the treaty. If the popular vote favored permanent union with Germany, the latter was to repurchase the mines of the basin at a price fixed by
three experts, a Frenchman, a German, and a representative of the League
of Nations.

To the west of the Saar Germany renounced her rights over the railways
of Luxembourg, and this grand duchy ceased to be part of the German
Customs Union. Slight changes in the German-Belgian frontier line were
made in favor of Belgium in the vicinity of Moresnet, Malmédy, and Eu-
pen. The last two were subject to a sort of plebiscite, which—although denounced by the inhabitants as unfair in its procedure—resulted in favor of
annexation to Belgium. The treaty also stipulated that the frontier between
Germany and Denmark should be fixed in conformity with the wishes of
the population, and provided for two plebiscite zones. This was because
northern Schleswig, when taken from Denmark in 1864, had been promised by Prussia that it would be reunited with Denmark if the inhabitants
"should express such a desire by a vote freely given." This "vote freely
given" Prussia never had permitted. In accordance with the plebiscites,
which were held in 1920, the northern zone was assigned to Denmark and
the southern to Germany.

It was in the east, however, that Germany suffered her greatest losses, for
here a considerable part of her territory, taken from Poland in 1772–1795,
was allotted to the new Polish republic. During the war the Allies had
committed themselves to the restoration of a "united and independent Poland." But how large this Poland should be or where her boundaries should
be placed none of the "Big Four" knew. The only thing that was definitely
known in the beginning was the Allied statement that the new Poland
should include the territory inhabited by a population indisputably Polish,
and "should be assured a free and secure access to the sea." To provide the
latter, experts recommended that a corridor through the province of West
Prussia, including both banks of the lower Vistula and the city of Danzig,
should be given to Poland.

But this recommendation was vigorously attacked, especially by Lloyd
George. He argued that such an arrangement would dismember Prussia,
that it would separate East Prussia from the rest of Germany and turn it
into "a German island floating in a Slavic sea." It would compel a German
going by land from Berlin to East Prussia to cross Polish territory. Furthermore, he pointed out, the population of the city and district of Danzig,
which exceeded 300,000, was overwhelmingly German, as was also the population in the narrow belt of territory around Marienwerder on the east
bank of the Vistula.

On the other hand, Polish statesmen, backed by Clemenceau, maintained that either Germans must cross Polish territory to go by land to East Prussia or Poles must cross German territory in order to carry their commerce to the Baltic. They pointed out that East Prussia's most important item in trade had always been the export of timber by ship, and that Germans could easily carry on their commerce with East Prussia by sea. Furthermore, they

DANZIG AND THE POLISH CORRIDOR

asserted, the rights and needs of the people in Poland ought to take precedence over those of the 1,500,000 in East Prussia. It was freely admitted that the population of Danzig and the Marienwerder district was predominantly German, but Wilson was quoted to the effect that every state had the right to conditions that would assure its economic life. Danzig was the natural port of Poland and of the Vistula river basin, and had been for many centuries outside the political frontiers of Germany. The possession of the Marienwerder district was necessary in order that Poland might control the lower Vistula and the one direct railway between Danzig and the Polish capital, Warsaw.

Ultimately it was decided that in order to ensure Poland's economic interests in Danzig without actually annexing it to that republic, a district of about seven hundred square miles around the port should be established as a free city under the protection of the League of Nations. The Allies undertook to negotiate a treaty between Danzig and Poland which should bring Danzig within the Polish customs lines, should ensure to Poland free use of all waterways and docks necessary for Polish commerce together with the control and administration of the means of communication between Poland and Danzig, and should give to Poland the conduct of the foreign relations of the free city. The executive of Danzig was to be a high commissioner appointed by the League of Nations.

In the treaty, therefore, Germany was compelled to recognize the independence of Poland and to renounce in the latter's favor about five sixths of the former province of Posen and the greater part of the former province of West Prussia. In East Prussia two plebiscites were to be held in districts in the vicinity of Allenstein and Marienwerder, chiefly to determine whether Poland should control territory on both banks of the Vistula. Both districts later voted for union with Prussia and were retained practically intact. In industrial Upper Silesia a plebiscite was likewise to be held; but in this case the final division of the district was favorable to Poland. Germany received a decisive majority of the votes of the inhabitants, but the region, though a closely integrated economic unit, was divided roughly in proportion to the number of votes each country received. The larger part of the population and territory went to Germany, but Poland was given by far the greater proportion of the economic resources. Germany also surrendered a small section of Upper Silesia to Czechoslovakia. The Baltic cities of Danzig and Memel, together with a certain area in the vicinity of each, were renounced in favor of the principal Allied and Associated Powers. The former, as discussed above, was established as a free city under the League of Nations; the latter was assigned in 1923 to Lithuania.

Before the peace conference, it was generally taken for granted among the Allies that Germany's conquered colonies would not be returned, and, when the question of disposing of them first came up in January, the great powers of Europe favored outright annexation. Wilson, however, opposed this procedure and pronounced in favor of a mandatory scheme which apparently had been conceived earlier by both General Smuts and Colonel House. This plan provided that to the various colonies which were "inhabited by peoples not yet able to stand by themselves under the strenuous conditions of the modern world, there should be applied the principle that the well-being and development of such peoples form a sacred trust of civilization." The various colonies should, therefore, be distributed among the powers as mandates which the powers should administer in trust for the League of Nations, to which they must make an annual report. The mandates might differ in character according to their conditions, but to all members of the League there should be equal opportunity for trade and commerce.

Wilson saw in this novel scheme an opportunity to increase the influence of the League of Nations and at the same time to prevent an out-and-out annexationist policy on the part of the European states. Others saw in it an opportunity to deprive Germany of her colonies without having to credit their value to the reparations account. Although French colonial circles were inclined to question the practicability of the proposal, the only open opposition came from Australia, New Zealand, and the Union of South Africa. In the end, however, the mandatory system was adopted, Germany renouncing overseas "all rights, titles and privileges whatever in or over territory which belonged to her or to her allies." Her former colonies were later distributed among Great Britain, France, Belgium, South Africa, Australia, New Zealand, and Japan as mandates of the League of Nations.

The fate of Germany's concession in Shantung caused an acute crisis at the conference. Early in the war Japan had joined the Allies and had captured the German fortress of Tsingtao; later, in 1917, Great Britain, France, and Italy had promised her Shantung and the German islands north of the equator. Definite engagements had thus been entered into which now arose to embarrass the conference. The Chinese government also had declared war on Germany, and at the conference the Chinese delegates demanded the restoration of Kiaochow to China. Wilson supported the Chinese in their demand and desired that Germany's rights in the Shantung peninsula should not be surrendered to Japan but should be returned directly to China.

But Japan was in possession of the district involved, and her delegates were inflexible in their demand for the concession. Taking advantage of the strained situation at the time of the withdrawal of the Italian delegation, they insisted that the Japanese claim to Shantung be granted at once, else they would leave Paris and refuse to sign the treaty or join the League. For a week the Shantung question monopolized the conference. Lloyd George and Clemenceau finally stated that they considered themselves bound by the pledges of 1917. Fearing that, in the face of these developments, the Covenant of the League of Nations might finally fail of adoption, Wilson yielded. It was agreed that the peace treaty should stipulate that Japan obtained the former German rights in Shantung. On the same day that the agreement was finally reached, however, Japan promised that she would return the Shantung district to China in full sovereignty, keeping only the economic rights which had formerly been granted to Germany, and the right to establish a settlement at Tsingtao. This promise was carried out by Japan in 1923.

LIMITATION OF ARMAMENTS

In the interest of the security of Germany's neighbors and of general disarmament, the peace conference deliberately sought to weaken Germany's military and naval forces and to limit her in the use of those which were actually left in her control. The treaty specifically stated that, after March 31, 1920, the army of the states constituting Germany "must not exceed one hundred thousand men, including officers and establishments of depots." There were to be neither military nor naval air forces. The great German general staff was to be abolished and might not be re-established in any form. The manufacture of arms, munitions, and other war material was strictly limited, and the importation or exportation of war material was forbidden. Neither the manufacture nor the importation of poisonous gases was permitted. Universal compulsory military service was abolished. In order to prevent the extension of military training to a greater number of men, by having a rapid turnover in the personnel of the army, the treaty stipulated that the enlistments of officers must be for at least twenty-five consecutive years and those of privates for at least twelve, and that the number of officers or privates discharged in any one year must not exceed 5 per cent of the total effectives.

Germany was definitely restricted in the use of her military forces even within her own frontiers. She was forbidden to maintain or construct any fortifications in her territory on the left bank of the Rhine, or on the right bank to a distance of fifty kilometers eastward. Those already existing were to be disarmed and dismantled. In this demilitarized area she was forbidden to maintain either temporarily or permanently any armed forces or to conduct any military maneuvers. Germany's violation of these articles would be regarded as a hostile act against the signatory powers. On the southern and eastern frontiers Germany must limit her system of fortified works to its existing state.

The German navy was restricted to six battleships, six light cruisers, twelve destroyers, and twelve torpedo boats, and she was forbidden to construct or acquire any warships except to replace units already in commission. Germany might not have any submarines, even for commercial purposes; and all existing submarines must be handed over to the Allied powers or destroyed. As in the army, so in the navy the personnel was limited. The fortifications and harbor of Helgoland were ordered destroyed, never to be reconstructed.

Inter-Allied commissions of control were provided for in the treaty to supervise the execution of the disarmament clauses. They were given the right to establish their organizations in Berlin, to send agents into any part of Germany, and to demand information and aid from the German government. The upkeep and cost of these commissions of control and the expenses involved in their work were to be borne by Germany.

REPARATIONS

In a prearmistice note of November 5, 1918, the Allies had demanded that compensation should "be made by Germany for all damage done to the civilian population of the Allies and to their property by the aggression of Germans, by land, by sea, and from the air." Nevertheless, in the opening weeks of discussion at the peace conference, the British and French delegates contended for the inclusion of all war costs in the amount which Germany should pay, arguing that only thus would the settlement really be based on justice. The American delegates, on the other hand, maintained that the demands which might be made upon Germany were limited by prearmistice agreements and that, consequently, only reparation of damage should be collected, and not the costs of the war. After Wilson had vigorously asserted that the inclusion of war costs was "clearly inconsistent with what we deliberately led the enemy to expect," the other three members of the "Big Four" gave way and agreed that Germany's reparations obligations should be limited to what might be called actual damage, the costs of the war being excluded.[4] The justification for the reparations demands was set forth in the later famous or infamous Article 231:

The Allied and Associated Governments affirm and Germany accepts the responsibility of Germany and her allies for causing all the loss and damage to which the Allied and Associated Governments and their nationals have been subjected as a consequence of the war imposed upon them by the aggression of Germany and her allies.

The next difficulty arose over the meaning of the term "damage" as distinct from "war costs." At first thirty-one different categories of damages were considered, but the number was gradually reduced to ten upon which there was general agreement except as to pensions and separation allowances. Lloyd George vigorously urged that these items should be included, arguing that there should be compensation for damage to families behind the front as well as for damage to houses and other property at the front. "Payment for a destroyed chimney was not to be placed above compensation for a lost life or a pension for a blinded or wounded soldier." The

---

[4] A single exception was made in the case of Belgium; Germany was to pay all of her war costs down to the signing of the armistice.

unanimous consent of the "Big Four" for the inclusion of war pensions and separation allowances was finally gained by a memorandum submitted by General Smuts.

Next came the question of the amounts, periods, and method of payment to be required. The American delegates contended for a fixed and reasonable sum. They argued that it would be well for the Allies to know exactly what they could depend upon to aid them in the rehabilitation of their own economic and financial situation and equally advantageous for the defeated powers to know exactly what they had to pay so that they could set about paying it. But the Allies could not agree on the amount which Germany could pay, and they felt that she should pay all that she could.

In the end it was decided that it would be unwise politically to fix any definite total in the peace treaty. Clemenceau asserted that whatever amount might be agreed upon would fall far short of the expectations of the French people and would bring the downfall of the government which accepted it. Lloyd George, recalling the campaign arguments of the election of 1918, readily fell in with this view. A provisional solution was therefore eventually agreed upon. Germany, by May, 1921, should pay in gold or its equivalent a total of $5,000,000,000, an amount which the experts in general asserted she could pay from her quick, realizable surplus assets. Out of this amount the expenses of the Inter-Allied army of occupation were first to be met, and the balance then applied to the reparations account. The question of further payments was left unsettled but was to be determined by that date, and the power to fix the final sum was to be vested in a Reparations Commission. In case of default by Germany in the performance of any of her reparations obligations, the commission should give notice of such default to each of the interested powers, and might make recommendations as to the action to be taken in consequence of such default.

The measures which the Allied and Associated Powers shall have the right to take, in case of voluntary default by Germany, and which Germany agrees not to regard as acts of war, may include economic and financial prohibitions and reprisals and in general such other measures as the respective Governments may determine to be necessary in the circumstances.

MISCELLANEOUS PROVISIONS

In addition to the provisions already discussed, the treaty when finally completed made a number of miscellaneous requirements of Germany. She consented to the abrogation of the treaties of 1839 which had established Belgium's neutrality, and also adhered to the termination of the regime of neutrality of the Grand Duchy of Luxembourg. She acknowledged and promised to respect strictly the independence of Austria, and agreed "that this independence shall be inalienable, except with the consent of the Council of the League of Nations."

In articles on waterways, the conference sought to provide access to the sea for landlocked countries of Europe by establishing international control over rivers which flowed through more than one country. International commissions were set up to control the Rhine, Oder, Elbe, Niemen, and Danube. In the control of three rivers considered as German—the Rhine, Oder, and Elbe—Germany was therefore placed in a minority. The treaty provided for free zones for Czechoslovakia in the harbors of Hamburg and Stettin. Finally, the Kiel Canal was to be free and open on terms of equality to the mercantile and war ships of all nations at peace with Germany.

In response to the aroused public sentiment in Allied countries during the war and just following it, the treaty publicly arraigned "William II of Hohenzollern, formerly German Emperor, for a supreme offense against international morality and the sanctity of treaties." A special tribunal was to be constituted to try the ex-emperor; but the Allied request for his extradition by the Netherlands was refused by the latter, and the trial never took place. In respect to German "atrocities," Germany recognized the right of the Allied powers to bring before military tribunals persons accused of having committed acts in violation of the laws and customs of war, and agreed to hand over such persons as the Allied powers should specify.[5]

Certain guarantees for the execution of the treaty of Versailles were stipulated in the treaty itself. German territory to the west of the Rhine, together with the bridgeheads, was to be occupied by the Allied troops for a period of fifteen years from the coming into force of the treaty. If the conditions of the treaty were faithfully carried out by Germany, the occupation would be gradually restricted. At the expiration of five years the Cologne area would be evacuated; at the end of ten years, the Coblenz area; at the end of fifteen years, the Mainz area and all other German territory under occupation. If before the expiration of the fifteen years Germany should comply with all the undertakings resulting from the treaty, the occupying forces would be withdrawn immediately. If, on the other hand, the guarantees against unprovoked aggression by Germany were not considered sufficient by the Allied governments, the evacuation of the occupying troops might be delayed to the extent regarded as necessary for the purpose of obtaining the required guarantees. Finally, it was provided:

In case either during the occupation or after the expiration of the fifteen years referred to above the Reparation Commission finds that Germany refuses to

---

[5] In the face of German protests, however, the Allies later gave way and permitted trials in Leipzig to be substituted for the trials established by the treaty. Only about a dozen of the hundred or more accused were ever brought to court, and most of them received merely light sentences as a result of the perfunctory trials conducted by the Germans themselves.

observe the whole or part of her obligations under the present Treaty with regard to reparation, the whole or part of the areas ... will be reoccupied immediately by the Allied and Associated forces.

THE SIGNING OF THE TREATY

On May 7, 1919, the draft treaty was presented to the German delegates who had at last been summoned to the conference, and they were informed that they would have three weeks in which to make written observations on the terms but that no oral discussions with the Allied delegates would be permitted. The counterproposals of the Germans reached the Council of Four on May 29, and were immediately submitted to ten Inter-Allied committees of experts for consideration. The Allied reply granted a few concessions, but in general left the treaty substantially unchanged. Germany was required to declare her willingness to sign the treaty, as modified, within five days, or the armistice would terminate and the Allies would take the necessary steps to enforce their terms. In Germany the feeling was most bitter, and the Scheidemann government resigned rather than sign the treaty. In the end, however, a new government, in which Gustav Bauer was chancellor and Hermann Müller foreign minister, agreed to accept it. Müller and Johannes Bell, minister for the colonies in the new German government, were appointed German plenipotentiaries for the formal signing.

Although none of the meetings of the conference had been held in the great palace of Versailles, arrangements were made to have the final ceremony in connection with the German treaty in the famous Hall of Mirrors in which, years before, the King of Prussia had been proclaimed German Emperor. There on June 28, 1919, the fifth anniversary of the assassination of the Austrian archduke, the final scene was enacted. When the delegates of all the Allied and Associated Powers—except China [6]—were seated, at three o'clock the German delegates were admitted. "Müller was pale and nervous, Bell held himself erect and calm. They were led to their seats just opposite the table of rose and sandalwood on which the book of the Treaty was placed." Upon Clemenceau's invitation the German delegates signed. After them the other delegates signed in the alphabetical order of their countries according to the French names, President Wilson signing first for *Amérique du Nord*. While the signatures were still being affixed the guns began to boom outside. At 3:40 P. M. the ceremony was over. In the gardens, whose gorgeous fountains were playing for the first time since the outbreak of the war, cheering throngs greeted the delegates as they came from the historic palace of Versailles.

[6] As a protest against the Shantung settlement, the Chinese delegates refused to sign the treaty of Versailles.

THE SIGNIFICANCE OF THE TREATY FOR GERMANY

The effects of the treaty upon Germany were far-reaching. Of her territory in Europe she was deprived of more than 25,000 square miles; of her population she lost about 6,000,000. But her loss of raw material was far greater and much more serious. Her prewar resources of iron, coal, oil, potash, lead, zinc, and foodstuffs were all greatly diminished. With Alsace-Lorraine went iron, petroleum, and potash; with the Saar basin went coal. With the removal of Luxembourg from the German industrial system went still more iron. With the lost regions in Upper Silesia, next to the Ruhr the most important industrial district in prewar Germany, went coal, zinc, lead, together with many foundries and mills. Altogether, Germany was compelled to surrender approximately 65 per cent of her iron-ore reserves, 45 per cent of her former coal wealth, 72 per cent of her zinc ore, 57 per cent of her lead ore, from 12 to 15 per cent of her principal agricultural products, and about 10 per cent of her manufacturing establishments.

Overseas, Germany lost an area of about one million square miles with a population of more than 12,000,000 natives. With this region went about 25 per cent of her prewar rubber supply, besides valuable oils and fibers. Her merchant marine, before the war totaling nearly 5,500,000 tons, was reduced to 400,000 tons. Many of the bases of her prewar foreign commerce, such as her special privileges, capitulations, and concessions in China, Siam, Morocco, Liberia, and Egypt, were destroyed. She forfeited many of her prewar commercial treaties with the Allied powers, was for a short period forbidden to discriminate against the commerce of any of the Allies, and in several respects had to grant without reciprocity most-favored-nation treatment to the Allies for a period of five years.

Possessing before the war the mightiest military machine in the world, she was reduced by the treaty to a peace army less than one eighth as large as her prewar establishment, and with no reserves. Her navy, from being second only to that of Great Britain, was reduced to comparative insignificance. Foreign armies were stationed in her territory, there to be maintained at her expense. Foreign commissions, likewise maintained at her expense, were given power to interfere in her economic and military life. On top of it all, she was committed to a reparations bill of unknown size which gave every indication of mounting into the tens of billions of dollars. It was a severe treaty, but it was in response to popular demand in the Allied countries, and should always be read in connection with the treaty which the Central Powers dictated to Russia at Brest-Litovsk.[7] Furthermore, it was President Wilson's idea that several of the treaty provisions were more

7 See pages 86–87.

or less temporary, while the League of Nations would endure and eventually operate to correct the evils which might later appear.

The Treaties with Austria, Hungary, Bulgaria, Turkey

After the signing of the treaty of Versailles,[8] other treaties were signed in 1919 with Austria and Bulgaria, and in the following year with Hungary and Turkey. In the drafting of the subsequent peace treaties, the treaty of Versailles served as the general model. Many of its clauses were transferred bodily into the later treaties, and many of its principles were simply modified to fit the other states.

THE TREATY OF ST. GERMAIN

The treaty with Austria took its name from St. Germain, near Paris, where it was signed. While the Germans were still considering their fate, the second of the peace treaties was presented to the Austrians on June 2, 1919. Like the Germans, they were given permission to make written observations. The Austrian delegates asserted that their state, "German Austria," was a new state, created after the armistice, and had never been at war with the Allies. It was just as much a successor state of the Habsburg empire, they declared, as Czechoslovakia, Poland, and the others. But they failed to convince the Allies, who insisted that Austria was an old state simply shorn of certain of its outlying provinces and endowed with a new government. Accordingly Austria was forced to drop the modifying "German" from her title and was further compelled to accept responsibility for the loss and damage inflicted upon the Allied powers "as a consequence of the war imposed upon them by the aggression of Austria-Hungary and her allies."

One reason why the Austrians had adopted "German Austria" as the official designation of their state was that it pointed the way toward their desired incorporation in the new German Republic. On racial and economic grounds the union seemed a natural arrangement, and, in general, it was approved by the American delegation. The French, Czechoslovaks, and Italians were all, for various reasons, opposed to Germany's annexing the Austrian territory, however, and they were able to influence the peace

[8] The departure of Wilson and Lloyd George immediately after the signing of the treaty of Versailles brought about the dissolution of the "Big Four." Subsequent negotiations and treaty-drafting were under the direction of the Council of Five, which now became known as the Supreme Council and which continued to sit in Paris until January 21, 1920, when, upon Clemenceau's resignation, the Supreme Council as such formally ended. It was succeeded by the Council of Ambassadors composed of the American, British, Italian, and Japanese ambassadors at Paris and of a French representative.

conference on this point. It was stipulated in the treaty that the independence of Austria was inalienable except with the consent of the Council of the League of Nations. It was further specified that Austria must "abstain from any act which might directly or indirectly, or by any means whatever, compromise her independence."

In dealing with central Europe, the peace conference was "placed in the position of executor of the Habsburg estate." Czechoslovakia, Poland, Rumania, Yugoslavia, Austria, Hungary, and Italy were the heirs, and by the time the conference assembled in January, 1919, they had already divided the territories of the Habsburgs in a rough, provisional fashion. But the heirs were in general so jealous, grasping, and quarrelsome that the statesmen at Paris had a dual task. They had to adjust the conflicts which had begun between the different nationalities before they developed into actual war; and they had "to effect a definitive division of the Habsburg inheritance that would be just, practical, and conducive to the peace and security of Europe."

The drawing of international boundaries is not easy, at best. The principles that may be adopted for such work are many, and include ethnic, economic, geographic, historic, and strategic considerations. Perhaps most important of all is the factor of national safety. But few indeed are the instances where boundaries which afford adequate national safety at the same time conform to historic and ethnic rights. In central Europe the lines of nationality were rarely so clearcut that boundaries could be drawn to the satisfaction of all involved. Few of the Habsburg races were separated from their neighbors by clearly marked natural frontiers. Lines of former administrative divisions were of little avail, for most of the provinces contained two or more races jumbled together. Questions of railway and canal communication as well as those of economic dependence had to be considered. It is little wonder, therefore, that the peace conference was obliged to work long and hard on this problem, only in the end to receive chiefly bitter criticism.

Again it must be emphasized that most of the provisions of the treaties were not drafted hastily by the statesmen of the great powers, but were rather the result of the careful investigation and study of a group of experts who were appointed for this purpose. Experts representing the United States, France, Great Britain, and Italy composed the commissions which drafted the new boundaries. When the report of a commission was unanimous, it was usually adopted without modification. Occasionally, however, when political considerations were involved or when a situation became especially acute, the "Big Four" took the whole problem into its own hands for settlement. Then "one might have seen President Wilson himself on all fours, kneeling on a gigantic map spread upon the floor and tracing with his finger a proposed boundary, other plenipotentiaries grouped around him, also on all fours."

The crisis which gained the greatest notoriety and which probably took up more time than any other one problem at the conference arose out of the need for allotting the former Habsburg territory. In the secret treaty of London Italy had been promised, in return for her entry into the war, the acquisition of certain territories around the head of the Adriatic and down the east shore, including the two ports of Trieste and Pola. Unfortunately, after the war the Italians were not content with the gains stipulated in the treaty of London. They demanded in addition the city of Fiume and territories of strategic and economic value which lay beyond the treaty of London line. A strong public sentiment was aroused in Italy to demand especially the annexation of Fiume, the population of which was declared to be for the most part of Italian blood. By many Italians it was believed that the acquisition of this city was necessary to complete, with Trieste and Valona, the "triple bridgehead for expansion in the Danubian and Balkan system" which was contemplated by Italy.

Furthermore, Italy had long aspired to the complete control of the Adriatic. It was partly to obtain the ascendancy in this sea that she had entered the war against Austria. Although Italy's former rival in the Adriatic had now disappeared, to many Italians it seemed that a new competitor for the control of that sea was being raised by the creation of Yugoslavia. Italy had no desire for another strong commercial or naval rival. If she could secure the port of Fiume in addition to Trieste, Pola, and Valona, she would obtain practically a monopoly of the maritime trade of the Dalmatian coast and would greatly handicap the commercial expansion of Yugoslavia, whose only practicable port was Fiume. Consequently, Orlando and Sonnino put forward the Italian claims to that city.

On the other hand, the Yugoslav statesmen were insistent that Fiume and the Dalmatian coast should be awarded to Yugoslavia. They based their claim on nationality and self-determination, quoting figures to show that the population of the region was overwhelmingly Yugoslav [9] and that before the war practically every popularly elected official had been Yugoslav. In respect to Fiume itself they based their claim particularly on the fact that it was their only practicable seaport. South of Fiume there was in Yugoslavia only one railway through to the coast, a winding rack-and-pinion road which came out at Ragusa but which would be very ex-

[9] In Fiume itself the census of 1910 showed 24,000 Italians and 16,000 Yugoslavs. Serbia asserted that, if the population of Šušak, a suburb of Fiume, were counted, the Yugoslavs would have a majority in the municipal area.

pensive to develop and operate as a first-class railway. Actually, nearly all the standard-gauge railways of Yugoslavia were in the latitude of Fiume and had their only direct outlet to the sea at that port. To hand over Fiume to Italy, it was maintained, would be an intolerable subjection of the Yugoslavs to foreign control.

President Wilson gave his support to the Yugoslavs. He not only opposed Italy's annexation of Fiume; he even opposed the complete execution of the Adriatic terms of the treaty of London, which he claimed was not in harmony with the Fourteen Points. In fact, he himself drew a boundary, known as the "Wilson line," which cut down the London terms though it conceded to Italy for strategic reasons the three key positions of Pola, Lissa, and Valona. A memorandum supporting this line was presented directly to the Italian delegation by Wilson, but, since it denied Fiume to Italy, Orlando and Sonnino refused to accept it, fearing to offend the aroused national spirit of the Italian people.

Finally Wilson gave to the press a statement of his reasons for opposing Italy's claim to Fiume. He concluded his statement with the assertion that the claim was contrary to the principles for which America had fought, contrary to the principles upon which she could consent to make peace, contrary to those upon which she hoped and believed "the people of Italy" would ask her to make peace. Orlando at once condemned Wilson's statement as an appeal "to the peoples outside of the governments which represent them, I should say, almost in opposition to their governments." Excitement reached a high pitch when, later in the same day, it was announced that the Italian delegation had decided to leave Paris. Although the Italian delegates actually returned to Rome, they realized that their continued absence from the conference would exclude Italy from the benefits of the treaty, and so, having found that the Italian people supported them in their opposition to Wilson, they returned to Paris. Orlando resumed his place in the Council of Four, but on June 19 his ministry fell, and he and Sonnino were succeeded in Paris by Nitti and Tittoni. The peace conference never succeeded in solving this problem but left it to be settled by direct negotiations between Italy and Yugoslavia.[10]

Aside from Fiume, however, the statesmen at Paris eventually succeeded in making some sort of provision for all the territory of the former Dual Monarchy. Austria lost not only her earlier subject peoples but even some

[10] In September, 1919, perhaps in imitation of Garibaldi's exploits in the nineteenth century, Gabriele d'Annunzio, an ultrapatriotic poet and soldier-aviator, seized Fiume with the aid of a small band of volunteers. In November, 1920, however, Italy and Yugoslavia signed the treaty of Rapallo recognizing Fiume as a free city, and Italian troops compelled D'Annunzio's forces to withdraw. Still later (1924), by another Italo-Yugoslav treaty, Fiume was annexed by Italy and Šušak, its chief suburb, by Yugoslavia.

of her own Germans as well. To Italy she ceded the Trentino, southern Tirol (although the latter included 250,000 Germans), Trieste, Istria, and two islands off the Dalmatian coast. To Czechoslovakia she lost part of Lower Austria, most of Austrian Silesia, Moravia, and Bohemia, with perhaps 3,000,000 Germans. To Poland she lost Galicia; to Rumania, Bukowina. The duchy of Teschen was divided between Poland and Czechoslovakia. To Yugoslavia she surrendered Bosnia and Herzegovina, together with the Dalmatian coast and islands. Austria shrank from an empire with a population of about 30,000,000 to a small landlocked state of only 6,500,000.

Most of the other provisions of the treaty were similar to those drawn up for Germany. Austria's army was reduced to 30,000 men and placed under various limitations. Her entire navy was surrendered, and in the future she was to have only three police boats on the Danube. She must make reparation, the amount to be determined by the Reparations Commission. States which contained territory of the former empire, however, were required to assume a proportional amount of the Austrian prewar national debt. In order that Austria might have free access to the Adriatic, she was given the right to transport goods over the territories and in the ports formerly in the empire and was to receive in those territories and ports national treatment in respect to charges, facilities, and all other matters. On the other hand, she was obliged to concede to Czechoslovakia the right to send her own trains over certain Austrian lines toward the Adriatic. Although the Austrian assembly vigorously protested against the detachment of Germans in Bohemia and Tirol and against the prohibition of Austrian union with Germany, it eventually changed the name of the state from "German Austria" to "Austria," assented to the new boundaries as outlined in the treaty, and agreed to safeguard the rights of the racial, religious, and linguistic minorities of the republic. The treaty of St. Germain was finally signed on September 10, 1919.

THE TREATY OF TRIANON

Although it had been intended to open the peace negotiations with Hungary at the same time as with Austria, the signing of the Hungarian peace treaty did not occur until June, 1920. The chaotic domestic political situation in Hungary was the cause of this delay, for it was not until late in November, 1919, that a government was organized in Hungary which the Supreme Council at Paris would recognize. In January, 1920, the first draft of the proposed treaty was presented to the Hungarian delegation headed by Count Apponyi.

Former Hungarian territory was awarded to every surrounding state— Yugoslavia, Rumania, Czechoslovakia, even Austria. To Yugoslavia went

Croatia-Slavonia and part of the Banat of Temesvar; to Rumania, the rest of the Banat, Transylvania, and some of the Hungarian plain to the west; to the Czechoslovak republic, Slovakia and territory to the east and south of the Carpathians inhabited by some 500,000 Ukrainians; to Austria, German West Hungary, the latter being the only case where one of the Central Powers was given additional territory. The fate of Fiume, Hungary's one direct outlet to the sea, was left to the negotiations of Italy and Yugoslavia, but at least it was lost to the Magyars. Hungary was reduced from a country with an area of over 125,000 square miles and a population of over 20,000,000 to a small landlocked state with only 35,000 square miles of territory and about 8,000,000 inhabitants; while outside these greatly contracted frontiers dwelt some 3,000,000 other Hungarians. The territorial adjustments were difficult to reconcile with any one clear-cut principle.

The rest of the terms of the treaty were substantially the same as those of the treaty of St. Germain. Hungary particularly objected to the settlement of her boundaries without recourse to plebiscites and to the treaty's prohibition of a restoration of the Habsburg dynasty. Count Apponyi resigned from the Hungarian delegation as a protest against the refusal of the Allies to make desired modifications, but the delegation was reorganized, and the treaty of Trianon was eventually signed by Hungary on June 4, 1920, in the Grand Trianon Palace, adjoining the park of Versailles.

THE TREATY OF NEUILLY

The peace treaty with Bulgaria was signed at Neuilly-sur-Seine on November 27, 1919. Although she suffered far less shrinkage in territory than any other of the defeated powers, she did not escape altogether. Her most serious loss was western Thrace, which she had gained from Turkey in 1913 and which provided her only direct access to the Aegean. This she was compelled to surrender to the Allies, who handed it over to Greece. In the west she was obliged for strategic reasons to cede three small areas to Yugoslavia. These were awarded to the latter in order that she might control certain mountain passes and thus obtain greater security in time of war for her Nish-Saloniki railway. Slight alterations were made also in the Greco-Bulgarian boundary line. In view of Bulgaria's loss of her coast line on the Aegean, the Allied powers undertook to ensure her economic outlets to that sea. Bulgaria's military establishment was limited, like those of Germany, Austria, and Hungary, and her navy was surrendered. She was obliged to recognize her liability to make reparation, the amount in this case being fixed at $450,000,000, payable in thirty-seven years from January 1, 1921. As a result of the war and the treaty of Neuilly, Bulgaria became one of the least of the Balkan states in area, resources, population, and military power.

THE TREATY OF SÈVRES

The last of the peace treaties to be concluded at Paris, and the only one never to be ratified, was that with the Ottoman Empire, signed at Sèvres on August 10, 1920. During the war several secret agreements had been made by the Allies looking to the eventual partition of the Turkish lands. Roughly, according to these, Russia was to obtain Constantinople and European Turkey from the Straits up to a line running from Enos on the Aegean to Midia on the Black Sea. In addition, she was to have the islands of Imbros and Tenedos in the Aegean, all the islands in the Sea of Marmora, territory on the Asiatic shore of the Bosporus, the provinces of Erzerum, Trebizond, Van, Bitlis, and part of Kurdistan. The other Entente powers were to share in the partition. Great Britain was to secure southern Mesopotamia with Bagdad, and the two Mediterranean ports of Haifa and Acre; France, the coastal strip of Syria, the vilayet of Adana, and an extensive hinterland; Italy, the Dodecanese in the Aegean, and an area in southwestern Asia Minor in the vicinity of Adalia which she hoped would include the coast from Adalia to Smyrna and the hinterland as far as Konia. Other agreements stipulated that the Arab population of the empire was to be freed and established as an independent Arab state, and that Palestine was to be internationalized. This disruptive program was never fully carried out, however, largely because of the Bolshevik revolution and the resultant uncertainty and differences of opinion which developed among the Allies as to the fate of those regions formerly assigned to Russia.

Eventually, under the provisions of the abortive treaty of Sèvres, Turkey surrendered sovereignty over practically all her non-Turkish populations. In Arabia the Kingdom of Hejaz was recognized as independent. Syria and Lebanon, Palestine, and Mesopotamia were to be entrusted to, or "advised and assisted" by, mandatory powers.[11] Smyrna and its hinterland were to be administered by Greece for five years, at the end of which a plebiscite was to decide their future status. The Dodecanese and Rhodes were ceded to Italy, which by another treaty agreed to turn over the former to Greece. Other Greek islands in the Aegean, together with eastern Thrace up to the Chatalja line, were surrendered by Turkey to Greece. Turkey agreed to recognize the independence of an Armenian state to be constructed in the area of Erzerum, Trebizond, Van, and Bitlis, the frontiers of which were to be decided by the President of the United States. Kurdistan was to receive an autonomous government or, if a plebiscite so decided, independence. The Straits were to be internationalized and the adjoining territory demilitarized. Constantinople and a region in Europe up to the

[11] On May 5, 1920, the powers at San Remo named France as the mandatory for Syria and Great Britain for Mesopotamia and Palestine. In July, 1922, the Council of the League of Nations formally assigned the mandates.

Chatalja line remained under Turkish sovereignty. Turkey was thus reduced to little more than a shadow of her former self, and became a small Asiatic state in the Anatolian uplands around Angora.[12]

The Minorities Treaties

In spite of the great advance toward nationalism which came as a result of the First World War, Europe was still far from organized into purely national states. So many considerations entered into the drafting of the new boundary lines that, even with the best of intentions, it was impossible to prevent the inclusion of racial minorities in some states. Along almost every frontier there were these minorities, a fact which gave considerable concern to the statesmen at Paris. To provide for this situation the "Big Four" decided to incorporate minimum guarantees for racial, linguistic, or religious minorities in the fundamental law of several of the European states. To this end, appropriate provisions were inserted in the peace treaties with Austria, Hungary, Bulgaria, and Turkey, and special treaties for this purpose were signed by the principal Allies with Poland, Czechoslovakia, Rumania, Yugoslavia, and Greece.[13]

Although the minorities treaties differed slightly in details, they were very similar. In general, the various states agreed to assure full and complete protection of life and liberty to all their inhabitants without distinction of birth, nationality, language, race, or religion. All inhabitants were entitled to the free exercise, public and private, of any creed, religion, or belief the practice of which would not be inconsistent with public order or public morals. Such minorities were further granted the free use of any language in private business and in private schools, and the right to instruction in the public primary schools in their own language if they constituted a considerable proportion of the population. In some cases particular privileges, such as the right of Jews to observe their Sabbath as a holiday, were guaranteed. The protection of minority rights was placed in the hands of the League of Nations, and the guarantees might be modified only with the consent of a majority of the Council of the League.

The states which were thus called upon to grant guarantees to minorities vigorously opposed the demand, insisting that they were being compelled to do something which the great powers themselves would never be willing to do. They pointed out that such exactions were an infringement of their own sovereignty and would only help to perpetuate the separatist

[12] For the treaty of Lausanne which in 1923 supplanted the treaty of Sèvres, see pages 405–407.

[13] Lithuania, Latvia, Estonia, and Albania later entered into engagements with the League of Nations to observe toward their minorities obligations more or less identical with those laid down in the minorities treaties.

tendencies which already existed among the minorities. The "Big Four," however, insisted that the demands were in the interest of the peace of Europe, and forced the acceptance of the various guarantees.

The Conflict of Ideas

The contents of the peace treaties drafted at the close of the First World War clearly disclose the conflict which was waged within the peace conference between the diplomats and statesmen of the old, "practical," Machiavellian school, on the one hand, and those of the new, idealistic, "forward-looking" school, on the other. A comparison of the terms of the peace settlement with President Wilson's Fourteen Points [14] will reveal the extent to which the idealistic parts of his program were defeated. Certain of the provisions of the treaties seem to indicate that the preceding century had seen little progress in the principles of treaty-making. If a fear-inspired desire to protect Europe against France was one of the basic principles in the Vienna settlement of 1814, it was far more so in respect to Germany at Paris in 1919. If the principle of "compensations to the victors" prevailed in 1814, it dominated in a degree only slightly less in 1919–1920. Many of the terms imposed in these later years were worthy of Metternich, Castlereagh, or Wellington.

Nevertheless, the statesmen of the new school left their impress on the settlement. If the victors' desire for spoils deprived Germany of all her colonies and Turkey of much of her territory, the idealists dictated that those who gained control of these regions must hold them as mandates of a world society to which they must render account as stewards. If the desire for compensation or protection against Germany led to the demand for territory inhabited by an alien people, it encountered vigorous opposition, for nationalism was as much exalted in 1919–1920 as it had been suppressed in 1814. Although the statesmen at Paris failed to usher in the millennium in respect to nationalist aspirations, an examination of the map of postwar Europe discloses the marked advance which was made toward the coincidence of national and political frontiers.

Despite the fact that there were some instances of arbitrary shifting of peoples from one state to another, which were reminiscent of the Congress of Vienna, such procedure was the exception rather than the rule. More frequently, when the will of the people was not fully known, it was determined through the use of a plebiscite. And in most cases where it was

[14] The Fourteen Points are enumerated on page 90. It is interesting to note that Professor Geoffrey Bruun believes that "it is scarcely an exaggeration to say that the betrayal of the Fourteen Points had already been half-completed, with Wilson's knowledge and House's acquiescence, before the armistice was signed." See Geoffrey Bruun, *Clemenceau* (1943), pages 174–175.

felt necessary, for strategic or economic or geographical reasons, to incorporate an alien people within the bounds of any state, the attempt was made to safeguard them in their political, religious, and linguistic rights by minorities treaties under the protection of the League of Nations.

Finally, the statesmen at Paris, in creating the League of Nations, succeeded in giving practical expression to something akin to that "Holy Alliance" which had been only vaguely conceived in the visionary mind of Alexander I, but which had been characterized by the statesmen of those days as a "sonorous nothing," a "piece of sublime mysticism and nonsense." Thus, in 1919–1920, though the statesmen failed to decide wisely and ideally in every instance, they took steps to provide a future means of correcting and remedying their own worst blunders. For the League of Nations was an integral part of the peace treaties, the keystone of the postwar settlement.

The United States and the Peace Settlement

The fact that the League of Nations was inextricably woven into the peace settlement largely accounts for the determined opposition which the treaty of Versailles encountered in the United States. Although many bitter "Hun-haters" in that country denounced it for its criminal leniency toward Germany, and many utopian idealists, on the other hand, condemned it for not being in full accord with Wilson's Fourteen Points, the attack on the treaty was directed chiefly against Part I, which constituted the Covenant of the League of Nations. Within the Covenant the most bitter assault was made upon Article 10, in which members of the League guaranteed the territorial integrity and existing political independence of all the other members.

Many Americans denounced this article as an infringement on the right of Congress alone to declare war and to authorize the use of the military forces of the United States. Many feared that it might involve the country in war without any choice in the matter, that it transferred to the League "the right to send our boys into wars overseas." There was undoubtedly much misrepresentation and misunderstanding of the League and its powers, and Wilson upon his return to the United States decided [15] to undertake a speaking tour throughout the country in behalf of the treaty and the League. In clear and eloquent addresses the President explained that the League could only advise members regarding steps to be taken against a recalcitrant state. Again and again he pointed out that, with the necessity for unanimous vote in the Council, the United States could not be led into a war against her will. In ratifying the Covenant, he explained,

[15] Despite the advice of his physicians and friends.

the United States did not assume any legal but only a strong moral obligation to enforce the sanctions of the League. Whether popular opinion would have been won to the support of the treaty had the President carried through his extensive speaking campaign will never be known, for on September 26, 1919, his strength failed him and he suffered a slight paralytic stroke.

Meanwhile, on September 5, the Senate had begun its formal consideration of the treaty, and in the course of the ensuing debates four points of view toward the League Covenant became evident: (1) nonratification, (2) ratification with far-reaching reservations, (3) ratification with mild reservations, (4) ratification without reservations. Wilson declared that the reservations proposed by Senator Lodge, chairman of the foreign relations committee, would seriously impair the League. Although willing to accept "reservations of interpretation" so long as they were not incorporated in the ratification,[16] he vigorously opposed reservations in the ratification itself, and urged Democratic senators to vote against the treaty with Lodge's reservations. Consequently, in November and again in March, 1920, when votes were taken in favor of ratifying with reservations, the opposing votes of those Democratic senators who followed Wilson's advice prevented the two-thirds vote necessary for ratification.

Wilson was confident, however, that the majority of Americans were with him and not with the Republican senators who had proposed the reservations. It was his hope that the presidential election of 1920 might be made a popular plebiscite on the League, and that the Democrats might win such a victory as to enable them to secure ratification of the treaty without reservations. By November, 1920, however, the American people had suffered a reaction from their war-time idealism, and were swayed chiefly by a feeling of disillusionment and discontent. Although the League played only a relatively minor part in the campaign, the Republicans interpreted their overwhelming victory in the election of President Harding as a popular mandate against the treaty and the League. The treaty of Versailles was therefore dropped, and the United States continued to be technically at war with Germany.

In July, 1921, Congress eventually passed a joint resolution which was designed to end hostilities immediately without waiting for a formal treaty. Early in the following month the treaty of Berlin was signed with Germany. This treaty was in reality little more than an "index treaty," for its provisions merely referred to specific terms of the Versailles treaty which were either accepted or rejected as applicable to the United States. The provisions of the treaty of Versailles which the United States rejected were chiefly those dealing with the League of Nations, the boundaries of Ger-

---

[16] This was the procedure followed in the case of the Briand-Kellogg pact (1928). See page 154.

many, the fate of Shantung, and the trial and punishment of Germans for war atrocities. The provisions accepted and ratified by the United States included principally those dealing with colonies and mandates, restrictions upon Germany's military, naval, and air forces, war guilt and reparations, the financial and economic clauses, provisions concerning German ports, waterways, and railways, and the guarantees of execution.

It is obvious that the clauses of the treaty of Versailles which the United States ratified in its own treaty of Berlin were among those considered most harsh and iniquitous by the Germans, while those which the United States repudiated were, in the case of those establishing the League of Nations, the very provisions which were designed to ameliorate the harshness of the peace settlement. Unfortunately, in the postwar years most Americans believed that the United States government had repudiated the whole Paris peace settlement. They therefore thought that their country was in no way responsible for the postwar situation in Europe and accordingly was not called upon to take any action regarding such problems as reparations, the French invasion of the Ruhr, Hitler's rearmament of Germany, and his remilitarization of the Rhineland.

Chapter VI

THE LEAGUE OF NATIONS, COLLECTIVE SECURITY, AND DISARMAMENT

ONE of the notable features of the Paris peace conference was its recognition that many of the problems which confronted it could be solved only by some form of permanent international organization. In consequence, the League of Nations, which was at first advocated chiefly as an instrument for the maintenance of peace among the nations of the world, was eventually seized upon by the statesmen at Paris and pressed into service as an agency for carrying out certain features of the peace settlement. The League's activities in this role, its financial rehabilitation of Austria and Hungary, and its handling of various international disputes are treated in connection with other topics.[1] This chapter discusses chiefly the organization and machinery of the League, its proposed role in the preservation of peace among the nations, and its efforts to provide international security and to bring about a general limitation of armaments.

The Structure of the League

The constitution of the League of Nations was the Covenant,[2] which comprised the first twenty-six articles of the various peace treaties drafted at the Paris conference. The Covenant might be amended by the unanimous vote of the members of the Council with a majority vote of the members of the Assembly, for the League was created to be not a fixed and static thing, but a living, growing organism. The original or "charter" members of the League were the signatory states named in the Annex to the Covenant and such of those "invited" states there named as acceded without reservation to the Covenant within two months of its coming into

[1] Consult the index under "League of Nations" or under the names of the countries or regions directly concerned.
[2] It may be found in Carnegie Endowment for International Peace, *The Treaties of Peace, 1919-1923.*

force. Any fully self-governing state, dominion, or colony not named in the Annex might become a member of the League by a two-thirds vote of the Assembly. At the time of the first meeting of the Council there were twenty-four members; ultimately the number increased to nearly sixty. A member might withdraw from the League after two years' notice of its intention so to do. Before the outbreak of the Second World War several had withdrawn, Japan, Germany, Italy, and Brazil being the most important.

The League functioned through the instrumentality of an Assembly, a Council, and a permanent Secretariat. The Assembly was the representative body of the League and as such somewhat resembled the representative legislatures of national states, but with the essential difference that it had no real lawmaking power. It was the instrument by means of which the nations of the League conferred, advised, and deliberated, and in it each member state had one vote and not more than three representatives. Meetings were held annually in Geneva beginning in September, the official languages being French and English. The Assembly was empowered to "deal at its meetings with any matter within the sphere of action of the League or affecting the peace of the world." More specifically, it controlled the budget [3] of the League, selected the nonpermanent members of the Council, admitted states into League membership, and participated in the election of the judges of the Permanent Court of International Justice.

The Council was composed of one delegate from each of the states entitled to representation. The Covenant of the League originally provided that the Council should have five permanent and four nonpermanent members, but the refusal of the United States to enter the League left only four permanent members. The total membership was thus only eight until in 1922 the Assembly increased the number of nonpermanent members to six. With the admission of Germany to the League in 1926, the number of permanent members was fixed at five and the number of nonpermanent members was increased to nine. In 1933 Japan and Germany gave notice of their withdrawal from the League and ceased to be represented in the Council. One of these two vacancies was filled in 1934 when the Soviet Union was admitted to the League and assigned a permanent seat, but another vacancy was caused when Italy announced her withdrawal in December, 1937. Meanwhile, in 1933, the number of nonpermanent members had been increased to ten. In 1939, therefore, the Council consisted of three permanent members—France, Great Britain, and the Soviet Union—and ten regular nonpermanent members. The latter held seats for three-year terms, and a certain number of terms expired each year. Representa-

[3] The annual budget of the League usually amounted to about thirty million Swiss francs.

tives of states not members of the Council might by invitation sit with the Council when questions concerning them were under consideration.

The scope of the Council's powers was the same as that of the Assembly's, but the Covenant delegated to it more specific tasks. It had the duty of formulating plans for the reduction of armaments, of advising on the means of protecting member states in time of foreign aggression, of mediating in case of international disputes, and of receiving reports from mandatory powers. In most cases the decision of the Council had to be unanimous. From 1923 the Council followed the procedure of meeting four times yearly, with extraordinary sessions as required, but in September, 1929, it decided to reduce the number of its regular sessions from four to three annually. Special emergencies and current work throughout the year were handled by the Council, which became to a certain extent the League's executive organ.

The permanent Secretariat comprised a secretary-general and a large staff. The first secretary-general, Sir Eric Drummond, was named in the Annex to the Covenant, but subsequent secretaries-general were to be appointed by the Council with the approval of a majority of the Assembly. Chosen in this way, Joseph Avenol, a Frenchman who had served the League in various capacities including deputy secretary-general, succeeded Sir Eric as secretary-general in 1933. The secretary-general was assisted by two deputy secretaries-general and three undersecretaries-general. These offices were distributed among the great powers, the first secretary-general being British, the deputy and undersecretaries being chosen from the other great powers. The body of the Secretariat was composed of eleven sections,[4] which varied in size from six or seven persons to forty or fifty, the total personnel of the sections numbering about two hundred. In addition to the sections, there were numerous other units known as services, offices, or branches. The Secretariat as a whole required a personnel of several hundred men and women, who were gathered from more than forty different countries. In general it dealt with what might be called the civil-service duties of the League.

The preliminary organization of the League began even before the signing of the treaty of Versailles. At the time the peace conference approved the text of the Covenant, on April 28, 1919, it authorized the appointment of an organization committee consisting of representatives of the powers constituting the members of the Council. Provisional headquarters of the League were established in London, and the secretary-general with the

---

[4] Political, information, legal, economic and financial, transit, administrative commissions and minorities questions, mandates, disarmament, health, social problems, international associations.

committee's approval selected the staff of the Secretariat. Permanent headquarters were later established in Geneva, which thus became the administrative center of the League. In 1936 the Secretariat moved into a
magnificent new League Palace, providing countless offices, numerous
conference chambers, a large library and reading rooms, and auditoriums
for meetings of the Assembly and Council.

The World Court

The Permanent Court of International Justice, commonly called the
World Court, was also in a sense an agency of the League. It was stipulated
in Article 14 of the Covenant:

The Council shall formulate and submit to the Members of the League for
adoption plans for the establishment of a Permanent Court of International
Justice. The Court shall be competent to hear and determine any dispute of an
international character which the parties thereto submit to it. The Court may
also give an advisory opinion upon any dispute or question referred to it by the
Council or by the Assembly.

The Council, at its second meeting, began the execution of this article by
naming a committee of eminent jurists to draft a plan for such a court.
This committee, under the leadership of Elihu Root, former secretary of
state of the United States, submitted its report to the League Council on
August 5, 1920. With slight amendment, the Council in turn presented the
report to the first Assembly, which, after adding a number of amendments,
adopted the plan. A protocol of signature, to which the project for the court
was annexed as a statute, was subsequently opened, and eventually it was
ratified by about fifty states. The statute became effective in September,
1921. The court was composed of fifteen judges [5]—not necessarily nationals
of members of the League—chosen for nine-year terms by an absolute
majority in the Council and the Assembly, each voting separately. The seat
of the court was at The Hague, where the first ordinary session began on
June 15, 1922.

The court had both "compulsory" and "voluntary" jurisdiction. Attached
to the protocol adopting the statute of the court was an "optional clause"
which pledged the states acceding to it to "accept as compulsory, *ipso facto
and without special Convention*" the jurisdiction of the court in all legal
disputes concerning the interpretation of a treaty, a question of international
law, or a breach of an international obligation. Only a few of the member
states adopted this clause immediately, but eventually more than forty

[5] The first judges elected were nationals of Brazil, Cuba, Denmark, France, Great Britain,
Italy, Japan, the Netherlands, Spain, Switzerland, and the United States.

states ratified it, some with reservations. In case of "compulsory" jurisdiction one state might summon another to appear before the court for trial, and, if the latter failed to respond, the court might give judgment by default. The jurisdiction of the court was "voluntary" when states having a dispute agreed to refer it to the court. All questions were decided by a majority of the judges present at the hearing. The court had also the function of giving advisory opinions at the request of the Council or the Assembly, though this use of the court was open to some criticism on the ground that such advisory opinions were somewhat in the nature of international politics.

The Permanent Court of International Justice should not be confused with the Hague Court of Arbitration, which was created by the Hague Convention of 1899 and still existed. The latter was not a permanent court to try cases, but existed only as a list of the names of 132 distinguished jurists from which disputing states might select arbitrators. The World Court, on the other hand, was a court of law and not of arbitration. Its decisions rested on legal principles and on the application of law and justice as found "in treaties, international practice and precedent, or accepted international teaching."

The International Labor Organization

To a certain extent the International Labor Organization, provided for by Part XIII of the treaty of Versailles and by similar sections in the other peace treaties of 1919–1920, was part of the machinery of the League of Nations. Although it was supported by the funds contributed by member states for the maintenance of the League, and although membership in the League entailed membership in the Labor Organization, the latter was completely self-directing. States might be members of the Labor Organization without being members of the League. The United States, for instance, became a member of the former in 1934, and various states which resigned from the League retained their membership in the Labor Organization. In 1939 there were about sixty member states.

The International Labor Organization (ILO) consisted of a General Conference, a Governing Body, and an International Labor Office. The General Conference met annually and consisted of four delegates from each member state, one representing labor, one representing the employers, and two representing the government of the state. In matters requiring a vote the delegates voted individually. The work of the conference generally took one of two forms. It might draw up a recommendation in the form of general principles for the guidance of national governments in drafting legislation, or it might formulate a draft convention in more precise and detailed terms for ratification by the member states. The governments of these states were pledged at least to submit the conference proposals to their respective competent authorities for action.

The Governing Body of the Labor Organization consisted of a group of thirty-two persons, eight of whom represented the workers, eight the employers, and sixteen the governments. Of the last group it was required (1939) that eight must represent the governments of Canada, France, Great Britain, India, Italy, Japan, the Soviet Union, and the United States, thus ensuring that half of the government representatives should be from the states of greatest industrial importance. The other eight states represented were chosen by the government delegates in the conference, and the representatives of the workers and the employers were chosen by the delegates representing those groups respectively. The Governing Body elected its own chairman, and its members held office for three years. It met at least once in three months and had the task of preparing the agenda for the conference.

The director of the International Labor Office was appointed by and subject to the control of the Governing Body, but he chose his own subordinates. The office was established at Geneva in a building erected for the purpose, the total personnel including about four hundred persons in Geneva and about fifty more located in branch offices in the principal cities of the world. The office collected information bearing upon the questions coming up for discussion, issued a journal dealing with labor matters, and kept in touch with governments and various voluntary organizations throughout the world. Obviously the structure of the International Labor Organization was very similar to that of the League of Nations. Its General Conference was analogous to the League Assembly, its Governing Body to the Council, and its International Labor Office to the Secretariat.

Up to 1939 some 133 recommendations and conventions had been drafted by the annual labor conferences. These had to do with working hours, woman and child labor, night work, sanitary conditions, unemployment, public labor exchanges, rights of combination among agricultural workers, conditions of employment at sea, protection against occupational diseases, and the like. Many of the conventions were ratified, many were not, at least by the industrial powers of the West, but before the outbreak of the Second World War more than 700 ratifications had been received from some fifty states. The greatest successes were achieved in the East—in India, Japan, China, and Persia. Although the International Labor Organization had no actual legislative or executive power, it made a strong appeal to public opinion and gave to labor such a vigorous leadership as it had never before known.

Mandates and Minorities

As already pointed out, the mandatory system created by the peace conference was placed under the supervision of the League of Nations. By the peace treaties Germany renounced in favor of the Allied powers all her overseas possessions, and Turkey renounced the possession of her Arab lands. All of the former and part of the latter were placed under the mandatory system, in accordance with which they were to be assigned to states which were members of the League, with the understanding that the mandates would be administered in the interests of their inhabitants.

As the territories were widely distributed over the globe, and as the peoples had reached varying degrees of civilization, the mandates were ranged into three classes, known as A, B, and C. Class A included the former Turkish possessions: Iraq, Syria and Lebanon, Palestine, and Transjordan. These territories were considered to "have reached a stage of development where their existence as independent nations can be provisionally recognized, subject to the rendering of administrative advice and assistance by a Mandatory until such time as they are able to stand alone." In Class B were the six mandates in central Africa, where a greater amount of supervision would be required, while Class C included Southwest Africa and the Pacific islands, which, "owing to the sparseness of their population or their small size, or their remoteness from the centers of civilization, or their geographical contiguity to the territory of the Mandatory, and other circumstances, can be best administered under the laws of the Mandatory as integral portions of its territory," subject to certain safeguards in the interests of their native population.

The distribution of the mandates was the work of the principal Allied powers. The allocation of the African and Pacific mandates was accomplished by the Council of Four at the peace conference in May, 1919. In general these areas were placed under the rule of the country nearest them. Thus, of the C group, Southwest Africa was assigned to the Union of South Africa; Samoa to New Zealand; Nauru to Great Britain, Australia, and New Zealand jointly; other former German islands south of the equator to Australia; and the former German islands north of the equator to Japan. Later in 1919 the Class B mandates were assigned. Kamerun (one sixth), East Africa (Tanganyika), and Togoland (one third) were allotted to Great Britain; Kamerun (five sixths) and Togoland (two thirds) to France; and Ruanda-Urundi to Belgium. The Class A mandates were not assigned until April, 1920. Palestine, Transjordan, and Iraq went to Great Britain, while France received Syria and Lebanon. The C mandates were approved by the League Council in December, 1920, the B mandates and Palestine and Syria in July, 1922, and Iraq in September, 1924.

Annually the mandatory powers presented reports to the League regarding their mandates. These were examined by the Permanent Mandates Commission, which was composed not of governmental representatives but of ten independent experts, the majority of whom were citizens of nonmandatory states. This commission, which met twice yearly, presented its observations to the Council of the League. Each year both the Council and the Assembly discussed the working of the mandates, and an opportunity was provided for the public opinion of the world to bring influence to bear upon the mandatory powers to protect the rights of the natives under their control. On three occasions the Mandates Commission felt called upon to intervene in the administration of mandatory powers, but in general the mandatories sought to receive the approval of the League, and suggestions of the Mandates Commission proved effective. After all, the mandatory system was a "great adventure in the difficult sphere of colonial government." It at least provided an effective means of exchanging experience and establishing co-operation between powers burdened with the task of governing backward peoples.

The reconstruction of Europe following the war still left some thirty million of its inhabitants constituting racial minorities in various countries. Most of these people lived under the protection of the minorities provisions of fourteen postwar treaties, in which the League of Nations was named as guardian. Violations of the rights of minorities might be brought to the attention of the Council, and petitions might be sent to the League. The usual procedure in these cases was for the head of the section of the League dealing with minorities to attempt to reach a settlement directly with the government involved, but more than once cases were taken to the Council, and on two or three occasions they were referred to the World Court.

The League's handling of the minorities problem did not always meet with the universal approval of its members. At the meeting of the League Council in December, 1928, the German representative, Stresemann, questioned the effectiveness of the League's action in respect to minorities, and at the next two meetings of the Council the minorities question occupied a prominent place on the agenda. The Council ultimately decided that all minorities petitions or communications should be submitted to minorities committees, consisting of the president of the Council and two (sometimes four) other members chosen by him. A new committee should be appointed for each petition, and this committee should decide whether any given petition should be placed on the Council's agenda. Individual members, however, still retained their right to call the Council's attention to any infractions of a minorities treaty. Nevertheless, dissatisfaction continued in some quarters, and in 1934 Poland announced that she would no longer feel obliged to co-operate with the League in respect to minorities until some new general system for their protection had been developed.[6] The whole system of protecting the rights of minorities was politically difficult, and the League, rather than try arbitrarily to impose its decisions upon the governments in question, sought to develop the spirit of toleration and conciliation.

Humanitarian Activities

Less spectacular and less widely acclaimed in the press than the activities discussed above were the League's efforts to promote co-operation in matters of general humanitarian interest and concern. It supervised, for instance, the safe return to their homes of several hundred thousand prisoners of war; it helped to care for hundreds of thousands of Greek and Armenian refugees expelled from Turkey; it organized Europe's medical services to prevent the spread of typhus from Russia to the rest of the continent. It brought about the financial rehabilitation of Austria and Hungary,[7] and gave financial assistance to other countries—notably Greece, Bulgaria, Estonia—in times of economic stress. It brought about regular international co-operation in the drafting of sanitary, antiepidemic, and quarantine regulations; in the suppression of traffic in women and in the study of comparative legislation for the protection of the life and health of children; in the reduction and restriction of the sale of opium; in the abolition of slavery and forced labor; in economic, financial, transit, and trade matters; in the extension of intellectual relations. In these fields of endeavor international effort was no longer feeble and spasmodic, for under the League's direction these questions were systematically and continuously studied.

The United States and the League

What the outcome would have been, had the American people been called upon to vote in a clear-cut plebiscite for or against the League of Nations in 1920, can never be known.[8] In the political campaign of that year no such opportunity was presented. Although the Democratic platform favored American adherence to the League, the corresponding plank of the Republican platform—drafted by Elihu Root, an enthusiastic sup-

[6] States bound by the minorities treaties felt aggrieved because certain other states with minorities—Germany and Italy, for example—were not bound to observe "as high a standard of justice" as they themselves were.

[7] See pages 340, 355.

[8] See Clarence A. Berdahl, "Myths about the Peace Treaties of 1919–1920," in *International Conciliation*, October, 1942, pages 411–422.

porter of the League—was ambiguous but seemed also to promise adherence to the League or to something like it. The Republican candidate for President, Warren G. Harding, himself at times interpreted this plank as pro-League and at other times as anti-League. But he promised to consult after the election with the best minds "to the end that we shall have an association of nations for the promotion of international peace."

Moreover, many of the most distinguished leaders of the Republican Party had been and were ardent advocates of American adherence to the League of Nations. Former President William Howard Taft, who was president of the League to Enforce Peace and a faithful worker for the League, supported Harding and certainly implied that there was nothing inconsistent in his doing so. Shortly before the election thirty-one eminent Republicans, including Charles E. Hughes, Elihu Root, Herbert Hoover, Henry L. Stimson, and President Lowell of Harvard, issued a statement in which they publicly announced their continued support of the League of Nations, publicly guaranteed the Republican platform and candidate as definitely pro-League, and publicly promised that the election of Harding would be the surest way of having the United States join the League. Furthermore, in October Herbert Hoover in a public campaign speech in behalf of Harding asserted:

The important thing is that the Republican Party has pledged itself by its platform, by the actions of its majority in the Senate, by the repeated statements of Senator Harding, that they undertake to put into living being the principle of an organized association of nations for the preservation of peace. The carrying out of that promise is the test of the entire sincerity, integrity and statesmanship of the Republican Party.

In view of these circumstances it can hardly be maintained that the American election of 1920 represented a clear-cut popular decision against the League of Nations. In 1921, however, the United States government definitely rejected the League by ratifying separate peace treaties from which the articles on the League were omitted. Moreover, the sweeping Republican victory in 1920 appeared to drive from President Harding's mind all thoughts not only of a free association of nations but even of the existence of the League itself. For several months the new Republican administration completely ignored the League of Nations and refused to acknowledge notes and communications to the United States government from that organization. Only after this situation had been exposed in the American press did the state department bring itself to acknowledge in a formal way the receipt of the League's communications.

Toward the Permanent Court of International Justice, as distinct from the League, President Harding was more sympathetic. In fact, he recommended that the United States should become a member of the World Court, provided she were given an equal voice in the election of the judges with those states which were members of the League. President Harding died suddenly on August 2, 1923, before the Senate had acted on his recommendation. Calvin Coolidge, who succeeded to the presidency, also urged the Senate to ratify the World Court Protocol, and the Senate, after much delay, in 1926 finally voted to approve it with five reservations. The states that were members of the World Court practically accepted all of these reservations except that which stated the court should not "without the consent of the United States entertain any request for an advisory opinion touching any dispute or question in which the United States has or claims an interest." This reservation, it was maintained abroad, would give the United States a privileged position.

Apparently discouraged by his inability to bring the Senate and the members of the World Court together, President Coolidge after 1926 ceased to urge adherence. In 1929, however, a committee representing the states that were members of the court, in a consultation with Elihu Root, formulated a series of amendments to the World Court Protocol to bring it into harmony with the American Senate's reservations. Herbert Hoover, who became President of the United States in 1929, thereupon authorized the signing of the Protocol and urged upon the Senate its ratification. Nevertheless, throughout President Hoover's term the Senate continued its dilatory policy and failed to take any action. Although in the presidential campaign of 1932 the political platforms of both Republican and Democratic parties advocated American adherence to the court, the Protocol was defeated by a close vote in the United States Senate in 1935.

Meanwhile, the policy of the United States toward the League itself had gradually undergone a change. From an attitude of complete aloofness the government of that country advanced by 1922 to a willingness to send "unofficial observers" to conferences where matters of concern to the United States—such as customs formalities, traffic in women and children, opium traffic, and communications and transit—were to be discussed. As the years passed, the American policy of co-operation expanded. The various disarmament and economic conferences called by the League were attended by American delegates. The United States eventually began to contribute a small amount toward the expenses of the League, and from time to time Americans were chosen to serve on League commissions. Four distinguished Americans—John Bassett Moore, Charles Evans Hughes, Frank B. Kellogg, and Manley O. Hudson—served as judges on the World Court. Beginning with the administration of President Coolidge, the United States government, as though a member of the League, voluntarily deposited with the League Secretariat copies of its treaties with other nations, and under Presidents Hoover and Roosevelt it made some effort to advance the cause of disarmament at the League's Geneva conference. Nevertheless, the lack of the official presence of the United States at the council tables of the League, and the ever-present uncertainty as to how far the United States might be relied upon to co-operate with the League, undoubtedly militated against the latter's successful mediation in international disputes as well as its efforts to apply sanctions against a warring nation.

The League and the Preservation of Peace

Undoubtedly the chief purpose in the minds of those who formulated the League of Nations was the prevention of future international wars. To this end, the member states in accepting the Covenant agreed "to respect and preserve as against external aggression the territorial integrity and existing political independence of all members of the League" (Article 10); to concede it "to be the friendly right of each member of the League to bring to the attention of the Assembly or of the Council any circumstance whatever affecting international relations which threatens to disturb international peace or the good understanding between nations upon which peace depends" (Article 11); to resort to arbitration or judicial settlement in case of failure to settle satisfactorily any dispute suitable for submission to arbitration or judicial settlement, to carry out in full good faith any decision that might be rendered, and not to resort to war against a member which complied with such a decision (Article 13); to submit to the Council any dispute likely to lead to a rupture which was not submitted to arbitration or judicial settlement (Article 15).

In the case of mediation by the Council, the parties to the dispute were to submit to the secretary-general statements of their case, together with relevant facts and papers. If the Council made a unanimous report (the votes of the interested parties not counting), it was considered conclusive, and members agreed that they would not resort to war against any state which complied with the decision. If the Council failed to obtain unanimity, the members were free "to take such action as they shall consider necessary for the maintenance of right and justice." If the Council authorized the Assembly to handle the dispute, a decision to be conclusive had to be concurred in by the representatives of all those states which were represented in the Council and by a majority of the other members of the League. In case the Council found that a dispute arose out of a matter which by international law was solely within the domestic jurisdiction of one of the states, it was forbidden to make any recommendation. In other words, the League had no right of intervention, no power within a state.

Penalties were stipulated for a member of the League which went to war in disregard of its agreements to resort to arbitration, mediation, or the World Court. All other members agreed "immediately to subject it to the severance of all trade or financial relations" (Article 16). This was the so-called "economic weapon" and applied not only to the states involved but also to the nationals of those states. When the Covenant was adopted, it was expected that the League of Nations would be a universal organization. By 1935, however, when Article 16 was first invoked,[9] not only the United States but Japan and Germany as well were nonmembers, so that at that time it was found to be exceedingly difficult to make economic sanctions as effective as expected. In addition to the "economic weapon" the Council might also "recommend" to the several governments concerned what effective military, naval, or air force the members of the League should severally contribute to the armed forces to be used to protect the covenants of the League. The members of the League agreed to adopt similar measures to protect a member state against a nonmember state which resorted to war against it.

The Geneva Protocol

The outbreak of the First World War had clearly demonstrated that great armaments did not secure peace. It had, indeed, convinced many that great armaments, by engendering international fear and suspicion, actually constituted an underlying or fundamental cause of war. Reflecting this state of mind, the statesmen at the Paris peace conference admitted in the treaties there drafted "that the maintenance of peace requires the reduction of national armaments to the lowest point consistent with national safety and the enforcement by common action of international obligations." They went even further than this, and made a beginning of compulsory disarmament by forcing Germany, Austria, Hungary, and Bulgaria to accept definite limitations upon their military and naval establishments. These limitations, the Allies informed Germany, were only "the first steps towards that general reduction and limitation of armaments which they seek to bring about as one of the most fruitful preventives of war, and which it will be one of the first duties of the League of Nations to promote."

Upon the Council of the League the statesmen at Paris imposed the duty of formulating plans for the reduction of armaments. Accordingly a commission was appointed in February, 1921, to make proposals, but the commission decided that no scheme for disarmament could be effective which did not provide some form of mutual security to be given in exchange. The third Assembly thereupon requested the commission to prepare a draft

---

[9] See pages 465–466.

treaty embodying this idea of mutual security. The result was a draft treaty of mutual assistance, unanimously adopted by the fourth Assembly in September, 1923.

The security provided in this proposed treaty consisted of the assurance given by the signatory powers that, if a state were attacked, the rest of the signatory powers would come to its assistance. The question of deciding which state was the aggressor in case of war was delegated to the Council of the League, which must render its decision within four days of its being summoned. In order to link together security and disarmament, the treaty further provided that no state should be entitled to claim the benefits of the mutual guarantee unless it had limited its armaments to a scale approved by the Council of the League.

This draft treaty was circulated to all states whether or not they were members of the League. The replies received indicated that sixteen states, including France, Italy, and Japan, accepted the treaty in principle, while twelve states, including Germany, Great Britain, the United States, and Russia, declared that they could not adhere to it. Nearly all the replies pointed out the absence of a definition of aggression and criticized the policy of giving full power to the League Council to determine the aggressor state. The various criticisms of the draft treaty convinced those interested in disarmament that such a treaty must include a definition of aggression and a clear-cut indication of the aggressor.

When, therefore, MacDonald and Herriot, premiers of Great Britain and France respectively, submitted to the fifth Assembly of the League a protocol for the pacific settlement of international disputes, they linked with disarmament and security a third feature, arbitration. This so-called Geneva Protocol (1924) provided that all legal disputes must go before the Permanent Court of International Justice and all nonlegal disputes must be submitted to arbitration. War was declared a criminal offense, and every state which resorted to war in violation of the undertakings contained in the Covenant or in the protocol became an aggressor. The definition of an aggressor state was thus made almost automatic, and one of the chief objection to the preceding treaty was overcome. The "sanctions" to be taken against an aggressor state remained those provided for in Article 16 of the Covenant—namely, economic boycott and possible military action. The definition of aggression, the system of arbitration, and the effective measures to be taken against an aggressor were supposed to create a threefold guarantee of security. The Geneva Protocol, however, had very much the same reception as the treaty of mutual assistance and failed of adoption. In the view of James T. Shotwell, this rejection "dealt the fatal blow from which the Protocol and the League never recovered."

The Locarno and Paris Pacts

Nevertheless, the general principles of the Geneva Protocol were almost at once adopted in an attempt to provide collective security within a limited region, when Gustav Stresemann, German foreign minister, in 1925 offered France a pact of mutual guarantee and nonaggression. In Aristide Briand, French foreign minister, he found a kindred spirit who admitted that such an agreement might be possible provided (1) Germany became a member of the League, (2) Belgium became a party to the pact, and (3) nothing in the pact should be construed to prevent France from going to the aid of Poland,[10] or the Allies from acting in accordance with the Covenant of the League. To draft such an agreement representatives of Germany, France, Great Britain, Italy, Belgium, Poland, and Czechoslovakia gathered in the little Swiss town of Locarno beside the blue waters of Lake Maggiore. After twelve days of negotiations the conference closed on October 16, 1925, with the initialing of a treaty of mutual guarantee, usually referred to as the Locarno pact, four arbitration treaties between Germany on the one side and France, Belgium, Poland, and Czechoslovakia on the other, and two treaties of guarantee between France on the one side and Poland and Czechoslovakia on the other.

By Article 1 of the treaty of mutual guarantee, Germany, Belgium, France, Great Britain, and Italy, as a group and individually, guaranteed the inviolability of the existing frontiers between Germany and Belgium, and between Germany and France, together with the demilitarization of German territory west of a line drawn fifty kilometers east of the Rhine. By Article 2 Germany and Belgium, and Germany and France, mutually agreed in no case to attack, invade, or resort to war against each other except (1) in case of legitimate defense against a violation of Article 2 of the treaty, (2) in case of a "flagrant breach" of the agreements regarding the demilitarized zone, (3) in case of being directed by the League against a state which had first attacked another member of the League.

In case of a "flagrant violation" of either Article 1 or Article 2, the signatory powers agreed to come immediately to the assistance of the injured party. In case of a doubtful violation, the question was to be considered by the Council of the League, and the signatory powers agreed to fulfill their obligations as above if the Council was satisfied that a violation or breach had been committed. The agreement was to come into force as soon as Germany became a member of the League of Nations, which she did in September, 1926, and was to remain in effect until the League Council

[10] France had defensive alliances with Belgium and Poland. See pages 309–310.

should decide that "the League of Nations ensures sufficient protection to the high contracting parties."

By the network of arbitration agreements Germany on the one side and Belgium, France, Czechoslovakia, and Poland severally on the other engaged to settle by peaceful means all disputes, of every kind, which proved impossible of adjustment by the normal methods of diplomacy. By the guarantee treaties which France signed with Czechoslovakia and Poland it was agreed that in case Poland or Czechoslovakia or France should suffer from a failure to observe the undertakings arrived at between them and Germany, France and reciprocally Poland, or France and reciprocally Czechoslovakia, should "lend each other immediately aid and assistance, if such failure is accompanied by unprovoked recourse to arms."

In 1927 Briand, desiring to extend the network of treaties of arbitration and nonaggression, proposed to the United States a declaration by the two powers condemning recourse to war, renouncing war as "an instrument of national policy," and agreeing that a settlement of all disputes arising between them should be brought about only by pacific means. The American secretary of state, Frank B. Kellogg, suggested that instead of a bilateral treaty a similar multilateral treaty should be drafted in order to extend "throughout the world the benefits of a covenant originally suggested as between France and the United States alone." In the course of negotiations which extended over the following months Kellogg's proposal was subjected to a number of reservations and interpretations, as a result of which it appeared that the nations were agreed that all war was to be renounced except (1) in self-defense, (2) against any treaty-breaking signatory state, (3) in the execution of any obligation consequent upon the signing of any treaty of neutrality, (4) in the case of Great Britain, in defense of certain strategic places which are considered vital to the safety of the empire, (5) in fulfillment of the obligations and responsibilities incurred by membership in the League of Nations and by the signing of the Locarno agreements.

Subject to these reservations, which were not, however, incorporated into the treaty, the plenipotentiaries of fifteen states gathered at the Quai d'Orsay on August 27, 1928, and there signed a general treaty for the renunciation of war, the so-called pact of Paris. In it the powers solemnly declared that they condemned recourse to war for the solution of international controversies, renounced it as an instrument of national policy in their relations with one another, and agreed that the settlement or solution of all disputes or conflicts which might arise among them should never be sought except by pacific means. Immediately following the signing of the treaty, it was opened to the adherence of all states, and ultimately it was accepted by practically every country in the world. The treaty was promulgated by President Hoover of the United States on July 24, 1929.

The succeeding years witnessed various attempts both to bring the League Covenant—which permitted war under certain circumstances—into harmony with the pact, and to strengthen the latter by linking it with some sort of consultative agreement. In the tenth Assembly of the League in 1929 an amendment was proposed to Article 12 of the Covenant, providing that disputing nations should "agree that they will in no case resort to war." The amendment, however, was not officially adopted. The effort to negotiate a consultative agreement for the pact of Paris was primarily connected with the general problem of disarmament.

The Limitation of Naval Armaments

Although the Geneva Protocol, the League's projected preliminary to general disarmament, had failed of acceptance by the powers, the League had not lost interest in the problem or abandoned its efforts to advance toward that goal. Late in 1925 the Preparatory Commission for the Disarmament Conference was organized, consisting of representatives of all the great powers, including the United States and eventually Germany and Soviet Russia. The commission began its work at Geneva in May, 1926. During the succeeding years it struggled with the difficult problem of drafting a convention in which various blank spaces regarding the strength of effectives and matériel should be filled in later by the Disarmament Conference.

Meanwhile, however, some progress had been made in the limitation of navies by direct negotiations between the principal naval powers themselves. At the close of the First World War, with certain groups in the United States demanding that their country should have a navy second to none, it appeared for a time that Great Britain, Japan, and the United States were embarked upon a race for naval supremacy. With a view to preventing such a development, the United States invited Great Britain and Japan to a conference to consider the possibility of limiting naval armaments. Since this question was found to be bound up with questions and problems concerning the Far East, the United States extended the scope of the conference to include these matters also, and invited not only Great Britain and Japan to send delegates, but France, Italy, China, Belgium, Portugal, and the Netherlands as well.

The Washington conference, in session from November 12, 1921, to February 6, 1922, resulted in the adoption of seven treaties which were designed to put an end to naval rivalry and to solve some of the difficulties in the Far East. Following the American proposal for a ten-year "naval holiday," two treaties were signed between the five most important naval powers: Great Britain, the United States, Japan, France, and Italy. The first treaty called for the scrapping of approximately 40 per cent of the capital ships already built or being constructed by the three great naval powers. For the future definite limits were placed upon the quota and tonnage of capital ships and aircraft carriers permitted to each state, the total tonnage being fixed at a ratio of approximately 5:5:3 for Great Britain, the United States, and Japan, and 1.67 for France and Italy. No new capital ships were to be constructed for ten years, and those built after 1931 were specifically limited in their tonnage and in the maximum size of their guns. The second treaty outlawed the use of poison gas in warfare and restricted the use of submarines.[11]

At the Washington conference Great Britain accepted the principle of "parity" with the United States, but, when the latter sought to extend the 5:5:3 ratio to all types of naval craft, an agreement was prevented largely by differences of opinion regarding the size of cruisers and the abolition of submarines. Another conference met in Geneva in 1927, upon the invitation of the United States, but again it was found impossible to reconcile the British program of a great number of small cruisers and the American program of a small number of large cruisers.

The failure of the Geneva conference engendered suspicion and ill will between Great Britain and the United States to such an extent that Anglo-American relations became more strained than they had been for a generation. In 1929, however, after Herbert Hoover had become President of the United States and Ramsay MacDonald had become prime minister of Great Britain for a second time, something of a *rapprochement* was effected between the two countries. Following MacDonald's visit to Washington, the British government invited the United States, France, Italy, and Japan to participate in a five-power naval conference in London in January, 1930. As the Washington conference had abolished the competitive building of capital ships, so it was hoped that the London conference might abolish or allay competition in all other categories.

Although Great Britain, the United States, and Japan ultimately succeeded in reaching an agreement regarding the size of the various categories of their naval establishments, it proved impossible to conclude a five-power agreement because of differences between Italy and France. The former demanded the right to have in all categories the parity with France which had been granted her in capital ships at the Washington conference. This France steadily refused to concede, asserting that to permit Italy parity

[11] The naval treaties also provided for restrictions on fortifications in the Pacific. Great Britain, the United States, and Japan agreed to maintain the *status quo* in the defenses on a number of their insular possessions and naval bases, with the exception of Hawaii and Singapore. In some regions, notably the Aleutian Islands and Japan's mandated islands, there were to be no fortifications whatsoever.

with France would be to give Italy actual superiority in the Mediterranean, since France had two seacoasts to defend. Back of the French attitude was France's desire for security, as was revealed when France stated that she would recognize the Italian claim to parity if Great Britain would underwrite a "Mediterranean Locarno." The latter was willing to do this provided, in turn, the United States would agree to a consultative agreement for implementing the pact of Paris. This proposal was rejected by President Hoover, however, so that France and Italy declined to be bound by the general treaty which was signed on April 27, 1930.

By the London naval treaty the existing holiday in capital ships was extended until 1936. The total tonnage of the three principal powers in cruisers, destroyers, and submarines was fixed, the United States being granted substantial parity with Great Britain in all categories. Japan gained parity in tonnage with these two in submarines, and in other categories was permitted a ratio slightly better than the 5:5:3 agreed upon for capital ships at Washington. The Anglo-American dispute over cruisers was solved by a compromise which permitted a greater number of large cruisers to the United States and a greater number of small cruisers to Great Britain. These terms, it was believed, gave each of the three powers sufficient naval strength to make a successful invasion of its home waters by either of the others practically impossible. The London conference resulted not so much in the reduction of armaments as in their limitation. Parity with Great Britain was granted to the United States, but as a matter of fact actual parity would entail the expenditure of more than a billion dollars by 1936 if American tonnage was to equal that of Great Britain.

The Geneva Disarmament Conference

During these years the League's Preparatory Commission for the Disarmament Conference had been working to pave the way for the calling of a general disarmament conference, and eventually, on February 2, 1932, the conference convened in Geneva with sixty nations, including the United States and the Soviet Union, represented. A number of difficult problems immediately confronted the conference.

One was how to estimate effectives. The countries that employed conscription in general objected to the counting of trained reserves as effectives, while those which had volunteer armies maintained that reserves should be included in this category. Another problem was that of international supervision. France and her allies desired to have an elaborate system of international control established, but the other states maintained that the execution of any disarmament program must in general depend upon the good faith of the nations involved. The United States would not consent to any limitation of expenditures for armaments; Germany refused to approve any limitation of effectives unless trained reserves were included, and rejected the articles stating that existing treaties providing for the limitation of armaments should remain in force; Italy maintained that an agreement must be reached by all the naval powers on the proportions and levels of maximum tonnage.

France, still insistent upon her postwar thesis that security must precede disarmament, proposed that an international force, principally aircraft, should be created and placed at the disposal of the League for use in case sanctions had to be applied under Article 16 of the Covenant. This proposal found little favor among the other great powers. Germany, in turn, demanded general recognition of her "equality of right" to possess the same armaments as other countries. Soviet Russia suggested a progressive and proportional reduction of armaments with a view ultimately to their complete and rapid abolition. As none of these proposals was generally acceptable, a deadlock ensued.

In June President Hoover of the United States sought to break the deadlock. "The time has come," he declared, "when we should cut through the brush and adopt some broad and definite method of reducing the overwhelming burden of arms which now lies upon the toilers of the world." He proposed that land forces should be differentiated into "police components" designed to maintain internal order and "defense components" designed to resist attack from abroad. The latter, he suggested, should be reduced by approximately one third. President Hoover's program received strong support from Germany, Italy, and Russia, but Great Britain, Japan, and France raised so many objections that the plan failed of adoption. When the conference adjourned in July, the German delegation let it be known that it would not return to the conference until Germany's demand for equality had been granted. In December, 1932, the German claim to equality was recognized by the powers.

In the following month Adolf Hitler, one of whose cardinal points was the repudiation of the treaty of Versailles, became chancellor of Germany. Nevertheless, when the delegates resumed their labors at Geneva in February, 1933, Germany was again represented. But by the end of the month, chiefly because of disagreements between the Germans and the French, another deadlock had resulted. To many it appeared that the disarmament conference was about to collapse. Such a disaster was prevented at the moment by the decisive action of Prime Minister Ramsay MacDonald, who came to Geneva with new proposals.

According to the British plan, which was to be effective for five years, all European armies should be recruited on a uniform basis of conscription with a short-term period of service. Soviet Russia would be allowed an army of 500,000 men; France, Italy, Germany, and Poland, each 200,000; Rumania, 150,000; Spain, 120,000; Czechoslovakia and Yugoslavia, each 100,000; and the other countries from 25,000 to 60,000 each. Under this scheme the total number of men under arms in Europe would be reduced by approximately 450,000, while the existing armies of Germany, Austria, Hungary, and Bulgaria would be increased by about 177,000 men. Powers having overseas possessions were to be permitted supplemental colonial troops ranging in number from 15,000 for Belgium to 200,000 for France. Limitations were to be placed on the use of heavy guns, military and naval aircraft, and bombing, and a permanent disarmament commission was to be established.

Although Germany was at first inclined to criticize the proposals and to increase her own demands, ultimately the German delegate declared that his government accepted the British plan as a basis for the proposed disarmament convention. Later he announced that Germany was willing to accept equality in only those weapons which the conference should decide were defensive, provided those that were defined as offensive were completely abolished at the end of the five-year period. Disagreements persisted regarding the steps to be taken to achieve disarmament, however, and in June, 1933, the conference adjourned until the following October. In the meantime, it was hoped, informal discussions between the representatives of the great powers might eliminate some of the difficulties which prevented a general agreement.

Such discussions were actively carried on during September and October. Eventually a tentative agreement was reached by Great Britain, France, Italy, and the United States, providing that for a period of four years no powers—Germany included—should increase their armaments. At the end of that period, however, Germany should be permitted to have such tanks, military airplanes, and other weapons forbidden by the treaty of Versailles as the other powers retained. Naturally, perhaps, the chauvinistic utterances of the Nazis had so alarmed France and the various succession states that they were unwilling to permit Nazi Germany to increase her armaments at once. The latter, on the other hand, was determined to secure immediately the right to have a limited number of such "defensive" weapons—tanks and military airplanes—as the other great powers possessed. She asserted, furthermore, that the former Allies were by the treaty of Versailles bound to reduce their armaments as they had compelled the defeated powers to do.

On October 14, 1933, two days before the disarmament conference was to reconvene, the world was startled by Germany's announcement of her withdrawal from the conference and of her intended withdrawal from the League of Nations. It had become evident, the German foreign minister declared, that the conference would not bring about general disarmament in accordance with "the contractual obligations" of the powers, and that the "satisfactory fulfillment of Germany's recognized claim to equality" was therefore impossible. Since the latter constituted the condition upon which the German government had agreed to return to the conference in December, 1932, it was now compelled to withdraw.

In view of Germany's spectacular move the other powers decided to postpone the meeting of the conference temporarily and in the meantime to resort to diplomacy in an effort to overcome the impasse. It was generally agreed to be futile to attempt to draft a general disarmament treaty before Germany and France had come to an agreement on the basic questions. The next four months, therefore, were devoted to an exchange of views between France and Germany, in the course of which each country submitted plans, only to have them rejected by the other.

Despite the failure to reconcile the differences between the two countries, however, the conference again convened on May 29, 1934. The views expressed by the leading speakers fell generally into two categories. On the one hand, British, American, Italian, and other delegates made clear their desire to place disarmament first and to consider defensive security as resulting from it. On the other hand, the French and Russian delegates argued for security first and disarmament second. On June 11 the conference, in despair of an agreement, again adjourned, and Arthur Henderson, chairman, openly charged France with responsibility for its failure to accomplish any practical results. After more than two years of effort the League's disarmament conference had not succeeded in scrapping a single gun, tank, or airplane.

Chapter VII

REPARATIONS, WAR DEBTS,

AND WORLD DEPRESSION

O NE part of the peace settlement which immediately received severe criticism and denunciation was that dealing with the highly technical and deeply perplexing problem of reparations. No other feature of the peace treaties so intimately affected the lives of so many millions of people. Probably no other provisions were so much discussed on the platform, in the street, and in the press, and generally with so little understanding of the real problems involved.

Germany's Total Obligation

It will be recalled that on the subject of reparations the final decision of the peace conference was that Germany must make compensation, in gold or in certain goods, for all damage done to the civilian population of the Allied powers and to their property during the war, but that the treaty did not stipulate the total amount which must be paid. This was left to be determined by a Reparations Commission,[1] but in the meantime Germany was to pay, in gold or otherwise as the Reparations Commission might determine, the equivalent of $5,000,000,000,[2] to be applied first on the expenses of the Allied armies of occupation, and then on the reparations account.

After the peace conference, therefore, the first problem was to determine the total amount which Germany must pay and the system of payments which she must adopt. Negotiations were carried on between the Allies and Germany—in the course of which the former demanded $56,500,000,000 —but no agreement was ever reached through the channels of diplomacy. When the negotiations broke down, the Allies proceeded to take both mili-

---

[1] The Reparations Commission was originally intended to have one representative each from the United States, France, Great Britain, and Italy, with a fifth representative from time to time as the interests of other powers were directly involved. But the United States, because it did not ratify the treaty of Versailles, was not represented on the commission.

[2] The reparations figures given in this chapter in dollars are only approximate, for the German mark and Reichsmark (normally worth 23.81 cents) are here counted as four to the dollar.

tary and economic sanctions by occupying the industrial cities of Düsseldorf, Duisburg, and Ruhrort and by sequestrating German customs receipts on the western frontier.

When high politics failed to bring an agreement upon a definite total, the Reparations Commission took up the task and finally notified Germany, on April 28, 1921, that the amount of damage for which reparations were due was $33,000,000,000, in addition to Belgium's war debt. According to the "London schedule" drawn up later, $12,500,000,000 of this amount was to bear interest at 5 per cent, and payments were to be made in fixed annuities of $500,000,000 plus variable annuities equal to a tax of 26 per cent on Germany's exports. Furthermore, despite Germany's claim to the contrary, the commission announced that Germany's total payments to date had not been more than sufficient to cover the expenses of the various Allied control commissions and armies of occupation, exclusive of the expenses of the United States army. According to the Reparations Commission, Germany had as yet paid nothing which could be credited toward reparations, and the total indebtedness therefore still remained intact.[3] An ultimatum was dispatched to Germany requiring her to accept without reserve the proposals of the commission under threat of Allied occupation of the Ruhr. On May 11, 1921, accordingly, Germany agreed to the total amount of reparations set by the commission and undertook to make payments according to the schedule the Allies had outlined.

Germany's Default

A number of circumstances made it almost impossible for the German government to fulfill the obligations which it had assumed. In the first place, postwar Germany had no international credit; and, even if she had had, no countries in the world, with the possible exception of the United States, were in a position to advance her any large amounts immediately. She could not, therefore, settle the reparations demands at once by foreign loans. In the second place, owing to the Allied blockade which had so long cut her off from sources of raw materials and at the same time destroyed her prewar commercial system, Germany was faced with the necessity of buying extensively abroad, but was unable immediately to export an equivalent amount of goods. Her foreign trade, therefore, failed to bring into the country gold or foreign exchange which might have been used to make reparations payments. On the contrary, the adverse balance of trade was draining from Germany the little gold that she had. The necessity of

---

[3] The Allies had agreed that of the reparations payments, France should receive 52 per cent, Great Britain 22 per cent, Italy 10 per cent, Belgium 8 per cent, all other participants 8 per cent. Belgium's right to preferential treatment was fixed at $500,000,000.

buying gold and foreign currencies to meet reparations obligations led, in turn, to increased inflation of German currency.

In the third place, Germany was handicapped by a tremendous "flight" of capital from the country. Capitalists were fearful lest their wealth be attached for reparations payments, and hastened to put as much of it as possible safely out of the clutches of the tax-gatherer. Considerably more than a billion dollars was thus placed beyond the reach of the government. The "flight" of German capital led to a still further inflation of the currency. This, in turn, coupled with the then existing inefficient fiscal system, resulted in a continuous national deficit which again compelled a resort to still greater inflation. Thus a vicious circle was created in the matter of currency inflation and depreciation. Finally, there existed in Germany a very definite lack of "the will to pay." This was especially true of the great industrialists, who with the depreciation of the mark waxed in power and arrogance. They appeared to defy the Allies, and refused to co-operate with their own government in any serious attempt to fulfill the terms of the treaty.

The combination of circumstances just discussed resulted eventually in Germany's failure to meet the cash payments or even to make full deliveries in kind according to the London schedule. Although the first payment of $250,000,000 was made, it was accompanied by a very decided decline in the value of the paper mark. By the end of the year Germany concluded that she could not continue to make full payments without the assistance of foreign loans or a resort to much greater inflation of the currency. She therefore raised the question of a moratorium. A partial moratorium was granted for 1922, but when Germany attempted to make her revised payments, the mark again sank rapidly in value. In July, 1922, Germany requested a moratorium on all cash payments until January, 1925.

As a result of Germany's demand for a total moratorium, the reparations problem for a time ceased to be merely a question between the Allies and Germany, and resolved itself into a diplomatic conflict between the British and French governments. Fundamentally, the view of each in respect to the policy to be adopted toward Germany was based upon the economic situation in its own country, and the divergence which developed in the viewpoints of the two governments was caused chiefly by the changed economic situation in Great Britain.

For some time following the armistice, business had boomed in Great Britain, thanks to the immediate demand from European countries which had been cut off from the outside world by the war. But for various reasons which will be discussed later,[4] the boom collapsed in 1920. Exports fell off in that year approximately 50 per cent, and during the succeeding years

[4] See page 273.

Great Britain's foreign trade remained far below the prewar figure. With the decline in exports, the volume of shipping fell off, and factories curtailed production. Business stagnation ensued, accompanied by wide-spread unemployment. The latter, in turn, entailed the payment by the government of millions of dollars in unemployment "doles." British statesmen, therefore, were confronted with the task of rebuilding the nation's prosperity, and, since this was dependent chiefly upon the ability of foreign markets to consume British goods, they were particularly eager that Germany, normally Great Britain's best customer, should regain her prosperity and with it her ability to purchase British commodities. Therefore, while British statesmen willingly conceded the French right to receive and the German duty to pay reparations, in 1922 they began to put forward the view that the economic restoration of Germany must precede the adequate payment of reparations.

On the other hand, France had emerged from the war with a devastated region of nearly thirteen thousand square miles to be restored. This region, which in prewar days had contained about one eighth of the total population of the country, had been both an agricultural and an industrial area. Approximately three fourths of the land had been under cultivation or in pasturage, while at the same time it had yielded about 55 per cent of the coal production and more than 90 per cent of the ore production of France. Furthermore, it had been an important manufacturing region. The chief economic problem for France after the war, consequently, was to restore this devastated area to its former wealth-producing capacity. By the middle of 1922 France had spent $7,500,000,000 in reconstruction and pensions. It was expected that this would ultimately be recovered from Germany, for the latter by the treaty of Versailles had agreed to make compensation for such expenditures. But, up to May 1, 1921, France, because of the expenses of the Allied armies of occupation and because of priority payments to Belgium, had received nothing in reparations from Germany, and had been compelled to finance her reconstruction work mainly through short-term internal loans.

French statesmen, therefore, did not look with favor upon Germany's demand for a moratorium. They believed that the German fiscal difficulties were chiefly caused not by the payment of reparations, but by Germany's bad administration of her finances and by the bad faith of her nationals, who were deliberately evading taxation and sending millions of dollars in gold and securities out of the country. Poincaré, speaking for France, asserted that no moratorium should be granted unless "productive guarantees" were secured. Furthermore, the French premier asserted that no greater amount of the reparations debt would be remitted to Germany than the amount of the French war debt which Great Britain might remit to France.

When, therefore, Germany on November 14, 1922, once more demanded a total moratorium for three or four years and a grant of bank credit from the Allies in order that she might stabilize the mark, it was practically inevitable that the Allies at their London conference in December would come to a deadlock. Poincaré was determined to have Germany declared in default in order that further sanctions might be exacted. On the other hand, Bonar Law, the British prime minister, believed that no step like the occupation of the Ruhr could possibly bring a satisfactory settlement of the reparations problem. Germany could not be declared in default in cash payments because she had been granted concessions in this respect by the Reparations Commission. She had, however, failed to meet all the requirements of deliveries in kind. The French government concentrated its attacks on deliveries of timber and coal, and by a vote of three to one, the British government dissenting, the Reparations Commission declared Germany in default in these respects. On January 10, 1923, the French government announced that a mission of control would be sent into the Ruhr.

The Struggle in the Ruhr

The French and Belgian governments, with the support of Italy, now sought a solution of the reparations problem through direct action. Within a few days the whole Ruhr and Lippe region was occupied as far east as Dortmund by French and Belgian troops. Although the occupied area was only about sixty by twenty-eight miles in extent, it constituted the industrial heart of Germany. It was estimated that, at the date of the occupation, 80 to 85 per cent of Germany's coal, 80 per cent of her steel and pig-iron production, and 70 per cent of the goods and mineral traffic on her railways came from this territory. Owing to the fact that almost all of her gun steel during the war had been produced here, the Ruhr had come to be called the "German arsenal." As might be expected, it was one of the most thickly populated regions in Europe, containing 10 per cent of the German people. These facts constituted the basis of Poincaré's policy. By holding this small area, France and Belgium would either secure reparations payments at first hand or so paralyze the industrial life of Germany as to force her to agree to their terms.

The German government now faced two alternatives: either to accept the French demand and make new proposals for the payment of reparations, or to refuse to co-operate with France and passively resist all French efforts. The German chancellor, Cuno, believed that without German assistance France would be unable to operate the Ruhr industries, that the cost of the profitless occupation would force the French treasury into bankruptcy, and that thus the French would be compelled to withdraw in defeat from the territory. His unhappy guess as to the outcome led him to choose a policy of passive resistance, and the German government now proceeded to do everything that it could, short of open resistance, to oppose French efforts. It stopped all deliveries of reparations in kind to France and Belgium. It ordered the inhabitants of the occupied area to pay no customs duties, coal taxes, or export duties which could come into French hands, and forbade them to render any assistance to the French under threat of severe penalties. Finally, it entered upon a program of financial aid to all those—officials, railwaymen, miners, and industrial workers—who by reason of passive resistance lost their means of support.

The French and Belgian authorities countered these measures by declaring a state of siege and by prohibiting the export of all manufactured goods from the occupied district. The economic isolation of the Ruhr became complete. Furthermore, they imposed heavy fines and prison sentences, placed a censorship on the press, seized private property and private funds, and expelled countless officials and leaders. Altogether, some 147,000 German citizens were expelled during the first eleven months of the occupation. Nor was this all. The French estimated that seventy-six Germans were killed and ninety-two wounded by the Allies, while twenty Allied soldiers were killed and sixty-six wounded by the Germans.

Large numbers of men in the Ruhr were thrown out of employment, and food became scarce, the French allowing only sufficient to come into the district to ration the population. The German government was ruining itself to sustain passive resistance by paying allowances to expelled officials, to miners "on strike," and in a multitude of other ways. The deterioration of the mark was catastrophic. Not only the workmen in the Ruhr but, because of the decline of the mark and the cutting off of goods from that district, millions outside the Ruhr suffered as well. Nevertheless, the German people rallied about their government largely because they believed that Poincaré was actuated not by a desire to secure reparations but by fear of the economic recovery of Germany, by the wish to tighten the French hold on the Rhineland and the Rhine frontier, and by the hope of building up a great industrial trust under French control, combining French iron ore with the Ruhr coal.

But the stranglehold which France held on German industry began to tell. France might not secure enough out of her occupation to pay for the cost of maintaining that occupation, but Germany could not go on indefinitely without free access to this great center of her national industrial life. Unemployment in other parts of Germany soon resulted from the loss of products from the Ruhr. The mark continued its precipitate decline. By the middle of June it stood at 100,000 to the dollar, a month later it had sunk to 200,000, and on August 8 it finally reached 5,000,000. Popular dissatisfaction with the complete failure of the policy of passive resistance brought the downfall of the Cuno ministry on August 12, 1923. A new cabinet was organized under Gustav Stresemann, who now had the unenviable task of extricating Germany from her embarrassing situation by the only possible course—the cessation of passive resistance. On September 26 the German government announced that resistance had been abandoned.

The effect of the occupation of the Ruhr was far-reaching. In Germany it brought a change in the attitude of the great industrialists. Formerly indifferent or hostile to the payment of reparations, they had been too often defiant in the face of the Allied demands for fulfillment. With the seizure of their industries in the Ruhr, however, their attitude gradually underwent a change, and with the utter collapse of the German currency they came to the place where they themselves were willing to make sacrifices to pay reparations in order that the French might be got out of the Ruhr and the way cleared for currency stabilization in Germany. The German people as a whole learned that France was really in earnest and had the upper hand. All this, in turn, made it easier for the German government to carry through the reparations program as later outlined.

In France the effect of the Ruhr occupation was equally important, for it revealed the fact that mere force could not wring from Germany the money so much desired. Although in the fall of 1923 the occupation actually did begin to prove profitable, the net returns for the first year were not great, and were accompanied by a decline in the value of the franc. The majority of the French were again ready to try the method of peaceable adjustment if there appeared to be any likelihood of its success. And in the negotiations which must precede a new program of fulfillment, France would no longer stand as a weak suppliant begging for her rights; she now held something with which to get them. The German need for relief from the situation caused by the Ruhr occupation now matched the French need for reparations payments.

The Dawes Plan

On October 24, 1923, in a note to the Reparations Commission, Germany declared her willingness in principle to resume payments under the treaty of Versailles, and requested an examination of her capacity to pay. The Reparations Commission thereupon appointed two committees of experts, one to consider the means of balancing the German budget and stabilizing the German currency, the other to estimate the amount of capital which had been exported from Germany and to recommend the means of bringing it back. In this nonpolitical investigation the United States government consented to the participation of American experts.

The first committee of experts, headed by Charles G. Dawes of the United States, came to be known as the Dawes Committee, and included two representatives each from the United States, Great Britain, France, Italy, and Belgium. The second committee was headed by Reginald McKenna of Great Britain, and had one representative each from the abovementioned countries. On April 9, 1924, the two committees simultaneously submitted their reports to the Reparations Commission. The McKenna Committee's report estimated that the total amount of German capital abroad at the end of 1923 was about $1,687,500,000 and that the amount of foreign currency held in Germany was about $300,000,000. It stated that the return of the capital could be hastened by permanently stopping German inflation and in general by carrying into effect the recommendations of the Dawes Committee.

The task originally assigned to the latter was to recommend ways and means of balancing the German budget and stabilizing the German currency. But the committee stated that, unless the amount of reparations which was to be contributed from the ordinary budget resources was known, financial and currency stability could not be assured. It thus cleared the way for recommendations in regard to German reparations payments.

In brief, the Dawes report embodied the following recommendations: (1) the Ruhr should be evacuated; (2) Germany should pledge certain revenues as security for payment of reparations; (3) the annual reparations payments should start at $250,000,000 and rise gradually over a four-year period to a normal figure of $625,000,000; (4) future payments should be increased or decreased according to an index of prosperity; (5) a foreign loan of $200,000,000 should be made as a foundation for Germany's fiscal system; (6) a central bank should be established with a fifty-year monopoly for the issue of paper money, subject to the control of an international board of seven Germans and seven foreigners. No change was made, however, in the total obligation for reparations payments placed upon Germany by the Reparations Commission in 1921.

Two days after receiving the report, the Reparations Commission notified Germany that it considered it a practical basis for the solution of the reparations problem. Five days later Germany gave her full consent. In July a conference of the Allies, with American representatives participating unofficially, was opened in London for the purpose of drafting a protocol to put the Dawes plan into effect. On August 30, 1924, the protocol embodying the acceptance of the plan by the various governments and the Reparations Commission was signed in London. On September 1 the plan began to operate; on July 31, 1925, the last French and Belgian soldiers left the Ruhr.

The Inter-Allied War Debts

Meanwhile, not unrelated to the problem of reparations was that of the Inter-Allied war debts, which were also a legacy of the First World War. During the early years of the conflict Great Britain, as the wealthiest of the Allies, advanced some billions of dollars in loans to Russia, France, Italy, and the lesser powers, and, after the United States became a belligerent, the latter loaned approximately $10,338,000,000 to the Allies, including Great Britain, in return for their demand notes bearing interest at 5 per cent.

At the Paris peace conference the British proposed a general cancellation of all Inter-Allied debts; that is, Great Britain asserted her willingness to cancel the amounts owed her by the Allies if the United States would do the same. Such a step would of course have been to the advantage of Great Britain, for her loss in canceling the Allied debts to herself would have been more than offset by the cancellation of her debt to the United States and by the general stimulation to world trade which would have followed such a reduction of international debts. On the other hand, such a step would, for all practical purposes, have placed a war indemnity of over ten billion dollars on American taxpayers.

Nevertheless, it was argued by many Europeans and even by some Americans that, since the war against Germany had been a common struggle, and since the United States had entered the conflict late and lost relatively very few men, she should consider the loans to the Allies as her contribution to the common cause. It was further pointed out that an amount even greater than that advanced in loans was spent in the United States by the Allies during the war and hence that the United States should be satisfied with the great wealth which had come to her from her war-time activities and should not try to collect the war debts. Finally, it was asserted that, since Europe could not pay her war debts without flooding the United States with foreign commodities, collection of the debts would greatly harm American manufacturers and merchants.

At the peace conference President Wilson declined the British proposal, however, and the American attitude during the succeeding decade was later succinctly summed up by President Coolidge when he explained that the Allies had "hired the money" and that they were therefore obliged to repay it with interest. In defense of the American position, it was argued that the war debts should be collected in order that European countries might learn that they themselves must pay for their wars even though they temporarily financed them by borrowing from abroad. Moreover, public opinion demanded that the war debts be collected in order to prevent the shifting of this heavy burden to the shoulders of American taxpayers, who otherwise would be obliged to retire the war bonds floated by the United States to obtain funds for the Allies. In 1922 the United States government, accordingly, officially requested all its debtors to take the necessary steps to fund their debts to the United States.

Once again the British attitude was shown in the Balfour note of August 1, 1922. In that note the British government declared that, although it still favored a general cancellation of both war debts and reparations claims, it was forced to adopt a different policy by the stand of the United States. The British government, according to the note, would seek to collect from its debtors only such sums as would in their aggregate equal the amount which Great Britain must pay to the United States. In other words, if the United States would reduce the amount of the British indebtedness, the British government would reduce the amount owed to it by the other Allies. The latter maintained, in general, that they could pay Great Britain and the United States only as they themselves received reparations from Germany.

This connection between reparations and war debts the American government consistently refused to admit, and in the end the debtor states entered into funding agreements with the United States. As a rule, no interest had been paid on the loans since their contraction, so that to each original loan was added, at the time of funding, the accrued interest. Consequently, the amount actually funded totaled approximately $11,500,000,000. The United States had earlier declared that, when final arrangements were made, each debtor nation's capacity to pay might be taken into consideration in determining the rate of interest. Such consideration was given, and, although the principal of each debt was maintained intact, the interest rate was in every case reduced from the original 5 per cent, that of Great Britain being reduced to an average of 3.3 per cent and that of Italy to as low as 0.4 per cent. In principal and interest the debtor nations agreed to pay the United States over a sixty-two-year period a total of approximately $22,000,-000,000. Figured on the originally contracted rate of interest, approximately half of the total debt was remitted by the United States.

The Young Plan

With Germany regularly making her reparations payments to the Allies under the Dawes plan, the Allies were able in turn to make their war-debt payments to the United States. Between September, 1924, and September, 1928, about $1,350,000,000 was paid to the Allies by Germany without any noticeable strain on the Dawes machinery or upon the external value of the German mark. Although the fact was not generally recognized at the time, Germany was enabled to make these reparations payments largely be-

cause during these years huge sums were being loaned to German interests by foreign bankers, chiefly American. With the opening of the fifth
year the first standard annual payment of $625,000,000 fell due, the experts
having assumed that by this time the financial and economic situation in
Germany would have become normal.

The Dawes report had, of course, limited itself merely to pointing out
the amount which Germany could pay annually over a period of years.
It had said nothing about how long she should pay nor what the total
should be. So far as Germany was concerned, she was still legally bound
to pay $33,000,000,000 by the agreement which she had been forced to accept
in May, 1921. But no one now considered it possible to exact any such
amount, and the fact that there was still no real final determination of Germany's reparations liabilities left an element of uncertainty in the affairs
of all the states concerned. The next step in the reparations problem, therefore, was to reach some new decision either as to a revised total which Germany must pay or as to the specific number of years over which the Dawes
plan was to operate.

During the sessions of the League Assembly in September, 1928, conferences were held between representatives of France, Great Britain, Belgium,
Italy, Japan, and Germany, which led to an agreement on the opening of
official negotiations with a view to a complete and final settlement of the
reparations problem. A new committee of experts was accordingly appointed which included in its personnel some of the best financial brains
of the nations concerned and of the United States as well. Beginning in
February, 1929, sessions of the committee were held in Paris under the
chairmanship of Owen D. Young, one of the American delegates, who had
played an important role in the drafting of the Dawes plan. As in the latter
case, the committee soon became known from its chairman as the Young
Committee.

On June 7, after nearly four months of struggle and compromise, what
has been characterized by one of its participants as "the grimmest conference on record" came to a close with the signing of the final report. The
experts had, of course, been acting independently, and their decisions had
to be approved by the governments concerned. To facilitate the ratification
of the plan, diplomatic conferences met at The Hague in August and again
in the following January. The final act was signed on January 20, 1930,
and in the succeeding months it was ratified by the various governments.

The Young plan provided for thirty-seven payments by Germany averaging $512,500,000, to be followed by twenty-two further payments averag-
ing $391,250,000. These were the equivalent of a cash payment of $9,000,-
000,000, in contrast with the $33,000,000,000 originally stipulated by the
Reparations Commission. Of each annuity, $165,000,000 was to be uncon-

ditional, that is, payable without any right of postponement of any kind; and of this amount $125,000,000 was assigned to France in order to allow her to mobilize a substantial part of her share in the total settlement. On the ground that the system of deliveries in kind had come to play an important role in the economic life of Germany and that its immediate cessation would not be in the interest of Germany or of the creditor powers, the plan provided for the continuance of the system for a period of ten years. Actually, however, the payments in kind were reduced to approximately half of what they had been.

The Dawes plan had begun the process of removing the reparations problem from the political to the financial sphere; the Young plan carried the process still further by the creation of the Bank for International Settlements. This institution was to perform the banking functions necessary in the sequence between the initial payment of the annuities and the final distribution of the funds. It was placed outside the field of political influences, and its powers and facilities were sufficiently broad to enable it to deal freely and promptly with the problems involved in the settlement of Germany's obligations. It was authorized, for example, to deal with the question of postponement of the conditional annuities if raised at any time by the German government. The control of the management of the bank was placed in the hands of the central banks of the countries involved in the reparations settlement, including Germany. Obviously, the reparations problem was lifted out of the political sphere, and the former political method of handling what was purely an economic problem now became obsolete.

In contrast with the Dawes plan, the Young plan definitely fixed the number and the amounts of the annuities necessary for a final settlement. It removed the uncertainty attendant upon the operation of the index of prosperity. It abolished the system of external controls, gave Germany full financial autonomy, and left to her the obligation of facing her engagements on her own responsibility. The system of deliveries in kind was greatly limited, and on the other hand the annuities were to be paid in a form lending themselves to mobilization. Finally, the whole scheme was placed in charge of a purely financial institution in the management of which Germany was to have an appropriate part.

Germany's payments, moreover, were fixed in relation to the sums owed by the Allied countries in war debts, and the *de facto* relationship between war debts and reparations was clearly recognized. If any of the creditor powers received any relief in its payments of war debts, during the first thirty-seven years Germany should benefit two thirds, and during the last twenty-two years the whole relief should be applied to the reduction of Germany's liabilities. Thus was destroyed the fiction that the problems of war debts and reparations were unconnected. Furthermore, it was agreed that the Inter-Allied occupation of the Rhineland should end. Evacuation began in September, 1929, and was completed by June 30, 1930. With the Allies and Germany at last in agreement regarding the number and amounts of the latter's future reparations payments, it was hoped that the settlement was "complete and final," and that at last the tortuous problem of reparations had been successfully solved.

The World Economic Depression

The financial experts of the Young Committee had based their scheme for reparations payments on the assumption that world trade would expand both in volume and in value. Unfortunately, however, almost simultaneously with the inauguration of the Young Plan there came an economic depression on an unprecedented scale, bringing in its train a drastic shrinking in the volume of world trade and a rapid and steady fall in commodity prices.

The causes assigned for the depression were about as varied as the interests and outlooks of those who examined the situation. By many the inadequacy of the world's relatively small supply of gold as a basis for national and international exchange was held responsible for the catastrophic decline in the price of commodities. By others the blame was placed upon the oversupply and consequently decreasing value of silver. This development, it was asserted, greatly lessened the purchasing power of, and therefore the international trade with, those countries—particularly China and India—which were on a silver basis. A world-wide surplus of agricultural products, it was further pointed out, inevitably brought a decline in the price of these commodities and therefore diminished the farmers' ability to purchase manufactured goods; while, at the same time, the postwar revolution in industry by the introduction of labor-saving machines decreased the man power needed in certain types of manufacturing and so through unemployment brought a decline in the purchasing power of the proletariat. The new machinery, on the other hand, vastly increased the output of manufactured goods, so that inevitably there came an overproduction and the closing down of factories, with further loss of purchasing power on the part of those who were dismissed. Extreme nationalism, with its erection of high protective tariffs and its resultant interference with the flow of international trade, also came in for bitter criticism. But, whatever were the causes of the depression, the year 1930 witnessed a marked slowing down of industry and an alarming increase in unemployment.

In 1931 the continued economic depression at last brought the financial collapse of certain countries of Europe, which found themselves unable to dispose of their surplus products at prices that would enable them to meet their international obligations. The latter were of three types: (1) payments on reparations and war debts, (2) payments of interest and amortization charges on huge long-term loans which had been made for rehabilitation work, (3) repayments of short-term credits which had been lavishly advanced by American and British banks in order that Europe might be able to continue her importation of commodities from their countries.

From 1924 to 1929 Germany had been enabled to make her reparations payments largely because she had been advanced huge sums from abroad, chiefly by American bankers. The Allies, having received reparations payments from Germany, had in turn also been able to meet their war-debt payments to the United States. In 1929, however, the sources of these foreign loans had begun to dry up,[5] and Germany had been forced to resort to short-term loans and to her own budget in order to meet her international obligations. During 1930–1931, despite the strenuous efforts of the government to curtail expenditures and increase receipts, the German budget became more and more unbalanced, and another financial debacle seemed imminent.

The incident which precipitated the financial crisis in central Europe occurred in Austria, where in June, 1931, the Creditanstalt, by far the largest private bank in the republic, came to the verge of collapse and had to be rescued by the Austrian government. The difficulties of the Creditanstalt shook foreign confidence in the solvency of central Europe as a whole and reacted on Germany, where a banking crisis was already developing, largely because American bankers were recalling their short-term credits.[6] Once again Germany seemed to face national bankruptcy. To prevent such a catastrophe, with all its attendant evils to the world, President Hoover, on June 20, 1931, proposed a suspension of all payments on reparations and intergovernmental debts for one year beginning July 1.

The situation in Germany, nevertheless, grew worse in July with the continued calling of short-term loans and the export of capital. Germans themselves, withdrawing money to hoard or to transfer abroad, precipitated a further crisis when on July 13 the Darmstädter und National-Bank, one of the largest financial institutions in the country, was forced to close its doors. This in turn evoked a governmental decree temporarily closing all banks and stock exchanges. In August a committee, headed by an American banker, Albert H. Wiggin, was convened by the Bank for International Settlements to study the German situation. This committee recommended that the existing short-term loans should be continued for a period

---

[5] Especially after the Wall Street crash in October, 1929.

[6] In July, 1931, the short-term credits of Germany totaled approximately $3,000,000,000.

of six months, and its recommendation was at once adopted by Germany's creditors, who negotiated a "standstill agreement" extending until February 29, 1932, all short-term credits.[7]

This "freezing" of short-term loans in turn reacted disastrously on Great Britain, whose bankers were fatally handicapped by their inability to recall the short-term credits they had advanced to Germany. During August and September gold was rapidly withdrawn from London, particularly by Dutch, Belgian, and Swiss bankers who feared that British banks would not be able to meet their obligations, and that the British government might even be forced to abandon the gold standard. On September 21 continued withdrawals finally forced Great Britain to go off the gold standard, a step in which she was soon followed by many other countries both in Europe and throughout the world.

World economic conditions in general and German conditions in particular soon convinced the German government that it would be impossible to resume reparations payments at the end of the Hoover moratorium. In November, 1931, therefore, availing itself of a provision of the Young plan, it requested the Bank for International Settlements to convene a special advisory committee of financial experts to investigate Germany's capacity to resume reparations payments in July, 1932. This committee on December 23 reported that Germany would be justified in declaring that she would not be able, in the year beginning in July, 1932, to transfer the conditional part of the reparations annuity. The committee also took occasion to point out that a prompt adjustment of all intergovernmental debts to the existing world situation was the only lasting step capable of re-establishing economic stability and real peace, for the tremendous fall in commodity prices had obviously greatly increased the burden of all intergovernmental payments.

The End of Reparations and War-Debt Payments

On June 16, 1932, a reparations conference once more convened—this time at Lausanne—to decide upon "a lasting settlement" of the questions raised in the report of the most recent committee of financial experts, and to consider measures necessary to solve the other economic and financial difficulties which, it was felt, were responsible for and might prolong the existing world crisis. So far as the reparations problem was concerned, Germany, of course, sought to secure the complete cancellation of all reparations payments. France, on the other hand, desired to have the Young plan

[7] In February, 1932, and yearly thereafter through 1939, the "standstill agreement" was extended. In 1940 short-term credits advanced by American banks had been reduced to less than $40,000,000.

formally continued but with the payments specified therein greatly reduced. In the end an agreement was reached (July 9) that the reparations payments stipulated in the Young plan should be set aside and replaced by an obligation upon Germany to pay into a general fund for European reconstruction the sum of $750,000,000. To meet this obligation, the German government was to deliver to the Bank for International Settlements bonds to that amount.

The Lausanne agreement constituted one more recession in the series of ever-diminishing demands upon Germany for reparations. An Allied demand in 1921 that Germany assume an obligation to pay $56,500,000,000 was followed in the same year by the Reparations Commission's decision that the total figure should be $33,000,000,000. This stood legally as Germany's obligation until the Young plan reduced it to an amount which was equivalent to a cash payment of approximately $9,000,000,000. Two years later came the Hoover moratorium, and then in July, 1932, the Lausanne agreement drastically revised Germany's obligations to a total cash payment of only $750,000,000, with the possibility that even this amount might never be paid.[8] Altogether, according to a competent and disinterested American calculation, Germany had paid under her reparations obligations a total of $5,396,250,000.

On the same day on which the Lausanne treaty was signed, Great Britain, France, Italy, and Belgium came to another agreement. By this so-called "gentlemen's agreement" these powers undertook not to ratify the Lausanne treaty until a satisfactory settlement had been reached between them and their own creditors. If such settlements were not obtained, the agreement with Germany was not to be ratified and Germany's position in regard to reparations would be legally that which existed before the Hoover moratorium. An effort was thus once more made to link the reparations question with the problem of Inter-Allied war debts, and to make the final solution of the reparations problem rest upon the willingness of the United States either to cancel or to reduce the debts due it from the Allies.[9]

Although the Hoover moratorium in 1931 suspended all payments on war debts, the United States expected that with the expiration of the one-year period these payments would be resumed. Congress, in approving the moratorium in December, 1931, expressly declared that cancellation or re-

[8] Early in 1937 Chancellor Hitler announced the German government's repudiation of these reparations bonds.

[9] In accordance with a suggestion of the Lausanne conference, a world monetary and economic conference convened in London in June, 1933. From the outset, unfortunately, the nations differed regarding the steps necessary to economic recovery. As the discussions proceeded it became clear that the settlement of the currency question was a prerequisite for agreement on other matters. When the United States declined to agree upon currency stabilization at that time, the conference came to an end without taking any notable step toward ending the world economic depression.

duction of any of the indebtedness of foreign countries to the United States was contrary to the policy of that body. On the other hand, the Allied governments maintained that the Lausanne agreement practically canceling Germany's reparations payments was made in the belief that the United States would consent to a revision of war-debts payments. In November, 1932, accordingly, Great Britain and France presented notes to the United States raising the question of debt revision. Both linked the questions of reparations and war debts, and both requested postponement of the payments due on December 15 as a preliminary to a general review of the debt agreements.

In reply, President Hoover pointed out that the American government still held that "reparations are a solely European question in which the United States is not concerned," and that it refused to recognize that the Lausanne settlement of German reparations "was made in reliance upon any commitments given by this government." He furthermore asserted that as President he had no jurisdiction to grant either a postponement of the payments due on December 15 or a review of the debt situation.

Although in both Great Britain and France strong minorities favored default, in neither country was the government willing to go so far. In the former the government was able to carry through its policy and on December 15 made its payment in full. Italy, Czechoslovakia, Finland, Latvia, and Lithuania followed Great Britain's example. Developments in France, however, were quite otherwise. The French had always strongly opposed the payment of war debts and had ratified the funding agreement with the United States with the reservation that the debt to that country was to be paid "exclusively by the sums that Germany shall pay France." Although Premier Herriot asserted that the honor of France required that she should make the debt payment as agreed, his request for authorization to pay the amount due on December 15 was voted down by the Chamber of Deputies, and he himself was obliged to resign. The payment was, in the words of the Chamber of Deputies, "deferred" until the United States should agree to enter a conference for the purpose of adjusting all international obligations and of putting an end to all international transfers for which there was no compensating transaction. Poland, Belgium, Estonia, and Hungary took the same stand as France.

On June 15, 1933, when payments again became due, Finland alone made her payment in full. Great Britain, Italy, Czechoslovakia, Rumania, and Latvia made "token" payments, the British payment being accompanied by a note indicating that the payment was to be considered "as an acknowledgment of the debt, pending a final settlement." France again defaulted completely and was joined in this step by Belgium, Poland, Yugoslavia, Estonia, Lithuania, and Hungary. Six months later only six of the countries scheduled to make payments to the United States actually did so, and five of them made merely "token" payments. Finland alone paid her full installment in December, 1933. Although, in an effort to bring pressure on the debtor governments, the United States Congress, in April, 1934, passed the Johnson Act forbidding nationals of the United States to make loans to foreign governments in default on their debt obligations to the United States, on June 15, 1934, the only payment received was from Finland. And in the succeeding years she was the only country to make any payments whatever to the United States.[10]

By 1934 it was becoming evident to most observers that the effort of the United States to collect some $22,000,000,000 of war debts and interest on the basis of settlements calling for payments over a period of sixty-two years had broken down. Just as the attempts of the former Allies to collect reparations payments from Germany in amounts ranging from $33,000,-000,000 to $9,000,000,000 had collapsed in the face of the impossibility of transferring such tremendous sums, so, it appeared, had American efforts suffered a similar fate. As the year 1932 saw the practical ending of the payment of reparations, so the year 1934 saw apparently the ending of payments of war debts to the United States by the Allied countries.

For this eventuality the United States was not entirely blameless. In the first place, although most of the original ten billion dollars had been transferred to the Allies in the form of commodities, the United States had refused to accept payment in kind from the debtor nations. In the second place, she had raised high tariff barriers against foreign commodities and had thus greatly handicapped the debtor powers in their efforts to secure American currency with which to make payments. In the third place, she had vigorously sought to increase her own export trade and in so doing had inevitably lessened the sale of goods abroad by the debtor nations. Finally, by subsidizing the American merchant marine, she had indirectly reduced the income of foreign shipping. All of these things the United States had a right to do, but in doing them she went far toward preventing the European powers from being able to meet their war-debt obligations. To many it seemed that the United States had as yet an incomplete understanding of her new position as a creditor rather than a debtor nation.

Political Effects of the World Depression

Meanwhile, the world economic depression had done more than merely smash the system of reparations and war-debt payments. It had profoundly affected the economic, social, and political life of most of the countries of the Western world. In the first place, one inevitable result of the depression

[10] During these years Finland had a favorable balance of trade with the United States.

was a tremendous increase in the number of unemployed, caused primarily by the closing down of factories as a result of the overproduction of goods and the inability of the masses to purchase them at the prices demanded. Although the unemployment problem affected every country—with the possible exception of Soviet Russia—it was more general in the industrial countries, and most keenly felt in those which had most thoroughly rationalized their industries. Naturally, not only the millions actually unemployed, but also millions of their dependents as well, suffered deprivation and want and provided a fertile field for discontent with existing institutions.

But others felt the stern hand of the depression, too. Earnings and profits of practically all types of business enterprises seriously decreased or disappeared altogether. Dividends were reduced materially or were wholly omitted. Not only the great capitalists, who owned and controlled vast business interests, but also the more numerous members of the middle class—who had invested modest sums in shares of industrial companies—became alarmed at the threat to their economic security.

In most countries efforts were made by the governments to assist the unemployed. In some countries aid was given directly through unemployment payments or "doles"; in others, governments sought to aid the unemployed indirectly by the inauguration of projects calling for the construction of extensive public works. Efforts were made to "prime the pump" of business by giving employment directly to millions who would then become purchasers of goods, or by undertaking enterprises which, in the course of their construction, would create a demand for goods and thus indirectly give employment to various subsidiary industries.

Obviously, such government policies entailed severe drains upon national budgets, especially at a time when the ordinary channels of revenue were inclined to dry up. Accordingly, governments were forced to seek new sources of revenue whenever possible or to increase existing tax rates. This, of course, caused discontent among those classes upon whom the taxes fell. Furthermore, in efforts to maintain balanced national budgets, governments in some cases reduced the salaries of state employees and the interest on government bonds. Such policies inevitably created discontent among bondholders and state employees. Finally, in some countries the national budgets remained unbalanced and national debts increased enormously. The resultant popular fear of currency inflation or repudiation caused widespread alarm among the classes which would be most adversely affected.

With discontent so general, with so many different classes dissatisfied with conditions arising from the depression, it was inevitable that politics should be affected. As the succeeding chapters show, in practically every country where popular opinion was allowed to express itself and where

the mass of the people had an opportunity to vote, the governments functioning at the time the depression began were turned out of office. The
extent of the resultant political upheaval ranged from a mere change in
the parties controlling the government to a veritable revolution such as occurred in Germany when the Nazis came into power. Furthermore, economic difficulties at home and the desire to get back to "normalcy" go far
toward explaining why political leaders in the democratic countries were
reluctant to resort to drastic measures to stop the aggressor nations in the
early stages of what turned out to be the preliminaries of the Second World
War.

Part Three

NATIONAL PROBLEMS AND EXPERIMENTS BETWEEN TWO WORLD WARS

Chapter VIII

SOVIET RUSSIA

THE national reconstruction which occurred in so many countries as a result of the First World War saw the inauguration of a number of new experiments in the political and economic life of Europe. The first of the great powers to embark upon a new course was Russia, where, with the establishment of the Soviet regime, there developed a "dictatorship of the proletariat." In the succeeding years sweeping political, social, and economic changes were made. In the end private enterprise largely disappeared from the economic life of Russia, to be succeeded by a system which may be described as state capitalism or state socialism. It was in order that they might be free to inaugurate undisturbed their extensive political, economic, and social reforms that the Bolsheviks had signed the humiliating treaty of Brest-Litovsk in March, 1918.

Failure to Dislodge the Bolsheviks

The Bolshevik hope of being left in peace to introduce their new regime in Russia was soon blasted, for both within and without the country numerous movements were at once begun for the purpose of driving the Bolsheviks from power. Many Russians—soon called White Russians because of their opposition to the Red Bolsheviks—believed that Bolshevism was but a passing phase in the Russian upheaval and hoped, by counter-revolutionary measures supported by the Allies, to be able to overthrow the Bolshevik regime. The Allies were at first not averse to intervention. Great stores of military supplies had been landed at Murmansk, Archangel, and Vladivostok for use against the Central Powers. Unless preventive measures were at once taken, it seemed likely in 1918 that these might be seized by the Germans and turned against the Allies themselves. Furthermore, France particularly was eager for the downfall of the political regime which had repudiated both the highly valued Franco-Russian alliance and the gilt-edged government bonds in which billions of francs had been invested by the French people.

After Russia's signing of the treaty of Brest-Litovsk, therefore, Allied expeditionary forces were dispatched to Murmansk, Archangel, and Vladivostok. In November, 1918, after the collapse of Turkey, French forces seized Odessa, and British forces occupied the various Transcaucasian republics. Each of the regions seized by the Allied armies served as a rallying ground for anti-Bolshevik Russians who were plotting to overthrow the Soviet government. With White armies planning to advance from the east, from the south, and from the west, it was hoped in anti-Bolshevik circles that the year 1919 would see the final downfall of the Soviet government.

Menaced by innumerable revolutionary plots from within and threatened by Allied armies of intervention from abroad, the Bolshevik leaders depended for defense chiefly upon two agencies—the Cheka and the Red Army. The Cheka was organized immediately after the November revolution to maintain order in the capital, but it was soon transformed into an agency of terror which was used to force the population into passivity or active support. In order to purge Russia of all elements dangerous to the revolution, the Cheka was empowered to arrest, try, and shoot all who were considered dangerous. In August, 1918, an organized Red Terror was begun which in the following years surpassed the bloody Reign of Terror in France. Thousands of tsarist sympathizers and bourgeois were ruthlessly put to death. But while Red Terror might suppress internal opposition, it could not unaided defeat the advancing White armies, subsidized and equipped by foreign powers. For a short time the Soviet government had almost no organized forces at its command. A volunteer Red Army was soon organized, however, by Trotsky, commissar for war, and it was developed during 1918 into a well-equipped, well-trained force of more than 100,000 men, commanded for the most part by former tsarist officers whose loyalty to Russia led them to fight against what they looked upon as foreign invasion.

In 1919 the simultaneous advance of the White armies began. Some of the forces actually got within sight of Leningrad (the name given to Petrograd by the Soviet government on April 22, 1920), only to be defeated and driven back. Perhaps the greatest single cause of the miserable failure of the White armies was the fact that the Russian people, especially the peasants, came to view them as the agents of reaction who were seeking to restore lands to the landlords and the old system of privileges to the aristocracy. The Russian peasants were not anxious to be "liberated" by armies of the landlords. The advance of the White armies had been accompanied, too, by looting, disorder, and a White Terror almost as ruthless as that of the Reds; and, as between Bolshevism and extreme military reaction, the Russian masses preferred the former temporarily as the less of two evils. The conduct of the counterrevolutionary armies and the bloody repressive measures of the White leaders also alienated popular sympathy in the Allied countries. By the close of 1919 all Allied forces had been withdrawn from European Russia, though the Japanese remained for a time in Vladivostok.

But the Soviet government was not yet freed from the need for military campaigns. The White forces of the south were actively supported by the French government, and during the early months of 1920 they once more moved northward in the Ukraine. At the same time the Poles, recalling the medieval grandeur of their state and desiring to push their Russian frontier as far east as possible, began an invasion of Russia. In May they succeeded in occupying the city of Kiev. Again the Russians rallied to support the Soviet government, and the Poles were hurled back almost to Warsaw. Only the timely aid of French men and munitions prevented a debacle. In October a preliminary treaty brought peace between the two countries and a settlement of the boundary question. By this time the Soviet government had concluded similar treaties with Estonia, Lithuania, Latvia, and Finland, and was finally free to give its attention once more to the White armies in the south. By the close of the year 1920 European Russia was cleared of active counterrevolutionary armies.

The Russian Soviet Federated Socialist Republic

Meanwhile, the Bolsheviks had profoundly altered the political life of Russia. In 1918 a new constitution, adopted by the fifth All-Russian Congress of Soviets, established the Russian Soviet Federated Socialist Republic (R.S.F.S.R.), with Moscow as the national capital instead of Leningrad. Russia became a federal state in which all power belonged to the workers "united in urban and rural Soviets." The new republic was declared to be "a free socialist society of the working people of Russia." The right to participate in the government was given to citizens of both sexes who were eighteen years of age, provided they were productive workers, the housekeepers of productive workers, or soldiers or sailors.[1] Local government was entrusted to rural and urban soviets. In villages the peasants, together with the home workers and local teachers and doctors, met and elected the deputies of the local soviet. In cities deputies were elected to the urban soviet from the factories and shops according to the different types of industry. Representation was in general by vocation, people of different employments voting separately, the ironworkers in one group, the miners in another, the soldiers in another, and so on. Housewives and independent

---

[1] Numerous classes were deprived of the right to vote or be voted for: (1) persons who employed hired labor for their own profit; (2) persons who had an income from some other source than their own labor; (3) private merchants, trade and commercial brokers; (4) monks and clergy of all denominations; (5) employees and agents of the former tsarist police, gendarmerie, or secret service; (6) members of the former reigning family; (7) criminals, lunatics, and those under guardianship.

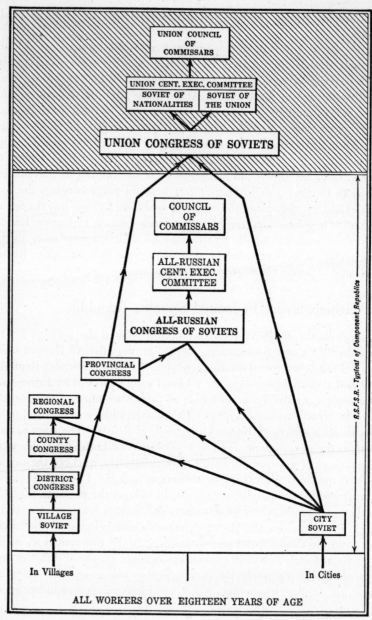

UNION COUNCIL
OF
COMMISSARS

UNION CENT. EXEC. COMMITTEE
SOVIET OF   SOVIET OF
NATIONALITIES   THE UNION

UNION CONGRESS OF SOVIETS

COUNCIL
OF
COMMISSARS

ALL-RUSSIAN
CENT. EXEC.
COMMITTEE

ALL-RUSSIAN
CONGRESS OF SOVIETS

PROVINCIAL
CONGRESS

REGIONAL
CONGRESS

COUNTY
CONGRESS

DISTRICT
CONGRESS

VILLAGE
SOVIET

CITY
SOVIET

R.S.F.S.R. - Typical of Component Republics

In Villages   In Cities

ALL WORKERS OVER EIGHTEEN YEARS OF AGE

POLITICAL STRUCTURE OF THE U.S.S.R. UNTIL 1936

handicraftsmen met ordinarily by districts. Until 1936 voting in these local elections was by show of hands rather than by secret written ballot. All representation above the village and city soviets was indirect, as shown in the accompanying diagram.

Supreme power in the R.S.F.S.R. resided theoretically in the All-Russian Congress of Soviets, composed of representatives chosen directly by the urban soviets in the ratio of one for every 25,000 voters, and by the provincial congresses in the ratio of one for every 125,000 inhabitants. A discrepancy in regard to representation was made in favor of the urban centers, where Communism had its greatest strength. The All-Russian Congress was originally supposed to meet twice yearly, but after 1921 it held only annual sessions. Its principal function was to elect the All-Russian Central Executive Committee, which was in theory responsible to it. This Central Executive Committee was "the supreme legislative, executive and controlling organ of the R.S.F.S.R." It convoked the All-Russian Congress and appointed the Council of People's Commissars, which was "entrusted with the general management of the affairs of the R.S.F.S.R." The Council of Commissars was a small group of about seventeen members which resembled the ministry in a parliamentary state. It had authority to issue decrees and to take the necessary measures to secure prompt and orderly administration, but its action was subject to annulment or approval by the Central Executive Committee.

The Union of Soviet Socialist Republics

For a time, after the November revolution of 1917, it appeared that Russia might be reduced in size to a territory little larger than that ruled by Ivan the Terrible in the sixteenth century. By the treaty of Brest-Litovsk she had been compelled to renounce her sovereignty over a great strip of territory in the west and over the whole of the Ukraine in the south. In the Transcaucasus her rule had been repudiated by Azerbaijan, Georgia, and Armenia, which had established themselves as independent states. In September, 1918, all Siberia had been organized under an anti-Bolshevik directorate at Omsk.

Nevertheless, with the exception of Poland and the new Baltic republics, which the Soviet government definitely recognized as independent in 1920, all of these apparently lost territories were soon regained. The reintegration of the Ukraine and the Transcaucasus was achieved by bringing into existence in those states governments organized on the soviet model, which, while nominally independent, entered into close relations with the R.S.F.S.R. In Siberia the Red armies succeeded in capturing Omsk, Tomsk, and Irkutsk, and all the territory west of Lake Baikal was incorporated into the R.S.F.S.R. The region to the east, however, remained independent and in 1920 was established as the Far Eastern Republic. When two years later a constituent assembly of the Far Eastern Republic declared its absorption into the R.S.F.S.R., Russia's control once more extended to the Pacific.

During the years of civil war and reintegration the constitution of the R.S.F.S.R. had been modified to meet the expanding territory and new needs. In December, 1922, conditions were deemed propitious for taking a further step. The tenth All-Russian Congress of Soviets in the R.S.F.S.R. accordingly declared in favor of a Union of Soviet Socialist Republics and appointed a delegation to collaborate with delegations from the other members of the proposed federation in the drafting of the terms of union. Shortly thereafter a declaration of the Union of Soviet Socialist Republics (U.S.S.R.) and a treaty of union were signed in Moscow, the latter being in reality the federal constitution of the union which it established. During the following months the treaty was ratified by the constituent states and became effective on July 6, 1923.

The U.S.S.R. became a federation of republics which varied in size and population from the R.S.F.S.R. with its more than 100,000,000 inhabitants to the smallest with less than one million. Its political machinery consisted principally of a Union Congress of Soviets, a Union Central Executive Committee, and a Union Council of Commissars. The Union Congress consisted of some 1500 members elected indirectly as shown in the diagram on page 186, and met for about a week once in two years to decide on general policies. It also elected the members of the Union Central Executive Committee.

The latter was a bicameral body composed of a Soviet of the Union representing the republics in proportion to population and a Soviet of Nationalities representing the ethnic units of the union on the basis of approximate equality. The Soviet of Nationalities was created to reflect the needs and consciousness of the innumerable ethnic units within the union, and it was so constructed that it might easily be expanded to include other and different ethnic groups which might later be sovietized. The two chambers co-operated in the drafting of legislation and administrative ordinances and in the exercise of political control in the union; and they had a joint presidium of some twenty members, which, between sessions of the Union Congress or Central Executive Committee, acted as the supreme authority.

The Union Council of Commissars, appointed by and responsible to the Union Central Executive Committee, consisted of a president, a vice-president, the chairman of the Supreme Economic Council, and the commissars for foreign affairs, war and marine, foreign trade, ways and communications, posts and telegraphs, workers' and peasants' inspection, labor, food, and finance. The first five commissars had sole jurisdiction throughout the union; the others had to do with matters in which the union and the constituent republics had concurrent jurisdiction. Since, however, the administrative ordinances of the union usually prevailed, the union had practically a monopoly of political power except as to local government. The union government had the right to abrogate any decisions of the congresses of soviets, central executive committees, and councils of people's commissars in the constituent republics which infringed the treaty of union. The federal character of the union, therefore, was extremely limited, one Russian scholar asserting that the constituent republics retained merely the right to legislate on social insurance, public health, education, minor courts, and agriculture except for land distribution.[2]

The Soviet system of government as found in the separate republics and in the union had three distinguishing characteristics. In the first place, the Soviet state was controlled by only one class—the proletariat. During what was expected to be merely a transitional stage from capitalism to pure communism the government of the Soviet Union was a dictatorship of the proletariat. That is to say, only the industrial workers and poor peasants had political power. The ultimate goal, of course, was the abolition of all classes and the destruction of the causes of class struggle. A second characteristic of the soviet system was the extensive use of indirect representation and the great distance which separated the voters from the supreme seat of authority. The peasants, who constituted perhaps 80 per cent of the people, were six steps removed from the Union Council of Commissars, and the urban proletariat were four. The third characteristic of the soviet system was the complete lack of separation of powers. The same set of agencies was used to perform all the functions of government—legislative, executive, administrative, and even, at times, judicial. The judiciary in the Soviet Union was "not an independent organ of the government, but an administrative department charged with the defense of the social order established by the proletarian revolution."

The Role of the Communist Party

Behind the formal machinery of the Soviet government and so interwoven into its fabric that it was not always easy to disentangle the two was the political organization of the Bolsheviks, the Communist Party,[3] which was the real power in Russia, although it was itself not mentioned in either constitution. "Without instructions from the Central Committee of our

[2] On February 1, 1944, the Supreme Soviet of the U.S.S.R. decreed that the constituent republics of the union (1) might enter into direct relation with foreign states, conclude agreements with them, and exchange diplomatic and consular representatives with them, and (2) might organize separate military formations.

[3] In 1918 the Bolsheviks changed their name officially to the Russian Communist Party.

party," once declared Lenin, "not one state institution in our republic can decide a single question of importance as regards matters of policy and organization." Higher offices in the government and in the party were largely interlocking.

This control of the higher offices was made possible largely because of the close organization of the Communist Party and the political activity of its members. Out of a population of approximately 160,000,000 in the U.S.S.R., only 2,500,000 were included in the party. But these members were subjected to a rigorous discipline. They were bound by the decisions of the party and might be expelled from the organization for failure to accept them. They were expected to be active in the trade unions and other organizations. In every soviet their aim was to organize the Communist members into efficient, disciplined groups for the purpose of winning control by the election of Communist members to the higher positions. Candidates for membership were required to pass through a probationary period before admission. The Communist Party, therefore, was "a carefully selected body of active workers with a definite goal, who are willing to make great sacrifices for its success and who are bound together by a centralized discipline." The party, too, had various youth organizations. For the purpose of perpetuating the enthusiasm and sacrificial quality of the older Communists who suffered exile or imprisonment for their principles, three junior Communist societies were created. The Octobrists (eight to ten years of age), the Pioneers (ten to sixteen), and the Communist Youth (sixteen to twenty-three) ultimately came to have millions of members, drawn from both sexes.

Aside from the Communist Party no other parties were permitted. All opposition was suppressed. Freedom of speech and of the press was abolished. Even "movies" were subject to government censorship. Although the Cheka was formally abolished in 1922, a state political department was created to take its place. The new organization of espionage was usually referred to by its initials as the Ogpu, and according to some the only difference between it and the Cheka was the change of letters. In 1934 the Ogpu, in turn, was abolished, and its functions were entrusted to a commissariat of internal affairs which was supposed to be organized along civil instead of semimilitary lines. Opposition continued to be crushed from time to time, however, by arbitrary imprisonment, exile to Siberia, or death.

Early Economic Experiments

Far more revolutionary than the changes introduced into the political system were those made in the economic life of Russia by the Communists during the first three years of their regime. The fundamental concept of their economic thought—prevention of the exploitation of the workers by the capitalists and landlords—demanded the nationalization of all land, forests, and minerals, together with all means of production, transportation, trade, banking, and insurance. These would then belong to the state, and under the soviet system the workers constituted the state. All profits which formerly went to landlords and capitalists would accrue to the state —in other words, to the workers. The surplus products of both peasants and proletariat would be turned over to state agencies from which each would in return secure those commodities which he needed; that is to say, money and wages would be abolished, and the state would take all output and in turn reward each according to his needs. In greatly simplified form, this was the economic system envisaged by the Communist leaders.

It had been the original intention of the Communists to nationalize only large industrial establishments at first, and then only after they had been concentrated in trusts. But this plan for gradual and systematic nationalization broke down almost immediately. Instead, there began a haphazard and punitive nationalization of all sorts of industries. The effect of this procedure upon Russia's economic life was disastrous. The workers were prepared neither by education nor by training to take over the responsibilities of management. The efficient conduct of the factories, the procuring of regular supplies of raw materials, and the distribution of the finished products were beyond their ability. There was little effort at co-ordination; each factory was run by its own committee independently of all others. Industrial chaos naturally ensued.

Because of the collapse of industry, an attempt was made in June, 1918, to escape further haphazard nationalization and to develop a system of industrial administration under centralized control. Practically all industry was nationalized. Furthermore, all agencies of domestic and foreign trade, the merchant marine, and the banks were nationalized and their total assets confiscated. To control and co-ordinate the industrial life of the country the Supreme Economic Council was established. It was to see that all factories were supplied with necessary raw materials, fuel, and machinery, as well as the money and food needed for their workers. As might have been expected under the circumstances, the Supreme Economic Council proved altogether unable to accomplish so gigantic a task. Industrial production fell off alarmingly. Moreover, costs of production everywhere rose because of increased demands of the workers, scarcity of raw materials, and uneconomical management.

Meanwhile, the government had become involved in a struggle with the peasants. In accordance with the Communist economic plan, as briefly outlined above, the Soviet government in May, 1918, established a food dictatorship and ordered every peasant to turn over to the state all grain above a certain minimum needed for seed and for the consumption of his family. This at once encountered the opposition of the peasants, who either failed to understand or refused to adopt the role which had been assigned to them in the Communist economic scheme. If in return for the grain which they surrendered to the state they could have received an equivalent value in the manufactured goods which they needed for their farms and their homes, they might have acquiesced. But this was impossible, both because of the cutting off of the importation of manufactured goods from abroad and because of the demoralization of Russian industries at home. The peasants, therefore, refused to surrender their grain. When the government seized grain by force, the peasants were further antagonized and thereupon resorted to passive resistance.

In 1920 the peasants reduced their acreage under cultivation until it was 29 per cent less than it had been in 1913. The smaller area sown and the decrease in available fertilizers and in effective agricultural tools, coupled with an unusually prolonged drought, combined to bring a tremendous reduction in available food supplies. The harvest in 1921 was only 42 per cent of the average in the four years immediately preceding the war. A severe famine resulted. Soviet authorities estimated that 30,000,000 people would need relief. The government fed millions, and appealed for foreign aid in the task. Some forty different foreign agencies, including the American Relief Administration, undertook to feed the starving millions. But many died from starvation or epidemics.

The first large-scale communist experiment in history was headed for disaster. The industrial workers had failed to produce the manufactured goods needed by the peasants. The peasants, failing to obtain tangible goods in exchange for their grain, had curtailed their planting. This had contributed to produce a shortage of grain, and the government was now unable to provide adequate food supplies for the industrial proletariat. And unless the urban workers were supplied with food, they would certainly turn against the government, for hunger is ever a powerful provocative of revolution. Outbreaks began to occur not only among the peasants but even among the proletariat, whose sympathy the government was beginning to lose. Cries of "Down with the Soviet Government!" began to be heard in workmen's meetings and demonstrations. Pure communism was doomed.

The New Economic Policy

In 1921 the Communists thus faced the possibility of losing their political power as a consequence of having antagonized the great body of peasants. They had made practically no headway in their efforts to win this class to their economic scheme, and so were forced to conclude that it was "easier to change their policy than to change the peasants." They decided that, while retaining complete control of the administration of the government, the means of transport, large-scale industry, and foreign trade, they would make a number of minor concessions in other phases of economic life. They began their economic retreat by inaugurating a "New Economic Policy" (Nep).

Perhaps the most important feature of this Nep was the abandonment of the system of requisitioning grain from the peasants and the substitution of a fixed tax. Whatever a peasant produced over and above the amount of his tax was his to retain or to dispose of freely in the open market. The incentive which had been destroyed by the communistic scheme was thus restored, and there at once followed a gradual increase in the area under cultivation. Existing conditions of land ownership were stabilized. Although the Soviet government continued to insist that the state was the sole owner of the land and that the peasants were merely tenants, the right of usage and the right to dispose of products became so unrestricted that for all practical purposes the land belonged to the peasants. In 1925 the Nep was extended to permit the renting of land for limited periods of time and the employment of a certain number of wage laborers. Some of the richer, more enterprising peasants (the *kulaks*) at once benefited by renting land to increase their holdings and by farming intensively with hired labor. As the years passed, therefore, just as before the revolution some peasants added to their wealth, while others became impoverished and sought employment once more as hired agricultural laborers.

In industry the Nep brought the denationalization of establishments employing fewer than twenty workers. With the exception of small factories and shops, however, the state still reserved to itself the monopoly of industrial production, though it introduced the principle of sweeping decentralization. Industries were organized into large independent units or "trusts," each with its board of managers acting as trustee of the state. These trusts were given freedom to dispose of their products and to obtain their raw materials and fuel in the open market, subject only to prices fixed by the state and to the obligation of preferred service to the state. In order to overcome the lack of liquid capital, the Soviet government even granted foreign capitalists concessions for mining, manufacturing, transportation, trade, and agricultural activity.

In the realm of commerce, foreign trade remained fundamentally a state monopoly, carried on through a number of organizations to which the government gave the right to conduct export and import operations within prescribed limits under its own control. Domestic trade was opened to private capital but was subject to taxation and, as it revived, to more and more state regulation. Private trade developed so rapidly that the government, beginning in 1924, began to exert great pressure against it in favor of state and co-operative agencies, with the result that many Nep-men were forced out of business.

The re-establishment of banking and credit operations began with the opening of a state bank in November, 1921. This was followed after 1924 by the opening of other banks—municipal, agricultural, co-operative, savings—throughout the union. In 1921 insurance of private property was instituted as a state monopoly, and three years later life insurance was restored. A new currency was introduced (the *chervonets*), a gold reserve was accumulated, and in 1924 the new currency was stabilized on a gold basis. Money wages were once more paid, and the system of governmental rationing of the cities was abandoned. A capitalistic system of taxation was inaugurated and eventually a balanced national budget obtained.

To summarize, then, under the Nep the state retained control of production in the large and middle-sized industrial plants and completely monopolized foreign trade, but restored agriculture, small industrial establishments, and domestic trade to private enterprise, subject to some degree of state control. Russia's economic life, as a consequence, came to present a strange picture of intermingled state socialism, state capitalism, and private capitalism. Nevertheless, under it that economic life came to be almost fully restored; some branches indeed even rose above prewar levels of production.

The Rise of Joseph Stalin

Meanwhile, a bitter conflict had been going on within the ranks of the Communist Party. So long as Lenin was able to take an active part in the direction of Russian affairs, this conflict had been held in abeyance, for his prestige and influence were of such magnitude that his policies found ready acceptance among his followers. But after illness had removed him from active participation in Russian affairs early in 1922, and especially after his death in January, 1924, differences between the Communist leaders became pronounced and constituted the basis of a struggle to determine who should assume Lenin's position as head of the Communist Party.

Prominent among those who became involved in the struggle over policies and power were: Trotsky, the first commissar for foreign affairs and later organizer of the Red Army, a brilliant revolutionary leader, orator, and writer, the one looked upon by most foreigners as the logical successor of Lenin; Zinoviev, the organizer and head of the Communist or Third International, enthusiastic in his plans to carry out the international propaganda of Communist ideas in order to achieve the world proletarian revolu-

De Cou, From Ewing Galloway, N. Y.

THE SUCCESSOR TO LENIN
Joseph Stalin

tion; Dzerzhinsky, a descendant of Polish-Lithuanian nobility, the organizer and head of the Cheka, skilled agitator and organizer of strikes who had twice suffered exile to Siberia under the tsarist regime; Stalin, the son of a Georgian shoemaker, a stalwart of the Communist "Old Guard" who had frequently suffered imprisonment and exile for his beliefs, former editor of the Communist newspaper *Pravda,* characterized by Lenin as "too cruel" and "too brutal" and as having concentrated too much power in his hands as general secretary of the Communist Party; Rykov, who as a young man had early come under Lenin's influence and had repeatedly suffered imprisonment and exile in his service, Lenin's private secretary, at one time head of the Supreme Economic Council, the successor of Lenin as president of the Council of People's Commissars; Kamenev, a former law student under President Millerand in France, vice-president of the Union Council of People's Commissars and chairman of the Council for Labor and Defense, suspected by Lenin of not being 100-per-cent Communist; Bukharin, an ardent supporter of Lenin, characterized as the "evangelist" of Communism, who from the words of his master had created "the gospel of Communism," yet considered by Lenin as having "stuffed his head too full of books." Within this small group there developed a powerful triumvirate composed of Stalin, Zinoviev, and Kamenev, the political genius of the group being Stalin. From this inner circle Trotsky was excluded, for he had joined the party only in 1917 and was looked upon as a newcomer by the "Old Guard," who consistently sought to discredit him.

Lenin's death at once precipitated a conflict within the party between a group led by the triumvirate and another led by Trotsky. The Stalin group believed that the capitalist regime outside Russia had become stabilized and that it was not likely to be overturned in the immediate future; the Trotsky opposition still clung to the hope of a world revolution "in our time." The former desired to cater to the interests of the peasants on the ground that their support was necessary for the success of the great Communist economic experiment; the latter wished to emphasize the interests of the urban workers as being paramount in a proletarian state. The group led by Stalin maintained that Russia's welfare demanded the assistance of foreign capital; the opposition denounced such a policy as treason to the Communist ideal. Briefly, the policies of the Stalin group were in the direction of stabilization; those of the opposition, in the direction of revolution. Late in 1924 Trotsky was defeated in the Communist Party congress. Early in 1925 he was dismissed as commissar for war and removed from the Council for Labor and Defense, and his active adherents were expelled from the army and navy.

Next the members of the triumvirate began to quarrel among themselves. Stalin was alarmed by the continued unrest among the peasants and advocated further concessions to win their support. He also advocated additional measures to attract foreign capital. Such concessions and measures were vigorously opposed by a Left group led by Zinoviev and Kamenev. In the party congress in 1925 Stalin, supported by Rykov, Dzerzhinsky, and Bukharin, succeeded in winning the support of the majority, and Zinoviev and Kamenev were ordered to discontinue their opposition. As they had humiliated Trotsky in the preceding year, so they themselves were now humiliated.

Trotsky then joined forces with Zinoviev and Kamenev in an attempt to oust Stalin and his group from control of the Communist Party. But again the Stalin group won out. In 1926 the Trotsky-Zinoviev opposition was ordered to submit to the party discipline or withdraw from the organization. When in the following year the opposition once more began its attacks, Trotsky, Zinoviev, Kamenev, and some fourscore of their associates were expelled from the Communist Party and sent into exile. But Trotsky from his place of exile in Turkestan continued his opposition, and during the winter of 1928–1929 his influence with the urban workers resulted in spasmodic agitation in the factories in his behalf. Eventually, on the ground that Trotsky was still carrying on illegal propaganda against the government, the latter exiled him from the union. Had it not been for the danger of creating a martyr to Trotskyism, it is possible he might have been executed. In April, 1929, the Communist Party once more approved Joseph Stalin's leadership.

This heir to Lenin's power in Russia was born in 1879 in Gori, a town in the Caucasus. The son of a Georgian shoemaker, he had been christened Joseph Visserionovich Dzhugashvili. Destined by his parents for the priesthood, he had been sent to a theological seminary, but from this clerical institution he had been ultimately expelled because of his Marxian ideas. Soon thereafter he became a member of the Social Democratic Party, and in 1902 he was arrested and exiled to Siberia for his part in a demonstration at Batum. Although an exile in 1903, when the Social Democratic Party split, Dzhugashvili sided with Lenin and thus at once entered the ranks of the Communists.

In 1904 Dzhugashvili escaped from Siberia and returned to his home district under an assumed name, and during the ensuing decade his career was filled with repeated arrests, exiles, escapes, and new aliases. Of the latter, the one by which he became best known was Stalin (Steel), conferred upon him by his fellow Communists because of his strength, coolness, ruthlessness, and taciturnity. Always plotting, agitating, writing, or editing, he persistently worked against the tsarist regime from within Russia. Six times arrested and exiled, he five times escaped, thanks to his cleverness and to his physical powers of endurance. During the years after 1913, however, he was successfully kept in exile in northern Siberia within the Arctic Circle. Isolation, prison tortures, forced labor, and severe deprivation were the lot of this "man of steel."

Freed by the March revolution of 1917 with its political amnesty, and permitted to return to Petrograd, Stalin at once became active in organizing soviets. Not an impassioned and eloquent orator, he interested himself primarily in the practical affairs of organization and thus helped to rebuild the Communist Party. When the November revolution occurred, he became one of the first commissars in the new Communist government. During the period of White invasions, he played a prominent part in defense of the Communist regime, and to commemorate his success at Tzaritzin on the lower Volga, that city was rechristened Stalingrad. From 1920 to 1923 he was commissar of nationalities and left his impress upon the constitution of the U.S.S.R. with its Soviet of Nationalities. As secretary-general of the Russian Communist Party, Stalin directed and maintained discipline within that organization and ruthlessly eliminated all disruptive personalities. Quietly but solidly he built up a political machine which enabled him to dominate the party—and through it the Soviet Union.

The Five-Year Plans

During the struggle between Trotsky and Stalin the former had frequently denounced the latter on the ground that his policies were threatening Russia with a reversion to capitalism, permitting as they did the growth of Nep-men and kulaks. Although Trotsky and his followers were expelled from the party and in some cases even arrested or exiled, their attitude toward kulaks and Nep-men was actually adopted by the victorious Stalin, and a program of swift industrialization and ruthless elimination of these classes ensued in the years after 1928. Stalin's new policies became effective through the so-called Five-Year Plan (*Piatiletka*), which sounded the death knell of both Nep-men and kulaks.

As early as 1925 the Soviet government had contemplated the introduction of a more organized and planned system of national economy. Eventually, on October 1, 1928, an official Five-Year Plan, prepared by the State Planning Commission (*Gosplan*), was inaugurated for the years 1928–1933. The fundamental aims of this first Five-Year Plan were: (1) to introduce modern technology; (2) to transform Russia from a comparatively weak agrarian country into a powerful industrial country which could be largely independent of capitalist countries; (3) to eliminate completely private capitalism; (4) to create a socially owned heavy industry which could provide machinery for industry, transport, and agriculture; (5) to collectivize agriculture and thus remove the danger of a restoration of capitalism inherent in the continued existence of individual farms; (6) to increase Russia's ability to defend herself in time of war.

The plan laid down a schedule for practically every phase of the country's activities—production, distribution, and finance. It called for an enormous amount of new industrial construction—huge tractor factories, gigantic agricultural machinery factories, immense steel plants, extensive hydro-electric works, and new railways. Capital investments during the five-year period were to amount to billions of dollars. Control figures for each of the five years included quantity and quality of products, cost of production, efficiency of labor, wages, cost of living, and so forth.

Agriculture was to be reorganized on a large-scale mechanized basis through the institution of huge state and collective farms. Through the organization of such farms it was planned to mechanize and socialize the agrarian system and thus at last bring agriculture, which had long been a stumbling block in the way of socialism, into the sphere of planned economic life. The state farms were to be experiments in the application of the most modern mechanized methods of agriculture to huge expanses of fresh land. Managers were to be appointed by the grain trust, a state organization, and labor was to be hired on a wage basis. The state farms were to be financed by the government, and their total agricultural product would belong to the state.

The collective farm, on the other hand, was to result from the combination of a number of peasants' small holdings into one large farm. Although there might be different types of such collective farms, in general the peasants were to retain their homes, gardens, cows, pigs, and chickens, but were to surrender their lands, machinery, and horses to common ownership. The peasants would then work together under the direction of an elected managerial board. After certain amounts were set aside for seeds and fodder, taxes and insurance, purchase of new machinery and construction of new buildings, debt payments, contributions for education and charity, and administrative expenses, the balance of income from the collective farm would be divided among the peasants in proportion to the amount of property which each contributed and the amount and quality of the work each had performed. This type of collective was called an "artel." By eliminating the ditches which separated the small individual plots, thousands of acres could be combined into huge fields in which tractors and modern agricultural machinery could be used to advantage.

The adoption of the Five-Year Plan marked a shift from the relatively loose and easygoing system of the Nep to a much more strictly regulated and definitely socialist phase of the revolution. Various earlier concessions to private initiative were to be annulled or rigorously restricted. The two principal capitalist classes which had grown up under the Nep—the private traders in the towns and the kulaks in the villages—were to be "liquidated." Ultimately, it was hoped, the Five-Year Plan, with its emphasis on all phases of industrial development and with its anticipated expansion of agricultural production, would bring Soviet Russia close to the goal of self-sufficiency in basic and essential commodities. In this sense, the Five-Year Plan was "a declaration of economic independence against the outside world."

The inauguration of the plan inevitably raised a number of serious problems. Obviously, one was the matter of finance. The government planned to finance its undertakings chiefly by means of taxes, internal loans, profits from state trusts, and capital savings resulting from the reduced costs of production. To pay for the necessary importation of machinery and other needed articles from abroad, the government proposed to rely largely upon the export of the country's increased surplus of grain. In this connection a second problem was raised by the drastic decline in the world price of grain. Although in 1929–1930, for example, Russia's exports rose almost 50 per cent —thanks to increased production of grain—the world decline in prices prevented this increase from being reflected in the country's monetary income. To meet this unexpected crisis, the Soviet government ruthlessly stripped the country of articles which had export value, and the world beheld the curious anomaly of a people forced to live on short rations while millions of tons of grain were being exported from the land.

Another problem in connection with the successful execution of the plan was that of securing an adequate number of well-trained engineers, technicians, and skilled workers. The plan called for the introduction of new specialized courses in schools and universities and for the establishment of many new technical and vocational schools. To solve the immediate problem, the services of foreign engineering firms and individual specialists were engaged. Foreign engineers and technicians became important, almost indispensable, cogs in Russia's industrialization machine. Still another problem was that of securing industrial efficiency from untrained or ill-trained workers. Machines were often injured and products ruined. The factory management itself was seriously handicapped by the necessity of discussing first with the workers any new plans they wished to inaugurate or orders which they wished to give. In the early period all incentive to speed and efficiency was largely lacking because of the policy of treating all workers alike.

The inevitable result of all these factors was that the scheduled decreased cost of production, increased efficiency of labor, and improved quality of goods were not attained. Although the quantity of goods produced in the ensuing years was frequently in excess of the control figures, the quality was usually below the required standards. Beginning with the year 1930, efforts were made by the government to remedy this situation. The Supreme Economic Council threatened severe punishment for individuals responsible for producing goods of low quality. Differential wage scales and piece work were introduced as an incentive to greater effort, and the work day was lengthened. To improve the efficiency of factory managements, their control over the workers was increased, and the authority of workers' committees was lessened.

Nevertheless, despite all handicaps and obstacles, the Five-Year Plan for industry moved steadily forward. In the case of many production schedules the five-year goal was attained within three years. In April, 1930, the 1100-mile Turkestan-Siberian Railway was completed more than a year ahead of schedule. The year 1932 saw a 900,000-horsepower hydroelectric plant, built at a cost of more than $100,000,000, dedicated at Dnepropetrovsk, and the first blast furnace fired in the Magnitogorsk steel works, which was destined to become one of the largest steel plants in the world.

In agriculture astonishing changes were introduced. Principally in southeastern Russia, Siberia, and Kazakstan huge state farms were established on previously unused lands. These great farms averaged between 100,000 and 200,000 acres, and the largest, the "Giant," located in the northern Caucasus, put under the plow nearly 300,000 acres in 1930. Tens of thousands of tractors and hundreds of combines—great machines which reaped and threshed the grain at the same time—were put into service.

Great advances were made, also, in the collectivization of peasant holdings. Special inducements—such as lower taxes, easier credit facilities, precedence in the acquisition of machinery and manufactured goods—were offered to those who joined the collectives. On the other hand, heavier taxes and a ruthless requisitioning of grain at fixed prices were the lot of the more prosperous peasants, who were loath to merge their holdings in a collective. The houses, livestock, and tools of thousands of these kulaks were confiscated, and they themselves were torn from their homes and banished to remote regions where they were compelled to work at hard labor. Thousands more were arrested and thrown into prison. The government was determined to liquidate the kulaks.

But collectivization by such methods had its evil side. Occasionally the persecuted kulaks united to defend themselves and precipitated uprisings which resulted in attacks upon the collectives and in the destruction of crops. Such revolts, however, were speedily suppressed. Much more serious than these peasant uprisings was the widespread slaughtering of livestock which occurred during the winter of 1929–1930, when peasants killed some 25 per cent of their cows, 33 per cent of their sheep, and 50 per cent of their hogs. This they did partly because they expected to lose them anyway as a result of forcible collectivization, and partly because the government's ruthless requisition of grain had the twofold effect of causing a shortage of foodstuffs for the peasants and fodder for their animals.

This situation precipitated another conflict within the Communist Party. In 1929–1930, a Right group, led by Rykov, Bukharin, and Tomsky, attacked Stalin on the ground that his ruthless liquidation of the kulaks and his rapid and compulsory collectivization of peasant estates was altogether too radical. This so-called Rightist deviation was in turn crushed, however, much as had been the earlier Left opposition led by Trotsky. Though in this case the leaders were not actually driven out of the party, their political power was greatly weakened and they were definitely subordinated to Stalin. In 1932, too, Zinoviev and Kamenev were once more expelled from the organization—along with a score or more of others—because of their subversive activities in creating within the party a faction opposed to official policies regarding the Five-Year Plan.

Nevertheless, Stalin saw the dangers of the situation and in 1930 called a halt. Government decrees eliminated the worst abuses of the program of forcible collectivization. The attempt of extreme enthusiasts to establish "communes," collectives in which the peasants were required to surrender all property except a few articles of personal use, was rejected in favor of the more moderate "artel." Peasants who had been collectivized by force were permitted to take back their property and become individual farmers once more if they wished. Additional inducements were soon held out to those who would voluntarily join, however, and it was decided that 5 per cent of the net income of each collective should be set aside yearly as a fund to reimburse peasants for animals and machinery which they had contributed to the enterprise. Gradually the tide turned again, and by the spring of 1931 more than 45 per cent of the peasant families were in collectives. The effectiveness of the new large-scale farming was shown in 1930 when, after a lapse of four years, Russia was once more able to export grain in substantial quantities.

In 1930 the government decided that the Soviet economic year should coincide with the calendar year, and so it was decreed that the Five-Year Plan should include only four and one quarter years in order that it might close on December 31, 1932. With the official ending of the plan it became possible to form some judgment regarding its success. Great strides had certainly been made toward transforming Soviet Russia into a powerful industrial country. The Union was dotted with enormous new factories and magnificent new power plants. No other important country could show a rate of quantitative industrial progress to compare with that of the Soviet Union during these years. In the production of machinery, tractors, and petroleum the original plan had been exceeded. On the other hand, in certain industries like iron, steel, and coal, and in some of the consumption industries like textiles, the production had failed to meet the schedule of the original plan. Furthermore, it had been discovered that huge industrial plants were far easier to construct than to operate efficiently.

In agriculture the plan, so far as acreage in state and collective farms was concerned, had been far exceeded. Nearly 30,000,000 acres had been organized into state farms, and more than 15,000,000 peasant households had been brought into the collective farms. Mechanization and collectivization of agriculture had made great advances. Nevertheless, here, too, not all the goals set up by the plan had been attained, for it had been found easier to bring the peasants into collective farms than to make them efficiently productive. As a stimulus to hard work and careful handling of tools and animals no adequate substitute had been found for private ownership.

For the great mass of the Russians, perhaps the worst failure of the plan was in the matter of wages and living standards. Although money wages went up faster than had been contemplated, a number of factors prevented a reduction of the cost of living and a corresponding rise in living standards. In the first place, when expected economies in production did not materialize and when the export income of the government did not reach the desired figure because of the decline in world prices, the currency was inflated by a resort to the printing press. Prices, therefore, became high in terms of the rubles which the Russians received for their products or labor. In the second place, there was a very real shortage of foodstuffs and of manufactured articles for daily consumption. The great majority of Russians were worse off in 1932 so far as food supply was concerned than they had been in 1927. In fact, the year 1932–1933 saw severe famine conditions in parts of Russia. Furthermore, consumption goods were sacrificed to the production of factories, power plants, and basic articles like steel, petroleum, and coal, with the result that many manufactured necessities of daily life became so scarce that they could not be generally obtained at any price. The Five-Year Plan, nevertheless, undoubtedly constituted a landmark in Russian industrial history.

Early in 1934 the Communist Party congress approved an outline of a second Five-Year Plan covering the years 1933–1937. Under the second plan more attention was to be given to consumers' goods. Greater emphasis was to be laid, also, upon the efficiency of labor, the reduction in production costs, and the improvement in the quality of goods. The material welfare of the masses was one of the major concerns of the second period. Thousands of houses and apartments were to be erected in the industrial centers, together with theaters, clubs, stadiums, and parks. The crying need for such construction was caused by the great shift in population from

A PRODUCT OF THE FIRST FIVE-YEAR PLAN

The dedication of the dam at Dnepropetrovsk in 1932

farms to the cities, the number of industrial wage-earners having increased from 11,500,000 in 1928 to 23,500,000 in 1934. These figures likewise explain the Soviet problem of increasing efficiency in industrial production with workers many of whom were inexperienced. To help solve this problem provision was made in the second Five-Year Plan for still greater expansion of facilities for vocational and technical training. In the interests of greater efficiency a decree in 1934 abolished fixed minimum wages and ordered reductions for inefficient workers.

The results obtained under the second Five-Year Plan were distinctly encouraging. In the basic heavy industries—mining, iron and steel, petroleum, machinery, railroad equipment, and the like—the specifications of the plan were generally exceeded. In fact, in 1934 the Soviet Union occupied second place in the world production of pig iron and third place in steel production, in each case ranking ahead of Great Britain. More encouraging still, perhaps, was the increase in workers' efficiency and the reduction in production costs; it was officially stated that labor productivity in 1937 was double that of 1929. Apparently the Russians had begun to master industrial technique. In agricultural production the gains were also notable. The grain harvest for 1933 was the largest in Russian history, that for 1934 was still larger, and that for 1935 again set a record. The last year saw record harvests in other products than cereals, too. Sugar beets, tobacco, fruit, cotton, and flax also established new records. The increased production of cotton was particularly significant in view of Russia's enlarged facilities for textile manufacturing. In 1937 agriculture was reported to be 93 per cent collectivized.

In contrast with the first Five-Year Plan, which imposed many privations upon the masses in order that the foundations might be laid for an industrialized country, the second Five-Year Plan began to bring to the Russian people some of the fruits of their long and arduous toil. This was evident, for instance, in the matter of foodstuffs. In 1935 the whole food-rationing system was abandoned, and all foodstuffs—meat, potatoes, butter, eggs, sugar, and the like—were made available to purchasers without restrictions. Moreover, prices were reduced by government decree. Nor were improvements in living standards limited to the matter of food. Since the industries producing textiles and footwear had exceeded their quotas under the plan, articles of wearing apparel were both more plentiful and lower-priced. In general, the retail stores were better supplied with goods than in previous years.

The peasants, too, participated in the rising standard of living. Higher official prices for farm products and freedom to sell surplus produce in the open market naturally increased their purchasing power. They thus found themselves in a position to buy in the village stores many consumers' goods which they had been unable to obtain in preceding years. And—what was equally important—more consumers' goods were available for purchase. It may therefore be stated with a fair degree of certainty that the real incomes of the Russian people and consequently their general standard of living rose during the early years of the second Five-Year Plan. The rate of improvement was checked in 1936, however, because of increased emphasis upon military and naval armaments to meet the increasing Nazi menace.

In 1936 the Communist leaders announced that the Soviet state had largely achieved the first of its objectives in its march toward communism. The productive means of the country, it was asserted, had at length been almost entirely socialized. Private producers—both handicraftsmen and peasants—constituted only 5.6 per cent of the population in 1937. Thus, it was pointed out, with the socialization of industry and the collectivization of agriculture, there remained in Russia only one class—the workers. Among the peasants—the most difficult of the Russians to be absorbed into the communist state—there were, it was reported, no longer rich, middle-class, and poor. All had become "members of a collectivized and socialized agricultural society." Although the Communist leaders were doubtless slightly overenthusiastic about the extent of their achievements, it seemed fairly clear in 1936 that the struggle to establish in Russia a collectivized and mechanized system of agriculture had been largely won.

The Constitution of 1936

In view of this situation, apparently, the Communist leaders decided that it would be safe to remove some of the political restrictions and discriminations which were originally designed to protect the Communist regime from those classes which were unsympathetic. In February, 1935, therefore, the Union Congress of Soviets voted that the constitution of the Union should be amended to give more direct popular control of the political machinery. The Union Central Executive Committee, accordingly, appointed a constitutional commission with Joseph Stalin as chairman. This commission, instead of merely preparing amendments to the existing constitution, drafted a complete new document which was approved by the presidium of the Union Central Executive Committee, and ultimately adopted with amendments by the Union Congress on December 5, 1936.

The new constitution changed the political machinery slightly. The Union Congress of Soviets was abolished, and supreme power was lodged in the Supreme Soviet of the U.S.S.R., a bicameral legislature which is practically the former Union Central Executive Committee under a new name. A similar change was proposed for each of the constituent republics

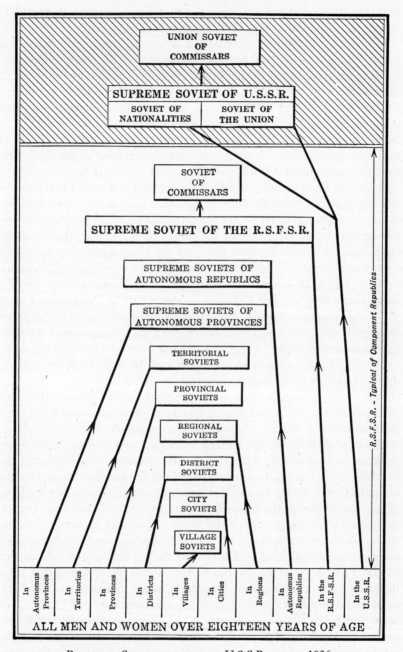

UNION SOVIET
OF
COMMISSARS

SUPREME SOVIET OF U.S.S.R.

| SOVIET OF NATIONALITIES | SOVIET OF THE UNION |

SOVIET
OF
COMMISSARS

SUPREME SOVIET OF THE R.S.F.S.R.

SUPREME SOVIETS OF
AUTONOMOUS REPUBLICS

SUPREME SOVIETS OF
AUTONOMOUS PROVINCES

TERRITORIAL
SOVIETS

PROVINCIAL
SOVIETS

REGIONAL
SOVIETS

DISTRICT
SOVIETS

CITY
SOVIETS

VILLAGE
SOVIETS

R.S.F.S.R. – Typical of Component Republics

In Autonomous Provinces · In Territories · In Provinces · In Districts · In Villages · In Cities · In Regions · In Autonomous Republics · In the R.S.F.S.R. · In the U.S.S.R.

ALL MEN AND WOMEN OVER EIGHTEEN YEARS OF AGE

POLITICAL STRUCTURE OF THE U.S.S.R. AFTER 1936

also. Much more significant were the modifications made in regard to franchise, method of voting, and system of representation.

In the new constitution every citizen at least eighteen years of age was given "the right to elect and be elected irrespective of his race or nationality, his religion, educational qualifications, residential qualifications, his social origins, property status and past activity." Candidates might be nominated by Communist Party organizations, trade unions, co-operatives, youth organizations, and cultural societies. Voting at elections was no longer to be by show of hands but by secret ballot. Moreover, the old system of indirect representation was completely abolished in favor of the direct election of deputies in all political units. That is to say, the peasant would now vote directly for those who should make his laws and would no longer be five steps removed from the supreme legislative body of the Union. Furthermore, the former discrimination against the peasants in favor of the proletariat was ended. Deputies to the Soviet of the Union, the popularly elected branch of the Supreme Soviet of the U.S.S.R., were to be elected from single-member constituencies (each of approximately 300,000 population) in which all citizens whether peasants or urban workers had the same electoral privileges. Deputies to the Soviet of Nationalities were also to be chosen by popular election on the basis of twenty-five deputies from each constituent republic, eleven from each autonomous republic, five from each autonomous province, and one from each national region.

A study of the diagrams on pages 186 and 205 will reveal the striking differences between the system of representation before and after 1936. The changes seem to indicate that the Communist leaders believed that class divisions within the Soviet Union had been practically wiped out, that there remained in Russia only one class—the workers.

The new constitution, too, seemed to indicate some change in economic doctrines and policies. It still stated that the "economic foundation of the U.S.S.R. consists in the socialist ownership of the implements and means of production" (Article 4), and that socialist ownership has either the form of state ownership or the form of co-operative and collective-farm ownership (Article 5). But alongside the socialist system of economy "the law allows small private economy of individual peasants and handicraftsmen based on individual labor and excluding the exploitation of the labor of others" (Article 9). That the Soviet Union had by 1936 departed from the ideals of pure communism is apparent in the statement that the "personal ownership by citizens of their income from work and savings, of home and auxiliaries pertaining thereto, of objects of domestic and household use, of objects of personal use and comfort, as well as the right to inherit private property are protected by law" (Article 10). This departure is further revealed by the declaration that in the U.S.S.R. "the principle of socialism is being realized: 'From each according to his ability, to each according to his work'" (Article 12). Apparently the earlier communist ideal of taking from each according to his ability and giving to each according to his needs has been abandoned.

Although the Communist leaders repeatedly emphasized the democratic features of the constitution of 1936, the first national election held in the Soviet Union, on December 12, 1937, disclosed that Russia's so-called democracy was far different from that of the United States, Great Britain, and France. In practically every one of the more than one thousand electoral districts, the voters were confronted with only one candidate. Most of the 91,113,153 voters who went to the polls therefore had no choice when they cast their secret ballots. When the Supreme Soviet of the Soviet Union convened for its first meeting on January 12, 1938, members of the Communist Party held 855 of the 1143 seats in the two houses.

The contrast between Russian Communism and Western Liberalism was further revealed by party purges in Russia before the Second World War. The fate of those who might dare to challenge Stalin's supremacy was startlingly revealed in 1934 when Sergius Kirov, a prominent member of the Communist Party and one of Stalin's close associates, was assassinated on December 1 in Leningrad. The Soviet authorities struck with terrifying speed. Within a few weeks the assassin and nearly a hundred others who were charged with complicity were executed. The conspirators were represented as consisting of remnants of the old Trotsky-Kamenev group who were seeking to prepare the way for Trotsky's return. Accordingly, a thoroughgoing purge of the party was at once inaugurated. A considerable number of Communists were arrested and, on the ground of their heretical beliefs, were ordered imprisoned for terms varying from five to ten years. As the result of new trials inaugurated in 1936 prominent Communist leaders, including Zinoviev and Kamenev, were condemned to death; while Tomsky, who was among the accused, committed suicide before the trial ended.

In 1937 hundreds more, including several prominent generals in the Soviet army and some high officials in the state governments, were summarily tried and executed on the ground that they were either Japanese or German spies. In 1938 twenty-one more Communist leaders were brought to trial on charges of plotting to overthrow the Soviet government and to dismember the Soviet Union. Included in the number, in addition to Bukharin and Rykov, were a former head of the Ogpu, a former head of the State Planning Commission, and former commissars of foreign trade and of agriculture. Bukharin, Rykov, and sixteen of the accused were shot, and the other three were sentenced to prison terms ranging from fifteen to twenty-five years.

Doubtless some of the condemned men were guilty of the crimes of which they were accused. Nevertheless, the suspicion was strong that Stalin and his associates in the government had deliberately rid themselves of many of their most dangerous rivals by recourse to these treason trials. Apparently the struggle for control of the Communist Party and the Soviet government, begun even before Lenin's death and greatly intensified after 1924, had continued. And personal rivalries and disagreements between Stalin and his associates, on the one hand, and other Communist leaders, critical of the new bureaucracy, on the other, instead of being left for peaceful settlement by the popular vote of the Russian people, were liquidated with increasing frequency by resort to the firing squad. These events, many believed, revealed the wide gulf between the reputed democracy of the Soviet Union and that of the liberal countries of the West. Others maintained that they were proof, rather, that many of Stalin's enemies were willing to work with the Nazis, if necessary, to overthrow his regime and that those executed therefore had constituted what would have proved later to be "fifth columnists."

Education and Religion

Not unrelated to the political and economic life of Russia was the attitude of the Soviet government toward public education. Upon the schools the Communists relied for two important achievements. By them must be prepared the well-trained, skilled technicians who were expected to assume in the economic and administrative life of the Union the places left vacant by the overthrow of the bourgeoisie. In this sense there was in Russia a "race between education and catastrophe." Then, as Lenin pointed out, the Communist economic scheme was not possible without "an intellectual revolution." From this point of view the Communists looked to the schools to produce a generation which should be thoroughly versed in and loyal to the Communist ideal.

Just how these aims should be accomplished the Communists were not altogether sure, so that the Soviet Union came to constitute a great laboratory for educational experiments. On one thing they were determined, however: that the illiteracy of the tsarist period should be wiped out, that no more generations of Russian children should grow up in ignorance. Under the old regime the higher schools and in many places the secondary schools were closed to the workers and peasants. This the Soviet government would change. In the old days education was for the privileged classes only; henceforth it must be for the masses.

In general the Soviet educational program called for free,[4] obligatory, and universal education between the ages of three and sixteen, and for the right of every Russian citizen to a higher education, though financial bankruptcy, civil wars, famine, and economic disorganization all contributed to prevent much progress until after 1921. The school system was secularized and "communized" to the extent that nothing contrary to Communist principles might be taught. Much progress was made, too, in educational work among the minority populations of Russia. Under the tsarist regime most of the different nationalities in the country had no schools, and many of them no written language. With the aid of anthropologists and linguistic scholars the Soviet government had the different languages reduced to written forms. It then provided textbooks in these local languages and laid the foundations of a school system in these scattered districts.

As already pointed out, the Five-Year Plans outlined programs of educational as well as industrial expansion. During the years 1928–1932 great strides were made in developing the public-school system, the aim being to make compulsory elementary education a fact and not merely a theory. By the close of the first Five-Year Plan nearly 22,000,000 children—three times the number in tsarist days—were enrolled in elementary schools; four fifths of all children between the ages of eight and fourteen were receiving education at the hands of the government; and illiteracy in the adult population had been to a considerable extent eliminated. An extensive system of vocational and technical training had also been developed, with factory schools to give instruction in the operation of machines and technical colleges for the training of engineers.

With the Communist Party officially atheistic and believing that religion is an "opiate of the people," it is not surprising that the position of the Orthodox Church in Russia was profoundly altered by the Soviet government. All lands belonging to the church or to monastic institutions were at once nationalized, and it was decreed that no ecclesiastical or religious association had the right to possess property. All church buildings became the property of the state. Many were transformed into schools or clubrooms, and some of the most famous cathedrals were turned into national museums. In general, however, buildings needed specifically for purposes of worship were turned over to associations of twenty or more persons for use free of charge.

The church was separated from the state, and government subsidies were abolished. The church was forced to depend henceforth, as in the United States, upon the voluntary contributions of its adherents. Public religious

---

[4] In 1940 tuition fees were instituted for the last two years of secondary schools except for needy students with excellent grades.

processions were forbidden, and the old church calendar—thirteen days behind that in use in the Western world—was abolished in favor of the latter. The church was deprived of its control of marriage and divorce, registration of births and deaths, and cemeteries. The control of all these was confided to the civil government. The schools were separated from the church, and it was originally decreed that Christian churches might not give organized religious instruction to minors under eighteen years of age. No religious instruction was permitted in any public or private school, but children in groups of three or less might receive religious instruction, provided it was given outside the schools and churches. Although the influence of the government was thus thrown against religion, attendance at religious services was unrestricted, except to members of the Communist Party.[5]

Soviet Foreign Policy

For the sake of convenience and clarity the history of the Soviet Union's foreign policy will be discussed in relation to the different aims which seem to have predominated in successive periods since 1917. In the first three years after the November revolution the dominant aim of the Soviet government was to bring about the overthrow of all capitalist governments. During this period the Communist leaders were far from confident of their ability to retain control in Russia. To them a world proletarian revolution which should everywhere supplant capitalism by a Communist regime seemed absolutely essential to their own continuance in power. The Soviet government's foreign policy during these early years, therefore, may be characterized as primarily that of revolutionary propaganda.

To facilitate the carrying on of this propaganda the Communist leaders in March, 1919, founded the Third or Communist International (*Comintern*).[6] This new organization was designed (1) to carry on an international propaganda of Communist ideas, (2) to unite and strengthen the Communist parties in all countries, (3) to win the leadership of all labor and socialist movements, and (4) "to accelerate the development of events toward world revolution." Once the revolution had been accomplished, the Third International was to direct the future efforts of the working classes. In the meantime it was to constitute the "headquarters for the

[5] During the Second World War the Soviet government permitted the synod of the Orthodox Church to meet and elect a patriarch, and also permitted the establishment of religious publications and of seminaries to train adult candidates for the priesthood.

[6] The "First International," officially the "International Workingman's Association," was organized in 1864 under the influence of Karl Marx to advance the rights of labor in all countries. As a result of the reaction against socialism in Europe a decade later, it fell to pieces about 1874. With the gradual revival of socialism came in 1889 the founding of the "Second International," with which the various Socialist and Labor parties of the world soon became affiliated. The First World War temporarily put a stop to its activities.

world army of the proletariat." Its headquarters were set up in Moscow, and it was liberally subsidized by the Soviet government.[7]

Sometimes through its own officials, but more often through the instrumentality of the Third International, the Soviet government during its first years attempted to launch anticapitalist offensives in various countries of Europe. It played a part in the Communist uprisings in Germany in 1918 and 1919, in the establishment of the Béla Kun regime in Hungary (1919), in the communistic experiments in Italy (1920), and in spasmodic outbreaks in some of the Baltic republics. Its efforts to establish strong connections with the workers of Great Britain, France, Austria, and Czechoslovakia, however, proved futile. Equally futile, too, were the government's efforts to win the good will and co-operation of the Asiatic peoples in the hope that they might be converted to Communism and a gigantic coalition be created against Western capitalism. Despite all efforts of the Soviet government and of the Third International, the world proletarian revolution failed to materialize.

At home, after three years of almost constant fighting against the forces of counterrevolution, the Communists found themselves at last in complete control, but in control of a Russia which, because of their communist experiments, was fast sinking into economic chaos. The New Economic Policy which Lenin thereupon decided to inaugurate has already been discussed. This change in economic policy at home was accompanied by a change in the Soviet government's policy abroad. In order to rescue Russia from its complete industrial and commercial collapse, there was need for the influx of capital, machinery, and experts from abroad. But these could hardly be obtained so long as Russia remained isolated among the nations. Early in 1918 the diplomatic representatives of all the powers had been withdrawn because of Communist policies, and until the opening of the year 1921 the only states which had recognized the Soviet government were the Baltic republics—Finland, Latvia, Estonia, and Lithuania. While not abandoning completely its purpose of undermining the capitalist governments by Communist propaganda, the predominant aim of the Soviet government next came to be the opening of trade relations with foreign countries as a means of hastening Russia's economic revival. A provisional trade agreement between Russia and Great Britain was signed on March 16, 1921, and by the end of the year the Soviet government had succeeded in obtaining similar agreements with Germany, Norway, Austria, Italy.

But one serious obstacle in the way of Russia's complete re-establishment of diplomatic and commercial relations with other countries was the Soviet government's repudiation of all Russia's foreign debts. Late in 1921, accord-

[7] In May, 1943, the executive committee in Moscow issued a declaration announcing the dissolution of the Communist International.

ingly, the Soviet government notified the powers that, though it was neither legally nor morally bound by the debts of the former regime, it was willing to consider what could be done toward meeting foreign claims. It proposed that an international congress should be held for the purpose of recognizing the Soviet government, devising some means of bringing about Russia's economic revival, and considering the problem of repudiated debts. In April, 1922, such a conference opened at Genoa with representatives of thirty-four states in attendance, all of Russia's creditors being present except the United States. After a number of weeks of negotiation, however, the conference finally broke down because the demands and counterdemands were so far apart as to prevent an agreement. The only immediate gain for the Soviet government was the fact that it had at least won the *de facto* recognition of Europe. During the negotiations at Genoa, moreover, Russia, by the treaty of Rapallo,[8] did secure *de jure* recognition by Germany.

Nevertheless, Russia had made little real progress toward regaining her former place in the states system of Europe. Six years after the November revolution she was still largely an outlaw nation. Her government was recognized *de jure* in Europe by only Poland, Germany, and the Baltic republics, and elsewhere in the world by only Turkey, Persia, and Afghanistan. The Soviet government became increasingly anxious to remedy this situation.

In 1924 the dominant and openly declared aim of its foreign policy became, therefore, *de jure* recognition. It let it be known that it was prepared to conclude a commercial treaty on especially favorable terms with the first great power to grant it such recognition. On February 1 Ramsay MacDonald, head of the new Labor government in Great Britain, telegraphed unconditional *de jure* recognition of the Soviet government. Italian recognition came officially six days later, and in the following months the U.S.S.R. received the *de jure* recognition of Norway, Austria, Greece, Hejaz, China, Denmark, Mexico, Hungary, and even France. At the close of the year 1924 the Soviet government had been recognized by fifteen European states as compared with only six at its beginning, and every European great power had re-established diplomatic relations with it. In the succeeding years *de jure* recognition was eventually obtained from most of the important states of the world, including the United States.

Meanwhile, the year 1925 had seen the successful conclusion of the Locarno negotiations among the other great powers of Europe.[9] The Locarno treaties were looked upon in Moscow as a serious menace to Russia's position, and from 1926 to 1933 the Soviet government's primary aim in for-

8 See page 243.
9 See page 153.

eign affairs was the creation of a protective barrier of states which could not be drawn into any concerted attack upon Russia. So successful were the Communists in this phase of their foreign policy that by the summer of 1933 they had concluded pacts of neutrality and nonaggression not only with all their neighbors to the west and south but with a number of the other powers of Europe as well.

After 1933, because of alarm over the aggressive policies of Nazi Germany in the west and imperialistic Japan in the east, the Soviet government ceased to be content with nonaggression pacts and sought instead to obtain definite promises of aid in certain contingencies. In 1934, despite the fact that the Communists had professed to believe the League of Nations an organization of capitalist states conspiring against them, the Soviet Union joined the League, and thus on paper obtained the benefit of collective security. In the following year it concluded defensive military alliances against Germany with both France and Czechoslovakia.

In 1938, however, after the failure of Great Britain and France to prevent the dismemberment of Czechoslovakia, the Soviet government apparently became suspicious that these powers were attempting to turn Hitler's aggression eastward toward Russia. In these circumstances, it appeared, the Communists decided to take such steps as might be necessary to postpone the Nazi-Soviet conflict as long as possible and accordingly signed a non-aggression pact with Nazi Germany in August, 1939. This step had, in Communist eyes, the double advantage of giving Russia added time to perfect her military preparations and at the same time of weakening Germany by leading her to become embroiled in a war with Great Britain and France.

The Eve of the Second World War

Shortly before the outbreak of the Second World War Russia launched her third Five-Year Plan (1938–1942), originally designed to raise the standard of living further by an expansion of the production of consumers' goods. The outbreak of war in Europe, however, forced changes in the plan. Although some increase in consumers' goods was permitted prior to 1941, greater emphasis was laid on the expansion of war industries. Efforts were made to develop regional economic autonomy, to utilize local resources to their utmost, and to eliminate wherever possible long hauls by train. These steps were designed not only to raise the country's general industrial efficiency but to enable it to continue its resistance in the face of any extensive invasion. As a result of this planned dispersal, by 1941 a considerable portion of the Soviet Union's industry was located east of the Volga; in fact, some 15 per cent of it was located east of the Urals. Furthermore, in answer to the increasing threat of war, the working day was lengthened to eight hours and the working week to six days.

Thanks to the three Five-Year Plans, the Soviet Union by 1940 was well on the way to becoming the second most important industrial country in the world. In that year its gross industrial output was reported as being five times as great as in 1929, twelve times as great as in 1913. In its production of railway locomotives, freight cars, trucks, tractors, and agricultural machinery it claimed to surpass any other European country. Its petroleum output was four times as much as that of the rest of Europe combined. It stood first in superphosphates, copper, and iron ore, and second only to Germany in the production of steel. Furthermore, it was claimed, of the ten important food and industrial crops, it led the world in acreage except in rice, corn, and cotton. During the Five-Year Plans the production of sugar beets and flax had increased nearly 200 per cent, potatoes nearly 300 per cent, cotton almost 400 per cent, and citrus fruits 160 times. Between 1932 and 1941 the production of milk had risen 50 per cent, and that of wool had doubled. In the latter year, too, the grain crop was 50 per cent greater than it had been in 1913.

In 1941 the Soviet Union, with its sixteen soviet socialist republics,[10] had a total population of 193,000,000. During the preceding fifteen years, according to semiofficial estimates, some 11,000,000 men had received full military training under the Soviet peacetime selective service law, and another 11,000,000 had received partial training. In 1939, as the war clouds darkened, the age of induction had been lowered from 20 to 19, and to 18 for those who had completed their high school education. During the thirties special attention had been given to mechanizing the army and to providing it with tanks, airplanes, and antitank and antiaircraft guns. At the same time, personnel was being trained in 63 schools for the land forces, 32 for the air forces, and 14 military academies. Russia in 1941 was much better prepared in leadership, man power, military equipment, and industrial and agricultural resources to withstand attack than she had been in 1914.

---

[10] These were the R.S.F.S.R., and the Ukrainian, White-Russian, Azerbaijan, Georgian, Armenian, Turkmen, Uzbek, Tadjik, Kazakh, Kirghiz, Karelo-Finnish, Moldavian, Lithuanian, Latvian, and Estonian soviet socialist republics.

Chapter IX

FASCIST ITALY

THE second of the great powers to inaugurate a sweeping program of political and economic reform during the postwar years was Italy, where Fascism launched a counteroffensive against Communism and established what many called a "dictatorship of the middle class." Fascism was often represented as "the last stand of capitalism," and it is true that in Italy the means of production, though extensively regulated and regimented, did remain for the most part in private hands with the profit system continuing. Nevertheless, it will become obvious to the reader of this chapter that the regime which Fascism introduced in Italy had many characteristics in common with that which Communism established in Soviet Russia.

Postwar Dissatisfaction with the Government

Probably the chief reason for Italy's embarking upon a new course in 1922 was that in the years immediately following the armistice a great portion of the Italian people came to feel that their existing political regime was able neither to preserve and defend Italy's just national interests abroad nor to provide law, order, and efficient government at home. More than the people of any other power, perhaps, the Italians entered the First World War for the purpose of securing certain definite additions of territory, and during the conflict their territorial ambitions further increased. They emerged from the war with the high hope and confident expectation of territorial acquisitions which should meet their nationalistic and imperialistic aspirations. Their first disappointment came in the case of Fiume. The failure of the statesmen at Paris to award that city to Italy bitterly disappointed the Italian people, and, when the Italian government later signed with Yugoslavia the treaty of Rapallo (November, 1920), recognizing "in perpetuity" the independence of the Free State of Fiume, and used the Italian army to expel D'Annunzio's legionaries from that city, the nationalists of Italy denounced the government for its weakness and pusillanimity.

Their second disappointment had to do with Albania, where the plan to make of the Adriatic an Italian lake called for the establishment of Italian control. But the Italian forces which had entered Albania during the war were gradually forced back into Valona by the Albanians, and the Italian government was obliged to withdraw its troops and recognize Albanian independence. This withdrawal constituted for Italian nationalists an "inglorious page of our political and military history." A third disappointment came in the colonial sphere. After the war Italians aspired to territorial acquisitions in the eastern Mediterranean and in Africa. But by the treaty of Sèvres and complementary treaties, Smyrna with its hinterland was allotted to Greece, and Italy was forced to agree that the Greek-inhabited Dodecanese Islands, which she had occupied since 1912, should likewise be surrendered to Greece. In Africa Italy fared little better, for the German African colonies were granted as mandates to Great Britain, France, and Belgium, while Italy, with her lack of raw materials and her scanty colonies, failed to obtain one square inch of German territory.

These disappointments and humiliations in foreign affairs led many Italian nationalists to believe that "the sacrifices made in the war were in vain," that the Allies "were robbing Italy of the fruits of the victory." The bitter hostility which was thus aroused against Italy's "faithless allies" was turned eventually even against their own government itself because of its inability to protect Italian national interests. Discontent and exasperation brought at length a strong nationalist reaction.

Nor were conditions within the country such as to win popular support for the government. Like so many other European countries, Italy faced a serious economic situation immediately after the war. Her national fiscal system was in a hopeless state. Staggering national deficits succeeded one another yearly, and the national currency fell steadily to less than a third of its face value. Living costs, in terms of paper currency, rose to six or seven times their prewar level. Furthermore, many soldiers, returning to civil life at a time of industrial crisis, failed to regain their old jobs or to obtain new ones.

Socialism profited by these circumstances. The Socialists from the beginning had denounced the war and had repeatedly prophesied ultimate disaster. Demobilized soldiers, contrasting their actual conditions with the extravagant promises made to them by politicians in the last months of the struggle, were profoundly disillusioned and went over to socialism almost *en masse*. In the parliamentary elections of November, 1919, the Socialists practically doubled their numbers in the Chamber of Deputies, where they constituted a controlling force and helped to paralyze the government. Meanwhile, the emissaries of Russian Communism had been preaching strikes, the seizure of factories and the land, and the dictatorship of the proletariat. Influenced by the Russian revolution, the extreme

Socialists abandoned their prewar law-abiding character and evolutionary methods and planned by revolution to transplant into Italy the soviet system. During the winter of 1919-1920, it is asserted, a good third of Italy was "Red." Thousands of the most flourishing communes were seized by extreme Socialists. Soon in the parliament itself Socialists were "singing the 'Red Flag,' giving cheers for Lenin, and hissing the King."

The extremists sought to accomplish their ends by direct action, and as early as August, 1919, disorders broke out in the rural districts. During the war many had advocated land for the peasants, and it was in an attempt to bring this about by direct action that land-raiding was begun. In some instances former service men sought to obtain plots of idle land for cultivation; in others tenants refused to pay rent to the owners; while in still others rural laborers sought to introduce the eight-hour day. Outrages were perpetrated—people were killed, houses were burned, cattle were slaughtered, harvests were destroyed. Although the total amount of land seized was relatively small, the psychological effect on the property-owning classes was great.

In industry, too, strikes became frequent and occurred in such essential services as the railways, tramways, and postal and telegraph systems, and even in the light and food-supply systems of the large towns. Enterprises dependent upon such services became demoralized. The strike movement reached its peak in August and September, 1920, when more than 600 factories involving some 500,000 employees were suddenly seized by the workers. Throughout the country the "dictatorship of the proletariat" was hourly expected. The government, paralyzed by divisions in the parliament and embarrassed by difficulties abroad, was powerless to intervene. Anarchists and Communists sought to extend the scope of the movement and to give it definitely revolutionary aims, but their proposal was vigorously opposed by the more moderate element. Ultimately the factories were returned to their owners, the trade unions accepting the government's proposal to bring in a bill for the establishment of factory councils.

Although the crisis passed, sporadic strikes continued, and the fear which the short Communist experiment had engendered remained. The proletariat had failed to carry through its program, in fact had abandoned its attempt; but it had succeeded in further demoralizing the already unstable commercial and industrial life of the country. Without permanently injuring the other classes, it had aroused their fear, hostility, and exasperation. Landlords and industrialists, who had looked in vain to the state for protection, denounced the supineness and inability of the government. All Italians who felt they had anything to lose by a Communist revolution urgently desired a firm government, and were ready to support any movement which might promise to provide it. And that there was dire need of some step to assure political stability seemed indicated by the fact that between June, 1919, and March, 1922, Italy had two parliamentary elections and four different prime ministers. The Chamber of Deputies as then constituted appeared to many to be utterly incapable of producing a stable majority which would maintain a strong government.

Mussolini and the Rise of Fascism

The group which benefited most from this situation was the new organization which had been founded by Benito Mussolini. This vigorous Italian was born in 1883, the son of a village blacksmith in northern Italy. His mother was a school teacher, and at the age of eighteen he himself became a teacher. Deciding that he needed further education, he later went to Switzerland, where he attended the Universities of Lausanne and Geneva, working to pay his expenses. While in Switzerland his innate organizing ability and his interest in socialism led him to participate in the founding of trade unions and the fomenting of strikes, activities for which he was ultimately expelled from the republic by the Swiss government.

Back in Italy he once more took up teaching. His continued interest in socialism, however, led him to become involved in agrarian disorders, and in 1908 he was arrested and temporarily imprisoned as a dangerous revolutionary. Later, after having been expelled from Trent by the Austrian government because of his irredentist propaganda, he drifted into journalism and in 1912 became editor of *Avanti*, the official organ of the Italian Socialist Party.

Upon the outbreak of the First World War Mussolini advocated Italian neutrality, urged the workers to resist being drawn into a "bourgeois" war, and preached preparation for a social revolution. Suddenly, in October, 1914, he changed his views and began to urge Italian intervention in the war. The Socialists thereupon repudiated him and forced him to resign from *Avanti*. In the following month he established in Milan the daily paper, *Il Popolo d'Italia*, which under his editorship became an interventionist organ. In September, 1915, when his class was called to the colors, Mussolini entered active service and served as a private on the Isonzo front. Early in 1917 he was wounded by the explosion of a trench mortar, and upon his recovery he procured exemption from further military service on the ground of being indispensable to the management of *Il Popolo d'Italia*. In the days following the Caporetto disaster its columns were used to combat the spirit of national depression.

At the conclusion of the war Mussolini, in March, 1919, issued a call for a meeting of former service men who "desire to express their attitude toward the country's postwar problems." A small group gathered about him—chiefly young men, mostly ex-Socialists—and under his leadership was founded the *Fascio di Combattimento* (Union of Combat). Its program of proposed political, economic, and religious changes was extremely democratic, even revolutionary, but at the same time strongly nationalistic. At first Fascism made little headway. In the parliamentary elections of 1919 it put forward two candidates—Mussolini was one—but neither was successful. Nevertheless, through pamphlets, speeches, and patriotic demonstrations the Fascisti denounced the government for its weakness both at home and abroad.

During the occupation of the factories Mussolini took no sides, though in the previous year he had approved a similar step. Following the collapse of the occupation, however, he threw the weight of his organization into a drive against the Communists. In northern and central Italy Fascist branches were established by ex-officers of the army and agents of the industrial and landowning classes. While Mussolini aroused enthusiasm by articles in his newspaper, *squadristi* of young men—wearing black shirts—were sent out to combat Communism. Guns, clubs, and castor oil were their weapons. The Giolitti government, wishing to destroy Communism, apparently connived with the Fascist forces. They were quietly supplied with arms, given free transportation on the railways, and rarely punished for their misdeeds. The growing strength of the Fascisti was revealed in the parliamentary elections of 1921, when they secured thirty-five seats in the Chamber of Deputies.

In 1921, too, Mussolini secured more followers when many of D'Annunzio's legionaries joined the Fascist movement. They added a more pronounced military and nationalistic element to Fascism and contributed certain Roman terms, symbols, and war cries. The fighting groups of "Black Shirts" rapidly increased during the first half of this year. Punitive expeditions, with their beatings, attacks on Communist and trade-union headquarters, and destruction of printing establishments continued. The Communists countered with ambuscades and mass attacks. Much blood was shed on each side during the conflict.

Great numbers now welcomed the new organization. To the employers it meant the restoration of discipline among workmen and the reduction of wages; to landowners, possible protection against further peasant outbreaks; to helpless and terrified professional men, middle classes, and intelligentsia, the restoration of law and order; to patriots, the purification of the civil life and the strengthening of the state. From all these classes young men hastened to enroll in the *squadristi*. Tired of violence and factional fights, the majority of Italians began to look to Mussolini to bring in an era of social peace. The failure of the Communist experiment, the weakness of the government, the subsidies of the rich, the revival of the middle class, the spread of patriotism, and the longing for a strong government, all these—together with Fascist willingness to resort to violence to attain its ends—contributed to bring success.

In November, 1921, the Fascist movement was transformed into the Fascist Party. A new and more elaborate as well as less radical program was drawn up. The succeeding months were spent in strengthening the party and in winning public opinion. The idea was spread abroad that Fascism had been responsible for the defeat of Communism, and that it alone stood between Italy and the return of that dread evil. The classes which had rallied to Fascism in order to rid the country of the threat of Communism now continued to support it for fear that the danger had not been permanently removed. The government remained unstable, weak, and inefficient. Its services were overstaffed, its budget unbalanced. Tremendous fiscal deficits piled up, and further currency inflation followed. Disorders continued at home, and the path of empire in Asia Minor and northern Africa was beset with difficulties. Ministerial instability discredited parliamentary government. During the summer of 1922 Fascism began its conquest of political power by the ejection of executive officials in the outlying provinces.

The "Fascistization" of the Government

During the fall of 1922 Mussolini repeatedly demanded that Facta, the premier then in office, either dissolve the parliament or resign in favor of a new cabinet which should include five Fascist ministers, but Facta refused to do either. In October, at a great congress of Fascisti in Naples, Mussolini delivered his ultimatum: "Either the government will be given to us or we shall seize it by marching on Rome." A ministerial crisis ensued. A tardy attempt was made to bring the Fascisti into the ministry by offering them certain positions. They declined. Instead they began their "march on Rome." The Facta government proclaimed a state of siege, but the king, in order to avoid civil war, refused to sign the decree. Instead he called upon Mussolini to form a new ministry. The government which the latter established on October 30 was a coalition in which the Fascisti were predominant.

Immediately upon assuming the premiership Mussolini demanded and received from the parliament what practically amounted to dictatorial powers until the end of 1923. Then followed the "fascistization" of the administrative offices of the government. Eventually a law was enacted giving the government authority to dismiss any civil servant who held political views contrary to those of Mussolini. Next came the "fascistization" of the parliament. An electoral reform bill was forced through the parliament, under the provisions of which the party obtaining the largest vote in a parliamentary election would receive two thirds of all the seats. In April, 1924, the plan was tested in a general election. The Fascist Party won over 60 per cent of the seats regardless of the provisions of the new electoral law, though the opposition declared that this was not accomplished without violence and intimidation. However that may be, the parliament was at any rate "fascistized." During 1925-1926 popular control of local government was also gradually abolished. Local machinery of government was suppressed in all municipalities of less than 5000 population, and these districts were placed under the control of *podestas* appointed by the government at Rome. Later all provincial, communal, and municipal elections were indefinitely suspended, and *podestas* took the place of popular government in all towns and cities.

Meanwhile, Mussolini's position as premier had been transformed into that of a dictator. He was freed from dependence upon the parliament and made responsible to the king alone. He was given permanent control of the national military, naval, and air forces. No item might be placed on the order of the day in either house of the parliament without his consent. The authority to issue governmental decrees with the force of law was placed in his hands. His title was changed to "Head of the Government," and the members of the ministry were made definitely subordinate to him, his relation to the ministry coming to resemble that of the President of the United States to his cabinet.

All these changes were not accomplished without opposition, but wherever it appeared drastic steps were immediately taken to suppress it. Newspapers were so rigorously censored that eventually nothing but a Fascist press remained. University presidents and deans and public-school principals were required (1930) to be chosen from the Fascisti, and professors were dismissed for holding views contrary to Mussolini's. A secret police, the OVRA (*Organizzazione Volontaria per la Repressione dell' Antifascismo*), was established to ferret out those who plotted against the existing regime, and military tribunals were set up to try such offenders. Many were exiled to the Lipari Islands off the north coast of Sicily for holding political views contrary to Mussolini's. Many who desired to leave the country were prevented from going. In general, freedom of speech, of the press, and of association—the pillars of liberal government—were destroyed.

In addition there was, especially in the early years, frequent resort to violence to suppress the opposition. Doubtless much of this was carried on by irresponsible elements in the party, for all sorts of men had been drawn into the movement from a variety of motives. On the other hand, on at least one occasion members of the party in high standing became involved.

In June, 1924, Giacomo Matteotti, a Socialist member of the Chamber of Deputies, was abducted and murdered, apparently because he had announced that he was going to expose the corruption of the Fascist minister of the interior. Although Mussolini, in an attempt to "purify" Fascism, at once removed from office all those known to be involved in the crime, they were later defended by high officers of the Fascist Party and escaped with almost no punishment.

Fascism Constitutionalized

The Fascist Party was a centralized, hierarchical organization. At its apex was the Fascist Grand Council presided over by Mussolini, *Il Duce* (the Leader). This council was the supreme Fascist organ, and, since Mussolini had the right to add to it at will any who had been of special service to Fascism or the nation, he was able to control a majority. The party consisted of some ten thousand branches (*fasci*), which were grouped into provincial federations with councils similar to the Grand Council. The secretary-general of the party was appointed by the king upon the nomination of Mussolini; the provincial secretaries were appointed by Mussolini on the nomination of the secretary-general; the local secretaries were appointed by the provincial secretaries. The control of the party was thus exercised from the top down rather than from the bottom up as in American political parties.

In order that Italy and Fascism might have a well-trained and disciplined youth, Fascism established four auxiliary organizations, the Fascist Wolf Cubs, the *Balilla,* the *Avanguardia,* and the *Giovani Fascisti,* for boys from six to eight, eight to fourteen, fourteen to eighteen, and eighteen to twenty-one respectively; and two, the *Piccole Italiane* and the *Giovane Italiane,* for girls under and over twelve years respectively. In 1928 the government ordered the suppression of all non-Fascist institutions for the physical, moral, or spiritual training of Italian youth, and the ranks of Fascism were eventually closed except to "graduates" of the *Balilla* and *Avanguardia.*

The militant character of Fascism during the early years expressed itself through *squadristi* of "Black Shirts." These were the armed forces of the movement in the years when it was fighting for existence and crushing opposition. It was the Black Shirts who conducted the "march on Rome." In 1923 the *squadristi* were disbanded, and from them was recruited the Voluntary Militia for National Security, which ultimately became part of the armed forces of the state. It was open to all citizens from seventeen to fifty years of age who possessed certain "physical, moral, and political" qualifications. It had charge of the preliminary training of the *Avan-*

guardisti, and some of its number were assigned to duty in connection with railways, ports, and postal and telegraph offices.

Although, from 1923 on, the policies which were enacted into law by the Italian parliament were in general formulated and enforced by the leaders of the Fascist Party, the latter as such had no constitutional place in the Italian government. In 1928, however, the Fascist Party was written into the Italian constitution. By the provisions of the Electoral Reform Act of that year, discussed below, the Fascist Grand Council was given the legal right to draw up the list of candidates for the Chamber of Deputies. Later it was also given the right to nominate candidates for the office of prime minister and for the other high government positions. At the same time it was made the chief advisory body of the government on all questions of a constitutional character, such as proposed legislation affecting succession to the throne, the royal powers and prerogatives, the composition of the two houses of the parliament, the powers of the prime minister, and the relations between church and state. International treaties which involved changes in the national territory became subject to its deliberation. The Fascist Grand Council was changed, therefore, from a mere organ of the Fascist Party unofficially consulted by the prime minister into an openly recognized *de jure* part of the political machinery of the state.

Fascist Syndicalism and the Corporative State

At the very beginning of the Fascist movement Fascist trade unions were organized in opposition to the existing Socialist unions. In 1923 a Federation of Fascist Syndical Corporations was created, and two years later the Fascist syndicates were recognized by the Italian Industrial Employers' Federation as the sole representatives of their employees. In 1926 the Legal Discipline of Collective Labor Relations Law, utilizing the syndical system, set up a vertical organization of producers. Under the provisions of this law as later modified there were in Italy nine national confederations, four for employers and four for employees in the fields of agriculture, industry, credit and insurance, and commerce, and one for professional men and artists. Each confederation had subdivisions or syndicates for regions, provinces, and municipalities.

These syndicates were given authority to enter into collective contracts regulating hours of labor, wages, apprenticeship, and the like. They had power over all workers and employers in a given industry and district regardless of whether the latter were members of the syndicates. The contracts which the syndicates made were binding upon all, and each syndicate had the right to exact an annual contribution to the common fund from all, whether members or not. Strikes and lockouts were illegal. When trouble arose between employer and employees, the syndicates to which they belonged sought an amicable settlement. In case of failure, the dispute was referred to the minister of corporations, an appointee of Mussolini. Failure here was followed by an appeal to one of the sixteen Italian courts of appeal, each of which had a labor section. From its decision there was no appeal. This vertical syndical system was designed to regulate the relations between workers and employers with a view to increasing the productive forces of the nation.

In 1934 Italy's economic life was further organized on a horizontal basis when Mussolini announced the formation of twenty-two corporations or guilds designed to represent every phase of Italy's economic life. The corporations, each of which had Mussolini as president and members of the Fascist Party among its officers, included representatives of employers and employees, and technicians in the twenty-two branches of Italy's economic life.[1] They were based on "cycles of production," and each corporation was to concern itself with the whole process by which a raw product was transformed into a finished article. Each was charged with the task of analyzing costs of production, reducing them whenever possible by rationalization, and establishing a price which must: (1) assure a profit for the employer, (2) give proper remuneration to the worker, (3) safeguard against overcharging the consumer, and (4) permit Italian exports to compete successfully abroad.

The councils of these twenty-two corporations, which included representatives of the nine national confederations of syndicates, were, in turn, grouped together to constitute the National Council of Corporations, described by Mussolini as the "general staff of Italian economy." In this body the decisions of the individual corporations were examined in the light of their possible repercussions on the cycles of production and upon the national economy as a whole. The permanent executive organ of this National Council of Corporations was the Central Corporative Committee, which served as the supreme command of the corporative system and was entrusted with the task of devising plans for Italy's economic self-sufficiency. It was composed of representatives of the twenty-two corporations, most of the government ministers, and all the members of the Fascist Grand Council.

That the corporative system was thoroughly subordinated to Mussolini and the Fascist Party is obvious. At the top of the pyramid was the minister of corporations under Mussolini. Next below came the National Council

---

[1] The twenty-two corporations were: Cereals; Horticulture, Flowers, and Fruit; Vines and Wine; Oils; Beets and Sugar; Zootechnics and Fisheries; Wood; Textile Products; Metallurgy and Engineering; Chemicals; Clothing; Paper and Printing; Building and Public Works; Water, Gas, and Electricity; Mining Industries; Glass and Ceramics; Insurance and Credit; Professions and Arts; Sea and Air; Internal Communications; Theater; Tourist Industry.

of Corporations, of which Mussolini was the head. Then came the twenty-two corporations, each of which had the Duce as its president. Below them came the nine national confederations of syndicates, the president and council of each of which were appointed by the government. The local syndicates, in turn, were subject to the control of the provincial prefect if their activities were limited to a single province, or to that of the minister of corporations if they included two or more provinces. Although in theory the syndicates and federations were elective bodies, actually all syndical officials were appointed by the Fascist Party, subject to ratification by the minister of corporations, and might be removed whenever their work was unsatisfactory to party leaders.

Meanwhile, the syndical and corporative system had been linked with the nation's political system. By the Electoral Reform Act of 1928 the right to nominate deputies was given to the national confederations of syndicates and to certain legally recognized "cultural, educational, charitable, or propagandist" associations. The national confederations were authorized to propose 800 candidates and the other associations 200 more. These names were then to be sent to the Fascist Grand Council, which, with full power to accept or reject any name or even to choose one outside those submitted, should draw up a list of 400 candidates. This list was finally to be submitted to a plebiscite of the voters who, as a single national constituency, must vote "yes" or "no" on the list as a whole. Men twenty-one (or eighteen if they were married and had children) might vote if they paid syndicate dues or 100 lire in taxes, if they received pensions from the government, or if they belonged to the clergy.

The electoral scheme was given its first test early in 1929 when an election or plebiscite, as it was called, was held on March 24. During the preceding two weeks a campaign in favor of the Fascist nominees was conducted by means of speeches, proclamations, and posters. No opposition speeches were permitted. The question which was put to the electorate was: "Do you approve of the list of deputies chosen by the Fascist Grand Council?" Of the 9,460,727 male voters who composed the electorate, 8,663,412 voted in favor of the Fascist list. Only 135,761 had the temerity to cast their votes against it. Five years later a second election (March 25, 1934) had similar results. Of the 10,041,998 votes cast, only 15,265 were in the negative.

The final step in transforming Italy into a corporative state was taken in March, 1939, when the Chamber of Deputies was supplanted by the Chamber of Fasces and Corporations. This new legislative body consisted of the Duce, the members of the Fascist Grand Council and the Fascist National Council, and the members of the National Council of Corporations. It thus represented politically the Fascist Party and economically the Italian corporative system. Members of the new national legislature had no fixed terms and surrendered their seats when they were no longer members of the constituent bodies.

The corporative system, according to Mussolini, was an attempt to advance in constitutional legislation along lines best calculated to promote smooth collaboration of all classes of society for the good of the state. "Herein," he declared, "lies the Fascist revolution's greatest legislative novelty and herein lies its great originality." Power was given to the "productive forces of the state" rather than to the mere representatives of territorial divisions. Each art, craft, trade, and profession was represented in this, Europe's first legislative body to be based on full economic representation.

The Fascist "Doctrine"

Meanwhile, Fascism had been compelled to formulate a doctrine in order that it might have some articles of faith, for Mussolini repeatedly asserted that Fascism was a faith, "one of those spiritual forces which renovate the history of great peoples." He did not hesitate to claim that, "if every age has its own doctrine, then innumerable signs point out Fascism as the doctrine of our age," and proclaimed that "never before have the nations thirsted for authority, direction, order as they do now." Fascism, he predicted, was "bound to become the standard type of civilization of our century for Europe—the forerunner of European renaissance."

Politically, the essence of the Fascist doctrine was the all-inclusive omnipotence of the state. "Everything in the state, nothing outside the state, nothing against the state." Apart from the state, according to Fascism, there was no scope for independent action either of individuals or of groups. Just as the past age had been that of the individual, the new age was to be that of the state. Fascism was thus the antithesis of democracy; it repudiated the right of the majority to rule. In place "of majorities and quantities" it sought to substitute the figure of *Il Duce,* "the Leader," which, of course, was but a euphemism for "dictator." According to Mussolini, in contrast with democracy, where the executive is reduced to being a mere instrument of elected parliaments, Fascism "rescued it from the weight of faction and party interest and the egoism of classes," thus conferring dignity upon the executive as the representative of the personality of the state. In other words, Fascism stood for autocracy, not democracy.

Economically, Fascism's doctrine was colored by its early fight against the Communists and Socialists. It openly repudiated Marxian collectivism and denied the doctrine of historical materialism. It asserted that political, not economic, factors made history. Furthermore, it rejected the doctrine of the class struggle, which, it claimed, was "the natural outcome of the economic conception of history," and sought instead the fusion of all classes into "a single ethical and economic reality." In the corporative state, Fascism asserted, a unity of classes is realized, for in it the divergent interests are co-ordinated and harmonized. Obviously, Fascism was definitely opposed to the doctrine of *laissez-faire,* and asserted that the age of *laissez-faire* was nearing its end. In taking this stand it, of course, repudiated the liberalism of the nineteenth century. In fact, Mussolini declared that, just as the nineteenth century had been the century of liberalism and *laissez-faire,* the twentieth century would be the century of authority.

Economic and Fiscal Problems

Perhaps the most pressing problem which confronted Fascism immediately upon assuming control of the government was the threatening state of the national finances. The budget was tremendously out of balance, the national debt was rapidly increasing, and the inflated national currency stood at twenty-four (normally five) to the dollar. Bankruptcy faced the state unless remedial measures were taken. Fascism at once began an extensive reorganization and modernization of the fiscal system in the interest of efficiency. Expenditures were rigorously scrutinized, and superfluous bureaucratic offices were abolished. The national railways, which had a deficit of over one billion lire in 1922, were made self-supporting and were even able to turn over a surplus to the national treasury. Taxes were increased until, in proportion to national income, they became heavier than those of any other country. The effects of these reforms soon became evident in the national balance sheet. Finally, after heroic efforts in 1926–1927, the national currency, which had declined to 31.6 to the dollar, was raised to 19 to the dollar, where it was legally stabilized on a gold basis in 1928.

Nevertheless, the most difficult and at the same time the most fundamental problem with which Fascism had to wrestle continued to be Italy's general economic situation. The seriousness of the problem rested chiefly on two basic facts: (1) the denseness of Italy's population, and (2) her lack of those natural resources which are essential to the upbuilding of a great industrial country. The population of Italy had a density of 323 to the square mile in contrast with about 184 for France; the coal and iron which France had in abundance, Italy was obliged to import; even her agriculture failed to produce sufficient foodstuffs for her people. The pressure of Italian population against Italian resources was great, and it seemed likely to increase, for the nationalist philosophy of Fascism demanded a powerful Italy, and this, it was believed, was dependent upon a populous Italy. Numerous measures were taken to encourage large families. Mussolini's aim was a nation of 60,000,000 inhabitants by 1950.

With so dense a population and such inadequate natural resources, it is not surprising that Italy was far from self-sufficient economically. She had long had a deficit in her foreign trade. To overcome this situation, Mussolini mapped out a program which called, in the first place, for a decrease in Italy's dependence upon foreign raw products. To this end, efforts were directed toward increasing the home production of foodstuffs by increasing the tillable area of the country, by draining swamplands and putting grasslands under the plow, and by increasing the yield through more intensive farming and the use of more modern scientific methods. By 1938 nearly twelve million acres had been reclaimed or were in the process of being reclaimed. At the end of the first decade of the "battle of the wheat," the production of wheat in Italy had increased by 70 per cent over that in 1922. At the same time, increases in the production of rice, corn, and oats ranged from 40 to 60 per cent, and further lessened Italy's need to import foodstuffs. Nevertheless, in the years just prior to the Second World War Italy still had a deficit in her production of foodstuffs. The possibility of freeing the country from dependence upon foreign fuel was no more favorable. Although hydroelectric projects were advanced until Italy stood first in Europe in this type of development, she was still forced to import large quantities of coal.

As a second part of his economic program, Mussolini sought to increase the production and export of Italy's manufactured goods, to expand her merchant marine, and to attract tourist trade. Under his new syndical system the number of days lost by strikes was greatly lessened, and the material forces of the nation were largely fused into "a single dynamo of production." As a result, Italy's industries expanded and her exports increased. Unfortunately, however, despite some increase in Italian mineral output, the country's dependence upon foreign metals rose with the acceleration of industrial production. To assist in the expansion of the Italian merchant marine, the government advanced subsidies to new lines. Fascism's restoration of economic and political stability, together with its fiscal reforms, restored foreign investors' confidence in Italy, and much-needed foreign capital began to flow into the country. In order to hold out further attractions, legislation was enacted abolishing inheritance taxes and exempting foreign capital for a time from various other kinds of taxes. By the opening of the second decade of Fascist rule Italy had advanced to the place where she had, at least temporarily, a favorable balance of trade.

Inevitably, however, despite Mussolini's efforts, the world depression took its toll. In 1933 Italy once more had an adverse balance of trade. This disturbing situation, which grew steadily worse in 1934, was further aggravated by decreased income from tourists and from remittances from Italians living abroad. To make the matter still worse, the country was confronted with serious budgetary problems caused by increasing national deficits. These circumstances, taken together, threatened to impair Italy's international credit, for during the year the country suffered increasingly heavy losses of gold. The situation became so menacing that the government in 1935 ordered that all foreign credits, foreign securities, and foreign currencies held by Italian nationals should be deposited with the National Exchange Institute, the holders to receive thereafter their interest and other payments in lire. Finally, in the summer of 1935, when Mussolini was preparing to conquer Ethiopia, the struggle to maintain the gold coverage was abandoned, and the law requiring 40 per cent was suspended. Thereafter the Bank of Italy's gold reserves steadily diminished until in October, when the publication of the monthly financial statements of the Bank of Italy was discontinued, the gold coverage stood at 28 per cent. Later, as a result of Mussolini's Ethiopian venture and his taking Italy into the Second World War, the Italian economic and fiscal system was of course completely wrecked.

The Settlement of the Roman Question

Fascism inherited from its predecessors the long-standing problem of Italy's relations with the Vatican. The pope, once the temporal ruler of the states of the church, which comprised a considerable portion of central Italy, was deprived of his last remaining territory when troops of the Italian government seized Rome in 1870. The former papal capital was made the capital of the Italian Kingdom, and in an effort to conciliate the Holy See the government in 1871 enacted the Law of Papal Guarantees to serve as the basis of relations between the papacy and the Italian Kingdom.

By the provisions of that law the pope and his successors were guaranteed possession of St. Peter's, the Vatican and its gardens, the Lateran Palace, and the Villa of Castel Gandolfo. The head of the church was accorded sovereign rights within these possessions, including the inviolability of his own person and the authority to receive and send ambassadors. He was further granted free use of the Italian telegraph, railway, and postal systems, and guaranteed an annual subsidy from the state of approximately $645,000.

Pope Pius IX refused to recognize the Law of Papal Guarantees, however, because it was a simple legislative act of the Italian government, a unilateral arrangement rather than a concordat. He and his successors refused to accept the annual subsidy, declared that they had been deprived of sovereign territory and were unable to exercise their legitimate prerogatives as sovereigns, and proclaimed themselves "prisoners of a usurping power" which they refused to recognize. At first the Holy See forbade

Italian Catholics to participate in national elections, but later it removed this prohibition and a sort of *modus vivendi* was reached. The Roman question, however, still remained.

In October, 1926, Mussolini through an intermediary expressed to Pope Pius XI his strong desire to enter into negotiations for the purpose of eliminating the existing state of hostility between the church and the state. The delicate negotiations which ensued eventually resulted in an agreement between the papacy and the Italian government, and on February 11, 1929, a treaty, a concordat, and a financial convention were signed in the Lateran Palace by Cardinal Gasparri, papal secretary of state, and by Mussolini.

By the terms of the treaty Italy recognized the state of Vatican City under the sovereignty of the pope. The Vatican City—the smallest of sovereign states, with an area of only slightly more than a hundred acres and with less than five hundred citizens—thus took its place among the states of the world. It was to have its own coinage system, postage stamps, wireless, and railway station, and the right to send and receive ambassadors. Its territory was always to be considered neutral and inviolable; freedom of access to the Holy See was guaranteed for bishops from all parts of the world; and freedom of correspondence with all states, even with states which might be at war with Italy, was assured. Furthermore, the privilege of extraterritoriality was granted outside the Vatican City to certain churches and buildings used by the Holy See for its administration. Finally, the person of the pope was declared to be as sacred and inviolable as that of the king.

In the concordat Italy recognized the Holy Catholic Apostolic and Roman religion as the only state religion in the country. The Italian government bound itself to enforce within its territory the canon law—that is to say, the laws relating to faith, morals, conduct, and discipline prescribed for Catholics by church authority. Matrimony was recognized by the state as a sacrament regulated by canon law, and thereafter, if certain regulations were observed, the state would recognize the legality of marriages performed by priests. Religious instruction, formerly excluded from the secondary schools, now became compulsory in both elementary and secondary schools, and was to be given by instructors selected by the bishops and maintained by the state. The election of bishops was also further regulated. Formerly they were appointed by the church subject to the approval of the state, which paid their salaries; thereafter the state's role would be restricted to the right of objecting to an appointee for political reasons. Ordained priests, moreover, were exempted from military obligations.

In the convention the pope accepted 750,000,000 lire ($39,375,000) in cash and 1,000,000,000 lire ($52,500,000) in 5-per-cent government bonds "as a definite settlement of all its financial relations with Italy in consequence of the fall of temporal power." Finally, the "Holy See . . . declares the Roman question definitely and irrevocably settled and therefore eliminated, and recognizes the Kingdom of Italy under the Dynasty of the House of Savoy, with Rome as the capital of the Italian State."

On June 7 ratifications of the treaties comprising the settlement were exchanged in the Vatican by Cardinal Gasparri and Mussolini. A papal nuncio was at once appointed to the Quirinal and an Italian ambassador to the Holy See. A few weeks later a pope left the Vatican for the first time in almost two generations, thus recognizing the settlement of the Roman question. Then followed a number of efforts to emphasize the new spirit which existed between the Italian government and the Vatican. In December, 1929, the king and queen paid their first visit to the pope. On the twelfth of the same month the Chamber of Deputies voted that September 20, the anniversary of the taking of Rome in 1870, should be supplanted as a national holiday by February 11, the anniversary of the signing of the Lateran treaties.

Recovery of International Prestige

Whether or not Mussolini improved the economic and political condition of Italy, there is little doubt that, during the first decade of his dictatorship, he raised her international prestige. In the early years of the Fascist regime he was fortunate enough to recover for Italy some of the territories and concessions which had been lost through the "weakness" of preceding Italian governments. The first gain came with the Dodecanese Islands which Italy had agreed to surrender to Greece by the Italo-Greek treaty of 1920. Mussolini maintained that this agreement was no longer valid because the treaty of Sèvres, with which it was linked, had lapsed. In the treaty of Lausanne (1923) Italy obtained legal recognition of her possession of the Dodecanese. A fortified naval base was at once constructed, and the foundation was laid for Italy's hoped-for predominance in the eastern Mediterranean.

Later in the year 1923 Mussolini delighted Italian nationalists by his spectacular action in the crisis arising out of the murder of an Italian who was head of the Delimitation Commission engaged in locating the boundary between Greece and Albania. On August 27 the head of the commission and four companions, of whom three were Italians, were killed on Greek soil near Janina. The Italian government at once presented an ultimatum to Greece, demanding among other things a strict inquiry with the assistance of the Italian military attaché and the payment of an indemnity of 50,000,000 lire. The other demands Greece offered to accept, but these two she regarded as "outraging the honor and violating the sovereignty of the state." The answer of the Italian government was the bombardment and occupation of the Greek island of Corfu on August 31. Mussolini announced that the occupation of Corfu was only temporary, but many saw in the affair a strange similarity to the events of July, 1914.

Greece, acting under Articles 12 and 15 of the Covenant, immediately appealed to the League of Nations, but Salandra, the Italian representative on the Council, denied the competence of the League to deal with the affair. He asserted that the Delimitation Commission had represented the Council of Ambassadors, which should therefore handle the matter. Mussolini at first contended that the affair would be settled without outside interference, but popular indignation throughout the world led him to retreat to the position already taken by Salandra.

The League Council thereupon urged the Council of Ambassadors to find a solution of the crisis. The latter stipulated that an Inter-Allied commission should supervise the preliminary investigation undertaken by Greece and complete its work by the date which Mussolini had set for the evacuation of Corfu, and that, if the Council of Ambassadors considered the commission's report sufficient, it should at once assess damages. The commission reported that the persons guilty of the crime had not been discovered, and the ambassadors ordered Greece to pay to the Italian government 50,000,000 lire. The money was paid, and Corfu was evacuated on September 27. The government's seeming defiance of the League of Nations convinced Italian nationalists that the whole affair had been a distinct triumph for Mussolini.

The Duce's settlement of the Fiume question, while no less satisfactory to Italian nationalism, was much more skillfully and quietly accomplished. By the treaty of Rapallo (1920) Fiume had been made an independent free city. The arrangement was satisfactory neither to the Italians nor to the Yugoslavs, and it proved unworkable. Mussolini made suggestions regarding a new solution of the Fiume question, and eventually his suggestions were incorporated in the treaty of Rome, signed on January 27, 1924. By the provisions of this treaty the Free State of Fiume was divided between Italy and Yugoslavia. Fiume proper went to Italy. Port Baros, which had been originally constructed especially to handle the trade of Croatia and which is separated from Fiume by only a small stream, went to Yugoslavia. On March 16, 1924, final Italian annexation of the city was officially celebrated at Fiume in the presence of King Victor Emmanuel. Another "catastrophic abandonment" of Italian interests was rectified.

The settlement of the Fiume question brought about an improvement in Italo-Yugoslav relations, and a five-year pact of friendship and co-operation was entered into between the two countries. This was followed in 1925 by the Nettuno convention, in which Yugoslavia in return for certain commercial advantages in Italy recognized the right of Italians to buy land within thirty miles of the Yugoslav frontier and the right of Italian firms in Yugoslavia to import Italian labor. In accordance with this general policy of eastward orientation, Italy in 1926 signed the treaty of Tirana with Albania, gaining economic concessions in return for guaranteeing "the *status quo,* political, juridical, and territorial, of Albania." The latter, furthermore, agreed not to conclude with other powers political and military agreements prejudicial to Italian interests. During 1927 internal improvements were carried out in Albania under Italian supervision and with Italian loans, and the Albanian army was reorganized by Italian officers. Later in the year Italy signed with Albania a twenty-year defensive alliance in which each agreed that, "when all the means of conciliation have been exhausted," she would come to the aid of the other in case of unprovoked attack. At last, it appeared, Italy had obtained the protectorate over Albania which Italian nationalists had been seeking ever since the outbreak of the First World War.

In 1927, too, Fascism sought to assert Italy's position as a great power in the western Mediterranean by securing the right to participate in the international regime at Tangier, a port in Morocco near the Strait of Gibraltar. In October of that year, on the eve of the opening of negotiations between France and Spain regarding the modification of the international regime in Tangier, three Italian warships made an ostentatious visit to that port. From Rome came the unofficial announcement that Italy as a Mediterranean power considered herself to be vitally concerned in the status of Tangier. There were not lacking those who perceived in Mussolini's gesture a striking similarity to the action of the German Kaiser William II when he precipitated the first Moroccan crisis in 1905. Briand's policy of conciliation was in the ascendancy in Paris at this time, however, and Italy was invited to participate in the ensuing conference. A new agreement concerning Tangier was reached in 1928, and by it Italy was given a larger share in the administrative machinery of that city. Italy's position as a great power had been protected, and in Rome the outcome was looked upon as a great diplomatic triumph for Mussolini. His attempts to advance Italy's position in the Mediterranean still further by demanding naval parity with France at the London naval conference in 1930 [2] and in negotiations during the succeeding years were not, however, so successful. Nevertheless, Mussolini in the decade after 1922 undoubtedly did succeed in strengthening Italy's hold on the Adriatic, in increasing her prestige in the Mediterranean, and in extending her diplomatic and commercial influence in southeastern Europe.

[2] See pages 156–157.

Fascism's Exaltation of War

The political and economic tenets of the Fascist "doctrine" have been discussed. A few words must now be said about its attitude toward international affairs. In international politics, Fascism exalted war instead of peace, maintaining that only war could keep man's energies at their highest pitch. War, it held, sets the mark of nobility on those nations which have the courage to face it. A nation must have "a will to power" and the desire for expansion. Life for the Fascisti must be "a continuous, ceaseless fight," and their aim must be to "live dangerously." According to Fascism, the pursuit of peace ran counter both to past experience and to "the tendencies of the present period of dynamism." "Equally foreign to the spirit of Fascism, even though they may be accepted for their utility in meeting special political situations, are all international or League organizations which, as history amply proves, crumble to the ground whenever the heart of nations is stirred deeply by sentimental, idealist, or practical considerations."

It is not surprising that Mussolini, dominated by such ideas, launched an offensive war and defied the League of Nations in his Ethiopian venture,[3] sent his troops to intervene against the legitimate republican government in the Spanish Civil War,[4] turned against the Western democracies and aligned himself with Hitler in the Rome-Berlin Axis,[5] sent his troops into Albania and annexed that country,[6] and seized what appeared to be an easy opportunity to expand the Italian empire by attacking France when the latter lay helpless before Hitler's blitzkrieg in 1940.[7] But the irony of the outcome was that Fascism's "will to power" brought not glory and empire but the end of Fascism and the execution of *Il Duce*.

[3] See pages 461–469.
[4] See pages 329–330.
[5] See pages 470–471.
[6] See page 487.
[7] See page 518.

Chapter X

LIBERAL AND NAZI GERMANY

GERMANY emerged from the First World War defeated but with a new political regime which was distinguished for its liberalism and democracy. Although compelled to wrestle with almost insuperable problems, the liberal republic survived until it was fatally hit by the world-wide economic collapse of 1929. During the depression years which followed, conditions in Germany came to be not unlike those existing in Italy from 1920 to 1922, and the popular reaction in the former was very similar to that which had occurred in the latter. In 1933 Germany finally came into the control of the Nazis, who in their so-called Third Reich inaugurated a regime in many ways like that of the Fascists in Italy, one which was vastly different from that set up by the German constitution of 1919.

The Weimar Constitution

For a time, after the downfall of the empire,[1] it looked as though Germany might adopt a soviet form of government, for tens of thousands of Communists—called Spartacists in 1918—were determined to establish in Germany the rule of the proletariat on the Russian Bolshevik model. Karl Liebknecht was the "voice," Rosa Luxemburg the "brain," of this group during the early weeks of the republic. In December, 1918, they stirred up a revolt among the sailors stationed in Berlin, but the Majority Socialist Friedrich Ebert, who had succeeded Prince Max as chancellor, successfully suppressed the uprising by calling upon the veteran troops of the old regime. A month later the Communists and Independent Socialists together attempted to overthrow the republican government, but after ten days of bitter fighting their movement collapsed. Liebknecht, "while attempting to escape," was shot; and Rosa Luxemburg, attacked on the way to prison, was likewise killed. The political future of Germany, it appeared, was to be decided not by street fighting but by the legally chosen representatives of the German people.

As the time for the election of the National Assembly approached, political parties became active. The German Nationalist Party, composed of the

---

[1] For the collapse of the German Empire, see pages 99–104.

conservatives, the Pan-Germans, the militarists, and the majority of the Junker class, succeeded to the old Conservative Party. During the election campaign its leaders openly avowed their monarchical sentiments. The Right wing of the old National Liberal Party organized itself into the German People's Party, which posed as the champion of liberalism in the new state. Although it preferred monarchy, it announced its acceptance of republican government. It specifically denounced all class rule, strikes, socialization, communism, and anarchy. It was the party of "big business" and was ably led by Gustav Stresemann. The Center Party supported the democratic republic but was strongly opposed to all attempts to establish a socialistic regime. It favored the maintenance of the federal character of Germany, universal suffrage, proportional representation, opening of all offices to all classes, and the adoption of a bill of rights. Its outstanding leader was Matthias Erzberger.

The Left wing of the old National Liberals united with the former Progressive Party to form the German Democratic Party, the first bourgeois party to organize after the revolution. In addition to supporting the republic it advocated the partial socialization of industry, the prosecution of war profiteers, and the adoption of a single progressive capital tax. It denounced the "divine right" of kings, the "squirearchy," and the military bureaucracy. The Majority Socialists proposed a scientific and gradual policy of socialization to be accomplished through the ordinary channels of parliamentary government. Of all the parties in opposition to the existing provisional government, the Independent Socialists conducted the most bitter campaign, accusing the Majority Socialists of treason to the cause of socialism. The Communists, because of their aversion to parliamentary tactics in any form, refused to take part in the election.

On January 19, 1919, national elections were held, with over 30,500,000 men and women voting in this first German election under universal suffrage. Because of the system of proportional representation the strength of each party was fairly represented in the number of seats it obtained. The Majority Socialists stood first, followed by the Centrists, the Democrats, the Nationalists, the Independent Socialists, and the People's Party. Although the Majority Socialists elected by far the largest number of delegates to the assembly, they did not control a majority, so that a coalition now became necessary. When the National Assembly met at Weimar in February, 1919, the Majority Socialist government therefore gave way to the "Weimar Coalition," composed of Majority Socialists, Centrists, and Democrats, under the chancellorship of the Majority Socialist Scheidemann. Friedrich Ebert, who since the preceding November had served as chancellor, was then elected the first president of the German Republic.

Following the establishment of a temporary government, the National

Assembly at once turned its attention to constitution-making. It could not, however, devote its whole attention to this task, for it was called upon to maintain internal order, to provide food for the starving population, to re-establish the national economic life, and to conclude peace with the Allies. Nor was it left to fulfill these arduous duties in peace and quiet. A Communist revolt in Berlin early in March was put down only after twelve hundred persons had been killed and property to the value of millions had been destroyed. In Munich another Communist uprising, provoked by a Nationalist's murder of Kurt Eisner, the Bavarian premier, led to the proclamation of a soviet republic which was not suppressed for two months.

Eventually, however, a constitution was drafted and accepted on July 31 by a vote of 262 (Majority Socialists, Centrists, Democrats) to 75 (Independent Socialists, People's Party, Nationalists). On August 11 it received the signature of President Ebert, and three days later it came into force by presidential proclamation. On August 21 President Ebert took the oath of office required by the new constitution before the last session of the National Assembly at Weimar. The assembly, however, did not dissolve with the conclusion of its constituent work but constituted itself a legislative body, which from September 30, 1919, sat in the Reichstag building in Berlin.

It has been said that "the constitution of a nation is its apparel, its mantle." The German people replaced their former royal robe with the latest mode of the plainer garb of democracy, choosing a republic in which political authority was derived from the people.[2] Every member state had to have a republican constitution, and representatives had to "be elected by the universal, equal, direct and secret suffrage of all German citizens, both men and women, according to the principles of proportional representation." The chancellor and the ministers required for the administration of their offices the confidence of the Reichstag and had to resign if the latter by formal resolution withdrew its confidence. The republic was therefore a truly representative democracy.

The executive of the republic consisted of the president and the cabinet, composed of the chancellor and other ministers. The president was elected by the direct vote of the people, held office for seven years, and might be re-elected. Like the French president and the British king, the German president had little real power, every executive order requiring the countersignature of the chancellor or some other minister. The chancellor, responsible to the Reichstag, was the one who determined the general course of policy and assumed responsibility therefor.

The national legislature consisted of two houses, the Reichstag and the

[2] The government as here discussed is that which existed prior to the drastic changes which were introduced in consequence of the National Socialist revolution of 1933. For subsequent modifications, see pages 258–260.

Reichsrat. The former was composed of members elected for a term of four years by the direct vote of all men and women over twenty years of age. It might be dissolved by the president, but only once for the same cause. The Reichsrat, like the former Bundesrat, represented the states. In it each state had at least one vote, the larger states having one vote for each 700,000 inhabitants; but no state might have more than two fifths of all the votes. The Reichsrat functioned merely as a sort of "brake on legislation," and contrary to the condition under the empire, the Reichstag was by far the more powerful branch of the legislature.

The constitution contained many compromises, but in general it reflected the more moderate desires of the Democratic and Social Democratic parties, with numerous concessions to the Centrists in matters relating to education and religion. The finished document was, as might have been expected, far too conservative to please the Independent Socialists and much too liberal to suit the parties of the Right.

The Defense of the Republic

To draft and set up a republican form of government for Germany was one thing; to defend it against the onslaughts of domestic foes of the Left and Right was quite another. From the day of its proclamation the republic encountered the bitter opposition of the Communists, who believed, not in democracy, but in the rule of the proletariat organized in soviets on the Russian model. The first open attempts to overthrow the republic came from this group, but their numerous riots, strikes, military uprisings, and political *coups d'état* during 1919 were eventually quelled by the government. Although the Communists continued to exist and fluctuated in political strength according to the exigencies of the republic, it was not until after 1930, when economic conditions became critical, that their numbers became so great as to be an important political factor.

Somewhat in proportion as the threat from the Communists declined in the early years of the republic, that from the reactionaries of the extreme Right increased. So long as Germany was actually threatened by communism, the reactionaries delayed their attack on the republic, for they feared communism more than bourgeois republicanism. But by 1920 the immediate danger from communism seemed to have passed, and the Junkers, Pan-Germanists, irreconcilable militarists, and remnants of the prewar Conservative Party took heart. If the Germans rejected communism, perhaps they would accept monarchism.

In March, 1920, the reactionaries struck their first blow against the republic in what is known as the Kapp-Lüttwitz *Putsch*. General Baron von Lüttwitz, commander-in-chief of Berlin, suddenly seized the capital, and his confederate, Wolfgang von Kapp, was proclaimed chancellor. But, though President Ebert's government fled precipitately to Dresden and then on to Stuttgart, the *Putsch* proved a miserable failure. Some of the monarchist leaders refused their active support, and the bulk of the army and of the propertied classes failed to rally to it. At the same time it encountered the determined opposition of the working classes, to whom President Ebert issued a passionate appeal to inaugurate a general strike. Necessities like water, gas, and electricity were suddenly shut off; railway and tramway services ceased. The revolutionary government was paralyzed and collapsed within a week, Kapp fleeing to Sweden.

During the next three years events in connection with the fulfillment of the peace treaty provided numerous opportunities for the reactionary monarchists to criticize the republican regime and to seek to weaken and discredit it. The losses of territory by plebiscites, the Allied demand for the punishment of German "war criminals" (many of whom were looked upon as national heroes in the fatherland), the reparations and disarmament demands, the forced disbandment of the Bavarian *Einwohnerwehr* (citizen guard), all presented points of attack for the monarchists. A "stab in the back" legend was developed to the effect that all Germany's postwar ills arose from the military defeat, which in turn had been caused by the prearmistice revolutionary intrigues of the present republicans. The past glories of the Hohenzollern monarchy were constantly placed over against the existing ills of the democratic republic. A campaign of agitation, centering in Bavaria, was directed against all who had played a part in the events leading to the signing of the Versailles treaty, and a series of political murders began which eventually claimed such distinguished figures as Matthias Erzberger, the Centrist leader, and Walther Rathenau, a Democrat who at the time of his assassination was minister for foreign affairs.

In 1923, when Germany was in chaos as a result of French occupation of the Ruhr and German passive resistance, various plots were hatched in Bavaria looking toward the overthrow of the Berlin government. One reactionary group under the leadership of Gustav von Kahr plotted the establishment of a directory which, backed by the military, would assume control of the Reich. Another group led by Ludendorff and Adolf Hitler, the latter destined to become the Nazi dictator of Germany, planned to march on Berlin, where Hitler would be proclaimed president under the military dictatorship of Ludendorff. Hitler's plans conflicted with those of Kahr, with the result that the two factions consumed their ardor in quarreling between themselves, and the "beer-cellar rebellion" of November 8 collapsed without having seriously threatened the republic. The chief conspirators were arrested and tried, but friendly courts let them off with lenient treatment.

In the midst of the republic's struggles against domestic foes of the Left and the Right its territorial integrity was seriously threatened. Almost simultaneously with the Hitler-Ludendorff *Putsch* in Bavaria came a separatist movement in the Rhineland which aimed, not to overthrow the German Republic, but to bring about its disintegration. The first blow was struck in September, 1923, when the separatists seized Düsseldorf in the Ruhr. During the following month Aachen, Coblenz, Bonn, Wiesbaden, Trier, and Mainz were occupied by separatist forces. The "Autonomous Government of the Palatinate" was proclaimed at Speyer in November and was at once officially recognized by the French high commissioner. Approximately 19,000 officials who refused to make declarations of loyalty to the Palatinate government were deported. But the unnatural Rhineland movement failed. Its leaders soon fell to quarreling with one another; the great majority of the lawful officials and population of the region refused to support it; the Belgian and British governments opposed it. In January, 1924, the president of the "Autonomous Government of the Palatinate" was assassinated. In February the French officials withdrew their support, and by the end of the month the separatist regime in the Rhineland had ended.

The Currency Debacle

While statesmen of the Weimar Republic were engaged in a life-and-death struggle to prevent the destruction or disintegration of the republic, they were forced to deal also with the reparations problem, which has already been discussed. At the same time they were compelled to wrestle with the perplexing and baffling problem of a currency rapidly depreciating toward the vanishing point. The republic had inherited a currency which was already greatly inflated, thanks to the former imperial government's unwillingness to impose heavier direct taxes during the First World War. And the exigencies of the period of demobilization and readjustment, together with the necessity of making reparations payments, had brought further inflation, largely because German statesmen were reluctant to increase taxes. In the years immediately after the war the burden of taxation in Germany was only a quarter as heavy as the burden in Great Britain, only half as heavy as in France.

By May, 1921, the mark had declined to 60 (normally 4.2) to the dollar. On June 1, 1921, the Reichsbank for the first time began to pay a premium for gold coin, thus officially recognizing the inflation. This depreciation of the mark in turn operated to keep the national budget unbalanced, for taxes assessed with the mark at one figure were paid later with a mark depreciated below that figure. The continued deficits which resulted led to still more inflation. By November, 1922, the mark had sunk to 7000 to the dollar. The occupation of the Ruhr by the French and the Belgians and the adoption by Germany of the policy of passive resistance, with the accompanying need for subsidizing the idle workers, started the mark upon its toboggan slide. By the close of January, 1923, it stood at 50,000 to the dollar. By July it stood at 160,000, and during the month it declined to 1,100,000 to the dollar. From this date began the so-called repudiation of the mark. By the middle of November it had become practically worthless, being quoted in Berlin at 2,520,000,000,000 and in Cologne at about 4,000,000,000,000 to the dollar.

Many of the great industrialists of Germany tremendously increased their wealth and power during this inflationary period. Availing themselves of artificially cheap labor, extensive Reichsbank loans, and a rapidly falling currency, they piled up tremendous paper profits. With these they purchased substantial assets abroad, enlarged and modernized their plants at home, or paid off loans and bonded indebtedness. Thus the mighty capitalists and industrialists profited enormously by the inflation and showed no great concern to check it until the mark had become worthless.

When, however, farmers and merchants began to refuse to sell food for worthless currency, when "the catastrophe of currency developed into a catastrophe of the food and other supplies, which was worse than in the worst periods of the war," when plunderings and riots began to be of daily occurrence, the German government in desperation decided to create a new bank of issue and a new currency. On October 15, 1923, a decree for the establishment of the bank was issued. In November Hjalmar Schacht, general manager of one of Germany's largest banks, was appointed special currency commissioner with the task of stabilizing the mark and introducing the new currency. His first step was to stop the printing presses in order to prevent further inflation. Simultaneously he issued a new currency, which was stabilized at the old rate of 4.2 to the dollar and circulated along with the old mark at the ratio of one to one trillion. At the same time Finance Minister Luther by heroic measures balanced the budget and ended the need for inflation. Eventually, in October, 1924, the Dawes plan loan [3] added to the working capital of the country and provided the economic backing which the situation required. With the organization of the new Reichsbank, the new currency became known as the Reichsmark. Provision was made that the old depreciated marks might, until July 5, 1925, be converted into the new Reichsmark at the ratio of one trillion to one.

The economic and social results of this practical repudiation of the mark were terrific. The obvious effect of the devaluation was the destruction of savings, pensions, and insurance. Those who had laid by or inherited a sum

[3] See page 168

sufficient to maintain them in comfort according to the standards of their class suddenly discovered that their capital was gone. Of what value were 100,000 marks invested in banks, bonds, or fixed annuities when the mark declined until it took 1,000,000,000 to buy a dollar's worth of food? The inevitable consequence of such a declining currency was the forced transfer of wealth from the creditor to the debtor class. Mortgages were lifted, bonds retired, and notes paid off with currency worth only an infinitesimal fraction of its face value. Undoubtedly the most lasting of the disastrous results of the currency inflation was the destruction or disintegration of a great part of the previously prosperous middle class. This vital class was, in the words of one German, "economically guillotined," and many of its members were forced into the ranks of the working people. The support which the middle class later gave to Hitler was in no small measure the result of suffering and discontent engendered by the currency debacle.

Stresemann's Policy of Conciliation

Meanwhile, German statesmen had been compelled to formulate a national foreign policy. The latter was inevitably based upon certain specific features of Germany's postwar situation. To begin with, an important part of her national territory was occupied by alien troops. Her military and naval forces had been drastically curtailed and were under the supervision of Inter-Allied commissions of control. Her Rhineland had been demilitarized. Her overseas colonies had been taken from her, and in Europe her territory had been dismembered and reduced by cessions to other countries. She had been denied the right to have her Austrian kinsmen unite with her even when they so desired. Furthermore, she was weighted down with the burden of an indefinitely large reparations obligation and with the odium of "war guilt." She found herself isolated, almost an outcast among the powers of Europe. Her former Habsburg ally had been utterly destroyed; her lesser allies had been defeated and rendered insignificant in European affairs. She had been refused an invitation to become a member of the League of Nations.

These fundamental facts practically dictated Germany's foreign policy, the fundamental aim of which was to throw off the various limitations on her sovereignty in order that she might regain her prewar position of power and influence in world affairs. More specifically, she sought (1) to reduce and ultimately to escape from the reparations indemnity which she was obligated to pay, (2) to liberate her territory from foreign occupation, (3) to secure the removal of the Inter-Allied commissions of control, (4) to regain her freedom in military and naval matters, (5) to restore her right to fortify and protect the Rhineland, and (6) to emerge from isolation and once more hold a place as an equal among the great powers. Ultimately, she sought to redeem the Saar, to secure a union with Austria, to bridge the gap between Germany and East Prussia, and to regain at least some of her colonies.

Immediately after the war many German statesmen were inclined to look to the east for their country's salvation. They cordially hated the victorious Allies, spurned any move toward reconciliation with them, repudiated their dictated peace treaty, declined to adopt a policy of fulfillment, and hoped eventually, by forming an alliance with Russia, to be able to defy them and overthrow the treaty. The economic recovery of Germany they would hasten by re-establishing trade relations with Russia and by extending German economic control over the boundless resources of the Soviet Union. The most spectacular step taken in this policy of eastern orientation was the signing of the treaty of Rapallo with Russia in April, 1922. Germany accorded *de jure* recognition to the Soviet government, and each renounced all war claims and prewar indebtedness. Probably the most important articles of the treaty, so far as Germany was concerned, were those providing for the extension of mutual facilities of trade. The results of the attitude of defiance were unfortunate, however. Not only were none of the immediate ends of her foreign policy attained, but in 1923 Germany found herself further limited and weakened by the Franco-Belgian occupation of the Ruhr.

Those in Germany who favored a policy of western orientation believed that the republic's salvation was to be found only with the aid and co-operation of the Allies. They demanded a "policy of fulfillment and reconciliation." The one who more than all others developed a constructive foreign policy for Germany based on the idea of western orientation was Gustav Stresemann, who assumed the office of foreign minister in the critical days of August, 1923, and held it through ten shifting ministries down to his regrettable death on October 3, 1929. A member of the bourgeoisie, associated with big business, he belonged before the war to the National Liberal Party. During the revolutionary days he formed the German People's Party and became its leader. Content during the early years of the republic to follow a more or less negative policy of opportunism, his assumption of a share of the governmental burden of responsibility in 1923 led him to become increasingly constructive in his policies. Under his guidance the republic chose the path leading toward fulfillment and reconciliation.

Real gains came to Germany from Stresemann's policy. The Dawes Committee's investigation brought the settling of the method and amounts of reparations payments in accordance with the views of impartial experts, and the introduction of the Dawes plan brought financial assistance which made the economic rehabilitation of Germany possible. It led within a year to the military evacuation of the Ruhr area and the cities of Ruhrort, Duisburg, and Düsseldorf. It secured for Germany admission to the League of Nations (1926) with a permanent seat on the Council. Early in the following year it brought the abolition of the Inter-Allied commissions of control, their duties being transferred to the League, of which Germany was now an influential member.

In 1928 Stresemann secured the initiation of negotiations looking toward a new settlement of the reparations problem and the early evacuation of the Rhineland. As a result, the definite total which was fixed for German reparations liabilities was placed far below that originally fixed by the Reparations Commission in 1921; and it was agreed that all Allied forces of occupation should be withdrawn from the Rhineland by June 30, 1930. But the influence of Stresemann's policy of fulfillment and reconciliation did not end with his death. It continued for a number of years to affect the Allied attitude toward Germany and undoubtedly played a part in the practical cancellation of reparations payments at Lausanne in 1932.

Economic Recovery and Decline

Not unrelated to Stresemann's successful foreign policy was the rapid economic recovery which the republic experienced during the five years after 1924. Prewar Germany had been the third most powerful wealth-producing organism in the world, possessing an abundance of coal and iron, a closely unified and efficient railway system, a profitable merchant marine, extensive colonies, and large foreign investments. It has been pointed out how the treaty of Versailles drastically changed all this.[4]

But Germany set resolutely to work to rebuild or adapt her economic machine to the new situation. In this task she was aided by the fact that her territory had not been devastated by the war and that she had, consequently, no great reconstruction problem such as burdened France. Germany's factories, within her postwar frontiers at least, were intact. She was aided in the second place, strange to say, by her currency debacle, which in no sense diminished the real wealth of the country but rather contributed to the industrial recovery of Germany in several ways. By the sale abroad of German currency, drafts in marks, banknotes, and other securities which became worthless as a result of the inflation, real wealth estimated as high as $2,000,000,000 came into German hands. Inflation enabled Germany to compete for a time in the markets of the world with goods produced at home by labor unusually cheap, while at the same time it enabled her industrialists to expand and modernize their plants with loans which were repaid with an almost worthless currency. By 1924, as the Dawes experts

[4] See page 126.

GERMANY BEFORE AND AFTER THE FIRST WORLD WAR

Legend:
— Postwar Germany
▨ Areas lost by Germany
⫶ Demilitarized zone

D - DANZIG FREE STATE
S - SAAR BASIN

MANHATTAN DRAFTING CO., N.Y.

NORTH SEA
NETHERLANDS
Amsterdam
BELGIUM
Brussels
LUXEMBURG
FRANCE
Paris
LORRAINE
ALSACE
Rhine
SWITZERLAND
AUSTRIA
HUNGARY
Budapest
Vienna
Danube R.
Munich
CZECHOSLOVAKIA
Prague
Frankfort
Coblenz
Mainz
Cologne
Essen
Ruhr R.
Weser R.
Bremen
Hamburg
Elbe R.
GERMANY
Berlin
Stettin
Oder R.
POLAND
Warsaw
Vistula R.
EAST PRUSSIA
Königsberg
Niemen R.
LITHUANIA
Memel
DENMARK
Copenhagen
KIEL CANAL
BALTIC SEA

pointed out, Germany's industries and transportation system were in admirable physical condition. All that she needed was international credit, and, as a result of the introduction of the Dawes plan, abundant credit became available.

It is not surprising, therefore, that Germany's economic recovery was rapid in the years that followed. She had lost a considerable proportion of her coal resources; to compensate for this, she resorted to the more extensive use of electricity. She possessed water power whose total potential output, it is calculated, would produce in power annually the equivalent of 32,000,000 tons of black coal; this she began to develop. She had vast beds of lignite or "brown coal"; these she began to transform into electricity, constructing in their vicinity great generating plants. In her steel industry new methods of furnace construction and better utilization of coal brought lower costs. She soon reached the place where she again had a surplus of coal for export, and by 1927 her production of steel ingots was back nearly to the prewar figure. The rolling stock in her railroads became superior in quality and condition to that of prewar days. The gross tonnage of her merchant vessels rose from 400,000 to 3,738,067 by 1928, and possessed the great advantage of being nearly all new.

German industrialists felt confident of their ability to achieve success. They planned to resume their prewar commercial and industrial relations and hoped to regain the place in the world's markets which they had held in 1914. To hasten the republic's economic recovery they introduced into German industrial life the "rationalization movement," to which they ascribed the rapid rise of American industry. Mass production and industrial efficiency became their watchwords. Standardization of products and materials, scientific planning and management, elimination of duplication and useless competition by the formation of trusts and combines—these became their goals. Undoubtedly greater efficiency was achieved. The average output per man was considerably increased in various types of industry and even in agriculture. Furthermore, greater protection was given to home industry by modifying the German customs tariff act, and German interests abroad were advanced by the conclusion of commercial treaties with all of the important powers. By 1929 the total volume of industrial output in Germany exceeded that of 1913.

In 1929, however, it began to be apparent that the republic's rapid economic recovery could not continue. That recovery had been facilitated in part by extensive loans which had been obtained from foreign bankers. In 1929 the sources of these loans began to dry up. Continued economic recovery required a further extension of German markets abroad. But the high tariff walls raised by other countries, the successful competition of the United States, Great Britain, and France, and the inability to regain to any great extent the prewar markets in Russia, operated to prevent that necessary extension. Moreover, the loss of wages by those who were rendered superfluous in industry by the introduction of "rationalization," and the decrease in prices of agricultural products resulting from world over-production, both brought a noticeable decline in the purchasing power of the home market. In 1929 German industrial activity began to decline, and unemployment began to rise. The resultant situation raised serious problems for the German government and inevitably reacted upon the political situation.

The First Decade of Politics

During the first decade of the republic Germany had one presidential campaign and four parliamentary elections. On February 28, 1925, President Ebert died. As chancellor or president he had been at the head of the government ever since the proclamation of the republic on November 9, 1918. Although originally favoring a democratic parliamentary monarchy like Great Britain's, he had accepted the republic after its proclamation by the proletariat and had used the influence of his unselfish patriotism to strengthen and stabilize it. An artisan and the son of an artisan, lacking the academic training so highly esteemed in Germany, a plain man of the people, his presence at the head of the state had gone far toward winning the radical proletariat from Bolshevism to the support of the republic. President Ebert's term of office had been provisional. The unsettled conditions during the early months of the republic had convinced the members of the Weimar assembly that it would be unwise to hold a popular election at that time. They had therefore elected Ebert president without referring the question to the people. His death precipitated the first popular presidential election, for the German constitution made no provision for a vice-president.

German electoral procedure called for one or two elections to determine the popular choice. In the first balloting a candidate to be successful had to receive a clear majority of all votes cast. If no candidate received such a majority, a second election had to be held in which the candidate receiving the largest number of votes, whether a majority or not, was elected. Seven candidates were presented in the election of March 29, 1925, and none received the requisite majority. A second vote therefore became necessary, and party coalitions were the result. The Centrists, Democrats, and Social Democrats, who together had polled over 13,000,000 votes in the first election, finally agreed to support Wilhelm Marx, leader of the Centrists. The Communists refused to join this coalition and persisted in running their own candidate, Ernst Thälmann. The combined vote of the parties of the Right in the first election had been less than 12,000,000, so that they were now confronted with a serious problem. They solved it unexpectedly by dropping all their earlier nominees and naming as their common candidate the aged Field Marshal Paul von Hindenburg, the idolized hero of the German people.

In the first poll some 12,000,000 qualified voters had failed to participate. In the final election on April 26, between three and four million of these lethargic citizens were galvanized into action by the dynamic magic of Hindenburg's name, and nearly three million of them cast their ballots for the war hero—enough to turn the scale in his favor. By many it was feared that the election of Field Marshal von Hindenburg to the presidency by "militarists" and "monarchists" would lead to the overthrow of the republic. But the new president took the oath of loyalty to the republic without qualification and apparently sought sincerely to fulfill it—at least until 1932.

In the early parliamentary elections the voting usually resolved itself into a contest between the so-called Weimar parties, which had been responsible for Germany's liberal constitution, and the parties on the Right and Left, which were theoretically opposed to the acceptance of the democratic republic. The outcome of the elections varied with the exigencies of the economic situation. In June, 1920, and again in May, 1924, the parties of the extreme Right and the extreme Left gained at the expense of the middle groups, although the latter, with the aid of the People's Party, were able to retain a bare working majority. In a special election of December, 1924, the Nationalists on the Right increased their Reichstag representation so much that they stood second only to the Social Democrats. The cabinet which assumed control of the government after this election was a Right-Center group consisting of members of the Nationalist, People's, and Center parties.

The number of ministries which the German Republic had during the first decade of its existence was in marked contrast with the few which served during the period of the empire. Germany had a multiparty system. The multiplicity of parties was a direct advantage to the chancellor under the old imperial regime, since he was responsible only to the Kaiser and could play off one party against another. But now that the chancellor had to have a majority of the Reichstag behind him, the multiparty system resulted in frequent changes of the ministry. In the shifting of the ministries the Center Party well exemplified its name. Its strong sense of moderation and responsibility made it the nucleus of practically all of the coalition governments of the postwar period. Its chief task was to determine whether it would ally itself with the Left or the Right. The trend, however, during the first nine years was steadily toward the Right. Although the first four ministries, beginning in November, 1918, were headed by Socialist chancellors, during the eight years after June, 1920, there was not a single Socialist chancellor, and only twice during that period were Socialists even included in the ministry. On the other hand, the People's Party four times had the chancellorship, and Nationalists were twice included in the government. In other words, the drift in German politics during these years was distinctly toward bourgeois control.

The fourth general elections for the Reichstag, in May, 1928, when Germany was economically prosperous, brought a swing back from the Right. The Nationalists lost heavily, while the Social Democrats and the Communists both increased, the latter outnumbering the People's Party and becoming the fourth largest group in the Reichstag. A Socialist, Hermann Müller, became chancellor and a "grand coalition," consisting of the People's Party, Centrists, Bavarian People's Party (an offshoot of the Centrists), Democrats, and Social Democrats, was organized under his leadership. But Social Democratic dissatisfaction with financial reforms which were pushed through the Reichstag in an effort to solve the republic's pressing economic problems after 1929 brought the downfall of the Müller government in March, 1930. In the new government, headed by Heinrich Brüning, leader of the Centrists, the Social Democrats refused to participate. It consisted, therefore, of only the middle parties, and marked a renewed swing back toward the Right.

The chief task of Brüning's government was to secure the adoption of a budget which would wipe out the steadily increasing national deficit, but conflicts between party, class, and local interests in the Reichstag constituted a serious handicap. Finally, in July, 1930, after the Reichstag had rejected the government's budget, President Hindenburg dissolved that body and called for new elections to be held in September. In the meantime, availing himself of the "emergency clause" (Article 48) of the constitution, the president inaugurated a financial program which differed little from the one the Reichstag had rejected.

Hitler and the National Socialists

The political group which benefited most from the economic depression and the growing spirit of unrest in Germany was the National Socialist Party, whose chief was Adolf Hitler. This fanatically nationalistic German leader was born (1889) not in Germany but in Austria, and was the son of a humble customs inspector of the Dual Monarchy. His formal education was somewhat limited, for he had been obliged to leave school at an early age because of financial difficulties. While yet a mere youth he went to Vienna for the purpose of studying architecture, but finding himself unable to enter the Painting Academy, he had had to be content with a position as draftsman and decorator. The Austrian capital Hitler had abhorred as a "racial Babylon," and it was during his years in Vienna, apparently, that he developed his bitter anti-Marxist and anti-Semitic hatreds.

Shortly before the First World War began, Hitler moved to Munich, where he worked as a house painter. During the war he fought in the Bavarian army as a private and later as a corporal, and acquitted himself so well that he was awarded the Iron Cross. Soon after the war he helped to organize in Munich the National Socialist German Workers' Party, and in February, 1920, a program of twenty-five points, formulated by Gottfried Feder, was adopted by the party.[5] This early program, somewhat analogous to the early platform of the Italian Fascists, was modified by later pronouncements of Hitler and was ultimately much expanded in a volume of memoirs entitled *Mein Kampf* (My Struggle). In 1921 Hitler began to harangue the crowds in the Munich beer gardens, especially denouncing the Jews, the capitalists, the French, the treaty of Versailles, and the Weimar Republic. In 1923, as already pointed out, he co-operated with Ludendorff and others in an unsuccessful attempt to overthrow the German government, and was consequently sentenced to five years' imprisonment. After a prison term of only a few months, he was released but was forbidden for a time to make public speeches.

Hitler then devoted himself primarily to the task of organizing his followers, and in this work he closely followed the plans of Mussolini. The swastika, or hooked cross (卐), was adopted as the emblem of the National Socialist Party, which was further provided with an elaborate ritual and a military organization. Party members were required to pay small monthly dues and were permitted in turn to wear the party uniform—a brown shirt with a black swastika on an armband. Like Mussolini's *squadristi,* Hitler had his "storm troops" (*Sturmabteilungen*), whose duties in the beginning were to protect Nazi meetings and to interfere with Communist gatherings. In addition, the organization had its smaller group of "defense squads" (*Schutzstaffeln*), which constituted a sort of party police for protecting Nazi leaders and for executing unusually difficult tasks. In order to reach the whole German people with the Nazi program the country was organized into twenty-six districts, each in turn subdivided into "cells" to which a number of trained Nazi speakers were assigned.

So far as organization was concerned, therefore, the National Socialists, or Nazis, were in a position to make great gains in the election of 1930. Their program, too, was of such a nature as to attract large numbers of adherents in a time of national humiliation and economic depression. They were extremely nationalistic in their aims, seeking to stimulate German

[5] The text of this document may be found in *Current History,* Volume XXXVI, pages 170–172.

patriotism, to unite all Germans (those in Austria, Czechoslovakia, Poland, Holland, and Alsace included) in a common state, to regain for Germany her lost colonies and her parity with the other great powers in national armaments, to secure the cancellation of the peace treaties and thereby the refutation of war guilt and the repudiation of reparations obligations. They advocated, too, certain social and economic reforms such as the abolition of all unearned income, the confiscation of war profits, the nationalization of the great trusts and large department stores, the guarantee by the government of employment and decent living conditions for German citizens (Jews could not be citizens), the abolition of speculation in land, the inauguration of agrarian reform, and the shifting of tax burdens from the workers and lower middle classes to the rich. All these reforms and achievements were to be the fruits of the "Third Reich" [6] which the National Socialists aimed to establish.

At a time when the number of unemployed in Germany was close to 4,000,000, when the burden of taxation was becoming constantly heavier, when no ray of hope for a way out of the economic depression was visible, it is not surprising, perhaps, that great numbers were won to the National Socialist standard by the magnetic oratory of Adolf Hitler. Although labor, in general, remained deaf to the Nazi leader's siren song, millions of others who were alarmed at the prospect of pauperization responded. From the German youth great numbers of university students and university graduates, moved by their discontent with a situation which failed to provide employment for the educated classes, joined the Nazi ranks. From the professional classes many who suffered from the keen competition of the Jews in medicine, law, banking, and trade were cheered by the promise of the National Socialist anti-Semitic program. Unorganized retail shopkeepers and lesser capitalists, fearful of the encroachments of the great trusts, department stores, and chain stores, found hope in the Nazi plan to nationalize such enterprises. Even the peasants, burdened with debt and prevented by their concept of private property from supporting the Communists or Socialists, in many cases as a protest threw their support to the Nazis. Finally, the great ranks of the white-collar classes, unemployed or poorly paid, joined the Hitler movement almost *en masse*. When the votes were finally counted at the close of the election of September 14, 1930, therefore, it was found that the National Socialists had made tremendous gains. The 12 seats which they had held in the Reichstag at the time of its dissolution were now increased to 107, thus giving to the Nazis a strength in the national legislature second only to that of the Social Democrats.

[6] According to the Nazis the first Reich was the Holy Roman Empire and the second was created by Bismarck in 1871.

The Collapse of Parliamentary Government

Despite the losses of the middle parties, Brüning's government was enabled to continue in office through the support of the Social Democrats, who threw their strength to it on a vote of confidence. Again in December, 1930, however, President Hindenburg was compelled to resort to emergency decrees in order to put into effect the financial program of the government. But Brüning was confronted by a national financial crisis which grew steadily worse, and in 1931 emergency decrees were once more issued in an attempt to increase income and reduce expenditures. The financial crisis which was precipitated in that year and the efforts of the powers through a moratorium and "standstill agreements" to prevent a complete debacle have already been discussed.[7] Nevertheless, the situation in Germany—both economic and political—continued to be so critical that late in 1931 President Hindenburg felt compelled to issue a new set of emergency decrees.

In order to spare the country the cost and excitement of a presidential election in a time of such political and economic distress, Brüning suggested to the various party leaders early in 1932 that Hindenburg's term be extended beyond the legal seven years. Hitler opposed the suggestion, however, and, since the president declined to use his emergency powers to prolong his own term, an election was called for March 13. Hindenburg and Hitler were the principal candidates for the presidency in an election which witnessed a notable shift in party loyalties when contrasted with the campaign of 1925. The Social Democrats and the Centrists, who on the former occasion had opposed Hindenburg's election as a menace to the republic, were now his most stanch and active supporters; while the Nationalists and the monarchists, who had put forward the marshal as their candidate in 1925, now became his most determined opponents.

The voting on March 13, 1932, failed to bring the election of any candidate, for President Hindenburg lacked by approximately one half of one per cent the necessary majority of the votes. In the second election, held on April 10, Hitler increased his vote—this time to more than 13,400,000—but Hindenburg received a majority of approximately 2,200,000 over the combined votes for Hitler and Thälmann, the Communist candidate, and thus in his eighty-fifth year began his second term as president of the German Republic.

Although the outcome of the presidential election was by many interpreted as a popular mandate in favor of Brüning's policies, gains by the

[7] See pages 174–175.

Nazis in state elections during the succeeding weeks indicated that there was a widespread and growing dissatisfaction with his government. Naturally, his attempts to enforce rigid economies in the government, coupled with his increases in taxation, reacted against his popularity. Furthermore, the feeling was becoming somewhat general that Brüning's system of governing by executive decree was a failure. In 1932 the unemployment figures rose to nearly 6,000,000, and the budgetary deficit mounted to $400,000,000. On May 30, 1932, Brüning finally resigned.[8]

The new chancellor chosen by Hindenburg was Colonel Franz von Papen, who as military attaché in Washington in 1915 had been recalled at President Wilson's request because of alleged violations of American neutrality.[9] The ministry which he selected was composed for the most part of nationalists and conservatives, and constituted a decided swing to the Right. Realizing that he could not hope to control a majority in the existing Reichstag, Chancellor von Papen had it dissolved immediately. Nothing, however, seemed to be able to stem the rising tide of Hitlerism. In the ensuing elections the Nazis more than doubled the number of seats in the Reichstag which they had obtained in 1930. Their new total of 230 seats gave them the largest number that any party had ever had in the history of the republic. Nevertheless, President Hindenburg rejected Hitler's demand that he be made chancellor. To escape a vote of no confidence Papen at once dissolved the recently elected Reichstag and again called for elections. On this occasion the Nazis lost some 2,000,000 votes, but still retained first place in the number of seats in the national legislature. On the other hand, the Communists increased their total number of seats to 100 and came within striking distance of the strength of the Social Democrats. It appeared that the workers were deserting the moderate Social Democratic Party to join the ranks of the more radical Communists.

President Hindenburg now invited Adolf Hitler to undertake to construct a government of national concentration, but the Nazi leader found himself unable to obtain the promise of majority support. The president in turn declined to entertain Hitler's proposal that he be appointed with dictatorial powers, and instead called to the chancellorship General Kurt von Schleicher, minister of defense in the Papen government. Schleicher's ministry, which was recruited largely from that of Papen, proved to be no more able to handle the situation than its predecessors. After less than two months in office General von Schleicher resigned on January 28, 1933.

[8] The immediate cause of Brüning's resignation was the president's refusal to sanction the chancellor's plan to provide relief by carving up into small farms some of the large estates of East Prussia.

[9] See page 65.

The National Socialist Revolution

Two days later Adolf Hitler was appointed chancellor at the head of a ministry in which two of the appointments were highly significant. The important post of minister of the interior was given to Wilhelm Frick, one of Hitler's Nazi colleagues in the Munich *Putsch* of 1923. An appointment as minister without portfolio went to Hermann Göring, next to Hitler the most powerful personality in the Nazi movement. Göring had also participated in the "beer-cellar rebellion," and to escape punishment at that time he had fled to Italy, where he spent two years in studying Fascism.

Regardless of the fact that they constituted a decided minority in the government, the Nazis at once set out to secure complete control. In the hope of gaining ascendancy in the Reichstag Hitler dissolved that body and called for new elections. During the ensuing five weeks Hitler's government resorted to strong-arm methods against the opposition, particularly the Communists, the Social Democrats, and the Centrists. Opposition newspapers were suspended or suppressed; opposition meetings were forbidden or broken up; opposition speakers were denied access to the radio, which became a Nazi monopoly. Five days before the elections a fire of incendiary origin nearly destroyed the Reichstag building.[10] The Communists were at once accused by the Nazis of being the perpetrators of this act of vandalism, and hundreds of Communist leaders were arrested. By dwelling upon the dangers of a Communist-Socialist plot to overthrow the government, the Nazis sought to cause a wave of anti-Communist hysteria to sweep the country. An emergency decree of the president suspended all constitutional provisions guaranteeing personal liberty, freedom of the press, liberty to hold meetings, and even secrecy of the mails.

On March 5, 1933, stirred by the propaganda and excitement of the preceding week, more than 39,000,000 German citizens went to the polls. Although the German workers still showed their militancy and strength by polling 7,000,000 votes for the Social Democrats and 4,800,000 for the Communists, although the Catholic Center parties showed their opposition to the Nazi program of suppression and intimidation by casting 5,500,000 votes and even increasing their Reichstag representation, the millions of ordinary "stay-at-homes" who participated in this election turned the tide in favor of the National Socialists. In the country as a whole the latter secured more than 17,000,000 votes, which, with the 3,000,000 votes of

[10] The Nazis have been accused of deliberately burning the building in order to arouse fear of the Communists.

THE DESTROYER OF THE WEIMAR REPUBLIC

Adolf Hitler

the Nationalists, gave the Hitler-Papen government about 52 per cent of the popular vote. With 288 Nazi representatives and 53 Nationalists, Hitler controlled a majority of the 648 seats in the new Reichstag.

Wearing his Nazi uniform, Chancellor Hitler appeared before the newly elected Reichstag at its first session and, much as Mussolini had done in 1922, demanded dictatorial powers for four years. In a single session the Reichstag rushed the enabling act granting these powers through the required three readings, and then adjourned indefinitely.[11] Adolf Hitler thus after more than a decade of fighting achieved by constitutional methods the great triumph toward which he had looked forward. He was now chancellor of Germany and possessed of power greater by far than even the "iron chancellor," Bismarck, had ever wielded.

Any attempt to appraise the forces which brought about the National Socialist revolution must take into account four or five major factors. Perhaps first in importance was the world economic depression. In the years from 1924 to 1929, when Germany was experiencing an economic recovery, the Nazi movement made relatively little headway. But the misery and suffering resulting from four years of economic depression inevitably caused in Germany as in every other country a reaction against those in power. A second factor was the resurgence of a militant German nationalism, carefully cultivated by Hitler's exaltation of German racial superiority. With the rise of nationalism came a strong reaction (1) against the sense of humiliation resulting from defeat in the First World War and from the harsh terms of the treaty of Versailles, (2) against the doctrines of men like Stresemann and Brüning, who had preached that the only pathway open to Germany was acknowledgment of defeat and fulfillment of the demands of the victors, (3) against the Weimar middle parties, which had pursued a policy of conciliation and fulfillment, and (4) in favor of the Nazis, who promised to repair for Germany the losses resulting from defeat and to regain for her that proud place among the powers of the world which she had held before 1914.

A third factor in the situation was the temporary collapse of parliamentary government caused by the German multiparty system and the adoption of proportional representation under the Weimar constitution. As already pointed out, for more than two years before the elections of March, 1933, there was a deadlock in the Reichstag resulting from the fact that no party or group of parties controlled a majority. German labor, which in its own interest should have presented a common front against the Nazi menace, unfortunately became more divided than ever and accordingly weakened its power and contributed to the breakdown of parlia-

[11] On January 30, 1937, the Reichstag extended this enabling act for four more years.

mentary government. When a resort to the "presidential" type of government failed to end the crisis, many became convinced that only a "strong man" could bring back to Germany the domestic peace and prosperity of prewar days.

This desire for a "strong man" was further increased by fear of the rising tide of Communism, which was winning millions of discontented and despairing workmen into its ranks. After the burning of the Reichstag building by alleged Communists, the anti-Communist feeling mounted almost to hysteria among the upper and middle classes, who saw in the Nazis a bulwark against the "Reds." Furthermore, fear of Communism and a desire to smash the power of German labor had led some of the great Rhineland industrialists, notably Fritz Thyssen, to subsidize the Nazi movement in the days when it might otherwise have collapsed.

Finally, Hitler's own contribution to the forces which brought the revolution must not be overlooked. The Nazi leader was apparently not particularly original in his methods or ideas, but he was certainly a skillful imitator. He undoubtedly understood the temper of the German people, particularly of the younger generation. He was an adept psychologist, a clever demagogue, and a master showman. At the same time, he was a resourceful agitator, a tireless worker, and an able organizer. Above all, he was a captivating and inspiring orator and knew how to sway people in the mass. With the conditions which existed in Germany and with Hitler's ability to exploit them to the full through popular propaganda, the outcome was almost inevitable, especially when the Nazis resorted to repression and intimidation in the weeks before the election.

Anti-Semitism

For years Hitler and his colleagues, in order to popularize their program and win members to the National Socialist Party, had carried on a bitter anti-Semitic campaign. Again and again in their efforts to whip up an anti-Semitic frenzy they had threatened the German Jews with physical violence, civil and political degradation, and economic repression once the Nazis should come into power. It was not surprising, therefore, that the Nazi political victory in March was at once followed by numerous attacks upon Jews by Nazi storm troopers. Apparently the government and the police made little effort to afford protection. "The police," said Göring, "are not a defense squad for Jewish stores or there to protect rogues, vagabonds, swindlers, profiteers, and traitors."

These early outbursts of physical violence were soon followed by many measures which, while not so violent, nevertheless made the Jews objects of persecution and deliberate discrimination. It was decreed that no person of non-Aryan descent [12] or married to one of non-Aryan descent could be eligible for appointment as an official of the national government, the states, the municipalities, or any kind of public or legal corporation, institution, or endowment. Non-Aryan civil servants were required to resign unless they had been already employed at the outbreak of the First World War or unless they had fought at the front or lost a father or son in the war. Likewise—subject to the same conditions—it was decreed that admission to the bar might be refused to Jewish lawyers, that Jews might be struck off the roll of patent-lawyers, that Jewish notaries should be "urgently advised" to refrain from exercising their calling. All Jewish judges were "invited" to apply for leaves without delay, and all Jewish court clerks and court attachés were ordered dismissed. Similar steps were taken in the medical profession, where Jewish doctors were deprived of the right to serve as panel doctors in the national health-insurance service [13] and were excluded from practice on clients of private companies insuring against illness. Various state and municipal authorities went so far as to issue orders expelling Jewish physicians from hospitals and forbidding Jewish nurses to practice.

In the realm of education it was decreed that Jewish students must not comprise more than 1.5 per cent of those entering schools, colleges, and universities, and that all Jewish students already attending such institutions should be dismissed in so far as their numbers exceeded 5 per cent of the total attendance. Jewish university professors and teachers in secondary schools were progressively dismissed from their positions and deprived of their licenses to teach or lecture.[14] Even such a world-renowned scholar as Professor Albert Einstein, the physicist, incurred the wrath of the German Nazis.

In an attempt to "extirpate the un-German spirit" from the public libraries a public burning of un-German books was announced for May 10, 1933, at which time the books of some 160 writers were burned at inquisitional stakes in various university towns. During the ensuing months measures were taken—too many to be enumerated here in detail—to bar Jews from an increasing number of activities—economic, social, and cultural. Tens of thousands of Jewish professional men, business men, teachers, writers, musicians, artists, and artisans felt the heavy hand of the Nazi regime as it ruthlessly deprived them of their accustomed means of livelihood. The seeds of anti-Semitism, so lavishly sown by Nazi agitators before 1933, thus bore abundant fruit.

[12] "Non-Aryan descent means descent from non-Aryan, and especially Jewish, parents or grandparents, even though only one of the parents or grandparents was of the Jewish religion."

[13] Great numbers of the younger physicians and many of the older ones received a large part of their professional income from their panel practice.

[14] So also were many liberals who were not Jews.

Additional steps were taken in 1935 to define the status of Jews in Germany and to restrict them further in their political and social life. Only three classes of persons were thenceforth to be recognized under German law: (1) Germans, (2) Jews, who were defined as those having more than two Jewish grandparents, (3) Jewish "mixtures" or "hybrids," those having less than three Jewish grandparents. Jews were specifically deprived of German citizenship. They were, however, to be subjects of the state; that is to say, although barred from voting and holding office, they would still have obligations to the state. Among the Jewish "hybrids" those might be citizens who were (1) only 25-per-cent Jewish, or (2) half-Jews who did not belong to a Jewish religious community, or (3) half-Jews who were not married to Jews. A decree "for the protection of German blood and honor" forbade marriages between Germans and Jews and between Germans and Jewish "hybrids" who were half-Jews. In 1938 it was announced officially that the number of persons affected by these laws was between 800,000 and 1,000,000. Of these, 450,000 were orthodox Jews, and 290,000 were half or quarter Jewish. In the first three years of the Nazi regime, it was stated, nearly 100,000 Jews had left Germany.

The government was apparently determined to do its utmost to hasten the emigration of Jews by bringing economic pressure to bear upon them. In April, 1938, for instance, all Jews possessing property worth more than 5000 marks in Germany or abroad were required to declare their holdings. This property, it was stated, would "be used in harmony with the needs of the German economy." Another decree forbade Jews to sell their property without official permission, or to open any new Jewish business or branch business. Later still another order deprived the Jews of access to their safe deposit boxes except in the presence of a Nazi observer. On August 3 still another decree deprived all Jewish physicians of their permits to engage in any medical practice after September 30, 1938.

In November, using as an excuse the assassination of a secretary of the German embassy in Paris by a Polish Jew, the Nazis subjected the German Jews to a brutal persecution. Thousands were arrested; many were reported executed. Jewish shops were looted, synagogues were burned, and the Jews collectively were fined one billion marks. Nazi decrees closed all universities, high schools, theaters, and movies to Jews, and forbade them to engage in retail trade or mail-order or commission business.

The Totalitarian State

Meanwhile, vigorous measures had been taken to create in Germany a totalitarian state in which there should be but one political party, the National Socialist. Some of the parties—notably the Communist, Social

Democratic, and Democratic—were forcibly outlawed by the government; the others voluntarily dissolved. On July 14, 1933, Hitler's government decreed that the National Socialist Party was the only legal party in Germany, and that the formation of any new parties would constitute high treason. Furthermore, in order that the administrative offices of the republic might be filled with Nazis, a new civil-service law, applying to the federal, state, and municipal services, was promulgated, making it possible to dismiss all civil servants who were not acceptable to the central authorities.

The Nazi government also inaugurated a program designed to centralize all political authority in Berlin. Within a year it had progressed so far that on January 30, 1934—the first anniversary of Hitler's appointment as chancellor—the Reichstag passed unanimously Hitler's measure transferring the sovereign powers of the various German states to the Reich government. The legislative functions of the states were definitely abolished, and the governors appointed over the states by the Reich government were placed under the jurisdiction of the Reich minister of the interior. The situation of the states and governors in Germany thus came to be not unlike that of the French departments and prefects. The act also empowered the Reich to dispose of the Reichsrat, which had originally been instituted to give the states parliamentary representation. The formal abolition of the Reichsrat occurred in February, 1934.

Even the municipal governments were "co-ordinated." The burgomasters of the cities and the presidents of the villages were made appointees of the Reich minister of the interior. Full power to make all decisions was to rest with these appointed executives. Members of the city and village councils—thereafter to be merely advisory bodies—were also to be appointed by the minister of the interior in agreement with local Nazi leaders. These various measures resembled in effect those taken in Italy by Mussolini in 1925–1926.

Steps were also taken to secure undisputed control of the German youth. In 1926 Hitler had organized the Hitler Youth, an organization which came to include boys from ten to twenty years of age. After coming into power Hitler created the position of "Leader of the Youth of the German Reich" and appointed to this office the director of the Hitler Youth organization. This new official was made head of all German youth organizations and was authorized to take over the administrative functions of all the governing bodies which had hitherto existed. Furthermore, no new youth organization or junior auxiliary of an adult organization might be formed without his consent. Membership in the Hitler Youth was eventually made a prerequisite for admission to the Nazi Party and for appointment to government offices. Late in 1936, in fact, it was decreed that all youth—boys and girls—within the Reich were to be included in the Hitler Youth organization.

Thus Hitler attained his goal of a completely centralized, totalitarian, or one-party, state. The federal, state, and local governments had been brought wholly under his control; the parliamentary system had been entirely destroyed; the various military organizations had been either absorbed into the Nazi ranks or suppressed; the German youth movements had been restricted and centralized under Nazi leadership. As in Italy all political life was centralized in and controlled by Mussolini's Fascist Party, so at last in Germany the political life of the republic was monopolized by the Nazis. "The National Socialist Party," Hitler announced, "is the state." The Nazi party flag—the black hooked cross in a white circle on a red field—in 1935 became the official flag of the Third Reich.

To expedite the creation of the totalitarian state, Hitler had utilized two different agencies: propaganda to popularize the Nazi regime, and force to suppress all opposition to it. The former was placed in the hands of Paul Joseph Goebbels as minister of propaganda and enlightenment; the exercise of the latter was confided to Göring, Prussian premier and minister of police. Freedom of speech and of the press was abolished, and even the secrecy of telephone conversations and of the mails was disregarded. The whole educational system was placed in the hands of the Nazis, and all teachers and officials known to be in opposition to the Hitlerite regime were removed. Many famous German scholars and scientists were deprived of their positions and forced to take refuge abroad. By a national decree of July 14, 1933, all critics of the government living abroad were made subject to loss of citizenship and seizure of property unless they returned to Germany, and their relatives in Germany might be held as hostages for their good behavior. The *Gestapo* (*Geheime Staatspolizei*), a secret state police independent of the regular police, was created and placed under the command at first of Göring, later of Heinrich Himmler. To trace and fight all political activities dangerous to the state was declared to be its peculiar task. Thousands of Germans were arrested and placed in "concentration camps."

The "Co-ordination" of Germany's Economic Life

But the Nazi program of co-ordination was not limited to the political realm alone. Steps were taken to bring Germany's economic life likewise into harmony with Nazi principles. In 1933 all the previously existing trade unions in Germany were suppressed, and in the following year the employers' associations were likewise dissolved. To replace these former organizations of workers and employers a new organization, the German Labor Front, was established to represent capital and labor in the realm of commerce, industry, and the professions. Under a new labor law, effective from May 1, 1934, the principle of the solidarity of capital and labor was accepted, and the idea of an inevitable conflict between the two was rejected. Collective bargaining, strikes, and lockouts were forbidden. The workers thus lost their ultimate safeguard against exploitation—the right to strike—and became dependent for their well-being upon labor trustees, political appointees of the Nazi government, who were given full authority to issue regulations, binding upon both workers and employers, "establishing the conditions for the concluding of wage agreements."

Under the law of 1934 the Nazi principle of "leadership" was introduced into the economic life of the Reich. In each enterprise with more than twenty employees the employer became the "leader"; the employees became the "followers." A "confidential council," chosen yearly, was authorized to advise on the running of the business, on working conditions, and on the maintenance of efficiency and a spirit of co-operation. The members of this council were nominated by the leader in consultation with the head of the Nazi cell organization among the workers. The list of nominees was then submitted to the workers. In case no satisfactory election could be made, the workers might then appeal to the labor trustee for their district to appoint the members of the council. To these trustees was confided the task of maintaining industrial peace. They had authority to interfere in cases where large dismissals of workers were contemplated. They had authority also to draft general regulations for the fixing of wages and to enforce existing contracts on both the employer and the workers. They even had power to oust the employer from his business if he were too inefficient or too inconsiderate of the welfare of his employees.

Private property and private initiative were thus still retained as in the orthodox capitalistic system. The owner or manager of an enterprise, as the leader, however, was made not only responsible for carrying on his business as efficiently as possible, but equally responsible for the welfare of his workers or followers. The latter in turn were to have confidence in their employer and assist him in every way possible. Reciprocal confidence, common responsibility, and Nazi leadership were expected to create an economic system in which the welfare of society should prevail over that of the individual.

Despite their earlier promises of agrarian reform, the Nazis made no attempt to confiscate or to divide the great landed estates of the Junkers of East Prussia and Pomerania. They did, however, introduce some changes in the German system of landholding. A law—called the Hereditary Farms Law—was promulgated with the purpose of elevating the independent farmers into a new "nobility." By this law estates of less than 278 acres, capable of supporting a family and owned by a German citizen of Aryan descent, became hereditary farms. A hereditary farm could not be sold, mortgaged, or attached for debt and must pass undivided upon the owner's death to the eldest son or nearest male heir. The new owner, however, was held responsible for the support and educational training of his younger brothers and sisters. The law was in a sense designed to create a peasant aristocracy, only the owners of hereditary farms being entitled to be termed peasants.

In its attitude toward agriculture the Nazi government was influenced to a considerable extent by its desire to realize national self-sufficiency (*Autarkie*). In view of Germany's experience during the First World War, the Nazis were particularly determined that the Third Reich should become completely independent of the outside world for its food supplies. In addition to measures designed to "ennoble" the independent farmer, the government established for agriculture an organization called the Food Estate (*Nährstand*) under the direction of the Reich minister of agriculture. This organization introduced a sort of planned economy for agriculture and regulated the price and distribution of most foodstuffs.

In the realm of foreign trade the Nazis encountered difficulties. The large export surplus which Germany had enjoyed at the time the Nazis came into power decreased—partly as a result of boycotts in foreign countries because of the Nazi anti-Semitic measures—until in 1934 it finally became an import surplus instead. The resultant drain on the gold reserves of the Reichsbank was so severe that they became depleted, and the gold coverage fell to the dangerously low figure of 2.1 per cent. Once more the fear of currency depreciation haunted the German people. Immediate and drastic steps were needed, and Hjalmar Schacht, president of the Reichsbank, was appointed minister of economics with dictatorial power.

Three types of measures were taken by Schacht to meet the threatening situation: (1) default in whole or in part on foreign interest payments in order to stop one of the drains on Germany's gold, (2) rigid curtailment of imports into Germany from abroad in order to reduce another drain on the country's gold reserves, and (3) extensive subsidies to industries manufacturing for export in order that they might reduce their prices, increase their foreign sales, and thus bring gold or goods into Germany. As a result of these measures, the year 1935 closed with a favorable trade balance of 111,000,000 marks, which rose to 550,000,000 marks in 1936.

The years after 1934 saw a rapid recovery in German industry, production rising until by the opening of the year 1937 it was running 12 per cent ahead of the boom year 1928. This improvement was largely the result of credit-financed programs of rearmament and public works. To secure the funds for these extensive programs the government resorted not to increased taxes or direct currency inflation but to what amounted to a system of forced loans from banks, industries, and various organizations which had funds that might be used for investment. In other words, the

German government went more and more into debt. The amount borrowed was not revealed, for after 1934 the Reich budget was not published. There was certainly, however, a growing credit inflation in Germany with a rise in the price of many commodities.

In September, 1936, Hitler announced the inauguration of a Four-Year Plan designed to increase Germany's self-sufficiency and at the same time to provide productive employment for those released by the gradual completion of the Reich's rearmament program. During the ensuing four years all of Germany's resources—land, labor, capital—were to be mobilized to serve the campaign for greater self-sufficiency. Since Germany was at that time largely dependent upon foreign countries for all important industrial raw materials except coal, the plan placed upon German scientists what Hitler called a "stupendous task." Göring, the Nazi strong man, was placed in charge with plenary powers to issue all decrees necessary for the execution of the plan.

In respect to raw materials Göring sought to hasten the development of certain synthetic products, notably rubber, oil, and fabric threads. A 100 per cent tax was placed on rubber imports, for example, and the use of rubber for some unessential commodities was restricted. In the interest of accelerating the rearmament program, efforts were made to increase the production of iron by the development of new methods for utilizing low-grade iron ore, by the more intensive exploitation of old mines, and by the salvaging of scrap iron. So far as trade and industry were concerned, Göring's attitude was expressed in his statement that there must be "cannon before butter."

In 1938, on the fifth anniversary of Hitler's accession to power, official figures were released showing that the total national income had risen since January, 1933, from 45,200,000,000 marks to 68,000,000,000. Savings bank deposits had grown from 11,400,000,000 marks to 16,100,000,000. The value of industrial production had doubled during the period; steel production had mounted from 5,650,000 tons to 20,000,000; and the number of employed had increased from 12,580,000 to 18,370,000. Labor's share of the national income had declined, however, for wages and salaries had fallen from 56.9 per cent of the total in 1932 to 53.6 in 1938.

The "Co-ordination" of the Church

In Germany there were, before the National Socialist revolution, some twenty-nine major Protestant churches, a situation which, according to the Nazis, tended to make for disunity and inefficiency. Hitler desired instead that Germany should have one national church (*Reichskirche*) with a national bishop (*Reichsbischof*) at its head, and that it should be subordinate to the state. Threats of "co-ordinating" the Protestant churches with the Nazi regime were made early in 1933. A preliminary step toward this end was taken by Nazi Protestants when they organized into a group known as "German Christians."

In order to forestall any possible interference by Hitler, the various Protestant churches took steps in 1933 to create a new organization which should bring them all into one German Evangelical Church. The new constitution provided that at the head of the new church there should be a Lutheran bishop and that he should have co-operating with him a spiritual cabinet representing the non-Lutheran evangelical bodies. There was to be also a national synod to co-operate in promulgating church legislation and in appointing church heads. Representatives of the twenty-nine Protestant churches chose as the first bishop of the new church Friedrich von Bodelschwingh, a clergyman widely known for his social-welfare work. The new bishop had never been actively identified with any political party, and it was hoped by those who elected him that his choice would satisfy Hitler and lead the government to keep its hands out of church affairs.

Unfortunately, Ludwig Müller, a Nazi army chaplain and one of Hitler's chief advisers on religious matters, desired to be bishop of the new church, and, when he failed to secure the position, he at once issued a statement announcing that the "German Christians" could not accept the election. His opposition to Bodelschwingh's election was seconded by the head of the "German Christians," and their attitude boded ill for the freedom and independence of the German Evangelical Church. Hitler appointed Wilhelm Frick, minister of the interior, to mediate between the two groups, and under his direction Müller, Bodelschwingh, and other representatives of the two Protestant factions sought a solution of the problem. In July, 1933, a new constitution for the German Evangelical Church was approved by the representatives of the Protestant churches of Germany. A referendum on the new constitution was ordered, at which time delegates to the national synod and members of local church boards were also to be elected.

In the days before the church elections the Nazis turned the full force of their political machine to the advantage of the "German Christians," who called themselves the "storm troops of Jesus Christ." Press and radio publicity was limited to the pronouncements of the latter, and the government ruled that all persons over twenty-four years of age, who had baptismal certificates showing them to be Protestants, were entitled to vote. On the eve of the elections Hitler, in a radio address, once more raised the specter of Communism and appealed to the Protestants to elect representatives who would support the new political regime. The result was a foregone conclusion; the "German Christians" won by a landslide. It was therefore not surprising that the national synod, when constituted, chose as Reich Bishop Ludwig Müller, the candidate of the Nazi "German Christians."

Extremists in this latter group now sought to make a number of radical changes. They advocated the rejection of the Old Testament, the removal of crucifixes from the churches, and even a revision of the New Testament in such a way as to repudiate the divinity of Jesus Christ. They further demanded the insertion in the church constitution of a so-called "Aryan paragraph" which was designed to force out of the pulpit all Christian clergy having Jewish blood in their veins and to segregate in a separate church all Christians with Jewish blood. To prevent such innovations in the church several thousand clergy, led by Martin Niemöller, organized the Pastors' Emergency League. Their opposition resulted in the elimination of the "Aryan paragraph" from the church constitution, but further efforts on the part of Reich Bishop Müller to co-ordinate the church led to continued conflict.

Although the Pastors' Emergency League was disbanded, its work was carried on by a Confessional Synod, to which, rather than to Müller, the opposition looked for direction in matters of doctrine and discipline. Hundreds of pastors were thereupon arrested, suspended, transferred, or deprived of their incomes because of their refusal to obey the Reich bishop. Eventually, in September, 1935, Hitler definitely placed the Evangelical Church under state control. Reich Bishop Müller was deprived of his authority, and Hanns Kerrl was made minister for church affairs with full control of all nondoctrinal church matters. Three months later Kerrl decreed that all groups which in the future attempted to interfere with state control of the church would be suppressed.

Throughout 1936 and 1937 the government sought to obtain unity within the Evangelical Church, but failed. The Nazi government thereupon renewed its campaign against the Confessional Synod. All five members of the executive committee of the synod's provisional church government, together with Niemöller, were suddenly arrested by the secret state police, and it was made a crime to collect or to contribute money for the work of the synod. In March, 1938, Niemöller was sentenced to a fine and to seven months' imprisonment, but the court held that his sentence had already been discharged by his eight months' detention since his arrest. Upon being released, however, Niemöller was at once seized by agents of the Gestapo and put in a concentration camp. At the outbreak of the Second World War the conflict between the Nazis and the Evangelical Church had not been settled.

Relations between the Nazi government and the Catholic Church were also far from peaceful. Soon after coming into power Hitler sought to secure a single concordat with the Holy See to replace the existing three concordats between the church and the governments of Prussia, Bavaria, and Baden. Ultimately, on July 20, 1933, a concordat was signed, by the terms of which Catholic clergy were forbidden to take any part in German politics, and the Vatican withdrew any support it had previously given to the German Center parties. The Catholic religion in Germany was placed on an even footing with the Protestant faith and was guaranteed the same rights and privileges as the latter. Catholic chaplains were to serve with the German armed forces and were to be placed under a military archbishop appointed by the pope. All bishops and archbishops in Germany were to be German citizens and were to be appointed by the Holy See after consultation with the German government. The latter, for its part, recognized the Catholic Action as a nonpolitical organization under the leadership of which the Vatican might concentrate its efforts on the development of nonpolitical Catholic groups. Catholic schools, youth organizations, workers' associations, and cultural societies were to be unmolested so long as they did not concern themselves with politics.

As might perhaps have been expected, friction soon developed between the Nazi state and the Catholic Church over the interpretation of certain articles of the concordat dealing with schools and youth organizations. In the last analysis, the Nazis were determined to limit the activities of the Catholic Action, to absorb the Catholic Youth Movement, to suppress the confessional schools, to destroy the Catholic workingmen's societies, and to abolish freedom of the Catholic press. On the other hand, prominent Catholic clergy publicly denounced the Nazi sterilization law and the Nazi attacks on the crucifix and on the Old Testament. Friction was further increased in 1935 when the Nazis charged that money and foreign exchange were being smuggled out of Germany by members of the Catholic secular and regular clergy contrary to German decrees. Millions of marks in fines were levied by the government.

During 1936, despite the provisions of the concordat, the government continued its efforts to enlist all Catholic children in the Hitler Youth and to put an end to education by Catholic schools. By pressure upon parents the Nazis succeeded in reducing registrations for Catholic schools in some parts of southern Germany almost to the vanishing point. Ultimately the pope was led to protest, and in an encyclical on March 21, 1937, he declared that the concordat had been both misinterpreted and openly violated by the Nazi government. At the same time he called upon German Catholics to rally to defend the freedom of the church. The government, on the other hand, sought to discredit the Catholic Church by bringing numerous priests and members of religious orders to trial on charges of immorality. Furthermore, in June, 1937, it went so far as to dissolve hundreds of Catholic schools in Bavaria, converting them into secular institutions. In the following year the chief Bavarian Catholic Youth associations were also dissolved, and it was announced that not only the elementary schools of the church but the secondary schools as well were to be closed.

Nazi Politics and Foreign Policy

It might reasonably have been expected that, after Hitler received dictatorial powers, he would not feel called upon to consult the German electorate. This proved not to be true, however. Three times, when the nationalism of the German people had been roused to a high pitch as a result of some step taken by the Führer, elections or plebiscites were held to prove the popular support of the Nazi regime. On one other occasion, after stirring events within the Reich, a plebiscite was held to show that Hitler's deeds were sanctioned by the German people. The latter, therefore, though ruled by a dictator, continued to have the privilege—the duty, according to the Nazis—of expressing themselves in favor of the dictatorship through popular elections.

The first of these elections was held to show that the Germans supported Hitler in the first step in his foreign policy. As already pointed out, when the Nazis came into power Germany had not yet attained some of the primary objects of her postwar foreign policy. Although she had escaped from reparations payments, liberated her territory from foreign occupation, secured the removal of the Inter-Allied commissions of control, and gained a permanent seat in the Council of the League of Nations along with the other great powers, she was still restricted in military and naval matters and still prevented from fortifying the Rhineland. Furthermore, she had not yet redeemed the Saar, and had made no apparent progress toward union with Austria or toward the reacquisition of the territory lost to Poland. But all of these aims and more were included in the Nazi program as proclaimed in the years before 1933. Whereas Stresemann's foreign policy had been based on conciliation and fulfillment, however, Hitler's was founded on recalcitrance, opportunism, and the threat of resort to force.

That Nazi Germany would not meekly submit to national inferiority was soon indicated when, in October, 1933, she withdrew from the Disarmament Conference, the League of Nations, and the International Labor Organization because of the delay in granting the Reich equality in armaments.[15] At the time that Hitler announced these steps the Reichstag was dissolved and new elections were set for November 12. In the weeks preceding the plebiscite Hitler pleaded with the Germans to cast their votes in such a way as to show the world that they were "solidly behind the stand formulated by me against our country's accepting a position of inferiority

[15] See page 159.

to other countries." Undoubtedly swayed by Hitler's masterful oratory and the popularity of the issue, some 43,000,000 Germans participated in the first national plebiscite and election under the Nazi regime. Of this number, more than 40,500,000 gave their approval of the policy of the Reich government, and more than 39,500,000 voted in favor of the Nazi list of Reichstag candidates.

Although on the surface the elections of November, 1933, appeared to indicate that Hitler's party was functioning efficiently and harmoniously, a dangerous cleavage was developing within the ranks of the Nazis, who had been drawn from widely differing economic and social groups. Anyone who seriously studied the Nazi program realized that it contained goals that were distinctly in conflict one with another, and that, when the time should come to put the program into effect, some of the groups that had rallied to Hitler's standard would inevitably be disappointed. During the first half of the year 1934, the Left elements of the party became restless because of Hitler's failure to carry into effect his earlier socialistic, anti-capitalistic, and anti-Junker promises. Apparently Ernst Röhm, chief of staff of the Nazi storm troops, assumed leadership among the discontented elements of the party, who desired a "second revolution" which should carry into fuller effect the socialistic features of the original Nazi program.

According to Hitler's official statement, issued later, Röhm and a small group of ambitious storm-troop leaders spent some months in preparing for action. They feared that Hitler planned to lessen the importance of the storm troops and therefore plotted to forestall Hitler's action by seizing power for themselves. The discontented Left elements, they hoped, would rally to their side against the existing regime. During the day of June 29, 1934, alarming messages reached Hitler informing him that the "plot" was about to be carried out. Instructing Göring to take vigorous steps in Berlin and elsewhere in Prussia, Hitler at once flew by airplane to Munich and proceeded against the alleged plotters. Apparently lists of those to be killed had been carefully prepared in advance, for Hitler's agents seemed to know exactly who were to be found. Within a few hours, in a reign of terror, seventy-four persons, according to the official statement, were summarily killed with little or no hearing. Prominent among those murdered, shot, or "permitted to commit suicide" were Röhm, former Chancellor Kurt von Schleicher and his wife, Erich Klausener, leader of the Catholic Action group, and three of Papen's secretaries.[16] The complete list was never published. Hitler's defense of his summary action was that "I was responsible for the fate of the German nation and therefore I myself was the German people's Supreme Tribunal for those twenty-four hours."

---

[16] For some days Papen's fate was in doubt. President Hindenburg came to his aid by ordering the Reichswehr to be responsible for his safety.

Germany had hardly had time to calm down when on August 2, 1934, President Hindenburg died. Hitler at once assumed the functions of the president in addition to those of chancellor and thus became probably the world's most powerful ruler. He declined to assume the title of president, however, and requested that he be addressed as in the past as "Leader" or "Reich Chancellor." Desiring that the cabinet's action in combining the presidency and the chancellorship should have the approval of the German people, Hitler ordered another plebiscite to be held. Once again all the oratorical artillery of the Nazis was brought into action. A document described as the "political testament" of the late president, indicating Hindenburg's approval of Hitler's policies, was published on August 15. Two days later the chancellor made an appeal to the people in a national broadcast. Of the 43,529,710 ballots cast in the plebiscite, 38,362,760, or approximately 88 per cent, were in the affirmative.

Meanwhile, the Nazis had attempted to advance toward their goal of bringing all Germans into the Third Reich. Apparently in order that Germany might be undisturbed in her efforts to consummate the *Anschluss* with Austria and to redeem the Saar, the Reich government in January, 1934, had signed with Poland a ten-year nonaggression pact recognizing temporarily the inviolability of Germany's eastern frontiers. The Nazis then concentrated their attention on Austria and sought to "co-ordinate" that little German republic by a Nazi terror which culminated in the murder of the Austrian Chancellor Dollfuss and the abortive Nazi *Putsch* of July, 1934.[17] But the failure of the Austrians to support the *Putsch* and more especially Mussolini's prompt action in rushing Italian troops to the Austro-Italian frontier prevented the Nazis from seizing the Austrian government. The Reich government hastened to deny any connection with these events in Austria. In the Saar plebiscite in the following January, however, the Nazis were more successful, and in March, 1935, that German territory was incorporated in the Third Reich.[18] In other territory lost to Germany by the treaty of Versailles Hitler's policy was at first one of "Nazification." In 1935 the governments of Danzig and of Memel both came under the control of local Nazi parties which were linked with the Hitler organization in Germany.[19]

In the following year a third plebiscite was held after Hitler had made spectacular moves to regain full sovereignty for the Reich. In March, 1935, after the return of the Saar Basin to Germany as the result of the League's plebiscite in January, Hitler repudiated the military and naval restrictions of the treaty of Versailles, and in 1936 he remilitarized the Rhineland in

[17] See page 343.
[18] See pages 457–458.
[19] See pages 371, 374.

defiance of the same treaty and of the Locarno pact as well.[20] In the latter year, too, he denounced the clauses of the peace treaty which internationalized the Rhine, Elbe, Danube, and Oder Rivers and the Kiel Canal. Confident, no doubt, that a plebiscite held under such conditions would be overwhelmingly favorable, Hitler called for elections in March, 1936. On this occasion 98.5 per cent of the eligible voters—nearly 45,000,000—went to the polls. As a matter of fact, Nazi storm troops saw to it that the electorate was mobilized. After the votes were counted, it was announced that 99 per cent had been cast in favor of the Führer's foreign policy.

Although the Nazi foreign policy undoubtedly had emancipated and strengthened Germany as a military power, it had had an unfortunate effect upon her international position. Before 1933 both Italy and Russia had been inclined to support Germany, and even Great Britain had been sympathetic with German policies. By 1936, on the other hand, the Nazi drive against Communists and the Nazi program for eastern expansion had driven Russia into a Franco-Soviet military alliance; the Nazi attempt to absorb Austria had alienated Mussolini and facilitated a Franco-Italian *rapprochement;* and the Nazi rearmament program had alarmed Great Britain and forced her into what was practically an Anglo-Franco-Belgian alliance against Germany. In 1936 Germany stood practically isolated among the great powers of Europe.

But Hitler soon removed the chief cause of friction between Mussolini and himself. In July, 1936, Germany signed an agreement with Austria recognizing the independence of the latter and pledging herself not to interfere in Austria's domestic political life. Thereafter Mussolini and Hitler co-operated to a large extent in their foreign policies. Germany joined Italy in aiding the Spanish Insurgents, and Italy in turn supported Germany by signing the anti-Comintern pact which Germany and Japan concluded in November, 1936. The Rome-Berlin-Tokyo Axis was thus created.

Despite the almost unanimous support which Hitler had received in the plebiscite of 1936, however, unanimity on matters of policy did not prevail within Germany. Although the merciless purge of June, 1934, had eliminated one Left group which had threatened to embarrass the Führer, in the succeeding years another Left group—with which apparently Hitler was this time largely in sympathy—had developed. Led by Heinrich Himmler, chief of the *Schutzstaffeln* and of the Gestapo, Joseph Goebbels, minister of propaganda, and Joachim von Ribbentrop, German ambassador to Great Britain, this Left group advocated a more revolutionary policy both at home and abroad. They favored the pursuit of more active policies in behalf of the Germans in Austria and Czechoslovakia, urged that more help be given General Franco in Spain, and wished to see the Rome-Berlin Axis

20 See pages 459–460.

and the anti-Comintern pact more forcefully implemented. In internal affairs the Leftists wanted an intensification of the anti-Jewish campaign and the extension of the control of the Nazi Party over the army. Most of these policies the Right group—supported by the conservatives of the general staff and of the foreign office and by the great industrial and financial leaders—strongly opposed.

Furthermore, the military looked upon Field Marshal von Blomberg, Hitler's war minister, as a political soldier, too closely associated with the Nazi Party to be good for the army. A clash between Hitler and the conservative army leaders was precipitated when General von Fritsch, the commander-in-chief, demanded that the war minister be retired because, contrary to the army traditions of "caste and class," he had married the daughter of a humble carpenter. At the same time Fritsch made other demands—that the army should have a status above politics, that it should not be subjected to the Nazi anti-Christian doctrines, and that the government should restrict its "activist" foreign policy. Thus the question was raised: was the army to be under the control of the Nazi Party or was it to stand above domestic politics?

Although the military were strong enough to force the removal of Field Marshal von Blomberg, Hitler struck back. On February 4, 1938, he suddenly dismissed General von Fritsch and thirteen senior generals in the army and air force, and announced that he himself had assumed "personal and direct command over all the armed forces." At the same time he removed from the foreign ministry Baron von Neurath, who had held that position since before the Nazis came into power, and appointed in his place the 100 per cent Nazi, Joachim von Ribbentrop. The "conservative" ambassadors to Italy, Japan, and Austria were also recalled. By this purge Hitler definitely strengthened the Nazi control of the Reich's army and foreign policy.

Evidence that the Left group was in control was soon forthcoming. On February 12 came the famous interview between Hitler and Chancellor Schuschnigg of Austria in which the former by threats forced the latter to admit Austrian Nazis into his government. One month later came the overthrow of Schuschnigg's government and the absorption of Austria into the Third Reich,[21] which was thus increased in population to 74,000,000. The "activist" policy seemed to be highly successful; one more objective in Hitler's announced policy had been attained. On April 10, 1938, another plebiscite revealed that more than 99 per cent of the voters in Germany loyally supported Hitler.

With the German people thus apparently lending their support, the Left-group Nazis continued their aggressive foreign policy in the succeed-

[21] See pages 476–478.

ing months. In September, 1938, they precipitated the Munich crisis,[22] as a result of which the Reich annexed the Sudetenland. Six months later, in March, 1939, Hitler destroyed Czechoslovakia altogether.[23] Bohemia and Moravia were for all practical purposes absorbed by the Reich, and Slovakia was made a dependent ally. In the same month, too, Hitler "redeemed" Memel by forcing Lithuania to cede that city to Germany.

Doubtless emboldened by these successes and confident of the superiority of the German military forces and *Luftwaffe,* Hitler and his Nazi associates next determined to continue the Reich's *Drang nach Osten* at the expense of Poland. Despite the warnings of Great Britain and France that they would enter the war if Germany attacked Poland, in September, 1939, the Nazis launched an attack against that state.[24] By so doing they precipitated the Second World War, which eventually brought upon the German homeland destruction worse than any suffered by that country since the Thirty Years' War.

[22] See pages 478–484.
[23] See pages 485–486.
[24] See pages 494–495.

Chapter XI

GREAT BRITAIN AND IRELAND

THE European great power which wavered least in its loyalty to the liberal tradition during the years following the First World War was Great Britain, which, more than any other country in Europe, displayed a deep attachment to political democracy and a continued concern for social justice. But the quest of the latter was made particularly difficult after the war because Great Britain found it impossible to increase her foreign trade to its prewar level. The chronic unemployment which resulted from this failure became such a serious problem that it repeatedly affected the policies of the British government both at home and abroad. Like a scarlet thread it can be traced through the history of the postwar period.

Trade Decline and Unemployment

For a time after the armistice, thanks to the great demand for commodities in European countries long isolated from the rest of the world by the war, British trade prospered. But toward the close of 1920 the business boom collapsed, and in the next year exports fell off by about one half. During the succeeding years, though some improvement occurred, Great Britain's foreign trade never reached its prewar figure.

Various circumstances accounted for this decline. Great Britain's foreign trade was obviously dependent upon world and especially European conditions. But the war had impoverished the world's purchasing power so that, after the first spurt in buying, purchases were greatly curtailed. The situation was further aggravated by the depreciation of so many continental currencies. At the very time when Great Britain was trying to deflate her own currency, most European countries were resorting to inflation. This situation worked to the great disadvantage of British manufacturers, who were forced to compete in foreign markets with goods produced where labor was relatively cheaper because of the depreciated currency in which it was paid. Furthermore, the war had ended in the creation of numerous new states, and each, led by an excessive national zeal, began to erect "political dams across the economic streams of Europe." National tariffs inevitably interfered with the flow of British goods to their accustomed markets.

The British coal industry was particularly hard hit. In prewar years Great Britain had been accustomed to export some 62,500,000 tons of coal annually, but the rapid development of new sources of power—hydroelectric plants, petroleum oil, and low-temperature carbonization of coal and lignite—decreased the demand for raw coal. Germany's delivery of coal to France and Italy as part of her reparations payments further lessened the demand for British coal. But the staple industries were also seriously affected, in this case chiefly because the spread of the Industrial Revolution was depriving British industries of long-monopolized markets. The expansion of cotton manufacturing in India, China, and Japan, for example, was seriously felt in Lancashire. Outside Europe, Britain's exports of cotton cloth in the postwar years were only about half as great as before 1914. Old plants and antiquated methods, furthermore, handicapped many British industries in meeting competition.

Because of the decline in export trade, factories were forced to curtail production. The volume of British shipping naturally decreased, and the demand for new ships for a time largely disappeared. The important shipbuilding industry was therefore also adversely affected. But the welfare of most of the British was bound up with industry and commerce, for only 6 per cent of the people of England were directly dependent upon agriculture for a living. Nearly 80 per cent (1921) of the population was urban in England and Wales. Anything affecting the industrial or commercial life of the country, therefore, was bound to affect to a greater or less degree the majority of the British people.

The reduction in British foreign trade was even more serious at this time because in the decade after 1913 the total population of Great Britain had increased by about two million. The natural increase in the number of workers which this brought was further augmented by contingents of women who during the war had entered the industrial field, and by part of the former "leisure class" who had been driven, by the increased cost of living and the relative decline in their incomes, to join the ranks of the workers. With the collapse of Britain's commerce in 1921, therefore, came a rapid increase in unemployment. At the beginning of the year over one million were out of work; by the middle of the year the number had considerably more than doubled; and in subsequent years it rose as high as three million. The various British governments as they succeeded one another were inevitably compelled to wrestle with this unemployment problem.

The Lloyd George Coalition

Great Britain emerged from the First World War with a coalition government. The exigencies of the war had brought a reorganization of the government in 1915, when Asquith had become the head of a coalition ministry composed of representatives of the Liberal, Conservative, and Labor parties. In 1916 a further change had occurred when Lloyd George forced Asquith out of the premiership and himself assumed the office. Politics had been "adjourned" in Great Britain for the duration of the war, so that the dissolution of Parliament which should regularly have occurred in 1915 had been postponed. When the armistice was signed, therefore, eight years had elapsed since the last election. It was high time for the electorate to be consulted. Parliament was at once dissolved, and new elections were set for December 14, 1918.

On a platform which called for the punishment of German "war criminals," the full payment of the Allied war costs by the defeated powers, the protection of "essential" British industries, the prevention of dumping in Great Britain of goods produced by cheap foreign labor, the improvement of housing and labor conditions, and the settlement of the Irish question, Lloyd George appealed for the continuation of the war coalition. Asquith, however, denounced the coalition and entered the lists at the head of a party known as the Independent Liberals, and the Labor Party, declining longer to participate in the coalition, waged a campaign to increase its own parliamentary strength.

The elections of 1918 were particularly notable, since they provided the first opportunity for nearly 8,000,000 new voters to register their views. Earlier in the year Great Britain had taken another great stride toward political democracy by passing the Representation of the People Act. Aside from certain temporary provisions this act conferred a parliamentary vote on all men twenty-one years of age who could qualify by six months' residence or by the occupation of business premises, and on all women thirty years of age who were local government electors or wives of such electors. The act also provided for the redistribution of representatives in accordance with the principle of single-member constituencies of approximately equal size, and the limiting of an elector's vote to not more than two constituencies. The number of electors participating in this election, therefore, was far greater than in any other in the previous history of Great Britain.

The result of the voting was an overwhelming victory for the Lloyd George coalition. Asquith's Independent Liberals managed to capture only 28 seats, but Labor increased its representation to 63. Lloyd George therefore had a large majority over all opposition groups. But the character of the majority must have given the Liberal leader pause, for it was made up five to two of Conservatives. In the reconstitution of the ministry in January, 1919, this fact was reflected. The proportion of Conservatives became so great that the coalition ceased to be predominantly Liberal in tone, and Great Britain was presented with the anomalous spectacle of an extreme Liberal at the head of a government consisting largely of Conservatives.

A number of steps were taken by Lloyd George's government in an effort to meet the unemployment situation. The Unemployment Insurance Act was modified to give greater relief, and the government itself contributed millions in "doles" to the unemployed. Such measures, however, could at best be only temporary palliatives. They did not strike at the root of the evil. Lloyd George therefore advocated the resumption of trade relations with Soviet Russia in order to rehabilitate British trade and industry. On March 16, 1921, a trade agreement was signed with Russia providing for the resumption of trade and commerce between the two countries pending the conclusion of a formal general peace treaty which should regulate their economic and political relations in the future. Later in the year the Safeguarding of Industries Act was passed. This measure was designed to protect key industries which would be vital in the event of future war, and to protect British workmen against the competition of cheap foreign commodities. For these purposes the act provided for a 33⅓ per cent duty to safeguard certain special industries, and for a tax on imports from countries with depreciated currencies. This partial abandonment of Great Britain's traditional policy of free trade aroused much opposition throughout the country.

Meanwhile, as the years passed, Lloyd George discovered that the Conservative portion of his coalition was becoming restless. The effect of the partial adoption of the old Conservative policy of protection in 1921 was nullified by his conclusion late in that same year of the Anglo-Irish treaty recognizing the Irish Free State.[1] Conservative leaders, notably Bonar Law and Stanley Baldwin, eager to secure freedom of action for their party, quietly fostered a movement looking toward secession. Finally, in October, 1922, the Conservative Party declared its independence and decided to enter the approaching electoral campaign as a separate party with its own leader and its own program.

With the defection of the Conservatives the coalition government was doomed. Lloyd George immediately resigned, and Bonar Law was called upon to head a new ministry. The government which the latter organized was drawn entirely from the ranks of the Conservatives and was the first homogeneous ministry since 1915. Parliament was dissolved, and new elections were called for November, 1922. In the ensuing campaign Lloyd

[1] See page 293.

George led what was known as the National Liberal Party, but Asquith and his Independent Liberals continued their active opposition and held aloof. The real struggle was between the Conservatives and the Laborites. Fear of the supposed radical tendencies of the Labor Party and hope of obtaining once more a one-party parliamentary government both helped to place the Conservatives in power with a majority over all opposition parties. Although the Conservatives won a great electoral victory, the achievement of the Labor Party was of even greater note. With the 142 seats which the Labor Party now controlled it became the second largest group in Parliament and therefore stepped into the position of "His Majesty's Opposition."

Free Trade or Protection?

The chief task of the Conservative leaders when they assumed control of the government was to formulate some program which would solve the unemployment problem. In May, 1923, Bonar Law resigned the premiership because of ill health, and was succeeded by Stanley Baldwin. The latter, haunted by the specter of unemployment, resolved that some drastic step must be taken to meet the situation. While he was in this state of mind, the extremists of his party apparently suggested protection as a solution. Without consulting his party as a whole, Baldwin suddenly announced his determination to introduce a protective tariff. But the Conservatives had taken office with the general understanding that they would embark upon no aggressive or radical program without further consulting the electorate. Such a radical departure from the long-accepted British policy of free trade, therefore, called for an appeal to the people, and Baldwin, recognizing this, dissolved Parliament and went to the country on the issue of protection. In order to relieve British unemployment and maintain a reasonable level of wages for British workers, he demanded the defense of the home market by means of a tariff on manufactured goods.

The Conservatives argued that the whole world was erecting tariff barriers against British goods and that British duties might be utilized as a means of forcing reductions in these foreign tariffs. They asserted that the British Empire was economically sufficient unto itself and advocated Joseph Chamberlain's earlier scheme of imperial preference. They promised to keep raw materials on the free list, to place no tax on such foodstuffs as wheat and meat, and to reduce duties on tea and sugar. The opposition parties argued, on the other hand, that in an exporting country like Great Britain protection could not cure chronic unemployment. Among the Liberals personalities were subordinated in the face of Baldwin's attack upon their cherished free-trade principle, and a reconciliation, at least superficial, was brought about between the followers of Asquith and the Welsh leader. Although as a result of the election of 1923 the Conservatives still retained the largest number of seats, their former safe majority over all opposing parties was transformed into a decided minority. Labor maintained its position as the chief opposition party by raising its total representation in the Commons to 192. The reunited Liberals stood third with 158. A majority of the electorate appeared to favor the traditional policy of free trade.

Britain's First Labor Government

The outcome of the election entailed a change in the government. Clearly Baldwin had been rejected on the platform of protection, but on the other hand no single party now controlled a majority. Either a coalition or a minority government therefore became necessary. But none of the parties appeared anxious to merge its identity in a coalition again. The final outcome was the resignation of the Baldwin ministry and the elevation of Ramsay MacDonald (January 22, 1924) to the premiership as the head of Great Britain's first Labor government, the highest point yet reached by Labor in its rapid rise from a minor parliamentary group with only twenty-nine seats in 1906.

But the change in government entailed no radical departure from well-established British policies by the introduction of anything suggestive of Bolshevism, for, in the words of MacDonald, "Our Labor movement has never had the least inclination to try short cuts to the millennium." In fact, one of the reasons why the Labor Party had increased so rapidly was the growing recognition by the British people of the essentially constitutional character of the movement. A second reason why nothing radical was to be expected in the way of legislation was the fact that Labor was dependent upon one of the other parties for the support necessary to enact any measure. Consequently Labor was compelled to defer its more far-reaching proposals such as the capital levy, for lack of an adequate majority. MacDonald's government was therefore bound to cut a rather sorry figure in domestic affairs, especially since the economic situation was largely out of the power of any British government to control.

The Laborites were almost immediately confronted with an epidemic of serious strikes, but by their firmness in handling the strikers, who came from their own ranks, they gained the confidence and respect of the country at large. This confidence was retained by their handling of the fiscal problem, in which nothing especially radical was undertaken. The tax on cheap amusements was repealed, and, in spite of the vigorous protests of the protected interests, the protective duties inaugurated by Lloyd George were abolished. No attempt was made to introduce a capital levy. In ac-

THE FIRST BRITISH LABOR PREMIER

Ramsay MacDonald

cordance with their platform a bill was passed providing a scheme for building inexpensive houses with the aid of government subsidies. They proved to be unable to lessen noticeably the number of unemployed, however.

It was in the realm of foreign affairs that MacDonald achieved his outstanding success. His most spectacular move was his unconditional *de jure* recognition of the Soviet government of Russia on February 1, 1924. This was in full accord with his earlier pronouncement that the first step in the process of settling affairs with Russia should be recognition, which was the key for reopening the markets of that country to British goods. The immediate sequel of this move was the Anglo-Russian conference, which opened in London in April, 1924, in an attempt to negotiate a general treaty of amity and commerce to replace the trade agreement of 1921, and to effect a settlement of the claims arising out of the Soviet government's repudiation of Russia's debts and the confiscation of private property. Two treaties were finally drafted and signed,[2] the immediate effect of which would be merely the favorable treatment of British goods in Russian markets.

The Russian treaties were immediately attacked not only by the Conservatives but even by Lloyd George, who had been responsible for the first trade agreement of 1921. In fact, the desertion of MacDonald by the Liberals at this time was the beginning of the end. A little later he was again attacked by them because his government had abandoned the prosecution of a Communist accused of inciting British soldiers to mutiny. Without a majority to support him, MacDonald dissolved Parliament and appealed to the electorate. For the third time in two years the British voters were called upon for a decision. In this campaign both the Conservatives and the Liberals directed their attacks against Labor. The latter's prospects were injured by the publication, shortly before the election, of a letter purporting to be from Zinoviev, the head of the Third International, urging British Communists to prepare the way for a revolution in Great Britain. Moderates were frightened by the specter of what might follow if the detested "socialists" were returned to power. At the same time many workers were disappointed by the continuance of unemployment even under a Labor government.

In the election of 1924, although Labor piled up a total of 5,500,000 popular votes, its parliamentary representation was reduced to 155. Since the Liberals elected only 36 members, the Conservatives were swept back into

[2] In a treaty of commerce and navigation Russia gave unconditional most-favored-nation treatment to British goods. In a general treaty she admitted liability for the claims of British bondholders and promised to negotiate with them, and agreed that such other claims as were established by a joint commission should be embodied in a subsequent treaty. The British government for its part agreed that, as soon as the British claims had been settled by a subsequent treaty, it would submit to Parliament a proposal to guarantee a loan to the Soviet government.

power with a top-heavy parliamentary majority of over two hundred, though they obtained less than a majority of the popular vote. With such a Conservative majority in the House, Baldwin of course returned to Downing Street, and MacDonald stepped down to his earlier position of leader of the opposition.

Five Years of Conservative Government

But the change in government brought no immediate improvement in Britain's economic situation. During the ensuing year the production of coal, iron ore, and pig iron, the basic industries of the kingdom, remained considerably below the prewar figure. In the hope of "safeguarding employment" and, incidentally, of satisfying certain British industrial interests, Baldwin returned to the tariff policy inaugurated by Lloyd George and afterward repealed by the Labor government. Over the protests of the opposition, who declared that he was violating his campaign pledges, a plan for partial protection was enacted.

The coal industry, in which the industrial depression was most pronounced, profited little from this scheme, however. The price of coal continued to fall, and the operators, in order to cut the cost of production, asked the miners to lengthen the working day from seven to eight hours and to accept a cut in wages. The miners refused to agree to these proposals, whereupon the operators availed themselves of a provision of the existing wage agreement to terminate it on July 31, 1925. In order to prevent a coal strike the government then subsidized the industry until May 1, 1926, pending a permanent settlement. Before that date a royal commission under Sir Herbert Samuel made an investigation of the coal industry. In its report it stated that three fourths of the coal raised was being produced at a loss. It recommended national ownership of the mines [3] and an extensive reorganization of the industry, including the closing of the pits which were permanently impossible of operation at a profit. It declared that the coal industry was facing disaster and that, to restore the industry to solvency, wage reductions were necessary.

When the mine operators notified the miners that the existing wage agreement would end on May 1, the latter decided to strike. The Trades Union Congress, in order to assist the miners, thereupon called a sympathetic strike in certain vital industries, including the transport services and the printing trade. In popular belief Great Britain faced a "general strike,"

[3] Eventually, in April, 1937, Prime Minister Baldwin announced that the government had agreed to pay the 4300 mine owners of the country £66,450,000 in return for the extinction of their claims to all future royalties. This nationalization of coal royalties was expected to clear the way for a systematic reorganization of the coal industry by a central government authority.

but this was hardly the case. Less than half of the six million trade-union members were called out, and it was specifically ordered that work should not cease in electric and gas, sanitary, and health and food services. The government at once declared a state of emergency and issued an appeal for volunteers to maintain the essential services. The generous response to this appeal more than any other factor contributed to the failure of the sympathetic strike.

The "general strike" lasted only nine days. On May 12 the Trades Union Congress announced the decision to end it with the understanding that negotiations would be resumed regarding the wages of miners. These, however, resulted in no agreement. The operators demanded lower wages; the miners refused to return to work. In July Parliament passed the Mines Act providing for an eight-hour day in the coal industry, but the act produced no coal, and it became necessary to import large quantities from Germany and the United States. Finally, after more than seven months, the strike came officially to an end on November 19, 1926, with the complete surrender of the miners' unions. Their submission was forced by the exhaustion of their resources and by their inability to prevent numbers of miners from returning to work. With winter coming on, longer hours and lower wages seemed preferable to no work at all.

The Conservative Party, never particularly sympathetic with trade unions or the labor movement, availed itself of the state of public opinion and the exhaustion of labor after the great strike of 1926 to pass the Trades Disputes and Trades Union Act in the following year. By the terms of this law, a general strike became illegal, picketing was forbidden, and no member might be disciplined by a trade union for refusing to participate in an illegal strike. The Trades Dispute Act of 1906 was repealed in so far as it exempted trade unions from legal suit, and trade-union funds might be enjoined by the attorney-general. A blow was struck at the Labor Party by including a provision that trade unions might make political levies on their members only if the latter gave specific permission in writing. Formerly the law had stated that such levies might be made unless a member formally protested.

In 1928 Baldwin carried out his campaign pledge to extend the ballot to all women on the same age basis as to men. Another five million voters, it was estimated, were thus added to the registers. An attempt to reorganize the House of Lords so as to increase its strength and importance had to be abandoned, however, in the face of the strong opposition which was aroused. A number of measures of social legislation were enacted, the most important being the act for widows', orphans', and old-age pensions. Based on the principle that the state, the employer, and the worker should each contribute to the fund, it provided that every insured worker should receive a pension at the age of sixty-five, and that, if he died before that age, his widow and children should receive pensions.

In foreign affairs the Conservative government largely continued the spirit of co-operation and conciliation so happily inaugurated by the Labor premier. Only in respect to Russia was the latter's foreign policy completely reversed. Baldwin refused to submit to Parliament the treaties which the Labor government had negotiated, so that both lapsed, and the trade agreement of 1921 remained the basis of relations between Russia and Great Britain. On May 12, 1927, in the belief that certain secret documents which had disappeared from the British War Office had come into Russian possession, the government raided the offices of Arcos, Ltd., the headquarters of Russia's trading agency in Great Britain. Although the lost documents were not discovered, the government declared that considerable evidence was found of Russian military espionage in Great Britain and of other revolutionary activities in the British Empire. As a result, Parliament voted to sever all relations with the Soviet government.

Meanwhile, despite the establishment of many new industries in southern England and the noticeable shift of industrial population into that region, and despite the fact that London in general was prosperous, the unemployment problem continued unsolved. The year 1928 saw a considerable increase in the number out of work, and ended with close to 2,000,000 unemployed—the highest number since the worst days of 1921–1922. The unparalleled distress and suffering, especially in the coal fields, aroused public generosity to supplement government grants in the work of alleviation.

So far as the government was concerned, the chief measures taken to meet the unsatisfactory economic condition of the country were designed to safeguard certain British industries from foreign competition and to relieve them from the burden of local taxation. By 1929 industries producing motorcars, silk and artificial yarns, clocks and watches, cinematograph films, gloves, cutlery, china, and rubber tires and tubes were being safeguarded or, as critics asserted, "protected by the back door." By the reform in local taxation the great basic industries were freed from the oppressive burden which they declared was strangling them. As a consequence of the new legislation they were relieved to the extent of 75 per cent of the local taxes. In general, however, Baldwin advocated a policy of *laissez faire* toward business as a cure for unemployment.

Inevitably the problem of unemployment and rehabilitation of British trade was again the outstanding issue in the general election of May, 1929. "The great need of the day," declared one influential journal, "is a positive policy for dealing with unemployment by promoting industrial recovery as well as by providing immediate work. The party that has the best unemployment policy deserves to be the next Government." This fact the leaders of all three parties well realized, and in the campaign to win public favor each stated its position in respect to this problem. The solution put forward by the Liberal Party was national works on a colossal scale, including roads and bridges, telephone and electrical development, land drainage, London passenger traffic, and housing. This program, Lloyd George asserted, would reduce the terrible figures of unemployment to normal proportions in a single year.

Labor, which was hopeful of obtaining a clear majority over both of the other parties, offered a much more extensive and detailed program. The Labor Party advocated nationalization of the coal, transport, and power industries and of life insurance; the fostering of the migration of miners into other districts and other occupations, and the prohibition of the recruitment of adults from other industries into mining; the immediate raising of the school-leaving age; and a great national scheme for development of electrical power. To the workingmen it specifically promised the repeal of the Mines Act (1926) and the Trades Disputes Act (1927), the creation of a superannuation scheme for aged miners, a forty-eight-hour week, and steeply graded inheritance taxes and high supertaxes on the rich. The Conservative Party was disposed to stand on its record and to appeal to the conservative electorate. "Safety first!" was its slogan, and it asked the voters to support it as the defender of the constitution against the threat of the general strike and against the perils of socialism, and as the only party which could secure stable conditions and ordered progress along sound, practical lines.

The elections of 1929 brought an increase in Labor's representation in the Commons from 160 to 289, while the Conservatives declined from 396 to 259. Owing to the fact that the Liberal Party elected 58 candidates, however, no party controlled a majority. But it was apparent that the Conservatives had been rejected, and Stanley Baldwin at once resigned the premiership. On June 5, 1929, Ramsay MacDonald for the second time accepted the king's invitation to form a government.

The Second Labor Government

The second Labor government, like the first, was handicapped in carrying out its domestic policies by dependence upon either the Liberals or the Conservatives for support. But of the various pledges which the Labor leader had made regarding domestic legislation, he was able to carry out a few. A widows' pension bill was enacted to extend a weekly pension to approximately 500,000 widows unprovided for by the original measure passed by Baldwin's government. A new unemployment insurance act was passed with provisions designed to care for 1,000,000 unemployed at any time. A bill for the rehabilitation of the coal-mining industry became law, providing for price-fixing agreements, compulsory marketing schemes, and the possibility of compulsory amalgamation of mining enterprises in the same area. A bill for raising the compulsory school age was introduced, but in the face of the determined opposition of the Catholics, whose schools could not accommodate the increased numbers, the measure was dropped. Similarly, an amendment to the Trades Disputes Act was introduced to restore to Labor its privileges under the act of 1906, but again MacDonald was unable to carry his measure through Parliament.

In foreign affairs MacDonald returned to his earlier policy toward Soviet Russia. In December, 1929, full diplomatic relations were resumed with the Soviet government, on the latter's promise to abstain from subversive propaganda within the British Empire. This step led in April, 1930, to an Anglo-Russian trade treaty which provided for most-favored-nation treatment in commerce between the two countries. The treaty further stipulated that the general offices of the Russian trading corporation in Great Britain should be inviolate, thus obviating the possibility of another raid like that on the offices of Arcos, Ltd., in 1927. Finally, the treaty provided that the British government would guarantee a credit of $150,000,000 to be employed in financing Russian purchases in Great Britain during the ensuing two years.

Meanwhile, general business conditions in Great Britain improved not at all. Exports of manufactured goods declined in 1929. In 1930 the iron and steel trade fell to the lowest point in four years, and the depression in cotton manufacturing was considered the worst since the American Civil War. In 1930 the country's foreign trade declined by over $1,650,000,000. Naturally, these figures were reflected in the growth of unemployment. When Labor took office the unemployed numbered approximately 1,000,-000; within a year the number had increased to over 1,700,000; and early in 1931 it reached the highest point since the war with more than 2,600,000 out of work. The government was, in general, helpless to remedy the economic situation. It did, however, take care of those without work. It not only contributed tens of millions of dollars, as its share, to the unemployment insurance fund, but advanced hundreds of millions more in the form of loans to the fund, which went steadily further into debt.

The severe drain upon the British budget, resulting from increasing expenditures and decreasing tax receipts, became evident when the fiscal year 1929–1930 closed with a deficit instead of the contemplated surplus. The deficit in the following year was still greater, and that for the year 1931–1932 appeared likely to reach $600,000,000. The prospect of such a seriously unbalanced budget caused alarm both within and without the kingdom. Gold began to flow in large amounts from Great Britain to the Continent.

London, which served as a bank of deposit for foreign funds, had over a long period of years built up the tradition of meeting every obligation promptly and in full. But on this occasion it was fatally handicapped by the "standstill" agreement following the Hoover moratorium,[4] which temporarily "froze" large sums that had been loaned by the Bank of England to Germany and other countries. With the British supply of liquid credit thus seriously impaired by inability to call in many short-term loans, it was imperative that steps be taken to increase confidence in British financial integrity.

At this point came the report of the May Committee of financial experts which had been appointed to make recommendations to the chancellor of the exchequer regarding the budget. In order definitely to balance the budget, the experts suggested some slight additional taxation, but particularly recommended severe reductions in expenditures for pensions, salaries, defense, public works, and social services. Laborites immediately denounced the report on the ground that approximately 90 per cent of the reductions suggested would be at the expense of the classes from which the Labor Party drew its chief support. Economies such as these, they claimed, did not constitute "a general sacrifice." They demanded, instead, that the deficit be met chiefly by increased taxation. When Ramsay MacDonald and Philip Snowden, chancellor of the exchequer, decided to accept the experts' recommendations, the Labor Party split, and the Labor government was forced to resign (August 24, 1931).

The National Governments

MacDonald, apparently placing loyalty to Britain's welfare above loyalty to party pledges, undertook to organize a new ministry. For the third time he became premier, this time in a coalition of Laborites, Conservatives, and Liberals which became known as the National government. Philip Snowden, J. H. Thomas, and Lord Sankey followed their leader into the new government, and for this step they and MacDonald were read out of the Labor Party, which chose Arthur Henderson as its official leader.

In September, 1931, Snowden submitted a supplementary budget which in general followed the recommendations of the May Committee. Drastic economies were effected in national expenditures by decreasing the amount spent on social services, on army, navy, and air forces, and on government salaries. More than half of the retrenchment was made by reductions in unemployment insurance payments and by increases in unemployment insurance premiums. Meanwhile, the flow of gold from London had continued. Fear that Great Britain might not be able to balance her budget,

[4] See page 175.

that she might be adversely affected by the critical financial situation in central Europe, that she might have to abandon the gold standard, that a new election might bring further instability, led many foreigners and even Britishers themselves to sell sterling. Speedy action was needed, and on September 21 Parliament suspended the gold standard.

In October the National government went to the country in a general election. This occasioned a split in the Liberal Party, for Lloyd George and a number of his free-trade followers refused to give the National government their support. On the other hand, Sir Herbert Samuel, acting leader of the Liberals, and Sir John Simon, who had long been restless under Lloyd George's leadership, both threw their lot in with the Nationalists and led what were called the National Liberals. A few of the Laborites, generally referred to as National Laborites, gave their support to MacDonald. The election, consequently, was a three-cornered struggle between the Nationalists (Conservatives, National Liberals, and National Laborites), the Laborites, and the free-trade Liberals.

The outcome of the election of 1931 was an amazing triumph for MacDonald's National government, which received 554 seats in a House of Commons of 615. This huge total was composed of 471 Conservatives, 68 National Liberals, 13 National Laborites, and 2 independents. The 267 seats which the Labor Party had held before dissolution were cut to 52. Lloyd George's free-trade Liberals captured only four seats. With the Conservatives so overwhelmingly returned it was thought that Stanley Baldwin might head a new government, but instead he gave MacDonald free rein to choose his ministers. The latter's fourth cabinet, as finally organized in November, 1931, consisted of eleven Conservatives, five National Liberals, and four National Laborites.

Three major domestic problems confronted the National government in the years that followed. The first was that of maintaining a balanced national budget. The year 1931–1932 closed with a balance in the treasury, and the following year would have done likewise except for the war-debt payment to the United States for which no provision had been made in the budget.[5] The next four years, however, closed with surpluses. At the same time taxes were slightly reduced, and the reductions in unemployment insurance and in government salaries were gradually restored. When the budget for 1936–1937 was introduced, however, the trend toward lower taxation was reversed. Germany's rearmament, Italy's aggressive policy in Africa and in the Mediterranean, and the apparent break-down of collective security compelled the government to inaugurate an extensive defense program. In the so-called defense or rearmament budget, therefore, tax increases were made, but, despite considerable increases in taxes in the

---

[5] The government had expected the Hoover moratorium to be extended.

following years, huge expenditures for armaments resulted in unbalanced budgets. By 1938 the national debt had risen to the all-time high of £8,000,000,000.

The second problem with which the government wrestled was that of reducing the country's adverse balance of trade. A committee of the cabinet, appointed to consider ways and means, concluded that imports into the country must be restricted, and recommended a 10-per-cent tariff on a very wide range of manufactured and semi-manufactured articles. The new tariff was finally approved, and on March 1, 1932, after some eighty years of free trade, Great Britain again became a protectionist country. As a result of this step there followed a considerable decrease in British imports.

In the matter of increasing British exports, one step had already been taken which it was hoped would help, namely, the abandonment of the gold standard with the subsequent depreciation of the British pound. This move was expected to lower the cost of production in Great Britain and thus enable British goods to compete on more favorable terms in world markets. In the hope of increasing still further the demand for British goods, the government sent a delegation to the Imperial Economic Conference which met at Ottawa during the summer of 1932. At this conference Great Britain made a number of treaties with various parts of her empire, as a result of which she gained slight advantages for some of her manufactured goods at the expense of non-empire countries. But the advantages which Great Britain extended to the dominions—particularly the duty on foreign wheat—aroused opposition in the cabinet and led in September, 1932, to the resignation of Lord Snowden,[6] Sir Herbert Samuel, and a number of others.

In subsequent years, by using the British protective tariff as a basis for bargaining, new reciprocal commercial agreements were negotiated with a number of countries for the purpose of increasing British exports, and these agreements were further supplemented by a system of import quotas designed to assure exports to some home industries and to control imports in favor of others. At the same time, to strengthen British business at home and to enable it to compete more efficiently abroad, the government adopted policies some of which strongly resembled those of the NRA and the AAA in the United States. Obligatory agreements to fix prices and wages, to control marketing, to abandon inefficient plants and out-of-date equipment, and to set up machinery for the self-regulation of industry were instigated or encouraged by the government. Financial assistance was granted to aid in the rationalization of some of the backward industries. Agricul-

[6] In 1931 Philip Snowden was created Viscount Snowden of Ickornshaw. and took a seat in the House of Lords.

tural subsidies, processing taxes, protective tariffs, and import quotas were used to preserve the home markets against foreign competition. In addition, the whole recovery movement was accelerated by an extensive slum-clearance and housing program. In the summer of 1935 the index of general business activity reached the 1929 level. But the new depression of 1937 had its effect, with the result that the adverse trade balances in that year and in 1938 were the largest in British history.

The third major problem which faced the government during these years was the perennial one of unemployment. Despite all the efforts of the government to improve the situation, at the end of 1932 the number of unemployed had risen to the highest point reached at any time since the war, over 3,000,000 being out of work. Improvement came in the succeeding years, however. By 1937 the number of unemployed had fallen below 1,500,000, but the depression of that year, referred to above, reversed the trend again. Not until men were absorbed in large numbers by expanding war industries and by the national military conscription act was the number of British unemployed materially reduced. Before the outbreak of the Second World War, in certain "depressed areas" in South Wales, in the north of England, and in Scotland the situation remained particularly bad.

Politically, the position of the National government appeared to be weakening in 1934. In by-elections the Labor Party was usually able to reduce the immense majorities received by the National government in 1931. Probably most spectacular was the triumph of the Labor Party in the London County Council election in March, when Labor won a majority for the first time in its history, and displaced the Conservatives who had controlled the Council for a generation. In November Labor repeated its victory by extending its control from four to fifteen of London's twenty-eight boroughs. In other parts of the kingdom somewhat similar shifts in electoral strength were evident, so that it appeared that the Labor Party would be a much stronger contender for power in the next parliamentary election than it had been in 1931.

On June 7, 1935, Ramsay MacDonald submitted his resignation because of his ill health, and was succeeded by Stanley Baldwin, head of the Conservative Party, which had dominated the National government. Four months later, the new premier cleverly seized upon a critical international situation to retain control of the government for another term of years. A huge unofficial peace ballot taken earlier in the year had showed that at least 10,000,000 voters favored the League of Nations and the use of economic sanctions against a warring nation. These millions might be expected to look with favor upon a government which had apparently dared to take the lead at Geneva against Italy's Ethiopian venture.[7] Moreover,

7 See page 464.

the Labor Party had just approved the use of sanctions, but at the cost of a split in the party and the loss of three of its outstanding leaders. Thus the most serious rival of the Conservatives was in no good position to wage an effective campaign. On October 25 Parliament was dissolved, and an election was called for November 14, 1935.

As was expected, the election resulted in an easy victory for the National government, although its previous majority was reduced. The Conservatives, however, themselves had a majority of more than 150 over all the other parties combined. As was also expected, the Labor Party increased its representation considerably, adding nearly 100 seats to the number it had had before the election. The Liberal Party secured only 20 seats. The situation in the House of Commons again came to resemble the two-party system which most Englishmen prefer. Although both Ramsay MacDonald and his son, Malcolm, were defeated, they were included in the new cabinet, which remained very much as it had been before the election.

Meanwhile, during the summer of 1935, various celebrations had been held in Great Britain to commemorate the twenty-fifth anniversary of George V's accession to the throne. The king held a high place in the affections of his people both because of his recognition of the limitations of his position as a constitutional ruler and because of his modesty, patriotism, and readiness to perform the duties which fell to him. During his Silver Jubilee the kingdom and empire had united to show their high esteem for the monarch. Not many months after the completion of the festivities connected with his jubilee, however, the king was taken ill, and a few days later, on January 20, 1936, he died at the age of seventy. His eldest son, the former Prince of Wales, at once succeeded him as Edward VIII. But before the date set for the new monarch's coronation a constitutional crisis had forced him from the throne.

The crisis was precipitated in December, 1936, when the Baldwin government resisted the king's desire to marry a twice-divorced American woman. Edward argued that his marriage was a private matter on which he was not limited by the advice of his ministers, but the cabinet maintained that it was a public act which was bound to affect seriously the monarch's standing not only in Great Britain but in the dominions overseas. Baldwin insisted that the elevation to the British throne of a twice-divorced woman would undermine the prestige of the crown to such an extent that he was doubtful "if anything could restore it."

The king's proposal that Parliament should legalize a morganatic marriage which would not raise his wife to the rank of queen and would exclude their children from the succession was also refused by the government. The House of Commons, realizing that the issue was fundamentally a question of whether the will of the king should prevail over the advice of the cabinet representing Parliament, supported Prime Minister Baldwin.

Faced by this impasse, Edward VIII on December 10 informed Parliament of his decision to renounce the throne. On the next day Parliament passed the Abdication Act giving effect to the king's abdication and regulating the succession to the throne. Edward VIII then gave his official assent to the measure, and that night left England. On December 12 the accession of King George VI and Queen Elizabeth was proclaimed in London. The new king's first act was to confer upon Edward a dukedom and the title of Duke of Windsor. Five months later (May 12, 1937) King George and Queen Elizabeth were crowned at Westminster Abbey in the presence of thousands of representatives of the kingdom, commonwealth, and empire.

Shortly after the coronation Prime Minister Baldwin, who had been so much responsible for the change in monarchs, tendered his resignation and that of his cabinet, and retired from public life.[8] A new ministry, dominated by the Conservatives but including also National Laborites and National Liberals, was organized on May 28 by Neville Chamberlain, son of the Joseph Chamberlain who had led the Unionist secession from the Liberal Party in 1886. Chamberlain at once announced a five-year plan of rearmament which called for an annual expenditure of £300,000,000 and which was to be concentrated on the production of aircraft, warships, air-raid shelters, and munitions. These expenditures seemed tremendous, but they were of course completely dwarfed by those of the Nazis, who since 1933 had been spending annually on an average five times as much for military preparedness. But Chamberlain's name is popularly connected not so much with his inadequate rearmament program as with his futile policy of "appeasement," a policy which is discussed in the later pages of this book.[9]

The British Commonwealth of Nations

According to Prime Minister Baldwin, the British government had been guided to a great degree during the constitutional crisis of 1936 by the advice of the various dominion governments. The fact that it had asked the assent of the dominion parliaments to the Abdication Act was in itself indicative of the change which had occurred since 1914 in the constitutional organization of the empire over which Great Britain had so long presided. During the First World War an imperial conference had recommended that the self-governing dominions be recognized as autonomous nations of an imperial commonwealth. Another conference in 1926 had actually de-

---

[8] Stanley Baldwin was made an earl and took his place in the House of Lords. Ramsay MacDonald was also offered an earldom but declined.

[9] See pages 478–484.

clared (Balfour Report) that Great Britain and the dominions were "autonomous communities within the British Empire, equal in status, in no way subordinate one to another,...though united by a common allegiance to the Crown." A committee representing the "autonomous communities" had been appointed (1929) to recommend the steps that should be taken to carry into effect this declaration, and its report had been adopted by an imperial conference in 1930. This report had then been transformed into law by the action of the parliaments of Great Britain and the dominions. In accordance with this procedure the Statute of Westminster had been passed in December, 1931, by the British Parliament.

By the terms of this statute it was agreed that (1) no law passed by a dominion parliament could in the future be declared void because it was contrary to a law of Great Britain; (2) no law of the British Parliament could apply to any dominion unless the latter specifically requested it; (3) no longer might the king on the advice of his British ministers set aside an act of a dominion parliament; (4) no change in the laws concerning succession to the British throne might be made without the consent of the dominion parliaments. As early as 1930 the dominions had successfully contended that their choice of governor-generalship should be accepted.

As the Statute of Westminster legalized the dominions' independence in their domestic affairs, custom and practice had brought a notable change in their status so far as international relations were concerned. Whereas before 1914 the foreign policy of the empire as a whole had been directed by a British ministry responsible to the Parliament in Westminster alone, in succeeding years it came to be directed to a large extent by the advice of the dominion ministers. At the same time, the dominions had gained practical independence in their own foreign relations, being represented individually in the League of Nations, being allowed to administer mandates of the League in their own names, and having their own diplomatic representatives in many foreign capitals. Furthermore, they had obtained the right to negotiate treaties for themselves and to refuse to ratify treaties entered into by Great Britain.

In other words, the British Empire in the years after 1914 had been transformed into something like a league of independent states bound together by a symbol, the crown, and co-operating through periodic imperial conferences of the prime ministers of the several states. Great Britain had thus ceased to be the ruling head of an empire and had become merely an equal member of the "British Commonwealth of Nations." That she still had the loyalty of these "independent states" in the Commonwealth was abundantly proved by the support which they gave her in the Second World War. Only Ireland remained neutral.

Ireland

From the time when Ireland was absorbed into the United Kingdom in 1801 there had existed in that island a persistent and insistent demand for Home Rule. During the nineteenth century this had meant to most people returning to the Irish the parliament of which they had been deprived. Twice during the latter part of the century Gladstone had introduced a bill to confer Home Rule upon the Irish, but twice the measure had been defeated, once in the House of Commons and once in the House of Lords. During the years 1912–1914, however, advantage had been taken of the Parliament Act of 1911 to pass a third Home Rule Bill. This measure had brought Ireland to the verge of civil war, because the Protestant Ulsterites of northeast Ireland, for economic and religious reasons, were determined never to be included in any Irish state in which they would constitute a minority; while the majority of the Irish people were equally determined that the restored Irish parliament should rule the whole island as it had formerly done. In 1914 both Irish groups had organized well equipped military forces to defend their views. Upon the outbreak of the First World War the British government, because of the serious situation in Ireland, had suspended the act for the duration of the war.

During the war the situation in Ireland had improved not at all. Irish demands became more radical, and, under the direction of Sinn Fein leaders, home rule came to mean for many not a parliament for an Ireland which would still constitute a part of the British Empire, but the establishment of a republic under which Ireland should be as independent of Great Britain as is the United States. This desire for independence resulted in an Irish revolt in 1916, planned in conjunction with the military leaders of Germany.

Although the rebellion was quickly suppressed, a very decided drift into the ranks of Sinn Fein continued. This was clearly revealed in the parliamentary elections of 1918 when the Sinn Feiners won an overwhelming victory outside Ulster. The newly elected Sinn Fein representatives thereupon asserted that the elections constituted a mandate in favor of an independent republic, and proceeded to organize themselves into an Irish parliament, the Dail Eireann. In January, 1919, the latter elected Eamon de Valera "President of the Irish Republic." During the following months what practically amounted to a state of war existed between the "Irish Republic" and Great Britain. The "Irish Republican Army" outnumbered the forces of the crown, which were almost powerless to restore order. Only after the government's forces had been strengthened by many auxiliary cadets were they able to defeat the Sinn Feiners.

THE FOURTH HOME RULE ACT

In December, 1920, a fourth Home Rule Bill was passed by the British Parliament. This measure provided for two parliaments in Ireland, one for the six counties in northeast Ulster and one for the rest of the island. It conferred greater powers upon the Irish legislatures than those given by the act of 1914, but reserved certain imperial services such as the army, navy, foreign relations, customs, and excise to the parliament at Westminster. In this latter body the two divisions of Ireland were still to be represented by duly elected though somewhat less numerous members. Northern Ireland at once accepted this plan as preferable to subordination to a parliament at Dublin, and proceeded to carry it out. On June 22, 1921, the parliament of Northern Ireland was formally opened by King George V. In Ireland, outside Ulster, however, the act was generally repudiated, for the Sinn Feiners refused to have anything to do with a scheme which seemed to make permanent the partition of the island.

Two days after the opening of the Ulster parliament Lloyd George invited De Valera to confer with him regarding the possibility of a settlement. But the proposals which the British prime minister made in the ensuing conference were characterized as unacceptable by De Valera and were also rejected by the Dail Eireann. Nevertheless, Lloyd George extended a second invitation, and in October, 1921, another conference met in the prime minister's official residence in London. Representing the Sinn Feiners were such Irish leaders as Arthur Griffith, Michael Collins, Eamon J. Duggan, and Gavan Duffy. De Valera did not attend. After eight weeks of intermittent negotiations the signatures of the plenipotentiaries were eventually affixed to a treaty providing for the establishment of the Irish Free State.

THE ANGLO-IRISH TREATY

Under this agreement the Irish Free State was to have "the same constitutional status in the community of nations known as the British Empire as the Dominion of Canada" and the other self-governing dominions. The crown was to be represented in Ireland by an officer "to be appointed in like manner as the Governor-General of Canada." The Free State assumed responsibility for a share of the British national debt, the amount to be determined later. It was to have its own military forces, and its own armed vessels for the protection of revenue and fisheries. Certain harbor facilities were conceded by the Free State to the imperial government, and the coast of Ireland was to be defended by the British fleet, pending an arrangement to be negotiated later. Northern Ireland was not to be included in the Free State if it declared its desire to continue under the act of 1920.

The treaty at once created a schism in the ranks of Sinn Fein. De Valera denounced it as in violent conflict with the wishes of the majority of the Irish and urged its rejection. Arthur Griffith, on the other hand, asserted that the treaty would lay the foundation of peace and friendship between Ireland and England, that the end of the conflict of centuries was at hand.

IRELAND TODAY

In the Dail the treaty, after much debate, was accepted. De Valera thereupon resigned from the presidency, and Arthur Griffith was chosen to succeed him. A few days later De Valera and his followers withdrew from the Dail. The bare majority which remained set up a provisional government under the chairmanship of Michael Collins.

De Valera next plunged Ireland into civil war. The "Irregulars," as the men in his Irish republican army came to be called, subjected southern Ireland to an orgy of destruction, in the course of which the country was desolated. Bridges and viaducts were blown up, railways and roads were destroyed, houses were burned, supplies were requisitioned, "traitors to the republic" were "executed." On August 12, 1922, came the unexpected death of Arthur Griffith, founder of Sinn Fein but since 1921 a loyal supporter of the Irish Free State treaty. Four days later Michael Collins, a Sinn Feinér who had turned his unbounded courage and energy to the defense of the Free State, was ambushed and killed. Ireland presented, in the words of Kevin O'Higgins, "the spectacle of a country bleeding to death, of a country steering straight for anarchy, futility, and chaos." But under the guidance of William Cosgrave and Kevin O'Higgins the provisional government resorted to vigorous measures to restore order. In the spring of 1923 De Valera finally admitted the impossibility of continuing the struggle, and ordered his followers to put aside their arms.

Some months before this the Irish Free State had been legally established. In September, 1922, a provisional parliament had met and elected Cosgrave president of the provisional government. The parliament at once gave its attention to its constituent duties and on October 25 adopted a constitution. As in the other dominions, the executive authority was vested nominally in the king, represented in the Free State by a governor-general. Actual executive power was placed in the hands of an executive council, directly responsible to the lower house of the legislature. The legislature (*Oireachtas*) was to consist of two houses, the Chamber of Deputies (*Dail Eireann*) and the Senate (*Seanad Eireann*). The latter was to be elected indirectly for twelve years, one fourth of the members being chosen every three years. The Chamber of Deputies was to be chosen by a system of proportional representation with universal suffrage.

THE IRISH FREE STATE

Early in December the constitution received the assent of King George, and on December 6, 1922, the Irish Free State was established by royal proclamation. In September, 1923, representatives of the Free State were received into the Assembly of the League of Nations; in October Cosgrave, president of the executive council, for the first time attended a dominion conference in London. Diplomatic representatives of the Free State were established in Washington, Geneva, Paris, Berlin, and Brussels, and a high commissioner took up his residence in London. In a reaction against the use of English, Gaelic was made compulsory for civil servants and for lawyers, and the Irish representative in the League of Nations Assembly was even instructed to make his speeches in Gaelic. Family and place names were Gaelicized, the best-known example being the change from Queenstown to Cobh. The difficulty of using Gaelic, however, prevented the universal adoption of the language. Irish nationalism did obtain some satisfaction, however, in the adoption of Irish coins and postage stamps.

In the summer of 1927, when it began to seem that Ireland was at last settling down to a somewhat ordered life, the world was shocked by the recurrence of assassination. On July 10 Kevin O'Higgins, vice-president of the executive council of the Free State and the "strong man" of the government, was deliberately shot and killed by three assailants. O'Higgins had been Cosgrave's chief lieutenant since the assassination of Collins and the death of Griffith. As minister of justice he had been largely responsible for the vigorous measures which had suppressed the Republican opposition. The "Irregulars" had long hated him. Although De Valera and his followers disclaimed any connection with the assassination of O'Higgins, popular opinion throughout the world was inclined to place part of the responsibility for the deed upon the obstructionist tactics of the republican leader.

Soon after this event De Valera changed his tactics. Until then he and his republican followers had refused to take the oath of allegiance to the British king and in consequence had been excluded from the Chamber of Deputies. In August, 1927, De Valera announced that he would take the oath and would undertake to become the head of a constitutional opposition. In parliamentary elections held in the following month his Fianna Fail Party increased its representation, but Cosgrave's Free State Party won the largest number of seats, and with the support of some of the lesser groups President Cosgrave was enabled to remain in office.

Nevertheless, despite the very real material and nationalistic gains which came to the Irish as a result of Cosgrave's administration, the world depression inevitably affected the popularity of his government. As sentiment in practically all countries where democratic government prevailed turned against the parties in power during the years of the depression, so it was in Ireland. Furthermore, De Valera constantly appealed to the Irish with a very definitely anti-British—and therefore popular—program. The extreme republicans were attracted by his demand for the abolition of the oath of allegiance to the British king. Small landholders were won by his promise to withhold the land annuities which they were compelled to pay to the British government under the land-purchase agreements of earlier years.

De Valera entered the political campaign of 1932 with a platform which called for the abolition of the oath to the British king, the retention by the Irish treasury of the land annuities which were due under agreements of 1921, 1923, and 1926, and the enactment of a protective tariff. In general, he advocated a policy of political and economic self-sufficiency for Ireland. The subsequent voting resulted in the election of 72 members of Fianna Fail and 65 followers of Cosgrave, but representatives of lesser parties held the balance of power. When the Laborites threw their support to De Valera, the latter was elected president of the executive council in March, 1932.

De Valera at once undertook to carry out his promises. In April, 1932, a bill was introduced in the Chamber to remove the oath from the Irish constitution, but opposition in the Senate, which Cosgrave's followers controlled, prevented the bill from becoming a law. On July 1 De Valera withheld the payment of £1,500,000 due on the land annuities. This action the British government declared was a violation of a binding engagement of the Irish Free State, and the British parliament passed a law empowering the government to levy a duty up to 100 per cent on Irish goods coming into Great Britain, in order to secure funds equivalent to the defaulted land annuities. De Valera retaliated with Irish duties which were almost prohibitive on certain British goods, and a tariff war therefore ensued. That De Valera's policy had the support of a majority of the Irish seemed apparent when new elections in January, 1933, returned the Fianna Fail Party with a clear majority over all opposition.

In an effort to make the Irish Free State less dependent upon Great Britain economically, De Valera encouraged the expansion of local industry. and sought to persuade farmers to strike a more reasonable balance between grazing and tillage. Undoubtedly a considerable development of industry occurred, and many commodities which formerly had to be imported came to be manufactured in the Free State. But the attempt to make Ireland economically more self-sufficient, although perhaps beneficial in the long run, had unfortunately the effect of raising the cost of living in the Free State. De Valera, nevertheless, stoutly asserted that Ireland was "prepared to take the full consequences of being an independent nation."

What these consequences might be economically was revealed when the annual trade reports were published. In 1933–1934 the country's adverse balance of trade was the highest in the history of the Free State; in 1934–1935 it was still higher. Indeed, the Free State's total foreign trade for 1934–1935 was only 60 per cent of that for 1930–1931, the year before De Valera became president. Obviously, no adequate substitute market for Free State produce had been found to take the place of Great Britain. By 1936 it was becoming apparent that De Valera's hope of making the Free State economically independent of Great Britain was destined to be blasted, and early in that year the Free State president practically admitted the failure of his plan. In a trade agreement signed in 1936 the Free State government removed the duty on British coal and gave the British practically a monopoly of the market for that commodity within its territory. It also reduced the duties on a great number of other commodities usually imported from Great Britain and agreed to purchase one third of its cement from British firms. In return Great Britain, although still retaining high duties on many Irish products, reduced them somewhat on livestock and meats.

Meanwhile, De Valera had been taking steps to emphasize the political independence of the Irish Free State. In May, 1933, the Chamber of Deputies again passed the bill abolishing the oath of allegiance, and this time it became law. Next the governor-general's approval was made unnecessary for the legalization of acts passed by the Irish parliament. Later in the year the right of appeal from Irish courts to the British Privy Council was abolished. In March, 1934, De Valera arranged that the new United States minister to the Irish Free State should present his credentials, not to the governor-general as the representative of the British crown, but to the president of the executive council. Later in the same year he introduced a bill in the Chamber to create a separate Free State citizenship and to abolish British citizenship in the Irish Free State. In 1935 no Free State delegate attended the celebration of the twenty-fifth anniversary of King George's accession to the throne. The absence of such a delegate was doubtless one more gesture designed to emphasize De Valera's determination to cut the Free State off from Great Britain. A similar gesture was made again in January, 1936, when King George died. The Irish Free State government took no step to proclaim King Edward VIII in Dublin and sent no official representative to the funeral of the deceased ruler. In December, 1936, during the constitutional crisis in Great Britain, the Chamber of Deputies abolished the office of governor-general and the British king's prerogatives in Ireland's domestic affairs. Although the Chamber gave its necessary official assent to the Abdication Act, the Free State government refused to proclaim the new king in Dublin or to send an official representative to his coronation in the following May.

EIRE

In April, 1937, De Valera published a new Irish Free State constitution which proclaimed the Irish nation's "indefeasible and sovereign right to choose its own form of government, to determine its relations with other nations and to develop its life, political, economic and cultural, in accordance with its own genius and traditions." Nowhere in the constitution was there any mention of Great Britain or the British king. The new constitution provided for a president who should be elected by direct vote of the people for a seven-year term and who in a sense was to occupy the titular position formerly held by the governor-general. Executive power was to be exercised chiefly by a prime minister and cabinet responsible to the Chamber of Deputies. The parliament was to consist of a popularly elected Chamber of Deputies and an indirectly elected or nominated Senate.

After consideration of the draft of the new constitution by the Chamber, the latter was dissolved and an election was called with De Valera's policies as the issue. At the same time the proposed constitution was submitted to the voters for their approval or rejection. Although the constitution was approved by slightly more than 56 per cent of those who voted, De Valera's Fianna Fail Party did not fare so well. Its representation in the Chamber was reduced and De Valera found himself dependent upon the Labor Party for a working majority in the Chamber of Deputies. He was, nevertheless, re-elected president of the executive council. The new constitution became effective on December 29, 1937, when the name of the Irish Free State was officially changed to Eire.

De Valera next turned his attention to the task of removing the causes of dissension between Eire and Great Britain and happily found Prime Minister Chamberlain equally desirous of restoring amicable relations. After somewhat lengthy negotiations, on April 25, 1938, three agreements were signed in London between Great Britain and Eire. In the first Great Britain agreed to transfer to Eire the admiralty property and rights at Berehaven and the harbor defenses there and at Cobh and Lough Swilly. British forces, which had been stationed at these places by the terms of the treaty of 1921, were thereupon withdrawn, and Eire became responsible for her own defense.

The second agreement provided that Eire should pay Great Britain £10,000,000 on or before November 30, 1938, as the final settlement of Britain's claim to land annuities. In addition Eire agreed to continue to pay £250,000 annually until 1987 in accordance with the Anglo-Irish agreement of 1925, which had to do with property damages incurred during the so-called "troubles." This convention also provided for the abolition of the special duties imposed by the British government in retaliation for the withholding of the annuities and for the abolition of the retaliatory customs duties levied by Eire. The third agreement, which came into effect on May 19, was a trade treaty designed to restore to each of the signatories the favorable commercial position held prior to the recent tariff war. According to De Valera, all causes of difference between Great Britain and Eire were thus removed except the question of partition, which he still hoped would ultimately be adjusted.

On May 27, 1938, Premier de Valera dissolved the Chamber of Deputies, doubtless with the expectation that, with Anglo-Irish relations thus happily adjusted, his party might secure a majority in the Chamber so that he would no longer be dependent upon the Labor Party and Independents. His expectation was fulfilled, for the election of June 17, 1938, gave Fianna Fail a decisive majority over all the opposition groups.

Meanwhile, provision had been made for Eire's first President. On April 22 De Valera and Cosgrave, representing the two largest Irish political parties, jointly offered the nomination for President to Douglas Hyde, the seventy-eight-year-old poet, historian, and retired university professor. The presidential nominee, the son of a Protestant clergyman and himself a Protestant, had long been an ardent nationalist. By many his nomination was looked upon as a gesture toward reconciliation with Protestant Ulster. On May 4, 1938, there being no other candidate, the new President was elected by acclamation.

The outbreak of the Second World War provided De Valera with another opportunity to emphasize that Eire was independent of Great Britain. In contrast with the other members of the British Commonwealth of Nations, Eire at once declared her neutrality and remained out of the war. Throughout the conflict the inability of the British navy to use the ports surrendered to the Irish by Chamberlain in 1938 constituted a grave handicap in the battle of the Atlantic.

Chapter XII

THE THIRD FRENCH REPUBLIC

FRANCE emerged victorious from the First World War only to find herself beset by numerous and perplexing problems. Some of these were solved without too great difficulty, but others produced such differences of opinion among the French people that stalemate and national paralysis at times resulted. Though the bulk of the French stood loyally by their liberal republic, the uncertainties, anxieties, and hardships of the postwar years gradually led many to desert to the ranks of the Communists on the Left or the fascists on the Right. A careful study of French affairs clearly reveals that the forces and circumstances which led to the collapse of France in the Second World War were present and increasingly effective in the years between 1919 and 1939.

French Politics

An appreciation of the political instability which handicapped France in the years before the Second World War requires some knowledge of the basic features of the political system of the Third Republic. The legislative power of the republic rested in a bicameral parliament consisting of a Chamber of Deputies, elected directly for a four-year term by universal manhood suffrage, and a Senate, elected indirectly for nine years, one third being retired every three years. The Chamber of Deputies was the more powerful of the two houses, for, though in theory the Senate had equal authority with the Chamber, in reality it acted more as a brake on hasty action of the popularly elected house. The Chamber was the body which usually controlled the rise and fall of ministries. When the Chamber and the Senate met in joint session, they constituted the National Assembly.

The President of the republic was elected for a seven-year term by the National Assembly. His powers were distinctly limited. He had no veto power over legislation passed by parliament, and all his acts had to be countersigned by a member of the cabinet. As has been pointed out many times, the President of France did not reign like the hereditary King of Great Britain, nor did he rule like the elected President of the United

States. He was the titular head of the republic, but neither ruled nor reigned.

The actual executive power of France was in the hands of a cabinet of ministers officially appointed by the president but actually named by the leaders of parliament and directly responsible to that body. France thus had a parliamentary government, but the parliamentary system operated quite differently in France than in Great Britain. Whereas some one party usually controlled the British House of Commons, the French ministry, because of the many political groups in France, had to rely on coalitions or blocs. Furthermore, the French political groups were neither so well organized nor so clear-cut in their differences as the British parties, with the result that blocs once formed were forever disintegrating and permitting a ministry to fall. By resorting to his right of "interpellation" a deputy might at any time force a vote of "lack of confidence" and the resignation of the ministry. Between 1870 and 1914 the Third Republic had had a kaleidoscopic succession of at least fifty different ministries. There was never any question in France of a ministry's dissolving the Chamber of Deputies to avoid resigning; the Chamber was supreme.

At the close of the First World War Georges Clemenceau, who had become premier during the critical days of 1917, was still head of the government. National elections had been postponed in France during the war, and not until after the treaty of Versailles had been ratified by the French parliament did Clemenceau call for general elections. Then the National bloc, a coalition of most of the Right and Center parties, was organized by Alexandre Millerand to support the government, defend the treaty, and combat Bolshevism. In the election of deputies in November, 1919, the National bloc won an overwhelming victory, and a similar result followed in the senatorial elections of January, 1920.

In the following month President Poincaré's term of office was to expire, and so on January 17 the National Assembly met to elect his successor. The two outstanding candidates were Clemenceau and Paul Deschanel, the latter long a member of the Chamber of Deputies and for years its president. Contrary to the expectations of many in foreign countries, Clemenceau was decisively defeated. Since the aged premier had made the presidential election a sort of vote of confidence on his work as premier, his defeat left him no alternative but to resign his office. He was succeeded by Millerand, the organizer of the National bloc. But the latter did not long retain the premiership. In September, 1920, President Deschanel resigned because of ill health and an unfortunate accident, and Millerand was chosen to succeed him. After some further ministerial changes the premiership was eventually assumed in January, 1921, by Aristide Briand, who was destined to play a prominent role in the diplomatic history of postwar Europe. Perhaps his most pressing immediate problem was to secure reparation payments from Germany commensurate with the cost of reconstructing northern France.

The Problem of Reconstruction

At the close of the First World War, throughout some 12,884 square miles of northern France chaos reigned. Here in prewar days had dwelt one eighth of France's population. Here had been concentrated the greater part of her industries and mines. But as a result of the war hundreds of towns and villages had become deserted wastes of shapeless ruins. Hundreds of thousands of homes had been wrecked or totally destroyed. Thousands of factories had been looted or blown up; mines had been allowed to fill with water or been deliberately destroyed; railroads had become dilapidated and worn out. Millions of acres of once smiling farmland had been cut and torn and scarred with trenches and shell holes. Orchards and forests had been shot to pieces or razed by the retreating Germans; thousands of wells had been damaged, contaminated, or destroyed; hundreds of thousands of cattle and other stock had been carried off; and everywhere mile upon mile of barbed-wire entanglements and heaps of debris had been left to encumber the ground.

The restoration of this territory to its prewar state constituted a gigantic problem for France. During the war the French government had promised to reimburse its citizens for all direct and material losses occasioned by the war; in other words, it took the stand that losses occasioned by war were to be reimbursed by the state as a matter of right. With the cost of replacement of damaged and destroyed property averaging five times its estimated value in 1914, partly in consequence of the decline of the franc, the French government was thus called upon to expend billions in the work of restoration. But it was hoped and expected that whatever was spent for this purpose would ultimately be recovered from Germany under the treaty of Versailles.

The procedure of the French government, therefore, was to create for the reconstruction of the devastated area a special budget known as the "budget of recoverable expenditures." To this budget were charged all expenditures for restoration, and for this purpose money was spent freely and, some said, not without fraud. Since reparations payments were not immediately forthcoming, however, income for the special budget was provided from loans floated by the French government with the understanding that they would ultimately be retired when German reparations payments began to come in. By the summer of 1921 great strides had been made in the work of restoration, in the course of which the French government had spent over 20,000,000,000 francs, but up to that time France had actually received nothing from Germany to apply on her reparations account.

The Problem of National Finance

It was inevitable that the reparations problem should become involved in French politics. Briand stood for a policy of reasonable moderation and conciliation. But with France's failure to receive reparations payments of any size, Frenchmen became restless. When at the close of 1921 Germany asked and was later granted a partial moratorium, the Nationalists, led by Raymond Poincaré and André Tardieu, took up cudgels against Briand, and in January, 1922, he was forced out of office and was succeeded by Poincaré. The latter's policy, culminating in the French occupation of the Ruhr [1] and the subsequent appointment of the Dawes Committee, has already been traced.

By 1924, however, a number of circumstances conspired to weaken Poincaré's position. The continued fall of the franc reacted against him, as did the accompanying rise in the cost of living. The failure to secure reparations from Germany, the increase in the national debt, the heavier taxes being laid upon Frenchmen, and the inability of the government to balance the national budget gave his opponents numerous opportunities to attack him. Through the efforts of Briand a Left bloc was finally organized with the purpose of defeating Poincaré, and in the general parliamentary elections in May, 1924, the parties of the Left were returned in a majority, the Radical Socialists constituting the largest single group in the new Chamber.

The immediate result of this reversal in French politics was the downfall of both Premier Poincaré and President Millerand. That Poincaré should be forced to resign was, of course, quite to be expected under the French parliamentary system. But the French president was constitutionally considered to be in somewhat the same position as the king of England relative to party politics, that is, not affected by the fluctuations in party strength or by the rise and fall of ministries. The leaders of the Left bloc, however, now resolved that Millerand must resign because he had overstepped his presidential prerogatives by pursuing a personal policy and by openly supporting the National bloc during the preceding electoral campaign.

When, therefore, after Poincaré's resignation, President Millerand called upon Édouard Herriot, leader of the Radical Socialists, to form a government, the latter declined. The president then invited another member of the Chamber to assume the premiership, but the latter's cabinet when presented failed to secure the support of the Chamber. An impasse was

1 See pages 165–167

thus created which was surmounted only when President Millerand resigned his office on June 11. Gaston Doumergue, president of the Senate and a member of the Left group, was elected president, and Herriot then accepted the new president's invitation to form a cabinet.

Herriot's most difficult problem was that of national finance. Four factors united to produce a serious crisis in the French fiscal system: the tremendous increase in the service charges on the debt of France, which had risen from 35 billion francs to 180 billion francs during the war; the enormous current expenditures required for the reconstruction of the devastated area in the early years of the postwar period; the relatively insignificant amounts actually received in reparations payments prior to 1926; and the failure of the government's system of taxation to bring in revenue sufficient to balance the budget. During the five years before Herriot came into power annual deficits had added a total of 150 billion francs to the already gigantic national debt. The national currency had become greatly inflated, and the franc, normally worth 19.3 cents, had depreciated until by March, 1924, it was worth less than 5 cents.

In 1924 the French people began to show a reluctance to make further loans to the government, and holders of short-term bills displayed an unwillingness to renew their loans as they came due. But the government was unable to increase the national revenue materially because of the bitter conflict in the parliament over the method of taxation. The Left groups demanded a capital levy on the rich, heavier direct taxes, and a reduction of expenditures by a lowering of the interest rate on government bonds. The Right groups, on the other hand, demanded the imposition of more indirect taxes, heavier taxes on the middle classes, and a reduction of expenditures by the lowering of government salaries and wages. Parliament's inability to enact either of these programs in effect decreed a policy of currency inflation, with the result that increases in paper currency continued until, in April, 1925, the Chamber of Deputies forced the resignation of Herriot by refusing longer to support this procedure. In the ensuing fifteen months no less than six ministries followed one another in rapid succession while the fiscal impasse remained.

By May, 1926, an acute financial crisis had begun which culminated in a panic in the following July. At that time French bonds were selling far below par, the treasury was practically empty, the budget was still unbalanced, an enormous floating debt was maturing at the rate of 7,500,000,000 francs a month, the franc had fallen to 48 to the dollar, and the confidence of the French people in the integrity of the financial measures of their government had become seriously impaired. The crisis brought a radical change in the government. Party lines were temporarily obliterated, and a ministry of National Union was organized to include six former premiers under the leadership of France's "strong man," Poincaré, who was given practically dictatorial powers in the realm of finance.

Drastic measures were at once taken. The budget of recoverable expenditures was absorbed into the national budget, which in turn was greatly simplified. New tax measures were enacted, increasing the amount of indirect taxes and shifting the burden somewhat from the wealthy to the middle classes. Extensive reforms in the administrative system reduced expenditures. The budget—the largest in the nation's history—was balanced, and the year 1926 closed with a surplus of over 1,500,000,000 francs in the treasury. The franc was gradually raised in value until, December 20, 1926, it stood at 25.19 to the dollar, where it was given *de facto* stabilization. With the franc at this value, the gold standard was restored in June, 1928. These measures brought a return of investors' confidence in the government, which enabled the latter to adjust its floating debt advantageously. Renewed confidence in the government made it possible to reduce interest rates so that by 1928 the service charges on the floating debt had been decreased by over 300,000,000 francs yearly. Furthermore, the reconstruction of the devastated area was practically completed so that extraordinary expenditures for this purpose became negligible, while income from reparations payments under the Dawes plan increased.

In 1928 France had an opportunity to pass upon Poincaré's achievements in the parliamentary elections which were held in April. As in the elections four years earlier, the chief issue was Poincaré and his policies, but on this occasion the elections constituted a victory for his government. Poincaré continued to hold the premiership until ill health forced his resignation in July, 1929, when the removal of his strong hand from the helm of state brought a return of the republic's traditional ministerial instability. Party politics again became active, and the succeeding years saw numerous ministries come and go, the most prominent premiers between 1929 and 1932 being André Tardieu and Pierre Laval.

The Problem of Alsace-Lorraine

Meanwhile, another problem which had confronted French statesmen after the war was that of assimilating into a unitary state the provinces of Alsace-Lorraine, whose institutions in the years after 1871 had come to differ from those of France. Friction soon developed between the inhabitants of the "redeemed" provinces and the French government because of political changes. Under Germany the provinces had constituted a single political unit which, though ruled arbitrarily by the imperial government until 1911, had in that year been granted a local legislature with considerable power. But in a unitary state like France there was no place for provincial legislatures. In accordance with the French system of government Alsace-Lorraine in 1919 was divided into three departments, and the legislature was ignored. Strasbourg ceased to be a capital with governmental powers and organs and became simply a prefecture. The inhabitants of the provinces were naturally reluctant to lose their local rights. Furthermore, they complained that officials sent out from Paris knew no German, the language most nearly akin to that spoken by the majority of the people.

The matter of language also caused ill feeling in the provinces. The great majority of Alsatians and Lorrainers spoke patois or dialects closely related to high German, which was used in printing and writing. Only German was taught in the elementary schools during the years in which the provinces were included in the German Empire, but with the return to France the official language of the schools of Alsace-Lorraine became French. It was required that during the first two years of the elementary schools French should be studied exclusively; after that three hours a week of instruction in German was also provided. The French government insisted that French should have a primary place in the school system and discouraged the use of German, despite the desire of many Alsatians for language equality.

The greatest dissatisfaction arose from the government's efforts to change the religious and educational situation in Alsace-Lorraine. At the time when the provinces were taken from France in 1871, these matters were regulated by the concordat which Napoleon had concluded with the pope in 1801. Under this agreement the salaries of the clergy were paid by the government, which had a voice in their appointment, and education was almost entirely under the control of the church. The German government had respected these arrangements in Alsace-Lorraine when it annexed the provinces and had permitted them to continue. The result was that in Alsace-Lorraine the salaries of the clergy were paid by the local government, and the children were permitted to attend Catholic, Protestant, or Jewish schools in accordance with the religion of their parents. In the rest of France, on the other hand, subsequent anticlerical legislation had meanwhile altered the situation. Church and state had been completely separated, all religious instruction had been removed from the schools, and teaching by religious orders had been forbidden.

France, a highly centralized unitary state, had no provision for local differences in such matters as education. Nevertheless, President Poincaré at the time of the recovery of Alsace and Lorraine had pledged the retention of their religious system, and the government of the National bloc had winked at the anomalous situation created in France when it permitted the religious and educational situation in Alsace-Lorraine to continue undisturbed. But the Left government which came into power in 1924 was definitely anticlerical, and determined to introduce in Alsace-Lorraine the same regime as existed elsewhere in France. When it attempted to disestablish the churches and to introduce secular schools, however, it encountered the active obstruction of the people. The Catholic school children of Alsace-Lorraine united in a great strike, and Catholics in many other parts of France vigorously protested. In the end the government had to recede from its stand. The churches were not disestablished, and the schools were not all secularized. In some places an "interconfessional" school system was introduced in accordance with which the children were to be sent for their academic instruction to a common school without regard to their religious beliefs but were to be separated for their religious instruction.

Many of those in Alsace-Lorraine who had welcomed French troops so enthusiastically as "liberators" who would bring in "a new era of liberty, prosperity, and happiness" later had serious doubts as to whether their return to France was altogether an unmixed blessing. In fact, stimulated by grievances and fears as well as by a highly financed propaganda, disgruntled elements of the Alsatian population were gradually won over to an autonomist movement which sought home rule or even separation from France. So serious did the situation become that in 1929 the Chamber of Deputies devoted itself for more than two weeks to a consideration of the problems connected with the administration of Alsace-Lorraine. In the succeeding years, however, and especially after the Nazis came into power in Germany, autonomist agitation largely ceased.

The Problem of Security

Meanwhile, too, French statesmen had been busily engaged in building a system of alliances to provide security for France. They were especially disturbed after the First World War by the specter of a discontented and revengeful Germany, for they perceived that the latter even within her postwar frontiers still had the largest population of all the states of western Europe. It took very little mathematical ability for a French statesman to prove that France's 39,000,000 would be no match for Germany's 62,000,000 and that each year would see the disparity grow greater if the French population continued to remain stationary while that of Germany increased. Great was their alarm lest the "fall in the French birth rate might undo the work of Foch in a single generation." Before the war, in order to counteract this situation, which had existed for many years, France had allied herself with populous Russia so that their combined man power and resources might be protection against their powerful neighbor, Germany. The loss of Russia as an ally, with the coming of the Bolsheviks in 1917, was a terrible blow for France, but at the peace conference her statesmen had sought to repair this damage by carrying through the program of security drawn up by the French government for their guidance as early as November, 1918.

Although the French had obtained a number of the points for which they contended at the conference, they had not obtained all. As protection against another German invasion they had been obliged to accept, instead of French military control of the Rhine, a compromise which included Allied military occupation of the left bank of the Rhine for fifteen years, the permanent demilitarization of this area together with a strip of territory fifty kilometers wide on the right bank, and a tripartite guarantee treaty promising that the United States and Great Britain would come to the assistance of France in case of a future unprovoked attack by Germany. But this bulwark of protection was soon weakened. Although Great Britain ratified the guarantee treaty, the United States refused to have anything to do with it, and consequently the whole scheme fell to the ground, for Great Britain's adhesion to the treaty was contingent upon that of the United States.

French statesmen lost no time in crying over spilt milk. If they must now construct their own security alliance, they would proceed at once to do so. There was one country of western Europe which was as much concerned as France in the problem of her future security against Germany. Belgium after her terrible experiences of the war would be only too eager to obtain protection against their repetition; therefore to Belgium France now turned in a conciliatory spirit. Military conversations between the French and Belgian staffs culminated on September 7, 1920, in the signing of a military convention.

But France with Belgium alone could still not hope to cope with Germany. She must seek some greater power to take the place of her lost ally, Russia. With this in mind she turned to the new Polish Republic, largest of all the new states of Europe. If France needed security for her eastern frontier facing Germany, to no less a degree did Poland need a similar security for her western frontier, which had been established at the expense of Germany. If France had reason to fear for the stability of her German frontier, twice justified was Poland, for the loss of Upper Silesia, Posen, and West Prussia with their mineral and agricultural resources and their large German minorities was felt by the German nation more keenly than the loss of Alsace-Lorraine. Fear of German attack thus created a strong common bond between Poland and France. In the summer of 1920 during the crisis of the Russo-Polish campaign the French government sent a military mission to Poland and helped to save Warsaw from the Bolsheviks. Diplomatic negotiations next ensued, and a Franco-Polish treaty of alliance was signed on February 19, 1921. The treaty system thus far created by France provided that, if Germany should attack her, France would be aided by Belgium in the west and by Poland in the east.

But France was not yet content with the security which had been obtained. In the following year she sought to obtain a defensive alliance with Great Britain. This time she failed, however, because Lloyd George and Poincaré, the prime ministers of the two countries, could not agree upon terms. Nevertheless, France persisted in her general scheme and turned next to Czechoslovakia, whose statesmen wished to guard against the union of Austria and Germany and against the restoration of either the Habsburgs or the Hohenzollerns. In 1924 a Franco-Czechoslovak treaty of alliance was formally signed in Paris.

In the succeeding years France sought to forge still more links for her chain of security treaties. In 1926 she signed with Rumania a treaty of friendship in which, among other things, the two states promised to consult each other in all matters which might threaten their external security or which might tend to subvert the situation created by the treaties of peace. If either state should be attacked without provocation, the two governments engaged immediately to consult each other as to the action to be taken by each "within the framework of the Covenant of the League of Nations" in order to safeguard their legitimate national interests and to maintain the order established by the peace treaties. The two states agreed to concert their policy in case of any attempted modification of the political status of the countries of Europe and to confer regarding the attitude to be taken in such an event. In 1927 France signed an almost identical treaty with Yugoslavia.

This extensive system of alliances and friendship treaties conferred upon France a position of leadership among those continental powers which were, generally speaking, beneficiaries of the Paris peace settlement and consequently vitally interested in the maintenance of the *status quo*. It was hoped that as a bloc they would outweigh any power which might seek by force to abrogate the terms of the peace treaties, and might therefore deter such a power from military aggression. Furthermore, these treaties, it will be recalled, were supplemented by the Locarno pact of mutual guarantee, which bound Great Britain and Italy to aid France in case of a German attack, and by the pact of Paris, which outlawed war as an instrument of national policy. Thus, on paper, at least, France greatly strengthened her national security during the years immediately following the First World War.

Much of the credit for these diplomatic successes belonged to Aristide Briand, who for more than seven years served as foreign minister. In 1931, when President Doumergue's term of office expired, a large group of senators and deputies of all parties united to urge Briand to stand as a candidate for the presidency, and, despite his reluctance to withdraw from active politics and to surrender control of his cherished foreign policy, he finally consented. Two days later the National Assembly elected not Briand but Paul Doumer President of France. Doumer, a venerable self-made man and a representative of the bourgeoisie, was at the time president of the Senate and had been president of the Chamber of Deputies. In theory he was a Radical Socialist, but he had apparently displayed no bitter partisan feelings and had aroused none among his political opponents. Briand's failure to be elected president, like that of Clemenceau in 1920, seemed to many an indication that French statesmen who play vigorous roles in politics arouse so many enmities that they have great difficulty in being elevated to the presidency. Others saw in the outcome the National Assembly's realization that Briand would still be for some time indispensable to the conduct of French foreign affairs.

From the days preceding Locarno, Briand as foreign minister had directed the foreign policy of the republic. For some time he had been in poor health, however, and on March 7, 1932, shortly before his seventieth birthday, he died. Almost exactly thirty years before, he had entered French public life. More than a score of times he had held portfolios in various cabinets, frequently being himself the premier. It was his role, during the postwar period, to advocate unwaveringly the policy of moderation and conciliation and to labor unceasingly in the interests of international arbitration and organization. His impress on the public mind is revealed by the fact that, though the international agreement to outlaw war (1928) is officially known as the pact of Paris, it is popularly referred to throughout the world as the Briand-Kellogg pact.

Deflation and Unrest

Although France was slower to feel the world depression than most countries, by the time of the parliamentary elections of May, 1932, its effects upon French economic life had become abundantly evident. During the weeks preceding those elections, therefore, Left speakers pointed out how the fruits of the existing Right government were unemployment, huge financial losses, and an empty treasury. Right speakers, on the other hand, tried to frighten French voters with the specter of a return to the "black days" of 1924–1926, should the Left bloc be elected. During the electoral campaign President Doumer was assassinated (May 6) by a Russian émigré, and Right speakers seized upon the crime in an effort to stampede voters away from Left candidates. But it was all in vain; as in other countries during the depression, the vote went against those in office. The Left bloc won, with Herriot's Radical Socialists the largest single group in the new Chamber. In June, 1932, Herriot assumed the premiership, as he had done eight years earlier after a similar swing to the Left. In the meantime, on May 10, Albert Lebrun, then president of the Senate, had been elected president of the republic.

In the succeeding years the rise and fall of ministries was generally connected with some phase of the republic's perplexing budgetary, fiscal, or economic problems. France, because of her adhering to the gold standard, found herself obliged to compete with devalued British pounds and American dollars. In consequence, her foreign trade greatly decreased, as did tourist expenditures which formerly brought into the country hundreds of millions of dollars. Industrial output declined in most categories, the railways incurred deficits, and unemployment from the autumn of 1934 on progressively reached new high peaks for the postwar period. By bankers, exporters, and those catering to tourist trade the government was urged to devalue the franc once more in order to enable France to compete more successfully with foreign currencies. On the other hand, the *rentier* class, having learned by experience the effect of currency depreciation upon it, was unalterably opposed to any further experiments of that nature.

In general, the policy of French statesmen during the ensuing four years was that of deflation. That is, they sought by reductions in the wages of government employees, in the pensions of war veterans, and in the interest rate on government bonds to lessen the national expenditures, while at the same time they attempted by higher taxes to balance the budget and thus remove the necessity for increasing the national debt or inflating the currency. Such a policy inevitably incurred the opposition of many taxpayers, government employees, and war veterans. Furthermore, many in France argued that the government's fiscal system should be balanced not by deflation of the budget but by inflation of the currency. There was, accordingly, much dissatisfaction with the various attempts at deflation. Moreover, the government's revenues regularly fell below budgetary estimates, so that deficits continued and the national debt mounted. Alarm at this latter development in turn occasionally created fear of monetary inflation and a consequent run on gold. Altogether, the position of the premiers who succeeded one another during these years was far from enviable. Édouard Herriot, Joseph Paul-Boncour, Édouard Daladier, Albert Sarraut, and Camille Chautemps, all Radical Socialists, held the premiership between June, 1932, and January, 1934.

During the winter of 1933–1934 the government became linked in the public mind with a pawnshop scandal which caused a loss of 200,000,000 francs to French investors. The failure of the police to find the absconder, Alexander Stavisky, led to charges of corruption against the administration of justice, and, when Stavisky killed himself, it was rumored that he had been shot by the police to prevent his revealing embarrassing information. Public demand for a complete reorganization of the government, accompanied by riots in the streets of Paris, eventually forced Chautemps out of office late in January, 1934.

But the disorders did not cease when he was succeeded by Daladier. Newspapers representing various elements in France, apparently seeking to embarrass the government, called upon their readers to gather for demonstrations on the day that the new cabinet was to appear before the Chamber of Deputies. On the one hand, royalists, war veterans, and members of various Right organizations were urged to gather for a demonstration "to oppose the thieves and this abject regime"; on the other, Socialists and Communists were incited to defend their interests against "the forces of fascism" which were said to be seeking to destroy democracy.

Daladier, feeling that the police might not be able to cope with the situation unaided, ordered some 3000 troops to Paris. Soldiers with machine guns were stationed on the steps of the Palais Bourbon where the Chamber of Deputies was to meet. On the night of February 6, 1934, while the crowds were milling about the Place de la Concorde and fighting the police, the floodlights suddenly went out. In the confusion that ensued police and troops, apparently without orders from their officers and under the impression that they were fighting in self-defense, began to use their pistols. Seventeen civilians were killed and more than six hundred were wounded. Of the police and military, one was killed and more than 1600 were wounded.

In view of these developments, the Daladier ministry was forced at once to resign. The situation was highly critical and demanded immediate and extraordinary steps if calm were to be restored. Prominent political leaders united in urging that former President Gaston Doumergue be made premier. In answer to their appeal this veteran statesman agreed to form a ministry on condition that he be given complete freedom in regard to his program and choice of ministers. Hailed as a "national savior," Doumergue arrived in Paris on February 8 and immediately organized a cabinet which included among its members six former premiers and Marshal Pétain. Nearly every shade of political opinion except the extremes was represented, only the royalists, Socialists, and Communists being omitted. The new ministry inspired confidence, political harmony was attained, and government economies were introduced.

But, when Doumergue sought to have the French constitution amended in order to increase his executive powers and to give the premier the right to dissolve the Chamber and call for new elections, fear of a movement toward dictatorial rule caused opposition and brought the fall of his ministry in November, 1934. Again came a rapid succession of governments, headed by Pierre-Étienne Flandin, Fernand Bouisson, Pierre Laval, and Albert Sarraut.

The reluctance of the Chamber of Deputies to vote new powers to the premiers during these years was caused, in part, by the fear that a movement toward a fascist dictatorship was under way in France. The one most suspected was Colonel François de la Rocque, leader of the *Croix de Feu,* an organization of war veterans, which was supported by many prominent French industrial capitalists. Colonel de la Rocque, in his program, had been content with such vague statements as "Take France away from the politicians and give it back to the French people," but he had been able by his oratory and personal magnetism to weld together an organization of several hundred thousand men. Although the *Croix de Feu* was the most important and most powerful of the various antirepublican organizations, there were several others, notably the royalist *Action Française* and *Camelots du Roi* and the nationalistic, anti-Communist *Cagoulards, Solidarité Française,* and *Jeunesse Patriote.*

Not unmindful of the way in which fascist dictatorships had arisen in other countries during the postwar period, the Socialists and Communists, in turn, began more effectively to organize their ranks. Clashes inevitably occurred between the Right and Left groups, and each side accused the other of preparing to overthrow the government. So strained did the situation become that a law was passed forbidding the carrying of arms to public meetings and authorizing the dissolution of semimilitary organizations with uniforms, insignia, and arms. Following an unprovoked assault on Léon Blum, leader of the Socialist Party, by members of the *Action Française,* President Lebrun on February 13, 1936, decreed the dissolution of the *Action Française* and the *Camelots du Roi.*

The Popular Front

In preparation for the parliamentary elections to be held in the spring of 1936 the Radical Socialists, the Socialists, and the Communists organized the Popular Front. Although the parties differed among themselves on many points, on one fundamental they were agreed—that a united and militant front must be set up against the threat of fascism. Apparently the French electorate felt similarly, for the elections resulted in a decisive victory for the Popular Front. For the first time in French history the Socialists secured the largest number of seats in the Chamber of Deputies.

Their leader, Léon Blum, was naturally anathema to the various political groups and organizations of the Right. A brilliant scholar, a literary figure, and a contributor to the Socialist paper, *L'Humanité,* before the First World

War, he had entered active politics only after the outbreak of that war and the accompanying assassination of the then Socialist leader, Jean Jaurès. Throughout the war and afterward, however, his influence with the Socialists had steadily increased. In 1919 he had been elected to the Chamber of Deputies by a Paris constituency, and in 1924 he had been chosen president of the Socialist Party. He was now called upon to assume the premiership. The opposition which he was bound to encounter was disclosed by a Rightist official circular: "This election clearly shows the extent of the Red menace and reveals the impossibility of parliamentary government."

Blum sought to construct a ministry which would include representatives of all of the Popular Front parties, but the Communists declined to enter such a coalition. His cabinet, therefore, when it finally took over the reins of government on June 5, 1936, consisted of only Socialists and Radical Socialists and was partly dependent for its continued life upon the support of the Communists.

At the time that the Blum government took office, France was seriously disturbed by "sit-down" strikes involving hundreds of thousands of workers who demanded collective labor contracts, wage increases, a forty-hour week, a two-week annual holiday with pay, and the right of the workers to present claims and complaints to the management. Immediately upon assuming office the new premier arranged a settlement between the workers and employers which granted wage increases. He also secured the enactment of legislation providing for a forty-hour week, holidays with pay, and collective labor contracts. The strike situation thereupon improved, although it was some months before all of the major labor disputes were settled. Eventually the parliament empowered the government to provide by decree for the compulsory mediation and arbitration of industrial conflicts. Meanwhile, on the ground that their members were precipitating clashes by interfering with strikers, Blum in June, 1936, ordered the dissolution of several Rightist leagues.[2]

This step had been included in the Popular Front platform, and during the summer legislation was enacted to carry out certain other items of that platform. The way was opened for the nationalization of the private armaments industry of France by a law providing that any concern engaged in the manufacture or sale of armaments could be expropriated at prices to be fixed by arbitration. Steps were also taken to "democratize" the powerful Bank of France by reducing the influence of the much-publicized "two hundred families." Legislation provided that each stockholder, regardless of the size of his holdings, should have a single vote, and that the composition and selection of the governing body of the bank should be

[2] Some of them appeared later with new names.

altered so that all classes of French economic life would be represented and a majority of its members would be appointed by the government. Finally, in order to protect the French farmer from disastrous fluctuations in the price of wheat, a special office was created with authority to fix the price of that commodity.

In September, in an attempt to solve the republic's economic and fiscal problems, the government took the important step of reducing the gold content of the franc by about 30 per cent in order to align it with British and American currencies. By depreciating the franc Blum hoped to stimulate business through the expansion of the French export trade. Unfortunately for his hopes, however, the economic situation did not respond to devaluation as favorably as had been expected. He had also hoped that devaluation would bring the return of French capital in sufficient amounts to enable the government to meet its needs by floating loans. But here, too, he met disappointment, largely because the wealthy classes were opposed to the Socialist premier. In June, 1937, France still had an unbalanced budget, her bonds were selling below par, and the republic's credit was at the lowest point since the fiscal crisis of 1926.

To meet the new crisis, Blum sought temporary dictatorial powers in the realm of finance like those conferred upon Poincaré in 1926. Although such powers were voted by the Chamber of Deputies, the more conservative Senate refused to pass the bill. In consequence, Blum resigned on June 20, 1937, after having established, in the words of one historian, "a record for energetic planning and parliamentary generalship unequaled in the history of the Third Republic." He was succeeded by Camille Chautemps, a leader of the Radical Socialists who had been a member of Blum's cabinet. The Socialists agreed to maintain the Popular Front government, and Blum and eight other Socialists accepted places in Chautemps' ministry. As in the case of Blum, the Communists gave the government their support.

On June 30 the parliament voted the Chautemps government, until August 31, 1937, the full powers which it had denied Blum. The new government thereupon gave up its attempt to maintain the French currency on a gold basis, and the franc immediately fell in value to about 3.75 cents. The budget deficit for 1937 amounted to about 8,000,000,000 francs, and the closing days of 1937 saw the franc again declining. The Socialists and the Communists demanded a controlled foreign exchange to solve the republic's monetary problem, but Georges Bonnet, the Radical Socialist finance minister, opposed such a solution. The Socialists then withdrew their support from the government, and Chautemps on January 14, 1938, resigned the premiership. For all practical purposes, the Popular Front was ended.

French Weakness in the Face of Nazi Germany

During the ensuing weeks, when Hitler launched his *Drang nach Osten* by seizing Austria, France passed through a period of ministerial instability caused by the Socialists' opposition to Chautemps and the Senate's opposition to Blum, for, though the latter had largely abandoned his program of reform and wished to concentrate on national armament, the Rightists refused to co-operate with him. Not until April 10, 1938, after the *Anschluss* had been safely consummated, was a stable government of Radical Socialists and representatives of certain moderate groups organized under Édouard Daladier. And it did not augur well for France that her new premier was weak and indecisive and that her foreign minister, Georges Bonnet, was hostile to Soviet Russia, France's new-found ally against Nazi Germany. But by this time many French patriots were becoming alarmed at the growing threat to French security from across the Rhine, and, when Daladier demanded that party politics should yield to national politics, the parliament at once voted his government special powers.

Many of the wealthy now threw their support to the government, so that a national defense loan of 5,000,000,000 francs was almost immediately taken up, and funds which had been sent abroad were repatriated to the extent of some 25,000,000,000 francs. Labor also rallied to the country's call. The forty-hour-week law was modified to authorize the minister of labor to call for extra hours in certain industries; in fact, the Left groups finally agreed that the law should be so modified as to assure national defense and the national economy. And when, after the "Munich crisis," the government called on the workers to work longer hours for less pay, they responded. The industrial production index rose from 83 in October, 1938, to 100 in June, 1939, when it was back to the predepression level.

Meanwhile, during the preceding decade, the government had been devoting special attention to the matter of national defense—and throughout this period the emphasis in France was on the word *defense*. Recalling the French success in holding back the Germans in the heroic battle of Verdun, the French high command had sought to transform the whole Franco-German frontier into a fortress more powerful even than Verdun. In 1930, under Tardieu's minister of war, André Maginot, French military engineers had begun the construction of the vast system of steel and concrete fortifications throughout Alsace-Lorraine which came to be known as the Maginot Line. The $500,000,000 expended on this line in the succeeding years seemed to indicate that the eyes of the French high command were turned toward the past, that French military leaders believed that in any future conflict the system of trench warfare and the slow war of attrition which had won in 1918 would inevitably win again.[3] They revealed, too, though it seemed not to be evident to many observers, that France had abandoned the strategy of attack, which was the inevitable and necessary corollary of all the mutual assistance treaties which she had signed in the twenties.

In January, 1938, an "extraordinary" budget of 18,500,000,000 francs had been adopted to provide further for French preparedness. Much of it was to be used to strengthen the navy, which in 1942 was expected to be 50,000 tons stronger than the Italian and 120,000 stronger than the German. In May, 1938, after Daladier came into office, plans were made to add some 2600 airplanes to the armed forces, and in the summer of that year a decree provided for the increase of the air force to 62,495 officers and men. Contracts were even signed for American fighting airplanes to be delivered by April, 1939. Feeble and tardy efforts—compared with the German— were thus made to modernize the French forces to meet the Nazi threat.

But it must be obvious to the reader of this chapter that conditions within France had already conspired to weaken that country almost beyond repair. In the first place, the political leaders of France had failed to grasp the significance of the Nazi revolution or the determination of the Nazi leaders to remake the map of Europe; and, in the years when they should have been devoting their united efforts to preparing their country for defense, they had kept France weak by their continual maneuvering for personal political preferment. Moreover, the bitter antagonism between the Right and the Left had prevented the carrying out of a strong, nationally supported foreign policy and had militated against the execution of adequate measures for national defense. In some Frenchmen loyalty to groups had become stronger than loyalty to France. In fact, certain groups and certain prominent politicians—some of them under the influence of Otto Abetz, a German agent in Paris—had become definitely enamored of fascism. Through their anti-Communist eyes even Hitler's Nazism looked good. Many of the bourgeoisie had come to feel that "fascism was a sort of insurance against proletarianism."

In the second place, during the period when capital and labor were sternly regimented in Germany in order that the nation's industry might pour out military equipment for use in a future war, French industrial and economic life had been repeatedly demoralized by strife between workers and employers, with disastrous results for the production of war supplies. Finally, those at the head of the French military forces had had little

---

[3] The distinguished British historian, Arnold J. Toynbee, has pointed out that history teaches that, once a nation wins wars or makes conquests by a particular ephemeral technique which may have been revolutionary in its formation, it ends by idolizing that technique and stubbornly adheres to it long after it has outworn its usefulness.

conception of the revolutionary changes introduced into warfare by airplanes and motorized equipment. They had failed to keep pace with Germany's production of these essential instruments of modern warfare, mis-
takenly putting their reliance in the defensive strength of a heavily fortified
line. Furthermore, despite the German blow through Belgium in 1914,
they had incredibly failed to extend the Maginot Line in its full strength
along the Belgian frontier.

The French commander-in-chief, General Maurice Gamelin, a cautious
and unimaginative military leader, overrated the strength of the Maginot
Line and underrated the striking power of the tank and the airplane. As
for the French people, during the first decade after Versailles they had
been impressed with the fact that France had the finest army in the world,
and they continued to believe this even after Germany's rearmament had
radically changed the situation. The outbreak of the Second World War,
therefore, was to find France unprepared politically, industrially, militarily,
and psychologically to fight through to victory.

Chapter XIII

SPAIN

IN the quarter-century after the First World War the Spanish experienced more changes in the political structure of their state than any other people in western Europe. Constitutional monarchy, military dictatorship, democratic republic, bloody civil war, and corporate fascism followed one another at short intervals. During the years 1936–1939, moreover, the Spanish people were plagued by foreign intervention, during which the fascist dictators of Italy and Germany used Spain as a proving ground for their own military tactics and weapons. Whether the regime established in Spain as the result of civil war and foreign intervention was that desired by the majority of the Spanish people was open to grave question. Fundamentally, the conflict in Spain was merely the continuation of the struggle between liberals and conservatives which had been going on in that country since the time of the French Revolution.

Military Dictatorship

The first of the revolutionary changes in the postwar period was brought about by a course of events which in Spain were somewhat analogous to those which led to Mussolini's dictatorship in Italy. During the war and early postwar years Spanish labor, plied with socialist and syndicalist propaganda, became more and more aggressive. Costly and sometimes bloody strikes ensued, particularly in the industrial region of Barcelona. The years 1919–1921 were especially disturbed by general strikes and street fighting; in March, 1921, the Spanish premier was even assassinated; and in the next two years hundreds were killed or wounded in the recurring industrial disputes.

In addition to widespread labor unrest, Spain was disturbed during these years by a growing autonomist movement in Catalonia, the northeastern section of the country including the populous city of Barcelona. The regional consciousness of this district was deep-rooted, for it had emerged as a separate entity back in the ninth century when Charlemagne created the Spanish March. Not until the fourteenth century had it been conquered and gradually merged into what became the Spanish monarchy, and during the intervening centuries it had developed a separate language and literature and its own parliament. Even down until the nineteenth century many of its liberties had been retained, though during this century the last vestiges of its former independent existence were destroyed by the highly centralized government at Madrid. Catalan nationalism survived, however, and even before the First World War a states' rights program had been drawn up.

During the war, when so much was said about nationalism and the rights of self-determination, the autonomist movement waxed stronger. One group, the autonomists, demanded that Catalonia should have its own parliament, its own executive, its own judiciary, and its own official language. It should be united with the other provinces of Spain only in a federal union. Another group, even more extreme than the autonomists, went so far as to demand complete independence. Regionalism and separatism, therefore, were seriously disturbing factors in the history of Spain during these years. Ministerial instability, caused by industrial strikes and autonomist agitation, was further increased by the repeated interference in political affairs of the military juntas, that is, councils of army officers.

The lot of the government was made still more difficult by the course of events in Spanish Morocco. Native resistance had begun as soon as Spain had attempted to extend her sway over that region, and, despite the vigorous military campaigns finally undertaken by the Spaniards in 1918, Abd-el-Krim, the Riffian chieftain, continued to defeat the Spanish forces. King Alfonso took it upon himself to meddle personally in the Moroccan situation, and thus became involved in one of the most disgraceful military disasters in Spanish history when some 20,000 Spanish soldiers were caught in a trap by Riffians and suffered a loss of 12,000 killed (1921). This debacle precipitated a crisis in Spanish affairs. Demands were made that those responsible should be summarily punished, and a parliamentary committee was appointed to investigate the tragedy. The committee's report was at once suppressed, but rumor said that a considerable number of high officials—even Alfonso himself—were implicated.

When the parliament, the press, and the populace began to protest against the action of the government in withholding the report, when they began to demand that punishment be meted out where punishment was due, King Alfonso seemingly decided to forestall the attempts to find scapegoats for the Moroccan disaster. At the same time, apparently, he hoped to strengthen the government to deal with the continuing industrial and regional unrest. Having given his consent to the establishment of a military dictatorship in the country, he tactfully arranged to be visiting in France when the blow was struck.

On September 13, 1923, General Miguel Primo de Rivera overthrew the ministry, suspended the constitution, organized a military directorate, proclaimed martial law, and established himself as military dictator of Spain. Rivera was an army man of long standing. He had served with the Spanish troops in Cuba and the Philippines during the Spanish-American War; he had fought in Morocco in later years; and after 1915 he had been military governor of various districts of Spain. At the time of his *coup d'état* he held this position in Barcelona. As dictator, he at once dissolved the parliament, suppressed freedom of speech and of the press, and abolished trial by jury. To prevent incriminating evidence regarding the Moroccan catastrophe from leaking out, he seized the documents resulting from the parliamentary investigation.

For the next two years Rivera ruled by strong-arm methods. Provincial legislatures were arbitrarily dismissed, leaders of the republican group were exiled, severe fines were exacted for minor offenses, and the censorship was tightened. In spite of these developments—or perhaps because of them—popular hostility toward the dictatorship increased instead of diminishing, and, unfortunately for King Alfonso, it tended to rise against the monarchy as well. After 1928 popular dissatisfaction grew rapidly. In 1929 a mutiny occurred in the army, and riots of university students and the working classes became frequent. Gradually Rivera was deserted by nearly all classes. Plans were made in some circles for a revolution which should usher in a republic early in 1930. The dictator became discouraged. Suffering from ill health, discovering that he had lost the confidence and support not only of his king but of the army as well, Rivera suddenly resigned his office on January 28, 1930, and left the country. On March 16 he died.

Upon Rivera's resignation, King Alfonso at once announced that the constitution of 1876 would be restored, the demands of university students and professors would be granted, all officers who had suffered at the dictator's hands would be given their former status, all political prisoners would be pardoned, and free and honest elections would be held late in 1930 for a new national parliament. The Socialists insisted, however, that the new government differed not essentially from that of Rivera, and before long shouts of "Down with the king and the monarchy!" began to be heard. The shouts were soon followed by the definite demand that a national assembly be called to draft a new constitution and to determine whether Spain should remain a monarchy or become a republic. In December a serious military uprising and a republican revolt were suppressed only after thousands had been arrested and martial law had again been proclaimed throughout the country.

In February, 1931, Alfonso restored the constitution and called for parliamentary elections to be held in March. So great was the popular demand for a constituent assembly rather than a parliament, however, that the government later suspended the call for the March elections. It announced instead plans for municipal and provincial elections in April, to be followed by the election of a constituent assembly. Apparently Premier Aznar and King Alfonso desired to learn popular sentiment by local elections before proceeding with plans for a constituent assembly. If so, they were not left in doubt. The municipal elections of April 12 constituted a veritable republican landslide. On the next day the Aznar government resigned, and a republican junta headed by Niceto Alcalá Zamora, leader of the unsuccessful republican revolt of December, 1930, issued an ultimatum stating that a revolution would be called if Alfonso refused to abdicate. That night the king without formal abdication left for France, merely suspending "the exercise of the royal power" until he should "learn the real expression of the collective opinion of his people."

The Establishment of the Republic

Following the flight of the king, Zamora at once proclaimed a republic with himself as provisional president. A carefully selected cabinet of the best moderate republican and Socialist talent available took charge of the government, which was soon recognized by most of the leading powers. The provisional government hastened to outline its program, for it faced the necessity of meeting the demands of the various groups which had been responsible for the development of the strong antimonarchical sentiment: the intellectuals, who denounced the church and deplored its medieval influence in Spanish affairs; the republicans, who sought a constitutional democracy in which the military should be subordinated to the civil authorities; the Socialists, who had as their goal a new economic and social order; and the autonomists, who wished to throw off the old detested centralized regime.

The republican government immediately guaranteed religious and civil liberty and recognized the rights of private property. It proclaimed an amnesty for all political prisoners and invited all exiles to return to Spain. It abolished all titles of nobility and arrested a number of former royal officials. It announced that it would inaugurate comprehensive agrarian reforms with a view to modernizing the system of land tenure and improving the methods of farming, which were hopelessly antiquated. It promised to hold elections for a national constituent assembly in the near future and modified the electoral system to make it conform with modern conditions. It extended the franchise to the clergy, but at the same time it abolished compulsory religious education in the public schools.

Elections for the constituent assembly were held in June, 1931, and resulted in an overwhelming victory for the Left Republicans and the Socialists. The assembly at once took up its task and, after nearly five months of consideration and debate, finally completed the republican constitution which on December 9, 1931, was adopted. Spain was declared "a republic of the workers of all classes," in which the franchise was extended to all men and women over twenty-three years of age. A single-chamber parliament (*Cortes*) was provided for, its members being elected directly for four years by popular vote. The president of the republic was to be chosen for a six-year term by an electoral college, consisting of the members of parliament and an equal number of electors chosen by the voters. No active or reserve army officer and no member of the clergy might be a candidate for the presidency. Executive power was placed in the hands of a ministry directly responsible to the parliament. In other words, Spain became politically a democratic, parliamentary republic. So far as decentralization was concerned, the constitution provided that any area which desired autonomy must submit for the approval of the parliament a regional charter, and that the parliament in turn might delegate to the local authorities power to administer certain national laws.

Wide as was the break between Spain's former political system and that established in 1931, the departure from the former regime in social, cultural, and economic matters was perhaps even more pronounced. Spain was to have complete religious freedom and no state church. Education was to be secularized. Divorce was to be made easy, and illegitimate and legitimate children were to have equal rights. The state was to have authority (1) to expropriate, with compensation, all kinds of private property, (2) to socialize large estates, (3) to nationalize public utilities, and (4) to "participate in the development and co-ordination of industries." In general, therefore, all the wealth of the country was to be subordinated to the interests of the national economy. Spain, it appeared, was to be transformed from a semi-feudal nation into a modern state with somewhat socialistic tendencies.

A special clause of the constitution provided that the first president of the Spanish Republic should be chosen by the national convention which had drafted the constitution. Accordingly, on December 10, 1931, Niceto Alcalá Zamora was elected to this office; on the next day he received the oath of office and took up his official residence in Alfonso's former palace. The provisional government at once resigned, and a new cabinet headed by Manuel Azaña took office. As has frequently been the case in the history of other countries, the constituent assembly did not resign upon the completion of its constituent duties, but continued to sit thereafter as the national parliament. The members of the assembly desired themselves to launch the program of reform which by laws should carry into effect the general principles laid down in the constitution. "We have finished the first step," said Premier Azaña. "We must now complete the revolution by drafting supplementary laws."

In January, 1932, the Jesuit order was dissolved; its property, valued at $30,000,000, was confiscated by the state and later ordered to be distributed for purposes of social welfare. In May, 1933, the drastic Associations Law was passed, stipulating that the heads of the various religious orders in Spain must be Spanish citizens and must submit to Spanish laws, and that the state reserved the right to pass upon their appointment. Members of religious orders were forbidden to teach anything except religion. Church schools were suppressed, and all teaching by members of religious orders was to cease. All church property was nationalized; although placed under the custody of the clergy, it was subject to the disposition of the government. All government support of priests—of whom there were 40,000 in Spain— was to cease after November 11, 1933. The pope at once issued a vigorous protest in an encyclical in which he condemned the separation of church and state and denounced the prohibition of teaching by religious orders.

The government also made a beginning of agrarian and labor reform. The great estates of Spain's grandees [1] were confiscated, for the most part without compensation, and the parliament enacted a measure for distributing over fifty million acres of land held before the revolution by the king or under his royal grant. It was expected that a million Spaniards would be settled on these lands, and that they would be assisted with government subsidies. Furthermore, in the interests of the peasants and industrial workers alike, a new charter of economic independence and freedom was adopted, providing for a national schedule of working hours and wages and for mixed courts to settle labor disputes.

Finally, the problem of Catalan autonomy was settled to the apparent satisfaction of most of the Catalans when in 1932 Premier Azaña presented an autonomy statute to the president of the Catalan *generalidad* in Barcelona. By the terms of this statute Catalonia secured the right to have its own state government, which was given power to tax and to enact social legislation within certain restrictions. The enforcement of law and order in Catalonia was left to the local government, and the execution of national laws was in general confided to Catalan authorities. Without destroying the integrity of the republic, a considerable measure of self-government was thus extended to Catalonia. As further concessions to the national sentiment of the Catalans, they were granted the right to have a national anthem and their own flag. The Catalan language was made official in the province and was given equality with Castilian in official communications with the

---

[1] A grandee was a person who had the right to appear in the presence of the king of Spain without removing his hat.

rest of Spain. On December 6, 1932, the Catalan parliament met for the first time since 1705.

The Struggle to Control the Republic

But not all Spaniards were content with the course of events in the new republic. On the Right were the clericals, the royalists, and the landed aristocrats, who looked back with longing upon their positions and privileges in the old regime and who fervently prayed for the collapse of the republic and the return of the monarchy. On the extreme Left were the Syndicalists and Communists, who felt that the Spanish revolution had stopped altogether too soon, that the republican government should be displaced by a regime more like that in Soviet Russia. Abortive attempts to overthrow the government were made by both the royalists and the Communists in the years 1932 and 1933.

In November of the latter year the republic had its first parliamentary elections. The result was a disastrous defeat for the moderate Left parties which had been in control of Spain since the overthrow of the monarchy. The combined opposition of the Catholic Popular Action Party, led by the brilliant young editor José María Gil Robles, of the commercial, industrial, and financial leaders, and of the landlord classes—plus the universal tendency to vote against any government in office in time of economic depression—had carried the day. The ensuing year was marked by a succession of minority governments which leaned more and more to the Right. The relations between the government and the Vatican were improved, legislation designed to ameliorate the lot of the clergy was passed, the educational measures and land reforms enacted in 1932–1933 were modified and weakened, and many grandees were permitted to return to their landed estates. The leaders of the Left became convinced that the parliament was undermining the republic and threatening to turn Spain back again to men who were monarchists at heart.

In October, 1934, a new ministry included three members of the Popular Action Party. This was particularly alarming to the Left groups, for in the national assembly those who later organized this party had been frankly antirepublican and hostile to nearly every article in the constitution which was adopted. They had refused to vote for the constitution and had from the day of its adoption been revisionists. In the elections of 1933 the Popular Action Party had been allied with the royalists, and, although Gil Robles had later announced his acceptance of the republic, the party was still suspected by those on the Left of remaining monarchist at heart. The Left parties at once called a general strike against what they claimed was a shift toward fascism in Spain. At the same time, President Companys of Catalonia proclaimed that state a free and independent republic. Open revolt spread rapidly through central and northern Spain, causing the death of thousands and the destruction of millions of dollars in property.

Unfortunately for the revolutionists, there was lack of solidarity among the Left elements and in many parts of the country relatively little support from the rural districts. The uprising in Catalonia was almost immediately crushed by the use of the army, the navy, and the civil guard. President Companys, former Premier Azaña, and hundreds of others were arrested and held for court-martial. In the reaction which followed, Socialist provincial governors and municipal councilors were throughout the country largely replaced by men loyal to the government at Madrid. The Catalan statute, moreover, was set aside and made subject to a thorough revision, while outstanding Catalonian leaders were held for trial by court-martial.

The Center and Right groups next sought to alter Spanish institutions to conform with their ideas, claiming that those who drafted the constitution had gone beyond the wishes of a majority of the Spanish people in matters relating to the church, education, and agrarian reform. In 1935 the government began to draft a number of constitutional amendments to carry out the policies of the Right. But ministerial instability continued, and when in December of that year the government was again overturned, President Zamora, who had apparently begun to fear for the safety of the liberal republic, passed over Gil Robles, who could have formed a government commanding a majority in the parliament, and instead appointed as premier Manuel Portela Valladares, a loyal moderate republican. In January, 1936, President Zamora dissolved the parliament and called for new elections.

In the ensuing elections the score or more of political parties in Spain combined into two major groups. On the Left the Syndicalists, Communists, Socialists, Left Republicans, and Republican Unionists fought together as the Popular Front. They were determined to prevent the Rightists from securing control of the parliament lest they should liquidate completely the achievements of the republic. On the Right the Conservative Republicans, the clericals, and the royalists combined in an effort to prevent the triumph of those who were suspected of desiring to introduce a proletarian regime. The election resulted in a decisive majority in favor of the Left; within this coalition the Socialists won the most seats. Of all the parties, however, Gil Robles' Popular Action still had the greatest number of deputies.

Manuel Portela, who was himself defeated in the election, at once resigned the premiership and was succeeded as head of the government by Manuel Azaña. The latter's ministry consisted of eleven Left Republicans and two Republican Unionists, the Socialists declining to participate in the government. Amnesty was at once proclaimed for 30,000 political prisoners and exiles, among whom was Louis Companys, former president of Catalonia. The Catalonian parliament, suspended since the revolt of October, 1934, reassembled, and steps were taken by the central government to restore Catalonian autonomy. Agrarian reform was again pushed, and thousands of tracts of land were distributed among the peasants. Anticlericalism once more surged to the front as scores of churches, schools, and convents were attacked and burned, and street clashes resulted in the death of some forty or fifty persons. In April, 1936, the parliament voted to remove President Zamora from office on the ground that he had exceeded his powers in dissolving the parliament, and Manuel Azaña was elected to succeed him as president.

Civil War

Meanwhile, the Popular Front government had been taking steps to rid the army of officers whose loyalty to the existing regime was suspected. In April a decree stipulated that all officers known to have been politically active should be retired at once upon pensions. Some with monarchist or conservative sympathies were transferred to Spain's overseas possessions; General Francisco Franco, who had been chief of staff when Gil Robles was minister of war, was sent to the Canary Islands. In July the government further ordered the removal from their posts of many of the officers of the Foreign Legion in Morocco. These various measures threatened the control of Spain's military forces by the ruling clique of officers, and apparently led the latter to decide to overthrow the government. They knew that in a rebellion they could count on the support of most of the royalists, clericals, Conservative Republicans, and great landowners; and, in view of later developments, it is probable that they had the encouragement of Fascist and Nazi leaders in Italy and Germany.

On July 17, 1936, a number of regiments in Morocco raised the standard of revolt, and General Franco, the leader of the insurrection, flew to Morocco to take charge. In Spain garrisons in various parts of the country at once mutinied under the leadership of their generals. The Insurgents, it appeared, had the support of approximately 90 per cent of the officers and two thirds of Spain's organized military forces. In August, furthermore, they began to receive aid from Italy and Germany; ultimately thousands of well-trained officers and men from these countries joined the Insurgents as "volunteers."

The government, with only a small part of the organized military forces loyal to it, was obliged to turn to the left-wing labor groups for assistance. In September, 1936, Francisco Largo Caballero, a left-wing Socialist, became premier in a cabinet which for the first time included Socialists and Communists. A Popular Militia of workers was hastily created, and thanks to its efforts Madrid and Catalonia were saved. But the Loyalist forces were unable to stop the advance of General Franco's disciplined units. In November the Insurgents were at the gates of Madrid, and the seat of the Loyalist government was transferred to Valencia. Germany and Italy thereupon extended *de jure* recognition to the Insurgent government which had been set up by General Franco at Burgos. But by this time the Popular Militia had been strengthened by antifascist volunteers from many foreign countries, and by supplies—particularly airplanes and tanks—presumably from Soviet Russia.

Although the Insurgents, or the Nationalists, as they came to call themselves, were unable to capture Madrid in either 1936 or 1937, on June 19 of the latter year, after a long and desperate siege, in which they were greatly aided by German and Italian planes, men, and munitions, they did succeed in capturing the Basque city of Bilbao on the Bay of Biscay. Late in August they also took Santander, to the west of Bilbao, and on October 21 they occupied Gijón, an important port. With the capture of Gijón the Nationalists completed their conquest of northwestern Spain, and made plans to concentrate all of their forces against the Loyalist lines in the eastern part of the republic.

Foreign Intervention

Meanwhile, there had been more or less constant fear that the Spanish struggle might precipitate a general European conflict. The fascist states— Italy, Germany, Portugal—were apparently determined to assist General Franco, on the professed ground that the triumph of the Loyalists would result in the establishment of another Bolshevik state in Europe. But both Italy and Germany were suspected of aiding the Nationalists in the hope of obtaining valuable economic concessions from Franco's government. Then, too, they apparently saw advantages for themselves in the establishment of a fascist state on the "other" side of France. To many it appeared that Mussolini by helping the Spanish Nationalists expected to advance Italy's program of controlling the Mediterranean, while Hitler, in view of later developments, was apparently using the Spanish civil war to provide an opportunity for his military leaders to experiment with mechanized and aerial warfare in order to discover the best methods for a future blitzkrieg.

Soviet Russia appeared willing to assist the Spanish Loyalists, but the British and French governments seemed to be chiefly interested in preventing the struggle from developing into a general European war. The British people were divided in their views. Although the Laborites and trade unionists generally sympathized with the Loyalists, many others because of their economic investments and views were inclined to look with tolerance upon a Nationalist victory. The British government appeared to be attempting to follow a neutral policy. In France the Left groups favored the Spanish Loyalists, but the government—even when headed by Léon Blum—desired to avoid any steps that might open the way to a general war. Not long after the civil war began, in August, 1936, France initiated negotiations looking toward a European agreement against intervention. Eventually twenty-seven countries, including all the great powers of Europe, agreed to set up a committee in London to apply a policy of nonintervention in Spain.

Early in 1937, on the suggestion of Great Britain and France, all of these countries further agreed to prohibit the flow of foreign volunteers to Spain and to this end decided to establish a system of international control. In March, by which time there were already 100,000 Italian soldiers in Spain, a naval cordon, consisting of ships provided by Great Britain, France, Italy, and Germany, was thrown around Spain, and inspectors were stationed along the French and Portuguese land frontiers. All went well with the international blockade until the latter part of May, when the German warship *Deutschland* and the Italian warship *Barletta* were bombed by Loyalist airplanes. Five German warships thereupon at once bombarded the Loyalist city of Almería in retaliation.

After these events Germany and Italy withdrew from the nonintervention patrol, and thereafter the fascist states tended to become more aggressive and recalcitrant. Although in June, following a new agreement between the four great powers, Germany and Italy rejoined the naval patrol, an alleged attempt of the Loyalists to torpedo the German cruiser *Leipzig* led the two fascist powers again to withdraw their warships and to intimate that they considered themselves freed of nonintervention obligations.

During the summer of 1937 a number of neutral merchant ships suspected of carrying cargoes to the Spanish Loyalists were attacked by submarines in the Mediterranean. Although the submarines were unidentified, they were widely suspected of being Italian, and in September the Soviet government openly charged Italy with responsibility for the torpedoing of two Soviet freighters. In order to consider measures for dealing with these acts of "piracy," a conference of all the Mediterranean and Black Sea powers and Germany was called to meet in September at Nyon in Switzerland. Italy and Germany, however, declined to attend because the Soviet Union was to be represented. Nevertheless, the powers at Nyon agreed to establish an antisubmarine patrol of warships and airplanes to protect neutral merchant ships in the Mediterranean and the Black Sea, and after the Nyon agreement the submarine attacks soon ceased.

On October 2 a Franco-British note to Italy pointed out that no improvement in the general European situation could be expected until the policy of nonintervention in Spain had been made fully effective by the withdrawal of foreign nationals from the Spanish armies. It emphasized the failure of the London nonintervention committee to solve this problem and proposed a three-power conference between France, Great Britain, and Italy. Italy, however, declined the invitation to such a conference and proposed instead that the question of foreign volunteers be dealt with by the London committee.

The question of the withdrawal of volunteers was therefore considered by the nonintervention committee, but the discussions were deadlocked by the fascist powers' demand that at the same time belligerent rights should be extended to the Nationalists. Eventually, however, Italy and Germany agreed to accept in principle the British plan to defer the grant of belligerent rights until after "token" withdrawals of foreign fighters had been made from both sides. As was expected, the drafting of the specific plans for the actual withdrawals required long negotiations, and it was not until June, 1938, that the British plan for counting and evacuating the foreign volunteers was accepted by the nonintervention committee. The Loyalist government accepted the plan which had been drafted, but Franco's government raised so many objections to it that its reply constituted a rejection. In other words, Franco continued to have the assistance of large numbers of foreign troops.

Victory of the Nationalists

Meanwhile, the Nationalists had pushed a threatening salient into the Loyalist lines defending Madrid, Valencia, and Catalonia, the point of the salient being only sixty miles from Valencia. Fearing that a Nationalist drive might divide Loyalist Spain and cut off Madrid and Valencia from Catalonia, the Loyalists late in October, 1937, had again moved the seat of their government—this time from Valencia to Barcelona. That they were justified in these fears soon became evident, for the Nationalists in the early months of 1938 drove eastward from Saragossa and on April 15 reached the sea south of Tortosa. The coast road connecting Barcelona with Valencia and Madrid was thus cut, and Loyalist Spain was divided.

For a number of months thereafter, thanks to the valiant efforts of the Loyalists, the military situation appeared deadlocked, but in December, 1938, the Nationalists with a well-equipped army of some 300,000 men again struck—this time toward Barcelona. The Loyalist forces, greatly inferior in guns, tanks, and airplanes, were unable to check the Nationalist advance. On January 13, 1939, Franco's forces crossed the Ebro, and twelve days later they reached the outskirts of Barcelona. Here they met no such determined fighting as they had encountered when they reached Madrid in November, 1936. The Loyalist government withdrew to Figueras, President Azaña fled to the Spanish embassy in Paris, and Barcelona surrendered without offering resistance on January 26. As the Nationalists pushed forward in pursuit of the retreating and demoralized Loyalists, the territory held by the latter in Catalonia rapidly contracted. Hundreds of thousands of refugees and Loyalist troops fled across the frontier into France after the downfall of Figueras early in February.

With the extensive industries, munitions plants, and harbor facilities of Catalonia in the hands of the Nationalists, President Azaña and most of the cabinet ministers realized the futility of further resistance and urged the opening of negotiations with General Franco. Premier Negrín, a right-wing Socialist who had succeeded Caballero as head of the government in May, 1937, was determined to continue the struggle, however, and in this determination was supported by the Cortes. But only central Spain with the two important cities of Madrid and Valencia still remained in Loyalist hands. To Madrid, therefore, Premier Negrín now returned by airplane, only to discover that the military leaders there believed that further resistance was useless.

On March 6 General Miaja, commander-in-chief of all remaining Loyalist forces, broadcast an appeal for peace. This broadcast precipitated a series of Communist uprisings within Madrid with the aim of overthrowing the Council of National Defense, but after more than a week of bloody fighting the Communists were eventually suppressed. Then, following futile attempts to obtain a negotiated peace, General Miaja withdrew from Madrid, and on March 28, 1939, General Franco's victorious troops entered the capital unresisted. Already, on February 27, Great Britain and France had extended recognition to the Nationalist government in Burgos. The specter of a general European war rising out of foreign intervention in the Spanish struggle seemed at last to be definitely laid.

But the civil war had exacted a terrific death toll. The most reliable estimates placed the number of those killed in battle or by firing squads at 1,200,000, to say nothing of the misery which was brought upon other millions of Spaniards who were not killed. In addition, an untold amount of wealth and property had been destroyed by the indiscriminate bombing of many Spanish cities.

The Fascist Corporative State

Although during the civil war General Franco had received support from diverse groups within the country—royalists, landed aristocrats, army leaders, clergy, fascists—as early as April, 1937, he had adopted most of the program of the fascist Phalanx (*Falange Española Tradicionalista*) as his official program. In March, 1938, the Phalanx had issued a labor charter, and at the conclusion of the war the Nationalist government announced that this charter was thereafter to be applied throughout Spain. Labor unions were abolished, and strikes and lockouts were forbidden. All workers, including executives, were incorporated in vertical syndicates, restrictions were imposed on workers and employers alike, and each industry was organized under supervision of the syndicalist state, somewhat as in Italy under Mussolini.

Politically, Nationalist Spain was organized about the Phalanx Party, in which by a decree of July, 1939, officers and men of the army were incorporated as "affiliated members." At the head of the state stood the *Caudillo* (Leader)—General Franco—who on August 4, 1939, assumed "absolute authority" and became "responsible only to God and to history." Assisting him was the Phalanx National Council, part of whose members were named by the Caudillo, and the Phalanx Political Junta, the permanent governing body of the Phalanx, which had the right to present to the Caudillo any proposals it might think fit. Wide powers were also conferred on the secretary-general of the Phalanx Party, a permanent official appointed by the Caudillo. In January, 1940, by the Law of Syndical Unity, all organizations representing economic or class interests—whether composed of employers or of workers—were incorporated in the Phalanx. The similarities between the Phalanx system of Spain and the Fascist system of Italy are readily apparent.

As might be expected, a number of decrees of a reactionary nature were issued. It was ordered, for example, that the grandees should be given back all land seized under the Agrarian Reform Law of 1932. The Catholic Church also regained many of the privileges which it had held in Spain before the downfall of the monarchy. Catholicism was made the official state religion, government subsidies were restored to the clergy, all confiscated property was returned to the Jesuits, civil marriage and divorce were prohibited, and religious instruction was required in all public schools, colleges, and universities.

While Franco took steps to reward his supporters, severe measures were invoked against those who had prominently supported the Loyalist government. A Law of Political Responsibilities, designed "to liquidate the political crimes of those who, through their acts or through their serious failure to act, have contributed to ... the present plight of Spain," outlawed twenty-six specified organizations, including supporters of the Popular Front, autonomist organizations, and Masonic lodges. Even before the war ended, General Franco had stated that he had "more than 2,000,000 persons card-indexed, with proofs of their crimes and names of witnesses," and tens of thousands of new arrests were made immediately following the fall of Madrid. A year after the close of the civil war it was reported that there were still some 500,000 political prisoners in Spain.

Nationalist Spain's leaning toward the Axis powers was evident not only in its political and economic organization but in its foreign policy also. At the close of the civil war Franco's government signed Hitler's anti-Comintern pact, and in May, 1939, Spain withdrew from the League of Nations. The occasional demands of Spanish imperialists for the return of Gibraltar indicated that Spain under favorable circumstances might join the totalitarian states against the "possessing" powers, though financial weakness and need for physical rehabilitation militated against the country's hasty entrance into war in the immediate future. Throughout the Second World War she remained—formally, at least—an uneasy neutral.

Chapter XIV

THE SUCCESSION STATES

OF CENTRAL EUROPE

THE disruption of the once powerful Habsburg empire and the distribution of its territory and people among seven different states was one of the most spectacular of the many results of the First World War.[1] Of the three great empires which had existed in Europe in 1914, the German was reduced in size and transformed into a democratic republic, the Russian was likewise diminished in territory and still more profoundly altered in political and social structure, but the Austro-Hungarian was completely obliterated from the map.

The New Central Europe

Obviously, therefore, central Europe differed radically from what it had been before the war. Although the former Habsburg empire had long been a political anachronism, yet, stretching from the plains of the Vistula to the shores of the Adriatic and from the heart of the Alps to the bounds of Rumania, it had constituted a strong economic unit. Within its confines had been found grain fields, pasture-lands, and forests; oil wells and coal mines; iron, copper, lead, silver, and gold ores; breweries, distilleries, and sugar refineries; steel mills and textile factories; glassworks and potteries. All had been included within a common tariff union. This relatively balanced and unified economic organism was utterly disrupted by the nationalistic upheaval which followed the war. Most of the periphery of what had been Europe's second largest country was absorbed into surrounding states— Italy, Yugoslavia, Rumania, and re-created Poland; the center fell to Austria, Hungary, and Czechoslovakia.

Austria,[2] now essentially a financial and industrial country, was left with inadequate food supplies for her population and insufficient raw materials for her industrial enterprises. On the other hand, she inherited the populous capital of a former empire of more than 51,000,000 inhabitants, a city which

[1] For the disintegration of the former Habsburg empire, see pages 96–99
[2] About 6,500,000 inhabitants in an area of 32,369 square miles.

contained thousands of officials, soldiers, and tradesmen, drawn there by former imperial institutions. Hungary [3] was reduced to little more than an agricultural plain, her former mountainous border being assigned to adjacent countries. She possessed almost no wood and very little water power, and was cut off from manufacturing centers, natural markets, and much-needed raw materials. Czechoslovakia [4] was more fortunate, for she obtained from 85 to 90 per cent of the soft coal, about 60 per cent of the iron ore, and nearly 80 per cent of the industries of the former empire. Furthermore, she had extensive agricultural districts. She, therefore, possessed the food, mineral wealth, and manufacturing establishments necessary for a somewhat balanced economic life.

These three states had numerous reasons for economic co-operation. Austria needed to import food supplies and raw materials; Hungary needed to import manufactured goods and to export surplus foodstuffs; Czechoslovakia needed markets for her manufactured products. Nevertheless, this free exchange of goods was prevented when each country, actuated by an excessive nationalism, at once erected tariff barriers against all its neighbors. The economic ills which resulted further embittered their political relations.

The new boundaries of central Europe cut almost recklessly across railways, rivers, canals, and highways, seriously interfering with the accustomed trends of commerce. The former empire had held two important seaports on the Adriatic, but each of these new states was landlocked. In an attempt to overcome this handicap, the peace conference internationalized the Oder from Czechoslovakia to the Baltic, the Moldau from Prague to the Elbe, and the latter to the North Sea. Hamburg on the Elbe and Stettin on the Oder were made free ports for Czechoslovakia. The Danube was internationalized from Ulm to its mouth and thus provided all three states with a water route to the Black Sea. Austria and Hungary, furthermore, were accorded free access to the Adriatic. This included the right to transport goods over the territories and in the ports severed from the former Habsburg empire, and to receive in them the same treatment as nationals of the states to which the territories belonged. To provide Czechoslovakia, also, with an outlet to the south she was given the right to send her trains over certain Austrian railroads toward the Adriatic.

The new boundaries not only cut across railway lines but cut across racial lines as well. Despite the fact that postwar central Europe presented a much nearer approximation to the ideal coincidence of political and racial boundaries than did the former polyglot Dual Monarchy, all of the heirs to Habsburg territory—except little Austria—still contained national minorities.

[3] About 8,500,000 inhabitants in an area of 35,875 square miles.
[4] About 14,500,000 inhabitants in an area of 54,207 square miles.

ETHNOGRAPHIC MAP OF THE FORMER DUAL MONARCHY, SHOWING THE SUCCESSION STATES, 1919–1938

For strategic, historic, or economic reasons, varying numbers of Magyars and Germans were included in Czechoslovakia, Rumania, and Yugoslavia. Some of the new *irredentas* thus comprised the former dominant races, groups of high intelligence and great initiative, not accustomed to submission.

Just as the Germans and Magyars, the ruling groups in the former empire, had bent all their efforts toward maintaining their predominance at the expense of the less fortunate nationalities, so now the liberated groups, particularly the Czechoslovaks, the Yugoslavs, and the Rumanians, directed their efforts toward protecting themselves against the vanquished. To check the outward thrust of Hungary's irredentism the surrounding states resorted to centripetal counteralliances. In this defensive movement the initiative was taken by Eduard Beneš, Czechoslovak foreign minister, who made his first objective an understanding between Czechoslovakia, Yugoslavia, and Rumania.

In 1920 Czechoslovakia and Yugoslavia signed a convention in which each agreed to assist the other in case of an unprovoked attack by Hungary. A Czechoslovak-Rumanian convention with practically identical terms was signed in April of the following year, and the so-called Little Entente was completed two months later by a Yugoslav-Rumanian alliance in which each agreed to aid the other if attacked by Hungary or Bulgaria. In 1933 a convention was signed with the purpose of transforming the Little Entente into a permanent "unified international organization." By the terms of this convention the earlier bilateral treaties between the members of the Little Entente were renewed for an indefinite period; a permanent council, consisting of the foreign ministers of the three states, was organized, and a permanent secretariat was established. Every political treaty and every economic agreement thereafter entered into by a member of the Little Entente was first to have the unanimous consent of the permanent council. This convention created in a sense—so far as international affairs were concerned—a new great power in Europe, with a population not far from 50,000,000 and with a combined military force of considerable size. By treaties which France signed [5] with Czechoslovakia, Rumania, and Yugoslavia the Little Entente was to some extent linked with that great power.

Austria

It will be recalled that on October 21, 1918, the German deputies of the former Austrian Reichsrat had constituted themselves a provisional national assembly, and had declared the independence of German Austria. The bourgeois parties favored the establishment of a constitutional monarchy,

[5] See page 310.

but the Social Democrats, backed by the working classes, demanded a republic and prepared to fight, if necessary, to get it. The effect of their determination was seen on November 12, when the Provisional National Assembly adopted a temporary constitution which provided that Austria should be "a democratic republic." At the same time the assembly announced that Austria was "an integral part" of the recently proclaimed German Republic, it being the fond hope of the Austrian leaders that an actual union with Germany might be effected at once and the peace conference later confronted with a *fait accompli*.

In the early months of 1919 vigorous attempts were made to bring Austria into the ranks of the soviet republics. In the midst of acute food shortage and widespread unemployment, emissaries from Soviet Hungary and Soviet Russia preached communism in the streets of Vienna. Disciples of Lenin invaded workmen's councils and waged a mighty struggle for control. But, thanks to the efforts of moderate Socialists like Otto Bauer and Victor Adler, there was in Austria no bitter communist conflict between the proletariat and the bourgeoisie. The issue was settled within the ranks of the workers. The forces of moderation won out; Bolshevism was rejected. Elections in February, 1919, gave the Social Democrats the largest representation in the National Constituent Assembly, whose first act was to announce that Austria was a democratic republic. The Habsburgs were banished from the country, and all possessions of the dynasty were confiscated.

On October 1, 1920, a constitution was adopted. Under it Austria became a federal republic with nine provinces, each with its own local diet. The national government had a bicameral legislature consisting of the Federal Council, elected by the diets, and the National Council, elected by popular vote. In 1929 provision was made for the popular election of the president also. Real executive power, however, resided in a ministry responsible to the National Council, which, furthermore, had authority to enact legislation over the veto of the upper house. The whole political structure rested on proportional representation and universal suffrage. On December 9, 1920, Michael Hainisch, a liberal bourgeois, was elected first president of the republic, which, in the same month, was admitted to membership in the League of Nations.

ECONOMIC AND FISCAL DIFFICULTIES

The disruption of the Habsburg empire had particularly unfortunate economic results for Austria. The latter, which inherited the populous capital of the former empire, was left with inadequate food supplies for her population and with insufficient coal and raw materials for her industries. She therefore faced the necessity of importing these commodities. But the free exchange of goods, which might have enabled her to pay for her imports by the exportation of her manufactured products, was prevented when each of the succession states of central Europe at once erected tariff barriers against its neighbors.

By 1922 Austria's plight was so serious that Chancellor Ignaz Seipel proposed a currency and customs union with Italy as a cure for the republic's economic woes. But this proposal was so distasteful to Czechoslovakia that Beneš, the Czechoslovak foreign minister, did his utmost to persuade the League of Nations to save Austria from bankruptcy. In September, 1922, Seipel made a personal appeal to the League, stating Austria's willingness to accept a system of control if assistance were forthcoming, but warning that Austria unaided would constitute a grave danger to the peace of the world, a danger which it was the duty of the League of Nations to avert.

The League decided to undertake the financial rehabilitation of the little republic, and on October 4, 1922, three protocols embodying the Council's scheme were signed by representatives of Great Britain, France, Italy, Czechoslovakia, and Austria. The first protocol contained a solemn declaration that all the signatories would "respect the political independence, the territorial integrity, and the sovereignty of Austria," while the latter agreed not to alienate her independence and to "abstain from any negotiations or from any economic or financial engagement calculated directly or indirectly to compromise this independence." Austria agreed to carry through a program of reform in order that her budget might be balanced by the end of 1924. The governments of Great Britain, France, Italy, and Czechoslovakia guaranteed a loan up to 650,000,000 gold crowns ($135,000,000) to cover the excess of expenditure over revenue available from normal resources during the next two years. A bank of issue was to be established under prescribed conditions, and the Austrian government agreed to surrender all right to issue paper money or to negotiate loans except by special authorization. A commissioner-general, in collaboration with the Austrian government, was to supervise the execution of the plan. In a sense Austria went into the hands of a receiver.

During November, 1922, the inflationary issue of notes was stopped. In December Alfred Zimmerman, a Netherlander who had been appointed commissioner-general, arrived in Vienna to take up his duties. From January 2, 1923, a new national bank of issue began to function independently of the state; the currency was stabilized at 14,400 paper crowns to one gold crown, and the monetary reform of 1924 established a new unit, the schilling, on a gold basis. Although the reforms occasioned considerable suffering by the dismissal of some 80,000 public officials, expenditures were not reduced sufficiently to balance the budget for 1924. By June, 1926, however, the work of reconstruction had progressed to such a degree that the League's control of Austrian finances came to an end with that month.

During the next four years Austria managed to get along without great financial difficulties, but with the coming of the world depression her troubles once more began. In an attempt to meet the situation a tentative agreement was reached early in 1931 for the establishment of a customs union between Austria and Germany. But the nationalists of France, Czechoslovakia, and Poland—envisioning the consummation of the political union of the two countries which they so much feared—were immediately aroused, for to them the plan seemed to resemble the customs union which had helped Prussia to create the German political union in the nineteenth century. They therefore denounced the Austro-German proposal as contrary to the treaty of Versailles, the treaty of St. Germain, and the Geneva protocol of 1922. France and Great Britain brought the matter before the League of Nations, which in turn referred the question—one of interpreting treaty obligations—to the World Court for an advisory opinion. On September 5, 1931, the latter by an eight-to-seven vote decided that the proposed customs union was incompatible with the Geneva protocol. But even before this, as a result of French financial pressure, both Germany and Austria had announced their abandonment of the plan.

In order to strengthen Austria's economic position, France in 1932 proposed that the five Danubian states should arrange among themselves a close economic collaboration based on preferential prices and quotas. The French plan was approved by the Little Entente, but Austria opposed it because it did not provide for the inclusion of Germany and Italy, Austria's best customers. France insisted that such a commercial union should exclude these great powers, and many believed that the French had in mind the creation of a Danubian economic unit under the domination of French financial and commercial influences. Antagonism between the Little Entente and France, on the one hand, and Austria, Germany, and Italy, on the other, prevented any tangible results.

Again Austria had to turn to the League of Nations for help, and in the summer of 1932 a twenty-year loan of $42,000,000 was made to the republic through the Bank for International Settlements. Certain conditions were attached to the loan. The national budget must be balanced, and the republic must once more submit to the financial supervision of a League representative. It must not, furthermore, enter into any economic union with Germany during the duration of the loan. This loan again rescued Austria from the economic abyss, but left her future still in doubt. Although to many the situation of the little republic appeared hopeless, some agreed with Chancellor Engelbert Dollfuss, who in 1933 asserted that, if Austria could obtain markets and reasonable facilities for the discharge of her debts, she could stand by herself "as Switzerland does."

THE ANSCHLUSS QUESTION

To many, however, the only solution for Austria's economic difficulties appeared to be union with Germany. Therefore, although Austria in the treaty of St. Germain had been compelled to agree not to alienate her sovereignty without the consent of the League Council, the desire for union with Germany persisted. Not all Austrians, to be sure, were thoroughly in sympathy with the movement. Some disliked the idea of being linked with a Germany so strongly Lutheran; others feared the dominance of aggressive and militaristic Prussia; while still others were disturbed by the prospect that their glorious Vienna might be relegated to the position of a second-rate provincial city like Munich. Those who favored the *Anschluss* argued, on the other hand, that all Germans should be in one state, that Austria's domestic markets would be greatly extended if she were part of Germany, and that, when it came to negotiating commercial treaties with foreign states, Austria as part of Germany could secure far better terms.

In 1921 an attempt had been made to circumvent the provisions of the treaty of St. Germain when two Austrian provinces held plebiscites and voted for union with Germany. Although the peace treaty forbade Austria to unite with Germany, it was argued, no restraint had been placed upon the individual provinces. Vigorous protests from the Allies, however, soon put an end to this movement. Nevertheless, the desire for union was not destroyed, and during the succeeding decade a number of steps, official and unofficial, were taken to bind the two peoples closer together both in spirit and in fact. Government officials and university professors exchanged visits. Austro-German cartels were established in various branches of production. Tariff concessions were granted to each other in respect to certain commodities. In many fields legislation and codes were made uniform. Thus a sort of "progressive assimilation" took place. But when an Austro-German customs union was proposed in 1931, it was, as pointed out above, prevented by the opposition of the powers.

After 1931 the *Anschluss* question developed a new phase, largely because of the spectacular rise of Adolf Hitler in Germany. Even before the Nazi leader came into power at Berlin, a subdivision of his National Socialist Party was established in Austria, and the situation in the little republic became complicated by the organization of Nazi "Brown Shirts." Hitler's success in Germany in 1933 at once had its repercussion in Austria, where Austrian Nazis immediately began to work for the *Anschluss*. German Nazis, doubtless realizing that the outright annexation of Austria—which they had always advocated—would cause international complications, apparently determined to achieve the same end indirectly. Since the Austrian Nazis belonged to Hitler's party and took their orders from him, a Nazi political victory in Austria would bring the *de facto* union of the two republics. That this might be accomplished, the German Nazis spent millions of dollars on propaganda in Austria. Skilled agitators were sent into the little republic, while German Nazis dropped from airplanes over Austria and broadcast from Bavarian radio stations attacks upon the Dollfuss government.

But in Chancellor Dollfuss they encountered a serious obstacle to their success. Although he was originally in sympathy with the *Anschluss,* the activities of the Hitlerites drove him into open opposition. Boldly and resolutely he struck back at the Nazis. He at once dissolved the parliament, abolished freedom of the press and of assembly, forbade Nazi propaganda over the radio, forced German Nazi agitators to leave the country, prohibited the wearing of the Nazi uniform and the display of any flag or political symbol except the Austrian flag, and finally, in June, 1933, outlawed the Nazi party in Austria altogether. During that summer Dollfuss sought to build up a spirit of Austrian patriotism by creating the so-called Fatherland Front, an organization designed to replace all political parties for the purpose of unifying the Austrian people.

The Nazis continued their activities, however, and on July 25, 1934, a small group of them seized the government radio station and forced the announcer to broadcast a statement that the Dollfuss cabinet had fallen. Another group seized the chancellory, mortally wounded Dollfuss, and held other members of the cabinet captive. Apparently their plan was to force a reorganization of the government in order to give the Nazis prominent places in the new cabinet. Their plot was not well organized, however, and quickly collapsed. By July 28 the Austrian government had the situation well in hand, and on the next day a new cabinet was formed, headed by Kurt Schuschnigg, a Christian Socialist colleague of the former premier and a member of Dollfuss's last cabinet. Between ten and fifteen of the Nazi leaders were eventually put to death, thus becoming Nazi martyrs, while hundreds were sentenced to prison terms of various lengths.

Events in Austria had their repercussions abroad, where it was widely believed that the German Nazis were back of the attempted revolt. Mussolini promptly mobilized troops along the Austrian frontier, as did also Yugoslavia. But Hitler's government carefully maintained a "correct" attitude, being as yet in no position to wage a war. It officially denied any connection with the Austrian revolt, closed the roads across the frontier into Austria, recalled the German minister in Vienna on the ground that he had overstepped his authority during the uprising, and dismissed the Nazi head of the radio station at Munich. Nevertheless, Austria's dependence upon outside support for the maintenance of her independence was made emphatically clear. Had it not been for Mussolini's swift dispatch of Italian troops to the Brenner Pass, the Nazi *Putsch* might have succeeded. The creation of the Rome-Berlin Axis and Mussolini's announcement in 1937 that Italy could not give military assistance to protect Austria against a German attempt to consummate the *Anschluss* were particularly alarming, therefore, to those who desired to maintain the independence of the little state.

HEIMWEHR VERSUS SCHUTZBUND

But Austria was not disturbed merely by the German Nazis. In the second decade of its existence the republic was shaken by bitter conflicts between the urban proletariat and the rural classes. The republic comprised roughly two districts which were nearly equal in population though not in area. The eastern end, including Vienna, the plain between the capital and Wiener-Neustadt, and the ore-bearing districts of Styria, constituted a great industrial region. The rest of the republic was agricultural and was largely in the hands of peasant proprietors. As a consequence of these differences there had developed in postwar Austria a fairly clear-cut antagonism between the socialism of the factory and the individualism of the farm, between the skepticism of the city and the clericalism of the province —more specifically, between the "Reds" of Vienna and the "Blacks" of the countryside. The federalization of the republic had been caused chiefly by these differences, for decentralization had been demanded by the conservative Christian Socialists as a means of protection against the radical Social Democrats of the capital.

Although the Social Democrats originally favored the unity of the state, federalism for a time worked to their great advantage in at least one respect. Vienna, a city of nearly 2,000,000 inhabitants, was detached from Lower Austria and established as a separate province. As such the municipality became wealthy, for one half of the taxes raised in each province went to the local government. Under Social Democratic control the capital raised and spent money freely on social welfare, public health, education, and city improvements. Large sums were devoted by the municipality to the construction of model tenements and public baths for the proletariat, the money being raised largely by confiscatory taxes levied upon property holders. Public utilities were taken over by the municipality, former palaces were transformed into office buildings or museums, and prewar royal gardens were opened as public parks.

The enmity between the proletariat of Vienna and the peasants of the provinces led to the creation of two hostile militant organizations, the *Schutzbund* and the *Heimwehr*. The former, with its strength in the industrial districts, came to have a well-disciplined membership of nearly 100,000 men, and managed to store in secret hiding places large quantities of arms and munitions for use in time of crisis. The rural Heimwehr, on the other hand, was a type of fascist organization which was not only strongly anti-Socialist but inclined to be monarchical as well. Financed to some extent by the wealthy Prince Ernst von Starhemberg, the Heimwehr ultimately enrolled some 60,000 well-armed men. Frequent clashes occurred between the rival bodies, and at times the government with its very small army had difficulty in maintaining order.

Ultimately the government's attitude toward this domestic conflict was influenced by its desire to prevent Austria from coming under the control of the Third Reich. At the close of the year 1933 Chancellor Dollfuss was looking for some way to strengthen his hand against the Nazis. The Social Democrats, the largest political group in Austria, would have been glad to unite with him in a common front against their common foe. But Mussolini, who had been supporting Dollfuss in his struggle to prevent the consummation of the *Anschluss*, apparently opposed an alliance with the Socialists and favored instead a government in Austria which should include the Heimwehr. The latter, in turn, made the destruction of the Socialists the price of their support. On February 12, 1934, police and Heimwehr men began raiding Social Democratic headquarters.

When a general strike was called by Social Democratic leaders, Dollfuss at once outlawed the Social Democratic Party, declared martial law, ordered civilians with firearms to be executed, and began military measures against the Socialists. Although the Heimwehr succeeded almost at once in getting possession of the city hall in Vienna, the Socialists held out until the government gave a promise of amnesty to all except certain of their leaders. In the end the Social Democratic Party was completely suppressed. Some of its leaders fled to Czechoslovakia; hundreds, including Mayor Seitz of Vienna, were arrested and thrown into prison; a few were hanged. On April 1, 1934, a new municipal constitution was decreed for Vienna, removing the last vestiges of self-government for that city, which had been governed since 1918 by the Socialists.

Four weeks later the Austrian parliament without opportunity for debate —and with more than half of its members, including the Social Democrats, absent—approved a new constitution submitted to it by the Dollfuss government. An authoritarian corporative state was outlined. The word "republic" nowhere appeared in the new constitution, which abolished universal suffrage and political representation of the people. In one more European state democracy had been crushed.

Beginning in 1935 there occurred in Austria a struggle for power between the extreme fascist and pro-Italian Starhemberg and the clerical and slightly less extreme Schuschnigg. The two leaders had not always seen eye to eye. Some years earlier Schuschnigg had organized the Catholic Storm Troops to counterbalance Starhemberg's Heimwehr, and, although their two private armies had co-operated in 1934 to crush the Socialists and the Nazis, the leaders differed on a number of policies. Schuschnigg was apparently willing to make some conciliatory moves toward the former Socialists and was even ready for a *rapprochement* with Germany if the latter would unreservedly recognize Austria's independence. Both of these policies were anathema to Prince Starhemberg.

On April 1, 1936, evidently after consultation with Mussolini, who desired to strengthen Austria against the increasingly more militant Germany, Chancellor Schuschnigg proclaimed the introduction of universal conscription in defiance of the limitations of the treaty of St. Germain. This step had been opposed by Starhemberg, for it was apparent that it would sound the death-knell of private armies like his Heimwehr. The conflict between the two leaders finally reached a climax in May when a bloodless coup ousted Starhemberg from the vice-chancellorship and from the headship of the Fatherland Front. Chancellor Schuschnigg himself assumed the portfolios of foreign affairs and the interior, in addition to those of war and public instruction which he had formerly held. He also assumed command of the Fatherland Front and of the Fatherland Front Militia, the only military force thereafter to be permitted in the republic.

With the support of Mussolini, Schuschnigg next sought that *rapprochement* with Germany which had been opposed by Starhemberg. In July, 1936, an agreement was ultimately reached with Hitler by the terms of which Germany reaffirmed her recognition of Austria's independence, Austria declared herself to be "a German state," and each agreed not to try to influence the other's internal affairs but to co-operate in the stabilization of the situation in central Europe. Hitler's seizure of Austria in March, 1938,[6] revealed how worthless this "scrap of paper" was.

Czechoslovakia

On one of the last days of the First World War, October 18, 1918, Thomas G. Masaryk, head of the Czechoslovak Provisional Government in Paris, had issued the formal declaration of Czechoslovak independence, a step taken by Karel Kramář, head of the Czech National Committee, in Prague on the next day. On October 28 a bloodless revolution had occurred in Prague as the result of which the administration of Bohemia and Moravia passed without opposition into Czech hands. On the following day the territory of the new state had been enlarged when the Slovak National Coun-

[6] See pages 476–478

CZECHOSLOVAKIA 347

cil declared for the union of Czechs and Slovaks into a single state. Fifty-five Slovak members were thereupon added to the National Council in Prague, which then constituted itself the Provisional National Assembly of Czechoslovakia. The two provisional governments, the one in Paris and the other in Prague, co-operated in plans for the meeting of the first National Assembly, which, on November 14, 1918, unanimously proclaimed the republic and elected Masaryk President, Kramář premier, and Beneš foreign minister.

Of the three succession states of central Europe, Czechoslovakia until 1938 enjoyed the most ordered and prosperous national development. The relative stability of this republic came chiefly from its advantageous economic situation as an industrial and agricultural country, from the Western outlook of its dominant races, and from the great ability, wisdom, and moderation of its leading statesmen. No other of the new states of postwar Europe enjoyed during its first decade of existence the continuous guidance of two such capable national leaders as Masaryk and Beneš. The former, rising above political and racial groups, steadily pointed the way toward co-operation and unity within the republic; the latter won and held for Czechoslovakia a prominent place in the councils of Europe.

On February 29, 1920, the Czechoslovak National Assembly approved a constitution, providing for a democratic parliamentary regime. Under this constitution the National Assembly consisted of a Chamber of Deputies and a Senate, both elected by universal, equal, secret, and compulsory suffrage. Real power in the government rested in the Chamber of Deputies, which had both the right to enact legislation over the veto of the Senate and the right to compel the resignation of the ministry by a vote of no confidence. The president of the republic was elected for a seven-year term by the National Assembly. On May 27, 1920, Masaryk was elected president.

Next to the revolution itself the greatest accomplishment of the republic, according to President Masaryk, was the land reform, which, in his words, constituted the "crowning work and the genuine realization" of the revolution. Before the reform, 2 per cent of the landowners of Bohemia owned more than 25 per cent of the land; less than one per cent of the landowners of Moravia owned nearly a third of the land; and in Slovakia about a thousand persons owned nearly half of the land. Most of these great estates owned by Germans had belonged to Czechs before the Bohemian Protestants were dispossessed by Emperor Ferdinand back in 1620. Land reform, therefore, had the double object of improving the lot of the peasants and righting a great historic wrong.

In April, 1919, a law providing for expropriation was passed. The maximum above which land might be expropriated was fixed at 375 acres for arable land and at 625 acres for other types. Peasant holdings were fixed usually at from 15 to 25 acres. Peasants might either lease or buy the land, but in the latter case they might not resell it within ten years without the consent of the state. The thinly settled sections of Slovakia presented a suitable field for colonization, and a number of colonies were planted in that province. Three months later a law providing for compensation was passed. All expropriated estates, except those belonging to the former royal family, were to be paid for at a rate based upon the average market price during the years 1913–1915, with a reduction from this price for estates of more than 2500 acres. The depreciated Czech crown was to be considered as the equivalent of the prewar Austro-Hungarian crown in compensating the landowners. Peasants were required to pay in cash only one tenth of the purchase price, the state extending credit for the rest. By 1935 some 4,395,000 acres had been transferred to new peasant proprietors. A total of 1913 estates, including some 27 per cent of the tillable land of the country, had been involved. In place of a few hundred large agrarians, more than half a million peasants had become owners of land.

Undoubtedly the most difficult domestic problem of the republic arose from the great number of its racial minorities, about a third of the total population being Germans, Magyars, Ukrainians, Jews, or Poles. The political and racial heterogeneity of parts of the country was well illustrated by elections for the Chamber of Deputies in March, 1924. In one province thirteen different parties contested the eight seats, five of them succeeded in electing candidates, and the oath of office was taken in Ukrainian by four, in Magyar by two, and in Slovak and in Czech by one each. The rights of these minorities were protected by a minorities treaty signed by Czechoslovakia and by specific provisions of the Czechoslovak constitution which guaranteed the rights of all citizens without regard to language, race, or religion. Special schools for the minorities were provided, and official business might be transacted in a minority language in districts where 20 per cent of the population belonged to that minority.

One phase of the minorities problem arose in Ruthenia, a province lying at the eastern tip of the republic. This province, providing Czechoslovakia and Rumania with the direct connections which were considered essential to complete the territorial ring about Hungary, was assigned to Czechoslovakia by the peace conference with the provision that it should be granted extensive local autonomy. The population was composed largely of Ukrainians, who in 1919 were for the most part illiterate as a consequence of prewar Magyar oppression. The Czechoslovak government feared that a Ukrainian diet, if established at once, would be dominated by the well-organized Magyars and Jews rather than by the Ukrainians, and therefore delayed establishing it. In the meantime the government began the rapid introduction of an educational system and instituted throughout

THE FATHER OF CZECHOSLOVAKIA

Thomas Garrigue Masaryk

the province special courses of instruction in the Ukrainian language for government officials. The first governor appointed was an American of Ukrainian extraction, but in 1923 a native Ukrainian succeeded to the office. Although in the beginning most of the state officials of the district were not Ukrainians, by 1922 more than half were natives of the district. Nevertheless, the government's delay in granting full autonomy to Ruthenia caused bitter complaints.

The Czechs and Slovaks were officially regarded as forming one Czechoslovak nationality and as such constituted the racial majority in the republic. Nevertheless, the differences between them were marked. The Czechs had a very high degree of literacy and were inclined to be both socialistic in politics and agnostic in religion. The Slovaks, on the other hand, had in 1918 a high degree of illiteracy and as a conservative peasantry were for the most part loyal and pious Roman Catholics. It is perhaps not surprising, therefore, that friction developed between them. In the early years of the republic the Slovaks complained that the Czechs were monopolizing the administrative offices. The Slovak Popular Party (Catholic) began to demand semiautonomy for the province, and in 1924 went even so far as to hold meetings calling for a boycott of everything of Czech origin until the demand should be granted. Eventually, in 1929, a new local autonomy law went into effect under which the country—except for Ruthenia, which by then had an elective diet—was divided for administrative purposes into three districts. Bohemia, Moravia and Silesia, and Slovakia were given three local councils which were partly elected and partly nominated.

The aim of the government, under the direction of Masaryk and Beneš, was not only fair treatment of the minorities but such a union of all groups of the population that distinctions of majority and minority would not be felt. At first that policy seemed to succeed. In October, 1926, two Germans became members of the government, and three months later they were joined by two representatives of the Slovak Popular Party. Nevertheless, continued unrest in Slovakia led in September, 1929, to the dissolution of the parliament and to the Slovak Popular Party's decision to co-operate with the German and Magyar minorities in an effort to throw off Czech domination. That the party did not reflect the viewpoint of all the Slovaks, however, became apparent when it emerged from the election of October, 1929, with a loss of six seats.

In 1932–1933 the German Nazi movement penetrated Czechoslovakia as it did Austria, and tended to interfere with the co-operation of the German parties in the parliament. The Czechoslovak government realized the menace of Hitlerism, with its Pan-German program, and sought, by restricting the use of the radio and prohibiting the circulation of many foreign newspapers from Germany and Austria, to handicap Hitlerite propaganda in the republic. In October, 1933, the Czech Nazi Party announced its own dissolution, just before a government order was issued proscribing it and the German National Party, with which it was apparently about to amalgamate. The Sudeten German (*Sudetendeutsch*) Party was organized to succeed the proscribed parties, and under the leadership of Konrad Henlein it polled the largest number of votes in the republic in the parliamentary elections of May, 1935. The Nazi movement, therefore, became a force to be reckoned with in Czechoslovakia.

Early in 1937 the government, in an effort further to conciliate the three million Germans, whose presence within Czechoslovakia constituted the republic's chief minority problem, reached an agreement with them providing for cultural autonomy, a fair share of government contracts, a greater proportion of German officials, larger appropriations for social services, and an extension of the official use of German. Although Henlein refused to approve these concessions on the ground that they fell short of the political autonomy which the Sudeten German Party demanded, they appeared to satisfy the million or more members of the German Social Democratic Party and the German Agrarian League.

Nevertheless, after Hitler's seizure of Austria in March, 1938,[7] Henlein called on all Germans in Czechoslovakia "to join the great political front of our people's party." The party, it was announced, would admit new members until May 31, 1938, and there was the thinly veiled threat that after that it would be too late to "get in" on the winning side. The intensive propaganda campaign soon bore fruit. On March 22 the German Agrarian Party withdrew its representative from the cabinet and joined the Sudeten German Party; two days later the German Clericals did the same; on March 26 the German Social Democrats withdrew their representative but did not join the Sudeten German Party. Henlein thereupon announced that the Social Democrats could no longer be included in the German race group.

On April 23, at the Sudeten German Party congress at Karlsbad, Henlein announced an eight-point program, three of the demands being legal recognition of the German areas within the state, full self-government for the German areas, and full liberty to profess German nationality and political philosophy. The fulfillment of these three points seemed to make possible the establishment within a democratic republic of a totalitarian state taking its orders from a foreign ruler. This the Czechoslovak government was unwilling to consider, and tension between it and the Sudeten Germans continued to mount.

Meanwhile, on December 13, 1935, after having held the office for seventeen years, Thomas Garrigue Masaryk, founder of the Czechoslovak Re-

[7] See pages 476–478

public, had resigned the presidential office. Eighty-five years of age, he felt that he was no longer strong enough for the task which he had handled so well in the difficult formative period of the republic. "Four times I have been elected president of the republic," he said. "This fact may give me the right to ask you ... always to remember that states can be maintained only by respecting those ideals which brought them into being." Justice, he emphasized, must "be equal for all citizens regardless of race and religion." Five days later, in Vladislav Hall of Prague Castle, where formerly the kings of Bohemia had been crowned, Eduard Beneš had been chosen by the National Assembly to be Czechoslovakia's new president. It was upon President Beneš and Prime Minister Hodža, accordingly, that the impossible task of satisfying Hitler and Henlein fell. The results of the Nazi attack upon Czechoslovakia are discussed later. Happily for the "Father of Czechoslovakia," he had died (September 14, 1937) before his country was dismembered.

Hungary

It has already been pointed out [8] that the Magyars considered Emperor Charles's manifesto of October 16, 1918, as the end of the Dual Monarchy. The Hungarian ministry had at once announced Hungary's independence of Austria. It was the fervent hope of the Magyar leaders that the territorial integrity of the monarchy might be preserved under the rule of the Habsburg Charles, and that the Kingdom of Hungary might yet play an important role in European affairs. This hope was soon blasted. On President Wilson's recognition of the independence of the Czechoslovaks and Yugoslavs (October 18), the movement toward disintegration began with a Croatian revolt against continued inclusion within the Hungarian realm. The discredited, aristocratic Magyar ministry thereupon fell from power.

Out of the political crisis which ensued there finally rose to power one of the very few liberal aristocrats of the country, Count Michael Karolyi. Despite his aristocratic position he had for years, even before the war, advocated such liberal measures as the division of the great landed estates and the granting of universal suffrage. He had later opposed the war, denounced German policies, repudiated the idea of conquest, and demanded a definition of peace terms. He had pointed out that the war was bound to end disastrously for Hungary, for, even if the Central Powers won, victory would bring only the future domination of Hungary by Prussia.

Realizing that the collapse of Hungary was impending, Karolyi, in October, 1918, had pronounced in favor of peace and a federalized, moderately socialized republic. He openly negotiated with leaders of the non-Magyar

[8] See page 98.

and Social Democratic groups and finally, in the latter part of October, succeeded in creating a Hungarian national council which became essentially a revolutionary body. This council, backed by the Budapest garrison, demanded Karolyi's appointment as prime minister, and, after revolutionary troops on October 31 had actually seized the government buildings, the king gave way and called upon Karolyi to head a ministry. Some two weeks later (November 13) King Charles issued a document—never countersigned—in which he renounced all participation in Hungarian affairs and recognized in advance future decisions regarding the form of the Hungarian state. With the way thus cleared, the National Council, perhaps hoping thus to obtain more lenient treatment from the victorious Allies, on November 16 proclaimed the Hungarian People's Republic.

With feverish haste long-overdue reforms were next initiated. Democratic federation, universal suffrage, secret ballot, proportional representation, freedom of speech and of the press, trial by jury, separation of church and state, genuine liberal education, expropriation of the large estates—all these were included in the aims of the new government. But Karolyi's program, liberal though it was, failed to win the support of the people. The concessions came too late. No longer would the subject races be content with federation within a Hungarian republic. They now demanded complete independence or union with their kinsmen in neighboring states. Moreover, the prospect of agrarian reform frightened many of Karolyi's followers, who thereupon withdrew their support. Finally, the Allies had no sympathy with Karolyi's plan to retain the subject peoples in a federalized Hungary and in March, 1919, ordered Hungarian troops to withdraw from Transylvania. Karolyi at once resigned his position as provisional president.

Meanwhile, radicalism had rapidly increased, fostered by the hardships resulting from the continued Allied blockade and by Bolshevik ideas brought back by soldiers returning from the Russian front. The Socialists and Communists decided to seize upon Karolyi's resignation as an occasion to set up a soviet state. Actual power came into the hands of the new commissar for foreign affairs, Béla Kun. This young middle-class Jew had been an active Socialist ever since his graduation from the Transylvanian University of Kolozsvár. During the war he had been an officer in the Austro-Hungarian army on the Galician front, where he had been taken captive in 1915. He was in Russia during the revolution of 1917 and became an ardent admirer of Bolshevism. Supplied with money from Russia, Béla Kun had returned to Hungary with the avowed object of overthrowing the People's Republic and of establishing soviet rule in its place.

All branches of the government now came into the hands of soviet officials, who assumed practically dictatorial powers. The immediate nationalization of large industrial establishments, railways, banks, and mines was ordered. A drastic land-reform scheme was adopted which nationalized the large estates without compensation. An elective soviet system was introduced, with the franchise limited to productive workers. Education was separated from church control and reorganized on a strictly proletarian basis. The Communists, comprising only a very small minority of the population, resorted to terror in order to maintain themselves in power. Revolutionary tribunals replaced the existing judicial system, and a Red Army was created. The press was muzzled, the right of public meeting was denied to all except Communists, hundreds were imprisoned, and political murders became frequent.

But even Red Terror could not maintain the Communists in power against the rising tide of opposition. The peasants refused to sell their produce for Bolshevik currency. The situation of the capital, blockaded by the Allies and boycotted by the peasants, became daily more and more desperate. The majority of the trade unionists, not extreme Communists at heart, turned against the new regime. The Allied powers demanded the resignation of the soviet government to make way for one elected by the people. A counterrevolutionary movement was inaugurated, and at Szeged in the French zone an opposition government was set up. A Rumanian army defeated the Hungarian Red Army and in August, 1919, captured Budapest. Béla Kun fled to Russia.

In November, 1919, counterrevolutionary forces, led by Nicholas Horthy, a rear admiral in the former Habsburg navy, entered the Hungarian capital. Early in 1920 elections were held for a national assembly to decide upon the future constitution of the country. Sentiment for a monarchy was once more strong, and the first law enacted by the assembly restored the former monarchical constitution. Although Charles IV had never legally abdicated the throne, his return was temporarily prevented by the attitude of the Allies. Consequently, on March 1, 1920, the National Assembly elected Admiral Horthy to act as regent during the enforced absence of the king. Three weeks later an executive order formally declared Hungary a monarchy. Reactionary legislation followed, and a White Terror continued for many months to punish those in any way connected with the soviet regime.

Influenced by the hope that the strong monarchical reaction in Hungary presaged an enthusiastic welcome to his return and by the belief that a *fait accompli* would receive no more than a formal protest from the Allied powers, King Charles suddenly returned to Hungary in 1921 and on March 21 demanded back his throne. The result was most disappointing and disillusioning to Charles. There was no outburst of popular acclaim; Horthy declined to surrender his power until ordered to do so by the National

Assembly; the Little Entente powers and the principal Allies vigorously protested. The Hungarian National Assembly joined Horthy in urging Charles to leave the country immediately. Confronted by great opposition and accorded little support, the ex-monarch reluctantly withdrew.

But Charles was neither convinced nor contented. On October 20, 1921, he escaped from Switzerland by airplane and made his second return to Hungary. There he placed himself at the head of a band of armed royalists and marched on the capital. Two days later Beneš, foreign minister of Czechoslovakia, announced that the return of Charles constituted a *casus belli*, that preparations for mobilization were going forward, that energetic measures would be taken in concert with the other Little Entente powers, and that military force would be used, if necessary, "to obtain the final settlement of the Habsburg question in Hungary."

Hungarian troops were dispatched against Charles, who was defeated and taken prisoner. Horthy's government then demanded that Charles abdicate, but he resolutely refused to comply. Upon representations from the Allies, the ex-monarch and his wife were eventually delivered on board a British monitor in the Danube for removal to a definitive place of residence. The Allies demanded the deposition of Charles, but the Little Entente powers went further and demanded the permanent exclusion from the throne of the whole Habsburg dynasty. The Hungarian National Assembly was obliged to pass a law carrying these demands into effect, and the government agreed to permit no election to the throne without previously coming to an understanding with the principal Allies. Hungary thus remained a monarchy, but with the election to the throne indefinitely adjourned.

Although Charles IV died in exile in April, 1922, there continued to be in Hungary a Legitimist Party which advocated the immediate coronation of his son Otto. As the day approached when the latter would reach his majority (November 20, 1930) and, in the eyes of the Legitimists, become entitled to rule at Budapest, some nervousness was felt among those opposed to a Habsburg restoration. The Hungarian government prepared to defend itself against a *coup d'état*, but when the day arrived no untoward events occurred. By the members of the Habsburg family Otto's headship was acknowledged; but the youthful archduke, following a picturesque ceremony at his mother's home in Belgium, returned to the University of Louvain to continue his education. Hungarian governments after 1930 showed little active interest in a Habsburg restoration.

Although Regent Horthy was more often in the limelight and was usually considered the "strong man" of Hungary, the statesman who really directed the policies of the monarchy during the decade after 1921 was Count Stephen Bethlen. The latter was the descendant of a wealthy noble family of prewar Transylvania, but the First World War and the treaty of Trianon had forced him to choose between Rumanian and Hungarian citizenship. As one of the Hungarian optants, he had lost his estates in Transylvania and had become relatively an impoverished man. Though of the conservative aristocracy, Bethlen recognized that the prewar order in Hungary could not be fully restored, and his Union Party—representing the interests of the landowners, the well-to-do peasants, and some of the clergy—constituted a middle group between the Socialists on the Left and the reactionaries on the Right.

Nevertheless, Hungary remained generally conservative in her institutions. Soon after proclamation of the monarchy an executive decree restricted the suffrage and called for open voting in most districts. In 1926 an upper legislative chamber was created, with forty life members and with the rest not popularly elected but drawn from the nobility, county and municipal councils, church organizations, universities, and commercial and industrial bodies. Although an agricultural country, Hungary experienced little in the way of agrarian reform during most of the postwar period, remaining a land of large estates. While nearly 40 per cent of the land was held in estates of more than 1400 acres each, the great majority of the peasants consisted of landless agricultural laborers or of owners whose tiny holdings placed them in practically the same category.

Among the lesser states of Europe, Hungary was probably the outstanding advocate of revisionism. From the day the treaty of Trianon was signed the spirited Magyars were ardent revisionists, for they deplored their loss of territory and the inclusion of some three million of their kinsmen within the frontiers of other states. Furthermore, they could not forget their prewar dominant position as rulers of millions of Slavs, nor could the former landed aristocrats reconcile themselves to the loss of their vast estates in Transylvania and elsewhere. Their denunciation of the treaty of Trianon was vigorous, and their determination to overthrow the settlement established by that treaty was openly proclaimed by such nationalist organizations as the "Awakening Magyars."

In the early postwar years Hungary, like Austria, had a difficult time with her finances, and in 1923 Bethlen's government had appealed to the League of Nations for assistance. In the following year the League inaugurated in Hungary a financial regime similar to that instituted in 1922 in Austria. Hungary's recovery was rapid, and by June, 1926, she was again possessed of a sound fiscal system, though the situation once more became difficult during the world depression. By the summer of 1931 the national budget was seriously out of balance. France then came to Hungary's assistance with a loan, but insisted in return that the government should cease its revisionist agitation.

In Hungary, as in other states, the world depression took its political toll. In August, 1931, Count Bethlen was forced to resign. The next outstanding personality was General Julius Gömbös, a personal friend of Regent Horthy and former minister of war. Gömbös had the distinction of being one of the very few commoners to become prominent in Hungarian political life. He had played an active part in elevating Horthy to the regency and had organized an officers' national defense society to support the Horthy regime. It was Gömbös with his defense society who had been chiefly responsible for preventing Charles's enthronement at Budapest in 1921. He had been a violent anti-Semitic in former years and had been closely connected with the propaganda of the Awakening Magyars. In the autumn of 1932 Gömbös became premier and head of the Union Party.

Although, upon becoming premier, Gömbös renounced his earlier anti-Semitic views, he did not hesitate to summon all Magyars to prepare for that day of Hungary's resurrection which should be ushered in by the peaceful revision of the treaty of Trianon. The economic rehabilitation of the Danubian area, he asserted, could not be accomplished without a revision of the postwar treaties. In the succeeding years he sought to link Hungary closely with Fascist Italy, but his career was cut short by death in October, 1936, before he had been able to alter the situation in central Europe. His place as premier was taken by Kálmán de Darányi.

As in Austria and Czechoslovakia, the Nazi movement penetrated also into Hungary, where, in October, 1937, the Hungarian National Socialist Party was organized. The Independent Small Farmers Party, the chief opposition group, thereupon began to advocate the restoration of the Habsburgs as the surest means to check the inroads of the Nazis, but the government continued to be indifferent to the restoration. Apparently the members of the Union Party were content to continue indefinitely under a regency. Earlier in the year, in fact, the parliament had passed an act increasing the powers of the regent and providing for the election of a new regent in case of Horthy's death. Some progress was made toward greater political democracy, however, as the result of the enactment of the Electoral Reform Bill of 1938, which extended the secret ballot to all constituencies and enfranchised all men over twenty-six years of age, provided they met certain standards of education, and all women over thirty years of age, provided they were self-supporting or married to men qualified to vote.

During 1938, too, active steps against the Nazis were taken by the government. In February all offices and branches of the party were closed by the police; in April the chief organizer of the proscribed Nazi party was sentenced to two years' imprisonment; and in May Darányi's government was overthrown because it had been too weak in dealing with the Nazis. The new premier, Béla Imrédy, former president of the National Bank, was a strong anti-Nazi. In August more than a hundred Hungarian Nazis were arrested in Budapest for attempting to cause disorders during the St. Stephen's Day celebrations.

The Hungarian government's excessive territorial demands upon Czechoslovakia after the Sudeten crisis,[9] although in accord with the country's revisionist program, were caused in part by fear of the Nazis—Hungarian and German. Throughout the crisis the Imrédy ministry was the target of strong attacks by the Hungarian Nazis, who denounced it for not defending the national interests with sufficient vigor. The premier dared not be too conciliatory lest he jeopardize the existence of his cabinet. At the same time, fear of the German Nazis and their *Drang nach Osten* led the government to put forth claims to Ruthenia in order to give Hungary a common frontier with Poland and thus strengthen these two states to resist German pressure.

In 1938 the Imrédy government, in order to lessen the political and economic influence of the Jews—especially of those who had entered the country during the preceding quarter of a century—had inaugurated a program of anti-Semitic legislation. Unexpectedly confronted with the fact that one of his own great-grandfathers had been born a Jew, the embarrassed prime minister submitted his resignation to Regent Horthy. On February 15, 1939, he was succeeded by Count Paul Teleki, a geographer of international note, who proceeded with the government's anti-Semitic program. He also emphasized Hungary's strong attachment to the Axis powers, and at once transformed his words into deeds by signing Hitler's anti-Comintern pact (February 24, 1939) and by announcing Hungary's withdrawal from the League of Nations (April 11, 1939). With Austria and Czechoslovakia safely within the Reich's grasp, it appeared in 1939 that Hungary, too, was rapidly being brought under the economic and political influence of the German Führer.

[9] See pages 485, 487.

Chapter XV

POLAND AND THE BALTIC REPUBLICS

DURING the years 1919–1939 a group of states—Poland and the Baltic republics—stretched across Europe from Czechoslovakia and Rumania on the south to the Arctic Ocean on the north, effectively cutting off the great Soviet Union from direct contact with most of western Europe. These states resembled one another not only in their proximity to the Soviet Union but in the fact that the territory of each was carved wholly or in part from prewar Russia. All of these states were newly created at the beginning of the postwar period, and each consequently faced the problem of establishing its government and building up its national economic structure. Each of them contained within its new frontiers the racial minorities of other nations to complicate its already difficult situation; each as an agricultural country was confronted with the problem of agrarian reform.

Poland

History, which is frequently said to repeat itself, occasionally has a way of reversing itself. In the closing years of the eighteenth century Poland, partitioned by powerful Romanov, Hohenzollern, and Habsburg monarchs, disappeared as a state from the map of Europe. When at the close of the First World War those same proud dynasties were hurled from their thrones, the three separated portions of the Polish people once more became united, and their state again assumed an important position in the political system of Europe.

The re-creation of Poland was not accomplished, however, without friction and ill feeling within the country and even more friction with adjoining states. On October 15, 1918, the Polish deputies in the Austrian Reichsrat declared themselves "subjects and citizens of a free and reunited Polish state," and on the same day the Polish Regency Council at Warsaw, a creation of the Central Powers, summoned the Galician Poles to co-operate in the formation of a new Polish government. To assist in the establishment of the new state there soon arrived in Warsaw one who was, perhaps, the

most outstanding Polish patriot of his day—Joseph Pilsudski. A veteran of
the Russian revolution of 1905, he had suffered exile for his activities at
that time. A determined opponent of the tsarist regime, he had left Russia
on the very day that war was declared and had organized Polish legions to
fight for the Central Powers in the First World War. Becoming convinced
in 1917 that the latter did not intend to permit the establishment of a
completely united and independent Poland, he had refused to fight longer
against Russia and, in consequence, had been thrown into a Prussian prison
in Magdeburg. From here he had been released by the outbreak of the German revolution.

Upon his arrival in Warsaw Pilsudski disarmed the German troops in
Poland and expelled them from the country. The Regency Council, deprived of its military support, thereupon resigned in favor of Pilsudski,
who was proclaimed head of the national provisional government. For a
time, however, it appeared that friction would develop between the provisional government in Warsaw and the Polish National Council in Paris.
The latter, headed by Roman Dmowski, represented and had the support
of the conservative bourgeoisie and peasants, and controlled the Polish army
in France commanded by General Haller. The Warsaw government, on
the other hand, was backed by the Socialists and radical peasants, and had
at its head Pilsudski with his rapidly growing Polish legions. It was imperative that this schism among the Poles should be healed.

At this point Ignace Paderewski did an inestimable service for his coun-
trymen. He had been in the United States at the time of the signing of the
armistice, but immediately afterward he set out for Europe with the aim
of reconciling and unifying the various political groups. After a conference
with Allied representatives and the Polish National Council in Paris,
Paderewski betook himself to Warsaw, there to confer with Pilsudski. Out
of his efforts came a compromise, on January 16, 1919, when Pilsudski was
made temporary chief of state, Paderewski premier and foreign minister,
and Dmowski one of Poland's representatives at the Paris peace conference.

THE PROBLEM OF BOUNDARIES

Probably no other postwar territorial settlement in Europe led to so
much actual fighting or to such bitter and prolonged controversy as did the
definition of Poland's boundaries. The difficulties in connection with the
problem of Danzig and the Polish Corridor have been discussed.[1] Just as
the acquisition of the Polish Corridor led to animosity between Germany
and Poland, the latter's seizure of Vilna caused bitter hostility in Lithuania.

Vilna had had a varied history. Capital of the medieval kingdom of Lith-

[1] See pages 117–119.

uania, it had passed under Polish influence when the two countries became united by the marriage of the Grand Prince of Lithuania to the young Queen of Poland in the fourteenth century. This union, further cemented by the Act of Lublin in 1569, lasted until the close of the eighteenth century, and during this period the Polish language and people came to dominate in the region about Vilna; in fact, the latter became a center of Polish culture. By the partitions of Poland, Vilna next passed under Russian control.

Following the overthrow of the tsar and the defeat of the Central Powers, the Lithuanians declared their independence and set up their own government in Vilna. In January, 1919, the Bolshevik army drove the Lithuanians out of Vilna, but the Bolsheviks in turn were driven out by the Poles, who then occupied the city themselves. No definite frontier between the two states was laid down by the peace conference, but the treaty of Versailles provided (Article 87) that the boundaries of Poland not established by that treaty should be "subsequently determined by the Principal Allied and Associated Powers." Acting under this authority, the Supreme Council on December 8, 1919, laid down a provisional boundary, the "Curzon line," which gave to Poland most of the territory in which the Poles predominated, but assigned the city and province of Vilna to Lithuania.

During the successful advance of the Bolsheviks in 1920, Vilna was again occupied by Russian forces. While the latter were still in possession of the city, the Russian and Lithuanian governments concluded the treaty of Moscow (July 12, 1920), by which Vilna and parts of the former provinces of Suwalki and Grodno were ceded to Lithuania. When the Poles again drove back the Russians, the former and the Lithuanians came into conflict over Vilna, and actual fighting began. Poland appealed to the Council of the League of Nations. In October the two governments were persuaded to sign an armistice agreement, accepting as a provisional boundary a revised "Curzon line" which still left Vilna to Lithuania. On the day before this agreement was to come into force, however, General Lucian Zeligowski, an independent Polish commander with a large body of irregular Polish troops, drove the Lithuanians out of Vilna and occupied the greater part of the province for the Poles.

The question once more came before the League Council, which eventually persuaded both countries to accept the principle of a plebiscite under the supervision of the League. A plebiscite commission was established, and preparations were made for the creation of an international force to ensure a proper vote. Numerous difficulties were encountered, however, and in March, 1921, the Council abandoned the idea of a plebiscite in favor of direct negotiations between the two governments; but a conference under the presidency of a representative of the League in turn failed to bring the two governments to an agreement. Finally, in January, 1922, the

Council withdrew the League commission at Vilna, thus practically admitting its inability to settle the problem with its existing powers. An assembly elected in Vilna under Polish supervision voted in favor of union with Poland. On February 3, 1923, the Council again laid down a provisional boundary between the two states which assigned to Poland the district occupied by General Zeligowski's forces, and with this act washed its hands of the whole affair. Lithuania protested, refused to accept the boundaries, and continued to regard herself as in a state of war with Poland.

In the meantime the League had also been called upon by the Council of Ambassadors, the successor to the Supreme Council, to extricate it from the embarrassing position in which it found itself while attempting to execute the provisions of the treaty of Versailles regarding Upper Silesia. The treaty stated that the results of a plebiscite conducted by an Inter-Allied commission should be reported to the Council of Ambassadors, which in turn should undertake to settle the boundary between Germany and Poland in accordance with the wishes of the people, and "with consideration for the geographical and economic conditions of the locality." An Inter-Allied commission, composed of representatives of France, Great Britain, and Italy, supported by an Inter-Allied force of French and Italian troops, arranged and supervised the plebiscite which was held on March 20, 1921. The official figures showed 707,605 votes for Germany and 479,359 for Poland, with 754 of the communes in favor of Germany and 699 in favor of Poland. The Poles at once claimed that they should be given those districts having Polish majorities, while Germany contended that the province was economically indivisible and that its fate as a whole should be decided by the majority.

While the controversy continued to become more and more acute, Korfanty, a Pole, at the head of a force of irregular troops, overran a large part of the territory. The French portion of the occupying troops openly favored the Poles, and six British battalions had to be sent to the scene to restore order. The Inter-Allied commission, being unable to reach an agreement upon a boundary line, referred the problem to the Council of Ambassadors, which proved to be no more successful in solving it. The latter then availed itself of Article 11 of the Covenant and laid the whole question before the League Council, requesting it to recommend a solution.

The Council appointed a committee of four members—representing Belgium, Brazil, China, and Spain—to study the Upper Silesian problem with the aid of experts. In accordance with the report of this committee, the Council recommended that Upper Silesia be partitioned and unanimously approved a line which divided the territory so that the number of electors assigned to each state did not differ appreciably from the total number given in its favor in the plebiscite. This awarded the larger part of the population and territory to Germany, but gave Poland by far the greater proportion of the economic resources. The Council further recommended that Poland and Germany should conclude a general convention which would place Upper Silesia under a special regime during a transitional period of fifteen years. The League's recommendations were adopted, and on July 9, 1922, the Inter-Allied troops left Upper Silesia, turning the region over to the Poles and Germans, who had already occupied those parts of the area to which they were entitled under the award.

The acquisition of eastern Galicia, like that of Vilna, resulted largely from the use of force. Although the inhabitants of western Galicia readily united in the establishment of the Polish Republic at the close of the war, the Ukrainians who constituted the bulk of the population in eastern Galicia were opposed to such a step. Many desired to unite with their kinsmen in the Ukrainian People's Republic, while others organized a national council in Lemberg and sought to establish an independent state.

The Poles refused to recognize Ukrainian self-determination, immediately invaded the region, occupied Lemberg on November 5, 1918, and during 1919 completed their conquest of the province. The peace conference at first planned to give eastern Galicia the right of self-determination, but finally decided that it should be granted autonomy for twenty-five years under a Polish protectorate, its status after that period to be determined by the League of Nations. Regardless of the peace conference, however, the Poles treated eastern Galicia as part of Poland and eventually, in March, 1923, succeeded in having the Council of Ambassadors settle the questions of Vilna and eastern Galicia by recognizing the *de facto* frontiers of the republic.

Between Russia and Poland the peace conference originally laid down a provisional frontier known as the "Curzon line," which was in general accord with the ethnographic situation. This, however, was not satisfactory to the Poles, who undertook a military campaign to regain their frontier of 1772.[2] The treaty which was finally signed with Russia at Riga in March, 1921, gave Poland an eastern boundary which, except for the territory that had become the new Republic of Lithuania, corresponded roughly with the one she had had just before the partition of 1795. The peace of Riga and the decision of the Council of Ambassadors to sanction the northern, eastern, and southeastern boundaries (1923) closed the period of acute controversy over Poland's frontiers. As finally stabilized, they included a territory four fifths as large as Germany, with nearly 29,000,000 inhabitants, many of whom, unfortunately, were of non-Polish nationalities. The frontiers were so drawn that in the first years of the republic, according to one

[2] See page 185.

Polish statesman, 75 per cent were "regarded as permanently menaced, 20 per cent insecure, and only 5 per cent safe."

POLITICAL DEVELOPMENT

Meanwhile, Poland had begun the organization of her political life in the hope of establishing a stable and efficient regime. In her efforts she was handicapped, however, by the lack of political experience on the part of most of her leaders, by the diversity of administration in the three formerly separated parts of the country, by the tendency of German and Austrian Poles to consider themselves the superiors of the Russian Poles, and by the great multiplicity of petty political parties which immediately sprang into existence. But eventually, in March, 1921, the Polish constitution was adopted. As in France, the president was to be elected for a seven-year term by a majority vote of the two legislative houses meeting together as a national assembly. The president was given no power over legislation, and in general his authority was greatly limited. All his official acts required the countersignature of some member of the ministry, which in turn was made responsible to the legislature. Both houses of the parliament were to be elected directly by universal suffrage with an age requirement of thirty years for electors of the Senate. Real power in legislation was placed in the Chamber of Deputies (the *Sejm*), which was empowered to pass any measure over the veto of the Senate by a bare eleven-twentieths majority of those voting.

Twenty months elapsed between the adoption of the constitution and the first parliamentary elections held under it in November, 1922. A score or more of political parties then presented candidates, and at least fifteen of them succeeded in obtaining representation in the first Chamber of Deputies. To Polish nationalists perhaps the most disturbing feature of the election was the fact that parties of various national minorities succeeded in winning 20 per cent of the seats in the lower house. In December of that year the two houses of parliament, meeting as the National Assembly, chose Stanislaw Wojciechowski as President of Poland.

Poland was now urgently in need of a strong, efficient government to deal with her serious economic and political situation. But the first parliament hindered rather than provided the efficiency needed. The multiplicity of parties produced ministerial instability, for no majority could be found that would consistently support a ministry. Governments changed in personnel and policies at frequent intervals, six ministries following one another within three and a half years. The policy of restricted expenditures, increased taxation, and cessation of inflation for the sake of fiscal reform was for two years prevented because the parliament would not support it.

Agrarian reform was sacrificed to the interests of the great landed proprietors, capitalists, and rich peasants.

National politics became a series of crises and personal and party struggles. Many became convinced of the incapacity of the parliament; many began to assert that it did not really represent the desires of the electorate. Demands for new elections were heard on many sides. But Poland's constitution made it impossible for the government to dissolve the legislature and hold new elections without the consent of the Senate, and the latter, reluctant to face a new election, withheld its consent. An obstructive legislature and an obstructive constitution seemed to stand in the way of a strong government, and there were not lacking those to point out that Poland's downfall in the eighteenth century had been due to causes of a similar type.

The political situation in Poland greatly disturbed Pilsudski, who became alarmed by the weakness of the government of the state which he had done so much to create. Eventually, in May, 1926, he decided that the situation called for drastic action, and he and his followers began a march on the capital somewhat in the manner of the Fascist march on Rome. They aimed by an armed demonstration to force the prime minister from office, but the latter was not at once persuaded. A three days' siege of Warsaw was necessary to convince him of the necessity of resigning, but his resignation finally came and with it that of President Wojciechowski. On May 15 a new government was established with Casimir Bartel as prime minister, Pilsudski as minister of war, and the other members chiefly professors and technical experts. Two weeks later the National Assembly elected Pilsudski President of Poland, but he declined to accept the office, suggesting instead that Professor Ignace Mościcki, a chemist of undoubted integrity, be elected.

In August the constitution was amended in order to strengthen the executive control of the budget, provide the president with authority to dissolve the parliament with the consent of his cabinet, and give him power within limits to issue ordinances with the force of law. By the use of such presidential decrees steps were at once taken to balance the budget, stabilize the currency, reorganize the Polish Bank, and improve the national credit. When in October, 1926, Bartel proved to be unable to command a parliamentary majority, Pilsudski himself assumed the office of premier, organized a strong ministry, and threatened the parliament with dissolution if it did not comply with his wishes. Finally, on November 3, 1927, he did order its dissolution to prevent discussion of the budget. In June of the following year Pilsudski resigned the premiership but retained the positions of minister of war and inspector-general of the army. He still dictated the policies of the republic, however, and constantly urged that the constitution

THE QUASI-DICTATOR OF POLAND
Joseph Pilsudski

be revised in order to increase the powers of the president. Ministries came and went, but the premiers were regularly lieutenants of Pilsudski.

Finally, in August, 1930, doubtless in the hope of attaining political stability for the republic, the marshal himself once more assumed the premiership. He immediately dissolved the parliament and called for new elections. With grim determination the government bloc set out to win control of the new legislature, a feat which no party or bloc had yet been able to achieve in the history of the republic. A systematic attempt was made to handicap and suppress the opposition. The rather natural outcome of elections held under such conditions was the victory of Pilsudski's national bloc, which won a safe majority in both houses. Having largely succeeded in the task which he had set for himself, Pilsudski, after the elections, again resigned the premiership, handing it over to one of his military colleagues.

Pilsudski's followers had long desired to reform the constitution in order to establish in effect a presidential dictatorship with a docile legislature. As early as 1929 they had submitted such a project, but it had been rejected by the parliament. They had hoped that the elections of 1930 would give them the necessary control to accomplish their ends, but in this they were disappointed. In the spring of 1931 the national bloc's project for constitutional reform was again presented and was again rejected. Once more in 1934 the government submitted its proposals, and this time, by methods which the opposition denounced as illegal, it secured the adoption of a new constitution, which was promulgated on April 23, 1935.

Under the new frame of government the president was elected by universal suffrage from two candidates, one nominated by the retiring president, the other by an assembly of eighty electors of whom fifty were chosen by the Chamber of Deputies and twenty-five by the Senate. Should the retiring president fail to make a nomination, however, the candidate of the Assembly of Electors was to be recognized as president without a popular election. The president appointed the ministers, who practically were responsible only to him; he convened, adjourned, and dissolved the parliament; he was head of the army, and appointed and dismissed the commander-in-chief and the inspector-general; he appointed one third of the members of the Senate, the others being chosen by a very limited electorate. The new basis of government obviously provided for a powerful executive. But the new electoral law provided for a complicated and far from democratic method of nominating and electing the Chamber of Deputies, and popular dissatisfaction with it led to a boycott of the elections of that year by a majority of the qualified electorate.

On May 12, 1935, less than three weeks after the promulgation of the new constitution, Marshal Pilsudski, the outstanding exponent of strong government for Poland, died on the ninth anniversary of the bold coup by which he had seized control of the government. In the years after 1926 Pilsudski had lived in semiseclusion, constantly watching over the welfare of Poland but content that others should have the titular authority. Firmly convinced that his country's woes in the eighteenth century had resulted from its military weakness and its inefficient government, he had patriotically sought to build up Poland's armed forces and to strengthen the republic's international position by favorable treaties and alliances. The new constitution provided more nearly the type of government which he thought Poland required than had the one which it supplanted. General Edward Śmigly-Rydz, inspector-general of the army, was elevated to the place formerly held by Marshal Pilsudski as the virtual dictator of Poland.

ECONOMIC PROGRESS

Meanwhile, progress had been made in the economic life of the country. Poland was primarily agricultural, 65 per cent of her inhabitants earning their living from the soil. Before the First World War a very large part of the land was in the hands of a few owners, most of whom belonged to the nobility. Only one third of the peasant farms were self-supporting, the peasants in most cases being obliged to work outside their own farms in order to earn a livelihood. This situation the peasants hoped to change under the republic. Some progress was made in land redistribution at the close of the war, but it was far from satisfactory to the peasant parties. Eventually, in December, 1925, however, a land act was passed providing for the distribution among peasants of some 500,000 acres yearly for a period of ten years. Compensation was to be based upon the existing value of the land, and payment was to be made partly in cash and partly in government bonds. Although not entirely satisfactory to any of those directly concerned, the agrarian legislation facilitated the recovery of the country. Practically all tillable land was again brought under cultivation, thousands of farm buildings were constructed, and farms were eventually restocked to the prewar level.

Industry was somewhat slower to recover from the war destruction and revolutionary disruption. By 1927, however, new postwar records were established in coal, pig iron, crude steel, and zinc production. The railways, completely demoralized after the war, were rebuilt and greatly extended. To free the republic from complete dependence upon Danzig, the construction of a new port was begun in 1925 at Gdynia on Polish territory in the extreme western corner of the Bay of Danzig. By 1929 what was formerly an obscure fishing hamlet had become a city of 15,000 inhabitants with a port capable of handling 2,000,000 tons of freight yearly.

Although Poland, like other countries, suffered from the effects of the world depression, she continued to develop her new Baltic port. In 1930 the government inaugurated regular steamship service between Gdynia and New York. In the fall of that year a new railway was opened between Gdynia and Bromberg on the southern edge of the Polish Corridor. In 1931 Poland turned to the bankers of her ally, France, and entered into an agreement with them to finance the building and operation of a railway to connect Upper Silesia with Gdynia. Such a direct line between the rich coal fields of Upper Silesia and Gdynia would greatly facilitate the exportation of Polish coal. By 1933 Gdynia had surpassed Danzig in total trading volume and had come to monopolize practically all of Poland's overseas passenger traffic. In 1939 its population totaled more than 125,000.

THE PROBLEM OF MINORITIES

But political and economic problems were not the only ones with which Polish statesmen had to wrestle. The republic contained within its borders the largest minorities population of all the countries of Europe. The most numerous minority group consisted of the Ukrainians. The Ukrainians insisted that the local autonomy which was extended in 1922 to eastern Galicia was greatly restricted and not at all consonant with that stipulated by the Council of Ambassadors. Furthermore, the Ukrainians asserted that Poland was not observing her obligations under the minorities treaty but instead was carrying on a campaign to "Polonize" the eastern provinces. Although in 1924 some concessions were made in matters of language and schools, the Ukrainians continued to complain of the way they were treated, and at times even resorted to passive resistance by refusing to pay their taxes.

The second largest minority group consisted of the Jews. Unlike the other minorities, they were not segregated in one area, but constituted a large percentage of the population in all towns and cities. In the early years of the republic they were subjected to harsh treatment at the hands of the Poles, who denounced them as not being good patriots on the ground that they put personal profit above national welfare. In 1925, however, the government negotiated with representatives of the Jews an agreement which became known as the "Declaration of Warsaw." In consequence of the Jews' recognition of their duties to the republic, measures were introduced giving them the same linguistic privileges as had been granted to the border peoples, legalizing their observance of Jewish religious holidays, and recognizing their schools. The agreement went far toward removing the causes of friction between the government and one of the republic's most numerous minorities. Nevertheless, in the succeeding years, and especially after the rise of anti-Semitism in Germany in 1933, there were occasional anti-Jewish outbreaks in Poland. In fact, in 1936-1937 Jews in foreign countries were active in calling attention to the woes of their kinsmen not only in Germany but in Poland as well.

The third major minority group in Poland consisted of Germans, and between Poland and Germany friction was occasioned by the former's treatment of these Germans within her territory. Poland was eager to regain as much as possible of the land which had passed from Polish into German hands while Posen was in the German Empire, and in 1920 decided to cancel all contracts of tenants who held land from the former German government unless they could show clear legal titles. Germany appealed to the League, and the question went finally to the World Court, which decided that Poland must respect private rights. Poland eventually agreed to compensate the German colonists who had been evicted.

A second cause of friction between Poland and Germany arose from the complaints of the German minority in that part of Upper Silesia which was awarded to Poland in 1922. Germans here asserted that they were being subjected to mistreatment and unfair discrimination. The Polish government, it was alleged, failed to provide adequate protection to the Germans, who were exposed to terrorism at the hands of the Poles, particularly during political campaigns. Germans in Poland sought the sympathy of the German Republic, which on several occasions brought the Silesian troubles before the League.

Poland claimed that she was attempting to live up to her obligations under the minorities treaty which she had signed, and submitted much evidence to prove her contention. She asserted, on the other hand, that the more than one million Poles in Germany were being consistently mistreated. What particularly irked Poland was the fact that, while the German minority in Poland had a statutory right to appeal to the League of Nations whenever they felt that they had been wronged by the Polish government, the Poles in Germany had no similar right. Eventually, at the meeting of the League of Nations Assembly in September, 1934, Poland announced that she found herself "compelled to refuse as from today all co-operation with the international organizations in the matter of supervision of the application by Poland of the system of minority protection" until "a general and uniform system for the protection of minorities" had been created. In 1937 the German-Polish treaty of 1922 governing each country's treatment of the other's nationals in Upper Silesia expired, and Poland announced her determination not to renew it. The way was thus opened for further friction with Germany over the question of Poland's treatment of her German minority. In fact, in 1939 Hitler used the "ruthless oppression of the Germans by the Poles" to whip up an anti-Polish hysteria in Germany on the eve of the Second World War.

Danzig, Poland, and the League

By the treaty of Versailles Danzig had been constituted a free city under the protection of the League of Nations. According to the provisions of the subsequently drafted constitution and the Danzig-Polish convention which supplemented it, the free city was given a popular Assembly of 120 members and a Senate of 22 members. The latter, which contained eight administrative heads, constituted the government. The city's foreign relations as well as the protection of its nationals abroad were committed to Poland. The control of the port of Danzig was entrusted to a commission composed of an equal number of Poles and Danzigers with a neutral chairman, and Poland was given "free use and service of the port."

A League high commissioner served as a court of first instance for disputes between Poland and Danzig, which had the right of appeal to the Council. A great number of disputes arose, owing to the complex intermingling of economic and political prerogatives in the free city. Many of the disputes were settled by direct negotiations between the two parties through the good offices of the high commissioner, but many others were referred to the high commissioner himself. Occasionally appeals were carried to the Council, and in one case the World Court was invoked to decide Poland's right to maintain a postal service in Danzig.

Economically, during the first decade of its new regime, the free city prospered. Its importance as a port increased. In 1925 the total tonnage of seagoing vessels entering and leaving Danzig was about twice as much as in 1912, and the total import and export trade of the port for 1927 was more than four times as great as for any prewar year. Poland's determination to create a great port of her own, however, caused considerable alarm in Danzig, which felt that its own economic position as the chief outlet for Polish commerce was threatened. In 1930 Danzig appealed to the League of Nations, seeking to have Poland compelled to use the port of Danzig either exclusively or preferentially for her sea-borne trade. But Poland refused to consider any arrangements involving the compulsory dependence of her trade upon Danzig, and steadily proceeded with the development of Gdynia. In 1933, however, a convention was signed between Poland and Danzig which stated definitely that Poland would direct 45 per cent of her foreign trade through Danzig and 55 per cent through Gdynia.

In the succeeding years the organization of a Nazi party in Danzig greatly disturbed the situation in the free city. The election of members of the Danzig Assembly on April 7, 1935, was preceded by an exciting electoral campaign in which the issue was the degree of success which the Nazis might attain. Their aim was to secure two thirds of the seats in order

THE BALTIC REPUBLICS AND CENTRAL EUROPE, 1919–1938

that the constitution of the free city might be amended to bring that territory into conformity with the totalitarian regime in Germany. Electioneering speeches were made by some of the outstanding Nazi leaders of the Third Reich, including Göring, premier of Prussia, Goebbels, minister of propaganda, and Hess, deputy chancellor. A Nazi campaign of terrorism, moreover, sought to intimidate the Socialists and Poles. Although the Nazis increased their representation in the Assembly, they fell slightly short of the two thirds which they needed to enable them to change the constitution.

In 1936 considerable friction developed between the League of Nations and the Nazi government of Danzig. In January of that year, Anthony Eden, British representative on the League Council, informed that body of the Danzig government's disregard of freedom of the press, election safeguards, and other opposition rights, and of its failure to execute certain Council recommendations. The Nazi president of the Danzig Senate, who represented the free city before the Council, was inclined to be recalcitrant. Under the threat of a League investigation and a possible resort to sanctions, however, the Nazi government gave in and promised to respect the Council's orders to obey the free city's constitution. Six months later, however, the head of the Danzig government appeared before the Council of the League and in the course of his address demanded that the Council should send a new high commissioner to Danzig with instructions to abstain from interfering in internal affairs and to deal only with external policy.

In Danzig it was officially announced that the government of the free city would thereafter ignore Sean Lester, the League high commissioner, and would have no more official dealings with him. Apparently the League felt that Lester's usefulness was seriously impaired by the Danzig government's attitude toward him, for in February, 1937, a new high commissioner—a citizen of Switzerland—was appointed, and it was generally believed that he had been instructed not to intervene in the free city's domestic affairs unless its government interfered with Poland's interests.

During 1936 and 1937 the Nazis by administrative measures transformed the government of the free city from a democratic to a totalitarian regime. The Communist, Social Democratic, German Nationalist, and Center parties were all dissolved or suppressed. After October, 1937, the National Socialist Party was the only German party permitted in the free city. Thus the Nazis eventually accomplished in Danzig that co-ordination with the Third Reich which they had sought but failed to achieve in Austria in 1934. But Hitler was not satisfied, and his determination to absorb Danzig into the German Reich was the immediate cause of the Second World War.

Lithuania, Vilna, and Memel

To the north of Poland lay Lithuania, a diminutive reminder and remnant of the once large and powerful grand duchy of the same name. The Lithuanians were so long merged with the Poles that the idea of their constituting a separate political entity was for a time forgotten. Gradually during the nineteenth century, however, the Lithuanians awoke to a consciousness of their separate nationality, and by 1905 they were demanding autonomy within a Russian federation. During the First World War their national sentiment increased. A movement for independence was begun, and Lithuanians living in other lands gave their efforts to a campaign of propaganda to advance the cause. National independence was finally and formally proclaimed on February 16, 1918. Powerful German influences succeeded in directing the political current into monarchical channels, and in July a German prince accepted the Lithuanian crown. The monarchy was but an ephemeral thing, however, and with the defeat of Germany it was speedily replaced by a republic.

The new Lithuanian state faced a difficult situation. It had to contend not only with the Russian "Reds" to the east but with the aggressive Poles to the south. Bolshevik armies were soon advancing into Lithuania, and the government was forced to retire from Vilna to Kaunas (Kovno). A few months of fighting eventually drove the Bolsheviks out of the country, but not until July 12, 1920, was peace actually obtained. In the treaty of Moscow the Soviet government recognized the independence of Lithuania and defined its boundary with the latter, ceding to it the district of Vilna. The struggle which immediately ensued with Poland over the possession of this capital of medieval Lithuania has already been discussed. Although the Council of Ambassadors, in March, 1923, confirmed Poland's possession of Vilna, the Lithuanian government continued to claim it on the basis of the treaty of Moscow. "The act of a sovereign state cannot be set aside by any Council of Ambassadors," declared the Lithuanian premier. The Vilna question remained a disturbing irritant constantly inflaming the Lithuanian body politic and preventing normal diplomatic relations between Lithuania and Poland.

The bitterness of defeat in the Vilna dispute was mitigated to some extent by Lithuania's acquisition of the former German city of Memel. The latter, a city at the mouth of the Niemen, which was the natural outlet for Lithuania and part of Poland, in the treaty of Versailles was surrendered by Germany to the Allies. At first it was administered by an Allied high commissioner supported by French troops, for at the time of the treaty of Versailles the future extent of Lithuania had not been settled, nor had the latter received full recognition from the Allies. Years passed, but Memel was not handed over to Lithuania. There were rumors that Poland desired the city as a Polish port in compensation for the loss of Danzig. Furthermore, there developed some feeling among the Allies that it might be better to give Memel a status like that of Danzig rather than to incorporate it in Lithuania. The Lithuanians became alarmed.

Early in January, 1923, Lithuanian troops entered the city, drove the French troops back, and set up a provisional government. Negotiations between the Council of Ambassadors and the Lithuanian government for a permanent settlement became deadlocked, and the whole problem was referred to the Council of the League. The latter appointed a special commission under Norman H. Davis, former undersecretary of state of the United States, whose report was approved by the Council and incorporated in a convention finally accepted by Lithuania and the Allies on March 15, 1924. Lithuania was given full sovereignty over the city, but the latter was accorded a large degree of autonomy in executive and legislative matters, and its port was to be administered by an international Harbor Board, composed of a Lithuanian, a Pole, and a citizen of Memel.

While the neighboring Poles were busy "Polonizing" Vilna, the Lithuanians were apparently engaged in an effort quietly to "Lithuanianize" the city and district of Memel. Their efforts in this respect were seriously checked after 1932, however, by the vigilance and activity of the Nazis of Germany, who extended their political organization into Memel. In February, 1934, the Lithuanian government outlawed two Nazi political parties in that city on the ground that they were treasonable. Later it arrested more than a hundred German Nazis in the Memel district on charges of plotting to restore the city to Germany by force.

In December, while the trials were being conducted, national sentiment in Germany was aroused, and demands that the "Saar of the East" be redeemed by the fatherland were frequently voiced. When, in March, 1935, the Lithuanian court condemned four of the accused to death [3] and eighty-seven to prison terms, indignation in Germany rose to great heights, with many popular demonstrations protesting the verdict. Fortunately the tension between Germany and Lithuania was lessened when the death sentences were commuted to life imprisonment and most of the prison terms were reduced in length.

Nevertheless, demands were made in Germany that the powers which had signed the Memel convention should see that the rights of Germans under Lithuanian rule were observed in accordance with that agreement. A directorate of five members responsible to a chamber of deputies was supposed to exist in Memel, but no chamber had functioned for prac-

[3] On the charge of murdering a so-called Nazi traitor.

tically a year, and no directorate existed. In April, 1935, the British, French, and Italian governments in a joint note to Lithuania declared that the latter should take steps at once to reintroduce representative government in Memel. In the ensuing election, which assumed somewhat the character of a plebiscite, the Germans won control of the Memel chamber of deputies. Consequently, a directorate controlled by German Memelanders was set up under the presidency of the Lithuanian-born head of the German group. Memel, like Danzig, thus came to be linked with the German Nazi Party.

Estonia and Latvia

To the north of Lithuania and Poland, along the east shore of the Baltic, lay territory inhabited chiefly by Estonians and Letts, who, after having been dominated by Danes, Germans, Swedes, and Poles, came in the course of the eighteenth century under the rule of the Romanov dynasty. Until 1819 they were serfs, tilling the soil on the great estates of the German barons, or Balts, the successors of the medieval Teutonic Knights who had originally conquered the territory and established there an "upper crust of Germanic civilization." Although both Estonians and Letts eventually rose from serfdom to the status of a free peasantry, the greater part of the land remained, until the First World War, in the hands of the Balts, who constituted an insignificant fraction of the population. Both peoples were filled with a bitter hostility toward these foreign masters of their soil, as well as toward their political rulers, the Slavs, who sought to "Russify" them.

As might have been expected, after the Bolshevik revolution in Russia the Estonians declared their independence on November 28, 1917. This action led to an immediate "Red" invasion from Russia, but in 1918 advancing German armies put the Bolsheviks to flight and subjected the country to German occupation. This was highly satisfactory to the Baltic barons, who were as eager as were the Germans to bring this territory under Teutonic control. But all attempts to force an Estonian representative assembly to elect a Hohenzollern duke were in vain. Finally the Balts, acting in the name of Estonia, invited the Kaiser to be their ruler, and in April, 1918, William II, through his chancellor, accepted the invitation. The defeat of the Central Powers, however, brought the collapse of monarchical and pro-German plans.

The withdrawal of German troops was in turn followed by a second Bolshevik invasion, which swept over most of the little country. Two months of severe fighting eventually freed Estonia of "Red" armies, but the war dragged on until an armistice was signed with the Soviet government in December, 1919. This was transformed into the definitive peace of Dorpat (Tartu) on February 2, 1920. By it Russia recognized the independence of Estonia, while the latter in turn granted Russia free transit to Estonian ports. On June 15, 1920, a permanent constitution was adopted establishing Estonia as an independent "republic in which the power of the state is in the hands of the people."

Meanwhile the Letts had fared in a somewhat similar way. From 1915 on, most of their territory had been occupied by the Germans, who planned to bring it permanently under Teutonic rule. In this they incurred the determined opposition of the Letts, and, as elsewhere in the Baltic regions, German influence and control were destroyed by the outcome of the war. On November 18, 1918, Latvian independence was proclaimed and a provisional government established. The new government, however, was soon confronted with a formidable task, for the Bolshevik armies began an invasion of Latvia and occupied most of the country. At the same time the Baltic barons seized the opportunity to intrigue with the remaining German forces to overturn the government in order to establish one favorable to their interests. But the Balts' attempts failed, and after a year's struggle the Bolsheviks were finally driven from the country in February, 1920. Six months later Russia by the treaty of Riga (August 11) recognized the independence of Latvia. In February, 1922, a permanent form of government was adopted which followed rather closely the Estonian constitution.

On January 26, 1921, Estonia and Latvia received the *de jure* recognition of the principal Allied powers, and in September of the same year both were admitted to the League of Nations. Both countries during their early years had to contend with Communist intrigues and uprisings fostered beyond their frontiers, and both in the end outlawed Communism. Because of the devastation wrought by German and Bolshevik forces and because of the cutting-off of the great Russian hinterland, the economic recovery of both countries was greatly handicapped. In order to hasten it and at the same time remove all need for Russia's plotting against them, both countries sought to foster the transit trade between their ports and Russian territory and provided every facility for Russian commerce.

Both Estonia and Latvia carried through a program of agrarian reform during the early years of their independence. In these two states the reform assumed the guise of a peasant revolt against the German Balt landlords, so that the movement was racial and national as well as economic and social. In the former, according to official statistics, 33,438 farms comprising some 2,560,000 acres were parceled out. In the latter approximately 125,000 new holdings—ranging from 25 to 55 acres each—were created.[4]

---

[4] Agrarian reform was also inaugurated in Lithuania. Before the war 36 per cent of the agricultural area of Lithuania had belonged to large landowners, chiefly Poles, most of whom held estates of more than 5000 acres. Of the agricultural population, on the other hand,

The close relations between these two republics and the fears which were common to them resulted in their concluding (November 1, 1923) a treaty of defensive alliance. Under its terms the two states agreed to pursue a purely pacific policy toward all nations, to concert together and lend each other political and diplomatic support in their international relations, and to give armed assistance to each other in case of unprovoked attack. Eleven years later Lithuania was linked with these two in the so-called Baltic Entente when the three powers signed (September, 1934) a ten-year treaty agreeing to settle by peaceful means such questions as might arise among them and to hold conferences at least twice a year for the co-ordination of their foreign policies.

Finland

The northernmost, the largest, and the strongest of the Baltic republics was Finland, a country nearly two thirds as large as France, lying just east of the Scandinavian peninsula and extending from the Baltic to the Arctic Ocean. Before the First World War the territory was under the control of the Russian tsars, and attempts were made to "Russify" the inhabitants. The latter, however, succeeded in preserving their own individuality, and reached a high level of literacy with a superior type of culture. They were thrifty and capable, and their educational and economic standards were far above those of the Russians. The Finns were therefore quick to seize upon the deposition of the tsar in 1917 as an opportunity for severing their union with Russia. In December, 1917, Finland formally declared her independence, and within a few weeks received the recognition of Soviet Russia, Sweden, France, Germany, Norway, and Denmark.

For a time it appeared that Finland, like Russia, might become a soviet republic. A radical wing of the Finnish Social Democrats attempted to introduce the soviet regime and was actively assisted with Russian soldiers, arms, and munitions. Early in 1918 "Red Guards" gained control of Helsinki, the capital, and all southern Finland. A class war ensued. The bourgeois and landowning classes took up arms to resist and organized "White" armies under Baron Mannerheim, a Swedish Finn who had been a cavalry commander in the Russian army. Foreign aid was sought by these Whites, and in April German troops landed, to be joyously acclaimed by the bourgeoisie as the "liberators" of their country. By the early part of May, 1918,

---

between 15 and 20 per cent was landless. By a law of February, 1922, lands in private estates in excess of 200 acres were expropriated, together with the church lands and those belonging to the former Russian nobles' and peasants' agricultural banks. These were added to the existing state lands to form a land reserve from which small holdings were formed for some 300,000 new proprietors.

the Red Guards had been defeated and expelled from the country. Then
followed a German attempt to bring Finland within the sphere of Teutonic
influence. After the end of the First World War, however, in June, 1919,
the Finnish diet decided in favor of a republic, and in the following month
a republican constitution was adopted. In December, 1920, Finland was
admitted to the League of Nations.

The peace treaty which was signed with Soviet Russia at Dorpat on
October 14, 1920, ceded to Finland a narrow strip of territory between
Murmansk and the eastern frontier of Norway so that the new republic
might have an ice-free port at Petsamo. In the treaty negotiations Finland
likewise sought the annexation of Eastern Karelia, a district lying outside
the frontiers of the old grand duchy but inhabited by people ethnically
affiliated with the Finns. The Soviet government refused to permit this
enlargement of Finland's territory, however, because the possession of Eastern Karelia was essential to Russia's control of the recently constructed
Leningrad-Murmansk railway. Finland was forced to content herself with
the Soviet government's promise to give political, economic, and cultural
autonomy to the district.

In the summer of 1921 Finland complained to the Soviet government
that it was not carrying out the stipulations of the treaty of Dorpat regarding Eastern Karelia. A few months later a rebellion against Russia broke
out in the district, but was suppressed. After having appealed in vain to the
League of Nations, Finland finally asked to have the case referred to the
Permanent Court of International Justice. Russia, however, refused to
recognize the court's competence, and the case gave the court an opportunity to hand down an important ruling, namely, that it could not express
an opinion in a dispute between a member of the League and a state not a
member, without the consent of the latter. Finland therefore was unsuccessful in her efforts to reopen the Karelian question.

In the Åland Islands controversy, historically significant as the first international dispute to be brought before the League of Nations, Finland fared
better. The Åland Islands, an archipelago of about three hundred islands
with a population of some 27,000, lay between Sweden and Finland and
commanded the entrance to the Gulf of Bothnia. They belonged for many
years to Sweden but were lost to Russia along with Finland during the
Napoleonic wars. From 1809 to 1917 Finland and the Åland Islands were
ruled by the Russian tsars as one administrative unit. Soon after Finland
became independent, the inhabitants of the Åland Islands, chiefly of
Swedish stock, began to talk of union with Sweden and even held two
plebiscites in favor of this step. Finland was naturally opposed, and, when
at length open revolt seemed imminent, Finnish troops were landed in the
islands and two of the separatist leaders were arrested. Public opinion in

Sweden thereupon became aroused and demanded some action on the part of the Swedish government.

At this juncture Great Britain, acting under Article 11 of the Covenant, had the matter brought before the Council in July, 1920. The latter first consulted a special committee of jurists regarding the question of jurisdiction and then sent a League committee to Sweden, Finland, and the islands to obtain evidence bearing on the case. As a result of the committee's reports, the Council, on June 24, 1921, decided: (1) that Finland should have sovereignty over the islands; (2) that she should guarantee autonomy and the protection of the political rights of the islands; (3) that she should preserve the rights of private property and the use of the Swedish language in the schools; (4) that the islands should be neutralized and not fortified, in accordance with the terms of the treaty of Paris (1856). A new international treaty neutralizing the islands became effective on April 6, 1922.

Despite the political and social struggle which accompanied the acquisition of her independence, despite the early need to suppress both the extreme Left with its sovietism and social revolution and the extreme Right with its monarchical tendencies, Finland soon became economically and politically stabilized. A sturdy race of yeoman farmers, an influential middle class, and an educated citizenry all helped to maintain a liberal bourgeois republic. Agrarian legislation paved the way to still further economic progress, for about two thirds of the population was engaged in agriculture and dairying.

Though the Finns had a short experiment with fascism during the years of the world depression, the spirit of social reform and general democracy were usually evident in the internal policies of the country. The same could not be said for the republic's foreign and military policies, however. More and more these came to be controlled by those who were strongly anti-Russian and noticeably inclined to be fascist. After Hitler came to power, the ties between the Finnish military leaders and the German Nazis became close, so that Finland's role in the Second World War should not have been a complete surprise to those acquainted with the Finnish situation.

Chapter XVI

THE TURBULENT BALKANS

THAT the Balkans before 1914 constituted the storm center of Europe and that the crisis which precipitated the First World War had its beginning in that quarter of the Continent, are notorious. Local nationalist aspirations and conflicting imperialist intrigues of the great powers for years kept the Balkans in an unsettled and chaotic state. When the war ended with the elimination of the long-standing Austro-Russian rivalry, when the victory of the Allies brought the final attainment of Yugoslav union, it was optimistically hoped that the Balkans might at last settle down to an orderly and peaceful existence. But repeated *coups d'état,* revolutions, dictatorships, border clashes, assassinations, and executions during the years 1919–1939 gave constant evidence of continued unrest in the turbulent Balkans.

Greece

For repeated and spectacular reversals of political life, no Balkan state better exemplified these unsettled conditions than Greece. The conflict between King Constantine and Venizelos during the war sharply divided the Greeks into two hostile groups, and after the king's forced abdication in 1917 [1] Greek politics became subject to sudden and unexpected shifts. For the most part the issues were in some way related to the outstanding Greek statesman of the period, Eleutherios Venizelos, and eventually all Greeks became either Venizelists or anti-Venizelists.

In 1919–1920 Venizelos's prestige was great as a result of the Allied victory and the territorial gains which were apparently to come to Greece. But during his prolonged absence in Paris in the interests of Greece, his numerous opponents at home were busily undermining his position. The royalists declared that his place at the head of the government was the result of Allied intervention, not popular choice, and accused him of resorting to dictatorial methods in order to maintain himself in power. Popular discontent was given an opportunity to express itself in the parliamentary elections of November 14, 1920—the first in more than five years. The un-

[1] See page 70.

expected death of King Alexander in the preceding month injected into the campaign the question of Constantine's return and made the elections a test of the immediate relative popularity of the premier and the ex-monarch. The premier's Liberal Party was decisively defeated, and Venizelos withdrew from Greece. In December a plebiscite was held on the return of Constantine, and, despite the announced opposition of the Allies, it proved to be almost unanimously in favor of the deposed monarch, who entered Athens amid great popular enthusiasm on December 19, 1920. The Allies refused to recognize the restored ruler and immediately ceased their subsidies to the Greek government.

Unfortunately for Constantine, he inherited a difficult military campaign in Asia Minor, a campaign undertaken on the assumption of Allied assistance which was now no longer forthcoming. His presence on the throne came to be connected in the public mind with the appalling Greek military disaster of 1922.[2] Disappointment at the loss of Smyrna, alarm over the threatened loss of Thrace, belief that the army had been betrayed by the government and that Constantine was the obstacle in the way of close relations with the Allies, all reacted against the king, whose abdication was at once demanded by the military chiefs. On September 27, 1922, Constantine surrendered his throne for the second time in a little over five years. In despair, the Greeks turned to Venizelos; the earlier repudiated statesman was recalled to the service of his country and sent to salvage all that was possible for Greece at the Conference of Lausanne.[3]

Although Constantine's eldest son succeeded to the throne as George II, sentiment in favor of transforming Greece into a republic grew rapidly. Venizelos opposed the parliament's desire to depose the king and advocated instead a popular plebiscite on the question. When the parliament persisted in its desire, Venizelos again withdrew from Greece, and in his absence the parliament voted to overthrow the Glücksburg dynasty. A popular plebiscite on April 13, 1924, then approved the establishment of a republic.

During the next four years conditions in Greece were far from stable. A succession of republican governments held office until, in June, 1925, General Theodore Pangalos seized power. Later he dissolved the parliament, proclaimed himself a temporary dictator, and made a feeble attempt to emulate Mussolini. But his career was in turn cut short by a *coup d'état* in August, 1926, and Greece once more had a series of republican governments. In 1927 Venizelos returned to his native land, and, disturbed by rumors of an intended royalist revolt, in May, 1928, he announced that he would again enter politics. In July he became prime minister, and in new

[2] See page 405.
[3] See pages 405-407.

The Balkans, 1923–1938

parliamentary elections his Liberal Party secured about 90 per cent of the seats. The electorate, apparently weary of the endless succession of weak governments, had turned again to the country's only dominant personality. During the next four years Greece enjoyed a period of political stability and progress.

Along with the problem of securing political stability, Greece after 1922 was compelled to wrestle with the necessity of assimilating some 1,200,000 refugees who came to her chiefly from Asia Minor and eastern Thrace as a consequence of the Greek military disaster of 1922 and the resultant treaties with Turkey in the following year. The exigency which arose when the population of the country was thus suddenly increased by one quarter forced the republic to appeal to the League of Nations for assistance, but in the course of succeeding years the refugees were accommodated.

Despite the misery and suffering which this forced migration brought to those involved, the ultimate result for Greece was undoubtedly beneficial. Most of the naturally industrious Greeks from Asia Minor were settled in Greek Macedonia and western Thrace, to whose long-neglected regions they brought benefits somewhat analogous to those brought to the sandy wastes of Brandenburg by French Huguenots in the days of the Great Elector. New territories were put under cultivation, new crops were introduced, new industries were established, and the economic center of gravity in the republic was shifted in the direction of Saloniki.

But the effect of the influx of Greek refugees was not alone economic. It conferred a predominantly Greek character upon the republic's territory in Macedonia and western Thrace and thus, it was thought, removed from the agenda of international disputes the question of the racial composition of those districts, where for economic reasons both Bulgaria and Yugoslavia had long desired to establish themselves. Furthermore, the exchange of Greek and Turkish populations ended, for the immediate future at least, the century-long Greco-Turkish territorial conflict. With the ancient feud between the Greeks and the Turks laid to rest, the two republics in 1930 signed a treaty of friendship and arbitration, reaffirmed their acceptance of the territorial *status quo,* and pledged neutrality in case of a war to overthrow the treaty settlement. Attached to the treaty was a protocol providing for the maintenance also of the *status quo* in naval armaments. Three years later the two powers signed a ten-year pact of nonaggression, mutually guaranteeing the inviolability of their common frontiers.

In Greece as in other countries the world economic depression had its effect upon politics. In parliamentary elections held in the autumn of 1932 the Liberals lost heavily and the royalist People's Party gained accordingly. In November Panagis Tsaldaris, leader of the latter party, became premier, but two months later he was forced out of office by an adverse vote of the

National Assembly, and Venizelos for the seventh time became the head of the government. New elections in March, 1933, however, gave the People's Party a clear majority, and Tsaldaris again came into power at the head of a royalist ministry.

Two years later fear that the Tsaldaris government was planning to restore the monarchy led to a republican revolt. Civil war broke out in Macedonia and Thrace, and the islands of Crete, Samos, Mytilene, and Chios went over to the revolutionists. Five warships in the harbor of Piraeus were seized by the rebels and forced to head for Crete, where the republican leader, Venizelos, was living. Vigorous measures were taken by the government, however, and in less than two weeks the revolt had been crushed. Venizelos fled from Crete. A few of the leaders were put to death, and a considerable number of the rebels were imprisoned.

That there was some basis for the fear of the republicans soon became evident, for Premier Tsaldaris soon announced himself in favor of a plebiscite on the question of restoring the monarchy. In July the parliament voted to have a plebiscite in which the electorate should decide whether to continue the republican regime. The republicans confidently declared that they would win if a fair vote was permitted.

Possibly that was what General George Kondylis feared, for he desired that the plebiscite should be held only after the republic had been abolished. On October 10, 1935, a military *coup d'état* led by Kondylis forced Tsaldaris to resign the premiership, and martial law was proclaimed. Bills were rushed through the National Assembly abolishing the republic and restoring the monarchical constitution of 1911. General Kondylis himself became premier and also regent until King George should return. On November 3 the plebiscite was held. Since the republicans felt that they could have little real influence on the outcome of the vote, in view of the fact that avowed monarchists were in control, they boycotted the plebiscite. The vote, therefore, proved to be almost unanimously monarchist. On November 25, 1935, George II, after an absence of some twelve years, returned to Athens as king.

The restored monarch's difficulties began almost at once. The king, who desired a general and inclusive amnesty, disagreed with Premier Kondylis, and, before a week had passed, the latter had resigned the premiership. Constantine Demerdjis, a professor at the University of Athens, thereupon organized a nonpartisan stop-gap government and immediately signed an amnesty pardoning several hundred prisoners and exiles, including even Venizelos. In the ensuing election of January 26, 1936, the Venizelist Liberals won a striking victory, but failed to secure a majority over all the other parties in the National Assembly. While attempts were being made to construct a new cabinet, General Kondylis died. The death of the one who was perhaps Venizelos's most bitter foe in Greece was followed within a few weeks by that of Venizelos himself. The veteran Greek statesman died on March 18, 1936, while still in exile in Paris. On April 13 the situation was complicated still further when Premier Demerdjis also died.

King George thereupon appointed as head of the government General John Metaxas, vice-premier and war minister in the preceding cabinet. On August 5, 1936, the latter, after announcing that Greece was threatened by a Communist uprising, declared martial law, dissolved the National Assembly, and postponed elections indefinitely. From then until their country was conquered by the Axis powers in 1941, the Greeks lived under a dictatorship which was in its essentials fascist.

Yugoslavia

The kingdom of the Serbs, Croats, and Slovenes—after 1929 officially called Yugoslavia—comprised principally the descendants of three Slavic tribes which had pushed their way into the Danube valley and into the northwestern part of the Balkan peninsula in the seventh century. Despite their proximity and their kinship in race and language, however, the three peoples had never before 1918 constituted parts of the same state. Furthermore, with the Serbs looking eastward to Constantinople, and the Croats and Slovenes looking westward and northward to Rome, Vienna, and Budapest, the three groups in the course of centuries had developed many differences in customs, culture, and religion.

Nevertheless, a common racial heritage as Yugoslavs, a common hatred of the Habsburgs, and a vigorous nationalist propaganda emanating from Serbia had gradually brought the three groups to believe in a common nationality and to envisage their future in a common Yugoslav state. Existing differences were recognized, and the Corfu Manifesto of 1917, the so-called "birth certificate of Yugoslavia," seemed to take them all into consideration when it proclaimed to the world that the three peoples constituted a single nation; that their future state would be called "The Kingdom of the Serbs, Croats, and Slovenes"; that it would be "a constitutional, democratic, and parliamentary monarchy" under the ruling house of Serbia; that the new state would have a flag of its own and the three constituent members would in addition have their own flags, which would "rank equally" and might "be freely hoisted on all occasions"; that the two alphabets and the three religions prevalent among the Yugoslavs would likewise be of equal rank; that suffrage in the new state would be universal, equal, direct, and secret; and that the future constitution would be framed by a special constituent assembly elected by universal suffrage.

But the spirit of conciliation and co-operation, which the Corfu Manifesto so happily seemed to promise, failed to materialize. One question that famous document left to be decided, and the inability to settle it to the satisfaction of all caused continuous political unrest and repeated crises in the kingdom. Should Yugoslavia be a unitary or a federal state? Immediately after the collapse of the Central Powers and the disappearance of the Habsburg menace, the Yugoslavs split into two groups: those advocating a centralized state which should be in a general way an expansion of the former Serbian kingdom, and those demanding a federal state with a considerable degree of local autonomy. The leader of the former was Nikolas Pashich, the "grand old man of Serbia"; of the latter, Stefan Radich, the "uncrowned king of Croatia."

The advocates of a unitary state argued that the former Hungarian territories were hopelessly backward politically, and that to create autonomous states of such districts would be most unwise. They pointed out that as a matter of fact Yugoslavia could not well be a federation of equals and that even in a federal system Serbian hegemony would inevitably result. They declared that the difficult and pressing task of national reconstruction and unification required the utmost use of all the forces at the disposal of the state, and asserted that these could best be marshaled under a strong central regime. But to all of these arguments the Croats, who had had a measure of self-government within the Habsburg empire, replied that the marked differences between the various territories composing the new state made a federal system the only possible solution.

For a time, after the First World War, the question remained largely in the realm of the academic, since Alexander, Prince Regent of Yugoslavia, refused to convoke a constituent assembly or to set a date for elections until the frontiers of the kingdom had been definitely decided. After the signing of the treaty of Rapallo with Italy had apparently settled the question of Yugoslavia's Adriatic territory, however, elections for a constituent assembly were held on November 28, 1920. Radich's Croatian Peasant Party succeeded in electing fifty deputies, but they refused to take their seats, so that Pashich was able to create a working majority. The Serbian statesman was determined to secure the adoption of a centralist constitution, and he succeeded in carrying through his program. The Yugoslav constitution of June 28, 1921, therefore, provided for a centralized government which should apply equally to all parts of the country in order eventually to do away with localism and obliterate regional differences. Historic frontiers were erased, and provincial diets were supplanted by one national parliament (*Skupshtina*) in Belgrade. Local officials were to be chosen directly by the people, but in the conduct of their offices they were to be subject to national supervision exercised by the minister of finance and by prefects appointed by him.

The first elections to the parliament were held in March, 1923, and resulted in large gains for the parties of the two opponents, Pashich and Radich. The former attempted to come to some agreement with the Croatian peasant leader, but his efforts were unavailing. Radich again refused to allow the Croatian Peasant deputies to take their seats, and Pashich was thus once more enabled to form a ministry. After another year of boycott, Radich apparently came to the conclusion that the only result of his party's abstention was to perpetuate Pashich in power. Accordingly, the deputies of the Croatian Peasant Party returned to the parliament and caused Pashich's resignation in March, 1924. The continued intransigence of the Croatian Peasant leader made parliamentary government difficult during the next four years, especially after the country was deprived of its most experienced statesman by the death of Pashich in December, 1926.

Affairs came to a crisis on June 20, 1928, when Radich attacked the government for its proposal to ratify the Nettuno convention with Italy,[4] which Croatians declared was inimical to their interests. Angered by the speech, a supporter of the government fired upon leaders and members of the Croatian Peasant Party, killing two and wounding several others. Among the latter was Radich himself, who died from the effects of his wound on August 8, 1928. The Croatian deputies thereupon withdrew from the parliament and set up a rival body at Zagreb, where they passed resolutions refusing to recognize laws enacted by the "rump" parliament at Belgrade. On October 1 delegates representing Croatia and Dalmatia met at Zagreb and decided to establish a close union to work independently of the Belgrade government and to boycott Serbia. Two months later the Croatians refused to participate in the celebration of the tenth anniversary of the founding of the Yugoslav state.

King Alexander decided to resort to drastic measures. Declaring that the nation's confidence in the parliament had been undermined by recent events, that parliamentarism, instead of developing and strengthening the feeling of national union, had begun to provoke moral disorganization and national disunion, the king on January 5, 1929, dissolved the parliament, abrogated the constitution of 1921, and called upon General Peter Zhivkovich, commander of the guard division stationed in Belgrade, to head the government. The new ministry, which was to govern the country by decree pending the complete reform of the constitution, was composed of representatives from Serbia, Croatia, Bosnia, Slovenia, and Dalmatia.

Yugoslavia was temporarily transformed into an absolute monarchy, the king assuming complete and sole authority over every officer of state. Very definite efforts were made to wipe out particularism in the kingdom and to replace it by a genuine national sentiment. The use of the names of the

[4] See pages 232–233.

separate races was frowned upon, the display of the flags of the separate peoples was prohibited, and the old historic boundaries were obliterated by the creation of nine new administrative districts—in six of which the Serbs constituted a majority—with entirely new boundaries and names. Finally, in October, 1929, even the name of the state was changed by royal proclamation to the "Kingdom of Yugoslavia." King Alexander hoped that the Serbs, Croats, and Slovenes would organize themselves nonracially into Yugoslav groups based on social, economic, and other class interests.

After nearly three years of arbitrary rule, during which some economic and cultural gains were undoubtedly made, Alexander announced on September 3, 1931, that the dictatorship was ended, and that the country would return to constitutional government. A new constitution—not the work of a popularly elected constituent assembly but the product of the king and his advisers—was proclaimed. According to this document the Kingdom of Yugoslavia was to have a bicameral parliament instead of its former one-house legislature. The Chamber of Deputies was to be elected for four years by the direct vote of all men and women at least twenty-one years of age. Half of the members of the Senate were to be elected for six-year terms in a similar manner, and the other half were to be appointed by the king. The administrative districts and municipalities of the kingdom were given a considerable degree of autonomy, but the governors of the nine districts were to be appointed by the king on the nomination of the premier.

But the electoral law, promulgated on September 12, caused great dismay. To participate in an election a party must have at least sixty supporters in each election district in the country, a condition which none of the former Yugoslav parties could fulfill. The voting was to be for national rather than district lists, and the party which received the largest vote in the kingdom was to receive two thirds of the seats in the Chamber of Deputies. Furthermore, voting was to be by open ballot; that is, each voter must declare his choice orally and in public.

The first parliamentary elections under the new constitution were held on November 8, 1931. Most of the former political parties, notably the Croatian Peasant Party and Serbian Peasant Party, were urged by their leaders to boycott the election. The only party which fulfilled the requirements of the electoral law was the National Party headed by Premier Zhivkovich. The election, of course, resulted in a "victory" for the government party. When the new parliament convened in January, 1932, it expressed its full approval of the government's work "from January 6, 1928, to the present day." The Croats, however, continued to resist the royal attempts to bring about the "Serbianization" of the government and the people.

The centralizing tendencies of King Alexander's government were apparently responsible for the assassination of the forty-five-year-old monarch on October 9, 1934. On that day, the king disembarked at Marseilles from the Yugoslav destroyer *Dubrovnik,* bound on an official visit to France. As he and Foreign Minister Barthou of France were riding together through the city, an assassin leaped upon the running-board and shot the king dead. The French foreign minister also received injuries from which he died shortly afterward. The assassin was killed on the spot even before he could shoot himself. Investigations disclosed that he had entered France under a forged Hungarian passport, and that the plot was the work of a Croatian terrorist organization headed by Ante Pavelich. Since the headquarters of the Croatian extremists were in Hungary, the assassination precipitated an international crisis. Peace was preserved, however, through the efforts of the League Council, which prevailed upon Hungary to promise to take all necessary measures against terrorist activities.

In Yugoslavia Alexander's oldest son, a boy of eleven years, was proclaimed King Peter II, and a regency council was established. In May, 1935, elections were held for a new parliament. Although opposition parties were permitted to present candidates, vigorous steps were taken by the government to prevent their having much success. Opposition leaders were arrested, and antigovernment meetings were broken up. On the other hand, considerable pressure was exerted in favor of the government party, which, as might be expected, won a decisive victory. When the parliament met, it was boycotted by all of the opposition members. Thanks, perhaps, to the conciliatory temper of Prince Paul Karageorgevich, the chief regent, the Croatian leader, Vladko Machek, was called to the capital to aid in settling the crisis.

A new ministry on a national basis—broad enough to include not only Croats but Serbian Radicals, Bosnian Moslems, and Slovene Clericals—was formed with the former finance minister, Milan Stoyadinovich, as premier. Stoyadinovich's statement of policy, however, was disappointing to the Croats, for, although he advocated a gradual transition from the dictatorship to a free parliamentary regime, he announced his adherence to the unitary rather than the federal form of government. When the premier organized a new political party—the Yugoslav Radical Union—pledged to maintain Yugoslav unity, the three Croatian members of the cabinet resigned, and Machek announced that the Croats would never be satisfied until Croatia was granted an autonomous position in Yugoslavia analogous to that of Hungary in the Dual Monarchy before the First World War.

Not until the Belgrade government became thoroughly alarmed at Hitler's *Drang nach Osten* and perceived how he had used disaffection within Czechoslovakia to encompass that country's destruction, did it decide to make concessions to the Croatians. But on August 24, 1939, an agreement was finally reached between the Serbian and Croatian leaders, under the terms of which about 26 per cent of the Yugoslav territory, with 4,423,000 inhabitants, was organized into the *banovina* of Croatia under a governor to be appointed and dismissed by the crown. Croatia was to have its own legislative body at Zagreb, and was to have full autonomy in all matters except foreign affairs, the army, foreign trade, state communications, public security, and religion. On September 23, 1939, the governor and the departmental heads of government of Croatia were appointed—nine Croats and two Serbs, none of them politicians—and Machek announced that he was completely satisfied with the new arrangement. The Yugoslav government was also reorganized, Machek becoming vice-premier and five members of his Croatian Peasant Party being included. Unfortunately for the unity of the kingdom, however, the radical element among the Croatians still remained dissatisfied, and Hitler in 1941 was able to utilize this situation to his advantage.

Albania

To the west of Yugoslavia and Greece was Albania, the smallest and weakest of the Balkan states, with an area equal to that of Denmark but with only a quarter of the latter's population. The country, which gained its independence in 1913, was at that time a most backward and primitive region, having no railways and very few roads. Schools and newspapers were exceedingly scarce, and illiteracy was general. The population was for the most part agricultural or pastoral, organized on an almost feudal basis, and largely lacking in national sentiment. In fact, the question was raised then, and was subsequently repeatedly raised, whether there should be an independent Albania. In 1913 Serbia and Russia, on the one hand, and Austria and Italy, on the other, had nearly come to blows on this point.[5] Albania's independent existence, therefore, resulted principally from the jealousies of her neighbors. Had it not been for the opposition of Italy and Austria, her territory might have been divided among Greece, Serbia, and Montenegro at the time of the Balkan wars.

During the First World War the dismemberment of Albania was contemplated, but at the peace conference President Wilson steadily opposed its partition. Italy sought a mandate for the region, most of which she had occupied in the course of the war, but the military opposition of the Albanians led the Italians to recognize their independence and to withdraw from the country in the fall of 1920. Despite the desire of Greece and Yugoslavia to partition the country, Albania's independence was recognized by her admission to membership in the League of Nations in December, 1920. During the following year, while the question of boundaries was still un-

[5] See page 18.

settled, repeated incursions into Albania were made by bands from Yugoslavia, and disruptive revolutionary movements were encouraged and assisted with money, arms, and ammunition sent in from that country. This menacing situation was eventually ended by the League of Nations, which threatened to consider the application to Yugoslavia of Article 16 relating to economic sanctions.

Meanwhile, within Albania the question of future government was being settled. A monarchical regime had been originally set up with a German prince as ruler, but he had been forced to leave the country soon after the outbreak of the First World War. Early in 1920 a temporary regency council of notables was elected in place of the monarch, and a struggle for control ensued. After frequent changes in the government during a period of three years, Ahmed Zogu, a young tribal chieftain who from the age of sixteen had been fighting in the cause of the Albanian mountaineers, at length won out. In 1925 a national assembly was convoked, a republic proclaimed, and Zogu elected president for a seven-year term. The constitution subsequently adopted provided for a bicameral legislature but placed the chief power in the hands of the president, who had an absolute veto on legislation, the sole right to initiate changes in the constitution, authority to dissolve the parliament at will, and the right to apply the previous year's budget in case of the parliament's failure to vote a new one. The president differed little from a dictator; in fact, in 1928 the National Assembly proclaimed him King Zog I.

The Albanian ruler's chief task was to create a modern state. To secure the capital which he so much needed, he entered into close relations with Italy. To secure an entering wedge for the economic domination of this weak state on the opposite shore of the Strait of Otranto, Italy gladly advanced the necessary funds. The treaty of Tirana (1926) granted Italy extensive economic concessions in Albania, and the Italo-Albanian defensive alliance (1927) drew the two states still closer together.[6] Albanian finances and the Albanian army were placed under the supervision of Italian experts. For all practical purposes Albania became an Italian protectorate and an outpost for Mussolini's desired economic penetration of the Balkans. In fact, in April, 1939, Mussolini swept away all pretense, drove out King Zog, and had Victor Emmanuel proclaimed King of Albania.[7]

Bulgaria

The political history of Bulgaria after the First World War, although not so kaleidoscopic as that of Greece, was far from calm and uneventful.

[6] For the terms of these agreements, see page 233.
[7] See page 487.

The military defeat of Bulgaria brought the immediate abdication and flight of King Ferdinand, who had been largely responsible for the country's joining the Central Powers, and the elevation to the throne of his young son, Boris III, who in succeeding years proved to be as democratic as his father before him had been autocratic. Military defeat likewise brought the downfall of the existing government and eventually (October, 1919) the elevation to the premiership of the leader of the Agrarian Party, Alexander Stambolisky, who had dared to oppose the royal proposal to join the Central Powers in 1915 and had been imprisoned for his temerity. Under his guidance the Agrarian Party won a decisive victory in the parliamentary elections of March, 1920, in consequence of which a homogeneous Agrarian ministry was established.

Then followed a three-year period of Agrarian rule in which the role of Stambolisky differed not materially from that of dictator. The great weakness of his regime was its devotion to the interests of practically one class, to the exclusion of the so-called upper classes. In 1923 the premier declared that the Agrarian Party would "keep at the head of national affairs until the country is rid of the old and pernicious parties, until the peasantry and the working classes get rid of their parasites, the lawyers, bankers, profiteers, idle politicians, and mischievous doctrinaires, and the people in general of its frenzied partisans." The Agrarian leaders became ever more overbearing and intolerant. Freedom of the press was abolished, leaders of bourgeois parties were imprisoned, and universities were closed.

Inevitably the neglected and oppressed classes drew together. The bourgeoisie, the intelligentsia, and the military discovered a common bond in their hatred of the Agrarian regime. A conspiracy was entered into, and on June 9, 1923, all the ministers were suddenly arrested except Stambolisky, who was absent from the capital. A new government representing all opposition parties but the Communists was formed with Alexander Tsankov, a professor in the University of Sofia, as premier. Stambolisky was later captured and shot, and his parliament, on the ground that it had been elected by fraud and violence, was dissolved.

A serious threat to the political stability of Bulgaria in the ensuing years came from the Communists. In September, 1923, they instigated a revolt in an attempt to replace the monarchy with a soviet republic, and thousands of peasants, bereft of their former leader, gave it their support. Although the uprising became so serious that at one time Sofia was practically surrounded, it was in the end successfully suppressed. In April, 1925, came a second Communist attempt when a bomb was exploded in the cathedral in Sofia at a time when it was crowded for the funeral of a recently assassinated general. Most of the members of the government were in attendance. More than a hundred persons were killed, and several hundred were injured, including Prime Minister Tsankov and some of his associates. A counterterror was at once inaugurated by the government; martial law was proclaimed; thousands were arrested; many were put to death.

In 1932 the Communists again surged to the fore. Naturally, the economic depression, resulting from the deflated prices of agricultural products, caused widespread and deep discontent. This reflected itself in successes of the Communists in municipal elections in February, 1932, and again in September of the same year when they won 19 of the 35 seats in the municipal council of Sofia. Fear of Communism again led the bourgeoisie to take defensive measures. The League of Reserve Officers, which had played a leading role in overthrowing Stambolisky, called for a rallying of all forces opposed to Communism, and in 1934 Bulgaria finally succumbed to a dictatorship when on May 19 the government was overturned by a *coup d'état* executed by a group of army officers and politicians.

Two major policies, it was announced, would receive the particular attention of the government, namely, the abolition of all political parties, and the complete suppression of the Macedonian revolutionary movement. The latter antedated the First World War. As early as 1893, when Macedonia was still included within the Ottoman Empire, agitation for autonomy had been begun by the Internal Macedonian Revolutionary Organization (IMRO). This agitation had eventually won the sympathy of the Bulgarians, who dreamed of a modern Macedonia which should be dependent upon Bulgaria for the defense of its territorial integrity, and be bound to her by ties of close kinship. But by the treaties of Bucharest (1913) and Neuilly (1919) Macedonia had been divided, most of it being allotted to Serbia and Greece.

After the First World War over 200,000 refugees and exiles from Greek and Serbian Macedonia had flocked into Bulgaria, where they formed a well-organized and well-armed group. These homeless masses constituted a grave domestic problem for Bulgaria, embarrassing the government's foreign policy by their constant demands for the redemption of their "Bulgaria irredenta," complicating the political situation by providing a fertile field for Communist propaganda, and frequently disturbing the ordered existence of the country by their brigandage. In that district of Bulgaria which was located near the convergence of the frontiers of Greece, Yugoslavia, and Bulgaria, the Macedonian *comitadjis* established a base of operations for guerrilla warfare, and their revolutionary activities repeatedly excited alarms and protests on the part of neighboring states.

Numerous clashes occurred along the Greco-Bulgarian and Yugoslav-Bulgarian frontiers, but the most serious occurred in 1925, when on October 19 shots were exchanged between Greek and Bulgarian sentinels. Reports reached Athens of a serious premeditated attack by the Bulgarians, and the

Greek minister of war ordered the Third Army Corps to march on the Bulgarian town of Petrich. Greek troops crossed the frontier and occupied some seventy square miles of Bulgarian territory. But Bulgaria at once appealed to the League of Nations, and the prompt action of Aristide Briand, president of the Council, not only prevented further armed clashes but brought the withdrawal of all Greek troops by October 28. For her unfortunate invasion Greece was obliged to pay Bulgaria an indemnity of some $220,000.

In the summer of 1926 an attack on a Yugoslav village by a band of *comitadjis* provoked a joint note of protest from Yugoslavia, Greece, and Rumania. The Bulgarian government did what it could to restore order on the frontiers, affirmed its sincere desire to keep the peace, pointed out the difficulties under which it labored, and invited the co-operation of its neighbors. The great numbers of unsettled refugees in Bulgaria who looked forward either to returning to their former homes across the border or to avenging themselves on those who had driven them out made the situation extremely difficult for Bulgaria to control. A year later renewed *comitadji* activities culminated in the assassination of a famous Serbian general. Yugoslavia thereupon closed her frontier against Bulgarians until February, 1929, when, after the establishment of the dictatorship in Yugoslavia, the Belgrade government took the conciliatory step of reopening the borders.

In the succeeding years the Macedonian revolutionists seriously weakened themselves by splitting into two warring and bitterly hostile factions, the Mihailovists and Protogerovists—the revival of a feud which dated back to 1907. Scores of members of each faction were assassinated, and in December, 1932, a miniature battle between the two groups occurred on the principal street in Sofia in front of the royal palace. In the early summer of 1933 Macedonian murders and abductions became so frequent in the Bulgarian capital that drastic steps had to be taken by the government to protect its citizens. Large numbers of suspected Macedonian terrorists were arrested and interned in concentration camps. All Macedonians having arms were ordered to surrender them, and leaders of the IMRO were imprisoned or ordered out of the Macedonian areas.

In 1934, faced by the new Bulgarian government's declared determination to destroy the IMRO, the Protogerovist organization announced its dissolution, and Ivan Mihailov with a number of colleagues fled across the border into Turkey. In proportion to the weakening of the Macedonians the good relations between Bulgaria and Yugoslavia were strengthened, and eventually, January, 1937, the two powers concluded a pact of nonaggression.

Meanwhile, the government established in Sofia by the *coup d'état* of

1934 had formally outlawed all political parties and had forbidden all forms of party activity. But gradually relations between King Boris and this government became more and more strained. According to reports, the premier insisted that the king should be deprived of his influence over government policies and converted into a figurehead. Boris naturally resented such plans, and in January, 1935, forced the resignation of the cabinet. A number of ministries followed one another until, in November, 1935, Kiosseivanov, a personal friend of the king, became premier. A royal dictatorship then ensued in which he and the king ruled Bulgaria without a parliament until March, 1938. At that time parliamentary elections were again held, with women voting for the first time. The opposition was seriously handicapped, however, because the former Radical, Liberal, Socialist, Old Agrarian, and Democratic Entente parties had been proscribed. The government therefore won a decisive majority of the seats.

As in so many of the states to the east of Germany, the Nazi movement penetrated Bulgaria. And, as in many other states, the government struck back; in 1938 and again in 1939 it ordered the dissolution of the Bulgarian Nazi Party. But, though officially suppressed, a pro-Nazi movement continued with another name under the leadership of former Premier Tsankov, who became increasingly revisionist in his views. Meanwhile, Hitler's government assiduously wooed Bulgaria. That it achieved some success seemed indicated by the announcement in Berlin on July 5, 1939, at the time when Premier Kiosseivanov was visiting Hitler, that Bulgaria and Germany realized they inhabited the same *Lebensraum* and understood the implications of that fact. The implications became more evident in 1940–1941.

Rumania

Rumania's acquisition of territory as a result of the First World War surpassed the fondest expectations of her extreme nationalists. That she might gain territory from either the Habsburgs or the Romanovs if she were fortunate in her choice of sides in the war was readily conceivable; but that she might in the end gain from both these mighty empires the territory which each had offered her at the expense of the other was, it seemed, utterly foolish to expect. And yet this was precisely what happened. Rumania emerged from the war with her territory practically doubled in extent, her frontiers very nearly attaining those of the province of Dacia to which Trajan sent the Roman colonists from whom the Rumanians love to trace their lineage.

In view of Rumania's joining the Entente powers in the war, the least-expected territorial acquisition was Bessarabia, the district between the river

Pruth, the river Dniester, and the Black Sea, which Russia had taken from Turkey in 1812. The population was chiefly Rumanian (Moldavian) in 1812, and in spite of a policy of "Russification" the largest element in it—the peasantry—remained Rumanian in 1914. In December, 1917, after the Bolshevik revolution, a Supreme Council in Bessarabia proclaimed an independent Moldavian republic and requested the Rumanian government to send troops to preserve order and to provide protection against the Bolsheviks. In April, 1918, the Supreme Council voted for political union with Rumania with the understanding that the district should retain a large degree of local autonomy. The Soviet government, claiming that this council was not a truly representative body and that it was intimidated by the presence of Rumanian military forces, refused to recognize the legality of this action. In November, after the defeat of the Central Powers, the Supreme Council, with only about a third of its members present, passed a new motion which canceled the conditions regarding local autonomy laid down in April and merged Bessarabia with Rumania. On the next day the council was permanently dissolved.

At the Paris peace conference Rumania included Bessarabia among her claims for territory, but the "Big Four" long delayed to take action. Not until October 28, 1920, did the principal Allied powers—France, Great Britain, Italy, Japan—sign a treaty recognizing Rumania's sovereignty over the district, and then they did so only in the face of Russia's protest and warning that she would not recognize the action. Rumania's acquisition of Transylvania, Bukowina, and part of the Banat of Temesvar by the treaties of St. Germain and Trianon has already been mentioned. In these regions there lived perhaps twice as many Rumanians as in Bessarabia, and they brought to the kingdom a higher culture and a greater political self-consciousness than the latter. The assimilation of all these territories taxed the Rumanian administrative system to the limit, and the succeeding years heard many complaints of inefficiency, corruption, and poor government, aggravated by dissatisfaction with economic conditions.

In 1917 universal suffrage had been introduced for parliamentary elections, and Jews had been admitted to citizenship rights. The political situation in Rumania was radically altered by this extension of the franchise to some millions who had previously not voted as well as by the addition of so much new territory. The Liberal Party, the organ of the industrial, commercial, and banking interests, centralistic, and nationalistic in its opposition to the influx of foreign capital, continued under the domination of the wealthy and clever John Bratianu. Another party, the People's Party, was organized by General Alexander Averescu after the enactment of the new franchise law, but its policies seemed to differ little from those of the Liberal Party, with which it became accustomed to co-operate. The political power of the peasants and minor nationalities was at once reflected in the organization of many new parties.

In the first elections held in Rumania after the war the peasant groups won a large majority, and a coalition government was organized under a Transylvanian leader. The conservative elements of the country at once became alarmed because of proposed expropriation of land and the fear of Bolshevik propaganda, and King Ferdinand, who maintained that he had the right to appoint and dismiss his ministers regardless of the parliamentary situation, dismissed the peasant government. General Averescu, leader of the People's Party, was appointed prime minister. During the next eight years, despite the undoubted numerical superiority of the peasant electorate, the government was kept almost constantly in the hands of Averescu or Bratianu, leaders of the parties whose chief strength was in the territory of prewar Rumania.

During these years a program of agrarian reform was inaugurated in Rumania. To bring about a wider distribution of land, legislation enacted between 1917 and 1921 provided for the expropriation of all landed property of absentee and foreign owners, all the arable lands of the crown, and all large estates in excess of 1250 acres. The original proprietors were to be compensated in state bonds on the basis of prewar values when the Rumanian leu was worth a gold franc. The greatly depreciated value of the leu after the war, however, made the compensation quite illusory, so that almost the entire burden fell upon the dispossessed landlords. By 1932 approximately 90 per cent of the land was in the hands of small peasant proprietors.

Meanwhile, despite agrarian reform, the peasants were becoming more and more restless because of their inability to obtain control of the government. In May, 1928, a peasant convention in Transylvania was attended by some 200,000 members of the National Peasant Party. Some had come equipped with arms, expecting that force would be employed, and the more spirited proposed a march on Bucharest. But their leader, Julius Maniu, wisely counseled moderation and, after resolutions demanding Premier Bratianu's resignation were passed, directed his followers to return to their homes. During the succeeding weeks the situation grew more tense. Plans for a rival National Peasant parliament and for a republican movement in Transylvania seemed to endanger not only the existing government but the monarchy itself. On November 4, 1928, the premier grudgingly laid down the reins of office, and the long rule of the Bratianus was broken. Two days later Maniu became premier. Parliamentary elections confirmed the peasants' victory by returning an overwhelming majority for the National Peasant Party. It appeared that the half century of almost continuous rule by aristocratic landed and capitalistic classes had come to an end, that Rumania's 14,000,000 peasants had at last come into their own.

The years 1929 and 1930 saw an increasing sentiment in behalf of Prince Carol, who in 1925 had renounced his right of succession to the throne, choosing instead to keep his mistress, Magda Lupescu. At that time the Rumanian parliament had recognized as crown prince five-year-old Michael, Carol's son by his wife, the former Princess Helen of Greece. Upon the death of King Ferdinand in July, 1927, Michael had succeeded to the throne, with a regency to govern during his minority. But the exiled Carol was popular with the army, and his return and accession to the throne were favored not only by his brother, Prince Nicholas, but by the veteran politician, General Averescu, and by the National Peasant Party as well. In fact, only his mother, Queen Marie, and Bratianu's Liberal Party very vigorously opposed his restoration. In June, 1930, following an announcement that he had broken with Magda Lupescu,[8] Carol arrived in Bucharest by airplane. The parliament at once annulled all acts which had been passed relating to his abdication, recognized him as having been the *de jure* king of Rumania since the death of his father in 1927, and proclaimed him as Carol II. Plans for the king's coronation were held in abeyance, pending a possible reconciliation with his wife, Helen. Such a reconciliation failed to materialize, however, and in 1931 Helen was obliged to renounce her queenly title and to agree to be known thereafter merely as Princess Helen of Rumania. Later she was exiled from the country.

For some months after Carol's return the government remained in the control of the National Peasant Party, but in April, 1931, the king forced the resignation of the ministry and replaced it with one headed by Nicholas Iorga. The latter, a prominent historian, had been Carol's personal tutor. The parliament, in which the National Peasant Party held an overwhelming majority, was at once dissolved. In the ensuing election the National Union, organized by the premier to support his announced program of economy and efficiency in government, secured only 48 per cent of the votes, but under the existing electoral law the National Union was given 75 per cent of the seats in the new Chamber. Carol and his premier then inaugurated a thinly veiled dictatorship, and it was feared by many that the peasants had again been definitely pushed aside.

Despite its party platform, however, the Iorga ministry proved to be far from efficient and economical. The government offices were overstaffed, expensive public works were lavishly initiated, expenditures regularly exceeded income, and the national deficit steadily mounted. Obviously, too, the world economic depression with its low price of grain constituted a serious handicap to the economic and financial recovery of the country. Ultimately the government's inability to secure a foreign loan did what the

---

[8] Subsequent events proved that this was not true.

peasants' votes had failed to do a year earlier. In May, 1932, the Iorga ministry was forced to resign. Alexander Vaida-Voevod, who had succeeded Maniu as leader of the National Peasant Party, became premier at the head of a cabinet consisting of members of his party. New elections in July gave the premier's followers control of the parliament. Rumania continued to be embarrassed by her financial difficulties, however, and in 1933 the government was obliged to accept the assistance of the League of Nations.

The Vaida-Voevod government's chief contribution to Rumanian history was the conclusion of a nonaggression pact with Soviet Russia. The active agitation for revision of the peace treaties, especially in Italy and in Germany, alarmed Rumania, which had made such large territorial gains by the peace settlement; and the rise of Hitlerism, with its subsequent vigorous suppression of the Communists in Germany, disturbed Russia. In self-defense the two countries moved closer together, and in June, 1934, they signed a pact mutually guaranteeing their existing frontiers. This amicable settlement of the Bessarabian question in favor of Rumania appeared to strengthen the position of the latter in relation to Hungary. Should a revisionist quarrel with Hungary occur, forces which might otherwise have been required to protect Bessarabia against Russia would be available for use in central Europe. To the extent that Rumania was thus strengthened, so also was the Little Entente.

Not all Rumanians favored cordial relations with the Soviet government, however. Opposition to the government's foreign policy was particularly strong from the Iron Guard, a violently anti-Semitic organization which had developed in the postwar period and which had come to be fascist and pro-German in its outlook. Vaida-Voevod's failure to curb the Iron Guard and other fascist organizations was largely responsible for Carol's dismissal of the National Peasant government in November, 1933, and for his appointment of a Liberal cabinet headed by Ian G. Duca. Elections for a new parliament were set for the following month, and in order to check the activities of the Iron Guard the new premier suppressed its meetings and publications and canceled its parliamentary nominations. Hundreds of those suspected of membership were arrested. The Liberals won the elections, but in retaliation for the repressive measures which had been used by the government a former university student assassinated Premier Duca in December, 1933. Three months later a plot was discovered to kill the king, the crown prince, and the members of the cabinet in order to set up a military dictatorship, but it was nipped in the bud, and those implicated were sentenced to prison.

In the ensuing years the Liberal government, headed by George Tatarescu, was compelled to wrestle with difficulties arising from the spread of fascism within the country. The fascist groups, subsidized by the German

Nazis, denounced the government's efforts to find a working basis with Soviet Russia and assailed Rumania's pro-French, pro-Soviet orientation. The fascist denunciations became louder than ever after the conclusion of the Franco-Soviet and Czechoslovak-Soviet alliances (1935) and the Rumanian government's decision to construct a strategic railway to connect the Soviet Union with Czechoslovakia, Rumania's ally. But neither King Carol nor Premier Tatarescu favored the fascist program of converting Rumania into a Nazi outpost against Russia. In 1937, with aid from France and Czechoslovakia, they carried forward their rearmament program. At the same time the government took drastic action to curb the activities of the fascists.

Nevertheless, in the following years, despite the opposition of Premier Tatarescu and King Carol, the fascist Iron Guard, supported by the German Nazis, continued to grow. This was startlingly revealed by the parliamentary elections of December, 1937, in which the government—contrary to all precedent—was defeated. Tatarescu was succeeded as premier by Octavian Goga, who was known to be anti-Semitic, antiparliamentarian, anti-Russian, and anti-French. But Goga's government was short-lived, for he in turn was forced to resign on February 10, 1938.

King Carol thereupon inaugurated something in the nature of a totalitarian state with greater authority in the hands of the king. A new constitution was proclaimed which provided for "a juster representation" of the farmers, workers, and other productive elements. At the same time the king was given the right to declare war and make peace, to conclude treaties, and to issue decrees when the parliament was not in session. Early in 1938 all political parties were ordered dissolved. Still another Balkan state thus succumbed to a royal dictatorship.

Cornelius Codreanu, leader of the Iron Guard, and hundreds of his followers were next arrested on charges of plotting to overthrow the government. The Iron Guard leader was sentenced to ten years' imprisonment, but on November 30, 1938, he and thirteen subordinates were killed "while attempting to escape from their prison guards." Thus the Iron Guard was deprived of its outstanding leader but at the same time provided with a "beloved martyr" whose death called for revenge. Thus, too, Rumania was weakened in the face of Hitler's *Drang nach Osten* by having among her citizens a considerable number who would be willing to co-operate with the German Nazis to bring about the downfall of Carol's government.

International Relations of the Balkans

It has already been pointed out how the activities of the IMRO disturbed good relations between Bulgaria and Greece and between Bulgaria and Yugoslavia.[9] Another question which disturbed the international relations of the Balkan states was that of adequate outlets to the Aegean for Bulgarian and Yugoslav trade. As a result of the Balkan wars of 1912–1913 Bulgaria had gained an outlet upon the Aegean by the annexation of western Thrace. This territory she lost, however, by the treaty of Neuilly, but in that treaty the Allied Powers undertook to assure her economic outlets to the Aegean. In the treaty which later gave western Thrace to Greece, the Allies stipulated that Bulgaria was to have freedom of transit over the territories and in the ports involved, and that in the port of Dedeagach she was to be granted a lease in perpetuity.

These provisions failed to satisfy Bulgaria, and at the Conference of Lausanne (1923) when the Near Eastern settlement was being revised, Stambolisky presented the Bulgarian case. He declared that it was impossible and inadmissible that Bulgaria's outlet to the Aegean should be across either Turkish or Greek territory, and demanded that western Thrace be transformed into a neutral zone which Bulgaria's railway system might cross and in which she might construct her ports. He definitely rejected the Allied proposal that a free port for all nations be constructed at Dedeagach and that the port and the railway connecting it with Bulgaria be administered by an international commission. He likewise refused to accept the Greek proposal of a Bulgarian free zone in Saloniki similar to that being arranged for Yugoslavia.

The Allies declared that at Lausanne they had done their best to carry out their obligations under the treaty of Neuilly, and that their failure had been caused by Bulgaria's attitude. They thereafter left the solution of the question to direct negotiations between Greece and Bulgaria. At Lausanne Venizelos had stated that Greece fully recognized Bulgaria's need for free access to the Aegean, and two years later (October, 1925) the Greek government voluntarily established a free zone in Saloniki for the use of all Balkan states, including, of course, Bulgaria. But the latter still maintained that its requirements had not been met, and continued to fret at the thin strip of Greek territory that shut her off from the near-by Aegean.

Greek territory likewise cut off Yugoslavia from her most natural and convenient access to the sea, which was at Saloniki. In 1906, when that port was still in Turkish territory, the Ottoman government had granted Serbia a lease on part of the harbor, and had conceded her the right of free entry and export. After the Balkan wars, Greece—which then controlled Saloniki —signed a treaty providing for a Serbian free zone, but the First World War had intervened before either state had ratified the agreement.

Fresh negotiations were undertaken in 1923 and resulted on May 10 in

[9] See pages 392–393.

the signing of a new convention which provided that an area in the port of Saloniki should be under Yugoslav customs administration (but under Greek law and police supervision), and that goods passing between the free zone and the Yugoslav frontier should be exempt from Greek taxes. But the Yugoslavs were still dissatisfied. They declared that the zone was too small for their needs, that such exports as cattle, horses, lumber, cement, and grain required more room for efficient handling. They complained that the disastrously slow and inefficient service on the forty-eight-mile section of the railway between Saloniki and Gevgeli on the Yugoslav frontier was detrimental to their export of such perishable goods as poultry, meat, cheese, and eggs. Furthermore, the traffic rates on goods shipped over this short Greek section of the railway, it was claimed, were four times as high as those on the Yugoslav section. But Yugoslavia's attempts to secure the removal of these handicaps to her foreign trade through Saloniki received little attention from Greece.

With the return to power in Greece of the statesman who had originally brought about close relations between that country and Serbia in the years preceding the Balkan wars, relations between the two states rapidly improved, however. Venizelos visited Belgrade soon after becoming premier and paved the way for the renewal of negotiations. Six protocols regarding the Yugoslav free zone in Saloniki and the administration of the Gevgeli-Saloniki railway were eventually signed in Geneva on March 18, 1929. All points at issue between the two states were settled, though quite apparently Yugoslavia surrendered some of her demands of 1926. The free zone was to remain restricted to the area stipulated in 1923, and Yugoslavia was to have no share in the administration of the Gevgeli-Saloniki railway. On the other hand, every facility was to be provided for Yugoslav commerce. Special direct trains were to run regularly between the Yugoslav frontier and the free zone. Disputes which might arise were to be settled by a jointly appointed arbitrator or, in case of nonagreement, by the League of Nations.

Meanwhile, Balkan diplomats had been busy in efforts to provide for the security of their various countries. The attempts of Rumania and Yugoslavia to obtain national security and to provide for the maintenance of the *status quo* in central Europe by uniting with Czechoslovakia in the Little Entente have already been discussed,[10] as has, also, the linking of the Little Entente with France.[11] But the Rumanian-Yugoslav convention of June 7, 1921, which finally completed the Little Entente, applied to the Balkans as well as to central Europe. Rumania and Yugoslavia had a common interest in Bulgaria's acceptance of the peace settlement, and the purpose of their

[10] See page 338.
[11] See page 310.

treaty was stated to be the maintenance of both the treaty of Trianon and the treaty of Neuilly. Each state undertook to assist the other in case of an unprovoked attack by either Hungary or Bulgaria.

But Rumania, in view of the fact that her annexation of Bessarabia, though eventually sanctioned by the principal Allies, was not recognized as legal by the Soviet government, desired security not only against Bulgaria but against Russia as well. Soon after the First World War, therefore, Rumania initiated negotiations with Poland—also fearful of Soviet Russia— and in 1921 a Polish-Rumanian defensive alliance resulted. By the terms of this treaty, an unprovoked attack on the eastern frontier [12] of either power would require the other to enter the war to assist the one attacked. When this alliance was renewed in 1926, it was extended to cover not only the eastern frontiers of the two states but all foreign aggressions.

The rise of Hitler and the success of the Nazis in Germany, the withdrawal of Germany from the League of Nations, and the subsequent collapse of the Geneva Disarmament Conference had their effect in the Balkans as they did in central Europe. As the result of negotiations initiated by Greece and Turkey, a movement was started to create an organization similar to the Little Entente in central Europe. What was envisaged was a general pact of nonaggression and guarantee to be signed by all the Balkan states. But Bulgaria, fearing that her adherence might prejudice her claim to an outlet on the Aegean Sea, declined to sign, and Albania, under Mussolini's influence, likewise declined.

On February 9, 1934, however, the foreign ministers of Greece, Turkey, Rumania, and Yugoslavia signed a pact agreeing to guarantee Balkan frontiers against aggression by any Balkan state, the pact to become effective against any Balkan state that might join an outside power that had committed an act of aggression against one of the signatories.[13] The Balkan pact was obviously much more in the nature of a defensive alliance than a mere nonaggression pact. In Greece it at once encountered vigorous opposition, and the Greek parliament ratified it only with the reservations that the boundaries guaranteed were those internal to the Balkans and that under no circumstances were obligations arising from the pact to be so construed as to involve Greece in a war with Italy or any other great power.[14] These reservations were accepted by the other signatories, though clearly they weakened the force of the pact. Provision was made for a permanent coun-

---

[12] The eastern frontier of Rumania was defined as that recognized by the principal Allied Powers in 1920, namely, the river Dniester; while Poland's was defined as that laid down by the Russo-Polish treaty of 1921.

[13] This would prevent an interpretation like that of King Constantine of Greece in 1915. See the footnote on page 51.

[14] In 1936 the Balkan Entente agreed that Albania should not be regarded as a Balkan state within the meaning of the Balkan pact.

cil, consisting, like that of the Little Entente, of the foreign ministers of the signatory powers.

Although Bulgaria had not joined the Balkan Entente in 1934, Hitler's seizure of Austria and the resultant fear of a Nazi *Drang nach Osten* drew Bulgaria and the Balkan Entente together in 1938. The former gave a pledge of nonaggression against any of the countries of the Balkan Entente, and in return the latter, on July 31, permitted Bulgaria to rearm and to remilitarize her frontiers with Greece and Turkey. This evidence of increasing solidarity in the Balkans was encouraging to those who hoped for continued peace in that part of Europe but, as in earlier times, that hope was eventually blasted by the interference of some of the great powers—in this case Germany and Italy in 1940.

Chapter XVII

THE NEAR AND MIDDLE EAST

AFTER the First World War a widespread revolt against the domination of the West swept through northern Africa, western and central Asia, India, China, and Japan—in other words, through those regions of the world which, because of their type of civilization, are usually referred to as the East. In consequence, certain European powers emerged from the war only to find themselves almost immediately confronted or threatened in distant parts of the world with uprisings of native populations. Where these powers were forced to resort to military operations, the efficiency of their modern weapons usually brought victory. In some cases, however, European countries, in preference to actual war, made sweeping concessions to discontented peoples, and occasionally even military success was followed by measures designed to placate the conquered. Full political independence, extensive national autonomy, or a measure of local self-government was obtained by various non-European groups, accompanied in some instances by the abolition of capitulations, the cancellation of foreign privileges, and the grant of economic freedom. At the same time, though revolting against the West, the East showed a pronounced tendency deliberately and voluntarily to adopt many features of the civilization of the West.

Turkey

One of the first clear indications of this revolt of the West was the Turkish nationalist movement which repudiated the treaty of Sèvres,[1] opposed the loss of Turkish territory, threw off the servitude of capitulations, and then sought to modernize Turkey.

THE "WARS OF FREEDOM"

Although the sultan, in Constantinople within range of Allied warships, was ready to accept the dictated treaty of Sèvres, the Turkish Nationalists were not. Back in the hills of Anatolia, far beyond the reach of Allied guns, the spirit of Turkish nationalism and Moslem fanaticism were aroused by a veteran army officer, Mustapha Kemal, who demanded the retention by

[1] For the provisions of the treaty of Sèvres, see pages 133–134.

Turkey of all territory "inhabited by an Ottoman Moslem majority," a plebiscite in eastern Thrace, the security of Constantinople, and, by implication, the abolition of the capitulations. When the sultan, doubtless under Allied pressure, dissolved the parliament and denounced the Nationalists, the latter held a grand national assembly at Angora and organized a government with Mustapha Kemal at its head. By June, 1920, Nationalist armies were threatening the British on the Ismid peninsula, the French in Cilicia, and the Greeks in the Smyrna area.

In these circumstances Venizelos proposed, and the Allies approved, a Greek offensive against the Turks to compel them to accept the treaty of Sèvres, and Great Britain advanced a loan to the Greek government. Greek armies at once began operations and before the end of the year succeeded in defeating the Nationalists and in occupying extensive regions of Anatolia, including the city of Brusa. During 1921 further military successes brought the Greek armies within two hundred miles of Angora, but their supreme attempt to capture the Nationalist capital failed.

Meanwhile, the Western powers had ceased to present a united front. In 1921 Soviet Russia recognized Mustapha Kemal's government and agreed to disavow the treaty of Sèvres. Italy, in return for the Nationalists' promise "to examine favorably Italian applications for railways, mines, and public works in Asia Minor," evacuated the district of Adalia.[2] And France, on October 20, 1921, signed a separate treaty with the Turkish Nationalist government, in consequence of which French troops were withdrawn from Cilicia. Furthermore, King Constantine's return to Greece alienated even the British government, which refused to recognize the restored ruler and cut off its subsidies to the Greek government. When, therefore, the Turkish Nationalists launched a determined drive against the Greeks in the summer of 1922, it is perhaps understandable why they won a decisive victory. On September 9, 1922, the Nationalists entered Smyrna. Within a short time every Greek soldier in Anatolia was captured or driven off the mainland. Faced by this situation, the great powers invited Greece and Turkey to a conference to draft a new peace treaty with Turkey. Mustapha Kemal accepted their proposal, and an armistice was signed at Mudania on October 11.

THE LAUSANNE PEACE SETTLEMENT

The "revisionary" peace conference opened in Lausanne on November 20, 1922, and was attended by delegates of Great Britain, France, Italy,

---

[2] On the same day that the treaty of Sèvres was signed, a tripartite agreement was made between France, Italy, and Great Britain by which spheres of economic and political interest were mapped out in parts of the new Turkey. The French "sphere" was Cilicia, north of Syria; Italy's was the southwest part of Anatolia outside the Smyrna area.

Japan, the United States, Russia, Greece, Rumania, Yugoslavia, and Turkey. The inclusion of Turkish delegates made this the only one of the peace treaties which was negotiated and not dictated. A draft treaty was finally completed and presented to the conference on January 31, 1923; but at the last moment the Turkish delegates asked for further time to consider, and at length on February 4 definitely refused to sign because of certain economic and judicial clauses. It appeared that the conference had failed; the delegates returned home. But it turned out that the conference had only been interrupted. Although the Turkish National Assembly rejected the draft treaty, it authorized the continuance of negotiations. On April 24, therefore, the conference resumed its sessions. Three months later, after the Allies had yielded on enough points to satisfy the Turks, the treaty of Lausanne was signed on July 24, 1923.

The territorial extent of Turkey was slightly increased over what it was to have been according to the treaty of Sèvres. Although Mesopotamia, Arabia, Syria, and Palestine were still recognized as independent of Turkey, the latter advanced her frontier in Europe to the line of the Maritza River, plus a small district to the west of it in one place in order that she might control Karagach and its railway station. In the Aegean Turkey retained the Rabbit Islands, off the entrance to the Dardanelles, and the islands of Imbros and Tenedos. The Dodecanese,[3] Rhodes, and Castellorizo, Turkey ceded to Italy; and all her other Aegean islands to Greece. Turkey renounced all rights and titles over Libya, Egypt, and the Sudan, and recognized Great Britain's annexation of Cyprus. She also accepted articles for the protection of minorities similar to those signed by several of the European powers. On the other hand, she obtained the recognition by the signatory powers of the complete abolition of the capitulations in Turkey, suffered no restrictions of her military and naval forces, and was released from any claim on the part of the Allied powers to reparations on account of the First World War.

In separate conventions a number of other agreements were entered into, which had the same force as the treaty itself. The "principle of freedom of transit and of navigation by sea and by air in the strait of the Dardanelles, the sea of Marmora, and the Bosporus" was recognized, and an International Straits Commission was to operate under the auspices of the League of Nations. Both shores of the Dardanelles and of the Bosporus were demilitarized, as were the islands off the entrance to the Dardanelles and all the islands in the Sea of Marmora except Emir Ali Adasi.

A Greco-Turkish convention stipulated that there should "take place a compulsory exchange of Turkish nationals of the Greek Orthodox religion

[3] On October 8, 1922, Italy had announced that she considered her agreement to cede the Dodecanese to Greece had lapsed because of the nonratification of the treaty of Sèvres.

THE MODERNIZER OF TURKEY

Mustapha Kemal Atatürk

established in Turkish territory, and of Greek nationals of the Moslem religion established in Greek territory." Exceptions were made in the case of the Greeks on the islands of Imbros and Tenedos and of those who were established in Constantinople before October 30, 1918, and of the Moslem inhabitants in the district in western Thrace which Greece had obtained in 1913 by the treaty of Bucharest. Other conventions provided for the demilitarization of a region on both sides of the Greco-Turkish and Turco-Bulgarian frontier lines, and for the withdrawal of British, French, and Italian troops from Turkish territory immediately after the ratification of the treaty by the Turkish National Assembly. A comparison of the provisions of the treaty of Lausanne with the aims announced by the Nationalists reveals that the Turks obtained nearly everything for which they had fought—ethnographic frontiers, freedom from international servitudes, and national independence.

One detail of the peace settlement, however, was not finally settled for some time, and in this case the ultimate outcome was not favorable to Turkey. The treaty of Lausanne stated that the frontier between Turkey and Iraq (Mesopotamia) should be "laid down in friendly arrangement to be concluded between Turkey and Great Britain within nine months," but that, failing such an agreement within the time mentioned, the dispute should be referred to the Council of the League of Nations. Representatives of the two states met at Constantinople in an attempt to settle the line but could reach no agreement, the chief difficulty arising over the vilayet of Mosul, which was rich in petroleum resources. On August 6, 1924, Great Britain referred the whole matter to the League of Nations.

A commission of inquiry was at once created to study the situation and to lay before the Council information and suggestions. In the meantime the *status quo* in the disputed territory was to be maintained. After clashes between Turkish troops and those of the mandated territory, however, the question came before the Council again in October, 1924. At that time a committee of the Council laid down a line which was accepted by both parties and adopted by the Council as representing the *status quo*. The "Brussels line," which left in British control practically all of the vilayet of Mosul, was intended as only a provisional boundary to be observed until the permanent frontier should be fixed.

The commission on the Turco-Iraqi frontier next proceeded to the scene of the dispute and spent weeks on a tour of investigation. Its report was submitted to the Council in September, 1925. Because of the backward state of most of the population of the area, the commission rejected the Turkish argument for a plebiscite. It reported that the majority of the inhabitants south of the "Brussels line" had sentimental leanings toward Turkey but calculated that their economic interests would be better served by a union with Iraq as a British mandate. In case Iraq were to remain under the effective mandate of the League for a number of years, such union appeared to be the best solution.

The Council next appointed General Laidoner, a distinguished Estonian soldier, to investigate the situation along the "Brussels line." In his report he stated that the Turks were driving Christians out of the provisional Turkish zone, and that atrocities were being committed similar to those which accompanied the Armenian deportations of 1915. Until the reading of this report certain members of the Council had favored a compromise division of the vilayet, on the ground that it would be unfortunate for the League to render a decision wholly favorable to a great power within the League against a small power outside. General Laidoner's report, however, produced unanimity. The Council decided on December 16, 1925, that the Turco-Iraqi frontier should be fixed at the "Brussels line," but that this decision was to be final only in case Great Britain undertook by treaty to ensure the continuance of the mandatory regime in Iraq for twenty-five years.

This decision was immediately accepted by both Great Britain and Iraq, which on January 13, 1926, concluded a treaty continuing the mandatory regime in the latter for the desired term of years. On March 11 the Council of the League of Nations pronounced definitive its previous decision. Although Mustapha Kemal had proclaimed, "Mosul is Turkish and nothing can ever change that fact, even bayonets," three months later Sir Austen Chamberlain informed the Council that a treaty between Great Britain and Turkey had put an end to the tension between them.

NATIONALISM AND WESTERNIZATION

Meanwhile, on November 1, 1922, the Turkish Grand National Assembly had deposed Sultan Mohammed VI. Some three months after the signing of the treaty of Lausanne that same body, on October 29, 1923, proclaimed Turkey a republic and unanimously elected Mustapha Kemal the first president.[4] Despite the name "republic," however, Turkey in reality became a dictatorship. Kemal's People's Party was for years the only organized political group permitted in the country; and after 1927 Kemal, as president-general of the party, had the right to name all of the party's candidates for the National Assembly. But though the general government remained a dictatorship, laws were enacted to bring its judicial system into step with the Western world. A Supreme Court was established, and in 1926 all the old law codes, based primarily on the Koran, were supplanted by new civil, penal, and commercial codes which were based on European models. In 1932 Turkey became a member of the League of Nations.

The strong national spirit of Kemal and his associates led to efforts to

[4] In 1927, 1931, and 1935 he was re-elected to the presidency.

free the Turks from non-Turkish influences. Cities were given new Turkish names, for example, Constantinople becoming Istanbul; Angora, Ankara; Smyrna, Izmir, and so on. The national capital was removed from the Bosporus, where it had been for centuries, and located at Ankara, which consequently grew from a small town into a modern city. To assist in the nationalizing movement, the language of the people was purified of Arabic influences. A national law in 1928 provided that in the course of the following fifteen years the Latin alphabet should supplant the old Arabic. Newspapers and books were ordered to cease publication in Arabic characters after January, 1929.

The religious institutions of the country also were fundamentally changed. In March, 1924, the National Assembly abolished the Turkish caliphate and exiled from the country all members of the former Osman dynasty. Four years later that same body decided that Islam should no longer be the state religion of Turkey, that in fact the republic thereafter should tolerate all religions on an equal footing. Although Islam continued to be the religion of the bulk of the Turks, republican officials were no longer required, upon taking office, to swear by Allah. Severe restrictions were placed on the teaching of religion—Mohammedan or Christian—in public or private elementary schools. Early in 1933, in order to force the Moslem clergy to have a more liberal training, the theological faculty and curriculum of the University of Istanbul were modified by the government. The next year the government again struck at the influence of the Moslem clergy by a decree forbidding the wearing of clerical garb except at religious rites. In 1935 Sunday rather than Friday, the Moslem's special day of prayer, was made the official day of rest.

Sweeping social changes were introduced by Kemal, especially in the position of women. In 1925 legal polygamy was abolished and divorce was made permissible. In the next year civil marriage was made compulsory, and the legal age for marriage was raised to seventeen for women and eighteen for men. Western clothing was introduced, the wearing of the fez was made illegal, and the wearing of the veil was made optional. Many occupations were opened to women. In 1929 women gained the right to vote in local elections and to hold office in municipalities; in December, 1934, an amendment to the constitution gave them the right to vote for and become deputies. In February of the next year seventeen women were elected to the Grand National Assembly. By another law passed in 1934 all persons were required to assume family names, which were to be registered with the authorities by January 1, 1935. The National Assembly suggested that Mustapha Kemal assume the surname "Atatürk" ("Father of the Turks"). This the president did.

In the realm of education considerable progress was made. Although handicapped by a shortage of money, teachers, and educational facilities, the government increased the number of schools to 7000 by 1936. Its goal was compulsory school attendance for all children between seven and sixteen years of age. Attempts were made to compel all Turks under forty years of age to take lessons in reading and writing, and beginning in June, 1931, literacy was in general necessary to obtain the full rights of citizenship. Nevertheless, although illiteracy, according to reports, had been reduced by half, in 1939 a considerable percentage of the population was still illiterate.

Some advance was made by Turkey in her economic life also. In this realm, too, Kemal's aim was modernization and Westernization. The government itself in many ways sought to assist directly in the economic upbuilding of the country. Special departments were established to study commerce, shipping, industry, and agriculture. Large appropriations for public works were made, railways and highways were constructed, and a strong central bank was established. To encourage infant industries, a protective tariff was adopted in 1929; and in succeeding years, in order to overcome the republic's adverse trade balance, a quota system of imports was inaugurated. State control or state ownership of various enterprises was secured. In 1936 a modern labor law was enacted requiring the compulsory arbitration of labor disputes, prohibiting strikes and lockouts, regulating woman and child labor, and providing for an eight-hour day, minimum wages, and social insurance.

To Westernize and industrialize the country further a five-year industrial plan was adopted in January, 1934, providing for the building of fifteen factories, twelve of which were to be owned and operated by the government. The new enterprises were designed, in part, to free Turkey from the need of importing certain types of manufactured goods. The government announced that it had decided upon the adoption of a form of state capitalism and that, as rapidly as the resources of the government permitted, private enterprises would be taken over. To make the raw materials of the country more available, 1681 miles of railway were constructed by 1937, and plans called for the building of some thousands of miles of additional railways in the ensuing years.

In 1934 the desire to free Turkey from foreign control again manifested itself in several ways. In March the government announced its decision to purchase the 450-mile Smyrna-Kassaba Railway, which was owned by French interests. Later in the year the government made arrangements to take over from the French companies their concessions for operating the port facilities at Istanbul, and in 1935 it acquired the Istanbul Telephone Company from British interests. Meanwhile, in 1934, the minister of public works had announced that, in the future, enterprises undertaken by foreign capital in Turkey must register as Turkish companies, that no new concessions would be granted to foreign companies having their headquarters abroad. Furthermore, in that same year a law went into effect ousting all aliens from the professions, the trades, and jobs involving manual labor. Only by becoming naturalized citizens of Turkey could the thousands of persons affected escape the provisions of the law, regardless of the fact that they might have lived in Turkey for years.

FOREIGN POLICY

Nationalism continued to exert an influence upon the republic's foreign policy, too. For a number of years Turkish newspapers strongly urged the government to secure again its prewar right to fortify the Straits. Eventually, in 1936, after having sounded out the other powers, Turkey laid before the states signatory to the treaty of Lausanne, and before the League of Nations also, a formal request for the revision of those clauses of the treaty relating to nonfortification of the Dardanelles and the demilitarized zones. The strong feeling against Italy because of the latter's high-handed conquest of Ethiopia in disregard of treaty obligations doubtless reacted in favor of Turkey when the latter sought thus to secure treaty revision in accordance with legal procedure. In July, 1936, an international conference, meeting at Montreux, Switzerland, approved a new convention authorizing Turkey to proceed with the fortification of the Straits immediately.

Nor were the Turks averse to seizing upon the exigencies of other states to advance their nationalistic program. For some years they had insisted that the Sanjak of Alexandretta in northwest Syria was inhabited chiefly by Turks and should therefore be detached from that Arab state. Eventually, in 1937, France, the mandatory power for Syria, so far gave way to Turkish demands as to establish the sanjak as an independent state, which adopted the name Republic of Hatay. But Turkey, having succeeded in detaching the district from Syria, next desired to add it to her own territory. When, in the summer of 1939, Great Britain and France were attempting to create a bloc of powers to oppose Hitler's *Drang nach Osten*,[5] Turkey availed herself of the international tension to attain this end. In order to secure a declaration of mutual assistance from Turkey, France was obliged to pay the former's price. On June 23, 1939, a Franco-Turkish convention ceded Hatay to Turkey, except for a small section inhabited by Armenians, which was returned to Syria. Turkey promised to respect the independence of Syria, as newly delimited, and to refrain from any form of revisionist propaganda within her borders. The latter protested against the cession, but the parliament of Hatay approved the transfer and voted itself out of existence. Alexandretta and Antioch thus became Turkish cities.

But Turkey's acquisition of these cities was not finally achieved by Kemal

[5] See page 489

Atatürk. On November 10, 1938, the "Father of the Turks" died. Since the proclamation of the republic he had been its president, and to many observers he had seemed to be a dictator no less than Mussolini. Others, however, maintained that his dictatorship was merely a transition period between the old regime of the sultans and the Western democratic system which Atatürk hoped to see ultimately established in Turkey. Immediately after Atatürk's death the National Assembly chose as his successor his close friend and coworker in building the new Turkey, Ismet Inönü. The new president was a distinguished Turkish general and statesman. He had played a prominent role in the war against Greece (1920–1922), had represented Turkey at the Lausanne conference (1922–1923), and had for many years been prime minister during Atatürk's presidency. There seemed little doubt that Inönü would vigorously continue Atatürk's nationalist policy, but some questioned his ardent loyalty to democratic republicanism.

Meanwhile, Turkey's interest in pacts of nonaggression and security, so far as they affected her European boundaries, had been revealed by her treaty with Greece (1933) and by her joining the Balkan Entente (1934), both of which have already been discussed.[6] But she was interested, too, in maintaining peace in Asia. In 1937 on Turkey's initiative a Middle Eastern Entente was established when a nonaggression treaty was signed by Turkey, Iraq, Iran (Persia), and Afghanistan. These four Moslem powers pledged themselves to guarantee security in the Middle East by fulfilling their obligations under the League Covenant and the Briand-Kellogg pact. They specifically promised to abstain from interfering in one another's affairs and undertook to prevent the formation within their territories of bands or associations seeking to disturb the peace of any of them. Thereafter Turkey was in a position to foster co-operation between the Balkan countries and those of the Middle East, for she was included in ententes with both groups of powers.

Egypt

British control in Egypt, inaugurated in 1882, had been in no way legalized when the First World War began, but on December 18, 1914, a proclamation was issued by the British government declaring a protectorate over Egypt. On the succeeding day the ruling khedive was deposed by a proclamation which stated that the succession had been accepted by Prince Hussein Kamel, whose title was to be Sultan of Egypt. The title indicated independence of Turkey, but actual control still rested in the hands of Great Britain.

[6] See pages 382, 402.

British rule during the war caused much discontent. Egyptians were forced to serve in the army labor corps under a form of conscription; grain and animals were commandeered; the supply of cotton was controlled. The natural discontent because of arbitrary foreign rule was further stimulated by the Arab movement for independence, the Wilsonian theory of self-determination, and Moslem dislike for Christians. General unrest gradually crystallized into an Egyptian nationalist movement against British rule. Led by Saad Zaghlul Pasha, the Nationalists in 1918 began demanding complete autonomy. Sporadic rioting, strikes, and continuous agitation throughout 1919 finally led the British government to send to Egypt a mission to investigate the situation and to suggest a form of constitution. The mission recommended that Great Britain recognize Egypt as a sovereign state, provided the latter would recognize Great Britain's special interests in the Suez Canal as a link in the system of British imperial communications. Such a proposal, however, was unacceptable to the Egyptian Nationalists.

At length, on February 28, 1922, the British government by proclamation terminated the protectorate, abolished martial law, and recognized Egypt as "an independent sovereign state," but reserved for future discussion (1) the security of British communications, (2) the defense of Egypt, (3) the protection of foreigners and minorities in Egypt, and (4) the Sudan.[7] This arrangement was characterized by Lord Allenby, British high commissioner, as equivalent "to the declaration of a British Monroe Doctrine over Egypt." Sultan Ahmed Fuad, who had succeeded Hussein Kamel in 1917, in order to give formal expression to Egypt's new international status, on March 15, 1923, assumed the title of King Fuad I, and in April a constitution was enacted by a royal rescript. In the first general elections for the Egyptian parliament Zaghlul's party won an overwhelming majority, and in January, 1924, he became premier. Zaghlul still demanded Egypt's complete freedom from Britain's control.

In November, 1924, Anglo-Egyptian relations were suddenly subjected to a severe strain when Sir Lee Stack, commander-in-chief of the Egyptian army and governor-general of the Sudan, was killed by assassins in Cairo. The act came as the culmination of a long campaign against British officers and British sympathizers. Both the king and Premier Zaghlul immediately expressed their profound sorrow and their horror at the crime, and in the

---

[7] The chief interest of both Great Britain and Egypt in the Sudan was economic, arising from the development of irrigation projects which make possible the extensive growth of cotton. Because the Assuan dam marked the limit of easy exploitation of the Egyptian Nile, and because of deterioration of the quality of Egyptian cotton in recent years, the Nationalists were eager to incorporate the Sudan in Egypt. This would entail the withdrawal of the British, for an Anglo-Egyptian condominium had governed the Sudan since 1899.

name of the Egyptian government Zaghlul pledged himself to put forth
every effort to bring the criminals to justice and to inflict exemplary punishment.

Nevertheless, on November 22 the British government presented an
ultimatum, demanding an apology, punishment of the criminals, prohibition of political demonstrations, and the payment of an indemnity of
$2,500,000. It further required the withdrawal of all Egyptian troops from
the Sudan within twenty-four hours, the removal of limitations which in
Egyptian interests had been placed on the area to be irrigated in the Gezira,
and the withdrawal of all opposition to Great Britain's wishes in regard to
the protection of foreign interests within Egypt. Zaghlul's government at
once accepted all the demands except those referring to the Sudan and to
the protection of foreign interests, and paid the indemnity within twenty-
four hours. Failure to accept all the demands, however, brought the British
announcement that the Alexandria customs office would be occupied. Zaghlul thereupon resigned, and a new premier accepted the British requirements in full.

But the Nationalists (*Wafd* Party) continued to win whenever parliamentary elections were held and likewise continued to reject Anglo-
Egyptian treaties when they were submitted to them. In 1930, apparently
in an attempt to weaken the Nationalists, the government issued a new
constitution, but the promulgation of this document had the effect of bringing about a union of the forces of the Nationalists and the Liberal Consti-
tutionalists, both of whom wished to retain the constitution of 1923. Preceded by the threat of a Nationalist boycott and by a resort to repressive
measures against Nationalist meetings, and accompanied by riots in which
hundreds were reported killed or wounded, the first elections under the new
constitution were held in May, 1931. In the following month King Fuad
pointed out in his speech from the throne that much had been done to
improve the economic condition of the country and that, in spite of the
depression, the national budget had been balanced. During the next three
years, however, the government continued to wield dictatorial powers,
resorting to severe measures to suppress the opposition, and calling and
proroguing the parliament about as it pleased. Nevertheless, after a protracted political crisis late in 1934, King Fuad's semiautocratic regime came
to an end with the abrogation of the constitution of 1930 and the dissolution
of the parliament.

Tension between Great Britain and Italy arising from the Italo-Ethiopian
conflict in 1935 gave the Egyptian Nationalists an excellent opportunity to
bring pressure to bear upon Great Britain. Their nationalism was further
aroused, moreover, by the apparent disregard with which Great Britain
treated the Egyptian government in the military and naval steps which the

former took in Egypt to prepare for a possible Italo-British clash, and by the fear that Egypt might be drawn into the Italo-Ethiopian conflict through Britain's actions. Anti-British demonstrations were staged in Cairo and other cities. Anti-British sentiment rose to new heights when Sir Samuel Hoare, British foreign secretary, admitted in a speech in London on November 9, 1935, that the British government had advised against the restoration of the constitution of 1923 on the ground that it was unworkable.

Three days later the Nationalist Party decided to withdraw its support from the government. In the succeeding days anti-British demonstrations of Egyptian students led to frequent riots and clashes with the police, in the course of which the British consulate in Cairo was stoned. Eventually all parties in opposition to the government organized a "united front" under the leadership of the former Nationalist premier, Mustapha Nahas Pasha, to force the restoration of the constitution. Faced by the possibility of political chaos in Egypt, so important a strategic spot for Britain's activities in the Mediterranean, the British government surrendered to the Nationalist demands. On December 12, 1935, King Fuad issued a royal rescript restoring the constitution of 1923. This was his last important official act, for in April, 1936, he died, and was succeeded by his sixteen-year-old son, who was proclaimed King Farouk.

In the parliamentary elections following the restoration of the constitution the Nationalists again won a decisive victory, and on May 10, 1936, Mustapha Nahas Pasha became premier in a ministry consisting entirely of Nationalists. Meanwhile, scenting the possibility of a still greater victory, the Nationalists had demanded a treaty of alliance with Great Britain which would recognize Egypt's complete independence. On August 26 such a treaty was signed in London, the terms differing little from those of the treaty of 1930 which the Nationalists had rejected. Apparently the attitude of the latter was influenced by the Italian conquest of Ethiopia, which emphasized Egypt's need of military protection against possible threats from Italian Libya and Italian East Africa.

By the terms of the treaty (1) the administration of the Sudan reverted to the prewar status, (2) Great Britain agreed to withdraw her troops from Egypt except from the vicinity of the Suez Canal, (3) Egypt gave the British the right to use Alexandria and Port Said as naval bases and the right to move their troops through Egyptian territory in the case of war or the threat of war, (4) Egypt agreed to have her army instructed by the British and equipped with British arms, (5) both agreed that should either be at war the other would come to its assistance, (6) in recognition of Egypt's complete independence Great Britain agreed to replace her high commissioner by an ambassador and to support Egypt in her request for the abolition of capitulations and for membership in the League of Nations. The treaty was ratified by the Egyptian and British parliaments in November, 1936.

In May, 1937, a convention was signed at Montreux, Switzerland, by the capitulatory powers, providing (1) that after October 15, 1937, foreigners in Egypt would be subject to Egyptian-made law and taxation, and consular courts would surrender most of their powers to mixed tribunals, and (2) that after a transitional period the mixed tribunals would be abolished and in 1949 foreigners in Egypt would be subject to the Egyptian courts and laws in all matters. In the same month Egypt was admitted to membership in the League of Nations.

Syria and Lebanon

In western Asia at the close of the First World War most of the non-Turkish regions of the former Ottoman Empire were entrusted to France and Great Britain as Class A mandates of the League of Nations. As such they were considered to have reached a stage of development where their existence as independent nations could be provisionally recognized, subject to the rendering of administrative advice and assistance by the mandatory power until they should be able to stand alone. The eagerness of the native peoples to secure complete independence and the reluctance of the advisory powers to recognize such a status at times precipitated serious armed clashes.

The political divisions of the Arab lands south of Turkey, as they were established by the great powers after the war, showed no close approximation to the political units of the former Ottoman Empire. Although the population of the region was largely Arab in language and culture, the territory was divided more or less to satisfy the desires of Great Britain and France. The allotment of the mandates was made by the Council of Ambassadors at San Remo in April, 1920. Syria and Lebanon went to France. Great Britain received Palestine, Transjordan, and Iraq.

The territory assigned to France, popularly referred to as Syria, stretched along the Mediterranean coast from Alexandretta to Tyre, and extended inland to the Jebel Druze in the south and northeastward across the Euphrates and Tigris rivers to a point north of Mosul. Although the whole region was placed under one French high commissioner, it was divided for administrative purposes. In accordance with the Franco-Turkish agreement of 1921, the Sanjak of Alexandretta—which included a considerable number of Turks—was given an autonomous regime. Lebanon, because of its large Christian population, had had a special administrative treatment under the Turks, and the French not only perpetuated this status but also enlarged the territory included in Lebanon.

The original hostility of the Moslems of Syria, increased by their impression that the French government was supporting the Christians against them, was still further aroused by the introduction of a depreciating French currency, the use of French in the law courts, and the long continuance of martial law. The iron-handed methods of the French administration ultimately led in 1925 to open revolt by the Druse tribesmen. The French retaliated by bombarding some of the native villages, and the uprising in consequence spread rapidly. When natives in the vicinity of Damascus attempted to cut the French line of communication, French forces countered by burning several villages. In fact, they ultimately subjected the city of Damascus to a bombardment and to bombing by airplanes, causing the loss of a thousand lives. The revolt continued, however, and in 1926 a second bombardment of Damascus, with the loss of another thousand lives, led the Mandates Commission of the League to remonstrate. In the guerrilla war which ensued, the French maintained control of the cities but for a time made little headway in the rural districts. The high commissioner continued to refuse to recognize the tribesmen as belligerents, and the latter continued to demand independence, with admission to the League of Nations.

Eventually, in 1928, the French permitted elections to be held for a constituent assembly which should draft a Syrian constitution, the understanding being that the adoption of the constitution would be followed by a Franco-Syrian treaty defining the relations between the two countries and giving Syria her place among the nations of the world. In the constituent assembly which opened on June 9 of that year a substantial majority was held by the Syrian Nationalists, who wanted a completely independent republic. But the French were unwilling to permit the adoption of such a constitution, and so the high commissioner at first suspended and then adjourned the constituent assembly *sine die*.

In May, 1930, a constitution promulgated by the high commissioner himself established a republic, subject only to the mandatory powers of the French government and to the latter's control of its foreign policy. Syria was to have her own president and her own parliament. The president was to be elected for a five-year term by the parliament and was to be a Moslem. Not until January, 1932, were popular elections held under this constitution, and then they were accompanied by considerable disorder. Thanks, many claimed, to French pressure, a majority of moderate Nationalists was returned. In June the parliament elected as president of Syria a wealthy Arab who had been practically nominated by the French.

Late in 1933 France negotiated and signed a Franco-Syrian treaty of friendship and alliance, apparently as a step preliminary toward ending her mandate over Syria. The treaty was strongly denounced by Syrian patriots, however, because it did not include all the territory which they desired to see incorporated in Syria, and because for twenty-five years Syria's foreign policy as well as her financial and military affairs were to be under French supervision. When it became clear that the treaty would not be ratified, the French high commissioner withdrew it and prorogued the parliament.

But the success of anti-British agitation in Egypt had its effect in Syria, where early in 1936 the Syrian campaign for independence was revived. When the French authorities sought to prevent trouble by ordering the dissolution of the Syrian Nationalist Party, violent street fighting broke out which brought the death of a number of persons and the arrest of hundreds more. A general strike by the Syrians finally compelled the French authorities to permit the establishment of a Nationalist cabinet. Léon Blum's government, which came into power in France in the summer of 1936, at once sought to bring about better relations with the natives and in the fall of that year signed with the Nationalist governments of Syria and Lebanon treaties of alliance and friendship which closely resembled the Anglo-Egyptian treaty of August, 1936. By the terms of these treaties both were to become independent nations at the end of a three-year transition period, and France was to sponsor their admission to the League of Nations. The French, however, were to maintain troops in the republics for a time and to train and equip their armies.

But the French parliament delayed its ratification of the Franco-Syrian treaty. The grave dissatisfaction which resulted in Syria was further increased when France consented to the handing over to Turkey of Alexandretta and Antioch. On July 7, 1939, the president of Syria resigned his office in protest against French policies. On the next day the French high commissioner in Syria dissolved the Syrian parliament, suspended the Syrian constitution, and ordered the establishment of a council to exercise executive authority under his supervision. On the eve of the Second World War Franco-Syrian relations seemed as far from an amicable settlement as at any time since 1920.

Palestine

Meanwhile, the British in Palestine had encountered great difficulties because of the apparently irreconcilable differences of the Arabs and the Jews. In 1917 the British government, in the famous Balfour Declaration, had promised to establish in Palestine a national home for the Jewish people. Five years later the League of Nations assigned Palestine to Great Britain as a Class A mandate, the terms of the mandate confirming the Balfour Declaration. On September 1, 1922, Sir Herbert Samuel, the first British high commissioner, promulgated a constitution for the mandated

The Near and Middle East Between the Two World Wars

territory. Palestine was to be governed by a high commissioner, an appointed executive council, and a legislative council, part of whose members were to be appointed by the high commissioner and part elected by the people. The Moslem Arabs, who constituted about 80 per cent of the population, refused to participate in the elections for the legislative council, however, so that the high commissioner was compelled to resort to an appointed advisory council. For a time serious riots occurred.

Although the Moslems failed to become reconciled to British policy, their open opposition abated for a time, owing to the improvement of the economic condition of the country and to the fact that the British government showed no hostility to the Arabs. Nevertheless, as the years passed, the latter became restless. Despite a certain degree of government control of immigration, the number of Jews in Palestine steadily mounted until there were by 1929 some 160,000 in the territory—nearly twice the number there when the mandate was established. Furthermore, the Arabs claimed that most of the newcomers—being refugees from Rumania, Poland, or Russia—were poor and inclined to be radicals. In addition to these grounds of complaint, the Arabs denounced the agrarian legislation which had been enacted. Laws making it possible for the Jews to purchase large sections of the somewhat restricted area of arable land, so the Arabs declared, menaced the very foundations of their own economic existence.

Late in August, 1929, the Moslems broke out in open rebellion and began an attack upon the Jews in Palestine which resulted in the death of more than two hundred and compelled the British government to rush forces to Palestine to restore order. The cause of the rioting, reported the Simpson commission of inquiry, was the Arab feeling of animosity and hostility toward the Jews, consequent upon the disappointment of their political and national aspirations, and fear for their economic future. Investigation brought to light the fact that while, by the natural increase in population, the number of Arabs was mounting, the land available for their sustenance, because of the area which had passed into Jewish hands, had decreased by about 250,000 acres. In the light of Arab methods of cultivation, there was, it was reported, no margin of land available for agricultural development by new immigrants. It was further pointed out that the Jewish National Fund, which rented land to the Jews, forbade the employment of Arab labor on its soil, and that the policy of the General Federation of Jewish Labor was to import Jewish workers rather than to hire landless Arabs.

Despite the protests of the Jews, the British authorities for a time suspended immigration. In 1931, therefore, the Arabs became more conciliatory and displayed a willingness to co-operate in the election of a legislative council. When the project of such a council was accordingly revived, it next encountered the opposition of the Jews, who declared they would have nothing to do with it unless they were guaranteed at least an equality in membership with the Arabs. Once more the project had to be dropped.

Although some attempts were made by the British authorities to control the type of Jewish immigrant, by 1933 there were in Palestine, according to Jewish authorities, more than 200,000 Jews, and the amount of land held by the latter had increased twelvefold since the close of the war. One new Jewish city, Tel Aviv, was reported to have a population of 60,000 in 1933 and to be increasing at the rate of 12,000 a year. Meanwhile, in 1925, a Hebrew University had been opened in Jerusalem. Thanks to the influx of capital from abroad, to the increased application of scientific methods to agriculture, industry, and business, and to the aid of the Palestine Foundation Fund, Palestine was relatively unaffected by the world depression. Millions of dollars of Jewish capital flowed into the country, projects for electrification were started, Haifa was improved into a deep-water port, a pipe line was begun to connect this port with the rich Mosul oil fields, and a survey was completed for a future Haifa-Bagdad railway. Many believed that, when these various projects were completed, Palestine would come to play an important role in the trade of the Near and Middle East.

Nevertheless, the opposition of the Moslems continued. When in February, 1933, the high commissioner declined to place further restrictions on Jewish immigration or to forbid the sale of Arab lands to Jews, Arab leaders once more announced a policy of non-co-operation with the British authorities. Three years later anti-Jewish outbreaks on the part of the Arabs again became serious. Clashes occurred which caused over three hundred fatalities, and increased British forces were sent to Palestine in an effort to restore order. To enforce their demand that further Jewish immigration be halted, the Arabs resorted to widespread strikes and to a campaign of civil disobedience.

In May, 1936, the British government again decided to send a royal commission to Palestine to investigate Arab and Jewish grievances. The Peel commission's report, published in July, 1937, declared that the aspirations of the 400,000 Jews and the 1,000,000 Arabs in Palestine were irreconcilable and the existing British mandate unworkable. It therefore recommended that Palestine be divided into three parts. Nazareth, Jerusalem, and a corridor from the latter to the Mediterranean at Jaffa should continue to be a British mandate; a section including about one third of Palestine should be converted into a Jewish state; and the rest of the territory should become an Arab state linked with Transjordan. The Jewish state would have ports at Haifa and Tel Aviv, the latter having by 1937 a population of 125,000. The Arab state would have an outlet to the Mediterranean at Gaza. Both states would have to enter into military alliances with Great Britain, and the important naval base and pipe-line terminus at Haifa would be left temporarily under British control. The commission's proposals were at once vigorously denounced by both Arabs and Jews, though the Zionist Congress eventually empowered its executive to negotiate for partition.

Although the British government at once approved the Peel commission's report, opposition was so strong in the House of Commons that it was voted to have the plan for partition studied further before final parliamentary action. Accordingly, early in 1938, the Woodhead commission was sent to Palestine to work out in consultation with the local communities there some detailed scheme.

Almost without cessation, while the Woodhead commission was working, Palestine was subjected to a reign of terrorism and interracial fighting. Riots, sniping, bomb explosions, assassinations, banditry, and other outrages were of almost daily occurrence. It is futile to give all the details. Suffice it to point out that in July, 1938, for example, 148 Arabs and 60 Jews were killed and 256 Arabs and 201 Jews were injured. The government vainly sought to restore order by imprisonments, hangings, and executions. British marines were landed at Haifa, and additional troops were ordered to Palestine. In October both Bethlehem and Jerusalem were seized by the Arabs, who were dislodged only after strong British forces had been dispatched against them. By the middle of the month Great Britain had in Palestine more than 17,000 men, with artillery, armored cars, and airplanes. The grand mufti of Jerusalem, the leader of the Arabs, announced, however, that fighting would continue until Great Britain had accepted the Arab demands.

In October, 1938, the report of the Woodhead commission was published rejecting the plan for partition on the ground that the practical difficulties in the way of such a division were insurmountable. The British government thereupon also rejected the partition scheme and announced that it would once more attempt to bring about an understanding between the Arabs and the Jews. For this purpose a round-table conference of Arabs and Jews was convened in London in February, 1939. But the Palestinian Arabs declined to sit with the Jewish delegates or to discuss the Palestine problem in any joint session Naturally, under these circumstances, the conference failed to reach an agreement.

In May, 1939, the British government issued a new "Statement of Policy" which envisaged the establishment within ten years of an independent Palestine. The new state was to be linked with Great Britain in treaty relations; the Jews and Arabs were to share in the government, and the essential interests of both were to be effectively safeguarded. During the transitional period of ten years land sales were to be restricted. During the first five years 75,000 Jewish immigrants would be admitted into Palestine, but after that no more Jewish immigration was to be permitted unless the

Arabs in Palestine agreed to it. After the Jews and Arabs in Palestine had finally established good relations between themselves, representatives of the people of Palestine and of the British government would together draft a constitution for independent Palestine.

These proposals were satisfactory to neither Jews nor Arabs. Violence and terrorism continued unabated in Palestine, and on July 12, largely because of the disturbed conditions and because of the number of Jews illegally entering Palestine, the British government announced the suspension of all immigration into Palestine for six months, beginning October 1, 1939. When the Second World War broke out, therefore, after twenty years of repeated efforts Great Britain seemed to be about as far as ever from a final settlement of the Arab-Jewish question in Palestine.

Iraq

Although the British met little opposition in assuming their mandate over Transjordan, where they confided the local government to Abdullah (son of Hussein, the first king of Hejaz), in Iraq, where they installed Feisal, another son of Hussein, as king, they encountered open revolt. Hostility to British rule was so great that, despite the suppression of open resistance, the mandate had to be transformed into an Anglo-Iraq treaty of alliance (1922). Not until 1924 was the treaty ratified by the constituent assembly of Iraq, and then only after Great Britain had threatened to bring the matter before the League Council. Late in 1925, in accordance with the League's decision in the Turco-Iraqi boundary dispute, Great Britain and Iraq negotiated another treaty, which was to run for twenty-five years or until Iraq should become a member of the League of Nations. This treaty was signed on January 13, 1926.

Iraq, however, was eager to throw off the mandatory status as soon as possible. In 1927 the Iraqi government attempted to persuade Great Britain that Iraq should be admitted to the League at once. Although the British were unwilling to support this step so soon, they did sign a new treaty (December, 1927) agreeing to recognize the independence of Iraq within five years and—if Iraq's existing rate of progress continued—to support her candidacy for admission to the League in 1932. Iraq, on her part, agreed to lease three new air bases to Great Britain and to turn over to a British military commission the training of the Iraqi army, which would use British equipment. It was further agreed that Great Britain should be represented in Iraq by an ambassador who should have precedence over all other diplomats.

Five years later the British mandate was ended, and Iraq became independent. The Mandates Commission in 1932 drew up a list of guarantees which Iraq had to accept before she could become a member of the League. These included protection of minorities, freedom of conscience and religion, recognition of rights acquired and debts contracted during the mandatory regime, and the guarantee of the rights of foreigners before the courts. Iraq promised, furthermore, in case of actual or imminent war, to aid Great Britain to the extent of her ability. On October 3, 1932, Iraq was admitted to the League as an independent power, and the European states surrendered their privileges under the capitulations.

Unfortunately for the orderly political progress of Iraq, King Feisal died in 1933. His son, who became King Ghazi, was less capable and less responsible, and the political situation thereafter deteriorated. In 1936 a *coup d'état,* brought about by the military, installed a Pan-Arab ministry, and Iraq became for all practical purposes a military dictatorship. The political situation was not improved when in 1939 King Ghazi was killed in an accident and was succeeded by his three-year-old son, who became Feisal II. It is not surprising that in the opening years of the Second World War Iraq became the scene of numerous plots and counterplots of the various belligerents.[8]

Iran (Persia)

Meanwhile, to the east of Iraq, the Persians had become imbued with the same nationalistic spirit which had led the Turks to rebel against the West. They had every reason to fear the extinction of their independence as a sovereign state, for the Anglo-Russian treaties of 1907 and 1915 had practically divided Persia between these two great powers. The withdrawal of Russian forces after the Bolshevik revolution gave little encouragement to Persian nationalists, since their place was taken by the British, and in 1919 an Anglo-Persian treaty made Persia dependent upon Great Britain in political and military matters.

The weak Persian government which consented to this treaty came to be regarded by Persian nationalists as an instrument of foreign rule. In February, 1921, this government was overthrown by a military revolution led by Riza Khan, who, like Mustapha Kemal, was a soldier who had risen from the ranks to be head of a small and efficient military force. Riza Khan at once became commander-in-chief of the Persian army and the real power in the government, which promptly denounced the Anglo-Persian treaty. Soon after the *coup d'état* of February, 1921, Riza Khan became minister of war, and, after making and unmaking several ministries, he finally assumed the premiership in October, 1923. The shah was induced to leave

[8] See pages 542-543.

Persia for Europe, and on December 12, 1925, a Persian constituent assembly made Riza Khan hereditary shah with the title Riza Shah Pahlevi.

By this time the reconstruction of Persia had been largely accomplished. The Russian-officered Cossacks, British-officered South Persian Rifles, and Swedish-officered gendarmerie had given way to a well-organized and well-equipped national Persian army of some 40,000 men. With this force Riza Shah had succeeded in restoring order and in asserting the authority of the Teheran government over many tribes which had been enjoying *de facto* independence. In 1921 the Persian government had sought foreign assistance in its task of remodeling its public finances and promoting the economic development of the country, and in the succeeding years Riza Shah sought further to modernize Persia. The legal age for marriage for girls was made sixteen years, and women were given an equal right with men to secure a divorce. Railway construction was begun, highways were extended, an air force was created, and in 1932 a small Persian navy was placed in the Persian Gulf. The latter was connected with the Caspian Sea when the Trans-Iranian Railway was officially opened shortly before the outbreak of the Second World War.

The attempt to throw off outside control continued. All foreign capitulations in Persia were abolished, and national tariff autonomy was secured. Foreign mission schools in the country were forbidden to teach Persian children in the primary grades. In 1931 the Persian government took over control of all the country's telegraph lines, which were formerly in the hands of the Indo-European Telegraph Department of the British India Office. In the next year the Junkers Aircraft Company, a German concern, was forced to discontinue its air services in Persia, largely because the Persian government placed difficulties in the way of a renewed concession; at the same time the government refused to allow the Imperial Airways Company of Great Britain to have landing fields in Persia on the route to India.

Finally, in November, 1932, the Persian council of ministers, presided over by Riza Shah, decided to cancel the concession of the Anglo-Persian Oil Company, a majority of whose stock was held by the British government. Great Britain at once denied Persia's right to cancel the concession, but proposed that the whole question be referred to the World Court. Persia refused to admit the competence of the court in a dispute between herself and a commercial company. Thereupon Great Britain requested that the matter be submitted to the League Council. At the meeting of the Council in February, 1933, however, the two countries agreed that the League proceedings should be suspended for three months while direct negotiations regarding a new concession were carried on between Persia and the Anglo-Persian Oil Company. This step marked a distinct victory for Persia, for throughout the dispute she had steadily maintained that the company should negotiate directly with Persia.

The Persian government ultimately won a victory in its dispute with the powerful British company. On April 30, 1933, a new sixty-year lease was signed with drastically altered terms. In place of the former 16 per cent of the net profits of the company, Persia was to receive one dollar per ton of oil extracted regardless of the price and, in addition, was to receive 20 per cent of the company's total net profits above a stated minimum. Furthermore, the company was to pay Persia in taxation about $1,125,000 annually for the first fifteen years and about $1,500,000 for the second fifteen years. Persia gained much better financial terms than she formerly enjoyed. Moreover, she made other nationalistic gains. The company's area of exploitation was drastically curtailed; it was to replace progressively its foreign employees by Persians; it was to spend some $50,000 annually educating Persians in Great Britain; and it was to sell oil to Persians and to the Persian government at a discount from the world prices. By many it was considered that Persia's victory in this dispute constituted an important precedent in the relations between "backward" nations and powerful concessionaries.

In 1935 Riza Shah officially changed the name of his country from Persia to Iran. Developments during the Second World War,[9] however, raised the question whether Iran was actually any more able to maintain its independence of the great powers than Persia had been a generation earlier.

India

The First World War directly affected India, for nearly a million and a half men were sent overseas, more than a third of them actually becoming combatants. As a consequence of the war, India incurred or assumed a financial burden of about $700,000,000. Out of this contact with the war came a sense of added prestige and an increased desire for freedom from European control, for a place as an equal among the states of the world. A great impetus was thus given to the nationalist movement which had already begun in India before 1914.

In December, 1916, a meeting of representatives of both Hindus and Moslems in India drafted a scheme of reform for which the National Party in India should stand, and the British government soon took steps to recognize the national awakening. Two Indians were included among the four delegates from India at the imperial conference of 1917. In August of that year E. S. Montagu, secretary of state for India, announced that the British government was planning to increase the association of Indians in the ad-

[9] See page 520.

ministrative branches of the government and to develop gradually self-governing institutions. In July, 1918, came a report on the reforms which had been drafted as a result of consultations between Montagu and Lord Chelmsford, the viceroy of India. The moderate parties in India accepted the scheme outlined, but in December the National Congress Party, now the organ of the extreme nationalists, wholly condemned the proposals and demanded immediate and full autonomy.

For the time being, however, the constitutional question was eclipsed by the course of events in India, where Mohandas K. Gandhi, a Hindu social and religious reformer, became the spokesman and leader of the agitation and initiated a movement of passive resistance. The Indian government, alarmed by the unrest and revolutionary agitation, hurriedly passed certain emergency measures. These the Congress Nationalist press and politicians at once denounced as attacks upon popular liberties and as instruments of tyranny and oppression. A wave of excitement spread over the Punjab and reached its height when on April 13, 1919, the "Amritsar massacre" occurred. Military forces employed to disperse an unlawful gathering in Amritsar caused the death of about 400 Indians and the wounding of three times that number.

In Great Britain it was hoped that the admission of Indian claims to self-government would alleviate Indian unrest and Indian hostility. The Montagu-Chelmsford scheme of constitutional reform was accordingly pushed through Parliament and became the Government of India Act in December, 1919. This act applied not to the three hundred or more Indian principalities which have relations with the British government, but only to the 230,000,000 people living in British India.

The Government of India Act fundamentally altered the political situation in India. In the first place, it provided for decentralization through the establishment of provincial governments which should have charge of such matters as education, public health, agriculture, irrigation, criminal law, prisons, and labor legislation. For most administrative purposes, the provinces were treated as separate states within a kind of federation. Each of these provinces had a legislative council in which at least 70 per cent of the members were elected and not more than 20 per cent were officials. All men over twenty-one years of age had the vote, provided they met certain property or occupational requirements, but these were of such a character that only about 5,350,000 persons had the franchise.

Within each province the functions of government were divided, under a system known as dyarchy, into reserved and transferred subjects. The reserved departments, including irrigation, land revenue, factory inspection, and police, were administered by the provincial governor and his executive council; the transferred departments, including public health, education, public works, and agriculture, were administered by ministers chosen from the provincial assembly and responsible to it. In this way it was planned to provide a field in which Indian leaders could be trained in the actual practice of government; and the dyarchical scheme was intended to be only transitory and experimental.

No dyarchy was provided for the central government, however, which consisted of the governor-general in council and two advisory bodies—the Legislative Assembly and the Council of State. The governor-general and his executive council remained directly responsible to the British Parliament for the government of India, but the two advisory bodies were chosen by very restricted Indian electorates. Those entitled to vote for the Legislative Assembly numbered less than a million men, while the electorate for the Council of State included less than eighteen thousand. The Legislative Assembly developed into the chief agency for crystallizing and voicing Indian opinion, and came to be something of a parliament without power.

The Government of India Act stipulated that ten years after its passage a parliamentary commission should go to India to inquire into the working of the plan and to report on the desirability of extending or modifying the degree of responsible government already existing. Two years before the expiration of the designated decade, the British government appointed an interparty parliamentary commission under Sir John Simon to consider possible amendments to the act of 1919. The exclusion of Indians from the commission led to dissatisfaction among the Congress Nationalists, who demanded that responsible Indians should themselves devise the future system of government in India or at least be treated as equal co-operators. The commission attempted to give Indian statesmen an opportunity to help construct the future constitution of India by proposing that Indians should work with them "on equal terms in joint conference."

During the early months of 1929 the Simon Commission continued its investigations, while Indian radicals did their utmost to awaken a widespread distrust of it and its objects. Gandhi again conducted a vigorous campaign against the use or sale of British cloth in India, resulting in the seizure and burning of such cloth, and in subsequent riots and arrests. In 1930 he inaugurated a new campaign of civil disobedience. Setting an example by himself violating the laws establishing a government salt monopoly, he brought about a general defiance of laws in India. The collection of taxes was resisted, railway and street traffic was obstructed, and many Hindu officials resigned. Although Gandhi counseled his followers to avoid violence, disorders broke out, and in May, 1930, the government finally took the step of arresting and imprisoning Gandhi and a number of his more important followers.

In 1930 the report of the Simon Commission was published. The document carefully avoided any mention of dominion status or independence and appeared to seek an increase in the executive powers of the secretary of state for India, the governor-general, and the various provincial governors. It was thoroughly unsatisfactory to the Congress Nationalists. In an attempt to work out some compromise solution of the Indian problem the British government next called a number of round-table conferences to meet in London. The first, which assembled in November, 1930, was attended by representatives of the three British political parties, the native Indian states, and various groups in British India. In September, 1931, a second conference convened, and this time Gandhi himself attended. This conference was notable chiefly for its disagreements. Hindus and Moslems disagreed on means of protecting the latter; British Indians and the native princes disagreed on the type of federation to be adopted; high-caste Hindus and the "untouchables" disagreed on the future status of the latter; and, finally, Britishers and Indians disagreed on the extent of self-government which India was to have. The conference ultimately adjourned in December, after Premier MacDonald had pointed out that disagreements among the Indians themselves constituted a serious handicap to the drafting of a constitution.

Meanwhile, during 1931, India had been greatly disturbed by violence on the part of the Nationalists. So serious did the situation become that the governor-general issued a number of ordinances of a severely repressive nature. Upon his refusal to recall them, Gandhi once more launched a campaign of civil disobedience. The Nationalist leader, in consequence, was again imprisoned, and during the first half of 1932 nearly 50,000 Indians were arrested for violation of special ordinances. Ultimately the British government announced that it would itself work out a plan to solve the minorities problem, and that when it had done this it would summon a third round table to draw up a new constitution for India.

In November, 1932, this conference convened in London for a final consideration of the projected Indian constitution. When it adjourned late in December, a complete and definite form of government had at last been drafted. In March, 1933, the British government issued a white paper containing the new Indian federal constitution. This was in turn submitted for consideration and revision to an India Joint Select Committee, chosen from both houses of the British Parliament. Although many Labor members of the British Parliament and some extreme Conservatives were opposed to the projected scheme of government—though, obviously, for far different reasons—the Government of India Bill was passed by the House of Commons, and on August 2, 1935, it became law. The Marquess of Linlithgow, chairman of the India Joint Select Committee, was thereupon appointed to be the new viceroy of India and entrusted with the task of putting the act into effect.

Under her new constitution India still failed to attain dominion status, for the British viceroy was to control defense and foreign relations and was to possess a number of emergency powers in case of domestic crises arising from conflicts over religion, minorities, currency, or justice to foreigners. British India was to have a central government and eleven provincial governments, and the general purpose of the constitution seemed to be to place the chief responsibility for domestic administration on the latter. In each of the self-governing provinces a ministry, selected from its legislature, was normally to conduct all provincial affairs, including even the maintenance of law and order. Over the ministry, however, was to be placed a British governor, as formerly, with special responsibilities. If circumstances demanded, the governor might take charge of any branch of the provincial government, might issue ordinances with the force of law, might even override the provincial legislature on appropriation bills. The electorate for the provincial legislatures, according to figures which were published, was to include some 38,000,000 men and women, and therefore marked a considerable extension of the franchise over that existing under the act of 1919. The Council of State, the upper house of the national legislature, was to have 150 members elected by the provincial legislatures, 100 members appointed by the princes, and 10 appointed by the government. The Legislative Assembly, the lower house, was to have 250 members elected directly by the voters, and 125 members appointed by the princes. The national electorate was to consist of some 6,000,000 voters, which likewise constituted an advance over the provisions of the act of 1919. Nowhere, of course, was universal suffrage provided. The new constitution, being a compromise, naturally pleased nobody. In general, the Indian view was that it in no sense substantiated agreements reached at the first two round tables. The Congress Nationalists at once decided to boycott the new regime.

When elections were held in the eleven provinces in January and February, 1937, however, the Congress Party participated and won a decisive victory, securing an absolute majority in six and a plurality in three of them. In March the All-India Congress Committee resolved that Congress ministers should accept office only if each governor would agree not to "use his special powers of interference or set aside the advice of ministers in regard to their constitutional activities." The provincial governors, however, declared it constitutionally impossible for them to accept this formula. On April 1, when the new constitution was formally introduced, a general strike and a protest demonstration were organized against it, but in seven provinces Congress leaders organized governments and in the succeeding

THE NATIONALIST LEADER OF INDIA
Mohandas K. Gandhi

months showed a desire to make their administrations function successfully.

A flare-up occurred in February, 1938, when the British viceroy, availing himself of his statutory powers to issue orders to provincial governors
"for the purpose of preventing any grave menace to the peace or tranquillity of India," advised the governors of two provinces not to carry out the
orders of the provincial ministries to release all political prisoners. The Congress ministries thereupon resigned, but the moderation of the leaders of
the party was revealed when they accepted Gandhi's suggestion against
extending the political crisis to the other provinces where Congress ministries were in office. Ultimately, in July, compromise agreements were
reached between the provincial governors and the resigned premiers, and
the latter resumed their offices.

In 1939, upon the outbreak of the Second World War, the Working Committee of the Congress Party asked the British government to set forth
Britain's war aims in regard to democracy and imperialism and to state
their application to India. This request was endorsed on October 10 by the
All-India Congress Committee, and Jawaharlal Nehru, a prominent Indian Nationalist, declared that only two courses remained open—agreement with the British government or conflict. One week later the viceroy
disappointed Indian Nationalists with his statement that at the close of the
Second World War the British government would be willing to enter into
consultation with representatives of the various groups in India with a view
to securing their aid and co-operation in framing modifications to the act
of 1935. The Working Committee thereupon called upon all Congress ministries to resign their offices, and on November 23, 1939, it declared that the
recognition of India's independence and the right of her people to frame
their own constitution was essential to enable Congress Nationalists to
consider future co-operation. Obviously the various steps taken by Great
Britain between the two wars to extend a measure of self-government to
India had failed to satisfy Indian Nationalist leaders.

Chapter XVIII

THE FAR EAST

ALTHOUGH native unrest and nascent rebellion in French Indo-China, the Dutch East Indies, and the American Philippines were phases of the East's revolt against the West, the chief exponents of this movement in the Far East were the Chinese and Japanese. The former persistently sought to rid themselves of Western domination and exploitation, but unfortunately were seriously handicapped by their own inability to unite and present a common front. The latter, nationally united and militarily modernized, ultimately revolted against Western interference in their imperialistic plans, and even before 1939 successfully defied both the League of Nations and the United States.

China in 1914

In China conditions existing in 1914 were such as inevitably to provoke a strong nationalist reaction against the West. China had long been deterred by prejudice, self-sufficiency, and conservatism from embarking upon a program of modernization in the Western sense. Her armies and navies, therefore, had been helpless before the powerful military and naval machines of modern imperialism, and unable to prevent the exploitation and spoliation of the country. As the result of wars waged against the Chinese Empire by Great Britain and France in 1840–1842 and in 1856–1860, eleven ports had been opened to foreign traders, foreign ministers had secured the right to reside in Peking, Europeans had been granted the privilege of traveling in the interior, Christian missionaries had been assured the protection of the Chinese government, and Great Britain had acquired the island of Hong Kong and a foothold on the mainland adjoining. During the succeeding years the vast Chinese Empire with its hundreds of millions of inhabitants was a constant temptation to the imperialistic powers of the West.

It was a temptation, too, to the virile Japanese, whose empire in the years after 1867 had passed through a veritable political and economic revolution. In 1867 the youthful Emperor Mutsuhito had been freed from the domination of his chief officer or *shogun,* whose family had ruled Japan for more

432

than two hundred and fifty years. The young emperor, who reigned until 1912, had then proceeded to inaugurate a regime of progress and enlightenment. Feudalism was abolished, the government was centralized and made more efficient, and a national army and a modern navy were established under the direction of European officers. In an attempt to make Japan the equal of the Western powers, foreigners were invited into the country and Japanese commissions were sent abroad to study European institutions. Western learning was introduced, Western codes of law were adopted, religious toleration was granted, and in 1889 a written constitution based on a study of European governments was promulgated. Western methods of industry were also introduced, so that in the last quarter of the nineteenth century Japan became a modern industrial power. And, as happened in Europe, so in Japan imperialists were soon demanding colonial expansion to obtain markets, foods, raw materials, and outlets for the country's dense population.

In 1894–1895 the Japanese had waged a war against China and, after their victory, had forced the latter to make important territorial concessions. Although the intervention of imperialistic European powers, especially Germany, Russia, and France, forced Japan to relinquish most of her ill-gotten gains, she did succeed in retaining the important island of Formosa. A decade later it became evident to the Japanese that if they were going to advance their own interests on the Asiatic mainland they must check the apparently irresistible eastward march of Russia. The result was the Russo-Japanese War of 1904–1905 in which, to the amazement of the world, the vast Russian Empire was decisively defeated by the little island kingdom. Japan compelled Russia to cede to her the southern half of the island of Sakhalin, to recognize Japan's ascendancy in Korea, and to relinquish in favor of Japan Port Arthur and the various privileges in South Manchuria which Russia had wrested from the Chinese. Korea, with its name changed to Chosen, was shortly afterwards annexed to Japan, and the latter in South Manchuria began her active penetration of Chinese territory.

Meanwhile, an intense resentment against Westerners had developed among the Chinese, resulting, toward the close of the nineteenth century, in popular attacks on missionaries and other foreigners who were accused of undermining the ancient traditions of China. In 1900 the local riots grew into an anti-European rebellion, led particularly by members of the secret society of Boxers, who called upon all patriotic Chinese to rise in defense of their country. European legation quarters in Peking were soon crowded with frightened foreigners besieged by the fanatical Chinese, and troops were immediately rushed to their rescue by Great Britain, Germany, Russia, Japan, and the United States. The speed with which the Boxer rebellion was suppressed deeply impressed upon many of the Chinese the futility of attempting to cope with Western powers without first borrowing from them the political, economic, and military methods which gave them their superiority. Chinese students, returning from study in Western lands, began to agitate for the modernization of China.

In 1905 the Dowager Empress gave up her opposition to the Westernization of China, and began the reorganization of the Chinese army in accordance with European practices. The building of railways under Chinese control was encouraged. The ancient classical system of education was abolished, and Western science and modern languages were substituted. In 1907, yielding to pressure from the progressive group, the Dowager Empress promised a constitution and announced that representative government would be gradually introduced. Unfortunately, she died in 1908, leaving the throne to a two-year-old boy, Henry Pu-yi. The regent who was appointed was a weakling, incapable of handling the National Assembly which was convened in 1910. The government's attempt to suppress certain radicals in the South, where secret societies had been organized to work for the establishment of a democratic republic, led to the outbreak of revolution in the Yangtse valley. In 1912 the struggle resulted in the deposition of the boy-emperor and the proclamation of a republic. Sun Yat-sen, who for years had worked to bring about the republic, was elected provisional president.

In the interest of Chinese harmony and unity, however, Sun resigned in favor of Yuan Shih-k'ai, the last premier under the empire. The Chinese liberals, organized as the Nationalist (*Kuomintang*) Party, were from the beginning suspicious of the new president and soon came into open conflict with him. While the Nationalists sought to establish in China a democratic regime, based upon a broad franchise, a strong parliament, and a relatively weak executive, Yuan aimed to set up a powerful executive and a weak parliament. In fact he would have preferred no parliament at all. Friction developed between the two groups, and after an attempt had been made to overthrow Yuan, the latter ordered the unseating of the Nationalist members of parliament (1913), and took steps looking toward the reestablishment of a monarchy. In 1916, before he had succeeded in doing this, he died, and after his death a succession of presidents held office in Peking. Although the Nationalists, denouncing the Peking government as illegal, in 1917 proclaimed a new provisional government in Canton, and asserted that the latter was the only constitutional government in China, foreign powers continued to recognize and deal with the authorities in Peking. In the meantime the real power in China fell more and more into the hands of various military chiefs (*tuchuns*) who devoted themselves primarily to the advancement of personal rather than national interests.

Foreign powers had also taken advantage of the confusion in China to improve their positions. Russia compelled the new Chinese government to recognize most of Mongolia, referred to as Outer Mongolia, as an autonomous province under conditions which made it practically a Russian protectorate. When Tibet revolted against the Chinese Republic, Great Britain forbade the Chinese to suppress the revolt, and China accordingly lost actual authority in that great province, which tended more and more to become a British sphere of influence. By 1914, as a result of foreign encroachments both before and after the revolution, China's tributary kingdoms of Burma, Annam, Tonkin, and Korea and the great island of Formosa had been wrested from her. Four important ports had been leased to foreign powers as naval and commercial bases. The three provinces of China south of the Yangtse River had been converted into a French sphere of interest. Shantung and the Hwang Ho valley had become a German sphere; the Yangtse valley and the province of Shansi, a British sphere; North Manchuria and Outer Mongolia, a Russian sphere; and South Manchuria, a Japanese sphere.

Moreover, foreigners residing in China had the privilege of extraterritoriality, that is, were exempt from Chinese laws and were subject only to the jurisdiction of their own government. China's national tariff was regulated and administered by the Western powers rather than by the Chinese themselves. In many important Chinese cities extensive districts had been acquired by foreigners, and had been converted into foreign concessions. The latter constituted municipalities which were free from Chinese control and in which the government was in the hands of foreigners. Troops of various Western powers were stationed in China, and the country's resources were being largely exploited by foreign capital.

Japan, China, and the First World War

In August, 1914, as has already been pointed out,[1] Japan demanded that Germany surrender her leased territory of Kiaochow "with a view to the eventual restoration of the same to China," and, when Germany refused to comply with this demand, Japan declared war upon her. In November the German base was surrendered to the Japanese. Not content with the acquisition of this former German stronghold on Chinese soil, the imperialistic Japanese in January, 1915, presented to President Yuan a list of twenty-one demands designed to transform China into a Japanese pro-

[1] See page 35.

tectorate. Although the Chinese president was warned to keep the negotiations strictly secret, news of the demands ultimately became known, and foreign powers with interests in China protested that they would not recognize any Sino-Japanese agreement which violated their own treaty rights.

Menaced by a Japanese threat of war and, well aware that the European powers were too preoccupied with their own affairs to intervene effectively in her behalf, China on May 25, 1915, finally signed two treaties which in a modified form embodied most of the points of Japan's original demands. The latter obtained special concessions in South Manchuria and Inner Mongolia. Included among these were the right to develop coal and iron projects, ninety-nine-year leases of the South Manchuria and the Kirin-Changchun railways, and options on all loans and on the construction of all railways in these two regions. The Chinese Nationalists denounced the treaties and declared that they would never recognize their validity; the agreements, in fact, were never ratified by the Chinese parliament. Japan, nevertheless, claimed that her rights were valid because the treaties contained clauses providing that they should become effective on the date that they were signed.

In 1917 Japan further strengthened her position in China when she persuaded Great Britain, France, and Russia to agree to support at the peace conference Japan's claims to Shantung. Even the United States, after entering the war, became a party to an interchange of notes with Japan which resulted in the so-called Lansing-Ishii agreement. The two countries agreed that the Open Door policy should continue to be respected in China, but the United States was persuaded to recognize, in addition, that Japan had "special interests in China, particularly in that part to which her possessions are contiguous." Japan, it appeared, was trying to create a Monroe Doctrine of her own for the Far East.[2]

In the early years of the war China had three times contemplated entering the conflict on the side of the Allies, but on each occasion the Japanese government—reluctant to have China build up an efficient army or participate in the eventual peace conference—had managed to prevent the step. After Japan's position in China had been strengthened by various agreements in 1917, however, she began to urge the latter to enter the struggle, and in this she was seconded by the United States. Eventually, in 1917, the authorities at both Peking and Canton declared war on Germany and Austria-Hungary. The attempts of the powers to obtain China's entry into the conflict gave Chinese leaders a more exalted opinion of their country's position, and aroused the hope of an improvement in its international status.

At the peace conference, consequently, China presented demands which

[2] On the request of the United States the Lansing-Ishii agreement was canceled in 1923.

THE FAR EAST, 1920–1931

included tariff autonomy, the abolition of extraterritoriality, the cancellation of foreign spheres of influence, the withdrawal of foreign troops, and the surrender of leased territories. The statesmen at Paris, however, held that they had no power to deal with these questions. On the other hand, the peace conference, shackled by secret treaty agreements, awarded the former German rights in Shantung to Japan. In China a violent popular movement against foreigners resulted, and numerous student demonstrations were organized in protest. A widespread and vigorous boycott of Japanese goods was instituted, and Japanese trade in China suffered severely. China scorned the direct negotiations with Japan concerning Shantung which the peace conference recommended, and refused to sign the treaty of Versailles.

Nevertheless, some nationalist gains came to China as a result of the war. She obtained membership in the League of Nations by signing the treaty of St. Germain, and by a separate treaty with Germany she secured the cancellation of the latter's extraterritorial rights. Furthermore, China saw to it that treaties with the new states of Europe made no extraterritorial concessions.

The Washington Conference

The next real gains for China in her struggle for the recognition of her integrity and independence and for the abolition of all special privileges of foreigners in her territory came at the Washington conference on the limitation of armaments. In 1921 the United States government, besides wishing to check a possible naval race with Great Britain, desired to secure the satisfactory settlement of certain questions in the Pacific and the Far East. It therefore invited Japan, China, Great Britain, France, Italy, the Netherlands, Belgium, and Portugal to a conference at Washington. The conference sat from November 12, 1921, to February 6, 1922, and as a result of its deliberations a number of treaties were concluded. The two which had to do with naval disarmament have already been discussed.[3] The others dealt with questions which concerned the Pacific and the Far East.

Although China failed to obtain all that she demanded in the way of national rights, she made a number of gains. The nine powers agreed to respect her territorial integrity and independence and again proclaimed the policy of the "open door." They also agreed to respect China's rights as a neutral in time of war and promised not to support any agreements between their respective nationals which were "designed to create spheres of influence or to provide for the enjoyment of mutually exclusive opportunities in designated parts of Chinese territories." China, for her part, promised not to exercise or permit unfair discrimina-

[3] See pages 155–156.

tion of any kind on her railways. A second nine-power treaty permitted China to make an increase in her tariff rates and gave her greater control of the expenditure of the proceeds. Provision was also made for the appointment of two commissions to study the problems of Chinese tariff autonomy and extraterritoriality. A separate agreement between China and Japan, signed outside the conference, provided that Japan should return Shantung and all former German property rights in that province, and that China should reimburse Japan for the amounts which the latter had spent for railway and other improvements since 1914. In December, 1923, Shantung was restored to Chinese control.

The commission on customs, decided upon at Washington, eventually met in Peking in October, 1925. It passed a resolution agreeing that Chinese tariff autonomy ought to be restored, but, in view of the chaotic conditions within China, it adjourned without taking positive action. The commission on extraterritoriality met in Peking early in 1926. Although China during the four years after the Washington conference had been laboriously attempting to introduce judicial reform, the commission reported that the republic was not yet in a condition to administer justice in accord with Western ideas. It therefore recommended the postponement of the abolition of extraterritoriality until a later date. The Peking government, nevertheless, began denouncing all treaties granting extraterritoriality as they expired.

Nationalist Efforts to Unite and Emancipate China

In the years after 1921 it appeared for a time that the Nationalists, who had established a constitutional government at Canton, might be the salvation of China. Their aim was not only to unite the whole country under one administration, but to emancipate it from all foreign restrictions as well. For assistance against both Western imperialism and the opposing Chinese forces in the north they turned to the Soviet government, which in those days was eager to assist in the fight against Western capitalism. Early in 1924 a Nationalist congress offered party membership to all Chinese Communists who were willing to accept the Kuomintang program.

By 1926, however, a serious schism had developed among the Nationalists, for the Right wing of the party was opposed to communism and desired to break with the Soviet government. Chiang Kai-shek, a successful general who became leader of the Nationalists after the death of Sun Yat-sen in March, 1925, threw his lot in with the Right wing of the party, repudiated communism, and began to persecute the Communist members of the Nationalist Party. Nevertheless, despite division within their ranks, the Nationalists successfully carried on their northward advance against the opposing military chiefs. In September, 1926, they captured Hankow and early in the following year Shanghai and Nanking. In April, 1928, Chiang moved his Nationalist government to the latter city, and, after Nationalist troops captured Peking in June of that year, the northern government was abolished, and Nanking was made the new national capital of China. The name of Peking (Northern Capital) was thereupon changed to Peiping (Northern Peace). In August the Nanking government was recognized *de jure* by the League of Nations, which accepted its representative at the meeting of the League Council in that month.

In October, 1928, the central executive committee of the Nationalist Party issued an organic law for the national government of China. This document provided that the supreme administrative body in China should be a Council of State; and on October 10 the central executive committee, under whose supervision the organic law was to be executed, chose Chiang to be chairman of this council. Chiang thus came to hold in China a position analogous to that of president. By the close of the year 1928 the Nanking government had secured recognition from Japan and most of the Western states.

By this time the Nationalist government had begun its campaign to emancipate China from her international servitudes and had announced that it would abrogate all the "unequal treaties" as they expired. In 1928 the United States concluded a treaty restoring to China complete national tariff autonomy. Other Western powers took the same step, and the year closed with practically all countries recognizing Chinese tariff autonomy. Early in 1929 a new national tariff was put into effect by China, raising the basic rate from the former 5 per cent to 12½ per cent. A new criminal code and a new code of criminal procedure in accordance with Western ideas were introduced in September, 1928, and in October the Chinese government sent identical notes to all powers which still held extraterritorial privileges, asking them to take steps to abolish such privileges as soon as possible. Germany and Russia had already surrendered their extraterritorial rights, and late in 1928 Belgium, Italy, Denmark, and Portugal did the same. Again in April, 1929, the Chinese foreign minister, in a note to the foreign powers, requested action toward the relinquishment of the rights then held under treaties, so that steps might "be taken to enable China, now unified and with a strong central government, to rightfully assume jurisdiction over all nationals within her domain."

Unfortunately for China, she was neither so unified nor possessed of so strong a central government as the Nationalist foreign minister asserted. Although Chiang earnestly sought to create a united and powerful Chinese state, his handicaps were great. South of the Yangtse, in Kiangsi, Hunan, and North Fukien provinces, Chinese Communists, taking advantage of the hardships resulting from floods and famines, won great numbers into their ranks and endeavored to establish a soviet regime. In other parts of China rival military leaders still sought to benefit from the central government's weakness by securing control of one or more valuable provinces for their own advantage. Worst of all, perhaps, was the fact that the Nationalist Party itself definitely split in the spring of 1931. Because of dissatisfaction with what they termed Chiang Kai-shek's "dictatorship," Kwantung and Kwangsi provinces joined in a rebellion against the Nanking government and set up a separate regime at Canton. Once more, it appeared, China was headed toward chaos.

Japanese Penetration of Manchuria

Meanwhile, the Japanese were availing themselves of every opportunity to strengthen their hold upon Manchuria. In 1931 what was described on maps as Manchuria consisted of the three eastern provinces of China—Liaoning, Kirin, and Heilungkiang—with a total area about equivalent to that of France and Germany combined, and with a population of approximately 30,000,000. The region was not closely integrated with the Chinese Republic but enjoyed a great degree of autonomy. The control of the district rested in the military power of the local war lord and not in the central government of China. The war lord and governor of Manchuria, Chang Tso-lin, had repeatedly declined to take orders from those who seized authority in Peiping, and had actually declared Manchuria's independence of China at various times. Chang apparently looked upon Manchuria as possessing extensive autonomy under his personal rule, though his son and successor, Chang Hsiao-liang, after 1928 recognized the sovereignty of the Chinese national government.

Manchuria is rich in mineral resources—such as iron, coal, gold, silver, copper, lead, and asbestos—and numerous agricultural products are raised in abundance. It had therefore long been looked upon as a rich prize by the imperialistic powers of the world. Japan, in demanding the Liaotung peninsula at the close of the Sino-Japanese War of 1894-1895, had sought to wrest from the Chinese this southern gateway to Manchuria, but had been thwarted by the intervention of Germany, Russia, and France. Russia, in turn, had then persuaded China to grant her the right to build the Chinese Eastern Railway through Manchuria—thus making possible a shorter route from Chita on the trans-Siberian railway to the Russian port of Vladivostok on the Sea of Japan—and had secured from the Chinese government a lease of the Kwantung peninsula at the southern tip of Liaotung, with the right to build a naval base at Port Arthur.

Russia's attempt to exploit South Manchuria and to penetrate into Korea had led, as already explained, to the Russo-Japanese War. In the treaty of Portsmouth, at the close of the war, Japan secured Russia's lease of Kwantung, including the naval base at Port Arthur and Dairen, the chief port of entry for Manchuria, and thus opened the way for her own active penetration of Manchuria. In 1907 Japan had largely removed foreign opposition to her exploitation of South Manchuria when she and Russia divided Manchuria into two spheres of influence—Russia to dominate in the north, Japan in the south. In 1915 she had further strengthened her hold upon South Manchuria by her demands upon China in that year. Steadily the Japanese increased their economic interests in the region until by 1931 their investments in Manchuria amounted to approximately a billion dollars. The foreign banking business of the district was practically a monopoly of the Japanese, who also controlled the South Manchuria Railway, a seven-hundred-mile line connecting Dairen with the Chinese Eastern Railway at Changchun. Much of the foreign trade of Manchuria was diverted from the Russian port of Vladivostok to the Japanese-controlled port of Dairen.

By 1931, therefore, Japan had acquired or claimed in Manchuria rights the effect of which was to restrict the exercise of Chinese sovereignty in a manner and to a degree quite exceptional. She governed the leased territory of Kwantung, exercising therein what amounted to practically full sovereignty. Through the medium of the South Manchuria Railway, she administered the railway zones, including several towns and important parts of populous cities such as Mukden and Changchun. In these areas she controlled the police, taxes, education, and public utilities. She maintained armed forces in certain parts of the country—the army of Kwantung in the leased territory, railway guards in the railway zones, and consular police in the various districts.

The Japanese were eager and determined to strengthen their hold on Manchuria in order that they might continue and increase their exploitation of that region. Japan's own natural resources were not over-abundant and her population was relatively dense. Less in area than California, Japan proper had a population of approximately 65,000,000, more than forty per cent of which gained its livelihood directly from the soil. Unfortunately, however, less than one fifth of the country's area was tillable, so that the number of inhabitants in proportion to cultivated area was nearly four times as great as that in England. Even including Korea, the Japanese Empire had an area less in extent than Texas; yet it had to support a population of over 90,000,000, a population which was increasing by about one million annually. Obviously there was in Japan, therefore, a heavy pressure of population upon resources. The introduction of modern industrialism had afforded some relief from this pressure; but machines—if they were to be kept running—required plentiful supplies of raw products and profitable markets. Hence the Japanese were vitally interested in the future development of Manchuria.

Meanwhile, however, in the years after the Chinese revolution of 1911, the social and economic ties uniting Manchuria with the rest of China had grown stronger. Manchuria had been thrown open to the immigration of Chinese from other provinces so that by 1931 it was estimated that the Chinese and assimilated Manchus constituted some 93 per cent of the population. Moreover, with the passing of the years, the Chinese population and Chinese interests came to play a much more important part than formerly in the development and organization of the economic resources of Manchuria. After 1928, as pointed out above, Marshal Chang Hsiao-liang, head of the civil and military administration of the region, formally recognized the authority of the Chinese national government and this step tended to bring Manchuria into a closer union with the Chinese nationalist movement.

It was almost inevitable, therefore, that friction should develop between the imperialistic Japanese and the nationalistic Chinese. The interconnection of respective rights, the uncertainty at times of the legal situation, the increasing opposition between the conception held by the Japanese of their "special position" in Manchuria and the claims of the Chinese nationalists were a source of numerous disturbing incidents and disputes. Japan consistently sought to advance her interests in Manchuria by taking advantage of rights open to question. The Chinese authorities, on the other hand, repeatedly put obstacles in the way of the exercise of rights which unquestionably belonged to Japan.

Although there were a number of minor causes of friction between the Japanese and Chinese—such as Chinese oppression of Japanese subjects (especially Koreans) in Manchuria, Japanese taxation of Chinese nationals living within the area administered by Japan, and Chinese resentment at the presence of Japanese troops in Manchuria—the real reasons for dispute were more important. Japan claimed that the Chinese were placing obstacles in the way of the former's leasing of land and exercising of other treaty rights. Undoubtedly the Chinese, refusing to admit the validity of the agreements of 1915, were seeking to prevent the South Manchuria Railway from steadily increasing the amount of land being brought under its administration by leases. Moreover, the Chinese after 1925 were more than ever determined to develop in Manchuria their own railway system with the port at Hulutao as an outlet. The rapid development of this system and port caused alarm among the officials of the South Manchuria Railway, who became equally determined to prevent the Chinese from "strangling" their railway.

In 1931 various efforts were being made to settle the questions outstanding between Japan and China by the normal method of diplomatic negotiations. Nevertheless, the tension between Chinese and Japanese in Manchuria continued to grow, while a movement of opinion in Japan began to advocate the settlement of all outstanding questions by the resort to force if necessary. That the group advocating a resort to force ultimately gained the ascendancy in Japan is made abundantly clear by events recorded in the next chapter.

Part Four

THE SECOND WORLD WAR

Chapter XIX

THE COLLAPSE

OF COLLECTIVE SECURITY

ALTHOUGH the great mass of people in Europe and the world had emerged from the First World War fervently hoping that the system of collective security which the League of Nations was to establish would forever banish war from the face of the earth, developments during the years 1931–1939 clearly indicated that forces were once more operating which might plunge the world into another bloody conflict. Just as in the decade before 1914, these forces, beginning in 1931, produced international crises with monotonous regularity. But the statesmen of the major world powers, instead of effectively utilizing the machinery of collective security to check the aggressor states, ignored or evaded their responsibility and resorted to the policy of "appeasement." But "appeasement" did not satisfy the aggressors or remove the threat of war, and tension between the powers constantly increased. This chapter discusses the successive crises which were precipitated by aggression in different parts of the world, and reveals how by September, 1939, international relations were finally strained to the breaking point and the nations plunged into the Second World War.

Japan's Seizure of Manchuria

The crisis which lighted the powder train of events leading to the Second World War was occasioned by Japan's seizure of Manchuria in 1931–1932. The former's interest in and penetration of Manchuria were discussed in the preceding chapter, as was also the increasing alarm of the Japanese at the large Chinese immigration into that territory and at the closer integration of the latter with Nationalist China. Japanese alarm as well as imperialistic plans and aspirations was revealed in the so-called Tanaka Memorial,[1] which, though its authenticity was denied by the Japanese government, purported to be a report to the emperor drawn up by General Baron Giichi Tanaka after a conference of high Japanese military and civil officials in Manchuria and Mongolia. Supposedly Baron Tanaka, who

[1] See Carl Crow, *Japan's Dream of World Empire: The Tanaka Memorial* (1942).

447

had become premier as the head of the Japanese militarists, sent this document to the emperor on July 25, 1927.

The memorial pointed out that Japan's national existence would be endangered if obstacles to Japanese development of Manchuria were not removed. But the imperialism of the memorialists was not confined to Manchuria; it envisaged, also, the conquest of China. A grandiose program was outlined:

In the future, if we want to control China, we must first crush the United States just as in the past we had to fight in the Russo-Japanese War. But in order to conquer China we must first conquer Manchuria and Mongolia. In order to conquer the world, we must first conquer China. If we succeed in conquering China the rest of the Asiatic countries and the South Seas countries will fear us and surrender. Then the world will realize that Eastern Asia is ours and will not dare to violate our rights. This is the plan left to us by Emperor Meiji [Mutsuhito], the success of which is essential to our national existence.

Whether or not the Tanaka Memorial was authentic, it appears to have generally reflected the viewpoint of the Japanese militarists. And the latter were in a position to exert great influence upon the course of events, for in Japan the army and navy departments were practically independent of civil authorities and had the right to go directly to the emperor without regard for the cabinet. The army leaders had little sympathy for parliamentary rule and little respect for civil government, and looked upon many of the politicians as scheming individuals who were primarily concerned in advancing the interests of certain business groups. Beginning in 1931 the military succeeded in largely dominating the Japanese civil government, even to the extent of forcing it to defy the world. In fact, they did not hesitate upon occasion to resort to the assassination of high officials in order to advance their own policies.[2] With this situation and state of mind in Japan, with China apparently on the verge of lapsing again into chaos, with the world as a whole in the throes of a disastrous economic depression which was hitting Great Britain and the United States particularly hard, it was small wonder, perhaps, that Japanese militarists should decide that the time was ripe for further advancing Japan's position in Manchuria.

In the late summer and early fall of 1931 the situation in Manchuria reached a crisis. On the night of September 18 a section of the South Manchuria Railway near Mukden was destroyed by explosives, placed there—the Japanese army leaders asserted—by Chinese soldiers from neighboring barracks. The Japanese army had already carefully prepared a plan of

---

[2] In 1932 the Japanese premier was deliberately killed in his home by a group of cadets and army officers as a "patriotic protest" against the government's policies.

action in case of possible hostilities between the Japanese and the Chinese in Manchuria, and this plan was at once put into operation with swiftness and precision and without any prior consultation with the government in Tokyo. The next morning the population of Mukden awoke to find their city in control of Japanese troops.

The Nanking government at once made strong protests at Tokyo, and on September 19 the Chinese representative at Geneva, invoking Article 11 of the Covenant, placed the Manchurian situation before the Council of the League of Nations. The Japanese representative advised against any League action, however, maintaining that the incident was unimportant and could be settled by direct Sino-Japanese negotiations. The Council was loath to embark upon a course of vigorous action against Japan without assurance of the collaboration of the United States, but this was not forthcoming. The British representative, moreover, was also opposed to drastic action. Consequently, on September 22 the League Council merely called upon both China and Japan to withdraw their troops from the zone of conflict and to abstain from acts liable to aggravate the situation, and on the next day the United States sent identical notes of the same tenor to the two governments.

Although the Japanese member of the Council promised that his country's troops would be withdrawn to the railway zone as soon as possible, Japanese military operations continued in Manchuria. When the Council reconvened on October 13, the United States government urged the League not to fail to exert all pressure and authority within its competence toward regulating the action of China and Japan; it stated that, acting independently through its diplomatic representatives, it would endeavor to reinforce what the League did; and it offered to appoint an observer to sit with the League Council if invited to do so. The Council, with only the Japanese representative opposing, thereupon invited the United States to participate in its deliberations.

From the very outset Japan maintained that her military operations in Manchuria had no relation to anything but self-defense, and that she could not allow either their necessity or their appropriateness to be the subject of discussion.[3] When it came to instituting Sino-Japanese negotiations regarding the situation, however, China and Japan were diametrically opposed. China insisted that evacuation must precede any negotiations; Japan main-

---

[3] During the negotiations leading to the pact of Paris the American secretary of state, Frank B. Kellogg, had stated not only that the right of self-defense was inherent in every sovereign state and implicit in every treaty but that "every nation is free at all times and regardless of treaty provisions to defend its territories from attack and invasion, and it alone is competent to decide whether circumstances require recourse to war in self-defense." The United States Senate went even further by declaring that measures of self-defense might also involve military operations outside the territorial boundaries of the state.

tained that negotiation must precede and provide the bases for evacuation. The Council seemed to be more in sympathy with the Chinese viewpoint and on October 24 passed (Japan dissenting) a resolution calling upon Japan to evacuate the occupied territory in Manchuria by November 16, 1931, "on the basis of Chinese guarantees for the safety of Japanese nationals." The American "unofficial observer," Prentiss Gilbert, had been instructed to participate in the Council's deliberations only when the Briand-Kellogg pact was involved, and accordingly did not vote on the resolution. In fact, the United States disapproved of this step as likely to antagonize Japan. Regardless of the resolution, the Japanese continued their military operations in Manchuria.

On November 16 the Council once more convened, but, apparently as a concession to Senate isolationists in the United States, the American government declined to have an observer sit with it. This change in policy appeared to indicate that the United States was faltering in its support of the League. During the ensuing three weeks futile efforts were made to draft a resolution which would reconcile the conflicting demands of the Chinese and Japanese governments. Finally, on December 10, 1931, the Council, acting on a proposal made by Japan, resolved to appoint a commission which should investigate the Sino-Japanese conflict in the Far East. This commission, which was composed of representatives of Great Britain, Italy, France, Germany, and the United States, with the British Earl of Lytton as chairman, soon became known as the Lytton Commission.

On January 7, 1932, the United States secretary of state, Henry L. Stimson, in identic notes to Japan and China, stated that the United States "does not intend to recognize any situation, treaty or agreement which may be brought about by means contrary to the covenants and obligations of the pact of Paris of August 27, 1928," and thus formulated the so-called Stimson doctrine of nonrecognition. The United States had invited the co-operation of the British and French governments in the promulgation of this doctrine, but the invitation had been declined. The British, having extensive investments in the Far East, were reluctant to send challenging notes to Japan unless there was a determination to back up the words by force. There was no indication that the United States was prepared to do this; in fact, it was opposed to the application of even economic sanctions. Accordingly, Great Britain did not join the United States at this time in announcing the doctrine of nonrecognition, and it again became obvious to Japan that no common Anglo-American front existed. And without the whole-hearted support of the United States and Great Britain the League of Nations was practically powerless.

Although Japan, in reply to Stimson's note, disavowed any intention of violating the territorial integrity of China, Japanese military authorities in

Manchuria, apparently with political motives and often without authorization from Tokyo, steadily extended the area of occupation. Following each occupation the civil administration was reorganized, loyal Chinese officials being replaced by friends of Japan. A separatist movement was encouraged by the Japanese military authorities, who capitalized grievances held against the former administration by certain minorities among the inhabitants. With this encouragement from the Japanese, an "administrative committee" in Manchuria in February, 1932, issued a formal declaration of the independence of Manchuria and Inner Mongolia. On March 9, 1932, Henry Pu-yi—who as emperor had been deposed by the Chinese in 1912—was inaugurated as regent of the new state of Manchukuo.[4]

Meanwhile, the Chinese had once more resorted to their powerful economic weapon, the boycott. Since Japan's interest in trade with China was much greater than China's interest in trade with Japan, this weapon could be extremely effective. In the four months from September, 1931, to January, 1932, Japan's exports to China fell to one third of what they had been in the corresponding period of the preceding year. In response to the plea of Japanese residents of Shanghai, the most important foreign-trade center of China, Japan demanded a cessation of the boycott and of other anti-Japanese activities and the dissolution of the Chinese organizations responsible therefor. To support this demand a score or more of Japanese warships were dispatched to Shanghai. Faced by this demonstration, the Chinese accepted the ultimatum and acquiesced in the Japanese demands. Nevertheless, the Japanese admiral decided to occupy certain sections of Shanghai in order "to protect" the Japanese residents there. When marines were landed, late in January, a clash with the local Chinese garrison resulted, and fighting began.

Once more China appealed to the League, this time invoking Articles 10 and 15 of the Covenant, but the Council delayed taking action. The United States, in February, 1932, attempted to effect a concert with Great Britain for invoking the nine-power treaty of 1922, but the British government again declined, knowing that the United States was not prepared to back up the note by sanctions or force. In March, China, in desperation, summoned the League Assembly. In this body many of the smaller states demanded the condemnation of Japan and the imposition of sanctions, but Great Britain objected. The extent of the Assembly's action, therefore, was a demand that Japanese troops be withdrawn from Shanghai, and the formal adoption by the League of Stimson's doctrine of nonrecognition.

---

[4] On March 1, 1934—the second anniversary of the creation of Manchukuo—Henry Pu-yi was enthroned as Emperor of Manchukuo, with the title of Emperor Kang Teh. Regardless of his title, however, real authority in Manchukuo continued to rest in the hands of Japanese military authorities.

Eventually, in May, after weeks of stiff fighting, accompanied by artillery duels and air bombings in the course of which property damage estimated at over half a billion dollars resulted, an armistice was signed providing for the evacuation of the Japanese troops from Shanghai and the abandonment of the boycott.

Many of the Japanese troops withdrawn from Shanghai were sent to reinforce those in Manchukuo, where an attempt was being made to pacify the country and to extend the area of effective occupation. Japanese operations in Manchukuo were greatly facilitated by an agreement made with the government of that new state on September 15, 1932. In a protocol signed on that date Japan recognized Manchukuo as an independent state, and in return secured not only the right to station in Manchukuo "such Japanese forces as may be necessary" for the maintenance of the national security of either country, but Manchukuo's promise "to confirm and respect ... all rights and interests possessed by Japan or her subjects within the territory of Manchukuo by virtue of the Sino-Japanese treaties, agreements, or other arrangements, or through Sino-Japanese contracts, private as well as public." Manchukuo, it appeared, was to be a profitable Japanese protectorate.

Meanwhile, the Lytton Commission, with a group of expert advisers, had spent several months visiting Japan, China, and Manchuria, and had received extensive memoranda prepared by both the Japanese and the Chinese governments. In Manchuria, however, its investigations were gravely embarrassed by the fact that no one was allowed to come near it without a permit from the police. Thus, under the guise of protecting the members of the commission, Japan evidently sought to prevent it from obtaining first-hand information from those opposed to the new regime.

But eventually, on October 2, 1932, the Lytton Report was published at Geneva. A number of conclusions were the result of its investigations: (1) no wish to separate from China had ever been expressed by the population of Manchuria; (2) to cut off Manchuria permanently from China would create a serious irredentist problem; (3) the maintenance and recognition of the existing regime in Manchuria would be in the interests of neither China nor Japan; (4) a Sino-Japanese conference, with the League standing behind to help, but keeping hands off as much as possible, should work out a new status; (5) Sino-Japanese relations as a whole were much more important to Japan than Manchuria alone; (6) the disruption of China—of which a separate Manchuria would be the beginning—would lead to bitter rivalries between many powers; (7) Japan required the good will of China and would find better, less costly security against Chinese nationalism in friendly co-operation and enforcement of treaties; (8) China needed the help of the whole world, especially Japan, and should curb its intolerant nationalism and co-operate with the latter; (9) the considerations producing the Washington treaties of 1922 still held good. In view of these conclusions the commission recommended, among other things, that, although Japan's special interests must be recognized, Manchuria should be autonomous under Chinese sovereignty and should be policed only by gendarmerie.

On December 6, 1932, a Special Assembly of the League of Nations met to consider the Sino-Japanese dispute, and before that body the Chinese and Japanese representatives presented the views of their respective governments. After considerable general discussion, the Assembly referred the dispute to a committee of nineteen with the request that it draw up a plan of settlement. This committee eventually came to the conclusion that it could not formulate any plan which would be acceptable to both China and Japan, and proceeded to draw up a report on the dispute in accordance with Paragraph 4 of Article 15 of the League Covenant.[5] On February 17, 1933, the report was broadcast to the world in a spectacular manner by radio. Four recommendations were made for settling the dispute. These provided in essence that the principles laid down by the Lytton Report should be executed through a committee which should supervise the subsequent Sino-Japanese negotiations. All League members were urged to continue nonrecognition of Manchukuo and to refrain from any action liable to prejudice the situation.

On February 24 the League Assembly met to consider the report of the committee of nineteen. When the rollcall on approving the report was finally taken, forty-two member states, including all the great powers, voted "Yes"; Japan alone voted "No." By this action the Assembly exonerated China of blame for the course of events, denied that Japan's military measures as a whole could be regarded as measures of self-defense, asserted that the sovereignty of Manchuria belonged to China and that the "Government of Manchukuo" was made possible only by the presence of Japanese troops, declared that the presence of Japanese troops outside the zone of the South Manchuria Railway was incompatible with the legal principles which should govern the settlement of the dispute, and recommended the evacuation of all Japanese troops outside the treaty zones. Never before had such a universal vote of censure been passed upon any sovereign state. Yosuke Matsuoka, the Japanese representative, thereupon read a brief statement in which he expressed profound regret at the vote which had just been taken and emphasized that Japan had "reached the limit of endeavors to co-operate with the League regarding the Sino-Japanese dispute." With firm

[5] This article reads: "If the dispute is not thus settled, the Council either unanimously or by a majority vote shall make and publish a report containing a statement of the facts of the dispute and the recommendations which are deemed just and proper in regard thereto."

step he then walked down the center aisle and withdrew from the Assembly, followed by the other members of the Japanese delegation. On March 27, 1933, the Japanese government gave notice of Japan's intention to withdraw from the League.

In that same month Japan's troops added still a fourth province—Jehol in Inner Mongolia—to her puppet state. Early in April they next launched a drive against the Chinese and advanced south of the Great Wall to within a few miles of Peiping and Tientsin. In May the Nanking government ordered the Chinese troops to evacuate Peiping, and shortly thereafter the "Peiping Political Council," composed of men holding moderate or pro-Japanese views, was constituted with administrative authority over an undefined area in North China. Negotiations were opened between this council and the Japanese, and on May 31, 1933, a truce was signed at Tangku, near Tientsin. By the terms of this truce it was agreed that Chinese troops should withdraw south and west of a line running roughly from Tientsin to Peiping and that Japanese troops should withdraw north of the Great Wall. These measures resulted in the creation between Manchukuo and China of a demilitarized zone administered by Chinese friendly to Japan—the possible future nucleus of another state with pro-Japanese sympathies. A few weeks later an agreement regarding the administration of this demilitarized area was signed at Dairen between representatives of China, Manchukuo, and Japan. Apparently the Chinese had been driven to realize the futility of struggling against Japanese military forces and had come to the conclusion that, to prevent the possible spoliation of China proper, they would have to recognize that Manchuria had gone the way of Burma, Annam, Tonkin, Formosa, and Korea.

Doubtless a punitive war, conducted jointly by all of the great powers of the West, might eventually have crushed Japan, compelled her to observe her treaty obligations, and forced her to withdraw from Manchuria. But such a conflict would have been a costly struggle and would have entailed sacrifices far greater than the peoples of the West were willing to make at that time. Possibly, had the great powers been able to suppress their economic rivalries long enough to subject Japan to the rigors of a general worldwide financial and commercial boycott in accordance with Article 16 of the Covenant, they might have compelled her to surrender her ill-gotten gains. But in 1931–1932 the whole world was in the depths of an economic depression of the first magnitude, and the statesmen of none of the great powers wished to embark upon a policy which would aggravate the economic distress within their own countries. Furthermore, even had the statesmen of the great powers within the League been willing to impose sanctions upon Japan, they would probably have been deterred from effective action by the knowledge that the United States was not a member of the League and would not participate in such sanctions. Finally, it is probably true that in the years 1931–1933 no Western people sufficiently resented Japan's conquest of Manchuria to be willing to wage war to prevent it, and no responsible statesman of the great powers went so far as to urge measures which might conceivably have precipitated such a war.

Even Soviet Russia, which might have been expected to take a strong stand against Japanese domination of all of Manchuria, was primarily concerned in 1931–1932 with the success of her domestic economic program. Although she massed troops in eastern Siberia during the early weeks of the Manchurian crisis and in December, 1932, showed her good will toward China by resuming diplomatic relations with her, she pursued during these years a policy which was distinctly pacific and defensive. To Japan she made a number of concessions during the conflict. She granted her the privilege of transporting Japanese troops over the Chinese Eastern Railway; she tolerated Japanese occupation of large areas of northern Manchuria which had formerly been considered a Russian sphere of influence; she acquiesced in the replacement of Chinese by Manchukuo railway officials; she recognized Manchukuo consuls.

In the light of subsequent events it seems clear that the failure to enforce collective security in behalf of China was a fateful blunder and probably started the train of events leading to the Second World War. It is obvious now that the "appeasement" of Japan at the expense of China in 1931–1932 did not deter the former from further plans and acts of aggression. On the other hand, it seems likely that, if the great powers, including the United States, had resorted to an economic and financial boycott, supported if necessary by the might of their combined navies, Japan would have suffered an economic collapse, her military leaders would have been discredited, and her forces would have been withdrawn from Manchuria. Had these developments occurred, a great triumph for collective security would have been scored, and other potential aggressors would have been given reason to pause. But the inaction of the great powers in the face of Japan's aggression weakened the world's faith in collective security, encouraged other would-be aggressors to embark upon their plans, and brought upon the world a further series of international crises.

Germany's Rearmament

The next country to break its treaty obligations and to flout the collective action of the great powers was Nazi Germany, whose dictator, Adolf Hitler, already inclined to be aggressive, was doubtless encouraged in this direction by the pusillanimous attitude of the powers in the face of Japan's seizure of Manchuria. Germany's withdrawal from the Disarmament Conference and her notice of withdrawal from the League of Nations late in 1933 have already been discussed.[6] These steps gave warning that Hitler was determined to abandon Stresemann's earlier policy of apparent collaboration in favor of a policy of recalcitrance and possibly of aggression.

The realization of this change in the spirit of German foreign policy at once had its effect on Europe's international relations. In 1934 various European powers moved to strengthen themselves against the threats of Nazi Germany. Since Hitler had openly announced a program of German expansion to the east, it is not surprising that Soviet Russia was among those states which were active. In June, 1934, Russia and Rumania completed a triangular understanding by which the Soviet Union, Poland, and Rumania mutually guaranteed their existing frontiers and thus ended—temporarily—the years-old friction caused by Russia's refusal to recognize Rumania's title to Bessarabia. Three months later the Soviet Union, apparently in order to be linked with fifty-seven other states in an organization for the defense of the *status quo,* accepted membership in the League of Nations. Russia was now linked with the so-called satiated powers.

France, too, became active. In 1934 she proposed for eastern Europe the adoption of a pact of mutual assistance similar to the Locarno pact of 1925. In this so-called eastern Locarno agreement, the Soviet Union, the Baltic states, Poland, Germany, and Czechoslovakia were to be included. Although Russia agreed to sign such a pact, Germany declined. Poland also refused to be drawn into an eastern Locarno. Her statesmen felt that such a step might arouse the resentment of Germany and that it might even require her to defend Russian territory. Furthermore, in time of crisis, Poland might become the battlefield of eastern Europe. The French plan for blocking German aggression in eastern Europe therefore met with failure.

The French next set out to weaken Germany's position by winning Italy away from any possible alliance with the Reich. In the years after Versailles relations between France and Italy had not been particularly cordial. The former, a beneficiary of the peace settlement, had been the leader of the bloc of powers which were ardent defenders of the *status quo.* On the other hand, Italy, an unsatiated and ambitious power, had thrown her influence on the side of the so-called revisionists who insisted with ever-increasing vehemence upon changes in the peace treaties. Prior to 1933 Italy was inclined to align herself with unsatiated Germany.

Nevertheless, in 1934 France opened negotiations with Italy in an effort to remove the postwar causes of friction between the two states. These negotiations were successfully concluded by Pierre Laval and resulted in the signing of a number of pacts and conventions in January, 1935. France agreed to cede to Italy territory adjoining the latter's Libyan colony on the

[6] See page 159.

south and a strategic triangle of territory on the southern edge of Italy's Eritrea, so that the latter might have direct access to the Strait of Bab-el-Mandeb connecting the Red Sea and the Gulf of Aden. In addition, France also agreed that Italy should have a share in the railway from Jibuti in French Somaliland to Addis Ababa, the capital of Ethiopia. Another convention, dealing with the rights of Italians living in Tunis, was designed to remove Italy's dissatisfaction with the status of her citizens there. The two powers further agreed to consult in case Austrian independence should be seriously threatened. These various agreements went far toward removing the causes of ill feeling and friction between Italy and France, and resulted in Mussolini's moving from the revisionist group into the French camp. Later developments seemed to indicate that as his reward for this shift he obtained France's benevolent tolerance of his plans for the conquest of Ethiopia.

Meanwhile, it was widely suspected that Nazi Germany was secretly rearming despite her treaty obligations. That she did not openly defy the Allies in this matter may have been due to her belief that she should first accumulate a quantity of military supplies and to her fear that if she acted too soon the Allies might not permit the return of the Saar basin to Germany in accordance with the terms of the treaty of Versailles. It will be recalled that by the peace settlement Germany had been required to surrender political control of the Saar to a League commission for fifteen years, at the close of which period a plebiscite was to be held to determine the future status of the district. In 1934 the League Council set January 13, 1935, as the date of the plebiscite.

In the succeeding months an international plebiscite commission was established to supervise preparations for the plebiscite. Action was taken, also, to set up a plebiscite tribunal to decide any disputes regarding the voting. Both Germany and France agreed to abstain from pressure of any kind which might affect the outcome. Nevertheless, friction developed in the Saar, largely because of the aggressive tactics and terroristic activities of the German Front, an organization in sympathy with the Nazis of Germany. Because of the disturbed conditions, the chairman of the Governing Commission of the Saar requested the League Council to provide for a stronger police force. Eventually the Council arranged for a League army of 3300 men—supplied by Great Britain, Italy, the Netherlands, and Sweden —to enter the Saar for the maintenance of law and order during the plebiscite.

Although the atmosphere in the Saar was somewhat tense in the days immediately preceding the plebiscite, the explicit rules laid down by the plebiscite commission and the presence of the League army discouraged serious outbreaks of violence. On January 13 approximately 98 per cent of those registered participated in the plebiscite. Of the 528,005 votes cast, more than 90 per cent were in favor of returning the Saar to Germany. Only 46,513 voted in favor of continuing League rule, and only 2124 advocated annexation to France. Not a single voting district returned a majority against reunion with Germany. The Council of the League of Nations on January 17 awarded the entire Saar basin to Germany, and on March 1, 1935, the formal transfer of the district occurred.

A fortnight later, on March 16, Hitler proclaimed the rearmament of Germany. The Reich, he stated, would at once reintroduce compulsory military service and would increase the peace size of her army to more than 500,000 men. In justification of Germany's unilateral action in thus abrogating the treaty of Versailles, Hitler claimed that the treaty had already been nullified by the failure of the former Allies to carry out its promise of general disarmament. Furthermore, he asserted, Soviet Russia's huge peacetime army and France's proposed restoration of two-year military service required Germany to take measures for her own national defense. Protests against Germany's action were at once filed in Berlin by the British, French, and Italian governments. One month later the Council of the League of Nations formally condemned Germany for her unilateral repudiation of the disarmament clauses of the treaty of Versailles. But no steps were taken by the powers either singly or collectively to compel Germany to observe her treaty obligations.

In fact, the British government by its own action soon showed the world that it acquiesced in Germany's illegal action. An Anglo-German agreement was reached (June 18, 1935) giving Germany the right to a navy 35 per cent as large as that of Great Britain. Germany, which already had three powerful "pocket-battleships" limited to 10,000 tons each in accordance with the treaty of Versailles, would now be allowed to add a total of nearly 200,000 tons in capital ships. The treaty recognized, also, Germany's right to have submarines, contrary to the limitations imposed upon her by the treaty of Versailles. To observers it appeared that Great Britain, while taking steps to safeguard her own preponderance of power on the sea, was willing to permit Germany once more to become a military threat on the Continent.

France and the Soviet Union, meanwhile, had taken steps to meet the increased Nazi menace by signing (May 2, 1935) a five-year pact of mutual assistance. According to the agreement, France and the Soviet Union undertook to give each other mutual aid against unprovoked aggression involving violation of either's territory in case the League Council had failed to reach a unanimous decision in the dispute which led to the attack. The pact stated, however, that its provisions should not be carried out in any way inconsistent with existing treaty obligations, thus recognizing, apparently, that under the Locarno treaties France could not attack Germany without the consent of the League Council. A similar treaty of mutual assistance was signed between the Soviet Union and Czechoslovakia a little later.

Before the Franco-Soviet treaty was ratified, Germany called the attention of the powers signatory of the Locarno treaty of mutual guarantee to the fact that France was about to commit herself to obligations which were not reconcilable with the Rhineland pact. Germany maintained that the Franco-Soviet treaty was directed solely against herself and that, in the last analysis, France reserved the right to decide at her own discretion who the aggressor might be. There seemed to be much justice in Germany's claim that the French agreement to aid Russia if the League Council did not agree on the aggressor was in contravention of the French promise in no case to attack, invade, or resort to war against Germany unless directed by the League. The French denied the German contention, and pointed out that Germany might herself join in this defensive agreement, for the pact had been left open for her inclusion.

In March, 1935, Hitler had given his solemn promise to observe the Locarno agreements which had been voluntarily initiated and signed by Germany ten years earlier. Nevertheless, the natural corollary of Germany's rearmament was that she should seize upon some favorable occasion to remilitarize the Rhineland. Such an occasion presented itself during the Italo-Ethiopian conflict when the Locarno front was broken. Timing his act to fall when the international situation was particularly tense because of contemplated petroleum sanctions against Italy,[7] Hitler on March 7, 1936, announced Germany's repudiation of the treaty of Versailles and the Locarno mutual-guarantee treaty. Simultaneously with his announcement, 20,000 German troops marched into the Rhineland.

So far as the treaty of Versailles was concerned, Hitler asserted that the German people could not, should not, and would not bear the injustices of that dictated treaty. As to the Locarno treaty, he declared that it had been in effect nullified by the Franco-Soviet treaty of mutual assistance. Germany, therefore, no longer considered herself bound by its provisions, and accordingly "restituted full, unmitigated sovereignty of the Reich in the demilitarized zone of the Rhineland." A memorandum to this effect was dispatched to the other signatories of the Locarno treaty—that is, to Belgium, France, Great Britain, and Italy. On March 12 the signatories of the Locarno treaty—minus Germany—met and unanimously agreed that Germany's action was "a clear violation of Articles 42 and 43 of the treaty of

[7] See page 467.

Versailles and the Locarno pact." One week later the Council of the League of Nations also voted that Germany was guilty of infringing the Locarno treaty.

Although demands for economic and financial sanctions against Germany were made by France, Poland, the Little Entente, and Soviet Russia, Great Britain opposed such a step. Under the Covenant sanctions were applicable only against a state which had illegally embarked upon a war. This Germany had not done. Furthermore, since Laval had joined Hoare in opposing effective sanctions against Italy when the latter had deliberately launched an invasion of Ethiopia, France was at this time in no position to make a strong case for sanctions against Germany. Many felt, moreover, that morally, if not legally, Germany had much to support her attempt to regain a status of national equality with the other great powers. Therefore, despite the fact that the Locarno treaty of mutual guarantee specifically stated that the signatory powers would come to the aid of the injured party in case of just such a "flagrant" violation of the demilitarized zone, no steps were taken to force the German troops out of the Rhineland. Once more it was shown that the great powers were unable to agree on collective action to compel a state to observe its treaty obligations. This time the net result was a rearmed and militant Germany.

But Germany was not the only great power to object to permanent inferiority in the matter of national armaments. Japan also was determined to escape from a position of inferiority. The Washington and London naval treaties, which were scheduled to expire at the end of 1936, provided for the holding of another conference in 1935. In preliminary negotiations carried on in preparation for a new conference, Japan proposed that she should have the right to naval equality with Great Britain and the United States. But the United States was unwilling to grant parity to Japan, and in this stand was supported by Great Britain. These two powers argued that the 5:5:3 ratio gave Japan perfect equality for defense, that what should be sought was not equality in the size of navies but equality in security. They claimed that Japan's demand for parity was in reality a demand for effective superiority. This the Japanese denied, asserting that technical advances in the years since the Washington conference had increased the range of fleets and left Japan feeling no longer secure with her proportion of three to the five each for the other two great naval powers. Back of the Japanese proposal many saw, however, the desire to be prepared for a more aggressive policy on the Asiatic mainland as well as the desire to be able to enforce her new "Monroe Doctrine for the Far East." With a deadlock very soon reached on the matter of naval parity, the preliminary negotiations were finally adjourned.

Although there seemed to be little likelihood of success, a new naval conference did convene in London on December 9, 1935, with representatives of the five powers in attendance. The early discussions concerned themselves with Japan's proposal that the new treaty should be based upon the fundamental idea of setting up a common limit of naval armaments which the signatory powers should not be allowed to exceed. This, of course, was merely another way of saying parity among the great powers. On January 8, 1936, the Japanese declined to engage in further discussion until Japan's demand for parity had been granted. One week later, after the other four powers had rejected their demand, the Japanese announced that they could no longer "usefully continue" in attendance, and withdrew from the conference.[8] Japan had already notified the powers that she would not be bound by the Washington naval treaty after December 31, 1936. With Germany and Japan both refusing longer to be limited in their military and naval establishments, the way for a new armaments race among the powers was obviously wide open.

Italy's Conquest of Ethiopia

In the meantime the powers in the League of Nations had been engaged in a half-hearted attempt by collective action to prevent Mussolini from seizing Ethiopia. On December 5, 1934, Italian and Ethiopian border patrols had clashed at Ualual, an oasis in a disputed area between Ethiopia and Italian Somaliland. Ethiopia had immediately filed a protest with Italy and had requested that the affair be arbitrated in accordance with an Italo-Ethiopian treaty of 1928. Italy, however, had refused to arbitrate and had demanded instead a formal apology, an indemnity for Italian soldiers slain, and the arrest and punishment of the Ethiopian officers involved. There were not lacking those who believed that Mussolini was about to seize upon this incident to right another Italian "wrong" and to open the way for further Italian expansion.

Italians had been interested in the region about Ethiopia for more than half a century, and the latter had long been coveted by Italian imperialists. In the eighties of the nineteenth century Italy had secured footholds on the East African coast in Eritrea and in Somaliland. In 1889 she had aided Menelik, a local Ethiopian chieftain, to usurp the imperial throne of Ethiopia, and in return had persuaded him to sign the treaty of Ucciali, which Italy at once interpreted as transforming Ethiopia into an Italian pro-

---

[8] Despite Japan's withdrawal, the other four powers continued the conference and reached agreements on a number of points. Late in February, however, the Italian delegation announced that Italy would not be bound by the treaty. Consequently, the naval treaty which was drafted was in the end signed on March 25, 1936, by only three powers—France, Great Britain, and the United States. The terms of the treaty are of only academic importance.

tectorate. In 1891 Great Britain signed a treaty with Italy recognizing Ethiopia as within Italy's sphere of influence.

Two years later Menelik, becoming suspicious of Italy's intentions, denounced the treaty of Ucciali. France had encouraged him to take this step, and in return a French company was given the right to build a railway from Jibuti through Ethiopia to the Nile. Italy, in turn encouraged by Great Britain, decided to force her protectorate upon Ethiopia, and in 1895 Italian armies began an advance into that country from Eritrea. Menelik long delayed giving battle, but eventually near Adowa (March 1, 1896) he disastrously defeated the Italian forces. Italy made peace with Ethiopia, paid Menelik an indemnity of some $2,000,000, recognized his absolute independence, and withdrew from the province which the Italian forces had occupied. Thereafter Adowa was to patriotic Italians a synonym for humiliating disaster.

Although during the succeeding years various powers recognized the independence of Ethiopia and sent envoys to Addis Ababa, the desire for economic advantages in that country still intrigued imperialists. In 1906, for example, a tripartite treaty was signed by Great Britain, France, and Italy, promising to preserve the political and territorial *status quo* of Ethiopia if possible, but agreeing that, should it be disturbed, the three powers would act in concert to protect their special interests. Other agreements entered into by the three powers provided that the French railway from Jibuti was to extend only to Addis Ababa, that west of the capital the line should be continued by the British, and that if any line should be built connecting Eritrea and Italian Somaliland, it should be an Italian enterprise.

In 1923, with the support of Italy, France, and Great Britain, Ethiopia was admitted to the League of Nations and thus was again recognized as independent. Nevertheless, two years later Great Britain and Italy apparently made another imperialistic bargain in regard to Ethiopia. Great Britain was to have the right to build a dam across Lake Tana, the headwaters of the Blue Nile, and a motor road from the Sudan to the lake; Italy was to be permitted to build a railway through Addis Ababa, connecting Italian Somaliland and Eritrea. When Ethiopia protested against the encroachments on her sovereignty, the two powers disclaimed any such intentions, and the British foreign secretary emphasized that the Anglo-Italian agreements did not reserve any part of Ethiopia to Italian economic influence. In 1928 Italy concluded a treaty with Ethiopia in which each country pledged itself not to take any action detrimental to the independence of the other, and to submit to conciliation and arbitration all disputes arising between them. In the Italo-French treaty of January, 1935, it will be recalled, Italy was given a share in the French railway from Jibuti to Addis Ababa, and it was suspected that Laval had given Mussolini a free hand in Ethiopia.

It is obvious, therefore, that Italy had never entirely given up her hope of territorial or economic expansion at Ethiopia's expense.

Mussolini in his decision to use the Ualual incident as an excuse for a colonial advance into Ethiopia may have been influenced by several factors. There is little doubt that in the preceding years he had attempted to impregnate the Italian people with a militaristic and imperialistic spirit both by his actions and by his speeches. A colonial enterprise might afford an opportunity to give concrete expression to these impulses and at the same time take the minds of the Italian people away from the troubled economic situation in Italy. By "avenging" Adowa he might arouse still greater enthusiasm for the Fascist regime; by conquering a considerable portion of Ethiopia he might acquire for Italians more room for expansion and much-needed raw materials and natural resources. Since the League of Nations had failed to take any effective step to prevent Japan from seizing Manchuria or to interfere with Germany's rearmament, he may have believed that a weaker League—minus both Japan and Germany—would not dare to interfere with his venture. Possibly he felt doubly sure that the powers would not interfere because of their need for his support in Europe against an increasingly powerful Nazi Germany. Whatever the factors influencing his decision, however, it seems fairly clear that Mussolini began definitely planning to embark upon a military campaign against Ethiopia. By midsummer of 1935 more than 240,000 troops and laborers had been sent to Italy's East African colonies.

Efforts were made to settle the dispute by peaceful means, however. On January 3, 1935, Ethiopia formally appealed to the League under Article 11 of the Covenant, but the League Council in its January meeting postponed its consideration of the incident until its next session, hoping that it might in the meantime be settled by direct negotiations between the two governments in accordance with their arbitration treaty. In May the League Council was informed that the two governments had agreed to arbitrate. But when the arbitration commission failed to agree upon the fifth arbitrator, the Council again met, instructed the commission to proceed to the choice of a fifth member, and set September 4 as the date upon which the Council would begin a general examination of Italo-Ethiopian relations. The arbitration commission's unanimous decision, announced on September 3, 1935, was that neither side was to blame for the Ualual clash, since each believed that it was fighting on its own soil. Obviously this report eliminated the incident as a pretext for Italian reprisals.

Meanwhile, on the suggestion of the League Council, Great Britain, France, and Italy had entered into negotiations for the purpose of facilitating a solution of the differences between Italy and Ethiopia. The negotiations were brought to a sudden end, however, when Mussolini rejected the

Anglo-French proposal to entrust to Italy an economic mandate under the League for the financial and administrative organization of Ethiopia. Thereupon the British government decided to leave the dispute to the League and to invoke collective action and the use of sanctions against Italy if the latter attacked Ethiopia in violation of the League Covenant. Although France desired if possible to retain the newly won friendship of Italy even at the cost of permitting her to take part of Ethiopia, she wanted the support of Great Britain even more than that of Italy in case of another German war. Consequently, after the British government definitely determined to support collective action at Geneva, France was practically forced to take the same stand. When the League Council met in September, therefore, sanctions against Italy appeared to be almost inevitable unless Mussolini was willing to withdraw from his Ethiopian venture.

One more effort was made, however, to settle the dispute without war and yet at the same time to meet Italy's economic needs in Ethiopia. After hearing statements by the Italian and Ethiopian delegates, the Council appointed a committee to find a way to a peaceful settlement. This committee on September 18 recommended that far-reaching international assistance be extended to Ethiopia through the League, with foreign advisers nominated by the League Council with the consent of Emperor Haile Selassie. To facilitate the acceptance of the plan by both governments, Great Britain and France announced that (1) they were ready to aid in territorial adjustments between Italy and Ethiopia by themselves consenting to certain sacrifices in the region of the Somali coast in order to give Ethiopia an outlet to the sea, and (2) they would look with favor on the conclusion of economic agreements between Italy and Ethiopia, provided the two powers recognized and safeguarded the existing rights of Great Britain and France. Ethiopia at once accepted the proposals in principle, but Mussolini again rejected the plan on the ground that the concessions to Italy were inadequate.

On October 3, 1935, the Italian forces began their advance into Ethiopia. Adowa and Adigrat were bombed by Italian airplanes, and within three days both were taken without resistance, thus "avenging" the defeat of 1896. The Italian forces continued their advance and on November 8 captured Makale—about sixty miles southeast of Adowa—without resistance. Meanwhile, in the south other Italian forces under General Rodolfo Graziani had captured Gerlogubi, near Ualual, on October 6 and later had occupied Gorahai and Gabredarre. Thereafter the Italian advance slowed down. Time was required apparently to construct roads through the wild and mountainous country. Roads were necessary to make possible the bringing up of powerful heavy artillery and to prepare the way for the future advance of mechanized and motorized forces.

When her troops advanced into Ethiopia, Italy embarked upon a struggle not only against the Ethiopians but against the League of Nations as well. In world history the latter was much more important than the former in so far as the issues at stake were concerned. In the ensuing months was tested whether the nations through collective action but without resort to military measures could successfully protect a weak country against a strong and aggressive power.

On October 7 the League Council decided that "the Italian government has resorted to war [9] in disregard of its covenants under Article 12 of the Covenant of the League of Nations," and thus, for the first time, declared a European great power to be an aggressor. The Council's decision was then referred to the Assembly, which at once concurred in the verdict and appointed a committee to consider what measures should be taken under Article 16 dealing with sanctions. By October 19 five proposals had been drafted. The first provided for immediately placing an arms embargo against Italy and lifting any existing embargo against Ethiopia. The second provided for financial sanctions. The third forbade the importation —directly or indirectly—of all Italian goods. The fourth forbade the exportation to Italy—directly or indirectly—of a list of key war materials, and the fifth provided that League members would try to replace imports from Italy by imports from states which normally had profitable markets in Italy. These proposals were accepted by most of the member states, and the Assembly committee eventually declared that all sanctions against Italy should be in effect by November 18, 1935.

Although, under Article 16, members of the League agreed immediately to sever *all* trade and financial relations with an aggressor state, unfortunately for the success of the League's first attempt to prevent aggression by the imposition of economic sanctions, the latter were not applied with full force. The export to Italy of certain commodities of which she had special need was not forbidden. The Canadian delegate to the League proposed that petroleum, coal, iron, and steel should be embargoed, but Pierre Laval, French foreign minister, and Sir Samuel Hoare, British foreign secretary, had already agreed to limit the application of sanctions even before the time came to apply them. Both were disturbed by Germany's rearmament and hoped to avoid giving Mussolini an occasion for collaborating with Hitler. Publicly, however, it was argued that an embargo on these special commodities could not be effective so long as the United States and Germany did not co-operate with the League. Accordingly, although the Canadian delegate's proposal was adopted "in principle," the embargo was not to come into force "until conditions for rendering it effective appear to be realized."

[9] As in the case of Japan in Manchuria, Italy did not actually declare war upon Ethiopia.

But, although President Roosevelt of the United States in October had placed an embargo on arms shipments to both Italy and Ethiopia, it was vigorously asserted in the United States that the neutrality resolution passed by Congress in 1935 gave him no authority to embargo petroleum, iron, or steel. Despite the cutting off of trade in war munitions, American exports to Italy for the first three months of 1936 were practically the same in dollar value as in the corresponding period of the preceding year. And in Europe it was argued that to forbid British and Dutch oil companies to ship oil to Italy would merely result in increased sales of oil to Italy by American companies. Furthermore, Mussolini had announced that the extension of sanctions to include petroleum would be regarded as an unfriendly act, that is, an act involving war; and the statesmen of England and France were determined to avoid war. Consequently, those supplies which Italy most needed for the successful prosecution of her war were not cut off.

Nevertheless, in November, 1935, a League subcommittee decided that an oil embargo should be applied as soon as arrangements could be made, though Laval managed to postpone final action at that time. He still hoped that some way might be found to satisfy Mussolini; and Sir Samuel Hoare, who apparently feared that a general European war might develop out of a more vigorous application of sanctions, co-operated with him in seeking a solution. The result of their joint efforts was the notorious "Hoare-Laval proposals" which were made in December. These envisaged the cession to Italy of areas in Ethiopia in the vicinity of Eritrea and Somaliland and the establishment of an extensive zone of expansion and colonization in southern Ethiopia in which Italy should have a monopoly of economic rights.

On the surface it at once appeared that Italy for her aggressive actions against Ethiopia was to be rewarded by being given territory and rights far beyond those which she had as yet been able to conquer by force of arms. Public condemnation of the plan was widespread and vigorous even in Great Britain and France. In the former Sir Samuel Hoare was forced to resign as foreign secretary and was succeeded by Anthony Eden, who was known for his loyal support of League measures and for his advocacy of the policy of sanctions. In France Laval hastened to explain that the Anglo-French proposals had been made only because it was believed that they were the sole means of preventing the spread of the Italo-Ethiopian conflict to Europe. On the eve of his departure for the League meeting the French premier managed to win a vote of confidence, but his position was so undermined that he was obliged to resign the premiership a few weeks later. At Geneva the League of Nations politely shelved the Hoare-Laval proposals in a resolution which provided that in the future the Council should have charge of peace-making efforts.

According to Sir Samuel Hoare, the British government had joined in the proposals because the League appeared to be about to put an embargo on petroleum, which Mussolini had declared he would consider an act involving war, with the possible result that Italy might attack the British fleet in the Mediterranean. There was, he said, no certainty that the other League powers would fight along with the British. By January, 1936, however, armed support had been promised Great Britain by France, Yugoslavia, Greece, and Turkey in case of an attack by Italy, and Great Britain had promised the same to the others in return. Yugoslavia's promise to Great Britain was made "in full agreement" with Czechoslovakia and Rumania; apparently the Little Entente was willing to line up with the British. In January, too, the French Atlantic fleet went to Casablanca in Morocco not far from Gibraltar, and the Mediterranean fleet left Toulon for Corsica near Italy.

Late in January, therefore, Anthony Eden, the new British foreign secretary, urged the adoption of oil sanctions. But again there was delay because of events in England and France. Eventually the new French foreign minister, Pierre Flandin, persuaded the League committee on sanctions to make one more attempt at conciliation before resort to the embargo. Consequently, action on the oil sanction was deferred for forty-eight hours in order that a League committee might make a fresh appeal to Italy and Ethiopia to end the war on terms "within the League Covenant's framework." This appeal was sent on March 3, 1936, and stated that the committee would meet one week later to consider the replies. Before that date, however, Hitler's announcement (March 7) of the remilitarization of the Rhineland introduced a new element into an already complicated situation and definitely ended the possibility of France's supporting an oil embargo.

In Ethiopia, by this time, the Italian forces were again advancing after nearly three months of inaction. In the middle of January Graziani's troops suddenly launched an attack northwest from Dolo on the border of Italian Somaliland. With mechanized and motorized forces and with little resistance they pushed rapidly forward until they reached Noghelli, some 250 miles distant. From here they were in a position to strike at the chief caravan routes between Addis Ababa and Kenya. Later in the same month the Italian armies near Makale resumed operations. Within a few weeks they had routed the last well-organized Ethiopian army in the north. Developments seemed to indicate that the period of seeming inaction had been advantageously used by the Italians to create disaffection among the enemy chieftains through the judicious bestowal of large cash bribes.

In April, 1936, the primitive Ethiopian resistance completely collapsed in the face of Italian heavy artillery, tanks, airplanes, bombs, and poison gas. Haile Selassie, his armies demoralized and his retreat to the west cut off by disaffected tribal chiefs, on May 2 fled to French Somaliland, where he boarded a British warship. Meanwhile, 30,000 Italian troops in what was perhaps the greatest motorized column yet organized rolled slowly and steadily on by two main routes toward Addis Ababa. On May 5, with fifty airplanes roaring overhead, they entered the Ethiopian capital and hoisted the Italian flag.

THE ITALIAN CONQUEST OF ETHIOPIA

In Rome, on the same day, Mussolini, in addressing a great victory celebration, announced "Ethiopia is Italian." Four days later the Duce decreed that all of Ethiopia was "placed under full and complete sovereignty of the Kingdom of Italy," and that the "title of Emperor of Ethiopia is assumed for himself and for his successors by the King of Italy." By a further decree on June 1 Ethiopia, Eritrea, and Italian Somaliland were organized into a single unit to be known as Italian East Africa. Marshal Badoglio, commander of the army which had captured the Ethiopian capital, was made the first viceroy.

Italy's annexation of Ethiopia presented a new problem—should the League recognize Italy's conquest as a *fait accompli* which it had failed to prevent, and now remove sanctions, or should it maintain that Italy had gone to war in disregard of her League obligations and continue economic sanctions against her, regardless of her victory? The British government appeared to favor the "common-sense" policy of abandoning sanctions. On the other hand, the Little Entente, the Balkan Entente, and the so-called neutrals all pronounced in favor of continuing sanctions. When the Council convened on May 11, it decided that further time was necessary "to permit its members to consider the situation created by the serious new steps taken by the Italian government," and voted to resume its discussion of the Italo-Ethiopian conflict on June 15. In the meantime sanctions would continue. It appeared to be the general opinion, however, that, if on June 15 the Council failed to abandon its sanctionist policy, Italy would quit the League.

On June 2 Argentina formally requested the League to convoke the Assembly to examine the situation brought about by the annexation of Ethiopia, and four weeks later a special meeting of the Assembly opened in Geneva. On July 4 the Assembly adopted a resolution in which, while "remaining firmly attached to the principles of the Covenant . . . excluding the settlement of territorial questions by force," it recommended that its committee on sanctions should make the necessary proposals to bring the sanctions to an end. Two days later this committee fixed July 15, 1936, as the date on which economic and financial sanctions against Italy should be suspended. Italy, it appeared, had won, and another crushing blow had been dealt to the belief in the efficacy of collective action to stop aggression.

The Rome-Berlin-Tokyo Axis

It was probably natural and perhaps even more or less inevitable that the three unsatiated great powers which had been disturbing the world by their aggressive acts in the years 1931–1936 should draw together for mutual support, especially in view of the fact that at the opening of the year 1936 each stood practically isolated as the result of its policies. Japan, because of her seizure of Manchuria, had been unanimously condemned by the League of Nations, from which she in turn had cut herself off by resigning in 1933. Italy, because of her invasion of Ethiopia, had been not only condemned but subjected to sanctions by the League, and these acts, in which Great Britain and France participated, had driven a wedge between Italy and them.

By 1936 Germany, too, had alienated the great powers of Europe. The Nazi attempt to absorb Austria by overturning Dollfuss's government in 1934 had led Italy to welcome a *rapprochement* with France in January, 1935. Hitler's remilitarization of Germany in 1935 had resulted in a Franco-Soviet defensive alliance. And Germany's remilitarization of the Rhineland in 1936 had had the effect of driving Great Britain into the arms of France. The former at once agreed to assist Belgium and France in case of a possible attack by Germany. In April, 1936, the general staffs of the three countries were instructed to consult regarding the best means to make their joint operations effective. Italy, also, had moved to strengthen her position against possible Nazi aggression in central Europe. A conference between Mussolini and Chancellor Schuschnigg of Austria and Premier Gömbös of Hungary led to the decision to form a permanent council composed of the foreign ministers of the three countries to consult periodically on problems of mutual concern. Their immediate and fundamental aim was the maintenance of the *status quo* in central Europe by safeguarding the independence of Austria.

Other states of Europe took similar steps. In June, 1936, the powers of the Little Entente renewed their decision to oppose the union of Austria and Germany, and arranged to have their military staffs meet to discuss co-ordinated military action in central Europe. To make it easier for Soviet Russia to co-operate in blocking Germany if the latter should forcibly attempt to carry through her *Drang nach Osten,* Rumania in the following month agreed to construct—with the aid of a loan from Czechoslovakia—a military railway to facilitate the transport of Russian troops across Rumania to Czechoslovakia. In 1936, too, an exchange of visits by the Polish and French chiefs-of-staff bore witness to the fact that the Franco-Polish alliance was far from dead, even though Poland and Germany had in January, 1934, signed a ten-year nonaggression pact.

But in 1936 Germany took steps to emerge from her state of isolation. On July 11, 1936, she recognized the full sovereignty of Austria and agreed that the latter's political structure was an internal affair with which she would neither directly nor indirectly interfere. During that summer, moreover, Germany joined Italy in sending aid to General Franco in Spain, and their co-operation in a conflict which was described as one between fascist and communist ideologies further facilitated a *rapprochement* between Hitler and Mussolini. Finally, on October 25, 1936, Italy and Germany reached an accord which provided for (1) collaboration of the two states in all matters affecting their "parallel interests," (2) the defense of European civilization against communism, (3) economic co-operation in the Danubian region, and (4) the maintenance of Spain's territorial and colonial integrity. Germany recognized Italy's Ethiopian empire and in return was promised

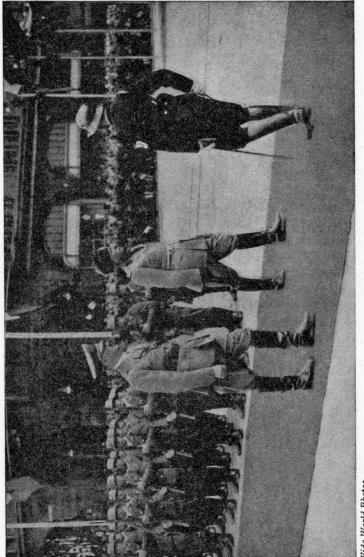

THE ROME-BERLIN AXIS
Hitler and Mussolini in 1937

economic concessions in that part of Africa. In December an Italo-German trade agreement implemented the October accord by extending to Italian colonies the economic privileges which Germany already enjoyed in Italy and by dividing the river and rail traffic of the Danubian states in such a way as to benefit Hamburg and Trieste. Thus was created the so-called Rome-Berlin Axis.

But Hitler was not yet content. Further to strengthen the Reich's international position, especially with reference to Soviet Russia, Germany on November 25, 1936, signed a pact with Japan in which each promised to inform the other concerning the activities of the Comintern (Third International), to consult with the other concerning measures to combat its activity, and to execute these measures in close co-operation. There were many, especially in the Soviet Union, who believed that the anti-Comintern pact was not so innocuous as it appeared, that it perhaps contained secret clauses providing for military co-operation against Russia. However that may be, when, on November 6, 1937, Italy also adhered to the anti-Comintern pact, three of the important totalitarian and unsatiated powers were brought together in the so-called Rome-Berlin-Tokyo Axis.

Evidence of the spirit of co-operation which developed among these authoritarian states was forthcoming on several occasions. Italy's adhesion to the Rome-Berlin Axis was confirmed in 1937 by the Duce's statement that Italy could not give military assistance to protect Austria against a German attempt to consummate the *Anschluss,* by Mussolini's visit to Germany as Hitler's guest in September of that year, and by Italy's announcement of her withdrawal from the League of Nations in the following December. The cordial relations between the two Western powers and Japan were confirmed by Italy's recognition of Manchukuo as an independent state in November, 1937, and by Germany's similar action on May 12, 1938. Further evidence of the operation of the Rome-Berlin-Tokyo Axis seemed indicated in 1938 by Hitler's order that all German military advisers to the Nationalist government in China should leave that country. Thus it is evident that by 1938 the great powers, as in 1914, were once more coming to be divided into two increasingly antagonistic groups.

Japan's Invasion of China

Meanwhile, in the years after 1933, Japan had continued to strengthen her dominant position in the Far East and to announce with ever-increasing clearness and decision her thesis "that Japan, serving as only a cornerstone for the edifice of peace in eastern Asia, bears the entire burden of responsibilities." In April, 1934, the Japanese foreign office emphasized this viewpoint once more when it announced that the activities of the League of

Nations for the rehabilitation of China, American loans to China, and the presence of foreigners as instructors in the Chinese army were considered by the Japanese government as tending to support in China resistance to Japan which threatened the peace of Asia. All of these measures, it was declared, were objectionable to Japan, and, if they were continued and supported by force, then "Japan herself may be compelled to resort to force." It seemed clear that Japan was determined to assert her exclusive right to control China in the interests of Japanese security and Japanese economic penetration.

During 1935 Japan began to encroach upon several of the northern provinces of China. In consequence of demands made upon the Nanking government, the governors of Hopei and Chahar provinces were removed, all branch offices of the Nationalist Party in North China were closed, all anti-Japanese organizations in Chahar were abolished, troops of the Nanking government were withdrawn from Hopei province and from the Chahar-Jehol frontier, and a new mayor, police commissioner, and garrison commander—all acceptable to the Japanese—were installed in Tientsin. On November 25, 1935, eighteen counties in and near the demilitarized zone along the Great Wall declared their independence and set up an autonomous state under the pro-Japanese administrative commissioner of the demilitarized zone. In the following month the Nanking government agreed to the establishment of a semi-independent regime in Hopei and Chahar provinces, which included Peiping, the old Chinese capital, and Tientsin, North China's commercial city. The newly organized government had as its head General Sung Cheh-yuan, a North China military leader, and consisted chiefly of pro-Japanese members. During 1936 this government permitted the smuggling of Japanese goods into North China upon payment of only one eighth of the national tariff dues, and agreed to the principle of joint Sino-Japanese economic development of that region.

Despite measures taken by the Nanking government to guard against the possibility of popular opposition to its policy of capitulation, a strong nationalist and anti-Japanese sentiment developed in 1936 in China, thanks largely to the activities of Chinese students. So strong did this nationalist movement become that even the semi-independent Canton government in South China demanded that the government in Nanking should resist Japanese aggression with armed force. Of China's important military leaders, Chiang Kai-shek alone appeared to remain opposed to the adoption of a strong anti-Japanese program. Possibly he believed that no effective resistance could be offered until China was thoroughly united and militarily prepared. Whatever his motives, however, an emergency law was issued in 1936 by the Nanking government authorizing Chinese troops and police to use force or any other effective means to dissolve meetings and parades, to suppress anti-Japanese propaganda, and to punish those who aided violators of these provisions. In December, 1936, it was revealed that the Nationalist government had accepted further Japanese demands: to suppress anti-Japanese movements, to engage Japanese advisers, and to reduce Chinese tariffs. In that month Nanking ordered twelve of the provincial governments to inaugurate an anti-Communist campaign in accordance with the Japanese desire to check the growing strength of the Communist forces in the northwest provinces of China. General Chiang himself proceeded to Shensi province because he was dissatisfied with General Chang Hsueh-liang's conduct of the campaign against the Communists.

But on December 12 by a sudden *coup d'état* Chang Hsueh-liang captured General Chiang and held him a prisoner at Sian, the capital of Shensi. As conditions for release he demanded a declaration of war against Japan, the Nanking government's promise to recover all lost territories, and the readmission of Chinese Communists to the Nationalist Party. Although much about the coup remained a mystery, after a detention of two weeks Chiang Kai-shek was released, and he returned to Nanking bringing General Chang as a prisoner. In January, 1937, however, the latter received a full pardon for his part in the rebellion, and later in the month an agreement between the rebellious Shensi forces and the Nanking government permitted occupation of northern Shensi by Communist troops. During the succeeding months negotiations were carried on between the Nanking government and the Communist leaders. The latter declared their willingness to modify their social program and to place their armies under Chiang Kai-shek's command, if the Nationalist government would adopt an anti-Japanese policy and introduce a more democratic regime in China.

During the first half of 1937 the Nanking government, with the whole of China united at least temporarily by a wave of nationalism, sought increasingly to assert its influence over North China officials. It also interfered with the Japanese-protected smuggling into North China, and it even ordered the suspension of a new Tientsin-Tokyo air line which had been established without Chinese consent. Undoubtedly the strong anti-Japanese sentiment in China and the apparently growing military strength of the latter were disturbing to Japanese military leaders, who evidently planned to establish a pro-Japanese regime in China's five northern provinces.

As in Manchuria in 1931, the Japanese were able to arrange an "incident" at the appropriate time. On the night of July 7, 1937, a clash occurred a short distance west of Peiping between Japanese troops and units of the Chinese army. After some diplomatic temporizing by both the Chinese and the Japanese, the latter on July 19 demanded (1) the withdrawal of the Chinese army from its position west of Peiping, (2) the punishment of the Chinese responsible for the clash, (3) the suppression of all anti-Japanese activities in North China, and (4) the enforcement of measures against the Communists. Chinese acceptance of these demands would obviously go far toward giving the Japanese that ascendancy which they sought in North China. The Nanking government refused to accept the Japanese demands.

Late in July, after an ultimatum, Japanese troops began an advance in the coveted northern provinces. Within a few days the eastern part of Hopei province, including Tientsin and Peiping, had been effectively occupied, and provisional governments favorable to Japan had been established. In August Japanese troops moved southward in Hopei province and northwestward toward Chahar. In Japan there was every indication that preparations were being made for war on a large scale. The Nanking government called for resistance to Japanese aggression, and Chiang Kai-shek announced that China would surrender no more territory "even though this means fighting inadequately and to the death." By the close of 1937 the Japanese had captured the capitals of Shansi and Shantung provinces and were well on their way to control of the five provinces north of the Yellow River. On December 14 a new pro-Japanese government was set up in Peiping, whose name had already been changed back to Peking (Northern Capital).

But the fighting had not been confined to North China. In August a campaign was also launched against the important commercial city of Shanghai, which, after three months of hard fighting, was captured on November 8, 1937. The Japanese next advanced up the Yangtse, and in December captured Nanking, the political capital of China. In an attempt to prevent the escape of fleeing Chinese soldiers, the Japanese resorted to indiscriminate attacks on all traffic on the Yangtse River above Nanking. During these attacks the United States gunboat *Panay,* although clearly marked to show that it was American, and three vessels of the Standard Oil Company were bombed and sunk by a Japanese airplane on December 12, and four vessels of British registry were shelled. The survivors of the *Panay* were even attacked by machine-gun fire while they were attempting to reach shore.

Sharp protests and strong demands for satisfaction, made by President Roosevelt and by the British government, brought immediate and profuse apologies by Japanese officials, and on December 14 the Japanese foreign office stated its readiness to pay compensation and to give guarantees against the recurrence of such incidents. In a note to the United States the Japanese government, although firmly maintaining its contention that the attack on the *Panay* was an unintentional mistake, cited the orders given to its armed forces to prevent a recurrence of similar attacks. The United States government thereupon accepted the amends. In a note on December 28 the Japanese government gave final satisfaction to the British, also, for the shelling of their ships.

But the relative indifference of Americans generally to the significance of the *Panay* incident may have convinced Japanese militarists that they had little to fear from the West. The Japanese military in China continued to violate the rights of Americans and other foreigners residing in that country. They also continued their conquests in China. By the close of the year 1938 they held the great commercial cities of Tientsin, Peiping, Shanghai, Nanking, Hankow, and Canton, and had installed the "New Government of the Republic of China" in Nanking, the former Nationalist capital. The Nationalist government of Generalissimo Chiang Kai-shek had, perforce, been moved to the interior city of Chungking.

Meanwhile, as in 1931, the Chinese government had appealed to the League of Nations against Japan. When the Assembly convened in September, 1937, China's appeal had been referred to the League's Far Eastern advisory committee, which unanimously condemned Japan as an invader and a treaty-breaker. It recommended that the Assembly should invite those members of the League which were signatories of the Washington nine-power treaty to meet as soon as possible to initiate consultation regarding the agreement to respect China's sovereignty, independence, and territorial integrity. On October 6 the League Assembly adopted the advisory committee's resolution, expressed its moral support of China, and recommended that League members should refrain from taking any action which might weaken China's power of resistance and should consider how they could individually extend aid to her. On the same day the United States government announced that its conclusions were "in general accord with those of the Assembly of the League of Nations."

Upon the League's invitation the representatives of nineteen nations convened at Brussels on November 3, 1937, to consider what might be done under the nine-power treaties to safeguard peace in the Far East. Japan declined to be represented at the meeting, however, and insisted that China was responsible for the existing conflict, that China, not Japan, was "violating the spirit of the pact against war." Japan further maintained that "the most just and equitable solution" could be reached through direct negotiations between herself and China. The delegates thereupon adopted a declaration expressing regret over Japan's refusal to participate in the conference, and characterizing Japan's military action in China as illegal. But China's appeal for the withholding of war materials and credits to Japan went unheeded. Late in November, just before adjourning indefinitely, the conference admitted that for the time being it could do nothing to reestablish peace. No group of states was willing to pay the price in life or wealth which would be necessary to save China from the invading armies of the Japanese.

In September, 1938, China again appealed to the League of Nations for assistance under the terms of Article 17 of the Covenant, which provided for the handling of disputes between a state in the League and one outside. The Council thereupon decided that Japan's invasion of China was a violation of the Briand-Kellogg treaty and of the nine-power treaty of 1922. It further decided that Article 16 regarding sanctions became applicable, but held that the time was not suitable for collective action. The net result of China's appeal was merely the Council's invitation to members of the League individually to support China. Once more collective security had been proved to be a broken reed.

Germany's Annexation of Austria

In the West, by 1938, the situation both in Germany and in Europe was such as to encourage Hitler, too, to embark upon his program of territorial expansion. Early in that year changes had been made in the German army and foreign office which brought them more under the control of the Führer and more into harmony with the aggressive Nazis' idea of an "activist" foreign policy.[10] In Europe Mussolini, who had earlier opposed the Anschluss, was now linked with Hitler in the Rome-Berlin Axis, and had even announced that Italy could not give military assistance to protect Austria against a German attempt to absorb that country. Furthermore, Italy was deeply involved in Ethiopia and in Spain and was therefore in no position to break with her partner in the Axis. France was passing through a period of ministerial instability [11] and seemed also to be in no position to act effectively. In Great Britain a majority of the members of the Chamberlain government were in favor of a program of "appeasement" of Germany and Italy, so much so that Anthony Eden, who opposed "appeasement," was forced to resign as foreign secretary on February 20, 1938. In some quarters it was believed that the Chamberlain government looked with tolerance upon Hitler's desire to seize Austria. Hitler decided that the time had come when he could safely disregard the promises he had made in the Austro-German treaty of 1936, and could successfully consummate the Anschluss which he had apparently sought but failed to achieve in 1934.

The first step in Hitler's program of territorial expansion for Germany came on February 12, 1938, when an interview between the Austrian Chancellor Schuschnigg and Hitler occurred at the latter's Bavarian mountain chalet at Berchtesgaden. As the result of the Führer's threats, Schuschnigg

[10] See page 271.
[11] See page 317.

was forced to agree to admit members of the Austrian Nazi Party into his government. Four days later a new cabinet was organized in Vienna with Arthur Seyss-Inquart, the Austrian Nazi leader, as minister of the interior, and with other Nazis as ministers of justice and of foreign affairs.

While the Austrian Nazis speedily took advantage of their new position and freedom to urge and work for the early consummation of the *Anschluss,* many Austrians hastened to proclaim their loyalty to an independent Austria. Schuschnigg still hoped to maintain the republic's independence and on March 9 suddenly announced that a plebiscite on the question would be held in Austria four days later. Evidently he believed that the interval before election would be too short for the Nazis to mobilize their high-pressure speakers and terroristic methods effectively, and that the subsequent vote would prove to the world that the majority of Austrians had no desire to be absorbed by Germany.

But Hitler and the Austrian Nazis were determined that no plebiscite should be held under such conditions. Nazis riots against the vote at once began to occur. Then, on March 11, Seyss-Inquart presented Schuschnigg with an ultimatum demanding his resignation and the postponement of the plebiscite, threatening that otherwise German troops, already mobilized on the border, would invade Austria. Confronted by this situation, Schuschnigg, "in order to save bloodshed," canceled the plebiscite and resigned. Seyss-Inquart was thereupon appointed head of the new cabinet, which at once invited the German government to send troops into Austria "to preserve order."

On March 12 Hitler returned to Linz, his former home in Austria. On the next day the German government issued a law declaring Austria to be a state of the German Reich. President Miklas resigned, and Chancellor Schuschnigg was placed under arrest. On March 14 Hitler arrived in Vienna, preceded by German mechanized and air forces, and was given an enthusiastic reception. "All Germany is living through this hour of victory—seventy-four millions in one united Reich," he shouted. "No threats, no hardships, no force can make us break our oath to be united forever." Although France and Great Britain lodged formal protests with Berlin, no state raised a hand in defense of Austria's sovereignty. A particularly marked contrast with the swift mobilization of Italian troops on the Brenner Pass in 1934 [12] was Italy's immobility in March, 1938.

After Germany's absorption of Austria the lesser powers of central and southeastern Europe at once sought to put their relations with their neighbors on a friendly basis in order to check the *Drang nach Osten.* On July 31, 1938, the Balkan Entente permitted Bulgaria to rearm and to remilitarize her frontiers with Greece and Turkey in return for Bulgaria's pledge

[12] See page 343.

of nonaggression against the countries of the Balkan Entente. A few weeks later the Little Entente permitted Hungary to rearm in return for a similar pledge. While these lesser states were thus promising to live in good neighborliness together, Great Britain was drawn more and more into alignment with France. On April 28 and 29 the premiers and foreign ministers of the two states conferred in London, and decided to continue the contacts between their general staffs as arranged for in 1936.

The British government made, too, what appeared to be an attempt to "appease" Italy and thus to weaken or destroy the Rome-Berlin Axis. On April 16, 1938, Great Britain and Italy signed agreements regarding the *status quo* of the Mediterranean and Red Seas and the Suez Canal. Great Britain promised to take steps in the League of Nations Council to free states that were members of the League from their obligations not to recognize Italian sovereignty over Ethiopia. Italy in turn agreed to Great Britain's formula for the proportional evacuation of the foreign volunteers from Spain, promised that all Italian volunteers would be removed from Spanish territory at the close of the civil war, and disclaimed any territorial or political aims or desire for a privileged economic position anywhere in Spanish territory. Nevertheless, despite this apparent Anglo-Italian *rapprochement,* Hitler's visit to Italy as Mussolini's guest in May, 1938, indicated that the Rome-Berlin Axis was still very much alive.

The absorption of Austria had greatly strengthened Germany's position in central Europe and at the same time had advanced her *Drang nach Osten*. She was now in direct contact with Italy at the Brenner Pass and also in direct touch with Yugoslavia and Hungary. Furthermore, domination in Austria gave the Third Reich military and economic control of practically all the communications of southeastern Europe. Czechoslovakia was almost isolated. Her trade outlets through Germany were at the mercy of the latter, and her communications by rail and river to the south and southeast could be severed almost at will. More important still, from a military standpoint, Germany by annexing Austria had placed herself in a position to outflank the powerful Czechoslovak defense system along the German frontier. Despite Hitler's pledge of March 11, 1938, that he would respect the integrity of the Czech nation, it is not surprising that the German Nazis next turned their attention to "alleviating the wrongs" suffered by their 3,500,000 kinsmen in Czechoslovakia.

The Dismemberment of Czechoslovakia

It has already been pointed out [13] that the Nazi movement had entered Czechoslovakia, where it was organized politically as the Sudeten German

[13] See pages 349–350.

(*Sudetendeutsch*) Party under the leadership of Konrad Henlein. From 1935 on the latter had denounced the government at Prague for its treatment of minorities and had accused it of denying to the Germans their rightful economic and cultural opportunities. After Hitler's success in Austria the Sudeten German leader called upon all Germans in Czechoslovakia to join his party and succeeded in forcing various Germans to withdraw from the Czechoslovak ministry. Thereafter Henlein became ever more aggressive in his demands.

In May, 1938, the tension both in Czechoslovakia and in Europe reached a high point when elections were held in the republic. Preceding the elections a vigorous campaign against Czechoslovakia was waged in the German press, and it was feared by many that the Nazi government might avail itself of some of the clashes between rival nationals in connection with the elections to go to the aid of the Sudeten Germans. On May 19 there were rumors of German troop movements near the border, and the Czechoslovak general staff countered these by making military dispositions along the German frontier.

Although the French government urged Czechoslovakia to go to the limit of concession to the Sudeten Germans, it left no doubt that France would fulfill her military obligations if Czechoslovakia were attacked. Russia also stated her readiness to go to the aid of the Czechs, should the need arise. The British government kept in constant touch with Paris and sought to bring pressure at both Berlin and Prague in favor of peace. In the end the elections passed off without the feared German intervention. Of significance, however, was the fact that hundreds of thousands of Germans were at once put to work to construct a line of fortifications along the Rhine from Switzerland to the Netherlands. By many it was believed that these gigantic fortifications—called by Germans the West Wall, but by foreigners christened the Siegfried Line—were designed to halt France in the west, should Germany later launch her *Drang nach Osten* against Czechoslovakia.

Meanwhile, the Czechoslovak government had approved a nationalities statute, proposing a substantial increase of local autonomy for communes, districts, and even regions in matters such as education, social work, and communications, with local elected diets in which the minority elements would have their own representatives. The statute did not, however, provide for autonomy for the Sudeten areas as such. On June 7 the Sudeten German Party, in turn, submitted its demands, which were somewhat more detailed than their previously announced Karlsbad program.[14] A wide gap separated the two sets of proposals.

In July the British government, apparently adhering to Chamberlain's

14 See page 350.

policy of "appeasement," asked Premier Hodža whether the Czechoslovak government would accept a British adviser in the dispute with the Sudeten German Party, and was informed that it would. Lord Runciman was then appointed as such an adviser, and both President Beneš and Premier Hodža stated that Czechoslovakia was prepared to go to the full limit of Lord Runciman's advice, provided the sovereignty of the state was protected. On August 3, 1938, Lord Runciman arrived in Prague to assist in the negotiations between the Czechoslovak government and the leaders of the Sudeten German Party.

During August the international tension greatly increased. The German government arranged for fall maneuvers of its armed forces, with the result that fighting men variously estimated at between 1,350,000 and 1,500,000 would be ready for action when the annual congress of the Nazi Party was held in Nuremberg in September. Shortly before the congress opened, Hitler made an ostentatious inspection of the fortifications of the West Wall. France and Great Britain also took steps to strengthen their positions in case of a war. French reserves were moved up to man the powerful Maginot Line, and Great Britain concentrated forty warships—her biggest Home Fleet since the First World War—at the North Sea base of Invergordon for autumn maneuvers at the time when the Nazi congress would be in session.

In this strained atmosphere negotiations were meanwhile being carried on between the Czechoslovak government and the Sudeten German leaders. One by one the proposals made by the government were rejected by Henlein, after conferences with Hitler. It became perfectly obvious that fundamentally the negotiations were between the Führer and the Czechoslovak government. On September 7 the latter offered a fourth plan, which, according to Lord Runciman, granted practically everything in the Karlsbad program of the Sudeten Germans.

The world awaited with considerable concern what Hitler would say in reply to these proposals when, on September 12, 1938, he made his final address to the hundreds of thousands gathered at the Nazi congress. In an impassioned speech the Führer then demanded the "right of self-determination" for the Sudeten Germans of Czechoslovakia, and announced that, if the latter could not defend themselves, "they will receive help from us." The German Nazis, he declared, "will not remain indifferent for long if these tortured and oppressed creatures cannot defend themselves." Immediately after Hitler's address the Sudeten Germans, as though operated by a push-button from Nuremberg, began demonstrating in favor of union with Germany. Riots and clashes with the Czechoslovak gendarmerie ensued, and a number of casualties occurred. Events seemed to indicate that a situation was being created to provide an opportunity for German troops

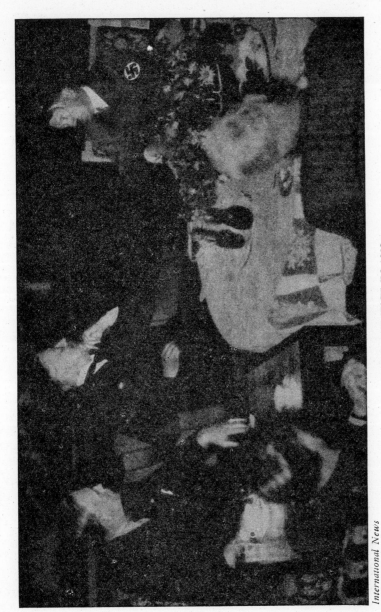

APPEASEMENT IN 1938
Chamberlain and Hitler at Berchtesgaden

to invade Czechoslovakia in order to protect the "tortured and oppressed" Germans living in that republic. Such an invasion would place upon France and Russia the obligation to go to the aid of Czechoslovakia and so might precipitate a general European war.

In this highly critical situation Prime Minister Chamberlain of Great Britain, hoping to prevent war by "appeasing" Hitler, took an unprecedented step; he asked the German Führer for a personal interview. Hitler was willing to hold such a conference, and so on September 15 Chamberlain, with the approval of France, flew to Munich and proceeded to the mountain chalet at Berchtesgaden where the fateful interview between Hitler and Schuschnigg had occurred seven months earlier. Here Chamberlain learned that Hitler had decided that the Sudeten Germans should have the right to unite with the Reich, if they wished, and that he would aid them if necessary even at the risk of a general European war.

Upon the prime minister's return to London the British and French governments decided, in accordance with Lord Runciman's conclusions, that the only way to avoid a general European war was to accept the principle of self-determination. On September 19 Great Britain and France therefore asked Czechoslovakia to agree to the immediate transfer to the Reich of areas inhabited by a population more than 50 per cent German. When Czechoslovakia suggested that the matter be submitted to arbitration, Great Britain and France, in what was practically an ultimatum, declared that she must accept the Anglo-French proposals at once or bear the consequences alone.

This Anglo-French decision to desert Czechoslovakia was the result of several factors. In the first place, there was in both countries a popular desire to escape the horrors of a general European war. Moreover, neither England nor France was then prepared to deal effectively with an attack from the air, and Chamberlain and Daladier apparently envisioned the quick destruction of London and Paris by the much-advertised German Luftwaffe, should a general war be precipitated. In the second place, in both England and France there were influential groups which opposed a war in behalf of Czechoslovakia. In the former, certain elements looked upon Czechoslovakia as an "artificial" creation of the Paris peace conference, and believed that, so long as it existed as then constituted, it would continue to be a constant invitation to dismemberment by neighboring national states. In the latter, certain Rightist groups felt that a war with Germany would open the way for the French Leftists to secure control of France, and they preferred "appeasement" of Hitler at the expense of Czechoslovakia to the possible triumph of the Communists at home. In the third place, there was undoubtedly still held in some quarters in both countries the belief, which had been so assiduously cultivated by Hitler, that

Nazism was a bulwark of strength protecting western Europe from Russian communism, and that therefore it should be upheld even at some sacrifice. Finally, Hitler had announced that once his demands upon Czechoslovakia were satisfied he would have no further territorial ambitions in Europe. Chamberlain and Daladier apparently still thought that some credence could be put in Hitler's pledged word, and consequently reasoned that the shift of the Sudeten Germans from Czechoslovakia to the Reich was not too high a price to pay for a satisfied Germany and a peaceful Europe.

Whatever may have been the reasons for Chamberlain's and Daladier's decisions, Czechoslovakia when faced by their final demand had little alternative but to give in. The Czech leaders had no wish to be blamed for precipitating a second world war. At the same time, they were reluctant to have their country saved by Soviet troops. On September 21 the Czechoslovak government accepted the Anglo-French proposals for the dismemberment of the republic. On the next day Chamberlain returned to Germany and at Godesberg in the Rhineland informed the Führer that Czechoslovakia had agreed to cede the German areas to the Reich. He then explained the plans which the British and French governments had worked out for effecting the transfer and for delimiting the new frontier. These plans Hitler at once rejected on the ground that they were too dilatory and offered too many opportunities for Czechoslovak evasion.

He, in turn, presented other proposals which called for the withdrawal by October 1, 1938, of all Czech armed forces, police, gendarmerie, customs officials, and frontier guards from the Sudeten German area as shown on an accompanying map, the evacuated territory to be handed over to Germany as it stood without any military, economic, or traffic establishments being damaged or removed. In certain areas, to be more definitely defined, plebiscites were to be held before November 25 under the control of an international commission, all persons residing in the areas on October 28, 1918, or who were born in those areas prior to that date, being permitted to vote.

On September 24 the government at Prague informed Chamberlain that Hitler's demands "in their present form" were "absolutely and unconditionally unacceptable," since they would deprive the republic of every safeguard for its national existence by admitting German armies deep into Czechoslovakia before the latter had been able to organize its defenses on a new basis, and because the whole process of moving the population would be reduced to panic and flight on the part of those who would not accept the German Nazi regime. Great Britain and France likewise held the demands to be unacceptable and agreed that no pressure would be exerted on Czechoslovakia to secure their acceptance. It appeared that Hitler might be compelled to carry out his threat to use force.

But Premier Daladier had stated that, if Czechoslovakia were the victim of an unprovoked aggression, France would immediately take the necessary measures to assist her, and on September 26 Great Britain, while declaring that she would guarantee the surrender of the Sudeten area to Germany if the latter did not go to war, announced that she and Russia would certainly stand by France if the latter went to the defense of Czechoslovakia. Meanwhile, Mussolini had declared that, should a general war break out over Czechoslovakia, Italy's place was already chosen at the side of her partner in the Rome-Berlin Axis. On September 27 it became known that Germany had decided to order mobilization against Czechoslovakia if the latter had not accepted the Hitler memorandum by 2 P. M. on the following day. Another general European war seemed imminent.

In these circumstances President Roosevelt of the United States made a direct appeal to Hitler urging an international conference to settle the controversy. At the same time Chamberlain, Daladier, and Roosevelt all appealed to Mussolini to use his influence with Hitler in the cause of peace. Apparently Mussolini, despite his warlike speeches, was at heart not eager to be drawn into a general war at a time when Italy was already involved in Ethiopia and Spain—especially when his partner in the Axis could secure what he desired without resort to arms. On the morning of September 28 Mussolini had a personal telephone conversation with Hitler, as the result of which the Führer agreed to an international conference to settle the Sudeten controversy. Chamberlain, Daladier, and Mussolini were invited to meet with the Führer at Munich on September 29. No representative of Soviet Russia, Czechoslovakia's most powerful ally, was invited. Nor was Czechoslovakia herself to be represented.

The meeting of the four statesmen in the Führerhaus at Munich must have been dramatic; Mussolini and Chamberlain had never seen each other, and Daladier had never met either Mussolini or Hitler. In less than nine hours, however, they had worked out an agreement regarding the Sudetenland which was essentially a surrender to Hitler's Godesberg demands. By the terms of this pact the Czechs were to begin to evacuate the Sudetenland on October 1, and on the same day the Germans were to begin their progressive occupation of four zones which were known to be predominantly German. An international commission representing Germany, Great Britain, France, Italy, and Czechoslovakia should decide by October 7 the remaining territory of preponderantly German character. This fifth zone should then come into German occupation by October 10. Great Britain and France promised to guarantee the new frontiers of Czechoslovakia against unprovoked aggression, and Germany and Italy promised to do the same "when the question of the Polish and Hungarian minorities in Czechoslovakia has been settled."

There was nothing for Czechoslovakia to do but submit to the Munich agreement. Early on the morning of October 1, 1938, German troops marched across the frontier into zone number one. Two days later Adolf

THE PARTITION OF CZECHOSLOVAKIA, 1938–1939

Hitler made a triumphal entry into Eger, which had served as the unofficial capital of the Sudeten Germans. On October 5 the international commission awarded Germany the fifth zone in Czechoslovakia, to be occupied between October 7 and October 10. This zone was by far the largest of those awarded Germany and brought the total area surrendered to approximately that demanded by Hitler at Godesberg.

But the territorial losses to Germany were not the only ones suffered by Czechoslovakia. On the eve of Germany's entrance into the Sudetenland Poland sent an ultimatum to Prague demanding the evacuation of Czechoslovak troops from an area about Teschen, where most of Czechoslovakia's Poles lived. Although inhabited predominantly by Poles, the Teschen area had been seized by Czech troops in January, 1919, primarily because of its economic and strategic value. The treaty of St. Germain had called for a plebiscite to decide the fate of the district, but Czechoslovakia and Poland in 1920 had agreed to let the Council of Ambassadors divide it between them. Poland had never been satisfied with the division of the territory. With a Polish army of some 200,000 men mobilized along the Czechoslovak frontier, the government at Prague on October 1, 1938, was forced to accept

Poland's demands. On the next day Polish troops crossed the Olsa River to begin the occupation of an area of some 400 square miles with a population of 240,000, of which 65 per cent were asserted to be Poles.

The Hungarian government did not act with quite the same decision and dispatch that Poland did, perhaps because Yugoslavia and Rumania threatened to assist Czechoslovakia if Hungary attacked her. Nevertheless, the government at Budapest demanded the cession of the area inhabited by Magyars, and on October 2 Czechoslovakia agreed to negotiate the question. Hungary then put forward claims which were denounced as excessive by Czechoslovakia, and the negotiations became deadlocked. Late in October, however, the two countries agreed that their territorial dispute should be arbitrated by Germany and Italy, and on November 2 the arbitrators awarded to Hungary approximately 4800 square miles of Czechoslovak territory with a population of about one million. Hungarian troops began their occupation of the ceded territory on November 5.

The crisis of September, 1938, had far-reaching effects on the international situation in Europe, for it largely wrecked the system of security which France had constructed on the Continent. Czechoslovakia, deserted by her strongest ally in the west, passed at once into the German orbit. Poland, Rumania, and Yugoslavia, with which France had long been linked in agreements to defend the *status quo* set up by the peace settlement, had every reason to question the value of collective security in general and of French commitments in particular. From Moscow came unofficial statements that the Soviet government considered its alliance with France as having come to an end. In fact, there are reasons to believe that after Munich the Soviet government strongly suspected that the British and French had deliberately surrendered to Hitler in order to facilitate Germany's *Drang nach Osten* and thus precipitate a war between the Reich and the Soviet Union.

And despite Hitler's assertion that with the acquisition of the Sudetenland his territorial ambitions in Europe would be satisfied, events soon proved the contrary. Within a few months he seized upon the internal situation in Czechoslovakia to push his *Drang nach Osten* once more. In that republic the Slovak Popular Party, which had long agitated for Slovak autonomy, had seized upon the crisis of 1938 to push its demands, as the result of which Slovakia was granted full autonomy within the framework of the republic. Joseph Tiso was at once appointed prime minister for Slovakia, and to his government was surrendered full control of all matters affecting Slovakia with the exception of foreign affairs, national defense, and national finance. As a result of the crisis, too, Ruthenia was made autonomous with its own premier and ministry. Czechoslovakia became, therefore, practically a loose federation of three states—Czechia, Slovakia, and Ruthenia. Slovakian and Ukrainian were declared the official languages respectively in the last two.

Despite this transformation of Czechoslovakia into a rather loose federation, relations between the Slovak government and the authorities in Prague continued to be strained. The Slovaks demanded further rights, and it was rumored that Slovak separatists were plotting to overthrow the Czechoslovak republic. In view of this situation, the Czechoslovak premier on March 10, 1939, took the drastic step of dismissing the Slovak premier, Tiso, and of proclaiming martial law in Bratislava. Tiso at once appealed to Hitler for aid, while the leader of the Germans in Slovakia proclaimed that the interests of the Germans were endangered and "must be protected." As in September, 1938, reports were circulated in Berlin of violent attacks on the German minority by Czech mobs or police.

On March 13 Tiso was summoned to Berlin by Hitler, and on the following day, after the former had given the Slovak diet an account of his conversations with the Führer, the governments of both Slovakia and Ruthenia declared their independence. On March 14 President Hacha, who had succeeded Beneš upon the latter's resignation in October, 1938, and the Czechoslovak foreign minister were also summoned to Berlin, and during discussions with Hitler which lasted till 4 A. M. on the fifteenth President Hacha was persuaded—by what threats one can imagine—to place "the fate of the Czech people and the land trustingly in the hands of the Führer of the German Reich," to quote the language of the German communiqué. Early on the morning of the fifteenth Nazi troops occupied western Czechoslovakia.

On March 16 Hitler announced that Czechia thereafter belonged to the territory of the German Reich and would be known as the "Protectorate of Bohemia and Moravia." Although the protectorate was permitted to retain its own government under the nominal presidency of Hacha, for all practical purposes it became an integral part of Germany under a "Reich protector," a position at first assigned to the former German foreign minister von Neurath. In the protectorate a one-party authoritarian system, based on the German pattern, was at once inaugurated.

Meanwhile Tiso, who had once more become premier of Slovakia, had invited Hitler to become the protector of that state. On March 23, 1939, a treaty was accordingly signed between Germany and Slovakia providing that the former would protect the political independence and territorial integrity of the latter. The German army was authorized to construct and use military works along the state's frontiers, and the Slovak government agreed (1) to organize its own military forces in close co-operation with those of the Reich, and (2) to conduct its foreign policy at all times in close agreement with the German government. Obviously Slovakia had become a vassal state of the Reich and possessed a degree of independence little greater than that of Bohemia-Moravia. One result of Germany's military occupation of both Czechia and Slovakia was crystal-clear—she was now in a stronger position than ever to continue her *Drang nach Osten,* for she now had new bases from which she could strike either northward against Poland or southward against Hungary.

While these events were following one another in swift succession, on March 14 troops of the latter country had crossed the Ruthenian frontier, and two days later the Budapest government had announced the incorporation of Ruthenia in Hungary. Thus the Magyars once more gained control of a people whom they had consistently oppressed in the years prior to 1914. Border clashes ensued between Hungarian and Slovak forces which eventually resulted in Hungary's further acquisition of some 400 square miles of Slovak territory, giving her full control of the Ung valley and of the railway connecting Hungary and Poland.

While Czechoslovakia was thus in the process of destruction, Hitler seized upon the confusion in Europe to redeem still another German area. On March 21, 1939, he presented an ultimatum to Lithuania demanding the immediate return to the Reich of the Memel territory. Lithuania was of course in no position to defy the Führer, and an agreement to this effect was at once signed in Berlin. Lithuanian troops and police were immediately withdrawn, and on March 23 Hitler arrived in Memel on board the battleship *Deutschland*.

Mussolini's Seizure of Albania

Hitler's partner in the Rome-Berlin Axis now decided that, regardless of pledges made in the Anglo-Italian treaty of 1938, he should strengthen Italy's position in the Balkans. For some time there had been serious differences of opinion between King Zog of Albania and Mussolini, and, persuasion having failed, the Duce decided to resort to force. Italian troops were landed in Albania, and on April 8, 1939, they captured Scutari and Tirana, from which King Zog and his family had already fled across the frontier into Greece. Count Ciano, Italian foreign minister, announced that the Italian forces had come merely to restore order, prosperity, and progress, and disclaimed any desire to interfere with the existence of Albania as a nation. An Albanian constituent assembly then met and voted to abrogate the existing constitution and regime and to offer the Albanian crown to the King of Italy. On April 15 the Italian parliament decided that Victor Emmanuel's title thereafter should be "King of Italy and Albania, Emperor of Ethiopia," and on the following day the Italian king accepted the Albanian crown at the hands of the Albanian premier. In theory, at least, Albania and Italy became united merely in a personal union, Victor Emmanuel being represented in Albania by a lieutenant-general resident at Tirana. But Albania was soon included in an Italian customs union, and by a constitutional statute her diplomatic services were taken over by Italy and her soldiers were absorbed into the Italian army. Obviously Mussolini had improved his position in the Balkans should he thereafter decide to push his own *Drang nach Osten.*

The End of "Appeasement"

In his proclamation of March 16, 1939, stating the terms of his protectorate over Bohemia-Moravia, Hitler had justified his action not on the ground of self-determination, as he had done in the case of Austria and the Sudetenland, but on the basis of history and the principle of self-preservation. "Bohemia and Moravia," he proclaimed, "have for thousands of years belonged to the *Lebensraum* of the German people." Further, he explained, "It is in accordance ... with the principle of self-preservation that the Reich is resolved to intervene decisively, to re-establish the bases of a reasonable Central European order, and to take all measures which in consequence arise." To many observers it began to appear that Hitler was determined not merely to bring all Germans in adjacent areas into the Reich but to construct something analogous to the Holy Roman Empire of the German Nation (the First Reich), which had been destroyed by Napoleon at the opening of the nineteenth century. And some were not slow to point out that Hitler's practical incorporation of Slovakia within his realm indicated that the Führer's ambitions were not even limited to the former Holy Roman Empire, for Slovakia had never been a part of that realm. In either case, however, there appeared to be plenty of cause for alarm to the statesmen of the other countries of Europe.

Certainly Hitler's repudiation of his own principles and of the formal pledges he had given Chamberlain in September, 1938, seems at last to have convinced the British prime minister that no reliance could be placed upon any assurances that might come from the Führer. At the time of the Sudeten crisis Chamberlain had asserted that he would fight if it became clear that any nation had made up its mind "to dominate the world by fear of its force." It now seemed apparent that Hitler had undertaken to dominate, if not the world, at least Europe by his might or the fear of it, and many believed that the next victim of his aggression would be Poland or Rumania. Consultations were accordingly at once begun by Great Britain, France, Russia, and some of the states of eastern Europe regarding measures to be taken in case of such an eventuality.

The first step in the new movement to "stop Hitler" came on March 31,

1939, when Great Britain and France announced that, "in the event of any action which clearly threatened Polish independence and which the Polish government accordingly considered it vital to resist with their national forces," they would at once lend Poland all support in their power. On April 5 Great Britain's unilateral commitment to Poland was transformed by a joint Anglo-Polish declaration into a reciprocal guarantee and took its place with the already existing Franco-Polish treaty of mutual guarantee. Consultations had meanwhile continued with other states, and, after Mussolini's seizure of Albania, Great Britain and France announced on April 13 that they had extended to Greece and Rumania guarantees identical with that given Poland two weeks earlier.

In May the number of states becoming linked together in the attempt to preserve their national security was further increased when Great Britain and Turkey declared that "in the event of an act of aggression leading to war in the Mediterranean area, they would be prepared to co-operate effectively, and to lend each other all the aid and assistance in their power." France sought to conclude a similar pact, but in her case Turkey seized upon the occasion to exact territorial concessions in the Syrian Sanjak of Alexandretta.[15] Eventually, on June 23, 1939, the French and Turkish governments signed a declaration of mutual assistance analogous to that made by Great Britain and Turkey.

Meanwhile, the indications pointing to Poland's becoming the next storm center of Europe increased. In a manner which experience had taught was the usual prelude to Hitler's execution of some new stroke, the German press in March had begun reporting attacks upon Germans in the Polish Corridor and denouncing the intolerable terror to which the German minority in Poland was subjected. Next, using the British-Polish declaration of mutual guarantee as a justification, Hitler on April 28, 1939, abrogated the German-Polish treaty of nonaggression of 1934 and the Anglo-German naval agreement of 1935. On the same day in a speech to the Reichstag he reiterated an earlier demand that Danzig be returned to Germany and that the latter be given a motor road and a railway line through the Polish Corridor possessing the same extraterritorial status for Germany as the Corridor itself had for Poland. In return he stated his willingness, among other things, to give Poland a free harbor in Danzig, to regard the existing boundaries between Germany and Poland as final, and to conclude a new nonaggression treaty with Warsaw. On May 5 Poland denied the German demands for Danzig and for extraterritorial rights in the Corridor, but suggested a common guarantee of the existence and rights of the Free City and pointed out that Poland already allowed German citizens to travel across the Corridor without customs or passport formalities.

[15] See page 411.

The Axis powers next made a countermove. In an apparent effort to strengthen themselves in the face of Great Britain's guarantee to Poland and the latter's resistance to German demands, or possibly in the hope of intimidating Chamberlain into returning to his policy of appeasement, Italy and Germany on May 22, 1939, signed a military alliance, which was at once implemented by conferences between German and Italian military leaders.

Meanwhile, it was obvious to most observers that the Anglo-French guarantees to Poland and Rumania were greatly weakened by the practical difficulty of sending military aid to eastern Europe. To solve this strategic problem the British government, under pressure from France, in April, 1939, had initiated negotiations for a mutual assistance pact with Russia similar to the Franco-Soviet pact of May, 1935. At the outset of the negotiations the Soviet government made clear that any such pact not only must provide for mutual assistance between Britain, France, and the U.S.S.R., but must also give to all the European states bordering on the Soviet Union a three-power guarantee against attack by aggressors. Furthermore, the pact must be accompanied by a military alliance, fully implemented by consultations of the general staffs of the three countries. Although the negotiations were continued until August, they failed to result in any Anglo-French agreement with Russia.

One of the principal reasons for this failure was the attitude of the Poles. The Warsaw government, fearful of Russia, was unwilling to accept any of the numerous proposals put forward as a basis for assuring effective Soviet-Polish co-operation in case of a German attack on Poland. The latter's attitude destroyed the possibility of any Anglo-Franco-Soviet agreement unless the Western powers were willing to proceed without regard to Poland's wishes. Though in 1938 they had done just that with Czechoslovakia in regard to Hitler's demand for the Sudetenland, they were unwilling to do so in 1939 in response to Russia's insistence that a military agreement with Poland was an indispensible condition for any Soviet pact with the Western powers.[16] The deadlock resulting from Poland's attitude lasted until August, when the political conversations were abandoned and the consideration of a military agreement was begun. The possibility of concluding such an agreement without a previous political understanding was remote, but the discussions continued until the announcement of the German-Soviet nonaggression pact in August.

For, while Russia had been negotiating—with little prospect of success— with Britain and France, she had also been seeking an understanding with Germany. On May 20 Foreign Commissar Molotov had proposed general political negotiations, and in June the Soviet government had let it be

---

[16] Finland, Estonia, and Latvia also rejected the idea of a three-power guarantee.

known that it desired a nonaggression pact with the Reich. Hitler had at first shown little interest and negotiations had lagged until August, when he began to push the matter urgently. By August 16 it had been agreed that a nonaggression pact would be signed and four days later Germany accepted the text as proposed by Russia. On August 23 a nonaggression pact and a secret accompanying protocol were signed in the Soviet capital. By the terms of the former, Russia and Germany agreed to refrain from any act of force against each other and to remain neutral should the other become "the object of warlike action on the part of a third power." The secret protocol divided Eastern Europe into German and Russian spheres, the dividing line running from the Baltic to the Black seas. In the north, Russia was to have a free hand in Finland, Latvia, and Estonia. In Poland, she was to annex the territory east of the Narew, Vistula, and San rivers. In the south, she was to regain Bessarabia which she had lost to Rumania at the close of the First World War. This agreement is more than faintly reminiscent of the one made at Tilsit in 1807 by Napoleon and Tsar Alexander I.

The motives which really actuated Hitler and Stalin in making these agreements cannot be known. Possibly Hitler hoped that an announcement of the signing of a Soviet-German nonaggression pact would cause Great Britain and France to repudiate their pledges to Poland as they had repudiated those to Czechoslovakia in 1938. Then he would be in a position either to gain a bloodless victory once more or to wage a short victorious war against the Poles. In view of his well-known disregard for his pledges, perhaps he planned that once he had consolidated his realm in western Europe he could deal with Russia as he pleased. There is no evidence that he ever abandoned his idea of bringing the Ukraine under his control. Stalin, on the other hand, had probably come to the conclusion that Russia could expect no tangible assistance from France or Great Britain if Russia were attacked by Germany. Possibly he had decided, also, that it might be to Russia's advantage to have Germany become involved in a long and costly war with the Western powers, and thus give the Soviet Union time to strengthen its own military and industrial position to meet the eventual conflict with Nazi Germany which he believed to be inevitable. He may have been influenced, also, by the hope that Germany, France, Britain, and Italy might exhaust themselves in a general war in the West, and thus leave the Soviet Union the dominant power on the Continent.

The Crisis of August, 1939

On August 22, as soon as it had become known that the German-Soviet nonaggression treaty was to be signed, Chamberlain warned Hitler that

that pact would in no way alter Great Britain's obligation to Poland, and stated that the British government was determined that there should be no misunderstanding on this point. He argued, however, that there was nothing in the German-Polish question which could not be settled without resort to force, and urged direct negotiations between Germany and Poland, possibly with the aid of a neutral intermediary. But he declared that any settlement which was reached should be guaranteed by other powers.

Hitler, in his reply on the following day, pointed out that Danzig and the Corridor were among the interests which it was impossible for the Reich to renounce. Germany was prepared to settle this problem with Poland "on a basis of a proposal of truly unparalleled magnanimity," but Britain's guarantee had made the Poles unwilling to negotiate and had encouraged them to unloose "a wave of appalling terrorism against the one and a half million Germans living in Poland." The British decision to assist Poland in case of war, Hitler maintained, could not change the Reich's determination to safeguard the interests of Germany. "The questions of Danzig and the Corridor must and shall be solved."

Two days later (August 25) Great Britain and Poland signed a five-year treaty for mutual assistance. On the next day Premier Daladier informed Hitler of France's determination to stand by Poland, but offered to cooperate in seeking a direct settlement between Poland and the Reich. Hitler replied that he saw no way of inducing Poland to accept a peaceful settlement, and once more restated his claims to Danzig and the Corridor. On August 28 Great Britain reiterated her contention that a reasonable solution of the German-Polish problem could be reached which would also safeguard Poland's essential interests, and declared that Poland had already agreed to enter into direct negotiations with the Reich on this basis, the settlement to be guaranteed by other powers. Great Britain hoped that Germany, too, would consent to such negotiations.

On August 29 Hitler declared that Germany was prepared to accept the British proposal for direct discussion, but explained that in the event of a territorial rearrangement in Poland, the Reich would no longer be able to give guarantees or to participate in guarantees unless the Soviet Union were associated therewith, and thus revealed that Germany had already made some commitment to Russia regarding the division of Polish territory. The German government, Hitler declared, accepted Great Britain's good offices in securing the dispatch to Berlin of a Polish emissary "with full powers," and it counted on the arrival of this emissary on the next day (August 30).

At 2:30 A. M. on August 30 the British government telegraphed its ambassador in Berlin to inform the Reich government that Hitler must not expect that the British government could produce a Polish representative in Berlin that same day. At 6:50 P. M. another telegram suggested that Germany adopt the normal procedure of handing the Polish ambassador the proposals for transmission to Warsaw. When Sir Nevile Henderson called on Foreign Minister von Ribbentrop to deliver this message, the latter "produced a lengthy document which he read out in German aloud at top speed." This document was a sixteen-point program [17] for the settlement of all German-Polish problems. When the British ambassador asked for the text of the proposals, he was informed that "it was now too late, as the Polish representative had not arrived in Berlin by midnight."

Apparently the German note of August 29 and the British reply of the thirtieth were not communicated to Poland until August 31. In the afternoon of that day the Polish government informed the British that it would authorize its ambassador in Berlin to inform the German foreign office that Poland had accepted Great Britain's proposals for direct negotiations. The Polish foreign minister stated, however, that the Polish ambassador would not be authorized to accept the proposals, which the earlier experience of the Austrian Chancellor Schuschnigg and the Czechoslovak President Hacha indicated might be accompanied by "some sort of ultimatum." Foreign Minister von Ribbentrop refused to see the Polish ambassador until the evening of the thirty-first. When at that time Ribbentrop learned that the Polish ambassador was authorized to receive Germany's proposals but had no plenary powers to negotiate, the interview was abruptly closed, and the German government at once broadcast its sixteen-point program, which had not yet been communicated officially to Poland. When the Polish ambassador tried to get in touch with Warsaw, he was unable to do so because all means of communication had been closed by the German government.

On that same evening Germany informed Britain that Hitler for two days had waited in vain for the arrival of a fully empowered Polish negotiator, and that therefore the German government regarded its proposals

[17] The following are the main points in the proposals: the Free City of Danzig to return to the Reich; the Corridor to decide by plebiscite whether it should belong to Poland or to Germany, all domiciled there on January 1, 1918, or born there up to that date having the right to vote; the territory to be evacuated by the Polish authorities and armed forces and to be placed under the supervision of an international commission on which France, England, Italy, and the U.S.S.R. would be represented; Gdynia to be excluded from the plebiscite area; the plebiscite not to take place before the lapse of twelve months, and the question of ownership to be decided by a simple majority; if the plebiscite area went to Poland, Germany to have an extraterritorial traffic zone, one kilometer wide, in which to lay down a motor road and a four-track railway; if the area went to Germany, Poland to have an analogous communication with Gdynia; in this case, Germany to have the right to proceed to an exchange of populations; Danzig and Gdynia both to have the character of exclusively mercantile towns; an international commission of inquiry to examine complaints of both sides as to treatment of their minorities; Germany and Poland to guarantee the rights of the minorities by the most comprehensive and binding agreement; in the event of agreement on these proposals, both countries to demobilize immediately.

as having been "to all intents and purposes rejected." Apparently, as the British foreign secretary later pointed out, Hitler conceived of a negotiation between Germany and Poland as nothing more than the summoning of a Polish plenipotentiary to Berlin, at twenty-four hours' notice, to discuss terms not previously communicated to him. At this time, too, Germany at last provided Britain with the sixteen points in full, but before these could be considered Hitler had ordered the German army to advance across the Polish frontier. At about 5 A. M. on September 1, 1939, German airplanes began raining bombs upon numerous Polish cities. Later in the day Danzig by Hitler's order was incorporated in the Reich, and the Nazi leader in that city was appointed head of the civil administration. Great Britain and France thereupon immediately presented ultimatums to Germany stating that unless the latter suspended all aggressive action against the Poles and withdrew her forces from Polish territory, they would at once fulfill their obligations to Poland.

At 9 A. M. on September 3, after having received no reply to the ultimatum of September 1, the British ambassador in Berlin notified Germany that unless satisfactory assurances had been received by Great Britain by 11 A. M., a state of war would exist between the two countries. Such assurances were not given, and at 11:15 A. M. Chamberlain announced that Great Britain was at war with Germany. France made a similar announcement at 5 P. M. the same day. The Second World War had begun.

Chapter XX

THE PERIOD

OF NAZI BLITZKRIEG

IN 1939 Hitler at last resorted to military measures to continue his policy of territorial expansion of the Third Reich. In the resultant Second World War his armies conquered or occupied one country after another until by the middle of 1942 his power extended almost unbroken from the Atlantic to the Volga and from the Mediterranean and the Caucasus to the North Cape. For a short time he controlled an area larger by far than Napoleon's empire at its height.

Nazi and Soviet Aggressions in 1939

On September 1 Germany's motorized armies advanced into Poland from East Prussia, Pomerania, Silesia, and Slovakia, while German airplanes at once subjected Polish airdromes to severe bombardments. Within a week the "eyes" of the Polish army had been blinded by the destruction of its airplanes and its bases. Meanwhile, German bombers ranged constantly far and wide, behind the Polish lines, disrupting Polish communications and interfering with Polish concentrations, while German Panzer (armored) and motorized divisions pushed steadily forward.

At the end of the second week of hostilities the Poles had lost almost all of their western provinces, and Warsaw was practically surrounded. During the third week, while the Germans were attacking such advanced points as Brest-Litovsk and Lwow (Lemberg), the Polish armies in desperation hastily withdrew to the east and south in the hope that they might establish a front along the Dniester River where they could possibly be supported through Rumania by aid from France and Great Britain. But suddenly, on September 17, Soviet armies began advancing into Poland from the east. This move brought the collapse of all effective Polish resistance except at Warsaw, which heroically endured terrific artillery and air bombardments until September 27, when an armistice was concluded. Thus in the unbelievably short period of twenty-seven days was completed the military destruction of a nation of 34,000,000 people, inhabiting a country 150,000 square miles in extent, defended by an army of 1,500,000 men.

On September 28 Germany and Russia signed a new treaty defining the

THE PARTITION OF POLAND, 1939

frontier of their interests in the former Poland. Generally speaking, the line roughly approximated the "Curzon Line" of 1919, and shifted to German control territory inhabited chiefly by Poles. In exchange for this additional territory, Hitler agreed that Lithuania should be considered in the Russian rather than in the German sphere. The territory given to Soviet Russia constituted an area of approximately 75,000 square miles, and, save in the province of Bialystok, a large part of the population was closely akin racially to the neighboring peoples in the Soviet Union. In October the newly acquired territory was organized as Western White Russia and the Western Ukraine, and in November the former became part of the White Russian Soviet Socialist Republic and the latter was absorbed by the Ukrainian Soviet Socialist Republic. Thus at last Russia regained the territory which Poland had taken from her when the Communists were fighting against "White" armies and foreign intervention in 1920.[1]

Meanwhile, the Soviet government had brought the Baltic republics largely under its control. During September and October the foreign ministers of Estonia, Latvia, and Lithuania successively had been summoned to Moscow for conferences as a result of which each of the republics granted the Soviet Union the right to maintain land, sea, and air armed forces within its territory. Obviously the Baltic republics—once they had carried out the terms of these agreements—were powerless to prevent their permanent occupation by Russia. As a matter of fact, during the summer of 1940 the three states were finally absorbed by the Soviet Union.

Undoubtedly by the acquisition of these air and naval bases Russia greatly strengthened her defensive position in the west. But Soviet leaders felt that the security of Leningrad was still menaced as long as Russia did not fully control the sea and land approaches to that city. The Soviet government therefore in October, 1939, initiated negotiations with Finland, apparently expecting the latter to make concessions similar to those which had been made by the Baltic states. Finland acceded to most of Russia's demands, but refused to lease or sell to Russia the port of Hangoe, which, the Finns contended, would give Russia complete domination of their country. Negotiations eventually reached a deadlock and the Finnish delegation withdrew from Moscow. On November 29 the Soviet government broke off diplomatic relations, and on the next day Russian troops and airplanes crossed the border. On December 2 Finland appealed to the League of Nations, which on the fourteenth condemned the Soviet invasion and expelled the Soviet Union from the League.

Military developments seemed to indicate that the Soviet government had not actually expected to have to wage a war in order to enforce its demands upon Finland, and had not made adequate preparations to do so. Although the Russians launched attacks at various points, at first relatively little headway was made anywhere against the heroic Finns. By January, however, the Russians seemed to have gotten their forces better organized for the attack, and in that month they turned their attention particularly to the Karelian Isthmus, across which the Finns had constructed the Mannerheim Line. The weight of man power and munitions gradually turned the scale. On February 26 the Russians finally captured the fortress which

[1] See page 362.

served as the western anchor of the Mannerheim Line, and a few days later they were approaching Viborg. With their most powerful line broken, their second largest city about to fall into the hands of the enemy, and little prospect of securing from abroad sufficient assistance to stop the Russian "steam roller," the Finnish government sued for peace. At Moscow on March 12, 1940, Finnish plenipotentiaries accepted the Russian-dictated terms, which were much more severe than the demands made in the previous October.

The Allied Policy of Defense and Attrition

Meanwhile, there had been relatively little activity on the western front, although by the beginning of October, 1939, some 158,000 men of the British Expeditionary Force had arrived in France and had taken up their assigned positions. At the outset of the war the Western democracies adopted the principle of a unified command, and the French General Maurice Gamelin was given supreme control of the forces in France. He made little effort to smash the German West Wall, and was reported as saying that he had no intention of starting "a new Battle of Verdun." Gamelin's attitude was exactly what Hitler had gambled on, for at the time he launched his Polish invasion he had left on the west front only six combat-worthy divisions, none of which was armored. Hitler had maintained, in opposition to his own general staff, that the French would not attack. Had Gamelin launched an all-out offensive at that time, according to the German chief of the operations division, he could have smashed through to the Rhine.[2]

On the sea the war proceeded more nearly in accord with expectations, though here, too, it was largely defensive in nature on the part of the Allies. As in 1914, the overwhelming British sea power drove German shipping into home or neutral ports. Except in the Baltic the German flag practically disappeared from the seas. And, as in 1914, the Germans struck back with submarines. Nor did they delay in starting their "unrestricted" campaign. As early as September 4, 1939, the British passenger ship *Athenia* was sunk with 1400 persons on board, of whom more than 300 were Americans. Thereafter neutral as well as Allied shipping was sunk without discrimination by submarines, mines, and airplanes. Also, to prey upon Allied and neutral shipping, German pocket battleships slipped through the British blockade and roamed the high seas. Occasionally spectacular engagements occurred. In December, 1939, the British cruisers *Exeter, Achilles,* and *Ajax,* despite inferior armaments, outmaneuvered and outgunned the Reich's

[2] O. J. Hale, "Adolf Hitler as Feldherr," *Virginia Quarterly Review,* Volume XXIV, page 210.

newest pocket battleship, the *Graf Spee*, and so damaged her that, on orders from Hitler, she was deliberately scuttled.

By this time it seemed to be clear that the Allies had decided to wage a war of attrition, relying upon the increasing pressure of economic strangulation to force Germany to her knees. To many observers there seemed to be a leisureliness about Allied long-range plans for the war that was extremely disturbing. The complacent assumption prevailed in high quarters that France was protected by the impregnability of the mighty Maginot Line and that Britain was safe behind her mastery of the sea. The eyes of most of those in authority appeared to be turned toward the past, and to believe that the system of trench warfare and the slow war of attrition which had won in 1918 must inevitably win again. They seemed blinded to the significance of the blitzkrieg which the German armored divisions and bombers had waged in Poland, and which was about to be unloosed against Norway.

Hitler's Seizure of Norway and Denmark

During the winter of 1939–1940 Hitler decided to seize Norway and Denmark, countries which had escaped being drawn into the First World War. These countries would provide him with valuable submarine and air bases for use against the British navy. Furthermore, their seizure would facilitate Germany's importation of much-needed Swedish iron ore by the use of the Norwegian port of Narvik and Norwegian territorial waters; would assure to Germans and deny to the British the foodstuffs which Denmark, particularly, produced; and, finally, would safeguard the Nazis against an attack from the rear when Hitler launched against the West the blitzkrieg which he was already planning.

On the night of April 9, 1940, German troops suddenly landed at the Norwegian ports of Narvik, Trondheim, Bergen, Stavanger, Egersund, and Arendal, and on the Oslo estuary, and early the next morning Denmark was similarly invaded by land and sea. Some of the "Trojan horse" troop transports, disguised as innocent merchant or ore ships operating through the territorial waters of Norway, had sailed from Germany at least a week before this blow was struck. Warships had been so dispatched as to reach all the Norwegian ports simultaneously, and the requisite air force had been carefully assembled to protect the troop transports against possible attack. But German military efficiency was not the sole explanation of the astounding success of the attack. Apparently the way had also been carefully prepared within Norway by the creation of a "fifth column" of Nazi sympathizers led by Major Vidkun Quisling and Colonel Konrad Sundlo.

The easy conquest of the almost impregnable Oslo fjord was made possible because fake orders were sent to garrison commanders and naval units not to resist the Germans. At Narvik, in fact, the port was turned over to the Germans by Colonel Sundlo without resistance. Once more the world was given an example of Nazi success in boring from within.

King Christian and the Danish government at once submitted to German control, and Denmark became, temporarily, a German protectorate. But King Haakon and the Norwegian government decided to resist and fled from Oslo to avoid capture by the Germans. On the next day Germany insisted on the creation of a new government headed by Major Quisling and other Nazi sympathizers. King Haakon declined to accede to this demand, and was thereafter forced to flee from place to place to escape pursuing German airplanes.

The initial stroke of the Germans gave them a tremendous advantage over the Allies in the subsequent struggle for the control of Norway. In Oslo they possessed an excellent port to which they could ferry reinforcements protected by submarines and by airplanes operated from captured Danish and Norwegian air fields. Although they lost some transports as the result of Allied submarines and mines in the Skagerrak and Kattegat, they were able to land sufficient men and adequate military equipment for a swift campaign. Their chief objective was to open a route between their Oslo forces and the German units at Trondheim.

The Allied expeditionary forces were handicapped from the very outset. All the better ports were in the hands of the Germans, and the Allied troops were compelled to land in small ports without proper harbor facilities for handling heavy military equipment and without neighboring air bases. The chief Allied objective was to isolate Trondheim from rail communication with the German base at Oslo. Despite German superiority in the air, Allied forces were landed north and south of Trondheim, but they lacked both antiaircraft guns and fighter aircraft and before long their bases were nearly destroyed by German bombers. German mechanized units moved swiftly up from Oslo, encountering relatively little resistance, and on April 30 these units met the German forces pushing southward from Trondheim. From that moment the fate of the 12,000 Allied troops in central Norway was sealed. By May 3 they had been evacuated and the German control of southern Norway was assured. On June 9, 1940, the war in Norway ended with the capitulation of the Norwegian army and the flight of King Haakon and his government to London.

Hitler's victory in Norway had immediate political repercussions in Great Britain, where Neville Chamberlain's government at once fell from power. On May 11 Winston Churchill, who during the preceding years had repeatedly pointed out the disaster that awaited Britain unless she awoke and

SCANDINAVIA AND THE BALTIC, 1939

prepared for the coming conflict with Hitler, became prime minister. Included in his new government were outstanding representatives of all three British political parties. It was generally believed that Churchill would inject new life into Britain's military, economic, and diplomatic efforts. That there was need for every effort, if defeat was to be avoided, was already apparent.

The Battle of the Low Countries

The day before Churchill became prime minister the Nazis unleashed another terrific attack which Hitler in a proclamation to his troops asserted would "decide the fate of the German people for a thousand years." At approximately 3 A. M. on May 10, 1940, German troops began to cross the frontiers of the Netherlands, Belgium, and Luxembourg. An hour later German parachute troops landed and seized the airport of Rotterdam, and before 5 A. M. seaplanes had alighted on the Maas (Meuse) River in the heart of that city and Nazi forces had occupied the bridges and two railway stations. Other parachute troops were landed at Dordrecht, at Delft, and near The Hague, and the airdrome at Amsterdam was heavily bombed. At the very outset of the invasion, therefore, the small Dutch air force was rendered useless by the capture or destruction of its landing fields.

While Dutch troops fought heroically near the frontiers to stem the tide of the invasion, bombing and parachute attacks destroyed large parts of Rotterdam, damaged Amsterdam and The Hague, and caused general confusion in the rear of the defending armies. Apparently there was again in this case, too, a certain amount of "fifth column" activity to assist the Nazis. German mechanized forces drove swiftly through the Dutch defense lines and on May 14 reached Rotterdam, while to the north the important city of Amsterdam was being bombed and attacked by parachutists. Overwhelmed by the sheer number of German bombers, tanks, parachutists, and troops, the Dutch on May 15 suspended hostilities. Queen Wilhelmina and the royal family had already fled to England.

Simultaneously with their attack on the Netherlands the Germans had struck at Belgium and Luxembourg. The latter was completely overrun on the first day of the attack. But the Belgians hoped that their strong defense line along the Meuse River and the Albert Canal would enable them to hold off the invaders until Allied forces could come to their aid. On May 10 British and French mechanized units were moving toward Belgium on a front extending from the North Sea to the Moselle River. On the next day, however, the powerful Belgian fort commanding the passage of the Meuse River and the Albert Canal fell to the Nazis, and their capture of bridges over the Albert Canal permitted the Belgian defense line to be outflanked. One week after the opening attack German troops marched into Brussels, and Antwerp was thereupon at once abandoned by the Belgian forces.

But it was farther south that the Allies suffered a gigantic military disaster. As soon as the French forces had been lured forward to assist the Belgians, the Germans concentrated the full force of their terrific attack against the relatively weak but vital Sedan-Montmédy sector. On May 15 the Nazis crossed the Meuse north of Mézières at three points. On the next day the battle from Namur to Sedan became open warfare with motorized units and aircraft participating. By May 19 the German forces had opened a sixty-mile gap through the weaker extension of the Maginot Line. The German mechanized forces then pushed on. Protected by swarms of bombers, they captured Amiens on May 21, and then sped on to Abbeville near the mouth of the Somme. By completing this advance the Germans succeeded in isolating the Allied forces in Belgium and northern France from the main body of the French armies, and the Nazis envisaged the complete annihilation or capture of these forces.

From the south the Germans swiftly began to close in. The important port of Boulogne was occupied by their mechanized forces on May 23, and Calais was attacked on the twenty-seventh. Meanwhile, other German armies were constantly pounding the Allied forces in Belgium, where the northern flank was held by the Belgian army led by King Leopold. This army was subjected to terrific punishment. General Weygand, who had replaced General Gamelin, flew to King Leopold's headquarters to discuss the situation and was informed that the Belgians could not hold out without "substantial new assistance." But such new assistance could not, of course, be given. On May 28 the Belgian king, against the advice of his ministers, finally surrendered unconditionally, and ordered the Belgian army to cease fighting.

The collapse of Belgian resistance exposed the left flank of the Anglo-French forces in Belgium and made desperate the efforts to withdraw them through Dunkirk before their annihilation. On May 26 German armored formations were poised only twelve miles from the beaches of Dunkirk, prepared to destroy the Allied forces crowded into the beachhead. But Hitler, contrary to the advice of both his commander-in-chief and the chief of his general staff, forbade the commitment of these armored formations and assigned the task of destroying the Allied forces to the Luftwaffe. The German ground forces—minus armored formations—were held up for four days by the British at Calais; the British air force, aided by foggy weather, gained a superiority in the air in a limited area around Dunkirk; and the

British navy mobilized some 220 war vessels and 650 other craft of all descriptions for evacuation purposes. Although the Allies admitted the loss of 12 destroyers and 20 other craft, War Secretary Eden announced that 350,000 of the 400,000 men in the British Expeditionary Force had been rescued before the Germans eventually captured Dunkirk on June 3. But the British army in Flanders had lost 30,000 men, 1000 guns, and all its mechanized equipment in what was characterized as a "colossal military disaster."

With the German capture of Calais and Dunkirk the first phase of the German drive on the western front was over. In twenty-four days Hitler's armies had overrun and conquered the Netherlands, Belgium, Luxembourg, and an important section of France extending from Montmédy to Abbeville north of the Somme and the Aisne. The victory was the most crushing German military triumph since Hindenburg's battle of Tannenberg. Not only had the channel coast opposite England fallen to the Nazis; all the ports in western Europe from Abbeville to Narvik beyond the Arctic Circle were now within their hands.

The Collapse of France

Meanwhile, the French had hastily prepared defensive positions extending roughly along the Somme, the Oise-Aisne Canal, and the Aisne to Montmédy at the western end of the Maginot Line. This new position was hopefully called by the populace the Weygand Line. On June 5, 1940, the Germans launched their new offensive against this line. The battle of France had begun. To meet the invader the French army stood practically alone, for most of the shattered British forces which had escaped from the Flanders trap were in England, recuperating and seeking new equipment to take the place of that abandoned in the hasty evacuation from Dunkirk. One British division held the extreme left of the French line south of Abbeville.

Although the French troops fought valiantly and tirelessly to stem the Nazi tide, they not only were decisively outnumbered by the attacking troops but were overwhelmed by German superiority in airplanes and tanks. By June 10 the Nazis had driven a wedge to the Seine near Rouen. On that day Mussolini, who had been becoming more and more bellicose with each advance of the Germans, took Italy into the war against France and Great Britain. This step removed all possibility of sending any of the million men guarding the Italian front to relieve the weary French soldiers before Paris. The Nazis began to encircle the capital, and the French government fled to Tours and then on to Bordeaux. In order that Paris might be spared the fate of Warsaw and Rotterdam, the government withdrew all troops and declared the capital an open city. German troops made a peaceful entry into the city on June 14.

Already on June 12 General Weygand had informed the French cabinet that the military situation was practically hopeless, and most of the minis-

KEY
Maginot Line.
●●●● Weygand Line on June 5.
▬▬ Battle line on June 17.
▬▬ Battle line when firing ceased June 25.
Area occupied by Germans under armistice terms.

THE COLLAPSE OF FRANCE, 1940

ters believed that the total occupation of France was therefore inevitable. Some urged an immediate armistice, but Premier Reynaud, who had succeeded Daladier in March, 1940, was determined that France should continue to fight as the ally of Great Britain, should never make a separate peace even if the government had to be transferred to northern Africa. But on June 16, after the German armies had captured Verdun, had begun to cut off the Maginot Line from the rear, and had penetrated it in frontal attacks from the north and east, Reynaud was forced to resign. His place as premier was taken by the 84-year-old Marshal Pétain.

Negotiations for an armistice were immediately begun, but it was not until June 21 that the French delegates were received by Hitler. On the afternoon of that day, in the railway coach at Compiègne in which Foch had handed the Germans the armistice terms in 1918, General Keitel read to the French the armistice terms of 1940. The French delegates signed these terms the next day, and two days later they signed another armistice with Italy. The order to stop hostilities was then given by Hitler, and fighting ceased on the battlefields of France on June 25, 1940.

By the terms of the Franco-German armistice, Nazi troops were to occupy all of France north and west of an irregular line from the Swiss frontier near Geneva to a point about twelve miles east of Tours, thence southwest to the Spanish frontier, the cost of the occupation and administration to be paid by France. This area constituted more than half of France and placed in German hands all French Atlantic ports. Except for the units required to maintain internal order, all French military and air forces were to be disarmed and demobilized. The French fleet was to collect in ports to be designated, there to be demobilized and placed under German or Italian control. All German prisoners held by France were to be surrendered, but French prisoners were to be held by Germany until the end of the war. France, furthermore, was to surrender any Germans on French territory whom the Reich government might designate, in order, apparently, that the Reich might arrest those anti-Nazi Germans who had sought refuge in France.

The Nazi blitzkrieg which demoralized and destroyed the French military forces at the same time destroyed the Third French Republic. On July 9, 1940, the two houses of the French parliament, meeting at Vichy outside the German-occupied zone, by overwhelming votes approved a draft resolution conferring upon Marshal Pétain full power to draw up a new constitution establishing an authoritarian regime. On the next day the same two houses, sitting as the French National Assembly, officially adopted the resolution, merely adding a proviso that the new constitution should be submitted to a national plebiscite.

On July 11 Pétain issued three constitutional decrees. By the first, he assumed the functions of Chief of the French State and abolished the position of President of France. By the second, he conferred upon the Chief of State plenary governmental powers both executive and legislative. By the third, he adjourned the Senate and Chamber of Deputies *sine die,* and de-

THE WEHRMACHT ON THE MARCH IN 1940

Nazi troops parading on the Champs-Élysées in Paris

creed that they should thereafter be convened only on call of the Chief of State. On the next day he appointed what was considered a strongly fascist cabinet, and named former Premier Laval—who favored French "collaboration" with the Nazis—as vice-premier. Later by still another decree all high officials in France were required to swear fidelity to Pétain's person, and the Chief of State was given authority to punish any official who betrayed his duties. Thus by legal steps the Third Republic was converted into the Pétain dictatorship.

But not all Frenchmen approved the actions and policies of Pétain. General Charles de Gaulle, Reynaud's undersecretary of war, was one who did not. He believed that France, though conquered on the Continent, should still fight as the ally of Great Britain, continuing to use her navy, her air force, and her vast colonial realm. At the time of the collapse of the French army he was on a military mission in London, where on June 22 he had issued a radio appeal urging all Frenchmen outside France to continue the war against Hitler. The interest of France demanded, he declared, "that all free Frenchmen should fight wherever they are." After the signing of the armistice, General de Gaulle appointed himself leader of the French outside France and established a Provisional French National Committee. During August and September revolts against the Pétain government in favor of continuing the war in conjunction with Great Britain occurred in Chad, French Kamerun, French West Africa, French Equatorial Africa, and some of the scattered French islands.

The United States the "Arsenal of Democracy"

In September, 1939, the great majority of Americans had had certain definite ideas regarding the war which had broken out in Europe. One was that there was little doubt as to where "war guilt" lay. They had watched Hitler's increasing disregard of Germany's treaty obligations and had seen him become ever more and more aggressive. At the same time they had seen the leaders of Great Britain and France make numerous efforts to appease the Führer in order to prevent the outbreak of another war, even when such appeasement had entailed the destruction or dismemberment of weaker states. Most Americans were convinced, therefore, that the war was the direct outcome of Nazi principles and technique, and, since they abhorred these, most Americans were openly sympathetic with the Allies and hoped they would win what was feared would be a long war. But the great majority of Americans fervently hoped that the United States would not be drawn into this war as it had been in 1917. President Roosevelt, in a radio address on September 3, 1939, to some extent expressed these two ideas when he stated that he could not "ask that every American remain neutral in thought," but at the same time stated his hope and belief that "the United States will keep out of this war."

These two fundamental ideas of the American people were further expressed in a new Neutrality Act which was passed on November 4, 1939. Under the Neutrality Act of 1937 the United States government was compelled to place an embargo on the shipment of implements of war to belligerent powers. Obviously, because of Britain's control of the sea, this act operated not to the detriment of Germany but to that of the Allies. Most Americans were willing to supply the Allies with the sinews of war if it could be done without involving the United States in war. The new act was designed to accomplish these two ends. The Allies were free to purchase war materials in the United States, but such materials might not be carried to a belligerent country in American ships. Furthermore, the act empowered the President to forbid American citizens and ships to enter combat areas in war zones. Thus, it was hoped, there would be no occasion for the United States to be dragged into this war as in 1917 because of the sinking of American ships by German submarines. Most Americans, it appeared, were willing to sit on the sidelines and watch the Allies defeat the Nazi dictator.

From this somewhat placid state the United States was rudely shaken by the startling developments in Europe in 1940. After the fall of France the feeling grew among Americans that Great Britain was their first line of defense against the Nazi and Fascist dictators, and that the British must be assisted with all aid "short of war." After Dunkirk the United States government turned back to American manufacturers—who rushed them to England—rifles, machine guns, field guns, and airplanes, which were needed to re-equip the evacuated British troops. In September, fifty over-age American destroyers were transferred to Great Britain in return for ninety-nine-year leases of naval and air bases in the islands of Newfoundland, Bermuda, the Bahamas, Jamaica, St. Lucia, Trinidad, and Antigua, and in British Guiana. By this transaction Great Britain was strengthened to defend her overseas lifeline and the United States secured advance bases for the defense of North America and the Caribbean.

While there was some difference of opinion among Americans regarding the policy of all aid to Great Britain "short of war," there were few who doubted that the United States should itself embark upon a sweeping program of national preparedness. In September, 1940, Congress passed and President Roosevelt approved the first American law to prescribe compulsory military service in time of peace. By the terms of the Selective Training and Service Act every male citizen who was between the ages of twenty-one and thirty-six was "liable for training and service in the land or naval forces of the United States." On November 18 the first groups of drafted men were inducted into the army. But men without weapons would, of course, be of little use in defending the country. During 1940 the government authorized the expenditure of more than $17,000,000,000 for a "two-ocean navy" and for all the latest and most efficient weapons for land and air warfare, and in the first six months of 1941 more billions of dollars were voted for similar purposes.

On December 29, 1940, President Roosevelt in a radio address pointed out that the American people faced the possibility of an Axis victory, which would mean "a new and terrible era in which the whole world, our hemisphere included, would be run by threats of brute force." In that address the President defined what many considered a doctrine worthy to rank alongside the Monroe Doctrine, namely, that the American people were determined not to permit control of the seaways leading to their coasts to pass into the hands of a power hostile to their own democratic way of life and bent on its destruction. British sea power in the Atlantic was recognized as a bulwark friendly to democracy, and in order that it should not be destroyed an administration bill "to promote the defense of the United States" was introduced in Congress in January, 1941.

This bill, which was popularly called the Lend-Lease Bill, after long debate in both houses of Congress finally became law on March 11. The act authorized the President to manufacture for, exchange with, sell, lease, lend, or in other ways make available any defense article to "the government of any country whose defense the President deems vital to the defense of the United States." Payment might be made by any means which the President deemed satisfactory. The United States was to become the great "arsenal of democracy."

The Battle of Britain

Meanwhile, spectacular though Hitler's military successes had been against Poland, Norway, the Netherlands, Belgium, and France, they had not attained for him his principal objective—the end of the war on his own terms. Though Great Britain had seen five states, including her chief ally, crushed in a few weeks by the mighty power of Hitler's war machine, she was determined to fight on. "Bearing ourselves humbly before God," Prime Minister Churchill had declared on July 14, 1940, "but conscious that we serve an unfolding purpose, we are ready to defend our native land against the invasion by which it is threatened. We are fighting by ourselves alone. But we are not fighting for ourselves alone. . . . Should the invader come to Britain," he warned, "there will be no placid lying down of the people in submission before him. . . . We shall defend every village, every town, and every city . . . ; we would rather see London in ruins and ashes than that it should be tamely and abjectly enslaved. . . . Thus only, in times like these, can nations preserve their freedom."

Already the British had struck one blow in an effort to protect themselves against Hitler's attack. Great Britain had reluctantly consented to France's withdrawal from the war on condition that the French fleet should be dispatched to British ports and remain there while negotiations were taking place. But the armistice terms which France signed stipulated, as already pointed out, that French warships should be collected in ports to be specified and be demobilized and disarmed under German or Italian control. The British feared that the situation on the seas might be seriously altered to Great Britain's detriment by the union of the French, Italian, and German fleets.

To prevent this eventuality, early on the morning of July 3, 1940, 2 French battleships, 2 light cruisers, 8 destroyers, a number of submarines, and about 200 smaller craft which lay in British harbors were seized by the British. At the same time, at the Egyptian port of Alexandria, a French fleet, consisting of a battleship, 4 cruisers, and a number of smaller vessels, had been immobilized as the result of negotiations with its commander. But at Oran, the French naval base in Algeria, the situation was not so easily handled. When the French admiral in command refused to comply with any of the alternatives offered him and declared his intention to fight, the British opened fire and all but destroyed his fleet. Thus Great Britain safeguarded her supremacy at sea, a supremacy which was to prove decisive in the battle of Britain.

In the ensuing struggle, Germany with a population of more than 80,000,000 held a distinct advantage over Great Britain, which without her overseas empire had only some 48,000,000. The British regular army at home consisted in July, 1940, of only 1,500,000 men. These were supported by another million "Home Guard" volunteers who had been hastily organized to destroy parachutists and other air-borne invaders. But the great bulk of the British troops were men who had never campaigned under actual war conditions, and many of them were incompletely armed and equipped. Moreover, the British suffered from a serious shortage of tanks, artillery, antitank guns, and even small arms. The German army, on the other hand, consisted of approximately 3,500,000 men, all well trained and fully armed and equipped. It was a veteran force, by most observers considered the best and most powerful in the world. It seemed rather certain that, if Great Britain in July, 1940, had been merely another country on the Continent, adjacent to France, she would have been invaded, overrun, and conquered by the Germans.

But, despite Hitler's declaration that there were "no more islands," Great

Britain remained separated from the Continent by a moat of water twenty miles or more in width. To cross that moat with sufficient men and equipment to assure a successful invasion the Germans needed thousands of suitable landing craft. And, unfortunately for Hitler's dreams of conquest, the Germans did not have them. To overcome this lack they made a tremendous effort to assemble from all occupied Europe craft of any and all types, but the latter were blasted by the RAF while they still lay in their harbors. On this occasion Hitler was uncertain and loath to take the risk of ordering a cross-Channel invasion of England. Although preparations for the invasion were made, D-day for this operation was twice postponed and finally cancelled in the fall of 1940.

But the English Channel could not stop an invasion by the Luftwaffe, and Hitler pinned his hopes upon it. Although in some categories British airplanes were superior to the German in quality, there seemed little doubt that at the opening of the battle of Britain Germany possessed an air superiority of three or four to one in the number of warplanes. But the Germans possessed not only the advantage of a superior number of planes. Thanks to the conquests they had made, they held a great advantage geographically. Scores of new air fields in southern Norway, Denmark, the Netherlands, Belgium, and France gave German planes admirable bases for attacking the southern and eastern coasts of Britain. As a result, the latter was geographically and industrially much more vulnerable to air attack than Germany. Although the British had a highly organized air-defense system, consisting chiefly of fighter planes, antiaircraft guns, and balloon barrages, the effectiveness of these defenses against mass attacks by thousands of airplanes had yet to be proved.

Marshal Göring, head of the German Luftwaffe, believed that German planes by terrific offensives in which thousands of bombers would be used might overwhelm and eliminate the British air forces as they had those of Poland and the Netherlands. Then, once British air fields had been destroyed and British airplanes had been grounded or wrecked, the Germans would do to the industrial cities of Great Britain what they had done to Warsaw and Rotterdam. Factories, power plants, warehouses, business centers, means of communication, if necessary the homes of the people, would be destroyed, and Britain would collapse internally.

On the night of June 18–19, 1940, Göring launched his attack upon Britain when German warplanes bombed the Thames estuary and southern England. On the following night British airplanes struck back, bombing Hamburg, Bremen, Cologne, Düsseldorf, Frankfort, and other places. Thus was inaugurated the long-expected and much-dreaded air war between the Reich and Great Britain. Nightly the air-raid sirens screamed, and not only British civilians, who had never experienced the horrors of modern war on their own soil, but Germans, whose country had not known foreign invasion for more than a century, came to feel the terrors of war in the homeland. During the latter part of July the Germans increased the intensity of their air attack, and in August Germany announced that "systematic destruction" would soon start. Beginning in September the Nazi bombing attacks were greatly increased, and special efforts were made to destroy or "erase" London. German bombers, directed personally by Marshal Göring, unleashed furious attacks upon the British capital, dropping incendiary as well as explosive bombs. Fires in various parts of the city illumined the skies almost nightly, and much destruction resulted, not only in the industrial and commercial sections of the city but in the residential areas as well. Berlin announced that waves of bombers would continue to strike at London until the British people set up a government which would be willing to accept German terms.

But the Germans succeeded neither in destroying British morale nor in eliminating the British air force. The British based their defensive strategy on the conservation and replacement of planes and crews. By scattering their planes they prevented great losses on the ground when air fields were attacked. Although they lost some 900 planes between September, 1940, and May, 1941, a steady though almost insignificant flow of new planes from British factories enabled the RAF to continue to fight. On the other hand, British daring and skill in combat and superiority in quality of planes and in tactics enabled RAF pilots to destroy some 3000 German planes during these critical months. Obviously the British inflicted a high rate of attrition on the Luftwaffe.

Experts have pointed out the serious error in Göring's strategy in failing to concentrate the Luftwaffe's attack on British war industries. Half a dozen factories, whose location was unquestionably known to the Germans, held, it is said, the key to Britain's Spitfire output. If the Luftwaffe had systematically bombed these factories, the production of British fighter planes could have been almost eliminated. But the Germans long held stubbornly to the plan which had been successful in Poland. Not until 1941 did they modify their strategy and attempt to strike the British war effort at its industrial roots. "Then it was too late. The destructive power of the Luftwaffe had been sharply reduced; new camouflaged plants had been completed, and production of critical parts widely decentralized; and American Lend-Lease was functioning, with hundreds of ... planes supplementing British output." [3] Although London, Coventry, Birmingham, Bristol, Liverpool, and other cities had suffered heavy property damage, they had not been "erased." Nor had the British air force been put out of the conflict.

[3] A. Carr, "The Five Fatal Mistakes of the Axis," *Harper's Magazine*, February, 1944, pages 219–223.

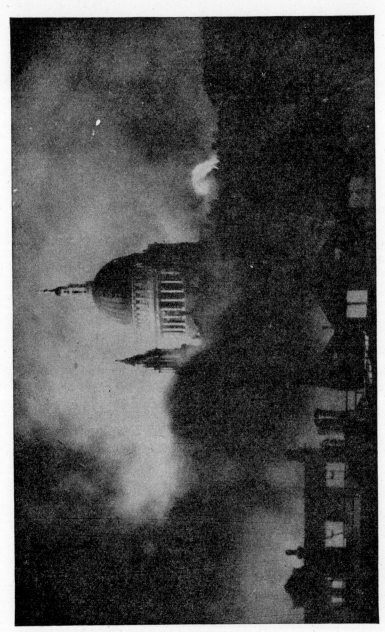

International News Photos

THE RESULT OF A VISIT BY THE LUFTWAFFE

London burning on December 29, 1940

The Extension of the War into the Balkans

By this time the war had engulfed the Balkans where the First World War had originated. The Soviet Union had struck first. Obviously disturbed by Hitler's spectacular successes in the West in 1940, Russia had swiftly availed herself of the German-Soviet secret agreement of 1939 regarding Bessarabia. On June 26, 1940, the day after fighting ceased in France, Foreign Commissar Molotov presented Rumania with a twenty-four-hour ultimatum demanding the immediate cession to Russia of Bessarabia and northern Bukowina. After frantically seeking the advice of Hitler and Mussolini, who urged acceptance in order to prevent a new war, the Rumanian government acceded to the demands, and Russian forces at once occupied these additional territories. In the succeeding weeks Russia took steps to strengthen her position in the Baltic, too. In August Estonia, Latvia, and Lithuania were absorbed into the Soviet Union as constituent republics.

Hungary and Bulgaria, also, both showed signs of a determination to regain the territories which Rumania had taken from them. Troops were rushed to both frontiers, and the possibility of another Balkan war seemed imminent. This Hitler and Mussolini at the moment wished to avoid at almost all costs. The leaders of the Hungarian, Rumanian, and Bulgarian governments were summoned for conferences, and out of them eventually came a further partition of Rumania. Bulgaria received that part of the Dobrudja which Rumania had taken from her in 1913; and Hungary received the northern half of the province of Transylvania, all of which had been awarded Rumania by the treaty of Trianon in 1920.

Within Rumania the fascist Iron Guard [4] at once sought to take advantage of the new situation to overthrow King Carol, who had been hostile to their movement. Despite Carol's efforts to ingratiate himself with the Iron Guardists—by cutting all ties with the Western democracies, withdrawing Rumania from the League of Nations, establishing a totalitarian state in Rumania, and appointing as premier General Ion Antonescu, who was an Iron Guard favorite—the king on September 6, 1940, was forced to abdicate in favor of his son, who for the second time became King Michael. Antonescu decreed the establishment of an Iron Guard totalitarian state whose foreign policy would be in complete accord with that of the Rome-Berlin Axis. Early in October German troops entered Rumania and began the occupation of that country with the permission of Antonescu's government. Another state thus succumbed to Nazi forces and Rumania's lot appeared to be little better than that of Denmark. At last Hitler had reached

[4] See pages 398–399.

the Black Sea, one of the principal objectives which he had outlined in *Mein Kampf.*

The next aggressive step in the Balkans was taken by Mussolini who, apparently expecting an easy victory, on October 28, 1940, ordered his troops in Albania to advance into Greece. But the Greeks first halted the Duce's

THE PARTITION OF RUMANIA, 1940

troops, then threw them on the defensive, and finally drove them back into Albania. During the first three months of 1941 the Greeks fought stubbornly on over difficult terrain toward Valona, Italy's chief Albanian port. The British, who had now secured naval and air bases on the Greek island of Crete, added to Mussolini's woes. British bombers and torpedo planes from Crete or from British aircraft carriers attacked Taranto and Naples and seriously interfered with the shipment of Italian troops and supplies across the Adriatic. By the spring of 1941 the Italian invasion of Greece had been turned into something of a debacle.

Meanwhile Hitler had been attempting through diplomacy to persuade the small states of central Europe and the Balkans to support the Nazis. In November, 1940, he had made some headway, for within a week Hungary, Rumania, and Slovakia had signed the tripartite agreement of September 27, 1940, which Germany, Italy, and Japan had made to facilitate the establishment of "a new order in Europe" and "in Greater East Asia." [5] Additional Nazi troops were soon sent to Rumania, and during the opening weeks of 1941 they were gradually concentrated on the frontiers of Bulgaria and Yugoslavia, apparently in the hope that pressure might force these states, also, to join the Axis powers and thus open the way to an attack upon Greece down the Struma and Vardar valleys. Hitler was eager to bring the Balkans entirely under his control in order to protect his southern flank during his projected invasion of Russia. On March 1, 1941, the Bulgarian government finally joined the Axis powers by signing the tripartite agreement in Vienna, and within a few hours Nazi forces were reported in occupation of Sofia.

After Bulgaria succumbed to Hitler's pressure and Nazi forces in consequence were able to concentrate on nearly all sides of Yugoslavia, the regent, Prince Paul, and Premier Cvetkovich apparently came to the conclusion that discretion would be the better part of valor. They knew that, if they defied Hitler and war resulted, the only route by which Yugoslavia could receive assistance and supplies was up the Vardar Valley from Saloniki—and this route might be speedily cut by German mechanized forces. Furthermore, they feared that going to war against the Axis might mean the end of Yugoslavia, for Bulgaria would be quick to demand the territory which she had lost in 1913 and 1919, Mussolini would undoubtedly seek to extend Albania at Yugoslavia's expense, and dissident Croats might throw their lot in with the Nazis in the hope that a dismembered Yugoslavia might result in an independent Croat state. On March 25, 1941, the Yugoslav government formally signed the Axis tripartite pact in Vienna.

The news of this capitulation to the Axis was received in Yugoslavia—at least in the districts which had constituted Serbia and Montenegro—with anger and resentment, which finally culminated in a bloodless coup d'état in the early morning hours of March 27. The regency of Prince Paul and the government of Premier Cvetkovich were both overturned. On the next day the seventeen-year-old son of former King Alexander was elevated to the throne as King Peter II, and General Dušan Simovich, commander of Yugoslavia's air force and leader of the coup against Cvetkovich, became premier. Although the new government announced that it would maintain a policy of strict neutrality as regarded the European war, it began to mobilize Yugoslav troops along the country's frontiers.

[5] See page 566.

But Hitler struck before the Yugoslavs had time to complete their mobilization. On April 6 the Nazis launched invasions into both Yugoslavia and Greece, using their usual blitzkrieg pattern. With their overwhelming superiority in mechanized equipment and air force, they were able to carry out a campaign against Yugoslavia very much like the one they had waged against France in 1940. At various points the Yugoslav lines were pierced by "mechanized infiltration"; the Yugoslav armies were separated from one another and then encircled. At the same time a powerful German thrust down the Struma and into the Vardar Valley effectively cut off the Yugoslavs from outside aid, even had such aid been available. Eventually the Germans, driving westward, made contact with the Italians fighting in Albania, and on April 17—after a twelve-day campaign—the defeated and disorganized Yugoslav army laid down its arms without conditions.

Meanwhile, the Germans had been pushing their invasion into Greece, which—aided by 60,000 British, Australian, and New Zealand troops and some heavy equipment from the Army of the Nile—was now compelled to meet blows from two major European powers. As in all their other campaigns, the Nazis possessed an overwhelming superiority in air and mechanized forces which inevitably weighed in the balance despite the more difficult terrain and the valiant stands of the Anzac troops. Almost at once the Nazis drove through Thrace from the Bulgarian frontier to the Aegean and thus cut off the Greeks from contact by land with Turkey. At the end of the third day of the campaign the defeat of the Yugoslavs in the lower Vardar Valley opened the way for a German advance upon the important Greek port of Saloniki, whose capture in turn entrapped the Greek army east of the Vardar. The German conquest of Greece now seemed inevitable, but the fierce resistance of New Zealand troops at historic Thermopylae Pass enabled the British Expeditionary Force to evacuate 45,000 of its men. Most of its heavy equipment, however, as at Dunkirk, had to be abandoned. On April 27, 1941, after a three weeks' campaign, the Nazis occupied Athens, from which King George II and the Greek government had already fled to Crete. In the ensuing days they completed their conquest of the Peloponnesus.

But the Führer was not content to stop with the conquest of the Balkans. On May 20 he launched the first completely air-borne invasion in history against the strategic British-occupied Greek island of Crete, some sixty miles from the European mainland. Following a terrific attack by hundreds of bombing planes which prepared the way for them, thousands of Nazi troops were landed in Crete by parachutes, gliders, and transport planes. After a day of fighting with the British and Greek forces the Nazis, though having suffered heavy casualties, had gained a foothold on the island. Then followed a contest between air power and sea power. The British navy, though repeatedly attacked by Nazi dive bombers, shattered all German attempts to land troops and heavy equipment by sea, but hundreds of airplanes, shuttling back and forth between Greece and Crete, carried men, supplies, and light equipment to the Nazi "bridgeheads" on the island. By early June the Nazis had occupied most of Crete, the British without aerial protection being almost helpless. For the third time, however, they were able to carry out an overseas evacuation with some degree of success. Meanwhile, George II and his government had again fled, this time to Egypt.

British Dominance in the Middle East

While the Nazis were conquering the Balkans, it was thought by many that Hitler might next turn his attention to Syria and Iraq, both in order to obtain the coveted Mosul oil fields and to secure a military base for an advance on the Suez Canal. In Syria the French high commissioner appeared to be wholly in accord with the Vichy government's policy of collaboration with Hitler; and in Iraq, on April 4, the pro-British government was ousted by a *coup d'état* when the pro-Axis Rashid Ali Beg Gailani seized control. The coup seemed to presage ill for Great Britain, and to counter possible Axis penetration in this important oil-producing country the British on April 19 began to land troops at Basra, the Iraqi port on the Persian Gulf. Although by the Anglo-Iraqi treaty of alliance the British had the right to use the Iraqi "railways, rivers, ports, airdromes, and means of communication" in case of war, Rashid Ali objected. Hostilities broke out on May 2 when Iraqi troops attacked the British air base at Habbania, some sixty-five miles west of Bagdad, and Rashid Ali appealed to Hitler for aid.

Although Hitler dispatched some bomber and fighter planes to Iraq, utilizing Syrian airdromes as bases, he was apparently already preparing for his conquest of Crete and failed to send sufficient aid to enable Rashid Ali to gain superiority in the air. British and "Fighting French" airplanes not only attacked the Iraqi forces but also repeatedly bombed the airdromes in Syria which were being used by the Germans. At the same time British motorized units pushed steadily on toward Bagdad. Rashid Ali's government collapsed, the pro-Axis premier himself fled to Iran, and on June 1 all fighting between the British and the Axis-inspired Iraqi came to an end. The pro-British government, which had been overthrown in April, returned to power and Basra, Bagdad, and Mosul—the only Iraqi towns of any size—came into the hands of the British, who thus secured possession of the "backdoor to the Near East." Next British imperial and "Fighting French" forces invaded Syria and succeeded in occupying that country. With Palestine, Transjordan, Iraq, and Syria under their control, the British thus retained their dominant position in the Middle East, a position which was further strengthened in so far as the control of the Red Sea was concerned, by their conquest of Italian East Africa, which was completed in May, 1941.

The Deterioration of Soviet-German Relations

Although from the moment the German-Soviet nonaggression pact was signed Stalin and Hitler had been suspicious of each other, it was not until after the collapse of France that relations between Nazi Germany and Soviet Russia had begun to deteriorate. Stalin had disliked the German troops' use of Finland as a base for operations against northern Norway, while Hitler had not liked the Russian annexation of northern Bukowina, which had not been mentioned in the secret protocol of 1939. Stalin had also resented the German occupation of Rumania and the Axis guarantee to that country, which he considered was contrary to the interests of Russia. But his unwillingness to accept Hitler's ideas of Russia's proper sphere of influence was probably the immediate reason for the final break in the peaceful relations of the two countries.

After the air blitz against Britain had failed, Hitler in an interview with Foreign Commissar Molotov in Berlin on November 12, 1940, had proposed that Russia should sign a four-power treaty with Germany, Italy, and Japan, and had further proposed that Russia should center her territorial aspirations in the region south of the Soviet Union "in the direction of the Indian Ocean." Apparently the Balkans were to fall chiefly within the German sphere. To anyone familiar with Russia's many efforts to secure dominance in the Balkans and control of the Straits, it is obvious that Hitler's proposals would be unacceptable to the Soviet government. The latter had finally replied on November 25 that it would sign such a four-power pact only if it were accompanied by secret protocols providing that: (1) Russia should be guaranteed a base for her light naval and land forces on the Straits: (2) Bulgaria, recognized as being within Russia's geographical security zone, should sign a mutual assistance pact with the Soviet government; (3) the focal point of Russia's territorial aspirations should be recognized as lying south of Batum and Baku in the general direction of the Persian Gulf; (4) German troops should be withdrawn immediately from Finland; and (5) Japan should renounce her rights to concessions for coal and oil in Northern Sakhalin. The conflict between Germany's longstanding desire for a drive into the Balkans and Russia's equally longstanding ambition to control that region was obvious, and it is doubtful that Stalin ever expected Hitler to agree to such terms.

The Soviet reply reached Berlin on November 26, and three weeks later the Führer issued to his military leaders his secret directive for "Operation Barbarossa," which was designed "to crush Soviet Russia in a quick campaign" and "to establish a defense line against Asiatic Russia on a line running approximately from the Volga River to Archangel." Preparations for the campaign were "to be completed by May 15, 1941." This directive was of course not known to the Soviet government. Nevertheless, although on the surface Russia and Germany continued to be friends, clashes in policy developed. On January 17, 1941, Russia warned that the entrance of Nazi armed forces into Bulgaria would be considered "as a violation of the security interests of the U.S.S.R." But Germany had disregarded the warning and had occupied Bulgaria in March. On April 4, Molotov had informed Germany that Russia was about to sign a treaty of friendship and nonaggression with Yugoslavia, and "hoped that the German government, too, ... would do everything to maintain peace...." On April 6, the Nazis had invaded Yugoslavia, an action which Molotov characterized as "extremely deplorable."

Meanwhile, Stalin seems to have become convinced that a Nazi attack upon Russia was only a matter of time, and he had taken special steps to prepare for it. Diplomatically he had moved to prevent, if possible, a war on two fronts; on April 13, 1941, he had signed a treaty of neutrality and nonaggression with Japan. Industrially he had also taken steps to increase the military strength of the country. Production of war materials had been speeded up; the work-day had been lengthened from seven to eight hours; some of the vital industries in western Russia had been ordered moved to safer locations east of the Urals. Finally, in May, 1941, as though in anticipation of a crisis, Stalin himself for the first time assumed the premiership of the Soviet Union.

The Nazi Invasion of Russia

In June, 1941, Hitler began to make Nazi troop concentrations on the eastern front. In the north, German men, guns, and tanks were sent to Finland; in the south, the Rumanians were persuaded to mobilize on the Russian frontier. The Luftwaffe was largely shifted from the west to the east. Then without warning, without preliminary negotiations or an ultimatum, the Germans on June 22 advanced into Russia. In a proclamation to the German people the Führer promised that in the ensuing campaign the movement of German troops would be "in its extent and magnitude the greatest that the world has seen." There is little doubt that this phase of the war constituted one of the most gigantic duels in history; millions of men and thousands of tanks were hurled against one another along a battleline of some 1800 miles, while overhead thousands of planes struggled for mastery of the air.

The Nazi attack on Russia had its immediate effect on other countries. Prime Minister Churchill at once announced that, though he had not changed his views on communism, "any man or state who fights against Nazism will have our aid." On July 13, 1941, Great Britain and the Soviet Union became formal allies. In July representatives of Great Britain and the United States flew to Moscow to ascertain what the Russians needed in the way of assistance, and late in September a formal conference in Moscow worked out plans for sending supplies to Russia by way of Archangel, Vladivostok, and Iran.

In order to safeguard a route to Russia by way of Iran the Allies were led to take drastic measures in that country. In August, 1941, Britain and Russia requested the shah to expel 3000 Germans from Iran. When the shah temporized, Russian and British troops entered the country and seized the railway lines and important oil centers. On September 9, the Iranian parliament finally agreed to surrender Axis nationals, expel the Axis legations, provide for transit facilities to Russia, safeguard the oil supply, and permit Allied military occupation of certain zones within the country. In the ensuing months the Trans-Iranian Railway and the motor highways were greatly improved by the Allies, and the routes through Iran came to play a vital part in providing Russia with much-needed British and American lend-lease supplies.

Meanwhile, the war in Russia had been proceeding. According to Hitler's original directive for the campaign, the zone of German operations was to be divided by the Pripet marshes into a northern and a southern sector. The main effort was to be made in the north. Soviet forces in White Russia and the Baltic states were to be annihilated and Leningrad and Kronstadt were to be captured. With the terrain in Russia generally similar to that in Poland, the Germans expected to execute on a much larger scale a blitzkrieg in which swift Panzer units would smash through the Russian lines in various places, then encircle the broken Red Army, and eventually annihilate it piece by piece. But the war in the north did not proceed "according to plan." Estonia was not completely overrun until September 5; Leningrad, although almost completely surrounded by besieging troops, never fell to the Nazis; and the Soviet armies were not encircled and annihilated.

In the area south of the Pripet marshes, according to the Führer's plan, German-Rumanian troops were to pin down the Soviet armies in Bessarabia while the main German force, advancing from Poland, was to capture Kiev and encircle and annihilate the Russian forces west of the Dnieper River. But here, too, operations did not proceed quite as the Nazis had expected. Nearly three months passed before Kiev was captured, and the Russian armies in the southwest were not enveloped and destroyed. But, during the period, the Soviet forces by their own admission lost 7000 tanks,

THE GERMAN INVASION OF RUSSIA, 1941-1942

8900 large-caliber guns, and 5300 planes. Russia, the Führer publicly exulted on October 3, "is already broken and will never rise again." If he had waited a few more weeks he might never have made such a statement.

Although in his original directive Hitler had declared that only after Leningrad had been taken should an attempt be made to capture Moscow, and that only a surprisingly fast collapse of Russian resistance could justify attempting to take Leningrad and the Russian capital simultaneously, on October 1 the Germans had launched a tremendous offensive against Moscow along a great semicircle some three hundred miles wide. By October 17 the Nazi forces had approached so close to the city that it was deemed advisable to move the Soviet capital to Kuibyshev, five hundred miles farther east. But the fierce Russian resistance, made possible by the ability of Russian factories to send an ever-swelling stream of fighting equipment to the front, not only surprised the German commanders but prevented their capture of the city. When this first Nazi offensive failed, Hitler, unmindful of the threat of a Russian winter, ordered another attack, which began on November 16. Seven of the eleven railways entering Moscow were cut, and at one point the Germans got within fifteen miles of the city. But, though the Germans meanwhile captured Odessa, Kharkov, and Rostov, Russia was not "broken," and Moscow was not taken. Instead, elsewhere on the far-flung battleline the Russians themselves launched an offensive.

A number of factors had contributed to the Nazi failure to put Russia out of the war with the same dispatch as Poland, France, and the lesser countries. For one thing, the Russians had plenty of space. Had any other country in Europe lost to an invader as much territory as the Germans conquered in Russia in 1941, it would have been completely overrun. Not so Russia. In the second place, Stalin was determined to permit no breakthrough by the German armies. The Soviet general staff, accordingly, had prepared a "defense in depth" into which the German armies repeatedly plunged, but through which they were never able to break. Though the Russian armies were pushed back and their lines were bent here and there, they avoided encirclement and remained intact. And the farther the Russians retreated, the farther the Germans advanced, the greater the strain became on German supply lines, especially since much of the territory through which the Germans advanced was deliberately devastated by the Russians themselves in accordance with a "scorched-earth" policy. Moreover, Russian guerrillas behind the invading armies menaced the German lines of communication. Soviet foresight in establishing many of Russia's newest and finest factories in eastern Russia or even east of the Urals and the swift transfer of some industries from the areas of invasion to safer regions to the east made possible the continued supply of Russian armies after the Germans had conquered regions previously considered the industrial heart of Russia. Space, time, weather, and Russian foresight and military skill all contributed to prevent the decisive victory which the Germans sought. In 1941 the Soviet armies punctured the myth of Nazi military invincibility.

When the German retreat in December, 1941, had threatened to become a rout, Hitler had summarily dismissed Field Marshal von Brauchitsch and had dismissed or relieved all but one of the older and experienced field commanders in the Russian theater of operations. He himself personally assumed command of the army, and thereafter held both the position of supreme commander of the German armed forces and commander-in-chief of the army. But the tasks which Hitler thus took upon himself were beyond his ability. Furthermore, in the succeeding years, which called for a greater effort on the home front than during 1939–1941, Hitler rarely left his military headquarters where he became less and less accessible. He lost personal touch with the military fronts, too, for between 1941 and 1945 he visited the armies at the front not more than twice. In the eyes of some military experts, Hitler's assumption of personal command in December, 1941, marked the turning point in the German conduct of the war.

The Battle of the Atlantic

Although the German attack upon Russia had compelled the Nazis to abandon their attempt to put Britain out of the war by the use of airplanes, they still hoped that the same end might be accomplished by their submarines. If the latter could successfully cut off the British from their overseas sources of supplies, England would be doomed.

To wage the battle of the Atlantic, Germany was more favorably situated than in the First World War. She had many more submarine and airplane bases, and they were more widely scattered—from Norway to the Pyrenees. It was much more difficult than in the previous conflict, therefore, for Great Britain to block German submarines by minefields, nets, and the like. Furthermore, many of the German submarines were larger and able to range farther than in the First World War. The Germans had still another advantage over 1917 in the ability of reconnaissance planes to inform submarine commanders of the location of British merchant ships which might otherwise escape detection.

On the other hand, the difficulty of the task of obtaining goods from abroad was greatly increased for Britain over what it had been in the First World War. In the first place, Hitler's conquest of Norway, Denmark, Holland, and France closed to the British some of their normal and near-by sources of supply. The longer hauls required to secure needed commodities from the New World or other overseas regions placed an added burden upon the British merchant marine. In the second place, Italy's entrance into the war against Britain practically closed the Mediterranean to British merchant ships, thus increasing the time and distance required for trips around the Cape of Good Hope to the Near and Middle East. At the same time Mussolini's determination to conquer Egypt and British East Africa made it more than ever necessary for the British to send supplies to those regions to meet the Axis threat. Great Britain, therefore, actually required more merchant ships than in 1917 to meet her needs.

Although British airplanes almost nightly bombed the most menacing German submarine bases on the Continent, the chief defensive measure against submarine attacks was the use of convoys protected by British warships. But the British were woefully short of destroyers, so that many convoys became relatively easy prey through lack of adequate protection. It was this desperate British need of added destroyers for convoy duty that led to the exchange of fifty over-age American destroyers for leases for United States air and naval bases in the western hemisphere in 1940. But the British were also handicapped in their convoy work by lack of some of the bases which they and the Americans had used effectively in the war against the German submarines in 1917. In 1938, Great Britain had surrendered all admiralty rights and harbor defenses in Eire, and, since Eire had declared her neutrality in the Second World War, the harbors of southern Ireland were closed to British warships.

By 1941 it was becoming apparent that the rate of destruction of British merchant ships was so great as to constitute a very real threat to Britain's ability to transport to her shores the foodstuffs and supplies without which she could not hope to continue the war. In May, 1941, the British admiralty revealed that German mines and air and sea raiders on British ships and ships in British service had, since the beginning of the war, sunk more than 1400 merchantmen, totaling more than 6,000,000 tons. Of this number 885 were British ships. It appeared that Britain's greatest difficulties in the battle of the Atlantic could be solved only if she obtained more merchant ships and more aerial and naval protection.

Meanwhile, the United States had begun to take steps to assist the British in the battle of the Atlantic. Early in 1941 the American Congress had passed the Lend-Lease Act to provide "the tools" for Britain to use in her struggle for existence. But it soon became clear to Americans that to produce the weapons of war was not enough. They must be put into Britain's hands if they were to be used in the fight in defense of democracy. The heavy toll of the German campaign against shipping, it appeared, might defeat the whole purpose of the Lend-Lease Act.

To assist in checking the ravages of the German submarines, the United States navy therefore inaugurated a "neutrality patrol system" to warn peaceful shipping of the presence of raiding submarines and airplanes. Then, on April 9, 1941, Secretary of State Hull and the Danish minister to the United States signed an agreement giving the United States the right to establish air bases and other military and naval facilities in Greenland. For all practical purposes the island was placed under the protective custody of the United States for the duration of the war. American bases in Greenland would flank the "Great Circle" shipping route between North America and Britain and would greatly strengthen the American naval and air patrol eastward to within three miles of the Nazi-proclaimed blockade zone. The increased efficiency of the American patrol made possible the shifting to other zones of some British naval vessels which had been operating in the western Atlantic. Furthermore, since British shipyards were overcrowded with new construction and repair work, many British ships, even warships, were repaired in American drydocks.

On June 9, 1941, it was learned that a German submarine had deliberately sunk an American freighter in the mid-Atlantic far outside the combat zone. Passengers and crew had been left in open boats far from land. On June 14, President Roosevelt ordered the immediate "freezing" of the assets in the United States of Germany and Italy and eight other states occupied or controlled by them. Two days later the American government ordered the closing of all German consulates and bureaus of information in the United States because their "improper and unwarranted" activities were inimical to the welfare of the United States. On June 19, both Germany and Italy ordered American consulates in their countries closed, whereupon the United States ordered the closing of Italian consulates also. In June, American troops landed in Iceland "to supplement and eventually to replace" British forces which had occupied that island since May, 1940. Shortly thereafter the United States navy extended its "neutrality patrol" as far as that island, some 3000 miles from New York.

Obviously the United States was determined to aid Britain in her struggle to prevent a Nazi-dominated world. But obviously Americans, as well as other peoples, desired to know what sort of world was envisaged in case the Nazis were defeated. An answer was given in the so-called Atlantic Charter, issued (August 14, 1941) by President Roosevelt and Prime Minister Churchill as the result of a meeting which they held at sea off the coast of Newfoundland. In a manner somewhat reminiscent of President Wilson's Fourteen Points, these two leaders set forth the common principles in the national policies of the United States and Great Britain on which they based their hopes for a better future for the world. They declared that:

First, Their countries seek no aggrandizement, territorial or other;

Second, They desire to see no territorial changes that do not accord with the .freely expressed wishes of the people concerned;

Third, They respect the right of all peoples to choose the form of government under which they will live; and they wish to see sovereign rights and self-government restored to those who have been forcibly deprived of them;

Fourth, They will endeavor, with due respect for their existing obligations, to further the enjoyment of all states, great or small, victor or vanquished, of access, on equal terms, to the trade and to the raw materials of the world which are needed for their economic prosperity;

Fifth, They desire to bring about the fullest collaboration between all nations in the economic field with the object of securing, for all, improved labor standards, economic adjustment, and social security;

Sixth, After the final destruction of the Nazi tyranny, they hope to see established a peace which will afford to all nations the means of dwelling in safety within their own boundaries, and which will afford assurance that all the men in all the lands, live out their lives in freedom from fear and want;

Seventh, Such a peace should enable all men to traverse the high seas and oceans without hindrance;

Eighth, They believe that all of the nations of the world, for realistic as well as spiritual reasons, must come to the abandonment of the use of force. Since no future peace can be maintained if land, sea, or air armaments continue to be employed by nations which threaten, or may threaten, aggression outside of their frontiers, they believe, pending the establishment of a wider and permanent system of general security, that the disarmament of such nations is essential. They will likewise aid and encourage all other practicable measures which will lighten for peace-loving peoples the crushing burdens of armaments.

A comparison of the Atlantic Charter and the Fourteen Points [6] reveals similarities and differences. One of the latter, especially significant, was the renunciation of any aim at territorial aggrandizement.

During the autumn of 1941 the United States further extended its aid in the battle against Nazi U-boats. In September its naval vessels began to assist in protecting convoys across the Atlantic. On the other hand, in order to prevent the increasing flow of lend-lease supplies to Great Britain, Russia, and the other Allies, German submarines redoubled their attacks on merchant ships, and began to seek out American destroyers engaged in patrol and convoy duty. When on September 4 an American destroyer was attacked by a German submarine, President Roosevelt announced that thereafter the navy "would shoot on sight" any Axis submarine observed anywhere in the Atlantic. In October, a second destroyer suffered some

[6] See page 90.

loss of life in an engagement with a German U-boat and another was sunk with the loss of about one hundred of her crew.

In November, Congress repealed part of the Neutrality Act of 1939 in order to permit the arming of American merchant ships and to give them permission to carry cargoes into ports of belligerent countries. As the year 1941 drew to a close, therefore, it seemed quite possible that war might be precipitated between the United States and Germany by the course of events in the Atlantic. It was not in the Atlantic, however, but in the Pacific that the events occurred which plunged the United States into the Second World War. Those events are discussed in Chapter XXII. It must suffice here to point out that, after the Japanese attack on Pearl Harbor, both Germany and Italy on December 11 declared war on the United States.

Chapter XXI

THE DEFEAT OF THE AXIS

IN EUROPE

U P to the autumn of 1942 Hitler's armies almost without interruption had continued their successful conquest of Europe. In the closing months of that year, however, thanks to the staying power of the British, finally supplemented by the tremendous man power and industrial resources of Russia and the United States, the German armies were halted. In 1943 they lost the initiative on all fronts. But Hitler conceived of no great strategic idea to alter this situation and fell back upon the policy of living upon "the capital sum of space" which the Germans had already conquered, insisting upon an inelastic defense of all territory held. In the succeeding years, however, they were driven out of their conquered lands and were ultimately forced back behind the Reich's boundaries. In 1945 the forces of the "United Nations" overran the devastated Fatherland, all German military resistance collapsed, and Hitler and some of his close Nazi associates died amid the flames and ruins of the German capital.

A United Front

Among the chief factors which had contributed to the Nazi victories in the first three years of the war were: (1) unity of command, which made possible quick decisions on the conduct of military operations; (2) a large and well-trained army, which enabled the high command to throw into any one theater of the war greater man power than the enemy; (3) superiority in aircraft and mechanized equipment, which provided the Nazis with the means to overwhelm their foes no matter how courageous the latter might be; (4) possession of the initiative, which allowed the Germans to choose where and when they would strike each overpowering blow. Until all or most of these advantages had been shifted to the Allies, the latter could have little hope of victory.

To this end the first step seemed to be the creation of a united front. On January 1, 1942, twenty-six states, which had declared war against the Axis, became the United Nations by signing in Washington a declaration in

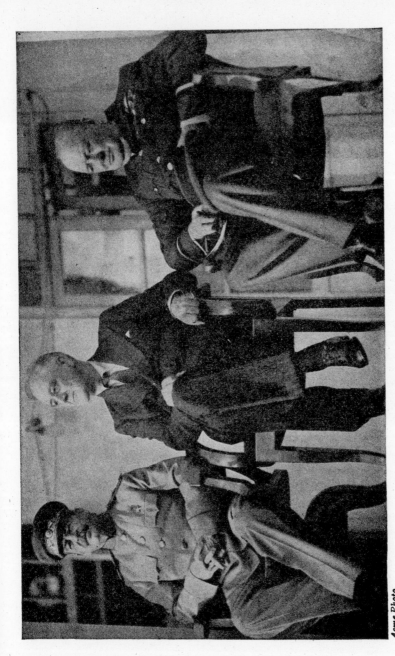

THE "BIG THREE" OF THE UNITED NATIONS
Stalin, Roosevelt, and Churchill at Teheran

which each subscribed to the principles set forth in the Atlantic Charter, promised to employ its full resources, military or economic, against those members of the Axis and their adherents with which it was at war, and agreed not to make a separate armistice or peace with the enemies.

The achievement of general unity in the strategic sphere was, of course, fundamental to the whole Allied war effort. Strategic decisions rested with the heads of the various governments, and during December, 1941, important diplomatic conferences were held in Washington by Prime Minister Churchill and President Roosevelt, in Moscow by British Foreign Secretary Eden and Premier Stalin, and in Chungking by the British General Wavell, the American General Brett, and Generalissimo Chiang Kai-shek. As the basis of the Allied strategy it was agreed, in general, that the major foe was Germany, for it was argued with reason that, whereas the defeat of Japan would not necessarily entail the defeat of Germany, the defeat of the latter would inevitably bring the ruin of Japan.

To maintain and increase the close co-operation of the four major anti-Axis powers, more conferences were held in the succeeding years: at Washington in June, 1942; at Casablanca, French Morocco, in January, 1943; at Quebec in August, 1943; at Moscow in October, 1943; at Cairo, Egypt, and at Teheran, Iran, in November, 1943; again at Quebec in September, 1944; and at Yalta, Crimea, in February, 1945. As the result of these various conferences, attended in most cases by Churchill and Roosevelt and their military staffs and at Teheran and Yalta by Stalin as well, definite plans were made for the invasion of North Africa, for the invasion of Sicily and the knocking-out of Italy, for the general advance against Germany, and for the defeat of Japan.

Prime Minister Churchill had early pointed out that the first period of the global struggle that was initiated at Pearl Harbor must be one of consultation, combination, and preparation until the Allies had acquired the necessary overwhelming superiority in man power and equipment and the shipping tonnage to give the Allied armies power to cross the seas and oceans separating them from the enemy. The length of this period must depend, he had said, on the vigor of the effort put into production in industries and shipyards.

Although Great Britain, Russia, Canada, and Australia bent every effort to the increasing of their national production of war materials, it was realized that it must be the production of the United States which would decisively tip the scales against the Axis powers. With that thought in mind President Roosevelt ordered the American war-production schedules for 1942 set at 60,000 aircraft, 45,000 tanks, 20,000 antiaircraft guns, and 8,000,000 tons of merchant ships. Moreover, in order to shorten the war and speed the day of victory, the United States decided to expand tremendously the already existing lend-lease system and to make greater efforts to meet the needs of Soviet Russia. By the northern route through Murmansk and Archangel and by the southern route through Iran supplies were forwarded to the Soviet armies so that by October 31, 1943, Russia had received under lend-lease arrangements 7000 planes, 3500 tanks, and 195,000 motor vehicles.

The United States also played a decisive role in tipping the scales against the Axis in the matter of fighting man power. In 1942 the armed forces of the United States increased from slightly more than 2,000,000 to 7,000,000 men. By the close of 1942 more than 1,500,000 United States troops were in service outside the American continent. A combined chiefs-of-staff organization was established in Washington by the United States and Great Britain as a step toward the creation of suitable machinery for co-ordinating their military efforts. Eventually Anglo-American military co-operation reached the point where the armies of the two countries were so meshed in the European theater of war that they constituted one fighting force. By the fall of 1942 that fighting force was large enough and well enough equipped to enable the Allies to enter the second phase of the war as outlined by Churchill, namely, the period of liberation, in which territories lost to the Axis would be recovered.

The Expulsion of the Axis from Africa

The first indication of a definite turn in the tide of the war came in North Africa. Events in that theater had been subject to swift and startling changes ever since Mussolini had taken Italy into the conflict and had started out to conquer an empire at the expense of Great Britain. In September, 1940, the Italians had advanced to Sidi Barrani within the frontiers of Egypt, only to be hurled back by the British, who between December, 1940, and February, 1941, advanced as far as El Agheila, to the west of Bengasi. Then, in April, 1941, the Italians, reinforced by German divisions and commanded by the German General Erwin Rommel, struck with superior force and within a few days were once more back within Egypt. Seven months later the tables had again been turned when the British, themselves reinforced by a new armored division, assumed the offensive in November, 1941, and by the end of the year they were again back at El Agheila.

But by January, 1942, Rommel had received enough supplies to counterattack, and he succeeded in recapturing the important port of Bengasi. Four months later the Axis forces, having in the meantime gained a superiority in heavy tanks, heavy guns, and antitank guns, again drove to the east. At first the British held fast, and Rommel lost heavily in tanks, but in June, 1942, the British tank force was successfully ambushed and lost some

THE MEDITERRANEAN AREA IN THE SECOND WORLD WAR

220 out of 300 tanks. Thus weakened, the British were forced to fall back. When they finally halted at El Alamein, they had retreated four hundred miles and had lost 80,000 men. The Axis forces were only sixty miles from Alexandria, whose fall was momentarily expected. In anticipation of a triumphal entry Mussolini hastened to North Africa.

But at El Alamein the British held a strong natural position, a front only forty miles wide protected on the north by the sea and on the south by the Qattara depression, in which tanks could not maneuver. Frontal attacks by Rommel's forces in July and again late in August, 1942, were successfully beaten back by the reinforced British. Meanwhile, the British Eighth Army had been given a new commander, General Sir Bernard Montgomery, and was being reorganized and re-equipped with the help of the United States. Huge convoys arrived with reinforcements and much-needed supplies, including heavier guns and heavier tanks. Rommel too received some fresh troops and added supplies, but by the fall of 1942 it was estimated that the Eighth Army had a superiority of four to one in guns and three to one in tanks and planes.

On the night of October 23, 1942, General Montgomery launched an attack designed to drive Rommel not only out of Egypt but out of Libya as well. It was no easy task to dislodge the Axis troops from their Alamein positions, and heavy losses were suffered on both sides. But on November 2 a furious armored battle was fought; Rommel's left flank was penetrated; and on November 3 a general Axis retreat began. By November 6 over 20,000 Axis prisoners had been counted, and 600 planes, 350 tanks, 400 guns, and thousands of vehicles had been captured or disabled. Four days later Rommel's forces had been driven back across the Egyptian frontier. Alexandria and the Suez Canal were again safe.

But General Montgomery did not halt his troops. On November 20 forces of the British Eighth Army entered Bengasi. Rommel tried to establish a line once more at El Agheila, the farthest point to which the British forces had ever penetrated in their previous advances into Libya, but, when Montgomery brought up his heavy guns and prepared for a second devastating barrage, the Axis retreat was resumed. On January 23, 1943, the victorious Eighth Army entered the port of Tripoli. The final battle for Egypt was over; the Italian empire in Africa was lost.

Meanwhile, far to the west the Allies had struck a surprise blow in accordance with plans decided upon at a conference between Churchill and Roosevelt in Washington in June, 1942. On November 7, shortly after Montgomery's break through the Axis position at El Alamein, the first of the great Allied amphibious undertakings was successfully carried through in French North Africa under the command of the American General Dwight D. Eisenhower. Convoys of more than 500 ships escorted by 350 naval craft arrived off the coast of Morocco and Algeria, bringing British and American troops from widely separated ports of embarkation, while airborne troops were flown from Great Britain to seize the French air field at Oran. In the early morning hours of November 8 Allied troops were landed at the port of Algiers, which surrendered that day. Other landings were made at Casablanca on the Atlantic coast of Morocco and at the strong naval base at Oran in Algeria.

It had been hoped that the French garrisons in North Africa, totaling some 100,000 men, would welcome and not oppose the Allied landings. President Roosevelt and "Fighting French" General de Gaulle made appeals to the French forces to co-operate. But their appeals were not everywhere heeded. At Oran the resistance was somewhat serious, and at Casablanca there was stiff fighting. In order to facilitate the occupation of North Africa, therefore, General Eisenhower recognized as head of the civil administration the Anglophobe, Vichyite Admiral Darlan, who happened to be in Algiers. On November 11 the latter issued orders to cease fire all over North Africa, but not before some 2000 casualties had been inflicted on the Allies by the French forces. Germany's reply to French collaboration with the Allies in North Africa was the occupation of hitherto "unoccupied France." An effort, too, was made by the Germans to seize the French fleet of some 75 warships and auxiliaries at Toulon, but in this they were balked by the French naval personnel, who on November 27 scuttled their ships in the harbor.

Meanwhile, the Anglo-American forces, once established in Algiers, had started a drive toward Bizerte and Tunis, the naval base and capital respectively of French Tunisia. At the end of November they were within fifteen miles of Tunis, but by then the Axis powers, under the command of the German General von Arnim, had established themselves in control. At the same time, in southern Tunisia General Rommel held the powerful defensive Mareth Line, which the French had built to protect Tunisia against an attack from Libya. In March, 1943, however, Montgomery outflanked and smashed this line and thereafter slowly drove Rommel's army northward until eventually his troops and Arnim's were concentrated in a small section of northeastern Tunisia. Rommel thereupon surrendered his command and withdrew to the European mainland. On May 7 both Bizerte and Tunis surrendered, and the Axis forces withdrew onto Cape Bon. But with the Allies in control of the sea there was no possibility of escape. On May 12, 1943, all resistance ended and General von Arnim and some 225,000 troops surrendered. Africa was cleared of Axis forces.

The Collapse of Italian Fascism

Stalin had for some time been calling for the establishment of a second Allied front in Europe to relieve the Nazi pressure on Russia. Although he would have preferred the second front in western Europe, Churchill and Roosevelt, in a spectacular conference held at Casablanca in January, 1943, had decided to invade Sicily, and four months later, in May, at a similar conference in Washington, they agreed that the principal Allied objective in 1943 should be the knocking out of Italy.

In May, accordingly, the Allied air force directed the full weight of its attack against the small Italian islands between Sicily and North Africa, against the ports and air fields of Sicily itself, and against Naples, the chief supply base for Sicily in southern Italy. On June 12, 1943, the first tangible results of these bombings came when the Italian key island of Pantelleria, which virtually commanded the sea passage between Sicily and Tunis, was forced to surrender by Allied bombers even before any troops had been landed to attack it.

Four weeks later the Allied invasion of Sicily began with the landing of parachute and glider troops several miles back from the southern and eastern coasts. On the morning of July 10 this air invasion was followed by large-scale landings from an armada of 2700 vessels of all descriptions. The invasion was made on the southeast corner of the island, and in the first two days some 80,000 men and 300 tanks were put ashore. Eventually the expeditionary forces consisted of 150,000 American, British, and Canadian troops. Axis resistance was weak; by July 15 the bridgeheads were firmly established, and the advance northward began, the British Eighth Army up the east coast and the American Seventh Army north and northwest from the south coast. On July 22, in a surprise thrust across the island against only half-hearted resistance, the Americans captured the important port of Palermo. By the close of July the Axis force of nearly 100,000 men had been compressed into a small triangle in northeastern Sicily. Progress was slowed by Axis mines and demolitions and by stiff German resistance from hill positions dominating the roads. But the Allies pushed steadily forward and finally entered the port of Messina on August 17, 1943, whereupon all organized resistance in Sicily ceased.

Meanwhile, military events in North Africa and Sicily had had political repercussions in Italy. Italian military authorities were in despair and asserted that only greatly increased aid from Germany could save Italy. But Hitler apparently refused Mussolini's plea for such assistance and insisted instead that the Axis must withdraw to northern Italy. Mussolini returned from his interview with Hitler to find Rome greatly disturbed by its first air attack, which had occurred on July 18. The political effect of Hitler's refusal to send additional aid, the Allied gains in Sicily, and the prospect of further air raids on Rome was not long delayed. On July 24 the Fascist Grand Council demanded Mussolini's resignation. On the next day he was summoned to the royal palace, informed of his dismissal by the king, and arrested as he left. Marshal Pietro Badoglio, the victor in Ethiopia, was appointed by the king to succeed Mussolini as premier, and he at once decreed the formal dissolution of the Fascist Party. But he also announced that Italy would continue in the war.

For a time the Allies suspended their air attacks upon the Italian mainland in the hope that Badoglio might open negotiations. But when he made no such move, the air attacks were resumed on August 1, and air and naval forces began preparing the way for a landing in Italy. Coastal defenses were shelled, and important communications centers—Naples, Salerno, Taranto, Foggia, and others—were bombed. On August 13 a second raid was made on Rome. Almost immediately thereafter the Badoglio government opened secret negotiations with the Allies, and ultimately, on September 3, 1943, at Syracuse, a representative of the Badoglio government agreed to the terms of an armistice laid down by General Eisenhower. At the latter's insistence it was agreed that the armistice should be announced at the time the Allies considered most advantageous.

The Allied Invasion of Italy

A few hours before the armistice was signed, General Montgomery's Eighth Army had crossed the Messina Straits, landed on the Italian "toe," and begun advancing northward and eastward. Five days later, on September 8, a daring amphibious landing of American and British troops, under the command of General Mark W. Clark of the United States Fifth Army, was made at Salerno, southeast of Naples. From Rome Badoglio announced the armistice, instructed the Italian forces to cease all opposition to the Allies, and then moved the headquarters of the Italian government within the Allied lines.

Meanwhile, the fate of General Clark's Fifth Army at Salerno hung in the balance. For two weeks the Germans had been preparing defensive positions above Salerno Bay, and they had five divisions of troops in the vicinity. Soon the weight of German reinforcements against General Clark threatened to drive his forces into the sea. The situation was critical. But Allied air power, operating from Sicily and North Africa, dropped thousands of tons of bombs on the enemy forces while British dreadnoughts poured in shells from their powerful guns. At the same time, from the south, the Eighth Army pushed rapidly northward against the weak resistance of the retreating Germans. Eventually, on September 17, the two Allied armies made contact and established a continuous front along 225 miles from Salerno to the Adriatic. Two weeks later they entered Naples, and on October 13 the Badoglio government formally declared war upon Germany.

Thus in three months the Allies successfully carried out two major amphibious operations against the Axis forces; conquered Sicily, Sardinia, Corsica, and the Italian mainland to a line some thirty miles north of Naples; and brought about the overthrow of Mussolini, the collapse of Fascism, and the surrender of Victor Emmanuel's government. These achievements had secured for the Allies the bulk of the Italian navy and valuable air bases in Italy, especially the one at Foggia, from which the Allies could readily bomb Hungary and the Balkans. Indirect but valuable results of these successes, of course, were the freeing of the Mediterranean for the use of Allied shipping engaged in carrying supplies to Egypt, to India, and, via Iran, to Russia; the release of Allied naval units in the Mediterranean for use elsewhere; the drain upon German man power as Italian forces in France, the Balkans, the Aegean, and even Italy had to be replaced by loyal Nazi troops; and the enhancement of Allied prestige.

For months after the capture of Naples the Allies were stalled before the Germans' so-called Gustav Line, constructed along the Rapido and Garigliano rivers. Late in January, 1944, they tried to outflank this line or to force a German withdrawal from it by an amphibious landing of American and British forces in the vicinity of Nettuno and Anzio, but Allied troops from this Anzio beachhead, as it was called, were unable to isolate the German armies fighting to the south. Heavy German reinforcements were rushed to attack the beachhead in an effort to drive the Allied forces into the sea, but the Germans in turn failed to dislodge the Allies, and a stalemate resulted in this sector. Similarly, against the Gustav Line, despite terrific air bombardments of the monastery and town of Cassino in February and March, the Allies failed to make much progress.

On the night of May 11, however, the Italian front was galvanized into action when an all-out attack was launched along the Rapido and Garigliano rivers. Both rivers were crossed; the Gustav Line was breached; and on May 18 Cassino was at last taken. Four days later the Anzio beachhead forces also launched an attack, and on May 25 contact was made between these forces and the Allied Fifth Army advancing from the south. On June 3 the German line in the Alban Hills was pierced, and the way was opened for an advance upon Rome. The German General Albert Kesselring thereupon proposed that Rome be considered an open city and agreed to with-

SWITZERLAND
Brenner Pass
AUSTRIA
Graz
HUNGARY
Bolzano
Udine
Postumia
Zagreb
Drava R.
Brescia
Verona
Trieste
Fiume
Milan
Padua
Venice
Mantua
Po R.
Sava R.
Parma
Ferrara
Pola
Genoa
Modena
Bologna
Ravenna
YUGOSLAVIA
La Spezia
Rimini
BATTLELINE SEPT. 5, 1944
Pisa
SAN MARINO
Zara
Florence
Ancona
Leghorn
Sebenico
Spalato
Siena
Perugia
ELBA
Bastia
San Benedetto
Grosseto
Tiber
Ragusa
CORSICA
Viterbo
Terni
Pescara
BATTLELINE NOV. 2, 1943
Ajaccio
Vatican City
Rome
ROME TAKEN JUNE 4, 1944
Ostia
Albano
Isernia
Cisterna
Cassino
Foggia
Terranova
ALLIES LANDED JAN. 22, 1944
Anzio
Nettuno
Formia
Capua
Bari
Littoria
Gaeta
Benevento
Brindisi
Caserta
Potenza
SARDINIA
Naples
NAPLES TAKEN OCT. 1, 1943
Castellammare
Salerno
Taranto
Gulf of Taranto
Leuca
Sapri
TYRRHENIAN
Sibari
Cagliari
ALLIES LANDED SEPT. 8, 1943
Cosenza
SEA
Catanzaro
LIPARI IS.
Messina
San Giovanni
MEDITERRANEAN
Reggio
Palermo
BRITISH LANDED SEPT. 2, 1943
Trapani
Bizerte
SICILY
Catania
Tunis
Agrigento
Syracuse
Vittoria
Ragusa
Scale of Miles
0 25 50 75 100
PANTELLERIA
TUNISIA
Sousse
LAMPEDUSA
MALTA
ADRIATIC SEA

THE ALLIED ADVANCE IN ITALY, 1943–1944

draw his troops. On June 4, 1944, in the face of only sporadic resistance, Allied troops entered the Eternal City, which thus became the first of Europe's capitals to be liberated from the Nazis.

In the succeeding weeks the Allies also liberated Perugio, Siena, Arezzo, and the important ports of Leghorn on the Ligurian Sea and Ancona on the Adriatic. The Germans, reinforced, made a determined effort to hold Pisa and Florence and the Arno River; they destroyed all the Florentine bridges across the Arno except one and blocked that by demolishing long-cherished buildings at each end. But on August 6, 1944, Allied troops stormed across the river into the heart of historic Florence. On September 2 Pisa, also, was captured, and the Nazis thereupon withdrew to their Gothic Line protecting the Po Valley where they prepared to make a desperate stand against the victorious Allies. Though little headway was made by the latter in the succeeding months, they continued to exert strong pressure against the Gothic Line in order to prevent the Nazis from shifting troops to their other hard-pressed fronts.

Stalingrad and the Great Russian Offensives of 1943–1944

While in 1942–1943 the Western Allies were conquering North Africa, invading Italy, and bringing about the collapse of Fascism, events of even greater importance had been occurring in Russia. In 1942 the Germans had launched a double-pronged offensive, aimed at the capture of Baku on the Caspian and Stalingrad on the Volga. If these could be taken, the important Volga communications would be cut, and the bulk of the Russian forces operating to the north would be deprived of their access to the rich petroleum resources of the Caucasus. By the last of August the Germans were in the Caucasus and their Panzer divisions had reached the suburbs of Stalingrad with a superiority in men, tanks, and planes. Constantly their heavy artillery and planes bombed the city until its factories and apartments became mere rubble. But Stalin had ordered his namesake defended to the death and the Germans never succeeded in taking it. Nor did they capture Baku or the oil fields of the Caucasus. The days when they could advance irresistibly were past.

Instead, the Russians, timing their operations with those of the Allies in North Africa and using reserves brought from Siberia, in November, 1942, launched a great counteroffensive both north and south of Stalingrad. Before the close of that month Soviet troops had cut off from retreat the twenty-two divisions of Nazis besieging that city. On February 3, 1943, the last units of the half-starved and abandoned German forces surrendered. The German loss of materials at Stalingrad was far greater than the Allied

SWEDEN

FINLAND

White
Sea

Medvezhegorsk

Lake
Onega

Helsinki

Stockholm

Vibor

Lake
Ladoga

Leningrad

Tallinn

Narva

Vologda

BALTIC SEA

ESTONIA

L. Ilmen

Pskov

Novgorod

U. S. S. R.

Riga

LATVIA

Staraya
Russa

Velikiye

Kalinin

Yaroslavl

Volga

LITHUANIA

Dvinsk

L.

Nevel

Rzhev

Moscow

Gorki

R.

EAST
PRUSSIA

Vilna

Polotsk

Vitebsk

Vyasma

Orsha

Smolensk

Minsk

Warsaw

Tula

Brest-
Litovsk   Pripet

Zhlobin

R.

Bryansk

Penza

POLAND

Gomel

Orel

Sarny

Korosten

Kursk

Tambov

Voronezh

Saratov

Lwow

Kiev

Shepetovka

R.

Volga

Zhmerinka

Vinnitsa

Smela

Kharkov

Jassy

Krivoi Rog

Kremen-
chug

Dniepropetrovsk

Donets

Stalingrad

R.

Don

Odessa

Nikolayev

Zaporozhye

Taganrog

RUMANIA

PEREKOP
ISTHMUS

Sea of
Azov

Rostov

Astra-
khan

Elista

CASPIAN SEA

Bucharest

CRIMEA

Sevastopol

Kerch

Armavir

Mozdok

Danube   R.   Constanta

Novorossisk

Maikop

BULGARIA

Tuapse

Makhach-
kala

TURKEY

BLACK   SEA

CAUCASUS MTS.

CARPATHIAN MTS.

Dniester

Bessarabia

THE RUSSIAN COUNTEROFFENSIVES OF 1942–1944

losses at Dunkirk. Meanwhile, in their winter offensive of 1942–1943 the Russian forces had driven more than 400 miles westward from Stalingrad, had cleared the Germans out of some 185,000 square miles of Russian territory, and had again shattered the myth of Nazi invincibility.

During the next summer the Soviet armies retained their initiative, met some 218 Nazi and satellite divisions, drove them back with heavy losses, and liberated still more tens of thousands of square miles of Russian territory. When their summer offensive of 1943 closed at the beginning of November, the battle line in Russia extended roughly southward from Leningrad, which had been relieved in January, 1943, to a point east of Vitebsk, then south to a point east of Gomel, then in general along the east bank of the Dnieper River to the Black Sea.

Without letup, however, the Russian winter offensive of 1943–1944 succeeded the summer drive. On November 6, Kiev, the capital of the Ukraine, was recaptured by Soviet armies, which drove relentlessly westward until in January, 1944, they crossed into pre-1939 Poland south of the Pripet marshes. Other troops, operating to the southwest pushed the Germans back until by the end of March, 1944, the Russians had reached the Carpathian Mountains, where for sixty miles they stood along the former Czechoslovak frontier. Still others had crossed the Dniester River into pre-1940 Rumania. In April, Odessa was liberated and in May, Sevastopol and the Crimea were cleared of Nazi forces. Meanwhile, in the Leningrad area the Soviet armies had recaptured the south shore of the Gulf of Finland nearly to Narva in former Estonia, had opened the main railway from Leningrad to Moscow, and had driven to the east shore of Lake Peipus. The map on page 539 shows the extensive gains made by the Soviet armies in their offensives from November, 1942 to May, 1944. Thanks to the fighting prowess of the Russian soldiers, the strategic ability of the Soviet high command, the efficiency of the Red Army railway battalions in restoring lines of communication, the ability of Soviet factories to provide military equipment, and the great assistance of lend-lease supplies, which during 1943 had increased "from a trickle to a torrent," the German armies had been driven almost entirely out of the Soviet Union.

D-Day

By this time the United States and Great Britain were ready to open the second front in France which Russia had so long urged. The Allies at length were well supplied with the weapons of war, for, in addition to British production, between May, 1940 and September, 1943, American industry had produced and delivered 123,000 aircraft, 349,000 airplane engines, 53,000 tanks, 93,000 artillery weapons, and 1,233,000 motor trucks, and in most of these categories more than half of the total production had come in the first eight months of 1943. During the same period the United States had completed 2380 fighting ships and auxiliaries, and 13,000 landing craft.

By the close of 1943, too, the German submarine campaign had been overcome. A number of factors had contributed to the defeat of the U-boats. Hundreds of destroyer-escort ships and corvettes had been built in the United States and Canada, and these had given increased protection to convoys. More effective patrols off the American coast and long-range patrol planes, operating from Newfoundland, Labrador, Greenland, Iceland, and the British Isles, had driven the submarines back into the mid-Atlantic. In this region, beyond the range of airplanes, squadrons of submarines, so-called wolf-packs, had for a time been very destructive, but eventually small escort aircraft carriers had been built and attached to convoys. Many new devices and techniques—radar, for instance—for detecting planes and ships had also been perfected by scientists and put into use. Despite German submarines, therefore, by the spring of 1944 tremendous quantities of all types of military supplies and millions of men had been gathered in Great Britain for the projected invasion of western Europe.

One of Hitler's boasts was that he had converted Europe into an impregnable fortress. But, as President Roosevelt pointed out, it was "a fortress without a roof," a fact which the Allied air forces had disclosed with increasing clarity from 1942 on. In that year the RAF had adopted the technique of saturation night bombing, that is, bombing by a large number of planes over a single target in a short space of time. On the night of May 30, 1942, for example, some 1043 bombers had dropped 1500 tons of bombs on Cologne in less than two hours, and in the hundred days following the Cologne raid, there had been 43 large-scale raids on German cities by forces of from 200 to 600 bombers.

During 1942 the tide of plane production had definitely and overwhelmingly turned in favor of the Allies. By the close of that year, British production was about equal to that of Germany and Italy combined, while American production was running ahead of that of all the Axis powers taken together. Furthermore, there had been a great increase in the production of heavy four-motor bombers capable of carrying bomb loads three times greater than earlier planes. By September, planes were dropping on German targets the so-called block-busters, huge two-ton and four-ton bombs which greatly increased the destruction. In 1942, the United States Army Air Force had also joined in operations against Nazi Europe.

In 1943 the Allied air forces had greatly increased their bombing offensives. Thousands of tons of bombs had been dropped on the German industrial cities of Essen, Düsseldorf, Cologne, Hamburg, Wilhelmshaven,

Rostock, Lübeck, Berlin, Nuremberg, Munich, Karlsruhe, Mainz, and Frankfort; on the French cities of Lille, Le Creusot, and Rennes, and on the industrial suburbs of Paris; on the submarine bases of Lorient, St. Nazaire, Brest, Cherbourg, Dunkirk, and Rotterdam. In the first half of 1943 the RAF alone had dropped thirty-five times the weight of bombs dropped by the Luftwaffe over Britain in all its 1940–1941 attacks. In ten days beginning on the night of July 24, the RAF and the USAAF in eight raids had dropped upon the single city of Hamburg a total bomb tonnage far greater than that dropped on London during a period of nearly a year at the height of the Nazi air blitz. Hamburg had been nearly eliminated as a functioning port and production center. The destruction of power plants, railway junctions, canals, synthetic-petroleum and synthetic-rubber plants, and factories producing munitions, airplane engines, and aircraft undoubtedly had constituted a "softening up" of Germany.

At a conference at Teheran (November 28–December 1, 1943) Churchill, Roosevelt, and Stalin and their military staffs had mapped out plans for a concerted attack on Hitler's Fortress Europe during 1944. According to the announcement made at the close of their conference, they had agreed upon the scope and timing of operations which would be undertaken from the east, the west, and the south with the aim of annihilating the German forces. "No power on earth," they proclaimed, "can prevent our destroying the German armies by land, their U-boats by sea, and their war plants from the air. Our attacks will be relentless and increasing."

The Allies during the ensuing months devoted themselves to preparation, organization, and the further aerial softening-up of Fortress Europe. Many changes were made in the high command to make ready for the coming invasion of Europe, but only a few can be mentioned here. General Eisenhower, the successful supreme Allied commander in the Mediterranean, was appointed supreme Allied commander in western Europe, and General Sir Harold Alexander was made commander-in-chief of all Allied forces in Italy. General Montgomery was transferred from command of the British Eighth Army in Italy to command of all British ground forces in western Europe, and General Omar N. Bradley was made the senior commander of the United States ground forces in the same area. General Clark continued to command the Anglo-American Fifth Army in Italy, but General Sir Oliver Leese was put in command of the British Eighth Army, which was operating on the Adriatic flank of the Italian front. The Germans, for their part, appointed Field Marshal Rommel to head the Nazi anti-invasion command. Under his direction efforts were made by the Germans to strengthen still further the already "impregnable" Atlantic Wall.

Against this Atlantic Wall, on June 6, 1944, American, British, and Canadian troops stormed ashore on the beaches of Normandy as the van-

THE ALLIED HIGH COMMAND FOR THE INVASION OF
WESTERN EUROPE

Seated, left to right: Air Chief Marshal Sir Arthur Tedder, deputy supreme
commander; General Dwight D. Eisenhower, supreme commander;
General Sir Bernard L. Montgomery, commander of British land armies

Standing, left to right: General Omar N. Bradley, commander of American
ground forces; Sir Bertram Ramsey, naval commander-in-chief; Air
Marshal Trafford L. Leigh-Mallory, air commander-in-chief; General
Walter B. Smith, chief of staff

guard of the greatest amphibious operation in all history. Brought to the
coast in an invasion fleet of 3200 transports and landing craft, they were
supported from the sea by 800 fighting craft of all sizes and from the skies
by thousands of planes. While landings from the sea were made in four
separate areas on the coast north of Bayeux and Caen, three divisions of
Allied troops were also dropped behind the beaches by parachutes and
gliders in what was probably the greatest air-borne operation yet under-

THE BATTLE OF NORMANDY, 1944

taken. By the close of D-day, that is, at the end of the first twenty-four
hours, 250,000 Allied troops had been successfully landed in Normandy.
Their immediate task was to hold and consolidate their beachheads. This
they did. By June 8 contact had been established between the sea-borne and
air-borne troops. Despite the much-vaunted strength of Hitler's Atlantic
Wall, it had been successfully breached. Allied sea, air, and land forces had
carried through the "greatest and most successful combined operation of
its type in military history."

It had been feared by many in Allied countries—and confidently believed
by the Nazis—that any invasion force which might land on the beaches of

western Europe could be wiped out or driven into the sea before it could consolidate its position or secure the necessary heavy mechanized equipment for a successful advance inland. What the outcome would have been had the Germans immediately rushed their armored divisions to the Allied bridgehead in Normandy can only be conjectured, for this they failed to do. Apparently Hitler and the high command believed that the landing in Normandy did not represent the main Allied effort. To this misconception the Allies had contributed in several ways. The pre-invasion bombings—carried on for a considerable period before D-day—had been deliberately scattered along the whole northwestern coast of France so as to give no accurate indication of the location of the projected landings. Then before and during D-day feints were made from England toward the Pas de Calais area by General George S. Patton's American Third Army, and on D-day an Allied naval demonstration was also made off that same coast. A feint was even made toward Norway by Allied planes and troops in Scotland. For weeks after D-day the Germans, in doubt as to the real purpose of the Allies, failed to transfer their troops from the Pas de Calais area to meet the invasion forces in Normandy.

It had also been feared in Allied circles that without an adequate harbor in Allied hands it would be impossible to land the heavy tanks and armored equipment that were necessary for a successful advance inland against an enemy who could easily and quickly move up such equipment over his land-based lines of communication. The ineffectiveness of landing forces without adequate harbor facilities had been strongly driven home by the Allied failures in Norway in 1940. And the terrible casualties which might accompany any attempt to capture a well-fortified harbor in enemy hands —even a futile attempt—had been startlingly revealed by an Allied attack on Dieppe in August, 1942. Furthermore, the disastrous effects which an Atlantic storm might have on the landing of men and supplies on open beaches was well recognized. To overcome these Allied handicaps, two artificial harbors had been constructed in England. Floating breakwaters and piers were towed across the Channel to anchorages off the newly won beaches in Normandy, and on the day after D-day thousands of men began constructing the harbors, which were designed for a total capacity larger than that of Cherbourg. Although a terrific storm on June 19–22 wrecked one of these harbors, the other continued to function and provided sheltered anchorages for Allied shipping and piers to expedite the flow of supplies and men. In the first four weeks after D-day more than 1,000,000 men, 183,500 vehicles, and 650,000 tons of supplies were landed despite German submarines, aircraft, mines, and other defensive weapons.

The Liberation of France and Belgium

Meanwhile, the Allied military operations had been proceeding ashore. In these operations the British and Canadian forces had been assigned a role which was primarily defensive while that of the Americans was offensive. The British seized and held the vital area around Caen, the hinge of the whole Allied position in Normandy. They thus protected the flank of the American troops, who struck inland across the peninsula and on June 18 reached the sea on the west side of the Cotentin peninsula. Cherbourg, on the tip of the peninsula, was thus isolated from the main German forces, and the American troops next stormed that city, which surrendered on June 26. Though the harbor had been wrecked by the Germans, Allied engineers here—as in Naples earlier—were soon at work preparing it for the use of Allied shipping. The capture of this important port made more secure the Allied foothold in Normandy and made more unlikely the success of any German attempt to expel the invaders from the Continent.

But for a time it seemed that the Nazis might manage to hold the Allies within the peninsula. For a month the latter made little apparent progress. Time was required, of course, for the Allies to build up reserves of men and matériel on the mainland. Nevertheless, even after they had landed more than a million men and hundreds of thousands of tons of supplies, the Germans continued successfully to localize the fighting within a small area. Allied casualties were heavy, and progress for a time was measured by yards. In the seven weeks after D-day the Allies suffered 105,765 casualties and gained only some 4800 square miles of territory.

Although the German armies appeared to be holding the Allies successfully, some disaffection and anti-Hitler sentiment had developed in the Reich, as indicated by an attempt to assassinate the Führer and the general staff on July 20, 1944. The plot was the work of a considerable number of military leaders, including a few generals on the general staff, and of certain key civilians. Although some of the generals present at the time of the bomb explosion died as the result of their injuries, Hitler himself escaped serious injury. The Nazis struck swiftly to purge Germany of anti-Hitler elements and to gain further control of the armed forces. Himmler, head of the Gestapo, was at once appointed "to make sure that there would be no second July 20." A court of honor was instituted "to inquire into the antecedents of field marshals and generals of the army to find out who took part in any way in the attempt," and during the succeeding weeks nearly 5000 persons—including some general staff officers and field commanders —were executed.

Meanwhile, on July 18 General Bradley's American First Army ultimately had captured strategically important St. Lô. It next blasted a corridor through the German lines between St. Lô and Periers to Coutances (July 25–28), and then held the gap open while armored divisions of General Patton's American Third Army poured through. Suddenly the entire situation in France was changed from a war of position to a blitzkrieg. American spearheads at once struck south across the Breton peninsula, which was cut off when they reached the Loire River near Nantes on August 6. Other spearheads turned westward and, since the Germans had practically stripped Brittany to send reinforcements to Normandy, they met little opposition. The ports of St. Malo, Brest, Lorient, and St. Nazaire were soon invested.

The American armies now had plenty of room in which to maneuver, and spearheads were soon striking eastward toward Paris and northward toward the Seine. In conjunction with the British forces to the north an attempt was made to encircle the German Seventh Army southwest of Caen, but the Nazi armored units escaped, though German casualties were estimated at between 50,000 and 100,000. The remnants of the German Seventh Army next endeavored to withdraw across the Seine and to establish a new line behind that river. But by August 27 the Allies had established four bridgeheads across the Seine, and these obviously made such a line untenable.

While the Germans were thus hurriedly withdrawing and the Allies swiftly advancing in northern France, another blow was struck (August 15) at the German positions in that country when the American Seventh Army, consisting of American, French, and British forces, landed from the sea and from the air along a 100-mile stretch of the Mediterranean coast of France between Cannes and Toulon. Their purpose was to advance up the Rhone valley and sever communications between the Germans in France and those in Italy, and they met relatively light opposition. Within two weeks the important ports of Toulon and Marseilles were both captured. Although this Allied landing in the south came too late to be of much assistance to the operations in northern France, it did serve to demoralize still further the German defense.

To that demoralization the French themselves also contributed. Almost from the moment of the Allied landings in Normandy the French Forces of the Interior (FFI), or the *Maquis* as they were sometimes called, had been active in sabotage. German lines of communications had been disrupted, munition dumps blown up, troops ambushed, villages and towns wrested from Nazi hands. On August 12 the commander of the FFI had urged the underground units to strike hard at once to prevent reinforcements from reaching the Germans, and his forces had responded with alacrity. By August 22, it was announced, twenty-two departments in Brit-

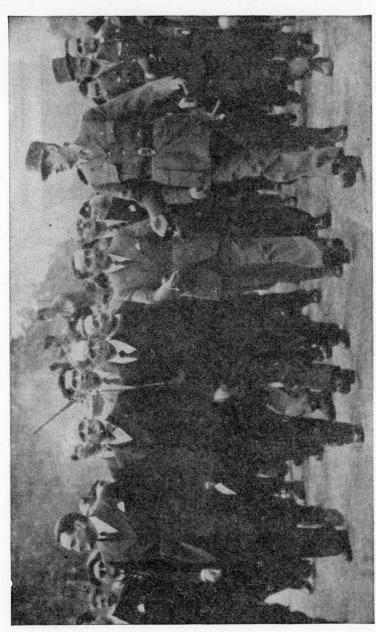

THE LIBERATION OF PARIS IN 1944

General Charles de Gaulle and General Jacques Leclerc leading a parade on the Champs-Élysées

tany and southern France had been liberated by the FFI, and all roads leading into Italy had come into their control. Everywhere the French tricolor
was being hoisted.

The most spectacular uprising of the FFI came in Paris, where a general
insurrection was ordered on August 19, when the Allied forces had advanced to within a score of miles of the capital. After four days of fighting
the German garrison in Paris was defeated. Although on August 23 the
German commander in the capital sought an armistice, on the next day
he repudiated it, resumed fighting, and threatened to destroy the city. The
FFI thereupon requested Allied aid, and General Patton sent to their
assistance the French General Jacques Leclerc with a French tank division
and some American troops. On August 25 the French capital, after four
years of Nazi occupation, was once more free.

But these stirring events in Paris did not retard the advance of the Allied
armies, which rushed to the north and the east. The very tactics that four
years earlier had swept the Germans on to Paris—plunging tank columns,
swarms of planes, mobile artillery, motorized assault forces—were now
turned against them. "Speed and power were welded into a weapon of
destruction. Tank columns kept thrusting far ahead, and it seemed a
mystery how they kept engines fueled, guns firing, men fed, and repairs
made." The roads of northern France, once the Allied vanguard had passed,
resembled vast conveyor belts, with trucks moving in endless streams, one
column going up and the other rolling back. Battlefields of the First World
War—the Marne, Château-Thierry, Verdun, Soissons, the Somme, Laon,
Reims, the Argonne, Sedan, Namur, Liége—where forces had been locked
in combat for weeks or months in the struggle of 1914–1918, were reached
and swiftly passed. Brussels was liberated on September 3 and the important port of Antwerp a few hours later. By the middle of September the
Allied armies had reached the German frontier in Belgium and Luxembourg and were facing the strong Nazi West Wall.

On the night of September 17 a bold attempt was made to outflank the
West Wall in the north when a large Allied air-borne force was dropped
in the Netherlands near Eindhoven, Nijmegen, and Arnhem. For days
these troops held on against heavy odds while the British Second Army in
Belgium battled its way northward toward them. Although the British
succeeded in moving the front up through Eindhoven and Nijmegen to the
south bank of the Lek River (the Dutch Rhine), German opposition was
so strong that they were unable to establish a bridgehead across this last river
barrier south of Arnhem. On the nights of September 25 and 26 the air-
borne force near the latter city was finally withdrawn, but, of the more
than 6500 men originally landed there, only 2000 got back. The failure of
this spectacular effort to outflank the West Wall appeared to leave the Allies

no alternative but to blast their way through the heavily defended, skill-fully constructed line. But that task was part of the battle of Germany, which is discussed later in this chapter.

At the close of what may be called the second battle of France, the com-bined operations of the Allied armies and the French Forces of the Interior had liberated nearly all of France, Belgium, and Luxembourg, and a part of the Netherlands. They had cost the Germans, according to Allied head-quarters, at least 750,000 men killed, wounded, and captured. Approxi-mately 400,000 prisoners had been taken, not counting the forces trapped in various invested ports. At the close of the battle the Allied forces stood, roughly speaking, on the German frontier from the Lek River in the north to the southern boundary of Luxembourg, and then on the west bank of the Moselle River south to the Belfort gap and the Swiss frontier.

The Collapse of Hitler's Satellite States

Meanwhile, in the east, terrific drives were being made by the Soviet armies on various sectors of their two-thousand-mile front extending from the Arctic to the Black Sea. Although at times during the summer and fall of 1944 the Russians were conducting several offensives simultaneously, for the sake of convenience and clarity each drive will be discussed as a unit as it was waged to the close of the year. In a general way, the eastern front was divided into four major sectors: (1) the Finnish front, extending from the Arctic to the Gulf of Finland, northwest of Leningrad; (2) the northern Russian front, extending from the Gulf of Finland southward to Vitebsk; (3) the central Russian front, confronting the German Fatherland Line and extending roughly from Vitebsk southward to the Pripet marshes; and (4) the southern Russian front, extending from the Pripet River west of the marshes south to Jassy in Bessarabia and then east to the Dniester River.[1]

On June 10, only four days after D-day in France, the Russians launched a strong offensive against the Finnish lines on the Karelian Isthmus. Nine days later the Finnish Mannerheim Line was breached, and on the next day Viborg (Viipuri) was captured. When it became obvious that Ger-many could not send aid to the Finns, President Ryti, who was committed to a continuance of the war, was forced to resign, and Field Marshall Man-nerheim was elected to succeed him. After the new government, on Russia's insistence, had broken relations with the Reich and had demanded the withdrawal of German troops from Finland, an armistice was signed on September 19 by the Soviet Union and Great Britain, acting on behalf of all

[1] See map on page 539.

the United Nations which were at war with Finland. The war was ended on that front.

Three days after the capture of Viborg, the second Russian offensive of the summer of 1944 was launched on the central front against the German Fatherland Line. With the fall of Minsk on July 3, the German defense system in White Russia was broken, and the weight and speed of the Russian offensive thereafter for a time swept aside all Nazi efforts to halt it. During August the Russians pushed on toward Warsaw but in the face of ever-stiffening resistance. The farther the Russians advanced, of course— and they had already advanced some four hundred miles on this front— the greater became their problem of supply and reinforcement, especially since the gauge of the railways in Poland had to be adjusted to accommodate Soviet rolling stock. Nevertheless, on September 14 they reached the Vistula and captured Praga, the Warsaw suburb on the east bank of that river. They failed, however, to establish a bridgehead across the Vistula, which the Germans were determined to hold as the last strong line of defense against an invasion of central Germany from the east.

One tragic result of the Russian failure to force the Vistula at this time came in Warsaw. As early as August 1, the Polish Home Army in Warsaw, an underground organization commanded by General Bor,[2] had risen against the Germans in that city. Whether General Bor's purpose was to liberate the city in the name of the Polish government in exile before the Russians reached Warsaw or whether he expected the speed of the Russian advance to continue so that aid would soon be forthcoming in the battle to free the Polish capital, is a matter of dispute. But long before the Russians had reached the Vistula, the Germans had launched strong tank attacks against the Polish Home Army. The failure of the Russians to force the Vistula again sealed the fate of the Polish capital for the time being. On October 2 the Home Army in that city gave up the struggle and surrendered to the Germans, who claimed that 200,000 Poles had lost their lives in the uprising. Many accused the Soviet government of deliberately failing to succor Warsaw in order to discredit and bring pressure upon the Polish government in exile, which was unwilling to recognize the Polish-Soviet boundary established in 1939.

However that may be, when the battle line in Poland became somewhat stabilized in September, it extended roughly from East Prussia to the Carpathians along the east banks of the Narew and Vistula rivers. Reserves of

---

[2] General Bor's real name was Komorowski. He had commanded a cavalry brigade in the campaign of September, 1939, and afterwards he helped to organize the Polish underground army, of which he was appointed commander-in-chief by Premier Sikorski in July, 1943.

men and supplies would have to be built up and lines of communication and transportation would have to be strengthened before Soviet troops could launch another effective drive on this front. A glance at the map, however, will reveal the vast extent of the Russian gains during some two months of fighting. The Germans had been hurled back in Poland beyond the line from which they had first launched their attack upon Russia in 1941.

The third Russian drive was launched on the northern front late in July. It had two major objectives: to push the Germans out of the Baltic republics and to protect the northern flank of the Soviet armies advancing into Poland. By the close of the year the Germans had been expelled from Latvia, from Estonia except for the Windau peninsula between the Gulf of Riga and the Baltic, and from Lithuania except for the district about Memel.

On the front south of the Pripet marshes the Soviet armies launched their fourth major offensive early in July. This offensive had two prongs. One struck southwestward with the apparent purpose of protecting the left flank of the armies advancing on the central front and of occupying Galicia with its extensive grain fields and oil wells. The second prong eventually turned southeastward into the Balkans with the purpose of driving the Germans out of that whole region, which Russia had for generations sought to make her own sphere of influence. By August 5, Soviet troops, driving southwestward, had captured Cholm, Lublin, Jaroslav, Przemysl, and Lwow (Lemberg), had taken the richest part of the Galician oil fields—thus depriving Hitler of one of his sources of natural petroleum—and Russian patrols were reported to be within thirty miles of Cracow, the gateway to central Germany. But as in 1915, so in 1944, the German defenses before that important industrial and strategic city held.

Stopped on the west, the Soviet armies on August 20 next launched a drive southeastward from Jassy in Bessarabia. The effect of the Russian advance was immediate in Bucharest. On August 23, King Michael dismissed the Antonescu government; appointed a new cabinet headed by his former aide, General Senatescu, and including both Maniu and Bratianu; ordered Rumanian troops to cease hostilities with the United Nations; and instructed them instead to fight at the side of the Allied armies to drive the Germans from Rumania and to liberate Transylvania from foreign occupation. Hostilities immediately broke out between German and Rumanian troops in Bucharest and Constanza and in the Ploesti oil fields, but on August 28 the Rumanian high command announced that all German resistance in Bucharest had ended. Three days later the Russians entered the Rumanian capital, and on September 13, 1944, an armistice was signed on behalf of the governments of the Soviet Union, Great Britain, and the United States.

In the meantime, Bulgaria had seen the handwriting on the wall and had been attempting to extricate herself from her position as a German satellite. On August 26 it was announced in Sofia that Bulgaria had withdrawn from the war, and on September 5, after a change in governments, Bulgaria proclaimed that she intended to carry out a "rigorous and unconditional policy of neutrality," that she would disarm all German forces in her territory, and that she considered as invalid her signature of the tripartite and anti-Comintern pacts. But these steps were not sufficient to satisfy Soviet Russia, which on the same day declared war on Bulgaria. The latter thereupon declared war upon Germany and asked Russia for an armistice. On September 16, Sofia was occupied by Soviet troops. On October 28, an armistice was signed with Bulgaria by representatives of the Soviet Union, Great Britain, and the United States. One more Hitler satellite state thus collapsed, and Bulgaria lost her gamble that she could secure Macedonia and Western Thrace by allying herself with Hitler's Third Reich.

The defection of Rumania and Bulgaria made the position of Nazi forces in Greece and the Aegean islands precarious. In September they began to withdraw and to move up the Vardar and Morava valleys toward Hungary. To hasten the Nazi withdrawal from Greece proper and, apparently, to prevent Russia from establishing a sphere of influence in that country, British forces landed at Patras in the northern Peloponnesus on October 4. They encountered only light German resistance as they advanced across the isthmus of Corinth, and ten days later Athens and its port of Piraeus were liberated. The northward advance continued, and with the help of Greek guerrilla forces most of the country was cleared of German troops by early November.

Meanwhile, the military forces of four countries had been co-operating to drive the Germans out of Albania and Yugoslavia. In the latter country patriot armies had never been completely suppressed by the Nazis, and now under the leadership of Marshal Tito they played a valiant role in the liberation of their country. They were assisted from the east by Bulgarian troops under Soviet command, from the Adriatic by British forces which were landed in Albania, Montenegro, and Herzegovina, and in the north by the Russian army moving west from Rumania. On October 20, Belgrade was liberated, and by the end of 1944, Albania, most of the Dalmatian coast, and eastern and southern Yugoslavia had been freed from Nazi domination. Only in the northwest, in Croatia and in Bosnia, did the Germans still retain control.

Farther north Russian and Rumanian armies had struck across the eastern Carpathians and the Transylvanian Alps into Hungary. With Soviet troops only fifty miles from Budapest, Horthy decided to seek an armistice. But Szalasy, leader of the Nazi Arrow Cross organization in Hungary, opposed such a step and was supported by German troops which had already occupied the capital. On December 16, Horthy was forced to resign and was interned in Germany. Szalasy thereupon headed a new government, appointed a regency council, and in an order of the day to the army announced: "Either we destroy or we will be destroyed." That the latter would be the outcome seemed indicated by the course of succeeding events, for the Russians continued to advance in Hungary and on November 4 the heavy guns of Soviet forces began to shell Budapest. The Nazis were determined to fight to the end in the Hungarian capital, however, and, though the city was ultimately surrounded and large sections of it were occupied by Russian troops, it was not until February 13, 1945, that Budapest was captured. Meanwhile, a Hungarian provisional government, chosen by a national assembly of delegates elected in the liberated territory, had announced a liberal political and agrarian policy and had promised to assist in the destruction of Hitlerism. On December 29 it had declared war on Germany. It also sought an armistice with the Allies, and on January 20, 1945, such a document was signed with Hungary by Russia, Great Britain, and the United States on behalf of the United Nations.

By this time, too, the liberation of Czechoslovakia had been begun. On the north Soviet troops from Poland had begun driving across the Carpathians into Slovakia and Ruthenia as early as September, 1944. Simultaneously other Soviet forces had advanced northward from Hungary. By the close of October, Ruthenia had been freed, and the Russians had begun to move westward into Slovakia. Operations here, however, were closely related to those in Hungary, and it was only after the fall of Budapest that substantial gains were made. But on April 4, 1945, the Russians captured Bratislava, the capital of Slovakia, and thus put the last and weakest of Hitler's satellite states out of the war.

Germany's Last Offensive

In the autumn of 1918, when it seemed likely that the Allies might soon be able to invade the Fatherland, German military leaders had forced the civilian government to sue for an armistice. If the decision had been left to the German high command in 1944, it is possible that in the fall of that year Germany might have again asked for a cessation of hostilities, for militarily the Third Reich was in a much more serious plight than the Kaiser's Germany had been in 1918. But the Nazi leaders well knew that their fate would be sealed when Germany surrendered, and consequently

FROM STALINGRAD TO CENTRAL EUROPE

A Red Army patrol in the outskirts of Stalingrad, and Red Army troops
crossing the Danube on the way to Budapest

reasoned that they personally had everything to gain and nothing much to lose by forcing the German armies to fight on. The Nazi forces would therefore have to be utterly defeated and the Reich overrun by the Allies before hostilities would cease. And before Germany could be invaded from the west, the allegedly impregnable West Wall would have to be smashed.

In the closing months of 1944 the Allies prepared for their eventual frontal attack. They lessened their supply problem by opening the Scheldt so that the extensive harbor facilities and railway connections of Antwerp could be utilized by the Allied armies facing the lower Rhineland. They cleared most of Alsace and Lorraine of German troops and reached the upper Rhine at Strasbourg. They captured Aachen and thus proved that important strategic bulwarks of the West Wall could be taken. The next stage in Allied activity in the west seemed likely to be a terrific smash across the Roer and Meuse rivers onto the Cologne plain. In fact, on December 16, 1944, General Bradley was at the supreme headquarters at Versailles for a conference on the details of the planned American winter offensive.

For some weeks, however, Hitler had been planning a counter-blow against the Allies, aimed at capturing Antwerp, driving a wedge between British and American armies, and annihilating the Allied forces to be surrounded in the area of Aachen-Liége. To the German commanders Hitler declared: "For months our entire industry has been working solely for this at the cost of the Eastern Front. . . . We must attack and start a war of movement once more." Surprise and speed, he declared, would be the most important factors, and the operation would be supported, he promised, by several thousand of the best and most modern German fighters which would secure, at least temporarily, air supremacy.

Thanks, in part, to their own careful planning and, in part, to failures of the United States military command, the Germans certainly achieved surprise when on December 16 they threw 250,000 men, 1200 tanks, and hundreds of new jet planes and V-bombs against a thin American line in the Ardennes held by only six divisions. German armored spearheads smashed through broken, difficult country and achieved a major break-through, advancing farther in a week than the Allied troops struggling toward Cologne had moved in the preceding three months of hard fighting. Despite the heroic resistance of American forces, especially at St. Vith and Bastogne, the Nazis drove on until they were within three miles of the Meuse near Dinant and Givet and less than that distance from the headquarters of the American First Army with its huge supply dumps and tanks of precious gasoline.

The Allied answer to this last gamble of the Germans was "the greatest and most rapid mobilization in history." All available reserves in the Central Army Group were used to strengthen the flanks of the penetration, and troops of the Northern Army Group were deployed to hold the line of the Meuse and the vital Liége area. When the German advance severed telephone communications between General Bradley on the south of the bulge and the headquarters of his First and Ninth Armies, the command of these armies and their supporting air forces was at once shifted to General Montgomery to the north of the bulge. The latter was able to contain the Germans and to prevent their advance upon Liége. At the same time the American Third Army was moved against the southern flank of the bulge and given the task of relieving the forces at Bastogne, which had refused to surrender. At the tip of the salient other American forces, aided by some units of the British Second Army, blunted the German attack and then turned it back. After the first week of the offensive, the weather cleared, and thousands of American and British planes assisted the Allied ground forces by bombing German concentrations and supply lines.

In less than two weeks the tide had turned. On December 28 Bastogne was liberated, and by the end of December nearly a third of the lost territory had been recovered. At the end of a month's hard fighting most of the bulge had been eliminated, though it was not until the end of January, 1945, that the lines were back where they had been on December 16. Both sides had lost heavily in men and equipment. Although the Germans had gained an initial tactical success and had imposed a delay of almost six weeks on the main Allied offensive in the West, they had failed to capture their primary objectives. They had lost 220,000 men, including 110,000 prisoners, and more than 1400 tanks and assault guns. To carry out the operation, moreover, the German high command had weakened the Reich in strategic reserves and resources which were needed to meet the powerful Soviet offensive which had begun.

The Battle of Germany

For, before the Belgian bulge had been completely obliterated, the Soviet armies had launched their expected winter offensive in Poland. The preceding four months had been utilized by the Russians to repair roads and railways through an area some 250 miles deep which they had conquered in their summer offensive of 1944. Time had been required, too, to bring up new weapons and men and to accumulate sufficient supplies for an extended offensive. At the close of their summer operations in Poland, it will be recalled, the Russians had stood roughly on a line running from the East Prussian frontier along the Narew and Vistula rivers to the Carpathians. On January 12, 1945, Stalin unleashed his new attack, which the Germans characterized as the "greatest of all time." Everywhere the Soviet forces, estimated at more than 3,000,000 men, seemed to move irresistibly forward.

GERMANY AND GERMAN-HELD TERRITORY, JANUARY 1, 1945

By the middle of March the Russians had invaded Germany and held a line extending along the Oder River from its mouth, opposite Stettin, up to the Neisse River and along the latter toward the Czechoslovak frontier. Silesia, except for beseiged Breslau, had been occupied, depriving the Germans of their second most important arsenal. Except for isolated forces near Gdynia, Danzig, and Königsberg, the Baltic had been cleared of Germans from Latvia to Stettin. According to Marshal Stalin, 800,000 Germans had been killed and more than 350,000 captured.

The next powerful blow against the Nazi homeland was delivered in the west, from which the German high command had transferred some twenty divisions to bolster the Reich's defense along the Oder River. With a decided superiority in men, supplies, mechanized equipment, and air power, the Western Allies—once the Belgian bulge had been eliminated—prepared to drive out or destroy the German armies on the left bank of the Rhine. Preceded and accompanied by terrific RAF and AAF blows, the initial attack was launched on February 8 by Canadian and British troops southeast of Nijmegen, who captured Cleve and Goch in the lower Rhineland. Immediately thereafter, on February 23, the American Ninth and First Armies swung into action, forced their way across the Roer, penetrated the German defense system, and made the whole West Wall vulnerable to envelopment from behind.

In the first of the ensuing envelopment movements the American Ninth Army cut behind the West Wall to the north, and on March 3 met the Canadians pushing southward. With the capture of much-battered Cologne three days later by the American First Army, the left bank of the Rhine from that city to the Netherlands was practically cleared of German troops.

The second enveloping movement began when forces of the American First Army struck up the Rhine from Cologne. So swiftly did they move that on March 8 they seized intact the Ludendorff bridge across the Rhine at Remagen just before the Germans planned to destroy it. This unexpected conquest was at once exploited by General Courtney H. Hodges to establish a bridgehead for the Allies firmly and securely on the east bank of the Rhine. In the meantime, the American Third Army west of the Moselle had been driving toward Coblenz, and on March 7 armored units reached the Rhine below that city. A junction was made by forces of the Third and First Armies with the result that the Rhine was cleared of German forces from Cologne to Coblenz.

The third of these enveloping movements came when the Third Army quickly drove to the west bank of the Moselle, crossed the river, and then slashed behind the German forces defending the Saar and the Palatinate against a frontal attack by the American Seventh Army. By March 23 the rich Saar Basin, the Reich's third most important coal and industrial dis-

TEN STEPS IN VICTORY OF THE RHINE

trict, had been seized, and German forces had been captured or driven out of the Palatinate except for a small bridgehead across from Karlsruhe.

The battle of the West Wall was one of the greatest Allied victories of the war. In a single month following the opening of the American offensive on February 23, the Allies had smashed through what was considered the world's most formidable defense system, over territory which the Germans had claimed was impassable and against fortifications which they boasted were impregnable. In the course of this achievement they had destroyed five German armies as military units. For 250 miles the Allied armies at last stood on the Rhine—the first time that any invading armies had achieved this feat since the days of Napoleon. Field Marshal Karl von Rundstedt was hastily removed, and Field Marshal Albert Kesselring was rushed from Italy to replace him as commander-in-chief of the German forces in the west.

But the Allies were not content merely to drive the Nazis out of the Rhineland. The American First Army already had one bridgehead across the Rhine at Remagen; on the night of March 22 the American Third Army stormed across the river in force south of Mainz and established a second. On the next night the Rhine was bridged again when the Canadian First, the British Second, and the American Ninth Armies crossed the river in the vicinity of Wesel, while the First Allied Air-borne Army in the greatest single air-borne operation of the war landed beyond the Rhine on the Westphalian plain. Thousands of Allied airplanes provided an "umbrella" for the crossing of the lower Rhine and struck behind the German lines at concentration points and communication centers. Within a week the American Seventh and the French First also joined the drive into Germany and established bridgeheads north and south of Mannheim. Apparently the German armies in the west, weakened to bolster the eastern front against the Russians, were powerless to hold the line. What had been considered the most formidable defense system in the world—the West Wall and the Rhine combined—was utterly destroyed.

As in France after the German break-through of the Weygand Line in June, 1940, there was in Germany in April, 1945, no longer any coherent front in the west. The German armies there did not retreat; they collapsed. During the first two weeks of April the Allies in the west took more than 550,000 prisoners. The Nazis who had started the Second World War with a blitzkrieg into Poland now saw that war being brought to a close with a blitzkrieg within the Reich. And the very superhighways which Hitler had built for his own armies were used to speed up the Allied advance. In less than three weeks from the night it crossed the Rhine, the American Ninth Army had crossed the Elbe River near Magdeburg, only fifty miles from Berlin.

Meanwhile, a number of enveloping movements had been successfully carried out by the Allied commanders. Spearheads of the American First and Third Armies enveloped the great industrial city of Frankfort, which was occupied on March 29. A second encircling movement was completed around the Reich's most valuable industrial area, the Ruhr, when units of the American First and Ninth Armies made a junction near Lippstadt on April 1. The Germans had made their largest concentrations of troops in the west in this region, and hard fighting ensued within the Ruhr pocket. On April 18, however, all organized resistance in the Ruhr ceased. The Americans captured 325,000 prisoners in the pocket, which made the Ruhr debacle the worst German defeat in the war, worse even than the disaster at Stalingrad. A third enveloping movement was carried out by the Canadian First Army, which struck north to cut off the German forces in the Netherlands. It reached the Ems River across from Emden and with the help of paratroopers successfully drove across the northern Netherlands to the North Sea. By April 19 the Canadians had compressed the German forces, estimated at 80,000 men, into the small but densely populated area south and west of the Ijsselmeer. In that area Amsterdam and Rotterdam were located, and apparently the Germans planned to deprive the Allies of the Dutch ports as long as possible.

By April 21, four weeks after their crossing of the Rhine in force, the Allies had conquered a large part of western Germany. The British Second Army was in the suburbs of Bremen and close to Hamburg. The American Ninth Army had captured Magdeburg and held a bridgehead east of the Elbe. The American First had captured Halle and Leipzig and stood along the Mulde River. To the south the American Third had crossed into Czechoslovakia, and farther south the American Seventh had captured the Nazi shrine city of Nuremberg. To the southwest the French First Army had taken Stuttgart. During this period German losses in men and matériel had been enormous. The central group of American armies alone had taken 842,864 prisoners since crossing the Rhine. During the first three weeks of April, Allied fliers had practically eliminated the Luftwaffe as an effective force. During these weeks, too, incontrovertible evidence of the inhuman cruelty, brutality, and depravity of German Nazi and military leaders was found in the prison and concentration camps captured by American forces. Claims made earlier by the Russians of what they had found in similar camps in the east were fully substantiated by the discoveries in the west.

In order not to interfere with the Russian drive upon Berlin, General Eisenhower ordered the American Ninth and First Armies to halt their advance at the Elbe and Mulde rivers to await a junction with the Russian forces from the east, a junction which was made by patrols at Torgau on

April 25. Meanwhile, during March and the first half of April, while supplies and reinforcements were being gathered on the front facing Berlin, the Soviet armies had been active elsewhere. The Baltic area east of Stettin had been practically cleared of German forces with the capture of Gdynia, Danzig, and Königsberg. In the south, at the same time, Soviet forces had been moving west after their capture of Budapest, and on April 13 they had captured Vienna, the former capital of Austria.

Upon the capture of Vienna the Soviet armies on the Oder at once launched their final drive upon Berlin. On April 21, the assault upon the German capital began. Nazi fanatics called upon the inhabitants of the city to fight to the last man, and the ensuing struggle was bitter and destructive. But the Soviet forces were definitely superior in men and matériel, and they could not be stopped. On April 25, Marshal Gregory Zhukov's First White Russian Army and Marshal Ivan Konev's First Ukrainian Army completed the encirclement of Berlin and thereafter pressed their attack toward the heart of the capital.

The End of the War in Europe

Apparently the Nazis realized that the end was near. On April 24, Heinrich Himmler asked the Swedish government to arrange for him to meet General Eisenhower in order that he might surrender all German forces on the western front. But this offer, Himmler stipulated, was only for the Western Allies and did not include Russia. On April 26, the United States and Great Britain informed Sweden that the only acceptable terms were unconditional surrender to the three Allied governments on all fronts, and stated that the German forces should surrender to local commanders in the field. The final Nazi attempt to split the Allies thus failed.

The first of the ensuing mass surrenders occurred in Italy, where the American Fifth Army and the British Eighth Army had already launched a vigorous attack designed to drive the Germans beyond the Alps. The coveted key city of Bologna was captured on April 21; three days later the Allies crossed the Po River. Thereafter the Allied advance was swift and general as German opposition disintegrated and anti-Fascist Italian "Partisans" raised the standard of revolt behind the lines. By the end of April all important Italian cities, including Verona, Genoa, Milan, Venice, and Turin, had been liberated by the Allies and the Partisans. The futility of further Nazi resistance was recognized by the supreme German commander in Italy, General Heinrich von Vietinghoff, who on April 29 authorized the signing of an unconditional surrender for all German and Italian Fascist armies in northern Italy and southwestern Austria. The collapse of German resistance in Italy brought the death of Mussolini. On

Acme Photo (above), Press Association, Inc. (below)

THE COLLAPSE OF GERMANY IN 1945

Above: The German surrender at Allied headquarters in Reims (left to right: Major Wilhelm Oxenius; General Gustav Jodl, German chief of staff; Admiral Hans Georg Friedeburg)

Below: The meeting of Allied commanders in captured Berlin (left to right: Field Marshal Sir Bernard L. Montgomery, of Great Britain; General Dwight D. Eisenhower, of the United States; Marshal Gregory Zhukov, of Soviet Russia; General de Lattre de Tassigny, of France)

April 28, he and a few former Fascist leaders were captured near Como by Partisans, who quickly tried and executed them. Mussolini's body was taken to Milan, where it was hung by the heels to receive the scorn and vilification of the city's crowds—an ignominious end for the once proud, powerful, and ruthless Duce.

Hitler escaped an end quite so shameful as this. During the last months of the war, however, he had become a mental and physical wreck without the power to make decisions. In his last days, in the bunker beneath his Chancellery garden in Berlin, he blamed the army, the Nazi Party, the German people—everyone but himself—for the catastrophe which was engulfing the Fatherland. Finally, on May 1 it was officially announced over the Nazi radio that, fighting to the last against Bolshevism, he had fallen for Germany. Apparently he had committed suicide. On the day before his death, Hitler, it was further announced, had appointed Grand Admiral Karl Doenitz, director of the German U-boat campaign, as his successor. The latter at once declared that he was "resolved to continue the struggle against the Bolsheviks." On May 2, however, the Russians captured Berlin, together with some 150,000 German soldiers, and avenged Stalingrad. On that same day, too, the British Second Army, which had taken Bremen, captured Hamburg and Lübeck. Two days later all German forces in the Netherlands, Denmark, and northwestern Germany, including Helgoland and the Frisian Islands, surrendered to Marshal Montgomery.

In southern Germany, meanwhile, the American Third and Seventh and the French First Armies had been driving steadily eastward into the so-called "National Redoubt." By May 5, Freiburg, Ulm, Regensburg, Augsburg, Munich, Innsbruck, Salzburg, and Berchtesgaden had all been captured, and the American Seventh Army had crossed the Brenner Pass to form a junction with the Fifth in Italy. The American Third Army drove on into Czechoslovakia and by May 6 had captured Pilsen and Karlsbad and was approaching Prague.

With practically all of Germany occupied by Allied forces and with most of the German armies already captured in the field, an all-inclusive unconditional surrender to the Western Allies and Soviet Russia was finally signed at General Eisenhower's headquarters at Reims in the early morning hours of May 7 by General Gustav Jodl on behalf of the German high command. The latter agreed to issue orders to all German military, naval, and air authorities to cease active operations on May 9 at 12:01 A. M. Greenwich time, to remain in positions occupied at that time, and not to scuttle or damage any ship, vessel, or aircraft. This surrender was formally ratified in Berlin on May 8 when a similar document was signed by Field Marshal General Wilhelm Keitel (who had presented the armistice terms to the

French in 1940), General Admiral Hans George Friedeburg, and General Hans Jürgen Stumpff, commanders-in-chief respectively of the German army, navy, and air force.

And so Europe's most terrible war was brought to an end. As yet it is impossible to give an accurate picture of the gigantic toll of lives and wealth which it exacted; it will require years to make the necessary investigations and computations. The most reliable estimates of battle casualties placed the death toll at more than ten million men, with perhaps another ten million permanently disabled. The heaviest losses were sustained by Germany and Russia. American battle deaths in the war against the European dictators were placed at more than 160,000. In addition to battle casualties, however, millions of civilians had succumbed to disease or starvation or been murdered in Nazi concentration camps. The monetary costs of the war mounted to astronomical figures. The direct cost of waging the war was estimated at more than one trillion dollars, and to that figure would have to be added the cost of replacing destroyed or damaged property throughout Europe. Russia's loss as the result of the German invasion, for instance, was estimated at more than $100,000,000,000. The war which Hitler unleashed in Europe in September, 1939, undoubtedly took a greater toll of human and material resources than any other conflict in history.

But the Second World War did not end with the armistice in Europe. In 1941 the conflict had become a global war, and even after V-E day the fighting continued in the Far East.

Chapter XXII

JAPAN'S EARLY BLITZKRIEG

AND ULTIMATE COLLAPSE

AS early as 1894 Japan had begun to have dreams of an empire on the Asiatic mainland, and in the twentieth century she had succeeded in extending her economic and political control over extensive areas in Asia. By 1939 she had annexed Korea, established a puppet government in Manchuria, and obtained a strangle hold on China. The outbreak of the Second World War in that year, her military and political leaders thought, afforded Japan an exceptional opportunity to fulfill her long-cherished dream without the successful intervention of the Western powers, and in a highly successful blitzkrieg during 1941–1942 Japan extended her control over the areas which she had long coveted. But, unfortunately for Japan, she had clashed in 1941 with the United States, with the result that she was ultimately crushed by the tremendous industrial resources and naval and military might of that country. Japan emerged from the Second World War completely shorn of the overseas empire which she had so ruthlessly created.

The Situation in the Far East, 1939–1940

At the time Germany invaded Poland, Japan had already been engaged for more than two years in an undeclared war against China. By the opening of the year 1939 the Japanese had captured the great commercial cities of Tientsin, Peiping, Shanghai, Nanking, Hankow, and Canton, and had gained control of most of the main railways of that country. Outside the great cities, however, in practically every "occupied" province, Chinese guerrilla forces were operating only a few miles from the railway lines.

During the first half of 1939 Japanese forces seized the large and valuable Chinese island of Hainan, which dominated the coast of French Indo-China and lay in a position to menace the sea lane from Singapore to Hong Kong, and annexed the Spratley Islands, lying midway between Indo-China and Borneo. By these annexations Japan moved prophetically nearer the Netherlands East Indies, rich in petroleum and rubber.

When Hitler launched his invasion of Poland, Japan declared that she did not intend to become involved in the European conflict, but would "concentrate her efforts upon the settlement of the China affair." The war in Europe, it seemed, would certainly offer the Japanese an opportunity for increased freedom of action in the Far East if they could only force the Chinese Nationalist government to make peace. Events in 1939 demonstrated, however, that the Chinese could fight if they could continue to secure munitions and war supplies in sufficient quantities, but there remained to them only two major avenues of importation—from Indo-China and from Burma. The former was rendered useless when late in 1939 the Japanese cut the Hanoi-Nanning-Kweilin motor road. The second was closed when, after France's collapse in 1940, the Japanese forced Great Britain to suspend the transit of goods to China over the so-called Burma Road.

Germany's successful blitzkrieg in western Europe in May and June, 1940, had pronounced repercussions in the Far East, where Japan at once moved toward establishing her hegemony not only over the East Asiatic mainland but over the South Seas, too. "The present international situation is developing in a manner advantageous to Japan's national policy," declared the Japanese war minister on June 25. "We should not miss the present opportunity or we shall be blamed by posterity." In June, 1940, at the moment when Marshal Pétain was seeking to obtain an armistice with Germany, Japan forced France to agree that Japanese inspectors might be stationed at key points in Indo-China with power to supervise and control all traffic through that French colony. Moreover, Japanese troops moved up to the frontier of Indo-China, Japanese warships began patrolling its coast, and the Tokyo government called to the attention of Hitler and Mussolini Japan's claims for consideration in the disposal of French possessions in the Far East. Japan continued to exert pressure upon France, and eventually, on September 22, 1940, the latter agreed to permit the Japanese to establish three air bases in northern Indo-China and to maintain a limited number of troops at Haiphong, the chief port in that region.

The Immediate Antecedents of Pearl Harbor

With the European powers deeply involved in Hitler's attempt to establish his dominance in Europe, it appeared that the United States constituted the chief obstacle to Japan's dream of empire. As early as April, 1939, the former, by transferring the American fleet from the Atlantic to the Pacific, had taken one step to indicate disapproval of Tokyo's apparent determination to become more aggressive. Then, on July 26, as a step to place the United States in a position to use economic pressure, if necessary, to retard

THE FAR EAST, 1939–1940

Japan's plan for the "new order in East Asia," the American state department had given the six months' notice necessary to abrogate the existing Japanese-American commercial treaty. It was well known that for some time the United States had been the economic "lifeline" for Japan in her effort to conquer China. Four days after the French had been forced to admit the Japanese armed forces into Indo-China, President Roosevelt on September 26, 1940, placed an embargo on the export of all scrap steel and iron except to the western hemisphere and Great Britain. According to the Japanese press this American embargo made inevitable a clash between Japan and the United States. If Japanese expansionists considered that war was inevitable, then it must have been clear to them that such a war must be fought in the not distant future, for in 1940 the United States had embarked upon the building of a powerful "two-ocean" navy.

Japan's move in the diplomatic chess game came at once. On September 27, 1940, in Berlin, representatives of Germany, Italy, and Japan signed a ten-year military alliance in which they undertook "to assist one another with all political, economic, and military means when one of the three is attacked by a power at present not involved in the European war or in the Chinese-Japanese conflict." A second move came six months later when, on April 13, 1941, the Japanese and Soviet governments signed a five-year pact of nonaggression and neutrality. Following these treaties, Japan exerted further pressure upon France and, in June, 1941, forced the latter to sign military agreements which gave the Japanese an undoubted supremacy in Indo-China.

Again the United States and Great Britain protested. But this time they backed up their protests by acts. On July 25, 1941, both governments ordered Japanese assets frozen, and thus ended any important trade between their countries and Japan. The British government further announced its intention to cancel the existing trade treaties between Japan and Britain, India, and Burma. The United States followed this up on August 1 by placing an embargo on the export of aviation oil and gasoline, thus cutting off Japan from her oil supply in the United States. For some months Japan had been negotiating with the Netherlands East Indies in an effort to increase her supply of oil from those islands. Her negotiations had proved fruitless; in fact, following the United States embargo, the Netherlands East Indies suspended their trade agreement with Japan, thus threatening a further reduction of the latter's oil supply.

In August, Prince Konoye, the Japanese premier, urged a resumption of the Japanese-American negotiations which had been broken off in the preceding month. It was soon apparent, however, that the two governments were no nearer an agreement than before. The Japanese refused to retreat from the stand which they had taken earlier or to alter their policy regarding Asia, while the United States continued to refuse to recognize changes brought about by force or in violation of treaty rights. Negotiations once more came to a deadlock.

Apparently the Japanese militarists decided that the deadlock could be ended only by war, and that for the advantage of Japan war must be precipitated soon. For Britain and the United States were already taking steps to strengthen their own positions in the Far East by assisting Chiang Kai-shek. The United States had dispatched a military mission to Chungking, was helping to improve the reopened Burma Road, and was sending American fliers to aid the Chinese. Lend-lease aid had been promised to China at the very time when vital supplies of oil and steel were being cut off from Japan. Furthermore, a common front against Japan was being created in the Far East. The United States and Britain not only co-ordinated their Far Eastern policy but broadened their consultations to include the Netherlands East Indies, Australia, and China. In October, 1941, representatives of these states held a military conference in Manila to discuss joint defense plans, and in the succeeding weeks British reinforcements were sent to Singapore and two British capital ships, the *Prince of Wales* and the *Repulse,* were rushed to the Far East.

The Japanese militarists pressed for action and forced the resignation of Prince Konoye on October 16 and the appointment of General Tojo to succeed him as premier. General Tojo's cabinet appeared to indicate that the extremists had finally obtained control. A special session of the Japanese diet was called to approve the government's expansionist policy and to vote additional expenditures totaling billions of yen. Meanwhile, apparently as a maneuver to gain time, a special envoy, Foreign Minister Saburo Kurusu, was sent to Washington to assist the Japanese ambassador to the United States in the deadlocked negotiations.

After preliminary discussions with President Roosevelt and Secretary of State Hull, the Japanese envoys on November 20 presented proposals which indicated the extent of the concessions which Japan was willing to make and which the Japanese foreign minister secretly described as an ultimatum. If the United States would (1) cease all aid to China, (2) cancel the order freezing Japanese assets and abandon all restrictions on trade with Japan, (3) supply Japan with as much oil as she desired and bring pressure on the Netherlands East Indies to do the same, then Japan would (1) promise not to make any new moves beyond Indo-China, (2) evacuate southern Indo-China upon the signing of the agreement, and (3) evacuate all Indo-China when peace with China had been attained. Obviously the Japanese militarists had no intention of withdrawing from China. Obviously, too, their abandonment of further expansion outside China was to be bought only at the price of American aid to Japan in her conquest of China.

Whether the Japanese, once they had conquered and gained control of the resources of China, would stand by this agreement was a matter of conjecture. Meanwhile, Japanese troop concentrations in Indo-China were increased.

On November 24 the British government announced that, should Japan attack the United States, the latter would find Britain by her side in the ensuing war. Two days later the American proposals for a comprehensive settlement in the Pacific were presented to the Japanese envoys. If Japan would (1) recognize the integrity of Indo-China, (2) withdraw her forces from that country and from China, (3) abandon the puppet government of Wang Ching-wei and recognize that of Chiang Kai-shek, then the United States would (1) remove the restrictions on American exports to Japan, (2) offer a favorable trade agreement, and (3) assist Japan in the stabilization of her currency. The United States further proposed a joint declaration recognizing the principles of nonaggression, international cooperation, and equality of opportunity in the Pacific. Any such program was, of course, anathema to the Japanese militarists. War seemed imminent.

Japan's complete occupation of Indo-China was by this time well under way, and the movements of Japanese transports indicated that developments in Indo-China were preparatory to further moves. By the close of November strong Japanese naval forces were reported in the vicinity of the Japanese mandated islands. President Roosevelt conferred with the heads of the armed forces, and warnings of the imminence of war were sent to Hawaii and to the Philippines. On December 6, Roosevelt in a final effort to avert war sent a personal message to Emperor Hirohito assuring him that the United States had no intention of attacking Indo-China and undertaking to secure similar assurances from China, Thailand, Malaya, and the Netherlands East Indies if Japan would withdraw her forces. On the next day the Japanese envoys presented to the American government their country's formal reply to the proposals of November 26. It was a lengthy document, but its conclusion was that Japan could not accept the proposals as a basis of negotiations and that it would be impossible to reach an agreement through further negotiations.

Japan's Conquest of Empire

On Sunday morning, December 7, 1941, before the Japanese envoys had presented their formal reply to Secretary of State Hull, the Japanese without a declaration of war and as the result of plans and operations which must have taken weeks to execute, suddenly launched an attack upon Hawaii, followed by other attacks upon Guam, Wake Island, Hong Kong, the Philippines, Thailand (Siam), and Malaya. The attack on the Amer-

Underwood-Stratton

THE JAPANESE ATTACK ON PEARL HARBOR

The destruction of the battleship *Arizona*

ican naval base at Pearl Harbor was the most important of these operations, and it was skillfully executed.

Despite the warnings of a possible surprise attack sent to the American army and navy commanders at Pearl Harbor, inadequate precautions had been taken to protect the sea and air forces stationed there. Admiral Kimmel and General Short apparently believed, as did high military and naval commanders in Washington, that the Japanese attack would probably be in the vicinity of Indo-China and the East Indies. A board of inquiry subsequently charged the commanders in Hawaii with being guilty of dereliction, and they were at once retired from active service. But this action could not compensate for the losses sustained by the United States navy. Nineteen naval vessels, including all eight of the battleships then in the harbor, were sunk or damaged so seriously as to be put out of action for some time. In addition 177 army and navy airplanes were destroyed, and 4575 casualties, of which 2343 were killed, were inflicted upon the navy and army personnel. The American aircraft carriers based at Pearl Harbor happened to be at sea and thus escaped damage. Nevertheless, at a cost of only a few aircraft and three midget submarines the Japanese in their first blow had succeeded in upsetting the naval balance in the Pacific to their great advantage.

On December 7, after the attack on Pearl Harbor, the Japanese government announced that it had been at war with the United States and Great Britain since dawn that morning, and on the next day it issued a formal declaration of war. On December 11, Germany and Italy gave their formal support to Japan's venture in the Pacific by declaring war on the United States, and on that same day the three Axis aggressors agreed to carry on war "in common and jointly," not to conclude either an armistice or a peace separately, and after the conclusion of the war to "collaborate closely . . . in order to realize and establish an equitable new order in the world." The Second World War had become indeed a global struggle.

A few hours after the attack on Pearl Harbor, Japanese planes from Formosa attacked Clark Field near Manila. Most of the American planes were caught on the ground, parked in rows, wing to wing, as they had been at Pearl Harbor. All the flying fortresses, recently arrived in the Philippines, and many of the pursuit planes were destroyed or severely damaged. Two days later Japan's air force further strengthened her hold on the sea by sinking the British battleships *Repulse* and *Prince of Wales,* which without air escort were seeking to intercept a Japanese convoy off the coast of Malaya. Thereafter, for some time, neither the United States nor Great Britain had naval or air power in the Far East capable of successfully challenging the Japanese. The two countries had been thrown back on their bases at Hawaii and Singapore, some 4000 miles apart.

With their control of the sea and the air the Japanese were able for a time to strike where and when they pleased with little fear of interference from the United States or Great Britain. The isolated American and British forces, which they thereafter attacked, could have no hope of aid or reinforcements from their homelands. Though they fought heroically, they were bound to be conquered or destroyed by the overwhelming naval, air, and military forces which the Japanese could concentrate where they

THE SCENE OF JAPAN'S BLITZKRIEG, 1941–1942

pleased. In December Guam, Wake Island, and Hong Kong were captured, and Thailand, after a token resistance, surrendered and became a Japanese ally.

The Japanese next struck at Singapore from the rear. Their planes, using bases in Indo-China and Thailand, systematically destroyed the few British planes in northern Malaya and by the destruction of air fields in that region made it impossible to send air reinforcements to the British operating there. The latter fought valiantly and repeatedly tried to establish and hold a line across the Malaya peninsula. But the Japanese controlled the sea, and were therefore able to conduct an amphibious campaign. Repeatedly they compelled the British to retreat by landing a force some miles behind the line which the British had established. For some 400 miles the British fought a hopeless rearguard action, but eventually, on January 30, 1942, they fell back on Singapore. This $400,000,000 British naval base had not been designed to hold off a land attack, and on February 15, 1942, a British force of some 70,000 men surrendered to the Japanese. The conquest of Singapore gave the Japanese control of the easiest passage from the Pacific to the Indian Ocean; it gave them control of what had been regarded as the main defense of Sumatra and Java; and it released troops and planes for use on other battlefields.

Even while one force of Japanese was driving southward toward Singapore, another, operating from Thailand, was advancing westward into Burma. The latter, part of the British Empire, had recently been separated from the administration of India, but the political regime established was unsatisfactory to many Burmese, and there was much disaffection. The local population in many places, in fact, actively aided the Japanese by guiding them through hidden jungle paths to outflank the British and by destroying the latter's supplies and communications. At best only about two divisions of British forces were available to defend this region—which was larger than Germany—when the Japanese launched their attack into Burma in January, 1942. On March 9, Rangoon was captured and the invaders secured a major port of entry for supplies and reinforcements.

During the succeeding weeks the Japanese advanced northward up the Irrawaddy, Sittang, and Salween rivers. In this period the British forces were supplemented by two Chinese armies led by Chiang Kai-shek's American military adviser, General Joseph W. Stilwell, to whom was entrusted the defense of eastern Burma. But the ensuing developments were very much like those in Malaya. Repeatedly outflanked by the Japanese, the defenders were constantly compelled to fall back. In April the Japanese launched an unexpected drive northward from Thailand which cut behind the Chinese defenders and captured Lashio, the southern terminus of the Burma Road. At the same time a frontal attack from the south up the Irrawaddy Valley split the Chinese forces, and on May 1, 1942, the Japanese captured Mandalay. Some of the British, at the sacrifice of their heavy equipment, managed to reach the security of India, and General Stilwell finally succeeded in extricating some of his forces, but Burma was lost and with it the last effective route for sending American and British supplies to Chiang Kai-shek.

By this time, too, the Japanese had largely conquered the rich Netherlands East Indies, one of their chief objectives. The forces which the Dutch could marshal to meet the invasion were none too formidable. They had an inexperienced army of 100,000 natives, built up from a nucleus of some 30,000 professional soldiers. This force was largely concentrated in Java. They also had some 400 planes, a few cruisers, and a number of destroyers and submarines. The American Asiatic squadron, consisting of one heavy cruiser and a number of destroyers and submarines, together with a British cruiser, an Australian cruiser, and some smaller British ships, had also been sent to the aid of the Dutch.

After capturing a few bases on islands to the north of Java, the Japanese

THE BURMA AREA

in January, 1942, set out to invade that island, which occupied a key position in the East Indies, and for this purpose they sent a fleet of about a hundred transports and warships. This fleet was met in the Macassar Straits by the Allied naval and air forces operating from Java, and in a six-day engagement (January 23–29, 1942), the latter succeeded in sinking or seriously damaging about a third of the Japanese ships. Temporarily checked in their direct advance upon Java, the Japanese next approached it obliquely. Immediately after the fall of Singapore they conquered Sumatra to the northwest of Java, and then, coming in from the other direction, they seized the island of Timor and the island of Bali at the eastern tip of Java.

Late in February the Japanese fleet again advanced on Java, and the Allied fleet once more challenged the Japanese navy. In the course of a three-days' running battle most of the Allied ships were sunk; only four American destroyers managed to escape. The way was now open to Java, and the conquest of the island was swift. By March 9, 1942, organized resistance had collapsed, and Japan was in possession of an empire rich in foodstuffs, minerals, petroleum, and rubber, commodities which she greatly coveted and vitally needed.

Longest to hold out against the Japanese in the regions mapped out by them for immediate occupation were the Americans and their Filipino allies. Although the ultimate fate of these forces had been sealed by events at Pearl Harbor and Clark Field on December 7–8, 1941, some of the defenders of the Philippines held out until May 7, 1942. This long defense was possible in part because, after Manila had been neutralized, the Japanese did not exert their full strength against the Philippines until Singapore had fallen. It was made possible in part, too, by the advantages which the defenders had in terrain. General Douglas MacArthur soon consolidated his forces in the Bataan peninsula of the island of Luzon, the central defense of the archipelago, abandoning Manila to the Japanese. Bataan, with its steep, jungle-covered hills and deep ravines, was connected with the island proper by only a narrow neck of land, and enemy penetration was difficult. Furthermore, it could be protected from the sea to a considerable extent by the guns of the strongly fortified island of Corregidor, only three miles away.

The Japanese recklessly and heroically charged the American lines in mid-January, 1942, and again early in February. On both occasions, however, the machine-gun fire of the defenders and the electrically charged barbed-wire obstructions halted them. But General MacArthur's 40,000 men, mostly Filipinos, no matter how valiant, could not fight on indefinitely without replenishment of food, drugs, and matériel, and they were completely cut off from any such possibility. Eventually the defense was weakened by malnutrition, malaria, and other diseases. The defenders, decisively outnumbered and almost dead of fatigue, slowly retreated to the sea. A few hundred were evacuated to Corregidor, but on April 9, 1942, a force of some 35,000 surrendered. Resistance was continued by the forces at Corregidor, although many of the men there were sick and half-starved. A war of attrition was carried on by the Japanese, who ultimately succeeded in landing on the naval base. Further resistance was futile, and on May 7, 1942, the garrison of 12,000 also surrendered.

The commander who surrendered, however, was not General MacArthur but General Jonathan Wainwright. On February 22, President Roosevelt had ordered the former to leave Bataan and to establish his headquarters in Australia, where he was assigned the task of organizing the defense of that island. General MacArthur and his family, traveling by devious ways, managed to evade the Japanese, and arrived safely in Australia on March 17. There he became commander-in-chief of the Allied forces, and it was hoped that this shift presaged also a change from the defensive to the offensive for the Allies in operations in the Southwest Pacific.

The Checking of the Japanese in the South Pacific

Within a few months after Pearl Harbor the Japanese had achieved a series of successes against the Western powers that would previously have been thought impossible. They had captured Guam, Wake Island, and Hong Kong. They had occupied Indo-China and Thailand, had swept down the Malayan peninsula, and had taken the supposedly impregnable British naval base at Singapore. They had driven the Allies out of Burma and had cut the Burma Road to China. They had seized nearly every strategic point in the far-flung Netherlands East Indies, and had finally destroyed all organized resistance in the Philippines.

For a time it was feared that the Japanese might next invade Australia, for their seizure of Rabaul and northern New Guinea, outer defenses of Australia, as well as of Timor to the west and the Solomon Islands to the east, seemed to presage an invasion of that great island continent. From these various bases they sought to "soften up" the Australian air fields at Port Moresby in southeastern New Guinea and at Port Darwin in northern Australia. The Australians became very much alarmed. Some Australian forces were recalled from the Mediterranean area, and Prime Minister John Curtin appealed to the United States for help. American troops and supplies were rushed to the Fiji Islands, the New Hebrides, New Caledonia, and New Zealand to guard the routes to Australia, and an American expeditionary force was dispatched to the latter itself.

In May, 1942, the Japanese suffered what was probably their first major reverse in the war. A great concentration of Japanese shipping appeared in the Coral Sea, lying between northeastern Australia and the Solomon Islands. Whether its immediate objective was the conquest of Port Moresby, the occupation of New Caledonia and the New Hebrides, or a landing in Australia was not known. But a strong task force of the United States navy sailed forth to meet it. Though the two naval forces never made direct contact in the ensuing battle of the Coral Sea (May 7–8), American carrier-based planes, aided by land-based planes of General MacArthur's force, administered a decisive defeat to the Japanese and compelled them to withdraw. This battle "marked the high tide of Japanese conquest in the Southwest Pacific."

But the Japanese made one more aggressive move before they were completely checked. In June the largest concentration of Japanese naval strength yet assembled sailed east with the capture of Midway as its preliminary objective. Diversionary forces were sent northeastward to attack the Aleutian Islands, where they seized Attu and Kiska, but the main Japanese force struck toward Midway. The Japanese fleet was sighted on June 3, 1942, and thereafter for three days American seaplanes and land-based flying fortresses bombed the invaders, inflicting heavy losses. "The battles of the Coral Sea and Midway restored the balance of sea power in the Pacific to the United States." The latter was at last in a position to seize the initiative.

On August 7, 1942, a strong force of American marines, protected by an American-Australian naval task force, launched an attack against the chief Japanese positions in the Solomons. The Japanese were apparently taken by surprise, and by the night of August 8 the marines had seized the air field on Guadalcanal. On that night, however, the Allied naval force covering the landing operations was attacked off Savo Island by the Japanese, and in the ensuing engagement three heavy American cruisers and one Australian cruiser were destroyed. As a result of this disaster no cover could be given the American beachheads except what could be provided fitfully and by daylight from the American carrier force to the south, for the United States had launched the campaign with an irreducible minimum of heavy cruiser strength, which had now been wiped out.

Bitter seesaw battles ensued on Guadalcanal. The Americans were bombed by planes from Japanese bases to the north; they were shelled at night by light Japanese naval forces; they were persistently attacked by the Japanese troops still on Guadalcanal. But American engineers rushed to completion the landing strip on that island, and on August 20 American fighter planes landed on what was christened Henderson Field. Air reinforcements followed in the succeeding days. This was exceedingly fortunate for the Americans, for to the north the Japanese had been making a counter-concentration of ships and planes for the purpose of retaking Guadalcanal before it became too strong. On August 24, 1942, this Japanese naval and air force, nearly as powerful as that sent against Midway, swept down from the north. The most violent air engagement of the Pacific war to that date took place, and as a result the Japanese attempt to retake Guadalcanal was frustrated by the attacks of American carrier-based planes and bombers from Henderson Field.

By October 11, American naval reinforcements had arrived, and in an engagement following a surprise attack that night they avenged the disaster off Savo Island by sinking three Japanese cruisers, four destroyers, and one transport at a cost of only one destroyer. But the Japanese persisted in their efforts to retake the island. Steadily at night under cover of darkness they shipped in more men and supplies, and there were times when it looked as though they might overwhelm the American forces. Then once more the Japanese attempted to recapture Guadalcanal by a sweep from the north with battleships, carriers, cruisers, destroyers, and planes. In the terrific battle of Santa Cruz, which began on October 26 and was fought chiefly by the air forces, both fleets suffered heavily in the loss of carriers. But the Japanese were turned back; their powerful naval force never got near enough to Guadalcanal to fire a gun at it. Still a third time the Japanese sent a tremendous force against Guadalcanal, but a third time they were frustrated in a battle which raged on sea and in the air during November 13, 14, and 15. Heavy losses were inflicted on the Japanese task force, and most of the Japanese transports, deserted by their protecting warships, were sent to the bottom. Japan's drive to the south was checked; she had lost the initiative in that direction.

This was further revealed by the course of events in New Guinea, where the Japanese had established bases at Gona and Buna from which they apparently planned to advance upon Port Moresby, Australia's outlying base on the southern coast of that island. They first tried an amphibious operation, landing troops at Milne Bay at the southeastern tip of New Guinea on August 26, 1942. But they were at once attacked by General MacArthur's forces, and by the end of the month the area had been cleared of the Japanese and all their heavy equipment had been either destroyed or captured. The Japanese also attempted to advance overland upon Port Moresby. In this case they not only failed but the Allies drove them back and even captured their bases at Gona and Buna.

The Reduction of Japan's Outer Defense Area

Nevertheless, as the result of her sweep of conquest during the six months after Pearl Harbor, Japan had extended her domination over a tremendous land and sea area whose perimeter curved from northern Burma and India in the west to the waters north of Australia in the south, to the seas beyond the Ellice, Gilbert, and Marshall Islands in the east, and to Attu and Kiska in the Aleutian Islands in the north. This vast region, according to strategists, was divided into three major zones: the outer, secondary, and inner defense areas.

The outer defense area consisted of a screen of small islands with air and naval bases. As each of these island strongholds was linked to all the others by air and sea, any conceivable enemy concentration against one, it was thought, could be crushed by swift reinforcements from the rest. They therefore served as advance patrols to protect the vital parts of the expanded

JAPAN'S DEFENSIVE AREAS

Japanese empire against any threat from American sea power. The secondary defense area consisted chiefly of southeast Asia—Indo-China, Thailand, Malaya, Burma—and the large islands of the Southwest Pacific. New Guinea, which the Japanese never succeeded in wholly occupying, lay partly in this zone. In this area were contained the rich and vital raw materials which Japan needed and had so long coveted. In a sense the Philippines, because of their strategic location between Japan and the Netherlands East Indies, constituted the key to this valuable island empire. But within this area, to the east, lay the Palau, Marianas, and Caroline Islands as outposts against an American naval invasion. And on the eastern perimeter of the area lay the island of Truk, considered an impregnable Gibraltar in the pathway of an American advance. The inner defense area consisted of the Japanese homeland, Korea, southern Manchuria, and eastern China as far south as Shanghai. The outer defenses of this zone were Formosa and the Ryukyu and Bonin Islands to the south and the Kurile Islands to the north. If these outposts could be held, the homeland, it was believed, would be protected against effective mass bombing by enemy airplanes.

The first two years of the Pacific war were for Americans chiefly years of preparation for their eventual offensive. The immediate task which confronted the United States was that of establishing new air and fleet bases to protect the supply route to Australia. During the early months of the war the United States rallied its forces and established bases on many South Pacific islands, including Jarvis Island, the Phoenix Islands, the Samoan Islands, the Fiji Islands, the New Hebrides, and New Caledonia. Thus a protective screen was erected to safeguard the flow of men and supplies to the Southwest Pacific and to provide bases of operation for future offensives against the Japanese.

A second pressing task was that of restoring the naval balance in the Pacific. After the disaster at Pearl Harbor the Japanese navy outnumbered the United States fleet in the Pacific in every category except, perhaps, submarines. By two methods, attrition and construction, the United States altered that situation. Work on the "two-ocean" program of naval construction was rushed with the greatest possible speed, and a new building program was initiated in 1942 with emphasis upon aircraft carriers and submarines. By a construction program unparalleled in history the United States modernized and expanded its navy to the point where it could successfully engage hostile fleets on several distant fronts at the same time.

The third task confronting the United States was that of gaining air supremacy over the Pacific, for war in that vast ocean, no less than in Europe, called for supremacy in the air if victory was to be achieved. The ordinary types of fighters and bombers could be used for some operations but, in view of Japan's strategic situation, it was obvious that for striking at the

Japanese homeland within the inner defense area something much more powerful and longer-ranged than ordinary bombers would be required. Fortunately for the effectiveness of the American air war in the Pacific, the United States army air force had approved—even before Pearl Harbor—plans for the so-called B-29 bombing plane or superfortress, capable of carrying heavy bombloads to targets 1500 or even 2000 miles distant. After Pearl Harbor American industrial genius devoted itself to the production and perfection of this giant war machine.

At the conference between Churchill and Roosevelt at Washington in May, 1943, it was decided that General MacArthur and Admiral Chester W. Nimitz should move against the Japanese outer defenses, ejecting the enemy from the Aleutians and seizing the Marshalls, some of the Carolines, the remainder of the Solomons, the Bismarck Archipelago, and the northern coast of New Guinea. At the conference at Quebec three months later the specific routes of the advance were laid out. General MacArthur, to whose strategic command the army forces in the South Pacific had been added, was to continue his operations along the New Guinea coast to reach the Philippines by the autumn of 1944. Admiral Nimitz was to advance across the tremendous reaches of the Central Pacific, taking the Gilberts, the Marshalls, and the Marianas. It was believed that by the spring of 1945 the American forces would be able to land in the Ryukyus, on the very threshold of Japan.

By August 15, 1943, the Japanese had been forced out of Attu and Kiska in the Aleutian Islands as the result of American and Canadian operations during the first eight months of that year. In November, Tarawa and Makin in the Gilbert Islands were captured. Preceded by days of bombing from the air and from surface craft, designed to reduce the island defenses, American marines on November 20 stormed ashore on Tarawa in the face of a murderous fire from Japanese guns which had not been silenced by the preliminary bombing. In three days of hard fighting the marines wiped out the Tarawa garrison, though at a cost to themselves of 913 men killed and more than 2000 wounded. The capture of Makin was less difficult and was completed on November 22.

Japan's outer defense area with its system of supposedly interlocked bases was thus proved to be highly vulnerable, for her fighters in the Gilberts had been prevented from receiving any assistance from other Japanese island bases. Tarawa had an excellent air field, and Makin had wharves, a good anchorage, and a seaplane base. The capture of these two islands, therefore, provided facilities for American land-based planes and brought the Marshall Islands within easy bombing distance. In January the Marshalls were bombed on twenty-two consecutive days, and then, on January 31, 1944, a powerful sea and air attack began. On the next day beachheads were established, and by February 8 the whole Kwajalein atoll had been occupied. Apparently the Japanese had been taken by surprise. Although more than 8000 Japanese were killed, the American losses on this occasion were only 286 dead and 82 missing. No American warships were sunk, and losses of aircraft were comparatively light. The next important step came on February 18 when Eniwetok, on the northwestern edge of the archipelago, was seized and with it a good air field extending American striking power some 300 miles farther toward the west. By the middle of April a score or more of the Marshall atolls were in American hands, and Japan's outer defense area in this part of the Pacific had been effectively reduced.

Four months later, on June 15, American marines and army troops landed on Saipan in the Marianas Islands, more than 3000 miles beyond Pearl Harbor. The Japanese here fought fanatically and not until after 21,000 men had been killed did their resistance collapse. The cost in American lives was heavy, too, for 2359 men of the invading forces were killed. By the close of July, Guam and Tinian had also been captured, and Truk and other Japanese bases in the Caroline Islands were largely isolated. On September 15, Admiral Nimitz' forces struck again, this time in the Palau Islands where marines and army troops landed on Peleliu, which had the best air field in the western Carolines and was only 500 miles from the Philippines.

Meanwhile, in the Southwest Pacific General MacArthur had been carrying on the campaign which had been committed to him. Without waiting for the final conquest of all of the Solomon Islands, which was not completed until early in 1944, MacArthur's American and Australian troops launched their drive westward. By the fall of 1943 the Americans in the Southwest Pacific had a superiority both on the sea and in the air, and it was MacArthur's intention to proceed along the coast of New Guinea by a series of envelopments. His forces were able to land where the Japanese were weakest and were able to isolate their stronger forces in places from which, because of American control of the sea and air, they could not be evacuated. By the end of May, 1944, Rabaul, Japan's strongest base in the Southwest Pacific, had been neutralized by landings on New Britain and in the Admiralty Islands (see map on next page), and all the Japanese bases on the north coast of New Guinea had been captured or isolated. In July, Noemfor Island was seized and on September 15, MacArthur's forces landed on Morotai, where they established a base less than 400 miles from Mindanao, the second largest island in the Philippines.

A glance at the map on page 577 will reveal that in consequence of American amphibious operations carried on in the Aleutians, in the Gilberts, in the Marshalls, in the Solomons, in the Bismarck archipelago, and in New

The Southwest Pacific in the Second World War

Guinea, Japan's outer defense area in the Pacific had been almost completely eliminated. Although she still had some centers of resistance in that region, the troops remaining there were trapped and doomed and unable to interfere with future operations of the Allies. Furthermore, a glance back over the military and naval developments in the Pacific makes clear how two giant arms had been steadily extended thousands of miles toward the same objective, the Philippines. The southern arm had moved slowly but steadily from the Solomons and the eastern tip of New Guinea toward the northwest, taking or immobilizing all the Japanese bases in the Southwest Pacific. The northern arm had pushed irresistibly into the central Pacific from the Gilberts through the Marshalls and the Marianas to the Palaus, acquiring a string of powerful American air and naval bases and isolating and neutralizing the few that remained to the Japanese. These two arms, with a mailed fist at the end of each, had struck simultaneously on September 15, 1944, at Peleliu and at Morotai, each roughly only some 500 miles from the goal. All that remained was to bring the two mailed fists together on a single objective in the Philippines.

The Liberation of the Philippines and Burma

At the Churchill-Roosevelt conference at Quebec in September, 1944, it was decided, upon Admiral William F. Halsey's recommendation—which received the approval of Nimitz and MacArthur—to advance the date of the projected invasion of the Philippines from December 20 to October 20, 1944. Preceded by ten days of heavy air raids over the Philippines—Luzon in the north, Mindanao in the south, and the Viscayas group in between—on that day an American landing was made on the east coast of Leyte Island in the central Philippines by a major amphibious operation. More than 600 ships participated in what was the most ambitious undertaking of the American offensive in the Pacific up to that time. Leyte lay between Mindanao and Luzon, the two largest islands in the Philippines, on which the Japanese were thought to have their chief troop concentrations. It had some air fields and offered numerous sites for others. It had an excellent harbor which would provide facilities for bringing in needed supplies. With Leyte converted into an American air and supply base, the Japanese forces in the Philippines would be cut in two, and either flank of their defensive position in those islands could be rolled up at will. The Japanese troops in Mindanao would, of course, become isolated.

The American landing on Leyte obviously threatened Japan's hold on the entire Philippine archipelago, which, in turn, was the key to her recently acquired empire in the Netherlands East Indies. By October 22 three strong Japanese fleets were steaming toward Leyte—two from the

BABUYAN
ISLANDS

Babuyan Channel

Aparri

Laoag

Buguey

Vigan

Tuguegarao

Bontok

Palanan

SOUTH

San Fernando

Baguio

LUZON

Lingayen

Dagupan

Baler

Tarlac

Cabanatuan

Olongapo

Malolos

POLILLO

CHINA

BATAAN

Infanta

CORREGIDOR

Manila

Cavite

Daet

PACIFIC

CATANDUANES

Lucena

SEA

Legaspi

OCEAN

MINDORO

MARIN-
DUQUE

Laoang

SIBUYAN

Bulan

Oros

San Jose

TABLAS

SEA

Allen

SAMAR

MASBATE

Borongan

Nabas

Capiz

Basey

PANAY

Ormoc

Tacloban

Iloilo

LEYTE

Dao

CEBU

Cauayan

Cebu

DINAGAT

SIARGAO

Puerto Princesa

NEGROS

BOHOL

PALAWAN

Siaton

*Mindanao
Sea*

Butuan

Cantilan

SIQUIJOR

Baliangao

Gingoog

Lianga

SULU

Katipuna

Cagayan

Hinatuan

Kabasalan

Iligan

Mailag

SEA

MINDANAO

Cotabato

Davao

Zamboanga

Santa Cruz

Davao Gulf

ARCHIPELAGO

Malita

Sandakan

SULU

CELEBES   SEA

BORNEO

JAPAN

Tokyo

CHINA

BONIN
IS.

IWO JIMA

FORMOSA

Hong
Kong

PHILIPPINE

MARIANAS

INDO-
CHINA

Manila

IS.

SAIPAN

GUAM

Singapore

MOROTAI

BORNEO

BIAK

NEW
GUINEA

JAVA

AUSTRALIA

San Bernardino Strait

Surigao Strait

THE PHILIPPINE ISLANDS IN THE SECOND WORLD WAR

west and one from home bases in the north. Although the two fleets from the west were discovered and vigorously attacked from the air as they crossed, the one the Sibuyan Sea, the other the Sulu Sea, they continued on their course, the ultimate objective of which could not be immediately known to the American naval commanders. On the twenty-third Halsey's Third Fleet and Kinkaid's Seventh Fleet disposed themselves to watch the two available approaches to Leyte Gulf—San Bernardino Strait to the north and Surigao Strait to the South. Late in the day came news of the approach of the Japanese fleet from the north, whereupon Halsey's Third Fleet dashed northward to engage it, leaving Kinkaid's fleet to guard Leyte. Early in the morning of the twenty-fourth, Halsey's fleet attacked in the open sea to the east of Luzon. The Japanese immediately fled but suffered heavy losses, losses which would have been still heavier if Halsey had not been halted in his pursuit by ominous news from the Seventh Fleet.

Admiral Kinkaid had disposed the bulk of the latter to meet the southern-most Japanese fleet should it emerge from Surigao Strait, and had left only a sparse defending force of destroyers, escort carriers, and destroyer escorts to guard against the supposedly unlikely contingency of the central Japanese fleet's emerging from San Bernardino Strait. Kinkaid's heavy ships did their work well, for, when the southern Japanese fleet reached the narrow channel opening into Leyte Gulf, the Seventh Fleet opened fire and "crossed the enemy's T." The Japanese fleet thereupon retreated, shattered and beaten. Its losses might have been still heavier, too, except that suddenly Kinkaid received word that the central Japanese fleet had emerged from San Bernardino Strait, to the north of Samar, and was speeding down the east coast of that island toward the helpless American shipping in Leyte Gulf. Only the weak American defending force lay between it and its goal, but that force, after broadcasting the vital news to Halsey and Kinkaid, at once closed in action with the more powerful Japanese fleet, using smoke screens, torpedoes, and planes. This heroic action gained time but at the sacrifice of two destroyers, one destroyer escort, one escort carrier, and many lives. The sacrifice was not in vain, however, for the Japanese admiral, delayed by the action and knowing that Halsey and Kinkaid were rushing toward him with their more powerful ships, decided to abandon the attack. The American beachhead on Leyte and the shipping in the gulf were saved.

The battle for Leyte Gulf (October 23–25, 1944) had disastrous results for Japan's sea power in the Southwest Pacific. According to the official figures published by the United States high command, Japanese losses were 3 battleships, 3 aircraft carriers, 6 heavy cruisers, 4 light cruisers, and 8 destroyers sunk, and severe damage to a considerable number of other ships of all categories. American losses were 1 light aircraft carrier, 2 escort carriers, 2 destroyers, and 1 destroyer escort sunk.

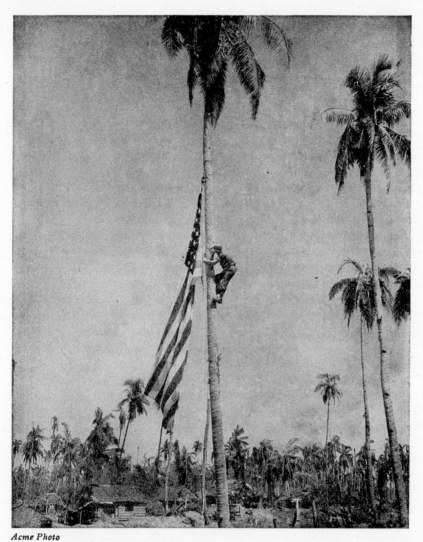

THE AMERICAN RETURN TO THE PHILIPPINES
Raising the first flag on Leyte

The defeat of the Japanese naval forces in their attempt to interfere with American landings on Leyte decided the fate of that island. Although there was still much hard fighting, General MacArthur on December 25 announced that, except for mopping up, the campaign for Leyte had ended.

But already another landing had been made in the Philippines by American forces. On December 15 an amphibious force, after a circuitous 600-mile cruise from Leyte Gulf through Surigao Strait, the Mindanao Sea, and the Sulu Sea past enemy-held islands, had made a surprise landing against little resistance on the southwestern tip of Mindoro, one of the larger Philippine Islands just south of Luzon. This landing seemed to point the way to the ultimate invasion of southern Luzon, which was separated from the northern coast of Mindoro by only a narrow strait. And indications of an approaching invasion of Luzon from the south continued to multiply. Other amphibious landings on Mindoro advanced American positions northward on that island, and on January 5, 1945, United States troops seized the island of Marinduque, within ten miles of the southern Luzon coast, and less than 100 miles from Manila. American superfortresses, meanwhile, severely bombed the Japanese home islands, while planes of the American Pacific fleet raided Formosa and the Ryukyu Islands. Every effort was bent toward isolating the Philippines from Japanese bases to the north.

Then, on January 9, 1945, United States troops, led personally by General MacArthur and protected by a terrific naval and air bombardment, landed from a convoy of more than 800 ships, not in southern Luzon, but along the southern and southeastern coasts of Lingayen Gulf, approximately 100 miles north of Manila. The Japanese, apparently deceived by American feints toward southern Luzon, were not prepared to repulse the landing here. The American troops met only light opposition, quickly established a firm beachhead, and began their advance inland. In less than three weeks the Americans had captured the big air base at Clark Field and had pushed to within forty miles of Manila. On February 4, American troops smashed into the city, capturing Santo Tomas concentration camp and Bilibid prison and liberating some 4800 American prisoners and internees. By February 23, the last Japanese resistance was being mopped up within Manila, and on the following day the liberation of the city was completed. On February 27, in the battle-scarred capital of the Philippines General MacArthur formally returned civil control of the islands to President Osmeña.

With their conquests in the Philippines the Americans had invaded Japan's secondary defense area, and had established strategically located bases for its reduction. But much still remained to be done. The island of Luzon—larger than Bulgaria—had to be cleared of the Japanese, and the garrisons on the many other islands had to be captured or exterminated.

The two tasks were carried on simultaneously. By the end of June the campaign in Luzon had been successfully ended and most of the larger and strategically important islands had been occupied. By that time, too, British, American, and Chinese troops as the result of long and difficult campaigns had succeeded in driving the Japanese out of Burma, and Lord Mountbatten's forces in southeastern Asia were closing in on Malaya and the Netherland East Indies. Australian troops were operating in southeastern Borneo, and Australian and Netherlands East Indian troops had seized Tarakan Island off northeastern Borneo. The Japanese secondary defense area was fast being overrun by the Allies.

The Attack on Japan

Even before the reduction of this secondary area had been completed, the Allies had begun carrying their attacks to Japan in the heart of the inner defense zone. As early as April, 1942, Tokyo and other Japanese cities had been bombed by American carrier-based planes commanded by General James H. Doolittle, but this attack had been an isolated exploit. It was not until more than two years later (June 15, 1944) that a "sizable task force" of American superfortresses flew from Chinese bases to make their first attack upon Japan, choosing as their target Yawata, the "Japanese Pittsburgh." But acceleration of these air attacks was painfully slow: two in June, two in July, three in August, two in September, four in October, and nine in November. One grave handicap was the arduous task of getting the necessary high-octane aviation fuel to the air bases in China, involving as it did transshipment in India and then a risky, gas-consuming 2400-mile round trip over the mountains by transport planes. The conquest of the Marianas, however, and the establishment of a superfortress base on Saipan greatly increased the possibility of bombing Japan.

On November 24, 1944, the superfortresses from Saipan inaugurated their attacks upon the Japanese home cities, and within eight days bombed aircraft factories and steel plants in Tokyo itself four times. Thereafter the number of attacks increased more rapidly: fourteen in December, and still more in January and February, 1945, when the Japanese homeland was attacked not only by B-29's but by hundreds of carrier planes of the American task force. During March the bombing of Japanese industrial centers—Tokyo, Nagoya, Osaka, Kobe—was particularly severe. Many square miles of the densely populated areas of these cities were laid waste by American explosive and incendiary bombs. The unpleasing prospect of having the industrial heart of their country scourged as other Allied planes had devastated Germany confronted the alarmed Japanese, whose industrial war machine was even more vulnerable than Germany's because it was more closely concentrated.

To secure additional bases from which to increase the air attacks upon Japan, American marines on February 18, 1945, had landed on Iwo Jima, an important island (*jima* means island) southwest of the Bonin group, after it had first been subjected to sixty-nine consecutive days of aerial bombardment and to four days of terrific naval bombardment. Nevertheless, because of the difficult terrain—its volcanic hills were honeycombed with caves which could not be reached by bombs or shells—and the fanatical resistance of the Japanese garrison of 22,000–24,000, the conquest of Iwo was a tough job. Although the island was only eight square miles in extent, nearly a month of furious fighting was required to capture it. The conquest of Iwo provided the American air force with a valuable advanced base. Fighter planes from Iwo could protect B-29 bases in the Marianas from Japanese bombers; they could also fly to the Japanese mainland to protect the superfortresses. The capture of Iwo was the first American conquest of territory within the Japanese inner defense zone, but the price paid by the marines was high—19,938 casualties, of which 4189 were killed, constituting, it was said, the marines' worst ordeal in their 168-year history.

Two weeks after the end of Japanese resistance on Iwo other American forces on April 1 landed on Okinawa in the largest amphibious operation yet undertaken in the Pacific. They were protected by the guns of the American Fifth Fleet and by carrier planes, land-based planes, and superfortresses. Okinawa was the strongest of the Ryukyu chain of islands joining Japan and Formosa. It was only half as far from Japan as Iwo. American air and naval forces based on Okinawa could sever Japan's route to her empire in the south and west, could transform the China Sea into an American lake. The significance of all these facts was not lost on the Japanese, who repeatedly sent large forces of "suicide" planes to attack the invasion fleet. Hundreds of Japanese planes were shot down, but by the middle of June 33 American ships had been sunk and 45 damaged, chiefly by these kamikaze or suicide attacks. Meanwhile, ashore American forces battled against the fanatical Japanese resistance which continued in the southern end of Okinawa. Not until June 21 did organized resistance cease, and then only after the American forces had suffered casualties more than twice those suffered in capturing Iwo Jima. But in Okinawa the Americans at last had a sizable strategic base within the shadow of the Japanese homeland.

In April, fleets of Marianas-based B-29's had begun striking at Tokyo, Nagoya, and other Japanese industrial cities, protected in their attacks by land-based fighter planes which took off from Iwo Jima. In July, after the capture of Okinawa, air fields on that island also began to be crowded with bombers and fighters, which joined in the aerial assault on the Japanese islands and what was left of Japanese shipping. Japanese industries and communications rapidly crumbled under the mounting tempo of aerial bombardment, supplemented by the destructive power of Allied naval forces.

The Japanese had already suffered another naval disaster. Shortly after the Americans had landed on Okinawa strong Japanese fleet units had been sighted proceeding southward from Kyushu. On April 7 they were attacked in the East China Sea by American carrier planes, which sank one cruiser, four destroyers, and Japan's newest and largest remaining battleship, the *Yamato*. This disaster, coupled with that suffered in the battle for Leyte Gulf, so weakened the Japanese navy that it was powerless to challenge the American battle fleets successfully thereafter.

In July the fast carrier forces of the American Third Fleet, comprising the greatest mass of sea power ever assembled, set out to complete the destruction of the Japanese fleet and to conduct a pre-invasion campaign to destroy Japanese industries. Strikes were made by planes from the fleet's carriers and heavy units of the fleet shelled shore installations. On July 17 the Third Fleet was joined by units of the British Pacific Fleet and the first combined American-British bombardment of the Japanese homeland ensued. The Japanese seemed powerless to halt either the air or naval attacks. Between July 10 and August 15 the Allied forces sank or damaged 148 enemy combat ships, including the *Nagato*, one of Japan's two remaining battleships.

Plans were meanwhile being made for the invasion of the Japanese homeland. An assault on southern Kyushu in the fall of 1945 was to be followed by a second invasion of the Tokyo plain of eastern Honshu in the spring of 1946. It was known that Japan had an army of 2,000,000 in the homeland which was being steadily enlarged by withdrawals from the Asiatic mainland. It was known that she had been husbanding her waning air strength and she was thought to have still some 8000 planes of all types. If casualties in the conquest of Japan itself were in proportion to those suffered in taking Okinawa and Iwo Jima, the price in American lives would inevitably be high. The American high command contemplated no early or easy victory over the Japanese by the use of ordinary weapons of war. Since 1940, however, the full resources of American and British science had been working on the principle of atomic fission, and by the summer of 1945 had produced a new and terrifically destructive atomic bomb. It was thought that the use of atomic bombs might persuade the Japanese not to fight to a last-ditch national suicide.

Official U. S. Navy Photo from Ewing Galloway

JAPANESE SURRENDER ABOARD THE U.S.S. MISSOURI

Japanese Foreign Minister Mamoru Shigemitsu signs for his Emperor, as General of the Army Douglas MacArthur, U.S.A., Supreme Commander for the Allies broadcasts the ceremonies.

The Atom Bomb and the End of the War

But before resort to atomic bombs, one last diplomatic effort was made by the Allies to secure an end to the war. On July 26, President Truman, Prime Minister Churchill, and Generalissimo Chiang Kai-shek, in a proclamation to the Japanese people, warned that prodigious forces were poised to strike final blows on Japan which would result in the utter devastation of the Japanese homeland. They demanded that the Japanese government should proclaim the unconditional surrender of its armed forces, and they stated the Allied terms: (1) the limitation of Japanese sovereignty to the islands of Honshu, Hokkaido, Kyushu, Shikoku, and minor islands; (2) Allied occupation of Japanese territory; (3) disarmament of Japanese military forces; (4) destruction of Japanese war industries; (5) trial and punishment of Japanese war criminals; (6) institution in Japan of freedom of speech, of religion, and of thought; (7) removal of obstacles to the revival and strengthening of democratic tendencies among the Japanese people. On July 29, however, the Tokyo radio reported that the Japanese Premier Suzuki had declared that the Allied proclamation would be ignored by the Japanese government.

To escape heavy casualties and to speed the end of the war, the American high command thereupon decided to use atomic bombs, and on August 6 one of these bombs was dropped on the military base of the Japanese city of Hiroshima. In a split second some 60 per cent of that city was obliterated. Said President Truman: "It was to spare the Japanese people from utter destruction that the ultimatum of July 26 was issued.... Their leaders promptly rejected that ultimatum. If they do not now accept our terms they may expect a rain of ruin from the air, the like of which has never been seen on this earth."

Thereafter the war came swiftly to a close. On August 8 the Soviet Union declared war against Japan in accordance with an agreement made at Yalta in February, and launched swift Red Army offensives into Manchuria and into southern Sakhalin. On August 9 a second atomic bomb was dropped on Nagasaki with even greater destructive force and fire than the Hiroshima bomb. On August 10 the Japanese government sued for peace. Four days later Japan declared her acceptance of the Allied terms, and on August 19 the instrument of surrender was presented to Japanese representatives by General MacArthur at Manila. On September 2 the formal surrender of the Japanese Imperial Government, the Japanese Imperial General Headquarters, and all Japanese and Japanese-controlled forces wherever located, was signed on board the United States battleship *Missouri* in Tokyo Bay. In a dramatic ceremony marking the final consummation of the victory of the United Nations, the last of the Axis powers laid down its arms, and the most extensive and destructive war in the history of mankind came formally to an end. The price of victory for the Americans was 170,596 casualties including 41,322 dead—almost as many in this one theater of operations as suffered by the American forces in the whole First World War.

Part Five

ANOTHER POSTWAR PERIOD

Chapter XXIII

THE UNFINISHED PEACE

SETTLEMENT AND THE

"COLD WAR"

IN contrast with the relative speed with which the Paris peace conference was convened at the close of the First World War, nearly fifteen months elapsed between the German signing of the armistice on May 7, 1945, and the convening of another Paris peace conference in July, 1946. And even then no peace treaties were drafted by the conference for the two major enemy states, Germany and Japan. This failure to complete the peace settlement was undoubtedly the result of the clash in ideologies and policies of the major Allied powers and to an increasing fear and suspicion which led ultimately to what was called the "cold war" between the Soviet Union and the United States. On the other hand, in marked contrast with the delay in restoring formal peace to the world was the speed with which a new international organization for the preservation of peace was launched at the close of hostilities.

The United Nations

The Second World War, with its incredible waste of lives and wealth, strikingly emphasized the shortsightedness of the world's statesmen in failing to utilize the machinery of the League of Nations to halt aggression in its initial stages. Moreover, it had brought to many Americans a growing conviction that by their own abandonment of the League in 1919–1920 they had contributed to the breakdown of collective security, a conviction that became even more general after the United States was engulfed in the war in 1941. To more and more Americans it became obvious that the "world was growing smaller" and that a third world war would involve the United States even more quickly and more disastrously than had the wars of 1914 and 1939.

Just as in the case of Woodrow Wilson, President Roosevelt became convinced that the war must lead to an international security system in which the United States must take an active part. Soon after Pearl Harbor the United States department of state took up the task of drafting proposals for such a security system, and at Moscow in October, 1943, Secretary of State Hull presented proposals for a world organization to Foreign Secretaries Anthony Eden and V. M. Molotov, of Great Britain and Russia respectively, and to the Chinese ambassador to Russia. The results of their conversations and negotiations were eventually embodied in the Moscow Declaration, in which the governments of these four leading powers stated that they recognized the necessity of establishing a general international organization.

To implement this declaration representatives of the United States, Great Britain, Russia, and China met at Dumbarton Oaks in Washington from August 21 to October 7, 1944. The results of seven weeks of negotiations, added to the years of study which had already been devoted to the problem, were embodied in the Dumbarton Oaks Proposals for the establishment of a general international organization. It was agreed that these proposals should in turn be formally submitted to the governments of the United Nations to serve as the basis of discussion at a full conference at which the charter of the international organization would ultimately be drawn up.

On March 5, 1945, the United States government, on behalf of itself, Great Britain, Russia, and China, invited the governments of the other United Nations to send representatives to a conference, called to meet at San Francisco on April 25. It had been planned to have President Roosevelt address the opening session of this world security conference, but on April 12, while resting at his home at Warm Springs, Georgia, where he had gone to prepare his speech, President Roosevelt died suddenly of a cerebral hemorrhage. He of all the world's statesmen had done most to create and hold together the United Nations. What effect his death might have upon the future of that organization and upon the plans for world peace, none could foretell. But his successor, President Harry S. Truman, at once announced that Mr. Roosevelt's policies would be continued and that the San Francisco conference would open as scheduled.

The United Nations Conference on International Organization was held at San Francisco from April 25 to June 26, 1945, and was attended by representatives of fifty states which were at war with either Germany or Japan or both. In the Charter of the United Nations which was there drafted and adopted, the core of the Dumbarton Oaks proposals was retained with few alterations, but one entirely new section was added dealing with trusteeship for dependent peoples. The Charter came into force on October 24, 1945, following the deposit of the necessary number of ratifications.

The international machinery outlined in the Charter in many ways re-

United Press photo

UNITED NATIONS GENERAL ASSEMBLY

President Eisenhower Speaking Before the Assembly on December 8, 1953

sembled that of the League of Nations.[1] The chief organs of the new organization are the following:

A General Assembly, composed of representatives of all member states, meeting in annual and special sessions, in which each state has one vote;

A Security Council, composed of representatives of eleven member states and so organized as to be able to function continuously. The United States, Great Britain, the Soviet Union, China, and France have permanent seats, while six states are elected for two-year terms by the General Assembly;

An International Court of Justice, to whose statute all members of the organization are parties;

A Secretariat, comprising an expert staff and headed by a secretary general as chief administrative officer;

A Trusteeship Council, consisting of the five great powers and such other states as administer trust territories, plus as many other states elected by the Assembly for three-year terms as may be necessary to ensure that the total number of members of the Trusteeship Council is equally divided between states administering and states not administering trust territories;

An Economic and Social Council, composed of representatives of eighteen member states chosen by the General Assembly for three-year terms;

A Military Staff Committee, composed of the chiefs of staff of the permanent members of the Security Council or their representatives with provision for the participation by other states when necessary.

The first five of these organs closely resemble in their composition and functions analogous bodies in the League of Nations, the Trusteeship Council being somewhat similar in purpose to the former Permanent Mandates Commission. The Economic and Social Council, however, is a new organ which was created to deal with matters which had formerly been handled by certain sections of the League Secretariat. Greater dignity and importance are given to economic and social questions by their being entrusted in this way to a special council elected by the General Assembly. The Military Staff Committee is, of course, something which the League of Nations did not have. The United Nations was expected to have military forces available for the maintenance of peace, and member states were expected to conclude agreements specifying in advance the numbers and types of forces to be made available to the Security Council. These armed forces would operate, when necessary, under the authority of the Security Council in accordance with plans made by it with the assistance of the Military Staff Committee. The new organization, it was hoped, would have more power to enforce its decisions than had the League of Nations. The primary responsibility for the maintenance of international peace and security was placed upon the Security Council, which would be in continuous session.

As might have been expected, the matter of voting in the latter body

[1] See pages 139–144.

caused considerable difficulty, but a compromise was finally reached which provided that: (1) each member of the Security Council should have one vote; (2) decisions of the Security Council on procedural matters should be made by an affirmative vote of seven members; (3) decisions of the Security Council on all other matters should be made by an affirmative vote of seven members, including the concurring votes of the permanent members, except that a party to a dispute should abstain from voting when the Security Council was engaged in the pacific settlement of disputes. In other words, the Security Council may informally discuss any dispute or difficulty without any power having a veto, and any member state may call that body's attention to a situation threatening the peace of the world without the veto interfering. But if a dispute moves beyond informal discussion to investigation or recommendation for peaceful settlement, there must be a formal vote in which the affirmative vote of seven must include the concurring votes of the five great powers unless one of the latter is a party to the dispute, in which case its vote is not counted.

The first session of the General Assembly convened in London on January 10, 1946, with fifty-one states represented. Paul-Henri Spaak of Belgium was chosen president of the Assembly and Trygve Lie of Norway was elected secretary general of the United Nations. The Assembly also elected six states—Australia, Brazil, Egypt, Mexico, the Netherlands, and Poland—as nonpermanent members of the Security Council, which held its first meeting on January 17 and immediately took up a number of important political problems connected with Iran, Greece, Indonesia, and Syria-Lebanon.[2] The Assembly, meanwhile, devoted itself to further organizational activities. Eighteen states, including the five great powers, were elected members of the Economic and Social Council; and fifteen judges were chosen, with the help of the Security Council, for the International Court of Justice, which met for the first time at The Hague in April, 1946. The Assembly decided that the Secretariat of the United Nations should be located in the United States, and eventually a permanent site was chosen in New York City. Thus a second experiment in world organization for the facilitation of international co-operation and for the prevention of war was hopefully begun.

Peace Negotiations and Another "Big Four"

Meanwhile, following the collapse of the Nazis and the military defeat of Germany, a three-power conference of the victorious powers had been held in Berlin (July 17–August 2, 1945) to consider the many problems

[2] For the United Nations' handling of various international problems, consult the index under "United Nations" or under the names of the countries or regions directly concerned.

arising from the outcome of the war. In the beginning the conference was attended by Premier Stalin, President Truman, Prime Minister Churchill, and their foreign ministers, Vyacheslav M. Molotov, James F. Byrnes, and Anthony Eden. Following Churchill's resignation as a result of the Labor Party victory in Great Britain,[3] however, Clement R. Attlee, the new British prime minister, and his new foreign secretary, Ernest Bevin, supplanted Churchill and Eden. Since the statesmen conferred at the Cecilienhof near Potsdam, their meeting came to be called the Potsdam Conference.

At this conference it was agreed to establish a Council of Foreign Ministers whose task should be the drafting of the peace treaties, first, with Italy, Rumania, Bulgaria, Hungary, and Finland, and eventually with Germany when the latter had established a government adequate for the purpose. At a subsequent conference in Moscow (December 16–26, 1945), Byrnes, Bevin, and Molotov agreed more specifically that the terms of the treaty with Italy should be drafted by the foreign ministers of Great Britain, the United States, Russia, and France; the terms of the treaties with Rumania, Bulgaria, and Hungary, by the foreign ministers of Great Britain, the United States, and Russia; and those of the treaty with Finland by the foreign ministers of Great Britain and Russia. The foreign ministers of France and the United States, it was further agreed, should have the right to attend all meetings of the council and to discuss treaty terms even in those cases in which they were not permitted to vote.

At the Moscow Conference it was also decided that, upon the completion of the draft treaties, a general peace conference consisting of representatives of the five great powers—Russia, Great Britain, the United States, France, China—and of the sixteen other states which had actively waged war with a substantial military force against the European states,[4] should be convened to consider the treaties and to make recommendations. Following this peace conference the states which had drawn up the original draft treaties should consider the recommendations of the conference and then formulate the final texts of the several treaties.

During the first seven months of 1946, therefore, the foreign ministers of the United States, Great Britain, Russia, and France, and their deputies, carried on negotiations in an attempt to reach agreement on the terms of the treaties to be presented to the future peace conference. Once more, as in 1919,[5] the peace negotiations were dominated by a "Big Four," which in 1946 consisted of Byrnes, Bevin, Molotov, and Georges Bidault, foreign minister of France, though the latter, like Orlando in 1919, played a some-

---

[3] See page 690.

[4] These sixteen states were Australia, Belgium, Brazil, Canada, Czechoslovakia, Ethiopia, Greece, India, the Netherlands, New Zealand, Norway, Poland, the Ukraine, South Africa, White Russia, and Yugoslavia.

[5] For the "Big Four" and peace negotiations in 1919, see pages 111–112.

what minor role. In the "Big Four" of 1946, however, there was probably a deeper distrust of one another's fundamental aims than in that of 1919, for Wilson, Lloyd George, Clemenceau, and Orlando had had at least one basic common bond in that they all represented capitalistic democracies. In 1946, on the other hand, the political and economic ideologies of the three "Western democracies" were far different from those of the Soviet Union. In consequence, the members of the "Big Four" in 1946 were soon caught in the vicious circle of fear and distrust—on the one hand, fear of Communism with its threat of "world revolution"; on the other, fear of "capitalistic imperialism" with its threat of "encirclement." Byrnes, Bevin, and Bidault accordingly sought national security against the alleged or suspected "plots of the Communists," while Molotov used his veto to try to check the "machinations of the greedy imperialists." Though not openly expressed, these fears were ever-present and the search for security by each side in turn only intensified national suspicions.

It is not surprising, perhaps, that, although agreement was readily reached on many points, the "Big Four" failed to come to a common understanding on several important matters, particularly the new Italian-Yugoslav boundary, the fate of Trieste, the disposal of Italy's colonies, Russia's claim to Italian reparations, the question of international control of the Danube, and the matter of withdrawing occupation forces from enemy states following the signing of the peace treaties. Usually the disagreement was between Molotov, on the one side, and Bevin and Byrnes, on the other.

The crisis which gained the greatest notoriety and which probably took up more time than any other one problem, in 1946 as in 1919, arose from the conflict over the boundary between Italy and Yugoslavia. In 1919, Italy, largely for strategic reasons sought a boundary which transgressed upon ethnic principles, and the city particularly involved was Fiume.[6] In 1946, Yugoslavia, from motives very similar to Italy's earlier, sought to push her boundary farther west in conflict with the ethnic situation, and the city involved was this time Trieste. In 1919, Wilson opposed Italy's demands and suggested a boundary which the Italians then denounced as grossly unfair but which in 1946 they themselves recommended as a just settlement. In 1946, Byrnes opposed Yugoslavia's demands for ethnic reasons and also, probably, because he was reluctant to see the important port of Trieste fall into the hands of a Russian satellite state.

The Trieste problem in 1946 likewise somewhat resembled the Danzig problem in 1919.[7] In the latter year Poland desired Danzig as an outlet to the sea, though Danzig's population of some 300,000 was overwhelmingly German. In 1946, Yugoslavia similarly desired Trieste as an outlet to

---

[6] For the Italian-Yugoslav crisis of 1919, see pages 129–130.
[7] For the Danzig problem in 1919, see pages 117–119.

the sea for her northwestern territories even though the city's 250,000 inhabitants were predominantly Italian. In 1919, France looked to Poland as a possible postwar ally, and Clemenceau therefore fought in the "Big Four" to have Danzig given to Poland. In 1946, Russia considered Yugoslavia as an ally and an outpost on the Adriatic, and Molotov consequently supported Yugoslavia's demand for Trieste. In 1946, as in 1919, a compromise was reached in the establishment of a Free City.

Ultimately in 1946, despite many disagreements in the "Big Four," full and almost complete peace treaties were drafted for each of the five minor defeated powers. Where agreement was not reached on any specific point alternative articles were prepared. The task of the peace conference of 1946, therefore, was to be that of accepting, rejecting, or amending articles already drafted by the "Big Four." The latter decided in advance, however, that the Council of Foreign Ministers must agree after the peace conference upon the specific and final terms of each treaty.

On July 29, 1946, the second Paris peace conference of the twentieth century was opened by French Foreign Minister Bidault. At the very first session of the plenary conference the smaller states revolted against domination by the "Big Four," but they won only slight concessions. In general, however, the small powers were better treated in 1946 than they had been at Paris after the First World War. For instance, in 1919 the full text of the treaty of Versailles was not presented to the small powers until the day before it was presented to the Germans, and then Clemenceau did not permit a vote on its acceptance or rejection. In 1946, the plenary conference, which included the small powers, was permitted to vote article by article on all five of the treaties. The defeated powers, too, were treated better in 1946 than in 1919, at least on the surface. Representatives of the five enemy states were invited to present their views to the plenary conference before the various commissions began their work, and speeches were accordingly delivered before the conference by the Italian and Rumanian premiers and by the Bulgarian, Hungarian, and Finnish foreign ministers. Although these speeches probably had little effect on the eventual treaties, the defeated powers were at least given a chance to be heard by the whole conference. Finally, the general public was better treated in 1946 than during the earlier peace conference. The 1919 meetings of the Council of Ten and of the "Big Four" were secret and even after the treaty of Versailles had been approved and presented to the German delegation, the full text was kept secret from people in the Allied countries. In 1946, on the other hand, the preliminary draft treaties were published at the time the peace conference opened, and all meetings of commissions as well as of the plenary conference were open to the press.

In 1946, as in 1919, most of the work of the peace conference was done by various commissions, but eventually on October 7 the latter had reports ready to submit to the plenary conference. In the ensuing days each national delegation was permitted one half-hour speech on each of the five treaties. Following these speeches the plenary conference started voting on the various articles of the peace treaties. Innumerable votes were taken and in general the outcome in each case was 15 to 6 in favor of the views of the Western powers and 15 to 6 against those of Russia or Yugoslavia. On the night of October 14 the last of the five treaties was approved, and on the next day the conference adjourned, following a farewell address by Bidault.

But it must be emphasized that the Paris peace conference of 1946 was only an advisory body and that the final treaties still had to be approved by those members of the "Big Four" which had signed the armistices with the respective enemy powers. About all that the conference had done, therefore, was to indicate by votes that, in general, those fifteen states which had capitalistic, democratic institutions uniformly supported Byrnes, Bevin, and Bidault against Molotov and that the Slav bloc of six states [8]—dominated by Russia with her communistic, totalitarian institutions—uniformly supported Molotov. The problem of unanimous agreement among the "Big Four" still remained unsolved.

In a last attempt to reach a solution another session of the Council of Foreign Ministers was held, this time in New York (November 4–December 12, 1946). On the majority of issues the agreements of the "Big Four" reached in that session were based upon recommendations made by the Paris peace conference. The five treaties were ultimately signed in Paris on February 10, 1947, by representatives of the enemy states and by representatives of the states which had participated in the Paris peace conference except the United States. Byrnes had already signed for the latter in Washington on January 20, the day before George C. Marshall succeeded him as secretary of state.

The Peace Treaties with Italy, Hungary, Rumania, Bulgaria, and Finland

The Italians, having signed an armistice with the Allies in 1943 and having indeed actually declared war on Germany in October of that year, were most unhappy over the peace treaty which they were obliged to accept. Under its territorial provisions Italy ceded four small and relatively unimportant areas along her northwestern boundary to France, the Dodecanese Islands to Greece, and her East Adriatic islands and most of the

---

[8] The Slav bloc consisted of Russia, White Russia, the Ukraine, Poland, Czechoslovakia, and Yugoslavia.

Istrian peninsula except Trieste to Yugoslavia. Trieste, which was to be established as a Free Territory, was lost to Italy. The latter further renounced all rights to Libya, Eritrea, and Italian Somaliland in Africa. The ultimate fate of these former Italian colonies was to be decided by the Council of Foreign Ministers, or, if the "Big Four" failed to agree, by the United Nations. But in the meantime they were to remain under British administration. Italy also surrendered all her rights in Albania, Ethiopia, and China.

Although no responsible statesman in 1946 had such fantastic ideas regarding reparation payments as were demanded from Germany after the First World War, Italy was required to make some payments in goods over a period of years: $100,000,000 to Russia, $125,000,000 to Yugoslavia, $105,-000,000 to Greece, $25,000,000 to Ethiopia, and $5,000,000 to Albania. She was also required to pay compensation for damage to Allied property in Italy to the extent of two thirds of its agreed value.

In the matter of war potential, Italy was drastically limited. Her army, including carabinieri, was reduced to 250,000 men, her air force to 25,000, and her navy to 22,500. She was permitted to have only 2 battleships, 4 cruisers, 4 fleet destroyers, 16 torpedo boats, and 20 corvettes, and she was forbidden to construct or acquire battleships, aircraft carriers, or submarines. Her air force was limited to 200 fighter planes and 150 transport and training planes, and she was forbidden to have any bombers. Extensive areas in Sardinia, Sicily, and Apulia, the strategic island of Pantelleria, and the Italian frontier areas along the boundaries with France and Yugoslavia were wholly or partially demilitarized. These restrictions were to remain in force until the treaty was modified by the Allies and Italy or, after Italy became a member of the United Nations, until agreement between Italy and the Security Council. The destruction of her empire and the limitation of her military, naval, and air forces, largely reduced Italy to the status of a third-rate power. In 1946 many Italians felt that for the second time in thirty years Italy had been betrayed by her "friends."

Many of the provisions of the peace treaties with Hungary, Rumania, Bulgaria, and Finland were in essence similar to those in the Italian treaty. The military, naval, and air forces of all four were strictly limited along the lines laid down for Italy. All four had to make reparation payments in goods over a period of years: Hungary—$200,000,000 to Russia and $50,-000,000 each to Czechoslovakia and Yugoslavia; Rumania—$300,000,000 to Russia; Bulgaria—$45,000,000 to Greece and $25,000,000 to Yugoslavia; Finland—$300,000,000 to Russia. Hungary surrendered all territorial gains made after January, 1938, and in addition ceded Czechoslovakia a small area on the right bank of the Danube opposite Bratislava. Rumania recognized her loss of Bessarabia and northern Bukowina to Russia and her loss

of the southern Dobrudja to Bulgaria in accordance with treaties signed
in 1940, but received back northern Transylvania which had been ceded
to Hungary at that time.[9] Bulgaria, despite repeated efforts, failed to obtain
a territorial outlet to the Aegean at the expense of Greece, but was allowed
to retain the southern Dobrudja. Finland by her treaty lost to Russia the
Karelian Isthmus, Viborg and its bay and islands, a number of islands in
the Gulf of Finland, territory west, north, and northeast of Lake Ladoga,
territory north of Markajaervi and Kuolajaervi, part of the Rybachi peninsula, and the district of Petsamo with its valuable mineral deposits and its
outlet to the Arctic.[10] Furthermore, Finland leased Russia territory and
water for a naval base on the Porkala headland in return for Russia's renouncing her earlier lease of Hangoe.

The European Recovery Program

The peace negotiations of 1945–1946 had repeatedly revealed the differences in ideologies and aims of Soviet Russia on the one hand and the
Western democracies on the other. During those same years ideological
clashes had also occurred over "democratic" elections in Bulgaria and Rumania, over Russia's removal of capital goods from Manchuria as "war
booty," over the granting of "freedom and independence" to Korea, over
Soviet pressure on Iran for oil concessions, and over Russia's demand for
control of the Straits. Soon after the signing of the peace treaties the tension
between Russia and the United States further increased as a result of the
announcement of the "Truman Doctrine." Disturbed by the growing evidence of Soviet influence in the states of eastern and central Europe and
by the possibility that Greece and Turkey might succumb to Communist
pressure, President Truman on March 12, 1947, declared that "totalitarian
regimes imposed on free peoples undermine ... the security of the United
States," and asked the Congress to appropriate funds to aid Greece and
Turkey to resist totalitarian pressure. Three months later the United States,
in order to hasten the economic recovery of Europe—and decrease the likelihood of more countries turning to Communism—offered the so-called Marshall Plan. Russia and her satellite states rejected the plan, denounced it as
American imperialism, and set out to wreck it. A "cold war" then ensued
between Soviet Russia and the Western democracies, particularly the
United States.

To anyone who knew the facts, however, the need for American economic aid to Europe was obvious. The physical destruction of European
industry, transportation, and agriculture by the Second World War was

[9] See page 513.
[10] See map on page 501.

terrific.[11] In addition to outright destruction, however, there was also an invisible devastation caused by the war in deterioration of capital and man power and in economic dislocations. Deterioration of industrial and transport equipment inevitably resulted from obsolescence and from over-exploitation during the war years without adequate maintenance and replacement. A parallel deterioration of agricultural tools and equipment also occurred, accompanied by a deterioration of soil fertility. Moreover, the productive capacity of the people was reduced by war exhaustion, under-nourishment, and loss of technical skills.

In the immediate postwar years, consequently, Europe suffered acutely from a number of shortages of basic commodities. One was coal. Whereas Europe [12] had been self-sufficient with respect to coal before the Second World War, in 1947 it produced only 84 per cent of its prewar average, and to meet its most urgent needs had to import high-cost coal from the United States. Steel was another commodity essential for Europe's reconstruction but in 1947 Europe produced only 63 per cent of its prewar volume and was therefore in no position to meet its reconstruction requirements in the matter of steel. Shortages of machinery and equipment were serious everywhere but particularly in the devastated countries. These shortages in turn contributed to the delay in the Continent's industrial recovery. The lack of mine equipment, for example, impeded the increase in production of both coal and steel; and the lack of coal and steel, in turn, handicapped the manufacture of machinery. Europe's system of transport and communication, too, had suffered extensive damage during the war. This was particularly true of motor vehicles, railway rolling stock, and merchant marine. "Thousands of miles of railway lines, a great many railway and highway bridges (well over half of the prewar number in some countries), large and small stations, locomotive sheds, construction facilities, repair shops and other buildings, and harbor installations, as well, were either destroyed or incapacitated."

Furthermore, Europe's shortage of food was critical in the immediate postwar years. The chief factors causing the lack of food were shortages of fertilizers, machinery, farm equipment, and draught animals. Although UNRRA provided 23,000 tractors and 260,000 draught animals, it was estimated that these replaced less than 5 per cent of the loss of draught animals. The deterioration and depletion of the latter and of machinery, in turn, necessitated more hand labor than before the war to produce the same quantity of food. In many of the devastated areas, therefore, there

---

[11] The material in the first five paragraphs of this section is drawn chiefly from *Salient Features of the World Economic Situation, 1945–47* (1948), an economic report of the United Nations.

[12] In these paragraphs "Europe" denotes Europe excluding the Soviet Union.

occurred a shortage of farm labor. Moreover, the sharp decline in the production of insecticides and allied products in the devastated areas and the reduction in the capacity of chemical industries in Germany and Italy created a lack of these commodities so essential to agriculture. Europe was therefore forced to increase its importation of food over prewar days in order to feed its people, and even before the Second World War 25 per cent of the imports of western Europe had been foodstuffs.

In the United States, on the other hand, over-all industrial production had increased 80 per cent and agricultural output had expanded 36 per cent. In the third quarter of 1947 the production of the durable goods industries in that country was almost double that of prewar production. It was to the United States primarily that Europe had to turn to procure its needed commodities, and during the first half of 1947 United States exports were five times the dollar value of those in 1938. American imports, on the other hand, did not increase at any such rate so that the United States balance of payments indicated a surplus on account of goods and services of $16,700,000,000 in the two years after the war ended with Germany. The European countries did not have the dollar credits to meet this tremendous adverse balance, and the United States government was called upon to furnish aid to many governments, chiefly European, aid which totaled $16,600,000,000 by October 1, 1947.

But by the end of 1947 normal economic conditions were still far from re-established in Europe, and it had become apparent that postwar economic reconstruction would require a longer period of time and be more difficult to achieve than had been expected. Agricultural production, in particular, had received severe setbacks as the result of unfavorable weather conditions. The standard of living of the population of Europe was still far below prewar levels. And to make matters worse, no state of equilibrium had yet been achieved in the economies of European countries, which continued to be subject to inflationary pressures arising from continuing shortages in the face of huge reconstruction requirements.

In the summer of 1947, United States Secretary of State Marshall declared that the United States could not proceed much further with its assistance to Europe unless the countries there reached some agreement as to their requirements and as to their own contribution to European recovery. Any further American assistance, he declared, "should provide a cure rather than a mere palliative." On June 27, 1947, Bevin, Molotov, and Bidault conferred in Paris regarding the Marshall offer. Molotov's views differed from those of the other two. He dismissed the idea of an "all-embracing European economic plan" as unacceptable, suggesting that each country should merely state what it required from the United States. He denounced any plan which provided that German resources should be used for general European reconstruction before the reparations question was settled. He declared that the Marshall Plan indicated that economic recovery must result from co-operation with the great powers by states under their domination, and asked how the small states would be able to safeguard their national economies and their independence. Bevin and Bidault maintained that the United States had reasonably asked, as a prerequisite of further American aid, that the European countries should now state what they could do to help themselves and one another, and asserted that Great Britain and France intended to pursue the Marshall offer in collaboration with any state which wished to join them. Molotov thereupon warned that such a step "would lead to Britain, France, and that group of countries which follows them separating themselves from the other states, and thus the American credits would result in dividing Europe into two groups of states and creating new difficulties in the relations between them."

The British and French governments, nevertheless, sent invitations to all European countries, except Russia, Germany, and Spain, to a conference in Paris on July 12, and stated their belief that a temporary organization should be set up to gather the data on which a program covering both the resources and needs of Europe would be based. This conference was attended by representatives of sixteen states—Britain, France, the Netherlands, Belgium, Luxembourg, Austria, Denmark, Norway, Sweden, Eire, Greece, Italy, Portugal, Switzerland, Iceland, and Turkey. But Russia and her satellites—Poland, Finland, Rumania, Bulgaria, Yugoslavia, Albania, Hungary, and Czechoslovakia—held aloof, though it was reported that strong pressure had to be exerted by Moscow to keep some of them from attending. In the report on the European Recovery Program (ERP), made on September 22, 1947, the sixteen countries pledged themselves to take all feasible measures to bring their budgets into balance, to reduce inflationary pressures, and to stabilize their currencies as quickly as possible. Proposals were submitted to abolish abnormal restrictions on trade and to aim at a sound and balanced multilateral trading system. The report further outlined a four-year program for recovery which called for the restoration of a sound European economy by 1951, but which would entail a total deficit of $22,400,000,000 of which $19,300,000,000 would be required from the United States.

On December 19, 1947, President Truman requested the United States Congress to authorize an appropriation of $17,000,000,000 for the European Recovery Program from April 1, 1948 to June 30, 1952. Although there was considerable opposition to the program in the Congress, it was ultimately approved by both houses on April 2, 1948, with the title "Economic Co-operation Act of 1948." Two weeks later representatives of the powers participating in the European Recovery Program signed a convention in

Paris establishing a permanent organization, the Organization for European Economic Co-operation (OEEC). In June the Congress finally voted an appropriation of $6,030,710,228 for the period from April 1, 1948 to June 30, 1949. On April 5 the first shipments under the Marshall Plan had left American ports. Subsequent shipments were to include food, steel, coal, cotton, petroleum, farm machinery, mining machinery, electrical equipment, and motor trucks.

The results were encouraging. By June, 1950, the Economic Co-operation Administration (ECA)—the United States agency responsible for administering the ERP—announced, industrial production in countries of the OEEC had risen 20 per cent above that of 1938. Intra-European trade had also mounted above the prewar level and, according to the OEEC, price stability had been achieved in virtually all its member countries. By 1951 it appeared that the ERP had accomplished in three years nearly everything which had been expected in four. In the years 1947–1950 the total deficit in western Europe's current balance of payments had been reduced from $8,000,000,000 to $1,000,000,000. While exports had increased 91 per cent by volume, imports had risen only 22 per cent. In July, 1951, the industrial production of the OEEC countries was 50 per cent above the 1947 level. By the summer of 1951 Great Britain, Ireland, Sweden, and Portugal had announced that they would no longer need ERP assistance.

Unfortunately, in 1951 the effects of the outbreak of the Korean War began to be increasingly felt in western Europe. The outbreak of that war started prices rising again, and the decision of the Western democracies to gird themselves for a possible future conflict with the Communist world led to new agreements for collective security and to increased and accelerated rearmament. The latter, in turn, put a heavier burden on western Europe's economy and the dollar gap once more began to widen. The ECA administrator stressed the need for the United States to import more from Europe to relieve the dollar shortage, and in Europe the slogan, "Trade not Aid," began to be heard.

The fate of the ERP after June, 1952, received increasing consideration both in Europe and in the United States, for it seemed clear that some form of American assistance to western Europe would have to be continued after its expiration. Ultimately, in September, 1951, the United States Congress created the Mutual Security Agency (MSA) to co-ordinate the administration of all United States economic, military, and technical aid programs, with emphasis, it was expected, to be placed chiefly on assistance to increase the military strength of the Western democracies. Europe's economic recovery, it was obvious to all observers, was seriously handicapped by the division of the world into two hostile camps.

The Cominform

That Europe was to become split into two camps had become evident as early as October 5, 1947, when it was announced that a conference of the Communist parties of Bulgaria, Czechoslovakia, France, Hungary, Italy, Poland, Rumania, Russia, and Yugoslavia, held in Warsaw, had decided to set up an Information Bureau. The name "Cominform" was soon applied to this new Communist international organization, which to many seemed to resemble the former Comintern. It was obvious from the resolution setting up the Cominform that it was designed to counteract the European Recovery Program, which it characterized as "only the European part of a general plan of world expansion being carried out by the United States." To counter "this front of imperialists and nationalists," it asserted, all democratic countries must oppose it. The "great task awaiting the Communist parties . . . is that of preserving freedom and peace."

The organization of the Cominform might, perhaps, be called Russia's negative reaction to the European Recovery Program. What might be called the Soviet Union's positive reaction came with the organization of the Council for Economic Mutual Assistance at a conference of representatives of Bulgaria, Czechoslovakia, Hungary, Poland, Rumania, and Russia in Moscow in January, 1949. The announcement of the new organization stated that it was formed because the United States, Britain, and certain other western European countries had been boycotting commercially "the countries of the people's democracy" and Russia because they had failed "to submit to the Marshall Plan dictate, as this plan violated the sovereignty of countries and the interests of their national economies." The announcement stated that the new organization might be joined by other European countries which shared the principles of the Council for Economic Mutual Assistance, and in February Albania was admitted into the Council. The division of Europe thus became clear-cut.

The effects of the ensuing "cold war" between Russia and the Western democracies are easily discernible in the Allied treatment of Germany, Austria, and Japan.

The Allied Treatment of Defeated Germany

One significant difference between peace-making in 1946 and peace-making in 1919 was that after the Second World War the Allies gave their attention first to the drafting of treaties with the minor powers rather than, as in 1919, to the most important task, namely, the peace treaty with Germany. In 1946 the crucial question for all Europe—the fate of Germany—

was postponed. The reason given for the postponement was that a peace settlement could not be made for Germany until that country had a government ready to accept it and adequate to execute it. But undoubtedly behind the announced reason for delay were also the fears and suspicions of the "Big Four" and their realization of the difficulty which would confront them in agreeing upon terms.

As early as the Yalta Conference the Allies had begun to make plans for dealing with postwar Germany and during the succeeding years many conferences of the "Big Four" concerned themselves with Allied treatment of that country. At the time when knowledge of the terrible war destruction and ruthless treatment of conquered peoples by the Germans was fresh and the general desire to ward off the horror of a third world war was paramount, the Allies mapped out a program which called for severe punishment, extensive reparations, swift and sure destruction of German militarism and Nazism, and the drastic restriction of German industry in order to prevent the future rebuilding of war potential. But as the years passed without a definitive peace settlement, memories of German atrocities and destruction dimmed, the problem of sustaining life in disrupted and restricted Germany proved a burden for the Western powers, and the latter's fears and suspicions of the aims of Soviet Russia became intensified. Gradually some parts of the earlier-adopted program for dealing with the Reich were modified in order to lessen the burden on the Allies and to improve the lot of the Germans enough to prevent them and the other peoples of western Europe from falling a prey to Communism because of their economic hardships and dissatisfaction. In the interests of clarity, the Allied treatment of Germany will be discussed topically.

OCCUPATION ZONES

At Yalta, Churchill, Roosevelt, and Stalin had agreed that defeated Germany would be occupied by military forces of the United States, Great Britain, Russia, and France, each country in a separate zone, and that a central control council, consisting of the supreme military commanders of the four zones, with headquarters in Berlin, would provide for co-ordinated administration and control. As finally worked out, the American zone consisted of southeastern Germany, including Munich, Nuremberg, and Frankfort, and a small region on both sides of the Weser estuary, including Bremen. The Russian zone comprised the states of northeastern Germany up to the Oder and Neisse rivers, excluding Berlin but including Leipzig, Dresden, Chemnitz, Halle, Eisenach, and Magdeburg. The British occupied northwestern Germany, including Hamburg, the Ruhr area, and Cologne but excluding the American enclave about Bremen. The French took over the Rhineland south of Cologne, including the Saar Basin, an area which, though much smaller than that of the other Allies, was of vital concern to France.

By the middle of August, 1945, the Russians had relinquished parts of Berlin for occupation by the other Allies, and on August 30 the Allies in a proclamation to the German people announced the establishment of the Allied Control Council in the former German capital.

New York Times

THE OCCUPATION ZONES OF GERMANY

FUTURE BOUNDARIES

At the Yalta Conference, also, the "Big Three" had agreed that Poland, while surrendering to Russia most of the former Polish territory east of the "Curzon Line," must receive substantial additions of territory in the north and west, although the final delimitation of the western frontier must await the peace conference. At Potsdam the three Allies agreed in principle that East Prussia in the vicinity of Memel and Königsberg should be transferred to Russia and that all other former German territory east of the Oder and Neisse rivers should be under the administration of Poland and should not be considered as part of the zone of occupation in Germany. Although at Potsdam it was again agreed that the determination of the Polish-German boundary should await the peace settlement, it was later generally assumed by Russian and Polish statesmen that the territory under Polish administration was to be permanently Polish, and that the Oder-Neisse rivers would constitute Germany's eastern boundary.

POPULATION TRANSFERS

At Potsdam, the three Allies had recognized that the transfer to Germany of German populations remaining in Poland, Czechoslovakia, and Hungary would have to be undertaken, and in November, 1945, Allied representatives approved a plan for the transfer of some 6,650,000 Germans from those countries into the various occupied zones in Germany. This step was deemed necessary because of these states' fears of having any German minorities within their bounds. The German policy of using slave labor in the Reich during the war created another gigantic problem of transferring populations. It was estimated that in the twelve months after the armistice the Allies handled between 20 and 25 million people, some moving east and some moving west. Only a few glimpses of what occurred can be given here. To Hungary, Czechoslovakia, and Yugoslavia 4,000,000 displaced persons were returned; to Russia 2,000,000; to Poland more than 2,000,000; to France, the Netherlands, and Belgium, 800,000. In addition, 1,000,000 prisoners of war were repatriated to France, and great numbers to Italy. Even within Germany great shifts occurred; for instance, 5,000,000 persons went from the British to the Soviet zone and 1,700,000 from the Soviet to the British zone. These population movements probably dwarfed anything which had ever occurred in Europe in so short a period.

WAR CRIMINALS

In contrast with the little that was done after the First World War,[13] the Allies had meanwhile taken steps to bring the chief German war criminals to trial. An International Military Tribunal was established by the "Big Four" and by October 18, 1945, twenty-four German leaders had been indicted with participating in the plot against peace and humanity conceived by Hitler. The International Military Tribunal held its hearings for many months in Nuremberg and eventually in the autumn of 1946 condemned twelve men to death, three to life imprisonment, and four to prison terms of from ten to twenty years. Ley, former head of the Labor Front, had committed suicide soon after his indictment, and Gustav Krupp's trial had been postponed because of his ill health. Göring com-

[13] See page 124.

mitted suicide before his sentence was carried out, but on October 16 ten former German leaders,[14] including Ribbentrop, Keitel, Rosenberg, Streicher, Frank, Frick, and Seyss-Inquart, were hanged. Hess was sentenced to life imprisonment, but Schacht, Papen, and Fritzsche were acquitted, contrary to the desire of many foreigners and Germans. The Nuremberg Tribunal also condemned as criminal four Nazi organizations: the Leadership Corps, the Schutzstaffeln (SS), the Gestapo, and the Sicherheitsdienst (SD).

In addition to this spectacular trial of prominent war criminals in Nuremberg, the military governments of the four zones also conducted trials of hundreds of lesser criminals. Some military commanders were punished for the war crimes of troops under their command, some members of Hitler's ministry of justice were sentenced to prison, and many men—and some women—were hanged or imprisoned for their roles in connection with the terrible atrocities perpetrated on some millions of inmates of German concentration camps. In 1947, Friedrick Flick, Thyssen's successor as head of the Vereinigte Stahlwerke, the directors of the I. G. Farben Industrie, and the directors of the extensive Krupp industries were also brought to trial on charges of conspiring with Hitler to wage aggressive war and on charges of participating in the German program of slave labor and the plundering of occupied countries. Although all were acquitted on the charges of conspiracy with Hitler, they did not all escape on the other two counts. The United States military tribunal sentenced Flick to seven years' imprisonment, Alfred Krupp to twelve years in prison and to the confiscation of all of his property, and ten former Krupp officials and thirteen former directors or officials of the I. G. Farben concern to prison terms ranging from eighteen months to eight years.

DENAZIFICATION

At Yalta, it had been decided to wipe out the Nazi Party, laws, organizations, and institutions, and to remove all Nazi influences from the cultural and economic life of the German people. At Potsdam, it had been further decided that Nazi leaders, influential Nazi supporters, and high officials of Nazi organizations and institutions should be arrested and interned, and that all members of the Nazi Party who had been more than nominal participants in its activities should be removed from public and semipublic office and from positions of responsibility in important private undertakings.

In pursuance of these aims, the Allied Control Council in 1945 issued

---

[14] Martin Borman was tried and condemned in absentia, his whereabouts being unknown. Hitler and Goebbels had died during the battle of Berlin and Himmler had committed suicide in 1945.

directives repealing Nazi laws, liquidating Nazi organizations, removing Nazi sympathizers from public office, and providing for the denazification of schools. The occupying governments in all four zones undertook to investigate and try millions of Germans suspected of having been active in the Nazi Party. Thousands were given prison terms, sentenced to hard labor, or debarred from office. In some cases the Allies were assisted also by German courts; those in the American zone, for instance, gave prison sentences of various lengths to some men who had been high in the Third Reich. But the Allies discovered that at least one disadvantage resulted from sweeping denazification; so widespread had been membership in the Nazi Party that practically all trained leaders, executives, and administrators in Germany's political, economic, and cultural life were included and their removal from office frequently made it necessary to put men of less knowledge, ability, and training in their places. As the desire for rehabilitating Germany increased among the Allies, and particularly after tension between Russia and the Western powers developed, the enthusiasm for thoroughgoing denazification declined, and men who were known to have been Nazis or sympathizers with Nazism were frequently permitted to resume their former duties. In 1948 denazification proceedings were largely discontinued in all the zones.

Meanwhile, efforts had been made to eliminate Nazi doctrines from German education. Many educators from the Allied countries were sent to Germany to attempt to remold that country's educational system and indoctrinate the German youth in democracy. They were handicapped, of course, by a shortage of classrooms, teachers, and books, but more particularly by German adherence to Nazi principles. In November, 1947, a popular poll taken in the British zone showed that most Germans still believed that Nazism was "a good idea, but badly carried out under Hitler." Said the American adviser on cultural matters in June, 1948: "It is evident to me that Germany will have recovered economically long before she has recovered spiritually. She will have great economic power long before she has developed a democratic sense of responsibility for the use of that power."

DEMILITARIZATION

At both Yalta and Potsdam the Allies had announced their determination to destroy German militarism in order to ensure that Germany should never again be able to disturb the peace of the world. To this end they planned to disarm and disband all German armed forces, break up for all time the German general staff that had repeatedly contrived the resurgence of German militarism, remove or destroy all German military equipment, and eliminate or control all German industry that could be used for military production. The first three of these objectives were largely attained in all the zones by 1947. The fourth objective caused some disagreement among the occupying powers because of the difficulty of drawing the line between industries that were valuable for peace production and those that could be used to produce war supplies. When the problem of rehabilitating German economic life became acute, Great Britain and the United States were inclined to become more lenient in their definition of peace industry and to permit the continuation of some industries in their zones which France and Russia considered ought to be dismantled.

The conflict between France on the one hand and the United States and Great Britain on the other was well exemplified in views regarding the treatment of the Ruhr. On November 10, 1948, the United States and British military governments announced that, in the interest of greater efficiency and increased production, limited and temporary control of the Ruhr coal, iron, and steel industries would be turned over to German trustees pending the final determination of ownership by a future German government. An international authority, however, would regulate the distribution of the Ruhr's products. France at once protested against this Anglo-American decision, and contended that, in the interest of her own security, international control must be extended also to production. She was apparently able to force some modification in the Anglo-American plans, for eventually, in December, a London conference of the six powers interested in the Ruhr agreed to set up "The International Authority for the Ruhr," with sweeping powers to supervise the Ruhr's industries for an indefinite period. The main organ of this authority was to be a council representing the United States, Britain, France, Belgium, the Netherlands, Luxembourg, and Western Germany, with the three great powers and Western Germany having three votes each and the lesser states one each.

The international authority was given power to ensure that the resources of the Ruhr would in the future be used not for purposes of aggression but solely in the interests of peace. To that end it was agreed that there should not be allowed to develop ownership in the Ruhr coal, coke or steel industries, or trade and marketing agreements among such industries, which would institute excessive concentration of economic power; nor should persons who had been or might be found to have furthered the aggressive designs of the Nazis hold positions of ownership or control in the Ruhr industries. The authority was to divide the coal, coke, and steel production of the district so as to ensure adequate access to supplies of these products by countries co-operating in the common economic good, taking into account the essential needs of Germany. Although these agreements did not go far enough to satisfy some French leaders and were bitterly denounced for different reasons by both the Germans and the Russians, they were in line with earlier agreements of the chief Allied leaders.

ALLIED ECONOMIC CONTROLS

At Potsdam the Allied statesmen had decided that controls should be imposed on German economy to the extent necessary: (1) to carry out industrial disarmament; (2) to assure the production required to meet the needs of the occupying forces and to maintain in Germany average living standards no higher than those of other European countries; (3) to ensure the equitable distribution of essential commodities between the several zones so as to produce a balanced economy throughout Germany and reduce the need of imports; (4) to control German industry and commerce with the aim of preventing Germany from developing a war potential. German economy, it was further decided, should be decentralized to eliminate the excessive concentration of economic power as exemplified by cartels, syndicates, and trusts. Furthermore, in organizing the German economy primary emphasis should be placed on the development of agriculture and peaceful domestic industries. Productive capacity not needed for permitted production should be removed as reparations or destroyed.

Early in 1946 the Allied Control Council published its plan for the future level of German industry, the general effect of which was expected to be a reduction by 1949 to about half the level of 1938. Exports were planned as 3,000,000,000 marks (1936 value) for 1949, and approved imports were not to exceed that figure, though they had amounted to 4,200,000,000 marks in 1936. Certain specific decrees were issued. The production of synthetic gasoline, rubber, ammonia, aluminum, magnesium, certain chemicals, agricultural tractors, and machine tools was forbidden. Germany's steel production capacity was limited to 7,500,000 tons and the production of steel was not to exceed 5,800,000 tons in any year without permission of the Council. Furthermore, Germany was forbidden to construct ocean-going vessels and forbidden to export basic chemicals, vehicles, tractors, and heavy electrical or metallurgical equipment. These limitations on Germany's industry and commerce largely deprived her of her former means of payment for imports. With more need than in 1936 to import food, she would be less able to pay for it.

Ultimately the statesmen of the United States and Great Britain reached the conclusion that the Germans could not export enough to buy for themselves the food and raw materials which they needed so long as their industries were thus drastically restricted and their country was arbitrarily divided. And if the Germans could not become self-sufficient, the United States and Great Britain would be compelled to advance huge sums in subsidies to enable them to exist. Furthermore, unless Germany was possessed of a sound economy, it appeared, there could be no sound economy in western Europe. These statesmen thus found themselves forced to choose between two policies: (1) the continued limitation of German industry in order to prevent the revival of German military might; (2) the restoration of German industry to a higher level than earlier contemplated in order to make Germany self-supporting and able to contribute to the economic life of western Euope. Bevin and Byrnes decided in favor of the second course.

In August, 1947, the United States and Great Britain decided to revise the level of industry in their two zones up to that of 1936, in contrast with the 70–75 per cent of 1936 production permitted by the Allied Control Council's plan of 1946. Their hope was to make their two zones self-supporting, and new totals of production in the so-called restricted industries and in the total export trade were permitted. In return for the United States' assumption of most of the cost of subsidizing the German economy, the United States received the controlling voice in the agencies for deciding production and export polic:es in the two zones. Russia denounced the Anglo-American plan as an abrogation of the Potsdam agreement and the French, still thinking of security, also questioned the wisdom of the Anglo-American policy.

NATIONAL ECONOMIC DISUNION

The Potsdam Conference had decided that during the period of Allied occupation Germany should be treated as a single economic unit, and that essential German administrative departments, headed by state secretaries, should be established, particularly for finance, transport, communications, foreign trade, and industry. Such departments were to function under the direction of the Allied Control Council. But the French government which had not been represented at Potsdam, claimed that it was not bound by these decisions, and refused to approve the establishment of the central administrative machinery agreed upon at that conference. No progress, therefore, was made toward establishing the five German administrative departments needed for an economically unified Germany and in consequence freedom of interzone transportation, communications, and commerce was lacking.

The French, ever mindful of the three German invasions of their country in the preceding century, were primarily concerned with their own national security. They asserted that 65,000,000 Germans in one state, much smaller in area than in 1937 and with its industrial life drastically curtailed, would surely explode politically within a generation and once more produce war. They argued that, until a solution was found of the problem of the economic existence of the German people, it was necessary in the interests of the French national security to prevent the political unification of Germany.

In July, 1946, at a meeting of the Council of Foreign Ministers, Bevin suggested a plan for treating the economic resources of Germany as a whole without establishing the central administrative departments to which the French objected. Bevin maintained that there should be an equitable distribution of German resources throughout the four zones, that surplus resources in one zone should be made available to meet any deficit in the approved requirements of the other zones. Because Germany was not being treated as an economic unit, he pointed out, the British zone was not obtaining the benefit of surplus German resources of other zones. Surplus from the Soviet zone, he declared, was being taken as reparations. On this occasion Byrnes and Bidault approved Bevin's plan, but Molotov rejected it, claiming that its operation would be contrary to the reparations agreement made at Potsdam. Meanwhile, the Russian zone was largely closed to outsiders and shrouded in obscurity. For all practical purposes rivers and nearly all railways and roads ended at the so-called "Iron Curtain." Nevertheless, it was generally known that Russia had removed, and was continuing to remove, large quantities of machinery, tools, and other equipment from its zone as reparations.

REPARATIONS

At Yalta the "Big Three" had agreed that justice demanded that Germany should make compensation in kind to the fullest possible extent for all damage caused to the Allied nations. This general statement was made more explicit at Potsdam where it was decided that Russia's reparation claims should be met, in the first place, by removals from the zone of Germany occupied by Russia and from appropriate German external assets in Finland, Rumania, Bulgaria, Hungary, and eastern Austria. In addition, however, Russia should receive from the Western zones in Germany 10 per cent of such usable and complete industrial capital equipment as was unnecessary [15] for the German peace economy and a further 15 per cent of such capital equipment in exchange for an equivalent value of food and other commodities. Russia, in turn, agreed to settle Poland's reparation claims from her own share of reparations. The reparation claims of the United States, Great Britain, and other countries entitled to reparations, except Poland, were to be met from the Western zones and from appropriate German external assets in countries other than those reserved for Russia. The payment of reparations, it was agreed, should leave enough resources in Germany to enable her people to subsist without external assistance.

In January, 1946, an Inter-Allied Reparation Agency was created and

[15] The determination of what industrial capital equipment was unnecessary was made subject to the final approval of the zone commander in the zone from which the equipment was to be removed.

designated as the central organization for allocating German reparation assets among the states, other than Russia and Poland, which were to receive reparation payments. According to the original agreement reparations were to come from industrial capital equipment, German external assets in countries other than those assigned to Russia, merchant shipping, inland water transport, captured enemy supplies, and current production. The work of the Reparation Agency was greatly handicapped, however, by the disagreement which developed in the "Big Four" over the political and economic future of Germany, and reparation assets made available to the Agency for allocation were comparatively small. In November, 1947, the Agency estimated the total number of plants declared available for reparations by the military governors of the three Western zones as 858, valued at only 800,000,000 to 1,100,000,000 Reichsmarks, and expressed disappointment at the low amount of reparations thus declared available. The Agency discussed the possibility of obtaining additional reparations from existing stocks, current production, and services, but dropped the discussion following the disagreement in the Council of Foreign Ministers at London (November 25–December 15, 1947).[16]

By this date the four great Allies had definitely split on the question of the economic treatment of Germany. Russia held that reparations were essential to repair the economic losses suffered by the United Nations, especially by herself, at the hands of Germany and her satellites. But they were essential, also, she maintained, in order to reduce Germany's industrial war potential. Furthermore, Russia had found that the removal of capital assets from Germany to the Soviet Union was not so efficient as she had expected and had concluded that it would in some cases be preferable to leave factories in Germany and take their products as reparations. In other words Russia had begun to press for reparation payments from current German production.

The Western Allies, on the other hand, had become more and more angered at Russia's unwillingness to permit the economic unification of Germany and more and more concerned at the disruption that the removal of reparations was inflicting on the German economy. In August, 1947, the United States and Britain finally gave notice that no more plants in their zones would be made available for reparations until Western Germany's production had been built up and until Russia had become more cooperative in the matter of German economic unity. Molotov thereupon

---

[16] Up to the end of 1947 the Reparation Agency had had 261 plants or parts of plants made available to it for reparations, of which equipment from 234 had been allocated to different countries by April, 1948. Better progress had been made in the distribution of the German merchant fleet; by the middle of 1947 some 274 ships had been distributed to eighteen nations. The remaining German vessels, suitable only for scrapping, had been sold to the highest bidders.

appeared willing to accept Germany's economic unification provided that Russia obtained reparations from the current production of the Western zones. Marshall and Bevin, on the other hand, held that German ability to pay for imports must have priority over reparation payments, otherwise the United States and Great Britain, which had each been subsidizing German imports with almost $500,000,000 yearly, would find themselves "paying for the imports necessary to keep Germany alive while others obtain the reparations." When Molotov ultimately agreed that Germany's industrial production might be raised to twice the total originally planned, but insisted that 10 per cent of it should go for reparations, regardless of the effect on German self-sufficiency, the London Conference broke down and adjourned *sine die*.

RESTORATION OF LOCAL SELF-GOVERNMENT

At Potsdam it had been decided that the administration of affairs in Germany should be directed toward the decentralization of the political structure of the country and toward the development of local responsibility. To these ends it was agreed that democratic political parties should be allowed and encouraged throughout Germany, that local self-government should be restored on democratic principles as rapidly as consistent with military security, and that the representative and elective principles should be introduced into regional, provincial, and state (Land) administration as soon as justified by the successful application of these principles in local government. It was further decided that for the time being no central German government should be established.

Although at first the Germans seemed to be politically apathetic, eventually, four major political parties again appeared: Social Democrats, Christian Democrats, Free Democrats, and Communists. The Social Democratic Party, led in western Germany by Kurt Schumacher—a former Reichstag deputy who had spent ten years in Nazi concentration camps—had three main aims: unification of Germany under a central government with local administrative power delegated to the states, nationalization of basic industries, and preservation of personal and political liberty. The Christian Democrat Union, on the other hand, desired a federal type of government and the protection and encouragement of free enterprise, and the Right-wing branch of the party had a bourgeois hatred of Russia. The Free Democratic Party, the weakest of the four, advocated a unified but decentralized Germany, free enterprise, and friendship with Soviet Russia as well as the rest of the world.

The Communist Party, whose spokesman, Wilhelm Pieck, had been an associate of Karl Liebknecht and Rosa Luxembourg [17] and had later spent

[17] See page 100.

some years in exile in Russia, sought a unified Germany under a centralized government, a planned economy based on nationalization, and friendship with the Soviet Union. In the Russian zone the Communist Party was particularly active and in April, 1946, forced the Social Democratic Party there to join it in the Socialist Unity Party of Germany. Although Social Democratic leaders in the other zones repudiated this step, the Socialist Unity Party sought, somewhat futilely, to establish branches throughout Germany.

In 1946 the Germans were given their first opportunity to participate in the political life of their country when elections were held for the governments of the smaller political units. Later in the year and in 1947 they were also given an opportunity to elect the members of the various state legislatures. But no steps were taken to restore the national government in Berlin. This was one of the causes of dissension in the "Big Four" at their meetings in Moscow (March 10–April 24) and in London (November 25–December 15) during 1947. Molotov urged the establishment of German political unity as a prerequisite of economic unity and the removal of zonal barriers. But the Allied ministers proved unable to agree on how or when a central government should be formed. This inability to agree, in turn, seemed to indicate an indefinite postponement of any peace conference to deal with Germany, for Molotov insisted that the formation of a central government was also the prerequisite of such a conference.

THE BEGINNING OF WEST GERMAN UNIFICATION

Meanwhile, the Western Allies, despairing of achieving complete economic unification of Germany, had taken measures to unify their zones. In December, 1946, an agreement was signed by the United States and Britain, providing that their two zones should be treated in economic matters as a single area—"Bizonia." France and Russia were invited to join in the project, but both declined. Nevertheless, in 1948, despite formal protests from Russia charging violation of the Potsdam agreement, the United States, Great Britain, and France held conferences in London, attended also by representatives of Belgium, the Netherlands, and Luxembourg, to consider the merger of the French zone with Bizonia. The Americans and British were eager to integrate Germany in the European Recovery Program through increased German production; but the French feared that German economic recovery might again jeopardize French security.

Ultimately, however, the six powers agreed that, pending the eventual re-establishment of German unity, it was desirable for the West German people to establish for themselves political institutions which would enable them to assume full governmental responsibility, subject to the minimum requirements of Allied occupation and control. The military governors were therefore instructed to authorize the heads of the several German states in the three Western zones to convene a constituent assembly in September, 1948, to prepare a federal constitution for the approval of the states.

THE "BATTLE OF BERLIN"

Meanwhile, on June 20 the three Western powers had introduced a currency reform in their zones, replacing the Reichsmark—which had been inflated by the Nazis and later by the occupying powers—with the Deutschemark at a ratio of 10 to 1. Immediately the Russian military governor forbade the use of the Deutschemark in the Soviet zone and also in Berlin, on the ground that the city, although actually divided among the Big Four, lay well within the Russian occupation zone and economically formed part of that zone. He also announced that a new currency would be introduced in the Soviet zone and that after June 26 all other currencies would be banned both there and in Berlin. On June 23 the Western military governors announced that they would introduce the Deutschemark into their sectors of Berlin; on the next day the Soviet authorities stopped railway traffic between Berlin and the west because of a "technical disturbance." Eventually they threw an economic blockade around the Western sectors of the city of Berlin by cutting all rail and water routes which the Western powers had been using to bring supplies into the city.

The so-called battle of Berlin followed. The Western powers countered the Soviet move by instituting a spectacular "air lift" to Berlin, using hundreds of airplanes to carry thousands of tons of cargo to the city daily. At the height of the Allied effort planes arrived in the capital on an average of one every two minutes. The Western powers also cut off from the Russian zone of Germany coal, steel, and other supplies which had been coming from the west. Although the Soviet government appeared to stay carefully within its legal rights, it sought to handicap or restrict the Western powers in Berlin to such an extent that they would withdraw from the capital or make concessions to Russia elsewhere—perhaps abandon the plan for a separate West Germany or grant the Soviet government a share in the control of the industrially rich Ruhr.

Although the Allied use of airplanes to supply Berlin was spectacular, it could not permanently meet the needs of the 2,300,000 Berliners in the Western zones. It could not, for instance, supply the necessary fuel and raw materials to maintain the city's industries. Some factories had to close, and unemployment resulted. At the same time, industries in Russia's zone were affected adversely by the Allied counterblockade. Eventually the Western governments sought to solve the impasse by instituting negotiations directly with Stalin. From July 31 to August 27 the Western ambassadors held conferences in Moscow with Molotov, conferences which Stalin himself twice attended. The Russians wished to discuss the whole German situation, particularly the London decision to set up a Western German government at Frankfort. The West demanded the lifting of the Soviet Berlin blockade as a prelude to such general discussions. The Russians as a prerequisite to lifting the blockade in turn demanded that their German currency be recognized as the sole legal tender in the capital. At length it was agreed in principle that the Soviet mark should be the only currency in Berlin, and the technical questions of currency and the blockade were then turned over to the Allied Control Council, that is, to the four Allied military governors.

While conferences were being held by the Allied generals, Communist-inspired attacks on Berlin's assembly, the only branch of the city's government which had continued to function on a city-wide basis, early in September destroyed that body. The Communist members retained control of the city hall, which was in the Russian zone, and the non-Communist members of the assembly were forced to meet in the British zone. In December the Soviet military commander formally recognized the city administration set up by the Communist members of Berlin's assembly as the only legal municipal authority in the city. Friedrich Ebert, son of the Weimar Republic's first president, became burgomaster of the Communist administration in the Soviet zone of Berlin and he in turn declared that the Soviet military commander was the only authority recognized by his regime. His administration denied access to the city hall to members of the former administration.

In the three Western zones of Berlin, despite Soviet objections, popular elections were held on December 5 for a new municipal assembly. More than 86 per cent of the electorate went to the polls and their votes were distributed roughly 65 per cent to Social Democrats, 19 per cent to Christian Democrats, and 16 per cent to Free Democrats. The new assembly unanimously elected a burgomaster who proposed that, pending the ultimate unification of Berlin, the three Western zones of the city should be merged into a single administrative unit, that the Western military commanders should organize an Allied Control Council for this unit, and that in this unit the Western currency should be the only legal tender. On December 21 the three Western military governors decided to resume the sittings of the Allied Control Council, declaring that if the Soviet authorities should later decide to abide by the existing four-power agreements, the quadripartite administration of Berlin could be reactivated.

Meanwhile, later in September, 1948, the Western Allies had submitted the problem of the Soviet blockade of Berlin to the Security Council of the United Nations. In the succeeding weeks that body had sought to find a solution which would be acceptable to the four Allied powers, but without success. Not until May, 1949, after the Western powers had carried on their airlift for months and had revealed no inclination to recede from their stand on the issues, was the impasse ended. It was finally agreed through diplomacy that the Soviet blockade should be lifted on May 12 and that the Council of Foreign Ministers should once more convene to discuss the German and Austrian situations. Accordingly, the blockade came to an end. But the meeting of the diplomats of the four powers in Paris (May 23–June 20, 1949) brought no tangible results so far as peace treaties with Germany and Austria were concerned.

THE FEDERAL REPUBLIC OF GERMANY

In accordance with the decision of the Western powers at London a constituent convention for West Germany had convened in Bonn in September, 1948, and in May, 1949, it adopted what was called the "Basic Law for the Federal Republic of Germany." By the provisions of this constitution, Germany continued to be a federal state. The national parliament is a bicameral body consisting of the Bundestag (Federal Diet), elected for four years by popular vote, and the Bundesrat (Federal Council), representing the governments of the constitutent states. In the latter each state has at least three votes; the larger states have four or five. The delegates in the Bundesrat are bound by instructions from their respective state governments and must vote as a unit. The Bundesrat is not so powerful as the Bundestag and, in general, exercises a delaying power through its provisional veto.

The executive branch of the government consists of the president and the cabinet, which includes the chancellor and other ministers. The president, definitely less powerful than under the Weimar constitution, is elected for five years by a federal convention composed of the members of the Bundestag and an equal number of delegates from the state diets. The president's position resembles that of the British ruler; the real executive power resides in the federal chancellor, whose position is much stronger than it was under the Weimar constitution. Special provisions are designed to make it difficult for the Bundestag to overthrow him. Forty-eight hours must elapse between a motion to censure the government and the vote on that motion; surprise votes are thus prevented and time is available for the opposing parliamentary groups to marshal their forces. Furthermore, the Bundestag may express its lack of confidence only after it has elected a successor by a majority vote of its members. Since the Federal Republic has a multiparty system the chancellor may not easily be overthrown; although he may be supported by only a minority, the majority may be unable to agree on his successor. On the other hand, the chancellor may ask the Bundestag for a vote of confidence and, if he fails to receive it, the president, at his request, may dissolve that body and call for new elections. Finally, if the Bundestag rejects a bill declared by the cabinet to be urgent, by

Article 81 the president at the request of the cabinet and with the approval of the Bundesrat may declare a state of "legislative emergency," and if the Bundestag again rejects the bill it may be enacted by the Bundesrat without the consent of the lower house. The sole safeguard of the Bundestag is the provision that there may be only one six-month period of "legislative emergency" during the term of office of the same chancellor.

In the first parliamentary elections under the new constitution, held on August 14, 1949, the Christian Democrats, including the Christian Socialists (their counterpart in Bavaria) won 139 seats and the Social Democrats 131. The two major groups secured slightly more than two thirds of the popular vote, the other votes being divided among some thirteen parties. Of the latter the Free Democrats (mildly Rightist) won 52 seats, the Bavarian and German parties (both distinctly Rightist) each 17, and the Communists 15. On September 12 the Bundestag and Bundesrat in joint session elected as the first federal president Theodore Heuss, a member of the Free Democratic Party, who had been a newspaper editor, a university professor, and a member of the Reichstag in pre-Hitler days. Konrad Adenauer, the 72-year-old leader of the Christian Democrats, was then confirmed as the new chancellor, with a coalition ministry consisting of Christian Democrats, Christian Socialists, Free Democrats, and members of the German Party. On September 21 in a formal ceremony at the headquarters of the Western Allies the latter recognized the Federal Republic, ended their military government in Germany, and replaced their military governors by high commissioners, who still retained some power to supervise German affairs under the new Occupation Statute which came into effect.

THE GERMAN DEMOCRATIC REPUBLIC

Meanwhile, in the Russian zone of Germany another state had been set up. In 1948 a People's Congress had been elected under the auspices of the Socialist Unity Party and it in turn had elected a smaller People's Council. The latter had adopted a draft constitution in September, 1948, which, it was announced, would go into effect for all Germany at some future time. In May, 1949, following the adoption of the constitution for the Federal Republic of Germany, a congress was elected in the Russian zone—only one list of candidates was submitted—which approved the already-drafted constitution, but no steps were taken to establish a government in accordance with its provisions until after the West German government had been set up in Bonn. Then, following a vigorous Russian protest against the Bonn constitution, the People's Council of East Germany promulgated the new constitution on October 7.

Under the constitution of the German Democratic Republic, which proclaimed Germany an "indivisible, democratic republic," authority was vested in the People's Chamber, elected by universal, secret suffrage, and in the State Chamber, with much less power, representing the states. Although the judiciary was described as independent, the People's Chamber was given the power to dismiss the Supreme Court. The People's Council, chosen in 1948, at once became the new People's Chamber and the state legislatures appointed the delegates to the State Chamber. Wilhelm Pieck, leader of the Socialist Unity Party, was elected president by the two chambers and Otto Grotewohl, a former Social Democrat but now a member of the Socialist Unity Party, was chosen premier. On October 11 the German Democratic Republic was formally inaugurated with Berlin as its capital, and a statement was read informing the two chambers that the U.S.S.R. was turning over to it "the administrative functions which have thus far belonged to the Soviet military administration." For all practical purposes the new German Democratic Republic became another Communist state with a People's Front government similar to those found in the other Soviet satellite states in eastern Europe. The latter and the Soviet Union at once exchanged diplomatic representatives with the Berlin government.

On the basis of these steps in 1949 it appeared that Germany as a consequence of the "cold war" had been at least temporarily partitioned, and that gradually the life of the two halves was being reorientated. On the one hand, the Federal Republic, including some 75 per cent of Germany's postwar territory and more than two thirds of her population, constituted a democratic, parliamentary state with the freedoms found in the Western democracies, with which it was linked economically and militarily. On the other hand, the Democratic Republic, with about 25 per cent of the German territory and approximately one third of the German people, had a regime which closely resembled that found in the Soviet Union and the other Communist states. Such a division of Germany was contrary to the nationalistic trend of the nineteenth and twentieth centuries and certainly was contrary to the desires of the German people.

The Allied Treatment of "Liberated" Austria

The situation in Austria in the years after the defeat of the Nazi armies in many ways paralleled that in Germany, although it had been expected that Allied treatment of that state would be more lenient than it was of the former Reich. As early as October, 1943, the three great Allies had decided that Austria should be re-established as a free and independent state, and had then agreed that an Allied Commission should be charged with the task of recreating a central administration for Austria as quickly as possible after the country's resumption of normal political activities. The liberation of the country came in April and May, 1945, and the control machinery of the Allied Commission was approved in July. The most important organ was the Allied Council, consisting of the commanders-in-chief of the four occupying powers (France to be included, as in Berlin), which was to exercise supreme authority in all matters affecting Austria as a whole and to ensure uniformity of action in the four zones of occupation. The Allied Council on September 11, 1945, officially sanctioned the resumption of political activities by the Socialist, Communist, and People's parties. The Socialists were the former Social Democrats and the People's Party consisted chiefly of the former Christian Socialists with some adherents from the former Landbund and Heimwehr.

On November 25, 1945, a general election for a National Assembly, with former Nazis debarred from voting, resulted in the People's Party securing 85 seats, the Socialists 76, and the Communists 4. The results of the elections, so far as the popular vote was concerned, were approximately the same as those in the last free election in Austria in 1930. The National Assembly unanimously elected Karl Renner, a Socialist and former chancellor, as President of the Republic, and a new government was organized with Leopold Figl, the leader of the People's Party, as chancellor. On January 7, 1946, the four Allies recognized Austria as an independent state with the same boundaries as in 1937. The National Assembly restored the democratic constitution which had existed prior to 1934.[18] Elections in 1949 and in 1953 brought some decline in the strength of the People's Party. Figl continued as chancellor until April, 1953, when he was succeeded by Julius Raab, another leader of the People's Party, who presided over a coalition government. On December 31, 1950, the revered President Renner died at the age of 80; Theodor Koerner, another Socialist, was chosen to succeed him.

Meanwhile, the Allied military occupation of Austria had been established. Styria, Carinthia, and southern Tyrol were occupied by the British; Upper Austria, Salzburg, and northern Tyrol, by the Americans; Lower Austria, Burgenland, and the province of Vienna, by the Russians; and Vorarlberg, by the French. Vienna, like Berlin, was also split into four zones. The arable lands producing the main crops of cereals, potatoes, and beets were chiefly within the American and Russian zones, while the French and British zones were mainly mountain lands where agriculture consisted chiefly in raising live stock. The British zone included the iron mines and the headquarters of the iron and steel industry, but most of the engineering works were in the Russian zone. The French zone had timber and copper which the others needed, and oil was found only in the Russian zone.

[18] For the Austrian constitution before 1934, see page 339.

Obviously, in both agriculture and industry the zones were complementary to one another and for economic recovery it was essential for Austria to function as a single unit.

Although in September, 1945, the Allied Council decided that freedom of transportation and communication should be restored throughout Austria in the near future, strict control on the demarcation lines continued. In January, 1946, the Allied Council decided that the free exchange between zones of surplus goods should be permitted but that each zone was to continue to be primarily responsible for its own self-sufficiency. The result was only a very limited movement of goods. Two months later it was decided that food rationing in all four zones should be identical, but neither the military nor political governments in the provinces were particularly ready to make available for Vienna foodstuffs from local resources. The old antagonisms between the "Blacks" and the "Reds" thus reappeared.[19] Hunger and starvation resulted.

As in the years immediately following the First World War,[20] Austria was forced to depend for her subsistence on aid from abroad. From April, 1945, to January, 1947, she received loans, credits, and relief assistance of about $281,000,000 from UNRRA, the United States, and Great Britain. After UNRRA came to an end on December 31, 1946, the country was dependent for assistance chiefly upon the United States. During 1947 numerous steps, official and unofficial, were taken in the latter country to help provide Austria with food, commodities, and foreign exchange, culminating in an emergency relief measure enacted by the American Congress to tide over France, Italy, and Austria until the European Recovery Plan— the so-called Marshall Plan—became operative. Austria was one of the sixteen states which had agreed to this plan, and benefited from the appropriation voted by the United States Congress in June, 1948.

The date of the final conclusion of a peace treaty with Austria seemed to retreat as the months and years passed. At a meeting of the "Big Four" in July, 1946, Byrnes proposed that a treaty should at once be drafted which would end the Allied occupation of Austria, but Molotov refused to accept his proposal, asserting that many Nazi laws were still in force in Austria, that the Pan-German movement there was still strong, and that hundreds of thousands of non-Austrians who had fought for Hitler had taken refuge in that country. Two years later the arrest of several hundred former Nazi Gestapo and SS men who had organized an underground Nazi movement in the British zone seemed to bear out these claims. At succeeding conferences of the "Big Four" one of the chief questions which delayed the Austrian peace settlement was that of determining what constituted German assets in that country. At Potsdam it had been decided that Russian claims

19 See page 344.
20 See pages 339–341.

to reparations should be met in part from appropriate German external assets in eastern Austria, but the four Allies proved unable to agree on a definition of German assets. During the period of the *Anschluss* German economic penetration of Austria had been far-reaching, and it was later estimated that, in all, Germans had seized about three fourths of Austria's total assets: mining, industry, banking, insurance, and property owned by Austrian state and public corporations. Russia insisted and the Western powers refused to concede that all these were legitimate German assets.

Again, at the Moscow Conference in 1947 the Allies failed to produce an Austrian peace treaty, being unable to agree on three major points: Russia's demand for $150,000,000 reparations from Austria, Russia's demand for the cession of Carinthia to Yugoslavia, and Russia's definition of German assets in Austria. A treaty commission was appointed to study these problems. But again at the London Conference which opened in November, 1947, the "Big Four" were no nearer agreement. By then it was obvious that Austria was strategically important in the struggle between Soviet Russia and the Western powers, and that the conclusion of a peace treaty with Austria was unlikely until the "cold war" should be ended. Although in the succeeding years Austria repeatedly requested the four Allied governments to resume work on the Austrian peace treaty and although from time to time the diplomatic representatives of the four powers did meet to discuss such a treaty, no apparent progress was made. Austria continued to be divided economically and occupied by Allied troops.

The Allied Occupation of Deflated Japan

There was much less difficulty in dealing with Japan at the close of the war than there was in the case of Germany or Austria, largely because, for all practical purposes, there was but one occupying authority, the United States.[21] The latter, immediately following the Japanese surrender, announced that though it would consider the wishes of the principal Allied powers "in the event of any differences of opinion among them, the policies of the United States will govern." The United States invited the powers directly interested in the postwar reconstruction of Japan to appoint members of a Far Eastern advisory commission, but Russia objected to its advisory nature and refused to participate. Byrnes, Bevin, and Molotov, at their conference in Moscow in December, 1945, eventually reached a compromise which provided for a Far Eastern Commission and an Allied Council for Japan.

The Allied Council sat in Tokyo and consisted of four members—one

[21] For an excellent brief discussion of the Allied occupation, see L. K. Rosinger, "The Occupation of Japan." *Foreign Policy Reports,* May 15, 1947.

each representing the United States, Russia, China, and one representing Great Britain, Australia, New Zealand, and India as a group. Its chairman was the American member—General MacArthur or his deputy. Its function was to consult with or advise the Supreme Commander for the Allied Powers (SCAP), General MacArthur, and it had no power to act. The Far Eastern Commission sat in Washington and included one representative from each of eleven governments concerned.[22] The functions of this body were to formulate policies, to review any directive issued to the supreme commander if requested by any member, and to consider other matters which might be referred to it by agreement of the participating powers. Theoretically the United States lost its predominant position, but actually directives to the supreme commander were issued according to the American interpretation of the commission's decisions, and General MacArthur generally applied the directives as he interpreted them. The irritation felt in some quarters over this situation was revealed by a speech made in Wellington, New Zealand, in February, 1948: "The Japanese emperor has renounced his divinity. It has been taken up by General MacArthur."

At Potsdam in July, 1945, the United States, Great Britain, and China had outlined their general aims for Japan [23] and these had later been accepted by Soviet Russia. Implicit in their announcement was the Allied decision to have the occupation authority operate through a continuing Japanese state and not, as in Germany, to displace the state. According to later American instructions to MacArthur, the Japanese emperor and government were to be subject to him, and he was to exercise his powers through them "to the extent that this satisfactorily furthers United States objectives." MacArthur might require changes in Japanese political machinery or governmental personnel or act directly if necessary. The American directive specifically stipulated that Japan was to be disarmed and demilitarized, the economic basis of her military strength was to be destroyed, and her war production was to cease. The large industrial and banking combinations which had controlled a great part of the country's trade and industry were to be dissolved. Democratic organizations in labor, industry, and agriculture were to be encouraged. Political prisoners were to be freed, ultranationalists were to be purged, civil rights were to be guaranteed, and the schools, laws, and government were to be reformed. Except for the decision to operate through the existing government, the program was much the same as that originally announced for Germany. This program was soon expressed in a series of directives issued by SCAP to the Japanese government.

---

[22] The states represented were: The United States, Great Britain, Russia, China, France, the Netherlands, Canada, Australia, New Zealand, India, and the Philippines.

[23] See page 589.

Immediately after the war the latter granted woman suffrage, lowered the voting age from 25 to 20 years, and permitted the organization of political parties, which had been dissolved in 1940. The most important of the new parties were the Liberal, Progressive, Social Democratic, and Communist. The first two represented the conservatives and sought to preserve as much as possible of Japan's old institutions. They had the support of most of the bankers and businessmen, the large landowners, the professional classes, and the peasant proprietors. The Social Democrats in their aims resembled the Labor Party in Britain. The Communists were not so extreme as those in Russia; they sought agrarian and industrial reforms but also promised the right of private ownership. The first postwar parliamentary elections in April, 1946, resulted in a conservative victory with the Liberal-Progressive bloc securing half the seats in the parliament.

Before the elections the government had issued the draft of a new constitution—reportedly drawn up by the staff of SCAP—to replace the undemocratic Japanese constitution of 1889. This was later ratified by the new parliament and was promulgated in November, 1946. Under this new constitution the emperor became merely the symbol of the state, deriving his position from the sovereign will of the people. All of his official acts required the approval of the cabinet which was made responsible to the parliament. A bill of rights was included, and war was "forever renounced as a means of settling disputes with other nations." On paper the constitution was a most liberal and progressive document. Whether under it the Japanese government would soon become the same, seemed open to some question. The first two premiers of the postwar period—Baron Kijuro Shidehara and Shigeru Yoshida—were members of the ruling circles which had long dominated Japan; the members of Japan's extensive bureaucracy of civil servants had, for the most part, been trained under the prewar regimes; and most of the Japanese apparently continued to revere the emperor despite his renunciation of divine status.

In the first general elections held (April, 1947) after the promulgation of the new constitution, although the conservative parties won more than a majority of the seats in each of the houses of parliament, the Social Democrats gained the largest number of any party. A shift in the ministry then occurred and Tetsu Katayama, the Socialist leader, became premier at the head of a coalition government. Because of dissension within his party, however, his ministry was forced to resign early in 1948 and Hitoshi Ashida of the Democratic (formerly Progressive) Party, who had been foreign minister under Katayama, became premier in a cabinet consisting of 6 Democrats and 8 Socialists. Although the Russian representative on the Allied Council demanded Ashida's dismissal on the ground that he had for seven years been president of a newspaper which was "one of the most notorious media for spreading the ideas of the Japanese military clique," Ashida remained in office until October, 1948, when, because of the indictment of two members of his ministry, he was forced to resign. Later Ashida himself was charged with accepting bribes. The Socialists refused to participate in a new coalition, and ultimately Shigeru Yoshida again became premier at the head of a conservative ministry of Liberals and Democrats.

Yoshida announced that his government contemplated the formation of a committee on un-Japanese activities and indicated that he meant activities of the extreme Left. The new premier dissolved the parliament and in the ensuing elections, held on January 23, 1949, his ultra-conservative Liberal Party won a decisive majority in the lower house. The moderate parties were rejected at the polls and Japan appeared to be dividing into ultra conservatives on the Right and Communists on the Left, for the latter increased their representation in the diet from 4 to 35 members. The Liberals were in a sense the successors to the men that had led Japan into war; they had shown their dislike of the Allied occupation and of the ideals of Western democracy; they had emphasized the necessity for a rebirth of Japanese nationalism. What their coming to power would entail for the occupation authorities remained to be seen.

Meanwhile, steps had been taken to demilitarize Japan. In 1945 military conscription was abolished as was also the general staff. Thousands of officers and men in the army, navy, or government were tried as war criminals and hundreds were convicted and put to death, including many generals and admirals. Ultimately, after a two-year trial, the International Military Tribunal for the Far East on November 12, 1948, sentenced seven Japanese to death by hanging, sixteen to life imprisonment, and two to prison terms. Included in the number were two former premiers, thirteen generals, one admiral, and former ministers and ambassadors. All but two were convicted of conspiracy to wage aggressive war for the domination of East Asia and the Pacific and Indian oceans. Those condemned to death were convicted, also, of breaches of the laws and customs of war. On December 22, after the refusal of the United States Supreme Court to intervene, the seven condemned to death were hanged. Some—Prince Konoye, for instance—saved the Allies the trouble of trials by committing suicide. Approximately 80,000 former army, navy, and military police officers were prohibited from holding public offices. Efforts were made, also, to remove from key positions in the government, the trades unions, and the school system those Japanese who had actively promoted war or who were considered subversive. By September, 1947, more than 570,000 persons had been "screened." In that month MacArthur announced the completion, too, of the purge of industrialists who had supported the militarists, though critics asserted that the top men had been often succeeded by their "lieutenants."

However that may be, the supreme commander declared in 1947 that the demilitarization of Japan had been largely completed.

Sweeping reforms were envisaged for Japan's economic life under the directives given to MacArthur by the United States government. Japan's prewar economy had been so organized as to reinforce militaristic concepts of government and foreign policy. The *Zaibatsu*, that is, the great financial-industrial-commercial holding companies, had controlled the country's economic life and had co-operated closely with the militarists in aggression. They had also largely prevented the rise of an independent middle class, which in most countries constitutes a liberalizing influence. In October, 1946, in accordance with the American directive and under plans drafted by SCAP, the stockholders of five of the most important *Zaibatsu*—Mitsui, Mitsubishi, Sumitomo, Yasuda, Fuji—voted to dissolve by transferring their securities to a commission which would sell them to the public. The companies in return would receive government bonds. A year later, in December, 1947, the parliament passed the Economic Decentralization Bill, designed to eliminate "concentrations of excessive economic power." It was estimated that some 500 of Japan's 93,000 corporations would be affected by this act but that these 500 controlled 65 to 75 per cent of Japan's industry. MacArthur believed that the free enterprise system could not be set up in Japan until the "traditional pyramid of economic power" had been destroyed. Whether SCAP could create a new financial-industrial ownership and prevent the new groups from repeating the *Zaibatsu* pattern remained to be seen. It could probably not secure much enthusiastic assistance in the task from the Japanese government.

Japan was of course expected to pay reparations and the first proposals were drafted by a commission headed by Edwin W. Pauley. These were used by the Far Eastern Commission to work out an interim program of removals which stipulated that arsenals, aircraft and light metal plants, steel capacity above 3,500,000 tons yearly, and much of the country's productive capacity in pig iron, shipbuilding, machine tools, and chemicals were to be removed. The problem of determining what each nation should receive was difficult, as was the question whether Russia's seizures in Manchuria should be considered "war booty" or reparations. A second reparations commission early in 1947 made milder recommendations than the Pauley commission, and in April of that year the United States announced that it would begin removals from Japan, with the largest share going at first to China.

As in Germany, the reparations problem was linked with disarmament and living standards. By a decision of the Far Eastern Commission in 1947 Japan's standard of living was to be that of 1930–1934, but her economy was to be changed to reduce her war potential much lower than in 1931.

As in Germany, too, the reparations problem was linked with American taxes, for the less Japan was able to pay for her necessary imports by her own exports, the more the United States would have to advance under its policy of deficit financing of occupied countries. With a population of more than 78,000,000 (1947) in an area less than that of California, Japan must necessarily be even more dependent upon exports to pay for her needed food supplies and raw materials than she was before the war. In 1947, however, her manufacturing output totaled only about 30 per cent of the 1930–1934 average, and in that year the United States began extending financial aid to Japan—in a sort of "small Marshall Plan"—for the purchase of needed raw materials and fibers for her textile mills. It seemed unlikely that the Japanese would have to make very heavy reparation payments.

Before the war Japanese industrial workers were denied the right to organize freely and worked in more or less enforced docility. The highest prewar union membership was only 420,000. By the close of 1946, however, the number of union members had increased to more than 4,400,000, most of them included in three different federations. Although the unions were deeply interested in politics—the Social Democratic Party won the most seats in the parliamentary elections of 1947—perhaps the chief cause of labor action was inflation. Despite the fact that it was the policies of SCAP which made possible the great increase in union membership, the infiltration of Communist leaders and the political pressure exerted by the unions apparently disturbed the supreme commander. In January, 1947, MacArthur forbade a proposed strike of some 2,500,000 employees, and in March, 1948, he announced that strikes such as the "co-ordinated work stoppage" planned by the union of communication workers could not be tolerated. Four months later the government announced that thereafter unions of government workers would possess neither the right of collective bargaining nor the right to strike, and in August, 1948, it further announced that all labor contracts and agreements concluded in the past were invalid. The Soviet delegate on the Allied Council protested to MacArthur and demanded that the ordinance be cancelled, and the American chief of the labor division of SCAP and some of his subordinates resigned in protest against what they considered MacArthur's new labor policy. Nevertheless, on November 30, the Japanese parliament passed legislation suggested by MacArthur outlawing strikes and collective bargaining by employees of the government or its enterprises, and in January, 1949, the Far Eastern Commission voted down the Soviet delegate's motion to condemn the law.

Although most Japanese landholdings were very small by American standards, before the war the landlord group dominated the rural economy. In 1936 nearly 70 per cent of the rural households consisted of tenants who, on an average, gave more than half their crops to the landlord as rent. In

December, 1945, MacArthur ordered sweeping changes "to destroy the economic bondage that has enslaved the Japanese farmers for centuries of feudal oppression." The Japanese parliament was dilatory, however, and not until October, 1946, were acceptable agrarian reform measures enacted. These provided that the government would purchase all tenant land owned by absentee landlords and all other landlord holdings above a certain size for resale to tenants, the latter to repay the government in thirty annual installments. Rural land commissions, which it was possible the landlords might dominate, were to decide what lands should be taken and to supervise the transfer. It was planned that more than 75 per cent of the land in tenancy would be sold, and by September, 1947, the government had purchased about 750,000 acres of land from absentee owners. But the Soviet delegate on the Allied Council characterized the land reform as only "a half-way measure" which was being unsatisfactorily administered because of opposition of the landowners. His view was supported by the British delegate and by an agricultural expert.

The Peace Treaty with Japan

In July, 1947, the United States had moved to secure a peace treaty with Japan by inviting the Far Eastern Commission to begin discussions under a two-thirds voting rule. Although the British Commonwealth nations accepted the American plan, Russia, probably realizing that she would be outvoted in the commission as she had been at the Paris peace conference in 1946, proposed that the Pacific "Big Four"—the United States, Great Britain, Russia, and China—should write the treaty as was done the year before for the lesser defeated powers in Europe by the Western "Big Four." But this proposal was rejected by the United States, probably for fear of a Russian veto. China offered a compromise that the Far Eastern Commission should draft the treaty with the "Big Four" holding a veto, but her proposal also was rejected.

For a time the matter of a peace treaty with Japan was allowed to drift, but Communist aggression in Korea revived the desire and determination of the United States to conclude a peace settlement for the Far East. In the autumn of 1950 the United States circulated an exploratory memorandum to the governments of fifteen countries particularly concerned in a Far Eastern settlement. This memorandum suggested that all nations at war with Japan might, if they wished, be parties to the treaty; that Japan should recognize an independent Korea and UN trusteeship under United States administration of the Ryukyu and Bonin Islands; that the future of Formosa, the Pescadores, South Sakhalin, and the Kuriles should be decided by Great Britain, Russia, China, and the United States, or, if they failed to reach a decision within one year, by the United Nations; that there should be co-operative responsibility between Japan and United States and perhaps other forces for the maintenance of internal peace and security in the Japan area; that reparations should be waived but that the Allies should keep Japanese property in their territory and be compensated for property lost in Japan.

Comments on this memorandum were received from most of the interested governments. As might have been expected, the Soviet government was the most critical. But the Chinese also expressed vigorous opposition to the suggested peace terms, and questions were likewise raised in Australia, New Zealand, and the Philippines, which all feared a resurgence of Japanese militarism. The Australian government declared that it would oppose any proposal permitting the unrestricted rearmament of Japan, although it agreed that Japan must be allowed "some capacity to defend herself against Communist aggression." The willingness of the United States to sign security pacts with Australia, New Zealand, and the Philippines, however, overcame the opposition of these states as far as it was based on the possibility of Japanese rearmament. By the summer of 1951 agreement on a draft treaty had been reached by most of the powers, though Russia, India, and the Philippines were not satisfied.

On July 12, 1951 a provisional peace treaty with Japan was published. It was immediately sent to the fifty-one countries at war with Japan, who were invited by the United States to a conference in San Francisco on September 4. India at once proposed that the treaty should be altered so that Japan should keep the Ryukyu and Bonin Islands, Formosa should go to China, and the clause permitting foreign troops to remain in Japan should be deleted. Although none of these proposals were incorporated, the text of a revised draft treaty, released on July 12, did contain a number of amendments resulting from other suggestions. With the release of this revised draft, the United States announced that, since the draft was the result of eleven months' negotiations with many nations, no further alterations of the text would be permitted at the San Francisco conference, which was for the conclusion and signature of the final text of the treaty and not for the reopening of negotiations on the terms. This conference, therefore, was to be of a quite different character from the one held in Paris in 1946.

On September 4 delegations from more than fifty states gathered in San Francisco for the Conference for the Conclusion and Signature of a Treaty of Peace with Japan. No delegates from India or Burma attended, and neither of the Chinese governments [24] had been invited to send representatives. On the other hand, contrary to general expectations, a Soviet delega-

---

[24] There was disagreement among the delegates as to which of the Chinese governments, the Nationalist government on Formosa or the Communist government on the mainland, represented China.

tion headed by Andrei Gromyko was present. At the outset, by a vote of 48 to 3 (Russia, Poland, Czechoslovakia), the draft rules of procedure submitted by Great Britain and the United States were adopted. In contravention of these rules, which forbade any further amendment of the draft, Gromyko immediately proposed a great number of changes in the treaty. In his speech he condemned especially the exclusion of the Ryukyu, Bonin, and other islands from Japanese sovereignty and the absence of provisions for the transfer of Formosa to China and for the return of Sakhalin and the transfer of the Kuriles to the Soviet Union. He argued that the treaty created conditions for the revival of Japanese militarism and opened the way for Japan's participation in aggressive alliances in the Far East. By an overwhelming vote, however, the conference overruled Gromyko's attempt to secure consideration of his proposals.

On September 8 the Japanese peace treaty was signed by the delegates of forty-nine states. But Gromyko and the delegates of Poland and Czechoslovakia declined to sign, Gromyko announcing to the press that the treaty was a draft for a new war which the Soviet Union could not support. Shigeru Yoshida, the Japanese delegate, on the other hand, expressed his people's "passionate desire to live at peace with their neighbors in the Far East and in the entire world." He did, however, appeal for the return to Japan of the Ryukyu and Bonin Islands and also of South Sakhalin and the Kuriles.

By the terms of the accepted treaty, (1) Japan recognized Korea's independence; (2) Japan renounced all claims to Formosa, the Pescadores, the Kuriles, Southern Sakhalin, and certain Pacific islands as well as her interests in the Antarctic and all special rights and interests in China; (3) Japan agreed to accept any United States proposal to the UN to place the Ryukyu and certain other American-occupied islands under UN trusteeship with the United States as sole administering authority; (4) all occupation forces were to be withdrawn from Japan within ninety days after the treaty came into force, but Japan might make bilateral or multilateral agreements with any Allied power or powers under which foreign troops could be retained within her territory; (5) Japan accepted the obligations of Article 2 of the UN Charter, that is, she agreed to settle all international disputes by peaceful means and to refrain from the threat or use of force against any state, but she was granted the right of self-defense which all UN members retained under Article 51 of the Charter; (6) Japan undertook to assist countries which had suffered war damage by making available Japanese skill and industry, but Japanese inability to pay reparations was recognized; (7) Japan agreed that China, though not a signatory, would be entitled to the benefits arising from Japanese renunciation of rights and interests in China; (8) Japan might conclude a bilateral peace treaty on the same or substantially the same terms with any state which, being a member of the UN and formerly at war with Japan, had not signed the present treaty; (9) the Allied powers recognized full Japanese sovereignty over Japan and its territorial waters; and (10) the return of captured Japanese military forces to their homes should be carried out to the extent not already completed.

In the absence of provisions stipulating heavy reparation payments and drastic limitations on national armaments, the peace treaty with Japan was in marked contrast with those concluded after the First World War, especially the treaty of Versailles. The treaty seemed to indicate that statesmen in 1951 realized better than they did in 1919–1920 the difficulties involved in exacting large reparation payments from any country. The treaty seemed to indicate, also, that the chief signatories were willing to take a calculated risk that the Japanese would not again become militaristic. It was hoped, apparently, that, if the treaty contained no restrictive provisions, the Japanese would have no reason to rebel against it and might therefore be willing to retain many of the reforms introduced under MacArthur's tutelage. In any case, rearmament would involve a very great burden for Japan, one which she would have great difficulty in carrying under her existing economic conditions. In fact, one of the unsolved problems seemed to be that of how Japan could survive economically without access to Manchuria's raw products and China's markets.

On the same day that the Japanese peace treaty was signed in San Francisco, the United States and Japan also signed a security pact agreeing (1) that the United States would have a right to deploy its land, sea, and air forces throughout the Japanese territory for the purpose of contributing to the maintenance of international peace and security in the Far East and to the security of Japan from armed attack from without; (2) that the United States would be allowed to help, at Japan's request, to put down any internal rebellions or disturbances instigated "by an outside power or powers"; (3) that Japan would not grant similar rights "of garrison or maneuver" to any third power without the prior consent of the United States; (4) that both governments would decide together when and how United States forces should be disposed; (5) that the pact would expire whenever both governments agreed that the strength of the United Nations or of other alliances was capable of maintaining peace in the area. The peace treaty and the accompanying security pact were both ratified by the Japanese parliament on November 18, 1951.

Chapter XXIV

SOVIET RUSSIA AND

HER SATELLITES

EAST of a line running roughly from Stettin on the Baltic to Trieste on the Adriatic, in the years immediately following the Second World War, were nine European states which came to follow in a general way the same foreign policy. The dominant state in this group was, of course, the Union of Soviet Socialist Republics. The others, which were forced or which chose to follow the Soviet foreign policy and even to adopt some of the features of Soviet internal institutions, constituted the so-called Russian satellite states.

The Union of Soviet Socialist Republics

As in so many other states in Europe, the period of the Second World War and the years following it saw several significant changes made in Soviet territory and institutions.

TERRITORIAL AND POLITICAL CHANGES

In 1939–1940 the Soviet Union was expanded by the absorption of Latvia, Estonia, and Lithuania, which became constituent republics in the Union, and by the addition of areas formerly in Poland, Finland, and Rumania. The latter areas were absorbed into already existing Soviet republics which were largely inhabited by populations of similar races. In 1945, following a plebiscite in Ruthenia, which was inhabited by Ukrainians, that territory, too, was transferred from Czechoslovakia to the Soviet Union and incorporated in the Ukrainian Soviet Socialist Republic.

At the close of the Second World War, therefore, the Soviet Union consisted of sixteen republics. In 1944, the Supreme Soviet of the Union had decreed that these constituent republics might enter into direct relation with foreign states and might conclude agreements and exchange diplomatic and consular representatives with them. They might also organize separate military formations. The armies which encircled Berlin in 1945, it will be recalled, were the First White Russian and the First Ukrainian. In international affairs, recognition of the change in the position of the constituent republics came with the admission of the White Russian and the Ukrainian Republics to the San Francisco Conference of the United Nations in 1945 and with their participation in the Paris peace conference in 1946.

In February, 1946, national elections to the two houses of the Supreme Soviet were held. Only one candidate was nominated for each seat and all were either Communists or representatives of a nonparty people's *bloc,* which appealed for a unanimous vote of confidence in the existing government. According to official statements, more than 96 per cent of the electorate voted and approximately 99 per cent approved the nominated candidates. Marshal Stalin tendered the resignation of his government to the new Supreme Soviet, which decided that thereafter the government should be called the Council of Ministers rather than the Soviet of People's Commissars. In the new ministry Stalin became prime minister and Molotov foreign minister.

WAR DESTRUCTION

The chief effect of the Second World War on Russia's economy was the vast devastation which it caused. The Soviet State Commission's report, published in September, 1945, revealed that the Axis armies had overrun an area inhabited by 88,000,000 people and, according to Marshal Stalin, had brought death to 7,000,000. The German-occupied territory included Russia's greatest single industrial region, her best agricultural land, and half of the nation's live stock.

Destruction by the invaders, moreover, was systematic and extensive in the entire Ukraine and in the Don Basin, for the Germans sought to deprive Russia of her newly created industries and to restrict her to the production of foodstuffs and raw materials for the great industrial empire which the Nazis intended to establish. They therefore methodically "destroyed industrial plants ... flooded mines, gutted oil refineries, stripped factories and laboratories of machinery and tools, leveled homes to the ground, and destroyed means of transportation." They wrecked or partly wrecked 1,710 towns, and 31,500 industrial enterprises, which had employed some 4,000,000 workers. They ruined a considerable part of the country's railway system by destroying some 40,000 miles of permanent right of way, 4,100 stations, 15,000 bridges, 15,800 locomotives, and 428,000 cars. According to official reports of the UNRRA mission to the Ukraine, the industrial plants of Kiev, Kharkov, Dnepropetrovsk, Dneprostoy, and Odessa had been almost completely stripped of modern machinery and their buildings either razed or shattered. At Zaponozhnie the largest steel and iron plant of the Ukraine had been so completely destroyed that it would take three to four years to restore it. Of the workers' houses, the UNRRA mission stated, only 8 per cent remained.

Agriculture was also hard hit. According to the State Commission some 98,000 collective farms, 1,876 state farms, and 2,890 machine tractor stations were "ruined and ransacked." The losses in agricultural machinery were appalling: 137,000 tractors (30 per cent of the prewar total), 49,000 harvester-combines, 4,000,000 harrows, plows, and other soil-cultivating instruments, and 1,150,000 seeders and threshers destroyed or stolen. Furthermore, the Germans had killed or stolen 7,000,000 horses (34 per cent of the prewar total), 17,000,000 cattle (30 per cent of prewar), 20,000,000 hogs (71 per cent of prewar), 27,000,000 sheep and goats (29 per cent of prewar), and 110,000-000 poultry. They had also destroyed or burned, wholly or in part, 70,000 villages. In the occupied area as a whole 6,000,000 buildings were destroyed and 25,000,000 people made homeless. As a result, according to one investigator, the average number of occupants for each five-room dwelling unit in 1947 was thirty persons, compared with twenty in 1937. This situation, coupled with the neglect of the consumer-goods industries during the war, resulted in living standards far below even the low standards of the prewar period.

Russia's total direct loss as a result of the German invasion was estimated as the equivalent of $128,000,000,000. These tremendous losses, especially of capital goods, went far to explain Soviet Russia's insistence upon reparation payments from the defeated Axis powers as well as her reportedly ruthless seizure of capital goods and other commodities in the countries occupied by her armies in the postwar period.

One has but to consider the fate of Stalingrad and its factories to realize that the Russians were faced by a herculean task of rehabilitation following the expulsion of the Axis forces from their land. Nevertheless, they set resolutely to work to bring their country back economically to the place it had been when "the enemy interfered with their long-range plans." In this task they were aided by the wartime expansion of industry, which had occurred in the region east of the Volga, where new plants had been constructed and to which, according to reports, some 1,300 large factories had been moved from the invaded areas. In the first half of 1945, for instance, the industrial output of the eastern areas—almost entirely in the heavy industries—was twice as great as in 1941; in the Volga area, 240 per cent greater; in the Urals, 260 per cent greater; in Siberia, 180 per cent greater.

NEW FIVE-YEAR PLANS

Not content with merely repairing the damage inflicted by the Nazis, however, the Russians in 1946 embarked upon another Five-Year Plan in which the immediate aim was to regain the ground lost as a result of the war and the long-term goal was a great increase in national production over the prewar period. The government still clung to its policy of giving primacy to heavy industry or, as Stalin phrased it, the "production of the means of production." By the final quarter of 1947 the country's industrial production as a whole equalled the average quarterly output of 1940, although in some categories—notably cement, timber, copper, steel, tractors, and steam turbines—this was not true. In 1948, the third year of the fourth Five-Year Plan, however, the prewar production level was reached in iron and steel, according to the State Planning Commission. In 1950, the final year of the plan, the production of basic materials and fuels had increased above that of 1940 as follows (in millions of metric tons): steel, from 18.3 to 27.3; pig iron, from 14.9 to 19.2; coal and lignite, from 166 to 261; petroleum, from 31 to 38. In the same period the production of electric power had increased in billions of kilowatt hours from 48 to 90. Shortages were still reported in iron and steel, however, and there were official complaints about slow progress in the Baku oil fields and in some individual industries. But according to official reports, the total national income for 1950 was 64 per cent above that for 1940, considerably above the goal originally set.

In the production of consumer goods and in agriculture the gains were not so striking. As in the first Five-Year Plan, consumer goods were deliberately sacrificed to produce capital goods. In agriculture only cotton, among the major agricultural products, exceeded the objectives of the fourth Five-Year Plan. Grain acreage in 1950 was reported as 20 per cent above that for 1940. Although the number of livestock was 4 per cent above 1940, it was below the planned goal. According to a study published by the UN Economic Commission for Europe, the agricultural production in Russia during these years had "probably not quite kept pace with the rise in population." In the hope of increasing it, steps were taken in 1950 to consolidate smaller collective farms into larger units. Initiated in the province of Moscow, where 6,000 farms were consolidated into less than 2,000, the movement spread into other areas to such an extent that by the end of the year the number of collective farms in the Soviet Union had decreased from some 254,000 to 215,000.

Although the fourth Five-Year Plan was completed in 1950, details of the fifth plan for the years 1951–1955 were not disclosed and approved until October, 1952, and they were then ratified, not by the Supreme Soviet, but by the Communist Party congress. The aim of the fifth plan was to increase the total volume of investment in industry to twice that made in 1946–1950, and to increase the gross industrial output by 70 per cent. But the planned production increases were not the same for all industries; heavy industries were to increase by 80 per cent but light industries by only 65 per cent. The number of industrial workers, also, was to expand from 39,200,000 to 45,100,000, and labor productivity was to increase by 50 per cent over 1950. In agriculture the plan called for an increase in the gross grain harvest from 125 million metric tons in 1950 to 175–190 in 1955. Most of this increase was expected to come from higher yields which, it was hoped, might be brought nearer to the best European levels in the more fertile Soviet regions. Large increases in the output of chemical fertilizer were therefore planned. The goals for livestock were percentage-wise more modest than for grain.

In October, 1952, Georgi Malenkov reported on the progress of the fifth Five-Year Plan. One can never be certain of the meaning of Soviet production figures and percentages, for the basis upon which calculations are made is sometimes altered without clear explanation. Nevertheless, even allowing for some exaggeration, the figures were generally encouraging to the Communists. According to Malenkov, the investment in industrial plants in Russia in 1952 was 77 per cent greater than in 1940 and the output of the heavy industries was 170 per cent above the prewar figure. The production of machines and equipment generally, which may include some military equipment, was reported as three times that in 1940. In some categories it was still higher. The output of petroleum equipment, for instance, was said to be 4.3 times that of 1940 and that of metallurgical machinery 5.4 times. In 1952 the number of industrial workers had increased to 41,700,000 and productivity had risen 18 per cent above 1950. The dispersion of industry had continued and the Volga valley and the Ural Mountains region had become the heart of Soviet heavy industry. In this connection the completion of the Volga-Don Canal in 1952 was significant. Since the Volga was already connected with the Baltic and White Sea, thereafter those seas and the Black and Caspian seas were linked together for water transportation. Toward the end of 1953 it was disclosed that steel production in the Soviet Union for that year would exceed 38 million tons.

In agriculture the consolidation of collective farms had continued and in 1952 the number had been reduced to some 97,000. There was, however, no great indication of increased efficiency resulting from the consolidation. Progress toward the livestock goals of the plan appeared to have been slow except for hogs. Nevertheless, according to the figures released, the number of cattle had increased by 1,800,000 head in 1951–1952 and the number of sheep and goats by 12,000,000. Meat production, it was reported, had increased by 709,000 tons in the years 1946–1951. But the Russian people were promised by 1955 a 90 per cent increase in meat supplies over those available in 1950 and a 300 per cent increase in dairy products. One large-scale agricultural project envisaged was the draining of the Pripet Marshes in White Russia which, it was estimated, would bring into cultivation some 12,000,-000 acres of high quality agricultural land.

In the summer of 1953, however, it was admitted that Russian agricultural production was insufficient for the population's food needs and the raw material needs of light industry. The most serious shortages were said to be in meats, potatoes, and vegetables. The central committee of the Communist Party attributed the situation to mismanagement on state farms and to lack of guidance by party, government, and agricultural bodies. A new directive set increased targets for livestock and poultry and for acreages of grass, corn, fodder, silage crops, and vegetables. At the same time, the directive moderated some of the government's policies for collective farms to provide incentives for more production. It also cancelled as from January 1, 1953, all arrears in deliveries to the state. Further to increase food production, it was announced, greatly increased investments would be made in the food industry in 1954 and a thousand new food factories would be built by 1956.

The percentage increases in consumer goods were not so impressive as those in the heavy industries. The total increase over production in 1940 was given as 60 per cent, but this was partly offset by an increase of some 8 per cent in population. Nevertheless, if the war or immediately postwar years are taken as a basis, improvement was marked. Consumer goods produced in 1952 were three times those in 1944 and 2.4 times those in 1946. There were considerable increases in fabrics and footwear and greater supplies of consumers' durables, notably furniture, radios, televisors, watches, bicycles, and cameras. Furthermore, in the view of one observer, the food supplies in state and co-operative stores in the towns and cities were perhaps more ample than at any time since 1928. Retail trade in 1952, it was reported, had doubled since 1948 and foreign trade, chiefly with the countries of the so-called democracies, was three times that of the prewar years.

In the matter of housing, Malenkov admitted that the Russians "still have an acute housing shortage everywhere." While the rate of home construction under the fourth and fifth Five-Year Plans was high in relation to prewar times, in view of the wartime destruction and the growth of population it was not enough to bring any rapid relief to the extremely overcrowded urban population of the country.

It was obvious to those who examined the figures released regarding the progress of the fifth Five-Year Plan that there were failures to reach goals and that in no way did the Soviet industrial and agricultural production match that in the United States. Nevertheless, as one careful student of Soviet affairs pointed out: [1]

The 1955 goals for basic industries speak eloquently against any complacency in the free world: 44 million tons of steel, 373 million tons of coal, 70 million tons of oil, 162 billion kilowatt-hours of electric power. Even if some of these goals,

[1] Oleg Hoeffding in *Foreign Policy Bulletin*, April 1, 1953, page 8.

and those of industries dependent on them, are not fully met, the fact remains that the U.S.S.R. is expanding its industrial potential at a rate not matched by the United States, let alone Western Europe.

THE NINETEENTH COMMUNIST PARTY CONGRESS

In the early years of the Soviet regime Communist Party congresses were held somewhat frequently; during the struggle for power after Lenin's death they had been held yearly. After Stalin had become the acknowledged dictator of Russia, however, these congresses had been held more infrequently, and up until 1952 none had been held since before the Second World War. In August, 1952, it was announced that the nineteenth all-Union congress of the party would be held in October to hear reports, pass on the fifth Five-Year Plan, and reorganize the party. During the intervening weeks regional party conferences elected some 1,200 delegates, among whom were Premier Stalin, all the members of the existing politburo, all the deputy premiers, and the principal members of the government. Present, also, when the congress convened, were delegates from the Communist parties of forty-four other countries so that this nineteenth congress somewhat resembled a meeting of the former Comintern.

The opening keynote address at the congress (October 5–14) was made by V. M. Molotov, and other major speeches were delivered by G. M. Malenkov, L. P. Beria, A. I. Mikoyan, N. A. Bulganin, and War Minister Vassilievsky. Seventy-two-year-old Stalin did not take an active part in the congress, but he did make a short closing address. The general tenor of the speeches was that the Soviet Union had only peaceful intentions, but that the Western democracies were imperialistic and aggressive, that the United States in particular was seeking world domination, and that the other states in NATO were only "unequal partners" and "poor relations" of the United States. But the delegates were assured that the Soviet Union was no longer isolated as it had been after Munich, since it now had as allies the Chinese People's Republic, the German Democratic Republic, and the people's democracies of Europe. They were further assured that the Union's domestic economy and foreign trade were expanding satisfactorily, and that, despite her peaceful intentions, Russia's economy could be quickly put on a war footing. Finally, they were told that the Soviet army had been revolutionized and its battle potentialities sharply increased, and that the fifth Five-Year Plan would provide for supplies of the most modern weapons "considerably greater than during the last war."

The congress adopted a number of proposed changes in party organization. On the ground that the Mensheviks had been annihilated and that therefore there was no longer rivalry between Bolsheviks and Mensheviks, the official name of the party was changed from "All-Union Communist

644 ANOTHER POSTWAR PERIOD

Party of Bolsheviks" to "Communist Party of the Soviet Union." The party membership, Malenkov announced, had increased from 2,500,000 in 1939 to more than 6,882,000 in 1952. Seventy-one new party statutes were presented, made necessary, it was explained, by various evils within the party which must be ruthlessly eradicated by expulsion of those guilty of them. The chief evils cited were lack of discipline among party leaders, the covering-up of mistakes and shortcomings, the frustration of criticism, nepotism, and favoritism. The proposed statutes were adopted.

In the party reorganization the politburo and the orgburo (organization bureau) were abolished and replaced by a single body, the presidium of the central committee, consisting of twenty-five members, among whom were Stalin, Molotov, Malenkov, Beria, Mikoyan, and Bulganin. A new and considerably enlarged central committee was elected which was headed by Stalin and included all the members of the former politburo. In the light of an article published by Stalin shortly before the meeting of the congress, the latter voted to set up a committee of eleven to reshape the party's program, which had not been revised since 1919. Among those appointed to the revision committee were Stalin, Malenkov, Beria, Molotov, and Kagonovich. The proposed fifth Five-Year Plan was unanimously adopted by the congress.

That Stalin still held the party reins seemed obvious. He was made chairman of the presidium of the congress, chairman of the new party presidium which supplanted the former politburo and orgburo, head of the party secretariat, and chairman of the committee to revise the party program. Furthermore, it seemed that the article which he had published shortly before the congress convened had more influence on the party than all of the speeches delivered at the congress.

THE PASSING OF STALIN

Nevertheless, it had been believed for some time that Stalin was not in good health, for his public appearances had become more and more infrequent. The world was not taken completely by surprise, therefore, when it was announced on March 4, 1953, that Stalin had suffered a stroke three days earlier which had affected his brain and that he was seriously ill. On the next day the seventy-three-year-old Soviet premier and head of the Communist Party of the Soviet Union died.

For a quarter of a century Joseph Stalin had been the practically unchallenged dictator of Russia. The son of a lowly Georgian shoemaker, he had risen to be probably the most powerful individual in the world. A non-Russian, he had become one of the greatest figures in all Russian history. By his policies and actions he had converted a backward agrarian country into the second strongest industrial power on earth. He had prepared the

Soviet Union to meet Hitler's "inevitable" attack and in the Second World War his armies and air force had eventually hurled back the Germans and freed Russia from possible Nazi domination. His achievements had been great.

On the other hand, he had oppressed the church and had forced scholars and scientists to conform to his edicts. In the years after he became dictator he had liquidated most of the leading figures of the November Revolution, who were still living, when they had dared to differ with him over policies. In the course of his collectivization program millions of peasants had been ruthlessly punished for opposition or had died as a result of the consequent famine. He had, according to reports, enslaved millions in his forced labor camps. Finally, at the end of the Second World War, when the Russians had won the respect and admiration of the United Nations by their heroic sacrifices and magnificent victories, he had turned these sentiments into suspicion and fear by his destruction of free governments in the states which his armies had overrun in eastern Europe. As the result of his policies, the world at the time of his death was engaged in a tremendously costly and threatening armaments race, which everywhere handicapped efforts to raise living standards.

Outside of Russia it was believed by many—perhaps hoped—that Stalin's death would weaken the Soviet Union from within, that a struggle for power such as followed Lenin's death might plunge the country into chaos. There was no immediate evidence of this, however. On March 6 a joint statement of the central committee of the Communist Party, the council of ministers of the Soviet Union, and the presidium of the Supreme Soviet announced a new government, the principal appointments being Malenkov, Stalin's right-hand man, premier, Beria, Molotov, Bulganin, and Kagonovich deputy premiers, Voroshilov chairman of the presidium of the Supreme Soviet (technically the president of the Soviet Union), Beria minister of internal affairs, Molotov foreign minister, Bulganin war minister, and Mikoyan minister of internal and external trade. It was also announced that the central committee of the Communist Party would thereafter have a single presidium of ten members instead of thirty-six. Among the ten were Malenkov, Beria, Molotov, Voroshilov, Bulganin, Kagonovich, and Mikoyan. Quite obviously those who had played leading roles in the nineteenth congress of the party were to carry on in Stalin's place, at least temporarily. The "big three" of the group appeared to be Malenkov, Beria, and Molotov.

On March 15 the government changes announced on March 6 were unanimously approved by the Supreme Soviet. In an effort, perhaps, to centralize power, there were many mergers of ministries, the number of ministries being reduced from fifty-one to twenty-six. In an address to the

Supreme Soviet at that time Premier Malenkov declared that the measures to reduce and unify the leadership had been agreed on while Stalin was still alive and that their execution had been merely accelerated by his death. On the question of the Soviet Union's foreign policy, he declared that it would aim at maintaining and consolidating peace, at insuring the defense and security of the country, at collaboration and trade with other countries, and at strengthening the ties of friendship with China and the people's democracies. He asserted, finally, that there was no question in Soviet relations with other states which could not be settled by peaceful means on the basis of mutual agreement.

In an attempt, perhaps, to win popular support for the new government, an amnesty decree issued on March 27 ordered the immediate release from prison of all persons serving terms up to five years, of persons serving longer terms if they were pregnant women or women with children under ten years of age, women over the age of fifty, or men over fifty-five. Also to be released were persons serving terms for "official" or "economic" crimes. Other persons serving terms longer than five years were to have their sentences reduced by half. Junior officials sentenced for exceeding their authority or failing to use it, state store clerks sentenced for cheating customers, factory directors sentenced for producing substandard goods, and workers sentenced for absence without leave were expected to benefit by the decree. In another apparent effort to win popular support, price reductions were ordered on items of food, cloth and clothing.

Nevertheless, despite surface indications of harmony among the top Communist leaders, on July 10 came the startling announcement that the central committee of the Communist Party had expelled Lavrenti Beria and that the presidium of the Supreme Soviet, in view of Beria's criminal anti-state actions, had removed him from his posts as deputy premier and minister of internal affairs and had referred his crimes to the supreme court of the U.S.S.R. Simultaneously, *Pravda,* the party newspaper, accused Beria of being "an agent of international imperialism," "an adventurist," and "a foreign hireling." Beria, a Georgian, who had joined the Bolsheviks in March, 1917, had since 1938 been head of the ministry of internal affairs. In other words, for some fourteen years he had been Stalin's right-hand man in control of the secret police. Obviously the accusation that he had tried to "subvert the Soviet state in the interest of foreign capital" was open to serious question. More plausible, probably, was the charge that he had attempted to "place the ministry of internal affairs above the government and the Communist Party." Even more credible, however, was not the charge but the fear of those associated with him in the post-Stalin government that he might use the secret police, as Stalin had done, to ensure the supremacy of one particular man. On December 15, 1953, it was an-

Sovfoto

STALIN'S IMMEDIATE SUCCESSORS
Molotov, Voroshilov, Beria, Malenkov

nounced that Beria and six other former officials in ministries of internal affairs—four of them from Georgia or the Ukraine—had been investigated and would be tried by the Soviet Supreme Court on charges of high treason and anti-Soviet activities. All, it was declared, had admitted their crimes. Eight days later the seven men were sentenced to death for high treason and were shot.

In the view of some competent observers, Beria's arrest and execution constituted a victory for "collective leadership," for those who were "determined to prevent the emergence of a new dictator à la Stalin." Whether or not this was true, in the opening months of 1954 Premier Malenkov seemed to be playing the prominent role in Soviet affairs formerly played by Stalin. Meanwhile, in the six months after Beria's arrest, numerous changes had been made in the governments and Communist Party organizations in many of the constituent republics, particularly in Georgia, Azerbaijan, the Ukraine, Moldavia, and White Russia. But even in the R.S.F.S.R. and in the U.S.S.R. shifts had been made in the top leadership of the party and the government. And a new man, Nikita Khrushchev, had been elected first secretary of the central committee of the Russian Communist Party. It appeared that those who had been or might be supporters of Beria were being replaced by men considered to be loyal to Malenkov and Molotov and their policies. On the surface, at least, these policies seemed more moderate and conciliatory both at home and abroad than had those of the Soviet government in the last years of Stalin's dictatorship. Whether these policies would be altered after the new leaders had consolidated their power was a question which only the future could answer.

RUSSIA AND MANCHURIA

During and after the Second World War it was repeatedly stated in Russia that the Soviet Union needed a long period of peace in order to rehabilitate its devastated regions and to carry through successfully its plans for further industrializing and modernizing the country's economy. The paramount aim of Soviet foreign policy, therefore, was said to be the safeguarding of the security of Russia in order that the country might be left in peace to accomplish these tasks. But, as Foreign Minister Molotov stated in May, 1946, it is difficult at times to draw a line between the desire for security and the desire for expansion. There seemed to be evidence to indicate that Russia's foreign policy was designed not only to extend the area indirectly dominated through the Communist parties of other states but to increase the area actually brought under the direct control of the Soviet government itself.

Russia's desire for open imperialistic expansion seemed to be most evident in Asia. At Yalta, in return for the Soviet promise to enter the war against Japan within three months after Germany surrendered, Stalin secured Roosevelt's and Churchill's promises that the rights lost by Russia in Manchuria by the treaty of Portsmouth in 1905 would be restored, that southern Sakhalin would be returned, that the Japanese Kurile Islands, off the east coast of Siberia, would be ceded to the Soviet Union, and that the existing status in Outer Mongolia, a Soviet protectorate, would be preserved. The Kurile Islands and southern Sakhalin—Japanese territory—were occupied by Russian troops in 1945.

So far as China was concerned, the agreements reached at Yalta were subsequently incorporated in treaties with the Soviet Union in August, 1945. In consequence of these treaties, the Chinese Eastern and the South Manchurian railways were united into the Chinese Changchun Railway, which became the common property of the Soviet Union and the Chinese Republic and was to be operated by them jointly under the management of a Soviet citizen. After thirty years the railway was to pass to Chinese ownership without compensation. Port Arthur was made a naval base for the joint use of the two countries. It was to be controlled by a commission dominated by Russia, which was entitled to erect the necessary installations for its defense and to maintain Soviet military, naval, and air forces there. In this case, too, after thirty years all Russian equipment and public property in the area were to be transferred to China without compensation. Dairen, which by 1945 had been enlarged to handle trade and shipping second only to Shanghai in Eastern Asia, was made a free port, open to the trade and shipping of all countries, and piers and warehouses were to be leased to Russia. The Soviet Union thus reacquired approximately the position in the Far East which imperialistic tsarist Russia had had prior to the Russo-Japanese War of 1904.

In August, 1945, the Soviet armies overran Manchuria with little opposition. Japan's capital investments in that region, valued at more than one billion dollars, were considered as war booty by the Soviet government, which proceeded to strip the region of machine tools and electrical equipment and, in some cases, of entire factories. Following the establishment of the Chinese People's Republic, however, Russian policy changed abruptly. The two Communist states became allies, former Japanese properties in Manchuria were turned over to China, and some of the Russian concessions gained in the treaty of 1945 were surrendered by the Soviet government (see page 809).

RUSSIA AND KOREA

In view of Russia's attempt to penetrate Korea prior to 1904, her activities in that country after the Second World War were open to suspicion of being imperialistic, though Russian statesmen declared that they were designed merely to establish in Korea "a true democratic and independent country, friendly to the Soviet Union, so that in the future it will not become a base for an attack on the Soviet Union."

On August 8, 1945, Russian forces landed in northern Korea and began mopping up the Japanese, whose regime was immediately liquidated. Korean committees of law and order were given authority to function under Soviet command, and on August 25 the "Executive Committee of the Korean People" took over the administrative powers of the former Chosen government-general. This Executive Committee, in turn, under the guidance of the Soviet authorities began to construct its organs of government. In February, 1946, the All-Korean People's Interim Committee of North Korea [2] was formally established in Pyongyang, the northern capital, to replace the Executive Committee. The final step in organizing the government of North Korea came in February, 1947, when a national assembly convened and approved the actions of the People's Interim Committee, adopted a national economic plan, chose a presidium and a supreme court, and confirmed the composition of the People's Committee of Northern Korea. In the meantime political parties had appeared, but in 1946 the United National Democratic Front was created, outside of which no political activity was permitted. Meanwhile, too, a people's militia of more than 100,000 men, armed with captured Japanese equipment and trained by Soviet officers, provided a force which could be used to maintain the Communist regime in power even if the Soviet army withdrew.

The economy of Northern Korea was largely copied from Soviet Russia. Lands and property of Japanese and Korean landlords were confiscated and transferred without charge to some 725,000 landless peasants or small holders. The new holders obtained their land in perpetual usufruct only, however, and it was not transferable. Banks, factories, and means of transport and communication which had belonged to "Japanese aggressors and to traitors to the Korean people" were also taken over by the people's committees and put under direct government control. Soviet technicians and managers directed and supervised the progress of economic rehabilitation. By the close of 1947, obviously, Northern Korea had become a Communist state. And this state contained some 88 per cent of all Korea's industries and practically all the timber, high-grade coal, nitrate deposits, and developed water power. Through its ability to control water power it was in a position to handicap the economic development of South Korea.

At the Cairo Conference (November 22–26, 1943) Roosevelt, Churchill, and Chiang Kai-shek had agreed that their three states were "determined

---

[2] At Yalta and Potsdam decisions were taken providing that the Soviet forces should accept the Japanese surrender north of the 38th parallel, and the United States forces should accept it south of that line. American forces did not land in Korea until September 8, 1945.

that in due course Korea shall become free and independent." Later, at the Moscow Conference (December 16–26, 1945), an agreement had been reached upon the procedure by which Korea was to gain her independence, but in the ensuing two years no implementation of the plan occurred because Russia and the United States could not agree on "the Korean democratic parties and social organizations" which their joint commission was supposed to consult. In September, 1947, the United States proposed an election in both zones of Korea, supervised by the United Nations, for a provisional legislature and government. The Soviet Union rejected this proposal and the United States then placed the case of Korea before the General Assembly of the United Nations. In November, 1947, the General Assembly voted that elections should be held in both zones under the observation of the United Nations and that a bizonal provisional government should be set up with United Nations assistance. The Soviet government's motion that the United Nations order both the Russian and American occupation troops out of Korea by January 1, 1948, was rejected, whereupon Russia declared she would not admit United Nations emissaries to the northern zone.

Nevertheless, in accordance with the United Nations resolution elections were held in Korea outside the Soviet zone on May 10, 1948, under the observation of a United Nations commission. The national assembly thus elected, representing about two thirds of the Korean people, drafted a republican constitution and elected Syngman Rhee as president. On August 15, the third anniversary of the country's liberation from Japan, the Korean Republic was proclaimed in Seoul, the capital.

The United States and China at once extended *de facto* recognition to the government of the Korean Republic, and on December 10 the United States agreed to provide at least $300,000,000 aid to the republic in the ensuing years through the Economic Co-operation Administration. Plans were made for the extensive nationalization of transportation, communication, and the major industries. In December the United Nations Assembly by a vote of 48 to 6 recognized the Seoul government as Korea's only legitimate government, and appointed a permanent commission to work for the unification of Korea and the withdrawal of occupation troops. In October the Soviet government had ordered the gradual evacuation of its troops from Korea and on December 30, 1948, it was announced in Moscow that all Russian troops had been withdrawn. Early in January, 1949, the United States took similar steps and by the end of June all American troops had been withdrawn except a small advisory mission.

But the government of neither of the Korean states was satisfied with the 38th parallel and both claimed jurisdiction over the entire peninsula. Each apparently had underground forces in the territory of the other, and after the withdrawal of American troops the rival Korean armies fought something of an undeclared war along the 38th parallel. How in June, 1950, the North Koreans, probably encouraged by Russia, finally launched an all-out invasion against the Korean Republic is discussed in Chapter XXVIII. Following the signing of the armistice at the close of the Korean War in 1953, the Soviet government expressed its willingness to help in the peaceful reconstruction of North Korea. It promised to make a one billion rouble grant to North Korea for the latter's use in the industrial construction and reconstruction of the country.

RUSSIA AND IRAN

The desire for territorial or economic expansion appeared to motivate, also, the Soviet government's policies toward Iran. As early as 1944 Russia asked for oil concessions in northern Iran at the same time that American and British oil companies were seeking new concessions in the southeastern part of that country. But Iran declined to grant such concessions during the war, whereupon Russia apparently brought pressure upon the government in Teheran and was accused of even encouraging a separatist movement in Iranian Azerbaijan. The problem was brought before the United Nations, but two agreements between Russia and Iran in April, 1946, seemed to settle the matter without action by that body. The first provided for the complete withdrawal of Russian troops from Iranian territory; the second, subject to ratification by the Iranian parliament, provided for the formation of a joint Soviet-Iranian oil company to operate as a monopoly for fifty years in developing the petroleum resources in a strip of territory across northern Iran.

Elections for a new parliament which should ratify or reject the Soviet-Iranian oil agreement were held early in 1947 and gave a substantial majority to the government which had signed the agreement. But in March came the announcement of the so-called Truman Doctrine, which committed the United States to combat the extension of Soviet influence throughout the world, and in the succeeding months pressure was applied on the Iranian government from all sides. During the summer it was announced that Iran would receive from the United States some $30,000,000 worth of surplus army equipment, together with a $25,000,000 credit with which to pay for it; and in September the United States ambassador to Iran stated that his country would defend Iran's freedom to make her own choice in matters of foreign commercial proposals. Finally, on October 6, 1947, the United States signed a pact with Iran providing for an American military mission to "enhance the efficiency of the Iranian army." Two weeks later the parliament in Teheran voted overwhelmingly against ratifying the Soviet-Iranian agreement for a joint oil company. The Soviet government at once declared that the Iranian government had "treacherously violated its undertakings," made a strong protest against its "hostile actions," and declared that it "must be responsible for any consequences." In February, 1948, the Iranian parliament voted to purchase $10,000,000 worth of arms from the United States.

RUSSIA AND THE STRAITS

What appeared to be a preliminary move to the demand for some concessions from Turkey, also, was the Soviet government's decision in March, 1945, to denounce the Turkish-Soviet nonaggression pact of 1925. Many suspected that the Soviet government was about to attempt to improve Russia's position at the Straits, a suspicion which was justified in August, 1946, when the Soviet government demanded that the Montreux Convention be modified to put the Dardanelles under the control of the Black Sea powers—Turkey, Russia, Rumania, Bulgaria—and that the fortification of the Straits be placed under joint Russo-Turkish control. Russia thus once more sought to realize her age-long desire to control the Straits, a control which had been promised her by the Allies during the First World War. Turkey opposed any Russian encroachment on the Straits and was supported in her stand by Great Britain and the United States. Turkey's desire to protect herself against pressure from Russia had led her to keep her army mobilized even after the end of the war, despite the heavy drain on her national treasury. To assist the Turks to maintain their military position, President Truman requested and the United States Congress approved in April, 1947, an appropriation of $100,000,000 to help Turkey in her military needs. As in the case of so many other world problems, Soviet-Turkish relations seemed destined to be involved in the "cold-war" between the United States and Russia. Six years later, however, after Stalin's death, the Soviet government in a note to Turkey on May 30, 1953, renounced Russia's claims to Turkish territory and to special privileges in the Dardanelles.

RUSSIA'S SATELLITE STATES IN EUROPE

Little effort was made by the Soviet government to conceal its desire to control indirectly through Communist parties the states lying along Russia's western boundary, for Stalin himself publicly justified it on the ground that the Germans had invaded Russia through Finland, Poland, Rumania, Bulgaria, and Hungary, and had been able to do so because governments hostile to the Soviet Union had existed in those countries. With the Red Army's successful advances in 1944 and the destruction of Germany's military and political power in 1945, the states in Eastern Europe which came to be characterized as "Russian satellites" fell almost inevitably within the Soviet sphere. Their economic and military weakness made it practically impossible for them to oppose Russia effectively just as it had prevented their successful resistance to the political, economic, and military pressure exerted earlier by Germany. In all of these satellite states except Finland, by the close of 1948, regimes had been established which were dominated directly or indirectly by Communists.

In the view of Soviet writers, three factors had helped to establish the new order in these Eastern European states. The first was the elimination of the former ruling groups because of their policy of collaboration with the Nazis. There is little doubt, certainly, that each of these countries at the outbreak of the Second World War was being governed by a political group which feared Communism and leaned more or less toward Fascism or Nazism. During the war their ruling classes had collaborated with Germany, and the latter's defeat inevitably involved them in total discredit. In fact, the strongly Leftist character of the resistance movements in some of the states was probably the outgrowth of popular revolt against the continuation of their Rightist, anti-Russian, often corrupt and inefficient governments. The second factor, according to Soviet writers, was the leading role played by Communists in the resistance movements, which produced national fronts against Fascism and its economic basis, big landownership and capital. Again, it is undoubtedly true that in all these satellite states, at the close of the war, there were set up coalition or "Front" governments of one kind or another in which Communists played important roles. Indeed, in some of the countries—notably Poland, Yugoslavia, Bulgaria, and Czechoslovakia— former Comintern officials actually returned during or in the closing days of the war to help organize the national Communist movements and to build strong party blocs around them of Leftist and patriotic resistance groups. The third factor which contributed to the establishment of the new order in these states, according to Soviet writers, was the moral, diplomatic, economic, and—they might have included—military support given by the Soviet Union. Without this factor, they admit, these countries would have succumbed to internal and external Fascist pressure.

In other words, the strongest factor in the creation of these "new-type democracies" was the influence of Communist Russia, exerted not through the revolutionary establishment of a Soviet system in the various states, as attempted in Germany and Hungary in 1919, but through a variety of "Front" coalition governments. In these "Front" governments a Communist usually took over the ministry of the interior, and then as unobtrusively as possible he gradually transformed the police and other security forces of the state into a Communist instrument. A similar process was usually carried out in the trade unions, also. At some point in the growth of Communist power and influence, the non-Communist ministers in the government became faced with the choice either of seeking to stop the

Communist expansion of power and thus opening themselves to the Communist charge of "disrupting national unity" or of finally acquiescing in the Communist seizure of power. In all the states except Finland they

RUSSIA'S NETWORK OF ALLIANCES, 1949

finally acquiesced. The liquidation of the chief opponents of Communism, on the ground that they were "traitors," "collaborators," or "conspirators," then followed and in the end the states for all practical purposes became Communist. Meanwhile, the satellite states had been linked together with

Russia and with one another by a network of alliances and mutual assistance pacts.

In 1948 the world was given a dramatic example of the value to Russia of her satellite states and of the close co-operation of the latter with the Soviet Union in international affairs. At Paris in 1946 the Western powers had insisted that an article should be included in the peace treaties with Hungary, Rumania, and Bulgaria stating that a conference of the interested states would be convened to establish a new permanent international regime of the Danube. Russia had maintained that the question of internationalizing the Danube should not be included in these treaties since it concerned other Danubian states also, but she had been voted down. It was decided that such a conference should be held and that it should be attended by representatives of Great Britain, France, Russia, the United States, and the six riparian states—Czechoslovakia, Hungary, Yugoslavia, Bulgaria, Rumania, and the Ukraine.

This conference eventually met in Belgrade from July 30 to August 18, 1948. At the very first session it became obvious that Russia would dominate the gathering. The Soviet government submitted the draft of a new convention which accepted the principle of free navigation for the commercial vessels of all countries, but which called for a revision of the international machinery for enforcing this principle and regulating traffic on the river. The prewar commission, which represented Belgium, France, Great Britain, Greece, Italy, Rumania, Yugoslavia, Czechoslovakia, Germany, Austria, Bulgaria, and Hungary, was to be replaced by one composed of representatives of the riparian states alone. Russia thus sought to exclude the Western powers from any control of the Danube, while the latter sought by opposing Russia's draft to retain some hold on that river as a means of penetrating the "Iron Curtain."

But just as the Western powers at the Paris peace conference had been able to carry through their program and defeat Russia's usually by a 15 to 6 vote, so now the Soviet government with a solid block of seven votes was able to defeat every proposal of the Western powers and force the adoption of the Russian Danubian convention. Great Britain, France, and the United States refused to sign the convention, and the United States government stated: "The unhappy subservience of the Danube peoples to Soviet imperialism was never more clearly manifest than at this conference. There was an evident Soviet determination to perpetuate its economic and political enslavement of the Danube peoples."

Poland

Perhaps the most conspicuous instance of Russia's determination to set up a friendly government in a neighboring state occurred in Poland. In prewar days the government of this state had usually been hostile to or suspicious of the Soviet Union. Poland had invaded Russia in 1920 and had pushed her boundary far east of the "Curzon Line" suggested by the Paris peace conference. She had formed an alliance with Rumania against Russia and had long declined to sign a nonaggression pact with the latter. After Hitler came to power she had even declined to participate in a French-sponsored Eastern Locarno, designed to safeguard the frontiers in eastern Europe, although the Soviet government expressed its willingness to do so. Finally, at the time of the Franco-British attempt to secure Russia's participation in an anti-Hitler pact in 1939, the Poles had resolutely refused to give the Soviet Union permission to send troops into their territory even to help defeat Germany in case the latter attacked Poland.

Following the collapse of Poland in September, 1939, a Polish government-in-exile was constituted in France, the creation of a Polish army of volunteers to fight on the side of the Allies was begun, and contact was soon established with an underground movement within Poland. When Germany conquered France in 1940 the Polish government moved its interim capital to London. Although the Poles were naturally more hostile than ever toward Russia because of the latter's participation in the partition of their country in 1939, it appeared for a time in 1941 that the basis for a future friendly collaboration might be laid. In July of that year, after the Nazi invasion of Russia, a treaty was signed between the Polish government in London and the Soviet Union in which the latter recognized that the Soviet-German treaties of 1939 regarding territorial changes in Poland had "lost their validity."

The Polish government in London at once interpreted this statement to mean that Russia's incorporation of Polish White Russia and the Polish Ukraine into the Soviet Union was invalidated, a view with which the Soviet government did not agree. The Moscow government apparently had in mind a settlement in which the territory east of the "Curzon Line" would remain in Russia and in which Poland would be compensated by the absorption of territory to the north and west which the Germans had taken from Poland in the eighteenth century. When the London government steadfastly refused to accept this view, relations between it and Russia deteriorated. The Soviet government did not long delay to take steps to create in Poland a regime friendly to Russia. During the winter of 1941–1942 a Russian plane dropped in Poland behind the German lines, Boleslaw Bierut, a former leader of the underground Communist organization in prewar Poland. In 1942 he helped create an organization in Poland in opposition to the underground movement directed by the Polish government in London.

In 1943, following the London government's request that the International Red Cross investigate the alleged slaying by Russia of some 10,000 Polish officers at Katyn near Smolensk in 1940, Moscow severed diplomatic relations with the Polish government. Russia maintained that the officers had been killed by the Germans and that the Polish government's request for an investigation indicated that the latter was only too willing to believe the "slanderous campaign hostile to the Soviet Union launched by the German Fascists." But in 1944 the Soviet government made one last effort to reach an agreement with the London Poles. On January 15, Moscow reaffirmed its view that the restoration of eastern Poland to Russia in 1939 had rectified "the injustice committed by the Riga Treaty of 1921," and again contended that "Poland must be reborn, not by means of the seizure of Ukrainian and White Russian lands, but through the restoration to Poland of lands which belonged to her from time immemorial and which were wrested from Poland by the Germans." The London Polish government's failure to accept Russia's proposals led the Soviet government to announce its belief that that government did not desire to establish good-neighbor relations with the Soviet Union.

Later in 1944, however, Prime Minister Stanislaw Mikolajczyk, leader of the Polish Peasant Party, who had become head of the London Polish government in 1943, went to Moscow to confer with Stalin regarding the re-establishment of friendly relations between their two countries. In the conference it became apparent that friendly relations would be resumed by Russia only if the London government repudiated the undemocratic Polish constitution of 1935, and agreed to Russia's proposals regarding Poland's new boundaries. Mikolajczyk, who had himself voted against the constitution of 1935, tried to persuade his government to accept these proposals but failed. He thereupon resigned the premiership and was succeeded in that office by a Russophobe Pole.

Meanwhile, early in 1944 Bierut and others of his pro-Russian underground group in Poland had gone to Moscow and had there set up the Polish National Council and the Polish Committee of National Liberation. When the Soviet armies rolled back the Germans in 1944, this Committee took charge of the areas liberated. Eventually, following the advance of the Red Armies, it established itself in the Polish city of Lublin. In January, 1945, following Mikolajczyk's futile efforts at a Polish-Russian reconciliation, the Polish National Council in Lublin announced the establishment of the Provisional National Government of the Polish Republic, with

Bierut as President and Edward Obsubka-Morawski as prime minister. On January 5 the Soviet government extended diplomatic recognition to the new regime, and following the liberation of Warsaw the new Polish government transferred its seat to the national capital. On April 21, 1945, the Warsaw government and the Soviet government signed a twenty-year defensive alliance against Germany.

With Russia recognizing the Lublin government and Great Britain and the United States recognizing the London government, it was imperative, in the interests of Allied military collaboration, that the two governments should be fused if possible. To this end, at the Yalta Conference in February, 1945, Stalin, Churchill, and Roosevelt agreed that the Lublin government should be broadened by the inclusion of democratic leaders from both inside and outside the country, and authorized the appointment of a three-man Allied commission to facilitate the reorganization. The new government would be pledged to hold free elections as soon as possible on the basis of universal suffrage and the secret ballot, with all democratic parties having the right to put forward candidates. Upon its reorganization, it was agreed, the United States and Great Britain would enter into diplomatic relations with the Warsaw government.

In June, 1945, the Allied commission held consultations in Moscow with representatives of the Warsaw Provisional Government, democratic leaders from Poland, and democratic leaders from abroad, including Mikolajczyk. As a result of these consultations Obsubka-Morawski's government resigned and was replaced by a Government of National Unity headed by him but including from abroad Mikolajczyk as vice-premier and minister of agriculture and Jan Stanczyk, a former leader of the Socialist Party, as minister of labor and social welfare. The new government, a majority of which consisted of men favorable to Soviet Russia, announced that it accepted the Yalta decisions and was prepared to hold free elections with a secret ballot, and the British and United States governments, accordingly, extended to it diplomatic recognition. The London government, no longer recognized by the three great powers, for all practical purposes ceased to exist.

Although the new ministry was called the Government of National Unity, its members were not united on the policies to be followed. The promised elections for the constituent diet were delayed until January, 1947, and then were accompanied by accusations of the government's use of terror, arrest, fraud, and suppression of freedom of speech and the press. Mikolajczyk's Peasant Party declined the invitation of the other parties in the government to form an electoral bloc with a single list of candidates. The Communists and Socialists thereupon began to accuse the leaders of that party of being reactionary, of being "Churchill's agents," and of having returned from London to conduct an opposition within the Government of National Unity. They further asserted that the Peasant Party had become the haven of those undemocratic Rightists whose own parties had been outlawed. The elections resulted in an 8 to 1 victory in the popular vote for the government bloc; Mikolajczyk's Peasant Party won only 28 out of 444 seats.

The new diet elected Bierut to be President of Poland and he, in turn, asked a leader of the Polish Socialist Party to form a cabinet. The latter included representatives of five political parties which were favorable to Russia. No member of the Polish Peasant Party was included. In October, 1947, because of alleged threats against his life, Mikolajczyk fled from Poland; thereupon the Left wing of his party, which had failed in an attempt to oust him from control earlier in the year, took complete charge. In February, 1948, the new leader of the party announced the abandonment of Mikolajczyk's policies and promised the fullest support of alliances with the Soviet Union and the other Slavic countries. Thereafter there was no important political group actively opposed to collaboration with Russia. The diet, meanwhile, had denounced Mikolajczyk as a traitor to Poland, deprived him of his seat in the diet, and banished him for life.

After 1948 the political situation moved closer to that of the Soviet Union when, after purging themselves of a number of Rightist leaders, notably Vladislav Gomulka, secretary of the Communist Party, and Edward Osubka-Morawski, former Socialist premier in the Lublin and Warsaw governments, the Communists and Socialists merged into the United Workers Party. In 1949 Soviet Marshal Konstantin Rokossovsky was sent to be Polish minister of defense and marshal of the Polish armies. Gomulka was thereupon dropped from the Communist central committee and was replaced by Rokossovsky. Later in the year he was expelled from the party, and in 1951 he and others were tried and ultimately imprisoned.

In 1952 a new Polish constitution was unanimously adopted by the diet, and the official name of the state was changed to the Polish People's Republic. The office of the president was abolished, his former duties being entrusted to a small State Council by which the diet was completely overshadowed. The State Council had authority to call elections, convene the diet, initiate legislation, issue decrees with the force of law, and declare martial law. Moreover, it supervised the national councils, which were the sole organs of state authority in all the political units of the republic. In October a new diet was elected from only one list of candidates, and in November, 1952, President Bierut was chosen premier. In many respects Poland's political situation thus came to resemble that of the Soviet Union, and thereafter as a satellite she followed more and more the "Moscow line."

Territorially, the new Poland was quite different from that which existed before 1939. The Yalta Conference had accepted Russia's contention that

Poland's eastern frontier should, in general, be based on the "Curzon Line." But in the Soviet-Polish treaty of August 17, 1945, settling the frontier, Russia ceded to Poland two districts—near Lwow and near Brest-Litovsk— besides several other small deviations from that line. It had also been decided at Yalta that Poland should receive substantial additions of territory in the north and west, though the final delimitation of Poland's western frontier should await the peace conference. At Potsdam, however, it was agreed that, pending this final determination, the former German territories east of a line running from the Baltic Sea immediately west of Swinemunde, and then along the Oder River to the confluence of the western Neisse River and along the latter to the Czechoslovak frontier (excluding only a portion of East Prussia around Königsberg and Memel, which was to be administered by Russia) should be under the administration of Poland and should not be considered as part of the zone of occupation in Germany. This boundary, which both Polish and Russian leaders soon considered permanent, gave the new Poland three fine outlets to the sea at Danzig, Gdynia, and Stettin, and gave her also all of the valuable industrial resources of Upper Silesia. These boundary changes, however, reduced Poland's prewar area by 20 per cent.

The territory added to Poland obviously contained a large German population, and the Potsdam Conference had decided that the transfer to Germany of the German population in Poland would have to be undertaken. By 1949 some 5,000,000 of the 8,000,000 Germans living within the new Polish boundaries had been transferred to Germany. Many of them had been allowed to take with them only such possessions as they could carry and a very small amount in currency. At the same time hundreds of thousands of Poles had been transferred into Poland from Germany and from former Polish territories incorporated in Russia. The transfer of both Polish and German populations inevitably occasioned grave hardships and losses to both. Probably the worst wartime sufferers in Poland, however, were the Jews, for in 1946 the Polish premier announced that of 3,200,000 Jews in prewar Poland, only 80,000 were left. Poland's heavy population losses during the war, together with the changes in boundaries, reduced her population from 35,000,000 in 1939 to 24,000,000 in 1945.

Following the Second World War, Poland was faced with problems of economic and social rehabilitation far greater than those which confronted her in 1919. These resulted primarily from the vast amount of material destruction which had occurred during the war [3] and from the forced transfer and shifting of a large part of the Polish population. Nevertheless, Presi-

---

[3] According to a United Nations economic report, in Poland 30 per cent of the railway lines, 70 per cent of the large bridges, 42 per cent of the locomotives, 92 per cent of the passenger cars, and 98 per cent of the freight cars were either destroyed or removed.

dent Bierut declared that the leaders of the new Poland aimed to change their country from an agricultural into an industrial power. According to him, before 1939 only some 1,500,000 persons had been employed in industry while 70 per cent of the population had "existed in misery" on their inadequate earnings from tiny farms and farm labor. To remedy the latter condition, a program of land reform was initiated in 1944 which entailed the confiscation of land belonging to Germans or to traitors and criminals and estates consisting of more than 125 acres of arable land. These confiscated lands were distributed to landless peasants and to those having less than 12½ acres, and by the 1931 census 1,900,000 peasant holdings were smaller than that. Bierut expressed the hope that eventually many of these smaller plots would be given up by persons who would be drawn into factory work.

The latter development was dependent, of course, upon the expansion of Poland's industry. This expansion, in turn, was greatly facilitated by Poland's acquisition of the relatively undamaged industrial resources of Upper Silesia. It was hoped that it might also be facilitated by the receipt of equipment received from Germany, for the Soviet government agreed to give Poland 15 per cent of all reparation deliveries from the Soviet zone of occupied Germany and 15 per cent of all usable industrial equipment which was delivered to Russia from the western zone of Germany. In return, Poland agreed to deliver to the Soviet Union specified amounts of coal yearly during the period of German occupation.

In January, 1946, all industries employing more than 50 workers (a limit subsequently raised to 100 and in some industries to 400) were nationalized. After nearly six years of German occupation all Polish industry, according to reports by some foreign observers, was disorganized and awaited government operation. Most of the former owners and managers had either refused to co-operate with the Germans and had therefore lost their factories and often their lives, or they had collaborated with the Nazis and had thus disqualified themselves as owners in the eyes of Polish patriots. Poland's postwar economy came to be a combination of state and privately owned enterprises, something like the situation which had existed in Russia under the Nep. Foreign trade was largely, but not wholly, controlled by state departments, co-operatives, or state-sponsored companies.

By 1950, as the result of the Three-Year Plan inaugurated in 1947, industrial production was reported as 100 per cent and agricultural production as 67 per cent above that in 1946. Socialization of industry and of retail trade had increased considerably, but collectivization of farms had lagged. In 1950 a Six-Year Plan was begun which called for a yearly output of 100,000,-000 tons of coal by 1955, an increase of industrial production by another 95 per cent and of agricultural production by 45 per cent. Particular emphasis was to be placed on collectivization in agriculture. Although the number of collective farms was said to have increased from 172 in 1949 to 2,872 in April, 1951, President Bierut complained a year later that peasant opposition was interfering with the success of the Six-Year Plan. By the close of 1953 only some 15 per cent of the country's arable land had been collectivized. The shift from agriculture to industry, however, was indicated by a 25 per cent decline in agricultural workers and an almost doubling of nonagricultural workers.

In the summer of 1953, as in some of the other satellite states, strikes and anti-Communist demonstrations occurred in Poland following the outbreak of violence in the German People's Republic in June of that year. Serious demonstrations were also reported three months later in consequence of the government's suspension or "deposition" of the Cardinal Archbishop of Warsaw and the arrest and imprisonment of other Roman Catholic clergy. In October, 1953, eight bishops of the Roman Catholic Church were reported to be in prison.

Czechoslovakia

Czechoslovakia is an example of a state which, although it willingly linked itself with Russia in foreign policy, nevertheless was ultimately forced to adopt institutions in its internal life which were in line with Communist ideology but distasteful probably to a majority of its own citizens. Its adoption of a Communist regime in 1948, like its loss of the Sudetenland ten years earlier, came as the result of the policies of the great powers who were maneuvering to their own advantage.

It will be recalled that following the Munich settlement of 1938, Eduard Beneš had resigned the presidency of Czechoslovakia and left the country. From then until the outbreak of the Second World War he lived abroad, chiefly in England and the United States. Upon the outbreak of the war in 1939, Beneš returned to Europe and, as he had done during the First World War, organized the Czechoslovak National Committee whose immediate purpose was to build up a new Czechoslovak army to fight against Germany. This National Committee refused to recognize the legality of either the Munich settlement or the government set up in Prague under Hitler's protection, and in 1942 it received British, Russian, French, and American recognition as the legal government of Czechoslovakia. In June of that year Beneš' government and the Soviet government signed a twenty-year defensive alliance against Germany and that treaty became the "central pillar" of Czechoslovakia's foreign policy.

After the German slaughter of Czech intellectuals in 1941–1942, no outstanding leaders arose within Bohemia and Moravia so that the Czechs were able to do little in the way of organized resistance during the war. But in Slovakia—supposedly an ally of the Third Reich—a resistance movement did arise against the Nazis. Delegates of the movement made contact with Beneš late in 1943 and plans were made for a rising to take place either when the Russian army called for it or when the Germans occupied Slovakia. Such a rising occurred in August, 1944, when German troops entered Slovakia. A large part of the organized Slovak army joined the patriots, and a Slovak National Council—50 per cent of whose members were Socialists or Communists—took over political control of liberated regions. Delegates of this Council conferred with the Czechoslovak government in London and announced that there was no fundamental difference of view between them and that government regarding the national future of their country.

In the spring of 1945, President Beneš returned to Czechoslovakia and set up temporary headquarters in Kosice. In April, after consultation with Stalin, he appointed a new government in which Zdenek Fierlinger, former Czechoslovak ambassador to Russia and a Left-wing Socialist with strong pro-Soviet leanings, was prime minister. Eventually, in May, 1946, elections were held for a constituent assembly, and as in prewar days several parties participated and elected candidates. Of the 310 seats, however, the Czech and Slovak Communist parties won the largest number (114), and President Beneš thereupon requested Klement Gottwald, the Communist leader, who had once been a member of the executive committee of the Third International, to organize a ministry. In June, Beneš was unanimously re-elected President of the Czechoslovak Republic, and in the following month the constituent assembly approved Gottwald's National Front ministry, which included representatives of the Communist, Social Democratic, National Socialist, People's, and Slovak Democratic parties.

The new Czechoslovakia differed from that existing before 1938 in area and population. Territorially, it was slightly smaller, for Ruthenia—inhabited by Ukrainians—in 1945 voted to join the Ukrainian Soviet Socialist Republic and was permitted to do so. Racially, the new Czechoslovakia was somewhat more homogeneous, for the great powers at Potsdam had agreed that the German population in Czechoslovakia should be transferred to Germany. These transfers were made, for the most part, in 1945 and 1946, and in the Sudetenland nearly 2,000,000 Czechs from other parts of the republic and from abroad were settled. Czechoslovakia also wished to have her Magyar population transferred to Hungary but, though Russia approved, the other members of the "Big Four" refused to assent and left the matter to be settled by negotiations between Czechoslovakia and Hungary. Since the latter was opposed to receiving into her territory all her kinsmen from across the border—perhaps because she wished to retain a basis for future "revisionist claims"—only some 20 per cent of Czechoslovakia's Magyars were transferred.

Minus its Ukrainians, most of its Germans, and some of its Magyars, it was hoped that the new Czechoslovak Republic might be less plagued than its predecessor by the problem of minorities. But the Slovak problem persisted. The attempt to draft a new constitution for the republic was blocked for more than two years by the Slovak demand for all the advantages of regional autonomy while having full participation in the central government's direction of national affairs. The Slovak Democratic Party, which received more than two thirds of the votes of Slovakia in 1946, contained former supporters of Tiso who had both separatist and fascist tendencies. In September, 1947, a widespread "plot" was discovered to assassinate President Beneš and restore an independent Slovak state with the co-operation of leading remnants of the former Tiso regime who had escaped abroad. Several prominent members of the Democratic Party were incriminated; some were arrested; others were forced to resign from government offices; and at least two had their parliamentary immunity suspended. In April, 1948, a number of members of the Slovak Democratic Party, including a former deputy premier of the republic, were given prison sentences.

The economic life of postwar Czechoslovakia came to differ markedly from that existing prior to 1939. Although the country's industrial system was practically unscathed by the war, its structure had been severely dislocated by the Nazis. Even before the Beneš government returned to Prague, it had announced a program of nationalization, and by four decrees in October, 1945, some 65 per cent of the country's industrial capacity was nationalized and Czechoslovakia was transformed into one of the leading socialist countries in the world. At that time, generally speaking, no business with fewer than 150 workers was nationalized but scarcely any employing more than 500 escaped. Small industries, retail trade, apartment houses, office buildings, and hotels were left in private ownership.

In October, 1946, a Two-Year Plan was adopted for the years 1947–1948 and had as its chief objectives a wider distribution of industry over the country and a shift in the balance of industrial development away from some of the light industries, in which highly-skilled German workers had formerly been engaged, to the heavy industries in which the Czechs hoped to play an important international role in southeastern Europe. The success of this Two-Year Plan, however, was contingent upon the receipt of foreign credits, especially from the United States, for it was largely from the latter that some of Czechoslovakia's basic needs for equipment must be filled. Unfortunately for the Czechs, the obtaining of further aid from the West was handicapped by the international struggle between the United States and the Soviet Union.

Meanwhile, during the first two years after the war the National Front had functioned with little difficulty. There was no Czechoslovak party which was fundamentally anti-Communist, those of prewar days having been liquidated and the bases of their power removed by nationalization decrees and population transfers. Furthermore, there was no Right wing in Czechoslovakia as there was in France and no anti-Communist Left wing like the Labor Party in Britain. The other parties in the National Front were primarily non-Communist rather than anti-Communist. The party which held the balance was the Social Democratic, and for two years it voted nearly always with the Communists.

There was in Czechoslovakia during these years what has been called a compromise between Eastern Socialism and Western Democracy. An Eastern orientation in foreign policy was dictated for the republic by all that had happened to it in the preceding decade. To the Czechs it seemed apparent that Russia was the only power that could guarantee them security against a resurgent Germany. At the same time a Western orientation in internal affairs, particularly in respect to political democracy and intellectual and personal freedom, was dictated by the history and temperament of the Czech people.

To many, however, it seemed obvious that this compromise within the republic could endure only if a similar compromise could be reached between the Western powers and Russia, and the deterioration which occurred in the international field in 1947 inevitably affected Czechoslovakia. Because the latter at the Paris peace conference in 1946 had voted on every major issue with the Soviet bloc, she apparently lost the good will of the United States government, which in September of that year cancelled $40,000,000 worth of credits already granted and suspended negotiations for an additional loan. Failure to obtain American credits in turn seriously handicapped Czechoslovakia's Two-Year Plan, for the Czechs aimed to overcome their serious man-power shortage by mechanization and had planned to buy much of their needed machinery in the United States with proceeds from loans.

When the Marshall Plan was offered, therefore, the Czechs at once announced their intention to participate in it and to send their delegates to Paris to join in the projected negotiations. In the Anglo-Saxon press suggestions were thereupon forthcoming that Czechoslovakia was going to disengage herself from the Slav bloc. Russia apparently feared that Czechoslovakia might indeed be won over to the side of the Western powers, in which case the Soviet Union would be deprived of an increasingly impor-

tant source of industrial goods at the very time when the United States was
determined that Russia should receive no further reparations in capital
goods from western Germany. The Soviet government, accordingly, insisted that Czechoslovakia refuse to attend the Paris conference and continue to align herself with the Slav bloc. "The Marshall offer brought down
Czechoslovakia as an independent, sovereign state."

The conflict between the Western powers and Russia next made itself
felt in the internal affairs of the little republic, for the Communist parties
of Czechoslovakia now launched upon a program of extra-parliamentary
steps and even direct action to secure greater control. Ministers who opposed their policies were denounced as "reactionaries," mass meetings of
factory workers were held, and strikes were even called in some of the
nationalized factories. For a time the Social Democrats resisted Communist
pressure and aligned themselves with the other non-Communist parties, but
in September, 1947, this alignment was broken when a Social Democratic
delegation, headed by Fierlinger, unexpectedly concluded a Socialist-
Communist pact. A crisis thereupon occurred in the Social Democratic
Party; Fierlinger was repudiated by the Western wing and was succeeded
as president of the party by the reportedly more moderate Bohumil Laušman, who was at once denounced by the Communists.

In 1948 the latter sought to tighten their control of the police, the army,
the trade unions, and the radio, probably with a view to controlling the
next parliamentary elections which were scheduled to be held in the early
summer. In an effort to prevent such steps, the non-Communist parties in
February demanded that the minister of the interior cease purging the police of non-Communists. When no reply was made by him, twelve members
of the ministry—representing the National Socialist, the People's and the
Slovak Democratic parties—resigned on February 20, apparently hoping to
force an immediate general election. Premier Gottwald at once denounced
these opposition ministers as "traitors" and demanded that President Beneš
permit him to form a new government. The latter recognized Gottwald's
right to head a new ministry but stated that he would not approve the exclusion from it of any party which had been in the previous government.
On February 24, Communist "action committees" seized the ministries
which had been held by the resigned ministers and a considerable show of
armed force was made by marching Communists in the capital. On the
same day the Social Democratic Party decided to support Gottwald and
thus assured him of a parliamentary majority. On the next day the General
Confederation of Labor—Communist-controlled—announced that it would
call a general strike unless President Beneš approved Gottwald's new ministry. Faced, he feared, by the prospect of national industrial paralysis and
perhaps even civil war, Beneš gave in, and accepted a cabinet consisting of

CZECHOSLOVAKIA'S LAST DEMOCRATIC STATESMAN

Eduard Beneš

twelve Communists, four Social Democrats—including both Laušman and Fierlinger, and eight others who were either members of minor parties or considered to be non-party. One of the latter, Jan Masaryk, son of the founder of Czechoslovakia, continued as foreign minister, declaring, "I have always gone with the people and I shall continue to do so."

Gottwald's new government set out to consolidate its power and to remove from the civil service, from government departments, from the judicial system including the supreme court, and from schools and universities those considered "not representative of the working classes." The minister of education decreed that a portrait of Stalin should be hung in every classroom, and announced that school teaching must be political throughout its course. The minister of justice declared that the "action committees" should be the supreme organs on cultural and political matters. Professors and even the rector of the 600-year-old Charles University were removed. Obviously the personal and intellectual freedom and the political democracy which both Masaryk and Beneš had cherished and sought to preserve in Czechoslovakia were being destroyed.

On March 10 came the startling news that Jan Masaryk had committed suicide by jumping from a window of his apartment. In Western countries some asserted that his death was the result of his depression over the destruction of democracy in his native land; others suspected that he had actually been murdered by Communists. Communist leaders in Czechoslovakia, on the other hand, attributed his death to illness and to depression caused by "recriminations from the West" for his part in the February crisis. It may have been caused by his belief that his failure to secure American economic assistance contributed to the collapse of the Czechoslovak democracy. At least it is known that a few weeks before his death Masaryk had lamented: "The United States treats us as though we had already been sold down the river, but we haven't—yet."

In the succeeding months events indicated Czechoslovakia's progressive conversion into a totalitarian socialist state. By April 6, it was announced, some 8,300 persons had been affected by the political purge. In April, further laws intensified the nationalization of the country's industry and trade until only about 8 per cent remained in private hands, and plans were made to confiscate land holdings in excess of 125 acres for allotment to landless peasants. In that month, too, the Social Democrats and Communists agreed to amalgamate into one party after the May elections. On May 9, the constituent assembly at its final session adopted a new constitution on the recommendation of Premier Gottwald, and three weeks later the National Front received nearly 90 per cent of the valid ballots cast in the parliamentary elections of May 30. Early in May, President Beneš had informed Gottwald of his intention to resign his office, partly because of political developments and partly because of his ill health. On June 7, he formally resigned—some said because he was determined not to approve the new constitution. One week later parliament by a show of hands elected Klement Gottwald to be the third President of the republic. Another Communist, Antonin Zapotocky, was chosen premier to succeed Gottwald and the two most important political positions in Czechoslovakia thus came into the hands of the Communists.

For some time Beneš had been in ill health. In the summer of 1947 he had suffered a stroke, and after the Communist coup of February, 1948, he had retired to his country home in Sezimovo Usti. During the summer his health continued to fail and he died on September 3. After a state funeral in Prague his body was buried, as he wished it to be, in a quiet corner of his garden in Sezimovo Usti. Thirty-four of his sixty-four years had been devoted to active service in behalf of the Czechoslovaks. For thirty years, except for a brief interlude following the Munich settlement, Beneš had served the republic as foreign minister or as President. During the period between the wars he had been one of the outstanding diplomats of Europe. Nevertheless, twice within a decade he had seen his country betrayed by great powers which were her professed friends or allies, first by France and Britain in 1938 and then by Soviet Russia in 1948. A firm believer in Western democracy, he had twice resigned after that type of democracy had been destroyed in his country by Nazis or Communists. Much as he was loved by the Czechoslovaks, some felt that he had lacked the necessary will power and confidence for effective political leadership in a time of great crisis. However that may be, the deaths of Beneš and Masaryk undoubtedly deprived Czechoslovakia of her two most notable exponents of true democracy.

In the succeeding years the Communists sought to belittle the roles of Masaryk and Beneš in Czechoslovak history, going so far, in 1953, as to order the destruction of all statues and monuments to former President Masaryk. Anti-government demonstrations at that time indicated the great difficulty which the Communists were having to crush the spirit of those who still clung to the ideals of Western democracy. That there was even a certain amount of anti-Russian nationalism within the Communist Party seemed indicated, too, by the repeated purges, treason trials, and executions which occurred. In 1949 President Gottwald admitted that an organized underground to "re-establish capitalism" existed in Czechoslovakia, and at that time more than 100,000 members were expelled from the Communist Party.

As in Russia, the Czechoslovak purges were no respecters of members in high standing. In 1950 Vladimir Clementis, an old-guard Slovak Communist, was dismissed as foreign minister on the ground of his anti-Soviet nationalism. In 1951 the powerful and ruthless secretary-general of the party, Rudolf Slansky, was arrested on charges of high treason. Finally, in November, 1952, fourteen purged Communists, including Clementis and Slansky, were tried and convicted. These two and nine others were hanged, and three were sentenced to life imprisonment. In March, 1953, the sudden death of President Gottwald brought further political changes. Premier Zapotocky was elevated to the presidency and Siroky succeeded him as premier. Both had been nominated by the central committee of the Communist Party.

Meanwhile, the success of a new Five-Year Plan (1949–1953) had been retarded by opposition and sabotage among workers and peasants. The unrest among the former was dramatically revealed by demonstrations and riots in Pilsen in June, 1953, which were so serious that the Czechoslovak security police with armored cars had to be called in to suppress them. It was less dramatically emphasized by the continued decline in the production of finished goods. At the same time, in 1953 President Zapotocky admitted that there was a serious shortage of foodstuffs in the country as a result of the low production of the new collective farms which constituted some 30 per cent of the arable land. In September of that year the Czechoslovak government was reorganized, and the new government promised concessions to the peasants and the workers. There was to be, according to announcements, less emphasis on heavy industry so that more consumer goods might be available.

At the close of the year 1953 one careful observer of the Czechoslovak situation declared that the Czechoslovaks were "so disgruntled and disillusioned that but for the unpleasant nearness of the Soviet troops, especially the tanks and airplanes, just across the borders of ... the country, Czechoslovakia might soon be in a state of revolutionary chaos."

Hungary

Hungary's first postwar government was organized in December, 1944, by a group of Hungarian Communists who had been living in Moscow, some of them since the fall of Béla Kun's regime in 1919. This government was a coalition, known as the Hungarian National Independence Front, which consisted of representatives of the Communist, Socialist, Smallholders, National Peasant, and Bourgeois Democratic parties, and of the trade unions. The Smallholders championed the interests of the lesser landowning peasants; the Socialists, those of the urban industrial workers; the National Peasants, those of the landless agrarian proletariat; and the Bourgeois Democrats, those of the "progressive bourgeoisie." The premier was General Béla Miklos, who had commanded the First Hungarian Army but had gone over to the Russians when Regent Horthy had issued his proclamation of surrender in October, 1944.

The program of the new government included the following points: recognition of all the orthodox democratic liberties; radical land reform and measures in favor of peasant proprietors and agricultural laborers; social legislation for industrial workers; nationalization of mines and sources of power; state ownership or control of some large industries; state support for artisans and small industries; and respect for the principle of property as such. In March, 1945, the government revoked all anti-Jewish laws, ordered the immediate release of all persons sentenced or on trial under these laws, and proclaimed the full equality of all citizens.

Miklos' Independence Front coalition governed Hungary during the difficult period while the war was being fought in that country. In April, 1945, following further Russian successes, the government moved to Budapest and a regular civilian administration was restored. Eventually, on November 4, 1945, general elections were held throughout the country. The parties of the original Independence Front—minus the Bourgeois Democrats, who had been relegated to the opposition—announced in advance that whatever the outcome might be, the four-party coalition would continue. The elections resulted in the Smallholders securing 246 seats, the Socialists 71, the Communists 67, and the National Peasants 22. They were therefore a distinct victory for the moderate, middle-class-farmer party and were considered to reflect something of a revulsion of feeling against the Communists who had created and largely dominated the Independence Front. A new coalition ministry was thereupon organized with Zoltan Tildy, leader of the Smallholders, as premier and with other representatives of the Smallholders receiving the important portfolios of foreign affairs and defense. In February, 1946, following the abolition of the monarchy and the proclamation of a republic, the National Assembly chose Tildy to be President of the Republic and Ferenc Nagy, Tildy's successor as head of the Smallholders Party, as premier.

In the elections of 1945 there had been no opposition parties of importance, with the result that most opposition votes had been cast for the Smallholders Party which was the one farthest to the Right. As a consequence, anti-government tendencies frequently found support within the ranks of the Smallholders Party, which in March, 1946, expelled nineteen members of parliament from the party as reactionaries. But the Communists were not satisfied with this purge and continued to demand the expulsion of all Right-wing members of that party. In January, 1947, the press reported a plot to overthrow the government in which many members of the Smallholders Party were involved. Premier Nagy asserted that the Smallholders, Social Democratic, and Communist parties had all been infiltrated by some of the plotters, but Communist leaders put the blame on the Smallholders entirely. Hundreds, including army officers and members of parliament, were arrested. In February twenty-five more deputies were expelled from the Smallholders Party, and Béla Kovacs, secretary-general of the party, was arrested by Russian military authorities, who later claimed that he had confessed his guilt as a conspirator, though they declined to submit copies of the documents to the Western powers. In March three ministers, members of the Smallholders Party, were dismissed from the government.

In May, while Premier Nagy was in Switzerland on a vacation, Moscow informed the Hungarian government that it was willing to hand over evidence of Kovacs and others which implicated many leading members of the Smallholders Party. Nagy became alarmed, resigned the premiership, and refused to return to Hungary, whereupon he was expelled from his own party which announced that it planned to rid itself not only of those implicated in the conspiracy against the state but even of those who might have given it moral support. Lajos Dinnyes, a member of the Smallholders Party and former minister of defense, was appointed prime minister to succeed Nagy.

On August 31, Hungary had parliamentary elections for the second time since the collapse of the Horthy regime. In addition to the four coalition parties, which decided in advance to maintain the Independence Front, there were six opposition parties, formed chiefly by members of parliament who had been elected in 1945 but who had subsequently been expelled or had seceded from their parties. A new electoral law disfranchised certain classes of citizens—Germans, sympathizers with the Nazis who had fled the country and not returned until after 1945, and those who were considered to have a fascist or counter-revolutionary past. Including the 150,000 Germans, the total number of disfranchised was announced as 330,000, or 6 per cent of the electorate. Despite Nagy's appeals—over the United States' radio—for Hungarians to boycott the elections, the number of votes cast was greater than in 1945, and of the votes 3,042,919 went to the four Independence Front parties and 1,955,419, or about 40 per cent, to the opposition parties. The Communists stood first with 1,113,050 votes but second place went to the opposition Democratic Peoples Party, supported by the lower clergy and by some of the religious orders. In view of its vicissitudes in the preceding six months, it is not surprising, perhaps, that the Smallholders Party stood third, slightly ahead of the Social Democrats. In the reorganized government, Dinnyes continued as premier but the Communists took over one more portfolio, that of foreign affairs.

The succeeding months witnessed some steps toward the destruction of non-Communist parties. In November, 1947, Zoltán Pfeiffer, leader of the extreme Rightest Independence Party, fled to the United States, and his party was ordered disbanded by the government. In the early months of 1948 arrests of those charged with disloyalty continued—political and business leaders, journalists, police officers. Right-wing members of the Social Democratic Party were expelled or resigned and ultimately in March, 1948, that party passed a resolution urging fusion with the Communists and the further exclusion of some forty more Right-wing leaders and officers. The program of the resultant United Workers Party called for an abandonment of the coalition government, an intensified war on capitalism, the nationalization of the schools, and the removal from them of all religious teaching.

Late in July, 1948, President Tildy's son-in-law, the Hungarian minister to Egypt, was arrested shortly after his return to Budapest on charges of spying and treason. Under the circumstances, Tildy announced, he himself felt that he could no longer command the confidence of his fellow citizens and accordingly resigned as President of Hungary. No attempt was made by the majority of parliament to dissuade him from this step, and in his place Arpad Szakasits, a pro-Communist Socialist leader of the new United Workers Party, who was then vice premier in the cabinet, was elected President on August 3. Thus another Smallholders Party leader was eliminated from the government and his place filled with one sympathetic with the Communists.

In the ensuing months the position of the Smallholders Party was further undermined. Early in December, 1948, it was revealed that the minister of finance, a Smallholder, had fled to Switzerland and resigned, and that five under-secretaries of state, also Smallholders, had also resigned. The party's political committee thereupon condemned Premier Dinnyes for his careless handling of double-dealing "bourgeois elements" within the party and forced his resignation, also. Dinnyes, a middle-class lawyer, was succeeded as premier by another Smallholder, Istvan Dobi, a "dirt farmer" who had been a resistance leader among the peasants during the Nazi occupation. The Smallholders political committee next declared that the party must be purged of all its bourgeois followers who had dressed themselves up as Leftists. A number of members of parliament thereupon resigned from the party, and it appeared that this once-dominant group might be largely liquidated. Finally, on February 2, 1949, the leader of the Democratic Peoples Party dissolved what had been Hungary's largest opposition group and fled the country, claiming that he had been threatened by Matyas Rakosi, a Communist leader, because he would not take a stand against Cardinal Mindszenty.

On February 1, the third anniversary of the proclamation of the Hungarian Republic, the official name of the state was changed to the Peoples Republic of Hungary. The government coalition likewise changed its name from Independence Front to Peoples Front. But Rakosi, the Communist deputy premier, apparently continued to wield the real power in Hungary.

Meanwhile, changes had been made in Hungary's economic life. The country had suffered severely as the result of both German and Russian military occupation. In the actual fighting Budapest, particularly, was hard hit and extensively damaged. Then, when the Germans were forced to retreat, they took with them food stocks, gold reserves, consumer goods, machinery, and railway equipment, and, so far as they could, wrecked what they were compelled to leave behind. One third of the country's capital in mining and industry, it was estimated, was destroyed during the war. Next, the exhausted and ravaged country was called upon to support a large Soviet army of occupation and to make reparations payments. Foodstuffs were requisitioned by the Russians as needed and factories producing materials desired by the Russian army were commandeered by them. On top of all other economic woes the country's monetary system was ruined; in May, 1946, the pengo, normally worth 20 cents in American money, was quoted at 400,000,000 to the dollar and was rapidly sinking in value. This fantastic inflation was finally ended in August of that year with the introduction of a new currency unit, the forint, which could be exchanged for 400,000,000,000 pengos. To insure the success of this new currency, the government announced, it would be necessary for the state to play a greater role in the economic life of the country.

Before the war the Hungarian government had owned the nation's railways, river and sea shipping, and some steel mills and factories producing machinery. During the years 1946–1947 the government had extended state ownership by nationalizing coal mines, power plants, heavy industry, and food-processing enterprises. After the political upheaval of May, 1947, the principal banks of the country were also nationalized, and in 1948 the nationalization of all industries employing more than 100 workers brought state ownership or control of the country's industry to 90 per cent.

Strong economic ties bound Hungary to the Soviet Union. In part this resulted from Russia's seizure of German assets in Hungary which she took as payments on German reparations. Using these German assets as its contribution, the Soviet government insisted on the formation of five corporations concerned with bauxite, oil, refining, railways, and civil aviation, owned jointly by the Russian and Hungarian governments. The board of directors of each corporation consisted of equal numbers of Russian and Hungarian citizens, but the general manager of each such joint enterprise was a Russian. But Russia's strong position in Hungary's economy was also the result of the latter's obligation to pay $200,000,000 in reparations to the Soviet government. In January, 1948, an estimated 15 per cent of the latter's current industrial production was going to the Soviet Union, but in June—in response to a plea from Hungary—the Soviet government cut its reparation demands by half.

In the meantime, long-delayed agrarian reform which was so much needed in Hungary had at last been brought about. Even before the war ended the provisional government had published a land reform act. Properties belonging to former members of Nazi or other Fascist organizations were confiscated, and all landholdings of others above 1,420 acres were ordered surrendered with some compensation. Smaller holdings were ordered reduced to a maximum of 142 acres. The land thus taken over by the state was to be distributed, first, to farm employees of the confiscated estates; next, to other landless agricultural workers; and the rest to small holders, the maximum area to be held being fixed at 21 acres. The land was to be paid for by the recipients over a period of twenty years. By 1948 about 640,000 families had received allotments, though many of them held only "dwarf farms."

It had been anticipated that the new small farms would prove to be less efficient economic units than the former large estates, and the government encouraged the development of agricultural co-operation. By 1949 there were said to be some 2,000 collective farms and a hundred state farms in Hungary. Although until 1949 no great pressure had been exerted on the peasants to join the collectives, the richer peasants—like the kulaks in Russia—had opposed the movement and some sympathy with the individualism of the richer peasants had existed in the ministry of agriculture. It was for this reason, apparently, that in October, 1948, scores of officials in that ministry were sentenced to punishment for sabotage and corruption. After 1949 pressure in favor of some kind of agricultural collectivization increased; by the close of 1953 some 25 per cent of the arable land was in collective farms.

Probably, in view of the government's agrarian policy, it was inevitable that state and church should clash after the Communists gained the ascendancy in Hungary. The Catholic Church had been the largest landowner in the country, possessing in 1944 some 1,370,000 acres, and it had lost more than a million of these acres by expropriation. Although the government agreed to pay the church an annual grant of some $8,000,000 for its religious, charitable, and scholastic establishments, the church never acquiesced in the state's agrarian policy. As late as 1948 Joseph Cardinal Mindszenty, the primate of Hungary, in a pastoral letter had referred to the injustices of the land reform. The Communists considered such a document an attack upon one of their most popular measures and resented the cardinal's action. They also resented his failure to recognize the republic and his openly avowed preference for the restoration of the Habsburgs.

The conflict between church and state finally developed into an acute crisis because of the government's educational reforms. In 1947 the government extended the prewar four-year elementary school curriculum to eight years and made these eight years of education compulsory, a big advance over the prewar situation. To meet the changed situation new textbooks were published by the state which, though accepted by the non-Catholic denominational schools, were rejected by the Catholic Church. The church's attitude therefore provided the government with a reason or an excuse for nationalizing all schools. The churches were invited to participate in negotiations, and the Calvinist and Lutheran churches, to which some 30 per cent of the Hungarians adhere, issued declarations in favor of such negotiations. Cardinal Mindszenty's reply, however, was considered uncompromising and unsatisfactory by the government. Ultimately the two Protestant churches approved a nationalization plan from which six Protestant secondary schools were exempted and under which the Protestant churches would receive financial grants from the state for twenty years. A similar compromise was suggested to the Catholic Church, but Cardinal Mindszenty in another pastoral letter rejected the principle of the scheme. Nevertheless, the school nationalization law was passed in 1948, affecting some 6,669 schools and 25,896 teachers. After the enactment of the law the minister of education again sought to negotiate—this time with the heads of various Catholic orders—but the primate declared that these heads had no authority and so the negotiations collapsed.

The uncompromising attitude of Cardinal Mindszenty in defense of what he considered the Catholic Church's traditional rights inevitably won for him the hatred of the Communists, who declared that the Catholic Church served as the protector of all those who were opposed to the government. Using the "confession" of a village priest that he had incited to murder under the influence of pastoral letters and instructions from the cardinal primate, the government launched an attack against the latter. Finally, on December 28, 1948, it announced that the cardinal and thirteen others, mostly churchmen, had been arrested on charges of treason, espionage, and foreign currency abuses. In February, 1949, Cardinal Mindszenty was tried before a people's court in Budapest and in the course of the trial he stated—whether voluntarily or under duress was a matter of dispute—that "I am guilty in principle and in detail of most of the accusations made, but I cannot accept the conclusion of having participated in a plot to overthrow the democratic regime." The court found him guilty on all charges, and sentenced him to life imprisonment, with the loss of civil rights and all property. In practically all countries outside the "Iron Curtain" strong protests were voiced against the trial and conviction of the cardinal, and the pope excommunicated all those connected with the prosecution. Nevertheless, by 1950 the Catholic Church in Hungary had lost both its landed estates and the right to maintain its system of schools.

In the succeeding years changes in the government eliminated Arpad Szakasits as president and Istvan Dobi as premier, the latter being succeeded by Matyas Rakosi, secretary-general of the Communist Party. Vigorous efforts were made to nationalize and collectivize agriculture and to exalt heavy industry. Both policies encountered great opposition and much sabotage, accompanied by arrests, an increase in concentration camps, and a decline in living standards. In July, 1953, however, after anti-Communist riots and demonstrations in East Germany had revealed widespread popular dissatisfaction with Communist policies, the Communist regime in Hungary suddenly moved to conciliate the masses. The politburo was reorganized and Rakosi's government resigned. The new premier, Imre Nagy, another Russian-trained Communist, announced a program subordinating industry to agriculture, permitting individual trade and individual farms, granting amnesty, liquidating concentration camps, and promising higher living standards—a sort of Hungarian Nep. But Rakosi still headed the party secretariat and politburo.

Rumania

Russia's increased influence in the Balkans is well exemplified by the course of events in Rumania. In August, 1944, when the Russians were rapidly advancing on Bucharest, King Michael dismissed the pro-Hitler government of General Antonescu and appointed a coalition cabinet consisting of the National Democratic Bloc under General Sanatescu. This bloc included the National Peasant, the National Liberal, the Socialist, and the Communist parties, and two smaller groups—the Plowmen's Front and the Patriots' Union—which co-operated with the Communists. The new government announced that it would purge the administration of all pro-Nazi elements, try war criminals, fulfill the armistice terms, and introduce agrarian reforms which would embrace all estates of more than 125 acres.

Inevitably the members of a coalition government such as Sanatescu's came to disagree over policies. The Peasant Party led by Julius Maniu and the Liberal Party led by Constantin Bratianu formed the moderate Right wing of the government and represented a large part of the Rumanian people. On the extreme Left were the Communists, representing some 5 per cent of the people, and the Plowmen's Front and Patriots' Union. These Left-wing groups desired to go much further than the moderates in introducing agrarian and financial reforms, and in general had the support of the Soviet government. The Socialist Party stood between the moderates and the extreme Leftists. Differences within the cabinet led eventually to the breakup of the National Democratic Bloc and the formation of the National Democratic Front by the Socialists and the three extreme Left groups. Although the Democratic Front was given increased representation in the cabinet, it did not secure majority control, and popular disorders organized by extremist leaders continued to embarrass the government. Suddenly, in February, 1945, A. Y. Vyshinsky, Russian vice-commissar for foreign affairs, arrived in Bucharest and demanded that the government be thoroughly reorganized. Although King Michael objected, he could secure no help from the Western Allies, and so on March 6 a new cabinet, with Petru Groza, leader of the Plowmen's Front, as premier, and George Tartarescu, a former premier under Carol, as deputy premier, came to power.

Under the Groza regime the Peasant and Liberal parties were permitted no part in the government and were prevented from presenting their views in the press or at public meetings. Although the Socialist Party was given cabinet posts, they went to members who were known to be pro-Russian, and ultimately, in March, 1946, the head of that party was ousted in favor of the pro-Russian leader, Stefan Voitec. Meanwhile, in 1945 the economic position of Russia in Rumania had been strengthened by a trade agreement and by the creation of five joint Soviet-Rumanian corporations interested in oil, transportation, civil aviation, banking, and lumber, the Soviet government taking over German assets in Rumania in accordance with the armistice terms. It is not surprising that on August 9, 1945, Russia recognized the Groza government.

But the United States and Great Britain delayed recognition and in August, 1945, King Michael requested Groza to resign so that a government satisfactory to the three great Allies might be created. When Groza refused to step down, Michael appealed to these great powers for assistance. The latter, as a result of their deliberations at Moscow in December, 1945, advised King Michael that the Rumanian government should be reorganized to include one member each from the Peasant and Liberal parties, that it should hold free parliamentary elections on the basis of universal suffrage and a secret ballot as soon as possible, and that it should guarantee freedom of press, speech, religion, and association. It was agreed that when the desired assurances had been received from the Rumanian government, it would be recognized by the United States and Great Britain.

Representatives of the Peasant and Liberal parties were admitted to the cabinet in January, 1946. The Groza government then pledged itself to fulfill the conditions set forth at Moscow and announced that elections would be held in May, whereupon it was recognized by the United States and Great Britain. But elections were not held until November 19, 1946, and then they were preceded by organized terrorism which brought, for instance, an attack upon the secretary of the National Peasant Party and the killing of a colleague when they attempted to hold a political meeting. The National Democratic Front, consisting of the Communists, the Plowmen's Front, the Socialists, and the Tartarescu National Liberals, won 80 per cent of the votes in an election which foreign observers asserted was based on "wholesale falsification of the results by the government authorities."

In the ensuing months hundreds were arrested in an attempt, apparently, to suppress all opposition to the government's policies. In July it moved against the strongest opposition group, the National Peasant Party, when it arrested its president, Julius Maniu, and five prominent National Peasant deputies on charges of plotting to overthrow the government. Ten days later the party was ordered dissolved. In November, Maniu and a colleague were convicted of treason and sentenced to life imprisonment, while other peasant leaders received lesser penalties. During Maniu's trial evidence seemed to implicate the National Liberal Party and its leader, Tartarescu. In November the chamber of deputies adopted a motion accusing the latter and the three other Liberal Party members of the cabinet of complicity in treason. All four at once resigned and Tartarescu later announced his withdrawal from public life. Of the four new ministers appointed, two were Communists and one a Socialist. Meanwhile, in October, the Social Democrats had approved a merger with the Communists to form the United Workers Party.

In December, Premier Groza utilized King Michael's request for the government's permission to marry a Danish princess to demand the king's abdication. On December 30, an announcement in Michael's name stated that, in view of the political, economic, and social changes which had occurred in Rumania, the institution of monarchy no longer corresponded to the new situation and that therefore the king was abdicating and resigning all his prerogatives not only for himself but for his successors. Parliament at once passed unanimously a law proclaiming for Rumania a "People's Republic" and chose a state council of five to act as executive pending the drafting of a new constitution. Elections for a constituent assembly in March, 1948, gave the government bloc 405 of the 415 seats. In April, a new constitution was approved, a Soviet-type of presidium was set up, and another government, headed by Groza and having only two of its twenty-one ministers non-Communists, took over. In August, 1948, a secret state police was established under the ministry of the interior, and all religious denominations and the teaching of religion were placed under state control. The new constitution provided for the nationalization of industry, transport, and means of communication, and in June, 1948, parliament transferred all industrial establishments, banks, insurance companies, and transport facilities to the state.

Economic conditions in Rumania continued to be bad. Her economy, already damaged by war destruction, was subjected to the further strain of having to produce sufficient quantities of specified commodities to fulfill her $300,000,000 reparations obligation to Russia, and to provide food for the Russian army of occupation. The joint Soviet-Rumanian corporations, too, by 1952 increased to thirteen, appeared to operate primarily "as a one-way conveyor belt for exports to Russia." Furthermore, the government's efforts to expropriate and collectivize the land met the bitter opposition and passive resistance of the peasants, though by the close of 1953 approximately 22 per cent of the country's arable land was reported as being in collective farms. On top of everything, between 1947 and 1953 inflation twice led to devaluation of the currency.

Whether to provide scapegoats for Communist failures in Rumania, or to tighten Communist control of the country, or to put into power those who would more ruthlessly execute Communist policies, significant changes were made in the government and party in 1952. Vasile Luca, vice premier and finance minister, who had forced upon Rumania the unfavorable trade treaties and the joint Soviet-Rumanian corporations and had in general been responsible for the country's economic policy, was removed from the ministry of finance and expelled from the central committee of the party. At the same time Ana Pauker, the foreign minister, was dismissed from that office, dropped from the politburo and the party secretariat, and eventually arrested. Teohari Georgescu, minister of the interior, was also expelled from the central committee. Vasile Luca and Ana Pauker were accused of obstruction because of their opposition to currency reform and collectivization. On June 2 the National Assembly supplanted Petru Grozu as premier by raising Gheorghe Gheorghui-Dej, secretary general of the Rumanian Communist Party, to the premiership. Thus, in 1952 in both Hungary and Rumania the head of the Communists openly took over political power.

Nevertheless, the year 1953 witnessed events which indicated both dissatisfaction with the Communist regime and efforts by the latter to placate the peasants and workers. In August the prime minister admitted that the attempted industrialization of Rumania had been at the expense of agriculture and promised that more attention would be given to the production of food and consumer goods in an effort to raise living standards. Increases in food rations were announced. To conciliate the peasants, a reduction of taxation was made and all deliveries from peasants to the state which were in arrears for the year 1952 were cancelled. Later in the year a reorganization of the ministries having to do with foodstuffs became effective.

Bulgaria

Soviet influence was also strong in Bulgaria in the postwar period. The arrival of the Russian army in Sofia had been followed by the overturn of the Bulgarian government and the creation of the Fatherland Front, a strongly pro-Russian coalition consisting of Communists, the Zveno National Union (a pressure group of army reserve officers and businessmen), the Agrarian National Union, and the Socialists. The Communists received the key ministries of the interior and justice, though the premiership went to Kimon Georgiev, leader of the Zveno National Union. The new government maintained the regency established after the death of King Boris in 1943, with a veteran Communist as one of the regents.

The Fatherland Front at once inaugurated a program which called for the liquidation of the legislation of the former pro-Nazi regimes and the institution of people's courts to try war criminals. The term "war criminal" was broadly interpreted and some 11,000 persons were brought to trial. The regents and cabinet members who served between March 1, 1940, and September 1, 1944, together with many former members of parliament, were among the more than 2,000 persons who were convicted and executed.

In their Yalta Declaration of February, 1945, the great powers offered their joint aid in the restoration of political order in the former Axis satellite states and pledged their assistance in the formation of democratic provisional regimes and the holding of free elections. The acts of the Fatherland Front in trying to destroy the Agrarian National Union and in depriving the leader of the Socialists of his newspaper were held to be inconsistent with the Yalta formula. So, too, was the scheme to have all political parties run as a single ticket in the elections scheduled for August 26, 1945. The Agrarians and Socialists felt sure that together they would win a majority in free elections, and in protest six members of the cabinet resigned. The United States and Great Britain thereupon stated that they would not recognize as democratic any government resulting from such elections, and the latter were accordingly postponed.

Three months later on November 18, 1945, elections were finally held but because of the electoral procedure and the police pressure of the government the Agrarian and Socialist parties refused to nominate candidates. The single Fatherland Front ticket therefore received some 88 per cent of the votes cast, the seats were distributed according to a prearranged bargain among the groups which had participated, and the composition of the ministry remained unchanged. But the United States declared that it would not accept elections held under such conditions as measuring up to the Yalta formula and both it and Great Britain withheld recognition.

At Moscow in December, 1945, the three great powers agreed that prior conditions for recognition were the inclusion in the government of two additional members of the opposition groups who were truly representative of those groups and willing to work with the government. The leaders of the Agrarian and Socialist parties, however, made their entering the government contingent upon two conditions: first, that the Communists should surrender the portfolios of the interior and justice and, second, that new free elections should be held. The Georgiev government refused to accede to these demands, whereupon the United States and Great Britain claimed that Bulgaria had not met the conditions laid down at Moscow. Russia supported the Georgiev government's action, however, and an impasse regarding recognition resulted.

At the time of the death of King Boris his young son had been elevated to the throne to succeed him as King Simeon II, but a regency council had been appointed to rule during the latter's minority. During 1945–1946 sentiment in favor of abolishing the monarchy began to develop, especially after a kindred South Slav state, Yugoslavia, proclaimed a republic late in 1945. Eventually the Bulgarians were called upon to vote on the question and in a referendum held on September 8, 1946, they voted decisively against the monarchy. A Bulgarian People's Republic was thereupon proclaimed. A few weeks later (October 27) in general elections for a constituent assembly, carried out in an atmosphere of terror, the Fatherland Front won 364 seats out of 465, the Communist Party alone obtaining 277. In the reorganized government George Dimitrov, a former secretary of the Comintern, became prime minister.

During 1947 steps were taken to destroy political opposition to the Communist regime. In June, Nikola Petkov, leader of the opposition Agrarian Party, was arrested on charges of "preparing for an armed *coup d'état*" and the assembly deprived twenty-three Agrarian deputies of their seats. Despite protests from the Western great powers, or perhaps because of them, Petkov was convicted and hanged. Others, including army officers, were given long prison sentences. In August, the assembly finally ordered the Agrarian Party dissolved because of its "terrorist, sabotage, and diversionary acts." Thus the Communists strengthened their dominant position in the republic. In December a new constitution was adopted and promulgated with a presidium, in which the Communists held a safe majority, as the supreme governing body. During 1948 the liquidation of the opposition parties continued, culminating in November in the arrest and imprisonment of nine Socialist deputies. By the close of the year, it was reported, not a single Bulgarian democratic leader remained at liberty.

The death of Premier Dimitrov in July, 1949, and that of his successor six months later led to the elevation of Vulko Chervenkov, the Communist

Party secretary general, to the premiership. The succeeding four years have been referred to as "Chervenkov's years," and apparently during them the economic structure of Bulgaria was radically altered. Collectivized farms, for instance, rose from 6.2 per cent to 60.5 per cent of the country's arable land, and the number of collectivized households increased to 53 per cent of all the peasant households. The "socialist sector" of Bulgarian agriculture came to be predominant in the country's production. But the extreme poverty of Bulgaria's peasants after four years of intense collectivization seemed indicated by the government's concessions in the autumn of 1953. Income-tax arrears and all taxes, fines, and other debts to the government up to December, 1952, were cancelled and all collective farm debts to machine and tractor stations were remitted up to August 31, 1952. At the same time, concessions were announced to the "private sector" of agriculture, contrary to the government's policy in preceding years. In fields other than agriculture, private enterprise in industry, transport, trade, and other forms of business was eliminated. According to official figures, the country's industrial production rose 250 per cent in the years 1948–1953, the period of Bulgaria's first Five-Year Plan. Unfortunately for the standard of living, however, emphasis was placed on the heavy industries, though in September, 1953, Chervenkov explained that the rates of development of heavy and light industry should be altered to increase the production of consumer's goods.

But Chervenkov's more conciliatory attitude in 1953 was revealed in other than economic affairs. In that year the Bulgarian Orthodox Church was permitted to elect a patriarch for the first time since 1395, and—still more amazing—it was allowed to elect a Western-educated Bulgarian bishop who was known for his anti-Communist views. The prime minister's conciliatory attitude was also revealed in his pronouncements on foreign affairs, when he expressed his willingness to establish friendly relations with Turkey, Greece, and Yugoslavia, and to resume diplomatic relations with the United States. In true Communist style, however, the elections for the Bulgarian National Assembly in December, 1953, presented the voters with a single list of candidates drawn up by the Communist-controlled Fatherland Front.

Albania

The course of events in Albania during the Second World War was somewhat like that in Yugoslavia. During the period of Axis domination resistance groups appeared and as they grew stronger these groups not only fought the Germans but inaugurated a civil war among themselves. Eventually the Communist-controlled forces, commanded by Enver Hoxha, emerged as the strongest element and when the Germans evacuated Albania in the fall of 1944, Hoxha was able to occupy Tirana and set up a government. In November, 1945, his regime was recognized as the provisional government of Albania by Great Britain, the United States, and Russia. In December Hoxha's Democratic Front Party won the national elections, and the resultant constituent assembly on January 11, 1946, formally deposed King Zog and proclaimed the People's Republic of Albania.

The new republic became a Communist state. In 1945 an agrarian law provided for the confiscation of all land and by the close of 1946 some 200,000 landless peasants or smallholders had received parcels of it. The constitution of 1945 declared that all mineral deposits belonged to the people and laws were subsequently passed nationalizing mining, industry, and banking. The little republic appeared too weak to stand alone economically, and in 1946 Albania and Yugoslavia signed a far-reaching agreement to co-ordinate their economies. Yugoslavia's expulsion from the Cominform (see page 765), however, brought a drastic change in this situation. Diplomatic relations between Yugoslavia and Albania were broken, and Albania sought aid by joining the Soviet Council for Mutual Economic Assistance. Although Albania is certainly one of Russia's satellites, perhaps because of her physical isolation from the Soviet Union the latter never signed a treaty of mutual assistance with her as it did with its other satellites. This isolated Communist bridgehead on the Adriatic, politically unstable and economically bankrupt, is now strategically almost useless to Moscow. Nevertheless, in an apparent effort to show its friendship with Albania, the Soviet Union raised its legation there to the status of an embassy in 1953.

Finland

Of all the Russian satellite states Finland was probably the most closely connected with Western thought and culture, and the principle of liberty governed by law was perhaps more deeply and generally rooted there than in the other seven. One of the main problems of Finnish statesmen in the years after 1944 was so to conduct themselves as to give Russia as little excuse as possible to intervene in Finnish internal affairs. Consequently when in 1944 the Soviet army had smashed the Mannerheim Line and captured Viborg, a political conflict had developed within Finland. President Risto Ryti was determined to keep Finland in the war on the side of Nazi Germany; the bulk of the Finns and Field Marshal Mannerheim, on the other hand, realized the futility of further resistance. Ryti had been forced to resign, Mannerheim had been elected President to succeed him, and in

September, 1944, Finland had signed an armistice with Russia. In fact, in the following March the Finnish government had even declared war on Germany.

Parliamentary elections held in the spring of 1945 appeared to reveal some desire to orient Finland to the new European situation. Less than half of the deputies in the preceding diet were re-elected and the Right group lost its majority control. On the other hand, the new Popular Democratic Union, a Communist organization, won 49 of the 200 seats and the Social Democrats won 50. The Agrarian Party, a conservative group, held the balance of power in the coalition government which Premier Juho K. Paasikivi formed, though ten of the eighteen ministers were chosen from the Left.

The Communists in their platform had demanded a partial nationalization of industry, but no drastic new measures were enacted. Even before 1939, however, the railways and important power plants were state-owned as also were the principal ore deposits and 40 per cent of the country's forest land. Despite the fact that 90 per cent of the land already belonged to individual farmers, the need for resettling some 45,000 Finnish families from the areas ceded to Russia led to further land reform. Owners of 62 acres or more were forced to turn over to the state portions of their holdings, ranging from 10 per cent for those in the lowest category to 60 per cent for those owning 500 acres. For all practical purposes, the land was confiscated, since it was paid for in inflated currency but at 1940 prices.

The Communists in 1945 had also demanded a limited prosecution of those responsible for Finland's joining the Axis in the war. This part of their program was carried out. A special People's Court was established to try Finland's war criminals, and in February, 1946, former President Ryti and seven former ministers, including Vaino Tanner, leader of the Social Democrats, were sentenced to imprisonment for terms ranging from two to ten years. The punishment inflicted, however, was far less severe than that meted out in most of the former Nazi satellites. In 1946 the Soviet prosecutor at the Nuremberg trials presented evidence of Field Marshal Mannerheim's collaboration with the Nazis, and soon thereafter, ostensibly because of his poor health, Mannerheim resigned as President of Finland. Paasikivi was elected to succeed him.

Aside from the resettlement of the Finns displaced by the cession of territory to the Soviet Union, Finland's chief postwar problem was the payment of reparations to Russia. As originally drawn up, more than half of the reparations payments were to be made by deliveries of machinery and ships. But the production of these commodities was dependent upon the import of raw materials which, in turn, was dependent upon Finland's ability to obtain foreign loans. The Soviet government did take some steps to assist the Finns. A trade treaty, made in August, 1945, was designed to relieve some of Finland's shortages, and concessions regarding rail and coastal transportation in the areas which Russia had annexed were designed to reduce Finland's transportation difficulties. In June, 1948, after the conclusion of a military assistance pact between Finland and Russia [4] and shortly before elections were to be held for a new diet, the Soviet Union reduced its remaining reparations claims on Finland by 75 per cent.

With the growing tension between Russia and the Western powers in 1948 there were evidences that the Communists might seek greater control in Finland, although President Paasikivi in April declared that no attempts to stage a Communist coup in that country had any chance of success. In May the diet passed a vote of no confidence in the Communist minister of the interior, Yrjo Leino, on the ground that he had been responsible for a police regime since 1945, and President Paasikivi dismissed him when he refused to resign. Some 100,000 workers, by strikes, attempted to force the appointment of another Communist to succeed Leino, and in the reshuffle of the cabinet a member of the Popular Democratic Union, favorable to the Communists, was appointed. The wife of Leino—who was, incidentally, the daughter of the president of the Finno-Karelian Soviet Socialist Republic—was also appointed minister without portfolio.

In the parliamentary elections in July, 1948, the Communist-dominated Popular Democratic Union fell from first to third place in the number of seats held in parliament. The Agrarians stood first with 56 seats; the Socialists were second with 55; and the Popular Democrats (Communists) elected only 38 members in contrast with the 51 which they had held before the elections. Not until four weeks later was it possible to organize a government. The Agrarians refused to join a two-party coalition for fear that the Popular Democrats would start strikes, and the latter declined to be in a coalition unless they received the foreign ministry and the ministries of interior and trade. Ultimately, on July 29, Karl Fagerholm, former president of parliament, became premier in an all-Socialist minority cabinet, which remained in office until March, 1950, when it was replaced by an Agrarian Party government headed by Urko Kekkonen. The latter believed in a neutralist policy for Finland, and for Scandinavia generally, in which the republic would have friendly relations with the Soviet Union. Meanwhile, in February, 1950, Paasikivi had been re-elected President of Finland. In the parliamentary elections of July, 1951, the Communists gained slightly in their number of seats but still had less than either the Social Democrats

[4] The pact provided that in case Finland, or the Soviet Union through Finnish territory, became the object of an armed attack by Germany or any state allied with Germany, Finland would fight within her frontiers to repel the attack, if necessary with the assistance of or jointly with the U.S.S.R. which pledged itself to help Finland. Each state further agreed not to conclude an alliance or join a coalition against the other and to observe the principle of nonintervention in the internal affairs of the other.

or Agrarians. Kekkonen continued as premier in a ministry in which these two parties predominated until November, 1953, when his government was succeeded by a nonparty cabinet headed by a director of the Bank of Finland. In 1952 Finland completed her heavy reparations payments to Russia, and the two states entered into a trade agreement as the result of which Finland was to exchange manufactured goods for needed raw materials from Russia.

East Germany

The German Democratic Republic, set up in the Soviet zone of occupation in 1949, must be included among Russia's satellites. This state with some 18,850,000 inhabitants, almost a quarter of whom were refugees from the regions east of the Oder-Neisse line, became organized politically very much after the Soviet pattern. In August, 1952, power was further centralized when the five existing provinces (*Länder*) were broken up into fourteen districts, each administered directly by the central government. Although, formally, there were four political parties besides the Socialist Unity Party, generally speaking they kept in step with the latter. In the parliamentary elections of October, 1950, for instance, there was but one slate of candidates and on the surface, at least, most of them were not members of the Socialist Unity Party. In practice, however, most of these elected representatives supported Communist policies. The most important government ministers and higher officials of the republic, moreover, were members of the Socialist Unity Party.

In 1950 the latter adopted a revised constitution along Communist lines, and the Moscow-trained Walter Ulbricht became secretary-general. As in Russia and the other satellites, there were party and government purges. By the middle of 1951 more than 200,000 members of the Socialist Unity Party had been expelled. The other parties, too, were apparently forced to do some purging of their own in 1952–1953.

Also, as in the Soviet Union, the Communists utilized youth movements to progress toward their goals. The Free German Youth (*Freie Deutsche Jugend*) was organized under the headship of Walter Ulbricht in close association with the Socialist Unity Party. By 1950 the FDJ included about a million young people aged 14 to 24 and nearly that many more aged 6 to 14 years. In the schools more and more Communists were placed as teachers. Books not in conformity with Communist ideas or programs were purged and others emphasizing the history of Communism, Leninism, Stalinism, and anti-Anglo-American imperialism were introduced. The aim of the government was to have enough young people pass through these Communist-directed schools to ensure soon a "correct Marxist atmosphere" in the German Democratic Republic. Church-maintained schools, however, were abolished and Christian youth organizations were forbidden. In fact, in 1952–1953 there were increasing evidences of Communist oppression of the church.

In foreign policy, too, the German Democratic Republic was a faithful follower of the Moscow line. In 1950 the republic joined the Soviet Council for Economic Assistance, and signed trade treaties with some of the other satellites. Its foreign minister in 1950 attended the Prague conference of East European foreign ministers where, under Molotov's direction, the satellite governments joined with the Soviet Union in formulating statements of policy regarding Germany. The German Democratic Republic cooperated with Russia in attempting to prevent West Germany from being rearmed and becoming more closely integrated with the West. On the other hand, in November, 1950, Premier Grotewohl in a statement reaffirmed the republic's close ties with the Soviet Union. The influence of the latter could be seen in the republic's agreements with Poland and Czechoslovakia. More Communist than German was the treaty (1950) with Poland in which the two states agreed on an "inviolable frontier of peace" at the Oder-Neisse line, the German Democratic Republic thus recognizing the loss of some 39,000 square miles of territory which had been German before 1939. In a similarly magnanimous spirit, the republic signed a joint statement with Czechoslovakia recognizing that the "resettlement" of Germans from Czechoslovakia was final.

As in Russia, after some preliminary preparations the German Democratic Republic eventually adopted a Five-Year Plan (1951–1955), designed to double the production levels of 1936 by 1955. Again, emphasis was placed on the development of heavy industry. In 1953 it was reported that Soviet stock companies, after having turned over to the republic sixty-six basic industrial enterprises in 1952, still owned 15 per cent of the republic's industrial capacity, nationalized companies 62 per cent, and private companies 23 per cent. The first two categories held the key positions in the economy; only in the production of consumer goods did private enterprise play much of a part. In April, 1953, however, private companies ceased to have the right to be represented in the Chamber of Industry and Commerce. Wholesale trade was reported in 1953 to be in the hands of state-owned distributing centers. In retail trade, as in Russia during the Nep, there were state stores, cooperative societies' stores, and privately-owned stores, the first two types accounting for about 60 per cent of the trade.

The Soviet Union exploited the German Democratic Republic as it did its other satellites. Part of this exploitation was in the form of reparations. According to Moscow the republic by May, 1950, had paid $3,658,000,000 on its $10,000,000,000 account. At that time the Soviet government announced that it was cutting in half the balance and that the remaining $3,171,000,000 might be paid in fifteen yearly installments. But the United States high commissioner claimed that the U.S.S.R. had already taken some $18,000,000,000 from East Germany as the result of looting, dismantling, seizure of current production, and recognized reparations. It seemed obvious that in 1953 the economic hardships of the people of the German Democratic Republic were much greater than those in the German Federal Republic. The most important foodstuffs were still rationed and, as in Russia in the early days of the Communist regime, the rationing was graded according to the types of work done.

Unsatisfactory conditions and the loss of freedom—economic, political, intellectual, social, and religious—undoubtedly accounted for the great stream of refugees who fled from the German Democratic Republic into Western Germany, a stream which accelerated in 1952–1953. They accounted, also, for the rather extensive demonstrations and riots which occurred in the eastern sector of Berlin and in other cities of the republic in June, 1953, riots which were serious enough to necessitate the use of Soviet troops and tanks to suppress them. The speed and smoothness with which they were suppressed, however, and the numerous executions and imprisonments which followed gave added proof that the German Democratic Republic was one of Russia's satellites.

In the succeeding weeks the Communists adopted a policy of concession and repression. Almost immediately the Socialist Unity Party promised increased wages, lower work norms, higher pensions, better housing, more schools, kindergartens, and theatres, relaxed travel restrictions, and reduced train fares for low income workers. At the same time Premier Grotewohl promised a revision of the republic's Five-Year Plan to place less emphasis on heavy industry and more on the production of consumer goods—a policy, in the words of the deputy premier, of "butter instead of cannon." A beginning was made, also, of returning some of the smaller nationalized enterprises to their former owners and some foodstuffs which had been hoarded by the government were released in an attempt to quiet the unrest. It was even reported that the Soviet Union would reduce substantially its demands for reparation payments from East Germany in order that the latter might the more readily raise the living standards of its people.

On the other hand, four weeks after the riots the minister of justice of the republic was arrested and replaced by one who had a record of imposing harsh punishments. The minister of transport was reprimanded by the politburo for his capitulation to the June rioters and an official associated with him was expelled from the party because he had actually supported the demonstrators. Wilhelm Zaisser, minister of state security, was dropped from the government and purged from the politburo because of his "defeatism," and the editor of the leading Communist newspaper in East Germany was similarly dropped from the party's central committee and purged from the list of "candidates" for the politburo. Finally, in conformity with the Communist party reorganization in Russia, the office of secretary-general of the Socialist Unity Party was abolished, though Ulbricht as first secretary of the central committee apparently retained his place as party leader. When in July United States President Eisenhower offered $15,000,-000 worth of food supplies to relieve food shortages in East Germany, Soviet Russia indignantly rejected the offer on the ground that it was an imperialist attempt to stir up trouble in the German Democratic Republic. And when hundreds of thousands of East Germans went to West Berlin to secure free food packages, the East German Communist government eventually brought pressure to bear upon its people to stop their going. Events seem to indicate how difficult it is to overthrow or rebel against a Communist government, with its monopolistic control of heavy armaments and its ubiquitous secret police.

On January 1, 1954, the most important of the provisions of an agreement signed on August 23, 1953, between Russia and East Germany came into effect. Thirty-three Soviet-owned industries were returned to East Germany, reparations payments were abolished, the occupation costs were reduced, and East German postwar debts to Russia were cancelled. It was estimated that the returned industries employed about 16 per cent of the East German workers and accounted for 32 per cent of the republic's industrial production. The great uranium works in Saxony, however, were not returned. Meanwhile, in October, 1953, Wilhelm Pieck, who had been president of the republic since 1949, was elected to another term in that office.

Chapter XXV

THE SO-CALLED GREAT POWERS

OF WESTERN EUROPE

IN the decade before the First World War most historians considered that there were six great powers in Europe, though Italy was usually included in the number more because of her ambitions than because of her potentialities. From this number the First World War definitely eliminated Austria-Hungary and the Second World War apparently removed Germany, Italy, and France. Though the latter was included in the "Big Four" discussions in the years after 1945, she usually played a secondary role. In fact, if present and future industrial and military power and not past history were taken as the sole basis for judgment, it is doubtful if there were in the world after 1945 more than two great powers, the United States and the Soviet Union. Aside from the latter, however, the European state which played the most important role in the postwar years was Great Britain.

Socialist Britain

The First World War seriously undermined Great Britain's economic position in the world; the Second weakened it so much more that the problem of paying for the needed imports of raw materials to sustain the country's industrial system and foods to preserve a reasonable standard of living for the country's population appeared to be almost insoluble. This problem was handed to the leaders of the Labor Party shortly before the Second World War ended.

THE LABOR PARTY IN POWER

In marked contrast with the victory which Lloyd George and his coalition won at the close of the First World War was the decisive electoral defeat which Winston Churchill suffered just after the end of the war with Nazi Germany. In the parliamentary elections held on July 5, 1945—the first since 1935—the Labor Party won 393 out of 640 seats, and for the first time in British history gained a clear majority in the House of Commons. Churchill was accordingly succeeded by Clement Attlee, leader of the Laborites, who included in his cabinet appointments Herbert Morrison,

Ernest Bevin, Arthur Greenwood, Hugh Dalton, Sir Stafford Cripps, and Sir William Jowett, all prominent Laborites.

The defeat of the Conservatives was nowhere considered a repudiation or denial of Churchill's incomparable services as wartime leader. There was in Britain, however, a widespread conviction that a fuller life was the reward which should come to the masses for their wartime sacrifices and that this fuller life should provide houses, social security, guaranteed jobs, agricultural reforms, greater educational opportunities, and adequate health insurance. Apparently the majority of the British felt that these objectives were more likely to be attained under a Labor government than under the Conservatives who had been in power since the crisis of 1931.

THE BAFFLING PROBLEM OF INTERNATIONAL PAYMENTS

The most difficult problem which the Labor government faced—profoundly important, too, because all others were directly or indirectly dependent upon it—was that of bringing into balance Britain's international expenditures and income. Britain's dependence on the import of foods and materials for her factories was long standing. These imports, before the Second World War, had been paid for by British exports, receipts from overseas investments, and by other items of invisible income—shipping receipts, and insurance and banking returns. Britain's war effort, however, not only had undermined the pattern of her peacetime production but had changed her from a creditor to a debtor nation. Furthermore, by June, 1945, she had sold £1,118,000,000 of her overseas capital holdings and had lost a large part of her merchant-marine tonnage. As a consequence of all these factors, in 1946 not only were Britain's exports reduced to 41 per cent of the prewar level, but her net invisible income was changed from a surplus of £232,000,000 in 1938 to a deficit of £176,000,000.

Only American lend-lease had enabled Britain to carry on during the war, and with the sudden end of lend-lease in 1945 she was faced with the necessity of paying for her imports. It was estimated that Britain would have to increase her exports at least 50 per cent above the 1938 figure to do so. Obviously, however, much time would be required to return the British productive machine to its normal peacetime pattern, to say nothing of increasing the production and export of goods above the 1938 level. Meanwhile, the gap between British overseas earnings and payments was bridged by United States and Canadian credits and by other temporary borrowings. But if Britain were not to live on foreign loans indefinitely, the gap between her expenditures for necessary imports and her income from exports would have to be narrowed.

In the first year and a half after the end of the war the British made rapid progress in the recovery of production and exports. By the middle of 1946 nearly 30 per cent more workers were employed in export industries than in 1938, and by the fourth quarter of that year the volume of exports had risen to 111 per cent of 1938. But in 1947 the unprecedented rise in world food prices hit Great Britain especially hard. The same volume of British exports bought less imports in 1947 than in 1945, and the purchasing power of United States credits declined rapidly as American prices became more and more inflated. The government made determined efforts to reduce imports. The importation of gasoline, newsprint, and American movies was reduced, and the importation of American tobacco was stopped altogether. In August, 1947, Prime Minister Attlee presented a so-called "austerity program" which called for substantial cuts in overseas expenditures, further restrictions on the consumption of goods in Britain, and an all-out drive to increase production and exports. Wartime rationing of food, gasoline, and foreign travel allowances was restored.

Nevertheless, largely because of an unexpected fuel shortage in February of 1947, the rate of expansion of British exports slowed down, so that the volume of exports in the fourth quarter of that year rose to only 117 per cent of 1938. The discouraging result was that whereas Britain had a total net deficit in international payments of £380,000,000 in 1946, it rose to £675,000,000 in 1947. Although in January, 1948, exports were 28 per cent above the 1938 figure, in February, Sir Stafford Cripps, minister of economic affairs, admitted that the export situation had become more critical for Britain in the preceding few months because it was proving more and more difficult for her to increase the sale of her goods abroad. Basically, in the years 1945–1948, the British people were living beyond their means, a fact which Cripps emphasized when he declared: "We must either export and earn enough to pay for our food and raw materials, or do without." Although the British in 1948 were being denied many of the products which they themselves produced, it seemed likely that a still greater per cent of the country's manufacturing capacity might have to be devoted to exports.

In 1949 it became obvious that the efforts to bridge the gap between exports and imports, though increasingly successful in much of the world, were failing so far as the United States was concerned. By the middle of that year Britain's gold and dollar reserves had fallen below the $2,000,000,000 considered to be the minimum safe margin. In July, therefore, the government ordered a halt in all new purchases from the United States and Canada in an effort to safeguard the nation's reserves. Finally, in September, 1949, when the gold and dollar reserves had fallen to $1,340,000,000, the government devalued the pound sterling from $4.03 to $2.80, in the hope that the cheaper pound would stimulate exports to the dollar area. In the ensuing months Britain's economic recovery was dramatic, partly because of the devaluation, partly because of renewed prosperity in the United States, and partly because of Marshall Plan aid. The country's gold and dollar reserves doubled in the year following devaluation, rising to $2,756,000,000 by October 1, 1950. Rearmament abroad created more demand for British goods and in November, 1950, exports reached an all-time record. With the dollar deficit gradually reduced and ultimately converted into a surplus Britain announced that she would no longer need Marshall Plan aid after January 1, 1951. On June 30 of that year the country's gold and dollar reserves reached a postwar peak of $3,867,000,000.

Unfortunately for Britain, circumstances beyond her control soon changed this happy situation. As a consequence of the wave of inflation which the Korean War caused, higher commodity prices raised the cost of British imports. Thus, since the prices of British manufactured goods could not be raised correspondingly, the basis for another payments and dollar crisis was laid. In the third quarter of 1951 Britain lost $598,000,000 of her gold and dollar reserves because of the renewed and increasing adverse balance of trade. Churchill's Conservative government, which had come into power on October 26, at once announced a program designed to cut imports drastically. Nevertheless, the dollar crisis grew progressively worse. By January 1, 1952, the gold and dollar reserves had fallen to $2,335,000,000, and four months later they were down to $1,662,000,000. But during the summer and fall of 1952, in consequence of the forced reduction of imports, the decline in reserves was halted. By October 1 they were back to $1,895,000,000 and six months later, on April 1, 1953, they had risen to $2,167,200,000.

But the problem was far from solved. Although Britain's industrial production reached a new high in 1953, provisional figures issued in January, 1954, revealed that the value of British exports in 1953 was only $7,229,600,000 (the same as in 1952) compared with imports of $9,371,-600,000 (4 per cent lower than in 1952). The OEEC in December, 1953, declared that Britain's problem was to achieve "a substantial increase of exports, particularly to countries outside the sterling area," a rather obvious conclusion. It further revealed that the rise in industrial production in Britain since 1950 had lagged behind that of other OEEC countries. Whereas the index of production in the other countries averaged 128 per cent of that for 1950, the index for Britain was only 105. It declared that British economic policy must be based on "an aggressive increase of exports, of industrial fixed investment, and of savings to match both."

This problem of international payments seemed likely to continue to be a baffling one for Britain, since it was largely affected by circumstances and conditions in other countries, particularly the United States, over which she had no control. Some felt that Britain's salvation lay, not in still better tillage of the land and still larger exports, but in large-scale emigration.

THE PROGRESS OF NATIONALIZATION

Linked with the plans to increase the production and export of British goods was the Labor Party's program of nationalization, for the Laborites contended that the modernization of industry and the attainment of full industrial capacity could be reached, in some cases, only through nationalization. Under private enterprise some of the older British industries had failed to remechanize as new machines were invented in the twentieth century, with the result that their products had been forced out of the world markets by those of more efficient competition in other countries. In the election campaign of 1945 the Laborites had therefore stated that their ultimate purpose was the establishment in Britain of a Socialist commonwealth. They had proposed to nationalize the Bank of England, the fuel, power, iron, and steel industries, and inland transport.

During its first year in power, the Labor government energetically pushed its program to convert Britain into a Socialist commonwealth. The Bank of England was nationalized, with compensation to its stockholders; government interest rates were lowered in order to give the state greater control over credit; and bills were passed to control investment. During the first year, too, Labor nationalized civil aviation and introduced a bill to nationalize the coal industry. The government maintained that the need to nationalize the coal mines was paramount, pointing out that since 1913 the industry had been declining, partly because of mine exhaustion but largely because of obsolete machinery and the use of antiquated methods. In July, 1946, the nationalization bill was passed and a National Coal Board took over the management of the mines on January 1, 1947. A national tribunal decided that the government should pay the owners some £165,-000,000, which the latter regarded as a reasonable figure.

In the first year of its ownership of the mines the government had a trying experience. When the latter assumed control, the stocks of coal on hand were nearly 3,000,000 tons less than they had been a year earlier, despite the need for more coal because of the increased scale of industrial production. This coal shortage, combined with the coldest winter in fifty years, and the partial breakdown of transportation, brought on a national crisis during the winter of 1946–1947. Many factories were closed, train services were reduced, street lighting was curtailed, and even many homes were deprived of electricity because of the lack of coal. Ultimately the crisis passed, however, and vigorous efforts were then made to increase the country's coal production to 200,000,000 tons in 1947. Although the goal was missed by only 300,000 tons, critics of socialism pointed out that the price of coal was higher in 1947 than in 1946 and that, even so, the government lost money on the year's operations. The Coal Board maintained, however, that the success of nationalization could not be decided in one transitional year. In 1948, Britain's coal production rose to 208,500,000 tons and the amount available for export was increased. The goal for 1949 was set at 223,000,000 tons.

In 1947, Parliament passed the Transport Act nationalizing the country's railways, canals, and trucking services. On January 1, 1948, the British Transport Commission took charge of all inland transport, and planned eventually to reorganize the country's entire transportation system by eliminating unnecessary duplication and arranging to have railways, trucks, and canals complement one another instead of competing for business. In November, 1947, the House of Commons had also approved the government's proposal to nationalize the iron and steel industry as of "May 1, 1950, or later." The act to nationalize Britain's iron and steel companies was eventually passed in November, 1949, but at that time the transfer date was not set. A year later a vote to proceed with the nationalization encountered strenuous opposition but was carried by a slim margin. The Iron and Steel Corporation was then organized and the nationalized companies were transferred to it in February, 1951. The individual companies as such were not dissolved but all the stock was transferred to the new corporation at prices fixed by the government. The original firms retained their own names and legal entity and, to a large extent, the same boards of directors. They were free to compete. Meanwhile, the progress of nationalization in Great Britain was a matter of considerable interest and concern to many outside that country, who were watching to see whether Britain could prove in practice that socialism and democracy could be compatible.

THE PROGRAM OF SOCIAL WELFARE

One thing at least was certain; under the socialist Labor government Britain greatly expanded the social insurance and social welfare programs which had been inaugurated by the Liberals in the years 1906–1914. During the Second World War the famous Beveridge Report, a study of social insurance in Great Britain, had been published in November, 1942. In 1944, the Churchill government had proposed to provide for unemployment and sickness insurance, health service, widows' pensions, retirement pensions, family allowances, orphans' allowances, maternity grants, and death grants by a scheme which would be compulsory for every citizen of Great Britain, so that all would have security "from the cradle to the grave." Before the election of 1945 a ministry of national insurance had been created to supervise the new program, though the program itself had not yet been adopted when the Churchill government fell.

In 1946, the Labor government introduced into Parliament the National Insurance Bill and the National Health Service Bill. The former expanded and strengthened the existing system of social insurance. The latter was designed to provide for socialized medicine and the program was ultimately inaugurated in July, 1948. By the provisions of the act all public hospitals and clinics were nationalized, and every Briton was assured medical and dental care, hospital treatment, home nursing, ambulance service, drugs, medical supplies, and other aids to physical well-being. Physicians and dentists were to receive from the government a basic salary plus a fee for each patient treated, and were to be permitted to continue some private practice if they desired. The so-called social-security charter, it was hoped, would free British citizens of their worst economic anxieties in sickness, in unemployment, and in old age.

Although the Labor government was not responsible for its enactment but only for its execution, another measure provided for improved educational facilities in Britain. Passed during the war, a new Education Act, effective on April 1, 1945, aimed to give British children and youth better schooling, better paid teachers, and better facilities. Those in the lower grades who showed outstanding ability were to receive scholarships to enable them to attend secondary school and college. More technical schools were established to provide the country with needed technologists, research specialists, scientists, engineers, and skilled machinists and electricians. In 1947 the school-leaving age was raised from fourteen to fifteen years.

The Labor government also sought to improve the housing situation in Britain. During the war some 500,000 houses had been destroyed and some 4,000,000 others had been damaged. Before 1939 over 300,000 houses were being built annually and this construction had stopped during the war, thus further creating a shortage. In addition, the great rise in the marriage rate during and just after the war increased the demand for shelter. Before Labor came to power the government had formulated a housing plan in which it was estimated that between three and four million new houses would be needed to satisfy shortages, and to eliminate slums, obsolescence, and overcrowding. Labor's task was to carry through the housing plan, but success here was handicapped to a considerable extent by the need to import lumber and other building materials at a time when the government was desperately seeking to reduce imports. Meanwhile, the national government and some municipalities embarked on extensive plans for slum clearance and the erection of new apartments and dwellings. To assist in this task the government passed another measure, the Town and Country Planning Act, which gave the state authority not only to control and restrict a landowner's freedom to build on his land but to prevent him from charging an unreasonable price for it in case it was needed for the site of government building projects. The national government also granted subsidies for houses built by local authorities.

POLITICAL DEVELOPMENTS

Although the postwar years were difficult for most Britons, the majority of them seemed to support the Labor government in its attempts to solve the nation's problems, if one may judge from the many by-elections which the party won following its coming into power. Inevitably, of course, hardships and privations caused some discontent, and the Conservatives tried to capitalize upon it. The coal crisis of 1947 they attributed falsely to the nationalization of the mines (which did not occur until January 1, 1947), and Churchill moved a vote of no-confidence. The motion was defeated. Later in 1947 the harshness of the government's austerity program apparently engendered more serious opposition. Municipal elections held in 388 towns and cities outside London resulted in a Conservative net gain of 625 seats and a Labor net loss of 652 seats. Churchill thereupon declared that the results showed that Labor had lost its popular support, and called for a general election. But the government pointed out that Labor had won all five of the by-elections in 1947, and refused Churchill's demand. On February 24, 1949, despite Churchill's active campaign in behalf of the Conservative candidate, the Labor Party won its forty-eighth successive by-election without losing a single seat to the Conservatives, a record unparalleled in British history.

One step which was taken by the Labor government appeared likely to alter the political situation in the country. In 1947 the House of Lords had delayed the enactment of the government's bill to nationalize the railways, even though the measure had been passed by the House of Commons. Apparently fearing that the Conservative Lords might use their existing right to hold up for two years Labor's contemplated measure for nationalizing the iron and steel industry, the government in the fall of 1947 introduced a bill to reduce from two years to one the period of time which the Lords might delay the enactment of any measure passed by the Commons. Despite strong opposition from the Conservatives, the bill was passed by the Commons on December 10, 1947, and was sent to the Lords who could constitutionally delay its enactment until December, 1949. At that time, however, the bill was passed by the Commons for the third time and, though also defeated by the Lords for the third time, it became a law. The power of the Lords to delay legislation passed by the Commons was thus reduced to one year.

Since the maximum term of the House of Commons is five years except in time of great national crisis, parliamentary elections were due during the first half of 1950. Early in February Parliament was dissolved and the election of a new House of Commons occurred on February 23. During the election campaign neither the Laborites nor the Conservatives frankly discussed the real economic remedies which Britain's situation called for. Generally speaking, the Laborites talked somewhat less about further nationalization, defended their program of social welfare, and sought to identify the Conservatives with British mass unemployment in the years before the Second World War. The Conservatives, on the other hand, consistently called the Laborites Socialists and talked much of the Socialist road to ruin. At the same time, however, they seemed to promise even more social benefits than the Laborites, and advocated no general reversal of nationalization except in the case of inland transport. Many expected the Conservatives to win control of the House of Commons, for, in an election in which more Britons voted than ever before, it seemed inevitable that some of the dissatisfaction caused by the country's difficulties and by the government's austerity program would be turned against the Labor Party. Although this expectation proved to be true and Labor's representation in the Commons was reduced from 391 to 315, the Labor Party still held an overall majority of six. The Conservatives increased their representation from 216 to 294, but this was not enough to enable them to take over the government. Labor's program, it appeared, still had wide support.

The smallness of the government's majority, however, militated against its embarking upon any comprehensive program of contentious measures. About the only step of this sort was the completion of the nationalization of the steel industry, which the Conservatives threatened to undo when they came into power. Meanwhile, the Labor Party was being weakened from within. Sir Stafford Cripps, chancellor of the exchequer, resigned because of ill health in October, 1950, and six months later Ernest Bevin, foreign secretary, resigned shortly before his death on April 14, 1951. Furthermore, the Laborites became divided over the urgency of the rearmament program which, it was estimated, would cost some $13,160,000,000 in the three years beginning April 1, 1951. With rearmament given top priority in the budget introduced in April the government sought to curtail some expenditures by placing ceilings on the cost of social services and on food subsidies and by imposing a charge on spectacles and dentures, which had previously been provided free under health insurance. In protest against these actions and against the scale and speed of rearmament, Aneurin Bevan, who had been health minister and director of the national health insurance program, resigned from the government, and was accompanied by two other ministers.

Meanwhile, too, conditions within the country were not conducive to the government's popularity. During the first half of 1951 the cost of living rose rapidly as a result of the resurgence of inflation following the outbreak of the Korean War. Moreover, the impact of rearmament and the reappearance of shortages of goods led the government to reimpose some of the controls which had previously been rescinded or relaxed. And, on top of all this, as pointed out above, another gold and dollar crisis was developing. It is not surprising, therefore, that when the government dissolved Parliament again in October, 1951, it was widely believed that the Conservatives would win a sweeping victory. Actually, however, in the election of October 25 the Conservatives received fewer popular votes than the Labor Party, though they did increase their representation in the House of Commons to 321 and secured an overall majority of seventeen. Though the Labor Party secured more popular votes, its representation fell to 295. Seventy-six-year-old Winston Churchill, therefore, succeeded Attlee as prime minister and thereafter he and the Conservatives had the task of trying to solve Britain's difficult economic problems.

The change in ministries could bring no startling change in Britain's economic situation, even though many Britons had been roused to expect better times if only the Laborites could be removed from power. Because of the country's international payments crisis, the Churchill government was compelled in 1952 to order further cuts in imports, lower rations, new controls, in a word, more austerity. In its first budget, in 1952, the government ordered a cut of some 40 per cent in food subsidies, by means of which British consumers since the war had been partly protected from the rising prices of basic food imports. The result was a sharp increase in the cost of living. But the budget introduced in 1953 was more encouraging. No new taxes were proposed, some reductions were made in income taxes and purchase taxes, and the excess profits tax was abolished as of January 1, 1954. At the same time, payments for old age relief and allowance for dependent relatives were increased slightly.

The Conservatives were pledged to denationalize the steel industry and truck transportation and to decentralize the nationalized coal mines, but they moved toward these goals slowly and cautiously. It was not until November, 1952—more than a year after they took office—that they introduced a bill to denationalize the steel industry. On May 14, 1953, the bill became law. Under the new act the securities of the companies which had been nationalized were transferred from the Iron and Steel Corporation to the Holding and Realization Agency which was to dispose of them to private bidders. The individual firms would then again be independent although the guidance on central policy enforced by the Iron and Steel Corporation was not entirely dropped. An Iron and Steel Board—similar to the board which had supervised general policy from 1946 to 1948—was set up to supervise the industry. The first chairman of the new board had been chairman of the earlier board and the first vice chairman had been general secretary of the steelworkers' trade union. The nationalized steel industry, meanwhile, had done well in production, establishing new high records for output in January and February, 1953, partly as a result of operations of a new steel plant in South Wales said to be the most modern in the world. Financially, in the year ending on September 30, 1952, the industry had earned a profit, before taxes, of £64,426,216.

The bill to denationalize road haulage (truck transportation) became a law on May 6, 1953, and freed long-distance haulage—forty miles or over— from restrictions on private ownership. The act was to be given effect by offering for sale to any bidder the 40,000 vehicles which the Transport Commission owned, after the undertakings operated by the government had been divided into "units." The purchasers would form road haulage firms or would expand their current haulage operations and would thereafter operate freely under the normal rules and regulations governing road haulage.

Meanwhile, on February 6, 1952, George VI had died at the age of fifty-six. Although he had been in ill health and had undergone an operation some months earlier, his death came unexpectedly and was a shock to the world. Never trained for the throne and handicapped physically for carrying out many of the royal duties, he had loyally assumed the kingship at the time of the crisis occasioned by the abdication of Edward VIII in 1936. He had been held in deep affection in Britain and the Commonwealth and, like his father before him, had been admired as a king who served his people to the end. His older daughter, who had been assuming many of her father's public obligations as his health failed, was in Kenya on her way to a royal tour of Australia and New Zealand at the time of his death. She at once returned to London by plane and was publicly proclaimed Queen Elizabeth II on February 8.

The twenty-five-year-old queen had been trained for years to fill the position for which she was destined. Intelligent, capable, and charming, her coronation on June 2, 1953, seemed to provide the British with the first great occasion for happiness and rejoicing since before Munich. A holiday spirit pervaded gayly decorated London where millions of coronation pilgrims, for days before and after the great pageant, gave the most sustained demonstration of loyalty to the Crown that the nation had ever seen. "For the first time the people as a whole, carried into Westminster Abbey by television and radio, seemed to realize that the coronation was not an event only of this time and of this country but ... 'the vivid repetition of a great historic act.'" Though in their hearts they probably knew that they still faced almost unsolvable economic problems, for the time being their morale was lifted and they were proud of the spectacle of unity, loyalty, and splendor which they presented for all the world to see.

BRITAIN'S NEW QUEEN
Elizabeth II, with Her Husband, the Duke of Edinburgh

BRITISH EMPIRE CHANGES

British economic difficulties together with the increasing strength of nationalism in the East forced many changes in Britain's imperial position in the postwar years. The need to reduce the financial burdens of empire was the cause of Britain's withdrawal from Greece and Turkey in favor of the United States [1] and, at least partly, the cause of her concessions to Egypt, her surrender of her mandate in Palestine, her grant of practical independence to India and Burma, of dominion status to Ceylon, and of greater self-government to the Federation of Malaya.[2] The maintenance of British troops in these territories had cost money. Winston Churchill denounced the Labor government for "scuttling" the British Empire, but Sir Stafford Cripps maintained that "only in the old conception of the word" was the empire being liquidated, that the British overseas territories were being developed, "which is a much better situation."

Although the great value of the Mediterranean-Suez Canal route to the Middle and Far East had been re-emphasized to the British by their temporary loss of control of this "lifeline" during the Second World War, the strategic importance of this route was lessened somewhat by the reduction of British imperial responsibilities. But that the British were not prepared to forego entirely their control of this lifeline their interest in the fate of the Italian colonies disclosed. Furthermore, although they lost some of their footholds in the eastern Mediterranean, they developed a new strategy which placed its principal reliance on a network of air bases in Kenya, Tanganyika, and Transjordan rather than primarily on naval bases as in the days before the development of air power.

The Fourth French Republic

Although France experienced the disaster of military defeat and occupation by enemy troops during the Second World War, thanks to the continued fighting of the British and to the entrance into the war of Russia and the United States she emerged from that conflict as one of the victorious powers. She found herself free to decide her own political future and free, too, to wrestle with her own national problems.

THE EFFECTS OF THE WAR ON FRANCE

Although France did not suffer from the war so grievously as many other countries, her life was disrupted and some of her institutions destroyed. Her population, already decimated by the First World War, was further

---

[1] See page 754.
[2] For these changes in the East, see pages 772, 779, 787–789, 792, 793, 794–795.

reduced. It was conservatively estimated that more than 1,500,000 French were killed as the result of military operations and subsequent bombing or died from hunger or other causes directly related to the war. This loss was a severe blow to a country which in 1939 was already suffering from under-population, and it resulted in a serious postwar labor shortage. Material war damage in France was estimated at $21,000,000,000, approximately twice that suffered in the First World War. Most serious were the destruction or dam-age to buildings, the disruption of the republic's transportation and com-munication systems, the depletion of the country's supply of industrial machine tools and agricultural equipment, and the loss of nearly 42 per cent of the nation's merchant shipping. The resultant problem of rehabil-itating the economic structure of the country was great and it was rendered still greater by the need to import heavily from abroad.

Furthermore, during the war the French currency became greatly inflated as a result of the payment of 631,866,000,000 francs to the Germans. The country's monetary circulation increased from 114,000,000,000 francs in 1939 to 620,000,000,000 francs in the fall of 1944. Postwar France accordingly inherited an inflated cost-of-living index which, aggravated by the country's inability to finance necessary imports and its decreased domestic production in the immediate postwar years, grew progressively worse. The price level at the end of the war was 3.7 times the prewar level; at the end of 1946 the figure was 8.5 times; in January, 1948, it was 13.5 times. Such changes in the cost of living inevitably caused labor unrest, strikes, and disputes over the relative merits of various policies proposed to halt inflation.

Finally, the war destroyed the French constitutional structure and the question of restoring that structure or creating another by means of a new constitution faced the French people. There was no unanimity of views regarding the nature of the political and economic structure which France should have in the postwar period. This clash of views was further accen-tuated as the result of developments within France during the period of German occupation.

THE RESISTANCE MOVEMENT DURING THE WAR

In the years 1940–1944 those who opposed the dictatorial Vichy govern-ment set up by Marshal Pétain in 1940, who rejected the policy of French collaboration inaugurated by Pierre Laval and others, and who fervently hated all Nazis, had sought to undermine and sabotage the German and Pétain regimes. Gradually within France eight or more resistance groups had been organized in different parts of the country. At the risk of their lives, indeed sometimes at the cost of their lives, leaders and members of these groups—men, women, young people—had carried on an unremitting campaign against the Vichyites and the Nazis.

By the spring of 1943 it had become obvious to the resistance leaders that their movements would be strengthened by union. Accordingly in that year the National Council of Resistance (CNR), representing eight resistance groups, was founded. In March, 1944, some three months before D-day in France, the CNR drafted a Resistance Charter as a program for postwar France. Politically, the charter called for the continued unity of the resistance groups after liberation, the punishment of traitors who had actively collaborated with the Nazis,[3] and the maintenance of freedom of the press, conscience, and assembly. Economically, it demanded the nationalization of large banks, insurance companies, and "the great means of monopolized production." The economic program of the CNR was not greatly different from that of the British Labor Party.

DE GAULLE'S PROVISIONAL GOVERNMENT

Meanwhile, following the Allied successes in North Africa in the fall of 1942, the "Fighting French" movement, which had been inaugurated by General Charles de Gaulle in 1940, had been crystallized into something resembling a provisional government when the French Committee of National Liberation, a sort of ministry, was established in Algiers under the chairmanship of De Gaulle. Later the French Consultative Assembly, a sort of unofficial legislative body, was also set up in Algiers. Félix Gouin, a Socialist leader, was chosen president of the Assembly, which made recommendations from time to time on matters relating to policy.

Immediately after D-day the name of the French Committee of National Liberation was changed to the Provisional Government of the French Republic. Following the liberation of Paris, General de Gaulle staged a triumphal entry on August 25, 1944, and was enthusiastically welcomed as *l'homme du 18 juin, 1940*—the symbol of courage, resistance, and hope." Political initiative appeared to lie with this "Fighting French" leader. Recognizing the strength and importance of the CNR, De Gaulle at once reorganized his Provisional Government to include six resisters, of whom Georges Bidault, chairman of the CNR, became foreign minister. This reorganized Provisional Government was then recognized as the *de jure* government of France by Great Britain, the United States, and the Soviet Union, and the administration of Paris and Central France was turned over to it. The membership of the Consultative Assembly was increased to 246, of which the CNR was given 149, a clear majority, and early in November it convened in Paris and again chose Félix Gouin as its president.

[3] In 1945 Pétain was sentenced to death, national degradation, and the confiscation of his property for intelligence with the enemy, but General de Gaulle, at that time Provisional President of France, commuted the death sentence to life imprisonment. Laval and some others were sentenced to death for treason and were executed.

During the ensuing months the Provisional Government was compelled to struggle primarily with the economic problems which faced France, and its chief objective was to obtain the man power, transport, coal, and other materials needed for the revival of production. But in attaining this objective it was handicapped by the continuance of the war until May, 1945. The fact that nearly all kinds of essential supplies became more scarce after the Provisional Government was established than they had been under the Nazi regime naturally caused disappointment, misunderstanding, and some discontent among the French. So, too, did the fact that De Gaulle's cabinet at first supported relatively conservative policies on nearly every important political and economic question which arose. Nevertheless, even his government eventually nationalized the commercial airlines, the factories producing airplane motors, some of the coal mines, the Renault automobile works, the Bank of France, and the big deposit banks. It also provided for the establishment of works committees in all factories employing more than 100 workers (the number was reduced to 50 in 1946). These committees consisted of representatives elected by the workers and presided over by the employer or his representative, and they were given extensive rights to deal with matters concerning increased production and the workers' welfare. They had also the right to know about the economic position of the enterprise—its profits, for example—and to have two representatives sit on its board of directors. The influence of the labor elements in the CNR was thus made felt.

With the ending of the war in Europe a growing sentiment in France demanded the re-establishment of government by elected representatives and the election of a President of the Republic. In response to this demand the election of a National Assembly by universal suffrage occurred on October 21, 1945. At that time the electors were also called upon to answer "Yes" or "No" to the question: Shall the National Assembly draft a new constitution for France? In this first national election with universal suffrage, 82 per cent of the registered electors voted almost unanimously in favor of a new constitution. By this action and by the overwhelming defeat which they administered to Rightist parties and to the Radical Socialists—long the chief party of the conservative middle class—the French repudiated "the political institutions and leaders associated with the defeatism that led to Munich and Vichy."

The three political parties which won most of the seats were the Communists, who advocated the Russian political and economic systems, the Socialists, who resembled the British Laborites, and the Popular Republicans, members of the *Mouvement Républicain Populaire* (MRP). The MRP was a new, predominantly Catholic party which had grown up during the period of resistance. Consisting in the beginning primarily of Catholic trade unionists and young Catholic Leftists, it had grown greatly in strength after liberation by adding many liberals and Rightists who had opposed the former collaborationists but who also opposed the goals of the Socialists and Communists. The MRP advocated the nationalization of certain key industries but with the retention of individualistic patterns of life based on private property. Since in the new Assembly the Communists held 151 seats and the Socialists and Popular Republicans each 142, it seemed clear that most of the French held views that were considerably to the Left of De Gaulle's. Nevertheless, the French Assembly unanimously elected the latter President of the Fourth Republic.

DISAGREEMENTS OVER A NEW CONSTITUTION

As soon as the Assembly's constitutional commission began its work, differences between De Gaulle and a majority of the Assembly developed. The general believed that in the Fourth Republic the President should be a strong executive and should have approximately the same powers as those possessed by the President of the United States. The MRP supported De Gaulle on this point, and also advocated a bicameral legislature which should be limited in its powers to overthrow the cabinet. The Communists, who opposed any system of political checks and balances, advocated an honorary President with an all-powerful unicameral legislature which should choose the ministry and designate its program. This would be more like the British than the American system of government. In January, 1946, the Socialists decided to support the Communist viewpoint. To De Gaulle it appeared that if the Communist-Socialist type of constitution were adopted he would become a mere figurehead as President, and on January 21, 1946, he resigned in protest. Félix Gouin was elected to succeed him. He at once organized a cabinet consisting of Socialists, Communists, Popular Republicans, and one Independent, with Georges Bidault as foreign minister. His government further advanced the policy of nationalization. In three months measures were enacted nationalizing all sizable coal, gas and electric, and insurance companies.

Eventually the constitutional commission completed its task and on April 9, 1946, the text of the new draft was laid before the Assembly. It provided for a one-house National Assembly which was empowered to enact laws, to elect the President of the Republic, and to choose the premier. The President was to have only honorary functions as under the Third Republic and the premier's powers were to be confined to the execution of the laws. The National Assembly was to be elected for five years by universal suffrage, and during the first half of its term it could be dissolved only by a resolution passed by a two-thirds majority of its members. The new document obviously provided a powerful legislature with little in the way of checks and balances. The proposed constitution was adopted by the Assembly by a vote of 309 to 249, the Popular Republicans opposing it and the Communists and Socialists approving it.

The draft constitution was next submitted to the people in a referendum on May 5, 1946. In this referendum less than 37 per cent of the electorate voted for it and more than 41 per cent opposed it, with nearly 20 per cent abstaining from taking any stand. The Communists had been the most vociferous campaigners for the new constitution, and apparently many of the French mistrusted their motives and suspected them of being too closely linked with Moscow. Many voted against the constitution, therefore, because they thought it did not provide sufficient safeguards against attempts to set up a single-party system of government as in the Soviet Union.

It had been expected that the elections on June 2, 1946, would be for a legislative body. As it turned out, however, it was again necessary to choose an Assembly not only to enact laws but to draft a constitution. As a result of the new elections the Assembly was somewhat less Leftist than its predecessor, for the Popular Republicans received 1,000,000 more votes than they had received in 1945, and secured the largest number of seats. The MRP held 161, the Communists 145, and the Socialists 115. The new Assembly elected Georges Bidault, a Popular Republican, President of France, over the opposition of the Communists. The latter agreed, however, to enter another coalition government under Bidault, who organized a ministry consisting of Popular Republicans, Communists, Socialists, and one Independent, with the Communist Thorez and the Socialist Gouin both deputy premiers.

In the second Assembly the Socialists co-operated with the Popular Republicans rather than with the Communists in the drafting of the constitution. The second draft provided for a bicameral parliament consisting of a National Assembly and a Council of the Republic. But the latter, chosen indirectly by a somewhat complicated system, was primarily a consultative body with chiefly delaying and supervisory functions. It could force the National Assembly to reconsider acts but could not stop their passage; and it could call attention to laws which it held to be unconstitutional but it could not force their repeal. The President of France was to be elected by the parliament for a seven-year term. Although he was largely a figurehead, he was given the right to request the National Assembly to reconsider a bill, and his advice had to be sought before the government could ask for a dissolution of parliament. On the matter of dissolution, the new constitution provided that after the National Assembly had been in existence eighteen months it might be dissolved if it passed two votes of no confidence within eighteen months. Fundamentally, however, the National Assembly was supreme, legislatively speaking; the cabinet was responsible to it alone.

A referendum on the second draft constitution was held on October 13, 1946, and the vote in metropolitan France resulted roughly in 9,000,000 for the constitution, 8,000,000 against it, and 8,000,000 abstentions. Actually, fewer voted for the second draft than had voted for the first. But since fewer also voted against it than voted against the first, it was adopted with the approval of about 36 per cent of the electorate.

Four weeks later elections for the new National Assembly gave the Communists and their allies 183 seats, the Popular Republicans 164, the Socialists 105, the Radical Socialists and their allies 64, the extreme Rightist PRL (*Parti Républicain de la Liberté*) 72, and other parties 23. After the Communist Thorez and the Popular Republican Bidault had both been rejected by the Assembly, on December 12 Léon Blum—generally regarded as a great and unselfish statesman of the highest integrity—was chosen almost unanimously to be premier in a stop-gap government. On January 16, 1947, Vincent Auriol, a veteran Socialist, was elected the first constitutional President of the Fourth French Republic, whereupon Blum submitted his resignation and was succeeded as premier by Paul Ramadier, another Socialist. The latter's ministry was a coalition of Socialists, Communists, and Popular Republicans. With a constitution, a President, a bicameral legislature, and a ministry, the Fourth French Republic was at last launched.

THE REAPPEARANCE OF OLD PROBLEMS AND OLD CONFLICTS

But the position of French premiers in the ensuing years was not an enviable one. As in prewar days the electorate was split into many parties or groups and political leaders were chiefly preoccupied with party struggles. Conflicts between the extreme Right and the extreme Left once more developed, fears of communism or fascism were again expressed, and ministerial instability in the Fourth French Republic resembled that in the Third. Between January 22, 1947, and May 21, 1953, for instance, France had thirteen ministries. The basic problem of each successive premier was to manage his multiparty cabinet in a way to offend none of the parties composing his government, which during the early years of this period consisted of Socialists, Popular Republicans and Radical Socialists, a coalition which came to be called the "Third Force." But since frequently, almost usually, the parties in his ministry were in conflict over some major policy, financial aid to Catholic schools, for example, or direct versus indirect taxes, attempts to hold them together often brought political inaction, if not national paralysis. No French leader seemed able to resolve the fundamental political and economic differences of the French parties. Consequently, in the words of one foreign observer, parliamentary government in France appeared as "an interregnum of dissent between spells of chaos."

There seems little value to be gained from tracing the rise and fall of every premier during these years.

Numerous problems, indeed, presented opportunities for conflict among the political parties. Many of them, in the last analysis, had a bearing on the national budget. For instance, the reconstruction of the devastated areas of the country, the cost of postwar social policies, the conduct of the long and ruinous war in Indo-China, and the rearmament of France to meet her obligations to the European Defense Community, all increased the total national expenditures (the budgets for 1952 and 1953 reached all-time highs) and, without some counter action, entailed an unbalanced budget. Thereupon inevitably ensued a conflict between political parties as to the proper method of balancing it, whether by decreasing expenditures in some other categories, the social service or the civil service, for example, in order to hold the total down or by increasing the income from taxes enough to cover the larger expenditures. And when it came to the consideration of increased taxes, as in the years between the wars [4] conflicts followed between the Left and Right as to the types of taxes to be imposed, and usually the budget went unbalanced. In consequence the government had frequently to resort to loans, the republic went more into debt in terms of francs, and the currency became further inflated. In 1952 the republic's monetary circulation reached the record figure of more than 2,000,000,-000,000 francs.

So, despite the government's repeated efforts to initiate deflation by imposing some price and wage ceilings, inflation therefore continued. For instance, from September, 1949, to the end of 1951 French retail prices rose 33 per cent, and one year later they were over 40 per cent higher than in December, 1951. The resultant lag of wages and salaries behind the rising cost of living in turn brought unrest among the workers and resulted in conflicts between labor and management and occasional strikes. The latter, in turn, were at times exploited by the Communists and, whether so exploited or not, contributed to handicap the rise of industrial production. Furthermore, the rise in prices of French goods led those engaged in export trade or in catering to tourists to demand measures to enable them to compete more successfully with other countries, and led to the devaluation of the franc. By 1953 the official rate of the franc stood at 350 to the dollar (in 1926 Poincaré had stabilized it at 25 to the dollar), though at times it was sold on the free market at as high as 475.

Despite ministerial and financial instability during the years after the Second World War, however, France happily experienced some economic recovery, thanks in part to aid from the United States. By the middle of 1952 the republic's industrial index was 39 per cent above that of

4 See pages 305 and 312.

1938. The production of coal in the restored and modernized mines reached a new high, though it was still insufficient for domestic needs. The steel produced in the first nine months of that year was 50 per cent more than for the same period in 1938, though the 7,000,000 tons seem pitifully small by American standards. The output of electricity, as a result of new hydroelectric plants, was far above the prewar level. Automobile factories, too, established new high records for the number of cars manufactured.

On a comparative basis, however, the French industrial situation was not so encouraging. "Since 1929," declared former Premier Reynaud in 1953, "American production has doubled. In Great Britain and Western Germany it has increased by over 50 per cent. Our production has increased by only 8 per cent." Whereas the basic industries, modernized and re-equipped under the Monnet plan, were efficient and capable of meeting foreign competition, the great bulk of France's industrial and commercial undertakings were small, under-equipped, and inefficient. As a result, their prices were too high to enable France to compete effectively in the export market. French agriculture, too, despite a 12 per cent increase in production since 1938, was still on the whole inefficient. A third of the farms were estimated in 1953 to be uneconomic. The French agricultural community was said to pay only about 13 billion francs in taxation but to receive 16 billion francs in subsidies and about 100 billion francs in the guise of legal privileges of various kinds. In 1953 French imports of agricultural products were twice the amount of her exports. That year saw France in a difficult foreign trade position. In the previous year her dollar deficit had almost doubled.

In the view of many observers, a thorough-going fiscal reform and the introduction of a system which would successfully prevent tax evasion would go far toward solving the republic's budgetary difficulties. A sound fiscal system might make it easier for France to improve her industrial plants further, which still suffered from undermechanized and antiquated methods of production. And such improvements, in turn, might bring sufficient reductions in the prices of French products to enable them to compete more successfully in world markets. But the state of public opinion, the political supremacy of the National Assembly, and an Assembly profoundly divided on economic policy made it practically impossible for successive premiers even to attempt to carry out any coherent economic policy.

And the course of French internal politics in the years beginning with 1951 gave no grounds for optimism regarding any improvement in the political situation. In the years during which the "Third Force" had been governing a new political party had appeared on the scene. This was De Gaulle's Rally of the French People (*Rassemblement du Peuple Français*). The RPF, as it was popularly called, was organized in 1947 and drew its support chiefly from parties of the Right, from the conservative clergy, and from prewar nationalists. It called, among other things, for a new constitution and "the re-establishment of authority in the state," and it was accused of being antirepublican.

In 1951 the "Third Force" in the hope of preventing the RPF from securing enough seats to control the Assembly and in the hope of reducing the number of Communist deputies, enacted a new electoral law. The latter stipulated that deputies were to be elected by majority votes from departmental lists, and provided for the possibility of alliances between parties something like the system introduced in Italy in 1953.[5] Since no party would associate itself with the Communists and De Gaulle announced that the RPF would make no alliance with any other party, the new law was expected to operate to the advantage of the parties of the "Third Force." This it did. In the election of June 17, 1951, fifteen political parties nominated candidates, though some of them formed blocs. A new grouping of moderate and Rightist parties was made, for instance, which called itself the "Fourth Force." As a result of the election, in which nearly 80 per cent of the electorate voted, although the Communist Party declined by only 2.1 per cent in its popular vote its representation in the Assembly fell from 187 to 103. The RPF secured 118 seats, but obviously not enough to control the government. The "Third Force" parties came through with 283 seats, and the new "Fourth Force" group won 98 seats.

A long ministerial crisis followed the elections of June, 1951, for the parties of the "Third Force" were deeply divided on at least two major issues. One was that of granting subsidies to Catholic schools, a practice initiated by the Pétain dictatorship but discontinued with the fall of the Vichy government. The Socialists and Radical Socialists, both long anticlerical parties, looked upon any such moves as an attack on the republic itself. The Popular Republicans, on the other hand, favored aid to the Catholic schools. But to complicate the situation still further, the Socialists were estranged from the Radical Socialists on economic and social policy. Ultimately the Socialists decided not to participate in the government though they were willing in general to lend their support. In the government which René Pleven formed on August 11, therefore, the Radical Socialists were the only lay party and the Popular Republicans constituted the most Left-wing party on economic and social questions. Eventually, in September, the "Third Force" came to an end; the usual political alignments were broken when the Assembly voted to re-establish the school subsidies. On this occasion the Socialists joined the Communists in opposition and De Gaulle's RPF united with the rest of the Assembly to pass the measure. Thereafter the political shift was more to the Right.

The longest ministerial crisis of the Fourth Republic occurred in 1953.

[5] See page 722.

In May of that year René Mayer, who had assumed the premiership in the preceding January, undertook to stop the constant increase in governmental expenditures which, he declared, would otherwise result in a budget deficit in 1954 of some 1,000,000,000,000 francs. He demanded not only no further increases but actual reductions. He envisaged reform of the administration of the nationalized industries, increased railway fares, and taxes on alcohol and commercial vehicles. He further demanded special powers to make administrative reforms and economies, something like those granted Poincaré in 1926.[6] When the Assembly's finance committee rejected his request for these special powers, the premier made the matter a question of confidence. He lost the support of the National Assembly on this vote, however, and was forced to resign on May 21.

In the ensuing crisis the Assembly refused to accept one man after another as the new premier. Each of the first three men who sought the support of the Assembly demanded long tenure in office and outlined in advance comprehensive programs in foreign and internal affairs. But the Assembly was reluctant to accede to the demand for long tenure and was not unmindful that, under the constitution of the Fourth Republic, the next premier would have the right, if he were defeated on a formal vote of confidence within eighteen months of his assuming office, to dissolve the Assembly and call for new elections. It was not until President Auriol had summoned eleven former premiers or designated premiers and nine leaders of as many political parties to meet with him to seek a solution of the political crisis that the Assembly finally approved Joseph Laniel as premier on June 26.

Laniel was a business man and a farmer. He had been one of the leaders of the *Maquis* during the war and had been a deputy for twenty years, having succeeded to the seat which his father had held for thirty-two years. He was a conservative leader of Reynaud's Independent Party and was definitely a compromise candidate. His policy statement to the Assembly was short; he made no promises and asked for no exceptional powers. It was believed that his government, which included Georges Bidault as foreign minister, would in foreign affairs continue to support NATO.

In internal affairs the new premier's most pressing problem was the national deficit. Laniel decided that the government would have to borrow 110,000,000,000 francs from the Bank of France. He proposed that this loan together with the 130,000,000,000 francs borrowed in the preceding three months should be repaid over four years by new taxes yielding 60,000,000,000 francs yearly. On July 8 the National Assembly approved the government's bill for financial reform and granted Laniel special powers until December 31 to issue decrees on many matters, including rent control, social security

[6] See pages 305–306.

administration, transport, and "the reintroduction of free competition in industry and commerce."

To win a vote of confidence from the National Assembly was one thing, to draft a program of financial and economic reform which would satisfy all Frenchmen was quite another. Even before the decrees were presented to the cabinet, however, popular dissatisfaction with rumored reforms made itself evident. Wine growers of southern France demonstrated and blocked road traffic because of the government's proposal to discontinue price supports. And in August, because of rumors that the government planned to dismiss many from government positions, to increase the age limit at which government employees could retire with pensions, and to introduce other reforms which would be at the expense of the government workers, some 2,000,000 of the latter went out on a nationwide strike—the most extensive since 1936.

Following the end of the wave of strikes the government in September issued many decrees covering administrative reform, taxes, and prices. In October, in response to the demand of the strikers, the National Assembly was reconvened to discuss the social policy of the government. One of its problems was to adopt the budget for 1954 which, introduced in November, again showed a deficit, estimated at 416,000,000,000 francs. Another problem was to choose a successor to President Auriol. The ensuing contest strikingly revealed the many cross currents and the resultant great difficulty in getting action in the French parliament in recent years. Thirteen ballots were required before a new president was elected on December 23, 1953; on no previous occasion since 1875 had more than two been necessary. None of the outstanding candidates could be elected. The new president was René Coty, a 71-year-old senator who was practically unknown before his election. Obviously as the Fourth French Republic entered the year 1954 it was plagued by many of the same problems and internal conflicts that had weakened the Third Republic in the years between the two world wars.

THE FRENCH UNION

Meanwhile, in the years after the Second World War French statesmen had had to wrestle not only with problems within continental France but with those arising in the republic's overseas territories. Throughout this world's third largest "empire," with its 73,000,000 inhabitants, swept the same dynamic nationalism which had manifested itself elsewhere in the worldwide revolt of the East against the West. In an effort to solve France's new imperial problem the constitution of 1946 created the French Union, based upon the principle that French overseas territories are a part of the French Republic, with which they are joined as more or less equal members.

Within the French Union four types of territories were recognized: (1) Overseas Departments, (2) Associated States, (3) Overseas Territories, (4) Associated Territories. The seven Overseas Departments include Algeria, which constitutes three departments, and Martinique, Guadeloupe, Réunion, and French Guiana. These departments have the same rights and privileges as those of continental France, and their inhabitants are full-fledged French citizens. The Associated States consist of Tunisia, Morocco, and Indo-China (Viet Nam, Laos, and Cambodia), which are considered semi-independent countries linked with France by treaties. The Overseas Territories include French West Africa, French Equatorial Africa, French Somaliland, Madagascar, French settlements in India, French settlements in the South Sea Islands, New Caledonia, St. Pierre and Miquelon, and the Comoro Islands, all of which are governed from Paris. The Associated Territories, Togoland and Kamerun, were received by France as mandates at the close of the First World War and are now held under trusteeship agreement with the United Nations.

The political machinery of the French Union consists of a President, a High Council, and an Assembly. The President of the French Republic is the President of the Union. The High Council, something like a ministry, is presided over by the President, and its members are appointed partly by the French government and partly by the overseas territories. Half of the deputies in the Assembly are chosen by the French National Assembly and half by overseas assemblies. The Assembly of the Union is not a legislative body, however. It has authority only to recommend legislation and to propose motions to the French National Assembly.

Despite their attempt to introduce a new type of "democratic colonialism," the French subsequently had serious trouble in their overseas territories. This was particularly true in Indo-China where the French were forced to conduct a disastrous and costly war against a nationalist, even though Communist-led, uprising.[7] But in North Africa, too, France was forced to stand on the defensive against the mounting nationalist movements in Tunisia, Algeria, and Morocco, each of which demanded liberation from colonial rule. Although Algeria was juridically considered "an integral part of France" and as such elected deputies to the French National Assembly, the Algerian natives became increasingly nationalistic and advocated the establishment of an Algerian republic. The fact that the former Italian colony of Libya was recognized as an independent kingdom by the United Nations in 1951 only contributed to French difficulties in Algeria.

Morocco, nominally a sovereign state over which France exercised a protectorate by virtue of a treaty (1912) with the Sultan of Morocco, became a serious problem when in 1950 the Sultan requested a revision of the

7 See pages 802–804.

protectorate treaty in order to hasten the independence of his country. Ultimately, in 1952, the French government accepted the principle of conversations looking toward the greater independence of Morocco—within the framework of the treaty of 1912. But a crisis developed in the latter part of the year when the Sultan, in a speech, demanded the formal abrogation of the protectorate. Riots broke out and the French on December 10, 1952, ordered the Nationalist and Communist parties in Morocco dissolved and their leaders arrested.

Continued disorders, however, led the French government to depose the Sultan in August, 1953, and to send him and his two sons into exile. On the next day a new Sultan, Mohammed ben Arafa, was enthroned and he announced that he planned to make Morocco a modern state. In September he signed decrees delegating part of his legislative power to a mixed council of viziers and French officials and later approved a new French program of reform. The latter was designed to provide municipal commissions consisting of an equal number of French and Moroccans and regional assemblies composed in a similar manner. These reforms gave the Moroccans a greater participation in their own affairs and at the same time gave French residents the same share in the management of Morocco as the Moroccans. In October the Sultan agreed to an entirely elective instead of a partly nominated Council of Government. Unrest continued, however, and by the end of the year 55 persons had been killed and 117 wounded by acts of terrorism since the Sultan's deposition.

In Tunis, although in 1951 the French, in collaboration with the leading nationalist party, introduced reforms aimed at bringing the nationalists into the actual administration of the protectorate, the latter considered these measures as only a beginning which should be followed by further steps toward autonomy. Subsequent Franco-Tunisian negotiations proved futile, however, and an impasse resulted. Eventually, in 1952, the Tunisian cabinet appealed to the United Nations to settle the Franco-Tunisian dispute. This step was considered illegal and contrary to the treaty of 1881 by the French, who arrested some of the nationalist leaders. Tunisian riots, in turn, led to the further proclamation of martial law by the French and to the arrest of the Tunisian premier and three of his cabinet members.

Shortly thereafter the Bey of Tunis disavowed the violence of the extremists and appointed a moderate premier who accepted in principle a plan of reforms proposed by the French, and the latter thereupon released the former premier and his associates. But this did not conclude the Tunisian affair. Thirteen Arab states decided to submit the problem to the UN even though the French delegate announced that the relations between Tunisia and France were purely an internal matter and not within the realm of the UN. Though the Soviet bloc threw its support to the Arabs, in

December, 1952, the UN General Assembly rejected the Arab motion of direct UN intervention. Tunisian unrest continued in 1953, however, accompanied by acts of terrorism, the assassination of the pro-French heir presumptive to the Tunisian crown, and French arrest of Tunisian nationalists.

The Italian Republic

During the years after 1943 the Italians threw off the Fascist yoke, joined the Allies in the war against Hitler, rejected their monarchy under the House of Savoy, drafted and put into effect a republican constitution, and by popular vote aligned themselves with the Western powers in the "cold war" which had developed between the latter and Soviet Russia.

BADOGLIO'S GOVERNMENT

Mussolini's downfall in July, 1943, it will be recalled, was followed by King Victor Emmanuel's appointment of Marshal Pietro Badoglio as premier. Badoglio's government at once set out to destroy the Fascist regime. The Fascist Party was dissolved and the Fascist Grand Council and the Chamber of Fasces and Corporations were abolished. The minister of finance was instructed to liquidate Fascist Party funds, and any assets which had belonged to the party were transferred to the state. Plans were made for the destruction of Mussolini's corporative state, with the retention of only the system of syndicates, which were to be reorganized on an elective basis. It was decided also to punish those who had been responsible for the suppression of freedom in Italy, members of Fascist organizations, and those who had taken part in the March on Rome, and a High Court for the Punishment of Fascist Crimes was set up for this purpose. In the succeeding months many were tried and sentenced to death or imprisonment for their activities under Mussolini. On the other hand, Mussolini's political prisoners were liberated and many who had lived in exile because of their views were permitted to return to Italy.

Badoglio's government was for all practical purposes a military dictatorship with the king's blessing. The dictatorial nature of the government was revealed in one of its first acts which forbade the activities of political parties. Despite the government's efforts, however, six major parties were organized in the autumn of 1943. From Left to Right these were: Communists, Socialists, Actionists, Labor Democrats, Christian Democrats, and Liberals. Confronted by a government which forbade all political activity, these parties temporarily ignored their differences and united in a common front in what came to be officially called the Committee of National Liberation (CLN). In October, 1943, Committees of National Liberation were set up in various cities and towns of liberated Italy. Ultimately the parties in the CLN agreed to oppose the dictatorial Badoglio government and to seek the abdication of Victor Emmanuel on the ground that he was responsible for the misfortunes of the nation. But Victor Emmanuel refused to abdicate voluntarily and the Allies, especially Britain, maintained that fundamental constitutional changes should not be made until the Italian people could be freely consulted at the termination of the war.

Badoglio next sought to organize an all-party government under his continued premiership. The Communists, Socialists, and Actionists refused to consider such a step, however, and an impasse resulted. This was solved by the return to Italy from Russia of Palmiro Togliatti, a founder of the Italian Communist Party, and by his insistence that the winning of the war should come first and that constitutional changes could wait. Victor Emmanuel, too, helped to solve the impasse by announcing that on the day the Allies entered Rome he would voluntarily withdraw from public life and appoint Crown Prince Humbert as Lieutenant of the Realm. This announcement by the king enabled the Socialists and Actionists to accept Badoglio's proposal of an all-party government, which was organized in April, 1944. But Badoglio's second government was not long in power. In May, the Allies launched their great offensive in Italy and on June 5, Allied troops entered Rome. On the next day, Victor Emmanuel, as he had promised, withdrew from public life and appointed his son Humbert as Lieutenant with power to exercise all royal prerogatives. When Badoglio for the third time attempted to form a new government to include representatives of the Roman CLN he failed because of the opposition of CLN leaders from Rome and Naples.

THE EMERGENCE OF ALCIDE DE GASPERI

Following Badoglio's failure, Ivanoe Bonomi, a pre-Fascist premier and more recently head of the Rome underground National Liberation Committee, formed a ministry which consisted of CLN nominees. Before accepting the premiership, however, Bonomi forced Crown Prince Humbert to guarantee that a constituent assembly would be summoned at the close of the war and secured a new formula for the oath of allegiance which did not commit the ministers to support the House of Savoy. Friction shortly developed within Bonomi's government when the Socialists and Actionists proposed that the Italian government should be built on the central, regional, and district Committees of National Liberation somewhat as the Communist government of Russia had been erected on the system of soviets. This idea Bonomi rejected, a ministerial crisis ensued, and in December, 1944, Bonomi formed a new cabinet with the Socialists and Actionists in opposition. It was not the opposition of these parties, however, but the end of the war which brought Bonomi's downfall.

The military successes of the Allies in 1945 and the collapse of the Third Reich brought the surrender of all Nazi and Fascist forces in Italy in May, 1945. The end of hostilities in Italy in turn brought a further reorganization of the government, for most of the parties in the CLN now wanted as premier one who had taken a leading part in the resistance movement. The North Italian Liberation Committee demanded one who had been active in the resistance movement in the North. The northern leader who enjoyed the widest prestige was Ferruccio Parri of Milan, who had been known to the partisans as "General Maurizio." The impact of the northern CLN upon the Roman CLN resulted on June 17, 1945, in the elevation of Parri to the premiership as the head of the first government of reunited Italy. All parties were represented in Parri's cabinet.

But with the war over and Italy liberated, it was natural that six parties holding such divergent views should sooner or later clash. In November, 1945, the Liberal and Labor Democrat ministers resigned and thus still another political crisis was precipitated. The Right and Left were fairly evenly balanced, and the crisis was finally solved by the elevation to the premiership of a leader from the center group, the Christian Democrat Party, the successor of the Catholic Popular Party of pre-Fascist days. The new premier was Alcide de Gasperi who had been a member of the three preceding governments. He had opposed Mussolini, had been imprisoned for a time, and after his release had worked under an assumed name in the Vatican library, writing an account of Leftist tendencies among Catholics. In December, 1945, De Gasperi formed a coalition government with the Socialist leader, Pietro Nenni, as deputy premier.

THE REJECTION OF THE MONARCHY

The way was now open for the promised opportunity to decide regarding the future of the monarchy in Italy. It was agreed that Italy's first democratic election since before the Fascisti came to power should be held on June 2, 1946, and that on that same day a referendum should be held to decide whether Italy should remain a monarchy or become a republic. Crown Prince Humbert, it was announced, would respect the free decisions of the Italian people. The outcome of the June elections, in so far as the monarchy was concerned, was to some extent foreshadowed by municipal elections in March which showed a decided republican trend. It seemed likely that the monarchy under the House of Savoy was doomed. Perhaps hoping that the elimination of himself as monarch might help change the trend toward a republic, Victor Emmanuel on May 9, 1946, signed a formal act of abdication and he and the queen sailed into exile in Egypt, where he died in December of the following year. Immediately after his father's abdication, the Crown Prince proclaimed himself King Humbert II, but De Gasperi's government in approving the title carefully omitted the traditional phrase "by the grace of God and the will of the people."

On June 2, 1946, the elections for a constituent assembly and the referendum on the monarchy were held simultaneously. The referendum showed that a slight majority of the men and women who voted favored a republic. King Humbert at first showed some reluctance to accept the results of the referendum as final but on June 13 he left for Spain whither his wife and children had already preceded him. In the elections for the constituent assembly, three parties captured most of the 556 seats; the Christian Democrats won 207, the Socialists 115, and the Communists 104. When the constituent assembly convened it elected Enrico de Nicola, a member of the Liberal Party before 1924, to be provisional President of the Italian Republic until a definitive head of the state should be chosen in accordance with the constitution which the assembly was to draft. Alcide de Gasperi was again chosen premier and foreign minister and the first Italian republican government—consisting of representatives of the Christian Democrats, Socialists, Communists, and Republicans—was sworn in by President de Nicola on July 14, 1946.

THE REPUBLICAN CONSTITUTION

At the outset the new Italian Republic was confronted with five major problems: (1) the conclusion of a peace settlement with the Allies; (2) the drafting of a republican constitution; (3) the attainment of political stability within the republic; (4) the choice between Western and Eastern orientation in its foreign policy; (5) the restoration of the country's economic life. The peace settlement with Italy has already been discussed.[8] Despite De Gasperi's pleas at the Paris peace conference in 1946, Italy by the peace treaty lost territory in Europe and all her overseas empire, was required to pay $360,000,000 in reparations, and was restricted in respect to her army, navy, and air force. Although many Italians were bitter over the treatment which their country had received at the hands of the Allies, Italy signed the treaty in February, 1947, and the constituent assembly ratified it on July 31 of the same year.

Meanwhile, the assembly in addition to legislating for Italy had been struggling with the problem of a new constitution. Party conflicts, ministerial changes, and labor unrest handicapped it, but ultimately, in December, 1947, it adopted the final text of the constitution of the Italian Republic, which came into force on January 1, 1948. This new constitution declared

[8] See page 600.

Italy to be "a democratic Republic founded on work," in which sovereignty belonged to the people. Popular sovereignty was to be exercised principally through universal suffrage and the direct election of both houses of the parliament. Members of the Chamber of Deputies were to be elected from single-member constituencies of approximately 80,000 population; those of the Senate, from each of the nineteen new large political units, the "regions," one senator for approximately every 200,000 inhabitants in each region. The President of the Republic was to be elected by the two houses of the parliament, sitting in joint assembly, with the participation of three delegates elected by the council of each region. The President constituted the titular head of the state, but the real executive power was lodged in a premier and ministry which required the confidence of the two chambers. The new constitution provided for a democratic, parliamentary, unitary republic.

ITALY IN THE "COLD WAR"

It was hoped by many that once the Italians had adopted a constitution for their republic, political stability might be achieved, for in the first five years after the overthrow of the Fascist regime Italy was plagued with ministerial instability. In the period between Mussolini's downfall and the referendum in favor of a republic the country had six different ministries, and during the first two years of the republican regime there were five more changes in the government. The latter were caused chiefly by the inability of the four parties represented in De Gasperi's government of July, 1946, to agree on national policies. In the beginning of this period the Communists and Socialists were bound by a unity-of-action agreement and seemed determined to use their position to turn Italy from the West toward Russia. In January, 1947, however, a split occurred in the Socialist Party when Giuseppe Saragat, president of the constituent assembly, and some forty Right-wing Socialist members of the parliament seceded from the party. The Saragat Socialists opposed continued close co-operation, amounting almost to fusion, with the Communists, and their refusal to support De Gasperi's government which included Communists led to the organization of a new ministry which the Saragat Socialists and the Republicans declined to join. The absence of these two groups, however, resulted in a government in which the opposing views of the Christian Democrats and Communists were evenly balanced and this situation, in turn, frequently produced a deadlock and prevented the government from taking decisive steps. But the fiscal and economic conditions in the republic called for action, and finally in May, 1947, De Gasperi again resigned.

Ultimately, on May 31, after both Nitti and Orlando had failed to form a government, De Gasperi resumed the premiership at the head of a ministry consisting largely of Christian Democrats and nonparty experts. For the first time since the collapse of Fascism there were no Communists or Socialists in the government. During the succeeding months, therefore, Left-wing criticism of the government greatly increased, doubtless fostered in part by the severe inflation which had pushed prices up to 58 times the prewar level by July, 1947. But in many cases criticism was accompanied by political violence, strikes, and the threat to use armed force. A general strike, called in Rome in December, proved a failure, however, and after its collapse De Gasperi organized his fifth government, increasing its strength in the parliament by including moderate Republicans and Saragat Socialists.

With the adoption of the new constitution a few days later, the life of the constituent assembly came to an end and preparations were made for electing the members of the two houses of the parliament on April 18, 1948. By this time the "cold war" between the Soviet Union and the United States was being waged with full force, and Italy inevitably became involved. The question was whether she would join the Western or Eastern bloc of powers. During the pre-election campaign Christian Democrats and others supporting De Gasperi emphasized the importance of Italy's' participation in the Marshall Plan and the advantages which the country had already obtained from generous American aid, and argued that a Communist victory in the elections would undoubtedly result in cutting Italy off from this much-needed foreign assistance. Indeed, statements made in the United States, as well as that country's policy toward Czechoslovakia, indicated quite clearly that Italy could expect little assistance from America if she "went Communist." Communist and other Left-wing speakers, on the other hand, declared that Italy would receive Marshall-Plan aid regardless of the outcome of the elections, and that, anyway, American economic assistance was actually only camouflaged penetration by American capitalists. On the eve of the election, apparently to swing the voting against the Communists, the United States, Britain, and France announced their readiness to discuss the return to Italy of Trieste. The Catholic Church, too, threw its powerful influence unreservedly against the Communists. The voting was unusually heavy, more than 26,000,000 Italians going to the polls, and the Christian Democrats received more than 12,000,000 votes. With 307 seats, they secured an absolute majority of the 574 seats in the Chamber of Deputies. To some extent the outcome was the result of the going to the polls of many voters, not normally interested in politics, who cast their ballots in favor of the middle parties and "law and order." On May 11, 1948, the two houses of the parliament elected, as Italy's first constitutional President, Luigi Einaudi, governor of the Bank of Italy, who had been vice-premier and minister for the budget in the existing government. Once more

De Gasperi formed a new ministry, in which the Christian Democrats held a majority of the posts but in which Saragat became vice-premier and Carlo Sforza, long an implacable foe of Fascism, minister for foreign affairs.

ITALY SINCE 1948

In the United States and Britain the Christian Democratic success in the elections of 1948 was interpreted to mean that the majority of Italians had decided that their country should be linked with the Western powers rather than with Soviet Russia, and in the succeeding years Italy did, in fact, become closely linked with the Western democracies. In 1949 she ratified the North Atlantic treaty and thus became a member of NATO. In the same year she participated in the drafting of the statute of the Council of Europe, and in 1952 she ratified the Schuman Plan for the pooling of the coal and steel output of Western Germany, the Netherlands, Belgium, Luxembourg, France, and Italy. She co-operated in the drafting of the treaty setting up the European Defense Community and early in 1951 announced that three divisions would be her initial contribution to the European army. In July of that year Italy formally requested the Allies to revise the arms clauses of the Italian peace treaty. These limitations, the treaty provided, were to remain in effect until modified by the Allies and Italy, or, after Italy had become a member of the United Nations, until agreement between Italy and the Security Council. Italy's admission to the UN, however, had been vetoed by Soviet Russia.

In September, 1951, the American, British, and French governments declared that the restrictions and disabilities to which Italy was subject under the peace treaty no longer accorded with the actual situation and stated their willingness to give favorable consideration to Italy's request to remove them. These restrictions and discriminations had no further justification, they asserted, and they affected Italy's capacity for self-defense. Despite Russia's denunciation of this action of the Western powers, it seemed apparent that Italy would be allowed and encouraged to rearm so that she could protect herself and play her assigned role in the North Atlantic Treaty Organization. In part because of increased military expenditures, the Italian government operated with budgetary deficits in 1952–1953 and 1953–1954.

During the years 1948–1953 De Gasperi's government sought to maintain financial stability, encourage industrial progress within Italy, and introduce some reforms. During this period, thanks to government policies, Italian currency remained stable. That there was industrial progress was indicated by a new national steel-production record of 3,000,000 tons in 1951, by the development and utilization of natural gas resources in northern Italy, by the rapid growth of petroleum refining, by the expansion of the country's chemical industry, and by the construction of new hydroelectric plants.

Although industrial production generally rose above the 1938 level, however, it apparently was not enough to compensate for Italy's increase in population or to overcome the republic's serious adverse balance of trade. But it was hoped that, as a member of the newly-organized European Coal and Steel Community, Italy might benefit from lower prices and more abundant supplies of those two key commodities.

Agrarian reform laws were passed in 1950, applying particularly to southern Italy where the need was both social and agricultural. As originally conceived, the program was to involve some 3,000,000 acres or 5 per cent of the country's arable land, on which it was hoped that 150,000 families might perhaps be settled. It was estimated that approximately 8,000 landowners might be affected but they were to receive compensation in cash and 5 per cent government bonds. There was to be no drastic abolition of private ownership and no compulsory collectivization. Rather, the aim was to break up large, poorly managed estates, to create numerous small peasant holdings, to encourage and support reclamation, and to introduce better land-use methods. But progress in carrying out the program was slow and the number benefiting directly was small. Peasant dissatisfaction and unrest continued, as was indicated by agrarian riots in 1952.

Politically, during these years, there seemed to be in Italy some contraction of the center elements and a polarization toward the extreme Right and Left. The strength of the Communists and Left Socialists has already been noted. The two Rightist reactionary groups which increased in strength during these years were the Monarchists, led by Achille Lauro, a Neapolitan shipping magnate, and the neo-Fascist Italian Social Movement (*Movemento Sociale Italiana* or MSI) in which the former Fascist, Marshal Rudolfo Graziani, was prominent. Local elections in 1951 and 1952 indicated a decline in the strength of De Gasperi's Christian Democratic Party.

In the hope of preventing a disastrous ministerial instability which might result if no party or working group of parties secured a safe parliamentary majority in the Chamber of Deputies to be elected in 1953, De Gasperi's government in October, 1952, introduced a bill to alter the electoral system. As later amended, the bill provided that, because of the increase in population since 1947, the number of seats in the Chamber should be increased from 574 to 590 and that, if any party or group of parties associated in a single list secured more than 50 per cent of the popular votes in a parliamentary election, it would receive 380 seats. The remaining 210 seats would be divided among the opposition parties in proportion to the popular vote each received in the national election. If there were no majority the seats would be divided among the several parties on the basis of a rough proportional representation. This bill was strongly suggestive of the Acerbo Act forced through parliament in 1923 by Mussolini.[9] Although there was great opposition to the bill in both the Chamber of Deputies and the Senate on the part of the Right and Left parties, De Gasperi eventually made its acceptance in both houses a question of confidence and it finally became a law on March 31, 1953.

Four days later both houses of parliament were dissolved, although Senate elections were not normally due until April, 1954, and general elections were set for June 7 and 8. The leaders of the Christian Democratic, the Democratic Socialist (Saragat Socialists), the Republican, and the Liberal parties, which had supported the electoral reform bill, agreed to fight the electoral campaign as a democratic center group and hoped as a bloc to receive at least 50.1 per cent of the popular vote and a resultant safe majority in the Chamber.

Conditions were not quite so favorable for a Christian Democratic victory in 1953 as they had been in 1948, however. In the latter year expectations of benefits from Marshall Plan aid were great; in 1953, despite continued economic assistance from the United States, many apparently failed to see how the aid had benefited them personally. In 1948 hopes were high that Trieste might be returned to Italy because the United States, Britain, and France had announced their readiness to discuss its return; in 1953, although the United States and Britain had transferred to Italy most of the civil administration in their occupation zones, Italy had not yet been able to annex the city and adjoining areas which she wished. And the fact that the United Nations had appointed Italy as a trustee of former Italian Somaliland for ten years seemed in no way to lessen the disappointment over Trieste. Furthermore, there was dissatisfaction with the government's failure to solve the persistent unemployment problem, to reform the national tax structure by reducing indirect taxes (which supplied about 80 per cent of the government's revenue), or to take adequate measures to meet the housing shortage.

In the elections of June 7 and 8, 1953, some 27,000,000 voters, or 93 per cent of the electorate, went to the polls. The center bloc, whose parties had received 62.7 per cent of the votes in 1948, received only 49.85 per cent in 1953 and thus failed by a few thousand votes to secure the necessary majority to give it the coveted 380 seats in the Chamber of Deputies. Each of the parties in the coalition declined percentage-wise from its vote in 1948. On the other hand, the Monarchists and the neo-Fascists increased their percentages from 4.8 in 1948 to 12.68 in 1953, and the Communists and Left Socialists increased their vote from 31.3 per cent of the total to 35.3 per cent. In the subsequent apportionment of seats the center bloc was allotted 303, the Left opposition 218, and the Right opposition 69, so that De Gasperi's coalition

[9] See page 221.

had a majority of 16 seats in the Chamber. In the Senate the center bloc won 125 of the 237 seats. Although the center bloc's majorities in each house thus appeared sufficient to enable De Gasperi to organize a new government, observers in the Western democracies were somewhat disturbed by the gains of the Right and the Left. Parties in both of these groups had opposed the Western policy of joint rearmament under NATO, though for different reasons.

On June 29 De Gasperi's government resigned but agreed to continue to deal with current affairs temporarily. A week later President Einaudi requested the former premier to try to form another government and on July 15 he submitted his eighth consecutive ministry, composed entirely of Christian Democrats. The Democratic Socialists, Liberals, and Republicans, perhaps because of their losses in association with the Christian Democrats in the June elections, declined to continue that association. But De Gasperi's government, in order to have a majority, needed the support of either their 38 deputies or that of the 40 Monarchist deputies. Consequently, when on July 28 a vote of confidence was taken and the Monarchists—who opposed De Gasperi's pro-Western foreign policy—voted with the opposition and the deputies of the three minor center parties abstained from voting, De Gasperi failed to secure a majority. He therefore at once resigned and President Einaudi was faced with the task of choosing another to try to organize a government.

To many observers it appeared that the next premier must be either a Left-wing Christian Democrat who might win the support of the Left-wing Socialists or a Right-wing Christian Democrat who might be satisfactory to the Monarchists. On August 2 President Einaudi asked former Vice Premier Attilio Piccioni, a Right-wing Christian Democrat to try to form a government. His choice apparently displeased the Democratic Socialists and Republicans but, since Piccioni strongly favored European integration and co-operation with the West, he could not win the support of the Monarchists. He therefore failed to form a government. Einaudi next invited Guiseppe Pella, minister of the budget in De Gasperi's last government, to organize a ministry. He formed a cabinet consisting, with one exception, of Christian Democrats, which he admitted was of a transitory nature but which lasted until January, 1954.

During this period Italy made a serious effort to regain control of Trieste. Premier Pella declared that the Allied tripartite declaration of 1948 stating American, British, and French willingness to discuss the return of that city to Italy should be implemented. On October 6, 1953, he announced that, while Italy's adherence to NATO remained the basis of her foreign policy, it might be difficult to get the EDC treaty ratified by the Italian parliament if Italy did not receive satisfaction over the question of Trieste. Two days later the United States and Great Britain sent a joint statement to Rome and Belgrade declaring that since it had been impossible to find a solution of the Trieste question acceptable to both Italy and Yugoslavia because of Soviet obstruction in the UN Security Council, they had decided to end the Allied military government in Zone A and to turn over its administration to the Italian government. The Anglo-American governments had come to the conclusion that the division of the Trieste area along the zonal border was the only practical course. They apparently expected protest and criticism but believed that Yugloslavia and Italy would ultimately acquiesce in the decision.

The Italian government at once accepted the Anglo-American proposal as an important step toward a definitive solution of the Trieste question but did not waive Italy's rights to territory outside Zone A. But Russia declared that the handing over to Italy of the administration of this zone would be a violation of the Italian peace treaty. Yugoslavia likewise asserted that such action would be a "unilateral violation" of the peace treaty and proclaimed that "in no circumstances" would she accept the situation which would result from the Allied withdrawal from Zone A. Yugoslav troops and tanks were ordered into Zone B, administered by Yugoslavia, and Marshal Tito stated that any movement of Italian troops into Zone A would be considered an act of aggression. In November the Italian flag was hoisted over the Trieste town hall in defiance of the Allied military government. When it was hauled down by the police, Italian riots started in the city—deliberately provoked and partly organized from Italy, according to the British foreign secretary—and six persons were killed and many injured before they were suppressed. In Rome, Milan, and other cities anti-American and anti-British demonstrations occurred. But the United States and Great Britain stood firm for law and order and regular diplomatic procedure, and ultimately Italy accepted an Allied proposal for a five-power conference on Trieste. Shortly thereafter Marshal Tito expressed Yugoslavia's willingness to attend such a conference and proposed that the city of Trieste should go to Italy and the Slovene-populated hinterland should go to Yugoslavia. In December Yugoslavia and Italy agreed to withdraw their troops from along the common frontier, and it was hoped in Allied circles that eventually the two countries would agree on a division of the territory.

So long as the Trieste crisis existed Premier Pella received the support of his parliament, but when that question was set aside for a solution by the diplomats, Pella was deserted by the Left wing of his party because of his failure to advance the Christian Democratic program of social reform, and had to resign on January 5, 1954. He was succeeded by Amintore Fanfani, a Left-wing Christian Democrat, who headed a government which, with two exceptions, consisted of Christian Democrats. But within a few days his government, too, was rejected by the Chamber of Deputies. The Christian Democrats having failed several times to get parliamentary support for a purely Christian Democratic government—Center, Right, or Left in political complexion—finally gave up the attempt at a one-party government, and agreed to a coalition with four Democratic Socialists and three members of other center parties in a government headed by the Sicilian, Mario Scelba, who had been minister of the interior. What the fate of his government might be was not immediately known, but to many it appeared that Italy was fast getting into a position where ministerial instability might come to be habitual as it was in France.

West Germany

On the basis of population, resources, industrial production, and military potential, the Federal Republic of Germany should probably be included among the so-called great powers of western Europe. Much smaller territorially than the prewar German Republic, it still had in the postwar period a population (about 50,000,000) exceeding that of either France or Italy. Although terrifically battered by Allied wartime bombing and deprived of valuable mineral and industrial resources, especially in Upper Silesia and the Saar, by October, 1952, West Germany had so far restored her factories that her industrial production was 59 per cent above that for the same area in 1936 and the German Federal Republic ranked next to Great Britain as an industrial power. There was certainly great need for Germany's industrial recovery, for, with the addition to her former population of ten million refugees and transferees from eastern Europe and the loss of former agricultural lands in eastern Germany, she was forced to import 40 per cent of her food supplies, and needed to export manufactured goods to pay for them.

From the day of its creation the German Federal Republic undoubtedly had three major goals: (1) to escape from the restrictions placed upon Germany as a consequence of her defeat by the Allies, or, in other words, to regain her national sovereignty; (2) to regain her former place among the great powers of Europe; (3) to re-unite Germany in a democratic state. In her attempt to attain these goals she was aided by the "cold war" which had developed between Russia and the Western democracies in 1947 and by Communist aggression in Korea in 1950 and the resultant desire of the Western powers to build up and strengthen collective security for the free world.

Within a few weeks after the outbreak of the Korean War the foreign ministers of France, Great Britain, and the United States in September,

1950, agreed: (1) to end the state of war with Germany by legislation; (2) to reinforce their troops there and to treat any attack against the Federal Republic or on Berlin as an attack on themselves; (3) to help in creating mobile police formations in the West German *Länder* (states) which would be at the call of the federal government in an emergency; (4) to empower the federal government to set up a foreign ministry and enter into diplomatic relations with foreign countries "in all suitable cases"; (5) to revise the Occupation Statute, and to remove or relax the Allied controls; (6) to revise the agreement on prohibited and restricted industries and in the meantime to allow cargo ships of any size to be built for export, and the steel production limit of 11,100,000 tons annually to be exceeded "where this will facilitate the defense of the West."

In March, 1951, a start was made in the execution of these agreements when the three powers authorized the German Federal Government to establish a foreign ministry and embassies in any country where it already had consulates, except in France, Great Britain, and the United States. In the latter the channel for relations between Germany and themselves would continue to be the high commission, and texts of all international agreements made by Germany would still be subject to high commission scrutiny and disapproval if found prejudicial to a German peace treaty. Within Germany federal and state legislation was freed from the necessity of prior high commission approval.

During 1951, too, nearly all restrictions on German industry were abolished except in respect to military equipment, atomic energy, and aircraft. The Allied high commission handed over to the federal government the control of all internal economic policies, requiring only that the republic complete the decentralization and decartelization programs already begun, and later transferred to the federal government the control of foreign trade, also. In 1952 the German Federal Republic achieved a favorable balance of trade. Following the lifting of all restrictions from West German shipping and shipbuilding, the republic once again began to participate in ocean trade and transport. By April, 1953, West Germany's merchant navy, almost totally destroyed as a result of the war, had risen to 1,840,000 tons, with nearly a million more tons of new ships being built in her shipyards.

For the republic's economic recovery the German people—resourceful, industrious, well educated, and trained in technology—were much responsible. But so, too, were the Western democracies, not only for lifting restrictions from West German economy but for giving much needed assistance. Between the end of the war and the middle of 1951, according to Chancellor Adenauer, the Western powers advanced some $4,000,000,000 (mostly from the United States) of which some $2,200,000,000 was a gift (again, mostly from the United States). Further to lighten West Germany's economic burdens, nineteen countries in February, 1953, agreed to scale down the republic's prewar foreign indebtedness from some $3,375,000,000 to $1,825,000,000.

Meanwhile, during 1951 various events had indicated West Germany's gradual return to her place among the nations. In May of that year the German Federal Republic was admitted to full membership in the Council of Europe [10] and Chancellor Adenauer attended the committee of ministers. In the next month it was also admitted to membership in the International Labor Organization. In July Great Britain ended her state of war with Germany and three months later the United States did likewise. By the end of the year the republic was a member of UNESCO and of OEEC.

In September, 1951, the Allied high commission had been instructed to negotiate agreements as soon as possible with the federal government to replace the Occupation Statute and to bring West Germany into the European Defense Community (EDC).[11] Because of conflicting national views and policies, however, many months were consumed in negotiations before the contractual convention between the Western powers and the German Federal Republic was signed in Bonn on May 26, 1952, and the six-power treaty creating the EDC was signed in Paris the next day. The linking of the general agreement with the projected European army was a concession to French desires, for obviously the German Federal Republic would acquire juridical equality with other nations and an end of the Allied occupation only by agreeing to enter the Atlantic defense community and by contributing armed forces to the proposed European army under NATO's control.

Although the powerful Social Democratic Party in Germany opposed ratification of these instruments, they were both eventually approved in 1953 by the federal parliament. To become effective, however, they required the ratification of all of the other signatory powers, and how long it would be before that had taken place was a matter of uncertainty. When the general agreement and the related conventions did come into force, however, the Occupation Statute with its powers of intervention in the internal affairs of the Federal Republic would be revoked, and the Allied high commission would be abolished. The three Western powers would retain only such special rights as could not at that time be renounced because of the special international situation of Germany, rights relating particularly to the stationing and security of Allied armed forces in Germany. The mission of these forces, it was stated, would be the defense of the free world, of which the Federal Republic and Berlin constituted a part. The final ratification of the Bonn agreement and the EDC treaty by the other signatories would mark a distinct advance of the Federal Republic toward

[10] See page 826.
[11] See pages 829–831.

national sovereignty and international recognition as "a powerful equal" among the Western democracies.

Undoubtedly one of the major desires of the German people after 1947 was a reunited fatherland. Social Democratic arguments against ratification of the Bonn and EDC agreements were that they would destroy the chances for German unification, because the Soviet Union would never permit the creation of a reunited Germany if that Germany were to be rearmed and allied with the West. On the other hand, Chancellor Adenauer argued that Western integration of the Federal Republic would create such a position of strength, politically and economically, that Eastern Germany would automatically be pulled into a unified, democratic Reich. Adenauer's government, moreover, sought not only the unification of East and West Germany but demanded the return of East Prussia, the area east of the Oder-Neisse line, the Saar coal basin, and small border districts annexed after the Second World War by Belgium and the Netherlands.

So far as the former Allies were concerned, both the Soviet Union and the Western democracies theoretically stood for a unified Germany. But the situation in Germany seemed to be similar to that in Korea.[12] On the surface there was inability to agree on what constituted democratic parties and free, democratic elections. But basically the Soviet government feared a unified, rearmed Germany allied with the West, and the Western democracies were determined to prevent the unification of Germany by any methods which might result in a reunited Reich, with all its resources and manpower, coming into control of a Communist government.

The Communist countermove to the Bonn and EDC treaties was to urge the unification of Germany and the withdrawal of all occupation troops. During the years 1951–1953 Soviet Russia and her satellite, the German Democratic Republic, took the initiative in keeping unification before the Germans in an apparent effort to influence the west Germans not to sign or ratify the Bonn and EDC treaties. Early in 1951 Premier Grotewohl of the East German government appealed directly to the West German Bundestag for a meeting of representatives of the two states to draft a constitution, arrange for elections, and establish a united Germany, which should be followed by a peace treaty and the withdrawal of all occupation troops. Nothing came of this appeal. In September of the same year the People's Chamber of East Germany made about the same appeal. But when the German Federal government laid down fourteen principles upon the basis of which it would accept the East German proposals and itself proposed that the territories east of the Oder-Neisse line be included in the voting, nothing came of this appeal either. In February, 1952, the Democratic Republic in its first formal note to the Big Four powers requested

12 See page 650.

that the United States, the Soviet Union, Great Britain, and France sign a peace treaty with Germany to speed unification.

Meanwhile, upon the request of Chancellor Adenauer, Great Britain, France, and the United States had asked that a UN commission should investigate the possibility of holding free elections in Germany. The East German government at once protested that German elections were a local matter in which the United Nations should have no concern. Ultimately Poland refused to serve on the UN commission and the East German government refused to reply to the commission's requests for opportunity to investigate conditions in East Germany. The Communist attitude toward the UN and German unification was similar to its attitude toward the UN and Korea in 1947.

In March, 1952, the Soviet government sent notes to the Western powers suggesting the bases on which a peace treaty with Germany should be drafted. During the exchange of notes in the ensuing weeks it became obvious that the United States objected to several of the bases laid down by Russia and also insisted that a treaty could be signed only with a government of unified Germany based on free elections. In August the Soviet government in another note to the Western powers accused them of violating agreements with Russia by signing a peace treaty with West Germany and by including the latter in an aggressive military alliance. But it suggested a four-power conference to discuss a German treaty and the creation of a government for all Germany. The Western powers, however, contended that such a four-power conference should limit itself to a discussion of free elections. Again nothing came from the exchange of notes. The year closed with all parties in the East German People's Chamber signing a declaration favoring four-power negotiations to achieve "a peaceful solution to the German problem."

In April, 1953, the East German People's Chamber in a message to the British House of Commons reiterated its desire for the early calling of a four-power conference to draft a German peace treaty and provide for German reunification "on the basis of peace and democracy." Whether influenced by this message or not, three weeks later Prime Minister Churchill in a speech on foreign affairs in the British House of Commons declared his belief that a conference on the highest level should take place in privacy between the leading powers without long delay. But President Eisenhower's view was that there should be more evidence of Russia's general good faith before the United States government committed itself to such a high-level international conference. Because of the latter's stand it was decided that a preliminary conference of the heads of the United States, British, and French governments should be held in Bermuda before a four-power conference including Russia should convene. A long ministerial crisis in

FEDERAL GERMANY'S FIRST CHANCELLOR
Konrad Adenauer

France, however, delayed the Bermuda conference and by the time the French crisis was resolved Prime Minister Churchill had been advised by his physicians to abandon his projected journey to Bermuda and to lighten his duties.

In view of Churchill's withdrawal from active duties, the idea of the Bermuda conference was abandoned and it was decided to hold instead a conference of the foreign ministers of the three states in Washington in July. This conference decided to propose a meeting of the foreign ministers, instead of the heads, of the Big Four states to discuss "the first steps which should lead to a satisfactory solution of the German problem." The three Western governments at once sent nearly identical notes to the Soviet government officially inviting Russia to such a conference, to begin about the end of September, to discuss the organization of free elections in all Germany and the conditions for the establishment of a free all-German government with freedom of action in internal and external affairs. Concessions were made to the United States in thus limiting the meeting to foreign ministers instead of heads of states and to a specific, limited agenda dealing only with Germany. The Soviet government did not reply to the three-power invitation until early in August and then, although it formally accepted the invitation, it made so many charges against the Western powers and suggested so many other subjects to be included in the agenda that it was impossible to arrange a conference in September. Eventually, in January, 1954, the Big Four foreign ministers did meet in Berlin, but no progress was made in plans for reuniting Germany.

The reason that the Western powers had suggested that the conference be held late in September was that it might come after the German parliamentary elections scheduled for September 6, so that nothing said or decided at that conference should embarrass or handicap Chancellor Adenauer in his efforts to hold his majority control in the Bundestag. Local elections in 1951 and 1952 had shown slight gains for the Social Democrats and for the Rightist parties at the expense of Adenauer's Christian Democrats. There was a mounting popular desire for German reunification upon which the opposition parties sought to capitalize. Kurt Schumacher, the aggressive postwar leader of the Social Democrats, had died in August, 1952, but the party, led by Erich Ollenhauer, carried on its same attack on Adenauer because, they said, he placed German integration with the West before German reunification.

A strong resurgence of German nationalism also apparently encouraged many former Nazis to re-enter politics and led some of the Rightist parties deliberately to seek Nazi support. In was reported, for example, that there was a distinct rise in pro-Nazi orientation among adherents of the Free Democratic and German parties. In January, 1953, British occupation authorities arrested Werner Naumann and seven other former Nazi leaders as ringleaders of a group which was anti-West in views and was plotting to regain power in Germany. Naumann had been nominated in Hitler's will to succeed Goebbels as propaganda minister. In February the federal government banned the German Free Corps as a neo-Nazi organization and arrested five of its leaders. But during the summer of 1953 the German Supreme Court released Naumann and his associates as well as the leaders of the Free Corps, and Naumann became a candidate for a seat in the Bundestag on the ticket of the German Reich Party. Labor's reaction was indicated by a statement released late in July by the chairman of the West German Trade Union Federation who attacked Chancellor Adenauer's coalition government not only for not meeting the demands of organized labor but for allowing too many "reactionaries" to return to positions of influence in the government.

Meanwhile, in an attempt to decrease the likelihood that a great number of splinter parties might elect members to the Bundestag and thus complicate the problem of majority rule, the Christian Democrats, Free Democrats, and Social Democrats in June had pushed through the Bundestag a new electoral law, somewhat as was done in Italy before the 1953 parliamentary elections. The German law was complicated but in essence it provided that no party should be represented in the Bundestag unless it received at least 5 per cent of the total popular vote or elected at least one candidate in the district elections.

The outcome of the parliamentary elections in West Germany on September 6, 1953, was quite different from that in Italy earlier in the year. Chancellor Adenauer's Christian Democrats secured an absolute majority over all other parties, and the government coalition won 307 of the 487 seats. Four political parties, including the Communist and the German Reich parties, secured no seats at all. Chancellor Adenauer interpreted the result of the election as a decision of the West German electorate that "Europe would come into being, that the European Defense Community would be realized, and that the cold war had been lost by Soviet Russia." In October Adenauer was re-elected chancellor by a decisive majority in the Bundestag and again organized a coalition ministry. He announced that his government's prime aim would be the restoration of German unity in collaboration with the Western powers, and declared that Germany would never recognize the Oder-Neisse frontier.

Chapter XXVI

THE LESSER STATES OUTSIDE

THE "IRON CURTAIN"

IN Europe outside the "Iron Curtain" there were after the Second World War a dozen so-called lesser powers. Most of them were inferior, however, only in respect to total resources, population, military and naval establishments, and ability to play important roles in international affairs. In personal liberty, economic well-being, achievements in science and literature, and progress in political, social, and economic institutions, some of them were not surpassed by any of the so-called great powers. In the postwar period efforts were made by the Western great powers to organize these states into some kind of a common front against Russia but they were not immediately successful. Although the Benelux countries (the Netherlands, Belgium, and Luxembourg) finally entered with Britain and France into a defensive alliance, some of the others—notably Switzerland and Sweden—preferred to follow a policy of neutrality.

The Scandinavian Monarchies

Among the more progressive states of Europe were the three Scandinavian countries—Denmark, Norway, and Sweden—which had much in common. The inhabitants of all three were "Nordics"; they spoke Teutonic languages which were closely related; and most of them were Lutheran Protestants in their religion. The economic life of all three was based primarily upon agriculture, commerce, and fisheries, though they differed slightly in the emphasis given to each. In all of them popular education was exalted and illiteracy reduced to the vanishing point. Although they all retained the monarchical form of government, they had introduced democratic principles and had been among the first to grant full political and civil rights to women. In all three countries the twentieth century had seen socialism become an influential force in their political and economic life. Their producers' co-operatives, consumers' co-operatives, and dairymen's associations were carefully studied and frequently imitated by even the great powers. The Socialists in these countries nevertheless believed firmly in the democratic process, in the fundamental freedoms of speech, press, assembly, and worship, and in the rights and dignity of the individual. In the years after the Second World War they were, therefore, among the strongest bulwarks in Europe against Communism.

DENMARK

In the Danish kingdom, the smallest of the Scandinavian countries, constitutional amendments had been adopted during the First World War providing for proportional representation and manhood and womanhood suffrage in the elections of both houses of parliament, thus converting the monarchy into a democratic state. Progress had also been made in the country's economic life. Although some attention was given to fisheries and, increasingly with the passing years, to industry, in the period between the wars the greatest percentage of the population derived its livelihood from agriculture. Danish peasants specialized in the production of butter, eggs, and bacon for export to neighboring countries, particularly to Great Britain and Germany. To aid the peasants in marketing their products, borrowing money, and securing expensive equipment, numerous co-operative societies had been organized. In the decade before the Second World War some 250,000 farmers were members of co-operative societies which handled the sale of their products. More than 90 per cent of the farmers, for instance, were members of a co-operative dairy. Through these co-operatives the small farmers were able to sell their products as advantageously as the large landowners. Also, with the increase in the number of employees in industry and commerce, social legislation had been enacted to provide labor exchanges and accident, sickness, old-age, and unemployment insurance.

Although Denmark did not suffer so much during the war as some of the other occupied countries, she did not escape unscathed. She lost half her merchant shipping, and her stocks of raw and finished industrial materials were nearly wiped out. In addition, the Germans drew heavily on the National Bank of Denmark for occupation costs. Altogether, it was estimated, the German occupation cost Denmark 12,000,000,000 crowns.

From the beginning of the occupation there had been some resistance to the Germans, but it was not until the last two years that the country's regular political parties joined the movement. Ultimately party leaders and other key persons made secret plans for a government to take over when the Germans should be obliged to withdraw. When that moment arrived in May, 1945, a new cabinet came into power and the prime minister declared that the Danish constitution was once more in force. Denmark had a multiparty system, and in the period after the war the same political parties were prominent as before 1940. Parliamentary elections were held in 1945, 1947, 1950, and 1953. In all of them the Socialists won by far the largest number of seats but not a majority. From 1947 to 1950 they constituted a minority government. During these years Denmark definitely aligned herself with the West, participating in ERP and NATO. Steps were taken also to increase the armed forces to meet the needs of EDC. In 1950 differences over the means of raising funds for the country's increased defense forces led to the resignation of the Socialist government, which was succeeded by another minority government consisting of Agrarians and Conservatives. This coalition, with the tolerent support of the Socialists, remained in office until after the plebiscite of May 28, 1953, in which the Danes voted on whether to change their constitution. At that time the voters adopted the recommendations of an all-party commission and by amendments to the Danish constitution (1) altered the provisions regarding royal succession so that King Frederick's daughter, Princess Margrethe, might succeed, (2) abolished the upper house of parliament, (3) lowered the voting age from twenty-five to twenty-three, and (4) converted Greenland from a colony to an integral part of Denmark. In the first elections held under the amended constitution in September, 1953, the Social Democrats won 74 out of a total of 175 seats, but none of the seven parties won a majority. A Social Democratic minority government was then again organized.

NORWAY

Norway even before the First World War had become a politically democratic state, with the members of both houses of its parliament chosen by manhood and womanhood suffrage. Although, compared with Denmark, Norway is a large country, most of it is barren and mountainous. More than 72 per cent of it is unproductive, and less than 4 per cent is under cultivation. Almost one fourth of the country is in forests, which constitute one of the kingdom's chief sources of wealth. In the period between the wars, wood pulp, paper and cardboard, and timber were among Norway's chief exports. Of her population some 30 per cent gained their livelihood from agriculture and forestry and 28 per cent from industries related largely to forestry. Navigation and transportation provided the economic basis for a further 10 per cent of the country's population, for Norway's merchant marine had long been important. Before the Second World War it was exceeded in total tonnage only by those of Great Britain and the United States. Approximately 100,000 Norwegians were also engaged in the fisheries industry, cod and herring constituting an important export commodity. Before the war the working people of Norway had gained considerable political influence and the Laborites had been by far the largest political party in the kingdom.

Norway suffered at the hands of Hitler much more than did Denmark.

Her losses resulted from the military campaigns of 1940, the Allied bombing of targets in the country, the sabotage activities of the resistance movement, the ruthless German devastation of Finnmark, and the sinking of some 43 per cent of the nation's merchant marine. It was estimated that Norway's real capital was reduced by about 5,600,000,000 crowns. Furthermore, the Germans, in order to finance their purchases of Norwegian goods and their extensive military works in the country, had forced the Bank of Norway to advance 11,200,000,000 crowns and had thus brought on inflation. During the war, Norwegian underground resistance to the Germans had grown steadily until it became a nation-wide movement under the direction of a secret central council. King Haakon's government in London had maintained a close and constant contact with this underground leadership on the home front, and at the close of the war the king, upon his return in 1945, was hailed by all the political parties as the symbol of the Norwegian fight against Nazism. The country's quislings were quickly arrested and in the succeeding two years tried in the Norwegian courts. Vidkun Quisling himself and some of his more notorious followers were condemned to death, and others received sentences ranging from fines to life imprisonment.

In the country's first postwar elections the Labor Party received 76 of the 150 seats in parliament, obtaining for the first time a clear majority of its own. The new Labor premier had been a distinguished leader in the underground home front during the war. He declared that the Labor Party was socialistic and aimed at a socialist society but admitted that it had no popular mandate authorizing a general socializing movement. Although the nationalization of existing businesses was not an immediate goal of the government, it did pursue a policy of establishing new enterprises and purchasing shares in existing ones. In the parliamentary elections of October, 1953, the Labor Party increased its popular vote but, because of a revised electoral system, its majority of seats over all other parties was reduced to six. On the other hand, the Communists—who lost in popular support—won three seats, whereas previously they had had none.

By 1952 Norway's recovery from the economic dislocations occasioned by the war was encouraging. Her merchant fleet had been more than restored, as had practically all of her war-damaged housing. By 1951 her industrial output had risen some 40 per cent above that of 1938, and her per capita consumption of electricity was said to be the highest in the world. In 1952 the parliament passed a number of laws designed to implement a ten-year plan for the economic development of northern Norway through the expansion of regional industries, particularly fishing, farming, mining, and manufacturing. Like Denmark, however, Norway was plagued by the problem of international payments. Before the war the country had obtained a large part of its imports from sources other than the western hemisphere, and until this pattern could be resumed the problem of international payments seemed likely to continue.

Like Denmark, too, Norway aligned herself with the West in NATO and the European Defense Community. Both countries extended the period of compulsory military service, Norway aiming at trained and fully equipped armed forces totaling 270,000 men.

SWEDEN

In Sweden in the years just before the First World War universal manhood suffrage had been introduced for the election of the lower house of parliament; the property qualification for electors of the upper house had been decreased; proportional representation had been provided for both houses; and ministerial responsibility had been inaugurated. At the close of that war the suffrage had been extended to women, also, on the same basis as to men. In the period between the wars, therefore, Sweden had been a democracy. It had also become increasingly industrialized, its industrial production capacity being increased by 50 per cent in the years 1929 to 1937. By 1933 nearly 400,000 workers were employed in factories. Politically, with the increase of industrial workers, had come the rise of the Socialist Party. In the parliamentary elections of 1914 it had obtained more than a third of the seats in the lower house, and eighteen years later the kingdom had had its first Socialist ministry. During the economic depression of the thirties Sweden had attracted the attention of the world by her experiment with a "managed" currency.

Sweden was one of the few European countries which escaped being embroiled in the Second World War. During that war the government became an enlarged coalition, and among the people a remarkable degree of national unity was preserved. There was no serious questioning of the government's policy of neutrality and all parties supported the substantial increases in national armaments. Nevertheless, Sweden did suffer some economic losses from the war. She lost 40 per cent of her merchant marine, an important source of earnings for balancing her international payments. There was, too, an excessive cutting of the nation's forests. The country's industrial plant and equipment also suffered deterioration, and its customary source of supply for much of its iron and steel, chemicals, and textiles—Germany—was lost. Sweden, therefore, had to rely more upon the United States for these commodities, and therefore was soon confronted with a dollar problem.

Although the Socialists won half the seats in the lower house of the Swedish parliament and a majority in the upper house in the elections of 1944, it was not until the summer of 1945 that the wartime coalition government gave way to a Socialist ministry headed by P. A. Hansson. The latter denied that his government had plans for complete socialization, insisting that the main principle of its program was that the means of production must be used as effectively as possible. "Whenever private enterprise proves to be used effectively, it will have our support," he declared, "but if it fails in any field, we shall have to find other forms of production or distribution." Following the death of Hansson in 1946, Tage Erlander—who was considered less conservative than his predecessor—became premier. The parliamentary elections of 1948 did little to weaken his position, but to broaden the base of his government in 1951 he persuaded the Farmers' Party to join it in a coalition. Parliamentary elections in 1952 gave this coalition a decisive majority over all other parties.

Even in the years before the First World War a considerable amount of socialization had existed in Sweden. The state had long owned some forest areas and waterfalls; the first railways had been constructed by the state; and the telephone and telegraph systems had been merged under government ownership. By 1948 the state owned about 20 per cent of the forests, a large share of the waterfalls, and the main electrical power lines. More of the private railway lines had been acquired and added to the state's system. All radio facilities, the domestic air service, the national bank, the munitions and armaments factories, and the telephone factories were also government owned. In addition, the state held all or most of the shares in a number of other industrial corporations, notably, pulp factories, saw mills, iron works, and mines. Sweeping agrarian reforms, designed to make agriculture more profitable, were enacted by the parliament in 1947, and additional family allowances and old-age pensions were made effective on January 1, 1948. In the postwar period, however, Sweden was increasingly confronted with economic difficulties, arising largely from the unexpectedly slow recovery of devastated Europe, the country's growing dependence upon the United States for essential supplies which its exports to that country did not pay for, and the impossibility of converting its earnings from other areas into hard currencies. In September, 1951, however, Sweden was able to dispense with Marshall Plan aid.

The difficult economic situation in which the Scandinavian countries found themselves after the war led them to consider the possibility of some kind of inter-Scandinavian economic co-operation. The foreign ministers of Denmark, Norway, Sweden, and Iceland [1] in 1947 did recommend the appointment of a committee of experts to investigate the possibility of some sort of economic union, but no tangible results followed. Nevertheless, a Scandinavian parliamentary council was established in 1952, consisting of

[1] In 1944, Iceland, whose inhabitants are of Scandinavian origin, had severed her union with Denmark under a common sovereign and had become an independent republic.

representatives of the cabinets and parliaments of the four countries, which was to meet annually and to make recommendations regarding the solution of common problems. The so-called Nordic Council, with fifty-three members, held its first meeting in Copenhagen in February, 1953.

During 1948 the Scandinavian countries considered, also, the possibility of establishing a defensive military alliance. All three were apparently willing to conclude such an alliance, but Sweden and Norway differed in their views regarding its relation to the North Atlantic pact. Sweden desired an alliance for Scandinavian self-defense but one which would be neutral in case of war among the great powers. Norway, in order to receive arms and assurances of aid from the Western powers, desired to have the Scandinavian alliance linked with the North Atlantic pact. In January, 1949, the projected Scandinavian alliance foundered on Sweden's determination to stick to her traditional policy of neutrality.

The Benelux Countries

After the Second World War Belgium, the Netherlands, and Luxembourg embarked upon a program designed to increase their mutual trade and to remove the obstacles to their eventual economic union. Before 1939 the tiny Grand Duchy of Luxembourg had been united with Belgium in a customs union, and on January 1, 1948, the Netherlands joined Belgium and Luxembourg in an enlarged customs union. The ultimate goal of the three states was a full economic and monetary union, which it was hoped might finally be brought into being. Beginning in 1947 the three states came to be referred to collectively as Benelux.

On March 17, 1948, the Benelux countries and Great Britain and France signed the treaty of Brussels in which all five states agreed to co-ordinate their economic activities, endeavor to raise the standards of living of their peoples, and afford all military and other assistance to any one of their number in case of an armed attack. For the purpose of better co-operating they further agreed to create a Consultative Council which should function continuously. Provision was made for other countries, also, to accede to the treaty. In January, 1949, the foreign ministers of these five states, meeting in London, issued a statement giving approval to the creation of a Council of Europe, which ultimately developed into a full scale attempt to integrate all western Europe (see pages 826–827).

The two dominant states in Benelux, of course, were Belgium and the Netherlands, the latter popularly referred to as Holland.[2] Although these countries are each smaller than Denmark, Norway, and Sweden, the popu-

[2] Holland is only one—but the largest and richest—of the eleven provinces in the Kingdom of the Netherlands.

lation of each is considerably larger than that of the most populous Scandinavian state. In fact, Holland and Belgium are the two most densely populated countries in Europe, the former having more than 9,000,000 inhabitants and the latter more than 8,000,000. In the period before the Second World War special circumstances accounted for the ability of these two small kingdoms to support such relatively large populations.

HOLLAND

Holland possessed an overseas empire of approximately 788,000 square miles with more than 60,000,000 inhabitants. Most of this empire was located in the East Indies, where the Netherlands controlled rich and populous Java, Sumatra, Celebes, most of Borneo, and approximately half of New Guinea, besides innumerable small islands. In the western hemisphere, she possessed Dutch Guiana on the northern coast of South America and Curaçao and a number of smaller islands in the Caribbean. The East Indian empire provided the Netherlands with a steady stream of wealth in the form of rubber, coffee, palm oil, tea, and tobacco. Moreover, the administration of the islands offered profitable careers to many Netherlanders, while the exploitation of their resources was profitable to Dutch merchants and bankers. All in all, the East Indies provided a livelihood for about 400,000 Netherlanders.

But Holland's economic life was based, in part, upon two other factors also. The country was strategically located not only from a military but from a commercial viewpoint. Rotterdam and Amsterdam served as *entrepôts* for a considerable amount of trade between central Europe and countries overseas. This exchange of goods across Holland's territory brought income to Dutch carriers and middlemen and provided a livelihood for many Netherlanders. Furthermore, Holland was also a rich agricultural land and was advantageously located between Great Britain and Germany. Neither of these countries produced sufficient foodstuffs for its population, and therefore they provided the Dutch peasants with ready markets for their agricultural and dairy products.

Economically, Holland suffered severely as a result of the Second World War, her loss of national wealth being estimated at one third, not counting losses in the Dutch East Indies. Within the Netherlands itself about 10 per cent of the arable land was inundated, nearly 100,000 houses were completely destroyed, about 50 per cent of the country's merchant marine and 40 per cent of the inland fleet were lost, and the transport system was almost completely disorganized. But postwar recovery was encouraging. Within a few months the flooded lands had been reclaimed; by the middle of 1946 transportation was again functioning; and by 1948 production in gas, electricity, and shipbuilding exceeded prewar levels. Full-scale revival, however, was hampered by the slowness of Germany's recovery, by the decline in British purchases, and by the disruption of trade with the Dutch East Indies, rent by civil strife.[3] Nevertheless, the situation so improved that in January, 1953—before the disastrous flood of that year—the Dutch announced that they could dispense with American financial aid.

Political democracy had been slower to develop in Holland than in some of her neighbors. It was not until 1917 that manhood and womanhood suffrage at the age of twenty-five was introduced for the election of the lower house of parliament. In the years between the wars the kingdom had had a multiplicity of parties which had made parliamentary government difficult. In the elections of 1937, for instance, twenty parties had entered candidates and ten had secured representation in the lower house. The three major parties were the Roman Catholics, the Socialists, and the Calvinist Anti-Revolutionaries. Prior to 1939 the Socialists were unwilling to join a coalition government so that during the interwar years Holland had had a series of Right-wing cabinets. During the Second World War, Queen Wilhelmina's government had functioned from London but after the country was liberated parliament lowered the voting age to 23 years in preparation for new elections.

In the parliamentary elections after the war the strength of the leading political parties changed relatively little. But the Labor Party (Socialist) gave up its earlier aversion to participating in a coalition government, and after the war joined with the Catholic Party to organize ministries. Until 1948 the premier was a Catholic but after that he came from the Labor Party. The co-operation of the Catholics and Laborites assured the government the two-thirds majority needed to enact constitutional changes in connection with the establishment of the Netherlands Indonesian Union.[4] It also ensured the continued influence of the Labor Party, with its social welfare program, on the government's policies.

Meanwhile, on September 4, 1948, the beloved Queen Wilhelmina, after a successful reign of fifty years, had abdicated in favor of her daughter, who succeeded her as Queen Juliana. The latter, in her speech from the throne in September, 1953, declared that the Netherlands considered economic integration one of the necessary steps in the creation of a European community, and asserted that her government would support the work of the Council of Europe, the OEEC, and other inter-governmental organizations. In fact, in January, 1954, the Netherlands parliament completed its ratification of the European Defense Community treaty.

[3] See pages 796–801.
[4] See page 800.

BELGIUM

The foundation of Belgium's economic life before the war was quite different from that of her neighbor to the north. Although some 60 per cent of the country was under cultivation and, thanks to the use of intensive methods and co-operative enterprise, agriculture had continued to be profitable, only a small percentage of the Belgians gained their livelihood from farms. For Belgium was not only the first continental country to become industrialized but was the most highly industrialized of them all. In the period between the wars those engaged in industry outnumbered those employed in agriculture by four to one. In trade and commerce, too, Belgium occupied an important place before the last war so that even in these fields the number exceeded that of agriculturists. Moreover, in the Belgian Congo the kingdom possessed a colonial realm which, though not so valuable as that of the Netherlands before 1939, was rich in rubber, gold, diamonds, copper, palm oil, cotton, coffee, and ivory. At the close of the First World War this empire had been further increased by the addition of a small part of German East Africa as a mandate of the League of Nations. Before the war Belgium's exports had paid for about 90 per cent of her imports, the deficit being covered by shipping and transshipment charges.

The country experienced a rapid economic recovery following the Second World War. Its valuable resources at home and in the Congo enabled it to move ahead with limited help from abroad. Successive governments carried out a rigorous deflation program, stabilized wages and prices, and expanded social legislation to include practically all workers. If currencies had been freely convertible into gold or dollars as in "the good old days," Belgium would have been on a self-sustaining basis. As it was, however, the country was handicapped by inability to convert sterling receipts into dollars and by the further fact that former nondollar sources of supplies for her foods and industrial raw materials were no longer available so that she had to turn to the United States for supplies. Since most of Belgium's exports were shipped to nondollar countries, she had in 1947 a trade deficit of $374,000,000 with the United States as compared with annual deficits of some $16,000,000 in prewar years.

The Belgians are not, like the people of the Scandinavian countries and Holland, homogeneous linguistically and racially. Those in the southern part of the kingdom are Walloons, who are closely akin to the French and speak French. Those in the north are Flemings, who are closely related to the Dutch in race and language. The Flemings are more numerous than the Walloons, but the Belgian bourgeoisie up to 1914 spoke only French, though Flemish was an official language to the extent that both French and Flemish had to be used in government publications. During the First

World War, Germany sought to weaken Belgian resistance by encouraging the Flemings to make more demands for cultural rights. King Albert thereupon promised the Flemings equality of language and the creation of a Flemish University of Ghent. In 1921, Belgium was divided into two parts; in one all administrative matters were to be conducted in Flemish and in the other, in Walloon. A later law provided that beginning with the academic year 1930–1931 all instruction in the University of Ghent was to be in Flemish. By that time, however, the Flemish nationalist movement had become a political force.

In the period between the wars, Belgium had had six political parties, of which the Catholic, the Liberal, and the Socialist were the largest. The Catholic Party included diverse economic groups but was dominated by conservatives; the Liberal Party was essentially bourgeois, but its Right wing was so strong that the Liberals often joined with the Catholics to form a government. The Socialist Party had originally been Marxist in its ideology, but under Émile Vandervelde in the twenties and Paul-Henri Spaak in the thirties it had abandoned its revolutionary program and had come to resemble the Labor Party in Britain. On the extreme Left was the Communist Party, created in 1923 by a militant group which had seceded from the Socialist Party. On the extreme Right there were two fascist parties; the Flemish Nationalist Party, which was financed in the thirties by Germany; and the Rexist Party, which included in its ranks high army officers and big businessmen, and which was generously supported by subsidies from many Belgian industrialists. As the result of parliamentary elections in 1939 the lower house consisted of 73 Catholics, 64 Socialists, 33 Liberals, 17 Flemish Nationalists, 9 Communists, and 4 Rexists. The government at the time of the Nazi invasion in 1940 consisted of Catholics, Socialists, and Liberals under the premiership of Hubert Pierlot, a conservative Catholic. This government, somewhat reduced in numbers, functioned from London during the period of Nazi occupation.

On February 17, 1946, Belgium had her first postwar parliamentary elections. The Flemish Nationalist Party and the Rexist Party had been outlawed and some 300,000 to 400,000 persons, condemned for or suspected of collaboration with the Nazis, were denied the right to vote in the elections. In the elections the Catholics obtained 92 of the 202 seats in the lower house. The Socialists won 69, the Communists 23, and the Liberals only 17 seats. After a considerable period of ministerial instability the government was temporarily stabilized in August, 1946, under the premiership of Camille Huysmans, a Socialist, who held the office until March, 1947, when Paul-Henri Spaak, the Socialist leader, organized a government which was an alliance between the Socialists and the Catholics. His cabinet rested on a coalition of the kingdom's two most powerful parties which together commanded nearly all the seats in the two houses of parliament. For the first time since 1915, except for a short interval, the Liberal Party was not in the government.

The question of King Leopold's restoration to the throne still remained to be settled. In September, 1944, after the Nazis had taken him as a prisoner of war to Germany, the Belgian parliament had elected his brother, Prince Charles, as Regent of the Kingdom. Following the liberation of Leopold III at the end of the war, conferences were held at Salzburg between the king and Belgian political leaders, during which the king apparently asked that the condemnation passed upon him in 1940 be retracted.[5] This the Belgian leaders refused to do and the king's return to Belgium in 1945 was prevented by the government with the support of the parliament. The Socialists, Communists, and most Liberals wanted Leopold to abdicate in favor of his son, Prince Baudouin, while the Catholics advocated a plebiscite on the question of his restoration. A referendum in 1950 showed 58 per cent of the voters favoring the king's return. When his return provoked strikes, riots, and the threat of civil war, however, Leopold agreed to permit his son to rule as prince royal until his twenty-first birthday. Leopold III finally abdicated on July 16, 1951, and his son succeeded him as King Baudouin I.

Switzerland

In the years between the wars Switzerland was probably the most democratic country in the world. This small republic was a confederation of twenty-two cantons [6] which had gradually come together for mutual protection during the preceding centuries. The confederation as a whole was not homogeneous in its population, however. Of its inhabitants approximately 65 per cent were German; 23 per cent French, and 12 per cent Italian. Besides differing in language and customs the Swiss also differed in religion, 57 per cent being Protestant and 41 per cent Roman Catholic. Finally, the Swiss differed noticeably in their economic activities. To the original herdsmen of the mountains and petty farmers of the valleys had been added the industrial workers of the cities.

The ability of these diverse groups to live together contentedly within one state was the result in part of three circumstances. In the first place, the cantonal governments had extensive powers, for in the confederation only certain delegated powers belonged to the national government. Although all of the cantons recognized the principle of popular sovereignty, they differed among themselves in the organization of their local governments.

[5] The Belgian cabinet, which had fled from the country, in 1940 had repudiated King Leopold's action in surrendering as traitorous.

[6] Three of the cantons were divided so that technically there were nineteen cantons and six half-cantons.

Whi'e some of the more populous adopted the representative type of government, some of the smaller cantons long retained a type of pure democracy —all the electors meeting at one time in one place to make political decisions by oral voting. Extensive local government, therefore, made it possible for each canton to manage its own local affairs as it chose.

In the second place, the confederation was divided into so many cantons that in each of them the population was fairly homogeneous racially and linguistically, and so there was lacking the feeling that one racial group was being dominated or exploited by another. In the third place, no one of the racial groups was distinctly favored by or in the national government. All three languages were recognized as official; any one of them might be used in discussions in the parliament; the presidency of the confederation went by rotation to the different nationalities; and the central government usually sought to exercise its authority in such a way as not to antagonize any of the cantons on racial, linguistic, or religious grounds.

The federal legislature consisted of an upper house with two representatives from each canton and a lower house popularly elected in proportion to population. The republic had a plural executive, called the Federal Council, which was chosen by the parliament, and the chairman of this council—though differing little from the other members in power—bore the title of President of the Swiss Confederation. But the legislative power of the national government was not entirely or finally in the hands of the parliament, for, by means of the referendum, laws passed by the parliament might be rejected by popular vote, and, by means of the initiative and referendum, laws might be popularly adopted even though not enacted by the parliament.

The economic life of Switzerland had for the most part a three-fold basis. Agriculture and dairying predominated in many of the cantons, and the manufacture of cheese and condensed milk constituted one of the republic's chief industries. In a number of the cities—notably Zurich, Basel, Geneva, and Bern—a considerable amount of modern industry existed and provided employment for some hundreds of thousands of Swiss workers. Silk and artificial-silk goods, watches, embroidery, coal-tar dyes, and electrical goods were among the exports from this little state. In addition to agriculture and dairying and industry and commerce, the third important source of income for the Swiss was the tourist trade. Hotel-keeping provided a livelihood for thousands of people, and it might well be said that one of Switzerland's chief businesses was the sale of scenery.

During the Second World War, Switzerland was eventually surrounded by Axis-controlled territory and her normal economic life was greatly disturbed. Although the republic's flourishing economy had largely been built on the principles of liberty, private property, and private initiative, economic planning became inevitable, emergency measures were inaugurated without popular approval gradually bringing the country's economy to a great extent under government control. At the end of the war the Swiss were divided in their views on this situation.

Two popular referendums were held in May, 1946, and a third in July, 1947, in an effort to reach some conclusion on the policy to be followed. In the first two the more radical and far-reaching program of the Socialists was repudiated; in the third, a compromise solution—favored by the Federal Council and the parliament—was adopted by a majority of the 87 per cent of the electorate voting. As a result, though the regime of emergency powers was ended, the state was constitutionally empowered to provide for the development of social welfare, the economic security of the community, and the equitable settlement of labor conditions. It was further authorized to take necessary measures to protect endangered parts of the country or branches of industry, to preserve the peasantry and agriculture from the harmful effects of cartels, and to deal with problems arising from unemployment, economic crises, and war. In economic matters *laissez-faire* was thus abandoned in favor of some degree of government control.

The dispute over centralization entered the field of taxation, also. Normally direct taxes were levied by the cantonal governments, which passed on to the federal government amounts fixed by quotas. During the Second World War, however, the federal government had been granted emergency powers to levy direct taxes, powers which had been extended until the end of 1949. There appeared to be much opposition to this levying of direct taxes by the federal government, but after some political maneuvers, the latter called for a popular referendum on the proposal to extend its authority to do so until December, 1954, by which time it was hoped that permanent financial reforms could be worked out to meet budgetary needs. This proposal was carried by more than a 2 to 1 vote. In December, 1953, however, the Swiss voters in a referendum rejected the government's proposed constitutional amendment providing that direct federal taxes be levied on a permanent basis. Apparently they preferred to return to their earlier long-established emphasis on the powers of the cantonal governments.

The Republic of Ireland

In Eire, as already pointed out,[7] the government had declared its neutrality at the outbreak of the Second World War. Twice during the conflict, moreover, De Valera had been able to block British conscription in Northern Ireland and when United States troops were landed in that territory in 1942, De Valera had protested. Throughout the conflict the government of Eire had maintained its normal relations with Hitler's Reich, and

[7] See page 300.

the latter's diplomatic staff in Eire had been of considerable assistance to the Nazis in obtaining information helpful in the struggle against Britain. Moreover, the cities of Eire by not dimming their lights at the time of Hitler's air blitz against the British had given the Nazis indirect assistance in locating their targets in Britain.

In 1948, after sixteen years in office, De Valera was finally forced to relinquish the premiership. Parliamentary elections held on February 6 of that year, though they gave his Fianna Fail Party the largest number of seats in the Chamber of Deputies, left his party in a minority. The other five parties and most of the Independents combined against him and on February 18 he was succeeded as prime minister by John A. Costello, a member of the Fine Gael Party, whose ministry was a coalition of all five parties. The new prime minister declared that social, economic, and educational matters would be his government's chief concern, and that economic conditions must take priority over all political and constitutional matters. Meanwhile, on June 16, 1945, Sean O'Kelly, a member of Fianna Fail, had been elected President of Eire to succeed Douglas Hyde.

Despite Costello's statement on the relative unimportance of constitutional matters for Eire, in the fall of 1948 his government took steps to repeal the External Relations Act of 1936, which constituted the last formal tie between Eire and the British king. Under the terms of this act, Britain's King George signed letters of credence of representatives of Eire going abroad. Costello asserted that under the act Eire was neither within the British Commonwealth nor an independent republic and that its repeal would clarify Eire's status as a sovereign independent state. On December 21, 1948, President O'Kelly signed the Republic of Ireland Bill, which repealed the External Relations Act, declared that the state should be described in English as the Republic of Ireland, and transferred to the President of the Republic the British king's function in connection with the state's external relations.

The reciprocal rights of Eire's citizens living in Britain and British citizens residing in Eire were provided for by actions of the British and Eireann governments. Representatives of both governments declared that everything would be done to develop the closest economic co-operation, but Eireann statesmen declared that there could be no military alliance with Britain so long as Ireland remained divided.

In June, 1951, De Valera returned to the premiership after new parliamentary elections had failed to give Costello's coalition a majority. In May, 1952, O'Kelly was re-elected President of the Republic of Ireland.

The Two Iberian "Police States"

It is probably something more than mere coincidence that among the states of western Europe the only ones that were "police states" in the years after the Second World War were Spain and Portugal.

SPAIN

Although the sympathies of Franco Spain were undoubtedly with the Axis powers during a great part of the Second World War, the country's political wounds and economic exhaustion prevented it from actively entering the conflict. Officially the Spanish government adopted a policy of neutrality at the start; then, with Hitler's spectacular successes in 1940, it changed to one of "nonbelligerency"; and finally, after the tide of battle had manifestly turned in favor of the Allies, in October, 1943, Spain readopted her policy of neutrality. During the period of nonbelligerency Spain illegally seized the international zone of Tangier, dispatched the "Blue Division" of some 17,000 to 18,000 men to fight against Russia, sent at least 20,000 Spaniards to work in Germany, permitted Axis submarines and destroyers to use Spanish ports, supplied Hitler with strategic war materials and used her own ships to transport these materials as well as Axis agents, allowed Germany to operate an extensive spy and sabotage system from Spanish territory, and secretly planned with Germany to attack Gibraltar and Morocco and to close the Mediterranean to the British.

On the other hand, Franco did give some assistance to the Western Allies, though for the most part it was of a negative character. He did not interfere with the Allied landings in North Africa; he twice refused to permit German troops to cross Spain. At the same time he let thousands of French volunteers cross the country to join the Allied forces in North Africa; he permitted an Allied spy system to operate in Spain; he allowed some 1,500 Allied airmen to escape internment and permitted Americans to retrieve secret equipment from downed planes; and, finally, under Allied pressure, he embargoed the export of wolfram—desperately needed by Germany for the manufacture of arms. After the war Franco surrendered to the Allies millions of dollars worth of official or semi-official German assets and returned to Germany for trial over three hundred Nazi officials, agents, or technicians.

After the end of the war Franco, on the surface at least, sought to push the Phalanx Party somewhat into the background; the party salute, for instance, was abolished as a form of greeting. In June, 1945, he declared that the Phalanx Party no longer wielded political power or made political decisions. In July he appointed the secular head of the Catholic Action foreign minister, and thus linked that well-organized group officially with his regime. The new foreign minister announced that Spain's system of government was moving toward new forms of popular representation and would eventually co-ordinate with the political systems of the Anglo-Saxon countries. Tens of thousands of political prisoners had been released during the war years, and on October 20, 1945, a government decree granted amnesty to all such prisoners convicted before the end of the civil war. In 1943 the Cortes had been re-established, but with all its members appointed directly or indirectly by the government, and in 1945 Franco in an official speech declared that he hoped the Cortes would examine and the nation approve a law for the monarchy's restoration. To many it appeared that the Caudillo (leader) was seeking to regularize his regime in the eyes of the Western world.

But apparently Franco's talk about the restoration of the monarchy was chiefly for effect. When Don Juan, the thirty-three-year-old third son of Alfonso XIII, sought to open negotiations with Franco in 1946, the latter proved to be unenthusiastic. In fact, five university professors and five members of the Cortes who had signed a letter supporting Juan, were at once dismissed. Unofficial negotiations between Juan and Franco eventually failed, apparently because the Caudillo refused to give up his powers. On March 31, 1947, Franco announced that Spain was to become a monarchy with a Council of the Kingdom and himself as Chief of State. The former was to consist of twelve members, most of them ex officio; only three members were to be chosen by the Cortes. In case of the incapacity or death of the Chief of State, the government ministers and the Council of the Kingdom, meeting jointly, should decide by a two-thirds vote who was to be proposed to the Cortes as king or regent. In effect the proposed law would make Franco virtual king of Spain and would give his appointees the right to choose his successor.

Don Juan at once denounced Franco's proposal as an attempt "to turn the dictatorship of an individual into his rule for life, consolidating his precarious claims and wrapping in the mantle of monarchy a regime based on arbitrary government." Gil Robles, leader of the earlier Catholic Popular Action Party,[8] from his residence in exile also denounced Franco's proposal, declaring that Catholicism was based on justice and truth, neither of which he could see in the existing Spanish regime. The Cortes, nevertheless, on June 7 passed the bill as proposed by the Caudillo, who called for a popular plebiscite on the law. A referendum was held on July 6, 1947, and resulted in 14,145,163 in favor of the law and 722,656 against it. Franco thus seemed securely settled in his position as Chief of State.

But Spain still remained a police state whose political opposition was

[8] See page 326.

ruthlessly hounded and summarily dealt with by military courts. In the early months of 1948 sixteen Spaniards were sentenced by a court martial to prison terms ranging up to twenty-five years on charges of attempting to re-establish the Socialist Party; seventy other Spaniards were sentenced by court martial to prison terms up to thirty years for being leaders in a quasi-military movement; the former chief of Franco's air force was sentenced to detention for expressing royalist views at a private gathering; and four high-ranking Spanish nobles were fined 25,000 pesetas each for holding or helping to organize private monarchist meetings without the permission of the police. In October of the same year eight men were sentenced to death and sixty-four others to terms of imprisonment on charges of activity against the state. Obviously, no challenge to the decisions of Franco and his advisers was to be countenanced.

Toward the close of 1948 Spain had what were called the first "popular elections" since 1936, when municipal councils were elected in three stages. On November 21 about one third of the councillors were chosen by heads of families and other adult males who were domestically and economically independent. One week later another third were elected by the officers of the syndicates, and one week later still, on December 5, those councillors already elected chose the remaining third from lists submitted by Franco's provincial governors. Obviously, "democracy" in Spain—even on the municipal level—differed from that found in Britain, France, and the United States.

After the Second World War, Spain found herself in a largely unfriendly world but a world which was reluctant to take any steps to remove the Franco regime. The United Nations Charter by indirection specifically barred Spain from membership in the United Nations. In 1946 the United States, Great Britain, and France declared that there could not be full and cordial association with Franco Spain and expressed the hope that the Spaniards might "soon find means to bring about the peaceful withdrawal of Franco." Poland charged in the UN Security Council that Spain was likely to endanger international peace and suggested that UN members should sever diplomatic relations with that state. Russia wished for drastic action to restore popular government in Spain, but the United States and Britain were reluctant to force Franco from power lest he be succeeded by a government under Communist influence. The attitude of the great powers continued to be similar to that shown during the civil war in 1936–1939.

The Security Council finally decided to appoint a committee to consider the situation and this committee reported that no act of aggression had been proved nor had any threat to peace been established. It recommended that the matter be submitted to the UN Assembly with the recommendation that diplomatic relations with Spain be severed by all UN members. Russia thought this action was too mild and vetoed it. Later in the year the Spanish question was raised in the UN Assembly. The United States and Great Britain argued against intervention in the internal affairs of a nation, and ultimately a compromise was adopted by the Assembly recommending that member nations should withdraw their heads of missions without severing relations and that Spain should be excluded from all UN functions. The UN action had little effect on Franco's position at home.

On the other hand, the intensification of the cold war after 1948 and the outbreak of the Korean War led to a distinct improvement in Spain's international position. In 1949 the United States lifted its embargo on private loans to that country, and shortly thereafter $35,000,000 was advanced by American bankers and businessmen, chiefly to finance the purchase of surplus American cotton. After the outbreak of the Korean War the United States Congress voted loans to Spain on a much larger scale. The changing attitude of many states was further revealed in November, 1950, when the UN General Assembly revoked its resolution of 1946 calling for the withdrawal of ambassadors and ministers from Spain and her exclusion from specialized agencies of the United Nations. Shortly thereafter both the United States and Great Britain sent ambassadors to Madrid. In 1952 Spain was finally admitted into UNESCO. In that same year, too, Franco was further forgiven for his past acts. In 1945 Great Britain, France, the United States, and Russia had sought to punish him for having unlawfully seized the internationalized city of Tangier in 1940. In 1952, however, the Control Council of that city, representing eight countries, yielded to Franco's demand and voted to return to the statute of 1923. By so doing they permitted Spain extensive participation in the rule of the city, including control of the police.

Meanwhile, United States military authorities had become convinced of Spain's strategic importance in the defense of Western Europe. In May, 1951, perhaps to test international sentiment on the subject, the American ambassador in Madrid expressed the hope that the Western countries would allow Spain to take her place in the common front against Communism. The general outcry which was raised against this suggestion in many western European countries and even in the United States, however, apparently convinced the United States government that Franco Spain's inclusion in the North Atlantic Treaty Organization or in the Western European Union was not likely to be soon welcomed or permitted. Subsequently, exploratory talks were initiated between the United States and Spain, aimed—according to the American secretary of state—not at Spain's association with NATO but at a bilateral agreement between the two powers. Six months later a United States mission was sent to Spain to survey air and naval bases which might be leased by the former. Finally, in September, 1953, three agreements were signed between Spain and the United States making Spain eligible for American economic, technical, and military aid from the Mutual Security Administration and authorizing the United States to develop, build, and use jointly with Spanish forces certain military airfields and naval facilities in Spain. The latter, however, were to remain under Spanish sovereignty and command. During 1954 assistance to Spain totaling $226,-000,000 would be furnished by the United States. Commenting on the agreements, which were to remain in force for at least ten years, Franco declared that Spain had emerged triumphantly from the international conspiracy to isolate her. The agreements were ratified unanimously by the Spanish Cortes in November, 1953.

Internally, in 1953 a further step was taken in the organization of management and labor when, on November 1, a decree was issued requiring an advisory council of employer and employed to be set up in all commercial undertakings having 1,000 or more employees. The councils were to consist of the owner or manager as chairman and from four to twelve employees, and were to be established eventually in all undertakings employing more than fifty persons in one place of business. These councils were strongly reminiscent of those set up in Germany by Hitler in 1934 (see page 261). Meanwhile, a great spread had developed between prices and wages, and the standard of living in Spain was recognized as the lowest in western Europe.

PORTUGAL

Portugal, Spain's neighbor in the Iberian Peninsula, must also be classified as a police state with authoritarian characteristics, though, compared with Franco's regime in Spain, that of Salazar in Portugal is mild and humane indeed. Salazar's regime, which has lasted a quarter-century, had its background in events which occurred in Portugal shortly before the First World War.

In 1910, a republican revolt had broken out in that country when both the army and the navy had mutinied and seized the capital. King Manuel II had fled, and a provisional government had proclaimed a republic. In 1911, a democratic constitution, closely resembling that of the Third French Republic, had been adopted, and Manuel Arriaga, long a leader of the Portuguese republicans, had been elected president. Then had followed a series of anticlerical laws, which resembled those enacted earlier in France. Diplomatic relations with the pope had been broken off; church and state had been separated; religious orders had been suppressed and their property confiscated; and a system of free, secular education had been introduced.

But the establishment of the republic had brought neither political stability nor general content. Socialists were dissatisfied with the bourgeois character of the new regime; monarchists intrigued to restore the old regime; and army leaders repeatedly meddled in political affairs. Great strikes, frequent riots, and occasional insurrections and coups prepared the way for the establishment of a military dictatorship. In 1926, the military marched into Lisbon, seized the government offices, disbanded the parliament, dissolved all political and trade-union organizations, suppressed freedom of the press, and imprisoned, banished, or deported to the colonies all who protested. General Antonio Oscar de Fragosa Carmona was elected to the presidency and ruled as dictator.

General Carmona was baffled by the national economic and fiscal conditions which confronted him, and in 1928 he persuaded Antonio de Oliveira Salazar, a university professor of economics, to come to his assistance. As minister of finance Salazar introduced drastic reforms and gradually became the dominant factor in the government, though Carmona continued as President. In 1932, Salazar assumed the premiership and in the next year he gave Portugal a new constitution which laid the legal basis for an authoritarian regime. Political nonconformists found themselves subject to special extralegal security police and were from time to time sent to detention camps without means of redress. Press censorship was continued. The general temper of Salazar's regime may be further judged by the fact that the Portuguese government sympathized and co-operated with Franco and his Insurgents during the Spanish civil war and by the fact that in 1940 it signed a concordat with the pope reconfirming the Catholic Church in possession of properties which had belonged to it before the separation of church and state.

Although as a neutral Portugal profited by the Second World War, the economic hardships following the war inevitably engendered criticism and discontent. By 1947, the currency had been inflated to about four times that of 1939. Prices rose and the cost of living increased to between 200 and 300 per cent of 1939. Wages, however, were not permitted to rise proportionately so that living costs were high out of all proportion to earnings. In 1947 strikes began to occur. In April a number of university students were arrested for having been involved in activities against the security of the state. In June, Admiral José Mendes Cabeçadas, the original head of the military triumvirate which sponsored the coup of 1926, and ten army officers and nineteen university professors and lecturers were dismissed from the service because of their part in conspiracies against the state. When the ex-officers were arrested and detained pending trial, Admiral Cabeçadas claimed for himself and his friends the benefits of habeas corpus, but in November, the government refused to grant the petition. Although the professors were later reinstated, the military men were held for trial by a court martial. Cabeçadas sought to inform his old colleague in revolt, President Carmona, that the Portuguese constitution was being consistently flouted, but apparently to no purpose. In June, 1948, a court martial sentenced the admiral to one year's imprisonment and nine others to eighteen months for their parts in the military revolt of April, 1947.

In 1949 Portugal had two elections. In the first the aged General Carmona, after the opposition candidate withdrew, was elected for his fourth seven-year term. In the second Salazar's National Union Party won all 120 seats in the national assembly; neither the monarchists nor the Left-wing groups had entered candidates. In April, 1951, President Carmona died at the age of eighty-one. In the ensuing presidential campaign two men opposed General Craveiro Lopes, the candidate approved by the National Union Party. One was disqualified by the supreme court nine days before the election; the other withdrew from the contest six days later. General Lopes was elected president. Again in November, 1953, as in the parliamentary election of 1949, the National Union Party won all 120 seats in the national assembly. Twenty-eight opposition candidates stood for election but were defeated.

Portugal is a member of NATO but not of the UN. Under the Marshall Plan she received some $50,000,000 which improved her economic situation. In 1951 she granted the United States more bases in the Azores and by the end of that year an American military mission was helping to equip and train the Portuguese armed forces.

The "Truman Doctrine" Countries

On March 12, 1947, President Truman of the United States in an address to the American Congress declared that "totalitarian regimes imposed on free peoples undermine the foundations of international peace and hence the security of the United States," and asserted his belief that it must be the policy of the United States "to support free peoples who are resisting attempted subjugation by armed minorities, or by outside pressure." At that time he asked the Congress to appropriate funds for the assistance of Greece and Turkey, and to give permission for American military and civil personnel to go to those countries. Actually, what the President was suggesting was that the United States should assume Great Britain's role in the Near East and seek to prevent Russia from reaching the Mediterranean by bolstering up the two non-Communist states which lay between her and that sea, namely, Greece and Turkey. These two countries, therefore, may well be classified as "Truman Doctrine" countries.

GREECE

That conditions in Greece were alarming in 1947, there was little doubt. The turbulent course of Greek history in the years immediately following that country's liberation from the Germans was the result primarily of the interplay of three forces: (1) the Greek resistance movement within the country, (2) the Greek government-in-exile, and (3) Great Britain's interest in Greece and the Near East.

Developments within Greece in the years 1941–1944 were very similar to those within France during the period of German occupation. In Greece, although there were several resistance movements, the largest and most effective organization was the EAM (National Liberation Front) with its military force, the ELAS (National Popular Liberation Army). Although in the beginning the EAM was organized and led chiefly by Communists, within a short time it had attracted such widespread support that it was in fact a National Liberation Front. At the peak of its power it was reported to have enrolled approximately one third of the population of the country. Its announced aim was to liberate Greece and assure the establishment of a truly representative and democratic postwar government. When Italy capitulated in 1943 the EAM obtained much war material from the surrendering Italian forces, with the result that ELAS greatly increased in numbers, became practically a regular army, and took over control of some three fourths of the country.

Meanwhile, after George II fled from Greece in April, 1941, he had eventually established his government, which was essentially a continuation of the Metaxas dictatorship, in Cairo. Metaxas himself had died, and the government in 1941 was headed by Premier Emmanuel Tsouderos. Though King George in 1942 announced the end of the dictatorship, the Tsouderos government remained strongly conservative, and it is not surprising, therefore, that when the three chief resistance groups made two basic demands upon it—that George II should not return to Greece until after a plebiscite and that the EAM should be represented in the government—Premier Tsouderos rejected both demands. The rejection was made contrary to the advice of the Greek cabinet but, it was said, on the advice of Churchill's government.

The policy of the British government toward Greek affairs appears to have been influenced primarily by two factors: extensive British investments in the Greek public debt and in Greek enterprises, and a British desire to check Soviet Russia's southward advance into the Balkans and the Mediterranean. Apparently Churchill and his advisers believed that British economic and strategic interests in Greece would be more likely to be advanced by King George's Rightist government-in-exile than by the Leftist

EAM. From 1943 on the British became increasingly anti-EAM and distributed arms and supplies to forces opposed to the ELAS.

Eventually, in September, 1944, a Greek government of national unity, which included representatives of the EAM, was formed in Cairo by George Papandreou, who was acceptable to the British. Three weeks later he, in turn, asked that British troops be dispatched to Greece, on the ground that an EAM–ELAS coup could be expected after the withdrawal of the Germans. On October 5 the British began their occupation of the country. Following the return of Papandreou's government to Athens a crisis arose because Rightists demanded the disarming of the ELAS. When the British General Scobie threw his support to the Rightists by calling for the disbandment of all guerrilla forces, the EAM ministers resigned from the cabinet, and the EAM central committee called for a protest mass meeting in Athens on December 3 and for a general strike on the following day. Government police fired upon the mass meeting, killing 23 and wounding 142. By December 5 British troops had begun fighting ELAS in Athens, and hostilities continued as heavy British reinforcements arrived. On January 11, 1945, however, a truce was concluded and subsequently the Varkiza Agreement was signed by representatives of the EAM and of the Greek government. By the terms of this settlement all arms were to be surrendered by ELAS within two weeks, the Communist Party and the EAM were to be recognized as legal political organizations, and the government was to grant an amnesty for all political crimes committed during the civil war.

But the amnesty was largely nullified by the harsh measures of the anti-Communist government forces and by local Rightist bands, so that—according to United Nations investigators—many guerrillas who might otherwise have laid down their arms and returned home were undoubtedly forced to retain them and flee to the hills in self-defense. Communist leaders, at the same time, urged their followers to keep their arms and to go underground or flee to Albania, Yugoslavia, or Bulgaria. As a result of this Communist policy, the military strength of ELAS was gradually re-established, and the subsequent internal conflict between the Greek Left and Right became linked with the general rivalry between Russia and the Western powers in the Balkans.

While the Greek people were still emotionally stirred by the civil war and further alarmed by fears of aggression by the pro-Soviet countries to the north, the government called for parliamentary elections. The EAM believed that a free vote would not be permitted and requested the Security Council of the United Nations to send a commission to Greece "to note that democratic conditions do not exist, and that the White terror continues." The Security Council took no action, but Great Britain, the United States, and France decided to send a mission of observers. In the elections on March 31, 1946, the royalist groups received the votes of about 710,000 of the 1,850,000 registered electors. So far as the parliament was concerned, Rightist parties won 234 of the 354 seats, the royalist People's Party alone securing 191 seats.

Eventually, on April 18, 1946, Constantine Tsaldaris, leader of the People's Party, formed a government consisting entirely of royalist ministers. On September 1, 1946, a plebiscite on the return of George II was held and resulted in a majority in favor of the return of the king. Most of the voters feared the Communists and hated the Bulgarians and their Slav supporters, the Russians; and apparently they hoped for strong Allied support against these foes if the king were restored. They therefore chose George II, despite his record of dictatorship, as the lesser of two evils. On September 28, 1946, the latter returned to Athens and for the third time mounted the throne of Greece.[9]

The land over which the king returned to rule was in dire straits. Before the war it was one of the poorest countries in Europe, and it had emerged from German occupation as one of the most thoroughly devastated areas in the world. In the period after the liberation it had received some $700,-000,000 worth of foreign aid, chiefly from UNRRA, Great Britain, and the United States, but the country had failed to show any significant signs of economic recovery. When, in December, 1946, the premier went to Washington seeking a new loan from the United States, he learned that such a loan would be contingent on the establishment of a more competent government in Greece. In January, 1947, Tsaldaris therefore gave way as premier to a more moderate member of the People's Party, Dimitrios Maximos, who formed a ministry representing the Right and Center parties in parliament.

Meanwhile, after the king's return the scale of guerrilla activities had increased, and during the winter of 1946–1947 the "Democratic Army," consisting primarily of former members of ELAS, grew steadily from some 3,000 men to an estimated 13,000 in February, 1947. The Greek army appeared to be unable to destroy the guerrilla forces, partly because it lacked equipment and training for guerrilla fighting and partly because the rebels fled into Albania, Yugoslavia, or Bulgaria when pursued. At this time, when the Greek government was having difficulty in handling the Communist-led rebellion, Great Britain on February 24, 1947, informed the United States that, because of her own difficult economic situation, she would be obliged to end her economic assistance to Greece and Turkey on March 31, and to withdraw her troops from Greece soon thereafter. American statesmen believed that Britain's withdrawal would create a vacuum which Russia would quickly fill unless the United States acted at once. President

[9] On April 1, 1947, George II died and was succeeded on the throne by Paul I, his brother.

Truman therefore asked the Congress for emergency legislation authorizing the expenditure of $400,000,000 to enable Greece and Turkey to survive as "free nations." More than half of the amount, it was planned, would go for military supplies.

But since Greece had failed in the past to progress toward economic recovery in a measure commensurate with the amount of foreign aid received, the United States required the Greek government to undertake a series of economic and social reforms and to consult American advisers before making decisions which might effect the American aid program. In May, 1947, the first contingent of the military section of the American mission was sent to Greece and on July 14, 1947, Dwight P. Griswold, chief of the mission, and the first group of 130 civilian experts arrived in Athens. In August the first installment of arms, munitions, planes, trucks, food, and clothing for the Greek army arrived at the Piraeus, and Griswold announced the award of contracts to American companies for the rebuilding of highways, railways, and the principal ports of Greece. While the United States disclaimed any desire to intervene in Greek political affairs, American spokesmen informed Greek leaders that the United States would welcome a broader political regime. On August 23, the Maximos government resigned, and eventually a new one was created by Sophoulis, the Liberal leader, which consisted about equally of Liberals and members of the People's Party, with Tsaldaris as vice premier and foreign minister.

The United States also took steps to make the Greek military forces more effective against the guerrillas. In September, 1947, it agreed to supply the necessary materials to increase the Greek army to 200,000 men. In October it was announced that United States officers would be attached not only to the general staff of the Greek army but also to operational units. In November an agreement was reached for a joint Greek–United States army staff. In February, 1948, General James Van Fleet was appointed chief of the United States advisory and planning group. Thereafter steady gains were made by Greek forces against the guerrillas until in August, 1948, the guerrilla chief was forced to flee across the frontier into Albania.

By the fall of 1949 the guerrillas were finally defeated. Three factors primarily accounted for the government's success: (1) American equipment and financial support, which enabled Greece to put a larger army in the field; (2) the appointment of General Alexander Papagos, the Greek leader in 1940–1941, as supreme commander; (3) Yugoslavia's break with the Cominform (see page 765) and the subsequent refusal of Marshal Tito to permit Yugoslav aid and asylum to be given the Greek guerrillas.

Following the end of civil war in Greece, American officials wished to begin rapid and extensive economic reconstruction. They desired a rigorous reduction of government expenditures in order that more funds might be available for investment in industry and agriculture, and that as a result some of the glaring inequalities between the rich and the poor might be alleviated. But this program encountered at least the passive resistance of the civil service employees, the army, and King Paul and an influential group of the Athenian ruling class. On top of all this, the outbreak of the Korean War interfered, for it at once led to the abandonment of the proposals to reduce Greek military expenditures, which had been an essential part of the American economic plan.

A continuing obstacle to Greek recovery was the ministerial instability which prevailed down to 1953. Because of innumerable political parties and jealousies and ambitions of Greek political leaders, the kingdom had had some twenty-five changes in the ministry during the postwar period. Partly in consequence of American pressure, however, the proportional system was replaced by the majority system in the election of November, 1952, which resulted in a landslide victory for the reactionary Greek Rally Party, led by General Papagos. The latter had pledged his government to an honest administration, wide national economies, the revival of provincial life, the improvement of agricultural conditions, and full employment. His contemplated reforms seemed likely to encounter the opposition of some of his most influential supporters, but if Premier Papagos could hold his majority in line for the four-year term economic benefits might result.

In 1953 provision for increased co-operation between the United States and Greece was made in a pact signed on October 12 authorizing the United States to improve and use jointly certain airfields and naval installations in Greece. The Soviet government protested that the pact changed Greek territory into a base for the "aggressive NATO *bloc*" and created a threat to peace and security in the Balkans. It further declared that Greece had begun to carry out measures in preparation for a new war by permitting United States armed forces to be based in her territory. Greece rejected the Soviet protest. Not only that but her general staff entered into defense talks with those of Turkey and Yugoslavia at Belgrade in November, 1953, which concluded with agreement on problems of defensive collaboration in event of aggression in the Balkans.

TURKEY

In the case of Greece the aid which President Truman called upon the American Congress to grant was to be used primarily to help the government of that country to suppress armed minorities within its borders, minorities which had the moral and material support of Communists in neighboring states. In the case of Turkey, on the other hand, there was no serious threat from any minority within the country. The aid which the United States was called upon to extend here was for the purpose of en-

abling Turkey to modernize and strengthen her armed forces so as better
to resist "outside pressure" which was being brought to bear to force her
to grant Soviet Russia a dominant position at the Straits.[10]

Throughout the war Russia had been dissatisfied with Turkey's attitude,
especially in regard to the Straits, and even before the war ended the Soviet
government had denounced its treaty of friendship and nonaggression with
that country. Soon after the end of hostilities Russia demanded a revision
of the Montreux convention governing the status of the Straits. During the
war Turkey had kept a large army mobilized as a deterrent to German
invasion, and after the threat from that country had passed she continued
to maintain her armies on a war footing because of the fear of Soviet Russia.
It had been possible for a nation of less than 19,000,000 inhabitants to sustain
an army of more than 500,000 men largely because it had sold chrome and
other critical materials to the belligerents for high prices and because it
had received extensive foreign aid, especially from Great Britain. In 1947
the latter's announcement of her intended withdrawal of economic and
financial support to Turkey was followed, as already indicated, by President
Truman's request for American aid to the Ankara government.

By the subsequently signed agreement between the latter and the United
States it was provided that an American mission by consultation with
Turkish representatives should determine the state of Turkish military
equipment in order that the United States should provide those military
necessities which Turkey herself was not in a position to procure. The
American mission decided that approximately $90,000,000 should be spent
on the armed forces, $5,000,000 on arsenals and repair facilities for motorized
equipment, and $5,000,000 on repairing and building roads. In September,
1947, American aid began to arrive—antiaircraft weapons, warning systems
for defense against air attacks, planes, tanks, motor vehicles, and supplies
of ammunition and ordnance equipment. Since, it was said, the United
States was supplying Turkey with war surplus material at 10 per cent of
its original cost, the latter was destined to receive a considerable quantity of
supplies. But in 1948 expenditures for defense still constituted 48 per cent
of Turkey's national budget.

Whether the Turks constituted one of the "free peoples" of the world
in the Western sense of that word, however, was in 1948 still open to question. In the quarter-century prior to 1946 Turkey had had only one political
party—the People's Party, founded by Mustapha Kemal.[11] Tentative experiments had once or twice been made with a two-party system, but they had
been abandoned. The Communist Party had been outlawed, and in 1946

[10] See page 652.
[11] For conditions in Turkey between the wars, see pages 404–412.

two attempts to establish Socialist parties had been suppressed. Nevertheless, there was in Turkey a growing popular opposition to the continuation of the one-party system, and in November, 1945, President Inönü proposed the replacement of the single-party rule by a parliamentary system. In 1946 a former premier was permitted to launch the Democratic Party, which criticized the restrictions on civil liberties and private enterprise, and demanded free, secret, and direct elections and the more rapid democratization of the country. The new party expected to be organized in time for elections in the spring of 1947, but the government unexpectedly advanced the date for voting to July, 1946. As the result of these elections the Democrats secured only 63 members out of 465 so that the People's Party still remained strongly entrenched in the government. A member of that party became premier, and Inönü, the head of that party, was re-elected President by the National Assembly.

The Democratic Party had drawn its support chiefly from the younger members of the People's Party who held moderate Left-wing views. Another opposition party was created by older Right-wing members. This was the Nationalist Party which, on the whole, was inclined to be economically, politically, and religiously reactionary. The Nationalists questioned the wisdom of the secularization policies introduced earlier by Atatürk and were apparently supported by the Moslem clergy. In new parliamentary elections held in May, 1950, however, the Democratic Party won an overwhelming victory, securing 408 seats in the National Assembly to 69 for the People's Party and only one for the Nationalists. Most of the Democratic victors were newcomers to the National Assembly. Djelal Bayar, the leader of the Democratic Party, was elected president to succeed Inönü, and Adnan Menderes was chosen to be premier in a cabinet in which eleven of the fifteen members had never sat in the National Assembly.

President Bayar was primarily a civilian, in contrast with Atatürk and Inönü, both of whom had been military men. As a young man he had been a banker but had given up his business career to participate in the Young Turk movement which had brought about the revolution of 1908. Under Mustapha Kemal he had been minister of economy until 1924 and again in 1932. Between times he had been head of a bank. In 1937 he had become premier but had resigned in 1939. He was concerned that Turkey should be further liberalized and that Turkish business should be freed from state control and allowed to develop under private enterprise. Premier Menderes had been educated at the American College at Izmir. He had served for many years in the National Assembly, had been considered a moderate, and because of his interest in agriculture, had been a member of the government commission on land reform. The political change in 1950 seemed to indicate that Atatürk's transition period for training new leaders and preparing the way for liberal parliamentary government had at length borne fruit in a middle-class government.

Premier Menderes announced four major aims: (1) the attainment of a balanced budget by economies in state expenditures; (2) the "acceleration" of the economic system; (3) the preparation of an over-all plan; (4) the liberation of production from governmental and bureaucratic interference. Much of the money saved by economies elsewhere was to be directed into agriculture, which still constituted the cornerstone of the country's economy. Tractors, better seeds, improved techniques, and the training of village leaders in agricultural institutes were needed. It was hoped that reductions could be made in the item of national defense, by far the largest item in the budget, and that the reductions might be made up by American aid. The republic had already received some $117,000,000 in Marshall Plan aid and in 1952 she received more than $58,000,000 from the Mutual Security Administration for military expenditures.

Considerable economic and social progress occurred in Turkey in the postwar period. In 1945 a land reform act transferred state and ecclesiastical lands, reclaimed and uncultivated lands, and private lands in excess of some 240 acres to landless peasants and Turkish immigrants from Soviet Russia and the Balkans. In 1947 the government reversed its earlier policy regarding the investment of foreign capital in Turkey, and removed all restrictions on the entry of such capital and on the withdrawal of profits. Premier Menderes' government planned to give foreign capital security and industry the incentive of free competition. By 1953 the manufacture of alcoholic beverages and 49 per cent of the state merchant shipping had been returned to private enterprise, the state match monopoly had been abolished, and salt production for export had been turned over to private companies. By 1949 the government's program of reclamation and irrigation had begun to show results in the added acres which were under cultivation. Compared with the average of 19,026,700 acres under cereal production in 1946–1950, for example, the area in 1952 was some 24,710,000 acres. And the yield in 1952 was 60 per cent higher than the average for the years 1934–1950. Turkey was, in consequence, converted from an importer to an exporter of cereals. But Turkey in 1953 was still plagued with an adverse balance of trade, diminishing though it was. In that year it curtailed the free list of imports, restricting them to those essential for the country's economic development. With a view to reducing the adverse balance of trade it imposed tariff duties on other commodities.

In the postwar years Turkey became closely integrated in the various organizations for collective security set up by the Western powers. In 1949 she became a member of the Council of Europe; in the Korean War she contributed troops in the interest of collective security; in 1952 she was admitted into the North Atlantic Treaty Organization; in 1953 she joined with Greece and Yugoslavia in planning for common military measures against aggression.

Yugoslavia, Ex-Satellite of the Soviet Union

Yugoslavia's refusal meekly to become an Axis satellite like Hungary, Rumania, and Bulgaria had led in 1941 to a German invasion, a ruthless crushing of the people, and dismemberment of the country. Italy and Hungary had both seized Yugoslav territory, Albania and Bulgaria had been given parts of the kingdom, and two puppet states—Croatia and Montenegro—had been established with Axis quisling governments. Particular vengeance had been wreaked on the Serbs; thousands had been put to death by Ante Pavelich (the Axis puppet in Croatia), by the Hungarians in the territory which they had seized, and especially by the occupying Germans.

Although the Yugoslav army had officially surrendered unconditionally to the Germans on April 17, 1941, fighting never completely ceased. The first resistance group to emerge was led by Dragha Mihailovich, and was known as the Chetniks. This group consisted primarily of Serbs, favored a continuation of the monarchy, and was bitterly anti-Communist. In the back country and in the hills the Chetniks continued the military struggle against the Axis and compelled the latter to keep a considerable occupation force in Yugoslavia. Mihailovich was eventually raised to the rank of general and was appointed minister of war by King Peter's government-in-exile.

Following the German invasion of Russia a second resistance group, the Yugoslav Army of Liberation or the Partisans, appeared in Yugoslavia led by Josip Broz, a Croatian Communist "trained in the university of revolution," who went under the nickname of Tito. The latter's group, too, came originally from the Serbian section of Yugoslavia but Tito's greater activity and uncompromising hostility to the Axis gradually drew adherents from other parts of the country. The Partisans were largely Communist in leadership but Tito tried to conceal this by an appeal to a progressive nonparty patriotism. Unfortunately for Mihailovich, his hatred for the Communists led him and his Chetniks to begin collaborating in 1942 with Italians against the Partisans and eventually in 1944 even with the Nazis. Because of Stalin's support of Tito and because of the greater effectiveness of the Partisans against the Axis forces—they tied down in Yugoslavia during 1943–1944 between ten and twenty German divisions—the Allies sent supplies chiefly to "Marshal" Tito.

With the spectacular Russian military successes of 1944 and the increasing prospect that his country might soon be freed of German troops, King Peter took steps to align the resistance movements in Yugoslavia with his government-in-exile and thus, incidentally, to improve the likelihood of his return as the country's monarch. On June 1, 1944, he appointed Ivan Subasich, former governor of Croatia, to head his cabinet and authorized him to negotiate with Tito and Mihailovich. Eventually an agreement was signed by Tito and Subasich which provided that a plebiscite would be held to determine whether King Peter should return, that in the meantime a regency council would be appointed by the king and a provisional government would be formed to include ministers from each federal unit of Yugoslavia, that a constituent assembly would be elected within three months after the liberation of the country, and that until the convocation of the constituent assembly all legislative functions in Yugoslavia would be exercised by the Council of National Liberation, a Partisan body. Although Peter objected to some of these terms, in March, 1945, he appointed the regency council and the latter called upon Marshal Tito to form a new government. The new ministry included representatives of all linguistic and religious groups in Yugoslavia with Tito as prime minister. Subasich was foreign minister and five other former ministers in Peter's government-in-exile were given portfolios.

It was not long, however, until Tito and Subasich, holding altogether different views regarding the political and economic future of Yugoslavia, were unable to co-operate in the government. In August, 1945, Marshal Tito declared that the monarchy was completely incompatible with the new regime which was being developed in the country; two months later, Subasich resigned from the government because of Tito's attitude. General elections, with universal suffrage for all over eighteen, in November, 1945, resulted in Tito's National Front candidates winning over 80 per cent of the seats in each of the two chambers of the new National Assembly. The latter thereupon unanimously proclaimed the Federal People's Republic of Yugoslavia, consisting of six states: Serbia, Croatia, Slovenia, Bosnia-Herzegovina, Montenegro, and Macedonia. It also passed laws prohibiting the return of the king, intrusting the functions of the President of the Republic to a presidium, and gave Marshal Tito's ministry a vote of confidence. In December, 1945, Great Britain and France recognized the new Yugoslav government and in April, 1946, the United States did the same. A year later King Peter and his close relatives were deprived of their nationality and their property was ordered confiscated.

In the trials of "war criminals," "collaborators" or "conspirators," which were conducted in Yugoslavia beginning in 1946, the one which attracted most attention was that of Dragha Mihailovich, who was condemned to death and shot on July 17, 1946, despite protests from Great Britain and the

United States. A number of others who had played prominent roles just prior to the Second World War were also shot or given prison sentences. In October, 1947, for instance, Dragoljub Yovanovich, leader of the Serbian Peasant Party, was sentenced to nine years' penal servitude for conspiracy against the government, and in the following February leaders of the Croatian Peasant Party, accused of being members of an illegal "Machek center," were similarly sentenced. Even leaders of the Catholic Church in Yugoslavia were arrested because of former collaboration with the Germans or because of opposition to the People's Republic. In 1948 the arrests of those accused of conspiring against the People's Republic still continued.

Yugoslavia's economy, which was backward before the Second World War, was completely disrupted by German occupation and exploitation, added to the inevitable war damage and looting. The systematic destruction of communications during the war by the resistance groups and by Allied bombing resulted in a situation which greatly hampered the rehabilitation of the country after hostilities ended. Even before the war a considerable part of Yugoslavia's economy had been state-owned; under Tito the state's part was greatly increased. By 1948 only about 10 per cent of the country's economic activities—limited largely to handicrafts, some retail trade, and agriculture—was left in private hands. Even in agriculture some steps had been taken to establish village co-operatives and the use of agricultural machinery rented by the state. In April, 1947, a Five-Year Plan for economic development during the years 1947–1951 was adopted, and like Russia's first Five-Year Plan it stressed the expansion of capital goods rather than the production of consumer goods. It was also designed to scatter industries into some of the less developed states, notably, Macedonia, Montenegro, and Bosnia-Herzegovina.

But the success of Tito's Five-Year Plan was very seriously endangered by the deterioration of relations between Yugoslavia and Russia which occurred in 1948. In the spring of that year the Russian Communist Party had criticized Tito and other Yugoslav Communist Party leaders because of their disregard of class differentiation in the peasant villages, their tolerance of unrestricted peasant landownership, their renunciation of the Marxist theory of classes and class war, and their behavior toward the Soviet Union in the same manner as toward bourgeois states. But, in the words of the Cominform announcement of June 28, the Yugoslav Communist leaders, "instead of honorably accepting this criticism and setting out on the road of Bolshevik correction of the errors committed, received the criticism with resistance and hostility, and set out on the anti-party road of categorical and general denial of their errors." Accordingly, the Cominform Bureau, meeting in Rumania, expelled Yugoslavia and moved the headquarters of the Cominform from Belgrade to Bucharest.

Fundamentally, the issues in the break between the Cominform and Yugoslavia seemed to be two. In the first place, Tito had evidently discovered that the success of his Five-Year Plan was dependent upon the peasants and had accordingly reversed his attitude toward them just as Lenin had done in introducing his Nep in Russia in 1921. In the words of the Yugoslav Communist Party statement, "to force collectivization on peasants while such tasks as industrialization are still in their early stages ...would provoke a political struggle that might disorganize the country's economy." But Tito's reversal of policy seems to have come at a time when Moscow was urging more drastic moves in the field of land policies, and a clash in policies therefore resulted. For reasons connected with his own country's welfare, Tito apparently refused to agree with the move planned in Moscow and imposed on the Cominform parties. In other words, Tito on this matter was in 1948 more a nationalist than an internationalist, and there was in Russia's program no place for the development of a strong nationalism in her satellites.

The second issue between Yugoslavia and the Cominform apparently was whether the governments of Russia's satellites were to be subservient to Moscow in their internal and foreign policies. The Russian Communists apparently expected the Communist leaders in their Cominform states to be obedient and, when criticized, to recant and submit. Early in 1948, for instance, Premier Dimitrov of Bulgaria had spoken favorably of an Eastern European Federation, but when he had been rebuked by *Pravda,* the Soviet Communist Party newspaper, he had thanked it for its "timely, valuable and useful warning" and had abandoned his idea. Similarly, in September, 1948, Vice Premier Wladslaw Gomulka of Poland, the active leader of the Polish Communist Party, after having been repudiated as leader by the party's executive committee because he supported a peasant policy in Poland similar to Tito's, recanted and adopted the "party line." It is possible that the Cominform's criticism and expulsion of Tito were designed to serve as a warning to any other Communist leaders who might be inclined to adopt a nationalist viewpoint.

In the ensuing months economic pressure was brought to bear against Yugoslavia by the members of the Cominform, which either reduced their trade with that country or boycotted it altogether. In January, 1949, for instance, Yugoslavia was excluded from the Council of Economic Mutual Assistance although she desired membership. Apparently the Soviet economic blockade was designed to bring Yugoslavia to her knees or at least to discredit Tito to such an extent that he might be driven from power by the discontented Yugoslavs. Tito was, perforce, compelled to turn to the Western democracies, particularly Great Britain and the United States, for aid. In the succeeding four years he received economic assistance to the extent of some $267,000,000, and obtained it without having political strings attached. Yugoslav trade, in consequence of the break with the Cominform, became completely reoriented.

But Tito's Five-Year Plan had to be scaled down and extended over a longer period. The cost of the import of capital equipment from the West, even with some assistance from the West, placed a heavy strain on Yugoslavia's economy. Furthermore, the need for increased rearmament after 1949 diverted manpower and materials from the original Five-Year Plan. In the ensuing years defense expenditures averaged twice what they had been before 1948, taking in 1953 some 20.5 per cent of the country's national income. Nevertheless, by 1952 a new machine-tool factory and a new steel plant were in production and in that year most Yugoslav industries had reached or surpassed the prewar level of production. By November, 1952, according to Tito, the state had invested $5,633,000,000 of its own funds in rebuilding and modernizing the country since the war. In June, 1953, however, it was announced that the great financial expenditures for heavy industries had caused stagnation in those producing consumers' goods and that a program of investment in industries producing the latter would be initiated.

As already pointed out, Yugoslavia did not follow Soviet Russia's lead in her agricultural program. Yugoslav land was not all nationalized. The size of holdings was limited, however, at first to approximately 85 acres but in 1953 to only 25 acres. A few state farms were established, and after 1948 some efforts were made by pressures of one sort or another to persuade or force peasants to organize collective farms, but in 1952 individual peasants still controlled 75 per cent of the agriculture. In that year, finally, the forced sale of agricultural products to the state at fixed prices was abolished and some controls and restrictions were removed in an effort to provide greater incentive to production. According to Marshal Tito, in the autumn of 1953, as a result of the government's decision to allow peasants to withdraw from the collectives and to sell their products in the open market the number of collective farms had decreased from about 6,000 to 2,000. But he pointed out the need for increased food supplies to take care of the country's increasing population and urged the peasants to "invest" their own efforts to match the government's investment in the manufacturing of farm equipment and in irrigation projects.

In January, 1953, Yugoslavia replaced her Soviet-type constitution of 1946 by one which was designed to remove the "tyranny of the administrative apparatus over the social initiatives of the workers" which was the root cause of "Soviet despotism," according to Yugoslav Communist leaders. The national parliament remained bicameral, with the lower house, the Federal Council, popularly elected. But the old upper house, the Council of

Nationalities, was replaced by the Council of Producers, representing the agricultural, industrial, and craftsmen's groups. The former presidium was abolished as was also the cabinet. The latter was replaced by the Federal Executive Council, chosen by the parliament. The new constitution provided for a President to be chosen by the two houses of parliament in joint session as in France during the Third Republic. The President of the Republic was also to be president of the Federal Executive Council, supreme commander of the armed forces, and chairman of the National Defense Council. On January 14, 1953, Marshal Tito was elected the first President of the Republic. Even before 1953 the federal government had transferred to the six constituent states direct control of heavy industry, public utilities, and social welfare within their borders, and had increased their control of education, finance, industry, and local transport.

In international affairs Marshal Tito after the break with the Cominform at first tried to pursue a policy of neutrality in the "cold war." But after the Soviet Union and its satellites renounced their alliances with Yugoslavia in 1949, and especially after the North Korean attack on the Korean Republic in 1950, he apparently reassessed Yugoslavia's international position. Events in Korea seemed to indicate that, though Soviet Russia might not wish to become involved in a general war, she might not be averse to having her satellites attack Yugoslavia, and the satellites in various ways constantly conducted a "war of nerves" against Tito's republic. Desire for economic and military assistance from the West undoubtedly prompted Tito to turn more and more toward the Western democracies, and the desire of the latter to build as strong a defensive bulwark as possible against any future Soviet aggression led the West to seek to strengthen Yugoslavia.

In 1949 the United States changed its economic policy toward Yugoslavia and lifted its embargo on all except military goods. In that year and the next it gave financial assistance to Tito through loans and through Marshal Plan aid. It supported the successful move in 1949 to seat Yugoslavia on the UN Security Council in place of the Ukraine. In 1949–1950 Great Britain also negotiated commercial agreements with Yugoslavia providing for the exchange of British manufactured goods for Yugoslav raw materials. In 1952 Great Britain, the United States and France advanced millions of dollars to Tito to cover Yugoslavia's trade deficit. At length, in 1951–1952, the United States undertook to provide military supplies, equipment, and service for the Yugoslav armed forces and to provide tanks, heavy artillery, and jet aircraft in 1952–1953. Yugoslavia, Tito declared in May, 1953, would never forget the support of the Western democracies in the most difficult moment of her history. But when, in January, 1954, Milovan Djilas, chairman of the Yugoslav Communist Party and a vice-president of Yugoslavia, was expelled from the central committee of the party because articles which he

Wide World photo

YUGOSLAVIA'S ANTI-RUSSIAN PRESIDENT
Marshal Tito

had written were charged with being of a "revisionist character" pleasing to certain quarters in the West, President Tito denounced his error and asserted that, though Yugoslavia was drawing closer to Western democracy, this was only in international matters and not on internal questions.

Meanwhile, Yugoslavia's relations with her non-Communist neighbors had improved. In 1949 Yugoslavia and Italy signed their first postwar trade treaty and reopened their frontiers which had been closed since 1949. On the other hand, in 1949, Yugoslavia gradually closed her frontiers to Greek insurgents and thus contributed to the end of the civil war in Greece. Eventually negotiations among Yugoslavia, Greece, and Turkey led to the signing of a tripartite treaty (May 25, 1953) creating a new defensive Balkan alliance, aimed at placing 70 military divisions in the field against any Soviet attempt to reach the Mediterranean. In urging the ratification of this pact Tito declared that any hesitation would be "a historic and perhaps irrevocable error." The extent to which Yugoslavia had become an ex-satellite of the Soviet Union is revealed by Marshal Tito's description of Russia as "the largest imperialist power with the most reactionary conceptions of relations between nations."

Nevertheless, the year 1953 saw—at least on the surface—a lessening of the tension between Russia and her satellites on the one hand and Yugoslavia on the other. Russia, Hungary, and Bulgaria resumed diplomatic relations with Yugoslavia, and in the Danube Commission the Russian and satellite delegates joined in electing a Yugoslav to the post of secretary, which had formerly been held by a Russian. The commission also approved a Yugoslav proposal to move the headquarters of the commission from Galatz in Rumania to Budapest.

Chapter XXVII

NATIONALISM IN THE EAST

IN the closing years of the nineteenth century, nationalism—which had played such an important role in the history of Europe—began to penetrate the East. In the period between the two world wars it had manifested itself in a growing revolt against the domination of the West, which had forced several European governments to make concessions to the natives of their overseas possessions. In the years after the Second World War this wave of nationalism became a veritable flood which swept away many of the long-established systems by means of which the West had ruled the East. Political independence, dominion status, or more self-government were won by many of the Eastern peoples, whose subsequent efforts to rule themselves were, however, in some cases complicated by Communist attempts to overthrow their new governments.

The Arab League

Even before the First World War the Arabs had begun to be imbued with nationalism, and during that war—encouraged by British promises of independence and the establishment of an Arab kingdom—the Arabs had fought on the side of the Allies to escape from Turkish domination. At the close of the war Arab nationalists were bitterly disappointed when, instead of being allowed to establish an independent Arab kingdom, most of the Arabs were distributed in various small states which were handed over to Great Britain and France as mandates of the League of Nations. In the years between the wars, Arab nationalists continued their struggle, now waged against their former allies, and made some gains. Iraq and Egypt were able to achieve their independence, but with the exception of Saudi Arabia and Yemen the rest of the Arab lands remained under European domination. Independence of all Arabs from foreign control and the formation of a united Arab nation continued to be the basic aims of Arab policy.

To advance these aims, on March 22, 1945, representatives of Egypt, Iraq, Transjordan, Saudi Arabia, Syria, Lebanon, and Yemen, meeting in Cairo, established the Arab League. The League, representing some 45,000,000 Arabs, would have a Council, in which each member state would have one vote, which would supervise the enforcement of conventions concluded among its members and would study means of collaboration with other international organizations. Recourse to force for the settlement of disputes between members was forbidden, and decisions of the Council in disputes brought before it—not affecting the independence, sovereignty, or territorial integrity of member states—would be binding. The League was to be open to other independent Arab states, and, until Palestine gained its independence, the League Council would appoint an Arab representative for Palestine. The permanent secretariat of the League was set up in Cairo.

The aims of the League were declared to be the strengthening of friendship between members, the co-ordination of their political action, and the safeguarding of their independence. In 1946 the Council approved a proposal to grant common citizenship to Arabs of all Arab states, and in the following year the states in the League concluded a cultural treaty designed to draw the Arab countries together. This provided for the exchange of students, professors, and teachers, for the encouragement of educational visits among the different states, and for co-operation in maintaining and revising the Arab cultural heritage.

The League sought to influence the course of political events by presenting the Arab viewpoint and, if necessary, by bringing pressure to bear on non-Arab states. In 1946 it voted to support Egypt's demands for the early withdrawal of British troops, and in the following year it supported that country's demands for the union of the Sudan with Egypt under the latter's king. It also resolved to work for the independence of Libya, and planned to co-ordinate the efforts of all nationalist parties to obtain full independence for Tunisia, Algeria, and French and Spanish Morocco. It tried to prevent the partition or federalization of Palestine and sought to establish it as an independent Arab state. It threatened to bring economic pressure to bear against states which voted for the partition of Palestine, using especially the power of certain of its member states to handicap foreign countries in their production or transportation of petroleum within Arab territories. The influence of the Arab League seemed to account, in part, for the vacillating policy of some of the great powers in regard to the future of Palestine.

The League, however, had internal weaknesses arising from the rivalry existing between the Hashimite family and the family of King Ibn Saud of Saudi Arabia. King Abdullah represented the aspirations of the Hashimites and he was supported by Transjordan and Iraq, which were ruled by his family. Ibn Saud, who in 1924 had added Abdullah's father's kingdom of Hejaz to his realm, represented the opposition to the Hashimites, and to some extent at least he was supported by Syria and Lebanon which were anti-Hashimite. The Arab situation was further complicated by King Farouk of Egypt who was anti-Hashimite but who also apparently had ambitions of his own. This inherent disunity of the Arabs helps to explain their ineffective war against Israel in 1948, which is discussed below. Although Arab unity appeared to have been weakened in 1949, the Arab League continued to play a role in international affairs, especially in the United Nations where its members usually constituted a bloc.

Egypt and the Sudan

At the close of the First World War, it will be recalled, Egyptians had insisted that their country be given its independence, and ultimately that independence had been recognized by the British government.[1] A treaty between Great Britain and Egypt had provided, however, for the stationing of British troops in the latter country. During the Second World War, Egypt had been saved from Axis subjugation largely by British empire troops operating within her borders in accordance with the terms of that treaty. But at the close of the war demands were made by Egypt that all British troops be evacuated and that negotiations should be initiated regarding the future of the Sudan.[2] Anti-British riots and violence occurred and the Arab League even announced that its member states would fight on the side of Egypt should war with Britain ensue.

In May, 1946, the British Labor government announced that it would withdraw from that country all British naval, military, and air forces. As evidence of its good intentions, on July 4, 1946, the Union Jack was lowered from the Cairo citadel where it had flown for some 64 years, and the Egyptian national flag was hoisted in its place. Three questions still remained, however, to be negotiated by the British and Egyptian governments: (1) the schedule to be followed by the British in evacuating their troops, (2) the future of the Anglo-Egyptian defensive alliance of 1936, and (3) the status of the Sudan. These negotiations were further complicated by Sudanese demands that they should be free to set up an independent democratic government of their own which would decide their country's future relations both with Egypt and with Great Britain.

Ultimately, in October, 1946, a draft treaty and two draft protocols were initialed by the representatives of Egypt and Britain. These so-called Sidkey-Bevin drafts provided for the cancellation of the treaty of 1936[3] and for the establishment of a new defensive military alliance between the two countries, by the terms of which Egypt assumed only limited obligation. Whereas Great Britain would come to the aid of Egypt in case of any armed attack, Egypt would assist the British only if they became involved in war as the result of an attack on countries adjacent to Egypt. In respect to the Sudan, they provided that Egypt and Britain would set up a joint council

---

[1] See page 413.
[2] For the importance of the Sudan, see the footnote on page 413.
[3] See page 415.

to watch the progress of the Sudanese toward self-government and to recommend eventually suitable arrangements for ascertaining the wishes of the Sudanese regarding their political status. Although the Egyptian cabinet and Chamber of Deputies approved the Sidkey-Bevin drafts, the Nationalists, led by Mustapha Nahas Pasha, declared that they would launch a passive resistance campaign against any government which signed them. Further negotiations were carried on until March, 1947, when they broke down because Egypt refused to accept Britain's proposal of eventual self-government for the Sudanese, who should then be free to choose independence or association or union with Egypt.

Following the collapse of Anglo-Egyptian negotiations the British took steps to facilitate the development of autonomous political institutions in the Sudan. In June, 1948, the British governor-general promulgated an ordinance enacting the recommendations of an Anglo-Sudanese conference. A legislative assembly was to consist of ten representatives named by the governor-general and sixty-five elected by territorial constituencies, and an executive council or embryonic cabinet, appointed by and responsible to the governor-general, was to consist of British and Sudanese ministers, with the latter constituting a majority. In the first elections under this ordinance the Independence Front, which represented chiefly the indigenous Sudanese and which demanded the ultimate complete independence of the Sudan, won a majority, partly because the National Front, representing the Sudanese Egyptians or pro-Egyptians, had boycotted the election. The latter desired to have the Sudan throw off British control but remain connected with Egypt.

In December, 1950, the legislative assembly passed a resolution calling for self-rule in the Sudan, and in response to this resolution a constitutional commission was appointed by the governor-general. Under the provisions of the self-government statute eventually adopted by the legislative assembly in May, 1952, the Sudan was to have a bicameral parliament. Of the fifty members of the upper house, twenty were to be named by the governor-general and thirty were to be elected. The prime minister was to be chosen from the members of the lower house and his cabinet was to be responsible to the parliament. The British governor-general, however, was still to retain wide powers, being responsible for foreign affairs, the civil service, and the approval of the speakers of the two houses of the parliament. In case of a constitutional breakdown, he was to have full legislative and executive authority. On October 22, 1952, the British government approved the statute.

By this time in Egypt the Nationalists had once more gained control of the parliament and Mustapha Nahas Pasha had become premier, with the avowed aims to abrogate the Anglo-Egyptian treaty of 1936, to drive the British out of the Suez Canal zone, and to unite the Sudan with Egypt. In fact, in 1951 the Egyptian parliament had unilaterally abrogated the treaty of 1936 and proclaimed Farouk "King of Egypt and the Sudan." The British had countered by increasing their military forces in Egypt and seizing the Suez Canal. Generally disturbed conditions within Egypt, coupled with widespread governmental corruption and an increasing antagonism to King Farouk, led in July, 1952, to a *coup d'état* by army officers under General Mohammed Nagib, which deposed Farouk, suppressed political parties, suspended the constitution, made Nagib virtual dictator, and ultimately proclaimed Egypt a republic.

General Nagib at once opened negotiations with all the leading Sudanese parties and ultimately reached a tentative agreement with them. He then re-opened negotiations with the British and a new agreement on the Sudan was signed in February, 1953. A Sudanese constituent assembly was to draft a permanent constitution and electoral law and to decide whether the Sudan should be linked with Egypt or be independent. In elections held during November and December, 1953, the National Unionists won a decisive majority of the seats, and on January 6, 1954, the leader of that party, Ismail el-Azhari, who had been educated at Beirut University and had served for many years in the Sudan ministry of education, was chosen the first prime minister of the Sudan. Under the agreement of February, 1953, the Sudan would now enter the transitional stage of self-government which was to end in union with Egypt or independence after a period of not more than three years, provided that by that time that country's army, police, and administration had been Sudanized. This solution still contained explosive possibilities, however, for Great Britain held that the second alternative would permit the Sudan's association with the British Commonwealth and Egypt insisted that this was precluded. In 1954 the Anglo-Egyptian situation continued tense, not only because of this difference but because of Nagib's determination to force the British out of the canal zone.

The United Kingdom of Libya

To the west of Egypt lies an area of some 700,000 square miles—mostly desert—with a population of some 1,250,000, which before the Second World War was part of the Italian "empire." Generally speaking, Libya consisted of two major divisions, Tripolitania and Cyrenaica, in both of which Islam is universal and Arabic the dominant language. In Italian efforts to conquer the region more protracted resistance was encountered in Cyrenaica than in Tripolitania, partly because Egypt offered the Cyrenaican fighting men a refuge when hard pressed. During the Second World War a Libyan Arab Force of Cyrenaicans was organized on its own initiative to fight the

Italians in the name of Emir Idris, leader of the Moslem religious fraternity of the Senussi. This force returned to Cyrenaica as "liberators" with the British Eighth Army in 1942. Because the Tripolitanians were liberated without much effort on their part, the Cyrenaicans regarded themselves as the more patriotic Libyans.

In the immediate postwar years the British set up separate military administrations for Cyrenaica and Tripolitania. In the peace negotiations the great powers were unable to agree upon the fate of Italy's former colonies and so, in accordance with the peace treaty with Italy, the question was referred to the UN General Assembly. The political committee of the Assembly in 1949 proposed that Libya should become independent after ten years, that in the meantime the British should administer Cyrenaica for that period and Tripolitania for two years, and that from 1951 to 1959 Italy should serve as trustee for the latter. Largely because of the opposition of the Arab states to Italy's return as a trustee, the proposals were defeated in the Assembly, however. Instead, the latter voted that a unified Libya should become independent by January 1, 1952, and that meanwhile a UN commissioner should administer the region.

A Libyan national assembly drafted a constitution providing for a federal democratic kingdom with Emir Idris as king. On December 24, 1951, final powers were handed over to the legally constituted Libyan government by the British administrators. Libya's first parliamentary elections were held on February 19, 1952, and the inaugural meeting of the parliament occurred in Benghazi, the capital of Cyrenaica, on March 25. To alleviate the rivalry between Tripoli and Benghazi, the parliament reconvened in the former city on April 27. Thus a people, who for two thousand years had been subjects of larger political organisms, had their national aspirations at last recognized.

Syria and Lebanon

In the years between the wars, Syria and Lebanon had been constantly disturbed by the struggle between Arab nationalism and French imperialism.[4] Although eventually, in 1936, France had signed treaties with the Syrian and Lebanese governments looking toward their full independence at the end of a three-year transition period, on the eve of the Second World War the French high commissioner had dissolved the Syrian parliament and suspended the Syrian constitution. In 1941, however, British imperial and "Fighting French" forces had launched an invasion of Syria to oust the pro-German Vichyite regime functioning there, and at that time the commander of the "Fighting French" in the Middle East, had proclaimed

[4] See pages 416–418.

the independence of Syria and Lebanon. Later in the year the "Fighting French" authorities had terminated the French mandate, and the two states had become sovereign, independent republics. In 1945 they were invited to attend the San Francisco Conference of the United Nations.

Nevertheless, contrary to the desire of the Syrian Nationalists, French and British troops continued to occupy Syria and Lebanon after the end of the Second World War, and in the summer of 1945 fighting occurred in Damascus and elsewhere between French troops and Syrians. Late in that year the French and British governments, which appeared to be suspicious of each other's motives in regard to Syria, signed an agreement providing for the withdrawal of their forces from both Syria and Lebanon, leaving only sufficient troops to guarantee security until the United Nations decided on the organization of collective security in that region. The Syrians and Lebanese were wholly dissatisfied with what they considered the dilatory nature of this agreement, and in February, 1946, they asked the UN Security Council to recommend the total and simultaneous evacuation of British and French troops from their countries. Although the Council took no decisive action, in the next month the French and British agreed to complete their evacuation by late summer. The evacuation was carried out as announced, and a national holiday was observed in Syria to mark the departure of all foreign troops. In November Syria was elected a nonpermanent member of the UN Security Council.

The Syrians, who are primarily Moslem Arabs, established a parliamentary government, but in the years immediately after the war were largely dominated by some twenty to forty families drawn from the four main towns. The Lebanese, a slight majority of whom are Arab-speaking Christians, also established a parliamentary republic. Their small state, only about a third the size of Belgium, owed its separate existence largely to memories of the ill-treatment of its Christians by Moslems in the nineteenth century.

Iraq and Jordan

Arab nationalism among the Iraqi, which in the period between the wars had forced Great Britain to recognize Iraq as an independent state rather than as a mandate, in 1948 was again aroused against the British. In a new treaty of alliance with Iraq, signed in January, 1948, Great Britain gave up her part ownership and management of the Iraqi railways as well as her rights in the management of the port of Basra. She also turned her air bases in Iraq over to the latter, though they were to be available for British use until peace treaties became effective with all ex-enemy powers—which might be a considerable time. A joint defense board, with equal Iraqi and British representation, was to co-ordinate defense policy, and Iraq agreed to standardize her armaments with those of Britain and to employ Britons if foreign military instructors were required. All facilities were to be given in Iraq to British forces in case of war or the threat of war. Although this treaty was readily signed by Iraqi representatives in Britain, in Iraq violent opposition to it appeared and the treaty was rejected. By 1953 Iraqi nationalists were demanding nationalization of Iraqi oil and the abrogation of Britain's right to maintain air forces in the country.

In Transjordan, too, concessions to nationalism had to be made. In the period between the wars this sparsely settled Arab state was a British mandate of the League of Nations, administered by the British high commissioner for Palestine and Transjordan. But the postwar period saw this small country transformed from a mandate to an independent kingdom linked with Britain merely in an alliance. An Anglo-Transjordan treaty, concluded in 1946 and modified in 1948, provided for a mutually defensive alliance between the two countries and for the stationing of British armed forces in Transjordan. On May 25, 1946, the independence of the country was formally proclaimed under King Abdullah. After the incorporation of the Arab remnant of Palestine the name of the state was changed to the Hashimite Jordan Kingdom, usually referred to as Jordan.

Palestine and Israel

The conflict which raged in Palestine from 1918 to 1939 between Jewish Zionism and Arab nationalism and which complicated Great Britain's task as a mandatory power there has already been described in some detail.[5] But after twenty years of repeated efforts to solve the Palestinian question, when the Second World War broke out Great Britain seemed to be about as far as ever from a final settlement of the Arab-Jewish conflict. In fact, from a strategic and diplomatic viewpoint the situation had become even more difficult for Britain. Further development of Arab nationalism, the growing solidarity of the Arab states as indicated by the organization of the Arab League and the latter's support of the Palestinian Arab demands, and the presence of millions of Moslems in India and Egypt, all these factors—plus Britain's need for bases and Moslem support in the Middle East—forced the British government to give careful consideration to Arab demands. At the same time, the continued propaganda of the Zionists, the terrible sufferings of the Jews at the hands of the Nazis, and the ardent desire of a million or more European Jews to find a haven of refuge somewhere, convinced world opinion that something must be done for the Jews. President Truman of the United States, for instance, in 1945 urged the British government to admit 100,000 Jews to Palestine at once, a step which was vigorously opposed

[5] See pages 418–423.

by the states in the Arab League and by Moslem organizations in India.

Britain was eager to associate the United States with her in the settlement of the Palestinian question, and consequently invited the latter to join in setting up an Anglo-American Commission of Enquiry to examine the question of European Jewry and to review the Palestinian problem in the light of that examination. The report of this commission was published as a British Blue Book on May 1, 1946. It recommended, among other things, that 100,000 Jews be admitted into Palestine as rapidly as conditions would permit, but pointed out that Palestine alone could not meet the emigration needs of Jewish victims of Nazi persecution. It therefore further recommended that Great Britain and the United States, in association with other countries, should endeavor immediately to find new homes for Jewish refugees. The report was at once denounced by both Jews and Arabs.

Palestine continued to be torn by acts of terrorism and violence, chiefly at the hands of the Jewish underground. These culminated on July 22, 1946, in the wrecking of the King David Hotel in Jerusalem, headquarters of the British Army in Palestine and of the secretariat of the Palestinian government. Scores were killed, including several high British officials. The Jews, Prime Minister Attlee contended, were adopting in Palestine "some of the very worst of the methods of their oppressors in Europe." In the late summer of 1946 the British were forced to take drastic military and naval measures to cope with Jewish terrorism as well as to prevent the illegal entry of Jews into Palestine.

During the summer of 1946 British and American officials met in London to examine and discuss the Anglo-American commission's report. Out of their discussion came a recommendation for a Palestinian constitution providing for federalization. This was followed by the British government's calling of a roundtable conference to meet in London, to be attended by representatives of the Palestinian Arabs and Jews and by representatives of the states in the Arab League. Since the Palestinian Arabs and Jews refused to attend the conference, nothing was accomplished. The British then made one more effort to reach an agreed solution by putting forward new proposals in February, 1947. When these were rejected outright by both Jews and Arabs, the British government decided to refer the whole problem of Palestine to the United Nations.

At a special session of the General Assembly of the United Nations a special committee was organized to investigate the Palestinian problems, and this committee, after visiting Palestine and a number of refugee camps in Europe, made its report on August 31, 1947. The majority recommended the establishment of two independent states, one Jewish and the other Arab, neither to include Jerusalem, which would be under international administration. During the General Assembly debates on the Palestine problem,

Great Britain announced that, regardless of the Assembly's action, she was surrendering her mandate and planning to complete the evacuation of her troops in the summer of 1948. Thanks largely to the support of the United States and Russia, particularly of the former, the Assembly on November 29, 1947, voted in favor of partition. There was rejoicing among the Jews but consternation and disappointment among the Arabs, who threatened to use force to prevent the execution of the plan.

Recruits for guerrilla operations in Palestine were enlisted in all the Arab countries, but the Arab League apparently decided not to use its national armies until after the British had withdrawn their forces. Although for some years the Jews had been directing their underground forces against the British troops and officials in Palestine, there had during this period been little conflict between the Jews and the Arabs. With the announcement of the partition and Arab opposition to it, however, open conflicts between the two groups began. During the next three months widespread disorders resulted in the gradual breakdown of economic life. Arab hostility to the United States and its possible effect on American oil and other interests in the Middle East apparently provoked an anti-Zionist reaction in Washington. Suddenly, on March 19, 1948, the United States representative in the Security Council announced that his country's support of partition was withdrawn. He proposed instead a temporary United Nations trusteeship for the whole country. The Security Council accordingly called another special meeting of the General Assembly for April 16.

Meanwhile, in Palestine the Jewish military position had steadily improved, so that by the middle of May there was a well-defined area of Jewish control which included the most important parts of the territory assigned to the Jewish state by the partition plan. On May 14, when a UN commission was attempting to negotiate a truce in Palestine and when the General Assembly was debating the idea of a trusteeship, the establishment of the State of Israel was proclaimed in Tel Aviv. At once, without even notifying the American delegation in the General Assembly, President Truman announced that the United States recognized this "provisional government as the *de facto* authority of the new state of Israel." At midnight of May 14 the British mandate in Palestine ended.

On the following morning the regular armed forces of Egypt, Transjordan, Iraq, and Syria advanced into Palestine. Within a week the Jews had been driven from the northern outskirts of Jerusalem, the Egyptians had occupied Gaza and Beersheba, the Syrians were fighting south of Lake Galilee, and Tel Aviv had been bombed several times from the air. An American demand that the Security Council should declare that a "breach of peace" within the meaning of Article 39 of the UN Charter existed in Palestine was rejected, but the Council did vote to call on all governments and authorities to issue cease-fire orders to their military forces. Open fighting in Palestine ended on June 11, when a four-weeks truce became effective. By that time the Arabs had occupied a substantial part of the area allotted them and had forced the unconditional surrender of the Jewish quarter of the Old City of Jerusalem. The Arab quarters of New Jerusalem remained in Jewish hands, however.

A tentative plan for a settlement, put forth by Count Folke Bernadotte, the United Nations mediator, was flatly rejected by both Jews and Arabs, and on July 9 fighting was resumed. This time the Jewish forces gained at the expense of the Arabs. The Security Council again issued a cease-fire order with threat of sanctions attached; the Arabs, under considerable pressure from Britain, complied, and fighting again came to an end. Some 300,000 Arabs had by this time fled for safety from Jewish areas to neighboring Arab states, and on July 22 the provisional government of Israel decided in principle not to allow the general return of these refugees to their homes. During the rest of 1948 fighting and cease-fire orders alternated with a monotonous regularity. Nonmilitary violence continued, too, and culminated on September 17 in the murder of the UN mediator, Count Bernadotte, by members of the so-called Stern gang of Jews. But by August, 1949, thanks largely to the efforts of Ralph Bunche, the acting UN mediator, armistices had been signed between Israel and each of her four Arab neighbors and hostilities had "officially" ended.

By this time it was obvious that the Arabs had failed, first, in their efforts to prevent the partition of Palestine and the establishment of an independent Jewish state, and, second, in their efforts to reduce the size of Israel to a minimum. The Arabs, especially those in Egypt, were inclined to blame the great powers for their failure. "The trouble is," complained one prominent Egyptian newspaper, "that every time we deal a crushing blow to the Zionists the big countries intervene and prevent us from continuing the fight." There was some feeling among the Arabs that they had been tricked and betrayed by Great Britain, influenced by the United States. But the Arab failure was certainly the result, also, of disunity among the Arabs. For a time the latter had been united by a common hostility to the Zionists, but after a few months this unity had been destroyed by internal rivalry and family disputes. This rivalry was brought out into the open when in September, 1948, one group of Arabs had announced the formation of a "Palestine Government" at Gaza which was recognized by Egypt, Iraq, and Syria but which was characterized as "strange and serious" by King Abdullah of Transjordan. The rivalry was further emphasized in December when a meeting of Palestinian Arabs in Jericho had proclaimed Abdullah as king of Palestine and Transjordan, and the parliament of Transjordan had unanimously approved the decision to unite the two. The Arab League

ISRAEL AND HER NEIGHBORS

was at least temporarily weakened when it denounced the action of the Jericho conference and the Transjordan parliament.

Meanwhile, the territory controlled by Israel had been enlarged by the military operations of Israeli troops. Meanwhile, too, preparations had been made to transform the provisional government of Israel into a permanent constitutional regime. On January 25, 1949, elections were held in Israel for a constituent convention. The moderate socialist Maipai Party, led by David Ben-Gurion, the provisional prime minister of Israel, won 46 of the 120 seats; the Leftist opposition Mapam Party, which opposed Anglo-American "imperialism" and favored an Eastern orientation, won 19; the United Religious bloc won 16; the Heruth Party, the political organ of the terrorist Irgun Zvai Leumi, won 14; and eight minor parties gained the rest. Israel, it appeared, would have to struggle with a multiparty system. On February 17, 1949, the Israeli constituent assembly elected as first President of Israel the veteran Zionist leader, Chaim Weizmann, who had been provisional president since the proclamation of the new state in May, 1948. By this time the Israeli government had received the recognition of more than thirty states, including most of the great powers. The interim constitution adopted for the new state provided for a democratic republic with a figurehead president, elected for five years by a unicameral legislature, and with ministerial responsibility to the national legislature. In May, 1949, Israel was admitted to the UN, and by the end of 1950 sixty-one states had recognized the Israeli government.

But the neighboring Arab states refused to grant recognition and so the boundaries between them and the new republic were not legally fixed. Israel barred Jordan's access to the Mediterranean and, after the latter incorporated the Arab remnant of Palestine, Jordan barred Israel's most direct route from Tel Aviv to Jerusalem and held the Jewish quarter of the Old City. Border clashes on the Jordan-Israeli border repeatedly occurred, becoming so serious that in April, 1954, the situation was brought before the UN Security Council. Arab-Israeli relations were further disturbed by Israel's refusal to permit the return of the Arabs who had fled from Palestine in 1948. These refugees, numbering 881,000 in 1952, were compelled to live on relief in the Arab countries where they had taken refuge.

Israel's chief domestic problem was to improve her economic life so that it could support an increasing population. In the five years after 1948 some 700,000 immigrants poured into Israel. Millions of dollars in aid were received from American and other agencies to assist in housing projects and in economic development. By 1953 the area under cultivation had been increased five-fold and food production four-fold; iron, copper, and phosphate mines had been opened; modern industrial establishments for the production of chemicals, textiles, and metal and food products had been built; and a merchant marine had been launched.

Iran

The nationalistic efforts under Riza Shah Pahlevi to modernize Iran and to force better terms from Western capitalism in the years between the wars have already been outlined (see pages 424–426). Although some progress was made, in the period after the Second World War most of the Iranians were still desperately poor, undernourished, and uneducated. Approximately 80 per cent of the country's 16,500,000 people were dependent on agriculture, but only 10 per cent of the land was cultivated and 15 per cent used for grazing. Agricultural development had been handicapped by scarcity of water and by unfavorable climate. But it had also been handicapped by an absentee-landlord system which took from the peasant some 80 per cent of his production and by agricultural methods which were wholly out-of-date.

Shah Mohammed Riza Pahlevi, who had succeeded his father on the latter's abdication in 1941, and some of his more enlightened advisers sought at the close of the Second World War to change some of these conditions. Eventually, with the advice of American consultant firms, a Seven-Year Plan to increase the country's agricultural and industrial production and raise living standards was adopted in 1949, and the parliament allocated all oil revenue for the ensuing seven years to finance the contemplated capital improvements. The next step was to secure the parliament's ratification of the 1949 supplemental agreement to the Anglo-Iranian Oil Company (AIOC) concession, by the terms of which Iran's share in the company's earnings would be about doubled.

But throughout 1950 the parliament deferred action and in the face of the determined opposition the government finally withdrew the agreement. The processing of oil at the AIOC refinery at Abadan, the largest refinery in the world, constituted Iran's largest single industry, employing in all its operations some 100,000 Iranians. But those who opposed ratification of the new agreement pointed out that the British government received more in taxes on AIOC profits than Iran did in royalties, and although the new agreement would increase Iran's share, opponents of ratification wanted Iran to obtain even more. Some demanded that Iranians should have a greater share in the management of the company; others demanded nationalization of the company altogether. Mohammed Mossadegh, leader of the National Front which had twice prevented ratification of the 1949 agreement by the parliament, proclaimed that nationalization would cure all the country's ills, that Iran's disasters lay solely in the existence of the Anglo-Iranian Oil Company. But Premier Ali Razmara, who shared the shah's reform ambitions, believed it necessary to co-operate with the West to implement the Seven-Year Plan and stanchly opposed all demands for nationalization. In consequence, on March 7, 1951, Razmara was murdered, "a martyr to reason and compromise." On April 28 the parliament then voted unanimously to nationalize the oil industry and two days later Mossadegh became premier. In his initial broadcast as the new premier he declared that all Iran could live in ease and affluence once the oil was nationalized.

The Iranian oil situation now became an international problem. The United States sought to persuade Great Britain to accept nationalization and attempt to work out some reasonable settlement with Iran, to take the long view—even at some sacrifice to herself—of the regional interests of the Middle East in order to prevent the extension of the Soviet empire into Iran. But the British believed that surrender to Iranian demands would only encourage extremists in the Arab oil-producing countries to denounce the oil agreements which had been negotiated with them, that it would open the way to endless blackmail of the West. The British did accede, however, to the American request not to use military force without prior consultation with the United States. Instead, Great Britain took the case to the International Court of Justice to try to force Iran to arbitrate with the oil company. She also appealed to the UN Security Council. Mossadegh flew to New York to present Iran's case, and the council postponed a decision. In June, 1952, Mossadegh presented Iran's case before the International Court, claiming that the court had no jurisdiction, and the court a month later ruled that the dispute did fall outside its jurisdiction.

Upon Mossadegh's return from The Hague, he demanded dictatorial powers from the parliament but was refused. His consequent resignation was followed by widespread riots, fomented by his supporters and by the Communist Tudeh Party, and a few days later he was reappointed premier and given special powers to rule by decree for six months. His first decree as dictator was to impose a 20 per cent tax on landowners, half of the tax to go to the tenant farmers and half to village councils for local needs and improvements. He further attacked the feudal agrarian system by forbidding work without wages and levies on peasants. On the other hand, he stopped the agrarian program of the shah, who wished to sell the royal estates to the peasants on easy terms. He became more autocratic as time passed. In September he purged the judges in the civil courts and dissolved all special courts; in October, 1952, he rid himself of the Senate, which had showed some opposition to him.

Meanwhile, after Anglo-Iranian negotiations had become deadlocked,

Iranian troops in September, 1951, had seized the Abadan refineries and those members of the British staff not already withdrawn were ordered to leave. During the early months of 1952 the International Bank for Reconstruction and Development attempted to find a basis for resuming the production of oil, but to no avail. Mossadegh, in turn, sought to find purchasers for Iranian oil and when the British announced that the oil was theirs and could not be sold, he closed the British consulates within Iran. In August the Iranian government informed Great Britain that it was willing to reopen negotiations with the AIOC within the framework of the nationalization law, but it attached conditions which the British would not accept. Counter proposals by Prime Minister Churchill and by President Truman were in turn rejected by Mossadegh, and in October Iran finally broke off diplomatic relations with the British. In February, 1953, new Anglo-American proposals were made to Iran, but they were rejected one month later by Mossadegh who, however, still left the door open for negotiations. Earlier in the year Mossadegh had informed the Soviet government that Iran, planning to nationalize the Iranian fisheries industry, would not extend the Soviet-Iranian fishery agreement which expired on January 31. Russia accepted the Iranian decision but reminded Iran of the latter's obligation not to grant a fishing concession to any other foreign power in the next twenty-five years.

In the first half of 1953 Mossadegh further increased his power. In January he demanded and received a one-year extension of his position as dictator. During February tension between the more moderate shah and his nationalistic premier increased to the point that the shah considered leaving the country, and for a time Iran was greatly disturbed by demonstrations— pro-shah or pro-Mossadegh. The premier sought to restrict the shah's authority, declaring that he should reign but not rule. By July, Mossadegh, through his National Front deputies, had managed to destroy the Chamber of Deputies' quorum and was thus able to rule about as he pleased. In August, a referendum held in the provinces resulted, it was announced, in an overwhelming demand for the dissolution of the Chamber.

But the Iranians had been promised that nationalization of the AIOC would bring them prosperity. Although in 1953 Iran sold some oil at 50 per cent discount to Japanese and Italian purchasers, the loss of the oil royalties had not only destroyed all gains expected from the Seven-Year Plan but had crippled the country's economy and contributed to a spiral of inflation. Even the United States showed its disapproval of Mossadegh's intransigence, when in July, 1953, President Eisenhower refused the premier's request for more economic aid on the ground that if Iran would settle with the British it could exploit its own rich resources and would not need outside help.

In August, after an abortive attempt of the shah to replace Mossadegh as premier by General Fazollah Zahedi, the monarch and his wife fled by airplane to Rome. Mossadegh at once sent troops to occupy the royal palaces and the parliament building and ordered the arrest of all opposition deputies and of about 100 others charged with complicity in the royal plot. But apparently the anti-Mossadegh, pro-shah sentiment was stronger than he expected. On August 19 the troops turned against their officers and the mobs shifted to the support of the shah. After pitched battles and mob violence, causing the death of hundreds and the burning of a number of buildings, the pro-shah forces gained control of Teheran and arrested Mossadegh. Three days later the shah returned to his capital, explaining that when the constitution was violated, the Chamber dissolved, the army disintegrated, and the treasury funds dissipated, then the law had to be carried out. It appeared that the hereditary ruler and the army sought to maintain the constitution whereas the prime minister, who began with a reputation as a democrat, had attempted to set up a personal dictatorship. In November the former premier was brought to trial on charges of defying the shah, attempting to overthrow the regime, and illegally dissolving the Chamber of Deputies. In the ensuing weeks the supreme court was re-established, the Senate was re-convened, the shah resumed the distribution of crown lands to the peasants, and in November Premier Zahedi announced that state lands also would be distributed to the peasants and workers.

Soon after his appointment the new premier had expressed the hope that the oil problem could be settled with due regard for the nationalization law and Iranian national aspirations, but pointed out that the fundamental reforms envisaged for Iran could not be carried through without oil revenues. Iran's failure to sell oil after it was nationalized, he estimated, had cost the government more than $100,000,000. He asserted, however, that no enmity existed between the Iranian and British governments, that Iran's dispute was only with the AIOC; the oil question was strictly economic. In December, 1953, diplomatic relations were resumed between the Iranian and British governments and it was announced that they would negotiate a settlement of the oil problem. When, in February, 1954, the Moslem leader in Iran criticized the government and appeared desirous of obstructing a settlement of the oil dispute, the government vigorously denounced him and declared "we will solve the oil problem in complete conformity with the spirit of the law and for the welfare of the Iranian people."

India and Pakistan

Under the Government of India Act, which became effective in 1937, Indians had reached the point where at the outbreak of the Second World War a limited electorate controlled the eleven provincial ministries and chose a majority of both houses of the Indian national parliament, but did not control the national government.[6] The act had failed to grant India dominion status, however, and was therefore unsatisfactory to the Congress Nationalists. Soon after the outbreak of the war, because they felt that Britain's assurances regarding India's future independence were too vague, the Congress Nationalists had instructed all Congress ministries to resign their offices and a policy of noncollaboration in the war effort was begun.

In 1942, after the Japanese had advanced nearly to the frontiers of India, Churchill sent Sir Stafford Cripps to that country to propose that at the conclusion of the war India should receive dominion status with the right of secession. Cripps nearly succeeded in bringing the Congress Nationalists and the Moslem League into agreement with Britain, but failed—many believed—because of Churchill's interference in the negotiations. Cripps' failure was succeeded by an outbreak of anti-British sentiment and violence which culminated in the government's arrest of all important Congress leaders. Not until 1945 were these political prisoners released. The Moslem League, which had not participated in the Congress Party's anti-British agitation, meanwhile inaugurated a campaign for the establishment of an independent Indian Moslem state, Pakistan. The situation in India which confronted the British Labor government when it came into power in 1945 was thus far from appealing.

Nevertheless, in September of that year Prime Minister Attlee announced that his government would act in accordance with the spirit and intention of the Cripps offer, and again in December the British government stated that it regarded as a matter of the greatest urgency the setting-up of an Indian constitution-making body, by which the Indians would decide their own future as an independent state. When only mutinies, strikes, and the defiance of authority ensued in India, a Cabinet mission was dispatched to that country, where it consulted with the leaders of the various important groups and ultimately convened a conference to discuss a possible constitution. But the Indian leaders were unable to agree upon the framework of their future government, so the Cabinet mission in May, 1946, put forward a plan of its own, by means of which a constitution could be drafted by the Indians for the Indians. An essential part of the new proposal was the im-

[6] See pages 429–431.

mediate establishment of an interim government to administer India while the new constitution was being drafted by a constituent assembly. With the exception of the viceroy, this new government was to consist of Indians, resting on the support of the popular parties as disclosed in the Indian elections of 1945.

Instead of proceeding at once to implement this plan for giving India dominion status, extremist Moslems and Hindus resorted to a bloody reign of terror against each other which brought the death of thousands of Indians. Jawaharlal Nehru and Mohammed Ali Jinnah, leaders of the Congress and Moslem groups respectively, were unable to agree upon an interim government, so that it was not until September, 1946, that such a government was created, and then it was selected by the Congress Party alone. Efforts of the viceroy, Lord Wavell, to persuade Jinnah to bring the Moslem League into the government failed, and ultimately the viceroy "virtually thrust the Moslem League into the cabinet." Friction between Moslems and Hindus continued, however, and the constituent assembly convened in December, 1946, without the Moslems, who feared that the Hindus would use their majority ruthlessly in the assembly. By February, 1947, it appeared that no compromise was possible and a new outbreak of violence was momentarily expected. On February 20, Prime Minister Attlee—apparently in the hope of breaking the impasse in India—announced that the British government intended to transfer power into responsible Indian hands and to withdraw from India not later than June, 1948. At the same time Lord Mountbatten was named to serve as Britain's "last viceroy" of India.

Attlee's startling announcement apparently forced some measure of cooperation upon the Moslem and Hindu leaders in India, for under Mountbatten's guidance the Congress Party, the Moslem League, and the Sikhs agreed upon a policy of partition. The British government thereupon announced that it intended to transfer power to Indian authorities on a dominion status on August 15, 1947. An Indian Independence Act, ratifying agreements thereafter rapidly reached between Mountbatten and Indian leaders, was passed by the British parliament in July to become effective on August 15. This act eliminated the word "Emperor" from the British king's title, removed British control from the whole of India, and provided for the partition of India into two dominions—the Union of India, in which Hindu majorities prevailed, and Pakistan, where Moslems constituted a majority. It returned paramountcy to the princely states of India and renounced all British treaties with their rulers. Pakistan was to include Baluchistan, Sind, the Northwest Frontier Province, West Punjab, and East Bengal. The provisional division of the last two provinces was made subject to revision by a boundary commission. The existing national legislature for all India was abolished, and the legislatures of India and Pakistan were to

THE FIRST PREMIER OF THE UNION OF INDIA

Jawaharlal Nehru

have all authority possessed by any dominion under the Statute of Westminster.[7] At the outset the constitution under which each dominion would function would be based on the Government of India Act of 1935,[8] but each would have authority to alter this act by legislative action. The two states had the option of seceding from the British Commonwealth after June, 1948. On August 15 the transfer of power occurred as planned, and six months later the last British troops left India.

In the Union of India, Lord Mountbatten served as governor-general until June, 1948, when he was succeeded by an Indian. Nehru became the first prime minister, and outlined a moderate socialist program of economic and industrial development, the abolition of the landlord system, the expansion of educational opportunities, and the enactment of a bill of rights. "Untouchability" for some 50,000,000 of the lowest social caste of Hindus was abolished, and all rights of citizenship in the dominion were granted them. New Delhi remained the capital of India and English was made the official language. India became a federal republic in which provincial governments and legislatures conduct local affairs. Nationally, there is a president but real executive power is in the hands of a cabinet responsible to the parliament which is elected by all aged 21 or over. In the UN the new dominion received the membership of the former empire.

In Pakistan, Jinnah, president of the Moslem League and author of the Pakistan plan, became the first governor-general and another Moslem the first premier. The port city of Karachi was designated as the temporary capital of Pakistan, and English was adopted as the official language of the government. But the plan of government envisioned by Jinnah for this dominion was non-Western, being based on Moslem religion and law as set forth in the Koran. Pakistan was at once admitted to membership in the United Nations and soon established diplomatic missions abroad. This dominion seemed to have one inherent weakness, however. It consisted of two separate blocks of territory, nearly a thousand miles apart, whose inhabitants were of different race and spoke different languages. Whether their common adherence to Islam would hold them together remained to be seen. The appointment of the premier of East Bengal to succeed Jinnah as governor-general, upon the latter's death in September, 1948, may have been designed to strengthen the ties between the two halves of Pakistan.

Most of India's hundreds of semi-independent princely states affiliated with either India or Pakistan in matters of defense, foreign affairs, and communications, with the princes continuing to govern locally. But not everywhere did events move smoothly. In Kashmir, where Moslems con-

[7] See page 291.
[8] See page 430.

stituted more than 75 per cent of the 40,000,000 inhabitants, a Moslem uprising, supported by invading tribesmen from Pakistan, proclaimed a provisional government which promised to hold a plebiscite on the question of joining India or Pakistan. The Hindu maharajah, Sir Hari Singh, however, acceded to India, and Sikh troops were flown from the latter to defend the Kashmir capital. When hostilities broke out India referred the matter to the UN Security Council which in the summer of 1948 sent a commission to investigate the situation. Although the commission persuaded both India and Pakistan to give a cease-fire order to their forces in Kashmir, the political question remained unresolved.

In the summer of 1952, however, an agreement was concluded between the Indian and Kashmir governments providing, among other things, that (1) Kashmir was to have a head of state elected by its constituent assembly instead of an hereditary maharajah, but his election was to be confirmed by the president of India; (2) Kashmir was to have a state flag but the Indian flag was to fly in Kashmir as the flag of the Union; (3) Kashmir was to be integrated financially into the Republic of India; and (4) Kashmir was to recognize the jurisdiction of the Indian supreme court. The Kashmir constitution was accordingly amended to provide for a head of state elected for a five-year term. The maharajah abdicated and his son was then elected head of state.

During 1953, however, a split developed among the leaders in the Kashmir government. The premier, Sheikh Abdullah, appeared to advocate more independence from India rather than closer integration; the deputy premier, after conferences with Nehru in Delhi, pronounced in favor of Kashmir's accession to India. In August the head of state suddenly dismissed Sheikh Abdullah as premier and appointed the deputy premier in his place. There was great agitation in Pakistan and the premier of that country immediately proposed a meeting with Nehru to discuss Kashmir. Shortly thereafter it was announced that the two premiers had agreed that a plebiscite administrator would be appointed for Kashmir by the end of April, 1954. But the new premier of Kashmir declared that Kashmir would feel safe only within the Indian Union, that Kashmir had no future in Pakistan, and that even a plebiscite would not be able to change the people's conviction. Kashmir appeared to be headed toward eventual assimilation into the Republic of India.

Hyderabad, another princely state with a population of some 16,000,000 and an area nearly as large as Great Britain's, was completely surrounded by the Union of India and from the geographical point of view should have acceded to that dominion. Although a large majority of Hyderabad's population was Hindu, the ruling prince was a Moslem. He apparently had no desire to join his state with Hindu India, while most of his subjects had no wish to be linked with Moslem Pakistan. The prince apparently sought to enter into friendly relations with India but to remain outside the Union with freedom to conduct his own foreign affairs. During the early months of 1948 negotiations were carried on between the Indian and Hyderabad governments, but to no avail. In June, Nehru declared that economically and geographically Hyderabad was an integral part of India which could not tolerate in its midst a unit which could not be assimilated. Three months later two Indian divisions began an invasion of Hyderabad which resulted in the prince's announcement (September 17) of his government's capitulation to India's demands.

As many observers had feared, the withdrawal of the British political and military forces from India was followed by the outbreak of violent conflicts between Hindus and Moslems. In each sector of the divided Punjab, for instance, the majority sought forcibly to expel the minority, and millions of persons were uprooted from their homes. Scores of thousands were reported killed in the mob violence which occurred. In an attempt to bring an end to the conflicts the aged Gandhi again embarked upon a fast which was broken on the sixth day when he received assurances from various communal leaders that peace would again prevail. But on January 30, 1948, Mahatma Gandhi was killed by a Hindu. Thus the great Indian leader, who more than any other person had dramatized for the world the struggle for Indian independence and who had always advocated the use of non-violent methods, died at the hands of an Indian assassin shortly after the attainment of Indian independence. Ultimately in 1950, however, an agreement was signed by the premiers of India and Pakistan guaranteeing the protection of religious minorities in both countries.

The Union of Burma

East of India, across the Bay of Bengal, lay before the Second World War the British dependency of Burma. This state, with an area three times the size of Great Britain and a population of some 15,000,000, had been separated from India and granted a degree of self-government by the Government of Burma Act in 1935. The political regime established at that time had failed to satisfy many of the Burmese, however, and when the Japanese invaded Burma in 1942 the local population in many places had actively aided them, lured on by the Japanese promise of "independence." Though Burmese enthusiasm for the Japanese soon evaporated during the period of occupation and though a Burmese patriot army of 10,000 men was eventually raised to aid the Allies in expelling the Japanese, extreme nationalists in the country at the close of the war were demanding independence. In June, 1945, the British governor of Burma assured the Burmese that one of his government's main objectives was to ensure that Burma attained full self-government as soon as possible. In December, 1946, Prime Minister Attlee declared that it was for the people of Burma to decide their own future and to draft their own constitution.

Thereafter political events moved rapidly. A constituent assembly was elected in Burma in April, 1947, and practically its first decision when it met in June was that Burma should be an independent sovereign republic to be known as the "Union of Burma." Three months later the constituent assembly unanimously adopted a new constitution drafted in accordance with this decision, and on October 17, 1947, a treaty was signed between Great Britain and Burma to regulate matters arising out of the transfer of power. Britain recognized the Union of Burma as a fully independent, sovereign state and agreed to remove all British troops from that country as soon as possible after the transfer of power. Burma, on her part, agreed that Great Britain should provide instructional and other staff for service with the Burmese military, naval, and air forces and agreed not to receive a defense mission from any state outside the British Commonwealth. She further agreed that British military aircraft should have the right to fly over and to use prescribed airfields in her territories. To assist Burma financially, Great Britain cancelled £15,000,000—about one third of Burma's debt to Britain—and Burma agreed to pay the balance without interest in twenty yearly installments. In December, 1947, the Burma Independence Bill was passed by the British parliament, and on January 4, 1948, Burma became an independent country. In the succeeding months the Union of Burma was admitted to membership in the United Nations and in the International Labor Office.

From the very beginning of its existence, however, the new republic was handicapped by revolts in various parts of the country. Communists denounced Burma's independence as a sham and sought to overthrow the government. The Karens, a racial minority of some 2,000,000 concentrated in a region northeast of Rangoon, demanded autonomy or independence. And the People's Volunteer Organization, consisting of former members of the anti-Japanese resistance forces who had not been rehabilitated, continued resistance tactics against the new Burmese government and tended to join the Communists. Finally, early in 1950, after the Communist successes in China, some 12,000 Chinese Nationalist troops took refuge in Burma where they plundered the countryside. By 1953 the government had largely reduced the native revolts to sporadic guerrilla activities, but the Chinese Nationalist forces were more difficult to defeat. In March, 1953, Burma brought their activities before the UN, which passed a resolution demanding their withdrawal. Subsequent negotiations among Burma, Formosa, and Thailand provided for their evacuation through Thailand. It was hoped, if the Chinese Nationalists withdrew, that the Burmese government would be able to re-establish peace.

The Dominion of Ceylon

Ceylon, an island in the Indian Ocean off the southern tip of India, with an area more than that of Belgium and Holland combined, and with a population of more than 5,000,000 at the time of the outbreak of the Second World War, had been taken from Holland by the British during the French and Napoleonic wars. From that time it had been ruled as a crown colony, and its exports of tea and rubber had contributed to British prosperity. In 1942 it was feared that the Japanese might seek to capture the island, and British empire forces were rushed to its defense. At the same time the British governor of Ceylon, seeking to rally the Ceylonese to the Allied cause, declared: "Ceylon has suddenly become a bastion ... of the sore-pressed citadel of freedom. It is not too much to say that the eyes of the world are upon us."

Perhaps the Ceylonese felt that if they were a bastion of freedom they should have more control of their own government. At any rate, when Sir Stafford Cripps was in India in 1942, the Ceylonese sought to send a deputation to discuss constitutional matters with him, but Cripps stated that the question of Ceylon's status was outside the province of his mission. A year later, however, the British colonial secretary declared his government's intention to examine the possibility of granting Ceylon full responsible government in matters of internal civil administration after the war. A royal commission subsequently recommended self-government for Ceylon with eventual full dominion status. On May 15, 1946, the British granted Ceylon a constitution providing for a bicameral parliamentary government with full powers to make laws except those discriminating against any community or religion. The British government's assent would be required, however, for bills relating to defense and external affairs, and the power to amend or revoke the constitution was retained by the British government.

Elections for the Ceylonese parliament were held on September 22, 1947; the first Ceylonese cabinet was sworn in four days later; and on February 4, 1948, Ceylon became a self-governing dominion in the British Commonwealth of Nations. Treaties between the Ceylonese and British governments provided for mutual military assistance for the security of their territories, for defense against external aggression, and for the protection of essential communications. Ceylon granted Britain the right to base such naval and air forces and to maintain such land forces in Ceylon as might be required for the above purposes. Obviously Ceylon's "dominion" status was not the same as that of Canada or Australia. But the developing nationalism in

Ceylon seemed to be indicated by an announcement in October, 1953, that thereafter at official functions the Union Jack would no longer be flown or the British national anthem played but only the Ceylon flag and the Ceylon national anthem.

The Federation of Malaya

In Malaya before the Second World War the British held a colony, the Straits Settlements (Singapore, Penang, Malacca), and had established a protectorate over four federated and five unfederated native states. During the war these states were all conquered and held by the Japanese. Shortly after the latter surrendered the British government announced its decision to form a Malayan Union of the nine federated and unfederated states and the two British settlements of Penang and Malacca. The fullest opportunities would be provided, it promised, to the peoples of Malaya to take a direct part in the civil administration, and facilities would be established to enable them to fit themselves for government posts. Singapore was to be established as a separate British colony. In January, 1946, Malcolm MacDonald, son of the first Labor prime minister, was appointed governor-general of the Malayan Union and Singapore, and Sir Edward Gent was appointed governor of the Malayan Union.

In March, 1946, however, a Pan-Malayan Congress resolved that the creation of a Malayan Union and Malayan citizenship would destroy nine sovereign states and was contrary to the principle of the sanctity of treaties. Moreover, it resolved, the new agreements made with the British government by the sultans of the native states were executed without the knowledge of their subjects, were contrary to democratic principles, and were null and void. At the request of the Pan-Malayan Congress the sultans did not attend the ceremony installing Governor Gent, nor did the Malay members attend the first meeting of the governor's advisory council. Later in the year the congress resolved that the transference of jurisdiction and sovereign rights from the states to the British crown was illegal, and at a conference of the sultans the latter decided to protest against the contemplated Malayan Union. They proposed instead a federation with a central body to decide matters of common interest to the nine constituent states but with each state having local autonomy. In May no sultans attended the ceremony of installing MacDonald as the first governor-general of the Malayan Union and Singapore.

During 1946 and 1947 negotiations were carried on by the British government with the sultans and the United Malays' National Organization, and ultimately an agreement was reached. The Federation of Malaya, a British protectorate, would be established to include the eleven states originally included in the proposed Malayan Union. The central government of the federation would consist of a high commissioner, a federal executive council, and a federal legislative council. The high commissioner would act as the representative of the British crown in matters of defense and foreign relations, and would advise the sultans in all matters of government except those relating to the Moslem religion and Malayan custom. The federal legislative council would consist of the high commissioner, 14 official members, and 34 unofficial members, selected to give the fullest representation to economic and social interests. Each of the constituent states would have a state executive council and a council of state with legislative powers. A British representative for each state would have the power of advice in state matters. The native rulers thus won some concessions from the British. On January 21, 1948, the nine rulers of the Malay states signed a treaty which established the Federation of Malaya, and on February first the new constitution was inaugurated and Sir Edward Gent was sworn in as the first high commissioner. The Federation had a population of 4,867,491, of which 2,130,493 were Malay and 1,880,452 were Chinese.

During the summer of 1948 Malaya was rocked by violent outbreaks which were ascribed to Communists, for there was an active Communist Party in Malaya, consisting chiefly of Chinese, and many organizations were said to have been subverted by it. On June 12, the federal government declared illegal the Pan-Malayan Federation of Trade Unions and ten other trade-union organizations. After many had been murdered and much property destroyed by guerrillas and terrorists, a state of emergency was declared throughout the federation and British aircraft and troops were sent in to restore order. Apparently the terrorists sought to paralyze the economic life of the federation, and their movement was aided by the widespread apathy or actual resentment of the Malayan Chinese, by the isolation of the plantations and mines, and by the almost limitless opportunities for ambush afforded by the jungle. In the succeeding five years, according to official figures, the terrorists suffered 8,363 casualties, the government forces 1,563, and civilians 4,095. The struggle was still going on in 1954, but it was believed the government was winning out. A Malayan army was being organized, full citizenship rights were offered to Chinese and Indians, settlements were being provided for Chinese squatters, greater self-government was being extended to rural communities, and programs for the social and economic betterment of the masses were being drafted.

Indonesia

Before 1939 the Netherlands East Indies, with an area of some 723,681 square miles and a population of 72,000,000, consisted of Java, Sumatra,

Borneo, Celebes, half of New Guinea, and many small islands. Even before the First World War a nationalist movement had developed in the islands and had been greatly influenced by the Congress Party of India. In the period between the wars, socialist and communist ideas had begun to influence the native workers, and labor disputes and strikes had resulted. By 1934 the Dutch had imprisoned all outstanding nationalist leaders, who did not secure their freedom until they were released by the Japanese when they conquered the Dutch Indonesian empire in 1942. During the period of Japanese occupation hatred for the white man was systematically and effectively cultivated by Japanese propagandists, and an intense nationalism was aroused. Perhaps to counteract the Japanese, Queen Wilhelmina in December, 1942, announced her intention, after the liberation of the Netherlands, to hold a joint consultation regarding the structure of the future Netherlands kingdom. She visualized, she said, a commonwealth in which all the Dutch colonies, together with the Netherlands, should participate, with freedom for each part to conduct its internal affairs.

Two days after the surrender of the Japanese forces in the Netherlands East Indies, Achmed Soekarno, a former political prisoner of the Dutch, who had collaborated with the Japanese occupation forces in Java because of their promise of independence for the Indonesians, proclaimed the Republic of Indonesia. The Netherlands government characterized this new state as a Japanese puppet government and refused to have any official relations with it. In Java extreme nationalists organized the Indonesian People's Army and, contrary to the desires of Soekarno's government, declared war on the Dutch. When the government at The Hague announced that it would not be forced into negotiations with the Indonesians, the Dutch governor-general of the Netherlands East Indies resigned. The progressive Lieutenant-Governor-General Hubertus van Mook thereupon announced that the Dutch realized that the old colonial system should go and that the Indonesians should have an ever-increasing share in the government. Fighting meanwhile continued between the Indonesian People's Army and British land, sea, and air forces, which had been assigned the task of reoccupying the islands.

In December, 1945, the Dutch lieutenant-governor-general returned to The Hague and in a broadcast explained that developments in Indonesia were "manifestations of an international spirit that will no longer tolerate subjugation by force of one people by another." Deeds were demanded, he declared, and a solution must not take too long. In February, 1946, the Netherlands government, under British pressure, published its proposal for the constitutional future of Indonesia, the main features of which were the establishment of the Commonwealth of Indonesia, in which the internal affairs would be managed independently by the Commonwealth's own institutions. The Commonwealth would be a partner in the kingdom, and the central institutions of the latter would consist of representatives of its constituent parts.

In September, 1946, a Netherlands commission arrived in Java to negotiate a settlement with the Republic of Indonesia; on October 1 a conference was opened; two weeks later a truce was agreed upon, based on the stabilization of existing military positions; and on November 15, 1946, the Dutch and Indonesian delegates initialed the so-called Linggadjati Agreement. The latter provided that (1) the Republic of Indonesia would include Java, Madura, and Sumatra; (2) by January 1, 1949, a United States of Indonesia, consisting of the Republic of Indonesia, Borneo, and the eastern part of the archipelago to be known as the Great East, would be formed on a federal basis, and its constitution would be drafted by a constituent assembly; (3) also, by January 1, 1949, a Netherlands Indonesian Union would be established, consisting of two parts—the Kingdom of the Netherlands and the United States of Indonesia—with the queen of the Netherlands at its head, to look after foreign relations, defense, and, so far as necessary, finance. This agreement marked a victory for the progressive section of Dutch opinion led by Lieutenant-Governor-General van Mook, but at The Hague it met a storm of opposition from the conservative and reactionary groups. Nevertheless, it was eventually signed in March, 1947, by the Netherlands and the Indonesian Republic.

It was one thing to reach an agreement, but it was quite another for the two parties to implement it when each distrusted the other. Negotiations were begun to set up an interim government to function until the establishment of the United States of Indonesia, but the discussions made little progress. On May 27, 1947, the Dutch commissioner-general presented five demands which amounted to a practical ultimatum, and the Indonesian government in reply suggested arbitration as provided by the Linggadjati Agreement. The Dutch refused to arbitrate. The Indonesian premier on his own initiative offered several concessions, but he was repudiated by his own party. The United States government then intervened and urged the Indonesian government to co-operate without delay in the formation of an interim government, and Great Britain urged the same. On July 8 and again on July 17 the new Indonesian premier accepted all the Dutch demands except one, and the British government suggested to the Dutch a compromise proposal on that one. But the Dutch adopted an increasingly menacing attitude, and on July 21 Dutch forces began military operations against the Republic of Indonesia to "end the intolerable situation" and to "guarantee" law and order.

On July 31, 1947, on the request of India, the UN Security Council began a consideration of the Indonesian situation, and on the next day the Council called on both parties to end hostilities and to settle their dispute by peaceful means. Both sides agreed to issue cease-fire orders. But a Security Council committee of observers reported that under the guise of mopping-up operations, the Dutch were continuing their advance and that therefore the cease-fire order had never been obeyed by either side. On August 25 an American proposal that the Security Council should tender its good offices to the Dutch and Indonesians for a peaceful settlement was adopted and accepted by both governments. A UN commission, consisting of the United States, Belgium, and Australia, was appointed, and in December it began discussions with the Dutch and Indonesians. The commission's proposals were accepted by the Indonesians, but the Dutch rejected them.

In January, 1948, the Dutch premier came to Batavia and announced that immediate steps would be taken to form an interim government, adding that "Holland reserves the right to resume her freedom of action if satisfactory results are not soon achieved." In the face of this ultimatum another agreement was reached on January 17, 1948. Five months later, however, the UN commission reported to the Security Council that the Dutch and Indonesians still remained divided by the same issues as formerly: (1) the ways and means by which the United States of Indonesia should come into being; (2) the place of the Republic of Indonesia in the federation; and (3) the allocation of powers between the federation and the Netherlands Indies Union. Negotiations between the Dutch and Republican delegations under the auspices of the UN commission broke down in June, 1948.

By December, 1948, the Dutch had created a number of states out of territory of the Republic of Indonesia, and to many it appeared that they were seeking to reduce the Indonesian Republic, which originally included 80 per cent of Indonesia's population, to the status of a relatively small and weak unit in a future federation. By military force and political action they had reduced the republic's territory to a fraction of its original size, and they continued to surround it with a naval blockade which, according to the UN commission's report in July, 1948, had prevented the economic rehabilitation of Indonesia.

The Dutch apparently believed that the UN Security Council was so divided that they could safely ignore its resolutions and its commission. Although the Soviet Union was strongly pro-republican and Australia, Syria, and Colombia were inclined to favor the republic, the colonial powers—Britain, France, and Belgium—seemed loath to support strong measures against another colonial power. The United States and China sought to maintain an intermediate position and strove to achieve some compromise. But the policy of the United States appeared at times to be vacillating, probably because that country was involved in the "cold war" with Russia and was committed to the economic recovery of western Europe and the creation of the North Atlantic alliance. Indirectly, the United States strengthened the Dutch in their struggle with the Indonesian Republic by granting $422,000,000 to the Netherlands and $84,000,000 to the Dutch-controlled area in Indonesia under the Marshall Plan.

On December 3, 1948, the UN commission reported that its efforts to bring about negotiations between the Dutch and the republic had been fruitless, that no political negotiations under its auspices had occurred in the preceding five months. Two days later the Dutch mission left Batavia for home. Two weeks later, in violation of the truce agreement of January, 1948 (the so-called Renville agreement), and after dispatching to the Republic of Indonesia an ultimatum with a time-limit so short that it could not be met, the Dutch launched a surprise air-borne invasion of the republic and captured President Soekarno and other high republican political and military leaders. The Dutch premier explained that republican truce violations had made any peaceful settlement impossible. Once again, as in July, 1947, "police action" was undertaken by the Dutch to "end an intolerable situation."

In 1949 the United States government gave its support to the Indonesians more whole-heartedly than it had done in 1947. When the Security Council reconvened in January of that year the United States representative condemned the Netherlands, and proposed the re-establishment of the republican government at Jogjakarta; the progressive withdrawal of Dutch troops to the Renville truce lines and later from all of Java, Sumatra, and Madura; the creation of a new UN commission; general elections in Indonesia by October, 1949; complete sovereignty for the United States of Indonesia by April, 1950. Meanwhile, a strong popular reaction against the attitude of the Dutch had made itself felt in most countries. In the Asiatic world this sentiment was crystallized when, on the invitation of Prime Minister Nehru of India, representatives of nineteen African, Asiatic, and Far Eastern states [9] convened at New Delhi to consider the Indonesian problem. By a unanimous vote these states, which represented approximately half of the world's population and a third of the members of the United Nations, on January 23, 1949, adopted a resolution similar to the January proposals of the United States but more drastic in that it called for a somewhat faster schedule to be followed.

Soon after the adjournment of the New Delhi conference the Security Council adopted a resolution calling for (1) the immediate release of the Indonesian political prisoners; (2) the immediate return of Jogjakarta and

[9] The states which sent representatives were Afghanistan, Australia, Burma, Ceylon, Egypt, Ethiopia, India, Iran, Iraq, Lebanon, Pakistan, the Philippines, Saudi Arabia, Syria, and Yemen. China, Nepal, New Zealand, and Siam sent observers.

its environs to the Indonesian Republic; (3) a three-power UN commission to supervise elections and recommend areas from which the Dutch should withdraw; (4) the formation of a federal interim government by March 15, 1949; (5) elections in October, 1949; and (6) the establishment of the United States of Indonesia by July, 1950.

The pressure of international opinion as exemplified by these resolutions, the desire of the other members of Benelux and NATO to have the Netherlands help increase the economic and military strength of Western Europe, plus the tremendous financial burden of maintaining an army of more than 100,000 men in Indonesia all combined to bring a change in Dutch policy. The imperialistic minister for overseas territories was forced to resign from the Netherlands government, which announced that it would convene a round-table conference with the Indonesians to consider the whole problem.

Under the mediation of a UN commission a compromise settlement was reached providing for the return of the Indonesian republican government to Jogjakarta, the discontinuance of military operations, and the release of all political prisoners arrested in the republic since December 17, 1948. President Soekarno and other members of the Indonesian government returned to Jogjakarta on July 6, 1949, and the cessation of hostilities occurred on August 1. Three weeks later the round-table conference opened at The Hague, with the UN commission in attendance. On November 2, 1949, the final act of the conference was signed. The solutions agreed upon were based on those originally reached in the Linggadjati and Renville agreements, but with one major difference—the new agreements provided for the immediate transfer of sovereignty.

The real, complete, and unconditional transfer of sovereignty to the Republic of the United States of Indonesia, consisting of sixteen states including the former Republic of Indonesia, took place in a formal ceremony at The Hague on December 27, 1949. The new state included all the former Netherlands East Indies except Dutch New Guinea, whose final status was left to be decided by future Netherlands-Indonesian negotiations. A Netherlands-Indonesian Union, under the Netherlands ruler, was created for the voluntary co-operation of the two states in fields of mutual interest, particularly foreign affairs and defense. The Union Statute stipulated that a permanent secretariat would be established and that conferences of ministers would be held at least twice a year. All decisions, however, would require unanimity and would have to be approved by the respective parliaments before becoming effective. For all practical purposes the Netherlands and the United States of Indonesia became two separate states with a common sovereign.

Achmed Soekarno was elected president of the new federal republic and Mohammed Hatta became its first premier. Almost at once, however, numerous revolts occurred in some of the constituent states, and in order to strengthen the new regime national leaders in August, 1950, adopted a new provisional constitution. This abolished the federal system of government and created a centralized unitary state for all Indonesia, with ten provinces instead of sixteen states. At the same time the name of the state was changed to the Republic of Indonesia. In September, 1950, the republic was admitted to membership in the United Nations. During 1951 most military remnants of the war for independence disappeared; the Dutch completed the withdrawal of their troops, and the UN commission which had been mediating between the Netherlands and Indonesia was discharged.

But Indonesian nationalism continued to have its effect on Indonesian affairs. In 1951 a premier was defeated because he was considered too moderate in his dealings with the Dutch in regard to New Guinea. He was succeeded by a Moslem leader who called for the nationalization of major industries and the Java Bank, all Dutch owned, and for agrarian reform so that Indonesians might take over land held by foreigners. But this premier was in turn rejected in 1952 because he accepted Mutual Security aid from the United States, which certain nationalist groups feared would compromise Indonesia's ability to pursue an independent foreign policy. And Ali Sastroamijojo, who became premier in July, 1953, declared that the most urgent question of foreign policy was revision of relations with the Netherlands. The status between the two countries must be changed to one of normal international relationship, he asserted, and agreements resulting from the 1949 round-table conference which were damaging to Indonesia would be revised or annulled.

Indo-China

In 1939 French Indo-China consisted of Laos, Cambodia, Tonkin, Annam, and Cochin-China. The first four were protectorates; Cochin-China was a colony. The population of Indo-China totaled about 23,000,000, of which the Annamites constituted about 72 per cent, although they inhabited only about 10 per cent of the area, chiefly the plain and coastal regions of Annam, Tonkin, and Cochin-China. As in the Netherlands East Indies, nationalism had gained a foothold in Indo-China even before the First World War. During the Second World War the Japanese occupied Indo-China, but they left the pro-Axis Vichy government in nominal control until March, 1945. At that time they interned the French and recognized an autonomous state of Viet Nam (the ancient name for Annam), consisting of Annam, Tonkin, and Cochin-China, with Bao-dai, the former emperor of Annam, as ruler.

Meanwhile, in 1942 the underground Annamite Communists had organized the Viet Minh, or League for Viet Nam's Independence, headed by Ho Chi Minh, a Russian-trained Communist. Following the collapse of Japan, the Viet Minh Party proclaimed Viet Nam to be a democratic republic and Emperor Bao-dai abdicated. In March, 1945, De Gaulle's government had approved a new statute for Indo-China, providing that it would become a federation of Indo-Chinese states with local autonomy within the French Union, and at the close of the war the French were prepared to put these plans into effect. In October, 1945, the French and Vietnamese leaders agreed to cease fighting in order that negotiations might be carried on, but the latter were determined that Indo-China should have not autonomy but independence within the French Union. Negotiations broke down, fighting was resumed, and French reinforcements poured into Indo-China.

But the unexpected strength of the Vietnamese forces led the French in March, 1946, to recognize the Republic of Viet Nam as a "free state" having its own government, parliament, army, and finances, but forming part of the Indo-Chinese Federation and French Union. As in the case of the Republic of Indonesia, however, when it came to implement this agreement, difficulties arose and negotiations broke down. Fighting became widespread in the north and the French poured in more reinforcements until some 150,000 troops were stationed in the country. During the ensuing years hostilities between the French and the Viet Minh forces continued without a decision.

Meanwhile, the French sought to organize a nationalist movement under former Emperor Bao-dai to counteract the Vietnamese movement led by Ho Chi Minh, and eventually an agreement was reached between the French and Bao-dai. Viet Nam was to be independent in internal matters, maintain a national army, and have limited diplomatic representation of its own, but was to remain within the French Union and permit France to have troops within its territory. In Cambodia and Laos, the two non-Annamite countries of Indo-China, the anti-French nationalist movement was not so strong. Both accepted autonomy within the French Union, with French officials serving as advisers and with French high commissioners possessing authority over affairs concerning French nationals.

It soon became apparent that Bao-dai, who in 1949 declared himself chief of state of Viet Nam and whose government was soon recognized by the United States and Great Britain, was failing to unite the Vietnamese under his leadership. The greater part of the nationalists remained either allied to Viet Minh or held aloof from the struggle. In an effort to impress the nationalists and to increase the prestige of the French-sponsored governments in Viet Nam, Laos, and Cambodia, the United States invited them to participate as independent nations in the signing of the Japanese peace treaty in San Francisco in September, 1951. Nevertheless, the attempt to organize all the progressive anti-Communist Vietnamese into an alliance with the French and Americans to repel the forces of Viet Minh proved unsuccessful, despite minor concessions made to the Viet Nam government by France from time to time. The fact that the former was not truly independent was strikingly emphasized in May, 1953, when the French without prior consultation with Bao-dai's government devalued the Vietnamese currency in terms of French francs.

In 1953 the pressures on the French government to grant full independence to the Indo-Chinese greatly increased. The premier of Viet Nam demanded that the treaty of 1949 be scrapped and that Viet Nam be given greater independence. The Cambodian government demanded independence as the price of Cambodian resistance to Viet Minh, and in June the king of that country went into voluntary exile in protest against French delay in granting independence. The United States apparently held the view that French colonialism was handicapping the fight against Communism and urged concessions to the nationalists. Finally, within France a powerful sentiment seemed to favor reducing the republic's commitments in Indo-China or withdrawing altogether. In July, therefore, France offered to begin round-table negotiations to increase the independence of Viet Nam, Cambodia, and Laos.

In August France and Cambodia signed an agreement for the transfer to the latter of the police and judicial powers formerly exercised by France. In October the two governments signed another agreement on the division of military authority within Cambodia, and in the next month the French high command handed over to the king of Cambodia military responsibility for those parts of his country formerly under French military control. In October, also, the king of Laos and the French president signed a treaty of friendship and association, by the terms of which Laos achieved "full independence" and affirmed her membership in the French Union.

In Viet Nam, however, probably because of Bao-dai's realization of the need of French military assistance against the forces of Ho Chi Minh, progress toward "complete independence" was somewhat slower. Conversations between Emperor Bao-dai and the French government in August, 1953, did result in the latter's pledge to grant Viet Nam full independence and in Bao-dai's pledge of Viet Nam's free association in the French Union. But pledges alone did not satisfy the Viet-Namese nationalists who in a congress in October resolved that the relations between Viet Nam and France should be based upon a treaty of alliance to be ratified by the Viet-Namese national assembly. In December the Viet-Namese premier resigned, complaining that he had prepared a list of powers which should be transferred to Viet Nam but that Bao-dai had neither allowed him to do anything with it nor permitted him to send a delegation to France to negotiate a new treaty. Bao-dai appointed his cousin to the premiership, and the latter then announced that the first task of his government would be to negotiate with France "for the total independence of Viet Nam," which should, however, continue to accept French help within the framework of an association based on equality.

But progress toward the military defeat of Ho Chi Minh's forces was even slower than that toward complete independence for Viet Nam. At the opening of the year 1954 the French-supported government of Bao-dai had effective control over only a small part of the country; Communists controlled from 75 to 85 per cent of the area. Despite more than seven years of bitter and sanguinary battles, despite French annual expenditures of close to one billion dollars to carry on the struggle, despite greatly increased military aid from the United States, despite France's weakening of her army in Europe and her appalling loss of officers, the French seemed in a worse position than ever. And the factor that particularly militated against French success was Viet-Namese nationalism. Ho Chi Minh's soldiers, apparently, were far less influenced by the fact that their leader was a Communist than by the feeling that they and he were fighting for home and country against foreign imperialist troops. In October, 1953, the foreign ministers of Great Britain, France, and the United States agreed, however, that the successful conclusion of the Indo-Chinese war was necessary for the re-establishment of peace in Asia.

The Chinese People's Republic

Although in 1943 Great Britain, the United States, the Netherlands, and Norway surrendered their extraterritorial rights in China, Chinese nationalism continued to be handicapped by a serious division among the Chinese people. The conflict between the Kuomintang, or Chinese Nationalist Party, and the Chinese Communists, as it had existed in 1929–1936, has been discussed.[10] For a time, beginning in 1937, the two groups had co-operated to present a common front against the Japanese, but during the Second World War Chiang Kai-shek's hostility to the Chinese Communists frequently led him to use a large portion of his forces against them rather than against the Japanese. When the war ended in the Far East the relationship between the Chinese Nationalists and Communists was one of "passive belligerency."

At the time of Japan's surrender, the Nationalist armies were largely concentrated in southwest China, and the Communist forces, being situated

[10] See pages 439–441, 473.

in the north and northeast, were able to take over Japanese equipment and to extend their positions before the Nationalist forces arrived. Furthermore, in 1945 the Chinese Communists moved into Manchuria to meet the advancing Russian armies and were consequently in a position to take over that region when the Soviet armies withdrew.[11] They were not inclined to give up their favorable positions to the "reactionary" Nationalists without a struggle, and open hostilities between the Chinese Communists and Nationalists resulted.

The United States recognized the Chiang Kai-shek government as the legitimate government of China, but it was eager for the cessation of hostilities there, and hoped that a conference between Nationalist and Communist leaders might work out a solution which would bring about national unification. To aid in the Chinese negotiations, President Truman, in December, 1945, sent General George C. Marshall, former army chief of staff, to China as his special envoy. Marshall succeeded in obtaining a truce between the hostile Chinese groups and the convening of an all-party consultation conference in Chungking. This conference rewrote and liberalized a draft constitution, originally drawn up in 1936, but never adopted, and agreed that a National Assembly should meet to consider it.

Although both the Nationalists and the Communists issued a cease-fire order in January, 1946, neither side apparently observed it. The efforts of the Nationalists to reoccupy Manchuria were handicapped by Communist control of the Peiping-Mukden railway and by Russia's refusal to allow Nationalist troops to land at Dairen or Port Arthur. Tens of thousands of Chiang Kai-shek's forces were ultimately flown in by United States transport planes, however, and after a vigorous campaign the Nationalists succeeded in occupying most of southern Manchuria. In June the Generalissimo announced a fifteen-day truce to permit negotiations for a settlement, with Marshall as arbiter, but the Communists rejected this proposal and accused the United States of interfering in China's internal affairs.

In July, 1946, Chiang Kai-shek's government, without consulting the Communist Party, announced that the National Assembly would convene in Nanking in November. Since the Communists did not attend the meeting, the Assembly was dominated by the Nationalists. The Right wing of the Nationalist Party sought to introduce some reactionary changes in the draft accepted earlier in the year by the all-party conference, but Chiang Kai-shek insisted upon the adoption of the agreed-upon draft, which was finally passed unanimously. On December 31, 1946, the Generalissimo promulgated the Republican Constitution of China, the eleventh to have been promulgated since the overthrow of the empire in 1912, to become effective one year later. In November, 1947, a general election was held to

11 For the Sino-Soviet treaty regarding Manchuria and Outer Mongolia, see page 648.

choose the first National Assembly under the new constitution, but Manchuria and North China except for Peiping and Tientsin did not take part because they were under Communist control.

The sessions of the Chinese National Assembly, the great majority of whose members were appointees of Nationalist Party organizations, were devoted chiefly to ratifying the constitution and to electing a new President and Vice President of the Chinese Republic. Attempts by the Assembly to exercise legislative power, to amend the constitution, and to impeach some high officials proved futile. The constitution was ratified unchanged, and Chiang Kai-shek, after announcing he was not a candidate, was elected President by an overwhelming vote. The only successful revolt on the part of the members came in the election of the Vice President when General Li Tsung-jen was finally chosen despite opposition of Chiang Kai-shek and the old guard Nationalists, who favored Sun Fo, the son of Sun Yat-sen. How far the son had departed from his father's democratic ideas seemed indicated by the former's demand, after his defeat, that the Nationalist Party should adopt the Soviet system of discipline and organization to restore the dominance of the party machine.

Meanwhile, the years 1947–1948 had seen disaster after disaster overtake the Nationalist army at the hands of the Communists. Manchuria was largely lost, and Communist forces occupied large areas in Hopei, Shantung, Shansi, Shensi, and Honan provinces. In the early months of 1948 some 110,000 Nationalist troops were captured or destroyed, and immense quantities of arms and munitions were thus secured by the Communists. Much, if not most, of the equipment used by the Chinese Communists consisted, it was said, of supplies captured from the Nationalists, whose armies seemed riddled with corruption, inefficiency, and nepotism. According to William C. Bullitt, a strong advocate of American military assistance to China, half the Nationalist generals and a third of the other officers were incompetent or corrupt or both.

General Marshall, at the time he was recalled as President Truman's special envoy to China in January, 1947, in order to become American secretary of state, declared that the chief obstacle to peace in China was "the complete and almost overwhelming suspicion with which the Chinese Communist Party and the Kuomintang regard each other." Although he believed that Chiang Kai-shek's government was in effect the National Party, which in turn was dominated by a group of military and political reactionaries who opposed the formation of a real coalition, yet the exigencies of the "cold war" with Russia led him as secretary of state to approve further American aid to the Generalissimo. There was among many groups in the United States a feeling that a non-Communist China was as essential for the welfare of the democratic countries as a non-Communist Greece and

Turkey. General Claire Chennault, commander of the China Air Task Force during the war, for instance, told the American Congress that China was the "key to peace" or to victory if war came. In response to this sentiment, President Truman in 1948 added to the European Recovery Program aid for China, and the Congress approved an appropriation of $420,000,000 to stop the deterioration of the Chinese economy.

Nevertheless, during the second half of that year and the first two months of 1949 the situation steadily deteriorated in so far as the Nationalist government at Nanking was concerned. By the end of October, 1948, Mukden had been captured by the Communist armies, and with it not only large stocks of arms but the general control of Manchuria. Three months later the Communists had also captured Tientsin, Peiping, and Suchow, and had advanced to the Yangtse River in many places. Meanwhile, in November, 1948, the Nanking government had been reorganized with Sun Fo becoming prime minister; the Chinese National Assembly had urgently appealed to the United States for aid; and Mme. Chiang Kai-shek had flown to Washington to place the situation before President Truman personally. But the Chinese Nationalist appeals proved fruitless. Apparently the United States government had decided to disengage itself from the policy of supporting Chiang Kai-shek, a policy which had been ineffective in stemming the tide of the Communist military advance, and had excited an Americanophobia among millions of Chinese. Apparently, too, it had come to feel that should the Soviet government seek to intervene in China, the Chinese nationalism which had become so anti-American would then be turned against the Soviet Union. In January, 1949, the United States terminated its program of military training of the Chinese Nationalist armies, and in February the United States Navy began the withdrawal of American marines from the Chinese mainland.

During the early weeks of 1949 political developments within China moved swiftly for a time. On January 14, General Mao Tse-tung, the Communist leader, broadcast his peace terms which among other things included the punishment of Generalissimo Chiang Kai-shek and prominent Nationalists as war criminals. One week later Chiang, who for more than two decades had headed the Nationalists, announced his retirement as president in "the hope that hostilities may be brought to an end and the people's sufferings be relieved." Following the Generalissimo's withdrawal to southern China, Vice President Li Tsung-jen became Acting President of the republic. Li sought to treat with Mao Tse-tung and eventually in April did succeed in opening negotiations with the Communists in Peking (the name restored to the city by the Communists), but to no avail.

Before the month was out Mao Tse-tung's forces again began to advance. On April 23 Nationalist troops and officials evacuated Nanking, which was at once occupied by the Communists. By the close of May the latter had also captured the important cities of Hankow and Shanghai. On September 30, 1949, while their troops were fighting their way toward Canton, the Chinese Communists proclaimed the Chinese People's Republic, with its capital at Peking and with Mao Tse-tung, chairman of the central committee of the Chinese Communist Party, holding a position equivalent to that of president in other republics. In October Canton fell to the Red armies, and by the end of 1949 effective Nationalist resistance on the Chinese mainland had ceased. Early in 1950 Hainan Island and the Chusan Islands were also captured by the Communists, whose government by the close of January, 1950, had received the recognition of India, Pakistan, Burma, and Israel in Asia and of the Soviet Union, Great Britain, Norway, Denmark, Sweden, and Finland in Europe. Finally, in May, 1951, by an agreement for the "peaceful liberation of Tibet" that vast region was also brought under effective Chinese Communist control.

In outward form the structure of the Peking government continued to conform with the coalition idea used by Mao Tse-tung during his earlier years. There continued to be a "united front" government which was called an alliance of "workers, peasants, petty bourgeoisie, and national bourgeoisie." In fact, however, the Chinese Communists soon established in China a thorough-going Communist totalitarianism, complete with political centralization, sweeping censorship, propaganda and indoctrination, ubiquitous security police, innumerable arrests and executions, confiscation and redistribution of land, tentative attempts at collectivization, a gradual destruction of private enterprise, and a five-year plan of industrialization. In January, 1954, however, the central committee of the Communist Party cautioned against too precipitate haste in the transition toward socialism. In agriculture the goal set for 1957 was set at 800,000 co-operatives to include some 20 per cent of the peasant households, but the immediate task for 1954 was much more modest—to increase co-operatives from the existing 14,000 to 35,000.

Meanwhile, evidence indicated that a working unity existed between the Chinese People's Republic and the Soviet Union. In 1949 the latter made vigorous but futile efforts to have the Peking government recognized by the United Nations as the legitimate government of China. In 1950 the two states signed a treaty of alliance in which it was agreed that they would act in concert in defense of China against Japan or against any power associated with Japan, a phrase which was thought to mean the United States. Both states guaranteed the independence of the Mongolian People's Republic, and they simultaneously recognized the Communist Viet Minh regime in Indo-China. Obviously the two Communist states co-operated in the Korean War, with the Soviet government supplying aircraft and other

RED CHINA'S DICTATOR
General Mao Tse-tung

weapons for the Chinese fighting forces. They co-operated, too, in plans for the rehabilitation of North Korea after the war. Finally, early in 1954, Soviet Foreign Minister Molotov persuaded the Western great powers to include representatives of Communist China in the five-power conference which was to meet in Geneva later in the year to discuss the whole Far Eastern question.

Also, in 1950, notes were exchanged between the Russian and the Chinese Communist governments recognizing that the Sino-Soviet treaty and other agreements of August, 1945,[12] were no longer valid. It was now agreed that after the signing of a peace treaty with Japan, and in any case not later than 1952, Russia would transfer to China all her rights in the administration of the Chinese Changchun Railway and that Soviet troops would be withdrawn from Port Arthur. Russia further agreed to hand over to the Chinese without compensation property acquired from the Japanese in Manchuria, and extended to the Chinese government a $300,000,000 credit at one per cent interest. In accordance with the agreements of 1950 the Chinese Changchun Railway was transferred to China in 1952 but, because "conditions dangerous for peace and favorable for the reiteration of Japanese aggression" had arisen, China agreed to permit Soviet troops to remain in Port Arthur until peace treaties with Japan had been concluded.

In various parts of China Sino-Soviet companies were established and Soviet technicians and advisers—estimated at 80,000—played an increasing role in the management of China's enterprises. To assist China in her five-year plan, inaugurated in 1952, Russia agreed to increase her shipments of capital goods. In September, 1953, Mao Tse-tung, expressed to Premier Malenkov China's gratitude for the Soviet government's agreement to extend economic and technical aid in the construction and renovation of many of the country's enterprises. Later in the year a Russian delegation joined in celebrations to mark the completion of steel mills and a new blast furnace which, it was claimed, would enable China to build her own ships, railways, and bridges. Meanwhile, on the death of Stalin in 1953 Mao Tse-tung had sent a telegram to Moscow declaring that the Chinese People's Republic would stand by the Soviet Union "definitely, forever, and with maximum resoluteness."

The Chinese Nationalists on Formosa

Late in 1949, after the Chinese Communists had captured the various cities on the mainland to which the Nationalists had successively moved their government, the latter finally withdrew to Formosa where Taipei was chosen as the capital of Nationalist China. Because the Chinese Reds then

[12] See page 648.

lacked effective air and sea power, it was believed that on Formosa—one hundred miles from the mainland—the Nationalists might maintain themselves. Early in 1950 Chiang Kai-shek again took over the political helm of Nationalist China, displacing Acting President Li despite the latter's objections. He also resumed control of the Nationalist military forces, consisting of some 600,000 men—defeated, disorganized, unpaid, and largely unequipped.

Formosa, with an area about one third that of Ohio, had been under Japanese rule from 1895 until 1945. But in the latter year, in accordance with the Cairo Declaration, the island had been transferred to China and a Nationalist general had been appointed governor. The population of Formosa was estimated as approximately 6,000,000 in 1949, and during that year it was increased by the influx of a million civilians from the mainland and the Nationalist army. Pressure of population on resources seemed inevitable. To lessen this pressure the government sought by agrarian reform measures to increase incentive and agricultural production. Land rentals were drastically reduced, land formerly owned by Japanese corporations was sold to tenants, and eventually holdings of absentee owners were purchased for sale to tenants. American ECA funds, moreover, were made available for the importation of fertilizer. Beginning in 1951 Formosa once more had rice to export.

Meanwhile, the Chinese Nationalist government remained practically as it was in 1948, with the terms of the legislative body being extended from year to year. Chiang continued as president and relatively few cabinet changes were made. The political future of Formosa, however, soon became a matter for heated debate. The United States government at first held the view that the issue should be settled by the Chinese themselves. In January, 1950, accordingly, President Truman announced that the United States would not give military assistance or advice to the Chinese Nationalists on Formosa. But this decision was extremely unpopular with many Americans, and it was ultimately changed after the outbreak of the Korean War, which is discussed in the next chapter.

Chapter XXVIII

COLLECTIVE SECURITY ON TRIAL

FIVE years after the conclusion of the Second World War collective security was once more challenged, this time by a military attack on a state established under the protection of the United Nations from an area outside that organization. Again, as in 1931, the challenge came in the Far East, but the subsequent course of events indicated that in 1950 some of the great powers, at least, were determined that such challenges should no longer be met by a policy of inactivity and appeasement. The succeeding years witnessed not only a resort to arms by the United Nations to throw back the forces of aggression but far-reaching and systematic efforts to strengthen and integrate the military and economic resources of the free world.

The Korean War

It has already been pointed out how, because of Soviet Russia's policy of obstruction in the United Nations and in Korea, the latter was not permitted to become a single unified state.[1] As a consequence, there were established in the peninsula the Republic of Korea, a democratic state which controlled the territory south of the 38th parallel and had its capital at Seoul, and the Korean People's Republic, a Communist state which controlled the area north of that parallel and had its capital at Pyongyang. The former was recognized by most of the states in the United Nations as the legitimate government of Korea and had the support of the United States; the latter enjoyed the recognition and support of the Soviet Union and its satellites. The governments of both republics claimed jurisdiction over all of Korea, and a state of undeclared war, with occasional minor clashes, prevailed along the 38th parallel. Although until the close of 1948 Russian forces had occupied the northern territory and the United States forces the southern, in 1949 the forces of both states were withdrawn, leaving the two republics to defend themselves with their own armed forces. It was generally recognized, however, that Russia had built up in the Korean People's Republic a far stronger and better equipped force than that possessed by the Republic of Korea.

Perhaps it was inevitable that sooner or later one of the Korean states

[1] See pages 649–650.

should seek to unify the peninsula under its own government. Several factors may have played a part in influencing the North Koreans to make the first attempt. They may have realized that, after the withdrawal of United States troops, the outnumbered and lightly armed South Koreans would be unable to withstand the Communist armies from the north. Statements of responsible persons in the United States that South Korea could not be successfully defended against an attack from the north and that Korea was not essential to the security of the American defense line in the Pacific may, also, have convinced them that the United States would not undertake a campaign to free South Korea if the Communists once conquered it in a swift campaign. Finally, the North Koreans may have been encouraged to make the attack by the Soviet Union. The latter may have hoped thus to extend Communist influence throughout Korea or, if prevented from doing this by the intervention of the democratic powers, to weaken the latter so much economically and involve their forces so deeply militarily in Korea that they would be seriously handicapped in their efforts to create a strong army under the North Atlantic pact.[2]

Whatever the motives behind the move, on June 25, 1950, North Korean troops in overwhelming force and strongly supported by Russian-made aircraft and tanks crossed the 38th parallel and pushed on toward Seoul. Once more collective security was challenged and the question was whether the states of the United Nations would remain inactive as those of the League of Nations had when Japan sought swiftly to occupy Manchuria in 1931. By many it had long been felt that the immediate train of events which led to the Second World War had started with the failure of the United States and the League of Nations to take up Japan's challenge at that time. In 1950 much depended upon the attitude of the United States.

President Truman at once decided that "the United States must do everything within its power, working as closely as possible with the United Nations, to stop and throw back this aggression," and at once took steps to bring the situation quickly before the UN Security Council. On the very afternoon that the war began in Korea the Council adopted a resolution declaring that North Korea had committed a breach of peace and calling for the immediate cessation of hostilities and the withdrawal of the North Korean forces to the 38th parallel. It further requested all UN members to give every assistance to the UN "in the execution of this resolution and to refrain from giving assistance to the North Korean authorities." [3]

The United States government believed that the attack on South Korea

---

[2] See page 823.

[3] At that time the Soviet government was boycotting the UN because of the latter's failure to recognize the People's Republic of China, so no Soviet delegate was present.

resembled the pattern of aggression which had led up to the Second World War. The possibility of active Russian or Chinese intervention to support the North Koreans was not ignored, but it was felt that the risks involved in stopping the aggression were less than the dangers involved in failure of the United States and the United Nations to take action. On June 26, therefore, the United States government decided that its navy and air force should be ordered to provide the fullest possible cover and support to the Republic of Korea (ROK) forces south of the 38th parallel. At the same time, in order to remove any temptation for the Chinese Communists to enter the war—and perhaps to placate Chiang Kai-shek's supporters in the United States—it was decided to order the United States Seventh Fleet to prevent any attack on Formosa and to call upon Chiang to cease any military action against the Chinese Communists. The American fleet was ordered to "neutralize" Formosa. On June 27 the UN Security Council adopted a resolution calling on the states members of the UN to give all necessary assistance to the South Korean Republic.

Meanwhile, the ROK forces had been driven back and were trying to form a line at the Han River just south of Seoul. On June 29 General Mac-Arthur, the Allied supreme commander in the Far East, reported that the South Koreans had already suffered casualties of nearly 50 per cent, and the United States joint chiefs of staff decided that stronger measures were needed, not only to help the ROK forces but to ensure evacuation of American nationals. United States ships and planes were thereupon authorized to strike military targets in North Korea, and the use of army service troops in South Korea and of certain combat units to protect a port and an airfield in the general area of Pusan was also authorized. These decisions were facilitated by the Soviet government's refusal to accede to the American request that it "use its influence with the North Korean authorities to withdraw their invading forces." Instead, Moscow had put all the blame for the situation in Korea on the South Koreans and "those who stand behind their back."

On June 30, after a personal reconnaissance in Korea, General MacArthur reported that the only assurance of holding the line of the Han River and regaining lost ground lay in the use of American combat troops. He urgently asked, and received the same day, the President's authorization to start the building up in Korea of two divisions from American troops in Japan for an early counter-offensive. Shortly thereafter American troops were being sent by airlift to Pusan in South Korea. Thus, six days after the start of the Communist aggression, orders committing United States troops to the struggle to provide collective security had been given to General Mac-Arthur. The attitude and actions of the United States government in this crisis were in marked contrast with those at the time of the Japanese aggression in Manchuria in 1931.[4]

On July 7 the UN Security Council approved an Anglo-French resolution which, among other things, recommended a unified command of United Nations forces and requested the United States—the country which had taken the lead in sending forces to combat the Communist aggression—to designate the commander. In compliance with the Council's directive President Truman at once named General MacArthur as commander-in-chief of all the UN forces in Korea. These consisted at first of only Americans and South Koreans, but ultimately ground, naval, or air forces were sent by Australia, Belgium, Canada, Colombia, Ethiopia, France, Great Britain, Greece, Luxembourg, the Netherlands, New Zealand, the Philippines, South Africa, Thailand, and Turkey. Hospital units were sent by Denmark, India, Italy, Norway, and Sweden.

Meanwhile, in Korea the first six weeks of the fighting had witnessed the steady retreat of the UN forces. The strength of the North Koreans had been underestimated by military observers, including even MacArthur, who had at first apparently thought that two United States divisions might be enough to turn the tide. But the superior numbers and the armored equipment of the North Koreans prevailed, and ultimately drove the UN forces into a 4,000 square-mile beachhead protecting the supply port of Pusan at the southern end of the Korean peninsula. It was feared that the forces of the UN might be driven out of Korea but this situation was swiftly changed on September 15 when some 50,000 United States marines and infantry made a successful amphibious landing at Inchon, on the west coast of the peninsula near Seoul. Ten days later the UN forces recaptured that capital city, and by the end of the month, all organized North Korean activities had ceased south of the 38th parallel. The aggressors had been hurled back.

On September 30 the South Korean parliament passed a resolution asking the United Nations to continue their advance beyond the 38th parallel. Whether to cross or not cross that parallel raised many questions. If the UN forces did not cross it and crush the aggressors, it was argued, the North Korean Communists would have an opportunity to reorganize their forces preparatory to another invasion. Moreover, not to cross it would appear to entail a divided Korea for an indefinite period. On the other hand, the crossing of the 38th parallel might provide an argument to bolster the Communist claim that the United States was embarked on an imperialist venture, an argument which might have considerable weight in the Asiatic world. Furthermore, such a crossing might incite the Chinese People's Republic to move its troops into Korea from Manchuria, might indeed precipitate a third world war.

[4] See pages 449–455.

THE SCENE OF THE KOREAN WAR

Even while the debate was being carried on, however, South Korean troops crossed the parallel and pushed northward. On October 7 the UN General Assembly approved a resolution which by implication authorized the crossing of the parallel by UN forces, and two days later UN forces crossed it in strength north of Kaesong. By October 20 they had captured Pyongyang, the capital of the Korean People's Republic, and a month later they were approaching the Yalu River, which constituted the boundary between Manchuria and Korea.

In North Korea along the Yalu River were power installations which had been started by the Japanese in 1937. After the Second World War these had become the joint property of Korea and China, and they supplied electric power for steel works, coal mines, and an aluminum plant in Manchuria. There were indications that the Chinese Communists were fearful that these power installations would fall into the hands of a hostile state and many observers believed that they would use their forces to protect them. From Western European governments came suggestions that a buffer zone be created along the Manchurian frontier and that no attempt be made to clear the North Korean troops from that border zone.

On November 24, however, General MacArthur announced a large-scale UN offensive, designed to "end the war, restore peace and unity in Korea, enable the prompt withdrawal of UN military forces, and permit the complete assumption by the Korean people and nation of full sovereignty and international equality for which the war was fought." But suddenly Chinese Communist troops in great numbers were hurled into the conflict on the side of the beaten North Korean army. Again the tide of battle turned. Outnumbered and outmaneuvered, the UN forces were halted and then thrown back. MacArthur at once notified the UN that Chinese Communist troops numbering more than 200,000 men now faced the UN forces in Korea, thus posing issues which would have to be resolved by the United Nations and within the chancellories of the world. The American representative on the UN Security Council thereupon denounced the Chinese People's Republic as an aggressor.[5]

In December, 1950, Pyongyang was recaptured by the Communists. The UN forces withdrew to positions near the 38th parallel and regrouped for a new defense of Seoul. But the weight of the Chinese Communist forces continued to be felt. Early in January, 1951, the United States Eighth Army was compelled to withdraw from Seoul in the face of overwhelming attacks by Chinese infantry, supported by tanks and artillery. The South Korean government again fled from Seoul to Pusan. Before the month was out the

---

[5] After much discussion and delay a United States resolution declaring the Chinese People's Republic was engaged in aggression in Korea was adopted by the UN General Assembly on February 1, 1951.

WAR IN KOREA
UN Troops on the Battle Line

Communist forces had once more crossed the 38th parallel. For a time it seemed that the long retreat of the summer of 1950 might be re-enacted, but ultimately the Communist advance was stemmed. The UN forces first halted their retreat and then gradually turned to the offensive again. On March 14, 1951, Seoul was recaptured for the second time by South Korean forces. By the end of the month UN troops were once more back approximately to the 38th parallel. In April that parallel was again crossed in a limited offensive.

For some time it had been apparent that General MacArthur's views on how to conduct the war in Korea and to provide American security in the Far East differed from those of the government of the United States and those of other members of the United Nations. The policy of the United States was to limit the war to Korea, to convince the Communist leaders by UN fighting that it was useless for them to continue their aggression, and thus lead them to be willing to negotiate. The bombing of Manchuria or China and the use of Chiang's Chinese Nationalist troops, it was believed, might result in the spreading of the conflict or even to a third world war. General MacArthur, on the other hand, felt that his conduct of the war was seriously handicapped by these restrictions, and although he had been instructed to clear all statements of a political nature with the government in Washington, he failed to do so. On April 11, 1951, President Truman unexpectedly relieved him of all his Far Eastern commands on the grounds that he did not agree with the official policies of the United States and the United Nations and was thus unable to give wholehearted support to them. General Matthew B. Ridgway, commander of the United States Eighth Army in Korea, was appointed to succeed MacArthur as the supreme commander in the Far East.

But the change in commanders had little effect on the military situation in Korea. Fighting continued, but General Omar Bradley, chairman of the United States joint chiefs of staff, announced in May that it was not the objective to drive the Communist armies out of North Korea but to inflict maximum casualties so that the Communists would be persuaded to negotiate. In June Trygve Lie, secretary general of the UN, declared that a new effort should be made to arrange a cease-fire approximately along the 38th parallel. This, he maintained, would fulfill the main purpose of the Security Council's resolutions of June and July, 1950. If no armistice could be arranged, he asserted, members of the UN should contribute additional forces for the war in Korea. It soon became obvious that both the Russian Soviet government and the Chinese People's government favored some such step, and ultimately, on July 10, 1951, cease-fire negotiations began at Kaesong.

But it soon became equally obvious that, though the Communists were ready to begin negotiations for a truce, they were in no particular hurry to reach an agreement on its terms. On question after question there were prolonged and seemingly futile discussions. Month after month passed without final agreement. And meanwhile fighting—but not all-out fighting—continued on the battlelines, with little result except to increase steadily the casualties on both sides. In some circles among the citizens of the free countries patience wore thin and demands for drastic action by the UN were vigorously voiced. But, seemingly, most of the free world preferred to negotiate as long as any hope of a cease-fire remained, and so intermittently the negotiations continued. Eventually, after some 158 meetings of the top negotiators and hundreds of meetings of their subordinates, the truce document was completed and signed by United Nations and Communist representatives. All military action in Korea and its surrounding waters halted at 10 P. M. on July 27, 1953, a little more than two years after the negotiations had started. As a result of the war the United Nations forces had suffered a total of 1,474,269 casualties (dead, wounded, captured, or missing), of which the South Koreans had suffered 1,312,836 and the United States, 144,173. The total Communist casualties were estimated at 1,540,000, of which the North Koreans had suffered 520,000 and the Chinese 900,000.

By the terms of the truce both sides, having ceased fire, were to withdraw two kilometers from the final battleline to form a neutral zone between the opposing armies. Both sides accepted restrictions on troop reinforcement and airfield construction, and a commission consisting of representatives of India, Sweden, Switzerland, Poland, and Czechoslovakia was to see that these restrictions were observed. All prisoners on both sides who wanted to return were to be repatriated at once and the others were to be placed in custody of a neutral commission, consisting of representatives of the above-mentioned states, with India providing troops to guard the prisoners. Communist and UN teams were to have opportunities to try to persuade reluctant prisoners to accept repatriation, with the neutral commission certifying any changes of mind. Finally, a high-level political conference was to convene within ninety days after the beginning of the truce to "settle through negotiation the questions of the withdrawal of all foreign troops from Korea, the peaceful settlement of the Korean question, etc." On August 5 the first prisoners of war were exchanged, and the exchange was completed on September 6. Four days later Indian troops began taking over custody of prisoners of both sides who had refused to be repatriated: 22,606 held by the UN and 1,578 held by the Communists. "Explanations" to the prisoners began on October 15 and ended on December 23. Neither side succeeded in changing the decisions of any large percentage of the men interviewed. More than 22,000 prisoners refused to be repatriated. On January 23, 1954, these prisoners were freed.

To most observers it appeared extremely unlikely that a final political

agreement regarding Korea could be easily reached. President Syngman
Rhee of the Korean Republic appeared eager to unify Korea by military
measures if diplomacy did not quickly achieve it, and, with the South Korean forces in 1953 far stronger than the North Korean (the reverse of the
situation in 1950), many believed that the Russian and Chinese Communists
would be reluctant to withdraw their forces. On the other hand, President
Rhee feared that should both the Chinese and the United Nations actually
withdraw their forces from Korea, the Chinese armies, just across the Yalu
River, might sometime again launch an all-out offensive and conquer all
Korea before the UN forces could effectively come to the Korean Republic's
assistance. To overcome Rhee's fears and possibly to deter the Chinese Communists from attempting any such coup, the United States on August 8
signed with the Korean Republic the draft of a mutual security pact with
a provision giving the United States the right to station troops in Korea
similar to that in the security pact between Japan and the United States.[6]
Furthermore, the sixteen countries which had fought under the UN flag
in Korea pledged themselves to take up arms again in case of any new Communist attack on Korea.

On the question of the political unification of Korea, both the Communists and the United Nations were in agreement. The problem appeared to
be whether in 1953 they could agree any better than in 1947[7] on the method
of achieving this end and on the meaning of "free elections." Finally, it appeared likely that the abbreviation, "etc.," in the truce agreement would
cause disagreements not only between the United Nations and the Communists but among the United Nations themselves. Involved in this abbreviation seemed to be the fundamental question of the relation between
the Western world and the People's Republic of China. Twenty-seven nations had recognized the Communist government in Peking and were
apparently willing to admit it into the UN, but in the United States a great
body of opinion, official and unofficial, opposed both of these steps. Shortly
before the signing of the truce the United States Congress had unanimously
adopted a resolution opposing Communist China's admission to the UN.
That the United States could indefinitely impose its views regarding these
two matters on Soviet Russia and Communist China as well as on most of
the United Nations, if its refusal to make any concessions would entail the
end of the truce and the renewal of fighting, seemed doubtful.

Meanwhile, on August 17, 1953, the General Assembly of the United
Nations had convened in order to arrange the political conference on
Korea provided for in the armistice agreement. At the outset a Russian
proposal to invite representatives of Communist China and North Korea

[6] See page 636.
[7] See page 650.

to participate in the debate on the political conference was rejected. Another Russian proposal that the conference should consist of representatives of the United States, Great Britain, France, Russia, Communist China, India, Poland, Sweden, Burma, North Korea, and South Korea was also voted down. A British proposal that India should be represented was likewise defeated, chiefly because of the opposition of the United States. In the end, the Assembly decided that all states which had borne arms under the UN flag, together with South Korea, should be entitled to representation. It then voted that the Soviet Union should be invited to take part in the conference, "provided the other side desires it." Arrangements regarding the place of meeting of the conference were to be made by United States and Communist representatives.

Talks between the United States and Communist envoys on the proposed Korean conference began in Panmunjom on October 26, 1953. Disagreements on many subjects at once arose. Eventually, on December 12, after the Communists had rejected a "final" plan proposed by the United States, the American envoy broke off the discussions. Although, a month later, the Communists proposed the resumption of the negotiations at Panmunjom, apparently both sides realized that the approaching meeting of the foreign ministers of the Big Four was the real place where a decision would be reached.

On January 25, 1954, the Big Four Council of Foreign Ministers—consisting this time of John Foster Dulles (United States), Anthony Eden (Great Britain), Georges Bidault (France), and Vyacheslav Molotov (Russia)—met in Berlin to discuss the whole complex of East-West differences. As was generally expected, the ministers failed to reach agreement on a plan to unify Germany, on an Austrian peace treaty, or on the question of European security. In fact, so far as Europe was concerned, no agreements were reached. Apparently the Russians had decided to hold fast to their positions in the West. In respect to the Far East, however, an agreement was reached, based on a proposal made by Molotov at the opening of the conference. When the meeting adjourned on February 18 the ministers had decided that a conference of representatives of the United States, Britain, France, the Soviet Union, and the People's Republic of China would be convened in Geneva in April for the purpose of reaching a peaceful settlement of the Korean question and of discussing the Indo-Chinese situation. In deference to Secretary of State Dulles' desire, it was at the same time announced that the Geneva conference in no way implied recognition of the Communist regime in China. What decisions regarding Korea and Indo-China might be made at a conference of the new "Big Five," only the future could tell.

Security Measures in the Far East

Communist aggression in Korea had worldwide repercussions. Without hesitation the foreign ministers of France, Great Britain, and the United States, meeting in New York in September, 1950, agreed that the most urgent problem before them was that of strengthening the defenses of the free world in Asia and in Europe. In the attempt to solve this problem the United States took the lead, seeking to bind countries together by mutual defense pacts and extending military and economic assistance to innumerable states in an effort to build up their ability to resist aggression. In some cases the desire to increase the effective strength of the anti-Communist world entailed a clear-cut reversal of former United States policies.

In the Far East, for example, the United States attitude of nonintervention in case of an attempt by the Chinese Communists to take over Formosa was completely altered. Immediately following the Communist attack on the Republic of Korea President Truman declared that since it had become clear that Communism had passed beyond the use of subversion to conquer independent nations and would now use armed invasion and war, a Communist occupation of Formosa would be a direct threat to the security of the Pacific area. He therefore ordered the United States Seventh Fleet to prevent any attack on that island. Then, early in 1951, the United States agreed to extend American military aid to the Chinese Nationalist government to enable it to ensure the internal security and self-defense of Formosa, and an American military mission was dispatched to supervise the use of that aid. In addition more than $200,000,000 in economic and technical assistance was provided Chiang Kai-shek in the two years following the outbreak of the Korean War. Apparently it was believed in Washington that in case a third world war should develop in the Far East Chiang and his Nationalist forces might be useful against Communist China.

Similarly, the United States attitude became more favorable to the French efforts to restore order in Indo-China, where for some years the French had been fighting a war against a native resistance movement led by the Russian-trained Communist, Ho Chi Minh. The French claimed that Ho Chi Minh's forces were being supported in part by the Chinese Communists, who provided training, technicians, and American equipment which had been captured earlier from Chiang Kai-shek's forces on the mainland. They argued that in Indo-China the French were fighting the battle against Communism the same as the UN forces were in Korea, and pointed out that they had paid and were paying a heavy price in lives and money in order that Communism might there be checked.

Immediately after the Communist attack on the Korean Republic President Truman announced that military aid to the forces of France and the "associated states" of Indo-China—Viet Nam, Laos, Cambodia—would be speeded up and that a military mission would be despatched to provide close working relations with those forces. In December, 1950, military aid conventions were signed between the United States and the "associated states," and it was announced that between $300,000,000 and $400,000,000 had been allotted for a two-year program of aid to Indo-China. Without the ever-increasing flow of war materials from the United States in the ensuing years, the French forces in Indo-China could probably not have held out.

Steps were also taken by the United States to create a network of mutual defense pacts in the Pacific area. On August 30, 1951, the United States and the Republic of the Philippines signed a treaty in which both nations expressed their common determination to defend themselves against attack and their joint recognition that an armed attack in the Pacific area on either would be dangerous to the peace and security of the other. Two days later Australia, New Zealand, and the United States also signed a mutual defense treaty, which provided that an attack on any one of the three states or on territories under their jurisdiction in the Pacific area would be recognized as a danger to all three parties and that each would act to meet it in accordance with its constitutional practices and with UN principles. In 1952 the Pacific Council of Ministers of Australia, New Zealand, and the United States (ANZUS) was established to carry out Pacific defense planning under the three states' mutual security pact. Finally, on September 8, 1951, at the time of the signing of the Japanese peace treaty, the United States entered into a far-reaching and long-time security pact with the Japanese government, the terms of which have been outlined.[8]

The North Atlantic Treaty Organization

During the discussions and debates which preceded and followed the dismissal of General MacArthur as the supreme commander in the Far East it was made abundantly evident that the United States and the states of Western Europe, although determined to oppose aggression in the Far East, were likewise resolved not to be turned aside from their endeavor to build up collective security in Europe. In fact, the war in Korea undoubtedly gave added impetus to the plans for the political, economic, and military integration of the states of the North Atlantic area.

Even before the outbreak of the Korean War it had begun to be felt both in western Europe and in the United States that military support by the latter was just as essential for world peace as its economic support was for European reconstruction. In June, 1948, the United States Senate adopted

[8] See page 636.

the so-called Vandenberg resolution which recommended, among other things: (1) that the United States encourage the development of collective security arrangements, (2) that it associate itself with such arrangements when they were based on full self-help and mutual aid and when they affected the security of the United States, and (3) that it make clear, in advance, that any armed attack by an aggressor nation upon a peace-loving nation whereby the security of the United States was affected would be combatted by the latter.

In October, 1948, the Canadian and the Brussels-pact governments [9] announced their readiness to negotiate a collective security treaty with the United States, and eventually, on April 4, 1949, the North Atlantic treaty was signed in Washington by the foreign ministers of twelve states—Great Britain, France, Belgium, the Netherlands, Luxembourg, Italy, Portugal, Norway, Denmark, Iceland, Canada, and the United States. The treaty contained six main points: (1) signatories renounced war as an instrument of policy except as provided by the United Nations Charter; (2) they were obligated to take military or other action forthwith in case of an armed attack against any signatory nation; (3) each signatory would decide for itself what constituted an armed attack and what immediate action it would take to fulfill its obligation; (4) the treaty would run for twenty years; (5) it would create a North Atlantic Council with powers to establish other committees; (6) the co-operation of certain other states would be welcomed.

In accordance with the terms of the North Atlantic treaty the North Atlantic Treaty Organization (NATO), consisting of one representative of each of the signatory powers, was established and held its first meeting in September, 1949. In that same month the Congress of the United States approved the creation of a military assistance program fund of $1,000,000,000, with which to finance shipments of arms to the pact countries from United States surpluses. In 1950 NATO approved integrated defense plans for the entire North Atlantic area and the United States signed bilateral agreements for arms shipments to all member countries which requested aid. It also agreed upon the necessity for concentrating on "the creation of balanced collective forces"; that is, the states agreed that each should concentrate on contributing its best resources for the common defense. It seemed to be expected that the United States would be responsible for strategic bombing, Great Britain and the United States for naval forces, France and Great Britain for tactical aviation, and the continental powers chiefly for ground forces.

The Communist attack on the Korean Republic in 1950 increased the desire to provide effective security through NATO. The United States Congress appropriated an additional $3,500,000,000 for the military assist-

[9] See page 739.

ance program, and NATO approved plans for the further integration of Western defenses and the appointment of a supreme Atlantic pact commander. In December, 1950, General Dwight D. Eisenhower, who had been supreme Allied commander in Western Europe in 1944–1945, was appointed to head NATO's armed forces. In April, 1951, he formally assumed command at the Supreme Headquarters of Allied Powers in Europe (SHAPE), which were located near Paris.[10] As the result of the decision of the North Atlantic Council meeting at Ottawa in September, 1951, Greece and Turkey, in whose defense against Soviet aggression the free peoples of the world were vitally concerned, were invited to become members of NATO. This invitation was ratified by the various governments and the number of NATO members was thus increased to fourteen. Despite the fears of some of the smaller Western European powers, the North Atlantic defense area was thus extended eastward to the Aegean and Black seas and to the Caucasus.

Various suggestions for further increasing the military potentialities of NATO were made from time to time. In December, 1950, the powers of the North Atlantic Treaty Organization agreed that a German contribution to Western defense was desirable, and France, Great Britain, and the United States were invited to explore the matter with the German Federal Government. Discussions were at once opened between the three Allied high commissioners and German Chancellor Adenauer, who agreed that the defense of Europe called for the inclusion of West Germany in the Western group of powers, but listed several prerequisites for West German participation. On the other hand, French statesmen were reluctant to permit the national rearmament of Germany lest German militarism be revived and France once again find herself confronted by a powerful and aggressive neighbor. The question of German rearmament became linked with the Pleven Plan for the creation of a European army.[11]

In February, 1952, the North Atlantic Council, meeting at Lisbon, decided to create a permanent operating organization, with a secretariat and an established headquarters, and subsequently the NATO headquarters were set up at Paris, near SHAPE. In the expanded organization the North Atlantic Council remained the most powerful organ, deciding upon the general policies of NATO in so far as the ministers had powers to make such decisions. A second organ was the permanent council, consisting of state ministers, which was to sit "continuously" at NATO headquarters.

---

[10] He was succeeded in 1952, after he had resigned to run for the presidency of the United States, by the American General Matthew B. Ridgway who, in turn, was succeeded in 1953 by the American General A. M. Gruenther.

[11] See page 829.

The secretariat would perform for NATO duties like those of the former secretariat of the League of Nations or that of the United Nations. A general military committee was established to represent all member states, but a special standing group, staffed by British, French and United States officers, to which the Supreme Allied Commander was responsible, was set up in Washington.

Meanwhile, progress was being made in the task of building up NATO's military force. Early in 1954 there were 28 or 29 ready active divisions under arms in Western Europe, plus 31 more in Greece and Turkey. Yugoslavia, which was not a member of NATO but seemed more and more inclined to co-operate with it, had about 32 small divisions. In air strength the goal of 4,000 tactical aircraft by the close of 1952 had been practically met, chiefly by contributions of the United States, though the figure included some 1,500 planes which were assigned to the home defense of France and Britain and were not technically under the control of the Supreme Allied Commander. Some 120 airfields and a large network of signal communications facilities were in use. The goals for air and naval forces for 1953 had been substantially met, and in December, 1953, the NATO Council had set goals for 1954 calling for some increase in the numerical strength of forces and a very substantial improvement in their quality and effectiveness.

According to military experts, the NATO forces in 1954 were strong enough so that the Soviet opportunity for a surprise attack had passed and the day of the "push-over" had ended. It was believed that, because of the West's superiority in both atomic and hydrogen bombs, any Russian attack on territories of the NATO countries would be punished severely and that Russians would pay heavily for any gains. It was hoped that this fact would serve as a deterrent to any Soviet attack. On the other hand, it was recognized that NATO strength was as yet inadequate to win a war against Russia or even to defend Europe for long. The great weakness in NATO's armed strength was reserves which were considered to be grossly inadequate.

Attempts to Integrate Western Europe

The Communist aggression in Korea gave added impetus, also, to the movement to bring about a closer political, economic, and military integration of Western Europe than yet existed. A slight beginning of political integration had been made in 1948 when the Benelux countries and Great Britain and France had signed the Brussels treaty and had given approval to the creation of the Council of Europe.[12]

12 See page 739.

THE COUNCIL OF EUROPE

On May 5, 1949, ten powers—Belgium, Denmark, France, Great Britain, the Irish Republic, Italy, Luxembourg, the Netherlands, Norway, and Sweden—formally signed the Statute of the Council of Europe, which inaugurated a sort of small-scale United Nations. In its organization the Committee of Ministers was analogous to the Security Council; the Consultative Assembly resembled the General Assembly; and a Secretariat was established at Strasbourg, the seat of the new international organization. In 1951 the German Federal Republic was also admitted to membership in the Council. It had become clear, said the chairman of the Committee of Ministers, that Europe could not exist without Germany, nor Germany without Europe. German Federal Chancellor Adenauer, attending the Committee of Ministers for the first time on May 2, 1951, declared that Germany would work in the Council toward the integration of Europe as the only way to resist pressure from Eastern Europe and from Asia.

In November, 1951, after American spokesmen had indicated that they hoped Western Europe might work out some plan for federation, Paul Reynaud of France proposed a union of all Western Europe, which, with the help of Great Britain and the United States, would be able to build a defense against the danger of encroachment by the Soviet Union. But some of the states in the Council of Europe were apparently reluctant to join a European federation unless Great Britain were included for fear it might come to be dominated by Germany. But the British government, even under Churchill—who had frequently preached European unity without specifying that he excluded Britain—reiterated its stand that Great Britain, because of her relations with her dominions, could not enter a European federation.

The development of plans for the European Coal and Steel Community (ECSC) and the European Defense Community (EDC), both discussed below, led the Council of Europe to concern itself with the task of deciding what its role should be relative to such specialized bodies. Beginning in 1951 two desires of the Assembly were discernible. First, it wished to emancipate itself from the control of the Committee of Ministers in order to have something more than a mere deliberative and advisory role. This desire of the Assembly, which in reality was a move toward the creation of a European federation, had the support of the United States but encountered the obstacle of the national sovereignty of its member states. The second desire of the Assembly was to make the Council of Europe the framework into which the various specialized bodies, the ECSC, the EDC, and any others which might be set up, could be fitted. The Assembly voted that all six-nation assemblies should be concentrated at the seat of the Council of Europe, that the six-nation communities should be asked to use the Secretariat of the Council of Europe, and that states members of the Council of Europe but not of the specialized bodies should accredit observers with the right to speak in the assemblies of the specialized agencies. Whether the desires of the latter to perpetuate their independence and the desires of all of the states to safeguard their national sovereignty would prevent the creation of a federation of Europe seemed likely to depend upon how serious the European states considered the threat of Soviet aggression to be. In November, 1953, however, the Committee of Ministers of the Council of Europe decided to set up a commission to draft a treaty establishing a genuine political community and requested it to prepare a report by March 15, 1954.

THE EUROPEAN COAL AND STEEL COMMUNITY

The possibility of an economic integration of Western Europe was chiefly connected with the so-called Schuman Plan, suggested by French Foreign Minister Robert Schuman in May, 1950. He proposed that the coal and steel production of France, Germany, and the other Western European nations should be pooled under a common authority. The Benelux countries and Italy joined with France and Western Germany to give shape to this proposal, but Great Britain declined to participate. A draft treaty embodying the plan set up the European Coal and Steel Community, and was ultimately signed on April 18, 1951.

Under the constitution of the European Coal and Steel Community executive power was entrusted to the High Authority, a sort of cabinet with nine members. A second organ, the Council of Ministers, consisting of one representative from each participating government, had the function of harmonizing the action of the High Authority with the general economic policies of the participating states. The High Authority was responsible to the Assembly, in which France, Germany, and Italy had eighteen delegates each, Belgium and the Netherlands ten each, and Luxembourg four. The Assembly might by a two-thirds vote censure the High Authority, and such a vote of censure would entail the resignation of all the members of that body and the immediate appointment of new members. Finally, the High Court of seven judges had power to adjudicate upon complaints brought against the High Authority by a member state, the Council of Ministers, an association of producers, or an enterprise. The court also had power to annul any decision or recommendation, should the High Authority abuse or exceed its powers or contravene the treaty or the law.

The primary concern of the European Coal and Steel Community was the creation of a single market within which free trade in coal and steel should prevail, and the powers conferred on the High Authority were chiefly designed to assure the six-country area free competition. Illegitimate competitive devices, particularly temporary or local reductions of price in order to secure a monopoly, were forbidden, as was also any price discrimination according to the nationality of the purchaser. Every enterprise was compelled to publish its schedule of prices and its conditions of sale, and the High Authority was given power to fix maximum or, in a time of a crisis, minimum prices for any coal or steel products. In case of a depression the High Authority had the right to fix production quotas, or to impose a tax on production by an enterprise in excess of an assigned limit and use the proceeds to subsidize enterprises which were underemployed. In its operations the ECSC would be somewhat like a cartel.

The importance of the projected European Coal and Steel Community seemed indicated to some extent by the fact that it was at once denounced by the Communists and characterized by them as the "pact of the cannon kings." Undoubtedly, a coal and steel pool of six West European countries under one administration would create a strong industrial potential in Europe to rival the Eastern bloc's Council for Economic Mutual Assistance.[13] The coal production of the six Western countries would equal Russia's production, and their joint steel production would exceed by several million tons annually that of the whole Eastern bloc. The Communists of Germany, France, and Italy at once undertook to defeat the ratification of the Schuman Plan.

Nevertheless, the Schuman Plan treaty was ratified by the six states involved, and came into force on July 25, 1952. It was decided that Luxembourg should be the ECSC's headquarters until the future of the Saar had been decided. In August the High Authority held its first meeting, with Jean Monnet, the French economic expert who with Schuman had been co-author of the plan, as chairman. In September the first meeting of the Council of Ministers was held under the chairmanship of Chancellor Adenauer of Germany, and the Assembly met and elected Paul-Henri Spaak, former Belgium premier, as president. The first task of this supranational organization was to level barriers within the ECSC, which had a total annual production of some 41,000,000 tons of steel and 235,000,000 tons of coal. In January, 1954, the High Authority revealed that, since the opening of the common market, deliveries of coal between countries in the community had increased by 20.4 per cent, of iron ore by 14.7 per cent, and of scrap iron by 66 per cent. At the same time the Assembly approved a four-year capital investment policy designed to reduce retail prices, especially of steel, and to improve working and living conditions.

But the ECSC was not interested in steel and coal alone. Some of the statesmen, notably Schuman and Adenauer, looked upon the ECSC as a means to overcome the long-standing Franco-German antagonisms. At its

[13] See page 607.

first meeting the Assembly converted itself into an *ad hoc* constituent assembly to draft a constitution for a political authority. The constitutional committee proposed that during an initial period the European Coal and Steel Community and the European Defense Community should be progressively merged into a political community. Drafts of a constitution were considered by the *ad hoc* Assembly in January and March, 1953, and on March 10, 1953, the Assembly finally adopted the draft treaty for the European Political Community. As envisaged, the six-nation community would have a bicameral parliament, the lower house popularly elected and the upper elected by the national parliaments, and a ministry responsible to the parliament. The Council of Ministers of the ECSC would also be part of the executive branch of the European Political Community, though what its role would be—unless to safeguard national sovereignties—was not clear. That national sovereignty was still much in the minds of most statesmen was indicated by the provision that the powers of the European Political Community would be defined by treaty and any extension of its powers would be subject to the unanimous consent of the national governments. Whether this draft treaty would ever be ratified and what the relation of the European Political Community would be to the Council of Europe remained to be discovered.

THE EUROPEAN DEFENSE COMMUNITY

To some extent, the movement to integrate the armed forces of Western Europe was launched by Winston Churchill who in a speech before the Consultative Assembly of the Council of Europe in August, 1950, had called for a real defensive front in Europe in which all members of the Council of Europe, including Germany, should bear their share. The Assembly had thereupon voted for "the immediate creation of a unified European army under the authority of a European minister of defense, subject to proper European democratic control and acting in full co-operation with the United States and Canada." But under the existing statute of the Council of Europe the Assembly was forbidden to discuss defense, so that its action on Churchill's proposal was ineffective.

In October, 1950 however, the so-called Pleven Plan was suggested by French Premier René Pleven in the hope of achieving some compromise between French fear of a remilitarized Germany and NATO's desire to have Western Germany contribute to its armed forces. Pleven proposed the creation of a European Defense Community (EDC) with a European army under a European minister of defense, who would be responsible to a European authority and would carry out the directives of a council of ministers composed of members of the participating countries. The European army, which would be financed by a common budget, would be used in accordance with obligations assumed under the North Atlantic treaty. The participating countries which already had national armies would retain control over that part of their armed forces which was not incorporated in the common force, but the Pleven idea was that a supranational army would gradually but irrevocably supersede the national armies.

The German Federal Republic was invited to participate in a conference at Paris on the formation of such a European army. Although Kurt Schumacher, the German Social Democratic leader, asserted that the Pleven Plan offered no basis for discussion, in February, 1951, a German representative attended the conference which included delegates also from France, Italy, Belgium, and Luxembourg. The French foreign minister emphasized the plan as a permanent solution of the "anachronistic and absurd divisions" of Europe, and asserted that Atlantic defense and European defense were not incompatible. The European army should be an integral part of the Atlantic force, and in the early stages of the plan decisions regarding the use of the European army would be the sole prerogative of the North Atlantic Treaty Organization. The conference decided that the heads of the five participating delegations should serve as a committee to work out the details of the plan.

In July, 1951, the delegations again met and agreed that the armed forces of the five countries set aside for European defense should be fused under a common supranational authority, political and military, the organs of which should be similar to those of the ECSC. Relations with NATO should be close and the military Authority should conform to the views and directives of SHAPE. Finally, in November, six countries—the Netherlands now joined the original five—agreed in a joint report, which they submitted to the North Atlantic Council, that a combined European army should be created as quickly as possible and placed under the command of General Eisenhower.

According to the EDC plan the six nations would pool all their ground, air, and sea forces—with certain specific exceptions—and would control this combined army by means of a European Authority staffed by and responsible, through a Council of Ministers, to all six powers. The European army would be paid and equipped from a common budget, made up of contributions from all six states augmented by United States aid. The forces to be excluded from control of the Authority would be (1) forces of the member states which were needed for service in their respective overseas territories, (2) forces engaged in "international" duties, as in Korea, Austria, and Berlin, and (3) forces needed for internal security. Each state, it was agreed, might exchange personnel between its troops in the European army and its overseas units, providing no diminution of the over-all European strength would result. In fact, it might, in case of an emergency in its overseas territory, detach some of its forces from the European army, provided the Supreme Allied Commander approved.

On May 27, 1952, the foreign ministers of France, the German Federal Republic, Italy, Belgium, the Netherlands, and Luxembourg signed the European Defense Community treaty, its military and financial protocols, and a protocol dealing with relations between NATO and EDC. The foreign ministers of the EDC states and of Great Britain and the permanent representatives of the NATO states also signed two additional protocols on the assistance to be given by EDC signatories to NATO members, and *vice versa,* in case of armed aggression. Generally speaking, all land and air forces of the six member states, except those needed in overseas territories and for special international commitments, would be under the control of SHAPE.

The European Defense Community would not come into force until all six states had ratified the treaty. The basic aim, of course, was to obtain German armed forces to aid in the defense of Europe without permitting the German Federal Republic to have a national army which might become dangerous to the peace of Europe again and which, as a national army, would undoubtedly raise French fears of a resurgent and aggressive Germany. Within Germany there was much opposition to the ratification of the EDC treaty. But the ratification of the latter was a prerequisite of the coming into effect of the convention between the Allies and Germany [14] providing for the abolition of the Occupation Statute with its authorization of Allied intervention in the internal affairs of the Federal Republic. Both houses of the German parliament approved the EDC treaty in 1953 but, despite considerable pressure from the United States government, both France and Italy delayed taking action. The grave concern of the United States over this delay was revealed by the American Secretary of State Dulles' statement to the North Atlantic Council in December, 1953, that if ratification of the EDC treaty were not forthcoming "soon," the United States would have to make "an agonizing reappraisal" of its own basic policies.

The Awaited Verdict

At the time this chapter was written collective security was still on trial, and the final verdict was far from certain. In the Far East the situation seemed to indicate a favorable outcome in the conflict between aggression and collective security. The Korean Communists, striking suddenly and with superior forces, in June, 1950 had overrun most of the Republic of Korea. Had the latter been left unaided to defend itself, there appears to be little doubt that it would have been conquered. But the armed forces of the United Nations went to its assistance, hurled back the invaders, and cleared the territory south of the 38th parallel of enemy troops. Then, in November, 1950, the Chinese Communists became aggressors. Their armies entered the fray in overwhelming numbers, and again the capital and some of the territory of the Korean Republic were occupied. But once more the United Nations armies stopped the aggressors, drove them north of the 38th parallel and apparently convinced them that a truce might be desirable. The truce obtained in July, 1953, constituted a victory for the United Nations. Though at considerable cost in men and money, they forced an aggressor to call off a war. Meanwhile, the United States, in the hope of discouraging further aggression in the Far East, had completed a series of security pacts with Australia, New Zealand, the Philippines, and Japan.

In the West the success or failure of collective security seemed to some to depend on the success or failure of efforts to bring about the political, economic, and military integration of Western Europe. The conversion of the Council of Europe into a West European Federation, however, appeared destined to be indefinitely postponed by the reluctance of member states to surrender national sovereignty to any superior federal authority. The best that seemed likely to be achieved was a close co-operation among a limited number of sovereign states in a small United Nations. But the prospects of some degree of economic and military integration seemed better. Both the Schuman Plan and the Pleven Plan, to be sure, were attacked by certain groups within Germany and France. National pride, national fears, and national suspicions were apparently exploited by some in each country for internal political reasons. But the European Coal and Steel Community became effective in 1952 and it was widely hoped that the European Defense Community treaty would be able to secure the necessary ratifications.

But even without political federation or the actual surrender of political sovereignty, considerable progress was being made in strengthening the forces of collective security through the North Atlantic Treaty Organization. To a large extent this was a consequence of the fact that Communist aggression in Korea had spurred the United States to make tremendous increases in its own armed strength and in its assistance to the armed forces of other nations. There seemed little doubt that at the close of the year 1953 the total armed forces of the free world were far greater, not counting those in Korea, than they had been when the aggressors launched their attack. And, in the words of General Eisenhower, the first Supreme Commander of NATO's armed forces, if the nations in NATO would stop their haggling over minor points of national interest or prestige and would achieve a closer unity—political, military, and economic—the collective security of the free world could be assured.

Although at times progress seemed painfully slow, it appeared possible that eventually through NATO the balance of Soviet and non-Soviet power would be improved by the linking together of more than 350,000,000 people, whose industrial and military potential for the conduct of modern war would be great enough to neutralize the strength of the Soviet world. And thus collective security—achieved through NATO—would, the free world fervently hoped, create, in the words of former President Truman, "a shield against aggression and the fear of aggression."

SELECT BIBLIOGRAPHY
and
INDEX

SELECT BIBLIOGRAPHY

As books dealing with history since 1914 pour constantly from American and foreign presses, the task of any author who desires to keep his bibliography somewhere within reasonable limits becomes more and more one of selection. And since in the selection of suitable books personal opinion inevitably plays a part, it is doubtful if any select bibliography in the field covered by this volume will be entirely satisfactory either in the books included or in those omitted. In the present case the bibliographer has sought (1) to list enough books on each topic so that some of them will almost surely be found in any college or public library; (2) to include the biographies, memoirs, and reminiscences of those who played roles in the history recorded so that readers may be able to humanize the necessarily brief outline in the text; and (3) to call attention, where possible, to books on both sides of various controversial questions so that those who wish may have an opportunity to form their own opinions on these questions.

Chapter I. The Background of the First World War

INTERNATIONAL RELATIONS 1870–1914: Anderson, E. N., *The First Moroccan Crisis, 1904–1906* (1930). Barlow, I. C., *The Agadir Crisis* (1940). Brandenburg, E., *From Bismarck to the World War* (1927); an account of German policy during this period. Carroll, E. M., *French Public Opinion and Foreign Affairs, 1870–1914* (1931); based on newspapers, documents, and periodical literature. Chang, C. F., *The Anglo-Japanese Alliance* (1931). Coolidge, A. C., *The Origins of the Triple Alliance* (1926). David, W. D., *European Diplomacy in the Near Eastern Question, 1906–1909* (1940). Dickinson, G. L., *The International Anarchy, 1904–1914* (1926). Durham, M. E., *Twenty Years of Balkan Tangle* (1920); hostile to Russia. Earle, E. M., *Turkey, the Great Powers, and the Bagdad Railway: A Study of Imperialism* (1923). Fay, S. B., *The Origins of the World War*, 2 vols. (1928); the first volume is an excellent discussion of the period 1870–1914. Gooch, G. P., *Before the War: Studies in Diplomacy*, 2 vols. (1936–1938). Gooch, G. P., *Franco-German Relations, 1871–1914* (1923); a brief survey. Gooch, G. P., *Recent Revelations of European Diplomacy* (4th ed., 1940). Goričar, J., and Stowe, L. B., *The Inside Story of the Austro-German Intrigue* (1920); explains how Austrian expansionist designs in the Balkans caused the war. Graves, P. P., *The Question of the Straits* (1931). Gueshoff, I. E., *The Balkan League* (1915); by a former Bulgarian prime minister. Haldane, R. B., Viscount,

3

Before the War (1920); discusses his efforts to secure a better understanding between Great Britain and Germany in 1912. Hammann, O., *The World Policy of Germany, 1890–1912* (1927); by a former chief of the press division of the German foreign office. Helmreich, E. C., *The Diplomacy of the Balkan Wars, 1912–1913* (1938). Hoffman, R. J., *Great Britain and the German Trade Rivalry, 1875–1914* (1933). Langer, W. L., *The Diplomacy of Imperialism,* 2 vols. (1935); continuation of the following work; comes down to 1902. Langer, W. L., *European Alliances and Alignments* (1931); one of the best volumes on the prewar diplomatic situation. Langer, W. L., *The Franco-Russian Alliance, 1890–1894* (1929). Michon, G., *The Franco-Russian Alliance, 1891–1917* (1929). Montgelas, Count M., *British Foreign Policy under Sir Edward Grey* (1928); based on an examination of British documents by a German historian. Neumann, R., *Zaharoff, the Armaments King* (1936). Porter, C. W., *The Career of Théophile Delcassé* (1936). Pribram, A. F., *Austrian Foreign Policy, 1908–1918* (1923). Pribram, A. F., *England and the International Policy of the European Great Powers, 1871–1914* (1931); a discussion of British continental policy by a leading Austrian authority. Schmitt, B. E., *The Annexation of Bosnia, 1908–1909* (1937). Schmitt, B. E., *England and Germany, 1740–1914* (1916). Schurman, J. G., *The Balkan Wars, 1912–1913* (1916). Seymour, C., *The Diplomatic Background of the War, 1870–1914* (1916). Shotwell, J. T., and Deák, F., *Turkey at the Straits* (1941). Sontag, R. J., *European Diplomatic History, 1871–1932* (1933); the first half deals with the period prior to 1914. Ward, A. W., and Gooch, G. P., *Cambridge History of British Foreign Policy, 1873–1919,* 3 vols. (1922–1923); an exhaustive collaborative study. Wedel, O., *Austro-German Diplomatic Relations, 1908–1914* (1932). Wolff, T., *The Eve of 1914* (1936); an admirable analysis of prewar diplomacy by the editor (1906–1933) of the *Berliner Tageblatt.* Woodward, E. L., *Great Britain and the German Navy* (1935).

THE CRISIS OF 1914: Barnes, H. E., *The Genesis of the World War* (1928); by one who finds Russia and France chiefly responsible. Benson, E. F., *The Outbreak of War, 1914* (1934); a dramatic and poignant account of the way events of July, 1914, appeared to a young Englishman of that day. Bloch, C., *The Causes of the World War* (1935); by a Frenchman. Durham, M. E., *The Sarajevo Crime* (1925); an indictment of the Serbs. Ewart, J. S., *The Roots and Causes of the Wars, 1914–1918,* 2 vols. (1925); by a Canadian. Fabre-Luce, A., *The Limitations of Victory* (1926); a discussion of the origins of the war by a French revisionist. Fay, S. B., *The Origins of the World War,* 2 vols. (1928); the second volume is a scholarly discussion of the crisis and reaches conclusions in general favorable to the Central Powers. Kautsky, K., *The Guilt of William Hohenzollern* (1920); a German indictment based on German documents. Lutz, H., *Lord Grey and the World War* (1928); by a distinguished German critic. Montgelas, Count M., *The Case for the Central Powers* (1925); the best presentation of the German viewpoint. Renouvin, P., *The Immediate Origins of the War* (1928); by a professor at the University of Paris. Rumbold, Sir H., *The War Crisis in Berlin: July–August, 1914* (1940). Schmitt, B. E., *The Coming of the War: 1914* (1930); an exhaustive and scholarly study by a leading authority whose conclusions are in general favorable to the Allies. Scott, J. F., *Five Weeks* (1927); traces the surge of public opinion in the European countries after the assassination. Seton-Watson, R. W., *Sarajevo: A Study in the Origins of the Great War* (1926); by a British specialist in Yugoslav history. Stieve, F., *Isvolsky and the World War* (1926); by one who had access to much of the correspondence of the Russian foreign minister from 1911 to 1914. Wegerer, A. von, *A Refutation of the Versailles War Guilt Thesis* (1930); one of the best presentations of the German view of war origins. Willis, E. F., *Prince Lichnowsky, Ambassador of Peace: A Study of Prewar Diplomacy, 1912–1914* (1942). Wilson, H. W., *The War Guilt* (1928); by a British publicist.

MEMOIRS AND RECOLLECTIONS: Asquith, H. H., *Genesis of the War* (1924); by the British prime minister in 1914. Bertie, F. L. B., *A Diary of Lord Bertie*, 2 vols. (1924); by the British ambassador at Paris in 1914. Bethmann-Hollweg, T. von, *Reflections on the World War* (1920); by the German chancellor in 1914. Buchanan, Sir G., *My Mission to Russia*, 2 vols. (1923); by the British ambassador to Russia in 1914. Churchill, W. S., *The World Crisis, 1911–1918*, 4 vols. (1923–1927); by the British first lord of the admiralty in 1914. Grey, E., Viscount of Fallodon, *Twenty-Five Years, 1892–1916*, 2 vols. (1925); by the British foreign minister in 1914. Haldane, R. B., Viscount, *The Autobiography of Richard Burdon Haldane* (1929). Knapland, P. (ed.), *Speeches on Foreign Affairs, 1904–1914, by Sir Edward Grey* (1932). Lichnowsky, Prince K. M., *Heading for the Abyss* (1928); reminiscences of the German ambassador to Great Britain in 1914. Paléologue, G. M., *An Ambassador's Memoirs*, 3 vols. (1924–1926); by the French ambassador to Russia in 1914. Poincaré, R., *The Memoirs of Raymond Poincaré*, 2 vols. (1926–1928); these volumes cover the years 1912–1914. Poincaré, R., *The Origins of the War* (1922); by the President of the French Republic in 1914. Sazonov, S. D., *Fateful Years, 1909–1916* (1928); by the Russian foreign minister in 1914. Schoen, W. E, Freiherr von, *The Memoirs of an Ambassador* (1922); by the German ambassador to France in 1914. Tirpitz, A. von, *My Memoirs*, 2 vols. (1919); shows the influence of the German naval staff. Wilhelm II, *The Kaiser's Memoirs, 1887–1918* (1922); throws a psychological light on the Kaiser but is of little historical value.

DOCUMENTS: Bridge, Major W. C. (ed.), *How the War Began in 1914, Being the Diary of the Russian Foreign Office* (1925); the diary of Baron Schilling, confidential assistant to Sazonov. Cooke, W. H., and Stickney, E. P., *Readings in European International Relations since 1879* (1931); an admirable selection of primary source material; Part I covers the period 1879–1914; Part II, the crisis of 1914; Part III, the war; Part IV, the peace settlement; Part V, the postwar years. Dugdale, E. T. S. (ed.), *German Diplomatic Documents, 1871–1914*, 4 vols. (1928–1931); selections from *Die grosse Politik der europäischen Kabinette, 1871–1914*, the monumental German publication of foreign correspondence. Headlam-Morley, J. W. (ed.), *Foreign Office Documents, June 28th–August 4th, 1914* (1926); this is Volume XI of *British Documents on the Origins of the War, 1898–1914*, edited by G. P. Gooch and H. W. V. Temperley.

Montgelas, M., and Schücking, W. (eds.), *Outbreak of the World War: German Documents Collected by Karl Kautsky* (1924). *Official Files Pertaining to Pre-War History,* 3 vols. (1920–1921); a fuller edition of the Austrian "Red Book" of 1914. *Official German Documents Relating to the World War,* 2 vols. (1923); documents dealing with the responsibility for the war, published by the Investigating Committee of the Reichstag. Pribram, A. F., *The Secret Treaties of Austria-Hungary, 1879–1914,* 2 vols. (1920–1922); excellent for a study of the Triple Alliance. Romberg, G. von, *Falsifications of the Russian Orange Book* (1923); reveals the deceptions by which the Russian government sought in 1914 to hide its responsibility for the war. Scott, J. B. (ed.), *Diplomatic Documents Relating to the Outbreak of the European War,* 2 vols. (1916); contains the official documents issued by the different European countries just after the outbreak of the war. Scott, J. B. (ed.), *The German White Book Concerning the Responsibility of the Authors of the War* (1924); notes exchanged between the German and Allied governments during the Paris peace conference relative to the responsibility for the outbreak of the war.

Chapter II. The Period of Teutonic Ascendancy

GENERAL: Buchan, J., *A History of the Great War,* 4 vols. (1922); very readable. Chambers, F. P., *The War Behind the War, 1914–1918: A History of the Political and Civilian Fronts* (1939). Cruttwell, C. R. M., *A History of the Great War, 1914–1918* (1934); by a trained historian who saw military service in the war. Frothingham, T. G., *A Guide to the Military History of the World War* (1920); a good synopsis with useful maps. Hayes, C. J. H., *A Brief History of the Great War* (1926). Liddell Hart, B. H., *A History of the World War, 1914–1918* (1935). McPherson, W. L., *A Short History of the Great War* (1920); emphasizes the role of the United States. McPherson, W. L., *The Strategy of the Great War* (1919); an American military critic discusses the major operations. Pollard, A. F., *A Short History of the Great War* (1928). Simonds, F. H., *A History of the World War,* 5 vols. (1917–1920); a good popular account. Stallings, L. (ed.), *The First World War: A Photographic History* (1933); probably the best volume for bringing to the lay reader the meaning of war. Thompson, P. A., *Lions Led by Donkeys* (1927); not so facetious as the title intimates. Woods, W. S., *Colossal Blunders of the War* (1930); mistakes on all sides.

SPECIAL AREAS OR BATTLES: Abbott, G. F., *Greece and the Allies, 1914–1922* (1922); a critical account of Allied activities. Ashmead-Bartlett, E., *The Uncensored Dardanelles* (1928); by a trained observer in touch with authoritative sources. Buxton, N. and C. R., *The War and the Balkans* (1915); has valuable documents. Churchill, W. S., *The Unknown War* (1931); an excellent account of the war on the east front. Emin, A., *Turkey in the World War* (1930); an excellent volume. Essen, L. van der, *The Invasion and the War in Belgium* (1917). Golovin, N. N., *The Russian Army in the World War* (1931); a careful study by a general of the Imperial Russian Army. Gordon-Smith, G., *From Serbia to Jugo-Slavia* (1920); an account of Serbian military campaigns. Graves, R., *Lawrence and the Arabian Adventure* (1928); reveals the importance of Lawrence's activities. Healy, T., *More Lives than One: An Account of the Author's Experiences with the Australian Army at Gallipoli and in France during the First World War* (1944). Heckscher, E., *et al., Sweden, Norway, Denmark, and Iceland in the World War* (1930). Ironside, Sir E., *Tannenberg: The First Thirty Days in East Prussia* (1925); an excellent account. Kannengiesser, H., *The Campaign in Gallipoli* (1928); by a former Prussian and Turkish major general. Kluck, A. von, *The March on Paris, 1914* (1920); by a German general. Lawrence, T. E., *Revolt in the Desert* (1927); by the young Englishman who won the Arabs to the Allied side. Liddell Hart, B. H., *Colonel Lawrence: the Man Behind the Legend* (1934); a brilliant and readable biography of the one who did so much to instigate the revolt of the Arabs against the Turks during the World War. Liman von Sanders, O., *Five Years in Turkey* (1927); excellent for the Turkish campaigns. McEntee, G. L., *Italy's Part in Winning the World War* (1934); by an American army officer. Noel-Buxton, E., and Leese, C., *Balkan Problems and European Peace* (1919); Allied diplomacy in the Balkans. Page, T. N., *Italy and the World War* (1920); by the American ambassador to Italy. Salandra, A., *Italy and the Great War: From Neutrality to Intervention* (1932); by the Italian prime minister. Seton-Watson, R. W., *Roumania and the Great War* (1915); an excellent analysis. Thomas, L. J., *With Lawrence in Arabia* (1924). Trevelyan, G. M., *Scenes from Italy's War* (1919); by the head of the British Red Cross in Italy. Tyng, S., *The Campaign of the Marne, 1914* (1935); the best account. Villari, L., *The War on the Italian Front* (1932); a good account by an Italian.

THE WAR ON THE SEA: Alexander, R., *The Cruise of the Raider "Wolf"* (1939); thrilling account by a prisoner aboard the raider. Carr, W. G., *By Guess and by God* (1930); a vivid account of submarine activities. Corbett, J. S., and Newbolt, H., *Naval Operations,* 5 vols. (1920–1931); British official history. Domville, C., *Submarines and Sea-Power* (1919). Dorling, H. T., *Endless Story* (1931); an account of the activities of British destroyer squadrons. Fawcett, H. W., and Hooper, G. W. W. (eds.), *The Fighting at Jutland* (1929); by some forty-five men who participated. Fisher, J. A., *Memories and Records,* 2 vols. (1920); by the first lord of the admiralty. Forstner, G. G. von, *The Journal of Submarine Commander von Forstner* (1917). Gibson, L., and Harper, J. E. T., *The Riddle of Jutland* (1934); one of the best of the many books dealing with this battle. Gibson, R. H., and Prendergast, M., *The German Submarine War, 1914–1918* (1931). Guichard, L., *The Naval Blockade* (1930); a scholarly account. Hashagen, E., *The Log of a U-Boat Commander, or U-Boats Westward!* (1931). Jellicoe, J. R., *The Crisis of the Naval War* (1920); discusses the antisubmarine campaign of 1917–1918. Jellicoe, J. R., *The Grand Fleet, 1914–1916* (1922); by its commander. Jellicoe, J. R., *The Submarine Peril* (1934). Lauriat, C. E., Jr., *The Lusitania's Last Voyage* (1915). Newbolt, Sir H., *A Naval History of the War, 1914–1918* (1920); probably the best one-volume history of British activities. Pochhammer, H., *Before Jutland: Admiral von Spee's Last Voyage*

(1931); discusses the battles at Coronel and the Falkland Islands. Puleston, W. D., *The Dardanelles Expedition* (1927). Scheer, R., *Germany's High Sea Fleet in the World War* (1920); by the commander of the German fleet at the battle of Jutland. Thomas, L., *Count Luckner, the Sea Devil* (1927). Thomas, L., *Raiders of the Deep* (1928); stories of the submarines.

THE WAR IN THE AIR: Lehmann, E. A., and Mingos, H., *The Zeppelins* (1928); by the director of the German raids over England. Raleigh, Sir W. A., *The War in the Air,* 6 vols. (1922–1937); British official history. Rawlinson, Sir A., *The Defense of London, 1915–1918* (1923); against raids from the air. Treusch von Buttlar-Brandenfels, H., *Zeppelins over England* (1932); by a German commander. Turner, C. C., *The Struggle in the Air, 1914–1918* (1919); the activities of the British air forces.

ESPIONAGE AND PROPAGANDA: Aston, Sir G. G., *Secret Service* (1930); by a British officer. Berndorff, H. R., *Espionage!* (1930); thrilling. Bruntz, G., *Allied Propaganda and the Collapse of the German Empire in 1918* (1938). Crozier, J., *In the Enemy's Country* (1931); a French account of espionage. Hardie, M., and Sabin, A. K. (eds.), *War Posters Issued by Belligerent and Neutral Nations, 1914–1919* (1920); with the stories connected with them. Landau, H., *All's Fair* (1934); the British secret service. Lasswell, H. D., *Propaganda Technique in the World War* (1927). Nicolai, W., *The German Secret Service* (1924); by the chief of the intelligence division of the German general staff. Playne, C. E., *Society at War, 1914–1916* (1931); a study of British national psychology in the first years. Ponsonby, A., *Falsehood in Wartime* (1928); discusses specific stories. Read, J. M., *Atrocity Propaganda, 1914–1919* (1941). Squires, J. D., *British Propaganda at Home and in the United States from 1914 to 1917* (1935). Stuart, Sir C., *Secrets of Crewe House* (1920); discusses the British propaganda organization. Thomson, Sir B., *The Allied Secret Service in Greece* (1931); a story of Allied activities. Viereck, G. S., *Spreading Germs of Hate* (1930); propaganda in the United States. Wild, M., *Secret Service on the Russian Front* (1932). Yardley, H. O., *The American Black Chamber* (1931); military intelligence and secret service.

SPECIAL TOPICS: Chamberlin, Waldo, *Industrial Relations in Wartime Great Britain, 1914–1918* (1940). Cocks, F. S., *The Secret Treaties and Understandings* (1918); throws light on the diplomatic intrigues of the war. Cook, E., *The Press in War-Time* (1920); in Great Britain. Dewar, G. A. B., *The Great Munition Feat, 1914–1918* (1921); with reference to Great Britain. Foulkes, C. H., *Gas! The Story of the Special Brigade* (1934). Fradkin, E., *Chemical Warfare* (1929). Fuller, J. F. C., *Tanks in the Great War* (1920). Liddell Hart, B. H., *Reputations Ten Years After* (1928); a postwar criticism of the military leaders of the war. Martin, W., *Statesmen of the War in Retrospect, 1918–1928* (1928); studies of the personalities and motives of twenty-three prominent statesmen of the war. Maurice, Sir F., *Lessons of Allied Co-operation: Naval, Military, Air, 1914–1918* (1942). Miller, H. W., *The Paris Gun* (1930); an account of the German gun that shelled Paris from seventy miles away. Molony, W., *Prisoners and Captives* (1933); by a war prisoner in Germany.

BIOGRAPHIES, MEMOIRS, RECOLLECTIONS: Asquith, H. H., *Memories and Reflections, 1852–1927*, 2 vols. (1928); the second volume deals with the war. Beaverbrook, Lord W. M. A., *A Politician and the War: 1914–1916* (1928). Brusilov, A. A., *A Soldier's Notebook* (1930); by the Russian commander on the Austrian front. Churchill, W. S., *The World Crisis, 1911–1918*, 4 vols. (1923–1927). Corday, M., *The Paris Front* (1934); diary of a middle-aged Parisian, 1914–1918. Djemal, A., *Memoirs of a Turkish Statesman, 1913–1919* (1922); by one of the controlling triumvirate during the war. Eisenmenger, A., *Blockade: The Diary of an Austrian Middle-Class Woman, 1914–1918* (1932). Falkenhayn, E. von, *General Headquarters and Its Critical Decisions* (1919); by the German chief of the general staff, 1914–1916. French, G., *The Life of Field Marshal Sir John French* (1931); based upon French's diaries. French, Sir J., *1914* (1919). Galet, E. J., *Albert, King of the Belgians, in the Great War* (1931); deals with the first three months of the war. Giolitti, G., *Memoirs of My Life* (1923); valuable for Italian policy in the war. Hamilton, Sir I., *Gallipoli Diary*, 2 vols. (1920); by the British commander. Hindenburg, P. von, *Out of My Life*, 2 vols. (1921); covers his entire military career. Hoffmann, M., *War Diaries and Other Papers*, 2 vols. (1929); by the German who is said to deserve much credit for success in the east. Joffre, J. J. C., *Personal Memoirs*, 2 vols. (1932); excellent for study of the first Marne campaign. Lloyd George, D., *War Memoirs of David Lloyd George*, 6 vols. (1933–1937). Ludendorff, E., *Ludendorff's Own Story, August 1914 – November 1918*, 2 vols. (1920); deals with political as well as military affairs. Mercier, D. J., *Cardinal Mercier's Own Story* (1920); the war in Belgium as seen by the courageous archbishop of Malines. Morgenthau, H., *Ambassador Morgenthau's Story* (1919); wartime Turkey as seen by the American ambassador. Recouly, R., *Joffre* (1931). Robertson, Sir W., *Soldiers and Statesmen, 1914–1918*, 2 vols. (1926); by the British field marshal. Speranza, F. C. (ed.), *The Diary of Gino Speranza: Italy, 1915–1919*, 2 vols. (1941); reflects conditions in Italy during the war. Townshend, Sir C., *My Campaign in Mesopotamia* (1920); by the leader of the ill-fated expedition against Bagdad. Wavell, General Sir A., *Allenby: A Study in Greatness* (1941). Whitlock, B., *Belgium: A Personal Narrative*, 2 vols. (1919); by the American minister to Belgium during the war. Witkop, P., *German Students' War Letters* (1929).

Chapter III. America's Intervention and Russia's Withdrawal

THE UNITED STATES AS A NEUTRAL: Baker, N. D., *Why We Went to War* (1936); by the American secretary of war, 1916–1921. Baker, R. S., *Neutrality: 1914–1915* (1935); the fifth volume of the *Life and Letters of Woodrow Wilson*. Bernstorff, J. von, *Memoirs of Count Bernstorff* (1936). Bernstorff, J. von, *My Three Years in America* (1920); by the German ambassador to the United States. Clapp, E. J., *Economic Aspects of the War:*

Neutral Rights, Belligerent Claims and American Commerce in the Years 1914–1915 (1915); shows anti-British feeling. Dumba, K., *Memories of a Diplomat* (1932); by the Austrian minister who was dismissed from the United States because of his activities. Gerard, J. W., *My Four Years in Germany* (1917); by the American ambassador to Germany. Gwynn, S. (ed.), *The Letters and Friendships of Sir Cecil Spring-Rice,* 2 vols. (1929); from the papers of the British ambassador to the United States. Hendrick, B. J., *Life and Letters of Walter H. Page,* 3 vols. (1922); the American ambassador to England during the war. Landau, H., *The Enemy Within: The Inside Story of German Sabotage in America* (1937). Lansing, R., *War Memoirs* (1935); by the American secretary of state, 1915–1920. Lyddon, W. G., *British War Missions to the United States, 1914–1918* (1938). Millis, W., *The Road to War: America, 1914–1917* (1935). Morrisey, A. M., *The American Defense of Neutral Rights, 1914–1917* (1939). Peterson, H. C., *Propaganda for War: The Campaign Against American Neutrality, 1914–1917* (1939). Robinson, E., and West, V., *The Foreign Policy of Woodrow Wilson, 1913–1917* (1917). Scott, J. B. (ed.), *President Wilson's Foreign Policy* (1918); a collection of important addresses, messages, and papers. Scott, J. B., *A Survey of International Relations between the United States and Germany, August 1, 1914 – April 6, 1917, Based on Official Documents* (1917). Seymour, C., *American Diplomacy during the World War* (1934); the development of American policy toward the European belligerents. Seymour, C., *American Neutrality, 1914–1917: Essays on the Causes of American Intervention in the World War* (1935). Seymour, C. (ed.), *The Intimate Papers of Colonel House,* 2 vols. (1926–1928); valuable for negotiations with the belligerents during the war. Seymour, C., *Woodrow Wilson and the World War* (1922). Sharp, W. G. *The War Memoirs of William Graves Sharp, American Ambassador to France, 1914–1919* (1931). Tansill, C. C., *America Goes to War* (1938). United States Department of State, *Diplomatic Correspondence with Belligerent Governments Relating to Neutral Rights and Duties,* 4 vols. (1915–1918). Viereck, G. S., *Spreading Germs of Hate* (1930); foreign propaganda activities in the United States.

THE UNITED STATES AS A BELLIGERENT: American Council on Public Affairs, *The Food Front in World War I* (1944). Ayers, L. P., *The War with Germany: A Statistical Summary* (1920); an interesting study by the chief of statistics of the United States general staff. Bailey, T. A., *The Policy of the United States toward the Neutrals, 1917–1918* (1942). Bassett, J. S., *Our War with Germany* (1919). Beamish, R. J., and March, F. A., *America's Part in the World War* (1919). Clarkson, G. B., *Industrial America in the World War: the Strategy Behind the Lines, 1917–1918* (rev. ed., 1924). Creel, G., *How We Advertised America* (1920); by the chairman of the Committee on Public Information. Daniels, J., *Our Navy at War* (1922); by the American secretary of the navy. Davison, H. P., *The American Red Cross in the Great War* (1919). Frothingham, T. G., *The American Reinforcement in the World War* (1927); an account of recruiting, equipping, and transporting the A.E.F. Frothingham, T. G., *The Naval History of the World War,* Vol. III (1926); an account of the United States in the war, based on data provided by the historical section of the U. S. Navy. Gleaves, A., *A History of the Transport Service* (1921); discusses the convoy system. Harbord, J. G., *The American Army in France* (1936); by a retired American general who had intimate contact with the A.E.F. Hurley, E. N., *The Bridge to France* (1927); building ships. Liggett, H., *A.E.F.: Ten Years Ago in France* (1928); by the commander of the American First Army. McMaster, J. B., *The United States in the World War*, 2 vols. (1918–1920); based largely on newspaper accounts. MacQuarrie, H., *How to Live at the Front* (1917); handbook published for American soldiers. March, P. C., *The Nation at War* (1932); by the American chief of staff. Mock, J. R., *Censorship, 1917* (1941); based on documents of the Committee on Public Information. Mock, J. R., and Larson, C., *Words That Won the War: The Story of the Committee on Public Information, 1917–1919* (1939). Moore, S. T., *America and the World War: A Narrative of the Part Played by the United States from the Outbreak to Peace* (1937). Mullendore, W. C., *History of the United States Food Administration, 1917–1919* (1941). Palmer, F., *Newton D. Baker*, 2 vols. (1931); biography of the American secretary of war. Palmer, F., *Our Greatest Battle* (1919); the Meuse-Argonne. Patrick, M. M., *The United States in the Air* (1928); by the chief of the air service of the A.E.F. Paxson, F. L., *America at War, 1917–1918* (1939). Pershing, J. J., *Final Report to the Secretary of War* (1919). Pershing, J. J., *My Experiences in the World War*, 2 vols. (1931). Sims, W. S., and Hendrick, B. J., *The Victory at Sea* (1920); the activities of the American navy. Thomas, S., *History of the A.E.F.* (1920). Van Every, D., *The A.E.F. in Battle* (1928). Viereck, G. S. (ed.), *As They Saw Us* (1929); the work of the American forces discussed by Allied and German generals.

THE RUSSIAN REVOLUTION: Alexandra, Empress Consort of Nicholas II, *Letters of the Tsarina to the Tsar, 1914–1916* (1923). Almedingen, E. M., *Tomorrow Will Come* (1941); a personal story of the Russian revolution by a young woman of the intelligentsia. Buchanan, Sir G. W., *My Mission to Russia*, Vol. II (1923); by the British ambassador to Russia in 1917. Bunyan, J., and Fisher, H. H. (eds.), *The Bolshevik Revolution, 1917–1918* (1934); valuable documentary material. Chamberlin, W. H., *The Russian Revolution, 1917–1921*, 2 vols. (1935). Carr, E. H., *The Bolshevist Revolution, 1917–1923*, 3 vols. (1951–1953); the most recent and thorough account. Chernov, V., *The Great Russian Revolution* (1936); by a minister in first provisional government. Florinsky, M. T., *The End of the Russian Empire* (1931); an admirable study of Russian history during the war. Fülöp-Miller, R., *Rasputin: the Holy Devil* (1928); the personality and role of Rasputin. Golder, F. A. (ed.), *Documents of Russian History, 1914–1917* (1927); extracts from diaries and letters. Hindus, M. G., *The Russian Peasant and the Revolution* (1920). Judas, E., *Rasputin, Neither Devil Nor Saint* (1942); by a former friend of Rasputin. Kerensky, A. F., *The Catastrophe* (1927). Kerensky, A. F., *The Prelude to Bolshevism* (1919); the Kornilov revolt. Kirby, L. P., *The Russian Revolution* (1940). Lenin, N., *Preparing for Revolt* (1929). Marcu, V., *Lenin: Thirty Years of Russia* (1928); perhaps the best biography. Marye, G. T.,

Nearing the End in Imperial Russia (1929); impressions of the American ambassador. Meyendorff, Baron A. F., *The Background of the Russian Revolution* (1929); by the vice-president of the Duma. Miliukov, P., *History of the Second Russian Revolution* (1920); by the foreign minister in the first provisional government. Mintz, J., *How Moscow Was Won in 1917: A Chapter in the History of the Revolution* (1941). Mirsky, D. S., *Lenin* (1931); by a former Russian prince. Nicholas II, *The Letters of the Tsar to the Tsarina, 1914–1917* (1929). Pares, Sir B., *The Fall of the Russian Monarchy: A Study of the Evidence* (1939); by a distinguished British historian who lived in Russia during the revolution. Rodzianko, M. V., *The Reign of Rasputin: An Empire's Collapse* (1927); by the president of the last Russian Duma. Trachtenberg, A. (ed.), *Lenin: Toward the Seizure of Power,* 2 vols. (1932); a collection of Lenin's articles and papers preceding the November revolution. Trotsky, L., *From October to Brest-Litovsk* (1919). Trotsky, L., *The History of the Russian Revolution* (1934). Trotsky, L., *Lenin* (1925); deals chiefly with the years 1900–1903 and 1917–1918. Trotsky, L., *My Life* (1930); very readable. Vulliamy, C. E. (ed.), *The Red Archives* (1929); documents which illumine the background of the revolution. Wheeler-Bennett, J. W., *Brest-Litovsk: the Forgotten Peace, March, 1918* (1939). Youssoupoff, F. F., *Rasputin* (1927); by one of his assassins.

Chapter IV. The Collapse of the Central Powers

In addition to the references for the two preceding chapters, the following are suggested:

BIOGRAPHIES AND MEMOIRS: Aston, Sir G. G., *The Biography of the Late Marshal Foch* (1929). Bruun, G., *Clemenceau* (1943). Charteris, J., *Field Marshal Earl Haig* (1929). Foch, F., *Memoirs* (1931). Lecomte, G. C., *Georges Clemenceau—the Tiger of France* (1919). Liddell Hart, B. H., *Foch, the Man of Orléans* (1932). Madelin, L., *Foch* (1929); by a distinguished French historian.

WAR AIMS AND PEACE EFFORTS: Andrassy, Count J., *Diplomacy and the War* (1921); by the Austro-Hungarian foreign minister at the close of the war. Czernin, O., *In the World War* (1920); by the Austro-Hungarian foreign minister during the latter part of the war. Dahlin, E., *French and German Public Opinion on Declared War Aims, 1914–1918* (1933). Dickinson, G. L. (ed.), *Documents and Statements Relating to Peace Proposals and War Aims, 1916–1918* (1919). Forster, K., *The Failures of Peace: The Search for a Negotiated Peace during the First World War* (1941). Harding, B., *Imperial Twilight* (1939); includes the Austro-French peace negotiations of 1917. Manteyer, G. de (ed.), *Austria's Peace Offer, 1916–1917* (1921). Nekliudoff, A. V., *Diplomatic Reminiscences before and during the World War, 1911–1917* (1920); useful for peace moves. Scott, J. B. (ed.), *Official Statements of War Aims and Peace Proposals, December 1916 to November 1918* (1921). Slice, A. van der, *International Labor, Diplomacy, and Peace: 1914–1919* (1941).

THE DISINTEGRATION OF AUSTRIA-HUNGARY: Baerlein, H., *The Birth of Yugoslavia,* 2 vols. (1922); a sympathetic account of the struggle for unification. Bauer, O., *The Austrian Revolution* (1925); by the leader of the Austrian Social Democrats. Beneš, E., *My War Memories* (1928); detailed story of the Czech revolutionary movement. Burian, Count S., *Austria in Dissolution* (1925); by the Austro-Hungarian foreign minister during the war. Čapek, K. (ed.), *President Masaryk Tells His Story* (1935); informal autobiography made up of reminiscences. Cohen, V., *The Life and Times of Masaryk, the President-Liberator: A Biographical Study of Central Europe Since 1848* (1941). Gillie, D. R., *Joseph Pilsudski: The Memories of a Polish Revolutionary and Soldier* (1931); contains Pilsudski's collected writings, speeches, letters, etc. Glaise von Horstenau, E., *The Collapse of the Austro-Hungarian Empire* (1930); by the director of the Vienna war archives. Jászi, O., *The Dissolution of the Hapsburg Monarchy* (1929); by one of Karolyi's ministers, an eminent Hungarian historian. Jászi, O., *Revolution and Counter-Revolution in Hungary* (1924). Karolyi, Count M., *Fighting the World: The Struggle for Peace* (1924); an account of conditions in Hungary during the war and at the outbreak of the revolution, by the head of the provisional government. Kerner, R. J., *The Jugo-Slav Movement* (1918); contains the Corfu Manifesto. Masaryk, T. G., *The Making of a State* (1927); an account of the Czech efforts during 1914–1918, by the first president of Czechoslovakia. Nowak, K. F., *The Collapse of Central Europe* (1924); a well-written and interesting survey of events in Austria-Hungary from December, 1917, to October, 1918. Opočenský, J., *The Collapse of the Austro-Hungarian Monarchy and the Rise of the Czechoslovak State* (1928); a detailed narrative of events, September–December, 1918. Papoušek, J., *The Czechoslovak Nation's Struggle for Independence* (1928); with interesting maps showing the journeys of the Czech leaders. Pilsudski, J., *The Memories of a Polish Revolutionary and Soldier* (1931); an account of the early phases of the war, by an outstanding Polish leader. Polzer-Hoditz und Wolframitz, A. Count of, *Emperor Karl (Charles IV, King of Hungary)* (1928); an Austrian nobleman, the emperor's chief private secretary, gives an account of the disruption of the monarchy. Selver, P., *Masaryk* (1940). Seton-Watson, R. W., *Masaryk in England* (1943); activities during 1915–1917. Steed, H. W., *Through Thirty Years* (1924); by one intimately connected with the disintegration of the Dual Monarchy. Street, C. J. C., *President Masaryk* (1930); discusses the Czech revolution. Strong, D. F., *Austria, October, 1918 – March, 1919: Transition from Empire to Republic* (1939). Tormay, C., *An Outlaw's Diary,* 2 vols. (1924); a thrilling picture of Hungary during 1918–1919, by a woman of the aristocracy. Windisch-Graetz, L., *My Memoirs* (1921); by a member of the Austrian foreign office in 1918.

THE DOWNFALL OF THE GERMAN EMPIRE: Baumont, M., *The Fall of the Kaiser* (1931); the best book on the subject. Bevan, E., *German Social Democracy during the War* (1919); thorough, dispassionate, interesting. Bouton, S. M., *And the Kaiser Abdicates: The German Revolution, November 1918 – August 1919* (1921); by the first enemy correspondent to enter Germany after the armistice.   Bruntz, G. G., *Allied Propaganda and the Collapse of the German Empire in 1918* (1938).   Frölich, P., *Rosa Luxemburg: Her Life and Work* (1940).   Lutz, R. H. (ed.), *The Causes of the German Collapse in 1918* (1934); authorized English translation of the documents of the German official committee appointed to investigate the cause of the German collapse.   Lutz, R. H. (ed.), *Fall of the German Empire, 1914–1918: Documents of the German Revolution,* 2 vols. (1920); a valuable collection of source material.   Lutz, R. H., *The German Revolution of 1918–19* (1922); an authoritative account. Maximilian, Prinz von Baden, *The Memoirs of Prince Max of Baden,* 2 vols. (1928).   Rosenberg, A., *The Birth of the German Republic* (1931); one of the best studies of the revolution.   Scheidemann, P., *The Making of New Germany: The Memoirs of Philipp Scheidemann* (1929); a valuable contribution by one of the leaders of the Social Democrats.   Ströbel, H., *The German Revolution and After* (1923); by a prominent German Independent Socialist.

THE END OF THE WAR: Maurice, Sir F., *The Armistices of 1918* (1943); the political and military negotiations involved.   Menne, B., *Armistice and Germany's Food Supply, 1918–1919: A Study of Conditional Surrender* (1944).   Rudin, H., *Armistice, 1918* (1944); chiefly from German sources. Scott, J. B. (ed.), *Preliminary History of the Armistice* (1924); a collection of documents.   Shartle, S. G., *Spa, Versailles, Munich: An Account of the Armistice Commission* (1941); by a member of the commission.

THE COST OF THE WAR: Bogart, E. L., *Direct and Indirect Costs of the Great World War* (1919).   Brittain, V., *Testament of Youth* (1933); effect of the war on a British family.   Clark, J. M., *The Costs of the World War to the American People* (1931).   Dumas, S., and Vedel-Petersen, K. O., *Losses of Life Caused by War* (1923).   Folks, H., *The Human Costs of the War* (1920). Grebler, L., and Winkler, W., *The Cost of the World War to Germany and to Austria-Hungary* (1940).   Hirst, F. W., *The Consequences of the War to Great Britain* (1934).   Kohn, S., and Meyendorff, Baron A. F., *The Cost of the War to Russia* (1932); in human lives and social disruption.   Shotwell, J. T., *What Germany Forgot* (1940); the cost of the war to Germany.

Chapter V. The Treaties Arising from the First World War

THE PARIS PEACE CONFERENCE: Albrecht-Carrie, R., *Italy at the Peace Conference* (1938).   Bonsal, S., *Unfinished Business* (1944) and *Suitors and Suppliants: The Little Nations at Versailles* (1946); from the diary of Colonel House's personal interpreter.   Dillon, E. J., *The Inside Story of the Peace Conference* (1920); by a journalist.   Harris, H. W., *The Peace in the Making* (1920); by a journalist.   Haskins, C. H., and Lord, R. H., *Some Problems of the Peace Conference* (1920); by two advisers to the American Peace Commission.   House, E. M., and Seymour, C. (eds.), *What Really Happened at Paris: The Story of the Peace Conference, 1918–1919, by American Delegates* (1921).   Huddleston, S., *Peace-Making at Paris* (1919); by a journalist.   Lansing, R., *The Peace Negotiations: A Personal Narrative* (1921); by the American secretary of state.   Luckau, Alma, *The German Delegation at the Paris Peace Conference* (1941); the German side of the peace negotiations. Marston, E. S., *The Peace Conferences, 1919: Organization and Procedure* (1945). Nevins, A., *Henry White: Thirty Years of American Diplomacy* (1930); one of the five American delegates. Nicholson, H., *Peace-making, 1919: Being Reminiscences of the Paris Peace Conference* (1933); by a member of the British delegation. Noble, G. B., *Policies and Opinions at Paris, 1919* (1935); describes the clash between the old and the new diplomacy. Palmer, F., *Bliss, Peacemaker: The Life and Letters of General Tasker Howard Bliss* (1934); one of the five American delegates. Riddell, G., *Lord Riddell's Intimate Diary of the Peace Conference and After, 1918–1923* (1933); by a representative of the British press. Schiff, V., *The Germans at Versailles* (1930); by the official press representative of the German delegation. Seymour, C. (ed.), *The Intimate Papers of Colonel House,* Vol. IV (1928); one of the American delegates. Shotwell, J. T., *At the Paris Peace Conference* (1937); by one of Wilson's technical advisers. Temperley, H. W. V. (ed.), *A History of the Peace Conference of Paris,* 6 vols. (1920–1924); scholarly and full. Thompson, C. T., *The Peace Conference Day by Day* (1920); by an Associated Press correspondent. United States Department of State, *Papers Relating to the Foreign Relations of the United States: The Paris Peace Conference,* 1919, 4 vols. (1942–1943).

THE BIG FOUR: Bailey, T. A., *Woodrow Wilson and the Lost Peace* (1944); emphasizes Wilson's mistakes. Baker, R. S., *Woodrow Wilson and the World Settlement,* 3 vols. (1922–1923); written from President Wilson's unpublished and personal material. Bruun, G., *Clemenceau* (1943). Clemenceau, G., *Grandeur and Misery of Victory* (1930); reveals the French premier's attitude toward the peace settlement. Dodd, W. E., *Woodrow Wilson and His Work* (1932). Johnson, G. W., *Woodrow Wilson, the Unforgettable Figure Who Has Returned to Haunt Us* (1944); the tragic hero of 1918–1919. Lansing, R., *The Big Four and Others of the Peace Conference* (1921); by the American secretary of state. Lloyd George, D., *Memoirs of the Peace Conference,* 2 vols. (1939). Loth, D., *Woodrow Wilson—The Fifteenth Point* (1941).

THE TREATY OF VERSAILLES: Baruch, B. M., *The Making of the Reparation and Economic Sections of the Treaty* (1920); by the economic adviser to the American Peace Commission. Birdsall, P., *Versailles Twenty Years After* (1941); an appraisal of the forces which determined the outcome of the struggle between Wilsonian principles and principles of reactionary nationalism. Burnett, P. M., *Reparation at the Paris Peace Conference from the Standpoint of the American Delegation,* 2 vols. (1940). Carnegie Endowment for International Peace, *The Treaties of Peace, 1919–1923,* 2 vols. (1924); the texts with maps. Ebray, A., *A Frenchman Looks at the Peace* (1927); an indictment of the treaty of Versailles. Jessop, T. E., *The Treaty of Versailles: Was It Just?* (1942). Keynes, J. M., *The Economic Consequences of the Peace* (1920); arguments for a revision of the treaty of Versailles, by a British economist. Miller, D. H., *The Drafting of the Covenant* (1928); the author, with Sir Cecil Hurst, drew up the final draft of the Covenant. Nitti, F. S., *The Wreck of Europe* (1922); an attack on the peace settlement by a former Italian

prime minister. Nowak, K. F., *Versailles* (1929); throws light on the acceptance of the treaty by Germany. Scott, A. P., *An Introduction to the Peace
Treaties* (1920); chiefly an analysis of the treaty of Versailles. Stegeman, H.,
The Mirage of Versailles (1928). Tardieu, A., *The Truth about the Treaty*
(1921); by a member of the French Peace Commission.

THE LESSER TREATIES: Almond, N., and Lutz, R. H. (eds.), *The
Treaty of St. Germain* (1934). Bethlen, I., *The Treaty of Trianon and European Peace* (1934); a plea for revision, by a former premier of Hungary.
Deák, F., *Hungary at the Paris Peace Conference: The Diplomatic History of
the Treaty of Trianon* (1942). Donald, Sir R., *The Tragedy of Trianon*
(1928); an indictment of the treaty of Trianon. Howard, H., *The Partition of
Turkey, 1913–1923* (1931); includes a discussion of the treaty of Sèvres. Seton-
Watson, R. W., *Treaty Revision and the Hungarian Frontiers* (1934); should
be read in connection with the volume by Bethlen listed above.

THE UNITED STATES AND THE PEACE SETTLEMENT: In addi-
tion to the books on President Wilson listed above, the following are valuable:
Bailey, T. A., *Woodrow Wilson and the Great Betrayal* (1945); by an American
diplomatic historian. Bartlett, R. J., *The League to Enforce Peace* (1944);
discusses the factors which caused the defeat of the League of Nations. Bur-
lingame, R., and Stevens, A., *Victory Without Peace* (1943); the campaign for
peace in 1918–1919. Dickinson, T. H., *The United States and the League*
(1923); bitter indictment of the men held responsible for defeating the ratification of the treaty of Versailles. Fleming, D. F., *The United States and the
League of Nations* (1932); an account of the conflict between President Wilson
and the Senate. Foley, H. (ed.), *Woodrow Wilson's Case for the League of
Nations* (1923); a collection of President Wilson's speeches in behalf of the
League. Lodge, H. C., *The Senate and the League of Nations* (1925); the Republican view set forth by one of Wilson's most determined opponents. Schrift-
giesser, K., *The Gentleman from Massachussetts: Henry Cabot Lodge* (1944);
includes much on the campaign against the League.

Chapter VI. The League of Nations, Collective Security,
Disarmament

THE LEAGUE OF NATIONS: Bassett, J. S., *The League of Nations:
A Chapter in World Politics* (1928); a detached and dispassionate work by an
American historian. Beer, M., *The League on Trial* (1933); brilliant but
satirical. Burton, M. E., *The Assembly of the League of Nations* (1941); historical. Cecil, E. A. R., Viscount, *A Great Experiment: An Autobiography*
(1941); a record of Lord Cecil's association with the movement for collective
security. Conwell-Evans, T. P., *The League Council in Action* (1929); a care-
ful study of twenty-three disputes. Davis, H. E. (ed.), *Pioneers in World
Order: An American Appraisal of The League of Nations* (1944). Howard-
Ellis, C., *The Origin, Structure and Working of the League of Nations* (1928).
Institute on World Organization, *World Organization: A Balance Sheet of the
First Great Experiment* (1943). Jones, R., and Sherman, S. S., *The League of*

Nations: From Idea to Reality (1927); development of the idea. League of Nations, *Ten Years of World Co-operation* (1930). Marburg, T., *Development of the League of Nations Idea,* 2 vols. (1932). Morley, F., *The Society of Nations* (1932); weaknesses and limitations of the League. Rappard, W. E., *The Quest for Peace since the World War* (1940). Slocombe, G. E., *Mirror to Geneva: Its Grandeur and Decay* (1938). Wilson, F., *The Origin of the League Covenant* (1928); an analysis of the Covenant, article by article, in the light of discussions at the time it was drafted. Zimmern, A., *The League of Nations and the Rule of Law, 1918–1935* (1936).

THE WORLD COURT: Bustamante, A. S. de, *The World Court* (1925); by a justice of the court. Hudson, M. O., *The Permanent Court of International Justice* (1934); an authoritative treatment of history, organization, and achievements. Lindsey, E., *The International Court* (1931); its history, organization, and activity. Wheeler-Bennett, J. W., *Information on the World Court, 1918–1928* (1929); a compact manual containing all the important documents.

THE INTERNATIONAL LABOR ORGANIZATION: Barnes, G. N., *History of the International Labour Office* (1926); a good brief survey by an official of the office. Oliver, E. M., *The World's Industrial Parliament* (1925); an excellent short popular account of the International Labor Organization. Shotwell, J. T. (ed.), *The Origins of the International Labor Organization,* 2 vols. (1934); authoritative; the first volume is historical; the second, documentary. Wilson, F. G., *Labor in the League System* (1935); perhaps the best study of the ILO available in English. World Peace Foundation, *The International Labour Organization* (1931); written by competent men.

MANDATES AND MINORITIES: Azcárate, P. de, *League of Nations and National Minorities: An Experiment* (1946); by the former director of the minorities section of the League. Gerig, B., *The Open Door and the Mandates System* (1930). Junghann, O., *National Minorities in Europe* (1932). Mair, L. D., *The Protection of Minorities* (1928); discusses the cases which have come before the League. Margalith, A. M., *The International Mandates* (1930); a general study of the origins and character of the system. Molony, W. O., *Nationality and the Peace Treaties* (1934); by a League official. Robinson, J., *et al., Were the Minorities Treaties a Failure?* (1943). Rouček, J. S., *The Working of the Minorities System under the League of Nations* (1929); one of the best general accounts. White, F., *Mandates* (1926); a popular survey of the individual mandates. Wright, Q., *Mandates under the League of Nations* (1930); the most thorough treatment.

THE UNITED STATES AND THE LEAGUE: Berdahl, C. A., *The Policy of the United States with Respect to the League of Nations* (1932). Fleming, D. F., *The United States and the World Court* (1945). Hudson, M. O., *The Permanent Court of International Justice and the Question of American Participation* (1925). Jessup, P. C., *The United States and the World Court* (1929); an objective record of the negotiations after 1926. Kellor, F. A., and Hatvany, A., *The United States Senate and the International Court* (1925); an account of the earlier attitude.

SECURITY: Ferrell, R. H., *Peace in Their Time; The Origins of the Kellogg-Briand Pact* (1952); good. Glasgow, G., *From Dawes to Locarno, 1924–1925* (1925); includes documents. Miller, D. H., *The Geneva Protocol* (1925); its legal aspects. Miller, D. H., *The Peace Pact of Paris* (1928); origins and purpose. Myers, D. P., *Origin and Conclusion of the Paris Pact* (1929); the negotiations. Noel-Baker, P. J., *The Geneva Protocol for the Pacific Settlement of International Disputes* (1925). Shotwell, J. T., *War as an Instrument of National Policy and Its Renunciation in the Pact of Paris* (1929); the most complete and careful discussion. Wheeler-Bennett, J. W., *Disarmament and Security since Locarno* (1932). Wheeler-Bennett, J. W., *Information on the Renunciation of War, 1927–1928* (1928). Wheeler-Bennett, J. W., and Langermann, F. E., *Information on the Problem of Security, 1917–1926* (1927); includes the most important documents.

DISARMAMENT: Boggs, M. W., *Attempts to Define and Limit "Aggressive" Armament in Diplomacy and Strategy* (1941). Buell, R. L., *The Washington Conference* (1922). Engely, G., *The Politics of Naval Disarmament* (1932). Harris, H. W., *Naval Disarmament* (1930). Hindmarsh, A., *Force in Peace: Force Short of War in International Relations* (1933). Hoag, C. L., *Preface to Preparedness: The Washington Disarmament Conference and Public Opinion* (1941). Ichihashi, Y., *The Washington Conference and After* (1928). Lefebure, V., *Common Sense about Disarmament* (1932); data for an understanding of the League's disarmament conference. Myers, D. P., *World Disarmament* (1932); a survey of the whole problem. Neumann, R., *Zaharoff, the Armaments King* (1936); an account of one who is supposed to typify in his activities all armament manufacturers who desire wars. Noel-Baker, P. J., *The Private Manufacture of Armaments* (1937). Sloutzki, N. M., *The World Armament Race, 1919–1939* (1941). Williams, B. H., *The United States and Disarmament* (1931).

Chapter VII. Reparations, War Debts, World Depression

REPARATIONS: Angas, L. L. B., *Germany and Her Debts* (1923); an early study with arguments for reduction. Bergmann, C., *The History of Reparations* (1927); the German viewpoint. Borsky, G., *The Greatest Swindle in the World: The Story of the German Reparations* (1942). Dawes, C. G., *A Journal of Reparations* (1939). Dawes, R. C., *The Dawes Plan in the Making* (1925). Frasure, C. M., *British Policy on War Debts and Reparations* (1940); an analysis of motives and public opinion. Keynes, J. M., *The Economic Consequences of the Peace* (1920). Keynes, J. M., *A Revision of the Treaty* (1922); suggests a way to solve the reparations problem. Kuczynski, R. R., *American Loans to Germany* (1927). Lichtenberger, H., *The Ruhr Conflict* (1923); by a French professor. Lloyd George, D., *The Truth about Reparations and War Debts* (1932); indictment of French and American attitudes. Long, R. E. C., *The Mythology of Reparations* (1928); examines the working of the Dawes Plan. Moulton, H. G., *The Reparation Plan* (1924);

a favorable analysis of the Dawes Plan. Moulton, H. G., and McGuire, C. E., *Germany's Capacity to Pay* (1923). Myers, D. P., *The Reparation Settlement* (1929); contains documents relating to the Young Plan. Schacht, H., *The End of Reparations* (1931); arguments for complete cancellation, by the head of the Reichsbank. Sering, M., *Germany under the Dawes Plan* (1929); one of the best treatments of the reparation problem from the German side. Street, C. J. C., *Rhineland and Ruhr* (1923); indictment of French occupation. Wheeler-Bennett, J. W., *The Wreck of Reparations* (1933); political background of the 1932 Lausanne agreement. Wheeler-Bennett, J. W., and Latimer, H., *Information on the Reparation Settlement* (1930); documents for the study of the Young Plan.

WAR DEBTS: Bass, J. F., and Moulton, H. G., *America and the Balance Sheet of Europe* (1921). Dexter, P., and Sedgwick, J. H., *The War Debts: An American View* (1928). Fisk, H. E., *The Inter-Ally Debts* (1924). Moulton, H. G., and Pasvolsky, L., *War Debts and World Prosperity* (1932). Moulton, H. G., and Pasvolsky, L., *World War Debt Settlements* (1926).

WORLD DEPRESSION: Einzig, P., *The Sterling-Dollar-Franc Tangle* (1933). Einzig, P., *The World Economic Crisis, 1929–1932* (1932); a popular account. Hodson, H. V., *Slump and Recovery, 1929–1937* (1938). Kranold, H., *The International Distribution of Raw Materials* (1939). League of Nations, *World Production and Prices, 1925–1933* (1934). Patterson, E. M., *The World's Economic Dilemma* (1930). Robbins, L. C., *The Great Depression* (1934); readable. Somary, F., *Changes in the Structure of World Economics since the War* (1931). Stamp, J. C., *The Financial Aftermath of War* (1932); for the general reader. Varga, E., *The Great Crisis and Its Political Consequences* (1935); the interaction of economics and politics after 1928. Wright, Q. (ed.), *Unemployment as a World Problem* (1931).

Chapter VIII. Soviet Russia

GENERAL: Basily, N. de, *Russia under Soviet Rule: Twenty Years of Bolshevik Experiment* (1938); by a liberal of the old regime. Best, H., *The Soviet Experiment* (1941); a sociological analysis. Chamberlin, W. H., *Collectivism, a False Utopia* (1937). Chamberlin, W. H., *The Russian Enigma* (1943). Chamberlin, W. H., *Soviet Russia* (rev. ed., 1931). Dallin, D. J., *The Real Soviet Russia* (1944). Davies, J. E., *Mission to Moscow* (1941); by the American ambassador to Russia, 1936–1938. Duranty, W., *Duranty Reports Russia* (1934); a vivid picture of the period from 1922 to 1934. Duranty, W., *The Kremlin and the People* (1941); a discussion of the "treason trials" of 1936–1938. Duranty, W., *USSR: The Story of Soviet Russia* (1944). Eastman, M., *Stalin's Russia and the Crisis in Socialism* (1940). Fischer, M., *My Lives in Russia* (1944). Florinsky, M. T., *Toward an Understanding of the U.S.S.R.: A Study in Government, Politics, and Economic Planning* (1939). Griffith, H., *This is Russia* (1944). Loukomski, G., *The Face of Russia* (1944). Lyons, E., *Assignment in Utopia* (1937). Utley, F., *The Dream We*

Lost: Soviet Russia Then and Now (1940). Webb, S. and B., *Soviet Communism: A New Civilization?* 2 vols. (1936). Webb, S. and B., *The Truth about Soviet Russia* (1942).

INTERVENTION AND COUNTERREVOLUTION: Aleksandrov, G. F., *et al., History of the Civil War in the U.S.S.R.,* 2 vols. (1946). Alioshin, D., *Asian Odyssey* (1940); by an officer in Kolchak's army. Bunyan, J. (ed.), *Intervention, Civil War and Communism in Russia, April–December 1918: Documents and Materials* (1936). Coates, W. P. and Z. K., *Armed Intervention in Russia, 1918–1922* (1935). Cudahy, J., *Archangel: The American War with Russia* (1924); by an American. Denikin, A. I., *The White Army* (1930); by one of its leaders. Graves, W. S., *America's Siberian Adventure* (1931); by the American general in command. Maynard, Sir C. C. M., *The Murmansk Venture* (1928); by the commander-in-chief of the British forces in northern Russia. Stewart, G., *The White Armies of Russia: A Chronicle of Counter Revolution and Allied Intervention* (1933). Strakhovsky, L. I., *Intervention at Archangel* (1944). Varneck, E., and Fisher, H. H. (eds.), *The Testimony of Kolchak and Other Siberian Materials* (1935). Wrangel, P. N., *The Memoirs of General Wrangel, the Last Commander-in-Chief of the Russian National Army.*

PARTY AND GOVERNMENT: Bukharin, N., and Preobrazhensky, E., *The A.B.C. of Communism: A Popular Explanation of the Program of the Communist Party of Russia* (1922). Gurian, W., *Bolshevism: Theory and Practice* (1932); an excellent book for serious study. Harper, S. N., *The Government of the Soviet Union* (1938). Popov, N., *Outline History of the Communist Party of the Soviet Union,* 2 vols. (1935); English translation of a standard Russian work. Rosenberg, A., *A History of Bolshevism* (1934); not confined to Russia. Strong, A. L., *The New Soviet Constitution: A Study in Socialist Democracy* (1937). Towster, J., *Political Power in the U.S.S.R., 1917–1947; The Theory and Structure of Government in the Soviet State* (1948); an extensive study by an American professor of government. Vishinsky, A. Y., *The Law of the Soviet State* (1948); published a decade earlier in Russia.

SECRET POLICE AND TERROR: Agabekov, G., *Ogpu* (1931); by an agent of the organization. Brunovskii, V. K., *The Methods of the Ogpu* (1931); by one who suffered at it hands. Cederholm, B., *In the Clutches of the Tcheka* (1929); by one who had such an experience. Popov, G. K., *The Tcheka: the Red Inquisition* (1925); by a correspondent who fell into the hands of the secret police. Tchernavin, T., *Escape from the Soviets* (1934); a personal account of escape from Soviet persecutions in 1930. Orlov, A., *The Secret History of Stalin's Crimes* (1953); the Moscow trials, 1936–1938.

LENIN AND STALIN: Barbusse, H., *Stalin: A New World Seen through One Man* (1935). Bigland, E., *The Riddle of the Kremlin* (1940). Graham, S., *Stalin: An Impartial Study of the Life and Work of Joseph Stalin* (1931). Hill, C., *Lenin and the Russian Revolution* (1947). Krupskaya, N. K., *Memories of Lenin,* 2 vols. (1930); by his widow. Landau-Aldanov, M. A., *Lenin* (1922). Levine, I. D., *The Man Lenin* (1924). Levine, I. D., *Stalin* (1931). Ludwig, E., *Stalin* (1942). Lyons, E., *Stalin: Czar of All the Russias* (1940).

Marcu, V., *Lenin: Thirty Years of Russia* (1928).   Mirsky, D. S., *Lenin* (1931); sympathetic.   Rochester, A., *Lenin on the Agrarian Question* (1942).   Shub, D., *Lenin: A Biography* (1948); scholarly, fair, readable; the best life of Lenin. Souvarine, B., *Stalin: A Critical Survey of Bolshevism* (1939).   Stalin, J., *Leninism,* 2 vols. (1933); important pronouncements of the Communist leader. Veale, F. J. P., *The Man from the Volga* (1932); Lenin.   Vernadsky, G., *Lenin, Red Dictator* (1931); excellent but unsympathetic.   Werner, M. R. (ed.), *Stalin's Kampf: Joseph Stalin's Credo Written by Himself* (1940); excerpts from Stalin's speeches and articles which the editor believes reveal his nature and purposes.   Wolfe, B. D., *Three Who Made a Revolution: A Biographical History* (1948); a thorough study of Lenin, Trotsky, and Stalin.   Yaroslavsky, E., *Landmarks in the Life of Stalin* (1942); may be considered official.

AGRICULTURE AND INDUSTRY: Baykov, A., *The Development of the Soviet Economic System* (1947); an excellent reference book.   Beauchamp, J., *Agriculture in Soviet Russia* (1931); an account of the state farms.   Chamberlin, W. H., *Russia's Iron Age* (1934).   Chamberlin, W. H., *The Soviet Planned Economic Order* (1931); the first Five-Year Plan.   Coates, W. P. and Z. K., *The Second Five-Year Plan of Development of the U.S.S.R.* (1934).   Dallin, D. J., and Nicolaevsky, B. I., *Forced Labor in Soviet Russia* (1947); based largely on accounts of those who escaped.   Dobf, M., *Soviet Economic Development Since 1917* (1948).   Fischer, L., *Machines and Men in Russia* (1932). Hirsch, A., *Industrialized Russia* (1934); by an American consulting engineer. Hubbard, L. E., *The Economics of Soviet Agriculture* (1939).   Hubbard, L. E., *Soviet Labour and Industry* (1943).   Iakovlev, I. A., *Red Villages: The Five-Year Plan in Soviet Agriculture* (1931).   Liberman, S., *Building Lenin's Russia* (1945); by a former manager of the Soviet timber trust.   Rukeyser, W. A., *Working for the Soviets* (1932); by an American engineer.   Russian Economic Institute, *U.S.S.R. Economy and the War* (1942).   Scott, J., *Behind the Urals: An American Worker in Russia's City of Steel* (1942); Magnitogorsk.   Turin, S. P., *The U.S.S.R.: An Economic and Social Survey* (1944).   Yugow, A., *Russia's Economic Front for War and Peace: An Appraisal of the Three Five-Year Plans* (1943).   Yugow, A., *et al., Management in Russian Industry and Agriculture* (1944).

EDUCATION AND RELIGION: Anderson, P. B., *People, Church and State in Modern Russia* (1944).   Bolshakoff, S., *The Christian Church and the Soviet State* (1942).   Casey, R. P., *Religion in Russia* (1946); originally delivered as the Lowell lectures.   Counts, G. S., and Lodge, N. P. (trs.), *"I Want to Be Like Stalin"* (1947); a training manual for Soviet school teachers.   Evans, S., *Churches in the U.S.S.R.* (1943).   Fülöp-Miller, R., *The Mind and Face of Bolshevism: An Examination of Cultural Life in Soviet Russia* (1928). Harper, S. N., *Civic Training in Soviet Russia* (1929); Soviet propaganda within Russia.   Harper, S. N., *Making Bolsheviks* (1931); how it is done.   Hecker, J. F., *Religion and Communism* (1935).   King, B., *Changing Man: The Soviet Education System of the U.S.S.R.* (1937).   Mehnert, K., *Youth in Soviet Russia* (1933).   Moscow Patriarchate (comp.), *The Truth about Religion in Russia: Compiled by the Moscow Patriarchate* (1944).   Timasheff, N. S., *Religion in*

Soviet Russia: 1917–1942 (1942). Woody, T., *New Minds: New Men?* (1932); an excellent account of the Bolshevik educational system.

FOREIGN POLICY: Beloff, M., *The Foreign Policy of Soviet Russia, 1929–1941*, 2 vols. (1946–1949); generally impartial. Borkenau, F., *et al., World Communism: A History of the Communist International* (1939). Coates, W. P. and Z. K., *History of Anglo-Soviet Relations* (1944). Dallin, D. J., *Soviet Russia's Foreign Policy, 1939–42* (1942). Davis, K. W., *The Soviets at Geneva: The U.S.S.R. at the League of Nations, 1919–1933* (1934). Degras, J. (comp.), *Calendar of Soviet Documents on Foreign Policy* (1948); valuable. Fischer, L., *The Soviets in World Affairs*, 2 vols. (1930). Florinsky, M. T., *World Revolution and the U.S.S.R.* (1933). Gankin, O. H., and Fisher, H. H., *The Bolsheviks and the World War: The Origin of the Third International* (1940). Harper, S. N. (ed.), *The Soviet Union and World Problems* (1935). Laserson, M. M. (comp.), *The Development of Soviet Foreign Policy in Europe 1917–1942: A Selection of Documents* (1943). Molotov, V. M., *Soviet Foreign Relations* (1940). Moore, H. L., *Soviet Far Eastern Policy, 1931–1945* (1945); from original Soviet sources. Murphy, J. T., *Russia on the March: A Study of Soviet Foreign Policy* (1941). Pares, Sir B., *Russia and the Peace* (1944). Pope, A. U., *Maxim Litvinoff* (1943); Russia's delegate to the League. Pusta, K. R., *The Soviet Union and the Baltic States* (1942). Ross, M., *A History of Soviet Foreign Policy* (1940). Taracouzio, T. A., *War and Peace in Soviet Diplomacy* (1940). Trotsky, L., *The First Five Years of the Communist International* (1946).

SPECIAL TOPICS: Asquith, M., *Famine: Quaker Work in Russia, 1921–1923* (1944). Binder, P., *Russian Families* (1942). Bulygin, P., *The Murder of the Romanovs* (1935). Field, A. W., *Protection of Women and Children in Soviet Russia* (1932). Fisher, H. H., *The Famine in Soviet Russia* (1927); authoritative record of the operations of the American Relief Administration. Halle, F. W., *Woman in Soviet Russia* (1933); a discussion not only of the present situation but of the position of woman in tsarist times also. Lorimer, F., *The Population of the Soviet Union* (1946). Newsholme, A., and Kingsbury, J. A., *Red Medicine: Socialized Health in Soviet Russia* (1933). Podolsky, E., *Red Miracle* (1947); a survey of the growth of medicine in Russia under the Communists. Serebrennikov, G. N., *The Position of Women in the U.S.S.R.* (1936). Smith, E. S., *Organized Labor in the Soviet Union* (1943). Struve, G., *Twenty-five Years of Soviet Russian Literature* (1944). Telberg, G. G., and Wilton, R., *The Last Days of the Romanovs* (1920). Trotsky, L., *The Revolution Betrayed* (1937).

Chapter IX. Fascist Italy

GENERAL: Binchy, D. A., *Church and State in Fascist Italy* (1942). Bonomi, I., *From Socialism to Fascism* (1924); by a former Italian premier who again became premier after Mussolini's fall. Borgese, G. A., *Goliath: The March of Fascism* (1937). Ebenstein, W., *Fascist Italy* (1939); institutions, policies, aspirations. Elwin, W., *Fascism at Work* (1934); condemns Fascism.

Finer, H., *Mussolini's Italy* (1935); objective. Hambloch, E., *Italy Militant: A Study in Economic Militarism* (1939). Hentze, M., *Pre-Fascist Italy: The Rise and Fall of the Parliamentary Régime* (1939). Hullinger, E. W., *The New Fascist State* (1928); a sympathetic account of Fascism's early achievements. King, B., *Fascism in Italy* (1931); a critical account by a distinguished authority on Italian affairs. McGuire, C. E., *Italy's International Economic Position* (1926); an illuminating study of Italy's problems. Massock, R. G., *Italy from Within* (1943); by a former head of the Associated Press bureau in Rome. Matthews, H. L., *The Fruits of Fascism* (1943); by a New York *Times* correspondent in Rome. Minio-Paluello, L., *Education in Fascist Italy, 1922–1940* (1946). Moore, T. E., *Peter's City* (1930); an account of the negotiation of the Lateran agreements. Morgan, T. B., *Spurs on the Boot* (1941); Italy, 1918–1941. Nathan, P., *The Psychology of Fascism* (1943). Nenni, P., *Ten Years of Tyranny in Italy* (1932); by a former associate of Mussolini. Nitti, F. F., *Escape* (1930); the experiences of a political prisoner on a Fascist penal island. Packard, R. and E., *Balcony Empire* (1942); Italy under Mussolini. Salvemini, G., *The Fascist Dictatorship in Italy* (1927); the classic formulation of the case against Fascism. Schneider, H. W., *Making the Fascist State* (1928). Schneider, H. W., and Clough, S. B., *Making Fascists* (1929); the creation of opinion in Italy. Sforza, C., *The Real Italians* (1942); by a former Italian foreign minister. Sillani, T. (ed.), *What is Fascism and Why?* (1931); a discussion of economic, social, and cultural achievements, by a number of Fascist leaders. Treves, P., *What Mussolini Did to Us* (1940); by an Italian. Walter, K., *The Class Conflict in Italy* (1938); sympathetic with Fascism. Williamson, B., *The Treaty of the Lateran* (1929); has pertinent documents.

THE CORPORATIVE STATE: Field, G. L., *The Syndical and Corporative Institutions of Italian Fascism* (1938); objective. Goad, H. E., *The Making of the Corporate State* (1932); sympathetic. Haider, C., *Capital and Labor under Fascism* (1930). Pitigliani, F., *The Italian Corporative State* (1934); the economic organization of the Fascist state, with an account of its achievements. Salvemini, G., *Under the Axe of Fascism* (1936); a bitter attack on the condition of the workers. Schmidt, C. T., *The Corporate State in Action: Italy under Fascism* (1939). Schmidt, C. T., *The Plough and the Sword: Labor, Land, and Property in Fascist Italy* (1938). Schneider, H. W., *The Fascist Government of Italy* (1936). Steiner, H. A., *Government in Fascist Italy* (1938).

BENITO MUSSOLINI: Fiori, V. E. de, *Mussolini, the Man of Destiny* (1928); eulogistic. Kemechy, L., *"Il Duce": The Life and Work of Benito Mussolini* (1930); eulogistic. Macartney, M. H. H., *One Man Alone: The History of Mussolini and the Axis* (1944). Megaro, G., *Mussolini in the Making* (1938); writings and speeches before the First World War. Mussolini, B., *My Autobiography* (1928); general and superficial. Mussolini, B., *My Diary, 1915–1917* (1925). Pini, G., *The Official Life of Benito Mussolini* (1939); written by an Italian Fascist journalist. Sarfatti, M. C., *The Life of Benito Mussolini* (1925); sympathetic. Seldes, G., *Sawdust Caesar: The Untold History of Mussolini and Fascism* (1935); hostile.

FOREIGN POLICY: Booth, C. D. G., and Bridge, I., *Italy's Aegean Possessions* (1928); the Dodecanese. Currey, M. I., *Italian Foreign Policy, 1918–1932* (1935); carefully written and sympathetic. Macartney, M. H. H., and Cremona, P., *Italy's Foreign and Colonial Policy, 1914–1937* (1938); sympathetic. Monroe, E., *The Mediterranean in Politics* (1938). Villari, L., *The Expansion of Italy* (1930); a Fascist defense of Italy's aspirations.

Chapter X. Liberal and Nazi Germany

THE WEIMAR REPUBLIC: Angell, J. W., *The Recovery of Germany* (rev. ed. 1932); Germany's economic progress during the Weimer Republic. Bieligk, K. F., *Stresemann* (1944). Brunet, R., *The New German Constitution* (1922); exposition of the Weimar constitution. Daniels, H. G., *The Rise of the German Republic* (1928). Fischer, R., *Stalin and German Communism: A Study in the Origins of the State Party* (1948); by a former German Communist. Gedye, G. E. R., *The Revolver Republic: France's Bid for the Rhine* (1930); an indictment of the French policy of separatism. Halperin, S. W., *Germany Tried Democracy: A Political History of the Reich from 1918 to 1933* (1946); by an American historian. Hoetzsch, O., *Germany's Domestic and Foreign Policies* (1929); by a German scholar. Knight-Patterson, W. M., *Germany from Defeat to Conquest, 1913–1933* (1945); argues that the Weimar Republic was only a façade for German nationalism. Ludwig, E., *Hindenburg and the Saga of the German Republic* (1935); an attempt to "debunk" Hindenburg. Luehr, E., *The New German Republic* (1929). Mendelssohn-Bartholdy, A., *The War and German Society: The Testament of a Liberal* (1937); the effects of the First World War on German life. Morgan, J. H., *Assize of Arms: Being the Story of the Disarmament of Germany and Her Rearmament, 1919–1939* (1945); an account of the Allied failure to disarm Germany. Mullins, C., *Leipzig Trials* (1921); war criminals. Olden, R., *Stresemann* (1930). Oppenheimer, H., *The Constitution of the German Republic* (1923); exposition of the Weimar constitution. Quigley, H., and Clark, R. J., *Republican Germany* (1928). Rheinbaben, R. von, *Stresemann, the Man and the Statesman* (1929). Schacht, H., *The Stabilization of the Mark* (1927); by the one who did it. Scheele, G., *The Weimar Republic: Overture to the Third Reich* (1946); a good discussion. Scheidemann, P., *The Making of New Germany: The Memoirs of Philipp Scheidemann* (1929); valuable for the early years of the republic. Schultze-Pfaelzer, G., *Hindenburg: Peace, War, Aftermath* (1931). Stresemann, G., *Gustav Stresemann: His Diaries, Letters and Papers*, 3 vols. (1935–1940). Tschuppik, K., *Ludendorff: The Tragedy of a Military Mind* (1932). Vallentin, A., *Stresemann* (1931); by one who knew him intimately. Weterstetten, R., and Watson, A. M. K., *The Biography of President von Hindenburg* (1930); treats of both civil and military affairs. Wheeler-Bennett, J. W., *Wooden Titan: Hindenburg in Twenty Years of German History, 1914–1934* (1936); discusses other leaders also. Ybarra, T. R., *Hindenburg, the Man with Three Lives* (1932).

THE DOWNFALL OF THE WEIMAR REPUBLIC: Abel, T. F., *Why*

Hitler Came into Power (1938); based on original life stories of 600 Nazis. Armstrong, H. F., *Hitler's Reich: the First Phase* (1933); the rise of Hitler. Brecht, A., *Prelude to Silence* (1944); an explanation of why the "good" Germans permitted Hitler to seize power. Butler, R., *The Roots of National Socialism* (1942). Clark, R. T., *The Fall of the German Republic* (1935). Deuel, W. R., *People under Hitler* (1942); explains how Hitler came to power and what life was like in Nazi Germany. Feder, G., *Hitler's Official Programme and Its Fundamental Ideas* (1934). Florinsky, M. T., *Fascism and National Socialism* (1936); an analysis and comparison of the two. Heberle, R., *From Democracy to Nazism: A Regional Case Study on Political Parties in Germany* (1945); scholarly. Hoover, C. B., *Germany Enters the Third Reich* (1934); an objective analysis of the forces and events leading to the Nazi revolution. Knickerbocker, H. R., *The German Crisis* (1932); by an American correspondent. Kraus, H., *The Crisis of German Democracy* (1932). Lengyel, E., *Hitler* (1932); the development of the Hitler movement. Lutz, R. H., *The Reichstag Election of March 5, 1933* (1943); a careful work. Menne, B., *The Case of Dr. Bruening* (1943); an indictment. Rauschning, H., *The Voice of Destruction* (1940); report of confidential talks with Hitler, 1932–1934. Reed, D., *The Burning of the Reichstag* (1934). Scandrett, J. J. M., *The Nazi Disease* (1939); explanation of the causes, influence, and spread of National Socialism. Strasser, O., *History in My Time* (1941); by a former Nazi. Thyssen, F., *I Paid Hitler* (1941); by one of the great industrialists who supported Hitler. Wheeler-Bennett, J. W., *The Nemesis of Power: The German Army in Politics, 1918–45* (1953).

THE THIRD REICH: Brady, R. A., *The Spirit and Structure of German Fascism* (1937). Cahen, F., *Men Against Hitler* (1939); the underground movement in Germany. Dodd, W. E., Jr., and M. (eds.), *Ambassador Dodd's Diary, 1933–38* (1941); impressions of the American ambassador. Ebenstein, W., *The Nazi State* (1943). Fraser, L., *Germany Between Two Wars: A Study of Propaganda and War Guilt* (1945); an analysis of German history as seen in official Nazi propaganda. Garratt, G. T., *The Shadow of the Swastika* (1938). Guillebaud, C. W., *Economic Recovery of Germany from March, 1933 to the Incorporation of Austria* (1939). Hambloch, E., *Germany Rampant: A Study in Economic Militarism* (1939). Holt, J. B., *Under the Swastika* (1936); interesting account of conditions in the Third Reich, by one who studied at Heidelberg, 1931–1935. Institute on Jewish Affairs, *Hitler's Ten-Year War on the Jews* (1943). Krieger, S., *Nazi Germany's War Against the Jews* (1947); a reference work. Kuczynski, J., *A Short History of Labor Conditions in Germany under Fascism* (1944). Landau, R., *Hitler's Paradise* (1941). Lichtenberger, H., *The Third Reich: Germany under National Socialism* (1939). Loewenstein, K., *Hitler's Germany: The Nazi Background of the War* (1939). Nathan, O., *The Nazi Economic System* (1944). Neumann, F. L., *Behemoth: The Structure and Practice of National Socialism* (1942). Pollock, J. K., *The Government of Greater Germany* (1940); a discussion of Hitler's government. Rauschning, H., *The Revolution of Nihilism* (1939); by a former Nazi. Roberts, S. H., *The House That Hitler Built*

(1938); sympathetic account by an Australian professor. Schuman, F. L., *The Nazi Dictatorship: A Study in Social Pathology* (1935). Shirer, W. L., *Berlin Diary: The Journal of a Foreign Correspondent, 1934–1941* (1941). Sington, D., and Weidenfeld, A., *The Goebbels Experiment* (1943); the Nazi propaganda machine. Spiecker, K., *Germany—From Defeat to Defeat* (1944); by an Anti-Nazi German. Warburg, G., *Six Years of Hitler: The Jews under the Nazi Regime* (1939). Williams, W., and Parry, A., *The Riddle of the Reich* (1941).

HITLER AND HIS ASSOCIATES: Bayles, W. D., *Caesars in Goose Step* (1940); interesting information about the Nazi leaders of Germany. Baynes, N. (ed.), *Hitler's Speeches*, 2 vols. (1942). Behrend, H., *Real Rulers of Germany* (1939). Bondy, L. W., *Racketeers of Hatred: Julius Streicher and the Jew Baiter's International* (1946). Combs, G. H., *Himmler, Nazi Spider Man* (1942). Dutch, O., *The Errant Diplomat: The Life of Franz von Papen* (1940). Dutch, O., *Hitler's Twelve Apostles* (1940); biographical and character sketches of Hitler's associates. Frischauer, W., *Himmler, The Evil Genius of the Third Reich* (1953); an account of the head of the ruthless Gestapo. Heiden, K., *Der Fuehrer: Hitler's Rise to Power* (1944). Heiden K. (ed.), *Der Führer: Speeches and Writings, 1919–1941* (1941). Hitler, A., *My Battle* (1943); a translation of Hitler's *Mein Kampf*. Koeves, T., *Satan in Top Hat* (1941); a biography of Franz von Papen. Lockner, L. (ed.), *The Goebbels Diaries* (1948); diaries of the Nazi minister of propaganda. Ludecke, K. G., *I Knew Hitler* (1937); by a disillusioned Nazi. Mühlen, N., *Schacht, Hitler's Magician* (1939); explains how Germany's creditors were exploited. Murphy, J., *Adolf Hitler: The Drama of His Career* (1934); a favorable interpretation. Papen, F. von, *Memoirs* (1953) by a prominent but controversial figure in recent German history. Riess, C., *Joseph Goebbels* (1948). Schwarz, P., *This Man Ribbentrop* (1943). Semmler, R., *Goebbels: The Man Next to Hitler* (1947). Singer, K., *Göring: Germany's Most Dangerous Man* (1940). Strasser, O., *Hitler and I* (1940); by one who was once intimately connected with him. Wagner, L., *Hitler: Man of Strife* (1942).

THE GESTAPO SYSTEM: Heiden, K., *The New Inquisition* (1939). Karst, G. M., *The Beasts of the Earth* (1942); experiences in the Dachau concentration camp. Lorant, S., *I Was Hitler's Prisoner* (1935); a gripping diary. Seger, G., *A Nation Terrorized* (1935); concentration-camp experiences of a former Reichstag member. Stein, L., *I Was in Hell with Niemoeller* (1942). Wallner, P., *By Order of the Gestapo: A Record of Life in Dachau and Buchenwald Concentration Camps* (1941). Winkler, E., *Four Years of Nazi Torture* (1942); experiences of a leader of the Catholic Youth Movement in Nazi concentration camps.

EDUCATION AND RELIGION UNDER THE NAZIS: Brennecke, F., *The Nazi Primer* (1938); required reading for Hitler Youth. Carmer, C. (ed.), *The War Against God* (1943); contains significant Nazi statements on religion. Duncan-Jones, A. S., *The Struggle for Religious Freedom in Germany* (1938); by an Anglican clergyman. Frey, A., *Cross and Swastika: The Ordeal of the German Church* (1938); by a German. Hartshorne, E. Y., *The*

German Universities and National Socialism (1937). Kneller, G. F., *The Educational Philosophy of National Socialism* (1941); the ideological basis and content of Nazi education. Micklem, N., *National Socialism and the Roman Catholic Church* (1939). Power, M., *Religion in the Reich* (1939); objective. Wolf, A., *Higher Education in Nazi Germany, or Education for World Conquest* (1944). Ziemer, G., *Education for Death: The Making of the Nazi* (1941).

Chapter XI. Great Britain and Ireland

BRITISH INTERNAL AFFAIRS: Benham, F., *Great Britain under Protection* (1941). Brand, C. F., *British Labour's Rise to Power: Eight Studies* (1941). Briffault, R., *Decline and Fall of the British Empire* (1938). Bromfield, L., *England: A Dying Oligarchy* (1939); severe criticism of Chamberlain's government. Cartland, B., *The Isthmus Years* (1943); social history of England between the two wars. Dalton, H., *Practical Socialism for Britain* (1935); a discussion of the official program of the Labor Party by one of its high officials. Davison, R. C., *British Unemployment Policy: The Modern Phase Since 1930* (1938). Dickie, J. P., *The Coal Problem, 1910–1936* (1936). Fyfe, H., *Behind the Scenes of the Great Strike* (1926). Graves, R., and Hodge, A., *The Long Week End: A Social History of Great Britain, 1918–1939* (1941). Greenwood, G. A., *England Today: A Social Study of Our Time* (rev. ed., 1926). Heaton, H., *The British Way to Recovery* (1934); proposals and actual policies. Hill, A. C. C., Jr., and Lubin, I., *The British Attack on Unemployment* (1934); the dole system. Hutt, A., *The Post-War History of the British Working Classes* (1938). Jennings, W. I., *The British Constitution* (1941). Lawrence, F. W. P., *The Gold Crisis* (1931); by a former financial adviser of the British Treasury. Loveday, A., *Britain and World Trade* (1931). Lubin, I., and Everett, H., *The British Coal Dilemma* (1927). McHenry, D., *His Majesty's Opposition: Structure and Problems of the British Labor Party, 1931–1938* (1941). Marriott, Sir J. A. R., *Modern England, 1885–1939: A History of My Own Times* (1943); by a distinguished English historian. Masterman, C. F. G., *England after War* (1922); the effect of the war on British society and culture. Morton, W. A., *British Finance, 1930–1940* (1943). Pigou, A. C., *Aspects of British Economic History, 1918–1925* (1947). Priestley, J. B., *An English Journey* (1934); a penetrating and readable description of England's "depressed areas" in 1933. Siegfried, A., *England's Crisis* (1931); a Frenchman's estimate of Britain's postwar difficulties. Snyder, R. K., *The Tariff Problem in Great Britain, 1918–1923* (1944). Somerville, D. C., *Between the Wars* (1948). White, J. L., *The Abdication of Edward VIII: A Record with All the Public Documents* (1937).

BIOGRAPHIES AND MEMOIRS: Arthur, Sir G., *Concerning Winston Spencer Churchill* (1941). Bolitho, H., *King Edward VIII: An Intimate Biography* (1937). Bolitho, H., *King George VI* (1938). Broad, L., *Winston Churchill* (1941). Buchan, J., *The People's King* (1935); George V. Edwards, J. H., *David Lloyd George, the Man and the Statesman*, 2 vols. (1929).

Feiling, K., *The Life of Neville Chamberlain* (1946); quotes extensively from his diary and letters. Germains, V. W., *The Tragedy of Winston Churchill* (1931); a bitter attack. Glasgow, G., *MacDonald as a Diplomatist* (1924); eulogistic. Gore, J., *King George V* (1941). Guedalla, P., *Mr. Churchill* (1942); the best biography. Hamilton, M. A., *Arthur Henderson: A Biography* (1938). Hamilton, M. A., *England's Labour Rulers* (1924); short biographies of members of the first Labor cabinet. Hodgson, S., *The Man Who Made Peace: Neville Chamberlain* (1938). Johnson, A. C., *Anthony Eden: A Biography* (1939); uncritical. Johnson, A. C., *Viscount Halifax* (1941). Kraus, R., *The Men Around Churchill* (1941). Kraus, R., *Winston Churchill* (1940). Mallet, Sir C. E., *Mr. Lloyd George: A Study* (1930); a Liberal criticism. Paneth, P., *King George VI and His People* (1944). Petrie, C., *The Chamberlain Tradition* (1938). Roberts, C. E. B., *Stanley Baldwin, Man or Miracle?* (1937); an unsympathetic political biography. Snowden, P., *An Autobiography*, 2 vols. (1934). Steed, H. W., *The Real Stanley Baldwin* (1930); an appreciation. Strauss, P., *Bevin and Co., the Leaders of British Labour* (1941). Thompson, E. R., *Mr. Lloyd George* (1922); popular. Tiltman, H. H., *J. Ramsay MacDonald, Labour's Man of Destiny* (1929).

BRITISH FOREIGN POLICY: Carr, E. H., *Britain: A Study of Foreign Policy from the Treaty of Versailles to the Outbreak of the War* (1939). "Cato," *Guilty Men* (1940); an indictment of the "appeasers." Coates, W. P. and Z. K., *History of Anglo-Soviet Relations* (1944). Eden, A., *Foreign Affairs* (1939); speeches in Parliament by Foreign Secretary Eden. Jerrold, D., *Britain and Europe, 1900–1940* (1941). Kennedy, J. F., *Why England Slept* (1940). Langford, R. V., *British Foreign Policy: Its Formulation in Recent Years* (1942). Medlicott, W. N., *British Foreign Policy since Versailles* (1940); excellent. Scarfoglio, C., *England and the Continent* (1939); an indictment. Seton-Watson, R. W., *Britain and the Dictators: A Survey of Postwar British Policy* (1938). Sipple, C. E., *British Foreign Policy since the World War* (1932); scholarly. Willert, Sir A., *Aspects of British Foreign Policy* (1928); by the chief of the press bureau of the British foreign office.

COMMONWEALTH RELATIONS: Dawson, R. M., *The Development of Dominion Status, 1900–1936* (1937). Elliott, W. Y., *The New British Empire* (1932); the changing relationships between the parts of the empire. Muir, R., *The British Commonwealth: How It Grew and How It Works* (1941). Wheare, K. C., *The Statute of Westminster, 1931* (1933).

IRELAND: Béaslaí, P., *Michael Collins, Soldier and Statesman* (1937). Collins, M., *The Path of Freedom* (1923); a discussion of the history and nature of the Irish treaty with Great Britain, by one of its signers. Curtis, E., *A History of Ireland* (1938). Good, J. W., *Ulster and Ireland* (1919); an Irish nationalist viewpoint. Gwynn, D. R., *De Valera* (1933); a critical and clear analysis. Harrison, H., *The Neutrality of Ireland: Why It Was Inevitable* (1942). Healy, T. M., *Letters and Leaders of My Day*, 2 vols. (1929); by the former governor-general of the Irish Free State. Hull, E., *A History of Ireland and Her People* (1926); special attention to the establishment of the Irish Free State. Ireland, T., *Ireland, Past and Present* (1942). Jones, F. P., *History of the Sinn*

Fein Movement and the Irish Rebellion of 1916 (1917). Kelly, R. S., *Ireland's Bloodless Revolution, 1932–1936* (1936). Kohn, L., *The Constitution of the Irish Free State* (1943); an analysis. McManus, M. J., *Eamon de Valera* (1946); a sympathetic biography. MacNeill, R., *Ulster's Stand for Union* (1922). Mansergh, N., *The Government of Northern Ireland* (1936). Mansergh, N., *The Irish Free State* (1934); its government and politics. O'Connor, B., *With Michael Collins in the Fight for Irish Independence* (1930); readable but partisan. O'Connor, F., *Death in Dublin: Michael Collins and the Irish Revolution* (1937). Paul-Dubois, L., and Gill, T. P., *The Irish Struggle and Its Results* (1934). Phillips, W. A., *The Revolution in Ireland, 1906–1923* (1926); excellent but unsympathetic. Quekett, Sir A. S., *The Constitution of Northern Ireland* (1928); by a government official. Ryan, D., *Unique Dictator: A Study of Eamon de Valera* (1936). Talbot, H. (ed.), *Michael Collins' Own Story* (1923). Wells, W. B., and Marlowe, N., *A History of the Irish Rebellion of 1916* (1916); a careful, detailed study.

Chapter XII. The French Republic

GENERAL: Bates-Batcheller, T., *France in Sunshine and Shadow* (1944). Daniels, H. G., *The Framework of France* (1937); by an Englishman. Davis, S. C., *The French War Machine* (1937). Fox, R. W., *France Faces the Future* (1936); the rise of the Popular Front. Fraser, G., and Natanson, T., *Léon Blum, Man and Statesman* (1937); the only authorized biography. Hale, R. W., Jr., *Democratic France: the Third Republic from Sedan to Vichy* (1941). Hayes, C. J. H., *France: a Nation of Patriots* (1930); French education for patriotism. Huddleston, S., *France* (1927); good general discussion. Huddleston, S., *Poincaré: A Biographical Portrait* (1924); by a foreign correspondent. Joseph-Maginot, M., *He Might Have Saved France* (1941); a biography of André Maginot, by his sister. Lazareff, P., *Deadline: The Behind-the-Scenes Story of the Last Decade in France* (1940). Leeds, S. B., *These Rule France: The Story of Edouard Daladier and the Men Around Him* (1940); a sympathetic treatment but reveals fascist tendencies in France. MacDonald, W., *Reconstruction in France* (1922); an interesting account of the work in the devastated area, showing the French need for reparation payments. Maillaud, P., *France* (1943); French life and problems on the eve of the Second World War. Peel, G., *The Economic Policy of France* (1937). Riethinger, A., *Why France Lost the War: A Biological and Economic Survey* (1940). Rogers, G. H., *The Process of Inflation in France, 1914–1927* (1929). Saposs, D. J., *The Labor Movement in Post-War France* (1931). Sharp, W. R., *The Government of the French Republic* (1939). Sieburg, F., *Who Are These French?* (1932); by a German journalist. Siegfried, A., *France: A Study in Nationality* (1930). Simon, Y., *The Road to Vichy 1918–1938* (1942); explains the reasons for French internal dissension. Spengler, J. J., *France Faces Depopulation* (1938); causes and results. Stokes, R. L., *Léon Blum: Poet to Premier* (1937); by an American journalist. Tissier, P., *I Worked with Laval* (1942); sidelights on French politicians. Torrès, H., *Pierre Laval* (1941); denunciation by a one-time friend and associate. Vaucher, P., *Post-War France* (1934); chiefly political. Werth, A., *France in Ferment* (1935); especially good for the years 1933–1934. Werth, A., *The Twilight of France* (1942); the last years of the Third Republic. Weyer, E., *The Decline of French Democracy: The Beginning of National Disintegration* (1940). Winter, G., *This Is Not the End of France* (1942); France from Versailles to Vichy.

FOREIGN POLICY: Cameron, E. R., *Prologue to Appeasement* (1942); French foreign policy, 1933–1936. Daladier, E., *In Defense of France* (1939); speeches delivered in 1938–1939. Micaud, C. A., *The French Right and Nazi Germany, 1933–1939: A Study of Public Opinion* (1944); helps explain the appeasement policy in France. Ormesson, W. d', *France* (1939); international affairs. Street, C. J. C., *The Treachery of France* (1924); a violent criticism of French postwar foreign policy. Thomson, V., *Briand, Man of Peace* (1930); exponent of collective security. Werth, A., *France and Munich: Before and After the Surrender* (1939); the causes of the French acceptance of Munich.

Chapter XIII. Spain

Alvarez del Vayo, J., *Freedom's Battle* (1940); by the foreign minister of the Loyalist government. Arraras, J., *Francisco Franco: The Times and the Man* (1938). Brandt, J. A., *Toward the New Spain* (1933); the growth of republicanism in Spain. Brenan, G., *The Spanish Labyrinth: An Account of the Social and Political Background of the Civil War* (1943). Casado, S., *Last Days of Madrid* (1939); by an officer in the Loyalist army. Davis, F., *My Shadow in the Sun* (1940); a foreign correspondent's experiences during the Spanish civil war. Deakin, F. B., *Spain Today* (1924); one of the best treatments of the period immediately preceding the revolution. Dundas, L., *Behind the Spanish Mask* (1943); background of the civil war. Elstob, P., *Spanish Prisoner* (1939). George, R. E. G., *Spain's Ordeal* (1940); a documented history of the civil war. Hamilton, T. J., *Appeasement's Child: The Franco Regime in Spain* (1943); conditions in Spain after Franco's triumph, as seen by a liberal foreign correspondent. Jellinek, F., *The Civil War in Spain* (1938). Knoblaugh, H., *Correspondent in Spain* (1938). Last, J., *Spanish Tragedy* (1939); by a Dutch volunteer in the Loyalist army. Loveday, A. F., *World War in Spain* (1939). Madariaga, S. de, *Spain* (1943); a brilliant study of the roots of the civil war. Manuel, F. E., *The Politics of Modern Spain* (1938); men, parties, and programs. Mendizabal Villalba, A. O., *The Martyrdom of Spain* (1938); the author, a liberal, a Catholic, a scholar, and a professor, condemns both sides. Morrow, F., *Revolution and Counter-Revolution in Spain* (1938); a Trotskyite interpretation, both anti-Loyalist and anti-Franco. Peers, E. A., *Catalonia Infelix* (1938). Peers, E. A., *Spain in Eclipse, 1937–1943* (1943). Peers, E. A., *The Spanish Tragedy, 1930–1936: Dictatorship, Republic, Chaos* (1936). Regler, G., *The Great Crusade* (1940); the Loyalist viewpoint. Rogers, F. T., *Spain: A Tragic Journey* (1937); defends Franco. Rolfe, E., *Lincoln Battalion: The Story of the Americans Who Fought in Spain in the International Brigades* (1939). Salter, C., *Try-out in Spain*

(1943); by a journalist. Smith, R. M., *The Day of the Liberals in Spain* (1938). Young, G., *The New Spain* (1933).

Chapter XIV. The Succession States of Central Europe

THE DANUBE BASIN: Basch, A., *The Danube Basin and the German Economic Sphere* (1943); by a Czechoslovak professor and economist. Crane, J. O., *The Little Entente* (1931). Evans, J. D. E., *That Blue Danube* (1935); racial, social, economic, and political conditions in the succession states. Fodor, M. W., *Plot and Counter-Plot in Central Europe: Conditions South of Hitler* (1937); by a foreign correspondent. Gedye, G. E. R., *Heirs to the Hapsburgs* (1932); by a British journalist. Hanc, J., *Tornado across Eastern Europe* (1942); diplomatic developments, 1918–1939. Hertz, F., *The Economic Problem of the Danubian States: A Study in Economic Nationalism* (1947). Lengyel, E., *The Danube* (1939); a survey. Macartney, C. A., *Problems of the Danube Basin* (1942). Machray, R., *The Little Entente* (1929); its origin and history. Pasvolsky, L., *Economic Nationalism of the Danubian States* (1929). Seton-Watson, R. W., *Eastern Europe Between the Wars, 1918–1941* (1945).

AUSTRIA: Ball, M. M., *Post-War German-Austrian Relations: The Anschluss Movement, 1918–1936* (1937). Basch, A., and Dvořáček, J., *Austria and Its Economic Existence* (1925); Austria's resources and economic structure. Bitterman, M., *Austria and the Customs Union* (1931); a Czech view. Buttinger, J., *In the Twilight of Socialism* (1953); the years 1934–1938. Frischauer, W., *Twilight in Vienna, the Capital without a Country* (1938); social conditions. Fuchs, M., *Showdown in Vienna: The Death of Austria* (1939); "inside" history of years 1935–1938, by a former aide to Schuschnigg. Germains, V. W., *Austria of Today* (1932); financial and political history. Gregory, J. D., *Dollfuss and His Times* (1935); a history. Gulick, C. A., *Austria from Hapsburg to Hitler*, 2 vols. (1948); from the viewpoint of the Socialists. Hardy, C. O., and Kuczynski, R. R., *The Housing Program of the City of Vienna* (1934); an account of the Socialist achievement in housing. Kleinwächter, F. F. G., *Self-Determination for Austria* (1929); the case for *Anschluss*. League of Nations, *The Financial Reconstruction of Austria* (1926). Macartney, C. A., *The Social Revolution in Austria* (1926). Macdonald, M., *The Republic of Austria, 1918–1934: A Study of the Failure of Democratic Government* (1946); brief, scholarly. Rothschild, K. W., *Austria's Economic Development Between the Two Wars* (1947). Rüdiger, E., *Between Hitler and Mussolini: Memoirs of Ernst Rüdiger Prince Starhemberg* (1942); by the leader of the fascist Heimwehr. Schuschnigg, K., *My Austria* (1938); a history by the last Austrian chancellor before the *Anschluss*. Schuschnigg, K., *Austrian Requiem* (1946); an attempt to defend his own and Dollfuss' policies. Sheridan, R. K., *Kurt von Schuschnigg* (1942).

CZECHOSLOVAKIA: Bartusek, L., *Happy Times in Czechoslovakia* (1940); life in a small Czech village. Beneš, E., *Eduard Beneš in His Own Words: Three-score Years of a Statesman, Builder and Philosopher* (1945). Bilek, B., *Fifth Column at Work* (1945); German activities in Czechoslovakia,

1936–1938. Borovicka, J., *Ten Years of Czechoslovak Politics* (1929); from 1918 to 1928. Čapek, K., *et al., At the Cross-Roads of Europe: A Historical Outline of the Democratic Czechoslovakia* (1938); general. Crabites, P., *Beneš, Statesman of Central Europe* (1936). De Colonna, B., *Czechoslovakia Within* (1938); critical discussion of the minorities problem. Grant Duff, S., *Europe and the Czechs* (1938). Hitchcock, E. B., *"I Built a Temple for Peace": The Life of Eduard Beneš* (1940). Holland, C., *Czechoslovakia: The Land and Its People* (1931); descriptive. Kerner, R. J., (ed.), *Czechoslovakia: Twenty Years of Independence* (1940); a symposium. Lechner, O., *As We Saw It in Prague: Twelve Discussions and a Letter, 1933–1939* (1943). Lowrie, D. A., *Masaryk of Czechoslovakia* (1938). Mackworth, C., and Stransky, J., *Czechoslovakia* (1944); brief. Polišensky, J. V., *History of Czechoslovakia in Outline* (1948); by a Czech historian. Seton-Watson, R. W., *A History of the Czechs and Slovaks* (1943); during past centuries as well as since 1914. Seton-Watson, R. W. (ed.), *Slovakia, Then and Now: A Political Survey* (1931); by twenty-five Slovak authors. Seton-Watson, R. W., *Twenty-Five Years of Czechoslovakia* (1945); by a British specialist on Central Europe. Street, C. J. C., *President Masaryk* (1930). Textor, L. E., *Land Reform in Czecho-Slovakia* (1923). Thomson, S. H., *Czechoslovakia in European History* (1943). Vondracek, F. J., *The Foreign Policy of Czechoslovakia, 1918–1935* (1937). Warren, W. M. P., *Masaryk's Democracy: A Philosophy of Scientific and Moral Culture* (1941). Wiskemann, E., *Czechs and Germans: A Study of the Struggle in the Historic Provinces of Bohemia and Moravia* (1938); one chapter deals with the Sudeten German movement. Young, P., *Czechoslovakia, Keystone of Peace and Democracy* (1938).

HUNGARY: Apponyi, Count S., *et al., Justice for Hungary* (1928); a typical Hungarian revisionist plea. Bethlen, I., *The Treaty of Trianon and European Peace: Four Lectures Delivered in London, November, 1933* (1934); by a former Hungarian premier. Deák, F., and Ujváry, D. (eds.), *Papers and Documents Relating to the Foreign Relations of Hungary, Vol. I, 1919–1920* (1939). Donald, Sir R., *The Tragedy of Trianon* (1928); a plea for revision of the treaty. Eckhart, F., *A Short History of the Hungarian People* (1931); an excellent introduction to Hungarian history. Gower, R., *The Hungarian Minorities in the Succession States* (1937); sympathetic discussion by an Englishman. Jászi, O., *Revolution and Counter-Revolution in Hungary* (1924); by a member of Karolyi's cabinet. Kaas, A., and Lazarovics, F. de, *Bolshevism in Hungary: The Bela Kun Period* (1931). Kosáry, D. G., *A History of Hungary* (1941); a general history by a Hungarian professor. League of Nations, *The Financial Reconstruction of Hungary* (1926). Macartney, C. A., *Hungary and Her Successors, 1919–1937* (1938); by an Englishman. Rothermere, H. S. H., *My Campaign for Hungary* (1939); a British argument for revision. Seton-Watson, R. W., *Treaty Revision and the Hungarian Frontiers* (1934). Street, C. J. C., *Hungary and Democracy* (1923); anti-Horthy. Kertesz, S., *Diplomacy in a Whirlpool: Hungary between Nazi Germany and Soviet Russia* (1953).

Chapter XV. Poland and the Baltic Republics

POLAND: Buell, R. L., *Poland: Key to Europe* (1939); a general survey. Devereux, R., *Poland Reborn* (1922); a good discussion of problems facing the new Poland. Dyboski, R., *Poland Old and New* (1926); three brilliant lectures by a Polish professor. Goodhart, A. L., *Poland and the Minority Races* (1922); the diary of a competent observer. Gorecki, R., *Poland and Her Economic Development* (1935). Halecki, O., *A History of Poland* (1943); through the centuries. Humphrey, G., *Pilsudski: Builder of Poland* (1936); eulogistic. Janowsky, O. I., *People at Bay: The Jewish Problem in East Central Europe* (1938). Machray, R., *The Poland of Pilsudski, 1914–1936* (1937). Mackiewicz, S., *Colonel Beck and His Policy* (1944); foreign affairs. Murray, K. M., *Wings over Poland* (1932); Poland's war against Russia. Murray, M. (ed.), *Poland's Progress, 1919–1939* (1944). Patterson, E. J., *Pilsudski, Marshal of Poland* (1935); a brief sketch, by an Englishman. Reddaway, W. F., *Marshal Pilsudski* (1939). Rose, W. J., *Poland* (1939); a brief history. Schmitt, B. E. (ed.), *Poland* (1945); an excellent symposium. Segal, S., *The New Poland and the Jews* (1938); by a Polish Jew. Shotwell, J. T., and Laserson, M. M., *Poland and Russia, 1919–1945* (1945); excellent. Slocombe, G., *History of Poland* (1940). Symonolewicz, K., *Studies in Nationality and Nationalism in Poland Between the Two Wars* (1944).

DANZIG AND THE POLISH CORRIDOR: Baginski, J., *Poland and the Baltic: The Problem of Poland's Access to the Sea* (1943). Donald, Sir R., *The Polish Corridor and the Consequences* (1929); hostile to Poland. Leonhardt, H., *Nazi Conquest of Danzig* (1942); its "nazification." Machray, R., *The Polish German Problem* (1942). Martel, R., *The Eastern Frontiers of Germany* (1930); the problem of the Polish Corridor. Mason, J. B., *The Danzig Dilemma* (1945); problems which arose while the Free City was under the League. Smogorzewski, C., *Poland, Germany and the Corridor* (1930).

THE BALTIC REPUBLICS: Bihlmans, A., *Latvia in the Making, 1918–1928* (1928). Borenius, T., *Field-Marshal Mannerheim* (1940). Harrison, E. J. (ed.), *Lithuania* (1928); descriptive. Jackson, J. H., *Estonia* (1941); a history. Jackson, J. H., *Finland* (1940); before and after 1914. Meiksins, G., *The Baltic Riddle: Finland, Estonia, Lithuania—Key Points of European Peace* (1943); sympathetic with Soviet Russia's policy in the Baltic. Norem, O. J. C., *Timeless Lithuania* (1944); a history. Reddaway, W. F., *Problems of the Baltic* (1940). Royal Institute of International Affairs, *The Baltic States: A Survey of the Political and Economic Structure and the Foreign Relations of Estonia, Latvia, and Lithuania* (1938). Ruhl, A. B., *New Masters of the Baltic* (1921); interesting, especially for social conditions after the First World War. Simutis, A., *The Economic Reconstruction of Lithuania after 1918* (1942). Soderhjelm, H., *The Red Insurrection in Finland, 1918* (1920). Strode, H., *Finland Forever* (1941); a sympathetic character study of the country and people. Van Cleef, E., *Finland, the Republic Farthest North* (1929); descriptive. Wuorinen, J. H., *Nationalism in Modern Finland* (1931).

Chapter XVI. The Turbulent Balkans

GENERAL: Armstrong, H. F., *The New Balkans* (1926); various problems. Armstrong, H. F., *Where the East Begins* (1929); a continuation of the preceding work. Konacs, F. W. L., *The Untamed Balkans* (1942); general and brief. Newman, B., *Balkan Background* (1944). Rouček, J. S., *Politics in the Balkans* (1939).

GREECE: Alastos, D., *Venizelos: Patriot, Statesman, Revolutionary* (1942). Andrew, Prince of Greece, *Towards Disaster* (1930); the reasons for the Greek military defeat in 1922. Eddy, C. B., *Greece and the Greek Refugees* (1931); by the last head of the Greek Refugee Settlement Commission. Gibbons, H. A., *Venizelos* (1920). Hibben, P., *Constantine I and the Greek People* (1920); a defense of the Greek king. Ladas, S. P., *The Exchange of Minorities* (1932); the exchange of populations by Greece, Turkey, and Bulgaria. League of Nations, *The Greek Refugee Settlement* (1926). Macartney, C. A., *Refugees* (1931); the Greco-Bulgarian exchange of population. Mavrogordato, J., *Modern Greece: A Chronicle and a Survey, 1800–1931* (1931). Mears, E. G., *Greece Today: The Aftermath of the Refugee Impact* (1929). Miller, W., *Greece* (1928); discussion of the years 1920–1927 by a specialist in Greek history. Morgenthau, H., *I Was Sent to Athens* (1929); by the first chairman of the Greek Refugee Settlement Commission. Phocas-Cosmetatos, S. P., *The Tragedy of Greece* (1928); an indictment of Allied policy towards Greece. Toynbee, A. J., *The Western Question in Greece and Turkey* (1922); a valuable work for understanding the Greco-Turkish War, 1919–1922.

YUGOSLAVIA: Adamic, L., *My Native Land* (1943); Yugoslavia, 1933–1943. Adamic, L., *The Native's Return: An American Immigrant Visits Yugoslavia and Discovers His Old Country* (1934); descriptive. Baerlein, H., *The Birth of Yugoslavia*, 2 vols. (1922). Beard, C. A., and Radin, G., *The Balkan Pivot: Yugoslavia* (1929); a study in government and administration. Buchan, J. (ed.), *Yugoslavia* (1923). Ellison, G., *Yugoslavia: A New Country and Its People* (1935); diary of a journey through Yugoslavia by an English woman. Graham, S., *Alexander of Yugoslavia* (1939); an account of events leading to and resulting from his assassination. Laffan, R. G. D., *Yugoslavia since 1918* (1929). Lodge, O., *Peasant Life in Jugoslavia* (1942). Sforza, C., *Fifty Years of War and Diplomacy in the Balkans: Pashich and the Union of the Yugoslavs* (1940); a chatty book by a former Italian foreign minister, a friend of Pashich.

ALBANIA: Bareilles, B., Durham, M. E., *et al.*, *Albania and the Albanians* (1920); a general survey of the country and its people. Chekrezi, C. A., *Albania, Past and Present* (1919); geographic, historical, political, and economic facts presented by an educated Albanian. Stickney, E. P., *Southern Albania or Northern Epirus in European Affairs, 1912–1923* (1926); includes a treatment of rivalries of the war and postwar periods. Swire, J., *King Zog's Albania* (1937).

BULGARIA: Anastasoff, C., *The Tragic Peninsula* (1938); a history of the Macedonian movement by one of Macedonian extraction. Christowe, S.,

Heroes and Assassins (1935); a pro-Macedonian view of the situation. Leslie, H., *Where East Is West: Life in Bulgaria* (1933). Logio, G. C., *Bulgaria Past and Present* (1936); before and after 1914. Londres, A., *Terror in the Balkans* (1935); the Macedonian Revolutionary Organization. Pasvolsky, L., *Bulgaria's Economic Position, with Special Reference to the Reparation Problem and the Work of the League of Nations* (1930). Swire, J., *Bulgarian Conspiracy* (1939); an account of Bulgaria's postwar history, written by an Englishman.

RUMANIA: Bolitho, H., *Roumania under King Carol* (1940); descriptive. Cabot, J. M., *The Racial Conflict in Transylvania* (1926). Clark, C. U., *Bessarabia* (1927); favors Rumania's claims. Clark, C. U., *United Rumania* (1932); sympathetic and well informed. Deák, F., *The Hungarian-Rumanian Land Dispute* (1928). Dragomir, S., *The Ethnical Minorities in Transylvania* (1927); a defense of Rumanian policy. Evans, I. L., *The Agrarian Revolution in Roumania* (1924); its results. Hoven, Baroness H. von der, *King Carol of Romania* (1940); authorized biography of Carol II. Ionescu, T., *Some Personal Impressions* (1920); by a Rumanian premier. Iorga, N. A., *History of Rumania* (1925); by a Rumanian professor and one-time premier. Janowsky, O. I., *People at Bay: The Jewish Problem in East-Central Europe* (1938). Rakovsky, C. G., *Roumania and Bessarabia* (1925); favors Russia's claims. Rouček, J. S., *Contemporary Roumania and Her Problems* (1932); the best general work in English. Szasz, Z., *The Minorities in Roumanian Transylvania* (1927); an indictment of Rumanian policy.

INTERNATIONAL RELATIONS: Geshkoff, T. I., *A Road to Peace in Southeastern Europe* (1940); the development of the Balkan Entente. Kerner, R. J., and Howard, H. N., *The Balkan Conferences and the Balkan Entente, 1930–1935* (1936). Padelford, N. J., *Peace in the Balkans: The Movement towards International Organization in the Balkans* (1935). Stavrianos, L. S., *Balkan Federation: A History of the Movement toward Balkan Unity in Modern Times* (1944).

Chapter XVII. The Near and Middle East

THE EAST IN REVOLT: Arberry, A. J., and Landau, R. (eds.), *Islam Today* (1943). Ben-Horin, E., *The Middle East: Crossroads of History* (1943). Boveri, M., *Minaret and Pipe-line: Yesterday and Today in the Near East* (1939); commerce and diplomacy. Breasted, J. H., *The New Orient*, Vol. I (1933); the Near East. Chirol, Sir V., *The Occident and the Orient* (1924). Dutcher, G. M., *The Political Awakening of the East* (1925); the influence of Western political ideas on the nations of the East. Hocking, W. E., *The Spirit of World Politics* (1932); the situation in Syria, Palestine, and Egypt. O'Leary, D. E., *Islam at the Crossroads: A Brief Survey of the Present Position and Problems of the World of Islam* (1923). Puryear, V. J., *International Economics and Diplomacy in the Near East* (1935). Spender, J. A., *The Changing East* (1926); deals chiefly with Egypt and India. Toynbee, A. J., *Survey of International Affairs, 1925: Part I, The Islamic World since the Peace*

Settlement (1927). Toynbee, A. J., *The Western Question in Greece and Turkey: A Study in the Contact of Civilizations* (1922); emphasizes the growing Oriental impatience with Western interference.

TURKEY: Allen, H. E., *The Turkish Transformation* (1935); social and religious changes. Armstrong, H. C., *Gray Wolf: Mustapha Kemal* (1933). Ellison, G., *Turkey Today* (1928). Hālidah Adïb, K., *Turkey Faces West* (1930); by a Turkish feminist. Ikbāl, Alī Shāh, *Kamal: Maker of Modern Turkey* (1934); by a Persian. Jackh, E., *The Rising Crescent* (1944). Jarman, T. L., *Turkey* (1935). Krüger, K., *Kemalist Turkey and the Middle East* (1932); Turkey's relations with her neighbors. Lengyel, E., *Turkey* (1941); the last chapter deals with the period since 1914. Luke, H., *The Making of Modern Turkey* (1936). Mikusch, D. von, *Mustapha Kemal* (1931). Ostroróg, L., *The Angora Reform* (1928); includes a brief discussion of the chief reforms. Price, C., *The Rebirth of Turkey* (1932). Toynbee, A. J., and Kirkwood, K., *Turkey* (1927); events after the Nationalist revival. Webster, D. E., *The Turkey of Atatürk* (1939). Wortham, H. E., *Mustapha Kemal of Turkey* (1931); a brief biography.

EGYPT: Elgood, P. E., *Egypt and the Army* (1924); the nationalist movement during the First World War. Harris, M., *Egypt under the Egyptians* (1925). Howell, J. M., *Egypt's Past, Present and Future* (1929); by a former American diplomat who lived in Egypt. Newman, E. W. P., *Great Britain in Egypt* (1928); during the First World War and the next decade. Royal Institute of International Affairs, *Great Britain and Egypt, 1914–1936* (1936). Symons, M. T., *Britain and Egypt: The Rise of Egyptian Nationalism* (1925). Young, G., *Egypt* (1927); stresses the period after 1914. Youssef Bey, A., *Independent Egypt* (1942).

PALESTINE AND SYRIA: Antonius, G., *The Arab Awakening* (1939). Armstrong, H., *Turkey and Syria Reborn* (1930). Hanna, P. L., *British Policy in Palestine* (1942). Kallen, H. M., *Zionism and World Politics* (1921); an interpretation of the movement. Lowdermilk, W. C., *Palestine, Land of Promise* (1944); reclamation work resulting from Jewish immigration. Luke, H. C., and Keith-Roach, E., *The Handbook of Palestine and Trans-Jordan* (1930). McCallum, E. P., *The Nationalist Crusade in Syria* (1928); the revolt of 1925–1927. Main, E., *Palestine at the Crossroads* (1937). Newman, E. W. P., *The Middle East* (1926); particularly Palestine and Syria. Preiss, L., and Rohrbach, P., *Palestine and Transjordania* (1926); surveys. Royal Institute of International Affairs, *Great Britain and Palestine, 1915–1936* (1936). Samuel, M., *On The Rim of the Wilderness* (1931); a Jewish viewpoint on the Jewish-Arab problem. Sereni, E., and Ashery, R. E., *Jews and Arabs in Palestine* (1936). Sidebotham, H., *Great Britain and Palestine* (1937). Stein, L., *Syria* (1926); racial and religious problems. Stoyanovsky, J., *The Mandate for Palestine* (1928); a technical study of the mandate. Van Ess, J., *Meet the Arab* (1943); by an American who founded a school for Arabs.

IRAQ AND PERSIA: Elwell-Sutton, L. P., *Modern Iran* (1941). Foster, H. A., *The Making of Modern Iraq* (1935). Ireland, P. W., *Iraq: A Study in Political Development* (1938). Main, E., *Iraq* (1935). Merritt-Hawkes,

O. A., *Persia: Romance and Reality* (1935); a traveler's impressions of Persia's transformation. Millspaugh, A. C., *The American Task in Persia* (1925); Persian problems discussed by the head of the American Financial Mission. Ross, Sir E. D., *The Persians* (1931); a brief survey.

INDIA: Andrews, C. F. (ed.), *Mahatma Gandhi: His Own Story* (1930); selections from Gandhi's autobiography. Andrews, C. F., *Mahatma Gandhi's Ideas* (1930); excerpts from his speeches and articles. Anstey, V., *The Economic Development of India* (1931). Coatman, J., *India: The Road to Self-Government, 1908–1940* (1943). Duncan, A., *India in Crisis* (1931); history of affairs, 1911–1931. Dutt, R. P., *The Problem of India* (1943); with suggestions for a solution. Fischer, L., *Empire* (1943); indictment of the British by an American liberal. Gandhi, M. K., *The Story of My Experiments with Truth,* 2 vols. (1927–1929); an autobiography. Mitchell, K. L., *India Without Fable* (1942); economic, political, and social background of Indian affairs and of the nationalist movement. Nehru, J., *Toward Freedom* (1941); by a leader of the Congress Party. Rolland, R., *Mahatma Gandhi* (1924); an appreciative biographical sketch. Simon, Sir J., *India and the Simon Report* (1930); by the chairman of the commission. Singh, A., *Nehru, the Rising Star of India* (1939). Whyte, Sir F., *India: A Bird's-Eye View* (1943); a British point of view.

Chapter XVIII. The Far East

GENERAL: Blakeslee, G. H., *The Pacific Area* (1929); by a leading American authority. Breasted, J. H., *The New Orient,* Vol. II (1933); the Far East. Buss, C. A., *War and Diplomacy in Eastern Asia* (1941); diplomatic and economic struggles during the past century. Close, U., *The Revolt of Asia* (1927). Hudson, G. F., *The Far East in World Politics: A Study in Recent History* (1937). Millard, T. F. F., *Conflicts of Policy in Asia* (1924); from 1918 to 1924. Park, No-Yong, *Retreat of the West* (1937); an informal review of the whole course of Occidental-Oriental relations. Vinacke, H. M., *A History of the Far East in Modern Times* (4th ed., 1941).

CHINA IN REVOLUTION: Berkov, R. H., *Strong Man of China* (1938); Chiang Kai-shek. Chang, H., *Chiang Kai-shek: Asia's Man of Destiny* (1944); reveals connection with Sun Yat-sen. Clark, E. T., *The Chiangs of China* (1943); also the Soong family. Clark, G., *The Great Wall Crumbles* (1935); by a former faculty member of the National University of Peiping. Gannes, H., *When China Unites: A History of China's Struggle for National Independence, 1840–1938: An Interpretive History of the Chinese Revolution* (1938). Hedin, S., *Chiang Kai-shek, Marshal of China* (1940); a sketchy biography, with reminiscences of the author. Holcombe, A. N., *The Spirit of the Chinese Revolution* (1930); scholarly. Hsü, L. S. (comp.), *Sun Yat-sen: His Political and Social Ideals* (1933). Lattimore, O. and E., *The Making of Modern China: A Short History* (1944); brief account of contemporary China and its background. MacNair, H. F., *China in Revolution* (1931). Peffer, N., *China: The Collapse of a Civilization* (1930). Pringle, J. M. D., and Rajchman, M.,

China Struggles for Unity (1939). Restarick, H. B., *Sun Yat-sen* (1931). Sharman, L., *Sun Yat-sen* (1934). Van Dorn, H. A., *Twenty Years of the Chinese Republic* (1932); excellent for nonpolitical changes. Wu Chao Chu, *The Nationalist Program for China* (1929); by a former Chinese minister to the United States.

CHINA AND THE POWERS: Buell, R. L., *The Washington Conference* (1922). LaFargue, T. E., *China and the World War* (1937). Norton, H. K., *China and the Powers* (1927). Pollard, R. T., *China's Foreign Relations, 1917–1931* (1933); a study of the movement for the revision of China's treaties. Willoughby, W. W., *China at the Conference* (1922); the best presentation of China's problems at the Washington conference. Willoughby, W. W., *Foreign Rights and Interests in China,* 2 vols. (1927); a standard work.

JAPAN BEFORE 1931: Carus, C. D., and McNichols, C. L., *Japan: Its Resources and Industries* (1944). Eckstein, G., *In Peace Japan Breeds War* (1943); personal impressions of an American scientist. Hishida, S., *Japan among the Great Powers* (1940). Ishii, Viscount K., *Diplomatic Commentaries* (1936); reveals the psychology of a leading Japanese statesman. Lederer, E., and Lederer-Seidler, E., *Japan in Transition* (1938). Lory, H., *Japan's Military Masters* (1943). Mitchell, K. L., *Japan's Industrial Strength* (1942). Moulton, H. G., and Ko, J., *Japan* (1931); economic development and problems. Norman, E. H., *Japan's Emergence as a Modern State* (1940); developments, 1867–1912. Penrose, E. F., *Population Theories and Their Application* (1934); with Japan as an illustration. Takeuchi, T., *War and Diplomacy in the Japanese Empire* (1935); by a Japanese professor. Tanin, O., and Yohan, E., *Militarism and Fascism in Japan* (1934); based on Japanese literature. Wildes, H. E., *Japan in Crisis* (1934); internal conditions. Young, A. M., *Imperial Japan: 1926–1938;* readable account by a former editor of *The Japan Chronicle.*

Chapter XIX. The Collapse of Collective Security

INTERNATIONAL RELATIONS, 1919–1939: Armstrong, G. G., *Why Another World War? How We Missed Collective Security* (1941); a survey, 1919–1940. Birdsall, P., *Versailles Twenty Years After* (1941). Butler, H., *The Lost Peace* (1942); the failure to use collective security, and why. Cuff, S. H., *The Face of the War, 1931–1942* (1942). Foot, M., *Armistice, 1919–1939* (1940). Graham, S., *From War to War, 1917–1940: A Datebook of the Years Between* (1940). Haines, C. G., and Hoffman, R. J. S., *The Origins and Background of the Second World War* (1943). Jordan, W. M., *Great Britain, France, and the German Problem: 1918–1939* (1944). Kain, R. S., *Europe: Versailles to Warsaw* (1939). Lee, D. E., *Ten Years: The World on the Way to War, 1930–1940* (1942). Marriott, J., *The Tragedy of Europe* (1941); a study of the years 1919–1939. Orton, W. A., *Twenty Years' Armistice, 1918–1938* (1938). Rayner, R. M., *The Twenty Years Truce* (1943). Schuman, F. L., *Design for Power: The Struggle for the World* (1941); the rise of the armed dictators and their drive toward world conquest. Schwarzschild, L.,

World in Trance: From Versailles to Pearl Harbor (1942). Spender, J. A., *Between Two Wars* (1943). Wolfers, A., *Britain and France Between Two Wars: Conflicting Strategies of Peace since Versailles* (1940).

JAPAN'S SEIZURE OF MANCHURIA AND INVASION OF CHINA: Bisson, T. A., *American Policy in the Far East: 1931–1940* (1940). Borton, H., *Japan since 1931* (1941). Byas, H., *Government by Assassination* (1942). Chamberlin, W. H., *Japan in China* (1940); covers 1937–1939. Chamberlin, W. H., *Japan over Asia* (1938). Crow, C. (ed.), *Japan's Dream of World Empire: The Tanaka Memorial* (1942). Grew, J. C., *Ten Years in Japan* (1944); by the American ambassador to Japan in 1941. Hindmarsh, A. E., *The Basis of Japanese Foreign Policy* (1936); the influence of domestic factors upon foreign policy. Kawakami, K. K., *Manchoukuo, Child of Conflict* (1933); a Japanese view of the origin, organization, and problems of the new state. Lattimore, O., *Manchuria, Cradle of Conflict* (1935); a revised edition of an excellent work. League of Nations, *The Verdict of the League* (1933); official documents of the verdict against Japan. Moore, F., *With Japan's Leaders: An Intimate Record of Fourteen Years as Counsellor to the Japanese Government, Ending December 7, 1941* (1942). Rea, G. B., *The Case for Manchoukuo* (1935); a defense of Japanese policy. Saito, H., *Japan's Policies and Purposes* (1935); by a Japanese statesman. Schumpeter, E. B. (ed.), *The Industrialization of Japan and Manchukuo, 1930–1940* (1940); a technical study. Tang Leang-li (ed.), *The Puppet State of Manchukuo* (1935); the Chinese viewpoint. Timperley, H. J., *Japan, a World Problem* (1942). Wang, Ching-chun, *Japan's Continental Adventure* (1941); begins with Manchuria. Willoughby, W. W., *The Sino-Japanese Controversy and the League of Nations* (1935); comprehensive and authoritative.

CHINA ON THE DEFENSIVE: Bate, D., *Wang Ching-wei, Puppet or Patriot* (1941). Bertram, J. M., *First Act in China: The Story of the Sian Mutiny* (1938); the kidnaping of Chiang Kai-shek. Carlson, E. F., *Twin Stars of China* (1940); by an American military observer. Chinese Ministry of Information, *China Handbook, 1937–1943* (1944). Clegg, A., *Birth of New China* (1943). Koo, V. K. W., *China after Five Years of War* (1943). Lin Yutang, *The Vigil of a Nation* (1945). Linebarger, P. M. A., *The China of Chiang K'ai-shek: A Political Study* (1941). McNair, H. F., *The Real Conflict between China and Japan: An Analysis of Opposing Ideologies* (1938). Smedley, A., *China Fights Back* (1938). Snow, E., *Red Star over China* (new ed., 1938); covers 1928–1937; sympathetic with Chinese Communists. Taylor, E., *The Struggle for North China* (1941).

ITALY'S CONQUEST OF ETHIOPIA: Badoglio, P., *The War in Abyssinia* (1937); by the Italian commander. Martelli, G., *Italy Against the World* (1937); the Italo-Ethiopian conflict. Potter, P. B., *The Wal Wal Arbitration* (1938); by one of the arbitrators. Rey, C. F., *The Real Abyssinia* (1935). Royal Institute of International Affairs, *Abyssinia and Italy* (1935); brief but reliable. Sandford, C., *Ethiopia under Haile Selassie* (1944); by one who lived there. Steer, G. L., *Caesar in Abyssinia* (1937); an account of the invasion. Work, E., *Ethiopia, a Pawn in European Diplomacy* (1935).

GERMANY'S *DRANG NACH OSTEN:* Armstrong, H. F., *When There Is No Peace* (1939); the Sudeten crisis. Beneš, V., *The Vanguard of the "Drang nach Osten";* the Sudeten crisis. Beneš, V., and Ginsburg, R., *Ten Million Prisoners* (1940); the Nazi invasion of Czechoslovakia and the results. Birchall, T., *The Storm Breaks: A Panorama of Europe and the Forces That Have Wrecked Its Peace* (1940). Brooks, C., *Can Chamberlain Save Britain? The Lesson of Munich* (1938); favorable to Chamberlain. Chamberlain, N., *In Search of Peace* (1939); speeches. Churchill, W. S., *Step by Step: 1936–1939* (1939). Churchill, W. S., *While England Slept: A Survey of World Affairs, 1932–1938* (1938). Dean, V. M., *Europe in Retreat* (1939); brief account of events leading to Munich. Einzig, P., *Appeasement before, during, and after the War* (1942). Fuchs, M., *Showdown in Vienna: The Death of Austria* (1939). Gedye, G. E. R., *Betrayal in Central Europe* (1939). George, G. J., *They Betrayed Czechoslovakia* (1938). Grant Duff, S., *A German Protectorate: The Czechs under Nazi Rule* (1942). Hadley, W. W., *Munich Before and After* (1944); a vindication of Chamberlain's foreign policy. Halton, M., *Ten Years to Alamein* (1944); a Canadian journalist's account of international affairs and military preparation from 1933 to 1943. Hodson, S., *The Man Who Made the Peace: Neville Chamberlain* (1938); eulogistic. Hutton, G., *Survey after Munich* (1939); political, economic, strategic. Johnson, A. C., *Anthony Eden* (1939); the British foreign minister who opposed appeasement. Lennhoff, E., *The Last Five Hours of Austria* (1938). Loewenstein, K., *Hitler's Germany: The Nazi Background to War* (1939); the Third Reich's power politics. Mendelssohn, P. de, *Design for Aggression* (1947); German political and military plans, 1937–1940, based on captured German documents. Namier, L. B., *Diplomatic Prelude, 1938–1939* (1948); a study of documents, memoirs, etc. Schuman, F. L., *Europe on the Eve: The Crisis of Diplomacy, 1933–1939* (1939). Walker-Smith, D., *Neville Chamberlain* (1940). Wheeler-Bennett, J. W., *Munich: Prologue to Tragedy* (1948); by a distinguished British historian. Wiskemann, E., *Czechs and Germans: A Study of the Struggle in the Historic Provinces of Bohemia and Moravia* (1938). Wolfe, H. C., *The German Octopus* (1938); Nazi penetration of neighboring countries. Churchill, W. S., *The Gathering Storm* (1948); critical but not always accurate. *Documents Relating to the Eve of the Second World War,* 2 vols. (1948); secret documents for the years 1937–1939 from the German archives. Gafencu, G., *Last Days of Europe* (1948); by the Rumanian foreign minister in 1939.

THE CRISIS OF 1939: Benson, O. E., *Through the Diplomatic Looking Glass: Immediate Origins of the War in Europe* (1939). Fisher, H. A. L., *et al., The Background and Issues of the War* (1940). Henderson, Sir N., *Failure of a Mission: Berlin, 1937–1939* (1940); by the British ambassador to Germany in 1939. Schuman, F. L., *Night over Europe: The Diplomacy of Nemesis, 1939–1940* (1941). Seton-Watson, R. W., *From Munich to Danzig* (1939); British view. Tolischus, O. D., *They Wanted War* (1940); Nazi aims and policies. Wegerer, A. von, *The Origins of World War II: A Brief Survey of the Beginnings of the Present War, on the Basis of Official Documents* (1941).

Wiskemann, E., *Prologue to War* (1940); Nazi activities in various European countries.

DOCUMENTS: France, *Papers Relative to the Events and Negotiations Which Preceded the Opening of Hostilities Between Germany on the One Hand, and Poland, Great Britain, and France on the Other* (1940). Gantenbein, J. W. (ed.), *Documentary Background of World War II, 1931 to 1941* (1948); valuable. Germany, *Documents on Events Preceding the Outbreak of the War* (1940). Great Britain, *Documents Concerning German-Polish Relations and the Outbreak of Hostilities Between Great Britain and Germany on September 3, 1939* (1939). Poland, *Official Documents Concerning Polish-German and Polish-Soviet Relations, 1938–1939* (1940). Royal Institute of International Affairs, *Documents on International Affairs, 1939–1946*, Vol. I. *March–September, 1939* (1951). Sontag, R. J., and Beddie, J. S. (eds.), *Nazi-Soviet Relations, 1939–1941* (1948); documents from the archives of the German foreign office. Toynbee, A. J. (ed.), *Documents on International Affairs, 1939–1946*, Vol. I. *March–September, 1939* (1951); also includes significant documents showing Nazi plans for aggression, 1936–1938. U.S. Department of State, *Documents on German Foreign Policy, 1918–1945.* Series D, Vols. I–V (1949–1953); from the archives of the German foreign office. U.S. Department of State, *Germany and Czechoslovakia, 1937–1938* (1949); official German documents. U.S. Department of State, *The United States and Italy, 1936–1946* (1946). Woodward, E. L., and Butler, R. (eds.), *Documents on British Foreign Policy, 1919–1939* (1951).

MORE RECENT BOOKS: Carr, E. H., *German-Soviet Relations between the Two World Wars, 1919–1939* (1951); a critical but brief study by a British political scientist. Ciano, Count G., *Ciano's Hidden Diary, 1937–1938* (1953); deals with the Spanish Civil War and Munich. Ciano, Count G., *The Ciano Diaries* (1946); covers the years 1939–1943. Esch, P. A. M. van der, *Prelude to War: The International Repercussions of the Spanish Civil War, 1936–1939* (1952); based on documents in European archives and on the press and periodicals of the chief states. Laffan, R. G. D., *et al., Survey of International Affairs, 1938*, Vol. II., *The Crisis over Czechoslovakia, January to September, 1938* (1951); excellent. Langer, W. L., and Gleason, S. E., *The Challenge to Isolation, 1937–1940* (1952); American diplomacy from Munich to the destroyer deal. Namier, L. B., *Europe in Decay: Study in Disintegration, 1936–40* (1950); excellent study by a British historian. Rossi, A., *The Russo-German Alliance, August 1939 to June 1941* (1950); a readable account by a former Italian Communist. Schmidt, P., *Diary of Hitler's Interpreter: The Secret History of German Diplomacy* (1951); by Hitler's and Ribbentrop's chief interpreter, 1935–1945. Wiskemann, E., *The Rome-Berlin Axis: A History of the Relations between Mussolini and Hitler* (1949); interestingly written. Craig, G. A., and Gilbert, F. (eds.), *The Diplomats, 1919–1939* (1953); by seventeen experts. Hilger, G., and Meyer, A. G., *The Incompatible Allies. A Memoir-History of German-Soviet Relations, 1918–1941* (1953). Langer, W. L., and Gleason, S. E., *The Undeclared War, 1940–1941* (1953); American diplomacy. Salvemini, G., *Prelude to World War II* (1953); an indictment of Britain's Conservative government. Tetens, T. H., *German Plots with the Kremlin* (1953).

Chapters XX–XXI. The Nazi Blitzkrieg and Defeat

GENERAL ACCOUNTS: Baldwin, H., *Great Mistakes of the War* (1950); by the military expert of the *New York Times*. Brown, F., and Manditch, L., *The War in Maps: An Atlas of the New York Times Maps* (1946). Churchill, W., *The Second World War,* 6 vols. (1948–1953); by the British wartime premier. Commager, H. S., *The Story of the Second World War* (1945); a selection of accounts designed to depict the war as it looked and felt at the time. Graves, P. P. (ed.), *A Record of the War* (1940 ff); published quarterly. Horrabin, J. F., *Atlas History of the Second World War,* 9 vols. (1941–1945). Hutchinson, W., *Pictorial History of the War,* 26 vols. (1939–1945). Ingersoll, R., *Top Secret* (1946); a postwar analysis of the Allied commanders and strategy in western Europe. Liddell Hart, B. H., *The German Generals Talk* (1948); based on conversations with surviving German generals. McInnis, E., *The War,* 6 vols. (1940–1946); written yearly during the war— excellent for contemporary atmosphere. O'Neill, H. C., *A Short History of the Second World War and Its Social and Political Significance* (1951); by a famous British military analyst. Root, W., *The Secret History of the War,* 2 vols. (1945); biased and undocumented. Sinderen, A. van, *The Story of the Six Years of Global War* (1946); a chronicle by months. Wilmot, C., *The Struggle for Europe* (1952); a history of World War II in western Europe by an Australian.

BIOGRAPHIES AND BIOGRAPHICAL SKETCHES: Bradley, O. N., *A Soldier's Story* (1951); valuable for its gallery of military portraits. Bullock, A., *Hitler: A Study in Tyranny* (1953); comprehensive, clear, well-written biography. Chatterton, E. K., *Leaders of the Royal Navy* (1940). Davis, K. S., *Soldier of Democracy; A Full Length Biography of Dwight Eisenhower* (1945); eulogistic. DeWeerd, H. A., *Great Soldiers of World War II* (1944); by an editor of the *Infantry Journal*. Frye, W., *Marshall: Citizen Soldier* (1947). Gilbert, F. (ed.), *Hitler Directs His War: The Secret Records of His Daily Military Conferences* (1950). Guderian, H., *Panzer Leader* (1951). Hagood, J., *et al., These Are the Generals* (1943); brief sketches of United States generals. Halder, F., *Hitler as War Lord* (1950); by the former chief of German general staff. Hart, W. E., *Hitler's Generals* (1944); by a former German officer who was anti-Nazi. Hatch, A., *General Ike* (1944). Hinsley, F. H., *Hitler's Strategy* (1951); based on records of his War Council. Karslake, H., *Leaders of the Army* (1940); British. Mellor, W. B., *Patton: Fighting Man* (1946); reveals an effort to be objective. Miller, F. T., *Eisenhower, Man and Soldier* (1944). Moorehead, A., *Montgomery: A Biography* (1947). Nicolay, H., *Born to Command: the Story of General Eisenhower* (1945). Payne, R., *The Marshall Story: A Biography of General George C. Marshall* (1951). Pollard, A. O., *Leaders of the Royal Air Force* (1940). Steel, J., *Men Behind the War* (1942); in Europe and Asia. Stokes, D. H., *Men Behind Victory* (1944). Wellard, J., *General George S. Patton, Jr.,*

Man Under Mars (1946); eulogistic. Weygand, M., *Recalled to Service* (1952); the story of both France and General Weygand from the outbreak of World War II until the Allied landings in Africa. Hitler, A., *Hitler's Secret Conversations, 1941–1944* (1953); reveals Hitler's confused mind.

THE WAR IN POLAND AND FINLAND: Anders, W., *An Army in Exile: The Story of the Second Polish Corps* (1949); by its commander. Bryan, J., *Siege* (1940); the Nazi attack on Warsaw. Elliston, H. B., *Finland Fights* (1940). Finland, *The Finnish Blue Book: The Development of Finnish-Soviet Relations during the Autumn of 1939, Including the Official Documents and the Peace Treaty of March 12, 1940* (1940). Hollingworth, C., *The Three Weeks' War in Poland* (1940). Langdon-Davies, J., *Invasion in the Snow* (1941); the Russo-Finnish war of 1939–1940. Mowrer, L., *Arrest and Exile* (1941); experiences of Poles transported from Lemberg to Siberia by Russia in June, 1940. Ullman, S. de, *The Epic of the Finnish Nation* (1940). Wierzynski, K., *The Forgotten Battlefield* (1944); the war in Poland. Wuorinen, J. H., *Finland and World War II, 1939–1944* (1948); by an American historian.

THE WAR IN NORWAY: Broch, T., *The Mountains Wait* (1942); by the mayor of Narvik. Buckley, C., *Norway: The Commandos, Dieppe* (1952). Curtis, M. (ed.), *Norway and the War, September, 1939–December, 1940* (1940); a collection of documents. Hambro, C. J., *I Saw It Happen in Norway* (1940); by the president of the Norwegian parliament. Johnson, A., *Norway, Her Invasion and Occupation* (1948); by an American professor. Koht, H., *Norway, Neutral and Invaded* (1941); by the foreign minister of Norway. Lapie, P. O., *With the Foreign Legion at Narvik* (1941). Torris, M. J., *Narvik* (1933); by one who fought there.

THE GERMAN CONQUEST OF HOLLAND AND BELGIUM: Belgian-American Educational Foundation, *The Belgian Campaign and the Surrender of the Belgian Army, May 10–28, 1940* (1940); exonerates the Belgian king. Belgian Ministry of Foreign Affairs, *Belgium: The Official Account of What Happened, 1939–1940* (1941). Cammaerts, E., *The Prisoner at Laeken: King Leopold—Legend and Fact* (1941). Chatterton, E. K., *Epic of Dunkirk* (1940). Divine, A. D., *Dunkirk* (1945); a thrilling account of the role of the ships and boats. Doorman, P. L. G., *Military Operations in the Netherlands from 10th–17th May, 1940* (1944). Falaise, H. de la, *Through Hell to Dunkirk* (1943). Kleffens, E. N. van, *Juggernaut over Holland* (1941); by the Dutch foreign minister. Masefield, J., *The Nine-Days Wonder* (1941); beautifully written account of the Dunkirk evacuation. Netherlands, *Netherlands Orange Book* (1940). Rhodes, A., *A Sword of Bone* (1943); the British retreat to the coast and evacuation of Dunkirk. Williams, D., *Retreat from Dunkirk* (1941); personal experiences.

THE COLLAPSE OF FRANCE: Armstrong, H. F., *Chronology of Failure: The Last Days of the French Republic* (1940). Barlone, D., *A French Officer's Diary (23 August 1939–1 October 1940)* (1942). Bloch, M., *Strange Defeat* (1949); an examination of the causes of defeat, by a history professor who joined the resistance movement. Blum, L., *For All Mankind* (1946); the Socialist leader's explanation of France's collapse. Bois, E. J., *Truth on the Tragedy of France* (1941); criticizes the government officials. Chambrun,

R. de, *I Saw France Fall* (1940); by Laval's son-in-law. Cot, P., *Triumph of Treason* (1944); by a former French minister. Draper, T., *The Six Weeks' War: France, May 10–June 25, 1940* (1944). Gerard, R. M., *Tank-Fighter Team* (1942); the battle of France. Giraud, A., *The Grave Diggers (I— Gamelin, Daladier, Reynaud; II—Pétain)* (1943). Lattre de Tassigny, Marshal de, *The History of the French First Army* (1953); by its commander. Malaquais, J., *War Diary* (1944); the French army before June, 1940. Marshall, S. L. A., *Armies on Wheels* (1941); a study of the significant campaigns from May, 1940 to the fall of 1941. Maurois, A., *Why France Fell* (1941); by a distinguished French writer. Simone, A., *J'Accuse!—The Men Who Betrayed France* (1940). Torres, H., *Campaign of Treachery* (1942); attacks pro-Nazi Frenchmen. Vilfroy, D., *War in the West: The Battle of France, May–June, 1940* (1942), by a French officer. Werth, A., *The Last Days of Paris* (1940).

VICHY FRANCE: Brooks, H. L., *Prisoners of Hope* (1942); report on life in Vichy. Flanner, J., *Pétain: The Old Man of France* (1944). Huddleston, S., *Pétain: Patriot or Traitor* (1951); a defense by a British journalist. Langer, W. L., *Our Vichy Gamble* (1947); an account of United States' relations with Vichy France, authorized by the State Department. Laval, P., *The Diary of Pierre Laval* (1948); Laval's defense, written while in prison before his execution. Lorraine, J., *Behind the Battle of France* (1943); the collaborationists. Marchal, L., *Vichy: Two Years of Deception* (1943). Martel, F., *Pétain: Verdun to Vichy* (1943); an indictment. Mikés, G., *Darlan: A Study* (1943). Montmorency, A. de, *The Enigma of Admiral Darlan* (1943). Sadleir, M. (tr.), *Pétain-Laval: The Conspiracy* (1942). Thomson, D., *Two Frenchmen: Charles de Gaulle and Pierre Laval* (1951); interpretative biographies. Tissier, P., *The Government of Vichy* (1942). Torres, H., *Pierre Laval* (1941); critical.

DE GAULLE AND THE FIGHTING FRENCH: Aglion, R., *The Fighting French* (1943). Barrès, P., *Charles de Gaulle* (1941). Cattain, G., *Charles de Gaulle* (1945). Gaulle, C. de, *The Speeches of General de Gaulle,* 2 vols. (1942–1943). Hassenstein, A. A., *A Giant in the Age of Steel: The Story of De Gaulle* (1944). Kerillis, H. de, *I Accuse de Gaulle* (1946); an indictment by a former member of the Chamber of Deputies. Riveloup, A., *The Truth about De Gaulle* (1944).

THE BATTLE OF BRITAIN: Ayling, K., *R.A.F.: The Story of a British Pilot Fighter* (1941). Beauman, B. (ed.), *The Airmen Speak* (1941): personal experiences told by officers and men of the RAF. Bolitho, H., *Combat Report: The Story of a Fighter Pilot* (1943). Bonnell, J. S., *Britons Under Fire* (1941). Dade, H. A., *To His Refugee Son* (1942); letters of an Englishman to his son in America during the blitz. Daniell, R., *Civilians Must Fight* (1941); concise, simple, dramatic description of an air attack on London. Eade, C. (comp.), *The War Speeches of the Rt. Hon. Winston Churchill,* 3 vols. (1953); they go back to 1938. Forbes-Robertson, D., *The Battle of Waterloo Road* (1941); the life of a typical London family during the blitz. Gleed, I., *Arise to Conquer* (1943); by a pilot of the RAF. Great Britain, Air

Ministry, *The Battle of Britain* (1941); from August 8 to October 31, 1940. Great Britain, Air Ministry, *Bomber Command* (1941); the British air offensive against the Axis, 1940–1941. Great Britain, Air Ministry, *Coastal Command* (1943); air force attacks on German ships. Great Britain, Ministry of Information, *Roof over Britain: The Official Story of Britain's Anti-Aircraft Defenses, 1939–1942* (1943). Grey, C. G., *The Luftwaffe* (1944). Lee, A., *The German Air Force* (1946); perhaps the best general discussion. Leska, G., *I Was a Nazi Flier* (1941); the diary of a German flight sergeant. Michie, A. A., and Graebner, W. (eds.), *Their Finest Hour* (1941). Michie, A. A., *The Air Offensive Against Germany* (1943). Pile, F., *Ack-Ack* (1950); the story of Britain's air defense. Reynolds, Q., *A Londoner's Diary* (1941). Robertson, B., *I Saw England* (1941); by the London correspondent of *PM*. Strachey, J., *Digging for Mrs. Miller* (1941); the story of an ARP warden. Underdown, T. H. J., *Bristol under Blitz: The Record of an Ancient City and Her People during the Battle of Britain, 1940–41* (1942).

THE WAR IN THE BALKANS: Amery, J., *Sons of the Eagle: A Study in Guerilla War* (1949); in Albania. "Athenian," *The Greek Miracle* (1942). Casson, S., *Greece Against the Axis* (1942); by a British officer. Easterman, E. L., *King Carol, Hitler, and Lupescu* (1942). Greek Office of Information, *The Campaign in Greece and Crete* (1943). Greek Office of Information, *Diplomatic Documents Relating to Italy's Aggression against Greece; The Greek White Book* (1943). Hetherington, J., *Airborne Invasion* (1943); the battle of Crete. Howell, E., *Escape to Live: Memoirs of the Campaign in Crete and Greece* (1947); by a British officer. Lavra, S., *The Greek Miracle* (1943). Mackenzie, C., *Wind of Freedom: The History of the Invasion of Greece by the Axis Powers, 1940–1941* (1943). Mitchell, R., *The Serbs Choose War* (1943). Montgomery, J. P., *Hungary: The Unwilling Satellite* (1948); of Nazi Germany. Papagos, A., *The Battle of Greece, 1940–1941* (1949); by a Greek general. Patmore, D., *Balkan Correspondent* (1941); an account of Rumanian politics, 1939–1941. St. John, R., *From the Land of Silent People* (1942); the campaign in Yugoslavia, Greece, and Crete. Tobin, C. M., *Turkey, Key to the East* (1944); explains Turkey's neutrality in the war. Waldeck, R. G., *Athene Palace, Bucharest* (1943); Rumania in 1940–1941. Wason, B., *Miracle in Hellas: The Greeks Fight On* (1943); by an American correspondent. White, L., *The Long Balkan Night* (1943); 1940–1941. Wisdom, T. H., *Wings over Olympus: The Story of the Royal Air Force in Libya and Greece* (1942).

THE WAR IN RUSSIA: Allen, W. E. D., and Muratoff, P., *The Russian Campaigns of 1944–1945* (1946). Borodin, G., *Red Surgeon* (1944); a biography. Caldwell, E., *All-Out on the Road to Smolensk* (1942); by an American correspondent. Cassidy, H. C., *Moscow Dateline* (1943); reports from Russia, 1941–1943, by an Associated Press correspondent. Ehrenburg, I., *The Tempering of Russia* (1944); the war to the battle of Stalingrad, by a Soviet correspondent. Fadeev, A., *Leningrad in the Days of Blockade* (1946); by a Russian. Fineberg, J. (tr.), *Heroic Leningrad: Documents, Sketches and Stories of Its Siege and Relief* (1945). Fischer, G., *Soviet Opposition to Stalin*

(1952); the story of Russian "defeatists" who aided the Germans. Graebner, W., *Round Trip to Russia* (1943); explains why and how the Russians fought so bravely. Grossman, V., *The People Immortal* (1944) and *With the Red Army in Poland and Byelorussia* (1945); by a *Red Star* correspondent. Hughes, P., *Retreat from Rostov* (1946). Isakov, I. S., *The Red Fleet in the Second World War* (1947); by a Soviet admiral. Kerr, W., *The Russian Army: Its Men, Its Leaders, Its Battles* (1944). Kovpak, S. A., *Our Partisan Course* (1947); the Russian guerrillas. Lesueur, L., *Twelve Months That Changed the World* (1943); October, 1941–October, 1942. Mehring, W., *Timoshenko: Marshal of the Red Army* (1942). Plievier, Theodor, *Stalingrad* (1948). Poliakov, A., *Russians Don't Surrender* (1942) and *White Mammoths: The Dramatic Story of Russian Tanks in Action* (1943); accounts of fighting in 1941–1942. Ponomarenka, P. K., *et al.*, *Behind the Front Lines: A Chronicle of Soviet Guerilla Activity Behind the German Lines* (1945). Skomorovosky, B., and Morris, E. G., *The Siege of Leningrad* (1944). Stalin, J., *The Great Patriotic War of the Soviet Union* (1945); Stalin's speeches and orders of the day. Stroud, J., *The Red Air Force* (1943). Thorwald, J., *Flight in Winter: Russia Conquers—January to May, 1945* (1951); a bitter book written from the German viewpoint. Tikhonov, N., *The Defense of Leningrad* (1943). Voyetekhov, B., *The Last Days of Sevastopol* (1943); a vivid account. Voznesensky, N. A., *The Economy of the USSR during World War II* (1948); based on official data. Weaver, D., *On Hitler's Doorstep* (1943); the German campaign in Russia to September, 1942, reported by a Swedish correspondent. Werth, A., *Leningrad* (1944); *Moscow War Diary* (1942); *The Year of Stalingrad* (1947); by an English correspondent. Zacharoff, L., *The Voice of Fighting Russia* (1942); a vivid picture of the war in Russia both on the battlefront and behind the lines. Anders, W., *Hitler's Defeat in Russia* (1953); a Polish general examines the reasons for it.

THE BATTLE OF THE ATLANTIC: Armstrong, W., *Battle of the Oceans* (1944); the British merchant marine. Cant, G., *The War at Sea* (1942); by a naval expert. Carse, R., *Lifeline: The Ships and Men of Our Merchant Marine at War* (1944). Chatterton, E. K., *Fighting the U-boats* (1942) and *The Royal Navy from September, 1939 to June, 1943*, 3 vols. (1942–1946). Coale, G. B., *North Atlantic Patrol* (1942). Edwards, K., *The Royal Navy and Allies from July, 1943 to September, 1945*, 2 vols. (1947–1948). Grenfell, R., *The Bismarck Episode* (1949); the exciting chase and destruction of Germany's most powerful battleship. Halstead, I., *Heroes of the Atlantic* (1942); a tribute to the merchant navy. Herman, F., *Dynamite Cargo* (1943); a convoy to Russia. Johnston, G. H., *Battle of the Seaways: From the Athenia to the Bismarck* (1942). Karig, W., *et al.*, *Battle Report*, Vol. II. *The Atlantic War* (1946); from U.S. official sources. Leeming, J., *Brave Ships of World War II* (1944); both British and American. Low, A. M., *The Submarine at War* (1942). Martienssen, A., *Hitler and His Admirals* (1949); a documented account of Germany's war at sea. Masters, D., *Up Periscope* (1943); British submarines. McCoy, S. D., . . . *Nor Death Dismay* (1944);

the merchant marine. Monsarrat, N., *Corvette Command* (1944). Morison, S. E., *History of United States Naval Operations in World War II*, Vol. I. *The Battle of the Atlantic: September, 1939–May, 1943* (1947); practically an official history. Puleston, W. D., *The Influence of Sea Power in World War II* (1947). Reynolds, Q., *Convoy* (1942). Rogers, S., *Enemy in Sight* (1943); stories of naval operations. Shaw, F. H., *The Merchant Navy at War* (1944). Spaight, J. M., *Blockade by Air: The Campaign Against Axis Shipping* (1942). U.S. Office of Naval Intelligence, *Führer Conferences, 1939–1940* (1947). Woodward, D., *The Tirpitz, and the Battle for the North Atlantic* (1953). Zim, H. S., *Submarines* (1942).

THE UNITED STATES AND THE WAR: Alsop, J., and Kintner, R., *American White Paper: The Story of American Diplomacy and the Second World War* (1940). Alsop, S., and Bradon, T., *Sub-Rosa—The OSS and American Espionage* (1946). Chamberlin, W. H., *America's Second Crusade* (1950); an attack on President Roosevelt's policies. Deene, J. R., *The Strange Alliance* (1947); an account of co-operation between the OSS and the NKVD, by the head of the U.S. military mission in Moscow, 1943–1945. Ford, C., *Cloak and Dagger: The Secret Story of the OSS* (1946). Hull, C., *The Memoirs of Cordell Hull*, 2 vols. (1948); the United States secretary of state. Hynd, A., *Passport to Treason* (1943); Nazi activities in the United States. Janeway, E., *The Struggle for Survival: A Chronicle of Economic Mobilization in World War II* (1951). Johnson, W., *The Battle Against Isolation* (1944); discusses the Committee to Defend America by Aiding the Allies. King, C., *Atlantic Charter* (1943). King, E. J., *Fleet Admiral King* (1952); memoirs by U.S. admiral. Lavine, H., and Wechsler, J., *War Propaganda and the United States* (1940); a study of pressure groups. Marshall, G. C., Arnold, H. H., and King, E. J., *The War Reports* (1947); by the heads of the U.S. armed forces. Morton, H. V., *Atlantic Meeting* (1943); background of the Atlantic Charter. Nelson, D. M., *Arsenal of Democracy: The Story of American War Production* (1946); by the chairman of the War Production Board. Riess, C., *Total Espionage* (1941); Axis espionage in America. Sherwood, R. E., *Roosevelt and Hopkins: An Intimate History* (1948); revealing. Stettinius, E. R., Jr., *Lend-Lease: Weapons for Victory* (1944); by the American administrator. Stettinius, E. R., Jr., *Roosevelt and the Russians: The Yalta Conference* (1949); by the then U.S. secretary of state. Treffousse, H. L., *Germany and American Neutrality, 1939–1941* (1951); a study of Germany's policies toward the U.S. U.S. Department of State, *Peace and War: United States Foreign Policy, 1931–1941* (1943). Welles, S., *Seven Decisions that Shaped History* (1951); wartime decisions by President Roosevelt. Cole, W. S., *America First; The Battle Against Intervention, 1940–1941* (1953).

THE WAR IN AFRICA: Aglion, R., *War in the Desert: The Battle for Africa* (1941). Austin, A. B., *Birth of an Army* (1943); the American Tunisian campaign. Belot, R. de, *The Struggle for the Mediterranean, 1939–1945* (1951); by a French admiral. Butcher, H. C., *My Three Years with Eisenhower* (1946); diary of Eisenhower's naval aide. Clark, M. W., *Calculated Risk* (1950); an account of the war in North Africa and Italy, by an

American general. Clifford, A. G., *The Conquest of North Africa, 1940–43* (1943); the British Eighth Army. D'Arcy-Dawson, J., *Tunisian Battle* (1943); the British First Army. Gerard, F., *Malta Magnificent* (1943); its two years of resistance. Great Britain, Ministry of Information, *The Army at War: Tunisia* (1944). Hill, R., *Desert Conquest* (1943); the British Eighth Army. Houghton, G. W., *They Flew Through Sand* (1943); the RAF in Libya. Liddell Hart, B. H., *The Rommel Papers* (1953); valuable. Marshall, G. C., *Report of the Chief of Staff of the U.S. Army to the Secretary of War (July 1, 1939 to June 30, 1943)* (1943). McMillin, R., *Rendezvous with Rommel* (1943); the British Eighth Army. Montgomery, Viscount, *El Alamein to the River Sangro* (1949); by the British commanding general. Morison, S. E., *History of United States Naval Operations in World War II*, Vol. II. *Operations in North African Waters, October, 1942–June, 1943* (1947); practically official. Pyle, E., *Here Is Your War* (1943); the American forces in Africa. Schmidt, H. W., *With Rommel in the Desert* (1952); by his aide de camp. Wordell, M. T., and Seiler, E. N., *Wildcats over Casablanca* (1943); American navy planes. Young, D., *Rommel, the Desert Fox* (1950); includes a discussion of the general's part in the plot to kill Hitler.

THE INVASION OF ITALY: Badoglio, P., *Italy in the Second World War* (1948); by the Italian chief of staff in 1940. Brown, J. M., *To All Hands: An Amphibious Adventure* (1943); the landing in Sicily. Gibson, H. (ed.), *The Ciano Diaries, 1939–1943* (1945); diaries of Mussolini's son-in-law who was Italian foreign minister. Heller, F., *Twilight of the Gladiators: Italy and the Italians, 1939–1943* (1944); by a Swedish journalist. Linklater, E., *The Campaign in Italy* (1951). Macartney, M. H. H., *One Man Alone: The History of Mussolini and the Axis* (1944). Majdalany, F., *The Monastery* (1946); an excellent account of the battle for Monte Cassino. Mussolini, B., *The Fall of Mussolini: His Own Story* (1948); written by the Duce after his downfall to justify his actions. Packard, R., and E., *Balcony Empire: Fascist Italy at War* (1942); by American correspondents in Rome, 1939–1941. Pyle, E., *Brave Men* (1944); Sicily and Italy. Shapiro, S. B., *They Left the Back Door Open* (1945); the Allied campaign in Sicily and Italy. Skorzeny, O., *Skorzeny's Secret Missions: War Memoirs of the Most Dangerous Man in Europe* (1950); by the Nazi who kidnapped Mussolini for Hitler. Starr, C. G., *From Salerno to the Alps: A History of the Fifth Army, 1943–45* (1948); by an American officer. Strabolgi, J. M. K., *The Conquest of Italy* (1944). Thruelsen, R., and Arnold, E., *Mediterranean Sweep* (1944); aerial warfare. Tregaskis, R., *Invasion Diary* (1944); Sicily and Italy.

THE ALLIED AIR OFFENSIVE AGAINST FORTRESS EUROPE: Ayling, K., *Bombers* (1944). Carlisle, N. V. (ed.), *The Air Forces Reader: An Account of the American Air Forces in Action* (1944). Charlton, L. E. O., *The Royal Air Force and U.S.A.A.F. from July, 1943 to September, 1945*, 2 vols. (1946–1947). Craven, W. F., and Cate, J. L. (eds.), *The Army Air Forces in World War II*, 4 vols. (1948–1951); with more to come. Hermann, H., *Luftwaffe: Its Rise and Fall* (1943). McCrary, J. R., and Scherman, D. E., *First of the Many* (1944); by one who bombed Germany. Pollard, A. O.,

Bombers Over the Reich (1941). Redding, J. M., and Leyshon, H. I., *Skyways to Berlin: With the American Flyers in England* (1943). Straubel, J. H. (ed.), *Air Force Diary* (1947); the U.S. Army Air Force. U.S. Army Air Forces, *Target, Germany: The Army Air Forces' Official Story of the VIII Bomber Command's First Year over Europe* (1943).

THE WAR IN THE WEST, 1944–1945: Allen, R. S., *Lucky Forward: The History of Patton's Third U.S. Army* (1947); by Patton's intelligence operations officers. Brown, J. M., *Many A Watchful Night* (1944); the Normandy landing. Chaplin, W. W., *The Fifty-two Days* (1944); following D-day. D'Arcy-Dawson, J., *European Victory* (1945); from the Normandy landing on. Edwards, K., *Operation Neptune* (1945); an account of the combined sea operations which covered the invasion of Europe on D-day. Eisenhower, D. D., *Report by the Supreme Commander to the Combined Chiefs of Staff on the Operations in Europe of the Allied Expeditionary Force, June 6, 1944 to May 8, 1945* (1946). Eisenhower, D. D., *Crusade in Europe* (1948); contains interesting material not in his official report. Guignand, F. F. de, *Operation Victory* (1947); by Montgomery's chief of staff. Gunther, J., *D Day: What Preceded It; What Followed It* (1944). Hagen, L. E., *Arnhem Lift: A Diary of a Pilot Glider* (1945). Harrison, G. A., *Cross Channel Attack* (1951); a detailed integrated account of D-Day. Heaps, L., *Escape from Arnhem* (1946); by a Canadian paratrooper. Lerner, D., *SYKEWAR: Psychological Warfare Against Germany, D-Day to V-E Day* (1950); valuable, but not easy reading. Marshall, G. C., *Report of the Chief of Staff of the U.S. Army to the Secretary of War (July 1, 1943 to June 30, 1945)* (1945). Marshall, S. L. A., *et al.*, *Bastogne: The First Eight Days* (1946); based on interviews with survivors. Melville, A., *First Tide: "D" Day Invasion, June 6, 1944* (1945). Merriam, R., *Dark December* (1947); the battle of the Bulge. Montgomery, Viscount, *Normandy to the Baltic* (1947); rather dry reading. Morgan, Sir F., *Overture to Overlord* (1950); the beginnings of the plans for the invasion of Normandy. Munro, R., *Gauntlet to Overlord: The Story of the Canadian Army* (1946); by a leading Canadian war correspondent. Norman, A., *Operation Overlord: The Allied Invasion of Western Europe* (1952). Patton, G. S., Jr., *War As I Knew It* (1947); reveals the temperament and viewpoint of the commander of the American Third Army. Pyle, E., *Brave Men* (1944). Rowan-Robinson, H., *Onward from D-Day* (1946). Speidel, H., *Invasion, 1944: Rommel and the Normandy Campaign* (1950); by Rommel's chief of staff. Tobin, R. L., *Invasion Journal* (1944); Normandy. Wallace, B. G., *Patton and His Third Army* (1946); by a military man. Wertenbaker, C. C., *Invasion* (1944); Normandy.

NAZI TREATMENT OF OCCUPIED EUROPE: Apenszlak, J. (ed.), *The Black Book of Polish Jewry* (1944); treatment by the Nazis. Basch, A., *The New Economic Warfare* (1941); Germany's manipulation of trade and politics in other countries. Berg, M., *Warsaw Ghetto* (1945); a diary. Christensen, S., *Norway Is My Country* (1943); life in Nazi-occupied Norway. Curie, E., *et al.*, *They Speak for a Nation: Letters from France* (1941); from those living under Nazi control. Davies, R. A., *Odyssey Through Hell*

(1946); treatment of the Jews in Eastern Europe. Goris, J.-A., *Belgium in Bondage* (1944). Gudme, S., *Denmark, Hitler's "Model Protectorate"* (1942). Hlond, August, Cardinal *et al.*, *The Persecution of the Catholic Church in German-Occupied Poland* (1941). Kernan, T., *France on Berlin Time* (1941); by an American who was publisher of the Paris *Vogue*. Lemkin, R., *Axis Rule in Occupied Europe* (1945); dispassionate. Lorraine, J., *The Germans in France* (1947). Malaparte, C., *Kaputt* (1946); evidence by an Italian Fascist on the brutal atrocities of the Nazis. Mentze, E., *5 Years: The Occupation of Denmark in Pictures* (1946). Moën, L., *Under the Iron Heel* (1941), a restrained, factual eye witness account of the Nazi occupation of Belgium. Nikitin, M. N., and Vagin, P. I., *The Crimes of the German Fascists in the Leningrad Region: Materials and Documents* (1946). Paulmer, P., *Denmark in Nazi Chains* (1942). Polnay, P. de, *The Germans Came to Paris* (1943); an account of life in Paris from June, 1940, to the latter part of 1941. Reveille, T., *The Spoil of Europe* (1941); Nazi methods of exploiting conquered countries. Shoskes, H., *No Traveler Returns* (1945); Poland. Shub, B., *Starvation over Europe: Made in Germany* (1943). Sledzinski, W., *Governor Frank's Dark Harvest* (1946); Poland. Somerhausen, A., *Written in Darkness: A Belgian Woman's Record of the Occupation, 1940–1945* (1946). *Soviet Government Statements on Nazi Atrocities* (1946); official. Weinrich, M., *Hitler's Professors* (1946); the part played by German scholars in the destruction of Jews and Poles. Zywulska, K., *I Came Back* (1951); by a Polish woman who spent 20 months in a Nazi extermination camp.

THE RESISTANCE MOVEMENTS IN OCCUPIED EUROPE: Brown, A., *Michailovitch and Yugoslav Resistance* (1943). Fast, H. M., *The Incredible Tito* (1944). Goffin, R., *The White Brigade* (1944); the Belgian underground. Höye, B., and Ager, T. M., *The Fight of the Norwegian Church against Nazism* (1943). Huot, L., *Guns for Tito* (1945); by an American officer who helped get supplies to Tito. Jones, W., *Twelve Months with Tito's Partisans* (1946). Jong, L. de, and Stoppelman, J. W. F., *The Lion Rampant; The Story of Holland's Resistance to the Nazis* (1943). Karski, J., *Story of a Secret State* (1945); the Polish resistance movement. Kessel, J., *Army of Shadows* (1944); French resistance movement. Liebling, A. J., *The Republic of Silence* (1947); resistance in France. Millar, G. R., *Maquis* (1945); French resistance movement. Myklebost, T., *They Came as Friends* (1943); Norway's reaction to the Germans. Nyquist, R. B., *Sons of the Vikings* (1943); underground warfare against the Nazis in Norway. Orska, I., *Silent Is the Vistula* (1946); experiences inside Warsaw during and after the abortive uprising of 1944. Padev, M., *Marshal Tito* (1944). Rootham, J., *Miss Fire: The Chronicle of a British Mission to Michailovich* (1946). Sava, G., *The Chetniks* (1942); Yugoslavia. Sudjic, M., *Yugoslavia in Arms* (1943); the resistance movement. Tenenbaum, J., *Underground: The Story of a People* (1952); the Polish Jews during German occupation. Wachsman, Z. H., *Trail Blazers for Invasion* (1943); underground activities of the Nazi-conquered countries. Woodman, D., *Europe Rises* (1943); resistance movements in Nazi-occupied countries.

NAZI GERMANY IN WARTIME: Andreas-Friedrich, R., *Berlin Underground* (1947); by a member. Boehm, E. H. (ed.), *We Survived: The Stories of Fourteen of the Hidden and the Hunted of Nazi Germany*. Burney, C., *The Dungeon Democracy* (1946); a German concentration camp. Deuel, W., *People Under Hitler* (1942); report by an American journalist. Dulles, A. W., *Germany's Underground* (1947); by the head of the U.S. OSS in Switzerland. Flannery, H. W., *Assignment to Berlin* (1942); Germany in 1941. Fraenkel, H., *The Other Germany* (1943); discusses the "good" Germans. Fredborg, A., *Behind the Steel Wall* (1944); by a Swedish correspondent. Gaevernitz, G. v. S. (ed.), *They Almost Killed Hitler* (1947); based on the personal account of one who made a daring attempt to kill Hitler. Gisevius, H. B., *To the Bitter End* (1947); the conspiracy against Hitler. Hassell, U. von, *The Von Hassell Diaries, 1938–1944* (1947); by a member of the German underground. Jansen, J. B., and Weyl, S., *The Silent War: The Underground Movement in Germany* (1943). Pihl, G., *Germany: The Last Phase* (1944); life within Germany as seen by a Swedish journalist. Rothfels, H., *The German Opposition to Hitler: An Appraisal* (1948). Rousset, D., *The Other Kingdom* (1947); the concentration camps. Seydewitz, M., *Civil Life in Wartime Germany* (1945). Smith, H. K., *Last Train from Berlin* (1942); the state of the German home front in the winter of 1941–1942. Trevor-Roper, H. R., *The Last Days of Hitler* (1947); the results of a careful investigation by a British scholar.

MISCELLANEOUS: Baker, R. L., *Oil, Blood and Sand* (1942); the Middle East. Denny, H., *Behind Both Lines* (1942); prison camps. Gordon, D. L., and Dangerfield, R., *The Hidden Weapon: A Story of Economic Warfare* (1947). Howe, T. C., *Salt Mines and Castles: The Discovery and Restoration of Looted European Art* (1946). Kirk, G., *The Middle East in the War: A Survey of International Affairs, 1939–1946* (1953); objective and documented. Linebarger, P. M. A., *Psychological Warfare* (1948). Loeffe, W., *Spionage* (1950); activities of a German counter-spy. *The New Yorker Book of War Pieces* (1947); some of the finest descriptive reporting of the war. Riess, C., *Total Espionage* (1941); the Nazi system. Sayre, J., *Persian Gulf Command* (1945). Singer, K. D., *Duel for the Northland* (1943) and *Spies and Traitors of World War II* (1945); the former is an account of German espionage in Scandinavia. Vail Motter, T. H., *The Middle East Theatre: The Persian Corridor and Aid to Russia* (1952). Weizsacker, E. von, *Memories of Ernst von Weizsacker* (1951); apologia of a German war criminal who participated in the Anschwitz atrocities.

Chapter XXII. Japan's Early Blitzkrieg and Ultimate Collapse

THE FAR EAST, 1931–1941: Abend, H., *Chaos in Asia* (1940). Clayton, E. L., *Heaven Below* (1944); by an eye-witness of events in China until early in 1942. Hanson, H., *"Humane Endeavor"; The Story of the China War* (1939). Harcourt-Smith, S., *Fire in the Pacific* (1942); the background of Japan's ambitions and military adventures. Hauser, E. O., *Honorable Enemy*

(1941); psychological analysis of the Japanese people. Matsuo, K., *How Japan Plans to Win* (1942); originally published in Japan in 1940 as *The Three-Power Alliance and a U.S.–Japanese War*. Maurer, H., *The End Is Not Yet* (1941); Chinese resistance. Quigley, H. S., *Far Eastern War, 1937–1941* (1942); a record of the war and a survey of American relations with China and Japan. Snow, E., *The Battle for Asia* (1941); the war in China, 1937–1941. Whelan, R., *The Flying Tigers: The Story of the American Volunteer Group in China* (1942); before the United States entered the war.

THE IMMEDIATE BACKGROUND OF PEARL HARBOR: Beard, C. A., *American Foreign Policy in the Making, 1932–1940: A Story in Responsibilities* (1947); critical of Roosevelt. Beard, C. A., *President Roosevelt and the Coming of the War, 1941* (1948); blames him for the war with Japan. Bisson, T. A., *America's Far Eastern Policy* (1945); a valuable survey. Davis, F., and Lindley, E. K., *How War Came: An American White Paper: From the Fall of France to Pearl Harbor* (1942); sympathetic with the Roosevelt administration. Feis, H., *The Road to Pearl Harbor: The Coming of the War Between the United States and Japan* (1950); chiefly an account of diplomacy. Hornbeck, S. K., *The United States and the Far East: Certain Fundamentals of Policy* (1942); by an authority on the Far East. Hull, C., *The Memoirs of Cordell Hull*, 2 vols. (1948); Roosevelt's secretary of state. Johnstone, W. C., *Why Japan Chose War* (1942); by an American professor. Kase, T., *Journey to the "Missouri"* (1950); the causes and influences leading to Japan's actions in 1941, by a Japanese diplomat. Millis, W., *This Is Pearl! The United States and Japan—1941* (1947); disagrees with Beard's books listed above. Mook, H. J. van, *The Netherlands Indies and Japan: Battle on Paper, 1940–1941* (1944); by the Dutch lieutenant governor-general. Morganstern, G., *Pearl Harbor: The Story of the Secret War* (1947); violently anti-Roosevelt. Rauch, B., *Roosevelt, From Munich to Pearl Harbor: A Study in the Creation of Foreign Policy* (1950); an able defense of Roosevelt's policy. Sanborn, F. R., *Design for War: A Study of Secret Power Politics, 1937–1941* (1951); maintains that Roosevelt plotted war. Tansill, C. C., *Back Door to War* (1952); a hostile account of Roosevelt's foreign policy. Taylor, G. E., *America in the New Pacific* (1942); explains how the United States became involved in the war. United States, Department of State, *Papers Relating to the Foreign Relations of the United States: Japan: 1931–1941* (1943) and *Prelude to Infamy: Official Report on the Final Phase of U.S. Japanese Relations, October 17 to December 7, 1941* (1943).

JAPAN'S CONQUEST OF EMPIRE: Bailey, D., *We Built and Destroyed: An Account of the Fall of Malaya and Singapore* (1944). Bayler, W. L. J., *Last Man Off Wake Island* (1943). Belden, J., *Retreat with Stilwell* (1943); from Burma. Braly, W. C., *The Hard Way Home* (1947); an account of Japanese prison camps in the Philippines. Brown, W., *Hong Kong Aftermath* (1943); a record of experiences in a Japanese prison in Hong Kong. Chennault, C. L., *Way of a Fighter: The Memoirs of Claire Lee Chennault* (1949); Commander of the Flying Tigers. Clark, T. B., *Remember Pearl Harbor!*

(1942); by an eyewitness of the attack. Devereux, J. P. S., *The Story of Wake Island* (1947). Donahue, A. G., *Last Flight from Singapore* (1943); by an American in the RAF. Franklin, A. and G., *One Year of Life: The Story of H.M.S. Prince of Wales* (1944). Gallagher, O. D., *Action in the East* (1942); Malaya and Burma. Glover, E. M., *In 70 Days: The Story of the Japanese Campaign in British Malaya* (1944). Hersey, J., *Men on Bataan* (1942); MacArthur's defense. Hotz, R. B., *With General Chennault: The Story of the Fighting Tigers* (1943); over Burma and China. Miller, E. B., *Bataan Uncensored* (1949); a former U.S. colonel tries to assess the blame for the catastrophe. Morrill, J., and Martin, P., *South from Corregidor* (1943); an account of navy men who escaped to Australia. Playfair, G., *Singapore Goes Off the Air* (1943); an account of the siege and fall. Raleigh, J. M., *Pacific Blackout* (1943); the war in the Netherlands Indies in 1942. Redmond, J., *I Served on Bataan* (1943); by an American army nurse. Romanus, C. F., and Sunderland, R., *Stilwell's Mission to China* (1953); also Burma and India. Romulo, C. P., *I Saw the Fall of the Philippines* (1943); by a Filipino officer. Scott, R. L., *God Is My Co-Pilot* (1943); by an American flyer in Burma and China. Stilwell, J., *The Stilwell Papers* (1948); by an American general in China and Burma. Thompson, V., *Postmortem on Malaya* (1943); an explanation of why it fell so quickly. Wagg, A., *A Million Died* (1943); the Burma campaign. Wainwright, J. M., *General Wainwright's Story* (1946); by MacArthur's successor as commander in the Philippines. White, W. L., *They Were Expendable* (1942); the Philippines campaign. Morton, L., *The Fall of the Philippines* (1953); official history of the defeat of the U.S. forces in 1941–1942.

GENERAL ACCOUNTS OF OPERATIONS AGAINST THE JAPANESE: Cant, G., *America's Navy in World War II* (1943) and *The Great Pacific Victory* (1945); from Pearl Harbor to Tokyo. Edmonds, W. D., *They Fought with What They Had: The Story of the Army Air Force in the Southwest Pacific, 1941–42* (1951). Eichelberger, R. L., *Our Jungle Road to Tokyo* (1950); by a U.S. general. Halsey, W. F., and Bryan, J., 3rd, *Admiral Halsey's Story* (1947); a first-hand but not unbiased account. Haugland, V., *The AAF Against Japan* (1948); from Pearl Harbor to Tokyo. Hough, F. O., *The Island War* (1947); by a major in the marines. Howard, C., and Whitley, J., *One Damned Island after Another: The Saga of the Seventh* (1947); air-force operations. James, D. H., *The Rise and Fall of the Japanese Empire* (1951). Jensen, O., *Carrier War: Task Force 58 and the Pacific Sea Battles* (1945); written during the war. Karig, W., *et al.*, *Battle Report*: Vol. I. *Pearl Harbor to Coral Sea* (1944); Vol. III. *Pacific War—Middle Phase* (1947); Vol. IV. *The End of An Empire* (1948); Vol. V. *Victory in the Pacific* (1949); from U.S. official sources. McInnis, E., *The War*, 6 vols. (1940–1946); written yearly during the war. O'Sheel, P., and Cook, G. (eds.), *Semper Fidelis: The U.S. Marines in the Pacific, 1942–1945* (1947); by the marine corps combat correspondents. Pratt, F., *The Marines' War: An Account of the Struggle for the Pacific from Both American and Japanese Sources*

(1948); by an American naval historian who had access to United States and Japanese documents. Wertenbaker, G. P., *5000 Miles Toward Tokyo* (1946); naval air force.

SPECIAL AREAS OR BATTLES: Appleman, R., *et al., Okinawa, the Last Battle* (1949); official account. Ayling, K., *Old Leatherneck of the Flying Tigers* (1945); General Chennault in China. Burchett, W. G., *Wingate's Phantom Army* (1947); in Burma. Cave, H. B., *et al., Long Were the Nights: The Saga of PT Squadron "X" in the Solomons* (1943). Coale, G. B., *Victory at Midway* (1944). Fergusson, B., *Beyond the Chindwin: Being An Account of the Adventures of Number Five Column of the Wingate Expedition into Burma* (1945); to expel the Japanese. Field, J. A., Jr., *The Japanese at Leyte Gulf* (1947); based on a cross-examination of Japanese officers. Ford, C., *Short Cut to Tokyo: The Battle for the Aleutians* (1943). Handelman, H., *Bridge to Victory* (1943); the reconquest of the Aleutians. Henri, R., *Iwo Jima: Springboard to Final Victory* (1945); excellent photographs. Hoffman, C. W., *Saipan: The Beginning of the End* (1950) and *The Seizure of Tinian* (1951); by a U.S. officer. Hough, F. O., *The Assault on Peleliu* (1950); by a U.S. officer. Johnston, G. H., *The Toughest Fighting in the World* (1943); New Guinea. Johnston, S., *Queen of the Flat-Tops: The U.S.S. Lexington and the Coral Sea Battle* (1942). Kahn, E. J., Jr., *G.I. Jungle* (1943); New Guinea. Matthews, A. R., *The Assault* (1947); an account of the first twelve days in Iwo Jima. Mears, F., *Carrier Combat* (1944); off Guadalcanal. Merillat, H. L., *The Island: A History of the Marines on Guadalcanal* (1944). Miller, J., Jr., *Guadalcanal: The First Offensive* (1949); an account of the ground operations. Morison, S. E., *History of United States Naval Operations in World War, II:* Vol. III. *The Rising Sun in the Pacific, 1931–April, 1942;* Vol. IV. *Coral Sea, Midway, and Submarine Actions, May 1942–August 1942;* Vol. V. *The Struggle for Guadalcanal, August 1942– February, 1943;* Vol. VI. *Breaking the Bismarcks Barrier, 22 July 1942–1 May 1944;* Vol. VII. *Aleutians, Gilberts and Marshalls, June 1942–April 1944;* Vol. VIII. *New Guinea and the Marianas, March 1944–August 1944* (1948–1953); official history. Mountbatten, Earl of Burma, *Southeast Asia, 1943–1945: Report to the Combined Chiefs of Staff* (1951); by the British commander in that area. Owen, F., *The Campaign in Burma* (1946). Rolo, C. J., *Wingate's Raiders* (1944); British efforts to expel the Japanese from Burma. Shalett, S., *Old Nameless* (1943); naval action off Savo and Guadalcanal. Sherrod, R., *Tarawa: The Story of a Battle* (1944) and *On to Westward* (1945); the fighting on Tarawa, Saipan, Iwo Jima and Okinawa. Tregaskis, R., *Guadalcanal Diary* (1943); by a war correspondent. Vetter, E. G., *Death Was Our Escort* (1944); early fighting in New Guinea. Wilson, E. J., *et al., Betio Beachhead: U.S. Marines' Own Story of the Battle of Tarawa* (1945); by marine combat correspondents. Wolfert, I., *Battle for the Solomons* (1943) and *Torpedo 8: The Attack and Vengeance of Swede Larsen's Bomber Squadron* (1943); both deal with the Solomon Islands fighting. Woodward, C. V., *The Battle for Leyte Gulf* (1947); excellent.

MISCELLANEOUS: Bell, F. J., *Condition Red: Destroyer Action in the*

South Pacific (1943). Cope, H., and Karig, W., *Battle Submerged* (1951); based on the activities of individual American submarines. Hubler, R. G., and DeChant, J. A., *Flying Leathernecks: The Complete Record of Marine Corps Aviation in Action, 1941–44* (1944). Huie, W. B., *Can Do! The Story of the Seabees* (1944). Kenney, G. C., *General Kenney Reports* (1949); by the head of MacArthur's air force. Lawson, T. W., *Thirty Seconds over Tokyo* (1943); by one who participated in the Doolittle raid. Olds, R., *Helldiver Squadron: The Story of Carrier Bombing Squadron 17 with Task Force 58* (1944). Pratt, F., *The Navy Has Wings* (1944); U.S. naval aviation. Rickenbacker, E., *Seven Came Through* (1943); experiences on a rubber raft for twenty-one days in the Pacific. Roscoe, T., *United States Submarine Operations in World War II* (1950); a definitive one-volume study. Sherman, F. C., *Combat Command: The American Aircraft Carriers in the Pacific War* (1950); by a U.S. admiral. U.S. Strategic Bombing Survey, *The Fifth Air Force in the War against Japan* (1947) and *The Effects of Air Attack on Japanese Urban Economy* (1947). White, W. L., *Queens Die Proudly* (1943); a flying fortress in the Southwest Pacific.

THE ATOM BOMB: Hersey, J., *Hiroshima* (1946); the moving stories of six survivors. Laurence, W. L., *Dawn Over Zero: The Story of the Atomic Bomb* (1946); by the science reporter of the *New York Times*. Miller, M., and Spitzer, A., *We Dropped the A-Bomb* (1946); by a radio operator who flew over both Hiroshima and Nagasaki. Magai, T., *We of Nagasaki* (1951); the story of eight survivors of the atom bomb.

Chapter XXIII. The Unfinished Peace Settlement and the "Cold War"

THE UNITED NATIONS: Arne, S., *United Nations Primer* (1945); the genesis of the organization. Besterman, T., *Unesco: Peace in the Minds of Men* (1951); aims and achievements. Dolivet, L., *The United Nations: A Handbook on the New World Organization* (1946); an excellent brief treatment. Evatt, H. V., *The United Nations* (1948); by an Australian statesman. Goodrich, L. M., and Hambro, E., *Charter of the United Nations. Commentary and Documents* (1946). Huxley, J., *UNESCO: Its Purpose and Philosophy* (1947). Murray, G., *From the League to the UN* (1948). United Nations, *Yearbook of the United Nations* (1948 ff); a valuable official source. Vandenbosch, A. and Hogan, W. N., *The United Nations: Background, Organization, Functions, Activities* (1952). World Peace Foundation, *International Organization* (1947 ff); a valuable quarterly containing an account of the activities of the UN.

PEACE NEGOTIATIONS, 1945–1946: Byrnes, J. F., *Speaking Frankly* (1947); by the United States secretary of state during 1945–1946. Dallin, D., *The Big Three* (1945); conflict in foreign policies of Russia and the United States and Britain. Holborn, L., *War and Peace Aims of the United Nations*, 2 vols. (1943–1948); official statements during the war of the political leaders of the Allies. Ivanyi, B. G., and Bell, A., *Route to Potsdam: The Story of the Peace Aims, 1939–1945* (1945); Allied peace aims and problems. Kalijarvi, T. V.

(ed.), *Peace Settlements of World War II* (1948). Laserson, M., *Russia and the Western World* (1945); optimistic. Nenoff, S., *Two Worlds, U.S.A.—U.S.S.R.* (1946). Neumann, W. L., *Making the Peace, 1941–45: The Diplomacy of the Wartime Conferences* (1949); brief, objective, based on documents and memoirs. Pick, F. W., *Peacemaking in Perspective* (1950); brief account of international conferences, 1945–1949. Ratchford, B. U., and Ross, W. D., *Berlin Reparations Assignment: Round One of the German Peace Settlement* (1948); by two Americans who helped decide on Germany's level of industry. U.S. Department of State, *Paris Peace Conference, 1946—Selected Documents* (1948); valuable source. Ziff, W. B., *Two Worlds; A Realistic Approach to the Problem of Keeping the Peace* (1946); the problem of Soviet-American relations.

EUROPEAN RECOVERY PROGRAM: Balogh, T., *The Dollar Crisis; Causes and Cure* (1950); by a British economist. Harris, S. E., *The European Recovery Program* (1948); by an American professor of economics. Kindleberger, C. P., *The Dollar Shortage* (1951), its nature, causes, and possible remedies, discussed by a British writer.

THE "COLD WAR": Burnham, J., *The Struggle for the World* (1947); advocates fierce opposition to Russia's program. Carr, E. H., *The Soviet Impact on the Western World* (1947); by a distinguished British writer. Clay, L., *Germany and the Fight for Freeedom* (1950); by the military governor of the U.S. zone in Germany. Dean, V. M., *Russia: Menace or Promise* (1947) and *The United States and Russia* (1947); by the Foreign Policy Association's expert on Russia. Dennett, R., and Johnson, J. E. (eds.), *Negotiating with the Russians* (1951); by negotiators for the West. Fisher, H. H., *America and Russia in the World Community* (1946); objective. Harris, S. E., *The European Recovery Program* (1948); by an American professor of economics. Lippmann, W., *The Cold War* (1947); a brief criticism of U.S. foreign policy. MacCurdy, J. T., *Germany, Russia, and the Future* (1945); a psychological study by a British professor. Morrell, S., *Spheres of Influence* (1946); an analysis of the Big Three struggle. Nenoff, S., *Two Worlds, U.S.A.—U.S.S.R.* (1946). Norborg, C., *Operation Moscow* (1947); believes Soviet-American agreement is impossible. Roberts, L., *Home from the Cold Wars* (1948). Ward, B., *The West at Bay* (1948); by a brilliant English writer. White, T. H., *Fire in the Ashes: Europe in Mid-Century* (1953); an appraisal of American policy since 1948.

THE ALLIES AND GERMANY: Davidson, B., *Germany: What Now? Potsdam, 1945—Partition, 1949* (1950). Friedman, W., *The Allied Military Government of Germany* (1947). Hill, R., *Struggle for Germany* (1947); urges the Western powers to build up Germany. Holborn, H., *American Military Government: Its Organizations and Philosophy* (1947). Morgenthau, H., Jr., *Germany Is Our Problem* (1945); the much-discussed proposals of the former U.S. secretary of the treasury. Noth, E. E., *Bridges over the Rhine* (1947); a French warning to the Allies not to let the Germans divide them. Plischke, E., *History of the Allied High Commission for Germany: Its Establishment, Structure, and Procedures* (1951). Pollock, J. K., and Meisel, J. H.,

Germany under Occupation: Illustrative Materials (1947); official documents and statements. Price, H., and Schorske, C. E., *The Problem of Germany* (1947); economic, social, and cultural. Riess, C., *The Berlin Story* (1952); from 1945 to 1952. Röpke, W., *The Solution of the German Problem* (1947); suggestions by an anti-Nazi German professor. Settel, A. (ed.), *This is Germany* (1950); a good analysis of conditions under the occupation. Stolper, G., *German Realities* (1948). U.S. Department of State, *Occupation of Germany: Policy and Progress, 1945–46* (1947); official report. Warburg, J. P., *Germany, Bridge or Battleground* (1947); an excellent account of the Allied policies in Germany. Zink, H., *American Military Government in Germany* (1947); by a professor of government who was a participant.

THE NUREMBERG TRIALS: Belgion, M., *Victor's Justice* (1949); critical of the trials. Calvocoressi, P., *Nuremberg: The Facts, the Law and the Consequences* (1948); by an English lawyer. Gilbert, G. M., *Nuremberg Diary* (1947); by an American who was prison psychologist at Nuremberg. Glueck, S., *The Nuremberg Trial and Aggressive War* (1946); by a Harvard professor of criminal law. International Military Tribunal, *Trial of Major War Criminals: Proceedings*, 40 vols. (1947–1949). Jackson, R. H., *The Case Against the Nazi War Criminals* (1946) and *The Nuremberg Case, As Presented by Robert H. Jackson, Chief of Counsel for the United States* (1947). Kelley, D. M., *22 Cells in Nuremberg* (1946); by the official United States psychiatrist. Mendelssohn, P. de, *The Nuremberg Documents: Some Aspects of German War Policy, 1939–1945* (1946). United States Chief of Counsel for Prosecution of Axis Criminality, *Nazi Conspiracy and Aggression*, 8 vols. (1946) and *Nazi Conspiracy and Aggression: Opinion and Judgment* (1947).

CONDITIONS IN POSTWAR GERMANY: Bach, J., *America's Germany* (1946); one of the better books on postwar Germany. Bourke-White, M., *"Dear Fatherland, Rest Quietly"* (1946); pictorial history of Germany in collapse. Byford-Jones, W., *Berlin Twilight* (1947); an account of postwar life in Berlin. Howley, F., *Berlin Command* (1950); by the commander of the United States sector. Joesten, J., *Germany: What Now?* (1948); includes sketches of German postwar political leaders. Klemme, M., *The Inside Story of UNRRA: An Experience in Internationalism. A First Hand Report on the Displaced Persons of Europe* (1949). Knappen, M., *And Call It Peace* (1947); German conditions described by an American historian in the AMG. Knauth, P., *Germany in Defeat* (1946); conditions in 1945. Kulischer, E. M., *Europe on the Move* (1948); a documented account of population movements. Lewis, H. O., *New Constitutions in Occupied Germany* (1948); discussion and documents. Peters, W., *In Germany Now: A Diary of Impressions in Germany, August–December, 1945* (1946). Rodnick, D., *Postwar Germans: An Anthropologist's Account* (1948); excellent. Schechtman, J. B., *European Population Transfers, 1939–1945* (1946); a careful study of the resettlement of Germans by the Nazis. Spender, S., *European Witness* (1946); an appraisal of German intellectuals by a British writer. Stern, J., *The Hidden Damage* (1947); the German civilians after the war.

THE ALLIES AND JAPAN: Brines, R., *MacArthur's Japan* (1948); by the

head of the Associated Press in Japan.   Busch, N. F., *Fallen Sun* (1948); an estimate of the results of U.S. occupation, by a writer for *Life*.   Cohen, J. B., *Japan's
Economy in War and Reconstruction* (1949); covers the years 1937–1948.   Col-
bert, E. S., *The Left Wing in Japanese Politics* (1951).   Farley, M. S., *Aspects of
Japan's Labor Problems* (1950); the labor movement under the occupation.
Fearey, R. A., *The Occupation of Japan: Second Phase, 1948–1950* (1950); by a
member of the U.S. State Department.   Gayn, M., *Japan Diary* (1948); experiences in Japan and Korea in 1945–1946.   Kato, M., *The Lost War* (1946); an
indictment of Japan's military leaders by a Japanese journalist.   Kelley, F. and
Ryan, C., *Star-Spangled Mikado: Japan under American Occupation* (1947);
a somewhat critical appraisal by an American and a British journalist.   La
Cerda, J., *The Conqueror Comes to Tea. Japan Under MacArthur* (1946);
readable, gossipy, but not documented.   Lauterbach, R. E., *Danger from the
East* (1947); critical of MacArthur's success.   Markham, E. M., *The Allied Occupation of Japan* (1948); official declarations and directives and their effects.
Reel, A. F., *The Case of General Yamashita* (1949); an indictment of the U.S.
military commission by one of the general's defense lawyers.   Reischauer, E. O.,
The United States and Japan (1950); a consideration of U.S. occupation policy
and the possibility of a democratic Japan.   Royal Institute of International Affairs, *Japan in Defeat* (1945); good discussion of Japanese institutions and possibilities.   Textor, R. B., *Failure in Japan* (1951); critical of the achievements
of the occupation.   U.S. Department of State, *Occupation of Japan: Policy and
Progress* (1946); official.   Van Aduard, E. J. L., *Japan: From Surrender to
Peace* (1953); a panegyric of MacArthur.   Wakefield, H., *New Paths for Japan*
(1948).

Chapter XXIV. Soviet Russia and Her Satellites

POSTWAR CONDITIONS IN SOVIET RUSSIA: Arakelian, A., *Indus-
trial Management in the USSR* (1950); a brief discussion.   Balzac, S. S., *et al.*
(eds.), *Economic Geography of the U.S.S.R.* (1949); a Soviet work.   Basseches,
N., *Stalin* (1952); a biography by a former Viennese correspondent in Moscow,
weak on period after 1937.   Beck, F., and Godin, W., *Russian Purge and the
Extraction of Confession* (1951); by a German scientist and a Russian historian.
Berman, H. J., *Justice in Russia* (1950); an analysis of the elements comprising
Soviet law.   Counts, G., and Lodge, N., *The Country of the Blind: The Soviet
System of Mind Control* (1949); by American students of Soviet Russia.   Crank-
shaw, E., *Russia and the Russians* (1948); a valuable interpretation by an Eng-
lishman.   Crankshaw, E., *Cracks in the Kremlin Wall* (1951); a penetrating an-
alysis of the weaknesses of the Soviet Union in the cold war.   Dallas, D., *Date-
line Moscow* (1952); a picture of the Soviet capital between 1947 and 1950.
Deutscher, I., *Stalin: A Political Biography* (1949) and *Soviet Trade Unions:
Their Place in Soviet Labour Policy* (1950); by a British specialist on Soviet
Russia.   Duranty, W., *Stalin & Co., the Politburo: The Men Who Run Russia*
(1949); by one who lived many years in Soviet Russia.   Ebon, M., *Malenkov:*

Stalin's Successor (1953); a careful preliminary study. Fischer, L. (ed.), *Thirteen Who Fled* (1949); life stories of Russian refugees. Frazier, R., *Malenkov* (1953); somewhat unrestrained. Herling, A. K., *The Soviet Slave Empire* (1951); based on testimony of Soviet victims. Inkeles, A., *Public Opinion in Soviet Russia* (1950); how the government seeks to control it. Jasny, N., *The Socialized Agriculture of the USSR: Plans and Performance* (1947); a critical analysis of Soviet farming since collectivization. Kalme, A., *Total Terror: An Exposé of Genocide in the Baltics* (1951); by a Latvian school teacher who suffered under both Russians and Nazis. Kirk, L., *Postmarked Moscow* (1952); bitter comments on everyday Moscow by a U.S. ambassador's wife. Lauterbach, R. E., *These Are the Russians* (1945) and *Through Russia's Back Door* (1947); experiences and conversations of an American correspondent in 1945–1946. Lipper, E., *Eleven Years in Soviet Prison Camps* (1951); by a German woman Communist. Magidoff, R., *In Anger and Pity* (1949); conditions in Russia described by an expelled foreign correspondent. Magidoff, R., *The Kremlin vs. the People* (1953); a discussion of tensions within Russia by a correspondent long in Moscow. Maynard, Sir John, *Russia in Flux* (1948). Members of the Overseas Press Club of America, *As We See Russia* (1948); chapters of varying value. Milhailov, N., and Pokshishevsky, V., *Soviet Russia: The Land and Its People* (1948); by Soviet geographers. Murray, N., *I Spied for Stalin* (1951); an interesting picture of Soviet society as seen by the daughter of a high ranking NKVD official. Nyaradi, N., *My Ringside Seat in Moscow* (1951); a picture of political and social life in Moscow in 1947 written by a former minister of finance in Hungary. Petrov, V., *Soviet Gold* (1949); by a former inmate of a slave-labor camp in the Kolyma gold fields. Pirogov, P., *Why I Escaped* (1950); by a Russian aviator who deserted in 1948. Rounds, F., Jr., *A Window On Red Square* (1953); excellent reporting and reflection resulting from a stay in Russia in 1951–1952. Schueller, G., *The Politburo* (1951); a comprehensive and detailed study. Schwartz, H., *Russia's Soviet Economy* (1950); a valuable factual survey. Schwarz, S. M., *Labour in the Soviet Union* (1951); a study of the transformation of the Soviet worker into a semi-serf. Schwarz, S. M., *The Jews in the Soviet Union* (1951); by a former member of the democratic Russian government of 1917. Shore, M. S., *Soviet Education, Its Psychology and Philosophy* (1947). Simmons, E. J. (ed.), *USSR: A Concise Handbook* (1947); excellent. Smal-Stocki, R., *The Nationality Problem in the Soviet Union and Russian Communist Imperialism* (1950); the Soviet problem of dominating non-Russian nationalities. Smith, W. B., *My Three Years in Moscow* (1950); experiences and reactions of the U.S. ambassador in Moscow, 1946–1949. Steinbeck, J., *A Russian Journal* (1948); with excellent photographs. Stevens, L. C., *Russian Assignment* (1953); the two years' experiences of a U.S. admiral in Russia. Baldwin, N. R. (ed.), *A New Slavery, Forced Labour: The Communist Betrayal of Human Rights* (1953). Curtiss, J. S., *The Russian Church and the Soviet State, 1917–1950* (1953). Deutscher, I., *Russia After Stalin* (1953); an attempt to forecast. Fainsod, M., *How Russia Is Ruled* (1953); a careful description and analysis of the power structure of

Soviet Russia. Gruliow, L. (ed.), *Current Soviet Policies: The Documentary Record of the 19th Communist Party Congress and the Reorganization after Stalin's Death* (1953).

POSTWAR SOVIET FOREIGN POLICY: Carman, E. D., *Soviet Imperialism: Russia's Drive Toward World Domination* (1950); since 1939. Communist International, *Blueprint for World Conquest: The Official Communist Plan* (1946); excerpts from documents. Dallin, D. J., *Soviet Russia and the Far East* (1948); before and after the Second World War. Ebon, M., *World Communism Today* (1948); a dispassionate report on the situation in the various countries. Laserson, M. M., *Russia and the Western World* (1946); seeks to provide historical perspective. Possony, S. T., *A Century of Conflict: Communist Techniques of World Revolution, 1848-1950* (1953); a penetrating analysis. Rothstein, A. (tr.), *Soviet Foreign Policy during the Patriotic War: Documents and Materials,* 2 vols. (1946); covers 1941-1944. Snow, E., *Stalin Must Have Peace* (1947); by a veteran American correspondent. Umiastowski, R., *Poland, Russia, and Great Britain, 1941-1945: A Study of Evidence* (1947); critical of Russia and Great Britain. Beloff, M., *Soviet Policy in the Far East, 1944-51* (1953).

THE SATELLITES—GENERAL: Bartlett, V., *East of the Iron Curtain* (1950); the fate of the peasants, aristocracy, and middle class. Beamish, T., *Must Night Fall?* (1950); a discussion of postwar developments in Poland, Rumania, Bulgaria and Hungary by a British Conservative. Betts, R. R. (ed.), *Central and South East Europe, 1945-1948* (1950); developments in the Soviet satellite zone. Dewar, M., *Soviet Trade with Eastern Europe* (1951); brief. Gluckstein, Y., *Stalin's Satellites in Europe* (1952); especially good for economic changes and for the Stalin-Tito conflict. Gyorgy, A. *et al., Soviet Satellites: Studies of Politics in Eastern Europe* (1949); a discussion of social reforms. Lehrman, H., *Russia's Europe* (1948); behind the "Iron Curtain" in Central Europe. MacEoin, G., *The Communist War on Religion* (1951); an indictment of Soviet policy toward organized religion, especially in the areas of postwar control in eastern Europe. Seton-Watson, H., *The East European Revolution* (1951); discusses developments in the "Iron Curtain" states. Shearman, H., *Finland—The Adventures of a Small Power* (1950); by an Irish economic historian. Stowe, L., *Conquest by Terror* (1952); an authoritative and readable account of satellite Europe. Waddams, H. M., *Communism and the Churches* (1950); a study of the situation in Russia, Albania, Bulgaria, Czechoslovakia, Hungary, Rumania, and Yugoslavia. Warriner, D., *Revolution in Eastern Europe* (1950); a brief British account dealing with Poland, Czechoslovakia, Hungary, Yugoslavia, and Bulgaria. Meyer, P., *et al., The Jews in the Soviet Satellites* (1953); scholarly and objective.

POLAND: Anderson, F., *What I Saw in Poland, 1946* (1946); by an UNRRA representative. Brant, I., *The New Poland* (1946); brief description of conditions in 1944-1945 by an American correspondent. Cary, W., *Poland Struggles Forward* (1949); conditions in 1947 described by an American. Ciechanowski, J., *Defeat in Victory* (1947); a denunciation of Anglo-American concessions to Russia, by the Polish ambassador to the United States, 1941-1945.

Czapski, J., *The Inhuman Land* (1952); a Polish study of Soviet treatment of the Poles. Gronowicz, A., *Pattern for Peace* (1951); a defense of the Oder-Neisse line as Poland's frontier. Jordan, Z., *Oder-Neisse Line: A Study of the Political, Economic and European Significance of Poland's Western Frontier* (1952). Kerstein, E. S., *Red Star Over Poland: A Report from Behind the Iron Curtain* (1947); conditions seen by an American. Kusnierz, B., *Stalin and the Poles* (1949); a Polish indictment. Lane, A. B., *I Saw Poland Betrayed* (1948); by the U.S. ambassador to Poland, 1945–1947. Mackiewicz, J., *The Katyn Wood Murders* (1951); a Polish journalist finds the Soviets guilty. Mikolajczyk, S., *The Rape of Poland: Pattern of Soviet Aggression* (1948); by the leader of the Peasant Party who fled from Poland in 1947. Scaevola, *A Study in Forgery: The Lublin Committee and Its Rule Over Poland* (1945); hostile account. Shotwell, J. T., and Laserson, M. M., *Poland and Russia, 1919–1945* (1945); contains a good discussion of the period 1939–1945. Strong, A. L., *I Saw the New Poland* (1945); sympathetic with the Lublin Poles. Umiastowski, R., *Poland, Russia, and Great Britain, 1941–1945: A Study of Evidence* (1946); hostile to Russia and Britain. Wojciechowski, Z. (ed.), *Poland's Place in Europe* (1947); Polish historians argue in favor of Poland's new western boundaries. Sharp, S. L., *Poland: White Eagle on a Red Field* (1953); a scholarly examination of the weaknesses of Poland's position as an independent state. Stern, H. P., *The Struggle for Poland* (1953); the years 1941–1947.

CZECHOSLOVAKIA: Brown, J., *Who's Next?* (1951); insights into Communist coup in Czechoslovakia in 1948, apparently by a Czech. Diamond, W., *Czechoslovakia Between East and West* (1947); developments, 1945–1947. Hindus, M., *The Bright Passage* (1947); optimistic account of Czechoslovakia written before the Communist coup. Lockhart, R. H. B., *Jan Masaryk: A Personal Memoir* (1951); a brief estimate by a friend. Mackenzie, C., *Dr. Beneš* (1946); perhaps the best biography in English. Ripka, H., *Czechoslovakia Enslaved: The Story of the Communist Coup d'État* (1951); by a Czech scholar and former cabinet minister. Schmidt, D. A., *Anatomy of a Satellite* (1952); how the Communists took power in Czechoslovakia. Stransky, J., *East Wind Over Prague* (1951); a former Czech official's attempt to show how the Red Army paved the way for the Communist coup.

HUNGARY: Fabian, B., *Cardinal Mindszenty: The Story of a Modern Martyr* (1949); by a Hungarian exile. Mindszenty, J. Cardinal, *Cardinal Mindszenty Speaks* (1949); official public letters and declarations collected by Mindszenty and ordered to be published if he should be arrested. Nagy, F., *The Struggle Behind the Iron Curtain* (1948); by the Hungarian premier who fled in 1947. Orme, A., *Comes the Comrade* (1950), a day by day record of Russian actions in Hungary in 1944–1945.

RUMANIA: Bishop, R., and Grayfield, E. S., *Russia Astride the Balkans* (1948); Soviet policy in Rumania. Lee, A., *Crown Against Sickle: The Story of King Michael of Rumania* (1950). Markham, R. H., *Rumania Under the Soviet Yoke* (1949); by a *Christian Science Monitor* correspondent. Roberts, H. L., *Rumania: Political Problems of an Agrarian State* (1951); since the First World War.

EAST GERMANY: Loewenthal, F., *News from Soviet Germany* (1950). Nettl, J. P., *The Eastern Zone and Soviet Policy in Germany* (1951); an excellent study. Schaffer, G., *Russian Zone of Germany* (1948); an eye-witness account of life in the Soviet zone. U.S. Department of State, *East Germany under Soviet Control* (1952). Klimov, G., *The Terror Machine: The Inside Story of Soviet Administration in Germany* (1953); by an escaped Russian official.

Chapter XXV. The So-Called Great Powers of Western Europe

SOCIALIST BRITAIN: Bocca, G., *Elizabeth and Philip* (1953); chatty. Brady, R. A., *Crisis in Britain: Plans and Achievements of the Labour Government* (1950); a good summary of the problems and achievements of Britain's "middle-way socialism." Clarke, C. F. O., *Britain Today: A Review of Current Political and Social Trends* (1951); an impartial account with considerable insight. Clemens, C., *The Man from Limehouse: Clement R. Attlee* (1946); deals particularly with the years 1939–1946. Cowles, V., *No Cause for Alarm* (1949); an account of social and political evolution under the British Labor government. Cowles, V., *Winston Churchill: The Era and the Man* (1953); a lively, shrewd, and original study. Dutt, R. P., *Britain's Crisis of Empire* (1950); a British appraisal of Britain's overseas problems. Estorick, E., *Changing Empire: Churchill to Nehru* (1950); a biographical approach to the problem. Estorick, E., *Stafford Cripps: Master Statesman* (1949); eulogistic but well-informed. Evans, T., *Bevin of Britain* (1946); brief biography of the former Labor foreign secretary. Hutchison, K., *The Decline and Fall of British Capitalism* (1950); an account of the rise of Labor from 1880 to 1949. Jenkins, R., *Mr. Attlee: An Interim Biography* (1948). Kahn, A. E., *Great Britain in the World Economy* (1946). Laffitte, F., *Social Security: The Fullest Summary of the Beveridge Proposals and Their Implications for the People of Britain* (1944). Mansergh, N., *The Commonwealth and the Nations* (1949); an analysis of changes in the British Commonwealth since 1939. Maillaud, P., *The English Way* (1946); penetrating appraisal of the British people by a Frenchman. McCallum, R. B., and Readman, A., *The British Election of 1945* (1946); excellent explanation and interpretation. Munro, D. (ed.), *Socialism, The British Way* (1948); a discussion of the achievements of Attlee's government. Murphy, J. T., *Labour's Big Three* (1948); Attlee, Bevin, and Morrison. Nicholas, H. G., *The British General Election of 1950* (1951); a study of the campaign, press attitude, forecasts and results. Paish, F. W., *The Post-War Financial Problem, and Other Essays* (1951); in Britain. Somervell, D. C., *British Politics Since 1900* (1950); a readable survey. Taylor, R. L., *Winston Churchill* (1952); entertaining and well documented, but suffers from being extremely laudatory. Watkins, E., *The Cautious Revolution: Britain Today and Tomorrow* (1950); a full and informative account of Britain, 1945–1950. Williams, F., *Socialist Britain* (1949); a study of England under Labor. Williams, F., *Ernest Bevin; Portrait of a Great Englishman* (1952). Windrich, E.,

British Labour's Foreign Policy (1952); the author believes that it is different from that of the Liberals or Conservatives. Broad, L., *Winston Churchill, 1874–1951* (1952). Fitzsimons, M. A., *The Foreign Policy of the British Labour Government, 1945–1951* (1953); critical. Nicolson, H., *King George the Fifth: His Life and Reign* (1953); excellent account of the king's public life.

THE FOURTH FRENCH REPUBLIC: Cowan, L. G., *France and the Saar, 1680–1948* (1950); objective. Earle, E. M. (ed.), *Modern France: Problems of the Third and Fourth Republics* (1951); an excellent collection of papers. Ehrmann, H. W., *French Labor From Popular Front to Liberation* (1947); deals chiefly with the period 1936–1941. Einaudi, M., *et al., Communism in Western Europe* (1951); particularly good for French and Italian Communism since World War II. Goguel, F., *France Under the Fourth Republic* (1952); by a professor at the University of Paris. Malraux, A. and Burnman, J., *The Case for De Gaulle* (1948); a biased account of the aims and possible effects of the Gaullist movement. Pickles, D. M., *France Between the Republics, 1940–1945* (1946); a brief guide to French politics. Rossi, A., *A Communist Party in Action: An Account of the Organization and Operations in France* (1951); by a former member of the secretariat of the Comintern. Russell, F. M., *The Saar: Battleground and Pawn* (1951); covers the period from 1914 to 1951. Taylor, O. R., *The Fourth Republic of France: Constitution and Political Parties* (1951); a concise and satisfactory coverage of the subject. Wright, G., *The Reshaping of French Democracy* (1948); excellent discussion by an American professor who was with the U.S. embassy in Paris, 1945–1947. Pickles, D., *French Politics: The First Years of the Fourth Republic* (1953); a careful and thorough study.

THE ITALIAN REPUBLIC: Croce, B., *Croce, the King, and the Allies: Extracts from a Diary by Benedetto Croce, July 1943–June 1944* (1951); throws light on the question of continuing the Italian monarchy. Einaudi, M., *et al., Communism in Western Europe* (1951); particularly good for French and Italian Communism since World War II. Grindrod, M., *The New Italy: Transition from War to Peace* (1947); a concise, factual account, published by the Royal Institute of International Affairs. Macartney, M. H. H., *The Rebuilding of Italy* (1945); the problems facing Italy after the war, discussed by a well-known British writer. Einaudi, M., *Christian Democracy in Italy and France* (1952). Hughes, H. S., *The United States and Italy* (1953); an excellent book on contemporary Italy.

WEST GERMANY: Clark, D., *Again the Goose Step: The Lost Fruits of Victory* (1949); observations of an American correspondent in occupied Germany. *Germany's Parliament in Action: the September 1949 Debate on the Government's Statement of Policy* (1950); gives a good idea of the atmosphere in West Germany at that time. Middleton, D., *The Struggle for Germany* (1949); the postwar German situation as seen by the head of the *New York Times* bureau in Berlin. Muhlen, N., *The Return of Germany: A Tale of Two Countries* (1953); a report on conditions in Federal and Communist Germany. Office of the U.S. High Commissioner for Germany, *Report on Germany* (1952); 9th quarterly report, covering Oct. 1 to Dec. 31, 1951. Tetens, T. H.,

Germany Plots with the Kremlin (1953); believes United States policy toward Germany is hazardous and ill-conceived.

Chapter XXVI. The Lesser States Outside the "Iron Curtain"

THE SCANDINAVIAN MONARCHIES: Arneson, B. A., *Democratic Monarchies of Scandinavia* (1949). Childs, M. W., *Sweden: The Middle Way* (1947). Cole, M., and Smith, C., *Democratic Sweden* (1939); an excellent discussion of Swedish social democracy. Friis, H. (ed.), *Scandinavia Between East and West* (1950); a comprehensive and authoritative account of social conditions. Galenson, W., *Labor in Norway* (1949); particularly industrial labor. Herlitz, N., *Sweden: A Modern Democracy on Ancient Foundations* (1939); excellent. Hinshaw, D., *Sweden: Champion of Peace* (1949). Howe, F. C., *Denmark: The Cooperative Way* (1936). Kenney, R., *The Northern Tangle; Scandinavia and the Post-War World* (1946); deals chiefly with the years 1939–1944. Larsen, K., *A History of Norway* (1948); by an American historian. Moller, J. C., and Watson, K., *Education in Democracy: The Folk High Schools of Denmark* (1944). Royal Institute of International Affairs, *The Scandinavian States and Finland* (1951); a concise informative report by specialists. *Social Denmark: A Survey of the Danish Social Legislation* (1946); authoritative. Strode, H., *Sweden: Model for the World* (1949); a readable survey. Walker, R., *A People Who Loved Peace: The Norwegian Struggle Against Fascism* (1946).

THE BENELUX COUNTRIES: Barnouw, A. J., *The Pageant of Netherlands History* (1951); an attempt to present the spirit of the peoples of the Low Countries. Goris, J.-A. (ed.), *Belgium* (1945); a symposium on its history and institutions. Hamilton, C., *Holland Today* (1950); brief. Kennedy, J. P., and Landis, J. M., *The Surrender of King Leopold, with an Appendix Containing the Keyes-Gort Correspondence* (1950); favorable to the king. Landheer, B. (ed.), *The Netherlands* (1944); a symposium by Dutch or descendants of Dutch. Landheer, B., *The Netherlands in a Changing World* (1947); by a Netherlands official. Mason, H. L., *The Purge of Dutch Quislings: Emergency Justice in the Netherlands* (1952); by an American professor who was a U.S. Army intelligence officer in the Netherlands, 1944–1946. Miller, J. K., *Belgian Foreign Policy between Two Wars, 1919–1940* (1951); a preliminary but incomplete account. Riemens, H., *The Netherlands: Story of a Free People* (1944); by a secretary of the Dutch embassy in Washington. Roberts, K., *And the Bravest of These* (1946); Belgian conditions, including a discussion of the problem of King Leopold.

SWITZERLAND: Brooks, R. C., *Civic Training in Switzerland* (1930). Rappard, W. E., *The Government of Switzerland* (1937); by a Swiss authority. Rougemont, D. de and Muret, C. T., *Switzerland: The Heart of Europe* (1941). Siegfried, A., *Switzerland: A Democratic Way of Life* (1950).

SPAIN AND PORTUGAL: Alba, V., *Sleepless Spain* (1948). Barea, A., *The Forging of a Rebel: An Autobiography* (1946); an excellent account of

Spanish history, 1923–1939, by a Spanish Socialist. Bragança Cunha, V. D., *Revolutionary Portugal, 1910–1936* (1939). Cleugh, J., *Spain in the Modern World* (1953); by a pro-Franco Briton. Feis, H., *The Spanish Story: Franco and the Nations at War* (1948). Foltz, C., Jr., *The Masquerade in Spain* (1948); discusses the group behind Franco. Hayes, C. J. H., *Wartime Mission in Spain, 1942–1945* (1945), by the United States wartime ambassador to Franco Spain. Hoare, S., *Complacent Dictator* (1947); by the British wartime ambassador to Franco Spain. Hughes, E. J., *Report from Spain* (1947); by an American Catholic who was a press attaché in the U.S. embassy in Madrid, 1942–1946. Livermore, H. V., *A History of Portugal* (1947); the best book in English. Lovejoy, A. F., *Spain, 1923–1948* (1949), a pro-Franco account by a British businessman. Pattee, R., *This Is Spain* (1950); a well-documented pro-Franco presentation. U.S. Department of State, *The Spanish Government and the Axis* (1946); official German documents.

GREECE AND TURKEY: Bisbee, E., *The New Turks: Pioneers of the Republic, 1920–1950* (1951); a sympathetic and informative account of post-Kemalist Turkey by a former professor at Robert College. Burr, P., *My Turkish Adventures* (1951); observations on present day Turkey by a school teacher at the American Girls College at Istanbul. Byford-Jones, W., *The Greek Trilogy: Resistance, Liberation, Revolution* (1946); by a British writer. Gomme, A. W., *Greece* (1945). Leeper, R. W. A., *When Greeks Meet Greeks* (1950); by the British ambassador to the Greek government, 1943–1946. McNeil, W. H., *The Greek Dilemma: War and Aftermath* (1947); an objective analysis of the Greek political situation, 1944–1946. National Liberation Front, *White Book, May 1944–March 1945* (1945); official and unofficial documents for the period 1944–1945. Paneth, P., *The Glory That Is Greece* (1945); events in Greece, 1941–1944. Sarafis, S., *Greek Resistance Army: The Story of ELAS* (1951); by a military commander of ELAS. Smothers, F., *et al.*, *Report on the Greeks* (1948); the situation after one year of American aid. Stavrianos, L. S., *Greece: American Dilemma and Opportunity* (1952); critical of American policy in Greece under the Truman Doctrine. Tomlin, E. F., *Life in Modern Turkey* (1946). Woodhouse, C. M., *Apple of Discord: A Survey of Recent Greek Politics in Their International Setting* (1948); by the chief of the Allied military mission. Kousoulas, D. G., *The Price of Freedom: Greece in World Affairs, 1939–1953* (1953); by a Greek who fought in the underground.

YUGOSLAVIA: Armstrong, H. F., *Tito and Goliath* (1951); Tito's rise, the break with the Cominform, and subsequent conditions. Bilainkin, G., *Tito* (1950); by a British correspondent who interviewed Tito. Clissold, S., *Whirlwind: An Account of Marshal Tito's Rise to Power* (1950); by a British press attaché in Yugoslavia. Dedijer, V., *With Tito Through the War* (1951); part of a Partisan wartime diary. Dedijer, V., *Tito* (1953); an authorized biography. Fotitch, C., *The War We Lost: Yugoslavia's Tragedy and the Failure of the West* (1948); criticism of the Allied policy toward Tito, by a former Yugoslav diplomat. Kerner, R. J. (ed.), *Yugoslavia* (1949); valuable. Korbel, J., *An Ambassador's Report on Tito's Communism* (1951); by the Czechoslovak ambassador to Yugoslavia, 1945–1948. Markham, R. H., *Tito's Imperial Com *munism* (1947); by a former correspondent of the *Christian Science Monitor*. Martin, D., *Ally Betrayed: The Uncensored Story of Tito and Mihailovich* (1946); strongly anti-Tito. Mihailovic, *General Mihailovich: The World's Verdict* (1947). Radin, G., *Economic Reconstruction in Yugoslavia: A Practical Plan for the Balkans* (1946); an account by experts. St. John, R., *The Silent People Speak* (1948); sympathetic with Tito's Yugoslavia. Ulam, A. B., *Titoism and the Cominform* (1952); based largely on material published in Yugoslavia and some of the satellite states. White, L., *Balkan Caesar: Tito versus Stalin* (1951); hostile to Tito. Pattee, R., *The Case of Cardinal Aloysius Stepinac* (1953); an indictment of Tito.

Chapter XXVII. Nationalism in the East

THE ARAB WORLD: Antonius, G., *The Arab Awakening* (1946). Graves, P. (ed.), *Memoirs of King Abdullah of Transjordan* (1950). Hourani, A. K., *Syria and Lebanon* (1945); a careful analysis. Issawi, C., *Egypt: An Economic and Social Analysis* (1947). Khadduri, M., *Independent Iraq* (1952); an account of politics since 1932. Rivlin, B., *The United Nations and the Italian Colonies* (1950); a brief but valuable discussion. Royal Institute of International Affairs, *Great Britain in Egypt* (1952). Stark, F., *The Arab Island: The Middle East, 1934–1943* (1945). Twictchell, K. S., *Saudi Arabia* (1947). Van Ess, J., *Meet the Arab* (1943); by one who lived among the Arabs for many years. Izzeddin, N., *The Arab World: Past, Present and Future* (1953); an Arab viewpoint toward world affairs.

PALESTINE AND ISRAEL: Barbour, N., *Palestine: Star or Crescent?* (1947); by a student of the Middle East. Bentwich, N., *Israel* (1953); an objective account by a former British mandate official. Crossman, R., *Palestine Mission: A Personal Record* (1947); by a British Laborite who was a member of the Anglo-American Commission appointed in 1945. Crum, B., *Behind the Silken Curtain* (1947); Palestine discussed by an American member of the Anglo-American Commission of 1945. Dunner, J., *The Republic of Israel: Its History and Its Promise* (1950); an introductory work. García-Granados, J., *The Birth of Israel* (1948); by a member of the UN Special Committee on Israel. Gaury, G. de, *The New State of Israel* (1952); a discussion of political, economic, and cultural conditions and problems. Hurewitz, J. C., *The Struggle for Palestine* (1950); a scholarly study of the problem since 1936. Joseph, B., *British Rule in Palestine* (1948). *Palestine: Land of Israel* (1948); excellent photographs. Matthews, C. D., *Palestine—Mohammedan Holy Land* (1949). *Palestine: A Study of Jewish, Arab, and British Policies,* 2 vols. (1947); by a number of scholars and experts. Rosenne, S., *Israel's Armistice Agreements with the Arabs States* (1952); a legal interpretation of the documents of 1949. Royal Institute of International Affairs, *Great Britain and Palestine, 1915–1945* (1947); a good survey. Schechtman, J. B., *The Arab Refugee Problem* (1952). Stone, I. F., *This Is Israel* (1948). Weizmann, C., *Trial and Error: The Autobiography of Chaim Weizmann* (1919); Israel's first president. Lilienthal, A. M., *What Price Israel* (1953); critical of the Zionists.

THE MIDDLE EAST: Bullard, R., *Britain and the Middle East: From the Earliest Times to 1950* (1951); a brief survey. Eliot, G. F., *Hate, Hope and High Explosives: A Report on the Middle East* (1948); by an American military commentator. Frye, R. N. (ed.), *The Near East and the Great Powers* (1951); a collection of papers presented at the Harvard conference on the Middle East in 1950. Lenczowski, G., *The Middle East in World Affairs* (1952); good for the period since 1914. *The Middle East: A Political and Economic Survey* (1950); a useful compendium of social, economic, and political information. Payne, R., *The Revolt of Asia* (1947). Royal Institute of International Affairs, *The Middle East: A Political and Economic Summary* (1948). Seton-Williams, M. V., *Britain and the Arab States: A Survey of Anglo-Arab Relations, 1920–1948* (1948); by a former member of the British ministry of information. Fisher, S. N. (ed.), *Evolution in the Middle East: Reform, Revolt and Change* (1953); a symposium.

IRAN: Haas, W. S., *Iran* (1946). Lenczowski, G., *Russia and the West in Iran, 1918–1948* (1949); provides excellent background. Mehdevi, A. S., *Persian Adventures* (1953); description of life in Iran by the American wife of an Iranian. Najafi, N., *Persia Is My Heart* (1953); sympathetic but revealing account of conditions by a member of the minor nobility. Thomas, L. V. and Frye, R. N., *The United States and Turkey and Iran* (1951). Wilber, D. N., *Iran: Past and Present* (1948); the latter part deals with the period since Riza Shah.

INDIA AND PAKISTAN: Ahmad, N., *The Basis of Pakistan* (1947). Bright, J. S. (ed.), *Selected Writings of Nehru, 1916–1950* (1950). Brown, W. N. (ed.), *India, Pakistan, Ceylon* (1951). Brown, W. N., *The United States and India and Pakistan* (1953); a pessimistic account of the two states by an American professor. Campbell-Johnson, A., *Mission with Mountbatten* (1953); by the press officer of the last viceroy of India. Choudhary Rahmat Ali, *Pakistan: The Fatherland of the Pak Nation* (1947); by the founder of the Pakistan National Liberation Movement. Cousins, N., *Talks with Nehru: India's Prime Minister Speaks Out on the Crisis of Our Time* (1951); a brief record of conversations held with Nehru. Fischer, L., *The Life of Mahatma Gandhi* (1950). Jones, G. E., *Tumult in India* (1948); a *New York Times* correspondent's description of conditions in India, 1946–1947. Joshi, G., *The Constitution of India* (1951). Kothari, S., *India's Emerging Foreign Policies* (1951); doubtful of the wisdom of India's having remained within the Commonwealth. Mellor, A., *India Since Partition* (1951); a brief account by a British newspaper man. Nehru, J., *Independence and After: A Collection of Speeches* (1950); by India's first prime minister. Roosevelt, E., *India and the Awakening East* (1953); based on a journey in 1952. Spencer, C., *Nehru of India* (1948). Symonds, R., *The Making of Pakistan* (1950); sympathetic. Vakil, C. N., *Economic Consequences of Divided India* (1950). Wallbank, T. W., *India in the New Era* (1951). Bowles, C., *Ambassador's Report* (1954); a competent and readable appraisal of India by a U.S. ambassador.

INDONESIA AND SOUTHEAST ASIA: Bailey, S. D., *Ceylon* (1952). Boeke, J. H., *The Evolution of the Netherlands Indies Economy* (1946).

Dobby, E. H. G., *Southeast Asia* (1951). DuBois, C. A., *Social Forces in Southeast Asia* (1949). Gerbrandy, P. S., *Indonesia* (1950); by a former Dutch premier who opposed granting independence. Jennings, I., *The Constitution of Ceylon: Ceylon as a Dominion* (1950). Lasker, B., *Human Bondage in Southeast Asia* (1950); helps one to understand developments in this area. Middlebrook, S. M., and Pinnick, W. A., *How Malaya Is Governed* (1949); a concise manual. Mills, L. A., *et al., The New World of Southeast Asia* (1949); by eight experts. Mook, H. J. van, *The Stakes of Democracy in Southeast Asia* (1950); by the former Dutch lieutenant-governor-general. Robequain, C., *The Economic Development of French Indo-China* (1944). Sjahrir, S., *Out of Exile* (1949); letters from a prominent Indonesian leader to his wife while he was imprisoned or interned, 1934–1941, by the Dutch. Talbot, P. (ed.), *South Asia in the World Today* (1950). Thayer, P. W. (ed.), *Southeast Asia in the Coming World* (1953); an outstanding symposium. Thompson, V., and Adloff, R., *The Left Wing in Southeast Asia* (1950); a study of the radical movements. Vandenbosch, A., *The Dutch East Indies* (1934). Wolf, C., Jr., *The Indonesian Story: The Birth, Growth and Structure of the Indonesian Republic* (1948); by a former American vice-consul at Batavia. Kahin, G., *Nationalism and Revolution in Indonesia* (1952); the most detailed study in English.

CHINA: Ballantine, J. W., *Formosa: A Problem for United States Foreign Policy* (1953); clear statement by a former State Department director of Far Eastern affairs. Bate, H. M., *Report from Formosa* (1952); sympathetic with the Nationalist cause. Belden, J., *China Shakes the World* (1949); a discussion of the social and political conditions which contributed to the victory of the Communists. Bodde, D., *Peking Diary: A Year of Revolution* (1950); diary of a United States student in Peking, 1948–1949. Chang, C., *The Third Force in China* (1952); by the anti-Chiang liberal who drafted the Chinese constitution of 1946. Compton, B. (ed.), *Mao's China: Party Reform Documents, 1942–44* (1952); party resolutions and policy-setting speeches by Mao Tse-tung and other party leaders. Elegant, R. S., *China's Red Masters: Political Biographies of the Chinese Communist Leaders* (1951). Fairbank, J. K., *The United States and China* (1948); a scholarly discussion of the problem of Sino-American relations. Fitzgerald, C. P., *Revolution in China* (1952); a penetrating examination of the Communist regime. Flynn, J. T., *While You Slept* (1952); denounces America's postwar policy toward China as responsible for Communist successes. Forman, H., *Report from Red China* (1945); somewhat sympathetic with the Chinese Communists. Hsiung, Shih-i, *The Life of Chiang Kai-shek* (1948). Hunter, E., *Brain Washing in Red China* (1951); a study of totalitarian re-education in China. Latourette, K. S., *The American Record in the Far East, 1945–1951* (1952); a brief objective account of policy and blunders. McCammon, D. S., *We Tried to Stay* (1953); experiences of a Mennonite missionary in Nationalist and Communist China. Moraes, F., *Report on Mao's Red China* (1953); by a lawyer who visited China in 1952. Payne, R., *China Awake* (1947); an account of conditions 1944–1946 by a former teacher in China. Payne, R., *Mao Tse-tung* (1950); an appreciative account of the Chinese Communist leader. Riggs, F. W., *Formosa under Chinese Nationalists Rule* (1952). Rosinger, L. K., *China's Wartime Politics, 1937–1944* (1944); good for Kuomintang-Communist relations. Schwartz, B. I., *Chinese Communism and the Rise of Mao* (1951); a scholarly study based largely on Chinese and Russian sources. Stockwell, F. O., *With God in Red China* (1953); by the last Methodist missionary to leave China. Strong, A. L., *The Chinese Conquer China* (1949); by a Communist sympathizer. U.S. Department of State, *United States Relations with China, with Special Reference to the Period 1944–1949* (1949); an official White Paper. Utley, F., *Last Chance in China* (1947); a pro-Chiang, anti-Soviet book. Vinacke, H. M., *The United States and the Far East, 1945–1951* (1952); a brief summary of events and an illuminating analysis of the historical forces which produced them. Feis, H., *The China Tangle: The American Effort in China from Pearl Harbor to the Marshall Mission* (1953); a brilliant discussion of a controversial subject. Hutheesing, Raja, *The Great Peace: An Asian's Candid Report on Red China* (1953); by the brother-in-law of Indian Premier Nehru. North, R. C., *Moscow and Chinese Communists* (1953); how Russia was related to the Communist success in China.

Chapter XXVIII. Collective Security on Trial

THE KOREAN WAR: Green, A. W., *The Epic of Korea* (1950); a brief survey of the first three postwar years. Gunther, J., *The Riddle of MacArthur: Japan, Korea and the Far East* (1951); readable and sometimes penetrating. Higgins, M., *War in Korea* (1951); by a war correspondent. Kahn, E. J., *The Peculiar War* (1952); the Korean War described by a newspaper reporter. Kim, A. D., *I Married a Korean* (1953); informative, first-hand account of life in rural Korea. Marshall, S. L. A., *The River and the Gauntlet: The Defeat of the Eighth Army by the Chinese Communist Forces November, 1950, in the Battle of the Chongchon River, Korea* (1953). McCune, G. M., *Korea Today* (1950); conditions prior to the outbreak of war in 1950. Meade, E. G., *American Military Government in Korea* (1951); by a participant in that government who claims that the U.S. failed to carry out effectively a reform program. Office of the Chief of Military History, Dept. of the Army, *Korea-1950* (1952). Oliver, T., *Why War Came in Korea* (1950); by a supporter of President Rhee. Riggs, R. A., *Red China's Fighting Hordes* (1951); by a U.S. Army officer. Rovere, R. and Schlesinger, A. M., Jr., *The General and the President* (1951); an account of the MacArthur controversy of 1951. Jacobs, B., *Korea's Heroes* (1953); the exploits of Medal of Honor winners.

NATO: *Atlantic Alliance: Nato's Role in the Free World* (1952); a brief study of aims, organization, and achievements. Boyd, A., and Metson, W., *Atlantic Pact, Commonwealth and United Nations* (1949); origins and significance of the pact. Hoskins, H., *The Atlantic Pact* (1949); an introduction. Middleton, D., *The Defense of Western Europe* (1952); an explanation of why NATO will be the pivot in Western Europe's turn against Soviet aggression. Royal Institute of International Affairs, *Atlantic Alliance: Nato's Role in the*

Free World (1952); excellent.   Roberts, H. L., and Wilson, P. A., *Britain and the United States, Problems in Cooperation* (1953); a joint report by British and Americans.

COUNCIL OF EUROPE: Boyd, A., and F., *Western Union: A Study of the Trend Toward European Unity* (1949).   *European Movement and the Council of Europe* (1949); the aims and steps leading to the Council of Europe.   Hawtry, R. G., *Western European Union* (1949).   Reynaud, P., *Unite or Perish: A Dynamic Program for a United Europe* (1951); by a former French premier.

INDEX

The following abbreviations are alphabetized as if they were spelled out: Aus.-Hun. (Austria-Hungary), 1WW (First World War), Gr. Br. (Great Britain), 2WW (Second World War), Sov. Rus. (Soviet Russia), Ts. Rus. (Tsarist Russia), U. S. (United States).

281, 282, 283-85, 288, 289, 329, 429, 690, 694, 697, 698, 699; Dutch, 741; Irish, 296, 299; Norwegian, 735, 736
Labor unions: in Czechoslovakia, 658; in Germany, 260; in Gr. Br., 280-81, 330; in Hungary, 353; in Italy, 217, 218, 219, 223; in Sov. Rus., 190, 206; in Spain, 333; in Ts. Rus., 76
Labrador, 541
Laconia, 66
Ladoga, Lake, 602
La Fère, 92
Laidoner, Johan, 408
Laissez-faire, 227, 282
Lancashire, 274
Land reform: in Albania, 683; in Bulgaria, 682; in China, 808; in Czechoslovakia, 347-48, 667; in Estonia, 375; in Finland, 378, 684; in Italy, 722; in Hungary, 351, 352, 353, 355, 674; in Japan, 632, 633; in Korea, 649; in Latvia, 375; in Lithuania, 375-76(n.); in Palestine, 420; in Poland, 364, 366, 661; in Rumania, 396, 679; in Sweden, 738; in Turkey, 762
Landlords: in Finland, 376; in Italy, 217, 219; in Spain, 326, 328, 332; see also Land reform
Laniel, Joseph, 711
Lansing, Robert, 110
Lansing-Ishii agreement, 436 (& n.)
Laon, 68, 69, 547
Laos, 713, 801-3, 822
Largo Caballero, Francisco, 328, 332
Lashio, 571
Lateran Palace, 229, 230
Lateran treaties, 230-31
Latvia: early history of, 374; in 1WW, 375; independent, 375; minorities in, 134 (n. 13); relations with other powers (except Sov. Rus.), 177, 375, 376, 490-91; in 2WW, 490, 491, 497, 513, 550, 556; & Sov. Rus., 211, 375, 490-91, 497, 513, 637
Latvian Soviet Socialist Republic, 214(n.)
Lauro, Achille, 722
Lausanne: conference at (1922–23), 380, 400, 405-6; conference at, on reparations, 175-76 (& n. 9); reparations agreement of, 176, 177, 244; treaty of (1923), 406-7
Laušman, Bohumil, 666, 667
Laval, Pierre, 306, 314, 456, 460, 462, 465, 466, 702, 703(n.)
Law, Bonar, 110, 165, 276, 277
Law: of Papal Guarantees, 229; of Political

Responsibilities, 333; of Syndical Unity, 333
Lawrence, T. E., 70
Leadership Corps, 611
Leadership, Nazi principle of, 261
League to Enforce Peace, 148
League of Nations: & Albania, 389, 390; & Argentina, 469; & armaments, 141, 150, 151-52, 155, 157-60; & Austria, 124, 128, 339, 340-41; & British dominions, 291; budget of, 140, 149; & Bulgaria, 393; & China, 438, 440, 449, 450, 451, 453, 471-72, 475, 476; & collective security, 447; Covenant of, 113-14 (see also Covenant of League of Nations); & Danzig, 119, 369, 371; & Egypt, 415, 416; & Estonia, 375; & Ethiopia, 462, 463-64, 466, 467, 469; & Finland, 377, 378, 497; & France, 450, 463, 467; & Germany, 242, 244, 267, 269, 361-62, 368, 450, 456, 457, 458, 460, 465; & Gr. Br., 407-8, 416, 418, 423, 425, 449, 450, 457, 463; & Greece, 232, 382, 393; & Hungary, 355, 357; & Iraq, 407-8, 423-24; & Ireland, 295; & Italy, 232, 234, 450, 457, 461, 463-64, 465, 466, 467, 469, 471; & Japan, 449-50, 453-54, 469, 471-72, 475, 476; & Latvia, 375; & Lebanon, 416, 418; & Lithuania, 360-61, 373; in Manchurian crisis, 449-50, 452-53; mandates of, 120, 133(n.), 141, 145-46, 291, 416 418; & mediation, 141, 150, 151; & Memel, 373; & minorities, 134 (& n.), 136 146-47, 424; & Netherlands, 457; & Palestine, 418; & peace, 150-55, 632; & Persia, 425; & Poland, 360-62, 368; & Rumania, 398; & Saar, 116-17, 269, 457-58; & sanctions, 150, 151, 288; & Sov. Rus., 213, 377, 456, 497; & Spain, 334; & the Straits, 406; structure of, 139-42; & Sweden, 377, 378, 457; & Syria, 416, 417, 418; & treaty of Versailles, 113-14, 127, 136; & Turkey, 407-8, 411; & U. S., 147-50, 151, 449, 450, 465, 475; & Wilson, 99(n.), 112; & World Court, 142-43; & Yugoslavia, 388, 390
League of Viet Nam's Independence, 802; see also Viet Minh
League of Reserve Officers, Bulgarian, 392
Leased territories, in China, 438, 441, 442
Lebanon, 133, 145, 416, 418, 597, 770, 775, 776
Lebensraum, 394, 488
Lebrun, Albert, 312, 314
Leclerc, Jacques, 547

France, 315, 708, 712; in Germany, 101, 239, 261; in Gr. Br., 278, 280-81; in India, 430; in Italy, 217, 218, 223, 228, 720; in Palestine, 421; in Spain, 320, 326, 333; in Syria, 418; in Ts. Rus., 77, 78; in U. S., 64
Struma valley, 515, 516
Stumpff, Hans Jürgen, 562
Sturmabteilungen, 250
Stürmer, Boris, 77
Stuttgart, 103, 239, 559
Styria, 344, 625
Subasich, Ivan, 764
Submarines: British, in 2WW, 500; & five-power treaty, 156; German, in 1WW, 39, 44, 51-53, 63-66, 88-89; German, in 2WW, 498, 523, 525-27, 541, 544; German, & treaty of Versailles, 121, 458; Japanese, in 2WW, 569; & London naval treaty, 157; in Spanish civil war, 330; U. S., in 2WW, 572, 578
Succession states, 127, 131, 159, 335-38; see Austria, Czechoslovakia, Hungary, Poland, Yugoslavia
Suchow, 807
Sudan, 406, 413 (& n.), 414, 415, 462, 771-74
Sudeten crisis, 485, 488
Sudeten German Party, 350, 478-79, 480
Sudeten Germans, 479, 481, 482, 483, 484
Sudetendeutsch Party (Sudeten German Party, *q.v.*), 350, 479
Sudetenland, 272, 483, 484, 485, 663
Suez Canal, 45, 70, 413, 415, 478, 517, 532, 773, 774
Suffrage: in Austria, 339, 345; in Czechoslovakia, 347; in France, 301; in Germany, 236, 237; in Hungary, 351, 352, 355; in India, 430; in Irish Free State, 295; in Poland, 363, 365; in Rumania, 395; for women, 101; in Yugoslavia, 384, 387; see also Franchise
Sulu Sea, 584, 585
Sumatra, 572, 740, 795, 797, 799
Sumitomo, 631
Sun Yat-sen, 434, 439, 806
Sundlo, Konrad, 499, 500
Sun Fo, 806, 807
Sung Cheh-yuan, 472
Superfortress, 579, 586, 587
Supreme Commander for the Allied Powers (in Japan), 628, 629, 631, 632, 824, 830, 831
Supreme Council: of Bessarabia, 395; of Paris

peace conference, 127(n.), 131, 360, 361; of U.S.S.R., 204, 206, 207
Supreme Court (U. S.), 630
Supreme Economic Council (Sov. Rus.), 188, 191, 195, 200
Supreme Inter-Allied War Council (1WW), 110
Supreme Soviet of the U.S.S.R., 189 (n. 2), 638
Supreme War Council, Allied (1WW), 75
Surigao Straits, 584, 585
Šušak, 129(n.), 130(n.)
Suwalki, 360
Suzuki, Kantaro, 589
Swastika, 250
Sweden, 376, 377-78, 457, 560, 737-39, 808, 814, 818, 820, 826
Swinemunde, 660
Swiss Confederation, 744-46
Switzerland, 4, 5, 82, 142(n.), 218, 606, 744-46, 818
Syndicalism, Fascist, 223-26, 228
Syndicalists, in Spain, 320, 326, 327
Syndicates: Italian, 223-24, 225, 700; Spanish, 333
Syracuse, 535
Syria: elections in, 417; & France, 133, 416-18, 517, 775-76; independent, 776; & League of Nations, 416, 417, 418; mandated, 133 (& n.), 145, 146, 416, 417; & Palestine, 779, 780; republic, 417, 776; revolt in, 417; in 2WW, 517; after 2WW, 596, 770, 775, 776, 779, 780, 798; & Turkey, 406, 411; & United Nations, 596, 726, 798
Szakasits, Arpad, 672, 676
Szalasy, Hungarian Nazi leader, 552
Szeged, 353

Tadjik Soviet Socialist Republic, 214(n.)
Taft, William Howard, 148
Taipei, 809
Tagliamento River, 74, 75
Tana, Lake, 462
Tanaka, Giichi, Baron, 447-48
Tanaka Memorial, 447-48
Tanganyika, 145, 701
Tangier, 14, 233, 748, 751
Tangku, 454
Tannenberg, 43
Tanner, Vaino, 684
Tarakan Island, 586
Taranto, 514, 535